April 18–23, 2015
Seoul, Republic of Korea

Association for
Computing Machinery

Advancing Computing as a Science & Profession

SIGCHI

CHI 2015
CROSSINGS

CHI 2015

Proceedings of the

33rd Annual CHI Conference on Human Factors in Computing Systems

Sponsored by:

ACM SIGCHI

Supported by:

Samsung, Golfzon, Google, Microsoft, NAVER, SK Planet, AutoDesk, Daumkakao, Disney Research, FuturePlay, Hyundai Motor Group, Language Grid, LG, NSF, Adobe Systems, H9Works, Yonsei University, KIPFA, and Samsung Art & Design Institute

Association for
Computing Machinery

Advancing Computing as a Science & Profession

The Association for Computing Machinery
2 Penn Plaza, Suite 701
New York, New York 10121-0701

ISBN: 978-1-4503-3145-6 (Digital)

ISBN: 978-1-4503-3773-1 (Print)

Additional copies may be ordered prepaid from:

ACM Order Department
PO Box 30777
New York, NY 10087-0777, USA

Phone: 1-800-342-6626 (USA and Canada)
+1-212-626-0500 (Global)
Fax: +1-212-944-1318
E-mail: acmhelp@acm.org
Hours of Operation: 8:30 am – 4:30 pm ET

Printed in the USA

From the General and Technical Program Chairs

Welcome to CHI 2015, the premier international forum for human-computer interaction (HCI). In its early days, HCI focused on optimizing interactions between a user and a computer. Today, computers pervade our world, impacting our lives in varied and subtle ways. By never focusing solely on technology itself but always on innovations and their effects throughout human lives, HCI has increasingly come to mean *human-centered innovation.*

The theme for the conference this year is *CROSSINGS* which represents our excitement about crossing into Asia and also reflects CHI's core principle of crossing disciplines, crossing people and technology, crossing research and business, crossing physical and digital, ... crossing you and me.

This year's conference brings CHI to Asia for the first time in its 33-year history, continuing the SIGCHI commitment to making CHI a truly international community. The city of Seoul represents one of many innovation centers in Asia and provides a fantastic opportunity to showcase groundbreaking content from across the region. In addition to an exciting technical program, we are holding four special symposia devoted to breakthrough insights and innovations from the Chinese, Japanese and ASEAN research communities.

The exciting keynote program features speakers who will bring fresh perspectives to CHI including Dean ***Lou Yongqi*** of Tongji University, China, a prominent global thinker on social and sustainable design; Executive VP ***Donghoon Chang***, MFA, head of Samsung Electronic's design strategy; Senior Research Fellow ***David Min***, PhD, head of the Software Center at LG Electronics; and ***PSY***, the media record breaker and innovator discussing creative methods and the impact of social media on to cross cultural boundaries.

CHI is honored this year to be the forum chosen by the recipient of one of ACM's top awards, the Athena Lecturer Award, ***Susan T. Dumais*** who developed novel algorithms and interfaces for interactive retrieval that have made it easier for people to find, use and make sense of information. She will present insights from her experiences at a special keynote session at the conference.

CHI 2015 includes two days of focused workshops and four days of technical content, including CHI's prestigious technical program, with 16 parallel sessions of rigorously reviewed research Papers, engaging Panels, Case Studies and Special Interest Groups (SIGs), an extensive Course program and invited talks from SIGCHI's award winners: Leysia Palen, Jean Scholtz, Michel Beaudouin-Lafon, Jim Hollan, Susan Dray and the new inductees to the CHI Academy.

We also host student research, design, and game competitions, and last-minute SIGs for discussing current topics. The popular alt.chi forum entered its tenth year of provocation to the HCI community. Interactivity's hands-on demonstrations showcase the best of interactive technology and innovation. The program also highlights more than 200 Work-In-Progress posters. Evening events include the CHI 2015 conference reception, Sponsors and University events, local performances and the Job Fair. Across all tracks, CHI received over 2800 submissions and accepted nearly 1000 that will appear in the ACM Digital Library.

We are deeply indebted to an enormous number of volunteers, without whom CHI 2015 would not be possible, including over 3800 reviewers, over 200 senior members of the program committee, nearly 100 members of the CHI 2015 conference organization committee and, of course, the more than 180 student volunteers. We are also deeply grateful to the ongoing support of the Korean HCI society who demonstrated incredible hospitality by moving their own conference's time and location to make room for

CHI in Seoul and who provided tremendous resources from their membership to support CHI logistically and in attracting novel content from around Asia.

We hope you will see fresh insights, strengthen connections and find new collaborators in Asia. *Above all, we hope you enjoy this unique experience of CHI 2015!*

General Conference Chairs

Bo Begole
Huawei, USA

Jinwoo Kim
Yonsei University, Korea

Technical Program Chairs

Kori Inkpen
Microsoft Research, USA

Woontack Woo
KAIST, Korea

From ACM SIGCHI's President and Vice President for Conferences

SIGCHI is proud to sponsor the premier annual conference in the field of human-computer interaction. We are extremely grateful to the CHI 2015 Conference Chairs Jinwoo Kim and Bo Begole, to Technical Program Chairs Woontack Woo and Kori Inkpen, and to their wonderful crew, who succeeded to build an impressive program and experience.

CHI 2015 is in Seoul, Korea, the first CHI ever in Asia. CHI started in Gaithersburg, MD, USA, in March 1982. That first conference in Gaithersburg drew over 900 attendees, and since then CHI, with the official name: "ACM Conference on Human Factors in Computing Systems" moved to annual, originally moving between the USA and Canada. Starting with 1993 CHI traveled between locations in Europe and North America. This year is another big step forward, made possible thanks to the Korean HCI Society that helped understand and navigate the local context, that moved its annual conference 3 months earlier to December 2014, and at the same time supported CHI's Technical Program meeting.

CHI has continued to grow and broaden its range of topics and contributing disciplines: the founding psychologists and software engineers began to meet new visions from ethnography, sociology, communication sciences and arts, among others. Relevant industries, as well as research institutes and academia, showed an increasing — and often long-lasting — interest and involvement (through volunteers and through sponsorship for conference expenses). This year's Conference Committee truly succeeded in crossing borders of all kind, providing new and unique opportunities for all participants to meet something entirely different.

CHI is an ideal forum for people to meet formally as well as informally, to exchange knowledge and views, to share experiences, and to learn. The CHI conference brings together professionals from research and practice; people from industry, academia, and from government; long-term veterans of HCI, young professionals and students; all in an environment designed to encourage interaction. We invite you to actively participate in that interaction: introduce yourself to people, interact with presenters and speakers, renew old friendships and make new ones

CHI is organized on behalf of ACM's Special Interest Group on Computer-Human Interaction (SIGCHI), an international community of professionals who share an interest in the many diverse facets of HCI. SIGCHI is committed both to advancing the field of HCI, to facilitate exchange of information within the SIGCHI community, and to support students to enter the domain.

The CHI conference is arguably the single most visible activity of SIGCHI, but we also sponsor and support a wide range of specialized conferences and workshops in areas ranging from interactive systems design to user interface technology to computer-supported cooperative work to "intelligent" user interfaces. Visit the SIGCHI website at **http://www.sigchi.org** to find our conference schedule, listing upcoming as well as past conferences.

SIGCHI and ACM produce some of the most respected publications in the field. All members receive interactions, a highly-acclaimed magazine covering the broad field of HCI and user interface design. ACM Transactions on Computer-Human Interactions (ToCHI), now in its 21st year, is our flagship journal – a quarterly publication with the top-quality archival research aimed at researchers and those translating research into practice.

SIGCHI is truly an international organization, with around 40 local chapters and 3 student chapters in 25 countries on 6 continents. We encourage all SIGCHI members to join their local chapter — or if there isn't one in your area, we would love to help you create one. And don't forget virtual communities! SIGCHI hosts dozens of electronic mailing lists on topics ranging from HCI and the Web, to HCI educations, to public policy and beyond. Those lists range from dozens of subscribers to thousands, and are an excellent way to keep up with the field and with friends and colleagues.

Finally, on behalf of ACM SGICHI, we again want to thank the conference committee and all of the hundreds of volunteers who make this conference possible. Their work makes this a rewarding experience for all of us.

Gerrit C. van der Veer
SIGCHI President

John "Scooter" Morris
SIGCHI Vice-President for Conferences

About SIGCHI

CHI 2015 is sponsored by ACM's Special Interest Group on Computer-Human Interaction (ACM SIGCHI). ACM, the Association for Computing Machinery, is an educational and scientific society uniting the world's computing educators, researchers, and professionals to inspire dialogue, share resources, and address the field's challenges. ACM strengthens the profession's collective voice through strong leadership, promotion of the highest standards, and recognition of technical excellence. ACM supports the professional growth of its members by providing opportunities for life-long learning, career development, and professional networking. ACM offers its more than 100,000 worldwide members cutting edge technical information through world class journals and magazines, dynamic special interest groups, and globally recognized conferences.

Visit www.acm.org for more information about the ACM.

SIGCHI is the premier international society for professionals, academics, and students who are interested in human-computer interaction (HCI). We provide a forum for the discussion of all aspects of HCI through our conferences, including our flagship CHI conference, publications, web sites, email discussion groups, and other services. We advance education in HCI through courses, workshops, and outreach, and we promote informal access to a wide range of individuals and organizations involved in HCI. Members can be involved in HCI-related activities with others in their region through local SIGCHI chapters. Come to the SIGCHI Town Hall meeting on Wednesday, April 22, at 12:50 to 14:30 in Room 308 or visit www.sigchi.org to learn more about SIGCHI.

Membership Information

Please contact ACM's Member Services Dept.
Online: www.acm.org
Tel: +1-800-342-6626 (USA/Canada)
+1-212-626-0500 (International)
Fax: +1-212-944-1318
Email: acmhelp@acm.org

Write:

Association for Computing Machinery, Inc.
General Post Office
P.O. Box 30777
New York, NY 10087-0777, USA

CHI 2015 Papers and Notes Chairs' Welcome

The CHI Papers and Notes programme is continuing to grow and this year! We are pleased that CHI continues to be the leading conference for research in human-computer interaction.

This year we considered more than 2120 submissions, ~600 of which were notes. This represents a continuation of ~4% annual growth in submissions. We accepted 486 submissions (~23%): 379 papers and 107 notes.

The CHI review process demands a tremendous amount of work from all areas of the human-computer interaction community. As co-chairs of the process, we are amazed at the ability of the community to organize itself to accomplish this task. We would like to thank the 2809 individual reviewers for their careful consideration of these papers. Every submission received at least three external reviews.

We also deeply appreciate the huge amount of time donated to this process by the 225-member program committee, who paid their own way to attend the face-to-face program committee meeting, an event larger than most ACM conferences.

We are proud of the work of the CHI 2015 program committee and hope that you enjoy these papers and notes, which represent the best research in human-computer interaction.

CHI 2015 Paper and Notes Chairs

Andy Cockburn
University of Canterbury

Janna McGrenere
University of British Columbia

Table of Contents

Visualizing Data

Session Chair: Christophe Hurter, *IRIT, France*

Interaction in 3D Space

Session Chair: Kening Zhu, *City University of Hong Kong, China*

Understanding & Evaluating Performance

Session Chair: Richard Davis, *Singapore Management University, Singapore*

Music & Art

Session Chair: Jonathan Hook, *University of York, UK*

Supporting Change in Developing Countries

Session Chair: Anirudha Joshi, *Indian Institute of Technology, Bombay, India*

Privacy, Security & Interruptions

Session Chair: Emilee Rader, *Michigan State University, USA*

Making & Sharing Assistive Technologies

Session Chair: Suranga Nanayakkara, *Singapore University of Technology and Design, Singapore*

Matching & Facilitating Social Interactions

Session Chair: Jofish Kaye, *Yahoo!, USA*

Family Communication

Session Chair: Siân Lindley, *Microsoft Research, UK*

Crowdsourcing Fans & Friends

Session Chair: Shaun Lawson, *University of Lincoln, UK*

Managing Personal Privacy

Session Chair: Sameer Patil, *Yahoo Labs, USA*

Health Sensors & Monitoring

Session Chair: Regan Mandryk, *University of Saskatchewan, Canada*

Kids Haptic, Wearable, Tangible Learning

Session Chair: Shuli Gilutz, *Interdisciplinary Center (IDC) Herzliya, Israel*

Motivation & Participation

Session Chair: Meredith Morris, *Microsoft Research, USA*

Sustainability & Recycling

Session Chair: Adrian Clear, *Lancaster University, UK*

Tangible Interactions

Session Chair: Otmar Hilliges, *ETH Zurich, Switzerland*

New Evaluation Approaches

Session Chair: David England, *Liverpool John Moores University, UK*

Evaluating Crowdsourcing

Session Chair: Bongwon Suh, *Seoul National University, Republic of Korea*

Smart Smartphone Authentication

Session Chair: Andrea Bianchi, *Sungkyunkwan University, Republic of Korea*

Healthcare Bias, Engagement & Adaptation

Session Chair: Tae-Jung Yun, *Samsung Electronics, Republic of Korea*

Storytelling in InfoVis

Session Chair: Charles Perin, *INRIA Saclay, France*

Grip, Move & Tilt: Novel Interaction

Session Chair: Jessica Cauchard, *Stanford University, USA*

Interactive Video & Collaborative Annotations

Session Chair: Amy Ogan, *Carnegie Mellon University, USA*

HCI for the Elderly

Session Chair: Maria Wolters, *University of Edinburgh, UK*

The Impact of Crowd Work on Workers

Session Chair: Jaime Teevan, *Microsoft Research, USA*

Social Media and Mobile Camera Privacy

Session Chair: Pam Briggs, *Northumbria University, UK*

DIY Healthcare: Apps & Wearables

Social Embodied Interaction

Innovation in Theories & Products

Design and 3D Object Fabrication

HMDs in Augmented & Virtual Reality

Session Chair: Shahram Izadi, *Microsoft Research, UK*

Tangible Interaction with Phones

Session Chair: Shengdong Zhao, *National University of Singapore, Singapore*

UI Impact on Performance & Decisions

Session Chair: Tom Gross, *University of Bamberg, Germany*

Player Performance & Experience in Games

Session Chair: Jan Smeddinck, *University of Bremen, Germany*

Neighborhoods & Disadvantaged Communities

Session Chair: Katharina Reinecke, *University of Michigan, USA*

Enhanced Security with Passwords & CAPTCHAs

Session Chair: Serge Egelman, *University of California, Berkeley, USA*

Accessibility at Home & on The Go

Session Chair: Hironobu Takagi, *IBM Research, Japan*

Visualizing Statistics & Graphs

Understanding Everyday Use of Mobile Phones

GUI Size, Resolution & Layout

Kids Social, Emotional & Special Needs

HCI for Civic Engagement

Session Chair: John Vines, *Newcastle University, UK*

Security Feedback & Warnings

Session Chair: Alexander De Luca, *University of Munich, Germany*

Wellness & Wearables

Session Chair: Marianna Obrist, *University of Sussex, UK*

Task Interruption & Resumption

Session Chair: Martin Halvey, *University of Strathclyde, UK*

Voting & Volunteerism

Session Chair: Andres Monroy-Hernandez, *Microsoft Research, USA*

Socio-Political Interactions

Session Chair: Liang Gou, *Almaden, USA*

Understanding Health through Online Behavior

Session Chair: Mary Czerwinski, *Microsoft Research, USA*

Natural User Interfaces for InfoVis

Session Chair: Bongshin Lee, *Microsoft Research, USA*

Interactive & Multi-Surface Maps

Session Chair: Brent Hecht, *University of Minnesota, USA*

Robot Personalities

Session Chair: Malte Jung, *Cornell University, USA*

Mid-Air Gestures and Interaction

Session Chair: Yang Li, *Google Research, USA*

MOOCS & e-Learning

Session Chair: Juho Kim, *Massachusetts Institute of Technology, USA*

Understanding Gamers

Session Chair: Toni-Jan Keith Monserrat, *National University of Singapore, Singapore*

Bridging Communities

Session Chair: Edward Cutrell, *Microsoft Research India, India*

Gender & Technology

Session Chair: Antonella De Angeli, *University of Trento, Italy*

Email & Social Media at Work

Session Chair: Pernille Bjorn, *IT University of Copenhagen, Denmark*

Understanding & Protecting Kids Tech Use

Session Chair: Svetlana Yarosh, *University of Minnesota, USA*

Social Media & Citizen Science

Session Chair: Elena Glassman, *Massachusetts Institute of Technology, USA*

CHI 2015 Organization

General Conference Chairs
Jinwoo Kim, *Yonsei University, Korea*
Bo Begole, *Huawei, USA*

Technical Program

Technical Program Chairs
Woontack Woo, *KAIST, Korea*
Kori Inkpen, *Microsoft Research, USA*

Papers
Andy Cockburn, *University of Canterbury, New Zealand*
Joanna McGrenere, *University of British Columbia, Canada*
Jun Rekimoto, *University of Toyko, Japan*

Case Studies
Danielle Cooley, *DGCooley Consulting, USA*
Joonhwan Lee, *Seoul National University, Korea*

Courses
Regina Bernhaupt, *ICS-IRIT, France*
Matt Jones, *Swansea University, UK*

Interactivity
Julie Rico Williamson, *University of Glasgow, UK*
Juhyun Eune, *Seoul National University, Korea*

Video Showcase
Jinwook Seo, *Seoul National University, Korea*
Rodrigo de Oliveira, *Google, USA*

SIGs
Enrico Rukzio, *Ulm University, Germany*
Simone Barbosa, *PUC-Rio, Brazil*

Doctoral Consortium
Si-Jung "Jun" Kim, *University of Central Florida, USA*
Jaime Teevan, *Microsoft Research, USA*
Sue Fussell, *Cornell University, USA*

Workshops
Juergen Steimle, *Max Planck Institute for Informatics, Germany*
Bongshin Lee, *Microsoft Research, USA*

Works in Progress
Shamsi Iqbal, *Microsoft Research, USA*
Shaun Lawson, *University of Lincoln, UK*
Shendong Zhao, *National University of Singapore, Singapore*

Student Research Competition
Seungyon "Claire" Lee, *Google, USA*
Geehyuk Lee, *KAIST, Korea*

Student Design Competition
Youn-Kyung Lim, *KAIST, Korea*
Anirudha Joshi, *ITT Bombay, India*

Student Game Competition
Floyd Muller, *RMIT University, Australia*
Alessandro Canossa, *Northeastern University, USA*
Soojin Jun, *Yonsei University, Korea*

alt.chi
Silvia Lindtner, *University of California, Irvine, USA*
Morgan Ames, *Intel, USA*
Henry Duh, *University of Tasmania, Australia*

TOCHI Papers
Jeffrey Nichols, *IBM Research, USA*

Best of CHI Awards
Mark Billinghurst, *University of Canterbury, New Zealand*

Panels
Khai Truong, *University of North Carolina, Charlotte, USA*
Elaine M. Huang, *University of Zurich, Switzerland*

Conference Theme Chair
Kyle Hyunsuk Kim, *Hongik University, Korea*

Industry Liaison
Garett Dworman, *TecEd, USA*

Operations

Chair's Assistant
Yoojin Lee, *Yonsei University, Korea*

Chair's Assistant
Nik Martelaro, *Stanford University, USA*

Student Volunteer
Jon Haber, *University of Calgary, Canada*
Siroberto Scerbo, *Virginia Tech, USA*
Jieun Wee, *Seoul National University, Korea*

Technology Liaisons
Sara Drenner, *University of Minnesota-Twin Cities, USA*
Scooter Morris, *University of California, San Francisco, USA*

Webmaster
Juho Kim, *MIT, USA*
TJ Monserrat, *National University of Singapore, Singapore*

Social Media
Max Wilson, *Nottingham University, UK*
Kwangsu Cho, *Sungkyunkwan University, Korea*

Data Managerment
Max Van Kleek, *University of Southampton, UK*
BoYu Gao, *Konkuk University, Korea*

Proceedings
Deana Brown, *Georgia Tech, USA*
Jaejeung Kim, *KAIST, Korea*

Infrastructure Accessibility Chair
Jongbae Kim, *Yonsei University, Korea*

Digital Accessibility Chair
Jeff Bigham, *University of Rochester, USA*

Scheduling
Christophe Hurter, *ENAC, France*
Juho Kim, *MIT, USA*

Mobile Apps
Stephen Oney, *Carnegie Mellon University, USA*
Eiji Hayashi, *Carnegie Mellon University, USA*
Jason Wiese, *Carnegie Mellon University, USA*
Célia Martinie, *Université Paul Sabatier, France*

Video Previews
Fanny Chevalier, *INRIA, France*
Stéphane Huo, *Université Paris-Sud, France*

Posters
Hyun Joo Song, *Seoul National University, Korea*

Translations
Sue Fussell, *Cornell University, USA*
Naomi Yamashita, *NTT, Japan*

Local Hospitality
Junho Choi, *Yonsei University, Korea*

Sponsors, Exhibits & Recruitment
Carol Klyver, *Foundations of Excellence, USA*

Registration
Yvonne Lopez, *Executive Events, Inc. USA*
Brooke Daley, *Executive Events, Inc. USA*

PCS Liaisons
Max van Kleek, *University of Southampton, UK*
Carol Klyver, *Foundations of Excellence, USA*
Scooter Morris, *University of California, San Francisco, USA*

Advancing Muscle-Computer Interfaces with High-Density Electromyography

Christoph Amma, Thomas Krings, Jonas Böer, Tanja Schultz
Karlsruhe Institute of Technology (KIT)
{christoph.amma, tanja.schultz}@kit.edu, {thomas.krings, jonas.boeer}@student.kit.edu

ABSTRACT
In this paper we present our results on using electromyographic (EMG) sensor arrays for finger gesture recognition. Sensing muscle activity allows to capture finger motion without placing sensors directly at the hand or fingers and thus may be used to build unobtrusive body-worn interfaces. We use an electrode array with 192 electrodes to record a high-density EMG of the upper forearm muscles. We present in detail a baseline system for gesture recognition on our dataset, using a naive Bayes classifier to discriminate the 27 gestures. We recorded 25 sessions from 5 subjects. We report an average accuracy of 90% for the within-session scenario, showing the feasibility of the EMG approach to discriminate a large number of subtle gestures. We analyze the effect of the number of used electrodes on the recognition performance and show the benefit of using high numbers of electrodes. Cross-session recognition typically suffers from electrode position changes from session to session. We present two methods to estimate the electrode shift between sessions based on a small amount of calibration data and compare it to a baseline system with no shift compensation. The presented methods raise the accuracy from 59% baseline accuracy to 75% accuracy after shift compensation. The dataset is publicly available.

Author Keywords
EMG; Muscle-Computer-Interfaces; Gesture recognition; electrode arrays.

ACM Classification Keywords
H.5.m. Information Interfaces and Presentation (e.g. HCI): Miscellaneous

INTRODUCTION
While body-worn computer systems become more and more popular, the question of the ideal input devices is still open. Since output devices are often decoupled from the input device, keyboard and touchscreen based solutions are inappropriate. A combination of speech and gesture interfaces seems most promising. While speech is the most intuitive way of entering information in situations in which the computer is perceived as communication partner, gestures are especially suited for spatial or silent and inconspicuous interaction. Gestures could be performed with the whole arm, the hand or the fingers: small sized gestures are generally more appropriate for wearable computing, since large scale gestures are tiring for the user and humans are specialized in fine-grained manipulation with their fingers. Therefore, interfaces allowing for fine-grained gestures and manipulation of virtual objects seem promising. Possible application scenarios are controlling smart glasses or watches with subtle finger motions and gestures.

The application of sensors directly at the fingers itself e.g., with data gloves, is inappropriate in daily-life situations. As a result, multiple approaches have been proposed to sense finger motion distantly. This includes body-worn cameras [12, 19], wrist-worn depth cameras [9], measuring the movement of the tendons [14] or directly measuring the muscle activity via Electromyography (EMG) [2, 10, 16, 17, 22]. The EMG approach and also the related tendon approach make use of the fact that most of the major finger muscles are located at the forearm and thus allow for sensing finger motion by attaching sensors around the forearm instead of the fingers. However, inferring the finger motion from the EMG is a challenging task. The positioning of the sensors is crucial for acquiring the right signals. Furthermore, there are interpersonal differences in the anatomy of the muscles and tissue layers. Wearable EMG based interfaces should not require exact positioning of electrodes and ideally autocalibrate themselves [18].

In contrast to earlier work we explore the use of high-density electrode arrays for EMG based gesture recognition. We analyze the impact of the number of electrodes on the recognition performance and show that such arrays can improve recognition accuracy and thus, an integration in future wearable devices would be beneficial. Additionally we introduce two methods for calibration across recording sessions of the same user and evaluate them on cross-session data. Furthermore the dataset is publicly available and can serve as a common ground for future research.

We do not present a readily wearable interface in this paper but rather want to lay the basis for follow-up work on high-density EMG based interfaces. Although technically challenging, it is possible to miniaturize all components and build devices with a high number of electrodes in the future.

CHI 2015, April 18 - 23 2015, Seoul, Republic of Korea

ACM 978-1-4503-3145-6/15/04$15.00
http://dx.doi.org/10.1145/2702123.2702501

Related Work

There have been numerous works on using EMG for Human Computer Interaction, in particular for recognizing hand and finger movement for gesture control and input. One can discriminate approaches which use electrodes that are precisely attached over the muscle [4, 10] and approaches that use array-like arrangements of electrodes to capture the activity under a certain area of the forearm [2, 16, 17, 18, 22]. Exact positioning of electrodes is in our opinion not a feasible method for wearable devices that need to be taken on and off quickly but is often used for controlling prostheses. Therefore we restrict our review mainly on related work that uses array-like electrode arrangements that do not require exact positioning of single electrodes.

Wheeler et al. [22] introduced a wearable EMG based controller which they used to recognize digits typed on an imaginary number keypad. Eight electrode pairs were arranged in two rings. One was placed distal (close to the wrist) and one proximal (close to the elbow) around the forearm in a regular grid. They applied hidden Markov models and performed cross-session evaluation of the keypad recognition reaching accuracies of 70% to 100% for the individual classes (overall mean accuracy is not reported). The differences of electrode placement between sessions lead to a degradation of performance. They propose the use of more electrodes for spatial oversampling. Saponas et al. [17] used an armband with 8 EMG channels at the proximal part of the forearm. They define 18 gestures which are divided in 4 smaller subsets (containing 4 to 5 classes each) and classified the gestures within each set using Support Vector Machines (SVM). The gestures include subtle motion like tapping of individual fingers. Accuracies from 78% to 95% were reached on the different sets. A preliminary evaluation for a person-independent setting revealed a strong degradation of the accuracy due to inter-individual differences and differences in the positioning of electrodes. In a follow-up work Saponas et al. [18] use a wireless armband and investigate performance under realistic conditions including cross-session evaluation on different days. Similarly to our work they only ask the study participants to try to attach the armband in approximately the same position than in the first session. For two gesture sets each containing three finger gestures they reach an accuracy of 86% and 76% for the within-session case and 86% and 66% for the cross-session case respectively using a calibration gesture to normalize the features. Assad et al. [2] also propose the use of a wearable EMG cuff for various control tasks. The cuff is equipped with 16 dry electrodes and an inertial measurement unit (IMU). In a small user study (N=3), SVMs are used for session-dependent classification of 17 static hand and finger gestures solely on EMG data, for which an accuracy of 96.6% was reached. A set of 9 dynamic gestures was classified with Dynamic Time Warping (DTW) using EMG and IMU data reaching an accuracy of 99%. Samadani and Kulić [16] use a prototype commercial wearable EMG device from Thalmic Labs to analyze person-independent recognition of hand gestures. On data acquired from 25 subjects performing 21 gestures they reach a person-independent accuracy of 49% (chance 4.8%). They use Hidden Markov Models to model the sequential patterns occurring during performing the gesture.

High-density EMG has mainly been used for research on how muscle activation patterns are composed and distributed [11] e.g., the identification and analysis of single motor unit action potentials (MUAP). Recently such electrode arrays have also been used to classify gestures and decode finger and hand motion. Rojas et al. [15] use electrode arrays at the upper arm and forearm to discriminate 12 motion classes, also involving large muscles like the biceps brachii. They reach accuracies of over 90%. Muceli et al. [13] decoded hand (not finger) kinematics from high-density EMG recordings by performing a regression on joint angles with artificial neural networks. They also evaluated the impact of using only a subset of the many EMG channels which revealed that a high number of electrodes increases performance. The evaluations were performed for the within-session case. Wand et. al [21] use EMG arrays attached to the face for silent-speech recognition. They analyze cross-session performance and successfully apply shift compensation by correlating all possible shifts within certain boundary conditions and choosing the shift with highest correlation.

Recently the open NinaPro database was established for myoelectric movement classification [3]. It aims primarily at researchers in the field of prostheses but includes EMG recordings of hand gestures which are of interest for HCI researchers. Besides individually placed electrodes, an armband with eight electrodes is attached around the proximal side of the forearm as it is common in HCI related EMG research. A total of 52 gestures and grasp types were recorded, on which a within-session accuracy of 76% is reached.

Generally, the performance of an EMG based recognition system strongly depends on multiple factors, the type and number of gestures, the type, number and placement of electrodes, and the conditions under which the subjects performed the recordings. Authors defined their own gesture sets and recorded data under varying conditions. Therefore, it is hard to compare different approaches to the problem based on numbers given in different publications. However, related work clearly indicates that competitive accuracies can be reached for the within-session case and a strong degradation of performance is encountered for the session and person independent case. How to deal with major changes in electrode positions across sessions or a generalization of the classifier across subjects are still open research questions.

Structure of the paper

In the remainder of the paper we will 1) give an introduction to forearm EMG, 2) introduce the used methodology, including EMG measurement, classification technique and the algorithms for estimation and correction of electrode displacement, 3) describe the conducted experiment, 4) discuss the results and 5) finally conclude the paper.

BACKGROUND

Figure 1 shows an illustration of the forearm muscles with the relevant finger muscles indicated by numbers. The muscles for the thumb are all located distal and the muscles which

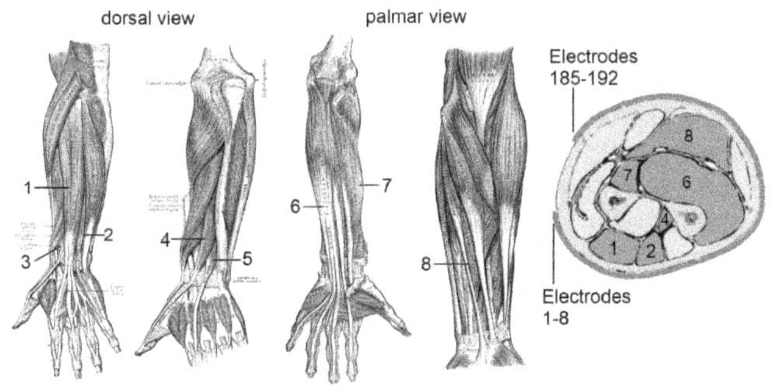

Figure 1. Illustration of the relevant forearm muscles. The dorsal view shows the extensors, the palmar view shows the flexors. The right most picture shows a cross section of the forearm in the middle between the distal and the proximal end. The red line around it indicates the approximate position of the electrode array. The muscles are 1: M. extensor digitorum communis, 2: M. extensor digiti minimi, 3: M. extensor pollicis brevis, 4: M. extensor pollicis longus 5: M. extensor indicis, 6: M. flexor digitorum profundus, 7: M. flexor pollicis longus, 8: M. flexor digitorum superficialis (pictures from Wikimedia Commons)

are in parts responsible for the pinkie and index finger are located distal as well. The main muscles for the fingers except the thumb are located proximal. In our experiment, we apply electrodes at the proximal part of the forearm, therefore we are able to capture at least parts of all finger's muscle activities except the thumb.

Electromyography

Surface Electromyography (EMG) denotes a technique for recording the electrical activity produced by muscles on the surface of the skin. Since the electrical activity correlates with the amount of force the muscle produces, it can be used to measure force and resulting motion.

Motion recognition based on EMG signals incorporates several challenges. One is the positioning of the sensors. In a real world day-to-day scenario, one does not want to narrow down the exact position for recording a certain muscle. Furthermore, there are inter- and intrapersonal differences in the signals. Interpersonal differences arise mainly from differences in anatomy, namely the actual size and position of the muscles and the properties and thickness of the skin and fat layer. In [3] Atzori et al., identify a negative correlation between EMG based gesture recognition accuracy and Body-Mass-Index. Intrapersonal differences arise from the dependence of the signal on parameters like skin conductance which vary with personal and environmental conditions.

METHODOLOGY

Within this section we describe the experimental setup, the applied classification pipeline, and the two methods for electrode shift compensation.

Experimental setup

We use an electrode array with 192 single electrodes arranged in a regular 8x24 grid with an inter-electrode distance of 10 mm. Both electrodes and the amplifier are from OT-Bioelettronica[1]. Figure 2 shows a picture of the array. The

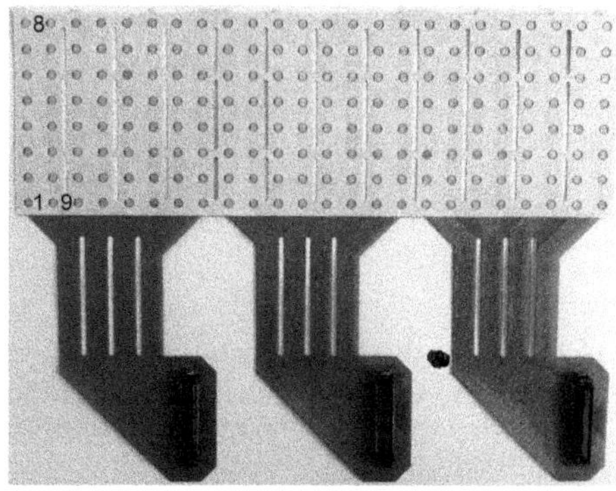

Figure 2. Picture of the electrode array used. The inter-electrode-distance is 10 mm. The electrodes are arranged in a 8x24 grid. Electrode numbering starts at the lower left corner and works columnwise.

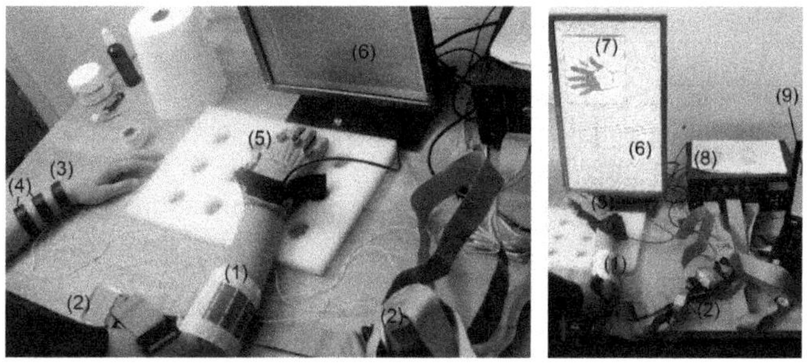

Figure 3. Picture of the actual setup used: (1) electrode array, (2) preamplifier, (3) Reference electrode, (4) DRL circuit, (5) data glove (not used), (6) real-time signal visualization, (7) guiding software, (8) amplifier, (9) recording computer

array is connected via three flat cables, each one with 64 wires. A pre-amplifier is attached to every cable closely to the electrodes to minimize noise caused by cable length. We made bipolar recordings, which means the amplifiers takes the difference between consecutive channels resulting in 192 channels in total. This means, every eights channel does not contain meaningful data, because it contains the difference of the last channel in one column and the first channel in the next column. These channels are therefore ignored for the data analysis, leading to a total of 168 channels of usable data.

The hardware setup we used is actually very bulky, however the works by Assad et al. show for example a wearable system with 16 electrodes. With further miniaturization and integration of components it should be straightforward to increase the number of electrodes. Furthermore our analysis shows that there is no need to use all 168 channels but that a number between 20 and 80 already gives a good trade-off between accuracy and complexity of the technical system.

All data was recorded with a sampling rate of 2048 Hz. The amplifier has an adjustable gain factor, which was set to 1000. The data is delivered via USB to a computer. We used BiosignalsStudio [7] to record the signals, which is a signal recording framework for multimodal data sources that offers synchronization facilities with other programs via timestamps. The data recordings were synchronized with the guiding software that presented the stimuli for the gestures to the user.

[1] http://www.otbioelettronica.it/

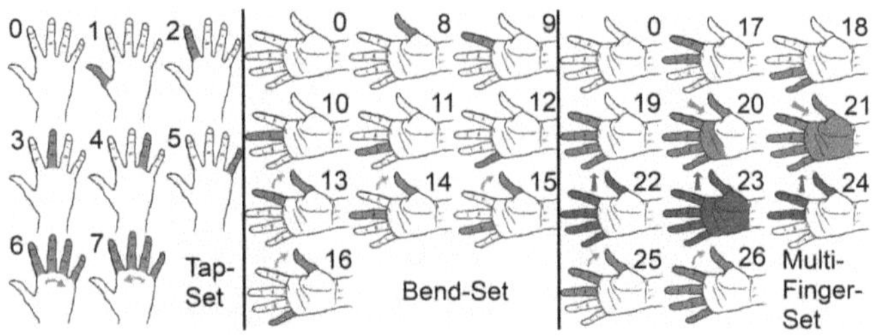

Figure 4. Iconic illustrations of the performed gestures. The gestures were divided into three sets: the tap-set, the bend-set and the multi-finger-set. The idle gesture (0) is contained in all three sets.

Figure 3 shows a picture of our actual recording setup. The subject was sitting on a chair in front of a screen. The screen showed the guiding software and the EMG signals in real-time. The screen was rotated to portrait format so that all 192 EMG channels could be visualized at once. This was done to be able to check the signals continuously for any anomalies e.g., if parts of the array were peeled off from the skin. The subject also wore a Cyberglove dataglove, which was intended to deliver accurate ground truth data for the finger motion. However, due to hardware synchronization issues, we unfortunately weren't able to use the acquired data.

Gesture set

We recorded a pre-defined set of 27 gestures, including an idle gesture. The set of gestures was chosen to cover extension and flexion of each individual finger and also incorporate some typical gestures that might be used in a HCI context. The gestures were organized in three sets, a set of tapping gestures, a set of bending gestures and a set of gestures including more complex multi-finger movements. Figure 4 shows iconic illustrations of the gestures that we recorded, which will be explained below.

Tapping gestures

The tap-set contains gestures which were performed with the hand lying flat on the desk in front of the subject (see left-hand picture in figure 3. For each of the gestures in the set, the subjects were asked to tap once with the finger(s) shown in red (gestures 1 to 5). In case of gestures 6 and 7, all four fingers should be tapped sequentially in the direction of the arrow. The tapping gesture set was designed to contain the muscle activity of the extensors. The actual tap motion after lifting the finger does not necessarily contain actual muscle activation, since it could be performed by simply relaxing the muscles involved in stretching. However this behavior was observed and not enforced.

Bending gestures

The bend-set was designed to contain activity of the flexor muscles. It contains bending of each of the fingers (gestures 8 to 12) and also pinch grips with the thumb (gestures 13 to 16) as these might be appropriate for interaction systems. Subjects were told to rest their hand with the ulnar side on the table (see right-hand picture in figure 3).

Multi-finger gestures

The multi-finger-set contains gestures that involve movement of multiple or all fingers in one gesture. These gestures were performed in the same hand position as in the bend-set. Gestures 17-19 correspond to a bending of two or four fingers similar to the gestures 9-12 in the bend-set. Gestures 20 and 21 correspond to making a fist, where gesture 20 means making a fist without applying force and gesture 21 means making a fist with force. Gestures 22 to 24 correspond to stretching out the fingers marked in blue. Gesture 22 means a light stretch of all fingers and gesture 23 means a stretch with force of all fingers. In gesture 24, thumb, index and middle finger are stretched while ring finger and pinkie are bent. Gestures 25 and 26 correspond to pressing the marked fingers against the thumb and are thus similar to the pinch grip gestures in the bend-set.

Classification Pipeline

We apply a standard classification scheme for our gesture recognition system. It consists of a segmentation step, in which we identify the actual segment of muscle activity within the recorded 3 s of data for each gesture. We then extract features on the segmented data and apply a naive Bayes classifier to discriminate all 27 classes. Before describing the individual steps in detail, we will shortly explain Root-Mean-Square (RMS) and baseline normalization, since both appear multiple times within the section. Root-Mean-Square (RMS) is a common measure of muscle activity. The RMS of an electromyogram has a high correlation to the force generated by the muscle and is therefore an adequate and widely used feature [6] for quantifying muscle activity.

By baseline normalization we mean the subtraction of the average activity measured during idle gestures from all gestures recorded. This allows for compensation of long-term artifacts leading to constant offsets in the activity patterns. Such offsets typically occur, if electrodes are partly or completely detached over multiple repetitions of gestures. Baseline normalization is done after computing the RMS for the data. We subtract the average RMS values acquired for the idle gesture from the RMS values of the desired signal. For each session and gesture set (tapping, bending, multi-finger) we compute the average RMS value over all repetitions of the idle gesture for each of the 168 used channels. The resulting vector is used for the baseline normalization of the data in this particular session and set.

We will now describe the individual steps of the classification pipeline:

Signal Preprocessing

EMG recordings typically suffer from different kind of signal artifacts e.g., powerline noise or skin motion. When recording such a high number of channels in parallel, it is hard to avoid any of these artifacts. Consequently, the presented dataset also contains different kinds of artifacts. Besides powerline and cable motion artifacts, the movement of the skin under the electrodes can lead to partial or complete detachment of single electrodes. The resulting artifacts are usually high amplitude, low frequency signal distortions. The signals were observed in real-time during experiments, to make sure artifacts appear only in a small amount of channels. The number of artifacts is typically higher in the multi-finger-set, since the forceful movement of all fingers leads to more skin deformation than gestures in the tap-set and bend-set. According to [8] and [13], we applied a fourth order butterworth band-pass filter with a pass-band of 20-400 Hz to attenuate dc offset, motion artifacts, and high-frequency noise.

Segmentation

In the segmentation step, we determine the segment containing the actual muscle activity within the 3 s window for each gesture. We use a thresholding approach on a sliding window and search the longest contiguous sequence of windows containing activity. We use non-overlapping windows of length 150 samples, which equates 73.2 ms. The last incomplete window is ignored. On each window, we compute the RMS for each channel. We then perform baseline normalization. Each window is therefore represented by a 168-dimensional vector of RMS values. We apply a spatial order 3 1-dimensional median filter on the vector to compensate local artifacts. As threshold for the segmentation, we compute the average of the summarized RMS values per window. If the sum of RMS vector elements of one window is greater than the threshold, we denote it as active. We then fill gaps in the sequence by setting every window to active whose direct predecessor and successor is active. Finally, the longest contiguous sequence of active windows is selected as the gesture segment.

Feature Extraction

The found segment is partitioned in N windows of equal length. We compute the RMS as feature for each channel on all windows and normalize the mean RMS over all channels. This results in a 168 dimensional feature vector per window. We concatenate the obtained RMS vectors resulting in a $168 \cdot N$ dimensional feature vector. Since the RMS is length normalized, it is irrelevant if the found activity segments do not have the same length.

Naive Bayes classifier

We use a naive Bayes classifier for classification. The feature distributions are modeled by kernel density estimation with Gaussian kernel function. The independence assumption of the naive Bayes classifier is clearly violated in our case since multiple electrodes span across the same muscle and different muscles do not act independently. However, Naive Bayes classifiers are known to work well under such conditions [23].

Estimation of Electrode Displacement

We introduce two methods to estimate the displacement of the electrodes between two sessions based on parts of the sessions data. Both methods are based on the idea to identify characteristic regions within two sessions and determine the shift between these regions. The first method tries to identify an area of low muscle activity over the ulna, the second tries to identify two regions of high muscle activity over the main flexor and extensor muscles. For increased robustness the coordinates of the regions are averaged over all gesture repetitions of one session.

Once the shift between two sessions is determined, data will be shifted accordingly. Since shifts usually are not aligned with the 10 mm inter-electrode distance, the shifted data is interpolated by bicubic interpolation. At the border of the

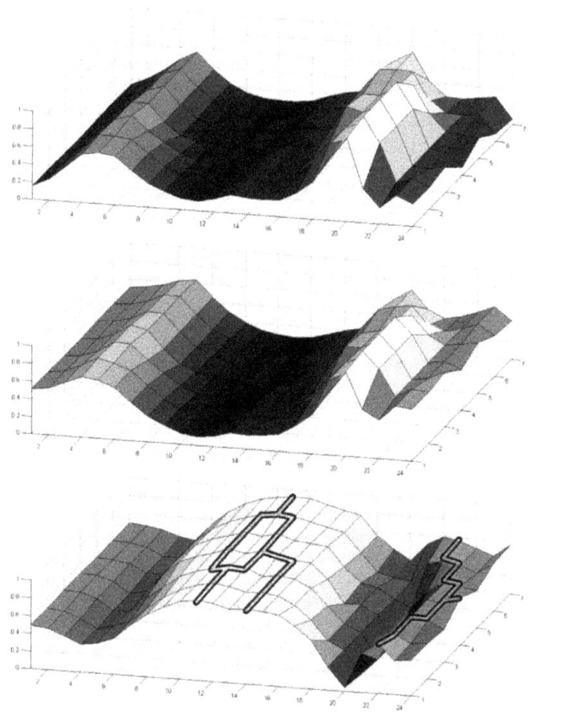

Figure 5. Example steps of identifying the ulna: 1) preprocessed normalized data, 2) data after application of the penalty function, low and high x values receive penalty, 3) found watersheds on the inverted data.

array, there will be a region of unknown data after shifting occurs. This region is filled with the marginal values.

Estimation of ulna position

Directly over the ulna is an area with no muscles and thus very low activity in the EMG. We try to identify the x position of the ulna and shift the array accordingly (only in x position). Since the electrode array is wrapped around the arm, we assume the ulna to be adjusted parallel with the y-axis. Therefore, estimation of the x position is sufficient. It should be noted that this method technically just identifies a region of low activity and we do not verify or claim that this is the actual position of the ulna.

The approach includes the following steps, of which 1-3 are illustrated in figure 5: 1) preprocessing and data normalization, 2) application of a penalty function to favor the region in the middle of the array's x range, 3) finding possible paths by applying the Watershed algorithm [20], 4) choose path with lowest cost using Dijkstra's algorithm [5].

We perform the same preprocessing as for classification. Before application of the penalty function, the data is scaled linearly to the interval $[0, 1]$. We base the penalty function on the density function $\varphi(x)$ of the normal distribution $N(\mu, \sigma^2)$ with $\mu = 12.5$ and $\sigma = 10$. The penalty function p is then computed as:

$$p(x) = 1 - \frac{\varphi(x)}{max(\varphi(x))}, x \in \mathbb{N}$$

It has the properties $p(1) = p(24) \approx 0.5$ and $p(12) = p(13) = 0$ resulting in no penalty in the middle of the array

subject	A	B	C	D	E
circumference in cm	25.5	26	26	30	27
length in cm	26	23	27	30	27

Table 1. Anatomical properties of the subject's forearms.

and a penalty of 0.5 at the borders. After applying the penalty function data is scaled linearly to $[0, 1]$ again and afterwards inverted to comply with the preconditions of the Watershed algorithm. The Watershed algorithm [20] interprets the data as a topographic relief and identifies watersheds (see figure 5, step 3). Since the algorithm identifies all watersheds, we need to find the one with lowest overall EMG activity connecting the distal with the proximal edge of the array. To find the watershed with lowest activity we use the Dijkstra path finding algorithm to find the shortest path in a weighted graph (see [5]). The arrays electrodes are interpreted as nodes and an edge between two nodes exists, if they are directly adjacent (not diagonally). The weight of an edge is the intensity value associated with the node it points to. An additional row of nodes and edges with cost zero is inserted at the top (distal edge) and bottom (proximal edge) of the array and the start and end nodes are chosen as the upper left and lower left corner of the resulting graph. This enforces equal costs for all entry or exit positions at the distal or proximal edges of the array on the x-axis. The mean x value of all nodes in the found path are taken as the position of the ulna, which allows also rational numbers.

Estimation of center of main muscle activity

We estimate the center and shape of the two main areas of muscle activity over the flexors and extensors by fitting a Gaussian Mixture Model (GMM) with two components to the data. That means, each activity area is modeled by one normal distribution. The initial mean values μ_1, μ_2 were set to both ends of the array, $\mu_1 = (1, 4)$ and $\mu_2 = (24, 4)$ to support convergence towards a left and right component of the GMM. Model fitting is done by Maximum-Likelihood estimation with the Expectation-Maximization algorithm. The mean values of the distributions are used to estimate the electrode shift. We compute the average mean values for the flexor and extensor models, compute the two shift values and take the mean as the final resulting shift.

EXPERIMENT

We performed an experiment with five subjects. All were in the age of 20 to 23, one of them female and four male. Every subject contributed five recording sessions on different days. Since every gesture was recorded 10 times (excluding idle gestures which were recorded 30 times) per session, a number of 6500 gestures plus 750 idle gestures were recorded, resulting in 7250 in total.

Experimental Procedure

The array was attached to the forearm at 2 cm to 4 cm distance to the bend of the elbow. The length of the array was less than the circumference of the arm of the subjects. The forearm circumferences ranged from 26 cm to 30 cm (table 1). Therefore it was not possible to completely wrap the array around the forearm. The array was attached in a way that the resulting gap was at the ventral side of the arm where no relevant finger muscles are located. Figure 1 illustrates the typical array position as red thick line around the cross-section of the arm. The different sessions per subject were recorded on different days. As a result, the array was attached at slightly different positions each time. We did this on purpose in order to get a realistic dataset. Invariance against positioning of the electrodes will be of major importance for every possible future wearable EMG system. The dataset allows for examining and evaluating methods to deal with this problem.

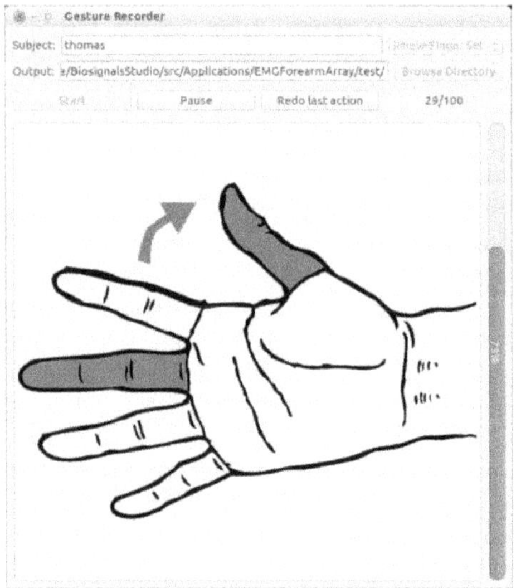

Figure 7. Screen shot of the program guiding the subject through a recording session.

The subjects were guided through the recording session by the guiding software. Figure 7 shows a screen shot of the program. The graphical representations of the gestures from figure 4 were shown to the subject. The subject was asked to perform the presented gesture within a time interval of 3 s. A vertical progress bar at the right indicated the remaining time to perform the gesture. In case of a gesture performance error, it was possible to redo the gesture multiple times. Typical errors were performing the wrong gesture, performing the shown gesture in an awkward way or not performing a gesture in the 3 s time frame. Usually subjects realized performance errors by themselves. Pausing of the procedure was also possible and subjects could pause at their will. The subject was also informed how many gestures he or she already had performed and how many are left (the two numbers in the upper right corner). The three different sets of gestures were recorded in sequence starting with the tap-set, then the bend-set and finally the multi-finger-set with short pauses in between. The main reason for not randomizing the order of the sets was that the multi-finger-set contains gestures with high activity of many muscles. This leads to a stronger skin deformation than the other sets. As these deformations sometimes lead to disconnection of one or more electrodes and robust reattachment is hard once it was disconnected, we chose to fix the order of the sets. Additionally the sets have growing complexity of gestures, so the subject could start with easy gestures and gradually get to more complex ones. Subjects

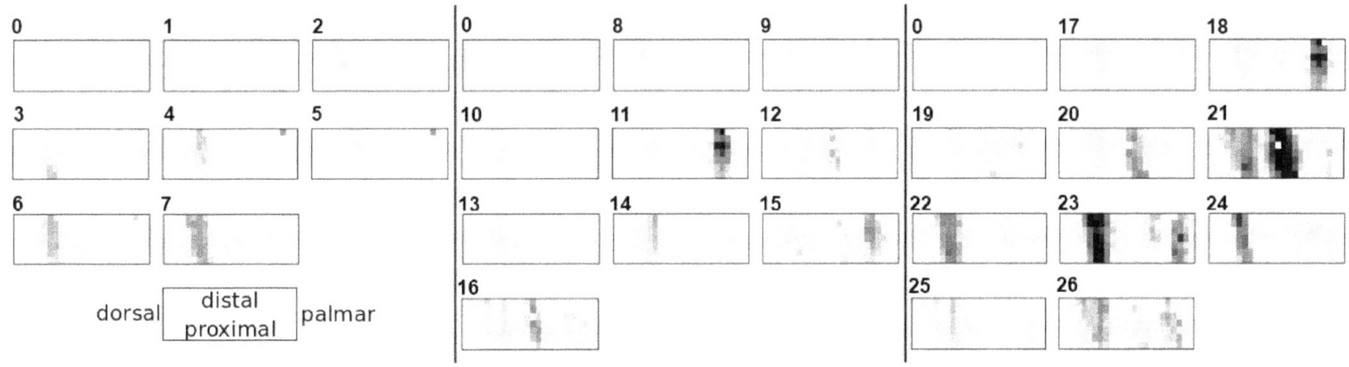

Figure 6. Average muscle activity per gesture for one selected session. The position of the graphs resembles the order in Figure 4. The color map encodes the average RMS value over the ten repetitions per gesture after segmentation and baseline normalization. Each pixel represents on channel. Single isolated channels with very high or low RMS values are defective channels which were not compensated by filtering and baseline normalization.

had to perform every gesture ten times, except the idle gesture, which is present in all three sets and therefore had to be performed 30 times in one session. Within the gesture sets, the order of gestures was randomized with a fixed seed value, resulting in the same order for every session and every subject. The complete *csl-hdemg* corpus is publicly available[2].

The synchronization works with timestamps on a software basis. The recording software and the guiding software run on the same machine and write timestamps on certain events (receive new data, present new stimulus). Afterwards, the recorded data is assigned to the corresponding gesture by comparing the timestamps. Due to buffering and latency in program execution, there is a small imprecision in this assignment. However the delay between stimulus presentation and start of motion by the user is much longer and therefore, the software synchronization is adequate.

Figure 6 shows averaged RMS values for each gesture of one selected recording session. Each of the 27 graphs corresponds with one gesture. The layout is the same as in figure 4. Each pixel represents the averaged RMS value over the ten repetitions of one gesture for one channel. The graphs exactly represent the electrode array layout i.e., every pixel represents the bipolar EMG between two consecutive electrodes and each graph can be read as activity map where white means no activity and black means high activity. The extensor activities can be seen in the left side of the graphs, whereas the flexor activities can be seen in the right part.

RESULTS AND ANALYSIS

Within-session classification

We report the results of within-session classification on the full gesture set of 27 gestures. Since the *idle* gesture is part of all 3 gesture sets, it was recorded 30 times per session. We selected 10 samples (numbers 2,4,7,8,11,13,19,25,26,30) out of the 30 repetitions to end up with a balanced dataset of 10 repetitions for each of the 27 gestures. We perform a leave-one-out cross-validation (LOOCV) on each session and report the average recognition performance. We did this for the case of one window ($N = 1$) and three windows ($N = 3$) per gesture segment. Table 2 shows the corresponding accuracies

[2]`http://csl.anthropomatik.kit.edu/cslhdemg.php`

Sub	S1	S2	S3	S4	S5	Avg	Std
A	83.7	90.0	95.9	94.4	84.4	89.7	5.6
B	89.6	94.4	90.0	88.5	88.2	90.1	2.5
C	87.4	91.5	90.4	88.5	83.3	88.2	3.2
D	90.4	95.6	82.6	90.4	88.2	89.4	4.7
E	93.3	88.9	94.1	92.6	88.2	91.4	2.7
						89.8	3.7

Table 2. Accuracies of the session-wise cross-validations with $N = 1$. Each row corresponds to one subject and the columns denoted by S1 to S5 correspond with session 1 to session 5.

Sub	S1	S2	S3	S4	S5	Avg	Std
A	85.2	90.7	95.2	94.8	90.7	91.3	4.0
B	83.7	92.2	94.1	88.9	90.0	89.8	3.9
C	88.9	93.3	92.6	92.2	88.9	91.2	2.1
D	87.8	92.2	87.0	85.4	84.8	87.4	2.9
E	91.5	89.6	96.3	94.1	90.4	92.4	2.8
						90.4	3.2

Table 3. Accuracies of the session-wise cross-validations with $N = 3$. Each row corresponds to one subject and the columns denoted by S1 to S5 correspond with session 1 to session 5.

of each session together with the mean and standard deviation for each subject and over the complete corpus for $N = 1$. Table 3 shows the results for $N = 3$. Overall, an accuracy of approximately 90% is reached, independent if only one window or three windows were used. We included the $N = 3$ case since this gave the best results in the cross-session evaluation reported below. The relatively low overall standard deviation indicates that the results are stable across subjects and sessions.

Figure 8 shows the accumulated confusion matrix over all subjects and sessions. It can be seen that the *idle* gesture is one of the most confused gestures. This is due to frequent confusion with gestures 1, 2 and 8. Gestures 1 and 8 are tapping and bending with the thumb, for which the flexors and extensors are not located under the area we recorded. A similar reason applies for gestures 2, tapping of index finger. Here the extension is performed by two separate muscles, of which one, the Musculus extensor indicis, is also not located under the area that was recorded. Gestures 22 and 23 are also often confused. They only differ in the amount of force

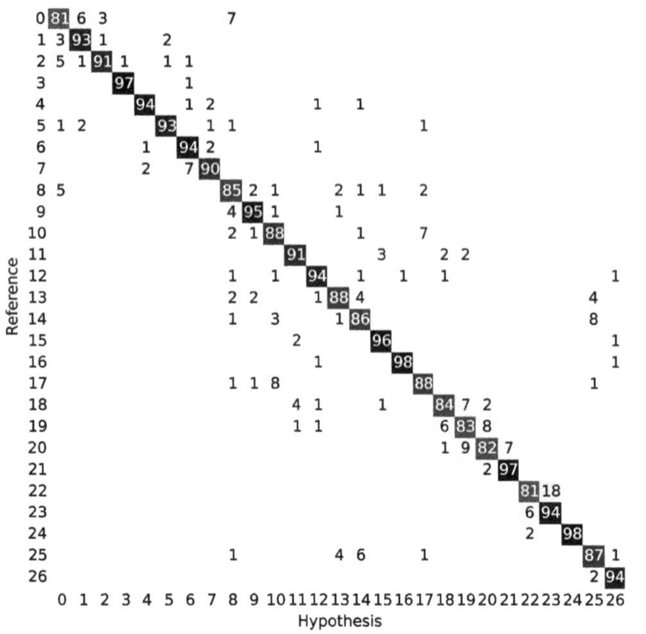

Figure 8. Accumulated confusion matrix for the within-session evaluation over all subjects and sessions. The numbers give the percentage of how often the pair of reference and hypothesis appeared in the classification results. Numbers were rounded and zeros were ommited.

applied and not in the movement itself. The same applies for gestures 19 and 20, which are also frequently confused. Further inspection of the confusion matrix shows, that most of the more frequent confusions relate to similar movements like e.g., gestures 13, 14 and 25 as well as gestures 18 and 19 and gestures 10 and 17. However, it should be noted that all gestures were clearly classified correctly in the majority of cases.

To analyze the impact of the number of electrodes on the recognition performance we evaluated the accuracy depending on the number of used electrodes. The actual electrodes that we used were chosen by maximizing mutual information with the labels on a per session basis. As feature selection method we compute the mutual information of each of the channels with the label vector. Mutual information is computed using kernel density estimation. A detailed description of this algorithm can be found in [1]. This results in different feature sets for each session. However since our aim here is to assess the relation between the number of electrodes and the accuracy and not to find the best overall reduced feature set, this is legitimate. Figure 9 shows the average accuracy for the number of used electrodes. Accuracy is improving when adding new electrodes up to about the number of 100, from where improvements get very small. The results indicate that classification accuracy benefits from a higher number of electrodes than usually used in state-of-the-art EMG based gesture recognition systems.

Shift compensation

We perform a leave-one-out cross-validation on the sessions of each subject to assess the cross-session classification accuracy. This means four sessions were taken as training set and

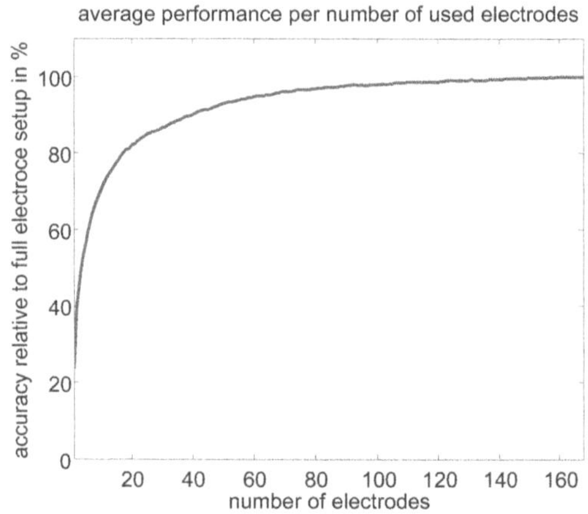

Figure 9. Average classification accuracy by number of used electrodes relative to full setup of 168 channels. Electrodes were selected by highest mutual information with the labels on a per session basis.

	Baseline		GMM		Ulna	
N	1	3	1	3	1	3
A	43.5	60.6	73.9	83.9	69.9	82.9
B	58.1	73.0	65.4	77.2	66.2	76.4
C	55.4	62.3	58.3	71.0	56.8	69.1
D	40.5	53.3	53.9	66.5	59.0	71.3
E	27.9	45.3	67.4	78.4	63.5	76.4
Avg	45.1	58.9	63.8	75.4	63.1	75.2

Table 4. Accuracies of the cross-session evaluation. Each row corresponds to one subject and the columns correspond to the different shift compensation methods including the baseline with no shift compensation and the number of windows used (parameter N).

one session as test set. Calibration was always done against the first session i.e., all data was shifted to the position of the first session before cross validation. Since the calibration gestures were also classified, the reported accuracy might be biased in favor of a higher accuracy compared to a independent set of calibration gestures from the same session. Since this effects only the calibration gesture, an upper bound of 10 biased classifications can be given. We believe the effect on overall results is negligible but want to point out that there might be a small bias.

As baseline system we report the results when performing no shift compensation at all. This resembles the use case of simply putting on a sensor sleeve and using the system without any calibration gestures. We compare the baseline to the two methods we introduced in the paper. Table 4 lists the results. For the GMM based system, we chose gesture 11 and for the ulna method gesture 23 for calibration. Results for all possible calibration gestures are given in the next paragraph. We set the number of windows to $N = 3$ since this gave best results and additionally report the results for $N = 1$ as a reference. Both shift compensation methods reach mean accuracies of around 75% versus 60% of the baseline system. Obviously the shift estimation methods work equally well and lead to a considerable improvement of accuracy although the within-session accuracy cannot be reached. Since all sessions have been taken on different days, it can be as-

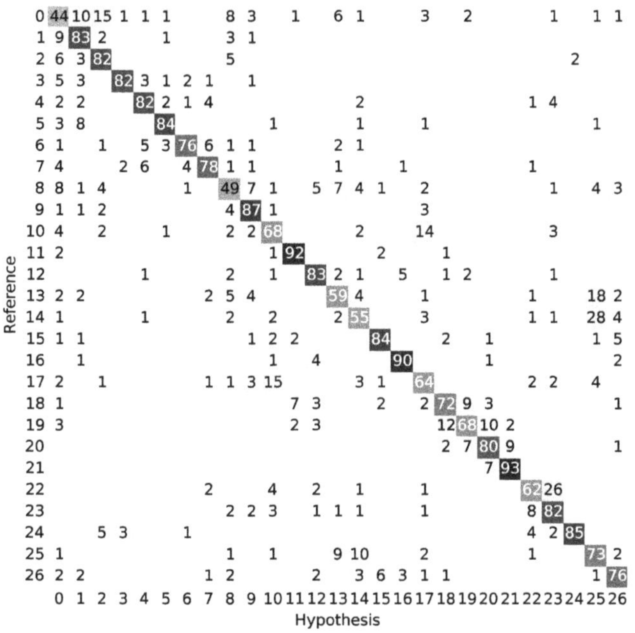

Figure 10. Accumulated confusion matrix for the cross-session evaluation over all subjects and sessions. The numbers give the percentage of how often the pair of reference and hypothesis appeared in the classification results. Numbers were rounded and zeros were ommited.

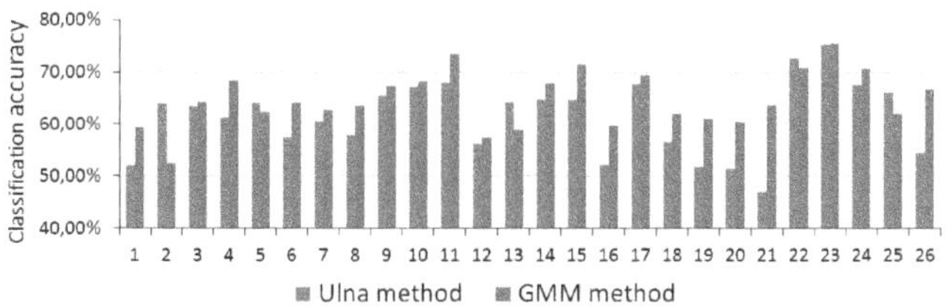

Figure 11. Classification accuracy for different calibration gestures.

sumed that additional factors degrade classification accuracy. These might include differences in skin conductance due to sweat, quality of electrode adhesion and gesture performance differences. Therefore, the within-session classification accuracy can serve as a gold standard though it seems unlikely to come very close to it. The accumulated confusion matrix for the ulna method is shown in figure 10. Pairs of gestures that were already often confused in the within-session evaluation get even more often confused for the cross-session evaluation. Additionally we observe an overall increase of smaller amounts of confusion for a variety of gestures.

Calibration gesture

We investigated which gestures are best suited to estimate the shift of the electrode array. We took each of the 26 non idle gestures as calibration gestures and determined the classification accuracy. Figure 11 shows the results for both methods of shift estimation. The ulna method works best for gestures 22 and 23 with 23 working best. Both gestures involve stretching of all fingers once with low force (gesture 22) and once with high force (gesture 23). Both gestures seem to lead to a distinct zone of inactivity along the y-axis. We didn't validate if the found path is actually consistent with the anatomical

Gestures	WS	CS
11,17,21,23,24	98.8	94.6
1,2,3,11,17,18,21,23,24,25	97.0	92.3
1,2,3,7,9,10,11,13,14,17,18,21,23,24,25	94.2	83.9

Table 5. Results for the restricted gesture sets given as mean accuracy for the within-session (WS) and cross-session (CS) case.

position of the ulna. For the GMM method, gestures 11, 14, 23, and 24 lead to highest accuracies with 11 performing best. Gestures 11 and 14 both consist of bending of the middle finger, once without any other finger involved (gesture 11) and once against the thumb (gesture 14). Both gestures lead to distinguished areas of activity that can be well modeled by two normal distributions.

Restricted gesture sets

We evaluated the classification accuracy on subsets of the complete gesture set to assess performance in more practical scenarios. Using the full set in a real HCI application is not feasible since a) the burden for the user to learn so many gestures is too high and b) we now know that some gestures are hard to recognize. We therefore chose subsets of size 5, 10, and 15 gestures, each containing the two calibration gestures and gestures that we chose based on the accuracy and possible suitability in a HCI context. This was done on a best guess base i.e., we did not evaluate the usefulness of our chosen subset in a real application. Table 5 lists the chosen gesture sets and the accuracies achieved. Restricting the gesture set increases the accuracy for both the within- and between-session case above 90% in all cases except one.

CONCLUSION AND FUTURE WORK

In this paper we investigate the use of EMG electrode-arrays for gesture recognition. We recorded a set of 27 gestures from five subjects in five different sessions. We introduce a baseline recognition system using a Naive Bayes Classifier that reaches an accuracy of 90% on the 27 classes, showing the feasibility of our approach to classify a large number of partly subtle finger gestures. We show that in our setup, best performance is reached for a number of 100 and above used electrodes. This shows that increasing the number of electrodes leads to performance gains. We also investigate the cross-session performance. Since sessions of one subject were recorded on different days with slightly varying electrode positions, this is more challenging. The accuracy for the cross-session case drops to 59%. We introduce two methods for calibration by estimating the shift in electrode positions across sessions by making use of anatomical characteristics. With both methods we achieve an accuracy of approximately 75%.

Currently the equipment to make such high-density recordings is still very bulky and not made for mobile use. However such devices might become ubiquitous in a few years and we believe that our results motivate that this is a direction which is worth to pursue. The dataset itself will allow for further analysis of the spatio-temporal distribution of the EMG activity during the recorded finger movements. Such high-density recordings enable for example the use of source-separation methods which we plan to investigate in the future. It might also serve as a common ground for future research and performance comparison of different approaches on EMG based wearable interfaces.

ACKNOWLEDGMENTS

This research was partly funded by Google through a Google Faculty Research Award.

REFERENCES

1. Ang, K. K., Chin, Z. Y., Zhang, H., and Guan, C. Mutual information-based selection of optimal spatial–temporal patterns for single-trial eeg-based bcis. *Pattern Recognition 45*, 6 (2012), 2137–2144.
2. Assad, C., Wolf, M., Theodoridis, T., Glette, K., and Stoica, A. Biosleeve: a natural emg-based interface for hri. In *Proc. HRI 2013* (2013), 69–70.
3. Atzori, M., Gijsberts, A., Kuzborskij, I., Heynen, S., Mittaz Hager, A., Deriaz, O., Castellini, C., Muller, H., and Caputo, B. Characterization of a benchmark database for myoelectric movement classification. *Neural Systems and Rehabilitation Engineering, IEEE Transactions on PP*, 99 (2014), 1–1.
4. Castellini, C., Fiorilla, A. E., and Sandini, G. Multi-subject/daily-life activity EMG-based control of mechanical hands. *Journal of neuroengineering and rehabilitation 6* (Jan. 2009), 41.
5. Cormen, T. H., Leiserson, C. E., Rivest, R. L., Stein, C., et al. *Introduction to algorithms*, vol. 2. MIT press Cambridge, 2001.
6. De Luca, C. J. The use of surface electromyography in biomechanics. *Journal of applied biomechanics 13* (1997), 135–163.
7. Heger, D., Putze, F., Amma, C., Wand, M., Plotkin, I., Wielatt, T., and Schultz, T. Biosignalsstudio: a flexible framework for biosignal capturing and processing. In *Proc. KI 2010* (2010), 33–39.
8. Hermens, H. J., Freriks, B., Merletti, R., Stegeman, D., Blok, J., Rau, G., Disselhorst-Klug, C., and Hägg, G. *European recommendations for surface electromyography*. Roessingh Research and Development The Netherlands, 1999.
9. Kim, D., Hilliges, O., Izadi, S., Butler, A. D., Chen, J., Oikonomidis, I., and Olivier, P. Digits: freehand 3d interactions anywhere using a wrist-worn gloveless sensor. In *Proc. UIST 2012* (2012), 167–176.
10. Kim, J., Mastnik, S., and André, E. Emg-based hand gesture recognition for realtime biosignal interfacing. In *Proc. IUI 2008* (2008), 30–39.
11. Merletti, R., Holobar, A., and Farina, D. Analysis of motor units with high-density surface electromyography. *Journal of electromyography and kinesiology 18*, 6 (2008), 879–890.
12. Mistry, P., Maes, P., and Chang, L. Wuw-wear ur world: a wearable gestural interface. In *CHI EA 2009*, ACM (2009), 4111–4116.
13. Muceli, S., and Farina, D. Simultaneous and proportional estimation of hand kinematics from emg during mirrored movements at multiple degrees-of-freedom. *Neural Systems and Rehabilitation Engineering, IEEE Transactions on 20*, 3 (2012), 371–378.
14. Rekimoto, J. Gesturewrist and gesturepad: Unobtrusive wearable interaction devices. In *Proc. ISWC 2001* (2001), 21–27.
15. Rojas-Martínez, M., Mañanas, M. A., Alonso, J. F., et al. High-density surface emg maps from upper-arm and forearm muscles. *J. Neuroeng. Rehabil 9*, 85.10 (2012), 1186.
16. Samadani, A.-A., and Kulić, D. Hand gesture recognition based on surface electromyography. In *Proc. EMBC 2014*, IEEE (2014), 4196–4199.
17. Saponas, T. S., Tan, D. S., Morris, D., and Balakrishnan, R. Demonstrating the feasibility of using forearm electromyography for muscle-computer interfaces. In *Proc. SIGCHI 2008* (2008), 515–524.
18. Saponas, T. S., Tan, D. S., Morris, D., Turner, J., and Landay, J. A. Making muscle-computer interfaces more practical. In *Proceedings of the SIGCHI Conference on Human Factors in Computing Systems*, ACM (2010), 851–854.
19. Starner, T., Auxier, J., Ashbrook, D., and Gandy, M. The gesture pendant: A self-illuminating, wearable, infrared computer vision system for home automation control and medical monitoring. In *Wearable computers, the fourth international symposium on*, IEEE (2000), 87–94.
20. Vincent, L., and Soille, P. Watersheds in digital spaces: an efficient algorithm based on immersion simulations. *IEEE transactions on pattern analysis and machine intelligence 13*, 6 (1991), 583–598.
21. Wand, M., Schulte, C., Janke, M., and Schultz, T. Compensation of recording position shifts for a myoelectric silent speech recognizer. In *Proc. ICASSP 2014* (2014), 2094–2098.
22. Wheeler, K. R., Chang, M. H., and Knuth, K. H. Gesture-based control and emg decomposition. *Systems, Man, and Cybernetics, Part C: Applications and Reviews, IEEE Transactions on 36*, 4 (2006), 503–514.
23. Zhang, H. The optimality of naive bayes. *AA 1*, 2 (2004), 3.

Proprioceptive Interaction

Pedro Lopes, Alexandra Ion, Willi Mueller, Daniel Hoffmann, Patrik Jonell, Patrick Baudisch
Hasso Plattner Institute
Potsdam, Germany
{firstname.lastname}@hpi.de

ABSTRACT

We propose a new way of eyes-free interaction for wearables. It is based on the user's *proprioceptive* sense, i.e., rather than seeing, hearing, or feeling an outside stimulus, users feel the pose of their own body.

We have implemented a wearable device called Pose-IO that offers input and output based on proprioception. Users communicate with Pose-IO through the pose of their wrists. Users enter information by performing an *input* gesture by flexing their wrist, which the device senses using a 3-axis accelerometer. Users receive output from Pose-IO by finding their wrist posed in an *output* gesture, which Pose-IO actuates using electrical muscle stimulation. This mechanism allows users to interact with Pose-IO without visual or auditory senses, but through the *proprioceptive* sense alone.

We developed three simple applications that demonstrate symmetric proprioceptive interaction, where input and output occur through the same limb, as well as asymmetric interaction, where input and output occur through different limbs. In a first user study, participants using a symmetric proprioceptive interface re-entered poses received from Pose-IO with an average accuracy of 5.8° despite the minimal bandwidth offered by the device. In a second, exploratory study, we investigated participants' emotional response to asymmetric proprioceptive interaction and the concept of the user's body serving as interface. Participants reported to enjoy the experience (*mean*= 4.6 out of 5).

Author Keywords: muscle actuation; proprioception; IO;
ACM Classification Keywords: H5.2 [Information interfaces and presentation]: User Interfaces. - Graphical user interfaces.

INTRODUCTION

Wearable interfaces, such as gesture-based watches [35, 26] allow users to interact with information anywhere, anytime. In order to minimize interference with the user's primary task, such as walking or having a conversation [1], many wearable devices are designed specifically for eyes-free use. Unfortunately, these devices typically use auditory feedback, which interferes with auditory tasks. Haptic interfaces, such as vibrating bracelets, show promise here [26], but are limited in terms of bandwidth [25] and are hard to learn because they lack mnemonic properties [21].

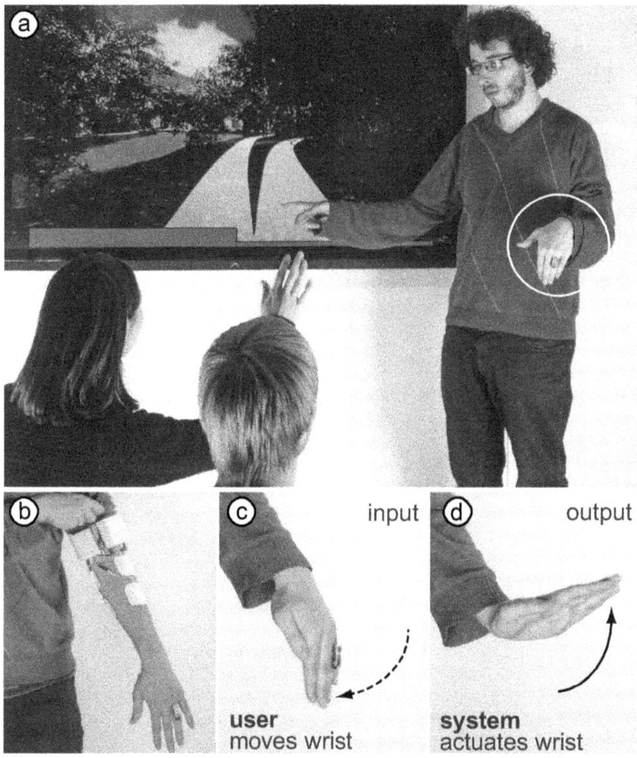

Figure 1: (a) Proprioceptive interaction allows users to interact eyes-free based on their sense of proprioception alone, allowing this user to rewind a video, while maintaining eye contact with his audience. (b) The user is wearing our proof-of-concept bracelet called Pose-IO. (c) It reads input by sensing the same wrist's flexion using an accelerometer and (d) it sends output to the user by actuating the user's wrist using electrical muscle stimulation.

We therefore propose a different type of modality for wearable interaction, namely *proprioception*, which is the users' sense of the relative position of neighboring limbs of the body. As we demonstrate in this paper, we can use proprioception for input *and output*.

PROPRIOCEPTIVE INTERACTION

Figure 1 illustrates the concept of proprioceptive interaction. Proprioceptive interaction allows for input and output by

CHI 2015, April 18 - 23, 2015, Seoul, Republic of Korea
Copyright is held by the owner/author(s). Publication rights licensed to ACM. ACM 978-1-4503-3145-6/15/04…$15.00
http://dx.doi.org/10.1145/2702123.2702461

posing one of the user's limbs, here the user's wrist. Users enter information by performing an input gesture, here flexing their wrists inwards. The device senses this using its accelerometer. Users can perform such a gesture eyes-free, as their proprioceptive sense informs them about the position of their wrist. Users receive output from a proprioceptive interface by finding their body posed in an output gesture, here again the wrist. Also, they perceive this eyes-free by means of their proprioceptive sense.

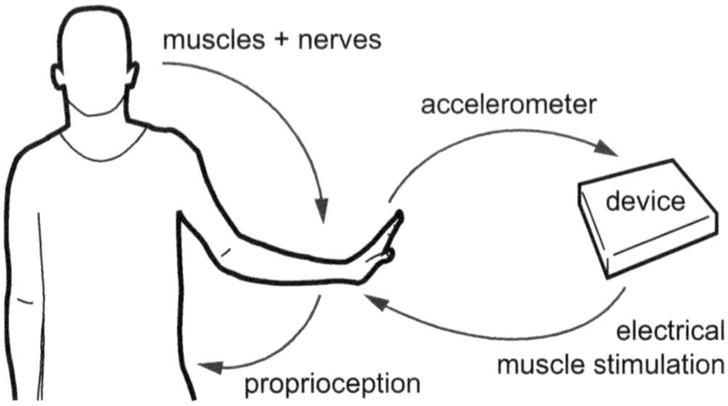

Figure 2: Symmetric proprioceptive interaction revolves around the pose of one of the user's limbs, here the wrist.

The interaction shown in Figure 2 is of the "purest" form in that input and output occur through the same limb, here the wrist. This "symmetric" interaction results in a particularly intuitive interaction [30]. However, proprioceptive input and output may also occur through different limbs, e.g., when the application requires more input than output or more output than input. We call this asymmetric proprioceptive interaction, which is depicted in Figure 3.

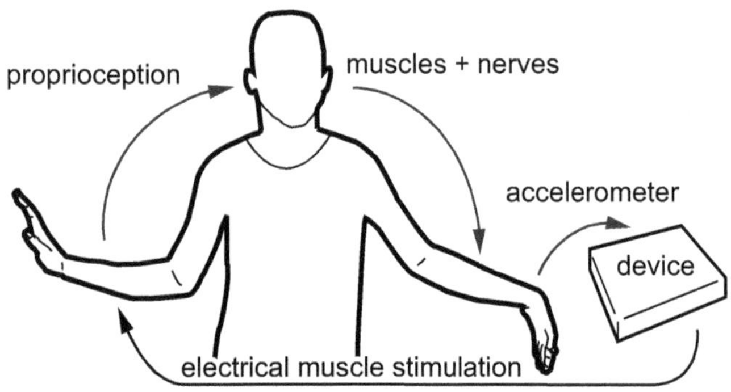

Figure 3: In an asymmetric proprioceptive interaction, input and ouput occur through different limbs.

The Pose-IO device

Figure 4 shows Pose-IO, the proof-of-concept proprioceptive device we have created. It offers input and output based on proprioception. We implemented Pose-IO in the form of a bracelet, which users wear under their clothing. Pose-IO receives input from the user by means of a wireless accelerometer attached to the user's hand. Pose-IO produces output by writing to the user's arm muscles using electrical muscle stimulation (EMS) through four electrodes attached to the user's arm.

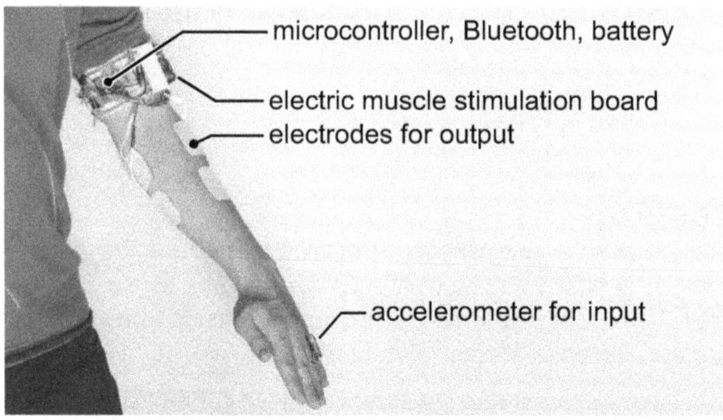

Figure 4: The main components of Pose-IO.

APPLICATIONS

We have implemented three simple applications, each of which highlights a different strength of proprioceptive interaction.

(1) Symmetric Proprioceptive Interaction

Figure 1a illustrates our video-scrubbing tool for presenters based on the Pose-IO device, which is an example of symmetric proprioceptive interaction. One of the audience members just asked whether the presenter could show the video one more time. Figure 5 shows how the presenter responds. (a) He invokes Pose-IO's video scrubber by performing an invocation gesture, here by shaking his wrist back and forth. (b) Pose-IO responds by posing the users' wrist, so as to represent the current video playback position, which the user perceives through his sense of proprioception. The user lets the video run for another moment during which Pose-IO keeps updating the user's wrist position, continuously extending it upwards, which again the user perceives through his sense of proprioception. (c) The user now rewinds the video by flexing his wrist back down to the desired play position. He uses sufficient force to override Pose-IO's control over the wrist. Pose-IO responds by scrubbing in real time, allowing the user to locate the intended position.

(b, c again) To emphasize his answer, the presenter replays the scene one more time. This time, he moves the video play head to its intended position without iterating, but by posing his wrist directly in the same position as before, based on his proprioceptive sense alone. (d) The presenter is just about to dismiss Pose-IO using a strong flick gesture, when one of the attendees throws him a marker. He catches the marker and Pose-IO interprets the abrupt movement as a dismiss gesture and deactivates itself. This is by design, so as to allow users' primary tasks to take priority whenever necessary.

This particular scenario uses the same limb for input and output, allowing us to implement a *symmetric* interaction, i.e., an interaction where the same modality and the same mapping are used for input and output, resulting in a particularly intuitive interaction that even allows users to learn input based on output [30]. This is a benefit of proprioceptive interaction over other wearable interfaces, for example, such as vibrotactile feedback, which has to be combined with a different input modality, such as a set of buttons.

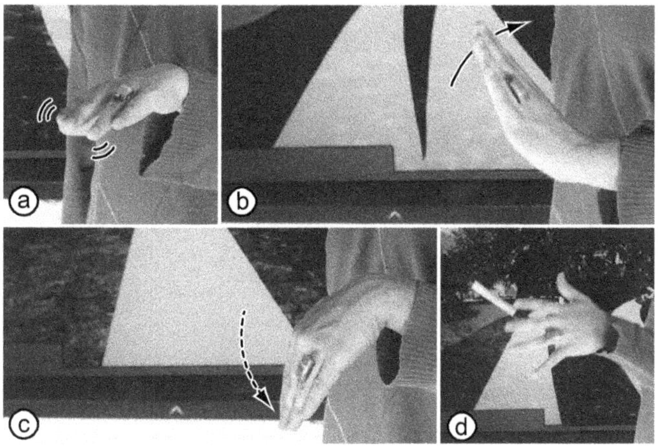

Figure 5: (a) The presenter from Figure 1 invokes the Pose-IO video scrubber by performing a shake gesture, which (b) causes his wrist to track with the video play head. (c) He scrubs backwards. (e) When someone throws him a marker, his abrupt hand movement automatically dismisses Pose-IO.

(2a) Asymmetric Interaction

Proprioceptive interaction does not have to be symmetric though. We demonstrate this at the example of the eyes-free reaction game *red hands* [29]. Traditionally, this children's game is played by two players, one of which is trying to slap the hands of the other. With the use of Pose-IO, we turn red hands into a solitaire computer game. We partition the user's body as depicted in Figure 6, which is why the interface is asymmetric. Here the user's right hand represents the computer opponent; the left hand continues to belong to the player. At every turn, the computer hand tries to slap the player's hand (i.e., game *output*); the player's objective is to evade the slap (i.e., game *input*). The red-hands application detects successful slaps based on *acoustic* recognition (similar to [13]), i.e., a wearable microphone in a small bracelet around the player's wrist.

Red hands is an example of asymmetric proprioceptive interaction in that output goes to the right hand, while the device receives input from the left hand.

To make red hands playable, it offers multiple levels of difficulty. The first level gives players several hundred milliseconds of advance warning before slapping. It does so by briefly flicking the computer hand before actually attacking. This warning period gets shorter on subsequent levels. Since Pose-IO talks directly to the user's muscles, it can actuate the hands surprisingly fast: if we set the warning period to zero, we found player's chance to evade the slap to be no better than random (see also Study 2). This ability for *very* fast interaction stems from talking to the user's muscles directly—a key strength of our approach.

Similar to the presenter tool, red-hands for one is played through the sense of proprioception. This allows playing eyes-free, which, interestingly, most of our study participants did even though they were allowed to look (see Study 2 for details).

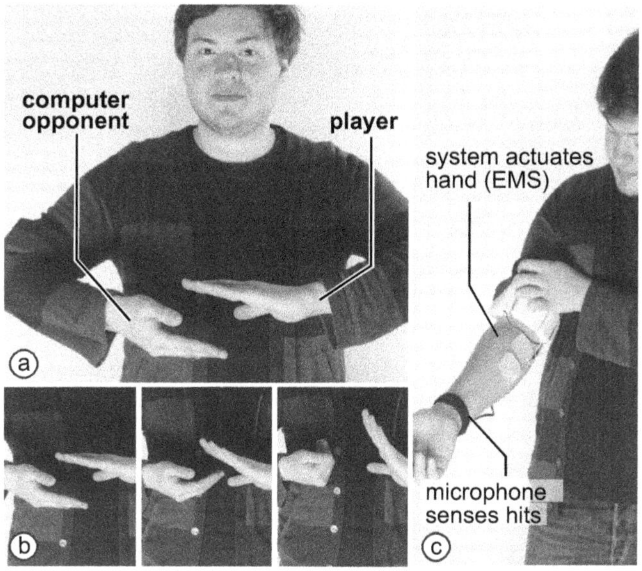

Figure 6: Red-hands for one: Under control of Pose-IO, the user's right hand is trying to slap the user's left hand. The goal is to evade getting slapped by his own hand.

(2b) Asymmetric Interaction with a Spatial Component

To demonstrate an interaction with a spatial component, we implemented *imaginary pong for one.* As depicted in Figure 7, we again partition the user's body so that the actuated hand forms the computer opponent, while the other belongs to the player.

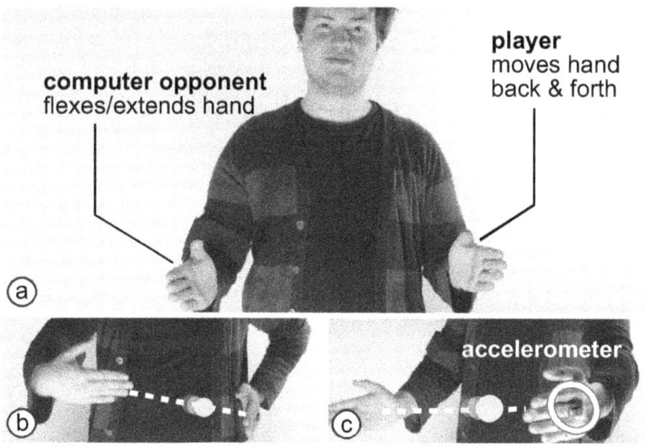

Figure 7: Imaginary pong for one: (b) The computer opponent plays the imaginary ball left by flexing its hand (c) The user returns the shots by moving his hand to where he feels the ball went.

There is no actual rendition of a ball. Instead, players have a notion where the ball should be based on their sense of physics (similar to [3]). The computer opponent may flex the user's hand to play the imaginary ball towards the player's body or it may extend the hand to play the ball away from the user's body. The user's task is to return the shots by moving his hand to where he feels the ball went.

In one version of the game, we added a second Pose-IO bracelet to the player hand in order to render recoil at the moment the imaginary ball hits his palm. This allowed us to add a timing element to the game. As with the two applications presented earlier, users play eyes-free through the sense of their proprioception alone.

CONTRIBUTION, BENEFITS, & LIMITATIONS

Our main contribution is the concept of proprioceptive interaction, here illustrated at the example of wrist pose.

In addition to being wearable, proprioceptive interaction offers four desirable properties: (1) It allows for eyes-free and ears-free use. (2) Instant invocation and dismissal allows users to invoke the device any time and also to return to their primary task immediately when necessary. (3) Symmetric setup allows implementing the same interaction "language" for input and output, resulting in a particularly intuitive interaction that even allows users to learn input based on output [30]. However, (4) this I/O symmetry is not mandatory, and we also explore an interaction modality in which input and output occur at different limbs; we denote it as asymmetric interaction. Thus, depending on the type of application, designers might place input and output freely to best fit their needs.

On the flipside, interaction based on the perception of poses is obviously very low in bandwidth compared to visual or auditory interaction. Its use is therefore only applicable for very simple tasks. Also, any solution that relies on EMS requires an initial step in which the system is calibrated. Furthermore, EMS is still undergoing improvements regarding comfort and ease-of-use (see Related Work).

HARDWARE IMPLEMENTATION

To help readers replicate our proof-of-concept device, we now provide a detailed description of it. As shown in Figure 8, Pose-IO's hardware design has the form of a bracelet with attached electrodes. The bracelet is comprised of 3D-printed sections, each housing the embedded electronics.

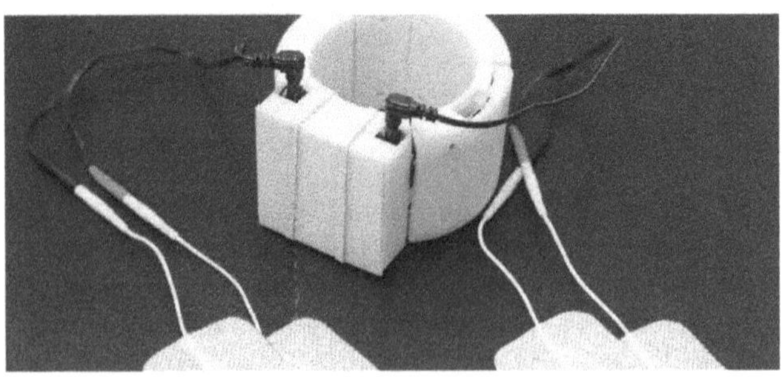

Figure 8: The 3D printed Pose-IO bracelet

Figure 9 shows the opened-up bracelet. Pose-IO writes output to the muscles using a medically-compliant electrical muscle stimulation unit (TruTens V3) connected to four pre-gelled electrodes (50x50mm). The amplification for the Electrical Muscle Stimulation is regulated by two CMOS digital potentiometers with non-volatile memory (X9C103, 10KOhm) controlled by an Arduino Nano using a three-wire serial interface.

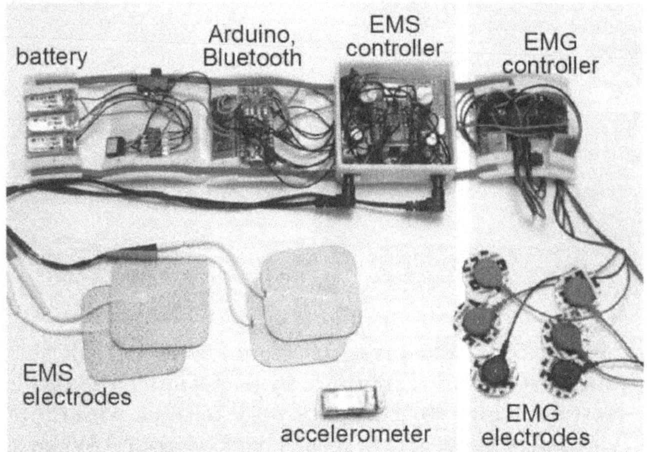

Figure 9: A Pose-IO bracelet unrolled and with the top enclosure removed. On the left side, the additional EMG unit.

Electrical Muscle Stimulation

Pose-IO creates its EMS signal as a biphasic waveform. Its signal pulsates at 120Hz with a pulse-width of 150μs. The current is limited to 100mA, allowing for safe operation. Given that the lowest power settings of the EMS unit did not achieve muscle actuation with the users we tested with, we stepped up the control curve by adding a 10K resistor in parallel to the EMS unit's variable output and input pins. This allows Pose-IO to achieve a smoother output current curve.

Upon first use, users calibrate Pose-IO's EMS device by specifying the lowest stimulus that still leads to a recognizable sensation (there is no visible hand motion at this level) as well as the maximum signal that the user perceives as comfortable. At all times, Pose-IO use is pain-free.

Figure 10 shows the placement of the EMS electrodes on the *extensor digitorum* (wrist extension) and on the *flexor digitorum superficialis* (wrist flexion).

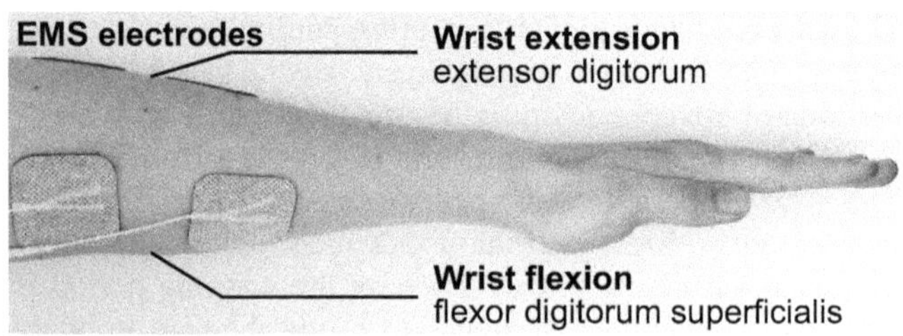

Figure 10: Placement for Pose-IO's EMS electrodes for wrist flexion and extension.

Accelerometer

Pose-IO uses the accelerometer's Y-axis to determine the user's wrist position as the tilt of the user's hand against the horizontal, sampled at 50hz. We also made an extended version of the device that determines the wrist pose with respect to a second IMU worn on the forearm. This allows users to operate Pose-IO in any body posture.

Users invoke and dismiss Pose-IO by holding the hand horizontally and then shaking it, which Pose-IO senses by looking for acceleration along any of the other accelerometer axes. Pose-IO sends commands to its applications, such as aforementioned games, which it runs on the Arduino microcontroller. Pose-IO talks to software running on other computers, such as the video player in the presenter tool scenario, via Bluetooth.

Depending on version, Pose-IO either uses an Axivity WAX3 or WAX9 3-axis wireless accelerometer that users wear on their ring fingers. After removing them from their casing, both measure 34.5mm × 16mm × 15mm and offer 4mg resolution [15]. The WAX-3 sends data over IEEE802.15.4 radio, which we convert using a laptop computer with a radio dongle; we resolved this issue with the newer WAX9, which sends data directly to Pose-IO's Arduino via Bluetooth.

Pose-IO is powered by a 9V power supply comprised of three 3.7V lithium ion rechargeable batteries connected in series and regulated using an L7809CV. Under continuous use, Pose-IO offers around 4 hours of battery-life on the bracelet and 8 hours on the accelerometer.

Control Loop for Symmetric Input & Output

When tracking an external signal, such as the video play position, Pose-IO actuates the user's muscles using a PID control loop. We obtain oscillation-free behavior using the gain factors: Kp=1.2, Kv=1.1, Ki=0.5 (Figure 11). Pose-IO calculates the error derivative on a moving average over the 10 last measured velocities.

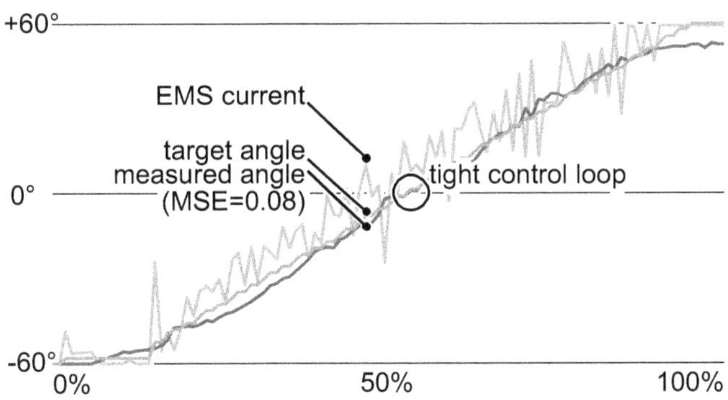

Figure 11: Behavior of Pose-IO's PID control.

If the accelerometer value deviates from the system state by 10°, Pose-IO assumes that the user intends to override the system state—in the video scrubbing scenario this allows users to override the video play head position.

Extended Version Based on Electromyography

The version of Pose-IO described so far relies on the accelerometer for input, which users wear visibly on their hand. For applications in which user control and a computer-control are distributed across two hands, e.g., the two games presented earlier, we achieve a fully hidden version of Pose-IO by dropping the accelerometer and instead using electromyography (EMG) for sensing. EMG senses muscle activity, which is what the two game applications require. Users invoke the EMG version of Pose-IO by over-extending their wrist for 1.5 seconds or longer (Figure 12).

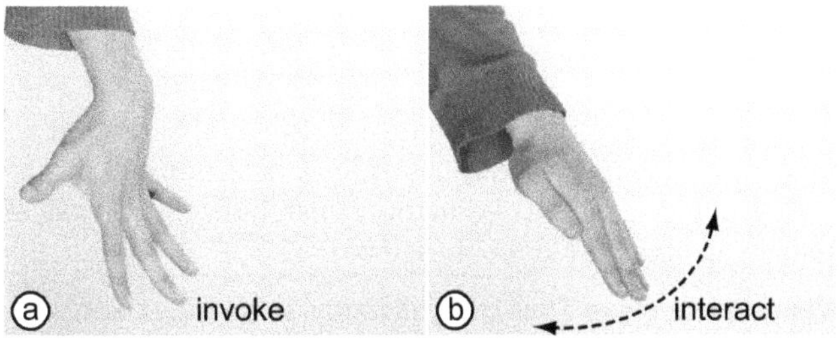

Figure 12: The Pose-IO version based on EMG uses hand-overextension as invocation gesture.

The EMG version of Pose-IO contains two additional electromyography boards shown on the right of Figure 9; they are based on the AD8221 differential amplifier. The EMG boards are connected to six electrode caps, four to sense and two references (20mm diameter), which are placed on the same muscles as for EMS, as depicted in Figure 13. The EMG boards are protected from the EMS current using two relays, which cut the EMG pathway if the EMS is active.

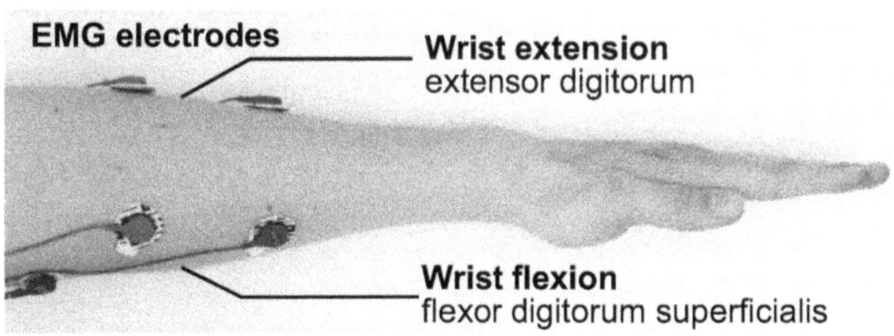

Figure 13: EMG electrode placed on wrist extensor and flexor.

RELATED WORK

The work proposed in this paper builds on proprioceptive feedback and wearable interfaces for eyes-free interaction. Furthermore it is inspired by different approaches to muscle-based input or output.

Proprioception

The human proprioceptive sense allows sensing the position, orientation, and movement of limbs, joints, and muscles [6]. Some debate has taken place whether proprioceptive and kinesthetic are two separate senses. However, the medical community points out that the term proprioception encompasses kinesthesia within [6].

More importantly, research suggests that proprioception is independent from the visual and auditory channels [6,7].

This is the reason why proprioceptive cues (position of limbs, sense of contracting muscles, etc.) are often elicited in bimanual interaction, as they provide users with a sense of where their wrists are relative to one another [19]. In our particular case, i.e., moving the wrist in mid-air, the sense of position of the wrist comes from the muscle spindles and golgi tendon organs which sense the position and movement of muscles, and the joint sensors provide a sense of flexion and extension [7,28].

Apart from research in cognitive and medical domain, proprioception has been often evoked in HCI with regards to haptic feedback. Bark et al. showed how the skin stretch sensation (part of proprioception), which is elicited once a muscle is moved, is superior to vibrotactile feedback for input tasks in which the user controls a cursor [16]. Ban et al. look at how proprioception provides a sense of weight for virtual objects, which the authors manipulate with visual hints in an augmented reality scenario [2].

Wearable Devices That Use the Body as an Input Surface

Skinput is a bio-acoustic sensor that captures the vibrations caused by users tapping on their arms [13]. *Imaginary Interfaces* are spatial non-visual input devices [11]. Users can operate them eyes-free by touching the palm of their non-dominant hand because the touch elicits tactile and proprioceptive senses [12]. *Imaginary Phone* by the same authors goes one step further and instantiates an input-device using the human hand with a small acquisition time because there is no need to reach for the mobile device in the pocket [11].

Non-Visual/Non-Auditory Output Using Mobile Haptics

For an interactive dialog to take place in an eyes-free manner, users need not only eyes-free input, but also output. The predominant eyes-free non-auditory type of output is vibrotactile output. Unfortunately, it is subject to a range of limitations. Karuei et al. found that vibrotactile output degrades in mobile situations, such as while walking [17]. Furthermore, vibrotactile output was found to offer only limited bandwidth [25] and is hard to learn because it lacks mnemonic properties [21].

The concept of unified I/O is common on touchscreen devices [38]. Recently, it was adapted to eyes-free interaction by Roudaut et al. [30]. Their prototype, *Gesture Output*, unifies input and output vocabularies in the form of 2D finger gestures on a mobile phone with an actuated touchscreen.

Reading Muscle Activity

More recently, researchers started measuring muscle activity as a means of achieving small wearable input devices that are controlled using finger flexion, such as the forearm electromyography input device by Saponas et al. [31]. This approach of sensing hand poses for input enables what Felzer et al. described as "hands-free control applications" [9]. We gathered inspiration from these findings and designed Pose-IO to be a wearable bracelet mounted onto the user's arm, which can read input signals from hand motion.

Actuating Users: Mechanically and using EMS

Actuating the user's body using mechanical actuators is common in haptics. The most common mechanical approaches actuate the body using pulley mechanisms. These mechanical actuators displace the user's body by pulling the limbs using motors; a notable example is the SPIDAR [24]. The aforementioned Gesture Output [30] is yet another example of such a system. Likewise, exoskeletons such as *Dextrous Hand* [14] or the *FlexTorque* [36] are a sub-class of pulley systems but attach the complete infrastructure to the user. While mechanical actuators are great for their accuracy and output power, they require attaching exoskeletons, motors and large batteries to the user.

As such, Electrical Muscle Stimulation (EMS) has been proposed as a mean of mobile actuation [22]. EMS originated from the field of rehabilitation medicine [33]. The technique is still under development and mostly used for rehabilitation and sports training [23]. The discomfort caused by the electrical fields passing through the skin ("tingling sensation") is being addressed by researching new tools such as multipath stimulation with large electrodes [23] or microelectrode arrays [4]. EMS found its way to artistic contexts, through Stelarc [32], and, more recently, into the field of HCI.

EMS has been applied in a range of interactive applications, ranging from gaming [8, 20] to assistive learning (e.g., *Possessed Hand* [34]). Lopes et al. demonstrated EMS as a means to implement force-feedback in mobile devices [22]. Since these systems do not use control loops, actuation works through pre-calibration [18].

STUDY OF PROPRIOCEPTIVE IN-/OUTPUT

The purpose of our first study was to verify our basic proprioception interaction concept, i.e., interaction by means of posing the wrist.

The study focuses on symmetric input/output. In the video scrubbing example presented earlier, Pose-IO informed users about the play head position by posing their wrists, allowed them to set the play head position by posing their wrist, and allowed them to recall a value by re-creating a known wrist pose. Since the first two have already been studied in the psychophysics literature [37] and [10], we decided to investigate the latter: *re-creating a wrist pose*. This interaction is particularly meaningful in the context of proprioceptive interaction in that it directly investigates symmetric input-to-output correspondence.

In this study, we used the Pose-IO device to pose participants' hands. Participants then dismissed this pose and after a pause tried to re-create that pose. Given that participants perceive both poses by means of proprioception, our expectation was to see close correspondence between the two poses.

Task

For each trial, Pose-IO posed the participant's wrist at a target angle (Figure 14) and held it stable for one second, played a sound, and dismissed the pose, causing the hand to drop. Then, the participants' task was to recreate the previous pose. When satisfied, participants pressed a keyboard button, which caused the system to record the trial. For each trial, we recorded Pose-IO's accelerometer reading during the target pose and during the recreated pose.

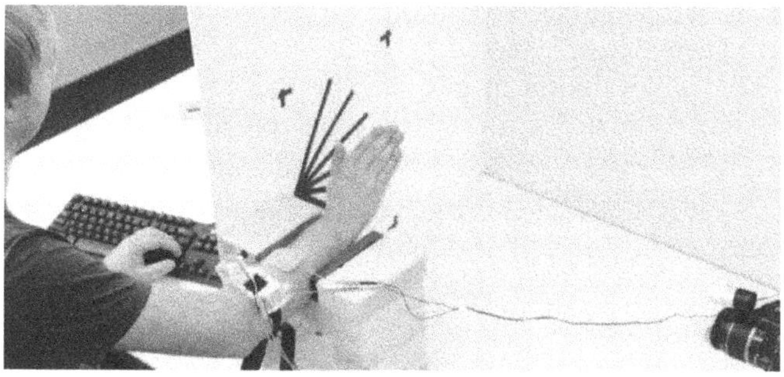

Figure 14: Apparatus for Study. A visual barrier prevented participants from seeing their wrist.

Apparatus

As shown in Figure 14, participants wore Pose-IO's electrodes on their dominant arm. The device was connected via USB to a notebook computer that ran the study script. A keyboard allowed participants to complete their trials. We recorded all trials using a camera.

An opaque screen prevented participants from seeing their hands. To make sure that participants would complete the task based on their proprioceptive sense alone, we also masked out the "tingling" sensation caused by EMS by (1) lowering skin resistance using conductive gel and (2) attaching two vibration motors to the electrodes to create a sensation similar to EMS feedback [27].

Procedure

There were 7 target angles in 20° steps between -60° (flexion) and +60° (extension) reflecting the biomechanical constrains of the human wrist [5]. Each participant performed (7 target positions × 4 repetitions) = 28 trials. Target angles were presented in random order.

Prior to the first trial, we calibrated the device for the respective participant. However, participants received *no* training on the task, as our expectation was that the unified correspondence between input and output would allow participants to complete the task based on their natural sense of proprioception alone. The study took about 30 minutes per participant.

Participants

We recruited 10 participants (3 female) from our local organization. All were right-handed.

Results

Participants recreated poses with an average error of 5.8° (*SD* = 5.1°) across all trials. A linear regression found the overall model fit to be R2 = 0.954. As shown in Figure 15, tilting the hand up further (shown on the left of Figure 15) resulted in slightly larger errors (*mean* = 6.49, *SD* = 5.93) (*mean* = 5.19, *SD* = 4.18). Furthermore, we found no statistical significant difference between any of the angles. For simplicity we present the results for the pairs with larger deviation, e.g., +40° vs. -60° (Z=-1.886; p=0.059) and +60° vs. -60° (Z=-1.274; p=0.203).

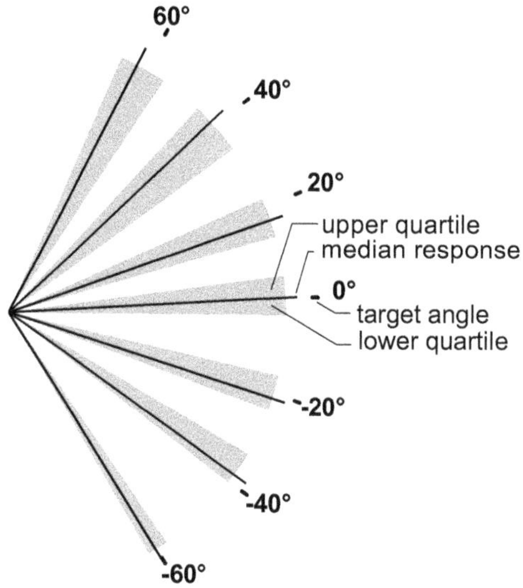

Figure 15: Differences in angle between target pose and recreated pose. Participants recreated poses with an average error of 5.8° (*SD* = 5.1°).

Interestingly, we observed several participants recreating not only the target wrist angle, but also the entire hand pose including the artifacts caused by electrical stimulation, such as the slightly overextended middle finger (Figure 16). This suggests that proprioception was at work on a broader scale.

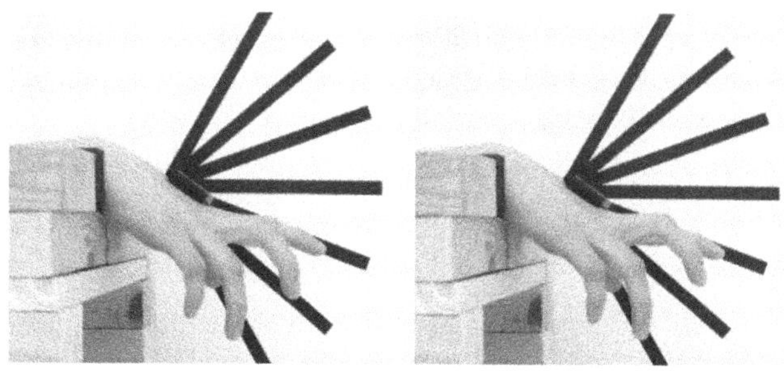

Figure 16: (a) Wrist actuated by Pose-IO (b) Pose recreated by participant in response.

Discussion

Our results show that the interaction did actually use and benefit from proprioception. As observed participants reposing was accurate and included reposing of fingers. The results suggest that proprioceptive interaction's ability to allow for symmetric input & output offers benefits when it comes to recreating poses, as users can perceive and re-pose their wrist using their proprioceptive sense.

On a practical level, participants acquired the target poses with comparably high accuracy, i.e., 5.8° error on average. With respect to the motion range of -60° to +60° = 120° this represents an error of under 5%. If we map these values back to the motivating example of video scrubbing, this means that Pose-IO would allow users to jump to a spot in a 1-minute video clip with ±3 seconds accuracy, which we argue to be a useful level of performance. Obviously, these values were obtained under idealized conditions, i.e., user was sitting down and immediately recreated the pose, and thus it should be interpreted as a lower bound for error.

AN EXPLORATORY STUDY OF THE PROPRIOCEPTIVE INTERFACES

While our discussion so far was focused on the technical aspects and abilities of proprioceptive interaction, one of its aspects that we are personally intrigued about is its way of representing the computer as part of the user's body. Very unlike traditional human computer interaction systems, where computers are outside and different from the user, proprioceptive interfaces make the user's limbs *themselves* serve as the interface, which we argue is the very essence of proprioception—after all, the word stems from Latin "proprius", meaning "one's own". Our video-scrubber application makes the hand partially "owned" by the user and partially owned by the machine. The two games we showed earlier push this approach even further by questioning that notion of "ownership" in that they cause one's hand to be fully owned by the machine.

We were wondering how users perceive this aspect of proprioceptive interaction and what emotional response it might produce. This is what we investigated in this second, exploratory study. We had participants play the red hands game described earlier. We recorded participants' response to the interface on video and had them fill in a questionnaire.

Setup

We recruited 12 participants (3 female) from our local organization, which did not partake in the previous study, and asked them to play the red hand game for about 5 minutes. As discussed earlier, participants' objective was to evade getting slapped by the computer-controlled hands. All participants received candy as a small incentive to participate and we promised additional candy to whoever would score highest.

The game offered levels of increasing difficulty. As mentioned earlier, these were implemented in the form of barely noticeable actuation of the slapping hand before the actual slap (750ms–50ms, depending on level). We did not tell participants about this "warning" mechanism, making it part of the game to either consciously or unconsciously figure it out. For this study we used an earlier Pose-IO prototype, i.e., same hardware but not wearable yet.

To make sure participants only responded to the pose interaction, we canceled out any auditory signals by making them wear noise-cancelling headphones that played music. Each study session started by participants calibrating Pose-IO, familiarizing themselves with the game mechanics, and playing one training level with 10 slaps. They then played 5 levels with about 10 slaps each. If they got hit less than 3 times per level, they proceeded to the next level and their score continued to go up. If not, their score stopped increasing, but we still let them finish the remaining levels to give them a chance to experience the complete game.

Findings

We had designed the game to be challenging and participants took the game quite seriously. All except one participant completed level 3; three level 4, and two made it to the fifth and final level. Participants rated the first two levels as easy (*mean* = 2.0 of 5; 1 = very easy, 5 = very hard) and the last levels as hard (*mean* = 3.92 of 5).

All participants rated the game as fun (*mean* = 4.6 of 5) as depicted in Figure 17 and further illustrated by Figure 18.

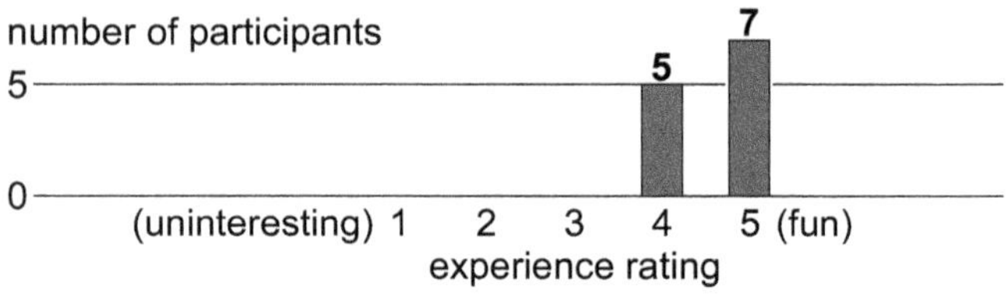

Figure 17: All participants rated playing red hands as fun (1: uninteresting, 5: fun).

When asked why, seven participants pointed to the fact that they felt as if they were "playing against themselves". Several participants went back and forth between referring to the hand wearing the device as "me" and as "computer", such as "it is weird that you lose against yourself" and "sometimes the computer hand was faster than I".

Figure 18: Participants playing red hands, an example of an asymmetric interaction.

In the last two levels, ten out of twelve participants stopped looking at their hands while awaiting the slaps. When asked about it, only two stated to have played by always looking at their hands, while five participants stated to play eyes-free and seven stated to have rarely looked. This suggests that participants operated our application by means of proprioception alone.

Most participants agreed that the muscle output had contributed to their excitement (*mean* = 4.91 of 5). One of the two participants who had continued to look at their hands explained: "it was so remarkable to see my hand moving without my intention that I could not look away".

In summary, watching the twelve participants confirmed that Pose-IO affords being operated eyes-free and that users perceived the "blurred ownership" of the user's body as compelling.

CONCLUSIONS AND FUTURE WORK

In this paper, we proposed the concept of proprioceptive interaction, which we instantiate through a wearable prototype. Proprioceptive interaction leverages the user's proprioceptive sense for both input & output, i.e., the use of pose as a bidirectional communication channel between human and computer. We demonstrated how proprioceptive interactions allows for (1) eyes-free and ears-free use; (2) invoking the device at any time and returning to their primary task immediately when necessary; and, provides (3) two modalities: symmetric, in which input and output occur in the same limb, and asymmetric (i.e., one limb for input, another for output).

A unique aspect of proprioceptive interaction is that it represents the computer using a part of the user's body, which our second study suggests that participants found this experience compelling. On a philosophical layer, this "blurred ownership" manifests itself because operating a device only through proprioception thins the boundary between human and computer, since the machine partially inhabits the human. In the case of the presented proprioceptive interface, the muscles which control the wrist are the interactive device, in contrast to most input & output devices which are external pieces of hardware, sitting outside the user's body.

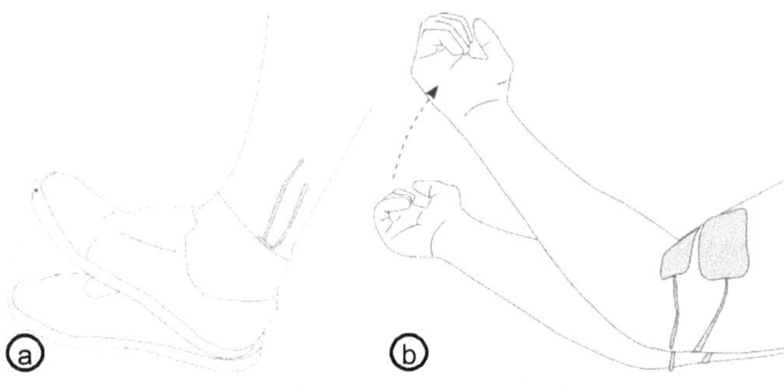

Figure 19: Extending proprioceptive interaction to other parts of the body: (a) the feet and (b) the upper arm.

Lastly, as future work, we believe the concept of proprioceptive interaction needs not to be restricted to the hands. In Figure 19 we depict two proprioceptive interaction designs, one for the upper arm (using the *biceps* for flexion) and one for the feet (using the *gastrocnemius* for plantar flexion). These additional possibilities open up interaction spaces for scenarios in which the hands are occupied with another task. Furthermore, other input & output mapping functions are of interest for further research, such as non-linear mappings.

ACKNOWLEDGEMENTS

We kindly thank the assistance of our colleague Uwe Hentschel (HPI), André Gonçalves (ADDAC), and Brian Kaminski (Advancer Technologies) with EMG circuitry.

REFERENCES

1. Ashbrook, D. *Enabling Mobile Microinteractions.* Ph.D. Dissertation. Georgia Tech, Atlanta, GA, USA.
2. Ban, Y., Narumi, T., Fujii, T., Sakurai, S., Imura, J., Tanikawa, T., and Hirose, M Augmented endurance: controlling fatigue while handling objects by affecting weight perception using augmented reality. *Proc. CHI '13*, 69-78.
3. Baudisch, P., Pohl, H., Reinicke, S., Wittmers, E., Lühne, P., Knaust, M., Köhler, S., Schmidt, P., and Holz, C. Imaginary reality gaming: ball games without a ball. *Proc. UIST'13*, 405-410.
4. Boven, K., Fejtl, M., Moeller, A., Nisch, W. and Stett, A. On Micro-Electrode Array Revival. In: Advances in Network Electrophysiology Using Multi-Electrode Arrays, 2006: 24-37.
5. Chao, E., An, K., Cooney, W., Linscheid, R. *Biomechanics of the Hand.* World Scientific Publishing, 1989.
6. Daniel, S., Gallagher, S., (Eds.), Handbook of Phenomenology and Cognitive Science, Springer; 2010 edition, ISBN-10: 9048126452
7. E. Gardner and J. Martin. Coding of Sensory Information, Principles of Neural Science. McGraw-Hill, fourth edition, 2000.
8. Farbiz, F., Yu, Z. H., Manders, C., and Ahmad, W. An electrical muscle stimulation haptic feedback for mixed reality tennis game. P*roc. SIGGRAPH '07 (poster).*
9. Felzer, T., and Nordmann, R. Using intentional muscle contractions as input signals for various hands-free control applications. *Proc. iCREATe'08*, 87-91.
10. Gandevia, S., Smith, J., Crawford, M., Proske, U., and Taylor, J. Motor commands contribute to human position sense. *Journal of Physiology,* 2006, 571(3) 703-710.
11. Gustafson, S., Bierwirth, D., and Baudisch, P. Imaginary interfaces: spatial interaction with empty hands and without visual feedback. *Proc. UIST '10*, 3-12.
12. Gustafson, S., Rabe, B., and Baudisch, P. Understanding palm-based imaginary interfaces: the role of visual and tactile cues when browsing. *Proc CHI'13,* 889-898.
13. Harrison, C., Tan, D., and Morris, D.. Skinput: appropriating the body as an input surface. *Proc. CHI'10*, 453-462.

14. Hollerbach J. and Jacobsen S. Haptic Interfaces for Teleoperation and Virtual Environments. *Proc. of First Workshop on Simulation and Interaction in Virtual Environments '95,* 13-15.
15. Hook, J., Nappey, T., Making 3D Printed Objects Interactive Using Wireless Accelerometers. Proc. *CHI '14 Extended Abstracts, 1435-1440.*
16. K. Bark, J. W. Wheeler, S. Premakumar, and M. R. Cutkosky, Comparison of Skin Stretch and Vibrotactile Stimulation for Feedback of Proprioceptive Information. *Proc. HAPTICS '08*, 71-78.
17. Karuei, I., MacLean, K., Foley-Fisher, Z., MacKenzie, R., Koch, S., and El-Zohairy, M. Detecting vibrations across the body in mobile contexts. *Proc. CHI'11*, 3267-3276.
18. Katoh, M, Nishimura, N., Yokoyama, M., Hachisu, T., Sato, M., Fukushima, S., and Kajimoto, H. Optimal selection of electrodes for muscle electrical stimulation using twitching motion measurement. *Proc. AH '13*, 237-238.
19. Ken Hinckley, Randy Pausch, and Dennis Proffitt. 1997. Attention and visual feedback: the bimanual frame of reference. *Proc. I3D '97*, 121-126.
20. Kruijff, E., Schmalstieg, D., and Beckhaus, S. Using neuromuscular electrical stimulation for pseudo-haptic feedback. *Proc. VRST '06*, 316–319.
21. Li, K, A. *Designing easily learnable eyes-free interaction,* Ph.D. Thesis. UC San Diego, 2009.
22. Lopes, P. and Baudisch, P., Muscle-Propelled Force Feedback: bringing force feedback to mobile devices, *Proc. CHI'13*, 2577-2580.
23. Maffiuletti, N., Minetto, M., Farina, D., and Bottinelli, R. Electrical stimulation for neuromuscular testing and training: State-of-the art and unresolved issues. In Journal of Applied Physiology 2011, 111:2391–2397.
24. Murayama, J., Bougrila, L., Luo, Y., Akahane, K., Hasegawa, S., Hirsbrunner, B., Sato, M. SPIDAR G&G: a two-handed haptic interface for bimanual VR interaction. *Proc. EuroHaptics '04,* 138-146.
25. Ni, T. and Baudisch, P. Disappearing mobile devices. *Proc. UIST'09*, 101-110.
26. Pasquero, J., Stobbe, S., and Stonehouse, N. A haptic wristwatch for eyes-free interactions. *Proc. CHI'11*, 3257-3266.
27. Pfeiffer, M., Schneegass, S., Alt, F., and Rohs, M., Let Me Grab This: A Comparison of EMS and Vibration for Haptic Feedback in Free-Hand Interaction, *Proc. AH'14.*
28. Proske, U., and Gandevia, S., The Proprioceptive Senses: Their Roles in Signaling Body Shape, Body Position and Movement, and Muscle Force, *In Physiological Reviews* 2012, Vol. 92 no. 4,1651-1697
29. Red Hands, http://en.wikipedia.org/wiki/Red_hands.
30. Roudaut, A., Rau, A., Sterz, C., Plauth, M., Lopes, P., and Baudisch, P. Gesture output: eyes-free output using a force feedback touch surface. *Proc. CHI'13*, 2547-2556.
31. Saponas, S., Tan, D., Morris, D., Balakrishnan, R., Turner, J., and Landay, J. Enabling always-available input with muscle-computer interfaces. *Proc. UIST'09*, 167-176.
32. Stelarc. From zombies to cyborg bodies: exoskeleton, extra ear and avatars. *Proc. C&C '99,* 23.
33. Strojnik, P., Kralj, A., and Ursic, I., Programmed six-channel electrical stimulator for complex stimulation of leg muscles during walking, *IEEE Trans. Biomed. Eng.* 26, 112, 1979.
34. Tamaki, E., Miyaki, T., and Rekimoto, J., Possessed Hand: techniques for controlling human hands using electrical muscles stimuli. *Proc. CHI '11*, 543-552.
35. Terrault, S., Lecolinet, E., Eagan, J., and Guiard, Y. Watchit: simple gestures and eyes-free interaction for wristwatches and bracelets. *Proc. CHI'13*, 1451-1460.
36. Tsetserukou, D., Sato, K., and Tachi, S. ExoInterfaces: novel exosceleton haptic interfaces for virtual reality, augmented sport and rehabilitation. *Proc. AH '10,* 1-6.
37. Walsh, L., Smith, J., Gandevia, S, and Taylor, J. The combined effect of muscle contraction history and motor commands on human position sense. *Journal of Experimental Brain Research*, 2009; 195(4): 603-10.
38. Wigdor, D., and Wixon, D, *Brave NUI World: Designing Natural User Interfaces for Touch and Gesture.* Morgan Kaufmann Publishers Inc., 2011.

AudioScope: Smartphones as Directional Microphones in Mobile Audio Augmented Reality Systems

Florian Heller
RWTH Aachen University
52056 Aachen, Germany
flo@cs.rwth-aachen.de

Jan Borchers
RWTH Aachen University
52056 Aachen, Germany
borchers@cs.rwth-aachen.de

ABSTRACT
Mobile audio augmented reality systems (MAARS) provide a new and engaging modality to present information or to create playful experiences. Using special filters, spatial audio rendering creates the impression that the sound of a virtual source emanates from a certain position in the physical space. So far, most of the implementations of such systems rely on head tracking to create a realistic effect, which requires additional hardware. Recent results indicate that the built-in sensors of a smartphone can be used as source for orientation measurement, reducing deployment to a simple app download. AudioScope presents an alternative interaction technique to create such an experience, using the metaphor of pointing a directional microphone at the environment. In an experiment with 20 users, we compared the time to locate a proximate audio source and the perceived presence in the virtual environment. Results show that there is no significant difference between head-orientation measurement and AudioScope regarding accuracy and perceived presence. This means that MAARS, such as audio guides for museums, do not require special hardware but can run on the visitor's smartphones with standard headphones.

Author Keywords
Virtual Audio Spaces; Mobile Devices; Audio Augmented Reality; Navigation.

ACM Classification Keywords
H.5.1. Information Interfaces and Presentation (e.g. HCI): Multimedia Information Systems

INTRODUCTION
Audio augmented reality systems overlay the physical space with a virtual audio layer that is perceived through headphones. Spatial audio rendering creates the impression that the sound of the virtual sources emerges from a certain location in the physical space. Such systems are used, e.g., to augment points of interest in museums, or to provide a navigational aid that does not put additional load on the visual sense [13, 15, 16]. While early audio augmented reality systems used external, dedicated hardware to render the spatial audio [15], today's smartphones provide enough processing power for individual, decentralized rendering [12].

CHI 2015, April 18–23, 2015, Republic of Korea.

ACM 978-1-4503-3145-6/15/04...$15.00.
http://dx.doi.org/10.1145/2702123.2702159

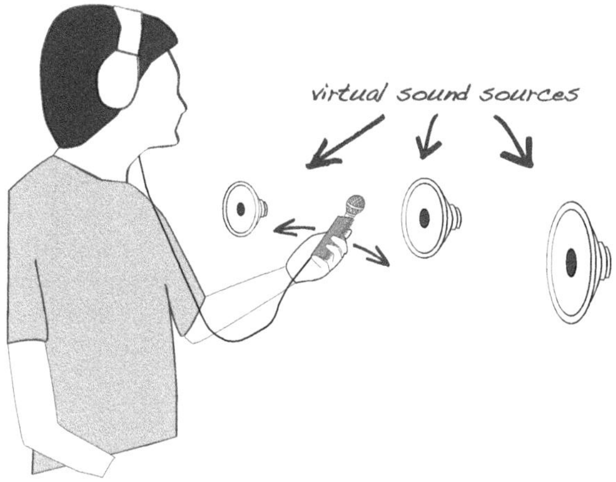

Figure 1. AudioScope uses the built-in sensors of a modern smartphone to create the illusion of a virtual directional microphone to explore mobile audio augmented reality environments.

To create a realistic experience in which the sources appear to be located in the physical space independent of the user's orientation, this orientation has to be measured. Most implementations rely on head tracking as the source of orientation for the spatial audio rendering algorithm, which requires additional hardware, such as a digital compass or intertial measurement unit (IMU). This hardware needs to be attached to the headphones, powered, and connected to the device rendering the spatial audio. The additional costs and handling slow down the distribution of mobile audio augmented reality systems (MAARS).

Recent results indicate that using the device compass is a feasible option [6], however, the resulting experience might not correlate with the users' expectations. We propose AudioScope, a metaphor that turns your smartphone into a virtual directional microphone. You can probe the audio space by simply pointing the device in different directions. If the sound source is to the left of the device, the sound on the left audio channel is louder and vice versa. By providing a well-defined mental model, we avoid disappointing users through a possible lack of realism as they discover that turning their head does not influence the audio output. We compared AudioScope with an implementation using a commercial head tracking system in a source localization experiment with 20 participants. While on average being 1.5 s slower in task completion time, AudioScope is on par with the headphone based measurement regarding accuracy and perceived presence in the virtual environment. This allows designers to deploy future MAARS as standard apps on unmodified smartphones, without the need for additional special sensor hardware.

RELATED WORK

Spatial audio rendering and the interaction with virtual audio spaces have been of interest to the research community for over three decades [2]. Most of the navigation tasks, however, included walking over a longer distance, which is reasonable for outdoor navigation, but not directly applicable to settings where the sources are close, e.g., in a museum.

Loomis et al. [8] examined the effect of spatial audio rendering algorithms on paths users take when walking towards virtual sound sources, and concluded that even simple algorithms that do not simulate pinnae effects can externalize sounds well enough to allow successful navigation. Mariette [10] later replicated this experiment with different rendering algorithms and head-tracker latencies and observed significant degradation of source stability ratings and effects in the recorded paths for an added latency of 800 ms and higher. At the same time, this only affected the better of the two tested rendering algorithms, while the simpler one covered the effects due to its lower angular resolution.

Heller et al. [6] analyzed differences in orientation between the head, the chest, and a smartphone while navigating in a virtual audio space. They found that, except for a large initial head-turn, the measures of head and device do not differ much. This suggests device orientation as a promising point of measurement for mobile audio augmented reality applications. However, even if results indicate that navigation performance is not affected, users might still be confused if the measurements are taken at a different point than they expect. During their trials, participants were not informed which source of orientation was used, and the results show that the device was aligned to the body most of the time, thus the participants did not take advantage of the device's mobility.

Marentakis et al. [9] successfully evaluated pointing as an interaction technique in virtual audio spaces. Participants had to point to an audible source with their arm while walking. A feedback sound was played whenever the arm was in certain range around the source to facilitate the task. Deo et al. compared pointing with a mobile phone to head tracking for multichannel audio conferencing [3]. Building on that, a gesture interface with a mobile phone was also tested to navigate trough a two-level spatial auditory menu [5] and the pointing metaphor was applied to this type of menu [7]. Results showed this technique to be feasible to interact with auditory menus where the items are arranged spatially around the head. While our interaction is similar, we do not focus on targeting a certain sound source, but on creating an auditory image of the source positions to navigate in an audio space.

IMPLEMENTATION

We measured head position at 34 Hz using a Ubisense (ubisense.net) location tracking system with an accuracy of around 5 cm. Head orientation was measured with the inertial measurement unit (IMU) of an Intelligent Headset (intelligentheadset.com), while device orientation was measured using the IMU of an iPhone 5S. We compared both IMUs,

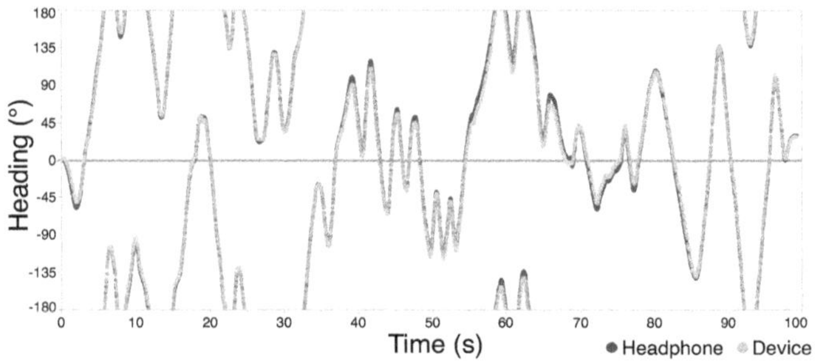

Figure 2. We compared the IMU of the Intelligent Headset (blue) and the iPhone 5S (green). Both report heading with a similar characteristic and update rate.

which report changes in heading with an update rate of around 40Hz, and found that they have a similar characteristic, with an average difference of only 4.8° (SD=3.4°) (cf. Fig. 2). The absolute average orientation error of the iPhone IMU is 4.25° (SD=3.05°). The specified overall latency of the headphone orientation measurement is around 100 ms, which is noticeable [4] but well below the limits of 372 ms defined in [10].

Spatial audio rendering was implemented using the OpenAL framework in iOS 7.1, with the `ALC_EXT_MAC_OSX` extension enabled. It uses a spatialization based on the spherical head model and includes interaural level and time difference, head filtering, and a frequency-dependent distance model as filters. To enhance front-back separation of sources, we added a low-pass filter to sources when they are behind the listener. The intensity increases linearly from 0dB to -36dB for azimuth angles between 90° (side) and 180° (back). The minimum audible angle of the rendering is around 4°. This method, although less realistic than algorithms using individual, natural body cues in form of head-related transfer functions (HRTF), is a good representative of spatial rendering on mobile devices.

EVALUATION

In our experiment, participants were instructed to navigate to single proximate sources with either head or device tracking enabled. We placed 24 loudspeakers spaced by 15° at a height of 150 cm forming a circle of 5 m diameter (Fig. 3). As in this experiment we only wanted to compare the impact of the orientation measurement using the same rendering in both conditions, the loudspeakers did not play any sound but were mere physical representations of the virtual sound sources.

In the two conditions of our experiment, the audio rendering algorithm used the orientation either from the *head* or from the *device*. Participants started every trial standing in the center of the circle facing source no. 1 and were instructed to identify the currently active source as quickly as possible. Correct alignment of the heading information with the physical setup was verified before each trial. In a real scenario, e.g., a museum or a public place, users might not be able to get close to the sources. To account for this factor, and to make sure that the experiment revealed the impact of orientation measurement, participants were instructed to move only in an inner circle of 3 m diameter, such that they had to determine the exact sound source from a distance of approximately

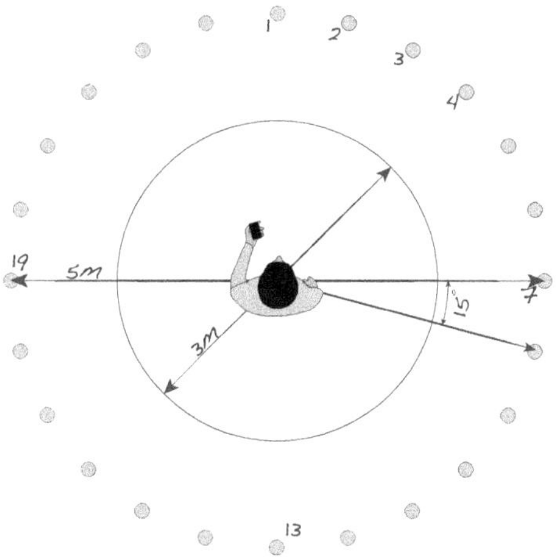

Figure 3. We placed 24 virtual sound sources, spaced by 15° in a circle of 5 m diameter. Participants had to start every trial standing in the center, facing source no. 1. They could move freely within the inner 3 m circle.

1 m. We used an audio sample of a male voice reciting colors at a fast pace[1].

We used a within-subjects design with a balanced order of conditions, and the order of active sound sources was randomized using Latin squares. Every participant had to navigate to all 24 sources in the *head* and *device* measurement condition and had to complete a 10-trial training before each condition. We measured the time from users starting each trial by pressing the start button on the smartphone, until they confirmed standing in front of the audible source by pressing a second button. Participants had to name the source that they assumed was playing. We recorded the paths the users took to walk to the sources, along with the orientation fed into the rendering algorithm. After each condition, participants had to fill out a questionnaire about their perceived presence in the virtual environment [18] on 5-point Likert scales.

In total, 20 users, 8 female, 12 male, aged 21 to 33 (average 26), participated in the study. None reported a hearing disorder or known problems with spatial hearing. Seven had prior experience with audio augmented reality systems.

RESULTS

The average time users took to navigate to the sound source was 15.71 s (SD=8.51) in the *head* condition and 17.22 s (SD=9.72) in the *device* condition. A mixed model repeated measures ANOVA revealed this difference to be statistically significant ($F(1, 916)$=14.79, p=.0001). At the same time, the rate of correctly recognized sources was 65% (SD=0.28) for head tracking and 69% (SD=0.26) for device tracking. This difference is not significant (p=.91) according to a Wilcoxon Signed Rank test. The recognition rates seem fairly low, but considering that the 15° spacing between our sources is in the range of the localization error of virtual sound sources [11, 17] and that we used a rather simple rendering algorithm, this is not surprising. Most of the errors were only off by one source to the left or right. If we count these "off-by-one" answers as correct, then the recognition rates climb up to 97% (SD=0.1) for head and 98% (SD=0.1) for device tracking. No front-back confusions occurred. While people without prior experience with audio AR where significantly slower in the device condition (M=14.3s, SD=7.5s vs. M=18.8s, SD=10.4s, p=.0003), no significant difference between conditions could be found for participants with prior experience. The average distance travelled only differs by half a step between conditions (*device*: M=9.00m, SD=5.4m, *head*: M=8.7m, SD=6.32m, p=.0335).

[1]http://hci.rwth-aachen.de/public/AudioScope/Colors.au

The median ratings from the perceived presence questionnaire did not differ by more than one item on the 5-point Likert scale. Not surprisingly, the headphone tracking was perceived more natural than the device (*head*: Mdn=5, IQR=1.75; *device*: Mdn=4, IQR=1). For both conditions, the experience was rated to be consistent with the real world (*head*: Mdn=4, IQR=1.75; *device*: Mdn=4, IQR=2), and participants felt able to localize sounds well (*head*: Mdn=4, IQR=0; *device*: Mdn=4, IQR=0.75). Wilcoxon signed rank tests only revealed the ratings for the *natural interface* to be significantly better (p=.022) for the *head* tracking, all other ratings did not differ significantly between conditions.

The tracking technology did not seem to interfere with the experience as both the responsiveness (*head*: Mdn=5, IQR=1; *device*: Mdn=5, IQR=1) and the perceived delay (*head*: Mdn=4, IQR=1.75; *device*: Mdn=4, IQR=2) received similarly high ratings in both conditions. After the experiment, the participants felt proficient with the interface both with head tracking (Mdn=4, IQR=1) and device tracking (Mdn=4.5, IQR=1). Again, no significant difference was found between the conditions.

DISCUSSION

Overall, the differences between both orientation tracking metaphors are fairly small. Out of the answers on the questionnaire, 85% of the ratings are above 3 out of 5 on a Likert scale (5 being the best). We are thus confident that the acceptance of the device orientation measurement is high. For people with prior audio AR experience, no significant difference in task completion time could be found which suggests that the metaphor is easy to adopt. The fact that the average task completion time was slightly longer (1.5 s) in the *device* condition is not critical in practice. Other studies have revealed that a longer task completion time can also be a result of people enjoying the experience [16], which in case of an audio guide for museums, is the primary focus. Furthermore, we observed that users experimented with the handling of the device tracking even though they completed the 10 training trials prior to the experiment.

The low recognition rates show that the distance between the sources was at the limit of what can be differentiated with our rendering. As stated above, the 15° spacing is in the range of the localization error of virtual sound sources. Participants spent more time in a 1.5 m radius around the active source than in the rest of the field, which indicates that they took a long time to differentiate between two candidate sources. This problem can be solved by either placing the sources further apart, or by providing additional context, e.g., a beacon sound that relates to the physical object.

Some participants stated that they felt faster with the device tracking, and one mentioned the head tracking being more difficult immediately after switching conditions. On the other hand, some participants mentioned being confused by the metaphor of the virtual directional microphone, since when moving the smartphone to the right of a source, the left channel becomes louder.

The focus of this paper is the evaluation of the interaction metaphor, for which the use of an external location tracking system is acceptable. However, indoor location tracking is currently a focus of both researchers and smartphone manufacturers. Technologies such as Estimote beacons (estimote.com) support that we can expect significant improvements in accuracy in the near future, making smartphones a complete platform for MAARS.

CONCLUSION & FUTURE WORK

We presented AudioScope, a system that uses the metaphor of a directional microphone to explore virtual audio spaces. The simple mechanism of pointing in different directions to locate sound sources is easy to understand and avoids confusion that might occur when simply replacing the head orientation measurement by device orientation without communicating this. Using built-in sensors of the device, AudioScope reduces the hardware requirements and allows deploying mobile audio augmented reality systems via a simple app download.

Together with the current integration of depth sensing cameras into smartphones, the implementation of assistive systems for the blind such as presented in [14] could be reduced to a simple download. Using AudioScope with an HRTF-based rendering that also simulates elevation, finding an item in a shelf can be done in a simple point-and-pick action.

Future studies should take a closer look at emerging indoor location technologies and measure their impact on navigation performance. For outside navigation, we can rely on assisted GPS which has been used successfully in a series of related projects. Furthermore, current spatial audio rendering algorithms for mobile devices usually do not simulate accurate rooms acoustics. Using these would make the implementation more difficult since the impulse response of the room would need to be measured, but the externalization of sounds and thus localization accuracy should increase [1].

ACKNOWLEDGMENTS

We would like to thank the participants of our study and Thorsten Karrer for his valuable feedback. This work was funded in part by the German B-IT Foundation.

REFERENCES

1. Begault, D. R., Wenzel, E. M., and Anderson, M. R. Direct Comparison of the Impact of Head Tracking, Reverberation, and Individualized Head-Related Transfer Functions on the Spatial Perception of a Virtual Speech Source. *J. Audio Eng. Soc* (2001).
2. Begault, D. R., Wenzel, E. M., Godfroy, M., Miller, J. D., and Anderson, M. R. Applying Spatial Audio to Human Interfaces: 25 Years of NASA Experience. In *AES Conference 40* (2010).
3. Billinghurst, M., deo, S., Adams, N., and Lehikoinen, J. Motion-Tracking in Spatial Mobile Audio-Conferencing. In *MobileHCI '07* (2007).
4. Brungart, D. S., Simpson, B. D., and Kordik, A. J. The detectability of headtracker latency in virtual audio displays. In *ICAD '05*.
5. Dicke, C., deo, S., Billinghurst, M., Adams, N., and Lehikoinen, J. Experiments in Mobile Spatial Audio-conferencing: Key-based and Gesture-based Interaction. In *MobileHCI '08*.
6. Heller, F., Krämer, A., and Borchers, J. Simplifying Orientation Measurement for Mobile Audio Augmented Reality Applications. In *CHI '14*.
7. Kajastila, R., and Lokki, T. Eyes-free methods for accessing large auditory menus. In *ICAD '10*.
8. Loomis, J. M., Hebert, C., and Cicinelli, J. G. Active localization of virtual sounds. *The Journal of the Acoustical Society of America* (1990).
9. Marentakis, G. N., and Brewster, S. A. Effects of feedback, mobility and index of difficulty on deictic spatial audio target acquisition in the horizontal plane. In *CHI '06*.
10. Mariette, N. Navigation Performance Effects of Render Method and Head-Turn Latency in Mobile Audio Augmented Reality. In *Auditory Display*. Springer, 2010.
11. Middlebrooks, J. C. Virtual localization improved by scaling nonindividualized external-ear transfer functions in frequency. *The Journal of the Acoustical Society of America* (1999).
12. Sander, C., Wefers, F., and Leckschat, D. Scalable Binaural Synthesis on Mobile Devices. In *AES Convention 133* (2012).
13. Stahl, C. The roaring navigator: a group guide for the zoo with shared auditory landmark display. In *MobileHCI '07*.
14. Tang, T. J. J., and Li, W. H. An Assistive EyeWear Prototype That Interactively Converts 3D Object Locations into Spatial Audio. In *ISWC '14*.
15. Terrenghi, L., and Zimmermann, A. Tailored audio augmented environments for museums. In *IUI '04*.
16. Vazquez-Alvarez, Y., Oakley, I., and Brewster, S. Auditory display design for exploration in mobile audio-augmented reality. *Pers. and Ubiqu. comp.* (2012).
17. Wenzel, E. M., Arruda, M., Kistler, D. J., and Wightman, F. L. Localization using nonindividualized head-related transfer functions. *The Journal of the Acoustical Society of America* (1993).
18. Witmer, B. G., and Singer, M. J. Measuring Presence in Virtual Environments: A Presence Questionnaire. *Presence: Teleoper. Virtual Environ.* (1998).

ScanShot: Detecting Document Capture Moments and Correcting Device Orientation

Jeungmin Oh, Woohyeok Choi, Joohyun Kim, Uichin Lee
Department of Knowledge Service Engineering, KAIST
{jminoh, woohyeok.choi, joohyun.kim, uclee}@kaist.ac.kr

ABSTRACT

Document capturing with smartphone cameras is performed increasingly often in our daily lives. However, our user study results (n=10) showed that more than 80% of landscape tasks had incorrect orientations. To solve this problem, we systematically analyzed user behavior of document capturing and proposed a novel solution called ScanShot that detects document capturing moments to help users correct the orientation errors. ScanShot tracks the gravity direction to capture document capturing moments, analyzes logged gyroscope data to automatically update orientation changes, and provides visual feedback of the inferred orientation for manual correction. Our user study results (n=20) confirmed that capturing moments can be recognized with accuracy of 97.5%, our update mechanism can reduce the orientation errors by 59 percentage points.

Author Keywords

Device orientation; automatic rotation; document capturing; smartphone camera

ACM Classification Keywords

H.5.2. [User Interface]: Input devices and strategies.

INTRODUCTION AND RELATED WORK

People use the built-in camera on a smartphone for various reasons, ranging from personal reflection to social experience and functional tasks [5, 8]. Our work considers the action of document capturing that occurs increasingly often in our daily lives (e.g., capturing a magazine or news article) [1].

Document capturing is typically done by configuring the angle of a smartphone camera to a top-down view (or bird's-eye view). However, orientation errors are often observed in the captured images. We discovered that this problem orginates from the phone's inferred orientation being different from the user's capturing orientation (hand posture). Smartphones typically have four orientation modes in 2D space (just as in a picture frame on a wall), namely portrait, upside down, landscape left, and landscape right (see Figure 1). For a given capturing orientation, there are three incorrect modes that cause orientation errors from the top-down angle.

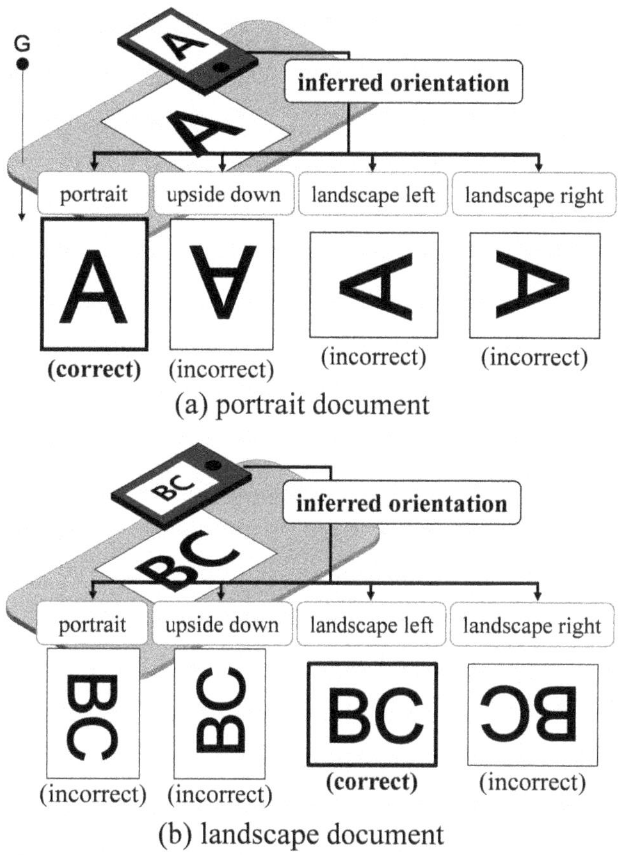

Figure 1: Orientation problem in document capturing

Why do such orientation errors happen? Smartphones typically use gravity-based screen rotation algorithms (e.g., using an accelerometer), assuming that users are standing or sitting upright while interacting with the device in their hands [7, 4]. That is, for orientation inference, the algorithms mainly consider two axes (X and Y axis) of the gravity vector. However, orientation inference fails to work properly if smartphones are close to the plane that is parallel to the ground, when the X and Y axes of the gravity are close to zero (e.g., taking a top-

ACM 978-1-4503-3145-6/15/04 $15.00
http://dx.doi.org/10.1145/2702123.2702440

down shot, or placing a phone on a table). If we rotate the phone parallel to the ground while taking a top-down shot, the phone's inferred orientation remains the unadjusted, and thus, an erroneous inferred orientation is obtained.

In the HCI literature, none of the earlier works have studied this problem systematically. Instead researchers have mainly focused on studying how to prevent unwanted screen rotation when users change their body posture (e.g., lying down). For example, a user's front facing camera was used to detect face orientation that is often consistent with the correct orientation [2]. Researchers showed that another good indicator is how the phone is grasped [6]. Cheng et al. demonstrated its usefulness by prototyping a touch-sensor based phone case (achieving about 80% inference accuracy) [3]. However, it is difficult to apply such techniques to top-down shots: a user's face cannot be captured consistently with this camera angle and the manner of grasping a phone is significantly different to regular smartphone use. For stable document capturing, users typically use both hands. Alternatively we can use optical character recognition (OCR) to detect the document's orientation for automatic correction, but its performance is heavily influenced by context (e.g., font, handwriting, language, and light conditions), and it poses significant processing overhead when compared to motion data processing.

The goal of this work is to systematically understand document capturing behavior in top-down shots and to design solutions that can mitigate orientation errors. We first perform a user study (n=10) to quantify the severity of orientation errors and analyze user behavior in typical document capturing tasks. We found that the error rates were surprisingly high particularly in the landscape document capturing (capture errors: portrait = 5% vs. landscape = 82%). Furthermore, nine out of ten participants were unaware of the concept of inferred orientation, thus failing to recognize orientation signifiers in a camera app (i.e., icon rotation).

Our task analysis of document capturing inspired us to propose ScanShot, a novel method to detect document capturing moments and fix the erroneous orientations. Our approach is composed of three steps. ScanShot first detects a document capturing moment (when a phone's body becomes parallel to the ground) by monitoring the gravity direction using an accelerometer. Secondly, when the document capture moment is detected, ScanShot attempts to automatically update the orientation by analyzing recorded gyroscope data. Finally, ScanShot provides visual feedback where a translucent paper icon is overlaid on the screen to visualize inferred orientation. Our user study results (n=20) showed that document capturing moments can be detected with accuracy of 97.5% and automatic rotation achieves accuracy of 82.16%. In addition, the participants noted the usefulness of visual feedback.

DOCUMENT CAPTURE BEHAVIOR ANALYSIS

Study Setup: We recruited 10 smartphone users who had experience in document capturing. Their ages ranged from 23 to 31 (mean: 26.80, SD: 2.39). Half of them were males, and there was one left-handed participant (P5). To understand document capture behavior, we carefully selected 20 parts in a National Geographic magazine. As shown in Figure 2, we

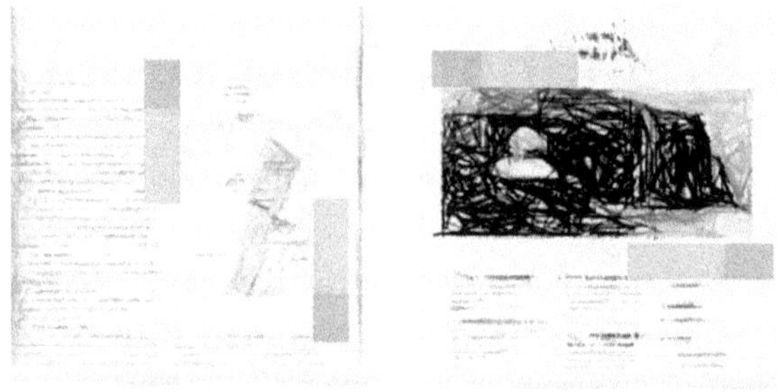

(a) Portrait document (b) Landscape document

Figure 2: Two types of documents to capture for experiment

highlighted the capture area using sticky notes. The sizes of chosen area ranged from a small portions of the magazine to entire pages. Two types of capture areas were investigated. Areas with large width corresponded to landscape tasks, and those with significant height corresponded to portrait tasks. We asked participants to always place the phone on the table after each capturing task so that every capture is treated as an individual task. We used Nexus 5, the current Android's reference phone and its pre-installed camera app in Android 4.4.4. Before this task, the participants engaged in a training session in which they took shots in order to become familiarized with the device and its camera app. After the experiment, the participants were asked if they were aware of the concepts of inferred orientation and rotation signifiers in a camera app (i.e., icon rotation). All sessions were videotaped for a subsequent behavioral analysis. Each participant was compensated with a gift card equivalent to $5.

Frequency of Orientation Errors: The error rates in the landscape and portrait tasks were 0.82 (SD: 0.27) and 0.05 (SD: 0.07), respectively. The landscape capture tasks had a significantly larger number of errors. The portrait capture tasks had only a 5% error rate because the portrait orientation is the Android device's default orientation. By examining video recordings and recorded sensor data, we found that the participants tended to hold the device orthogonal to gravity, which causes the gravity-based rotation system to be disorientated [4]. In Table 1, we present each participant's error rates in both portrait and landscape tasks. P7 and P10 showed relatively low error rates in the landscape tasks since both users tended to tilt the device toward their bodies to look at the preview images on the screen; P10 tilted more frequently than P7. For those two participants, gravity-based rotation sometimes worked, but we found that the majority of the participants had higher error rates due to erroneous orientation.

	P1	P2	P3	P4	P5	P6	P7	P8	P9	P10
Portrait	.0	.0	.1	.0	.1	.1	.0	.2	.0	.0
Landscape	1	1	.9	1	1	.9	**.6**	1	1	**.4**

Table 1: Ratio of orientation errors in capturing tasks

Most participants (9 out of 10) were not even aware of when and why the problem occured even though they were familiar with automatic screen rotation. The camera UI had visual indicators of the current orientation, but they did not notice that the camera's orientation also changed as they rotated. This may be due to the fact that users generally do not need to pay attention to the orientation problem in general photo taking as smartphone cameras typically perform well in this regard. Another factor of error comes from the user's failure to recognize changes in UI when the user's focal vision is on the target object on the preview screen during a top-down shot. The visual indicator is typically located in the peripheral screen area such as a rotating camera icon near the bezel frame.

Analysis of User Behavior: We investigated recorded videos in order to better understand document capturing behavior, which helped us design algorithms for automatic correction. The overall process consists of 1) launching a camera app, 2) adjusting orientation (optional), 3) composing a top-down shot (including zooming and panning), and 4) touching to focus (optional) and pressing a shutter button. In the case of landscape tasks, the participants adjusted the phone's orientation. Portrait capturing tasks do not require orientation adjustment because a phone's default orientation is the portrait mode (as it is the case of a smartphone's home screen orientation). Among four orientations, we observed only two orientation modes (portrait and landscape left) in the experiment. This pattern was consistent with that of the left-handed participant (P5). This important observation allowed us to reduce the number of possible states when designing an automatic algorithm. Note that this step generally came after launching the camera app, but we also observed that in a few landscape sessions, app launching was followed by device rotation. The participants then held their phones parallel to the plane where the document lies and tried zooming/panning to capture the target area. There were participants (P7, P10) who tended to tilt the device approximately up to 45° from the ground plane. Once the target area was determined, the participants touched to focus (occasionally) and pressed the shutter button to take a photo. In the landscape task, most participants grasped the phone with two hands. Likewise, in the portrait shot, two hands were typically used (sometimes one hand grasping the top, and the other hand the bottom).

SCANSHOT DESIGN

Our preliminary user study helped us design ScanShot. The key concept underlying ScanShot is that we can reliably detect whether a user is taking a top-down shot by tracking an accelerometer. Once a top-down shot is detected, we then analyze gyroscope data to fix any orientation changes (i.e., portrait to landscape posture). Finally, ScanShot displays a translucent paper icon overlaid on the screen to visualize the inferred orientation, which allows users to fix orientation errors if needed.

Detecting Document Capture Moments: To detect document capturing moments, we propose an accelerometer-based detection method. When a camera app launches, the accelerometer values fluctuate because of movements (switching to a top-down shot with zooming/panning). After a few seconds, the accelerometer values are soon stabilized because the user typically touches to focus and then presses the shutter button. When photo taking is about to happen, the accelerometer's Z-axis is close to the gravitational acceleration, or 9.8m/s^2.

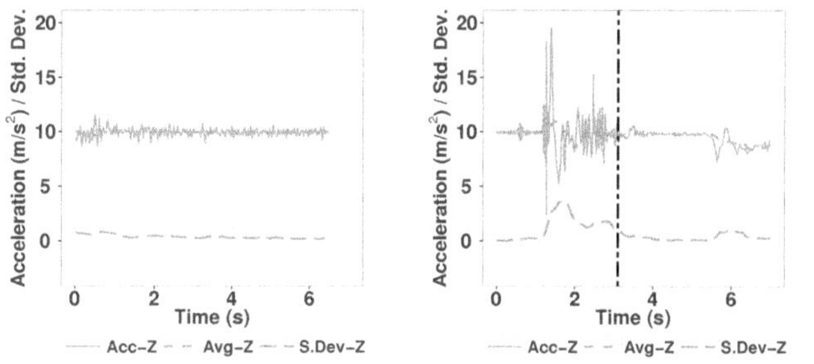

(a) Acceleration (portrait, no rotation) (b) Acceleration (landscape, rotation)

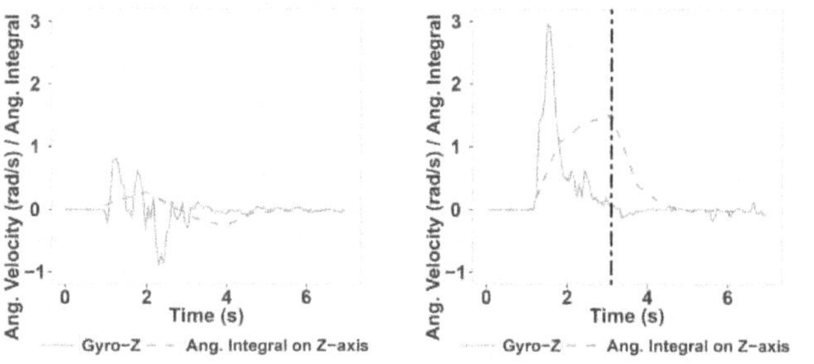

(c) Angular value (portrait, no rotation) (d) Angular value (landscape, rotation)

Figure 3: Accelerometer and gyroscope traces in the capturing tasks: portrait for (a),(c), and landscape for (b),(d) (vertical dotted lines in (c) and (d) represent the time mark that rotation has happened)

As shown in Figure 3, when taking a top-down shot, the participant's hands move with a maximum fluctuation value of ± 0.3. When a camera app is running, the document capture moment is detected when the Z-value is within the range from 9.5m/s^2 to 10.1m/s^2.

This mechanism prevents our algorithm from conflicting with the existing gravity-based orientation system because the Z-value of the accelerometer is nearly zero when taking a non-document photo. Thus, it is not influenced by the initial location of the device (e.g., on the desk or in the pocket).

Updating Orientation: We chose a gyroscope to detect an orientation change event because it can accurately sense device rotation. We used a moving window approach. For sensor data processing, the sliding window of size w seconds moved in time, with a segment size of s seconds. According to our user behavior analysis, rotating action typically took less than 2 seconds. Since the sampling rate was 15 Hz (one sample per 66ms), we set the segment size as $s = 0.66$s (10 samples per segment), and the window size as $w = 1.98$s (3 segments per window). For a given window, we integrated the Z-axis values of gyroscope samples. By carefully analyzing the data set, we set the threshold to detect a rotation event as $\pm$ 0.5, which corresponds to $\pm$ 28.6°. Thus, if this value was greater than 0.5, we classified it as a left rotation event; if it was lower than -0.5, it is classified as a right rotation event. Otherwise, we assumed that no rotation was made (see Figure 3). We used only two orientation modes (portrait and landscape left) for adjustment since these modes dominated in the user study.

```
SET adjustedOrientation to DEFAULT_ORIENTATION;
repeat
    if a new window is generated from sensor listeners then
        Calculate cummulative sum of gyroscope for the window;
        if the cummulative sum > 0.5 then
            adjustedOrientation = LANDSCAPE_LEFT;
        else if the cummulative sum < -0.5 then
            adjustedOrientation = PORTRAIT;
        end
        if 9.5 < avg. acc-Z < 10.1 and std. acc-Z < 0.3 then
            Use adjustedOrientation;
        else
            Use traditional gravity-based orientation;
        end
    end
until shutter button is pressed;
```

Algorithm 1: Pseudo code of ScanShot

Displaying Paper Overlay: According to the preliminary study, our participants generally did not notice orientation errors. When a top-down shot is detected, as a backup, ScanShot immediately provides a visual feedback by displaying a translucent paper icon overlaid on the screen (see Figure 4). For example, assuming that a user is taking a portrait shot, Figure 4(a) shows a correct overlay of a portrait shot. Figure 4(b) shows an incorrect orientation (landscape left). This design decision was made because when a user is taking a photo, the user's focal vision remains on the target object on the screen.

(a) Overlay with correct orientation (b) Overlay with incorrect orientation

Figure 4: Paper overlays for a portrait shot

EVALUATION

Setup: We recruited 20 participants to evaluate the performance of ScanShot. Their ages ranged from 22 to 34 (mean: 27.5, SD 3.25). The same tasks as the first experiment were given. Our ScanShot implementation took a user's input and automatically updated the orientation by modifying the output image file. Each participant was compensated with a gift card that is equivalent to $5.

Document	w/o ScanShot	w/ ScanShot	Diff.
Portrait	.08	.07	-.01
Landscape	.91	.32	-.59

Table 2: Error rate comparison between w/o and w/ ScanShot

Results: Our results showed that the accuracy of detecting document capture moments is 97.5%, thereby confirming the efficiency of our algorithm. We then tested the accuracy of detecting rotation events. Table 2 presents the detection accuracy. The error rate without ScanShot was similar to that of the previous study, and thus, we can assume that the nature of the two participant groups was similar. Overall, ScanShot fixed many instances of the orientation errors. In particular, there was significant decrement of error rates in the landscape tasks, from 91% to 32%. We manually studied failure instances and found that most errors were due to participants launching the camera app after rotation, which caused the algorithm to miss the sensor data corresponding to the rotation. This could be enhanced by continuously monitoring sensor prior to launching the app. The collected data are available online.[1]

CONCLUSION AND FUTURE WORK

We analyzed the problem of orientation errors in document capturing using smartphone camera. We proposed ScanShot, which automatically detects document capturing moment to automatically update orientation changes and then enables manual orientation correction with visual feedback. ScanShot supports these features solely with the use of built-in motion sensors, namely an accelerometer and gyroscope. Our user study results (n=20) showed that ScanShot detected capturing moments with 97.5% accuracy, and lowered rotation error rates to 32%. Our algorithm can be further improved by employing more sophisticated machine learning algorithms or adaptively changing window sizes.

ACKNOWLEDGEMENTS

This work was supported by ICT R&D program of MSIP/IITP [10041313, UX-oriented Mobile SW Platform].

REFERENCES

1. Brown, B. A., Sellen, A. J., and O'hara, K. P. A diary study of information capture in working life. In *Proc. CHI* (2000).
2. Cheng, L.-P., Hsiao, F.-I., Liu, Y.-T., and Chen, M. Y. iRotate: automatic screen rotation based on face orientation. In *Proc. CHI* (2012).
3. Cheng, L.-P., Lee, M. H., Wu, C.-Y., Hsiao, F.-I., Liu, Y.-T., Liang, H.-S., Chiu, Y.-C., Lee, M.-S., and Chen, M. Y. iRotateGrasp: automatic screen rotation based on grasp of mobile devices. In *Proc. CHI* (2013).
4. Hinckley, K., Pierce, J., Sinclair, M., and Horvitz, E. Sensing techniques for mobile interaction. In *Proc. UIST* (2000).
5. Kindberg, T., Spasojevic, M., Fleck, R., and Sellen, A. The ubiquitous camera: an in-depth study of camera phone use. *IEEE Pervasive Computing* (2005).
6. Lee, J., and Ju, D. Y. Defying gravity: a novel method of converting screen orientation. *IJSH* (2013).
7. Sahami Shirazi, A., Henze, N., Dingler, T., Kunze, K., and Schmidt, A. Upright or sideways?: analysis of smartphone postures in the wild. In *Proc. MobileHCI* (2013).
8. Sellen, A., Fleck, R., Kindberg, T., and Spasojevic, M. How and why people use camera phones. *Microsoft Technical Report* (2004).

[1] `https://github.com/ohtangza/chi2015-scanshot`

Mechanics of Camera Work in Mobile Video Collaboration

Brennan Jones[1], Anna Witcraft[1], Scott Bateman[2], Carman Neustaedter[3], Anthony Tang[1]
[1]University of Calgary {bdgjones, anna.witcraft, tonyt}@ucalgary.ca
[2]University of Prince Edward Island sbateman@upei.ca
[3]Simon Fraser University carman@sfu.ca

ABSTRACT
Mobile video conferencing, where one or more participants are moving about in the real world, enables entirely new interaction scenarios (e.g., asking for help to construct or repair an object, or showing a physical location). While we have a good understanding of the challenges of video conferencing in office or home environments, we do not fully understand the *mechanics* of camera work—how people use mobile devices to communicate with one another—during mobile video calls. To provide an understanding of what people do in mobile video collaboration, we conducted an observational study where pairs of participants completed tasks using a mobile video conferencing system. Our analysis suggests that people use the camera view deliberately to support their interactions—for example, to convey a message or to ask questions—but the limited field of view, and the lack of camera control can make it a frustrating experience.

Author Keywords
CSCW; collaboration; handheld devices; mobile computing; video communication

ACM Classification Keywords
H.5.3. Information interfaces and presentation: Group and Organization Interfaces – *CSCW*

INTRODUCTION
Recent advances in mobile technologies and networks are enabling new scenarios of video conferencing use—in particular, scenarios where one or more participants of a video call are out "in the real world" physically moving around (e.g., [12, 28]). For example, people now use mobile video conferencing to give tours of new places (e.g., [1, 20, 23]), share views of the outdoors or life experiences (e.g., [12]), provide directions to someone who is unfamiliar with a setting, help make decisions in retail outlets, and guide others during simple repair or construction tasks (e.g., [1]).

Mobile video conferencing differs from other video conferencing situations for two reasons: first, participants are away from a desk or a controlled environment (e.g., indoors, [12, 28]); second, that the video is being captured from a non-stable, moving camera. This presents an interesting paradox: on the one hand, manipulating the camera provides more control over the camera view; on the other hand, people must also actively attend to controlling the view, and the needs of the other party (e.g., [23]).

Figure 1: A mobile video conferencing scenario where one participant is out and about and the other is at a PC.

While others have explored the emerging social challenges and difficulties associated with mobile video conferencing (e.g., [26, 28]), our research is focused on the details of how people try to accomplish tasks using mobile video. Specifically, we are interested in the *mechanics of mobile camera work*—how people manipulate the handheld phone camera's position, orientation, the framing of objects, scenes, etc.—as a means of supporting collaborative interaction. For example: how do people help another person gain a sense of their spatial environment, and the objects in it? And, does this facilitate navigation? The overarching goal of our research is to articulate these mechanics, and challenges with existing technology, as a means of informing the design of new tools that support mobile video conferencing.

To help identify and articulate these mechanics, we designed and conducted a study where pairs of participants (connected via a mobile video call) were engaged in collaborative activities. To complete tasks, one partner used a mobile phone while 'out and about' to connect with their partner at a remote computer (Figure 1). We explore how the mobile device provides support for, and sometimes hinder, their actions and intentions through a variety of representative collaborative scenarios (e.g., [1, 11, 23, 26]).

Our results show that while video can help interaction by taking the place of or by supporting conversation, people compensate using a number of practices that are not ideal. In particular, camera work is hindered by the need for both good "overview" and "detail" views—often simultaneously. The imbalance of camera control means that one partner is

ACM 978-1-4503-3145-6/15/04...$15.00
http://dx.doi.org/10.1145/2702123.2702345

often left frustrated, and without the view they need to support collaboration. Furthermore, because deixis is such an important part of communication, the lack of gesturing mechanisms can be problematic. Based on these results, we suggest ways to provide overviews, awareness, and gesturing within mobile video calls, as well as tools to negotiate control of the camera view.

We make two main contributions in this paper: first, we provide the first detailed study of mobile camera work, articulating the exact mechanics of how people try to communicate using mobile video in common collaborative scenarios; second, we outline several issues that people face in these scenarios that can inform the design of future mobile video conferencing technologies.

BACKGROUND

Portable, Personal Video Conferencing in the Home

Research on personal uses of video conferencing has explored the use of fixed-location and handheld devices (e.g., [1, 14, 15, 20, 34]). Several researchers have described how "open connections" facilitate the sharing of life and routine in the home (e.g., [15, 20]). We have also seen novel systems address specific uses of video conferencing in domestic settings ranging from the use of physical proxies [32] to interactive storybooks [29] to media spaces [14, 15]. These explorations have focused primarily on video conferencing in the home using relatively stable camera views. In contrast, our work explores the use video conferencing in mobile contexts—where one participant can move around freely.

Mobile Video and Shared Experiences

Mobile video conferencing has not yet been well-explored. O'Hara's [26] diary study explored why people made mobile video calls, and the challenges they faced. In his sample, 28% of such calls were to show objects in a scene, while 22% of calls were for functional needs (e.g., asking for or providing assistance). Challenges included technical and environmental problems (e.g., ambient noise, poor lighting, etc.), and social challenges (e.g., embarrassing to use in public). Licoppe et al. [23] analyzed 100 mobile video calls from eight pairs of users, and discuss the use of mobile video as an interactional resource for conversation (e.g., pointing the camera at an object helps support that conversation). Brubaker et al. [1] provide vignettes based on the real life use of mobile video (e.g., providing help to perform an oil change or repairing airplanes), and describe how its use in establishing relationships with distant places (e.g., providing "house tours").

Recent work has explored novel mobile video conferencing prototypes where participants are "out and about" in the real world. Inkpen et al. [12] explore the use of video to share children's outdoor activities with a remote person at home. Here, multiple views (one of the scene, the other of the local parent) were beneficial to remote participants of the video chat: they could observe the activities while seeing reactions of the local parent. Procyk et al. [28] explore remote geocaching where pairs of people participate while streaming video to each other. The authors note the value of "micro shared experiences," but also discuss privacy concerns and dangers of being overly engaged with a remote person while navigating outdoors. Another type of activity is the 'virtual photo walk,' where a person shares video of an experience (e.g., a hike) with people who are unable to take part [33]. While commercial mobile video chat systems (e.g., FaceTime and Skype) are now widely available, few studies of their use exist.

While these explorations provide us with insight into the possibilities of mobile video calls (e.g., [12, 28]) and the social challenges of public use (e.g., [23, 26]), we are specifically interested in understanding the ways that people use mobile devices, the interactional challenges they face, and how they cope with these by using camera work.

Remote gesture in Collaborative Tasks

A principal challenge identified in explorations of video conferencing systems is being able to effectively refer to objects in the video scene (e.g., [10, 27]). So-called "deictic references" (e.g., pointing at an object and saying, "this one") are made problematic because each party in a video call does not typically share "physical co-presence" [28].

Gergle et al. [10] explore the role of visual connections that focus on a workspace (such as a desk), showing how being able to see the workspace supports interaction by taking the place of speech. Here, the visual space acts as a resource for interaction—there is no need to confirm that a particular action was taken (e.g., putting a LEGO block in place) when all participants easily view the action, and it is possible to refer to objects through deictic reference [21]. Kirk et al. [18] demonstrate that when the workspace that is captured includes a person's hands working in the space, people use their hands in surprisingly expressive ways to communicate. Gutwin and Penner [11] demonstrate that there is a temporal element to gestures, and that they are fleeting. Displaying gestures with visual traces that fade away slowly helps interpretation over remote connections [6]. Sodhi et al. [31] explore the problem of object referencing in video conferencing and add augmented reality. Their approach uses a symmetric mobile tool that captures a remote participant's gestures and hand postures and represents them using an avatar. While this seems like a promising solution, it is not yet widely available.

Although research has widely recognized the importance of gesturing, and provided some innovative solutions to facilitate gesturing over video, video conferencing systems still do not provide much support to facilitate gesturing.

Free-Moving Video in Collaborative Tasks

To ease remote gesturing and enable a greater range of expressive interaction and sharing, research has also explored novel video configurations. Fussell et al. [3] examine the combined use of head mounted and workspace-focused video for collaborative tasks. They demonstrate that head-mounted video provides a more detailed "work area," but has a limited FOV, and requires the helper to reorient himself as the worker moves head positions. In contrast, the scene camera provides the helper with a better sense of context, but a poorer sense of the specific activities being undertaken. Norris et al. [25] use a focus+context approach to give collaborators "focus windows" that provide detail in addition to the context window of the entire space. Yarosh et al. [34] explore the use of a mobile video camera condition in their study of child free-play, finding that movement and framing of children and scenes can be challenging.

We have a deep understanding of how video conferencing can support collaborative activities in work contexts where cameras are usually in fixed positions (e.g., [19]). Yet, we know comparatively little about mobile scenarios, where people need to manipulate the camera view.

OBSERVATIONAL STUDY

We designed a study of mobile video conferencing focused on two questions: first, what is the nature of the mobile camera work in supporting the communicative intentions of collaborators; second, what communicative problems do collaborators encounter trying to complete collaborative tasks, and how do they overcome these difficulties?

Participants

Nine pairs of adult participants (18 participants; 11 females) were recruited online and through printed ads. We recruited pairs of participants together, ensuring that one was familiar with our university campus while the other was not. With the exception of one pair (Pair 1), participants in each pair knew each other prior to participating in the study.

Method

We designed a set of four tasks to be completed by each pair. To mimic a typical mobile scenario where one person is 'out and about' and one is at home [1], we designed tasks where one participant needed to physically go to several parts of our university campus. Each task was designed so that participants needed to work together to exchange information to be successful. The desktop collaborator (DC) sat at a desktop computer with a high-resolution monitor, a webcam, a microphone, and a pair of headphones. The mobile collaborator (MC) used an Android smartphone with front and back cameras and a pair of earbuds. The MC was allowed to switch between landscape and portrait mode, and front and back cameras, as they liked. The pair was connected by video and audio using Google Hangouts.

We were interested in different behaviours given the different kinds of tasks, we limited participants to only ten minutes for each task. Even so, the entire duration of the study lasted about 90 minutes, owing in large part to the MC needing to move to different on-campus locations for each task. After completing all tasks, we conducted brief interviews with each pair to understand their experiences.

Tasks

Our tasks were based on the related work, where we aimed to keep the face validity high. These four tasks varied in three dimensions: (1) *knowledge*—in three tasks, one participant explicitly needs to share information with the other; (2) *physical movement*—in three tasks, the MC needs to walk between places; and (3) *target distance*—we anticipated that participants would use the video to share visual information, and so we varied the distance at which these targets would appear (based on each the task).

Task 1: Collaborative Physical Task. The MC constructs a MEGA BLOK structure (and has all the pieces), but only the DC has instructions on what to build. The DC's role is to guide the MC. The DC is given a set of six pictures showing the structure from different angles, but is not allowed to show these images to the MC. This task is based on the "collaborative physical tasks" commonly found in the literature (e.g., [10, 17, 21]). This task helps to provide a basis for comparison with prior work and our experiences with mobile video. Further, it mimics many of the scenarios in which a collaborator asks for help with a physical task, as seen in the related work (e.g., mechanical repair [1]).

Task 2: Campus Tour. The MC takes the DC on a brief tour of the central part of campus, showing the DC five key landmarks. The DC is to learn the spatial relationships between these landmarks. DCs were asked to sketch a map of this part of campus to illustrate their understanding of these spatial relationships. This task mimics a scenario in which one is spatially orienting or guiding someone through an environment (e.g., house tour [1]). We were interested in seeing how landmarks (and the spaces between them) would be shown and talked about in the video scene, and in particular, how MCs would move through space.

Task 3: Detail Search. The MC begins in the food court on campus, and together, the DC and MC construct a nutritious, three-day meal plan with a strict budget. The MC's role is to show the DC the different food outlets and help the DC make decisions about what would appear in the meal plan. We were interested in how participants would share different kinds of information, such as textual data (menu placards), as well as tangible objects (e.g., food items), and how this would relate to their movement through the food court.

Task 4: Negotiation – Shopping Together. The MC begins at the bookstore, and works with the DC to collect a set of gifts for a mutual friend's upcoming graduation. The team is given a strict budget, and each collaborator is given a short list of items that the friend likes or needs—each list containing items that the other list does not have. Both can share the knowledge they have, and together need to decide which gifts to buy under budgetary constraints. This task mimics help and assistance in retail shopping environments.

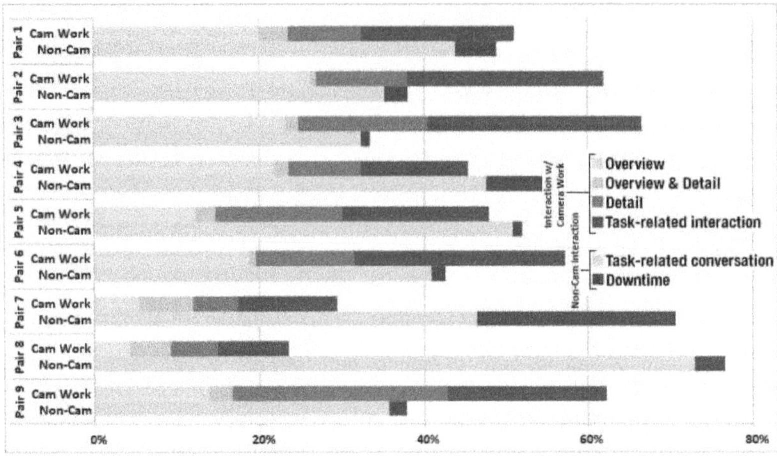

Figure 2: How participants used their time. About half of this interaction (blue-shaded) involved the camera in some way.

Data Collection and Analysis

Video and audio from both sides of the call were recorded, with an additional camera capturing the DC. We also collected field notes and videotaped interviews. These informed our analytic process.

We used *video-based interaction analysis* [13] to analyze the video data. Our analytic interests followed many of the foci outlined in [13]: specifically, the structure of events, the use of artifacts to structure events (namely, camera and objects being pointed at and referred to), how activity is organized, turn-taking, and participation structures. We applied this analysis framework by considering each of these concepts in relation to the video coding, iteratively and provisionally analyzing the data as it was collected. We reviewed this as a team, and concentrated on aspects of the framework where the mobility of the device made a difference in contrast to prior work in video-mediated communication spaces.

We observed participants' behaviours, such as how they communicated through the video connection, how the MC operated the camera, and how participants responded to the information they received. We looked for behaviours that were common across groups, as well as behaviours that were unusual. Raw videos from each session were synchronized and combined. We then iteratively annotated our videos, beginning with a small set of codes informed by interviews (e.g., showing overview/detail; using front/rear camera) and refining these codes by modifying, adding and removing codes as the process continued.

FINDINGS

We first report observations on how MCs held the phone. We then describe the basic mechanics of the MCs' camera work, in particular, how MCs try to provide overview and detail views. Then, we show how camera work supported communicative activity by supplementing speech. From here, we describe how MCs attempted to provide a sense of spatiality to DCs through movement and camera work. Finally, we discuss how the asymmetry in camera control affected participants' behaviours, and describe some of the social awkwardness experienced by our participants.

Camera Orientation. MCs held the phone in both portrait (63% of the time) and landscape (37% of the time) modes during the tasks. Landscape mode provides a wider FOV than portrait mode, and so it was surprising that MCs held the phone in portrait more often than in landscape—particularly in Task 2, where participants were explicitly trying to help orient the DC to the environment and where the larger FOV of landscape mode might have been more helpful (in this task, the split was 78%-22% in favour of portrait mode). According to participants' reports during the interviews, both social and ergonomic factors played into this decision. First, MCs found it awkward to hold the phone in landscape while walking around in public, because landscape typically signals to others that they were going to take a picture or video, whereas portrait mode attracted less attention. Second, participants found it physically awkward to hold the phone in landscape mode.

Front vs. Rear Camera. MCs used the back camera far more often than the front camera (81% of time using back camera vs. 19% front camera). Participants reported during the interviews that the DC does not usually need to see the MC's face while completing a task; instead, it was far more important to see what was in the environment. Only two groups used the front camera for more than one task; two other groups that tried using the front camera reverted to using the rear camera almost immediately.

With the exception of Task 1, MCs always held the phone in their hands; typically this was so the DCs could have a view of something (the environment, an object, or the MC—as a 'selfie'). Because MCs needed to complete a physical task in Task 1, some MCs would occasionally set the phone down or try to prop up the phone on the table.

Mechanics of Mobile Camera Work

As illustrated in Figure 2, most pairs made use of the cameras extensively to complete the tasks. We use *camera work* to describe how MCs operate the phone camera to capture the scene during the task. With the exception of Task 1 (where MCs were sitting at a table), MCs could freely manipulate the camera view—both by moving the camera phone and by physically moving. Here, we describe the basic mechanics of this camera work—first, we discuss how MCs tried to provide DCs with an overall sense of the environment (overview mechanics); second, how MCs try to give DCs an understanding of an object or landmark of focus (detail mechanics), and finally, task-related interaction, where MCs used the camera (through movement and positioning) to answer or ask questions, or to provide meaningful awareness into their action.

Camera Work: Overview Mechanics

Participants achieved overview shots in several different ways. In our analysis, we found that for these shots, either the camera was moving or held in a fixed posture, and either the MC was moving or stood still. While these practices were somewhat more fluid, the associated discussion would change depending on the overview mechanic being used.

Static overview: the MC provides an overview without moving the camera or physically moving through the space. We typically saw that MCs would show an object or several objects from far away. This occurred most frequently in Task 2, where MCs were trying to orient the DC through the space. Here, MCs would show a landmark from far away (approximately 10 to 150 metres) and keep the camera fixated while providing a verbal description of the landmark without approaching it. It seems that MCs were trying to allow DCs to "take in" the environment, as if it were a picture, allowing the DC to study features and aspects of the view. For example (Group 3, Task 2):

TIME	VERBAL	ACTION
14:28	**MC:** So, right there is the library.	*Cam:* Pointed at the library (~100 m).
14:32	**MC:** That's where you can check out books.	
14:34	**DC:** To the left of MacHall?	
14:35	**MC:** Yeah.	
14:42	**DC:** Alright. **MC:** Great!	

In Task 1, MCs would hold the phone away from the scene or step back from the desk a few feet to give an overview of the block structure at its current stage or of the available blocks. Similarly, in Task 3, MCs would point the camera at a restaurant or a picture menu board from far away to give an overview of the restaurant's offerings. In Task 4, MCs often pointed the camera at a set of items placed on a shelf and stepped back to show all of the items in frame.

Approach overview: the MC provides an overview by moving around in the environment, but holds the phone camera steady. This typically involved putting an object of focus in frame while approaching it and keeping it in frame. Usually, the MC starts doing this from far away—either because the object or landmark is simply far away, or it needs to be understood within the broader physical context—and approaches it until the viewer can see clear details of it. For example (Group 9, Task 1):

TIME	VERBAL	ACTION
12:21	**MC:** So this is Campus Security.	*Cam:* Facing entrance to the Campus Security office (~20 m).
12:26	**MC:** I'm just going to walk to it.	*MC:* Walks toward entrance; cam still has office centred.
12:30	**MC:** So if you have any security issues, you'll want to go there.	*MC:* Stops. *Cam:* centred toward on security office (~5 m).

Notice here that static and approach overviewing have different functional aims—whereas static overviewing allows the DC to take in the scene, approach overviewing is about setting an object (or its details) within context.

Camera-moving overviews: the MC provides an overview by moving or turning the camera. We identified two types of mechanics: *pan* overview and *spin* overview. *Pan* overview involves panning the phone camera across a set of objects or landmarks to give the DC a sense of what is there. This type of overview was especially common when the MC was trying to communicate a set of options to the DC. For example, MCs panned in Task 3 to show the food items a restaurant had on the counter, in Task 4 to show the items on a store shelf, and in Task 1 to show the set of available bricks. A related mechanic was the *spin* overview, where the MC provides a 180 to 360-degree overview of the environment from her current location by rotating the camera—usually while standing still. Spins were not very common (used by only three of nine MCs), but were notable due to being a means of providing a rich overview of an area. For example (Group 1, Task 3):

TIME	VERBAL	ACTION
22:25	**MC:** I'm in the food court right now.	*Cam:* Pointed at one side of the food court.
22:30	**MC:** So this is it.	*MC:* Physically spins steadily 270°. Many restaurants from both sides can be seen.

Walkthrough overview: the MC walks past a set of objects and points the camera left and right, at each one of them. For instance, in Task 4, MCs walking through clothing aisles would point the camera left and right to show the different types of clothes that were available. In Task 2, MCs also often showed DCs different landmarks as they walked past. Much like the pan overview, the purpose seems to be to provide the DC with a sense of the objects in the environment, but necessitates physically moving because objects cannot be captured all at once.

Camera Work: Detail View Mechanics

MCs also provided DCs with detail views whenever appropriate—for instance to discuss features of an item at a store, or to inspect specific food items. We saw this most frequently when there was substantial discussion of items, and a close-up view aided the interaction.

We typically described this behaviour as *centre-staging*, where a specific object or landmark is made the central focus by placing it in the centre of the frame and making it clearly visible to the viewer. For example, in Task 1, MCs centre-staged single blocks by picking them up and holding them in the centre of the frame (e.g., to ask whether the block was the correct one). In Task 2, MCs centre-staged landmarks while describing them. Similarly, in Tasks 3 and 4, MCs centre-staged restaurant signs, menu boards, store and food items, and price tags—for instance, one MC held the camera close to a package of sushi to give her partner a view of its contents. Another example (Group 9, Task 4):

TIME	VERBAL	ACTION
36:45	**MC:** It's called "Aquabee Sketchbook."	
36:53	**MC:** Here, this is the name.	*Cam:* Pointed at the label on the front of the sketchbook.
37:00	**DC:** Okay.	*Cam:* Moves away.

In some cases, the MC could pick up an object in question (e.g., in Tasks 1 and 4), and move it to the centre of the frame. In Task 1, six of nine MCs picked up the assembled set of bricks and rotated it to allow their partners to see it from different perspectives. This was done to both provide a view of the "current" state of the structure and to provide assistance in figuring out what steps to take next.

Camera Work: Technology Limits

Overview mechanics each had different purposes, but many involved trying to share something about the environment (e.g., where landmarks were relative to each other, the space of possibilities, etc.). MCs overcame the poor FOV of the camera (further exacerbated by MCs holding the camera in portrait mode) through the use of overviews constructed through movement (e.g., pan, spin, approach)—yet, there are obvious problems with these. In particular, they require the DC to integrate multiple scenes over time, remembering what they saw in relation to what they are seeing now. Furthermore, the video had substantial motion blur, as the camera could not focus quickly enough. Based on what we saw, it was clear that while the MCs were well intentioned in constructing overview shots, they were not always effective. For instance, DCs rarely got a complete sense of the entire spatial context. This was evident in the maps drawn by DCs in Task 2, which bore little resemblance to areas themselves. Similarly, with the walkthrough approach, it was easy to forget about objects that were no longer in view.

Because of the low resolution of the video feed from the mobile phone (and the lack of zoom controls and manual focusing), MCs also often had a hard time showing details from distances that would be appropriate if the DC were collocated. Instead, to accommodate the poor view of the camera feed, MCs needed to walk closer to objects of interest. For example, in Task 3, MCs would sometimes read restaurant menu boards aloud in addition to pointing the camera at them. They did this because they knew that it was hard for their partners to see the details of the menus or even read from them. In principle, with a high enough resolution, or the ability to bring attention to the area of interest, these extra movements would not be necessary.

Camera Work and Communication

While camera work supplemented speech, occasionally it also seemed to replace conversation altogether. Specifically, we saw all MCs ask and answer some questions solely through their manipulations of the camera view. For example, in Task 1, the MC asks where to place a block by hovering it over several possible spots (or in different orientations)—moving through options quickly enough that it is clear the MC is waiting for the DC to simply interrupt and say "that is where it should go," rather than waiting for a response to each possibility. Similarly in Task 3, the MC hovers the camera over several food items as a way of asking if the DC wants to try any of them. Again, the MC waits for the DC to interrupt the movement as a way of acknowledging positively which food item should be selected.

Similarly, MCs answered questions through camera work—responding, for instance, to questions from the DC by simply pointing the camera at an object or allowing the movement of the camera to indicate that an action is being taken. In Tasks 3 and 4, for instance, when DCs asked for the price or physical description of an item, some MCs would simply point the camera at the item or its price tag. For instance (Group 3, Task 3):

TIME	VERBAL	ACTION
19:28	**MC:** You want a muffin? It costs $1.43.	*Cam:* Pointed at the menu board (~5-7 m).
19:31	**DC:** Really? How big is it?	
19:33		*MC:* Slowly approaches the muffin on the display counter.
19:38	**MC:** This big. **DC:** Oh, okay!	*Cam:* Focused on the muffin on the display counter (~few cm).

To direct the DC's attention, MCs would sometimes point the camera toward an object of interest; however, this was sometimes inadequate—particularly if many things could be seen or the video scene was cluttered. Consequently, MCs would sometimes point through the frame (i.e., point their finger in front of the camera) to direct attention to certain things (e.g., Figure 3). While this was effective, it was very cumbersome for the MCs.

Conveying Spatiality through Movement in Space

MCs seemed to be aware that DCs would not be able to understand the spatial layout of the environment with a simple walkthrough. Consequently, many MCs adopted awkward movement and conversation strategies to help DCs understand the environment. For example, some MCs tried not to turn the camera around while moving (e.g., by pointing only in the direction that they were moving), while others would turn slowly while reporting loudly what they were doing. Other MCs moved only in a grid-like fashion (i.e., in simple directions such as left, right, forward, and backward, rather than diagonally), to make it easier for their partners to understand their movements. Figure 4 contains a sketch depicting an observed example of these actions.

MCs would also show new landmarks in relation to other familiar landmarks. There were two strategies that MCs used to accomplish this: *anchoring* and *backtracking*. With *anchoring*, the MC refers to a previously seen (or previously visited) landmark. This was done is a few ways:

Figure 3: Pointing with hands through the video frame.

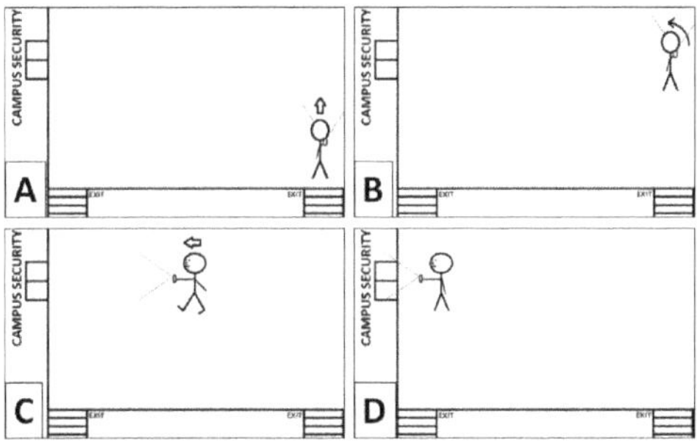

	TIME	VERBAL
A	11:15	**MC:** Okay, so I'm walking in [to the building].
B	11:23	**MC:** And then, I'm turning left.
C-D	11:30	**MC:** And this is what [the security office] looks like.

Figure 4: MCs often moved slowly and in a grid-like fashion; while pointing the camera forward and carefully describing their movements.

by pointing the camera at the landmark, by turning the camera at and pointing at the landmark, and by simply saying where the landmark was in relation to the MC. This technique was used at least once by every MC. Similarly, *backtracking* refers to when an MC goes to another location by walking backwards in a path that she took before. By doing this, the MC could recap the locations of previously seen landmarks while approaching a new landmark. Some MCs chose to backtrack rather than take a new path, even when a new path was available and more convenient, because they thought that it would be easier for their partners to understand. Both these strategies rely on camera work—on the MC's part to point and show physical relationships between landmarks, and again relying on the DC to be able to develop a mental model of the space based on the video.

In spite of all of these strategies, DCs generally developed poor (and incorrect) understandings of the spatial environment.

Asymmetries of Control, Participation and Awareness

The MC had complete control over the camera's location and orientation, meaning that the DC's ability to perceive the environment was strictly mediated by the MC. This had some interesting consequences for how the DC and MC interacted with one another—specifically when the DC wanted to direct either the action or the camera view.

Referring to Objects. In Task 1, only the DC knows how the final structure should look—as such, they explicitly need to provide information and instruct the MC on how to complete the task. In practice, this frequently amounted to describing a block and where to place it (along with the orientation). When participants are collocated, these instructional tasks tend to be fairly straightforward (e.g., [10, 17]). In our study, the explicit lack of access to the MC's workspace presented some serious problems for DCs.

DCs gestured at the computer screen (e.g., in Task 1 to refer to a specific block, or in other tasks to direct the action within the mobile frame). Unfortunately, as illustrated in Figure 5,

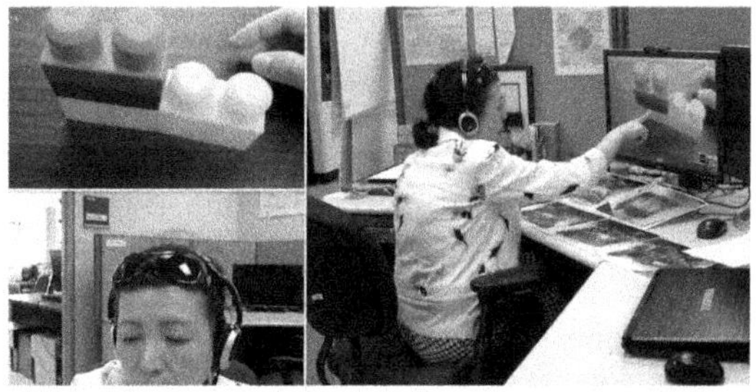

Figure 5: Right: The DC's gestures at the screen cannot be seen by the MC. Top left: The DC's view. Bottom left: The MC's view of the DC.

these gestures were not visible to the MC, meaning their communicative intent was lost. Nevertheless, these gestures were quite frequent—seven out of nine DCs made such gestures and, of these, averaged ten times during Task 1. The inability to view gestures (which included pointing, swiping, and rotating gestures) meant that the rich communicative intent was lost. DCs in Task 1 were frequently frustrated by their inability to articulate what is very easily communicated through gesture.

Negotiated Camera Control. DCs also had no control over the camera view—as such, if a DC wanted to see something in the view, they needed to negotiate with or ask the MC. There were a few instances when the DC interjected verbally and asked the MC to focus on or point the camera toward something specific in the environment. Some MCs seemed to provide opportunities for such interjections when panning slowly over a set of items or around the environment, sometimes asking questions while performing the camera movements. This was rarely smooth though. For example, in the vignette illustrated by Figure 6, while the MC is doing a walkthrough, the timing of the DC's requests are sufficiently behind with what is actually in the mobile frame that the DC's requests rarely get fulfilled. Here, while the pair is deciding on a shirt to buy, the DC says "the blue one"; however, at this point the blue shirt is out of frame and a white shirt is in frame. As the MC is turning around to point back at the blue shirt, the DC says "yeah, the white one"; but at that point the white shirt is out of frame and the blue shirt is in frame again. Note that the verbal references typically were in broad terms about what was seen (e.g., colour, shape,

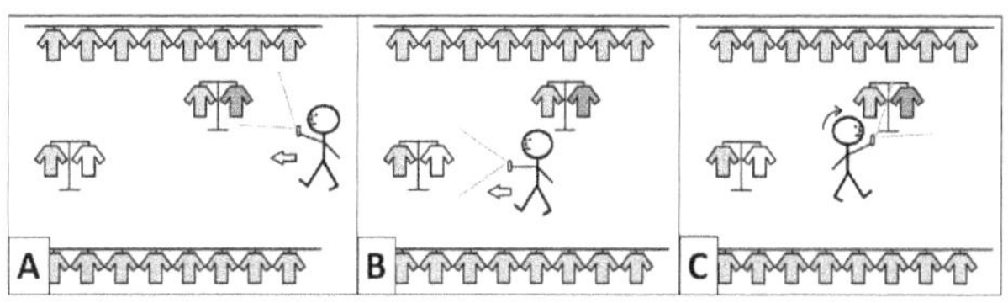

	TIME	VERBAL
A	12:49	
B	12:52	**DC:** The blue one!
C	12:53	**DC:** Yeah, maybe the white one! **MC:** This one? *(Referring to blue shirt.)*

Figure 6: MCs' attempts to allow the DC to interject do not always turn out smooth.

type of object, etc.). In three cases, the MC ignored these interjections or did not understand what the DC was trying to direct focus to.

Such interjections did not occur frequently—only occurring once or twice for six of the nine pairs. One reason could be that the DC gets a very limited view into the MC's environment and only interjects if something interesting shows up in frame. Another possibility (as illustrated in the vignette from Figure 6) is that ultimately such interactions are frustrating for both the DC and MC, and so participants may have been trying to minimize conflict.

MC Takes Over Completely. Because of the limited opportunities for the DC to interject or guide the MC's movement or focus, three MCs ended up completely taking the lead in one or more of Tasks 3 and 4 (Pairs 4, 7, and 8)—tasks designed for discussion and working together. For instance, one MC simply decided unilaterally what the DC was to order and eat from the food court in Task 3. Similarly, four MCs simply took on most of the shopping of Task 4 by themselves, going wherever they wanted and looking through items without showing or even describing them to their partners. In these cases, the DC ended up providing information only verbally or only discussing issues brought up by the MC.

Limited Awareness. The MC rarely paid close attention to the DC's view, and as such pairs would often miss opportunities to coordinate. In several instances, the MC tried to show something or do something expressly for the DC through camera work, but the DC did not notice. For example, in Task 3, while a pair was discussing healthy eating options, the MC slowly panned across a set of doughnuts (likely as a joke). Unfortunately, the DC was looking at her paper notes and did not notice.

Social Awkwardness and Distraction

Our MCs described feeling awkward holding the mobile phone in public while in the video call. In particular, many felt that holding the phone in landscape drew substantial unwanted attention as it implied or signaled the taking of a photo or video. As a consequence, MCs often held the phone in awkward ways (Figure 7): either close to one's body and away from the face (Figure 7 left and centre), making it difficult to see the screen; or close to one's chin (Figure 7 right), with the back camera pointed down at the floor and the front camera pointed up at the MC's chin.

An interesting consequence of the phone-holding postures was that MCs became very engrossed in providing their partners with a "good view." This meant that MCs frequently failed to notice other people or hazards around them. One participant was nearly hit by a vehicle passing by. Such incidents also suggest that, for at least some tasks, a wearable camera may be a good solution.

DISCUSSION

In articulating the mechanics of mobile camera work, our intention was to tease apart the goals of actions from the constraints placed on the MC by the design of the technology. Table 1 summarizes the observed goals participants had while completing the tasks, and the specific actions they would take to achieve these goals. Along with each goal, we present the informational challenges of the mobile and remote parties. This table acts as a tool in the discussion of mobile video collaboration practices and needs. Next, we discuss several implications of these findings. For simplicity, we continue to use DC and MC; however, more generally, DC refers to the party not controlling the camera view in question.

Many of the findings we outline here confirm prior findings from Gaver et al. [9]; however, the fact that a person is in explicit control of a mobile camera here adds substantial nuance. In particular, we see unpacking a user's *goal* with a particular camera angle (e.g., overview, detail, etc.) as adding something interesting to the overall discussion. In particular, if we can establish what people are trying to do, there may be opportunities for designing certain kinds of automation that can help address these goals.

Gesturing and Drawing Attention. Collaborators wanted to show details of the scene and reference objects to their partners during all of the tasks. We saw awkward attempts to gesture at the video scene (e.g., MCs putting their hands in the video scene), and the DC's gestures failing entirely (because their gestures could not be seen). Designs should provide effective and appropriate means to gesture. While this idea is not new (e.g., [6, 7, 8, 11, 16, 17]), most mobile video conferencing systems still do not provide this support. Further, even when gestures are observable, they might be missed, partly due to reduced awareness (e.g., because of the small mobile phone screen). In addition, while previous work has explored gesturing mechanisms that rely on explicit messaging (e.g., [6, 7, 8, 11, 17]), our findings suggest that it may also be important to support gesturing through social cues (e.g., by pointing, as in [16]). Furthermore, our findings also suggest that it is important for MCs to be able to read these cues while still maintaining high awareness of and concentration on the surrounding environment. This may be possible, for example, through vibrotactile wearables, where the vibrotactile device can be used to indicate which direction someone is interested in looking.

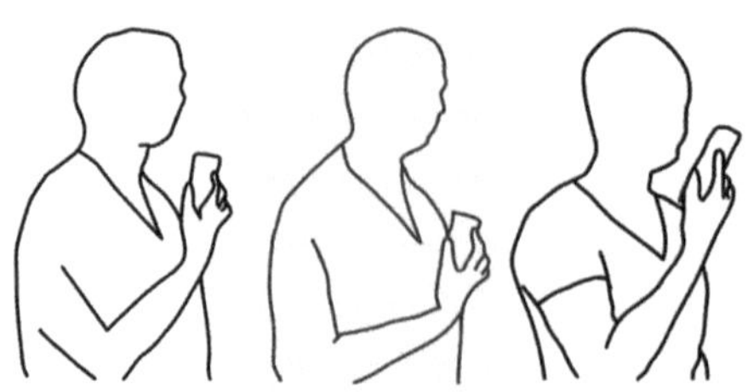

Figure 7: MCs held the phone in awkward ways.

Goal	Camera Work Mechanic
Show an environment/scene *Challenge:* DC should be able to explore the scene him/herself	Static overview, spin overview
Show a set of alternatives (objects) *Challenge:* DC should be able to remember all alternatives	Pan overview, walkthrough
Show detailed information *Challenge:* MC should be able to do this quickly and efficiently	Centre-staging, walking close to object, picking up object
Referring to an object *Challenge:* MC should be able to do this quickly and efficiently *Challenge:* DC may not be able to see the object	Pointing through the video scene, verbal interjection
Provide spatial awareness *Challenge:* DC cannot explore the scene him/herself	Backtracking, anchoring

Table 1: An MC's goal and the associated camera work observed.

Visibility of Objects. It was not always easy for either party to reference objects or scenes, either as a communicative act or to aid in memory. This was particularly true when the MC was very close to or far from a target object, or when a scene was not easily framed. This necessitated careful camera work to get close enough to an object to centre-stage it or to get in a position to correctly frame a scene. Two things make this procedure challenging: first, ensuring that the object of interest is in the scene (so the other person can see it); second, bringing the other collaborator's attention to the object, or the specific part of the object as necessary. Because the MC has control of the camera view, it is easier for them to accomplish this. Designers need good ways to provide DCs a means to convey what camera shot is needed. Allowing DCs to review recent scenes might save them from having to remember details or to request the MC to reframe a scene. This idea has been touched on to some extent by previous work (e.g., [7, 8, 16]).

Spatiality and Context. We also saw that both MCs and DCs are interested in understanding spatial context—to contextualize gestures and comments, and to understand what else is in the MC's environment that is not conveyed in the video scene. For DCs, because they did not have this context, they were unable to make coherent suggestions about what camera shot was necessary, or meaningfully help with decision-making (e.g., in the shopping scenario); instead, they were strictly confined to what the MC happened to be pointing the camera at. To address this, a larger FOV camera would likely again help (much like the workspace-oriented camera of [3]). This could provide the DC with better awareness of the MC's environment, allowing for more opportunities for the DC to interject and guide the MC's movement or focus. While our study did not lead to any concrete evidence that a limited FOV hinders collaboration, some participants did mention that they felt the limited FOV hindered their ability to complete certain tasks. We leave further investigation of this for future work.

Remote Control. We observed that MCs recognized that building a spatial awareness would be challenging for the DCs, and adopted a number of ways to accommodate (e.g., backtracking and anchoring). However, these failed to allow the DCs to build an accurate mental map of physical spaces. If the DCs had been local, this could have been easily achieved by looking around a space. However, this was not always possible because a particular view was not available when a DC needed it, and requesting it from the MC was awkward and cumbersome. We also saw that the lack of control for DCs led to frustration. Previous work has proposed and explored means to allow DCs to control their view of a mobile scene both directly (e.g., by controlling a camera [30] or a view of a reconstructed representation of the scene [7, 8, 16]) and indirectly (e.g., by providing means for DCs to request what direction to point the mobile camera in [16]). Our findings suggest that the social signals we use in day-to-day interaction should be respected while providing these means. In other words, approaches that rely on implicit and natural social cues such as pointing (e.g., [16]) are more favourable than approaches that rely on explicit user intervention (e.g., [7, 8]).

Avoiding Social Awkwardness. We observed participants holding their phones in awkward ways and avoiding the use of landscape mode because it communicated to others that they were taking photos or videos. Designers should consider ways to communicate to observers that a person is engaged in a video conversation, allowing others to understand what an MC is doing (e.g., by flashing the camera light at regular intervals). This might also communicate to people in the environment that this person's attention is divided and may allow others to accommodate (perhaps avoiding collisions).

Wearables. Collaborators had a difficult time manipulating the phone camera while completing Task 1, which required handling other physical objects. Hands-free mobile video conferencing technologies should be designed to support collaboration in tasks that require both hands. These types of technologies have been explored by other researchers (e.g., [22, 24, 30]). However, these technologies present interesting trade-offs in relation to the problems described above—as they are likely only able to provide detail views rather than good contextual overviews. Furthermore, being coupled strictly to a body part, be it a chest (as a pendant), or one's head (as a heads-up view) means that the FOV is strictly limited to what the MC is looking at, and we have observed that this can be frustrating for the person not holding the camera.

CONCLUSION

Current designs of mobile video conferencing technologies are mainly the mobile equivalent of their desktop counterparts. Very little work has gone into understanding exactly what changes in mobile video conferencing scenarios, particularly in support of shared tasks. Yet, mobile video enables a whole host of new applications and scenarios that were previously unavailable (e.g., aiding in mechanical repair, supporting navigation, etc.). As we have seen, it is likely that these scenarios are poorly supported by current tools. We saw that participants frequently found it difficult to effectively complete tasks—in part because of communicative breakdowns in relation to the camera view. Poor FOV and asymmetry of control mean that people cannot equally contribute to ongoing interaction.

Our study of mobile video conferencing has provided new insights on the ways in which camera views are used to help support communication across a video link. We have provided the first articulation of the mechanics involved in completing collaborative tasks using current mobile conferencing systems. Based on this new framework built from observation, we have outlined key challenges and several implications that could help designers build and improve mobile video conferencing tools in the future.

ACKNOWLEDGEMENTS

We thank all of our study participants, as well as Ray Sharma of XMG Studio, NSERC, SurfNet, GRAND NCE, Nokia, and AITF for their generous support of this work.

REFERENCES

1. Brubacker, J. et al. (2012). Focusing on Shared Experiences Moving Beyond the Camera in Video Communication. In *Proc. DIS 2012*, 96-105.
2. Clark, H.H., and Marshall, C.R. (1981). Definite reference and mutual knowledge. In *Elements of Discourse Understanding*, 10-63.
3. Fussell, S.R. et al. (2003). Effects of Head-Mounted and Scene-Oriented Video Systems on Remote Collaboration on Physical Tasks. In *Proc. CHI 2003*, 513-520.
4. Fussell, S.R. et al. (2003). Where do Helpers Look?: Gaze Targets During Collaborative Physical Tasks. In *EA CHI 2003*, 768-769.
5. Fussell, S.R. et al. (2003). Assessing the Value of a Cursor Pointing Device for Remote Collaboration on Physical Tasks. In *EA CHI 2003*, 788-789.
6. Fussell, S.R. et al. (2004). Gestures Over Video Streams to Support Remote Collaboration on Physical Tasks. *HCI 19(3)*, 273-309.
7. Gauglitz, S. et al. (2012). Integrating the Physical Environment into Mobile Remote Collaboration. In *Proc. MobileHCI 2012*, 241-250.
8. Gauglitz, S. et al. (2014). World-Stabilized Annotations and Virtual Scene Navigation for Remote Collaboration. In *Proc. UIST 2014*, 449-459.
9. Gaver, W.W. et al. (1993). One is not enough: multiple views in a media space. In *Proc. CHI 1993*, 335-341.
10. Gergle, D. et al. (2004). Action as Language in a Shared Visual Space. In *Proc. CSCW 2004,* 487-496.
11. Gutwin, C., and Penner, R. (2002). Improving Interpretation of Remote Gestures with Telepointer Traces. In *Proc. CSCW 2002,* 49-57.
12. Inkpen, K. et al. (2013). Experiences2Go: Sharing Kids'Activities Outside the Home with Remote Family Members. In *Proc. CSCW 2013,* 1329-1340.
13. Jordan, B., and Henderson, A. (1995). Interaction Analysis: Foundations and Practice. *Journal of the Learning Sciences 4* (1), 39-103.
14. Judge, T.K., and Neustaedter, C. (2010). Sharing Conversation and Sharing Life: Video Conferencing in the Home. In *Proc. CHI 2010*, 655-658.
15. Judge, T.K. et al. (2011). Family Portals: Connecting Families Through a Multifamily Media Space. In *Proc. CHI 2011*, 1205-1214.
16. Kasahara, S., and Rekimoto, J. (2014). JackIn: Integrating First-Person View with Out-of-Body Vision Generation for Human-Human Augmentation. In *Proc. AH 2014.*
17. Kirk, D., and Fraser, D.S. (2006). Comparing Remote Gesture Technologies for Supporting Collaborative Physical Tasks. In *Proc. CHI 2006,* 1191-1200.
18. Kirk, D. S. et al. (2005). Ways of the Hands. In *Proc. ECSCW 2005*, 1-21.
19. Kirk, D. et al. (2007). Turn It This Way: Grounding Collaborative Action with Remote Gestures. In *Proc. CHI 2007*, 1039-1048.
20. Kirk, D. et al. (2010). Home Video Communication: Mediating 'Closeness'. In *Proc. CSCW 2010*, 135-144.
21. Kraut, R.E. et al. (2003). Visual Information as a Conversational Resource in Collaborative Physical Tasks. *HCI 18* (1), 13-49.
22. Kuzuoka, H. (1992). Spatial workspace collaboration: a SharedView video support system for remote collaboration capability. In *Proc. CHI 1992*, 533-540.
23. Licoppe, C., and Morel, J. (2009). The Collaborative Work of Producing Meaningful Shots in Mobile Video Telephony. In *Proc. MobileHCI 2009,* 254-263.
24. Mann, S. (2000). Telepointer: Hands-free completely self-contained wearable visual augmented reality without headwear and without any infrastructural reliance. In *Proc. ISWC 2000*, 177-178.
25. Norris, J. et al. (2012). CamBlend: An Object Focused Collaboration Tool. In *Proc. CHI 2012*, 627-636.
26. O'Hara, K. et al. (2006). Everyday Practices with Mobile Video Telephony. In *Proc. CHI 2006*, 871-880.
27. Ou, J. et al. (2003). DOVE: Drawing over Video Environment. In *Proc. MULTIMEDIA 2003,* 100-101.
28. Procyk, J. et al. (2014). Exploring video streaming in public settings: shared geocaching over distance using mobile video chat. In *Proc. CHI 2014*, 2163-2172.
29. Raffle, H. et al. (2010). Family Story Play: Reading with Young Children (and Elmo) Over a Distance. In *Proc. CHI 2010*, 1583-1592.
30. Sakata, N. et al. (2003). WACL: Supporting Telecommunications Using Wearable Active Camera with Laser Pointer. In *Proc. ISWC 2003*, 53-56.
31. Sodhi, R.S. et al. (2013). BeThere: 3D Mobile Collaboration with Spatial Input. In *Proc. CHI 2013*, 179-188.
32. Tang, J.C. et al. (2013). HomeProxy: Exploring a Physical Proxy for Video Communication in the Home. In *Proc. CHI 2013*, 1339-1342.
33. Virtual Photo Walks. http://www.virtualphotowalks.org.
34. Yarosh, S. et al. (2010). Video playdate: toward free play across distance. In *Proc. CHI 2010*, 1251-1260.

Reducing the Stress of Coordination: Sharing Travel Time Information Between Contacts on Mobile Phones

Frank R. Bentley, Ying-Yu Chen, Christian Holz
Yahoo Labs, Sunnyvale, CA
{fbentley, yyc, christianh}@yahoo-inc.com

ABSTRACT

We explore the everyday use of a new abstraction for mobile location-sharing. By sharing the travel time between contacts calculated for walking, transit, and driving, we have enabled users to more easily coordinate meeting up and planning family obligations. Specifically, our participants reported that the information helped to lower the stress of these activities and provided reassurance of the arrival times of their close friends and family. In this paper, we describe our system, motivate its design, and explore results from a 20-user, 21-day field trial showing the usefulness of the abstraction as well as attitudes towards privacy when sharing travel times with close friends or family.

INTRODUCTION

For the past decade, the CHI literature has explored the topic of location sharing from a variety of different perspectives [2–6,8]. Much of this research has explored privacy-preserving ways of receiving the benefits of sharing location while limiting unintended or socially-undesirable disclosures. However, in this time commercial location-sharing systems have largely followed a different course, where absolute location is shared with a wider audience.

We wanted to revisit the topic of location sharing and return to the ideas behind some of the original privacy-enhancing location systems such as Motion Presence [3] or the Whereabouts Clock [5] but use today's smartphone technology to provide a more useful experience to users. We began by reviewing previous location sharing abstractions and chose to create a system that enhances coordination through sharing a new type of location-derived information: travel time between contacts.

We revisited the idea of sharing "in-motion" information from [3], but wanted to choose a location abstraction that was more useful for immediate coordination. Time-in-motion information works for standard commutes with fixed times, however quickly loses usefulness with traffic or deviations from normal behavior. In the years since that work, phones have evolved a rich set of precise location services and web APIs have become available for determining travel times via a variety of transportation options.

We chose to allow people to access the time-away (by foot, car, or transit) between themselves and a specific contact as a way to aid in the coordination process. To understand how this information could be used in daily life, we conducted a 21-day field study with a set of 20 diverse users. We discovered the details of how time-away data allowed participants to better plan meeting up in person, coordinate shared activities, and build awareness of each other's days. We will discuss our findings as well as their relevance to the design of services intended to aid coordination.

CHI 2015, April 18 - 23 2015, Seoul, Republic of Korea.

http://dx.doi.org/10.1145/2702123.2702208

BACKGROUND

As phones began to incorporate location-sensing capabilities in the early 2000s, researchers began exploring ways that people could share their locations with others to aid in coordination. With the emergence of modern smartphones, a wide variety of location-sharing applications have gained popularity. However, many of these applications tend to share absolute locations, which can be less useful in coordinating meet up times and can contribute to a larger loss of privacy than some earlier ideas from the HCI literature.

Among the earliest mobile location sharing systems was the Context Phonebook [7] which included icons to indicate if a contact was at home, work, or in transit. The Whereabouts Clock [5] displayed similar information, sensed from a mobile phone, on an ambient display in the home. However, in both of these systems, if the user was not at one of these pre-defined places they were only listed as "in-transit," making it hard to coordinate arrival times.

Later work began exploring ways to provide increased privacy over absolute location sharing while enhancing the utility of the data provided. The Motion Presence system [3] allowed users to see if a contact was currently "at a place" or "moving between places" as well as the number of minutes in transit. This allowed users plausible deniability about their absolute location, and was found to be useful for coordination by using the display of minutes in motion.

Today, many commercial smartphone applications allow for sharing one's location with friends. These applications tend to fall into one of two categories. Some systems allow for users to share location information ambiently in the background to a select group of people. For example, systems like Google Latitude showed the precise location of friends on a map. Other apps such as Foursquare's Swarm or the new Path Talk application share city or neighborhood names with friends. Glympse allows users to explicitly send their location and anticipated travel time to a set of people. Another set of systems allows for "check-ins" to specific venues, with the precise location of these venues shared with friends. These systems have enjoyed wide adoption, but in general do not follow many of the privacy enhancing strategies from earlier HCI studies.

People also share location manually in SMS. Battestini *et al.* [1] found that over 40% of text message conversations related to Planning or Places, both heavily used for coordination tasks. We have also observed that much of this communication adds stress to the tasks of meeting up. Having a friend not reply or receiving a text querying your ETA while driving, as two examples, can add undue stress to a hopefully pleasurable outing with friends or family.

Tang [8, 9] explored a variety of different geographical and semantic abstractions for location sharing. Among these, she looked at blurring or upleveling location as well as providing abstracted names for the places where people were located instead of geographic points. However, this work focused mainly on traditional location sharing and not abstractions (e.g. motion) that go beyond geographic entities. Consolvo *et al.*'s study of location abstraction [6] explored similar concepts of exposing different layers of a location hierarchy for a place (e.g. state or region level locations) to different users at different times.

We wanted to build a system that better supported the tasks of coordination and meeting up in strong-tie social relationships. We also wanted to move beyond sharing specific hierarchical descriptions of a location and focus on more actionable information. We decided to focus on time-away as the type of information that would be disclosed.

THE SYSTEM

Our time-away location feature was implemented as a part of our research prototype PairApp. The system allowed for users to create customized "apps" on their home screen that are each connected to a single important person in their lives. The app provided standard text and photo messaging with a similar look and feel to the native SMS application.

At the top of the chat window was a "location" button. Pressing this button would send the user's current location to our servers which would request the location of the pair's phone. The server would then call the API for Yahoo Maps to find the walking, driving, and transit times between the locations of the two phones and returned these to the devices. Both devices would then display the travel times in a drawer that would open in the chat window (see Figure 1).

We designed the system to explicitly engage in reciprocity. If a user requests another's time-away, the other person would see their location drawer open and travel times displayed. We hoped that this would engender trust and limit the unhealthy and voyeuristic practices explored in [4]. The application was implemented on both Android and iOS.

STUDY METHODS

To understand the use of this location feature, we conducted a field study in the Summer of 2014. We recruited ten main participants from the greater San Francisco Bay Area using a professional recruiting firm to ensure diversity. Each main participant then picked a friend or family member to use the app with over a period of 21 days. Main participants were selected to be diverse in many aspects. They ranged in age from 21-52, were half female, comprised a variety of ethnic backgrounds and had diverse occupations (e.g. lawyer, nurse, unemployed bartender).

We met with participants for an initial interview where we installed the PairApp on their phones (either Android or iOS devices). We then let them use the application for the next 21 days, with nightly voicemail diary entries to tell us about any use of the application that day. We finished with a final interview where we followed up on the voicemail entries as well as asked about general use of the application.

Participants were explicitly instructed that they did not need to use the application at all to be compensated for participation in the study. We asked them to act as if they just downloaded the application from the market, to use it how they saw fit, and to stop using it if they no longer found it useful. Our main participants could add anyone they chose as contacts in the application. Most chose to add significant others, while a few chose friends. We also interviewed the secondary participants at the end of the study.

All qualitative data from the initial and final interviews as well as from the voicemail diaries was transcribed and entered into grounded theory-based affinity analysis. Individual items of analysis were exact quotes from participants and the themes below emerged across participants' data.

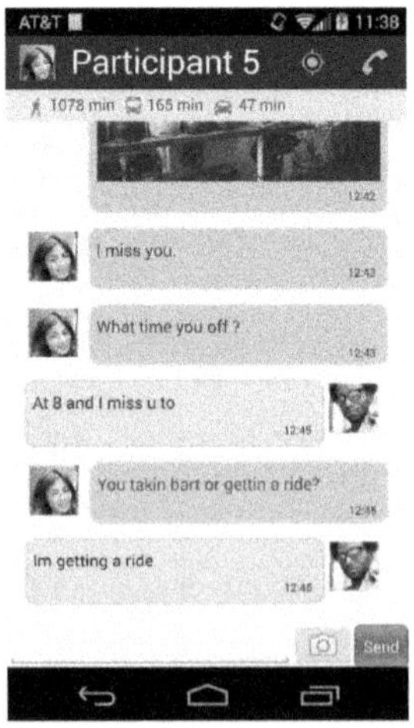

Figure 1: The location drawer in our PairApp shows walking, transit, and driving times to the contact. Participant names and photos have been anonymized.

FINDINGS

Our participants used the time-away feature with their pair an average of 12 times (median 9, s.d. 17) during the 21 days of the study. During this period they also sent an average of 78 text messages and 2.4 photos to each other.

Through analyzing data from the interviews and voicemail diaries, we were able to understand how our participants used the time-away feature of the application during the three weeks of the study. Themes emerged around using the feature to coordinate meeting up, to coordinate family tasks or activities, and around the level of privacy that the system enabled. As the analysis continued, we identified an overarching theme illustrating how the feature helped to reduce the stress of planning and coordination in daily life.

Coordinating Meeting Up

Participants used the time-away feature in a variety of ways to coordinate meeting up in person. Participants often knew that friends or family were on the way, but wanted to know exactly how long it would take them to arrive. P5 told us, *"I knew that he was coming from Oakland, and I wanted to see where he was in relation to [me]."*

Especially when their pair contact was driving or otherwise not using their phone, participants reported liking the time-away feature to see how far away their friend or family member was at a given time. P4 explained, *"I couldn't get a hold of her, 'Where are you? Where are you?' Trying to figure out what we're going to do for the night, try and figure out how far she is, I was like, oh yeah. I went into the app, said, 'Where are you?' But then I was able to pull up her ETA and ... was like, okay she's actually on her way. I think she was on her phone talking to somebody, she didn't want to talk to her husband."* P7 described a similar incident with his wife: *"She's calling me and I'm not answering, not responding to text, and she wants to see where I am, she can do that. ... If I said, 'I'm leaving work in 30,' and she doesn't hear from me for an hour and she does [a] location request."* These instances, and others in this theme, allowed for participants to feel at ease and know when their partner would arrive even though they could not get a hold of them synchronously via phone or text.

P1 appreciated that *"you don't have to interrupt them, like 'Oh, how far are you,' or get impatient. Just look."* This idea of "just looking" instead of potentially interrupting a spouse in a late meeting or while driving was a main factor in the stress relief that the system provided to participants.

Participants used this feature to understand when their contact would arrive at their location. P7 was coordinating with his wife on a busy day: *"She was coming from her office, to come pick up the dog, and I was in a hurry because I had a meeting and I needed her to come. I think we had tried to use it that way so I can see how close she was to me."* P4 also used it with his wife: *"I didn't even have to ask her, 'How far are you?' It just plopped up. That was a really nice feature we really liked."* He continued, *"Sometimes you don't know where this person's at ... For us it [helped] because then I knew how long it was going to take her to get to me. That helped."* In these cases, explicitly knowing the arrival time helped participants to feel at ease that the timing of complex handoffs could occur before they had to be somewhere else in their busy lives.

In addition to using the time to know how long it would take a contact to get to their location, participants also used the system to figure out their own ETA at the location of their pair. P3 saw how long it would take her to reach her boyfriend. P5 liked that *"it tells me my walking and my bus, when I don't have the car, how far away things are."* This helped participants to plan their arrivals at their contact's location and gave them piece of mind of arriving on time.

Coordinating Tasks/Family Activities

Beyond simply coordinating arrival times, participants used the time-away information to coordinate family tasks and activities. An extended look at P3's behavior around preparing dinner gives a detailed example. P3 was mostly unemployed, taking odd babysitting jobs to earn some money. Her live-in boyfriend worked a part-time job at a baseball stadium about an hour and a half away by train. She took great pride in having a hot meal prepared for him late at night as soon as he arrived home from work. However, baseball games do not have a set time duration and can vary in length by an hour or longer. In addition, transportation between the stadium and her home is quite sporadic late at night with 20 minutes or longer between trains. Thus P3 was never quite sure when her boyfriend would be home and when she should start cooking for him.

She told us that she would use the time-away feature whenever he was working and that: *"It made it so easy for me. I got to relax so much because I knew where he was ... If you already have like everything premade like you pre-seasoned your food and okay, I cooked the macaroni now but I just don't add cheese instead. Okay, by the time he gets here, I'm going to stir in the macaroni and tell him, 'Dinner's done. Here is your plate.'"*

She liked the accuracy of the time away in helping her to finish cooking the minute he would arrive. *"Yeah, I was very accurate with that way. The timing meant everything because it meant hot meals ... Imagine if I cooked the meal at 30 minutes before. I don't know about you guys but fried food cold is gross."* Before having this feature, she *"would kind of be off with the time a little bit, sometimes he'd get home sooner then I'm like, 'I'm still cooking. You aren't supposed to be here. You're supposed to come home 30 minutes later."* This information made her feel satisfied that she could demonstrate her love for her boyfriend by having a hot meal ready right when he arrived, greatly reducing her evening stress. In addition, this information also gave her time to do other things and *"just relax in the meantime."*

We observed other participants using the system to coordinate family tasks such as dog watching or child pickups.

Knowing when someone would arrive helped make these handoffs go more smoothly. P4 discussed meeting up for a play date for his kids, *"Yeah I was just on the [train], we were messaging back and forth. Instead of asking me the question she just popped it [the time-away] up. She's like, 'Oh you're here?' I was like, 'Oh yeah, I'm on the [train].' She was like, 'Okay, good.' … It was really nice to be able to connect that way. ... It just seems more fluid than a text."*

Privacy Concerns

Showing only the time-away helped to preserve privacy. Most participants felt quite comfortable using this more abstract form of location sharing. P3 said that it *"made me feel comfortable, more than [sharing a GPS] location ... Knowing a precise location would be good but then I think it'd be kind of be creepy because I wouldn't want someone to know like exactly where I was. That's a little weird."*

P6 would have preferred that he could enable or disable the features for specific conversations. *"Unless you explicitly want to tell somebody where you are at that moment, it's not cool with me. Yeah. Unless they're explicitly for that conversation able to enable it, to me that's ... stay away from that stuff."* Although he told us this, he was the most frequent user of the feature with an average of over two location requests per day. P6's concerns might stem from a specific event that happened during the study. His girlfriend had used the time-away feature and had discovered that he was driving past her home, yet he did not stop. P10 found a similar concern: *"I feel like I would be invading someone's privacy if I send them a text when they're just a minute away from me. I didn't know they're in my town. Sometimes I feel it might be knowing too much information."*

Overall, we saw that participants continued using the feature, despite having explicit instructions that use of any part of the system was not required. This, combined with the comments on how the time-away abstraction was useful and more privacy-preserving than sharing an absolute location, shows us that there is promise in the concept. However, our data indicates that the feature should be able to be enabled or disabled for specific times and people.

DISCUSSION

In exploring the design space of location-based abstractions that can be shared as real-time presence information, we chose a new point that we have not seen explored before. Our system lies in-between work such as Motion Presence [3] or the Whereabouts Clock [5], which only showed the act of being "in transit," and systems that share absolute location information such as Find My Friends or Latitude. The idea of abstracting sensor data to yield useful items to share with others is an area that is still quite rich to explore.

We have seen how displaying time-away information is more useful than simple motion or activity data as it allows people to plan more precisely for arrival times (of themselves or others) and produces a feeling of calm and control over coordination-based tasks such as food preparation or managing the care of children or pets. This put our participants at ease that their coordination task would work out, or if it would not, gave them added time to plan a contingency.

Similar to the work on Motion Presence, we have explored this type of sharing in strong-tie social relationships. Most of our participants chose their significant others as secondary participants and the remainder chose close friends. Clearly these relationships are much more amenable to sharing this type of private information than for other contacts [6]. Systems that enable these types of features should allow for users to easily enable or disable this type of sharing for specific people or time periods. The reciprocity of seeing a friend's time away when they request yours was an important part of our design, and the act of explicitly requesting another's time away distinguishes this work from existing push-based systems such as Glympse which also shares absolute location. This feature could also be useful in groups for specific meetup tasks and can be more useful than raw location in knowing when specific people will arrive, thus reducing the stress of unknown arrival times.

REFERENCES

1. A. Battestini, V. Setlur, and T. Sohn. 2010. A large scale study of text-messaging use. In Proc. MobileHCI '10.
2. L. Barkhuus, B. Brown, M. Bell, S. Sherwood, M. Hall, and M. Chalmers. 2008. From awareness to repartee: sharing location within social groups. In Proc CHI '08.
3. F. Bentley and C. Metcalf. 2007. Sharing motion information with close family and friends. In Proc. CHI '07
4. J. Boesen, J. Rode, and C. Mancini. 2010. The domestic panopticon: location tracking in families. In Proc. Ubicomp '10.
5. B. Brown, A. Taylor, S. Izadi, A. Sellen, J. Kaye, and R. Eardley. 2007. Locating family values: a field trial of the whereabouts clock. In Proc. UbiComp '07.
6. S. Consolvo, I. Smith, T. Matthews, A. LaMarca, J. Tabert, and P. Powledge. 2005. Location disclosure to social relations: why, when, & what people want to share. In Proc. CHI '05.
7. A. Schmidt, T, Stuhr, and H.W. Gellersen. 2001. Context-Phonebook - Extending Mobile Phone Applications with Context. In Proc. MobileHCI '01.
8. R. Schuler, S. Grandhi, J. Mayer, S. Ricken, and Q. Jones. 2014. The doing of doing stuff: understanding the coordination of social group-activities.
9. K. Tang. 2010. Sometimes Less is More: Multi-perspective exploration of disclosure abstractions in location-aware mobile social applications. PhD Thesis.
10. K. Tang, J. Lin, J. Hong, D. Siewiorek, and N. Sadeh. 2010. Rethinking location sharing: exploring the implications of social-driven vs. purpose-driven location sharing. In Proc. Ubicomp '10.

You Can't Smoke Here: Towards Support for Space Usage Rules in Location-aware Technologies

Pavel Andreevich Samsonov*, Xun Tang†, Johannes Schöning*, Werner Kuhn§, Brent Hecht†
*Expertise Center for Digital Media, Hasselt University - tUL - iMinds;
§Dept. of Geography, UC Santa Barbara;
†Dept. of Computer Science and Engineering, University of Minnesota
{pavel.samsonov,johannes.schoening}@uhasselt.be, kuhn@geog.ucsb.edu, {xuntang,bhecht}@cs.umn.edu

ABSTRACT
Recent work has identified the lack of *space usage rule* (SUR) data – e.g. "no smoking", "no campfires" – as an important limitation of online/mobile maps that presents risks to user safety and the environment. In order to address this limitation, a large-scale means of mapping SURs must be developed. In this paper, we introduce and motivate the problem of mapping space usage rules and take the first steps towards identifying solutions. We show how computer vision can be employed to identify SUR indicators in the environment (e.g. "No Smoking" signs) with reasonable accuracy and describe techniques that can assign each rule to the appropriate geographic feature.

INTRODUCTION
In 2013, a hunter started an illegal campfire that grew out of control and ended up damaging California's famous Yosemite National Park [4]. By violating a *space usage rule* (SUR) – a restriction against campfires – this hunter caused severe environmental and property damage and was a serious hazard to public safety.

SURs are not limited to constraints on campfires. Most of us encounter space usage rules frequently as we go about our day. From "no smoking" to "no fishing" to "no swimming", these rules maintain public health, enforce important laws, and protect fragile ecosystems. More generally, SURs are a critical mechanism through which governments and other stakeholders (e.g. landowners) manage our interaction with our environment.

However, despite their importance and ubiquity, space usage rules are absent from location-aware technologies. Schöning et al. [5] recently reported that while traditional paper maps frequently inform map readers of the space usage rules in the depicted area, no popular mobile or online map does the same. This omission is more than just a missing feature. As people become more and more dependent on their mobile devices as guides to unfamiliar spaces, the lack of support for SURs threatens to undermine the awareness of SURs and reduce their benefits.

CHI 2015, April 18–23, 2015, Seoul, Republic of Korea.
Copyright 2015 © ACM 978-1-4503-3145-6/15/04...$15.00.
http://dx.doi.org/10.1145/2702123.2702269.

Figure 1: An example of a "no-sign" showing a *space usage rule* (SUR), specifically "no dogs allowed".

The potential of SURs for location-aware technologies extends well beyond improvements to online and mobile maps: SURs can also enable an *entirely new class of context-aware applications*. For instance, it is easy to imagine a SUR-based app that tells smokers if it is legal to light a cigarette in their current location (and direct them to the nearest smoking area if it is not) and, similarly, an app that tells hunters where it is okay to start a campfire.

One can also easily imagine straightforward algorithms that provide routing instructions to help dog owners avoid "no dogs allowed" areas when walking their dogs and apps that generate vacation recommendations for specific areas that allow activities of interest (e.g. climbing, fishing, swimming). Along the same lines, SUR-based technologies could also help people negotiate complex issues with spatial components, such as laws that regulate where one can bring a concealed weapon in several U.S. states and laws that restrict the flight area of personal drones.

However, before these novel SUR-based technologies can be developed and before online/mobile maps can support SURs, a critical problem must be solved: *space usage rules must be mapped*. As we will show below, outside of a very small number of OpenStreetMap (OSM) tags, no dataset of SURs currently exists.

In this paper, we introduce the first techniques for the widespread mapping of space usage rules. Doing this mapping accurately and on a global scale is a challenging task that will require a variety of approaches. The goal of this paper is to demonstrate that the time is right to begin addressing the SUR mapping problem by demonstrating the feasibility of one family of approaches: those informed by computer vision. The objective of our computer vision-based technique is to mine publicly available geotagged photos for "no-signs" such as those shown in Figure 1 and Figure 2 and map the corresponding SURs to the appropriate spatial regions.

One major benefit of computer vision-based approaches is that they can be used on large datasets of geographically-referenced imagery, particularly those available to Google and Microsoft in their Streetview and Streetside corpora. While we show below that using publicly available image datasets allows us to increase the number of SURs available in OpenStreetMap by a significant amount, our methods below have been developed with an eye towards these larger corpora and the enormous increase in SURs that would result if similar methods were applied to them.

To summarize, this note makes the following contributions:

1. We introduce and motivate the *space usage rule (SUR) mapping problem*, discussing the need for SURs in existing technologies (e.g. mobile maps) and highlighting the technologies that could be enabled with a large-scale dataset of SURs.
2. We report the results of a small survey of SURs, finding that rules can be complex and can rely on indicators in the environment (e.g. "no-signs").
3. We show that the only public dataset of usage rules – SUR-like "tags" in OSM – is extremely limited in size, scope, and geographic extent.
4. We introduce a computer vision technique that can map SURs by automatically detecting "no-signs" (i.e. usage rules indicators) in geotagged photos. We also identify straightforward approaches to assign the corresponding SURs to the correct spatial features in OSM.

SURVEY OF SPACE USAGE RULES

To inform the design of our SUR mapping techniques, we first conducted a survey of SURs. Because Schöning et al. [5] found many SURs on public park maps, we surveyed the websites of 25 well-known parks in urban areas and 25 in rural areas using Wikipedia's lists of parks articles (e.g. "List of national parks of the United States"). Four to five parks of each type from every populated continent were selected.

Overall, we found that there was an average of 7 SURs listed per urban park website and 6.9 per rural park website. Over half (56%) of these rules applied not to the entire park, but to specific places in the park, and many of the rules were restricted to *types of areas* (e.g. paths, grass areas), adding complexity to SUR mapping efforts. In addition, in certain cases, the areas in which rules applied were not fully specified on the website. For instance, the website for New York City's Central Park lists several specific places where dogs must be leashed and adds that the rule also applies in "other areas where signs requiring dogs to be leashed are posted." Examining this "where posted" phenomenon in more detail, we found it to be common. For instance, in Minnesota, a business owner can ban guns in her business by posting a sign.

The complexity and non-specific nature of official usage rules led us to our computer vision-based "no-sign" detection approach as our first SUR mapping effort. This approach is robust against the "where posted" phenomenon, and can capture broader rules (e.g. park- or city-wide rules) as well in many cases. In the discussion section, we highlight other possible SUR mapping approaches and how they can complement the techniques described here.

USAGE RULE TAGS IN OSM

As noted above, the only public dataset of space usage rules of any size is embedded in OpenStreetMap. These rules are encoded by OSM contributors through the use of "tags" that are applied to spatial features. In order to understand the coverage of these tags, we examined the tags on all spatial features in the global OSM dataset. We focused on three SUR tags in particular: no-dogs, no-smoking, and no-fishing. These tags were selected as they were the top-used SUR tags.

The results of our mining of OSM for our three tags can be seen in Table 1, which shows that *OSM has very few SURs*. By far the most common is no-smoking, but there are only 13,976 spatial features total that have this tag. This represents less than 0.0006% of all features in OSM. The situation is even sparser for the other tags; only 57 water bodies in the entire world have been tagged with no-fishing.

Table 1 reveals that existing approaches based on crowdsourced volunteered geographic information have failed thus far to generate a dataset of SURs of a useful size. As such, other approaches like our computer vision-based technique are needed to develop the global or semi-global SUR dataset necessary to support SUR-based applications. It is important to note that more targeted crowdsourcing efforts may yield better results, something that we touch on in the discussion section.

MINING USAGE RULES FROM GEOTAGGED PHOTOS

The goals of our computer-vision based approach are (1) to identify "no-signs" in geotagged photos like those in Figures 1 and 2 and (2) to assign the corresponding SURs to the correct spatial features in OSM. In this section, we cover each of these goals in turn.

Region	no-dogs	no-fishing	no-smoking
Europe	137/1738/338	0/5/44	6858/37/3996
Asia	1/0/0	0/0/0	586/1/153
North America	5/472/11	0/4/3	1131/0/411
South America	0/4/2	0/0/0	214/0/43
Central America	0/0/0	1/0/0	68/0/58
Africa	0/1/0	0/0/0	107/0/90
Australia	5/20/1	0/0/0	171/0/52
Overall	**148/2235/352**	**1/9/47**	**9135/38/4803**

Table 1: OSM SUR tag distribution for points/lines/polygons.

To develop our computer vision approach, we used geotagged Flickr images. We focused specifically on the three SURs above, which means we concentrated on finding "no dogs", "no fishing", and "no smoking" signs in Flickr images. We developed datasets of Flickr images for these three tasks by downloading all geotagged Flickr images that had the terms "no dog", "no fishing", or "no smoking" in their titles, descriptions, and/or tags. In this way, we acquired 29,981 images for "no fishing", 28,921 images for "no dogs", and 17,268 images for "no smoking".

Our computer vision approach to "no-sign" detection occurs in two stages: (1) general sign detection and (2) the application of a sparse coding-based "no-sign" filter. It is important to point out that our work is not the first to address the more general "sign detection" problem. Several approaches that use visual salience detection to identify speed limit signs have been proposed (e.g. [2]). However, existing work assumes that a sign is the most salient feature in an image. We found that this was not true for most of the photos in our three datasets and, due to this assumption violation, it was necessary to develop our own approach.

Stage 1: General Sign Detection Algorithm

The aim of the first stage of our "no-sign" detection approach is to extract candidate signs from the original images, as the keyword search alone does not tell us if a "no-sign" is actually in the photo. Indeed, examining 3000 randomly-selected images in our three datasets, we found the "keyword-only" baseline precision to be less than 5%.

Object detection is well-studied in the computer vision community and we rely on prominent object detection techniques for this stage of the approach. Specifically, we apply the Viola-Jones object detection framework [6] with Local Binary Pattern (LBP) [3] image features. In our implementation, 159 "no-signs" cropped from the overall images are used as positive training data, while 1,060 "sign-free" random images are used as negative training data.

Using this dataset of 1,219 images, a 25-stage cascade classifier was trained. Example output can be seen in Figure 2. While the classifier was relatively robust against illumination variation and image tilting, the classification performance was not sufficiently high. Table 2 shows the precision of this stage of our approach. While precision for all types of signs was significantly higher than the 5% baseline, it was around or below 50% in every case. As such, in order to increase the performance of our approach, we added a second stage of processing, which is described below. Images in which our general sign detection algorithm finds "no-signs" get passed to the second stage.

Method	"No dogs"	"No fishing"	"No smoking"
Stage 1	.425	.364	.548
Both Stages	.840	.829	.915

Table 2. Detection precision for all three types of signs using the first stage of the algorithm only and both stages (general sign detection and filtering with sparse coding)

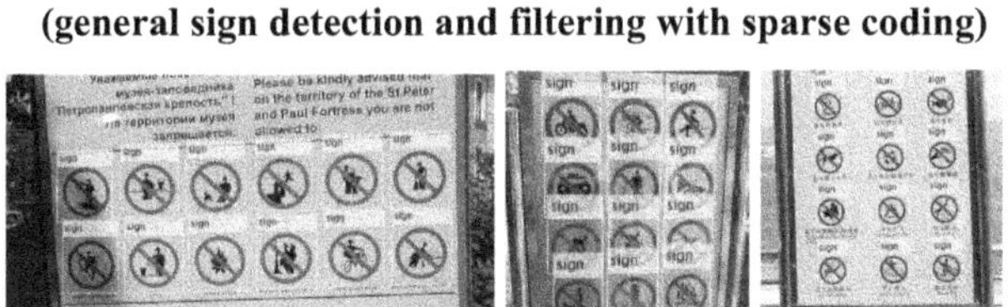

Figure 2: Sample results of the general detection algorithm.

Stage 2: Filtering with Sparse Coding

The second stage of our computer vision approach leverages sparse coding [7]. Using the sparse coding model, we developed a non-learning algorithm for detecting different "no-signs" through which most false positives among candidate signs are pruned, while most true positives are retained.

The sparse coding model tries to sparsely represent input objects. In the case that an input object is similar to a small number of bases, the representation residual is low, otherwise, the residual is high. The set of bases in a sparse coding model, therefore, should contain instances able to cover various kinds of the objects under consideration (true positive signs in our task). The bases in our approach contain edges of standard cropped signs having varying appearances as well as varying angles. The goal was to have our model be robust against different sign designs as well as color and background variation. In total, our basis set consists of eighty bases.

Following the application of sparse coding, we found that precision significantly increased (second row, Table 2). In total, after filtering out the relatively small number of false positives, our algorithm found 431 "no dogs" signs, 100 "no fishing" signs, and 638 "no smoking" signs. These photos were then passed on to the SUR-to-spatial feature assignment techniques described below. Although the total number of photos found was not enormous, if this type of approach were applied to a dataset like Google Street View (with some improvements, as described below), the number of extracted SURs would increase dramatically. In our work, we heavily biased precision over recall in order to ensure the entire pipeline – from photo to OSM tag – was effective. Future work will seek to increase recall, which was not possible to assess given the large numbers of photos involved (over 70,000).

ASSIGNING RULES TO SPATIAL FEATURES

The final step of our computer vision-based approach is to assign the SUR in a geotagged photo of a "no-sign" to the correct spatial feature in OSM (e.g. park region, building). In other words, the goal in this step is to take, for instance, a "no dogs" sign outside of a playground and tag the playground feature in OSM with the no-dogs tag.

To evaluate methods for accomplishing this task, we first downloaded all available OSM data in a 250m buffer around the geotags of the 1,169 identified "no sign" photos, excluding the small percentage of cases (<10%) where there was very little OSM data in this buffer zone (< 2KB). Next, we searched for pre-existing no-fishing, no-dogs, and no-smoking tags in each buffer zone and found 0, 1, and 51 tags, respectively. Because of the limited number of no-dogs and no-fishing tags, we focused on no-smoking tags for the remainder of our sign-to-region study.

We used the 51 no-smoking photo/tag combinations as ground truth for testing a variety of straightforward approaches for assigning a "no-sign" SUR photo to the correct spatial feature. It is important to note that the lack of a bigger ground truth data demonstrates there is very little overlap between geotagged photos of "no-signs" and tagged features in OSM. In fact, we found that just with our preliminary dataset of "no-signs" photos mined using the algorithm described above, we can boost the number of features with SUR tags in OSM by 15.0% for no-dogs, by 171.9% for no-fishing, and by 4.2% for no-smoking.

We evaluated four basic algorithms for assigning the no-smoking tag to the correct spatial feature (Table 3). The most elementary of the algorithms – simply choosing the nearest OSM feature – has the highest accuracy (97.6%). This suggests that assigning point-based SUR indicators to spatial features may be straightforward.

Method	Accuracy
Tag the closest OSM feature	97.6%
Tag the closest OSM node	87.8%
Tag the closest OSM polygon	12.2%
Tag the closest polygon belonging to the categories [Restaurants, Fast Food, Cafe, Pub, Bar] (which often have no-smoking tags), else select closest node belonging to these categories	85.4%

Table 3. The accuracy of various methods for assigning SURs in photos to the appropriate OSM feature.

DISCUSSION & CONCLUSION

In this paper, we have discussed the need for location-aware systems (e.g. mobile maps) to incorporate space usage rules (SURs) like "no smoking" and "no campfires", surveyed new location-aware technologies that would be enabled with SURs, and focused on the key problem of mapping SURs. We also demonstrated that computer vision approaches – combined with a straightforward technique to assign SUR indicators found in photos to spatial features – can help us address this problem. However, as noted above, a number of other techniques for developing SUR datasets can likely be effective, and our immediate future work involves investigating some of these techniques.

One promising approach involves using crowdworkers to capture SURs from official websites. We are developing an easy-to-use system that simplifies the encoding of complex SURs, e.g. Alaska State Parks' "Discharge of firearms within ½ mile of any developed park facility is prohibited". Major challenges include developing web mining techniques to identify SUR web pages (and to possibly automatically encode simple rules).

Another area of future research involves examining SUR-based applications with a lens informed by the interaction of law and technology. Because an incorrect SUR could lead to someone unintentionally breaking an important law, it may be possible that accuracy thresholds will be quite high for SUR mapping or that effective means of communicating uncertainty will need to be developed.

A limitation of this work is that we only tested our computer vision approach on "no-signs" that use a basic round shape (e.g. Fig. 2). In some countries, certain types of "no-signs" have different shapes, such as the polygon used in Brazil. While our approach in theory should work with any shape that is in the training set, we did not evaluate the approach's robustness in this respect.

Finally, it is important to reiterate that while we demonstrated that computer vision approaches can be used find SUR indicators (i.e. "no-signs") in geotagged Flickr images, the most significant value of this type of approach is in its application to large corpora of spatially-referenced imagery (e.g. Google Street View). In order for this to occur, several additional challenges must be addressed. In particular, our techniques must be tested on additional types of "no-signs", recall may need to improve, and methods for distinguishing between different types of "no-signs" must be developed. Early work on this latter problem suggests that similar approaches to those above can be effective. We were able to achieve 65.1% accuracy classifying images of four types of "no-signs" (the three considered above plus "no swimming") using sparse coding techniques.

ACKNOWLEDGEMENTS

This work was supported in part by the following grants: NSF IIS-0808692, BOF R-5209, and a Google Faculty Research Award.

REFERENCES

[1] Donoho, D.L. and Elad, M. 2003. Optimally sparse representation in general (nonorthogonal) dictionaries via ℓ1 minimization. *Proceedings of the National Academy of Sciences*. 100, 5 (Mar. 2003), 2197–2202.

[2] Itti, L., Koch, C. and Niebur, E. 1998. A model of saliency-based visual attention for rapid scene analysis. *IEEE Transactions on Pattern Analysis and Machine Intelligence*. 20, 11 (1998), 1254–1259.

[3] Ojala, T., Pietikainen, M. and Maenpaa, T. 2002. Multiresolution gray-scale and rotation invariant texture classification with local binary patterns. *IEEE Transactions on Pattern Analysis and Machine Intelligence*. 24, 7 (Jul. 2002), 971–987.

[4] Rogers, P. 2013. Rim Fire was started by hunter's illegal campfire. *San Jose Mercury News*.

[5] Schöning, J., Hecht, B. and Kuhn, W. 2014. Informing Online and Mobile Map Design with the Collective Wisdom of Cartographers. *DIS 2014* (Vancouver, B.C., Canada, 2014).

[6] Viola, P. and Jones, M.J. 2004. Robust Real-Time Face Detection. *International Journal of Computer Vision*. 57, 2 (May 2004), 137–154.

[7] Wright, J., Ma, Y., Mairal, J., Sapiro, G., Huang, T.S. and Yan, S. 2010. Sparse Representation for Computer Vision and Pattern Recognition. *Proceedings of the IEEE*. 98, 6 (Jun. 2010), 1031–1044.

Blended Recommending: Integrating Interactive Information Filtering and Algorithmic Recommender Techniques

Benedikt Loepp
University of Duisburg-Essen
Duisburg, Germany
benedikt.loepp@uni-due.de

Katja Herrmanny
University of Duisburg-Essen
Duisburg, Germany
katja.herrmanny@uni-due.de

Jürgen Ziegler
University of Duisburg-Essen
Duisburg, Germany
juergen.ziegler@uni-due.de

ABSTRACT

We present a novel approach that integrates algorithmic recommender techniques with interactive faceted filtering methods. We refer to this approach as *blended recommending*. It allows users to interact with a set of filter facets representing criteria that can serve as input for different recommendation methods including both collaborative and content-based filtering. Users can select filter criteria from these facets and weight them to express their preferences and to exert control over the hybrid recommendation process. In contrast to hard Boolean filtering, the method aggregates the weighted criteria and calculates a ranked list of recommendations that is visualized and immediately updated when users change the filter settings. Based on this approach, we implemented an interactive movie recommender, *MyMovieMixer*. In a user study, we compared the system with a conventional faceted filtering system that served as a baseline to obtain insights into user interaction behavior and to assess recommendation quality for our system. The results indicate, among other findings, a higher level of perceived user control, more detailed preference settings, and better suitability when the search goal is vague.

Author Keywords

Recommender Systems; Interactive Recommending; Information Filtering, User Interfaces

ACM Classification Keywords

H.3.3. Information Storage and Retrieval: Information Search and Retrieval – information filtering;
H.5.2. Information Interfaces and Presentation (e.g. HCI): User Interfaces – evaluation/methodology, graphical user interfaces (GUI), user-centered design.

CHI 2015, April 18–23 2015, Seoul, Republic of Korea.

ACM 978-1-4503-3145-6/15/04...$15.00.
http://dx.doi.org/10.1145/2702123.2702496

INTRODUCTION

Recommender Systems (RS) are a well-established technology that aims at assisting users with finding relevant information in large information spaces [25], thus reducing or avoiding the information overload problem. The goal of RS is to select from a large set of items—such as products, documents or movies—those items that best match the user's interests and preferences, and to present them in a suitable manner [25]. For this purpose, most RS rely on user profiles and use fully automated recommendation techniques. Successful RS minimize the interaction effort the user needs to invest to find relevant items, produce well-fitting recommendations, and may also reduce cognitive load [24].

On the downside, most RS afford little or no user interaction, and, in particular, lack options to control how recommendations are produced. A further problem is the lack of transparency that may hinder users in comprehending why a particular item is recommended [29]. As a consequence, acceptance of the recommendations and trust in the system may be reduced [33]. Since RS require the availability of a user-specific preference profile, they suffer from the cold start problem when no information about the current user's preferences is available. It is also possible that users do not want their preferences to be stored in the system, or their existing profile to be applied as it may differs from their current interests. All the issues mentioned may result in reduced usability, trustworthiness and user acceptance of RS [16,24,29,33].

While RS represent the upper end of the automation dimension, conventional information filtering systems [14] are positioned at the opposite end. Interactive search and filter techniques, including hierarchical navigation and faceted filtering [14,34], allow users to flexibly explore large item spaces while providing a high level of user control and transparency. However, the user's effort for searching and navigating is typically much higher compared to accepting recommended items. In addition, users may over-constrain their search in a filtering system, when strict logical query processing is applied [26]. Manual filtering also requires users to mentally form a more or less specific search goal which may be difficult in large or unknown domains. Alleviating this cognitive task is one of the strengths of RS.

Considering the respective advantages and shortcomings of fully interactive filtering and automatic recommending suggests that a closer integration of interactive approaches with recommender techniques may alleviate some of the issues described. Recommender systems research has up to now been mainly focused on optimizing the accuracy of recommender algorithms, i.e., how well the recommendations fit the user preferences. It is often overlooked, however, that the impact of improved algorithms on the overall success of a RS is decreasing [17]. Since existing algorithms are already very mature, only small and ever decreasing additional precision can be expected from further optimizing the algorithms [24]. Besides, the accuracy of recommender algorithms has typically been evaluated offline, without considering the actual user interaction with the system [16].

Only more recently, research has started to focus more on user aspects, e.g., the user's interaction behavior, user interfaces for RS, and the resulting user experience [16,24]. It has been shown, for instance, that users are not only interested in receiving precise recommendations and in lowering their search effort, but also in having a more active role in the entire recommendation process [33]. Users may be willing to invest more effort and even accept less accurate system recommendations if they are able to exert more influence over the system [17]. Considering these aspects in the development of RS seems an important research goal.

To overcome the limited extent of interaction, user control and transparency in conventional RS, we propose in this paper a novel approach we refer to as *blended recommending*, that combines the advantages of interactive information filtering and automated RS. Our approach expands the concept of hybrid RS, usually defined as combining different recommender algorithms to increase the accuracy [6], by additionally integrating several interactive filter techniques. However, our point of departure is faceted filtering [34] which has been shown to be an intuitive and efficient technique [18,28] for filtering and browsing large item spaces [14]. Users select concrete filter criteria from different facets which in our approach can represent hard (Boolean) as well as soft (fuzzy) constraints. In addition, facet values may serve as input for collaborative and content-based recommender techniques in a hybrid fashion.

To demonstrate the concept of blended recommending we implemented a movie recommender called *MyMovieMixer* (MMM). The system allows users to directly manipulate both setting and degree of influence of the different filters and recommender algorithms while the resulting set of recommendations is immediately updated and visualized. Based on the different filter criteria, the recommendation methods' output, and the weights set by the user, the system calculates each item's overall relevance, trying to optimally satisfy all user preferences. The system can cope with cold start situations or when conventional filtering may not yield useful results at all. By varying the settings and weights (with corresponding sliders) of a filter, users can easily explore the effect of each facet, thus increasing interactivity and transparency of the recommendation process.

In the following, we first discuss relevant related work regarding interactive RS and information filtering. Next, we describe the components of MMM and the methods used, its interaction concept and some algorithmic details. Then, we present a user study we conducted to compare MMM with a more standard filter interface. Finally, we conclude by discussing results and providing an outlook on future work.

INTERACTIVE RECOMMENDATION AND INFORMATION FILTERING APPROACHES

Popular recommenders like the ones used by Amazon [21] or Netflix [3] often produce recommendations that fit well the user's interest and can thus contribute to reducing the user's interaction effort and cognitive load [24]. Nonetheless, in many cases users are dissatisfied with the results since they may currently have a different search goal or feel too much dominated by the system. Current RS do generally not allow the user (or only in a limited fashion) to influence or control the recommendation process. More recently, the potential of interactive approaches to recommending has been discussed as a means to overcome these usage-related issues. Some systems, for instance, allow users to refine the result set by applying the Relevance Feedback principle [27]. While employing this principle in RS increases the perceived user control, basically, the already existing user interest profiles are just refined. Such long-term user preference data are central for most recommender algorithms, although they make it difficult to react to situational needs [9] and may lead to filter bubble effects [22]. Moreover, the necessary profile information is often not available, or the profile size is too small to generate precise recommendations. While several approaches exist to overcome such cold start problems algorithmically [15,37], a promising alternative can be seen in methods that capture the user's preferences interactively.

Critique-based RS [8] increase the interactivity by allowing users to criticize certain properties of the current recommendations. Users can iteratively refine the result set towards their search goal, e.g., by requesting longer movies or films by a different director. This is based on the assumption that users find it is easier to criticize recommended items with respect to certain product features than to formulate a search goal up-front. Visual support and direct manipulation of the criticized features can have a positive effect in terms of comprehensibility, user-friendliness and interaction effort [36]. Dynamically suggesting one or more features to be criticized can increase the efficiency [8]. However, as critique-based RS typically depend on predefined product dimensions, this principle is not applicable in all situations. Other approaches use, for instance, latent factors automatically determined with Matrix Factorization [19] to let users choose between item characteristics [20]. *MovieTuner* [31] is a system based on user-defined tags. The tags are automatically weighted by the system, and the most important ones are presented to the users. Users can then explicitly indicate a preference for movies with, e.g., more humor or less violence. While expressing preferences through tags or latent factors in these systems can be useful, there is no integration with other content information such as data on actors or movie genres. Users can thus not select and weight their preferences from a wider range of different feature types (e.g. predefined content information, tags and latent factors).

Only few approaches combine recommenders with interactive visualizations. *SmallWorlds* [13] is one example that embeds a graph-based interactive visualization in Facebook to simplify preference elicitation and to increase transparency. Whereas hybrid RS [6] are typically not controllable by users, *TasteWeights* [4], an interactive hybrid music recommender, is one of the few exceptions, providing possibilities to directly manipulate graphically connected widgets. By weighting the influence of different information types and social data sources, users perceived a higher recommendation quality and better understood how the results were produced. *SetFusion* [23] shows how a RS based on a common hybridization strategy [6] can be influenced by the user. Here, users can weight the influence of three different recommender algorithms individually. While several interactive features are provided (e.g. a Venn diagram visualizing the result set), user manipulations do not always have immediate impact on the results and explicitly selecting and weighting individual content-related filter criteria is not possible. The system also requires a persistent user profile. Nonetheless, user studies showed a high degree of perceived control and increased user engagement. Visualizing the results as well as explanations how they were generated also improved perceived transparency. Another example of increased interactivity in a hybrid RS is the browser plugin *MovieBrain* [10], that enhances the Internet Movie Database (IMDb)[1] with interactive settings and filters to generate movie recommendations that better match the user's situational needs. But, apart from filtering out particular genres, it also does not take further content information into account.

With information retrieval as their point of departure, there exist a broad range of information filtering techniques outside the RS field that are based on explicit user queries. Faceted filtering [34] is one of the most prominent and successful examples for iterative query refinement. It supports exploration and discovery [14,34] of large item spaces by selecting values from a set of facets, so that the item space is iteratively constrained until the desired result is found. Faceted search is also used to enhance conventional keyword search and to support more flexible navigation [14], e.g. in digital libraries or on commercial websites such as Amazon or eBay. While most simple variants use fixed filters and values from which the user selects in a stepwise manner, more dynamic approaches with complex filter settings were already introduced a long time ago. *FilmFinder* [1], for instance, established the concept of dynamic queries, supporting continuous manipulation of filters with immediate feedback in a visualization of the item space.

Early interactive filtering techniques mostly rely on predefined sets of filter attributes (facets) and typically implement only hard Boolean filtering. Also, it has been criticized that faceted search systems often only allow for conjunctive queries and consider all facets equally important for the user [26,28,30,32]. Furthermore, most approaches perform an exact matching to determine the result set. *DocuBrowse* [12] is one example that also employs fuzzy matching. The system supports faceted browsing of a large document collection. Document genres are automatically identified and when a corresponding facet value is selected, different coloring is used to express a document's relevance. The system also offers recommender functionality, but without integrating it with the filter methods. To deal with lacking metadata, the system utilizes information about the file hierarchy. Other approaches use, for instance, semantic [7] or social [30] data sources for that purpose. Most of these newer works also focus on automatic extraction and adaptive selection of facets and facet values [7,18,30]. Still, as facets and facet values are automatically inferred relying on user profiles (e.g. extracted from semantically enriched Twitter tweets [7] or social network data [30]) and observed user behavior, the user's influence on the current filter setting is limited. In addition, from a user's perspective, items may not be sufficiently described by content-related attributes [14].

The aforementioned approaches focus on ranking facets and facet values to suggest those that are likely to be most relevant for the user's search goal. *VizBoard* [32] is one of the few systems that allow users to change the influence of the selected criteria on the result set. The authors emphasize the importance of prioritizing facets to order the results appropriately, and to avoid excluding relevant items. Recent work has also concentrated on user experience of faceted search and has combined it with different visualizations. *IVEA* [28] uses a matrix visualization to display documents and their relevance according to the selected facets based on TF-IDF heuristics. The facets derived from a user-built ontology can be ordered by the users—although here, the main purpose is to compare document sets in large collections, and the item relevance is not considered for sorting the results.

Overall, the review of related work shows that blending interactive information filtering with recommender techniques seems to be a promising approach. Combining the benefits of hybrid recommending with incremental filtering may make recommenders more transparent and user-controllable while retaining the high level of usability and comprehensibility of faceted filtering [14]. Increasing the degree of user control in RS in general and improving interactivity of the

[1] http://www.imdb.com

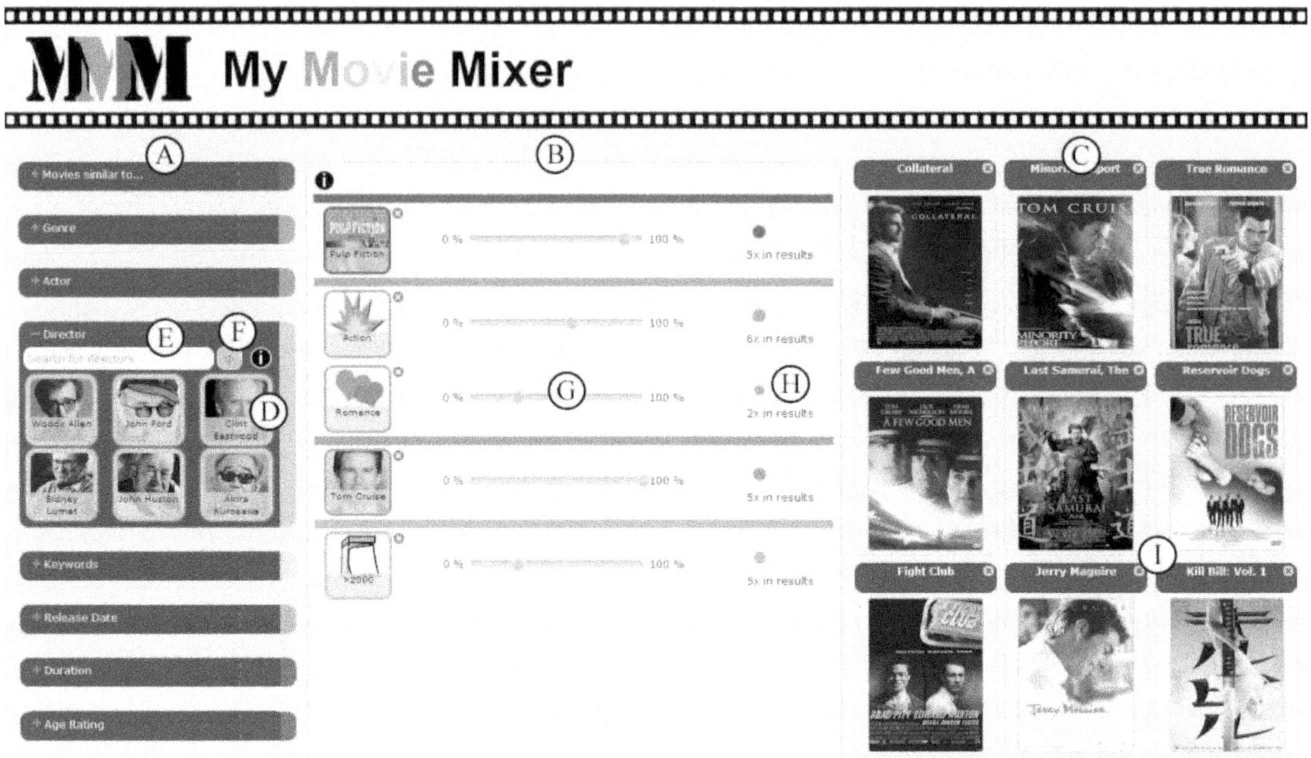

Figure 1. The MyMovieMixer application: widget area (A), work area (B), result area (C), tile representing a facet value (D), input field to search values (E), shuffle button to receive a new set of suggested tiles (F), slider to adjust a tile's weight for the recommendations (G), visualization of the number of movies fulfilling the criterion (H), button to dismiss a recommendation (I).

recommendation process have been described as important design goals [17] but are still not optimally realized in existing systems. It has also been requested that preference elicitation for RS should be more entertaining and attractive to motivate users to interact with the system [24]. Finally, fuzzy filtering with increased user influence in combination with intelligent recommender algorithms may overcome several drawbacks of conventional information filtering systems.

MYMOVIEMIXER: AN EXAMPLE APPLICATION OF BLENDED RECOMMENDING

In this section, we present *MyMovieMixer* (MMM, Figure 1), a web-based application we developed to demonstrate the concept of blended recommending. MMM integrates methods from the different approaches discussed before to recommend movies from the MovieLens dataset[2], a widely used collection of movie data with user ratings. To make the system flexible and useful in different contexts of use (e.g., for different moods, presence of different people or cold start situations), the recommendation process is entirely based on explicit user input given during a session. Although it would be possible to consider a user's long-term profile as well, this is not required for the approach.

MMM allows users to incrementally specify their preferences by selecting filter criteria from a set of facets. For facets with large number of values, a search function is provided. Users can also weight each criterion to change its influence on the resulting recommendations. The system calculates an overall relevance score for each movie by aggregating the movie's relevance values with respect to each criterion selected. Depending on the respective facet, Boolean and fuzzy filtering, as well as conventional collaborative and content-based recommendation algorithms are employed. For example, a user may indicate (as seen in Figure 1) that he or she would like to see movies similar to Pulp Fiction that also contain elements of the genres Action and Romance, although the latter criterion might be less important. In addition, the user may, for instance, love movies with Tom Cruise and would also prefer (at least to some extent) a movie from the last decade.

MMM combines the benefits of information filtering interfaces with the intelligence of RS. It allows to directly manipulate the different filters and weights and immediately shows the effect on the resulting recommendations, thus increasing user control and making it easy to understand the effect of the different settings. In the following, we first describe the

[2] http://grouplens.org/datasets/movielens/ (The MovieLens 10M dataset contains about 10 million ratings and 95 000 tags from more than 70 000 users for over 10 000 movies.)

different kinds of facets, and the corresponding filtering and recommendation methods used. Next, we elaborate on the interaction concept of MMM. Finally, we explain algorithmic details regarding the calculation of movie relevance scores.

Facet Types and Corresponding Filtering Methods

MMM offers a range of different facets, labeled: *Movies similar to…, Genre, Actor, Director, Keywords, Release Date, Duration*, and *Age Rating*. Depending on the facet type different methods are used to determine the relevance of movies with respect to the user preferences. In particular, we use Boolean filtering (for movie genres, directors and age ratings), fuzzy filtering (for a movie's release year and duration) as well as collaborative (for similar movies) and content-based (for actors and tags) recommender techniques:

- Boolean filtering: If the user selects a criterion from a facet such as movie genre, each movie with this genre will be considered in the results while the other ones will not be taken into account. The same procedure is used for directors and the age rating chosen by the user.
- Fuzzy filtering: We use Fuzzy Logic [35] to implement a soft filtering for criteria such as a movie's release year to avoid the need for exact matches as in most filtering systems. For instance, selecting a specific decade would also include, although with linearly decreasing relevance, movies released some years before or after that decade. This also applies to the length of a movie, where users can choose between "short", "normal" and "overlength" (corresponding to <80, 90–120 and >130 minutes duration). Movies falling within these time spans receive the full weight, movies in between receive lower relevance.
- Collaborative Filtering: From the *Movies similar to…* facet, users can select movies they like. Movies rated similarly by other users are then considered for the recommendations with increased relevance. For this purpose, we integrated Collaborative Filtering (CF), the overall most common recommendation method [25]. To determine similar movies, we utilize the ratings given by other users in the MovieLens 10M dataset and calculate the similarity between the selected movie and all other movies by means of their latent factor vectors (which are determined by a common Matrix Factorization [19] recommender[3]) using an Euclidean distance metric. This item-based CF approach allows users to take more than just content-related metadata of the items into account, what is often problematic or even not possible in information filtering systems [14,28,30].
- Content-based Filtering: For the actor and keyword facet we use conventional content-based recommender methods [25]. For instance, we calculate the relevance of a movie with respect to a certain keyword the user selects via TF-IDF heuristics [2]. Inspired by *MovieTuner* [31], we consider tags as terms and the set of tags associated with a movie as a document, and calculate the relative importance of each tag for this movie. This allows us to give those movies a high relevance value that are very specific for a certain keyword. Regarding the actor facet, relevance is determined based on the actor's importance (a value given by the dataset) in the particular movie.

While the choice of a concrete method depends on the underlying data, conceptually it is not important which method is used—any filtering method or recommender algorithm might be employed.

User Interaction Concept

The workspace of MMM consists of three main parts (Figure 1): The area on the left-hand side (A) presents the different facets from which the user can choose filter criteria. The work area (B) shows the selected criteria and the sliders by which users can change their degree of influence, while the resulting recommendations are shown on the right-hand side of the screen (C). We will now describe the interaction elements of these three components as well as the feedback mechanisms we integrated additionally in more detail.

Facets (A) are rendered as menu-like widgets, which in the uncollapsed mode show a number of rectangular tiles (D) representing possible criteria (facet values), visualized with images where possible. Users can drag tiles into the work area as input to the recommendation process. Since the number of values is typically large, users can add tiles by using a search box (E) with auto-completion [14]. Moreover, users can request a new set of values by pressing the shuffle button (F). The system then suggests tiles based on the frequency with which the corresponding criterion occurs in the current results. For example, when the user has dragged the genre tile Action into the work area, the result set is updated and actors most frequently occurring in action movies are shown in the actor facet. This allows the user to further filter the results with the most frequent values of other facets.

The work area (B) contains all tiles the user has dragged there as filter criteria. The weight of each criterion can be manipulated with the associated slider (G). Changing the weight of a criterion immediately updates the result set. In this way, users can interactively explore the effect of their preference settings on the recommendations. Since it may not be possible to fulfill all criteria specified, the system provides textual and graphical feedback (H) how often the criterion occurs in the current recommendations.

The ranked set of recommendations is presented on the right-hand side (C). Movies users are not interested in (e.g., because they do not like them or have already seen them), can be removed from the result set for the current session by clicking the x-button (I).

[3] *FactorWiseMatrixFactorization* from the MyMediaLite [11] recommender library.

Besides its explorative characteristic, MMM offers several means supporting the user's understanding of the recommendation generation. For example, users can open a dialog with detailed information about a recommended movie that also explains why it was recommended (i.e., which criteria were satisfied for this recommendation). In addition, recommendations related to a criterion are highlighted in color when the user moves the mouse over a tile in the work area or changes a slider's value, showing the correspondence of a criterion to the items in the result set. Considering how important it is for users to know the source of the recommendations in complex hybrid settings [23], this increases transparency and enables users at the same time to give the system feedback as in critique-based RS. Hence, they might use these hints to increase or decrease the weight of particular criteria to obtain better matching results.

Aggregating Facets for Relevance Calculation

Internally, MMM acts like a weakly coupled hybrid recommender [6]. This means, that it handles all criteria separately at first. We now describe the method used in MMM for aggregating the specified facet values, i.e., all criteria applied by the user by dragging tiles into the work area, for calculating the result set. For each movie m and each criterion c_i a value between 0 and 1 is determined. This value represents the degree with which m fulfills a criterion.

Depending on the type of criterion, the calculation of the fulfillment degree is done in different ways: As described earlier, for a criterion such as "Movie should be similar to movie x", a recommender based on Matrix Factorization [19] determines the similarity between the movies m and x by means of their latent factors. Other criteria, for instance, make use of Fuzzy Logic [35]. Assuming that a user prefers movies from a specific decade (e.g. the 1990s), a movie released in 1993 entirely fulfills this criterion and receives a 1. However, a movie from 1989 is not completely ignored—and therefore not mapped to 0, as it would be the case in Boolean filtering. In line with Fuzzy Set Theory [35] we apply a fuzzy membership function, so that a movie which only partly satisfies a criterion is (although not as strongly) considered in the results, too (and receives, e.g., a value of 0.5). In addition, we integrated a number of content-based recommending approaches [25], for example to determine how relevant a tag is with respect to a certain movie. In this case, we use TF-IDF heuristics [2] as described earlier. Boolean filtering as in conventional faceted search is applied when no other method can be meaningfully used, in particular for tiles from the genre or the director widget.

However, in some cases, especially where using Boolean filtering, a large number of items may receive a value of 1. Consequently, these items are ranked equally regarding their fulfillment degree. To avoid this, we apply an artificial ordering on these items based on the movies' average rating and the number of ratings they received. For this, we rely on the formula the Internet Movie Database (IMDb) uses for its top 250 movie charts[4]:

$$f(\mathrm{i}) = \frac{k * \bar{r} + |r_i| * \bar{r_i}}{k + |r_i|}$$

The function f basically corrects the average rating of an item towards the global mean. Therefore, it considers both the number of ratings $|r_i|$ for an item i, its average rating $\bar{r_i}$, the mean rating across all items $\bar{r}$, and a constant k we set to 100 as the result of earlier experiments.

As a consequence, the list of values for each tile can be sorted, e.g., by item similarities, fuzzy values, TD-IDF scores or at least by values returned by the formula described above. For each movie m and each criterion c_i we thus can determine the relevance value $rel_i(m, c_i) \in [0; 1]$ according to the movie's position in the sorted result list.

Subsequently, to get a relevance score rel for a movie with respect to all criteria, we aggregate the relevance values from all n tiles by means of the weights w_i the user has expressed by using the sliders with a weighted arithmetic mean:

$$rel(m, c_1, \ldots, c_n, w_1, \ldots, w_n) = \frac{\sum_{i=1}^{n} w_i \cdot rel_i(m, c_i)}{\sum_{i=1}^{n} w_i}$$

Finally, the movies are sorted in descending order with respect to these overall relevance values and the movies with the highest resulting values are presented to the user. Table 1 illustrates the calculations with a small example, where a user searches for a movie directed by Steven Spielberg (criterion c_1 with weight $w_1 = 100$) from the 1990s (c_2 with $w_2 = 50$). For demonstration purposes, we assume that the dataset consists of only three movies. We also dispense ordering the movies in case of equal relevance scores rel_i.

Movie	$\mathbf{rel_1(m, c_1)}$ *(Director)*	$\mathbf{rel_2(m, c_2)}$ *(Release)*	$\mathbf{rel(m, c_1, c_2, 100, 50)}$ *(Overall relevance)*
Indiana Jones 3 *(Spielberg, 1989)*	1.0	0.5	0.833
Jurassic Park *(Spielberg, 1993)*	1.0	1.0	1.000
Pulp Fiction *(Tarantino, 1994)*	0.0	1.0	0.333

Table 1. Relevance calculation for some example movies.

By applying the ranking technique described, we avoid the conjunctive application of filter criteria as it is used in most information filtering approaches [26,28], and allow users to fluently explore the results of different facet combinations. Nevertheless, there still may be filter settings that lead to too few results. In these cases, we extend the recommendation set dynamically with movies similar to the recommended ones by means of their latent factor values.

[4] http://www.imdb.com/chart/top

EVALUATION

Goals and Setting

Since blended recommending can be seen as an integration of faceted filtering and recommender techniques, we compared MMM with a conventional filtering interface to evaluate the effectiveness and the interaction quality of the system. We dismissed the idea of including a conventional RS in this comparison because we were particularly interested in the user interaction, whereas RS are usually based on existing user profiles and lack interactive features for expressing user preferences. Due to its high level of interactivity and controllability, a filter interface therefore appears to be a more natural competitor.

Thus, we developed a faceted filtering system (FFS, Figure 2) as an alternative condition that uses the same facets (except *Movies similar to...*), values and dataset as MMM. However, facets and values were fixed, users were not allowed to weight the different filters, and the filtering used only Boolean AND operations. Thus, in this condition, it was possible to over-constrain the search leading to empty result sets. While this general issue in faceted search can be circumvented by various means [14,26] we were interested in obtaining deeper insights into user interaction behavior. However, just as in MMM, the results are updated immediately. The system presents on the left-hand side the facets for filtering the result set, shown on the right-hand side. Additionally, the results can be sorted with respect to several criteria (e.g. movie title, release year, average rating). To further increase the fairness of the comparison, we adopted MMM's interface design, and implemented all features as similarly as possible. For the purpose of the study, we extended both interfaces with functions to add or remove items to/from a virtual shopping cart.

We hypothesized that users interacting with MMM would have a stronger feeling of control while the quality of the resulting item set would be at least as good as for the filter interface. On the other hand, the richer functionality in MMM might have led to lower usability. We therefore also evaluated usability for both systems. Moreover, we expected an influence of different situations and contexts of use. In particular, we hypothesized that MMM would be preferred in situations when users do not yet have a clear search goal or only a vague idea of what they want, which is often the case in large domains and, especially, for experience products such as movies. In contrast, we assumed that the filter interface would be preferred when the search target is known.

Method

We recruited 33 participants (20 male, 13 female, average age of 27, $\sigma = 6.46$) for the user study. The study was conducted over two weeks, and was designed as an experiment under controlled conditions. Participants used a desktop PC with a 24" LCD-display (1920×1200 px resolution) and a common web browser. The two different conditions (MMM and FFS) were tested in a between-subject design. We decided against the within-subjects option because searching

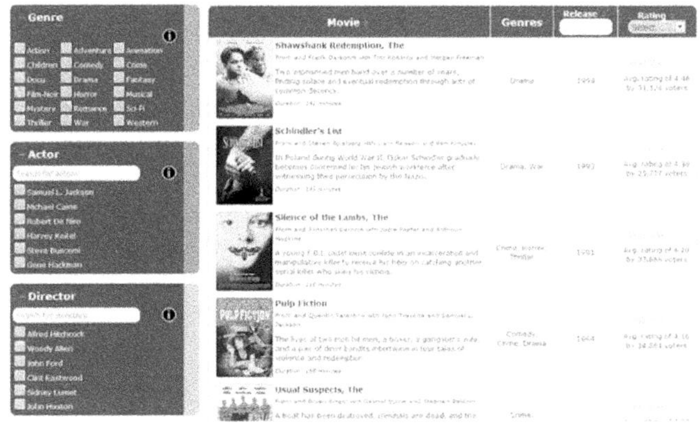

Figure 2. Screenshot of the conventional faceted filtering system we implemented to compare MMM against it.

movies the participants liked with the first system might have too much influenced their behavior with the second. In particular, participants might already develop a more specific search goal in the first trial, lowering the validity of the study for the intended usage scenarios of MMM. Thus, we randomly assigned each participant to one of the groups (MMM: n=17, FFS: n=16).

After a brief introduction by the moderator to the experiment and the system used, participants were asked to perform two tasks subsequently, which were equal for both conditions:

1. The first task can be seen as a training trial for the respective system, allowing participants to learn using its interface. Users were asked to assume that they want to buy a DVD as a gift for a friend who prefers movies from the genres Action and Romance, and especially likes the actor Brad Pitt.
2. The main task involved finding items matching the participants' personal interests. Therefore, they were allowed to use all features of the respective interface and were not restricted in time. While freely interacting with the system, they were asked to add movies (at least one) they actually would like to watch to the shopping cart.

We recorded the interaction as a screencast for later evaluation and measured task times as well. After performing the tasks, participants filled in a questionnaire comprising items we gathered from [16,24] for evaluating interaction and recommendation quality, using a positive 5-point Likert scale (1–5). Furthermore, we used SUS [5] to assess the systems' usability. Finally, we collected demographic data and asked about the participants' interests in movies, their familiarity with this domain, and their knowledge regarding movie portals and web product search.

Results

From the questionnaire data, we could identify significant differences between the two conditions: Participants reported a significantly higher feeling of control (*Control* construct from [24]) for MMM based on the impression that they were able to more flexibly adjust their preferences (MMM: $M = 4.43$, $\sigma = .50$; FFS: $M = 3.85$, $\sigma = .99$; $t(22) = 2.10$, $p < .05$). Also, the interaction (*Interaction Adequacy* construct from

[24]) was seen as significantly more adequate for generating recommendations in MMM (MMM: M=3.94, σ=.53; FFS: M=3.13, σ=1.00; $t(22)$=2.90, p<.01).

With regard to the constructs *Perceived Recommendation Quality*, *Perceived System Effectiveness* and *Perceived Recommendation Variety* from [16] the results for both conditions did not differ significantly (MMM: M=3.73, σ=.46; FFS: M=3.74, σ=.38). Also, the usability assessment with SUS [5] did not reveal any significant differences between the two systems (MMM: M=82.35, σ=14.80; FFS: M=83.59, σ=12.35).

We also asked participants to rate the suitability of the systems for different situations of use on a positive Likert scale (1–5). The results show that they found both systems suitable when users have an approximate search goal idea in mind (MMM: M=4.24, σ=.66; FFS: M=4.31, σ=.70). In situations where users are looking for a specific movie, they found the filter system significantly more appropriate (MMM: M=2.47, σ=1.46; FFS: M=3.50, σ=1.27; $t(31)$=-2.16, p<.05). In contrast, for situations with no clear search direction, participants rated MMM as more suitable (MMM: M=4.13, σ=1.09; FFS: M=2.80, σ=1.27; $t(29)$ = 3.13, p<.01).

For both systems, the number of selected movies (MMM: M=7.18, σ=5.81; FFS: M=7.21, σ=6.02), the duration of the main task (MMM: M=6.18 min, σ=2.25; FFS: M=5.37 min, σ=2.28) and the time per selected movie (MMM: M=1.25 min, σ=0.78; FFS: M=1.25 min, σ=1.23) did not differ significantly. The perceived interaction effort was rated highly acceptable on a positive Likert scale (1–5) for both conditions (MMM: M=4.47, σ=.73; FFS: M=4.25, σ=.68) without significant differences.

From the screencast, we extracted the number of criteria participants selected in task 2, including values which were used multiple times. In MMM the mean number was 8.21 (σ=2.91) and in FFS 9.92 (σ=3.73), with no significant difference between the conditions. However, the mean number of facet values selected when a movie was added to the shopping cart was significantly higher for the MMM condition (MMM: M=4.21, σ=2.51; FFS: M=2.22, σ=.83; $t(24)$=2.61, p<.05). The interaction analysis based on the screencasts also showed that in FFS participants often selected combinations of values that lead to empty result sets due to the hard filtering used. Then, users typically deselected and reselected some of the criteria in order to explore the results with different combinations of criteria. One participant even explicitly expressed the need for a Boolean OR operation. Analogously, also the participants in the MMM condition selected several criteria. But, as MMM always calculates the best matching rank order of items, users could not over-constrain their search as in FFS. Instead, they were able to immediately explore the results and adjust their preferences with the sliders. Typically, after exploring the result set and possibly adding movies to the cart, users started a new "iteration" with new or additional facet values.

Regarding further questionnaire data, in particular with respect to confounding factors such as the users' domain knowledge or prior experience with RS and filter techniques, we did not find any significant effects on our findings.

Discussion

A main finding of the study is that users feel more in control with MMM than with a standard faceted filtering system. While one might expect the level of control to be higher in the fully manual approach, the possibility to weight criteria, the soft ranking technique always leading to results ranked by how well they match the user preferences, and other interactive features of MMM seem to be the main contributors to this finding. Whereas the perceived overall quality of the results did not differ significantly, there were marked differences for different situations: The filtering system seems to be useful for more targeted searches whereas the blended RS is considered more appropriate when the user has no specific goal or the direction of the search is only vaguely known.

Despite the larger range of functionality in MMM, there were no significant differences in the usability ratings. Both interfaces received a high SUS score, indicating that the new concept is as easy to comprehend and interact with as the more well-known filtering approach. Also, task time did not differ significantly in the main task, following the short introductory task. Since also the number of items put into the shopping cart did not differ significantly this indicates that users spent a similar amount of time collecting the desired items (there was also no significant difference in the time to select the first item). Similarly, the perceived effort did not differ and was rated highly acceptable for both systems. This lack of differences on the efficiency dimensions will require some further, more in-depth analysis of the interaction behavior. An initial (weak) assumption of ours was that users would spend more time in the MMM condition since it has more functionality and might engage users more to explore the options before finally selecting a movie. Despite the lack of time differences this may still be true however. A qualitative analysis using screencasts of the user interaction with the filter system showed that users often over-constrained their search, forcing them to backtrack and change their filter settings. The time needed to correct the settings may have compensated the time gained due to the simpler filter technique. Forcing backtracking could of course be eliminated, e.g., by integrating query previews [14] or using dynamic taxonomies [26]. However, due to the underlying logic of filtering, even more advanced features would probably not have avoided that users had to try more combinations of filter settings to obtain appropriate results. In contrast, MMM always provides users with a ranked list of recommendations that match the criteria currently specified best, while they do not have to observe the logical implications of their query. However, this issue needs further investigation. Furthermore, while comparing MMM against a conventional filtering system served as a useful baseline to get insights into the user interaction behavior and the general quality of the results, it should be complemented with further comparisons against more advanced systems, both RS and filter interfaces.

An indication that users expressed their preferences more extensively in MMM can be seen in the fact that significantly more criteria were active when an item was added to the shopping cart. This is also supported by the fact that the total number of criteria set in the whole process was not different in both conditions. As this variable also includes changing and resetting criteria due to empty result sets which happened only in FFS, users of MMM may actually have applied more criteria to obtain the final result. These observations, together with the perceived high recommendation quality, indicate that users tend to specify their preferences in more detail—provided they have the option to do so—even if not all of them can be satisfied for each recommended item.

CONCLUSIONS AND OUTLOOK

In this paper, we have presented *blended recommending*, an approach that integrates conventional recommendation techniques with interactive faceted filtering methods. In blended recommending, the user is provided with a set of filter facets, the values of which can influence different recommendation methods including both collaborative and content-based filtering techniques in a hybrid fashion. Fixed filter facets as well as fuzzy filters are also used. User rating data may be used for Collaborative Filtering, supporting users even in situations where items are from a user's perspective not sufficiently described with content-related attributes. However, no stored preference profile for the current user is required, thereby circumventing the cold start problem. In principle, considering long-term interests is possible in our approach and will be subject of future work. In contrast to hard Boolean filtering, the user can select any combination of criteria and specify their degree of influence from which the system calculates a ranked recommendation list. The results of filter updates are shown immediately and can in turn be used to further refine the result set.

Besides the integration of (hybrid) recommender techniques with interactive filtering, a major goal of this work has been to provide the user with a higher level of influence and interactive control over how recommendations are generated. Active user involvement in the recommendation process has been identified by prior research as one of the major aspects in terms of user satisfaction. We achieve this by allowing users to interactively explore the results of different recommenders and filter settings by incrementally specifying preferences and manipulating their weights as well as by providing immediate visual feedback.

To demonstrate the approach, we implemented the movie recommendation system *MyMovieMixer*. We compared the system with a conventional information filtering interface in an empirical study in order to evaluate the interaction and recommendation concept of MMM. As MMM seems close to typical faceted filtering from a user perspective, such a comparison appears most natural as a baseline for a first evaluation, especially when focusing on HCI concerns. Nevertheless, we plan to also compare the system with other actual RS, in particular with interactive approaches. The results of the study show that allowing users to specify their preferences as input to different recommenders and filter techniques in combination with varying the influence of each criterion indeed leads to a high level of perceived user control. As a further result, MMM can be considered suitable for situations when the user already has a vague idea of the desired items as well as when no search goal has been formed yet. A conventional filter interface seems not very helpful in the latter case. However, as expected, the benefit of our approach is limited when the user already has a specific item in mind. In conclusion, the blended recommending approach allows users to interactively control the filtering of large item spaces while benefiting from the power of state-of-the-art recommender techniques. The approach gives users a strong feeling of control and is both effective in terms of recommendation quality as well as usability.

In future work, we plan to integrate more sophisticated visualizations, e.g., showing the result set in its entirety. In addition, we aim to investigate more intelligent facet selection techniques and different algorithmic implementations of the recommendation calculation. In this respect, it is worth mentioning that until now, our evaluation was focused on the user's perception of the interaction concept and the quality of the results, and thus should be complemented with more objective measurements. Moreover, we plan to compare MMM against other interactive recommending approaches and to implement the concept for different domains, in particular not only for experience products such as movies, but also for commercial search products.

REFERENCES

1. Ahlberg, C., and Shneiderman, B. Visual information seeking: Tight coupling of dynamic query filters with starfield displays. In *Proc. CHI '94*, ACM (1994), 313–317.
2. Baeza-Yates, R., and Ribeiro-Neto, B. *Modern Information Retrieval*. ACM, 1999.
3. Bennett, J., and Lanning, S. The netflix prize. In *Proc. KDD Cup and Workshop '07*, ACM (2007), 3–6.
4. Bostandjiev, S., O'Donovan, J., and Höllerer, T. Taste-Weights: A visual interactive hybrid recommender system. In *Proc. RecSys '12*, ACM (2012), 35–42.
5. Brooke, J. SUS – A quick and dirty usability scale. In *Usability Evaluation in Industry*. Taylor & Francis, 1996, 189–194.
6. Burke, R. Hybrid web recommender systems. In *The Adaptive Web. Methods and Strategies of Web Personalization*, P. Brusilovsky, A. Kobsa and W. Nejdl, Eds., Springer, 2007, 377–408.
7. Celik, I., Abel, F., and Siehndel, P. Towards a framework for adaptive faceted search on twitter. In *Proc. DAH '11* (2011).

8. Chen, L., and Pu, P. Critiquing-based recommenders: Survey and emerging trends. *User Mod. and User-Adapted Interaction 22*, 1-2 (2012), 125–150.
9. Chi, E. H. Transient user profiling. In *Proc. Workshop on User Profiling* (2004), 521–523.
10. Dooms, S., de Pessemier, T., and Martens, L. Improving IMDb movie recommendations with interactive settings and filters. In *Proc. RecSys '14*, ACM (2014).
11. Gantner, Z., Rendle, S., Freudenthaler, C., and Schmidt-Thieme, L. MyMediaLite: A free recommender system library. In *Proc. RecSys '11*, ACM (2011), 305–308.
12. Girgensohn, A., Shipman, F., Chen, F., and Wilcox, L. DocuBrowse: Faceted searching, browsing, and recommendations in an enterprise context. In *Proc. IUI '10*, ACM (2010), 189–198.
13. Gretarsson, B., O'Donovan, J., Bostandjiev, S., Hall, C., and Höllerer, T. SmallWorlds: Visualizing social recommendations. *Computer Graphics Forum 29*, 3 (2010), 833–842.
14. Hearst, M. A. *Search User Interfaces*. Cambridge University Press, 2009.
15. Karimi, R., Freudenthaler, C., Nanopoulos, A., and Schmidt-Thieme, L. Exploiting the characteristics of matrix factorization for active learning in recommender systems. In *Proc. RecSys '12*, ACM (2012), 317–320.
16. Knijnenburg, B. P., Willemsen, M. C., Gantner, Z., Soncu, H., and Newell, C. Explaining the user experience of recommender systems. *User Mod. and User-Adapted Interaction, 22*, 4-5 (2012), 441–504.
17. Konstan, J. A., and Riedl, J. Recommender systems: From algorithms to user experience. *User Mod. and User-Adapted Interaction 22*, 1-2 (2012), 101–123.
18. Koren, J., Zhang, Y., and Liu, X. Personalized interactive faceted search. In *Proc. WWW '08*, ACM (2008), 477–485.
19. Koren, Y., Bell, R. M., and Volinsky, C. Matrix factorization techniques for recommender systems. *IEEE Computer 42*, 8 (2009), 30–37.
20. Loepp, B., Hussein, T., and Ziegler, J. Choice-based preference elicitation for collaborative filtering recommender systems. In *Proc. CHI '14*, ACM (2014), 3085–3094.
21. Linden, G., Smith, B., and York, J. Amazon.com recommendations: Item-to-item collaborative filtering. *IEEE Internet Computing 7*, 1 (2003), 76–80.
22. Pariser, E. *The Filter Bubble: What the Internet is Hiding From You*. Penguin Press, 2011.
23. Parra, D., Brusilovsky, P., and Trattner, C. See what you want to see: Visual user-driven approach for hybrid recommendation. In *Proc. IUI '14*, ACM (2014), 235–240.
24. Pu, P., Chen, L., and Hu, R. Evaluating recommender systems from the users perspective: Survey of the state of the art. *User Mod. and User-Adapted Interaction 22*, 4-5 (2012), 317–355.
25. Ricci, F., Rokach, L., and Shapira, B. *Recommender Systems Handbook*. Springer, 2010, ch. Introduction to Recommender Systems Handbook, 1–35.
26. Sacco, G. M., and Tzitzikas, Y. *Dynamic Taxonomies and Faceted Search*. Springer, 2009.
27. Salton, G., and Buckley, C. Improving retrieval performance by relevance feedback. In *Readings in Information Retrieval*. Morgan Kaufmann, 1997, 355–364.
28. Thai, V., Rouille, P.-Y., and Handschuh, S. Visual abstraction and ordering in faceted browsing of text collections. *ACM Trans. Intell. Syst. Technol. 3*, 2 (2012), 21:1–21:24.
29. Tintarev, N., and Masthoff, J. *Recommender Systems Handbook*. Springer, 2010, ch. Designing and Evaluating Explanations for Recommender Systems, 479–510.
30. Tvarožek, M., Barla, M., Frivolt, G., Tomša, M., and Bieliková, M. Improving semantic search via integrated personalized faceted and visual graph navigation. In *Proc. SOFSEM '08*, Springer (2008), 778–789.
31. Vig, J., Sen, S., and Riedl, J. Navigating the tag genome. In *Proc. IUI '11*, ACM (2011), 93–102.
32. Voigt, M., Werstler, A., Polowinski, J., and Meißner, K. Weighted faceted browsing for characteristics-based visualization selection through end users. In *Proc. EICS '12*, ACM (2012), 151–156.
33. Xiao, B., and Benbasat, I. E-commerce product recommendation agents: Use, characteristics, and impact. *MIS Quarterly 31*, 1 (2007), 137–209.
34. Yee, K.-P., Swearingen, K., Li, K. and Hearst, M. Faceted metadata for image search and browsing. In *Proc. CHI '03*, ACM (2003), 401–408.
35. Zadeh, L. Fuzzy sets. *Information and Control, 8*, 3 (1965), 338–353.
36. Zhang, J., Jones, N., and Pu, P. A visual interface for critiquing-based recommender systems. In *Proc. EC '08*, ACM (2008), 230–239.
37. Zhao, X., Zhang, W., and Wang, J. Interactive collaborative filtering. In *Proc. CIKM '13*, ACM (2013), 1411–1420.

A Large-Scale Study of User Image Search Behavior on the Web

Jaimie Y. Park*
KAIST, Korea
jaimie@kaist.ac.kr

Neil O'Hare
Yahoo Labs, Barcelona
nohare@yahoo-inc.com

Rossano Schifanella
University of Torino, Italy
rossano.schifanella@di.unito.it

Alejandro Jaimes
Yahoo Labs, New York
ajaimes@yahoo-inc.com

Chin-Wan Chung
KAIST, Korea
chungcw@kaist.edu

ABSTRACT
In this study, we analyze user image search behavior on a large-scale query log from Yahoo Image Search, based on the hypothesis that behavior is dependent on query type. We categorize queries using two orthogonal taxonomies (subject-based and facet-based) and identify important *query types* at the intersection of these taxonomies. We study user search behavior on a large-scale set of search sessions for each query type, examining characteristics of sessions, query reformulation patterns, click patterns, and page view patterns. We identify important behavioral differences across query types, in particular showing that some query types are more exploratory, while others correspond to focused search. We also supplement our study with a survey to link the behavioral differences to image search intent. Our findings shed light on the importance of considering query categories to better understand user behavior on image search platforms.

ACM Classification Keywords
H.1.2 User/Machine Systems: Human Factors; H.3.3 Information Systems: Information Search and Retrieval

Author Keywords
image search; search strategy; user behavior; query analysis; click analysis; search intent

INTRODUCTION
Understanding user behavior in web-scale image search is important because it provides valuable insights on content relevancy, opportunities for advertising, and for the design of the interaction and user interface. There is strong commercial interest by content providers in determining what types of images people are looking for, and a deeper understanding of how people search also benefits user interaction designers and system engineers when fine tuning the search engine.

*This work was carried out while Jaimie Y. Park was visiting Yahoo Labs Barcelona for a research internship.

CHI'15, April 18–23, 2015, Seoul, Korea.

http://dx.doi.org/10.1145/2702123.2702527

With today's high volume traffic on web search engines, one of the most common approaches to gain insights into user behavior is the analysis of query logs. Previous studies on web image search [1, 5, 8, 17, 20] focused on characterizing overall characteristics based on aggregated search logs. These findings help us to gain an overall picture of how users search for images on the web, but do not capture variation amongst different types of image queries; it is likely that behavior varies across query types, since user behavior in search is heavily dependent on task or goal [12]. Understanding such differences, and how they relate to user intent, is the main focus of this work. For instance, we posit that searches for 'Britney Spears' would, in general, exhibit different search patterns from those for 'desktop wallpaper', with the former likely to lead to casual browsing of celebrity images.

In this study, we identify what users search for on web image search, and study how user search behavior varies with query type, based on the logs from Yahoo Image Search (`images.search.yahoo.com`). To study the variation in behavior based on differences in query type, it is first necessary to have a clear understanding of the important query types in image search, which also allows us to identify the important dimensions of images that search engines need to understand. This motivates our first research question:

RQ 1. What do users search for on web image search?

Information seeking is a complex process, and to properly understand it, we also need to study *how* users interact with image search results. Previous work on image search has not examined how such behavior relates to query type; the insights that we can gain from answering this question can have important practical implications for search engines, since user interaction signals are used as implicit evidence for relevance feedback from users (e.g. relevant images get more clicks), and these insights can also enable adaptive results presentation based on query type. This motivates our second research question:

RQ 2. How does image search behavior differ depending on query type?

Human interactions with computers never take place in a vacuum, but always occur in response to some user need or goal, and image search is no exception [13]. As with any information service, to provide the best possible service it is crucial to understand the underlying goals behind user behavior, motivating our final research question:

RQ 3. Can we associate query types with classes of search intent? How does search intent relate to behavior?

To summarize, the main contributions of this work are:

- We categorize a representative sample of image search queries using two complementary taxonomies, and identify a number of common image query types.
- We find a number of differences in search behavior based on query type; some query types are associated with exploratory, browsing-style behavior, while other query types users exhibit a more focused search.
- We emphasize three alternative sources of implicit feedback from search logs, *hovering over images*, *dwell time in the preview page*, and *click-through from image preview to referral website*. We show that position information is not always important for result clicks, and that click-through is heavily dependent on query type.
- We conduct a user survey to supplement our findings from the log-based analysis, and draw a connection between query type and known classes of image search intent.

In the next section we review related work, followed by a dataset description. We then characterize a sample of image search queries according to two orthogonal taxonomies, and identify important *query types* for further analysis. We then examine query type based differences in search behavior and present the results of a qualitative survey. Finally, we discuss the implications of our results and conclude the study.

RELATED WORK

'What' Images People Search for. Understanding what users search for allows us to identify the aspects of images that should be represented to support search, and several studies in the past have attempted to classify user queries on web image search engines. Pu [17] classified the 1,000 most frequent image queries based on a proprietary subject-based categorization scheme, and found that a majority of the queries were in the entertainment domain. Jansen [8] classified queries based on three existing non subject-based image query classification schema, focusing on whether users were searching for people, locations, etc., and on whether the search was about unique instances or non-unique instances, which is closely related to the facet-based Shatford-Panofsky categorization framework [18]. This framework was also used by Armitage and Enser [2] to classify image queries in offline multimedia archives.

The above studies, and other similar studies [6, 8, 17, 20], agree in their main findings that web image search is dominated by people queries or queries within the *Arts & Entertainment* category. They either explicitly focus on the most popular queries or do not reveal details of how they sample their queries, suggesting a possible bias towards popular queries. In this study we avoid such bias by taking a stratified sample from the entire query distribution; we further compare popular and rare queries to examine the differences between the two. The characterizations that emerge from subject-based or facet-based characterizations can be very broad (e.g. 'Arts & Entertainment'). To uncover more fine-grained categories that cover a significant amount of query traffic, we look at the query types that emerge at the *intersection* of subject-based and facet-based categorizations.

'How' People Search for Images. Following on from the work of Goodrum and Spink [5], researchers started working on characterizing image search behavior on web search engines [1, 5, 6, 8, 15, 17, 20]. These studies characterize the general behavior of users on image search platforms based on aggregated search log data, measuring features like session length, the number of result pages viewed, the number of results clicked per session and query reformulation patterns. They typically compare image/multimedia search behavior with general web (text) search behavior, finding that image searches lead to more clicks and deeper exploration of the search results (search depth), and conclude that image search tends to be more 'exploratory' and requires greater interactivity [1, 10]. Other work focus on search behavior on specialized image sharing platforms like Flickr [14].

Andre et al. [1] argue that, while image search tends to be more exploratory than text search, image searches can also be goal-directed. What factors affect this were not explored in the study, nor in any other study of web image search behavior. We posit that there should be significant differences in search behavior depending on the query type. Also, the above studies limit their behavior analysis to the statistics listed above (session length, number of result pages viewed, etc.), ignoring important interactions such as hovers on images, the relationship of clicks with rank position, and interactions with the image preview page (the page displayed after the user clicks on a result), all of which constitute a large portion of user interaction with image search engines. In our work, we address this gap by considering various user interactions with image search engines, and by conducting an in-depth study of behavioral differences based on query type.

'Why' People Search for Images. The general goals and tasks that motivate search provide the context for search behavior. Broder [3] proposed a taxonomy of *intent* for web search, which was adapted to image search by Lux et al. [13]. No previous work has attempted to link these classes of image search intent to specific query types, or to behavior observed in image search logs; in this work, we make a first attempt at linking intent, behavior and query type through a user survey that elicits the testimonials of real users.

DATASET

From the Yahoo Image Search server logs, we take as a sample all the queries issued in the U.S., across all device types (desktop, mobile, etc), during a continuous period in the fall of 2013[1]. We remove adult queries using an automatic classifier, and sessionize the data by partitioning a user's actions

[1]We do not reveal the exact time period, as revealing both volume and time period would disclose commercially sensitive information (i.e. volume of searches per day). However, the period under consideration does not involve major festivities, e.g., Christmas or Thanksgiving, that could introduce a problematic bias.

Number of Searches	102,534,341
Number of Unique Queries	36,103,126
Number of Sessions	34,715,204

Table 1: Dataset Description.

into separate *sessions* when the time between consecutive actions exceeds 30 minutes. The filtered, sessionized, sample contains approximately 102M searches, and 36M unique queries (Table 1). To group unique queries, we cast all queries to lower case and remove punctuation.

The query traffic distribution, as expected, has a long tail: 75% of unique queries (27M of 36M unique queries) were issued only once, and they account for approximately 25% of the traffic in the sample; the other 25% of queries account for 75% of all traffic. At the head of the distribution, the top 1% of unique queries (360K out of 36M) account for 46% of all traffic, and the top 10% account for 60% of all traffic.

From the logs, we extract data for events in two different page types: the *search results page* and the *image preview* page. The *image preview* page, a variation of which exists in the image search site of each of the major U.S. search engines, is an enlarged preview of an image, shown after the image is clicked on the search results page, with *next* and *previous* navigation buttons for further exploration of the results. A link to the referral website where the original image can be found is also displayed. We extract the following fields from each entry in the log: session id, timestamp, query string, anonymous user identifier, page type, and event type (i.e. pageview, click). For pageview events we extract the urls of all thumbnail result images displayed on the page, and the position they were displayed at. For click events, we have information about the type of click (e.g. click, hover), and the URL and rank position of the clicked image.

CATEGORIZATION OF IMAGE QUERIES

In this section we address *RQ 1*, *'What do users search for on web image search?'*. We begin by outlining our methodology, and then present our results in the section *'What Users Search for in Web Image Search'*.

Previous studies on what people search for either focus on only the most popular queries or do not give full details of how the queries were sampled, making it unclear if their findings are representative of all queries. Focusing only on popular queries would give a biased view (e.g. too much focus on celebrities), obfuscating the variety among less frequent queries. In this work, we take a sample that represents the entire distribution. Additionally, given that the long tail of rare queries takes up such a large portion of the traffic (e.g. singleton queries make up 25% of the traffic volume), we believe it is important that we understand what types of queries it consists of, and how this compares to the popular queries at the head of the distribution. This motivates our first subquestion:

RQ 1.1. Are there differences in the types of queries found in the head and the tail?

Previous studies conducted either subject-based classification or facet/aspect-based classification, leading to characterizations that are overly broad. For instance, a subject-based taxonomy may tell us that *Arts & Entertainment* queries are frequent, but this could refer to a wide range of instances, from a famous actor to a book title. By looking at the intersection of two taxonomy types, we can uncover finer-grained, but popular, query types. This motivates a second subquestion:

RQ 1.2. What are the frequent query types at the intersection of subject- and facet- based categorization?

Methodology for Query Categorization

For categorization, we take a sample of 1,000 queries to annotate manually. To reduce the sampling error that can arise from a random sample, we use a stratified sampling method. All search queries are partitioned into 1,000 equal-sized strata, where the nth stratum represents the nth permile[2] of the query traffic distribution[3]. In other words, each stratum is composed of queries that account for the same amount of traffic (i.e. the 1st stratum represents queries covering the top 0.1% of the traffic, etc.). We sample a single query from each of the 1,000 strata. This sampling strategy ensures that the set of annotated queries evenly covers the entire traffic distribution, and that by averaging over the annotated queries we get an average that represents all query traffic. It also allows us to separately analyze different portions of the query distribution (e.g. the first 100 query samples represent the top 10% of the distribution). We categorize the queries based on two complementary classification schemas described below.

IPTC Subject Taxonomy. Since there is no standard subject-based taxonomy for image queries, we chose the IPTC subject code taxonomy[4], which is often used for classifying online content, and has previously been used for images [21]. The taxonomy includes 17 top level subject-based nodes (e.g. *Arts, Culture & Entertainment*, *Lifestyle & Leisure*). Through the process of manual annotation, we identified an additional root category, *Nature*, not covered by the IPTC taxonomy. Also, the most frequent root categories, *Arts, Culture & Entertainment* and *Lifestyle & Leisure*, cover a range of subtopics, so we use IPTC subcategories for these. We also add three additional subcategories of *Lifestyle & Leisure* that we identified as important: (*Clothing & Accessories*, *Automobiles*, and *Graphics/Clipart*). The taxonomy is shown in Table 3.

Shatford-Panofsky Framework. The Shatford-Panofsky approach for image indexing was introduced by Shatford [18], based on a previous theoretical work [16], and was later adopted for classifying queries in image archives [2]. It was found to be useful in characterizing the way people formulate queries and revealing their visual information needs. The approach, summarized in Table 2, characterizes images/queries based on four *facets* (*who, what, where when*) and three *aspects* (*specific, generic, abstract*). Note that the *who* facet represents any entity, not just people, while the *what* facet

[2]permile = 1000-quantile

[3]Note that stratification was performed on all the searches, not on unique queries, so that a stratum may contain redundant queries (e.g. the first head stratum was entirely filled with 'miley cyrus').

[4]http://cv.iptc.org/newscodes/subjectcode (accessed Jan 14th, 2015)

	Specific	Generic	Abstract
Who	individually named person/group/thing (e.g. 'miley cyrus')	kind of person/group/thing (e.g. 'tiger')	mythical or fictitious being (e.g. 'pikachu')
What	individually named event/action (e.g. 'presidential election 2016')	kind of event/action/condition (e.g. 'commencement ceremony')	emotion or abstraction (e.g. 'cold')
Where	individually named geographical location (e.g. 'seoul')	kind of place: geographical/architectural (e.g. 'city')	place symbolized (e.g. 'paradise')
When	linear time: date/period (e.g. 'april 18th, 2015')	cyclical time: season/time of day (e.g. 'summer')	emotion symbolized by time (e.g. 'dark age (of life)')

Table 2: Facet/Aspect Categorization Schema.

represents actions, conditions and events (i.e. *what* that entity is doing). A query could instantiate the *who* facet and the *specific* aspect (e.g. 'miley cyrus') or the *who* facet and the *generic* aspect (e.g. 'tiger'). We further subcategorize the queries in the *what* facet as an *action*, *event* or *condition*. Similarly, we subcategorize queries in the *who* facet using the top level of the Schema.org entity type taxonomy[5].

Manual Annotation Procedure. To ensure an accurate categorization of our sampled queries, we manually annotate them into the two taxonomies. Manual annotation is especially important for the Shatford-Panofsky schema, where automatic classification is difficult. Three of the authors of this paper manually annotated the queries using an iterative process. Initially, a small test sample of queries, independent of the 1,000 sample, were annotated by all three annotators. The results were compared and conflicts discussed: this process was iterated until a stable set of annotation guidelines was agreed upon. Finally, each of the annotators annotated a random subset of the 1,000 query sample into both taxonomies. Any query identified as 'difficult to annotate' was discussed by the 3 annotators until a consensus was reached.

What Users Search for in Web Image Search

IPTC Categorization Results. Table 3 shows the IPTC subject categorization results. Subject categories covering less than 3% of the query volume are omitted from the table. *Lifestyle & Leisure* and *Arts, Culture & Entertainment* are the predominant subjects, covering more than 70% of queries, followed by *Sport* and *Nature*. Within *Lifestyle & Leisure* the most popular sub-categories are *clothing & accessories* (e.g. 'custom tuxedos'), *graphics/clipart* (e.g. 'android funky icons'), *automobiles* (e.g. 'ford explorer') and *house & home* (e.g. 'kitchen cabinets').

Shatford-Panofsky Categorization Results. Table 4 shows the Shatford-Panofsky classification results, with searches for specific people or things (*specific-who*) by far the most frequent, covering 57% of searches. Within this, people or product searches (e.g. 'miley cyrus', 'iphone 5c') are the most common. *Generic-who* queries (e.g. 'flower', 'wedding rings') are also very frequent, covering 41% of searches. The *who* facet is clearly the most important facet in image search, covering almost 93% of all searches. The next most frequent facet is *what*, covering 21% of searches. Unlike the *who* facet, *what* queries are more likely to be generic; users, in particular, often use generic conditions (7.4%) as modifiers for who queries (e.g. 'blue quilt'). It is also notable that the *when* and *where* facets mostly appear together with other facets, as modifiers of the terms associated with *who* and *what*. For example, the query 'flowers to plant in september' refers to a *generic-who* entity (flowers) modified by a *generic-what-action* (to plant) and a *generic-when* description (in september). 87% of *specific-where* queries, and 95% of *specific-when* queries, are multifaceted.

Differences between Head and Tail. Tables 3 and 5 also allow us to answer *RQ 1.1*, *'Are there differences in the types of queries found in the head and the tail?'*, by comparing

Category	All %	Head %	Tail %
Lifestyle & Leisure	**36**	2	43
Clothing & Accessories	**8**	1	10
Graphics/Clipart	**5**	0	4
Automobiles	4	0	5
House & Home	4	0	6
Gastronomy	3	0	4
Tourism	3	0	4
Others	9	1	9
Arts, Culture & Entertainment	**35**	85	16
Cinema	**15**	52	5
Television	**14**	39	4
Music	**7**	17	3
Fashion	4	13	1
Animation	3	0	1
Others	5	8	5
Sport	**7**	6	7
Nature	**6**	4	4
Science & Technology	4	0	3
International Interest	3	0	0
Health	3	0	4

Table 3: IPTC Categorization.

Category	Specific %	Generic %	Abstract %	All %
Who	**57.1**	**41.1**	5.1	**92.6**
Person	**28.2**	2.4	2.0	
Product	**15.5**	**14.6**	0.4	
Place	2.7	1.1	0.3	
Organization	5.3	0.4	0.0	
Animals/Plants	0.3	5.3	1.2	
Others	3.9	16.5	1.0	
What	2.6	**13.4**	5.4	**21.0**
Action	0.4	3.3	0.1	
Event	2.1	2.6	0.0	
Condition	0.1	7.4	5.1	
Others	0.0	0.2	0.1	
When	3.7	1.3	0.0	5.0
Where	5.4	0.5	0.0	5.8
All	**60.7**	**45**	10.3	

Table 4: Shatford-Panofsky Categorization.
(As queries can be multi-faceted, rows and columns do not sum to 100%, or to the values for 'all'.)

[5]http://schema.org/docs/full.html (accessed Jan 14th, 2015)

Category	Specific % (h)	Specific % (t)	Generic % (h)	Generic % (t)	Abstract % (h)	Abstract % (t)	All % (h)	All % (t)
Who	94	48	4	50	0	5	98	89.6
What	0	4	1	22	2	6	3	31.6
Where	0	12	0	1	0	0	1	6.4
When	0	5	1	6	0	0	0	12
All	94	54.4	5	56	2	11.2	-	-

Table 5: Shatford-Panofsky Categorization for Head (h) and Tail (t) Queries.

head and tail queries. We consider head queries as those in the top 10% of the distribution, and tail queries as those in the bottom 25% (we choose the bottom 25% because this is made up entirely of singleton queries). Significant differences emerge in the distribution of categories for head and tail queries. For IPTC subjects, the head is dominated by *Arts, Culture & Entertainment* queries (85%), followed by *Sport* and *Nature*. Tail queries cover a much more diverse set of topics, with *Lifestyle & Leisure* covering 43% of queries, followed by *Arts, Culture & Entertainment* covering 16%, and a non-negligible amount of queries related to *Sport*, *Nature*, and *Health*.

There are also differences in the Shatford-Panofsky categories between head and tail (Table 5), with the head dominated by *specific-who* queries (94%). In the tail this drops to 48%, with 50% covered by the *generic-who* facet. There are also more *what* and *where* queries in the tail, and a far greater proportion of *generic* queries.

These huge differences in the nature of head and tail queries emphasize the need to study the entire query distribution, and not just the popular queries.

Intersection of Subject and Facet Taxonomies. To answer *RQ 1.2*, *'What are the frequent query types at the intersection of subject- and facet- based categorization?'*, we look at the frequent query types at the intersection of the two taxonomies. We only consider the intersections of subjects and facets that cover at least 3% of the query traffic, and label each of these as a specific *query type* (e.g. *celebrity* queries have been annotated as cinema, television, movie or sports AND specific-who-person).

From Table 6 we see the following common *query types* at the intersection of the two schema, which between them account for 43.7% of traffic: *celebrities*, *graphics/clipart*, *fashion items*, *animals*, and *automobiles*. *Celebrity* and *automobile* queries both cover the *specific-who* facet, while the others cover *generic-who*.

A further inspection of the head and tail queries shows that *celebrities* queries, at the intersection of *Arts, Culture & Entertainment* or *Sport* and *specific-who*, are mainly drawn from the head of the distribution, while *graphics/clipart* and *fashion items* are more typical of the tail.

USER BEHAVIOR IN IMAGE SEARCH

In this section, we analyze user behavior in image search, focusing on behavioral differences between the query types identified in the previous section, addressing *RQ 2 'How does image search behavior differ depending on query type?'*.

Subject	Facet/Aspect	Query Type	%	Example
Cinema Television Music Sport	Specific/Who -Person	Celebrities	26.4	brad pitt kaley cuoco beyonce michael jordan
Graphics /Clipart	Generic/Who -Others	Graphics /Clipart	4.5	fall wallpaper, pumpkin clipart
Clothing & Accessories	Generic/Who -Product	Fashion Items	6.4	patent handbag, custom tuxedo
Nature	Generic/Who -Animals	Animals	3.4	dogs, wolf spiders
Automobiles	Specific/Who -Product	Automobiles	3.0	ford explorer, chevy malibu

Table 6: Popular Query Types Identified through Subject & Facet/Aspect Categorization.

Previous work has suggested that image search is more exploratory than web search [1]. Motivated by this, we are interested in understanding more fully to what extent this exploratory behavior applies to all query types:

RQ 2.1. For which query types can we find further evidence of exploratory behavior in image search?

Existing studies on web image search behavior focused on interactions with the search result page, dwell time on the results page, clicks on result images, and the number of result pages viewed. Other important interactions with search engines, such as image-hovers and interactions with the preview page, have not yet been explored. Given the large volume of such data (e.g. hovers are much more frequent than clicks), we also ask the following subquestion:

RQ 2.2. Do additional interaction features on modern search engines provide useful insights for understanding query type based behavior differences?

In the subsections below, we study session-level statistics, query reformulation patterns, and interactions with the preview page. The main research question *RQ 2* and the subquestion *RQ 2.1* are covered by all the subsections, whereas the subquestion *RQ 2.2* is covered in *Click/Hover-Through Rates*, *Click/Hover Entropy*, and *Comparing Clicks and Hovers*, which deal with result-interaction via hovering, and *Preview Page Interactions*, which deals with interactions with the image preview page.

To study query type based behavioral differences, we first examine the number of search pages viewed, query reformulation patterns, and number of result clicks, which were used in previous work to suggest that image search is more exploratory than web search [1]. In addition, we study features not explored in other studies, but which constitute a large portion of user interaction in image search, such as hover-through, the relationship between click-through and rank position, dwell time on preview page, and click-through from the preview page to the referral website.

For a large-scale analysis, we expand the set of queries associated with each *query type* identified at the intersection of subjects and facets. We run a named entity detector against the entire query sample to classify *celebrity* and *automobile* queries, and a text classifer for *animal* queries. We extract

Query Type	Searches	Unique Queries	Sessions	Searches/ Query
Celebrities	12,130,246	7,367	5,625,328	1646.5
Graphics/Clipart	1,487,864	643,299	574,299	2.3
Fashion Items	1,850,754	1,039,390	974,139	1.8
Animals	420,493	12,410	253,003	33.9
Automobiles	239,673	9,849	150,759	24.3

Table 7: Expanded Dataset by Query Type.

graphics/clipart queries as those containing a list of curated keywords[6] and *fashion item* queries based on the keywords from Google Product Taxonomy[7], under the *Apparel and Accessories > Clothing* category. Unlike our query characterization, which considered all device types, for this analysis we wish to to control for behavior differences based on device, so we only consider queries and sessions on desktop devices. The resulting dataset, which will be the testbed for our analysis in this section, is summarized in Table 7. As can be seen in the *Searches/Query* column, the query types in this dataset are a mixture of very popular queries (*celebrities*), moderately popular queries (*animals, automobiles*), and rare queries (*graphics/clipart* and *fashion items*).

Session Level Statistics

We start by looking at query type differences in session-based statistics, which give a high-level overview of search engine interactions.

Query Type	Session Duration (mins)	Queries per Session	Queries per Minute	Reformulation (%)	Search Depth (pages)
Celebrities	8.59	4.09	0.48	60.09	2.76
Graphics/Clipart	16.91	5.28	0.31	70.97	3.31
Fashion Items	15.29	4.99	0.33	61.44	2.96
Animals	13.55	4.88	0.36	60.31	2.32
Automobiles	10.87	3.78	0.35	54.04	2.66

Table 8: Session Statistics by Query Type.

From Table 8 we can see a clear difference in the duration of sessions containing *celebrity* queries, where the average length of a session is noticeably shorter than for all other query types. Table 8 also shows that *graphics/clipart* sessions have the largest number of queries and the longest average session length. Although longer sessions tend to contain more queries, queries are not issued at the same rate for each query type; for some query types, it takes longer for the same number of queries to be issued. *Celebrity* search sessions contain 0.48 queries per minute, which is the largest among all, suggesting that users spend less time interacting with the results, and move on to new/refined queries more quickly. Consistent with the greatest number of queries per session, there is a greatest tendency to reformulate queries for *graphics/clipart* sessions (70.97% of sessions contain more than one query) and least for *automobile* sessions (54.04%). Lastly, we compute search depth, based on how many pages of results a user explores, to see how deeply users explore the results: *graphics/clipart* and *fashion item* queries show the greatest search depth. These query types are associated with longer, deeper search sessions with more reformulations, suggesting they are relatively more focused, while other query types (*celebrities, animals, automobiles*) are characterized by shorter session lengths, less reformulations, and shallower search depths.

[6]the following keywords were used: 'graphic', 'clipart', 'clip art', 'wallpaper', 'background', 'icon', and 'illustration'

[7]www.google.com/basepages/producttype/taxonomy.en-US.xls (accessed Jan 14th, 2015)

Query Type	Adding %	Deleting %	Partial %	Complete %
Celebrities	15.4	0.6	25.1	58.8
Graphics/Clipart	18.3	3.8	47.0	30.9
Fashion Items	16.5	2.9	44.6	36.1
Animals	13.0	2.2	31.9	52.9
Automobiles	16.0	2.6	40.4	41.0

Table 9: Query Modification type by Query Type.

Query Reformulation

Previous studies show that query reformulation occurs frequently on image search platforms [1], and our data also provides evidence to support this, with approximately 60% of sessions involving more than one query. In this subsection, we look more deeply into the types of query reformulation used and how this relates to query type. Query reformulation is normally defined as any modification that a user makes to the initial query in hope of finding better results [7]. We adopt the approach of Jansen [9] and distinguish the following types of reformulation between consecutive queries: (i) *adding terms*, where one or more terms are added to the original query, (ii) *deleting terms*, where one or more terms are deleted from the original query (iii) *partial change*, where at least one term has been changed, but the updated query is neither a superset or a subset of the original, and (iv) *complete change*, where the two queries have no terms in common.

Table 9 shows the extent to which each type from reformulation occurs across different query types in our dataset. For all categories, many reformulations involve partial changes or complete changes to the preceding query. Term deletion is the least common type of reformulation, and adding terms is also relatively rare. We find noticeable differences in reformulation strategies for *celebrity* queries, which have a much higher proportion of complete changes, and lower proportion of deletions and partial changes, than other query types. *Graphics/clipart* queries have the most partial changes and adding terms, and the least complete changes. Table 10 shows some examples of the frequent query reformulations for each

Query Type	Popular Query Reformulations
Celebrities	*top:* elizabeth hurley → katherine webb charlie hunnam → dakota johnson christie brinkley → kate upton
Graphics/Clipart	*top:* school clip art → school clipart fall clipart → halloween clipart dallas cowboys → dallas cowboys wallpaper
Fashion Items	*top:* short haircuts → short hairstyles short haircuts → short haircuts 2013 short shorts → yoga shorts
Animals	*top:* eagle attacking deer → puppy doe cat → dog puppies → kittens
Automobiles	*top:* 2014 corvette → ferrari porsche 918 spyder → porsche carrera gt gold-plated lamborghini → kim zolciak

Table 10: Frequent Query Reformulations by Query Type. (The most frequent reformulation pair is denoted as *'top'*)

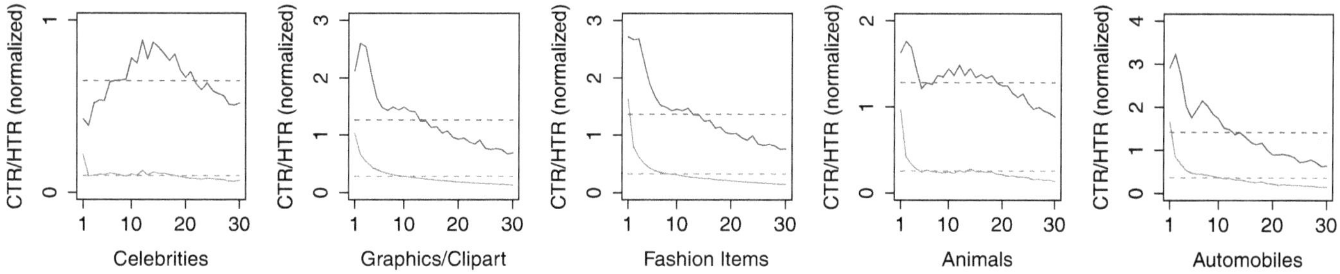

Figure 1: Click(bottom/red)/Hover(top/blue)-through Rate for Images for Top 30 Position Ranks by Query Type. (CTR/HTR are normalized to hide commercially sensitive data. Dotted lines denote the average over all positions.)

query type. The results suggest a more exploratory, browsing-like, behavior for *celebrity*, *automobile*, and *animal* queries, which have more complete changes to a different entity of the same type (e.g. 'puppies'→'kittens'). In contrast, for *fashion item* and *graphics/clipart* searches, users tend to refine queries through adding terms or partial changes, which serves as evidence of focused search behavior (e.g. 'fall clipart'→'halloween clipart').

Interaction with Search Results

In this section, we analyze how users interact with results after a query has been issued, based on explicit interactions with search results. Understanding this behavior is very important, as it can be an indication of user satisfaction as well as relevance of search results, and is heavily used by search engines as relevance feedback data. We focus on the following types of interaction with search results: *clicks* and *hovers*[8] on search result images, and interactions with the image preview page. We note that approximately 10% of our data consists of searches where no follow up action takes place whatsoever: the user inputs a query, views the first returned page, and ends the session with no further action.

Click/Hover-Through Rates. We now measure click-through rate (CTR), which has been shown to have a strong correlation with image relevance [4, 19], as well as hover-through rate (HTR). For each *(image,query,position)* triple, where position is the ranking of the image in the result list, we calculate CTR/HTR, the number of clicks/hovers on the image divided by the number of image views. In Figure 1, we plot the average CTR and HTR of images at the top 30 positions for each query type. HTR is significantly higher than CTR for all query types; indeed from the *click/hover ratio* in Table 11 we can see that it can be as much as 10 times higher for *celebrity* and *animal* queries. In terms of CTR (bottom/red lines), a sharp decay is observed over the top 5 images for all query types except *celebrities*, followed by a slower decay. For *celebrities*, the CTR stabilizes after the second result, and only starts to decay again after position 16. We also see a similar flat line for CTR on *animal* queries. For both *celebrity* and *animal* queries, the HTR is also somewhat unusual in that it increases with position, albeit after an initial drop in the case of animal searches. These CTR and HTR plots suggest that for *celebrity* searches, users want to browse a set of images; the relatively smaller impact of the ranking suggests that users are consuming the results (at least those in the top 30) as an unordered set, and not as a ranked list. The fact that CTR/HTR shows a gradual decrease for *graphics/clipart* and *fashion items* again suggests a more focused search, as position has more influence on CTR.

It is also very important to note that the overall CTR and HTR vary widely by query type. *Celebrity* searches, for example, have very low click-through in comparison with other query types; this suggests that these queries are often satisfied by the thumbnails on the results pages, without the need for further interaction, again suggesting a browsing-like behavior. These differences in CTR and HTR can also have very important implications for interpreting click data as an implicit relevance signal, as we will discuss later.

Click/Hover Entropy. To measure the amount of variation in the search results users click/hover on across query types, we calculate click/hover entropy, using the standard measure

$$Click/HoverEntropy(q) = \sum_{i,q} -p(i|q)log_2p(i|q),$$

where $p(i|q)$ is the probability of image i being clicked for query q. Since infrequent queries would have a low entropy and so generate bias, we compute entropy only for queries that were issued at least 20 times. Table 11 shows that hover entropy values are higher than click entropy values, which is to be expected since there are many more hover actions. The highest entropy is observed for *celebrity* and *animal* queries, which means it is harder to predict what image a user will click/hover on for these types. This again hints at the undirected, browsing-oriented nature of such queries in comparison to *graphics/clipart* and *fashion item* queries.

Query Type	Click Entropy	Hover Entropy	Click/Hover Correlation	Click/Hover ratio
Celebrities	4.75	6.47	0.49	0.09
Graphics/Clipart	4.03	6.07	0.44	0.13
Fashion Items	3.93	5.46	0.51	0.12
Animals	4.32	6.70	0.56	0.09
Automobiles	4.11	5.98	0.58	0.15

Table 11: Click/Hover Entropy, Correlation, and Ratio by Query Type.

[8]Hovers refer to a user placing the cursor on the thumbnail of a result image. Although this feature is not available on all image search engines, at the time of writing 2 out of the 3 top U.S. search engines (Bing and Yahoo) had implemented this user interface feature.

Comparing Clicks and Hovers. Given that there are many more hovers than clicks, and that clicks are highly correlated with relevance [4, 19], in this section we ask how similar hovers are to clicks, which will also tell us whether hovers are correlated with relevance. To measure the extent to which users hover over the same images that they click on for a given query, we first rank the images based on the number of times they were clicked or hovered on for a query, and compute the correlation between the click and hover ranks. We remove sparse data by only considering *(query,image)* pairs with at least 10 clicks, and only queries with at least 10 such images. Table 11 shows the correlation between clicks and hovers, which on average is moderate, at around 0.5. *Graphics/clipart* queries have the lowest correlation, consistent with our earlier interpretation that for this query type, users may be performing a more focused search, hovering over images for further inspection, without necessarily clicking on them. Finally, we calculate the click/hover ratio for each query type. The results in Table 11 show that, consistent with our other findings, *celebrity* and *animal* queries have the lowest proportion of clicks, compared with hovers, suggesting that hovers are more often used as a way to consume these images.

Preview Page Interactions. Modern search engines typically allow users to preview images after clicking on them, showing a maximized view of the image, along with next/previous buttons, on a new page which we refer to as the image preview page. This page also has a link to the referral website where the image can be viewed in its original context[9]. Table 12 shows that an average of 17 or more images are viewed on this page for every preview page visit (i.e. for every result click); this number is consistent across most query types, and the high volume of this interaction emphasizes the importance of exploring it further. *Graphics/clipart* searches, however, have half the number of images viewed per preview page visit compared with other query types, but a much higher average dwell time per image. *Celebrity* queries exhibit the shortest overall preview duration and image dwell time, which is consistent with the shorter total session length for these queries. This suggests that users spend more time inspecting images during *graphics/clipart* searches, while they take less time in viewing *celebrity* images possibly in a more casual manner. For *graphics/clipart* and *fashion item* queries, users are also much more likely to click on the referral website. The 'single image previews' column on Table 12 shows the proportion of cases where the user clicks on an image, views the image, and does not preview any other result images. It is largest for *graphics/clipart* queries, which also has the lowest number of images viewed per preview page visit. These results reinforce the query type based differences found in the previous section and, along with the analysis of hover behavior, provide a positive answer to *RQ 2.2*, showing that these additional interaction do, indeed, give further insights into image search behavior.

[9]All 3 major U.S. search engine provide variations of this type of image preview mechanism.

Query Type	Preview Duration (min)	# of Images Viewed	Dwell Time (sec)	Single Image Previews	Referral Page CTR
Celebrities	1.62	18	5.29	35.36%	1
Graphics/Clipart	2.12	9	14.34	49.71%	4.83
Fashion Items	2.32	17	8.38	39.16%	5.67
Animals	2.38	19	7.44	38.23%	1.67
Automobiles	2.17	17	7.50	33.52%	2

Table 12: Preview Page Characteristics by Query Type. (CTR is normalized to hide commercially sensitive data.)

LINKING BEHAVIOR TO SEARCH INTENT

To address *RQ 3 'Can we associate query types with classes of search intent? How does search intent relate to behavior?*, and to support our interpretations of user behavior with the testimonials of real users, we conducted a survey asking users about their most recent image search experience. All respondents, recruited through email, social media, and personal contacts of the authors, fall in the age range of 18 to 41, with 91% between 24 to 35. They completed an online survey (`http://goo.gl/gfO1Uh`), which is a mix of multiple-choice and open-ended questions, including questions specifically related to search intent. The open-ended questions allowed users to freely elaborate on their experience, and were especially useful in giving insights that were not available from the log analysis. To ensure veridicality, we asked the participants to rate, on a 5-pt scale, how confident they were in remembering their experience. We excluded those whose confidence rating was less then 3, as well as those whose last recalled search occurred more than a week previously, leaving 43 participants. As with any qualitative analysis, we acknowledge issues of limited generizability; while a more rigorous survey can further provide a deeper understanding of image search behavior, we believe these initial results are useful for interpreting the log analysis.

To link the user behavior with known classes of image search intent, we use 4 classes of image search intent proposed by Lux et al. [13]: *knowledge orientation*, *navigation*, *mental image*, and *transaction*. Our results suggest a link between the query type based behavior observed in our study and the *knowledge orientation* and *transaction* intent; the other two classes of intent were not referenced by our respondents.

Transaction-Intent Queries. A majority of the respondents stated they were searching for clipart, mostly for presentation slides. They were trying to 'illustrate an idea' using web images or were looking for images 'for further use', which corresponds closely with *transaction* intent [13]. They further responded that they were looking for a *set of images* on *generic* instances. Some signs of transactional intent for *graphics/clipart* searches found during the log-based analysis include: query refinement to improve the results, higher click-through rate compared to other query types, longer dwell time on the preview page (possibly due to image downloads), and higher click-through to the referral website. With regards to the motivation behind clicks and hovers, the main reason for clicking on images while searching for clipart appears to be to view a better-resolution image, or to visit the image webpage. Some argued that hovers were more convenient than clicks: "[Hovering is] similar to clicking but not that extensive". Since *fashion item* queries share many of these behavioral patterns, they may also be associated with transaction intent; in this case though, the user is likely to be viewing images of the items with a view to purchasing them, which would explain the high referral page CTR.

Knowledge Orientation-Intent Searches. Users searching for celebrities answered that they performed the search to 'inform themselves', which corresponds to *knowledge orientation* intent [13]. The log analysis showed that *celebrity* queries lead to relatively shallow interaction with results in the search results and image preview pages, suggesting that browsing the result thumbnails themselves is often enough to satisfy this intent. One respondent, searching for a famous basketball coach, stated that "just looking at the thumbnails (without clicking/hovering) was enough". This suggests that, for *knowledge orientation intent* queries, 'successful' queries may not always result in direct interaction with the results, and explains low click-through rates for this query type. *Celebrity* searchers also responded that they were looking for *a set of images*, which explains why users consume the top ranked images as a set (i.e. rank position was relatively unimportant for CTR). None of those who made celebrity searches responded that they rewrote the query, even though we detected many 'complete change' reformulations in the logs. We posit that complete changes are detected when users search for different celebrities from the initial search within the same session, but the respondents considered this a new query rather than a reformulation. The similar behavior associated with *animal* queries and, to a lesser extent, *automobile* queries, suggests a similar intent.

Is Image Search Exploratory? Previous work on image search log analysis suggested that image search is more exploratory than text search, mainly based on the number of results clicked and the search depth (number of result pages viewed) [1]. One of our research sub-questions, *RQ 2.1*, asked if we could *'find further evidence of exploratory behavior in image search'*. We have shown that *celebrity* queries and *animal* queries, which we are also associated with *knowledge orientation* intent, exhibit many features that suggest exploratory behavior: shallow interaction with the search results and image preview pages, complete query changes to other entities of the same type, more variety in terms of the images clicked/hovered on the results page, and the relative unimportance of rank position for CTR/HTR. The survey feedback also indicated that users were interested in a 'set of images', again indicating their interest in exploring a set of results, rather than finding a single result. *Graphics/clipart* and *fashion item* queries, on the other hand, which we have associated with *transaction* intent, exhibit a number of behavioral features that are more suggestive of a focused search: deeper interaction with the search results page and the image preview page, CTR that is heavily dependent on rank position, lower variety of images clicked and an emphasis on query refinement through partial changes. Andre et al. [1] interpret the *higher* result interaction and *greater* search depth in image search as an indication of image search being more exploratory than web search, while the query types that we interpret as exploratory exhibit *less* result interaction and *shallower* search depth, which would seem to contradict that. In fact, we agree with their interpretation that image search is generally more exploratory than text search; in our survey, a respondent also spoke about looking for *sets* of images for *transaction* intent image queries. We believe that image search has more result interaction than text search because it is inherently more exploratory, due to the large number of relevant images for most queries, and because users want to consume a set of images. Within image search, however, users need to interact with the results of focused queries even more deeply because they have a specific purpose in mind, meaning that it takes more effort to find what they are looking for.

PRACTICAL IMPLICATIONS

Our study has a number of important practical implications. The ways in which the insights from this work can be used to improve search relevance include, but are not limited to, the following:

(1) A query classifier for the query types we identify, along with a matching image classifier, can benefit relevance. For example, if we could classify a query as being a *graphics/clipart* query, and also classify images of the same type, this can be used to improve relevance. Also, the facet-based classification results suggest what types of image classifiers the community should work on (e.g. the *who* facet).

(2) We emphasize 3 alternative sources of implicit relevance feedback from search logs: hovering over images, dwell time in the preview page, and click-through from the image preview to the referral website. We have shown that hovers have a moderate correlation with clicks, which are already known to correlate highly with relevance. Given that there are many more hovers than clicks, this is a promising source of implicit relevance feedback. We also show that for most query types there is an average of at least 17 images viewed on the image preview page for every result click. Given this, interactions with the preview page (e.g. dwell time, referral page CTR) are very promising sources of additional implicit feedback.

(3) We show that CTR/HTR is heavily dependent on query type, as is dwell time and referral page CTR, which has important applications in click modeling [11]; the huge variation in CTR, HTR, dwell time, and referral CTR based on query type shows that, to effectively interpret implicit user feedback as a relevance signal, query type is essential. Similarly, the fact that position information is not always important for CTR/HTR can have important implications in interpreting click/hover feedback.

Overall, we find that only some query types are exploratory, and show which query types can be associated with *transaction* or *knowledge orientation* intent. This could motivate different ranking strategies, or results presentation, based on query type. Specific suggestions are out of scope of this paper, but our results can serve as useful evidence for design decisions or ranking strategies.

SUMMARY & CONCLUSIONS

In this paper we conduct a large-scale study of a web image search log, to understand what users search for and how their search behavior varies depending on query type. We categorize queries with respect to two orthogonal taxonomies. We show that the head of the query distribution is dominated by *Arts, Culture & Entertainment* queries and by queries for specific entities, mainly people: in other words, *celebrity* queries. The tail of the distribution exhibits much more diversity both in terms of the subject of queries (*fashion items*, *graphics/clipart* and *automobiles*) and their facets/aspects (specific and generic entities or actions). We also show that the following important *query types* emerge at the intersection of subject-based and facet-based taxonomies: *celebrities*, *graphics/clipart*, *fashion items*, *animals*, and *automobiles*.

We show that *celebrity* search sessions and, to a lesser extent, *animal* sessions, are shorter in duration and involve less interaction with search results than other query types, often leading to a browsing-like behavior where the user completely changes the query to a different entity within the same session. We also show that *graphics/clipart* queries in particular, and also *fashion item* queries, show more complex behavior, with longer sessions, more refinement of queries, and deeper interaction with search results. We also show that click-through rate (CTR) and image dwell time are much lower for *celebrity* queries than for other query types, and that CTR is much less dependent on the image rank position for *celebrity* and *animal* queries. These query type differences are sometimes very large, which suggests that we should be considering query type when using click logs as user feedback to improve image search relevance.

We further provide possible explanations of these differences in user behavior based on qualitative analysis of individual user experiences in searching for images, reported through a survey. The responses suggest that searches for *graphics/clipart* images are often associated with *transaction* intent, while *celebrity* queries are associated with *knowledge orientation* intent. We also show that the behavioral differences that we observe in our log analysis are consistent with such intent; for *transactional intent* queries, users often have a specific goal in mind that is difficult to articulate, and they take extra effort to view and select images, as well as to refine their queries. Similarly, survey feedback about *celebrity* queries supports our interpretation that such searchs tend to be more casual and exploratory.

For future work, we plan to analyze user behavior variation with respect to facets and aspects from the Shatford-Panofsky taxonomy. Also, while in this study we only deal with search behavior on desktops, it is also important to study the behavior across different device types, and to compare behavior differences between head/tail queries. Finally, it would also be beneficial to evaluate the effectiveness of hovers and preview page interactions for image search relevance.

REFERENCES

1. Andre, P., Cutrell, E., Tan, D. S., and Smith, G. Designing novel image search interfaces by understanding unique characteristics and usage. In *INTERACT 2009*, Springer-Verlag (2009), 340–353.
2. Armitage, L. H., and Enser, P. G. Analysis of user need in image archives. *JIS 23* (1997), 287–299.
3. Broder, A. A taxonomy of web search. *SIGIR Forum 36*, 2 (2002), 3–10.
4. Craswell, N., and Szummer, M. Random walks on the click graph. In *SIGIR 2007*, 239–246.
5. Goodrum, A., and Spink, A. Visual information seeking: A study of image queries on the world wide web. In *ASIS 1999*, vol. 36, ERIC (1999), 665–74.
6. Goodrum, A., and Spink, A. Image searching on the excite web search engine. *IPM 37*, 2 (2001), 295–311.
7. Huang, J., and Efthimiadis, E. N. Analyzing and evaluating query reformulation strategies in web search logs. In *CIKM 2009*, ACM (2009).
8. Jansen, B. J. Searching for digital images on the web. *JDOC 64*, 1 (2008), 81–101.
9. Jansen, B. J., Spink, A., and Narayan, B. Query modifications patterns during web searching. In *ITNG 2007* (2007), 439–444.
10. Jansen, B. J., Spink, A., and Pedersen, J. O. The effect of specialized multimedia collections on web searching. *J. Web Eng. 3*, 3-4 (2004), 182–199.
11. Joachims, T., Granka, L., Pan, B., Hembrooke, H., and Gay, G. Accurately interpreting clickthrough data as implicit feedback. In *SIGIR 2005*, 154–161.
12. Liu, J., Cole, M. J., Liu, C., Bierig, R., Gwizdka, J., Belkin, N. J., Zhang, J., and Zhang, X. Search behaviors in different task types. In *JCDL 2010*, 69–78.
13. Lux, M., Kofler, C., and Marques, O. A classification scheme for user intentions in image search. In *Ext. Abstracts CHI 2010*, ACM (2010).
14. Maniu, S., O'Hare, N., Aiello, L., Chiarandini, L., and Jaimes, A. Search behaviour on photo sharing platforms. In *ICME 2013* (2013), 1–6.
15. Ozmutlu, S., Spink, A., and Ozmutlu, H. C. Multimedia web searching trends: 1997–2001. *IPM 39*, 4 (2003), 611–621.
16. Panofsky, E. *Studies in Iconology: Humanistic Themes in the Art of the Renaissance*. Harper & Row, 1972.
17. Pu, H.-T. A comparative analysis of web image and textual queries. *OIR 29*, 5 (2005), 457–467.
18. Shatford, S. Analyzing the subject of a picture: a theoretical approach. *CCQ 6*, 3 (1986), 39–62.
19. Smith, G., Brien, C., and Ashman, H. Evaluating implicit judgments from image search clickthrough data. *JASIST 63*, 12 (Dec. 2012), 2451–2462.
20. Tjondronegoro, D., Spink, A., and Jansen, B. J. A study and comparison of multimedia Web searching: 1997-2006. *JASIST 60* (2009), 1756–1768.
21. Tsikrika, T., and Diou, C. Multi-evidence user group discovery in professional image search. In *ECIR 2014*, Springer (2014), 693–699.

DynamicMaps: Similarity-based Browsing through a Massive Set of Images

Yanir Kleiman[1], Joel Lanir[2], Dov Danon[1], Yasmin Felberbaum[2], Daniel Cohen-Or[1]
[1]Tel-Aviv University, Haim Levanon 55, Tel-Aviv Yafo, Israel
[2]University of Haifa, Mt. Carmel, Haifa, 31905, Israel
yanirk@gmail.com, ylanir@haifa.ac.il, dov84d@gmail.com, jas86f@gmail.com, dcor@tau.ac.il

ABSTRACT
We present a novel system for browsing through a very large set of images according to similarity. The images are dynamically placed on a 2D canvas next to their nearest neighbors in a high-dimensional feature space. The layout and choice of images is generated on-the-fly during user interaction, reflecting the user's navigation tendencies and interests. This intuitive solution for image browsing provides a continuous experience of navigating through an infinite 2D grid arranged by similarity. In contrast to common multidimensional embedding methods, our solution does not entail an upfront creation of a full global map. Image map generation is dynamic, fast and scalable, independent of the number of images in the dataset, and seamlessly supports online updates to the dataset. Thus, the technique is a viable solution for massive and constantly varying datasets consisting of millions of images. Evaluation of our approach shows that when using DynamicMaps, users viewed many more images per minute compared to a standard relevance feedback interface, suggesting that it supports more fluid and natural interaction that enables easier and faster movement in the image space. Most users preferred DynamicMaps, indicating it is more exploratory, better supports serendipitous browsing and more fun to use.

Author Keywords
Image browsing; Image search; similarity browsing; relevance feedback;

ACM Classification Keywords
H.5.m. Information interfaces and presentation (e.g., HCI): Miscellaneous. H.3.3. Information search and retrieval.

INTRODUCTION
As huge image collections become common in the Web and various digital libraries, it is increasingly important to allow users to easily search and browse these collections in fast and intuitive ways. Many commercial Web search engines have developed technologies to allow users to search for images, mostly focusing on keyword search with images presented in a grid ordered by some sort of relevance measure. While text-based directed search can be effective for many image search tasks, studies have shown that image search is often more exploratory in nature than Web search, and that browsing is an essential strategy when looking for images [1, 6, 21]. Still most commercial systems lack support for exploratory search and do not provide means for serendipity in the search process [13, 21].

To address this gap, various research systems have looked into browsing as a complementary tool to text-based search methods [8, 23]. One useful way of browsing through images is by using similarity. Users often look for images that are similar to a given image, and browsing according to similarity between images has been shown to be useful [20, 25]. A prominent method for browsing images according to similarity uses relevance feedback techniques, which refine search results according to a selection of preferred images made by the user [37]. At each relevance feedback step, the user is presented with a new set of images based upon past selections. However, the navigation experience with this approach is not continuous and it requires the user to go over a large collection of images and select the relevant or irrelevant ones at each step.

A possibly more intuitive approach is to lay out the images on a two-dimensional grid allowing users to navigate over them in a continuous manner. We present DynamicMaps, a novel system to intuitively navigate through a massive, dynamic set of images. Navigation is done with a metaphor of an infinite two-dimensional canvas, where the images are presented and browsed through according to similarity. Figure 1 illustrates the browsing process. The user views a local subset of images, ordered such that similar images are next to each other (A). The user decides to pan towards images on the bottom right corner (B), and new images similar to the ones on the boundaries of the images in (B) appear to reveal another patch of the map (C). The currently displayed map can be figuratively viewed as a window that shows a local patch of an infinite canvas.

CHI 2015, April 18 - 23 2015, Seoul, Republic of Korea

ACM 978-1-4503-3145-6/15/04...$15.00
http://dx.doi.org/10.1145/2702123.2702224

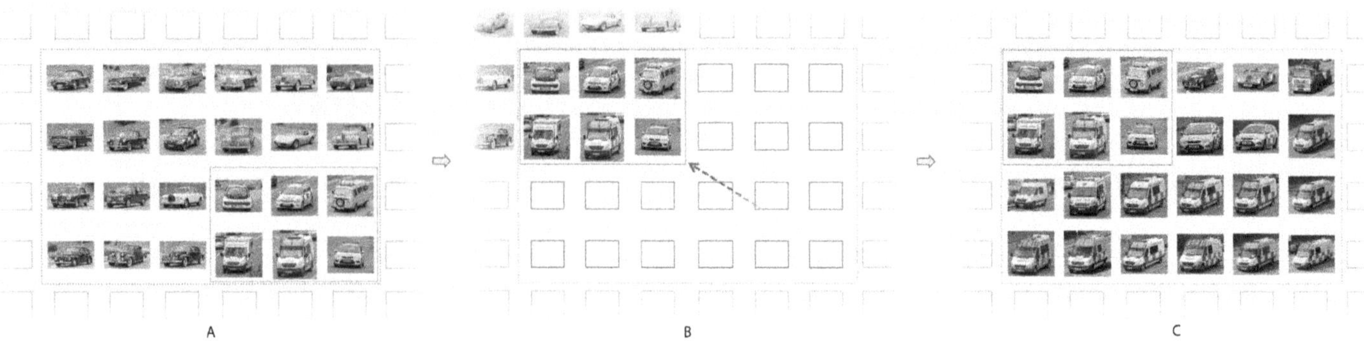

Figure 1. Browsing images using DynamicMap. A region of photos is displayed ordered by similarity (A). Dragging the map to the upper left corner (B) reveals new images which are similar to images in the dragging direction (C).

In order to support millions of images and more, given the high dimensionality of the image space (i.e., images have many different features that can be used: color, spatial structure, composition, texture, etc.), the challenge is in creating a cohesive grid that preserves the relations among all images. Conventional dimensionality reduction methods such as SOM, that can organize images on a 2D plane according to similarity, use global computations and are thus not scalable for a very large set of images [18]. We claim that for image-based navigation, the global requirements can be relaxed. In our solution, the local view is generated during navigation in response to user interactions, such that the relative positions of images respect only local high-dimensional relations.

We build on our previous work of browsing 3D shapes [19], extending and implementing it to support the browsing of images. The specific contributions of the current paper are as follows. First, images suggest a very different feature space than shapes. Dealing with images requires very different semantics and the variation between images is much larger. Second, we tested a significantly larger and richer collection of objects (1 million vs. 4500) enabling us to examine claims of supporting a massive set, as well as the behavior of the system when dense data is available. Third, image search is a much more ubiquitous domain than shape search. Forth and for most, we focus here on the UI considerations rather than the technical solution, reporting on a controlled empirical user study that evaluates the presented method and discuss its advantages and limitations, specifically in context of image search.

Evaluation of DynamicMaps, comparing it to a standard relevance feedback technique, showed that such similarity-based navigation enables an open-loop exploration, where users can quickly and seamlessly direct the search towards relevant images of their choice without the need to sequentially go over the images and select the relevant ones. Using DynamicMaps, users viewed many more images per minute compared to a relevance feedback interface, affording a quicker and more natural method of interaction. Our results indicate that most users preferred DynamicMaps thinking it is more exploratory, better supports serendipitous browsing in which the user explores unknown regions of a large dataset, and more fun.

RELATED WORK

The majority of work done on image retrieval focuses on the back end of the search in image indexing and content-based image retrieval (CBIR) (see survey in [9]). However, as our major contribution is with the design and evaluation of an image browsing user interface, we focus on the user experience side and first review systems that support image browsing and specifically similarity-based image browsing. We then briefly review related work on relevance feedback and dimensionality reduction methods.

Image browsing

Images have several characteristics that makes image search different than text-based search. Unlike text documents, the content of an image can be grasped at a glance, and a large number of images can be presented to a user at once. In image search, often the user does not have an exact target in mind [7]. Furthermore, images often lack textual cues and might have many different meanings embedded in a single image [30], making them difficult to support with only keyword-based search. For example, if the user is looking for a scenery image to add to a presentation, the user would not necessarily know how to phrase the search terms or even exactly which image he or she is looking for. Moreover, images presented in the first page of a text-based search result are not necessarily better than those presented in the following pages. Consequently, users have to sequentially scan these results spending considerable effort finding relevant images. Still, most current systems focus on providing text-based image querying rather than navigational support even though studies have shown that image browsing can improve in achieving user's search needs [8, 20, 23].

To address these needs, some research systems focus on supporting various browsing capabilities to enable navigating through images. For example, browsing specific clusters of images [23], browsing hierarchies that are automatically built according to visual and semantic similarities [17], or browsing along conceptual dimensions according to hierarchical faceted metadata [36]. Similarly, some commercial systems added interactive visual content-based search methods that allow browsing by similar shape and/or color. The "similar images" feature, allows users to search for images similar to a certain image, utilizing relevance feedback methods.

Laying out images on a large canvas allows users to browse the images according to some organization of their structure using pan and zoom interactions. In [8], the results of an initial query can be browsed on a zoomable user interface (ZUI). In [23], images were clustered into conceptual regions. The user can continuously pan across this plane and zoom in or out of any particular region. In JustClick [12] a topic network is first generated and browsed through. Representative images of a topic are then organized on a 2D hyperbolic plane according to similarity.

In the works above, the images are laid out according to some measure of distance (in similarity) between them. However, when browsing images, there is no need for an accurate representation of the original distances between images. In fact, an even spread of images over the canvas can be more beneficial than an accurate representation of the original geometry [25], especially in cases where the original data includes very distinctive clusters which may appear too far apart for easy navigation. Indeed, the most common way to lay out a set of images is on a two-dimensional grid. Studies have found that arranging a set of thumbnail images on a single-page grid according to their similarity can be useful for users in an image browsing task [20]. Strong and Gong [32, 33] employed this idea and organized a collection of images based on similarity using an SOM-based algorithm. Users could browse the image collection using pan and zoom interactions. According to the authors their system could support browsing with up to 10,000 images. Similarly, in PhotoMesa [3], images are laid on a large 2D grid. Users can browse through a large collection of images, panning to browse horizontally or vertically through the image collection. Here, zooming out enabled seeing the photos semantically grouped into pre-organized categories.

The systems mentioned above work with a limited number of images and are not scalable beyond several thousands of images. Thus, they are not suited for large repositories that exist in the Web today. Our work builds upon the idea of browsing images on a large 2D canvas, and the works in [20, 24, 32] that present similar images together on a grid. However, we apply it to a dataset of virtually unlimited size, finding solutions for interacting in such a large image space.

Relevance feedback

Many recent search and retrieval systems, including image retrieval, utilize relevance feedback [27], a method to refine search results using selection of preferred elements. Suditu and Fleuret [34] presented an image retrieval system that features iterative relevance feedback for a very large set of images. At each step, the user is presented with a set of images, and selects a single image that is the closest match to the desired query. Then a new set of images is displayed and the process is repeated.

While this process may be effective at filtering relevant images, the use of relevance feedback in commercial search interfaces is still relatively rare [28]. One possible explanation is that it requires users to make relevance judgments on each item, which is an effortful user task [28]. Relevance feedback tends to work best when the user selects multiple objects as relevant as well as some objects as irrelevant. However, selecting multiple objects is cumbersome for most users. This is amplified in image search where extractable low-level features (e.g., color, texture, shape) may not necessarily match high-level perception-based human interpretation [37].

Dimensionality reduction

Dimensionality reduction is a wide area that has been extensively researched over the years. Common techniques such as multidimensional scaling (MDS) [4] or locally linear embedding (LLE) [26] create a global map that aims to preserve the distances among the high dimensional data points. In image search, a similarity measure between images is first computed, after which a visual map of the image collection is constructed according to the projection of the features to a 2D space. A number of papers use these techniques to map and then browse an images space according to the global relations among images [5, 23]. In order to better organize images, layout methods have been applied to MDS results to put them on a 2D grid [24]. Self-organizing maps (SOM) [18] is a dimensionality reduction method that produces a grid which preserves similarity between elements without preserving the distance. Works such as [29, 32, 33] utilize SOM to visualize a relatively small set of images in a global cohesive map.

Dimensionality reduction methods such as MDS or SOM work very well for small datasets. However they do not scale well and are too computationally intensive to be effective for massive datasets. In [16], an SOM was used to organize millions of documents. Due to the large volume of the dataset, special tools and methodologies had to be developed, yet still, several weeks of computation time were required. In addition, in order to add or remove images to the dataset, the computation process needs to be redone. Since our method relies only on local relationships, our technique is computationally inexpensive and thus highly scalable, as well as dynamic, allowing the addition and removal of data during execution.

DYNAMICMAPS

We first describe the map generation process (for a detailed description see [19]). We then describe the way we computed the image nearest neighbors that is used in the map generation process. Next, we describe the zoom levels mechanism that was built to support browsing through different levels of similarity. Finally, we explain how users can focus on a single image.

Map generation

The grid-like map is instantly generated during user interaction to keep a sense of continuity. The generation of local neighborhoods in the map is based on the assumption that for high dimensional data such as images, short distances are more accurately measured than long distances. Even for a human observer, the task of deciding which images are more similar to each other is easier for a set of similar images than for a set of very different images. This carries over to automatically computed distance measures as well. We thus use only the shortest distances between images in our dataset. Only the distances to k nearest neighbors (with k being a small positive integer) of each image in the dataset are considered. Images farther apart relate to each other by a sequence of nearest neighbors that connect them, utilizing short distances in the whole set. The optimization problem becomes one of maximizing the similarity of nearby images, such that each image is surrounded by similar images. The result is a continuous map in which images show a gradual change over local neighborhoods. A dense set is expected to have shorter distances than a sparse set, hence our method is especially suitable for massive datasets.

The input to the map generation process is a precomputed list of nearest neighbors and their similarity score (see next section) for every image in the dataset. The map can be then seeded around a specific image or constrained by any number of images. As the user is navigating by panning the map, the map is extended locally to the region of interest, using previously placed images as constraints. The map is generated by iteratively filling in empty cells in the grid. Each cell is assigned with the most compatible image by calculating the best match of the closest neighbors of images that are already assigned to adjacent cells. Images that already appear on the map are excluded.

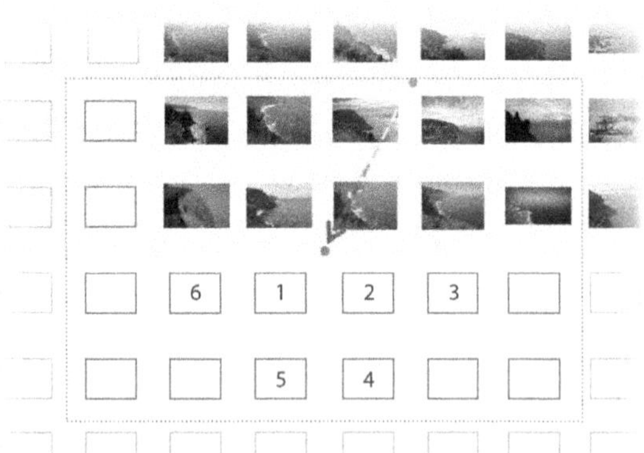

Figure 2: The order in which cells in the map are filled is relative to the direction of browsing. In this example, the user dragged the map two images up and one image to the right. The gray dot and red dot, respectively, mark the previous and new center of the viewport. The numbers state the order in which the first six images on the map are filled.

The order in which empty cells are selected has a great effect on the mapping. We select the vacant cells in accordance with the user's actions; in general, we give precedence to cells that have as many reference images as possible. However, since the map is a regular grid, often there will be ties and many cells will have the same number of reference images. We break ties by selecting the cell which is closest to the direction the user panned to. This causes the grid to start growing from the user's focus area on and outwards into the rest of the map. Figure 2 illustrates the order in which empty cells in the grid are filled. The user drags the map two images up and one image to the right. The center of the user's viewport thus moves on the map in the opposite direction; two cells down and one cell to the left. The cells marked with numbers 1 to 6 are closest to the direction of movement and therefore will be filled in their respective order, followed by the rest of the cells on the grid. Existing images which are closer to the panning direction effectively have more weight in the map generation, since their neighbors are selected first.

To maintain stability of view such that images that were already displayed are not repeated during browsing, we keep images that were placed on the map in their relative global position and prevent them from reappearing on the map again. That is, we save the 2D structure of the view of the created map, so if the user returns back to a previously visited location (e.g., pans right and then pans left), the map is not recreated but rather the previously shown map is presented. The 2D structure is kept until the map is rearranged around a new image. The stability of view supports the important guideline of reversal of actions [31], since users can easily return back on their steps.

Image nearest neighbors

The map generation is decoupled from the nearest neighbors computation. In our implementation, we find the k nearest neighbors of every image using three image metrics, or image *descriptors*. Each of the following three descriptors is computed for each image in the dataset. The distance between two images in each descriptor space is the Euclidean distance between the image descriptors. Average color and color histogram are popular descriptors used in image retrieval [10]. We used them as described below combined with a third descriptor. In other implementations, it is possible to choose different descriptors or different weights for each descriptor.

Average Color. The image is divided into 16 segments, a four by four grid, and the average color in each segment is computed. Similar images in this metric tend to have a similar composition. Of course, the image partitioning does not necessarily need to be four by four, but we find this partitioning appealing in the sense that it seems fine enough to distinguish between images with significantly different compositions, yet sufficiently coarse to ignore small changes in composition of similar images.

Color Histogram. A joint color histogram for RGB values is computed. Each color channel is divided into four bins, to create a total of 64 bins for every color combination. The number of pixels that fall in each bin is counted and divided by the total number of pixels in the image. Similar images in this metric have similar color distributions, which suggest similar atmosphere or surrounding. This descriptor is less sensitive to translation, rotation or reflection of the images compared with the average color descriptor.

Spatial Envelope. The spatial envelope was described in [22] and named gist descriptor since it captures the gist or context of a scene. The gist descriptor describes the spatial structure of a scene using a set of spectral signatures which are specifically tailored for the task of scene recognition. It was shown that in the gist descriptor space, scenes that belong to the same context are projected close to each other. We use the code provided by the authors to compute the gist descriptor of every image in the dataset.

The three descriptors are calculated for each image, and k nearest neighbors are found for each descriptor space separately. The distance from the image to each nearest neighbor in each descriptor space is kept as well. The three lists are then merged to a single list of k nearest neighbors by computing a normalized score for each candidate that appears in one or more lists.

Zoom levels

Our system supports semantic zooming by allowing zooming out to see a wider variety of images as well as enhance navigation capabilities, and zooming in to see more similar images. Zooming out brings the user to a higher level where images are less similar to each other, and thus it is possible to browse further away in the similarity matrix, and zoom back in whenever reaching an area of interest. This enables more diversity within the results, which was shown to be important in image search [14]. When the user zooms out, he or she browses through the higher level which is much smaller in size and thus much more diverse than the original level.

Zoom levels are implemented by automatically preselecting high-level delegates for every image in the dataset from its nearest neighbors list. To create a smaller, higher level delegate map, for each image in the dataset, we check whether one of its nearest neighbors is already a high-level delegate. If none of the nearest neighbors of the image is a delegate, the image itself becomes a delegate for all of its neighbors. The same process can be done when adding a new image to an existing dataset. We then create a higher level map using the chosen delegates. This process is repeated recursively to create multiple zoom levels. For example, if starting at a 1,000,000 images, and using k=20 nearest neighbors, since every delegate represents around 20 images, the second level will include 50,000 delegates, the third level 2500 and the fourth and final zoom level will include 125 images.

Zooming is always done according to a reference image. The user hovers over an image of his or her choice and uses the mouse scroll to change the zoom level. We regenerate the map around that image in a lower (or higher) zoom level, and vice versa for zooming out. To keep the user oriented, when zooming, the reference image does not get replaced by its delegate. Figure 3 illustrates the zooming out process. In addition, there is also a zoom widget in the control panel which, if chosen, zooms in or out according to a click with the center image as the reference image.

Focusing on an image

We provide the user with the option to focus on a single image by double clicking on it. This regenerates the map around the clicked image in the lowest zoom level (maximum similarity). The images in the rebuilt map are

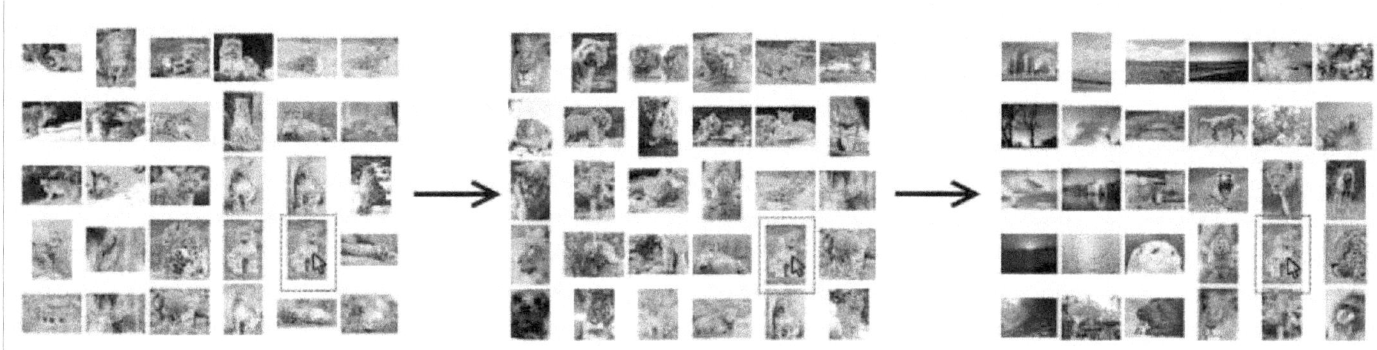

Figure 3. Zooming out. The user hovers over an image and uses the mouse scroll to zoom out. The image stays as a reference point and the images around it are retrieved from a higher zoom level (red box is only for illustration and is not part of the interface).

then more likely to be similar to the image in focus rather than the images around it. This option also provides the user with another way to quickly zoom in from higher levels.

EVALUATION

In order to evaluate DynamicMaps, we compared it to a standard relevance feedback method. Relevance feedback (RF) was chosen as the most prominent method for similarity-based browsing, and the only one we are aware of, that can support a corpus of millions of images. Another possibility was to compare DynamicMaps to another global approach (such as SOM). However, this would have limited the evaluation to the level of thousands of images (other global approaches do not scale more), not fully evaluating the utility of our system. For simplicity, we decided to implement a standard RF method rather than a more complex one (i.e., that might include negative feedback). We employed a within-subject design to compare performance and attitudes of participants. The main variable *interface* describes the search interface used: DynamicMaps (DM), or relevance feedback (RF).

Methodology

Participants. A total of 24 participants took part in the study, 11 were male and 13 were female with an average age of 27.1 (*SD* = 5.1). Participants were mostly students of a large university from a wide range of departments and faculties. All had normal or corrected-to-normal eye vision. 15 participants reported searching on the Web for images every week, while 5 participants reported searching every two weeks or so and 4 reported a lower rate. Image search task reported including finding images for presentations, looking for images for study purposes, looking for products and more. Most participants indicated using Google images as their main image search tool.

Interfaces. Both interfaces show a grid of 6x5 images at any given time. For the DM interface, we used the system as described above, initialized with the starting image at the center, around which the algorithm builds the initial screen grid of 30 images. For the RF interface, the system initializes showing the starting image on the upper left corner followed by the 29 closest neighbors on a grid. The user can then select up to 3 images and click a button (labeled "more images") to fetch the next set of images closest in similarity to the chosen images (ordered by similarity). At any time, the user can press the back button and return to the previous screen. Both interfaces included a "restart" button that returned the view to the initial screen formed by the starting image. As a starting point, users could enter an image number in a provided textbox around which the system initializes as mentioned above.

Tasks. Tasks were designed to be open-ended and reflect real-world search needs (similar to [24, 36]). Two general tasks were defined for the within-subject design. In each task participants were asked to find images that would best fit text slides of a given presentation. For example, the first presentation was on a non-profit organization titled "the society of preservation of nature". The initial slide was a title slide, the second slide talked about the organization's mission, the third slide talked about the history of the organization and the final slide talked about the major active projects the organization employs today. All slides included only text with no color or graphic design. Participants were asked to find up to three images that would best fit each slide. The second presentation was similar in nature and had to do with architecture. For each task, participants were given four starting points in the interface. This emulated four possible keyword search queries. The starting points were chosen as single images relevant to the task (for example, images of animals or nature for the previously mentioned task).

Dataset. We downloaded one million images from the free-to-use (creative commons) Flickr image hosting service. The image collection spans photos with an upload date within a range of 400 days, where for each day in the range a few thousands of random images were selected. This has resulted in a diverse dataset which contains images of many different types, such as landscapes, urban areas, people, wildlife, birds, vehicles and more. Computing the k nearest neighbors for each image was done as a preprocess using Matlab with k=20 and took a few hours for the entire dataset.

Procedure. Participants were seated in front of a 22" screen with 1440x900 screen resolution. Participants were then presented with one of the two interfaces. The user interface features were first explained to them, after which participants performed one practice task on which they were instructed to use the interface until they felt comfortable with it. Participants were then given one of the two tasks and were asked to perform the task as best as possible. No time limit was given for the task. After they completed the first task using the first interface participants were asked to fill in a questionnaire asking their subjective opinion of the interface they just used. Participants were then given the second interface on which they completed the same procedure using the second task. All interactions with the interfaces were logged and later analyzed. At the end of the experiment a comparative questionnaire was given and participants were asked to comment on each interface. The order of interfaces (which interface was first used), as well as which task set was used with which interface was fully counterbalanced, creating 4 different configurations (six participants in each configuration).

Results

Order effects

To rule out order effect (whether participants started with the DM or the RF interface), we performed a between-subject ANOVA with interface order as the independent variable on both task completion time and on number of unique images seen. No effect was found for both variables. Next, to ensure there were no differences between tasks we performed a within-subject ANOVA with task as an independent variable. Again, no effect was found for both task completion time and number of images seen.

Completion time

On average, it took participants 805.8 seconds (~13.5 minutes) to complete the task in the DM interface (*SD* = 334) and 761.5 seconds (~12.7 minutes) in the RF interface (*SD* = 348). A one-way repeated-measures ANOVA on task completion time did not find these differences to be significant, $F(1,23) = .55, p = .47$.

Amount of Interaction

We compared the amount of user interaction with each of the interfaces. In the DM interface, an interaction is performed either by dragging the mouse to pan the view in order to bring up more images (number of pans), by zooming in or out (number of zooms), or by double-clicking on a single image to bring it to the center. In the RF interface, an interaction translates into a "more images" or "back" press which brings up the next or previous set of images (number of presses). Thus, we compared the number of pans + zooms + double clicks in the DM interface with the number of combined "more" and "back" presses in the RF interface. Results indicate that there were many more interactions per task in the DM interface (*M* = 158.4, *SD* = 93.3) than in the RF interface (*M* = 35.9, *SD* = 31.4). A one-way within subject ANOVA on number of interactions showed these differences were significant, $F(1,23) = 90.9, p < 0.001$.

Amount of images seen

Analyzing the log files, we summed up the amount of images seen in each interface. We examined both the total amount of images seen in a specific task, and the total amount of unique images seen, since some images may appear several times during the same task. With the RF interface, the total amount of images seen is equal to the number of interactions (as listed above) plus 1 (for the initial screen) times 30 (each screen showed a grid of 6×5 images). In the DM interface, each pan adds a different amount of images to the screen depending on the pan position. We counted the 30 initial images, and then added the newly filled images in each pan. A zoom, restart, or doubleClick event brought 30 more images. For the unique images seen, in both interfaces, we counted the unique images presented from the beginning till the end of the task. Because there were large individual differences in task completion time, we normalized these results over time and measured the total number of unique and non-unique images seen per minute. Results, presented in Table 1, indicate a large, significant difference in both total and unique number of images seen per minute. Users using the DM interface have seen significantly more total images per minute than when using the RF interface, $F(1,31) = 98.2$, $p<0.001$. Users using the DM interface have also seen more unique images per minute than users using the RF interface, $F(1, 23) = 107.6, p < 0.001$.

	DM	RF	F	p
Task completion time (seconds)	805.8 (334.4)	761.5 (348.9)	0.55	0.47
Average number of images seen per minute	230.0 (51.9)	104.5 (51.0)	98.2	<0.001
Average number of unique images seen per minute	98.4 (21.1)	49.3 (18.6)	107.6	<0.001

Table 1. Task completion time and average number of unique and non-unique images seen per-minute (and standard deviation) per interface

Zooming

All participants used the zooming feature often, with an average of 39.6 times per session (or 2.94 zoom events per minute). To better understand the usage of DynamicMaps, we analyzed the use of the zooming levels. Figure 4 shows the number of pans made and number of (non-unique) images seen in each zoom level. As can be expected, most interaction was done in the first zoom level, with interaction dropping heavily after the first level.

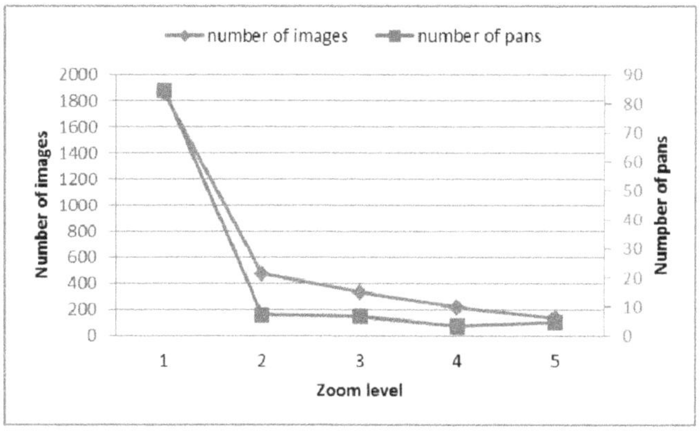

Figure 4. Average number of pans made and number of images seen in each of the five zoom levels (level 1 being images that are most similar to each other).

Subjective opinions

After using each interface, participants were presented with a set of statements and were asked how much they agreed with each one on a 7-point Likert scale ranging from strongly disagree (1) to strongly agree (7). Table 2 presents these statements and the visitors' responses with both interfaces. A Wilcoxon Signed Ranked non-parametric test did not find significant differences in ranking of any of the statements between the two interfaces.

At the end of the experiment, we presented participants with a final questionnaire asking them for their preference of interface on a list of criteria (Table 3). Results indicate a

Statement	DM	RF
The system was efficient for the search tasks	4.20 (1.14)	4.15 (1.22)
The system limited my options	4.75 (1.69)	4.91 (1.28)
The search was fun	4.63 (1.24)	4.33 (1.16)
I quickly understood how to use the interface	5.87 1.19)	5.87 (1.11)
During the search I felt frustrated	3.25 (1.64)	3.54 (1.84)
I am satisfied with the images I picked for the presentation	5.10 (1.25)	4.83 (1.00)

Table 2. Participants average ratings (and standard deviation) per interface on a 7-point Likert scale (N=24).

general preference toward the DM interface, although preference was not absolute. Most participants thought the DM interface was more efficient and preferred it overall. It is interesting to note that most participants thought the DM interface is better when there is a vague idea of the search target and for seeing a wide variety of images, while there was a general preference for RF when the target is clear.

DISCUSSION

Our results indicate that DynamicMaps provide a more interactive experience for the users and allows them to view a wider variety of images than previous methods. Participants viewed many more images (both unique and non-unique) per time with the DM interface compared to the RF interface. While the way of interacting in the two conditions is quite different, still, many more interaction events were measured in the DM compared to the RF interface. Thus, it seems that participants viewed more images by actively interacting more with the interface. It should be noted that we cannot be sure that participants actually saw all the images that were displayed on screen. RF actually forces the user to more closely examine each image, while DM better supports scanning through images. This may help to explain the large difference in the amount of presented images.

Statement	DM	RF	No pref
Which system was more efficient?	12	8	4
When you have a vague idea of the search target, which system is better?	15	7	2
When the search target is clear, which system is better?	7	15	2
Which system is best to see a wide variety of images?	16	5	3
Which system is easier to learn?	6	7	11
Which system do you prefer overall?	15	8	1

Table 3. Number of participants preferring each interface on a list of criteria (N=24).

DynamicMaps provides immediate and continuous interactive feedback that does not require the user to make conscientious sequential selections, but rather asks the user to visually choose a direction to follow based on general perceptive cues. Thus, it affords easier and faster movement in the image space, with less sense of commitment, enabling the user to see a wider variety of images (a fact also realized by participants in the subjective preference questionnaires). This can also be look at from a cognitive load perspective. Cognitive load in the information retrieval context can be seen as a measure of information processing effort a user expends to comprehend the visual stimuli and interact with the system [15]. Using the RF interface, the user needs to go over every image and explicitly provide a relevance judgment on the image, a process that requires a high state of cognitive load [2]. DynamicMaps is less cognitively demanding since the user does not need to make a decision regarding each and every image, but can rather follow general visual cues. As one participant wrote "*I prefer DM. Less mouse clicking. Dragging is easier then thinking of which images will bring me closer. In DM you can see a larger range of images at once without the need to choose and click over and over*".

Having easier interaction capabilities and viewing more images per time unit is more useful when the search is vague and it might be difficult to select specific images that lead directly to the target. It is then easier to experiment, and follow one or more visual search directions than to select specific images. Another advantage of faster and more interactive browsing is that it can better support serendipity in the search process, since users interact more and may stumble upon different areas. It is easy for users to explore regions they may not have envisioned. This was reflected in a statement of a participant: "*It is possible to reach different directions, thoughts and ideas that I have initially not thought about*".

Zooming was often used and was referred to by participants as being very useful. The Zooming option enabled the users to step back and get a wider view of the current corpus. It also supports getting a more diverse view, with the diversity level controlled by the user. Furthermore, using zoom out and pan, the user can view the different topics and content available in the current corpus using simple interactions. This can be useful to get an overview of the image corpus.

No overall significant difference between the interfaces was found for task completion time. Completion time is often looked at as a measure of efficiency. However, in the current study, the task was open-ended and participants were asked to take as much time as needed to find the best possible images. Thus, we do not think that in this case completion time is an indicator of efficiency or quality. On the contrary, it might be that more time spent on the task indicates that the interface was more engaging and caused users to search more thoroughly. Similarly, other studies have found no correlation between task completion time and quality of results or user satisfaction [24].

Finally, we note that many participants mentioned that DynamicMaps was enjoyable and the interaction with it was much more smooth and fun to use than the RF interface (e.g., "*The [DM] system is enjoyable, it is easy to operate and it naturally flows*"). We believe that this will be highlighted even more when using the system with touch-based interfaces. With its pan-based interaction, DynamicMaps should be ideal for searching images on a Tablet computer, for which the playfulness of DynamicMaps would be even more prominent.

Limitations and merits of the local solution

One of the most prominent features of our approach is locality. The k-nearest neighbors technique and the greedy map generation process are critical for accomplishing scalability, and as a result we are able to seamlessly work with massive data sets. However, there are certain attributes, such as distance, which are not preserved, and altogether from an algorithmic point of view, our solution technique does not seek a global solution of a well-defined optimization problem. Rather, we navigate through low dimensional representations of the image space, and rely on user input to scan through the images. A potential limitation of this approach is that it is difficult to assess the quality of the outcome, and we cannot rigorously prove optimality or near optimality. Work in the future will include further investigation of the effects of locality.

On the other hand, the local solution brings with it several strong merits: it is computationally inexpensive, highly scalable, flexible and dynamic. The local nature of the algorithm yields an efficient computational procedure. Computing a global solution may be computationally prohibitive and may present an over-constrained problem that leads to many conflicts, resulting in a solution that is not necessarily better than the one obtained by a local search. When considering massive sized image repositories, a computationally inexpensive approach which nonetheless produces high quality results is critical. DynamicMaps is also dynamic, and can easily handle frequent changes in the dataset. The local nature of the algorithm allows for a seamless addition of images, and other on-the-fly changes. This cannot easily be accomplished by other global feature-preserving techniques.

Another limitation of our system is that it may be difficult to find non-dominant concepts or particular images. If a concept rarely appears, the user will be unlikely to find it as it will be hidden within another area. This can be partly addressed by relaxing the stability of view allowing an image to appear multiple times in different contexts. However, a complete solution for this issue would have to involve combining our system with direct or faceted search.

Combining browsing with direct search

For browsing to be effective it needs to be complementary to direct keyword search, since using keywords is still the preferred method in image retrieval systems [11]. Furthermore, in order to browse, the user needs a way to approach the image space, which can be best done with direct search. One way to combine DynamicMaps with keyword search is by starting with a regular grid of images triggered by keyword search (such as provided by Google images), and allowing the user to choose an image around which the Map will be created to start browsing from. This is similar to how relevance feedback ("similar images") is combined with keyword search today. Thus, keyword search can be used to first reach an area of interest, and then the search can be refined using browsing according to similarity (similar to the orienteering strategy [35]). Another way, which we started experimenting with, directly embeds keyword search within the current DynamicMaps interface. The user types in the search query, and the system presents the results (that match the query) already ordered according to similarity. The challenge lies in seamlessly extending browsing to images that are not directly related to the search query.

ACKNOWLEDGEMENTS

We would like to thank Ofer Arazy for his insightful comments during the writing of the paper.

CONCLUSIONS

We have presented DynamicMaps, a system for browsing a very large set of images on a 2D grid according to similarity using a metaphor of an infinite canvas. DynamicMaps enables a smooth, fast and more interactive experience that is best suitable for exploratory search, when the search target is vague. It is also useful for serendipitous browsing in exploring image regions not envisioned by the user and for getting a wider view of the image corpus. Further work would explore using semantic information in the similarity measures as well as combine DynamicMaps with keyword search.

REFERENCES

1. André, P., Cutrell, E., Tan, D. S., & Smith, G. Designing novel image search interfaces by understanding unique characteristics and usage. *INTERACT* '09 (2009), 340-353.
2. Back, J., & Oppenheim, C. A model of cognitive load for IR: implications for user relevance feedback interaction. *Information Research 6* (2) (2001).
3. Bederson, B. B. PhotoMesa: a zoomable image browser using quantum treemaps and bubblemaps. *In Proc. UIST 2001*, ACM Press (2001), 71-80.
4. Borg, I. and Groenen, P. *Modern multidimensional scaling: Theory and applications*. Springer, 2005.

5. Chen, C., Gagaudakis, G., & Rosin, P. Similarity-based image browsing. *Int. conference on intelligent information processing* (2000), 206-213.
6. Chew, B., Rode, J. A., & Sellen, A. Understanding the everyday use of images on the web. *In Proc. NordiCHI'10.* ACM Press (2010), 102-111.
7. Chung, E., & Yoon, J. Image needs in the context of image use: An exploratory study. *Journal of Information Science* (2011).
8. Combs, T. T., & Bederson, B. B. Does zooming improve image browsing? *In Proceedings of Digital libraries'99.* ACM Press. (1999), 130-137.
9. Datta, R., Li, J., & Wang, J. Z. Content-based image retrieval: approaches and trends of the new age. *In Proc. of SIGMM.* ACM Press (2005), 253-262.
10. Deselaers, Thomas, Daniel Keysers, and Hermann Ney. Features for image retrieval: an experimental comparison. *Information Retrieval 11*, 2 (2008), 77-107.
11. Eakins, J. P., Briggs, P., & Burford, B. Image retrieval interfaces: A user perspective. *In Image and Video Retrieval,* Springer Berlin Heidelberg (2004). 628-637.
12. Fan, J., Keim, D. A., Gao, Y., Luo, H., Li, Z. JustClick: Personalized image recommendation via exploratory search from large-scale Flickr images. *IEEE Transactions on Circuits and Systems for Video Technology, 19*, 2 (2009), 273-288.
13. Hearst, M. *Search user interfaces*. Cambridge University Press. 2009.
14. Hoque, E., Hoeber, O., & Gong, M. Balancing the trade-offs between diversity and precision for web image search using concept-based query expansion. *Journal of Emerging Technologies in Web Intelligence*, *4*, 1 (2012) 26-34.
15. Hu, P. J. H., Ma, P. C., & Chau, P. Y. Evaluation of user interface designs for information retrieval systems: a computer-based experiment. *Decision Support Systems, 27*, 1 (1999) 125-143.
16. Igarashi T, Hinckley, K., Speed-dependent automatic zooming for browsing large documents, *Proceedings of UIST 2000.* ACM Press (2000), 139-148.
17. Jing, Y., Rowley, H., Wang, J., Tsai, D., Rosenberg, C., & Covell, M. Google image swirl: a large-scale content-based image visualization system. *Proceedings of WWW.* (2012), 539-540.
18. Kohonen, T. *Self-organizing maps* (Vol. 30). Springer. 2001.
19. Kleiman, Y., Fish, N., Lanir, J., & Cohen-Or, D. Dynamic maps for exploring and browsing shapes. *Computer Graphics Forum 32*, 5 (2012), 187-196.
20. Liu, H., Xie, X., Tang, X., Li, Z. W., & Ma, W. Y. Effective browsing of web image search results. *In Proc of SIGMM.* ACM Press (2004), 84-90.
21. Markkula, M., & Sormunen, E. End-user searching challenges indexing practices in the digital newspaper photo archive. *Information retrieval, 1*, 4, (2000) 259-285
22. Oliva, A., and Torralba, A. Modeling the shape of the scene: A holistic representation of the spatial envelope. *International Journal of Computer Vision 42*, 3 (2001) 145–175.
23. Pečenovic, Z., Do, M. N., Vetterli, M., & Pu, P. Integrated browsing and searching of large image collections. *In Advances in Visual Information Systems.* Springer Berlin Heidelberg. (2000). 279-289.
24. Rodden, K., Basalaj, W., Sinclair, D., & Wood, K. Does organization by similarity assist image browsing? *In Proc CHI.* ACM Press (2001). 190-197
25. Rodden K, Basalaj D W Sinclair, Wood K. Evaluating a visualization of image similarity as a tool for image browsing. *IEEE symposium on information visualization* (1999) 36–43
26. Roweis, S., and Saul, L. Nonlinear dimensionality reduction by locally linear embedding. *Science 290*, 5500, (2000), 2323–2326.
27. Rui, Y., Huang, T. S., Ortega, M., & Mehrotra, S. Relevance feedback: a power tool for interactive content-based image retrieval. *Circuits and Systems for Video Technology, IEEE Transactions on, 8,* 5 (1998), 644-655.
28. Ruthven, I., & Lalmas, M. A survey on the use of relevance feedback for information access systems. *The Knowledge Engineering Review, 18*, 2 (2003) 95-145
29. Sakamoto, Y., Kuriyama S., and Kaneko, T. Motion map: image-based retrieval and segmentation of motion data. *In Proc SIGGRAPH/ Eurographics symposium on Computer animation*, (2004).
30. Shatford-Layne, S. Some issues in the indexing of images. *Journal of the American society of Information Science. 45*, 8 (1994) 583-588
31. Shneiderman B. *Designing The User Interface: Strategies for Effective Human-Computer Interaction*, 4/e. Pearson Education India, 2003.
32. Strong, G., Gong, M.. Browsing a large collection of community photos based on similarity on GPU. *Advances in Visual Computing*. (2008), 390–399.
33. Strong, G., Hoeber, O., & Gong, M. Visual image browsing and exploration (Vibe): User evaluations of image search tasks. *Active Media Technology.* Springer Berlin Heidelberg (2010), 424-435.
34. Suditu, N., & Fleuret, F. HEAT: Iterative relevance feedback with one million images. *In ICCV 2011* IEEE (2011), 2118-2125.
35. Teevan, J., Alvarado, C., Ackerman, M. S., & Karger, D. R. The perfect search engine is not enough: a study of orienteering behavior in directed search. *In Proc CHI 2004.* ACM Press (2004), 415-422
36. Yee, K. P., Swearingen, K., Li, K., & Hearst, M. Faceted metadata for image search and browsing. *In Proc CHI 2003.* ACM Press (2003), 401-408.
37. Zhou, X. S., & Huang, T. S. Relevance feedback in image retrieval: A comprehensive review. *Multimedia systems*, *8*, 6 (2003), 536-544.

S.O.S.: Does Your Search Engine Results Page (SERP) Need Help?

Maximilian Speicher*
Technische Universität Chemnitz
09111 Chemnitz, Germany
speim@hrz.tu-chemnitz.de

Andreas Both
R&D, Unister GmbH
04109 Leipzig, Germany
andreas.both@unister.de

Martin Gaedke
Technische Universität Chemnitz
09111 Chemnitz, Germany
gaedke@cs.tu-chemnitz.de

ABSTRACT
Over the past 20 years, search engines have become *the* entry point of the WWW. Due to evolving needs for different and new kinds of information, the interfaces of search engine results pages (SERPs) change over time. Thus, their usability must be continuously evaluated to ensure user satisfaction and competitive edge. As no complete solution exists, we present *S.O.S.:* the *SERP Optimization Suite*. Our approach comprises (a) *WaPPU*, which is a near real-time tool for evaluating web interfaces based on usability scores, and (b) a *catalog of best practices* that maps bad scores to potential causes and corresponding adjustments for optimization. During a case study in which we assessed and optimized a real-world SERP, S.O.S. has proven its feasibility and effectiveness by significantly improving the SERP's usability.

Author Keywords
best practices; evaluation; metrics; optimization; scores; search engine results pages; usability

ACM Classification Keywords
H.5.2. Information Interfaces and Presentation (e.g., HCI): User Interfaces—*Evaluation/methodology, Style guides, User-centered design*

INTRODUCTION
Ever since the launch of *Archie*[1]—which is considered as the first of its kind—in 1990, search engines have become *the* entry point of the WWW. Numerous users do not even make use of the address bar of their browser anymore, but just type where they want to go into the search box of the default home page. For example, the *Start Page* of *Mozilla Firefox* is powered by Google[2] and simply shows their well-known search box. Also, the address bars of all modern browsers interpret non-URL input as search queries, which are forwarded to the default search engine defined in the browser settings. In this way, it is nowadays possible to browse the Web completely without URLs, thanks to *search engines*.

While the early search engines were relatively simple applications and provided limited functionality—i.e., they performed a full-text search on an index of HTML documents—, requirements towards search engines have evolved constantly. Nowadays, there is a demand for different types of results, such as news, images and videos. Search engines also more and more tend to answer queries directly on their *search engine results pages* (SERPs) and provide such answers in dedicated info boxes (cf. *Google Knowledge Graph*[3]). Finally, search engines as well have to somehow incorporate advertisements into their interfaces to ensure they can make profit and offer their services for free. All of this brings up numerous requirements concerning the delivery and arrangement of all different kinds of content. As a result, SERPs evolve continuously since they are the search engines' prime interfaces for ultimately presenting the desired information to the user.

To date, there is no form of a SERP interface that can be generally considered to be optimal. Although Google clearly stands at the top (number 1 in the *Alexa* top 500[4]), particularly trending search engines such as *qwant.com* and *duckduckgo.com* show different approaches towards SERP interfaces. To give just one example, besides other obvious differences, all three search engines feature completely different look & feels concerning the aforementioned info boxes (Figure 1). Thus, it is crucial for search engine owners to continuously evaluate the usability of their SERPs regarding the evolving needs of users and the introduction of new kinds of information.

In today's industry, SERPs are often evaluated using A/B testing set-ups that try to increase quantitative metrics like clicks on advertisements. These are popular due to their better efficiency compared to traditional usability evaluation methods, such as heuristic inspections [20] or lab studies. Yet, A/B tests usually lack effectiveness in determining usability [19]. For evaluating SERPs in an efficient *and* effective manner, we propose *S.O.S.:* the *SERP Optimization Suite*. S.O.S. comprises two interconnected components: (1) *WaPPU*, which is a tool for performing *usability-based* A/B tests, and (2) a

*The contents of this paper were developed while Maximilian Speicher stayed at Unister GmbH as an industrial PhD student.

[1] `http://people.lis.illinois.edu/~chip/projects/timeline/1990archie.htm` (Sep 1, 2014).

[2] `http://www.google.com/firefox` (Sep 1, 2014).

[3] `http://www.google.com/insidesearch/features/search/knowledge.html` (Sep 1, 2014).

[4] `http://www.alexa.com/topsites` (Sep 1, 2014).

CHI 2015, April 18 - 23 2015, Seoul, Republic of Korea

ACM 978-1-4503-3145-6/15/04...$15.00
http://dx.doi.org/10.1145/2702123.2702568

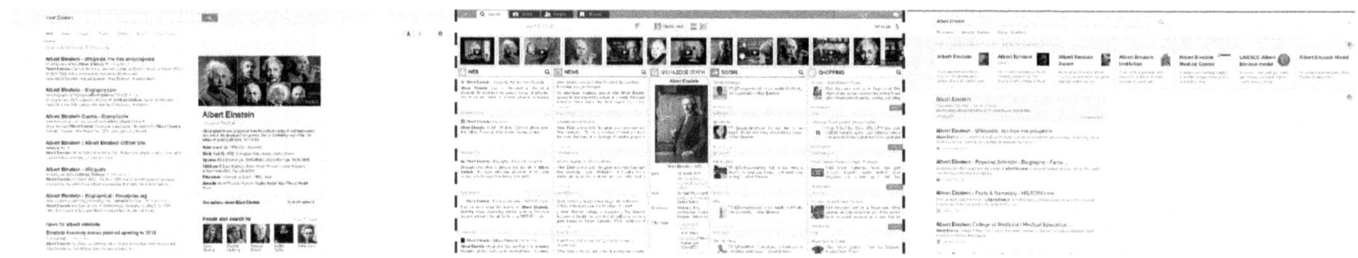

Figure 1. Comparison of the SERP interfaces of Google (left), Qwant (middle) and DuckDuckGo (right). They particularly differ concerning the look & feel and placement of the info box about "Albert Einstein".

catalog of best practices w.r.t. SERP usability. Our approach is able to determine usability scores of a SERP interface and for suboptimal scores automatically point out potential causes and corresponding countermeasures.

Speicher et al. have developed WaPPU ("*Wa*s that *P*age *P*leasant to *U*se") as a general tool for A/B testing based on quantitative usability scores [23]. Although existing work (e.g., [3, 8, 9]) already builds on user interaction analysis for better efficiency, *WaPPU* is the first approach to perform A/B tests based on seven usability factors as the target metrics (e.g., *readability* = -0.5 for Interface A). These metrics are based on a questionnaire as well as real users' interactions with the interface. Speicher et al. have proven the feasibility and effectiveness of WaPPU in a user test with two real SERP interfaces [23]. Yet, a major shortcoming of A/B testing approaches is the fact that improvements to an interface need to be performed *a priori*. That is, the old *and* the new version of the interface must be available before the usability-based A/B test starts. To date, there is no state-of-the-art tool that is able to propose optimizations to an interface based on usability scores or user interactions—like "Your rating for *readability* is negative, please adjust your font size"—, which would be highly desirable.

Therefore, we propose an extension to WaPPU to form S.O.S. Since the mapping between a usability score / vector of user interactions y and causes for bad usability x is *not* a bijective function $f(x) = y$, it is technically not possible to infer the exact necessary optimizations for an assessed interface. To give just one example, a bad score of readability might be caused by the wrong font size and line height while the font itself is good. Yet, it could also be caused by the wrong font while font size and line height are good. Thus, the proposed extension is a catalog of best practices that—in the context of SERPs—, maps a bad rating y of a usability factor to a *set* of potential causes C and corresponding countermeasures C': $f(y) = \{C, C'\}$. This catalog has been determined in a three-step process that followed the *find–fix–verify* pattern described by Bernstein et al. [5] to ensure it is well-founded. First, we have reviewed well-known SERP interfaces and extracted common best practices as well as potential problems from these. Second, we asked ten dedicated experts to review and revise this basic catalog. Third, each revision has been approved or rejected by three additional, independent experts. We have applied rules from the final catalog to a real-world SERP that had been evaluated using WaPPU. This case study suggests the effectiveness of S.O.S., as the redesigned SERP shows significant approvements for certain usability factors.

In the following, we discuss related work and motivate this paper by introducing WaPPU and shortcomings of A/B testing in more detail. In the subsequent section, we describe the development of the catalog of best practices. The workflow of S.O.S. is presented after that. Then, we explain the corresponding case study before discussing our work and giving concluding remarks.

BACKGROUND AND RELATED WORK

A/B testing [19] is a common method to evaluate changes to an interface. That is, the original version of the interface is compared against a modified version (e.g., advertisements vs. no advertisements) w.r.t. a pre-defined target metric (e.g., clicks on a specific link). The two versions that are compared are also referred to as the "interfaces-under-test" in the remainder of this paper.

Usability is a relative concept that can only be evaluated within a specified context. As Brooke [7] puts it: "Usability is not a quality that exists in any real or absolute sense." In this paper, the notion of "usability" is based on ISO 9241-11 [1], which we further specify as follows: We consider the usability *in use* [2] of a single webpage (which we refer to as the "web interface"), as perceived by real users. Moreover, we consider *do-goals* (achieving tasks) rather than *be-goals* (feeling special, being satisfied etc.) [13]. In accordance with [15], we remove "satisfaction" from the original definition of [1], as it has to be considered separate from usability in use.

Today, there are numerous approaches to **interaction-based usability evaluation**, such as [3, 8, 9] or the commercial tool *m-pathy*[5]. All of these try to infer usability / user experience issues from user's behavior on a website. This is partly done by visualizing interactions ([3], m-pathy) and partly by comparing users' logs to pre-defined optimal logs for a given task ([8, 9]). However, the above approaches still require manual inspection of the results by developers or experts. In particular, they do not provide the evaluator with a *quantitative* measurement of the performance of the investigated interface.

Contrary to the above, methods for **metric-based usability evaluation** intend to assess interfaces based on scores for usability. Nebeling et al. [16] developed a set of metrics specifi-

[5]`http://www.m-pathy.com/` (Sep 11, 2014).

cally aimed at large-screen contexts. Their metrics—which are determined based on a webpage's rendered layout—include small-text ratio and media-content ratio, to name only two. Speicher [21] has transferred these metrics to small-screen contexts and also provides an additional metric for a webpage's "overall quality". The *System Usability Scale* (SUS) [7] is a lightweight instrument for assessing arbitrary interfaces that provides a score between 0 and 100. It poses ten questions to the user that have to be answered on a 5-point Likert scale. *AttrakDiff*[6] is a similar tool that, however, assesses the user experience of a web application on a two-dimensional scale (pragmatic and hedonic quality), and thus builds on a different instrument. It is also specifically aimed at carrying out A/B tests. Although the above solutions provide different kinds of scores for evaluating interfaces, they are based on either static analysis of a rendered layout or users' answers to a questionnaire. None of them specifically aims at deriving such scores from user interactions.

The goal of the WaPPU tool contained in S.O.S. is to combine the two general approaches described above—i.e., evaluating interfaces based on user behavior and providing corresponding usability scores.

Concerning **usability optimization** of interfaces, *decision-theoretic optimization* [10] is a general approach. With this method, users' preferences are elicited using either *example critiquing*, i.e., giving the user the option to change parts of an interface, or *active elicitation*, i.e., explicitly asking a user for their preferences. In this way, it is possible to learn a cost function that can be optimized through linear optimization. Examples for systems implementing this technique are ARNAULD [10] and SUPPLE [11]. Similar to the above, *Crowd-Adapt* [17] gives users the chance to express their preferences by adjusting the layout of a webpage (rearranging elements, changing the font size etc.). In this way, interface optimizations are crowdsourced for different viewing contexts. *W3Touch* [18] also builds on the crowdsourcing idea, however, in the specific context of touch devices. The tool engages implicit feedback by, e.g., scaling text according to users' average zooming factor. While all of the above are promising tools for improving usability through interface optimization, with the exception of W3Touch they follow fundamentally different approaches compared to S.O.S. Also, none specifically aims at the case of optimizing SERPs.

When it comes to **SERP optimization**, [6] describe the *layout definition problem.* That is, given results from different domains and different result types, they try to compute an optimal layout. However, this is an *a priori* approach resulting in a complete *design strategy* for the SERP. Therefore, it is more likely involved in the early stages of the design process, e.g., before an A/B test is carried out.

Concerning **best practices**, there is a vast number of general checklists for web interfaces, such as *Userium*[7]. Also, *Userfocus* present a rather general, 20-item set of best practices for search usability[8]. However—to the best of our knowledge—there is no well-founded catalog of best practices for optimizing SERP usability. In particular, there is none that relates causes for bad usability and corresponding countermeasures to an actual usability evaluation.

The tool that is probably closest to our S.O.S. approach has been described in [12]. The proposed approach detects *bad usability smells* based on *a priori* assumptions and then provides the developer with a report of existing problems. Contrary to our work, Grigera et al. focus on rather high-level usability problems—like long navigation paths—in the context of complete web applications. Yet, their tool might be a useful complement to S.O.S., particularly if there occur intersections between bad usability smells and suboptimal usability scores reported by WaPPU.

MOTIVATION: WAPPU

WaPPU is an ongoing research project that has been introduced by Speicher et al. [23]. The prototype[9] has been developed as a general tool to (a) enable A/B tests that are based on *usability* as the prime target metric, and (b) enable the inference of the corresponding usability scores from user interactions. Its aim is to be more effective in determining usability than conversion-based[10] A/B tests while retaining most of their efficiency. In fact, A/B tests are popular in industry due to their advantages over traditional methods of usability evaluation, particularly concerning efficiency [19]. This is underpinned by a variety of available (commercial) A/B testing tools, such as *Google Analytics*[11] and *Visual Website Optimizer*[12], to name only two.

WaPPU evaluates seven usability factors: (1) Informativeness, (2) Understandability, (3) Confusion, (4) Distraction, (5) Readability, (6) Information Density, and (7) Accessibility.

These factors (or items) are taken from a usability instrument that has been specifically tailored to the needs of the tool [22]. That is, it is cost-effective and designed for inferring ratings of its items directly from user interactions [22]. In the context of WaPPU, the usability factors are what we refer to as usability *metrics* in the remainder of this paper. They also form an *overall metric for usability* by summing up ratings of all seven items.

User Interaction Tracking

WaPPU tracks a total of 27 features, among which are, e.g., *cursor speed, length of the cursor trail, number of hovers* and *page dwell time*. The developer has to include a client-side jQuery plug-in and define components (e.g., navigation, sidebar etc.) for which the features shall be tracked. All defined components have to be present in both interfaces-under-test

[6]`http://attrakdiff.de/index-en.html` (Sep 11, 2014).

[7]`https://userium.com/` (Sep 11, 2014).

[8]`http://www.userfocus.co.uk/resources/searchchecklist.html` (Sep 11, 2014).

[9]`https://github.com/maxspeicher/wappu-service` (Sep 2, 2014).

[10]For example, the number of clicked advertisements or the number of completed checkout processes.

[11]`http://www.google.com/analytics/` (Sep 2, 2014).

[12]`https://vwo.com/` (Sep 2, 2014).

of the A/B test, i.e., the high-level structure of both interfaces has to be the same. The collected interactions are then sent to the server-side WaPPU service in suitable time intervals.

Collecting Usability Judgments

WaPPU provides the option to automatically display a questionnaire when a user leaves a web interface. This questionnaire corresponds to the seven usability factors above and can be included in any of the interfaces-under-test included in an A/B test. It is necessary to display the questionnaire in at least one involved interface, as otherwise WaPPU is not able to predict usability scores from user interactions. In the current implementation, the user answers the seven questions based on a 3-point scale: ☹, 😐 or ☺ (bad–neutral–good). These seven *usability judgments* are then sent to the server side together with the tracked user interactions. In near real-time, the WaPPU service automatically learns one model for each usability factor based on existing machine learning techniques. Moreover, separate models are learned for different user contexts since factors such as the screen size have an impact on the tracked interaction features. The current prototype considers *screen size* and the presence of *ad blockers* as dimensions of user context and uses an incremental version of the Naïve Bayes classifier [14] for learning the models. This means that in total, seven models are provided per A/B test and detected user context. Once these models are of good enough[13] quality, the questionnaire can be removed and the usability of both involved interface versions is inferred from user interactions alone.

The WaPPU Dashboard

WaPPU summarizes the metrics and scores of an A/B test in a dedicated dashboard (Figure 2). For the seven individual factors, a score between -1 and $+1$ is given, corresponding to the bad–neutral–good scale (☹, 😐, ☺) described above. The score of the overall usability metric is then determined by summing up all factors, i.e., it has a value between -7 and $+7$ that is normalized to a value between 0% and 100%. All scores are visualized together with their standard deviations. The overall score is provided in analogy to SUS [7]. [4] found that the university grade analog (100–90 points correspond to an "A", 89–80 points to a "B" etc.) is a good rule-of-thumb for interpreting SUS scores. Moreover, they state that "products which are at least passable have [...] scores above 70" [4]. Thus, we set **70%** as the lower bound for a *good* usability score in WaPPU. This corresponds to individual factor scores of **0.4**, i.e., if all usability factors have a score of 0.4, we get an overall score of 70%.

If an interface-under-test features the questionnaire, the eight usability scores displayed in the dashboard are derived directly from users' answers. Otherwise, WaPPU predicts the scores based on the interactions collected on the respective interface and the available models. For example, if interface "A" displays the questionnaire, WaPPU learns the seven models M_i based on the corresponding answers and interactions $\vec{I}$ tracked on "A": $M_i \leftarrow \mathit{learn}(\text{answer}_i^A, \vec{I}^A)\ \forall i \in$ usability factors. The usability scores of interface "B" are then inferred from these models and the interactions collected on "B": $\text{score}_i^B = M_i(\vec{I}^B)\ \forall i \in$ usability factors.

[13]The definition of "good enough" is up to the developer in this case.

Additionally, the WaPPU dashboard features a traffic light indicating statistically significant differences between the interfaces-under-test. That is, WaPPU applies a *Mann–Whitney U test* to the (predicted) overall usability scores produced by all involved users. In case the usability scores of the two interfaces-under-test are statistically equal—i.e., no definite statement about which one is better can be made—the traffic light is yellow, otherwise it is red ("A" better) or green ("B" better).

Limitations

While WaPPU has demonstrated its feasibility and effectiveness in a user study [23], the tool has a major shortcoming. Because it follows the principle of A/B testing, both versions of the interface to be tested have to be present before the parallel A/B test starts. Particularly, improvements to an interface need to be performed *a priori*, i.e., before the developer is provided with quantitative evidence. This might lead to lots of test being carried out that cannot detect a significant difference between the two versions of the interface. Therefore, it would be highly desirable if WaPPU was able to propose improvements to an interface based on its measured usability.

A straightforward idea would be to use the interactions tracked by WaPPU for inferring the causes of bad usability scores. Once the specific causes would be known, corresponding improvements could be proposed. Yet, a bad score of a usability metric can have numerous different reasons, i.e., the mapping between the score y and the cause x is not a bijective function $f(x) = y$. As a representative example, let us consider bad *informativeness* on a SERP—i.e., the particular information the user is looking for is not present or only present in parts. Bad informativeness can have two main reasons: (1) the desired information is in fact not present on the SERP, and (2) the desired information is hidden in such a way that the user cannot find it (which might be due to a bad layout). In both cases, the user would give a rating of -1 (☹) for the item *informativeness*. Yet, they only consider the fact that the desired information is not present on the SERP from their point of view. Particularly, the user does not care about the specific cause for this lack of information. In [23], it is reported that on SERPs, bad informativeness is indicated by, e.g., a lower relative amount of hovers over the list of search results. However, in analogy to the given rating, the user's behavior would not change depending on the specific *cause* for a missing piece of information. This is because the user has no knowledge about this cause, which means that his interactions can only be influenced by the resulting higher-level fact that their desired information is not present.

Thus, we propose to extend WaPPU with a catalog of best practices for optimizing the usability of SERPs. For each of the seven usability metrics, this catalog maps bad scores y to a *set* of potential causes C and corresponding countermeasures C': $f(y) = \{C, C'\}$. Together, WaPPU and the catalog form *S.O.S.*—the SERP Optimization Suite. We will also describe a new workflow which ensures that developers can react to bad usability scores based on the catalog.

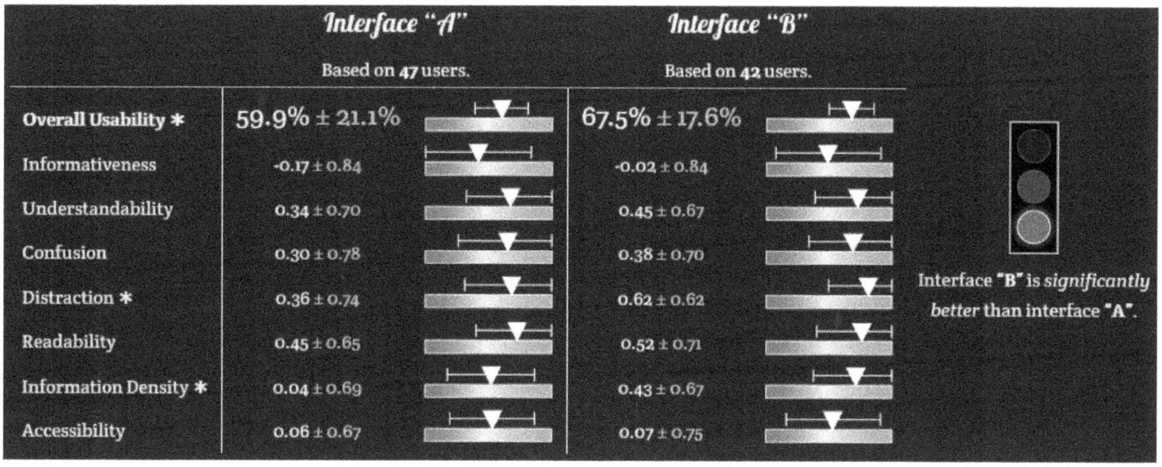

Figure 2. Screenshot of the WaPPU dashboard showing the evaluation of the A/B test carried out during the case study. It shows the scores (mean and standard deviation) of each usability factor and the overall usability metric for the two involved SERPs (Interface "A" = original SERP, Interface "B" = redesigned SERP, * significant difference).

BEST PRACTICES FOR SERP USABILITY

The catalog for optimizing the usability of SERPs has been determined in a three-step process. This process corresponds to the *find–fix–verify* pattern described by Bernstein et al. in [5]. In the first (the 'find') phase, we have reviewed SERPs of eight popular search engines and extracted common best practices and shortcomings. From these, we have compiled a first version of our catalog. In the second (the 'fix') phase, we have asked ten dedicated experts to review the catalog and propose adjustments as required from their point of view. Finally, in the third (the 'verify') phase, each adjustment from the second phase has been reviewed by another three independent experts, who could either approve or reject it. The final catalog has then been created by only making those adjustments that were approved by at least two experts from the third phase. By making use of a state-of-the-art pattern [5] and having our catalog thoroughly reviewed by a total of 20 experts—which according to [20] find more than 75% of present errors—, we believe the final outcome to be well-founded and a valid instrument for usability optimization on SERPs.

All resources, including the SERP reviews, the first version of the catalog, the anonymized revised catalogs, the anonymized reviews of the adjustments and the *complete final catalog* can be accessed at `http://vsr.informatik.tu-chemnitz.de/demo/SOS`. The three phases applied for creating the catalog will be described in detail in the following.

'Find' Phase

In the first phase, we have reviewed the top five search engines as ranked by Alexa[14]: (1) *google.com*, (2) *yahoo.com*, (3) *baidu.com*, (4) *yandex.ru*, and (5) *bing.com*. Moreover, we have considered three trending search engines that have been intensively and repeatedly discussed among friends and colleagues—i.e., (A) *qwant.com*, (B) *duckduckgo.com*, and (C) *ecosia.org*. These follow new approaches (all-in-one search, anonymous search and green search) and as of September 3, 2014, have considerable *Klout*[15] scores (A: 53, B: 81, C: 63) and numbers of *Twitter*[16] followers (A: 1,544, B: 32.4K, C: 5,095).

	Web/Interface Design		**Web Development/Engineering**	
Phase	work	skills	work	skills
'Fix'	4	3	3.5	3
'Verify'	3	3	5	4
	Usability / User Experience		**Search Engines**	
	work	skills	work	skills
'Fix'	4	2	2	2
'Verify'	3.5	2	2.5	3

Table 1. Experts ratings of how much their work/studies are concerned with each of the given fields (1 = not at all, 5 = very much) and how they rate their own skills (1 = no knowledge, 4 = expert). Numbers given are median values.

From these eight SERP interfaces, we have extracted common best practices (approaches that could be found in the majority of the investigated SERPs); and shortcomings (approaches followed only by a minority of the SERPs that we considered to be problematic from the usability perspective). Best practices included, e.g., search suggestions / related search queries, semantic results and generous use of white space. Shortcomings included not clearly identifiable advertisements, infinite scrolling and overloaded results, among others. From this, we compiled a first (basic) version of our catalog of best practices. This basic version contained a total of 40 potential causes for bad scores as well as 61 corresponding countermeasures for the seven usability metrics.

'Fix' Phase

In the second phase, the basic catalog was given to ten dedicated experts in the fields of web/interface design, web development/engineering, user experience / usability and search

[14] `http://www.alexa.com/topsites` (Aug 17, 2014)

[15] `https://klout.com/home` (Sep 3, 2014).

[16] `https://twitter.com/` (Sep 3, 2014).

engines. Each one was asked to review the catalog and make adjustments as necessary from their point of view—i.e., by adding new causes/countermeasures or by altering or removing existing ones. They were also provided with examples of SERPs for the query "Albert Einstein" (Google, Bing, DuckDuckGo).

The experts performed a total of 110 changes (additions, removals, alterations) to the basic catalog, which is an average of 11 changes per expert. In [20], Nielsen and Molich state that "evaluations from several evaluators [...] do rather well, even if they only consist of three to five people." In analogy to this, we assume that in the 'fix' phase with 10 experts ($\gg$3–5), *at least* 71% [20] of the errors/problems in the basic catalog were found. Particularly, as the setting of revising a catalog of best practices given interface examples is not fundamentally different from heuristic evaluation of interfaces.

The experts' ratings of their skills in each of the relevant fields is given in Table 1. Four of the experts worked in academia, four worked in industry and seven were (graduate) students (multiple answers possible). Five considered themselves to be a practitioner, one to be a researcher, three said "half/half" and one said "don't know". Nine of the experts were male (one female) at an average age of 27.1 (σ=1.85); five owned a Bachelor's and the remaining five a Master's degree.

'Verify' Phase

In the last phase defined by the *find–fix–verify* pattern [5], the catalogs from phase two were anonymized and randomly assigned to another ten independent experts (three per expert) who were disjoint from the experts above. In this way, every adjustment proposed for the basic catalog was reviewed three times. The experts were instructed to compare the revised catalogs to the basic version and approve or reject each adjustment individually. Thus, valid adjustments were found by majority decision (at least two approvals). In total, 44 adjustments (40%) were approved with a 3–0 vote, 37 (33.64%) were approved with a 2–1 vote, 9 (8.18%) were rejected with a 3–0 vote and 20 (18.18%) were rejected with a 2–1 vote. In case two contradictory adjustments to the same cause/countermeasure had been approved (a proposed change vs. a proposed removal), we counted the overall votes (by six experts), which happened four times. Moreover, in case of a draw (3–3), the item was—*in dubio pro reo*—not removed from the catalog, which was the case thrice.

The experts' ratings of their skills in each of the relevant fields is given in Table 1. Six of the experts worked in academia and five in industry (multiple answers possible). Three considered themselves to be a practitioner, one to be a researcher and six said "half/half". Nine of the experts were male (one female) at an average age of 29.5 (σ=3.47); eight owned a Master's and one a PhD degree (one stated "other degree").

Final Catalog

The final catalog is the semantic union[17] of (a) all approved adjustments from the revised catalogs, and (b) the remaining

[17] If two or more causes/countermeasures express the same meaning in a different way, they are included as one item in the final catalog.

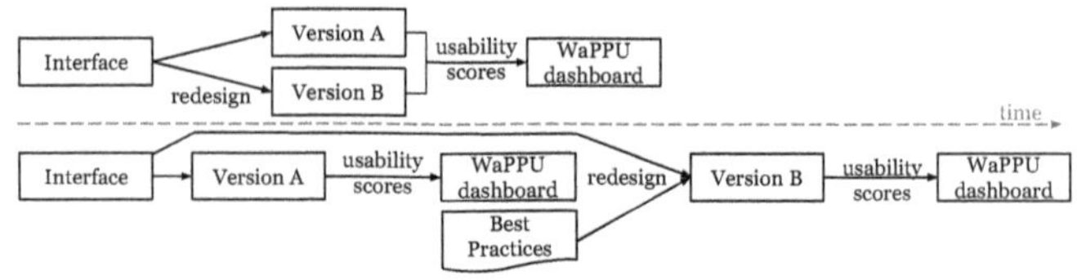

Figure 3. Usability-based A/B testing (above) vs. S.O.S.-supported sequential A/B testing (below).

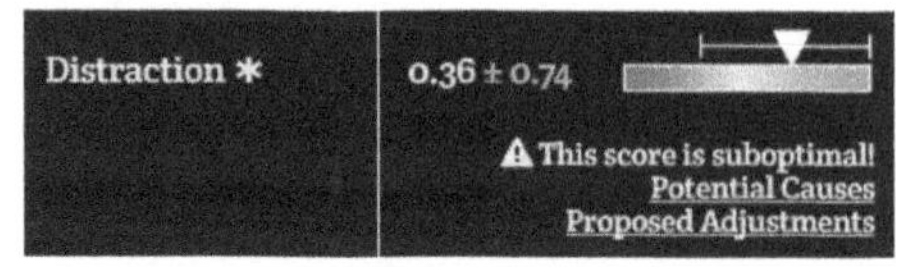

Figure 4. We have equipped the dashboard of the WaPPU prototype to display warnings next to suboptimal scores. Clicking the links leads to the corresponding parts of the catalog of best practices.

items from the basic catalog. Since we considered the *find–fix–verify* pattern [5] as well as Nielsen and Molich's findings [20], we believe that our catalog is well-founded and a valid extension to the WaPPU tool during search engine design and development. In Figure 5, we provide an *exemplary* excerpt of the final catalog that consists of the causes and countermeasures related to the case study described below. For each usability factor, the potential *causes* for a bad rating are numbered with *Roman* numerals and *countermeasures* are numbered with *Arabic* numerals. Items that were added or adjusted by the experts and approved in the 'verify' phase have their cumulative votes given in square brackets *[pro–contra]*.

S.O.S.: THE SERP OPTIMIZATION SUITE

The catalog (Figure 5) is intended to be an extension to the WaPPU service *in the context of search engine design and development*. Together, they form *S.O.S.*—the SERP Optimization Suite. Yet, when making use of S.O.S., there is the need for a different workflow compared to regular A/B testing. With the usual A/B testing workflow, both versions of the tested interface are available before the test starts. That is, the redesign intended to improve usability happens *a priori* and the two versions of the interface are evaluated in parallel (Figure 3). This is one of the main problems of standard A/B testing, as, e.g., Nielsen [19] points out. Contrary, when using S.O.S., we want to have empirical evidence of the original interface's usability first. Only *after* that, we identify potential causes for bad usability scores using the catalog and apply corresponding countermeasures, thus forming a redesigned interface. Then, also the new version of the interface is evaluated using WaPPU to investigate the changes made.

The WaPPU tool is technically not restricted to running A/B tests in parallel. Rather, the actual temporal distribution of users to the interfaces-under-test is completely up to the developer. That is, it is easily possible to direct 100% of the users to only one version of the tested interface. The A/B testing workflow to be used with S.O.S. is therefore to (1) first direct all users to interface A, (2) then consult the catalog of best practices and perform a redesign, and (3) finally direct all users to interface B to validate the redesign (Figure 3). To support this new workflow, we have already integrated according means into the WaPPU dashboard (Figure 4).

A. **Informativeness**
  I. bad index quality (desired result[s] not present on page)
  II. bad ranking quality (desired result[s] not present or ranked too low)
  III. desired result not clearly identifiable:
    a. inappropriate title and/or abstract
    b. too many other results
    c. too much content other than results
  2. ⑨ provide search suggestions / related search terms
  6. clarify layout:
    b. ①④⑧ clearly separate results from other content such as ads (or remove the latter) *[2–1]*
    c. ①②③ reduce amount of content other than results
    e. ④ clearly separate title from abstract *[3–0]*

B. **Understandability**

C. **Confusion**
  II. too many irrelevant results *[3–0]*
  III. too much content other than results
  IV. too many advertisements which are poorly marked as such; no clear separation between advertisements / sponsored results and real results *[6–0]*
  2. ⑧ clearly highlight results and mark other content as such
  5. ①②③ reduce amount of content other than results

D. **Distraction**
  I. too much content other than results
  III. too many images
  IV. non-results more salient than results *[2–1]*
  V. overloaded results (e.g., displaying secondary information, social media buttons etc.)
  1. ①②③ reduce amount of content other than results
  3. ③ reduce amount of images
  4. ③④⑤⑥⑦⑧ ensure that results are more salient than other content *[3–0]*
  5. clarify presentation of results:
    a. ② reduce to: title, URL, abstract

E. **Readability**
  I. wrong font size or character spacing (too small / too large) *[9–0]*
  II. wrong line height (too small / too large) *[6–0]*
  V. text not properly grouped (e.g., via white space or separation lines) *[3–0]*
  VII. inconsistent alignment of results and/or other elements of the page
  1. ⑤ adjust font size or character spacing (or offer according option to reader) *[11–1]*
  2. ⑤ adjust line height *[9–0]*
  5. add white space:
    a. ④⑦ between title, URL and abstract of result
    b. ④ between results
    c. ④⑦ between results and other content
  7. ⑥⑦ align results and other elements of the page consistently

F. **Information Density**
  III. too much content other than results; content that is not related to results *[3–0]*
  IV. too little white space
  V. missing visual hierarchy with salient results *[2–1]*
  VI. overloaded results (e.g., displaying secondary information, social media buttons etc.)
  3. ①②③ reduce amount of content other than results
  4. add white space:
    a. ④⑦ between title, URL and abstract of result
    b. ④ between results
    c. ④⑦ between results and other content
  5. ⑥⑦⑧ introduce contrast and visual hierarchy to separate results from content other than results *[3–0]*
  10. clarify presentation of results:
    a. ② reduce to: title, URL, abstract
  11. ③ remove unnecessary icons/abbreviations or add explaining tooltips *[3–0]*

G. **Accessibility**
  I. too much scrolling effort for user:
    a. too much content other than results, especially above results
    d. bad ranking quality (desired result[s] not present or ranked too low)
  II. desired result(s) not immediately identifiable:
    b. missing visual hierarchy *[2–1]*
    c. missing contrast between results and other content *[3–0]*
  1. reduce scrolling effort:
    a. ① reduce amount of content other than results, especially above results
  2. better highlight results / improve result presentation:
    b. ⑧ introduce contrast and visual hierarchy to separate results from content other than results *[2–1]*
    c. ③④⑤⑥⑦⑧ ensure that results stand out against other content

Figure 5. Excerpt of the final version of the catalog, showing the best practices applied during the case study (the circled numbers refer to Figure 7).

CASE STUDY

We made use of S.O.S. in a case study during which we evaluated a real-world SERP with the help of WaPPU.[18] The study was carried out in terms of a remote asynchronous user study with 81 users who triggered 198 search requests.

The catalog of best practices was taken into account for redesigning the original SERP, which reached only suboptimal usability scores in the evaluation. Our results show that, after identifying issues and taking appropriate countermeasures based on the catalog, the new version of the SERP performs significantly better concerning *distraction, information density* and also the *overall usability metric*. Furthermore, all remaining usability factors reached better scores after the redesign.

Evaluation: Original SERP

The case study was carried out with the SERP (for web search results) of a real-world search engine currently developed by the R&D department of the cooperating company. In the following, we report results for the largest and most representative group of users involved, i.e., novel users (they had never used the search engine before) with HD screens (N=89). During the A/B test, the original version of the SERP showed a suboptimal performance concerning its *overall usability*, with a score of 59.9% (σ=21.1%) based on 47 users. While this cannot be considered as "bad" in general, it is clearly below the threshold for good usability—which is 70% (cf. Section "The WaPPU Dashboard" above)—and thus not a satisfactory outcome from the company's point of view. Particularly, the evaluation revealed problems with respect to *informativeness* (m=-0.17, σ=0.84)[19], *information density*

[18] The case study has also been described by Speicher et al. [23], however, with a focus on evaluating the feasibility of WaPPU.

[19] The range of the score of an individual factor is $[-1, 1]$.

Figure 6. Results of the case study. The original SERP is given in orange, the redesigned SERP is given in dashed green (* significant difference).

(m=0.04, σ=0.69) and *accessibility* (m=0.06, σ=0.67). Contrary, the best-scoring factor was *readability* with a score of 0.45 (σ=0.65). In total, the scores of six out of seven factors were suboptimal, as they lay below the threshold of 0.4. The complete results for the original SERP are given in Figure 2 (left) and Figure 6.

Redesign

Based on the catalog of best practices, the original version of the SERP was evaluated by three experts in front-end design (one graphic designer, one interaction designer and one PhD student with focus on human–computer interaction). According to the workflow of S.O.S. and the usability scores provided by WaPPU, they identified a number of usability issues (the detailed items can be looked up in Figure 5):

- bad result quality (A.I./II., G.I.d.)
- relevant information not clearly identifiable (A.III., C.II., D.IV., G.II.)
- lack of white space (C.IV., E.V., F.IV./V.)
- too much other content above the list of results (A.III.c., C.III., D.I., F.III., G.I.a.)
- bad typography (E.I./II.)
- no clear structure (E.VII.)
- overloaded results (D.III./V., F.VI.).

To be able to apply a broader range of best practices in the case study, we also considered the factor *readability* for optimization, although its score was above the threshold of 0.4. Based on the identified causes for bad usability, the experts applied the corresponding adjustments given by the catalog (the circled numbers refer to Figure 7):

- ① reducing the amount of advertisements (A.6.b./c., C.5., D.1., F.3., G.1.a.)
- ②③ reducing results to title, URL and abstract; particularly by removing social media buttons (A.6.c., C.5., D.1./3./4./5.a., F.3./10.a./11., G.2.c.)
- ④⑤ adjusting results regarding white space, font size and line height (A.6.b./e., D.4., E.1./2., E.5.a./b./c., F.4.a./b./c., G.2.c.)
- ⑥ better aligning results (D.4., E.7., F.5., G.2.c.)
- ⑦ clearer separation between images and text (D.4., E.5.a./c., E.7., F.4.a./c., F.5., G.2.b.)
- ⑧ visualizing and separating results more clearly (A.6.b., C.2., D.4., F.5., G.2.b./c.)
- ⑨ optimizing the display of related search terms (A.2.)

A comparison between the old and the new SERP as well as details about the applied adjustments are given in Figure 7.

Evaluation: New SERP

Like the original version of the SERP, the redesign resulting from the above changes was evaluated using WaPPU. With respect to *overall usability,* the new version reached a score of 67.5% (σ=17.6%) based on 42 users. This was still below the threshold of 70%, but makes for a significant improvement ($p<0.05$, W=782)[20]. Furthermore, the item *distraction* raised by 0.26 points to a score of 0.62 (σ=0.62, $p<0.05$, W=798.5). A third significant improvement was achieved by the item *information density*, which gained 0.39 points to reach a new score of 0.43 (σ=0.67, $p<0.01$, W=692). Besides, the scores of all remaining usability items improved as well, however, not with statistical significance. Overall, four out of seven factors lay above the threshold of 0.4 after the redesign, which is an increase by three. The complete results for the redesigned SERP are given in Figure 2 (right). Moreover, Figure 6 illustrates that the redesign clearly dominates the original SERP across all usability factors.

Although only a fraction of the catalog of best practices was applied during the case study, the above results are a reasonable proof of effectiveness. The experts asked to redesign the SERP applied a set of rather subtle adjustments (Figure 7) that were particularly aimed at reducing *distraction* while improving *readability* and *information density*. The fact that two of these as well as the *overall usability* metric showed significant improvements is a clear indication of the feasibility and effectiveness of S.O.S. and the contained catalog of best practices.

DISCUSSION

S.O.S. has shown its good potential for evaluating and improving the usability of SERPs. While a first case study underpins the feasibility of the approach, it still has certain shortcomings.

First of all, our presented catalog is restricted to best practices for *SERPs*. Contrary, WaPPU serves as a *general* tool for evaluating the usability of any kind of web interface. Thus, it would be desirable and possible to also provide a general catalog that is applicable to a broader range of interfaces (cf. *userium.com*), or a collection of more specific catalogs for different types of interfaces. Besides rules that are specifically aimed at SERPs (e.g., A.I./II., C.2.), our catalog already contains a subset of general rules (e.g., E.I./II., F.11.). However, compiling a general catalog or a set of more specific

[20]All tests of significance were carried out in terms of *Mann–Whitney U tests* (α=0.05).

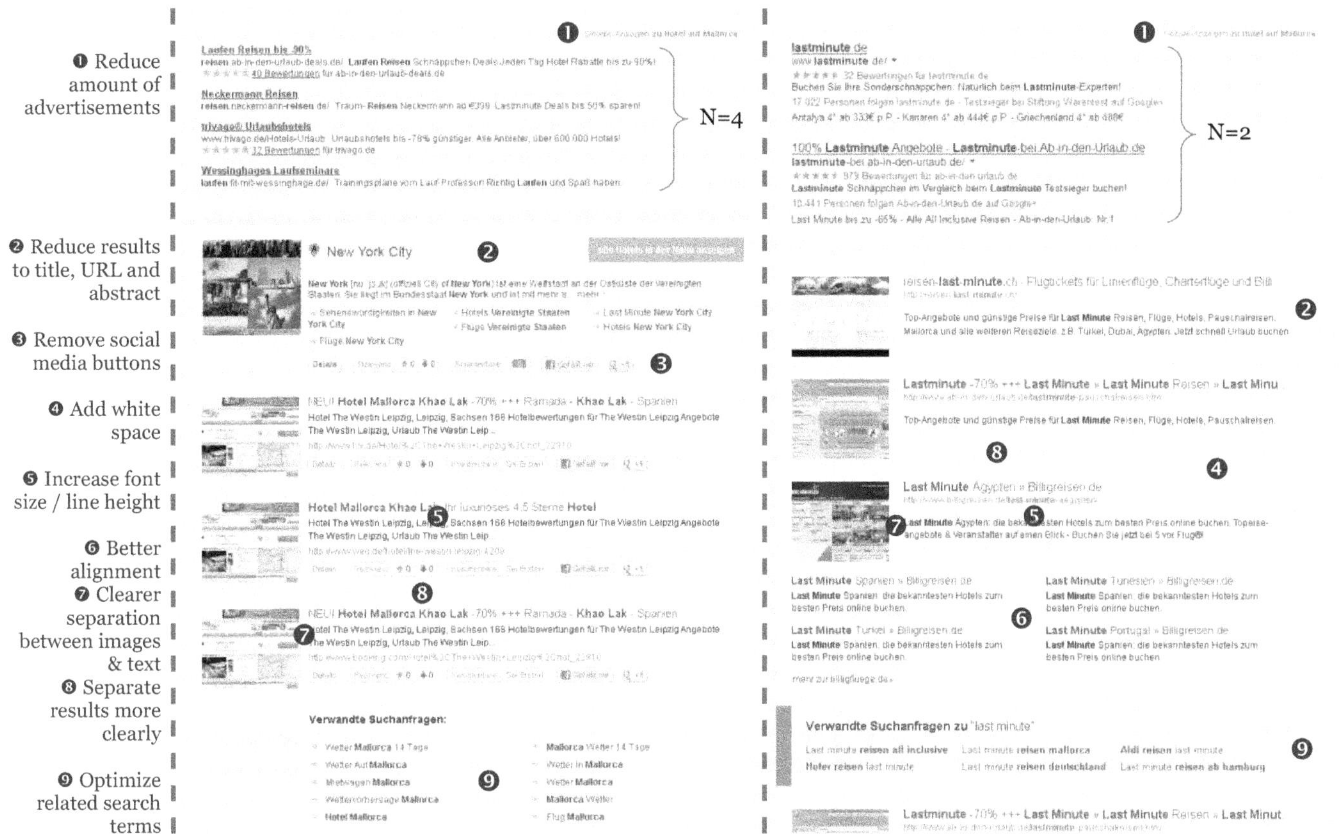

Figure 7. A visual comparison of the original (left) and redesigned SERP (right) evaluated during the case study. Please note that although in this specific image advertisements take more space on the redesigned page, the actual number of advertisements was reduced from four to two. The above are not screenshots of the actual interfaces in the browser, but the official models provided by the cooperating company's graphic designers.

ones is not a trivial process, as their validity must be ensured in analogy to the approach presented in this paper. This is planned as our prime direction of future work.

Second, we are only able to provide *best practices* for optimizing SERP usability. This means that identifying concrete usability problems and adequate adjustments still involves manual work by designers that is already done today without the help of S.O.S. Yet, Nielsen and Molich [20] found that even "good evaluators may sometimes overlook easy problems". Such "easy" problems (like a wrong font size) are often easily overseen and become obvious only when they are pointed out (by a colleague or, in our case, a catalog of best practices). Thus, we believe that S.O.S. is a valuable tool even for experienced designers. Another important point is that our suite facilitates communication with non-designers, as it relates concrete directives for optimization to usability metrics and scores. In this way, necessary adjustments to an interface can be better communicated towards superiors and other company officials.

Since during the case study we could only identify a fraction of causes for bad usability and corresponding countermeasures, not the complete catalog of best practices has been tested. Therefore, a more thorough case study involving each item of the catalog should happen as part of future work. However, it has to be noted that our catalog also includes a number of high-level instructions for adjusting the backend of a search engine—like improving the index or ranking quality—, which are not trivial to perform. Still, the results of the case study highlight the potential of our approach.

Finally, our catalog points out that advertising often stands in contrast to good usability. However, as one expert involved in verifying the catalog stated, "removing advertisements is unrealistic, as they are the only source of revenue [for search engines]". Therefore, although no advertisements would be optimal from the usability perspective, an adequate balance has to be found. This is necessary to ensure that search engines are able to provide free services to their users.

CONCLUSIONS

We have presented S.O.S.—the SERP Optimization Suite, which consists of the WaPPU tool [23] and a catalog of best practices for identifying and eliminating usability problems on SERPs. While WaPPU provides scores for seven different usability factors, for each of these our catalog contains potential causes for a suboptimal score (i.e., below 0.4) and proposes corresponding countermeasures. This relates necessary adjustments for optimization to usability metrics and scores and thus facilitates communication with non-designers and company officials. However, S.O.S.'s catalog of best practices can also be used as a standalone tool for designing user-friendly SERPs from scratch. During a case study, S.O.S. was used to evaluate and redesign the SERP of a real-world search engine. For the original SERP, WaPPU detected suboptimal scores for six out of seven usability factors as well as an overall score of 59.9%. After applying a selection of countermeasures from the catalog, the redesigned SERP yielded good usability scores (>0.4) for four out of seven factors. Also the overall score improved significantly to 67.5%.

Regarding future work, we particularly intend to apply our approach to web interfaces beyond SERPs. This includes the development of a general catalog as well as corresponding user studies. Also, S.O.S. could be integrated with crowdsourcing platforms (e.g., *Amazon MTurk API*[21]). In this way, tasks for identifying usability problems and selecting appropriate adjustments based on the catalog could be automatically posted to MTurk by WaPPU once the score of a factor drops below 0.4. This would be a considerable step into the direction of fully automatic usability evaluation *and* optimization.

ACKNOWLEDGMENTS

We thank all experts who contributed to our catalog of best practices. Special thanks go to R. Frankenstein, B. Freiberg, V. Nguyen, T. Stangneth and K. Zatinschikow, who helped with the case study. This work has been supported by the ESF and the Free State of Saxony.

Europa fördert Sachsen. ESF

REFERENCES

1. ISO 9241-11:1998 Ergonomic requirements for office work with visual display terminals (VDTs) – Part 11: Guidance on usability, 1998.
2. ISO/IEC 25010:2011: Systems and software engineering – Systems and software Quality Requirements and Evaluation (SQuaRE) – System and software quality models, 2011.
3. Atterer, R., Wnuk, M., and Schmidt, A. Knowing the User's Every Move – User Activity Tracking for Website Usability Evaluation and Implicit Interaction. In *Proc. WWW* (2006).
4. Bangor, A., Kortum, P. T., and Miller, J. T. An Empirical Evaluation of the System Usability Scale. *IJHCI 24*, 6 (2008).
5. Bernstein, M. S., Little, G., Miller, R. C., Hartmann, B., Ackerman, M. S., Karger, D. R., Crowell, D., and Panovich, K. Soylent: A Word Processor with a Crowd Inside. In *Proc. UIST* (2010).
6. Bozzon, A., Brambilla, M., and Comai, S. A Characterization of the Layout Definition Problem for Web Search Results. In *OTM Workshops* (2010).
7. Brooke, J. SUS: A "quick and dirty" usability scale. In *Usability Evaluation in Industry*, P. W. Jordan, B. Thomas, B. A. Weerdmeester, and A. L. McClelland, Eds. Taylor and Francis, 1996.

[21]`https://www.mturk.com/mturk/welcome` (Sep 10, 2014).

8. Carta, T., Paternò, F., and Santana, V. F. Web Usability Probe: A Tool for Supporting Remote Usability Evaluation of Web Sites. In *Proc. INTERACT* (2011).
9. de Vasconcelos, L. G., and Baldochi Jr., L. A. Towards an Automatic Evaluation of Web Applications. In *Proc. SAC* (2012).
10. Gajos, K., and Weld, D. S. Preference Elicitation for Interface Optimization. In *Proc. UIST* (2005).
11. Gajos, K., Wobbrock, J. O., and Weld, D. S. Improving the Performance of Motor-Impaired Users with Automatically-Generated, Ability-Based Interfaces. In *Proc. CHI* (2008).
12. Grigera, J., Garrido, A., and Rivero, J. M. A Tool for Detecting Bad Usability Smells in an Automatic Way. In *Proc. ICWE (Demos)* (2014).
13. Hassenzahl, M. User Experience (UX): Towards an experiential perspective on product quality. In *Proc. IHM* (2008).
14. John, G. H., and Langley, P. Estimating Continuous Distributions in Bayesian Classifiers. In *Proc. UAI* (1995).
15. Lew, P., Olsina, L., and Zhang, L. Quality, Quality in Use, Actual Usability and User Experience as Key Drivers for Web Application Evaluation. In *Proc. ICWE* (2010).
16. Nebeling, M., Matulic, F., and Norrie, M. C. Metrics for the Evaluation of News Site Content Layout in Large-Screen Contexts. In *Proc. CHI* (2011).
17. Nebeling, M., Speicher, M., and Norrie, M. C. CrowdAdapt: Enabling Crowdsourced Web Page Adaptation for Individual Viewing Conditions and Preferences. In *Proc. EICS* (2013).
18. Nebeling, M., Speicher, M., and Norrie, M. C. W3Touch: Metrics-based Web Page Adaptation for Touch. In *Proc. CHI* (2013).
19. Nielsen, J. Putting A/B Testing in Its Place, 2005. `http://www.nngroup.com/articles/putting-ab-testing-in-its-place/`, retrieved September 1, 2014.
20. Nielsen, J., and Molich, R. Heuristic Evaluation of User Interfaces. In *Proc. CHI* (1990).
21. Speicher, M. W3Touch: Crowdsourced Evaluation and Adaptation of Web Interfaces for Touch. Master's thesis, ETH Zurich, Switzerland, 2012.
22. Speicher, M., Both, A., and Gaedke, M. Towards Metric-based Usability Evaluation of Online Web Interfaces. In *Mensch & Computer Workshopband* (2013).
23. Speicher, M., Both, A., and Gaedke, M. Ensuring Web Interface Quality through Usability-based Split Testing. In *Proc. ICWE* (2014).

FeelSleeve: Haptic Feedback to Enhance Early Reading

Nesra Yannier [1,2] **Ali Israr** [1] **Jill Fain Lehman** [1] **Roberta L. Klatzky** [2]

[1] Disney Research Pittsburgh,
4720 Forbes Avenue,
Pittsburgh PA, 15213 USA
{israr, jill.lehman}@disneyresearch.com

[2] Carnegie Mellon University,
5000 Forbes Avenue,
Pittsburgh PA, 15213 USA
{nyannier, klatzky}@cmu.edu

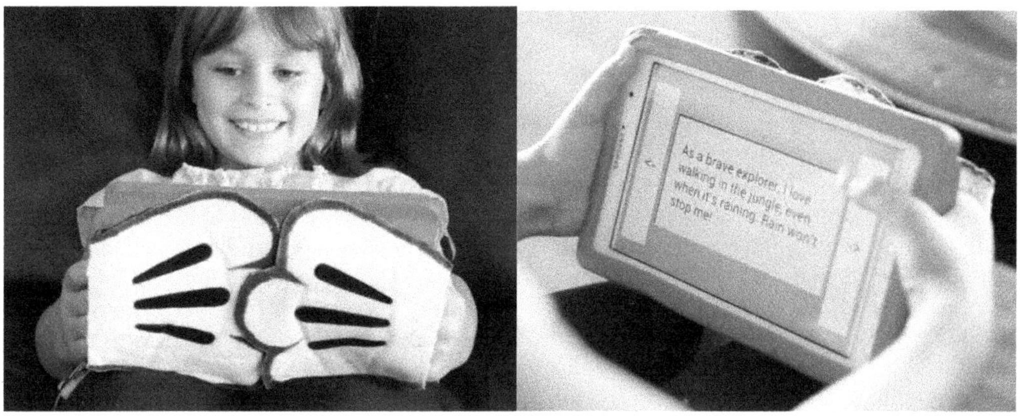

Figure 1. A child reading with FeelSleeve and feeling haptic effects associated with story events on her hands.

ABSTRACT
Engaging children with traditional approaches in education, especially reading, grows ever more difficult in the face of their attachment to tablets and computer games. We explore the possibility of making the story reading experience more interesting and memorable for children using haptic augmentation. In this paper, we present *FeelSleeve*, an interface that allows children to feel story events in their hands while they are reading on a mobile device. FeelSleeve uses transducers and audio output from the tablet within a gloved attachment to create vibratory effects that are meaningfully related to story content. We describe a study investigating whether embedding such haptic feedback into stories enhances reading for six to nine year olds. Our results indicate that story events accompanied by haptic feedback are better comprehended and appear to be more salient in memory. These results provide evidence that haptic effects have the potential to improve children's reading experience and make it more memorable.

CHI 2015, April 18–23, 2015, Seoul, Republic of Korea.

ACM 978-1-4503-3145-6/15/04...$15.00.
http://dx.doi.org/10.1145/2702123.2702396

Author Keywords
Haptic vocabulary; vibrotactile feedback; story reading technology; story listening technology; handheld technology

ACM Classification Keywords
H.5.2 [Information interfaces and presentation]: User Interfaces—Haptic I/O.

INTRODUCTION
As children transition from story listening to active reading, they undergo a fundamental and challenging transformation. Listening to stories sets the stage for reading by introducing children to a broad range of language, including new vocabulary and metaphorical extension, and establishing general skills of spelling and grammar [20]. Reading adds additional demands, not only in word decoding and oral language production, but in comprehension of ever more advanced language structure. To bridge the chasm from listening to reading, texts commonly introduce scaffolding in the form of alternative media, particularly illustrations. More recently, additional modalities and interactive media have been introduced even at the story listening stage [21, 24]. However, the integration of haptic feedback into the story listening and reading experience is not well explored. Furthermore, few controlled experiments investigate whether adding haptic feedback can enhance story reading for children by improving their comprehension and memory. The present research provides such an experiment

in the context of a mobile device. Relevant related work, discussed next, includes research relating haptic stimulation to language and memory and technologies that enable this approach.

RELATED HAPTIC TECHNOLOGY

Haptics and Language

Early efforts to show that language and meaning can be associated with haptic feedback were based on alphanumeric mapping, with limited success [9]. More recent work developed haptic phonemes, which can be combined to form haptic words [8], and a vocabulary of distinct haptic icons [29].

Still more recently, Israr and colleagues [14] integrated haptic feedback into a chair pad in order to convey the semantics associated with language phrases. They developed a haptic vocabulary for 23 *feel effects*—such as *rain*, *heartbeat*, and *creature walking*—that were created using spatially displaced, temporally interspersed pulses. Values for the actuators' parameters were based on a pair of studies in which, first, participants adjusted the intensity, duration, and inter-pulse interval of the actuators associated with a given phrase, and second, an independent group of participants validated the derived values [14]. The studies showed that feel effects led to reliable language/haptic associations, that synonym phrases could be substituted for the original language phrases, and that new effects could be constructed by inference.

There have also been some attempts to integrate haptic feedback into story listening. One such attempt was Sensory Fiction [11], where adults wore a vest that allowed them to feel artificial heartbeats that changed with the mood of the story. Changes in the temperature and pressure in the vest could also reflect story events. Another attempt involved a haptic vest to enrich children's story listening experience [32]. A study was conducted to test four to six year olds' ability to associate haptic effects with semantic interpretations. The results found that five and six year olds tended to assign lower agreement to incongruent versus congruent pairings of haptic effects and meanings, indicating effective communication of meaning by the haptic signal. The study further demonstrated that congruent haptic-meaning pairs could improve story comprehension and memory for that age group.

Reading with Other Modalities

Thus far we have reviewed research that attempts to use haptic effects to signal meaningful content. As our goal is to facilitate the incorporation of haptic feedback into the story reading experience, it is important to consider efforts of others to engage the young reader with nonverbal input, including haptic effects.

The use of nonverbal augmentation for children's reading is longstanding, of course. Typical children's books include visual illustrations along with text to convey information and meaning. Illustrations have been shown to enhance memory for story content, while also directly facilitating comprehension [21].

Some tangible interfaces have also been created to accompany storytelling and reading. Tanenbaum et al. created The Reading Glove, which allows users to extract memories, presented in the form of recorded audio, from ten objects by using natural grasping and holding behaviors [28]. The tangible, augmented-reality Magic Story Cube went further, integrating multiple modalities, including speech, 3D audio, 3D graphics and touch, in order to provide children with multi-sensory experiences in the process of storytelling [33]. Similar approaches combining tangible interfaces with storytelling include StoryMat [25] and ListenReader [2].

Effect of Haptics on Memory and Learning

The idea of using haptics to anchor memory and comprehension during reading is also supported by research in other contexts. Yannier et al., for example, found that students remember the cause-and-effect relationships in climate and geography better when presented with haptic feedback [31]. Research on embodiment has shown that memory for actions (e.g. performing a command such as "open the book") can be superior to memory for the verbal description of commands, suggesting that memory encompasses embodied information [7]. Haptic feedback has also been used to teach people who are visually impaired or dyslexic [15]. Jones et al. demonstrated that the use of a force-feedback device tended to support the development of 3-dimensional understanding of objects [15]. Together, these studies suggest that haptic feedback may also have the potential to enhance the reading experience.

Haptics and Mobile Devices

To take advantage of the current affinity for mobile devices, our aim is not only to integrate haptic effects into children's reading, but also to do so by means of the technology that they widely use. Thus research related to haptics on mobile devices outside the context of reading is also relevant.

A common use of haptics on mobile devices is to inform the user about incoming calls and messages. Early systems used a single unbalanced mass linear resonator, but more recent research has replaced the resonator with a speaker-like tactor, presenting tactile content that varies in both frequency and amplitude [5, 22]. In another approach, Yang et al. developed cues for hand-held devices via a system of 12 vibrotactile panels, each comprising a linear resonant actuator, a covering surface, and a vibration isolator [30]. Luk et al. also presented a handheld tactile display prototype to integrate haptics into mobile interaction, but used piezoelectric pins that stretch the skin laterally [19].

Other approaches have focused on creating illusory haptic sensations in order to increase resolution on the device. Such illusions work by introducing virtual actuators between real vibration sources. Seo and Cho, for example, demonstrated that vibrotactile flow could be reliably produced on a mobile device using phantom sensations in which spatially separated vibrotactile actuators stimulate different skin zones to induce a single tactile sensation midway between two stimulation points [26]. Lee and colleagues have also demonstrated use of a wide range of illusory percepts on handheld controllers, toys and mobile devices [17].

More recently, friction-based tactile technologies have been introduced to the touch screens of mobile devices [3, 18]. The level of friction is yoked to the location of the finger relative to the content on the screen.

Most of these technologies have focused on integrating haptic feedback into the screen of a mobile device or on vibrating or changing the friction of the device as a whole. In contrast, our FeelSleeve approach creates haptic sensations that are transmitted to the hands of a user who is simply holding the tablet in a natural position. This design, described in detail below, means that the reading experience does not need to be interrupted by an additional intentional action to trigger the haptic effect.

THE FEELSLEEVE STUDY

To help explore the question of whether haptics can improve children's reading experience, we created and tested a tablet-based FeelSleeve, a device that wraps around a handheld surface like a protective cover and provides localized vibrotactile stimulations on the hands. We programmed the FeelSleeve to coordinate with the display of text elements in our stories in order to produce feel effects (FEs): haptic patterns that, by virtue of their co-occurrence with a linguistic phrase, generate dynamic and expressive effects on the user's body [14]. In the study described below, we test whether the ability to feel events like rainfall, tapping, and heartbeats while reading about them can enhance memory for and comprehension of the story.

Experimental Method

Participants

Forty-four children from six to nine years old participated in our study. There were 16, 14, and 14 from First Grade to Third Grade, respectively.[1] Children were recruited from a participant pool and by giving out flyers. We excluded children who were reported as non-readers. The Institutional Review Board approved the recruitment methods.

Apparatus: Hardware

The FeelSleeve hardware used to deliver feel effects on the tablet during reading is shown in Figure 2. The device consists of a 3D-printed, soft cover sleeve embedded with two vibrotactile exciters (Tectonic Elements Ltd., model: TEAX19C01-8, Cambridgeshire, UK) and a simple electronic driver. The exciters are spaced 180 mm apart and enclosed in compartments in the sleeve. The moving ring of the exciter is pressed against the vibrating flap placed on the back of the sleeve so as to optimize the vibratory response of the embedded exciter and keep the stimulations localized and distortion free. When a user holds the FeelSleeve, it directly stimulates the skin of the hands. The exciters are driven by a custom electronic driver to amplify the stereo audio output of the tablet using two 1-Watt audio amplifiers (model LM4889, ti.com). The driver is powered either by a wall adapter or by a 6 V battery, and a switch is provided to turn the driver on and off. Fig 2(b) shows the location of exciters, vibrating flaps and the electronic driver.

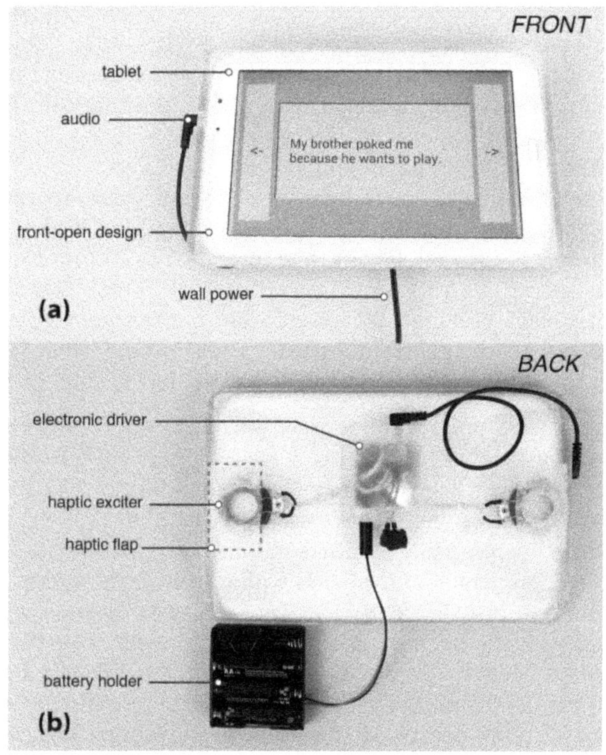

Figure 2. FeelSleeve hardware.

Our design objective was to create a tablet enclosure that could house two haptic transducers for stimulating the hands while allowing the user to interact with the tablet in a natural, comfortable way. The semi-flexible, cover-shaped sleeve with a minimal lip and open front holds the tablet securely, allows it to be inserted and removed easily, and leaves most of the screen surface available. Compartments holding the transducers and channels for wiring are unexposed once the sleeve is attached.

The two flaps pressed by their exciters are the haptic elements of the FeelSleeve that relay vibration from the exciters to the user's hands. The thickness, size and surface finish of the flaps are designed to achieve localized, smooth and noise- and distortion-free haptic stimulations. The thickness of the flap has a significant effect on its vibratory response. A thick flap dampens response, resulting in high

[1] We did not go beyond Grade 3 because pilot testing with 4th graders indicated that they performed at ceiling level.

power requirements, while too thin a flap wears down quickly, eventually delivering unreliable and uncomfortable stimulations. The prototype uses a safe thickness of 1.5 mm. The surface area of the flap is 50 mm x 30 mm with a 2 mm void layer directly below the flap. The void layer allows the flap to move freely in the open space, reduces stretch between the flap and sleeve, and amplifies vibratory response of the flap. Finally, a pilot evaluation of four users contrasting texture versus smooth flaps found that all participants preferred the smooth flap to the textured flap, which was found uncomfortable and distracting. Therefore the prototype uses flat flaps, as shown in the bottom of Figure 2.

FeelSleeve's flexible cover is made of a light and relatively soft rubber-like material (TangoPlus FLX930, www.stratasys.com, Shore hardness: scale A, 26-28), so that it is comfortable for users to hold over long durations. Correct placement of the hands with respect to the actuators is ensured in two ways. First, the short ends of the sleeve have protrusions that, when grasped, provide consistent contact between the hands and the vibrating flaps while leaving the thumbs available for navigation (Figure 3). Second, small pockets (in the shape of gloves) are attached to the back of the sleeve to guide users' hands to the right location to feel the haptic patterns (Figure 1). In order to make FeelSleeve visually appealing for children, we painted the sleeve and the gloves attractive colors. The weight of the sleeve is 400 g; combined with the tablet, the full weight is less than 750 g, typical of other sleeved devices.

Stimuli: The Language Component

Our stimuli are co-temporal linguistic/haptic pairings known as feel effects, or FEs. The linguistic component of each FE occurs in the context of one of two stories written in the first person by a professional storywriter for children.

The stories had different content but similar story arcs and were matched for word count. The protagonist of one story

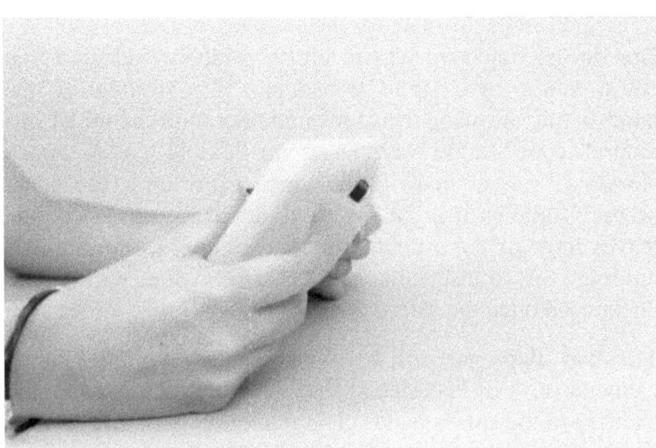

Figure 3. The back of FeelSleeve highlighting functional and ergonomic design.

(*Space*) was a child pilot who delivers "Very Important Packages" and is headed to Jupiter on his or her birthday. After going through a meteor shower, the child arrives on Jupiter to deliver a package; once there, s/he walks into a surprise birthday party and discovers that the package contains the cake. In the second story (*Jungle*), a child jungle explorer searches for a silver-striped tiger, which, according to legends, is as big as a building and very scary. After hiking through the jungle and having adventures with other animals along the way, the explorer finds the silver-striped tiger, which turns out to be as small as a squirrel and very friendly.

For purposes of tablet presentation, the stories were divided into *frames*: segments of one to four sentences that fit on a single screen. Each frame consisted of a maximum of 25 words (average: 16 words). The original versions of *Jungle* and *Space* were written for story listening, where the need to decode the text is not a factor [32]. Accordingly, we adjusted the original text for reading level using lexile-to-grade correspondences[2] to affirm that the reading difficulty of each segment was appropriate for the target age group of six to nine year olds. In their entireties, *Jungle* and *Space* had lexile scores of 480 and 420, respectively.

Each story contained twenty frames, ten of which were paired with appropriate haptic input to create the feel effects. Sample frames from each story and the name of the associated FE are shown in Table 1; the haptic components of the FEs are described in the next section.

Text in Frame	Associated FE
As a brave explorer, I love walking in the jungle, even when it's raining. Rain won't stop me!	Rain
I'm glad it stopped raining. But now my boots make a *squish-squish* with each step in the mud.	Squish Squish
Yipes! What's that? "Oh, Hammy! Get out of my space gloves silly!" My pet hamster loves to sleep in there.	Creature Walk
I start the engines, and they hum to life. 3…2…1… Blastoff!	Purr
But why is it so dark in here? My heart starts racing. Then suddenly I hear: SURPRISE!	Heartbeat
I feel a tap and look up to see my mom standing there.	Tap

Table 1. Feel Effects associated with the story text displayed on the screen.

[2] https://lexile.com/analyzer/

Space	Jungle
Ring *(Set 1 and 2)*	Rain *(Set 1 and 2)*
Creature Walk *(Set 1 and 2)*	Roar *(Set 1 and 2)*
Push *(Set 1)*	Poke *(Set 1)*
Purr *(Set 2)*	Creature Walk *(Set 2)*
Shake *(Set 1)*	Tap *(Set 1)*
Poke *(Set 2)*	Squish squish *(Set 2)*
Slap *(Set 1)*	Heartbeat *(Set 1)*
Rain *(Set 2)*	Shake *(Set 2)*
Heartbeat *(Set 1)*	Swipe *(Set 1)*
Tap *(Set 2)*	Purr *(Set 2)*

Table 2. FEs for *Jungle* and *Space* stories in sequence; participants felt either Set 1 or Set 2 effects, with counterbalanced story order across all users.

Table 2 shows how the full set of FEs were actually used in the study. The first two FEs in each story were always active (i.e., had the haptics played while the text was visible) in order to familiarize the child with the sensations and avoid simple effects of surprise or novelty. The remaining eight FEs were split so that those that were active in one condition were inactive (text shown without haptics) in the other; the within-subject comparison avoids conflation from reading variability. Active and inactive FEs alternated to maintain approximately equal spacing. Each child was randomly assigned to one of four conditions, which differed with respect to story order and which set of FEs was active.

Stimuli: The Haptic Component

The haptic component of a FE realizes the semantics of a story event using a composition of four parameter settings for each of the two tactors in the FeelSleeve: SOA (stimulus onset asynchrony), duration, ramp-up rate, and intensity. In order to increase the spatial resolution of the haptics, we employ parametric models of sensory illusions in our rendering schemes to create the perception of multiple points, moving points, hopping and modulating points, bumps, knocks, taps, etc.

More specifically, to expand on the intrinsic effects made possible by the resident transducers, we implement three common illusions on the skin: apparent tactile motion [16; 27], phantom tactile sensations [4, 1] and sensory saltation [10]. These illusions are well investigated in previous research and have been shown to reliably create illusory effects on the skin of the back [12, 13], hands [17, 26], arms and torso [6] and other parts of the body. The use of these illusions in the context of the FEs in our stories is illustrated in Figure 4.

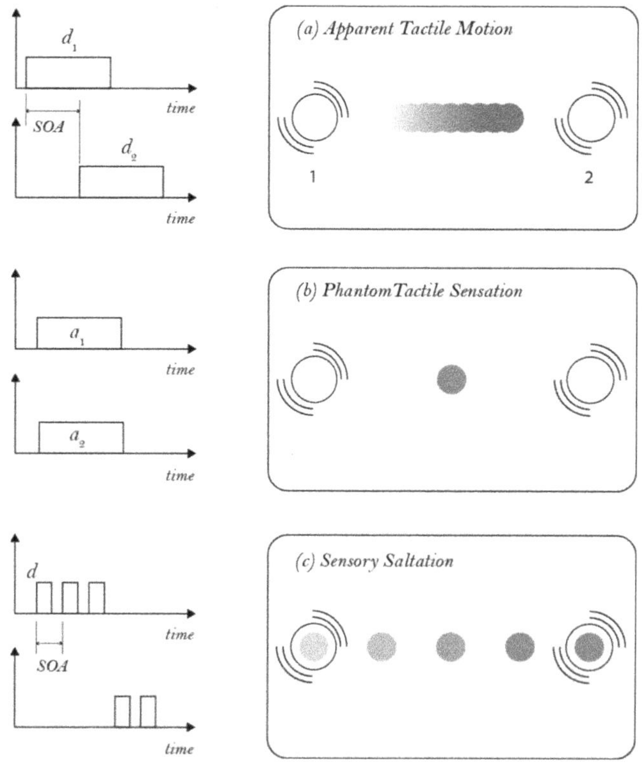

Figure 4. Sensory Illusions used for high-definition haptic rendering on FeelSleeve.

Although some new FEs were created specifically for this study, most of the FEs we used were adopted from a library tested in a previous study on adult participants [14], adapted for two actuators. The original forms of the adapted FEs had also been tested on children and shown to be effective for children of five years and older [32]. We organize FEs with related semantic meanings and haptic realizations into families. The families used in this study are:

- ***Rain*** (both stories): produced by random stimulation of ten vibratory points (two real and eight phantom sensations created as in Figure 4(b)). Duration defines size, intensity defines strength and SOA defines the frequency of drops.
- ***Heartbeat*** (both stories): produced by activating both transducers simultaneously for two pulses. SOA between pulses defines heart rate.
- ***Swipe*** and ***Squish squish*** (*Jungle*): produced using continuous apparent movement (see Figure 4(a)) from one transducer to another. In particular, *swipe* uses apparent movement from the left actuator to the right actuator, while *squish squish* uses two swipe motions in a row from right to left. Control parameters are SOA (speed), duration (continuity), intensity (size), direction and number of occurrences.
- ***Creature Walk*** (both stories): produced using five vibratory points moving from one transducer to another (see Figure 4(c)). Control parameters are intensity (size

of animal) and SOA (speed). The approach was used to create both the *lizard running* effect in *Jungle*, and the *hamster walking* effect in *Space*.

- ***Purr* and *Roar*** (both stories): produced by playing a purring sound through both transducers, with intensity (loudness) and tempo (rhythm) adjusted for use. *Tiger purring* in *Jungle* and *engine rumbling* in *Space* were created with this method.
- ***Tap* and *Shake*** (both stories): produced by activating both transducers simultaneously in pulses. Control parameters are intensity (strength), SOA (urgency), duration (size) and number of pulses. Used for *hands shaking* and *seeds tapping* in *Jungle* and *body shaking* and *mom tapping* in *Space*.
- ***Push*, *Poke* and *Slap*** (both stories): produced by activating both transducers simultaneously one time. Intensity (strength) and duration (size) are adjusted. Used for *branch poking* in *Jungle*, and *slapping a button, pushing a door* and *knob poking* in *Space*.
- ***Ring*** (*Space*): produced by playing a ring tone through both transducers simultaneously. Controls are intensity and pitch.

The haptic effects were created using an open-source dataflow programming language, Pure Data (aka Pd, puredata.info), and stored as stereo (dual) channel wav files. The FE stimuli were created by compiling the stories in an Android application that displays frame-by-frame sections on the tablet screen as it plays back associated wav files via the FeelSleeve. The haptics are played in a loop for the duration in which the frame is displayed on the screen, so that users can experience the FEs again if they miss them the first time. Navigation to a different frame is under the child's control via two big buttons on either side of the text which respond to a thumb tap while the rest of the hand remains correctly positioned by the gloves (see Figure 1).

Test materials

Twelve post-reading questions with three alternative responses were constructed for each story. One question was directly related to each of the 10 frames with FEs (whether active or inactive). Two additional questions were included to test children's understanding of the gist of the story, one querying content and the other asking for a best title, where the correct response was intended to capture the overall theme.

Each question was presented visually and read aloud, initially without multiple-choice alternatives. Spontaneous answers were recorded and scored as correct only if the child reported the specific content related to the associated FE, thus constituting a test of the saliency of the haptically-signaled event. After the spontaneous response, the child was given three answers to choose from as a more general test of comprehension and memory. Some example questions are presented in Table 3.

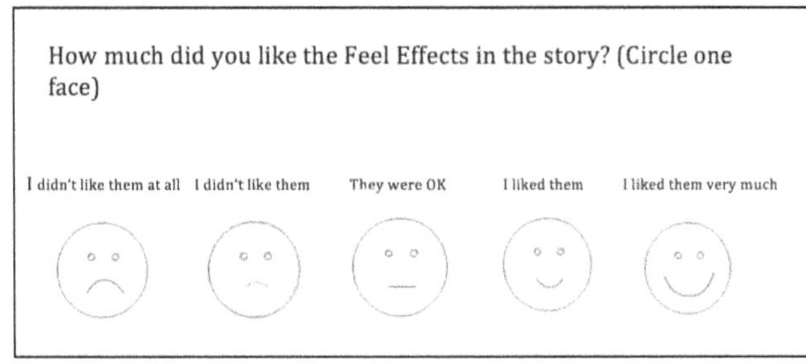

Figure 5. Post-reading question assessing FE enjoyment.

Procedure

The experimenter described the task to the child as reading text out loud on a screen while possibly feeling sensations on the hands. The child was shown that he or she could control the screen's forward (or if necessary, backward) advance with on-screen arrows. The child then put his or her hands into the FeelSleeve's gloves and was given two sample screens with active FEs. When the experimenter confirmed that the haptic pattern could be sensed, the experiment proper began. Children were told to read the sentences they saw on the screen out loud, pressing the arrow button on the right to go to the next screen when they were finished reading. They were informed that if they did not know how to read a word or what it meant they could ask for help, at which point the experimenter intervened with oral assistance.

After reading the first story, the child was asked to summarize it as a check on general attention. After summarization, questions were presented on paper and read aloud in two parts: the question alone, then the question with three alternative responses.

For most children the same procedure was repeated for the second story. Three children who were very poor readers were thanked and dismissed at this point.

What did the tiger do when it came up to you?

a) It sat on my lap.
b) It got into my jacket.
c) It lay at my feet.

(associated with *Jungle* FE: tiger purring in jacket)

How did you know your mom was there?

a) She called my name.
b) She tapped me.
c) She kissed my hair.

(associated with *Space* FE: mother tapping on child's hand)

Why were you surprised when you saw the tiger?

a) Because it was small.
b) Because it was silver and green.
c) Because it was scary.

(question about the gist of *Jungle*)

Table 3. Example comprehension questions.

After the second story, children were shown a five-point visual scale and asked how much they liked the FEs (see Figure 5) and whether they would prefer another story with or without them. Finally they were asked to report their favorite FEs and give general comments.

RESULTS

Comprehension Questions

Our primary analysis is based on the eight comprehension questions that corresponded to the FEs distinguishing Set 1 and Set 2. FE active (FE) and inactive (NoFE) scores were computed separately for each child as the percentage of correct responses for the four relevant questions in the condition. Figure 6 shows means for each story as a function of FE status.

An ANOVA was conducted for the multiple-choice results for the comprehension questions using within-participant factors of FE status (active, inactive) and Story (*Jungle*, *Space*), and the between-participant factor of Grade level. The analysis showed an effect of Story, $F(1, 37) = 36.62$, $p<0.001$. No other effects were significant. However, examination of the data by story indicated that children were essentially at ceiling when given the multiple-choice questions for *Jungle*. This pattern is consistent with previous research using a listening comprehension version of these stories with younger children, which found that *Space* produced lower comprehension scores [32].

Accordingly, we analyzed for FE and Grade effects in each story separately, using a two-factor ANOVA. For *Jungle*, no effects were significant. For *Space*, the effect of FE status was significant, $F(1,40) = 4.31$, $p = 0.04$, as was the effect of Grade level, $F(2,40) = 5.08$, $p = 0.01$ (Figure 7). The mean of the FE questions answered correctly was 2.72 out of 4 questions (68.2% with a standard error of 3.8%) while the mean for the NoFE questions was 2.32 out of 4 questions (58.3% with a standard error of 3.9%). Thus, across all grades, addition of an FE improved comprehension relative to the NoFE baseline by 17%.

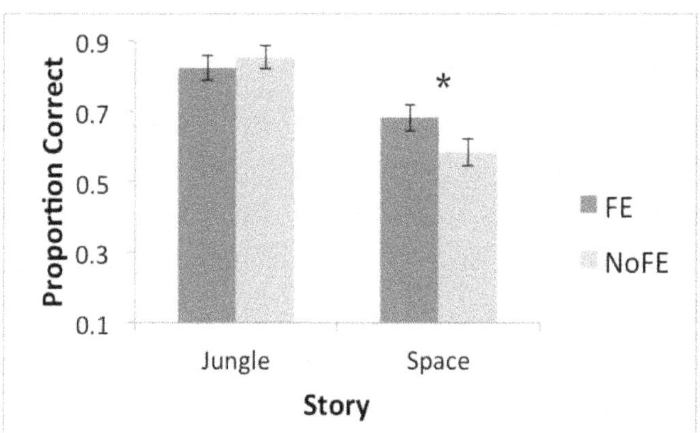

Figure 6. Proportion correct for comprehension questions by Story and FE status. Error bars are 1 standard error.

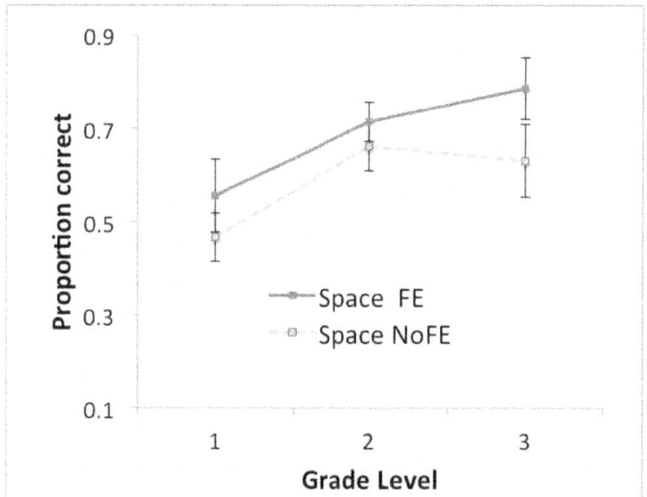

Figure 7. Proportion correct for *Space* comprehension questions by FE status and Grade. Error bars are 1 standard error.

Recall that gist questions were designed to check whether children understood the main idea of the story. An analysis of the multiple-choice responses for the gist content question indicated understanding was high, with 90% of children who read both stories responding correctly to *Jungle* and 95% to *Space*. The corresponding values for choice of the most thematic title question were 60% and 55%. All are significantly greater than chance ($p<0.01$).

Recall of FE events

We also analyzed the spontaneous answers to each question to see if, without seeing alternatives, children would recall the events related to the FEs. Because we were interested in assessing the saliency in memory for the specific event associated with an FE, a spontaneous reply was given credit in this analysis only if it mentioned that event, regardless of whether other details were correctly reported. For example, in response to the question about what the tiger did when it came up to the explorer, "it got in my jacket" would be a credited response because it referred to the FE event (tiger purring inside my jacket), but "it looked right at me," while correct, would not be credited. Figure 8 shows the mean proportion credited by story and FE status.

An ANOVA was conducted using within-participant factors of FE status (active, inactive) and Story, and the between-participant factor of Grade level. This analysis (which excludes four children who completed only one story) showed a significant effect of Story, $F(1,37)=15.50$, $p<0.001$. The effect of FE status was marginal, $F(1,37) = 3.36$, $p = 0.08$. No other effects approached significance.

Given the obvious difference between story performance levels, also evident in the comprehension measure, we analyzed each story separately, using a two-factor ANOVA with FE status as a within factor and Grade as between. The effect of FE status was significant only for *Space*, $F(1,40) = 4.60$, $p = 0.04$. For this story, the mean of the FE-related

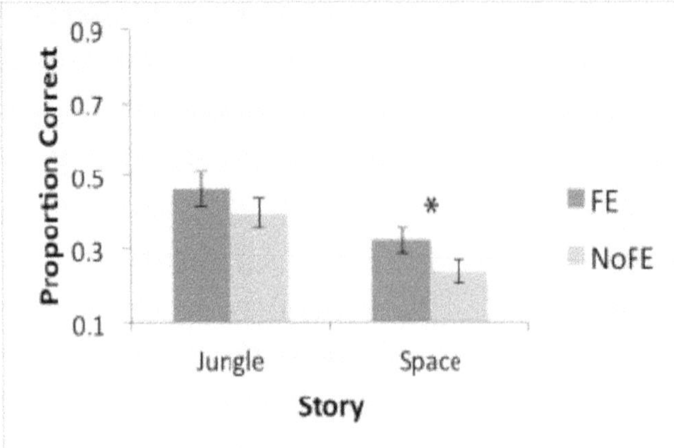

Figure 8. Score for Recall of FE events by story and FE status. Error bars are 1 standard error.

events recalled correctly was 1.28 out of 4 (32.2% with a standard error of 3.4%) while the mean for the NoFE questions was 0.92 out of 4 (23.8% with a standard error of 3.1%). The similar trend in *Jungle* did not reach significance. For the *Jungle* story, the mean of the FE-related events recalled correctly was 1.84 out of 4 (46.3% with a standard error of 4.7%) while the mean for the NoFE questions was 1.56 out of 4 (39.6% with a standard error of 4.1%). As the intrinsic saliency of story features is unknown, this cannot be characterized as a ceiling effect. However, the statistical unreliability of the trend may still reflect an effective limit on children's tendency to recall the particular story content signaled by the FE, in the face of other attractive alternative content. For example, when children were asked how they knew they were excited at viewing the tiger, the most common response was essentially, "because I was looking at a tiger." Failure to mention the heartbeat, signaled by the FE here, is hardly surprising.

Reading time

A t-test was performed on the reading time normalized by the number of words, to check if there was any difference between screens with and without FEs present. No significant difference was found between the reading times per word.

Post-reading Survey

Figure 9 shows the result of the survey question related to liking the FEs, where scores ranged from 1 (didn't like at all) to 5 (liked very much). Asked, "If you read a story again, would you like to read it with or without the Feel Effects?" 65% favored FEs. Not all participants wished to name their favorite FE, but among those who did, common favorites were *rain*, *lizard running across my hands*, *roar*, *alarm clock*, *heart beating*, and *mom tapping*.

In response to the request to comment about their experience, many children expressed that they liked the FEs and enjoyed feeling sensations in their hands. One of them said, "It felt really cool. If I was one of them [protagonist], I wondered how it would actually feel. It was like a preview about how it would actually feel." Another said, "It felt really cool in my hands. I just wish that there were more of them." Many children mentioned that they liked the gloves and thought that they were warm and comfortable. One of them said, "I liked that there were gloves and you knew where to put your hands. You didn't have to feel where to put your hands, you could just put your hands in the gloves." Another participant expressed that it felt like a video game with his thumbs clicking the buttons. Another said, "I thought that was really cool, like a leap in technology!"

DISCUSSION AND CONCLUDING REMARKS

The present results provide evidence for two promising influences of haptic FEs during story reading. One is to increase the memory salience of the events paired with FEs, making them more available for recall. The other is to enhance story understanding more generally. These effects emerged clearly in the *Space* story, where the impact on comprehension was a 17% increase in performance. The *Tiger* story was essentially at ceiling in the comprehension test and showed a similar memory-enhancement trend that failed to reach significance, which may also reflect practical limits on performance.

Our within-subjects, within-story experimental design was prepared specifically to minimize the effect of novelty in the study. Had we separated children into groups with and without FEs, those getting the haptic effects might simply be more motivated and pay more attention to the story. In contrast, each participant received the same number of haptic effects, distributed evenly throughout the story among sentences that were not augmented by touch. Furthermore, the first two haptic effects (excluded from the analysis) were always activated to familiarize the child with the sensations and avoid simple effects of surprise or novelty.

Further work is needed to investigate the long-term effects of haptic feedback and to establish the generality of the findings in this study. An important extension is to children who are relatively disadvantaged in reading preparation.

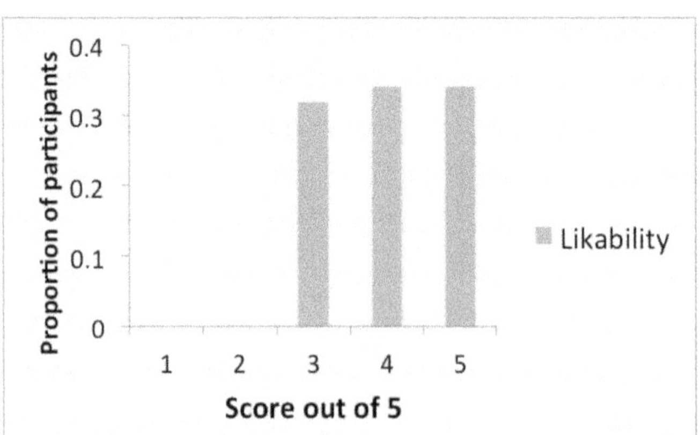

Figure 9. Proportion of children selecting each alternative on the likability scale (1-5, increasing).

The present subjects were generally competent readers, as evidenced by their understanding of gist and the high level of comprehension in the more accessible story. Given that the effect of FE emerged in the story that yielded lower performance overall, it seems possible that effects would be greater for children who are finding reading difficult.

The present approach is amenable to various instructional approaches to reading [23]. The limiting factor is not the reading theory *per se*, but the extent to which children's literary material lends itself to haptic effects. Consistent with approaches where children are encouraged to seek out practice that interests them, the greater engagement and motivation associated with FEs should promote reading activity. Phonics-based reading materials could likewise be enhanced with FEs.

The experiment reported here tested the effect of adding haptic feedback to stories presented as text alone. Another interesting direction would be to explore the effect of haptics in the context of different story materials. Integrating graphics into the stories along with feel effects may further enhance the reading experience. Furthermore, FeelSleeve could be used with other applications on tablets, such as comic books or games, to enhance children's experiences in education and entertainment. Ultimately, our goal is to engage young readers and promote their enjoyment of a variety of textual materials.

ACKNOWLEDGEMENTS

We thank Disney Research for supporting this work. We also would like to thank Matthew Glisson and Siyan Zhao for their help with the early prototyping.

REFERENCES

1. Alles, D. S. Information transmission by phantom sensations. *IEEE Transactions on Man-Machine Systems 11*, 1 (1970), 85-91.
2. Back, M., Cohen, J., Gold, R., Harrison, S., & Minneman, S. Listen reader: an electronically augmented paper-based book. In *Proc. CHI 2001*, ACM Press (2001), 23-29.
3. Bau, O., Poupyrev, I., Israr, A., & Harrison, C. TeslaTouch: Electrovibration for touch surfaces. In *Proceedings of the 23nd annual ACM symposium on User interface software and technology*, ACM Press (2010), 283-292.
4. Békésy, G. v. Human skin perception of traveling waves similar to those on the cochlea. *The Journal of the Acoustical Society of America* 27, 5 (1955), 830-841.
5. Brewster, S., Chohan, F. and Brown, L. Tactile feedback for mobile interactions. In *Proc. CHI'07*, ACM Press (2007), 159-162.
6. Cholewiak, R.W., Collins A.A., The generation of vibrotactile patterns on a linear array: Influences of body site, time, and presentation mode. *Perception & Psychophysics 62*, 6 (2000), 1220-1235.
7. Englekamp, J. & Zimmer, H. D. Memory for action events: A new field of research. *Psychological Research 51*, 4 (1989), 153–157.
8. Enriquez, M., Maclean, K.E. & Chita, C. Haptic Phonemes: Basic building blocks of haptic communication. In *Proc. of the 8th International Conference on Multimodal Interfaces*, ACM Press (2006), 302-309.
9. Geldard, F. A. Adventures in tactile literacy. The *American Psychologist 12* (1957), 115-124.
10. Geldard, F.A. & Sherrick, C.E. The Cutaneous "Rabbit": A Perceptual Illusion, *Science 178* (1972), 178-179.
11. Heibeck, F., Hope, A. & Legault, J. Sensory Fiction MAS S65 Science Fiction to Science Fabrication (2013). Retrieved from http://scifi2scifab.media.mit.edu/2013/12/19/sensory-fiction/.
12. Israr, A., & Poupyrev, I. Tactile brush: drawing on skin with a tactile grid display. In *Proc. of CHI 2011*. ACM Press (2011), 2019-2028.
13. Israr, A. and Poupyrev, I. Control Space of apparent haptic motion. In *Proc. of World Haptics Conference*, IEEE (2011), 457-462.
14. Israr, A., Zhao, S., Schwalje, K., Klatzky, R. L. & Lehman, J. Feel Effects: Enriching storytelling with haptic feedback. *ACM Transactions on Applied Perception 11*, 3 (2014), Article 11.
15. Jones, M. G., Bokinsky, A., Tretter, T., & Negishi, A. A comparison of learning with haptic and visual modalities. *Haptics-e: Electronic J. Haptics Res 4,* (2005).
16. Kirman, J.H. Tactile apparent movement: The effects of inter stimulus onset interval and stimulus duration. *Perception and Psychophysics 15*, 1 (1974), 1-6.
17. Lee, J., Kim, Y. & Kim, G. Funneling and saltation effects for tactile interaction with virtual objects. In *Proceedings of the SIGCHI Conference on Human Factors in Computing Systems* (CHI '12), ACM Press (2012), 3141-3148.
18. Lévesque, V., Oram, L., MacLean, K., Cockburn, A., Marchuk, N.D., Johnson, D., Colgate, J.E. and Peshkin, M.A. Enhancing physicality in touch interaction with programmable friction. In *Proc. CHI 2011*, ACM (2011), 2481-2490.
19. Luk, J., Pasquero, J., Little, S., MacLean, K., Levesque, V. & Hayward, V. A role for haptics in mobile interaction: initial design using a handheld tactile display prototype. In *Proc. of CHI 2006*, ACM Press (2006), 171-180.
20. Phillips, L. The Role of Storytelling in Early Literacy Development (1999). http://www.home.aone.net.au/stories/doc/childhd.htm

21. Pike, M. M., Barnes, M. A., & Barron, R.W. The role of illustrations in children's inferential comprehension. *Journal of Experimental Child Psychology 105*, 3 (2010), 243-255.

22. Poupyrev, I. and Maruyama, S., Tactile Interfaces for Small Touch Screens. In *Proc. of UIST 2003*, ACM Press (2003), 217-220.

23. Rayner, K., Foorman, B.R., Perfetti, C. A., Pesetsky, D., & Seidenberg, M. S. (2001). How psychological science informs the teaching of reading. *Psychological Science in the Public Interest 2*, 2 (2002), 31-74.

24. Ricci, C. M. & Beal, C. R. The effect of interactive media on children's story memory. *Journal of Educational Psychology 94*, 1 (2002), 138–144.

25. Ryokai, K., & Cassell, J. StoryMat: a play space for collaborative storytelling. *Ext. Abstracts CHI 1999*, ACM Press (1999), 272-273.

26. Seo, J., & Choi, S. Initial study for creating linearly moving vibrotactile sensation on mobile device. In *Proc. Haptics Symposium*, IEEE (2010), 67-70.

27. Sherrick, C.E. and R. Rogers, Apparent Haptic Movement. *Perception and Psychophysics 1*, 3 (1966), 175-180.

28. Tanenbaum, J., Tanenbaum, K., & Antle, A. The Reading Glove: designing interactions for object-based tangible storytelling. In *Proc.1st Augmented Human International Conference*, ACM Press (2010), 19.

29. Ternes, D., & Maclean, K. E. Designing large sets of haptic icons with rhythm. In *Haptics: Perception, Devices and Scenarios*, Springer Berlin Heidelberg (2008), 199-208.

30. Yang, G. H., Jin, M. S., Jin, Y. & Kang, S. T-mobile: Vibrotactile display pad spatial and directional information for hand-held device. In *Proc. Intelligent Robots and Systems (IROS)*, IEEE (2010), 5245-5250.

31. Yannier, N., Basdogan, C., Tasiran, S. & Sen, O. L. Using haptics to convey cause-and-effect relations in climate visualization. *IEEE Transactions on Haptics 1*, 2 (2008), 130-141.

32. Zhao, S. Feeling Stories: Enriching Story Listening Experience for Children with Haptic Feedback. Unpublished senior honors thesis, Carnegie Mellon University Dept. of Psychology (2014).

33. Zhou, Z., Cheok, A. D., Pan, J. & Li, Y. Magic Story Cube: An interactive tangible interface for storytelling. In *Proc. of CHI 2004*. ACM Press (2004). 364-365.

BodyVis: A New Approach to Body Learning Through Wearable Sensing and Visualization

Leyla Norooz[1], Matthew L. Mauriello[2], Anita Jorgensen[2], Brenna McNally[1], Jon E. Froehlich[2]
Makeability Lab | Human-Computer Interaction Lab (HCIL)
College of Information Studies[1], Department of Computer Science[2],
University of Maryland, College Park
{leylan, mattm401, bmcnally, jonf}@umd.edu

ABSTRACT
Internal organs are hidden and untouchable, making it difficult for children to learn their size, position, and function. Traditionally, human anatomy (body form) and physiology (body function) are taught using techniques ranging from worksheets to three-dimensional models. We present a new approach called *BodyVis*, an e-textile shirt that combines biometric sensing and wearable visualizations to reveal otherwise invisible body parts and functions. We describe our 15-month iterative design process including lessons learned through the development of three prototypes using participatory design and two evaluations of the final prototype: a design probe interview with seven elementary school teachers and three single-session deployments in after-school programs. Our findings have implications for the growing area of wearables and tangibles for learning.

Author Keywords
Wearables; interactive body learning; physiological sensing

INTRODUCTION
Learning the position, structure, and function of internal body parts is challenging for children [29,30,35]. Unlike fingers, arms, toes, and other external parts, internal organs remain hidden beneath layers of skin, muscle, and tissue and operate without conscious thought, making it difficult for children—and even adults [3]—to understand the internal workings of their bodies. This body knowledge is important. For pre-school and primary school children, higher body literacy corresponds to greater compliance with health care regimens, better self-care practices, and increased self-understanding [30,33]. For example, young children with asthma are more likely to take inhaled medications if they understand how their lungs function [30]. Other researchers emphasize the critical role of anatomy and physiology in teaching and understanding basic science (*e.g.,* biology) [11].

In pre-school and primary school education, human anatomy (body form) and physiology (body function) are traditionally taught using a mixture of techniques including 3D models and dolls, coloring and activity books, stories, audio-visuals, and video games [35]. With the advent of low-cost physiological sensing, ubiquitous computation, and electronic textiles (e-textiles), new approaches for body learning are now possible.

CHI 2015, April 18 - 23 2015, Seoul, Republic of Korea

ACM 978-1-4503-3145-6/15/04...$15.00
http://dx.doi.org/10.1145/2702123.2702299

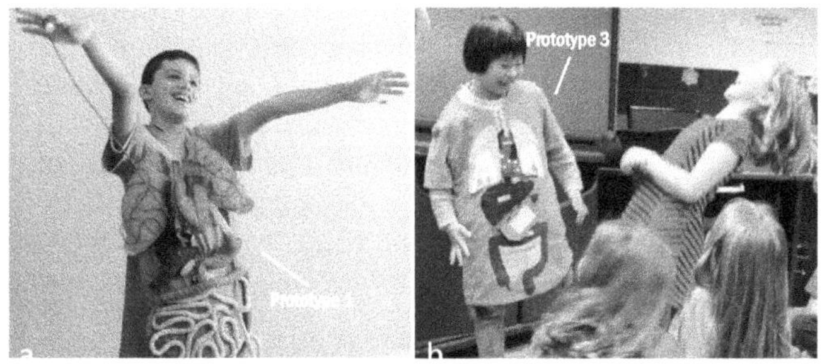

Figure 1: *BodyVis* is an interactive e-textile shirt for body learning that actively responds to the wearer's physiology and visualizes their body data on externalized anatomical models. Prototypes 1 and 3 shown above.

In this paper, we present *BodyVis*, a custom-designed wearable e-textile shirt that combines biometric sensing and interactive visualization to reveal otherwise invisible parts and functions of the human body (Figure 1). The wearer's physiological phenomena are visualized on externalized fabric anatomy, allowing the wearer and viewers to gain a unique view of the internal body. While past research has investigated wearables [22,23,24] and augmented reality [2,4,26] for body learning, BodyVis is the first exploration of a physical/digital manifestation that actively responds to the physiology of the wearer.

To investigate our approach, we iteratively designed and evaluated three BodyVis prototypes over a 15-month design cycle. While our long-term aim is to assess how a BodyVis-approach may impact learning, as an initial investigation, our research questions were exploratory: *e.g.,* identifying key design considerations, exploring the understandability, aesthetics, and approachability of our prototypes, and examining how BodyVis *engages* children in body learning topics. Our design iterations were informed by two participatory design sessions with children, a MakerFaire exhibit, an early demonstration at a children and technology design conference (*IDC'13*) [27], and relevant prior work (*e.g.,* importance of 3D models in learning [31], idea of bio-responsive e-textiles [21]).

The final prototype (Prototype 3) was evaluated in two ways: first, as a design probe in semi-structured interviews with seven elementary school teachers (Study 1); second, via three, single-session field deployments in local Boys and Girls clubs (Study 2). While the teacher interviews provide insight into how BodyVis may support classroom learning goals and new types of learning activities, the exploratory field deployments allowed us to assess children reactions to BodyVis (*e.g.,* engagement, playfulness, curiosity, social interactions, and general usability issues). Teachers were positive about BodyVis' ability to engage learners, to concretize otherwise abstract concepts, and to enable physical and collaborative learning although they expressed concerns about robustness, maintenance, and cost. Our Study 2 findings demonstrate BodyVis' potential to involve children in learning about their bodies, to engage them in self-inquiry and experimentation (*e.g., What happens to my heart if I jump up and down?*), and to support social interactions and peer learning.

The contributions of this paper are: (i) the introduction of a new approach and system called BodyVis for body learning, which combines wearable biometric sensors and on-body visualization to provide new insights into anatomy and physiology; (ii) results from our iterative, participatory design process creating three BodyVis prototypes; (iii) findings from two evaluations: interviews with seven teachers and three field deployments at out-of-school programs; (iv) design reflections and directions for the emerging area of wearables and learning.

RELATED WORK

We discuss body literacy and current teaching strategies as well as previous research on sensor-based learning and tangible interactive computing.

Body Literacy and Teaching Strategies

As noted in the introduction, body learning is challenging. By age four most children have a well-defined understanding of their external body and the relationships between body parts; however, their conception of the inner-body is comparatively weaker [35]. Children between the ages of four and eight can recall approximately three to six internal body parts, most commonly the brain, heart, and bones [*ibid*]. However, children often misconceive their size, shape, position, and function. For example, the heart is typically drawn as a playing card "valentine" heart (*e.g.,* [8,12]) and the stomach is considered a respiratory mechanism because it moves in and out with breath (*e.g.,* [13]). In addition, few children have a clear idea of how food passes through their body and how waste is eliminated [28]. Although these conceptions improve with age [30], some misconceptions can persist into adulthood [3].

Most researchers emphasize that because internal organs are not accessible, they are difficult for children to understand, observe, and experiment with in daily life (*e.g.,* [29]). Although few experimental studies have compared teaching methods for children's body knowledge, a few studies point to the benefits of using three-dimensional teaching aids [31,35,36]. Findings suggest that teaching artifacts should be engaging (*e.g.,* comprised of bright colors and different textures), realistic but approachable (not "scary"), and interactive. For example, Schmidt [31] discovered that children learn more from interactive lungs than their stationary counterparts. These results point to the benefits of an interactive tangible approach.

Sensor-Based Learning

Originally termed "microcomputer-based laboratories" and then later "probeware," sensor-based learning emerged in the 1980s to help children explore, experiment with, analyze, and visualize measured phenomena in the physical sciences (*e.g.,* sound [32], electricity [41], motion [5]). Researchers suggest that it is the tight coupling between an activity and the computer-mediated feedback that accounts for improvements in understanding [5].

Despite its long history, as Lee and Thomas note [24], there has been surprisingly little consideration of physiological and on-body sensors applied to learning contexts. The work that does exist (*e.g.,* [22,23,24]) explores off-the-shelf tracker tools rather than custom innovations (as we do here). Though on-body sensors have long been used in the health and medical sciences (*e.g.,* [9]) as well as human-computer interaction (*e.g.,* [7]), their potential to help children learn about their bodies remains largely unexplored. BodyVis represents a new generation of probeware where the "material" being measured is the human body and the visual representations are responsive, tangible, wearable models.

Tangible and Wearable Interfaces for Learning

Our work also relates to tangible interfaces [34]. Though conceptual and theoretical understandings of tangibles to support learning are still being developed [1,25], researchers suggest that tangibles: offer a natural and immediate form of interaction that is accessible to learners, promote active and hands-on engagement, allow for exploration, expression, discovery, play, and reflection, allow learning of abstract or complex concepts through concrete representations, and offer opportunities for collocated collaborative activity (as summarized by Antle and Wise [1]). In the domain of human anatomy, we could not find prior work in the tangible interactive space. However, augmented reality systems have been developed to allow users to "peer inside" a human body [2,4,26], for example, using a large-screen display [4,26]; however, these systems are aimed at medical students (not children), and the anatomical representations do not react to the sensed physiology of the user and are not tangible.

Finally, the way information is *represented* is a critical aspect of tangible interface design. In the science domain, such as molecular biology or astronomy, designers often represent microscopic or macroscopic forms as semi-realistic models imbued with computational behaviors; the computation is used to provide dynamism and augmented information (*e.g.,* [10,14]). Our work is similar in that we attempt to concretize the invisible structures and functions of the internal body by coupling tangible physical models (structure) with embodied digital forms (function). The abstraction of the look, function, and feel of an organ in our tangible representations and its effect on learning is an open research question, though we begin exploring it here.

DESIGN PROCESS AND GOALS

We pursued an iterative, human-centered design approach over 15 months. To help engage with and better understand children's perspective with our designs, we employed a participatory design method called *Cooperative Inquiry* (CI) [15]. Here, seven children (ages 7-11; four girls) and four adults (2 from research team) worked together at key points in the design process to co-design BodyVis features and to provide feedback on our prototypes. We conducted three CI sessions in total but report only on the first two due to space limitations (the third session focused on the future of BodyVis post-Prototype 3). All children had at least three months of general co-design experience. We also received feedback on Prototype 1 from the IDC community [27] and informal feedback from parents, teachers, and children at a MakerFaire exhibit midway through our design process. Our more formal qualitative studies with teachers and children were conducted after the development of Prototype 3 and are presented after the design section.

Design Goals. Before describing the three prototypes and lessons learned, we present seven high-level design goals in Table 1, which focus on user experience (*e.g.,* playful, multi-sensory, responsive), hardware and materiality (*e.g.,* lightweight and robust), and learning attributes (*e.g.,* personal relevance, support for peer learning). These goals were informed by related work, outcomes from the initial CI session, and our experience building the first prototype.

Anatomical Overview. Though our prototypes differ in how they sense the wearer's physiology and in anatomical representations, there are commonalties. Using a t-shirt as the visual medium, all three prototypes include the *thoracic region* above the diaphragm and the *abdominal region* below it (Figure 2). For the thoracic cavity, we include the lungs, heart, and esophagus. The abdominal cavity includes most of the digestive organs including the esophagus, stomach, liver,

BodyVis Design Goals	
Incorporate multiple senses: use touch, sound, vibration, visuals	**Promote active, playful, and hands-on** movement-based engagement that is situated in the physical world
Link action to representation: provide immediate feedback to bodily actions in the physical world	**Personal relevance:** to help provoke curiosity and engagement, data should be personalized either to the individual learner and their body or their peers/classmates
Multiple timescales: representations should convey that organ systems work at different timescales (*e.g.,* the circulatory system *vs.* digestive)	**Collaborative learning:** allow learners to compare their physiology to others & collectively engage in self-inquiry (*e.g.,* to provoke questions such as "*how are our bodies the same or different?*"
Robust & lightweight: the shirt should allow for and be robust to movement, encouraging the wearer to self-experiment and move about the world	

Table 1: Our seven BodyVis design goals.

(a) Prototype 1 **(b)** Prototype 2 **(c)** Prototype 3

Figure 2: Design evolution of the three prototypes.

gallbladder, pancreas, small intestine, and large intestine. Currently, none of our prototypes depict reproductive organs, the thymus gland, trachea, human waste orifices, or the interactions between organ systems. We return to the tension between abstractions and scientifically accurate representations in the Discussion.

ITERATIVE DESIGN OF THREE BODYVIS PROTOTYPES

We present our three BodyVis prototypes (Figure 2) along with lessons learned throughout the design process.

CI Session 1: Initial Ideation

In the initial ideation phase, we conducted a CI session to explore potential design options and gain insight into how children understand their bodies. The CI group used a low-tech prototyping technique, called *Bags of Stuff* [15], to create interactive t-shirts that represented their anatomy. Our bags consisted of art and textile supplies including markers, yarn, felt, and pom-poms. Children and adult design partners were split into groups and given 40 minutes to design interactive anatomical shirts. Afterward, all groups gathered to share and present their designs to the team. Following the *Big Ideas* CI approach [15], an adult design partner recorded group ideas on a whiteboard, and discussed surprising and related ideas with the team. Thus, ideas were analyzed and categorized *in situ*.

CI Outcomes. Though each group created unique designs, a set of overarching themes emerged around the use of color, sound, lights, and movement (Figure 3). Color was used to distinguish organs (*e.g.,* red for veins and heart). For sound, children used audio to increase the playfulness and reactivity of their shirts: *e.g.,* breakable ribs and spines with "cracking" sound effects, "talking" organs, and using the spine as a musical instrument. Lights mainly indicated an action such as a pumping heart, hunger, or blood moving through veins. Finally, the most popular design theme was illustrating movement within the human body: food traveling through the digestive system and dissolving in the stomach, physically pumping hearts, and "breathing" lungs. In summary, while the design ideas ranged in feasibility, there was a clear emphasis on dynamics, interactivity, and reactivity to the human form and function.

Figure 3: To help design BodyVis, we conducted two participatory design sessions with children ages 7-11. Above: the results of our first session where children co-designed interactive anatomy t-shirts.

Prototype 1: Plush, Colorful, interactive

Informed by our first CI session as well as prior work (*e.g.,* [21,33,35]), we designed and implemented our first prototype (Figures 1a, 3, and 4). Organs were created using two pieces of fabric, cut into anatomically correct shapes, sewn together, and filled with pillow stuffing. This approach resulted in a plush, tangible aesthetic designed to attract a child's attention and touch. We attempted to correctly shape and position each organ on the shirt; however, to avoid occlusion, some organs were slightly modified (*e.g.,* the stomach, liver, gallbladder, and pancreas were spread out, some organs were disproportional).

We selected a green t-shirt as the base, and bright and colorful fabrics to make each organ salient. Although our palette is not anatomically correct, the intention was to use distinctive colors that may help children remember the functionality and purpose of each individual organ. For example, one team in the CI session had a brown-colored large intestine in their design, as it represented the final stage of the digestive system, "where the poop comes out."

Heart and Lungs

The heart is made of red and blue fabric embedded with flashing red/blue LEDs, which represent blood entering and leaving the heart (Figure 3). The LEDs are connected to a pulse sensor (pulsesensor.com) controlled by an Arduino Uno, which uses infrared to detect the wearer's heart rate. Through experimentation, we found that the pulse sensor functioned best when attached to the finger (visible in Figure 1a). For the lungs, we used orange fabric with red and blue electroluminescent (EL) wire to represent veins. As veins, the EL wire animated blood moving through the lungs. Prototype 1 did not contain a respiratory sensor, so the wearer's breathing rate was not visualized.

Digestive System

The digestive system consists of the esophagus, stomach, liver, gallbladder, pancreas, small intestine, and large intestine. Though we had originally planned to infer eating automatically using a microphone-based machine-learning approach (*e.g.,* [39]), our early attempts were unsuccessful. Thus, the digestive system was made solely of low-tech materials and was not dynamically responsive to the wearer. The esophagus was created from the grooved portion of a suction pump, chosen because of its visual similarity to the human esophagus, which uses surrounding muscles to pinch inward and send food to the stomach. Connected organs are sewn together (*e.g.,* the esophagus is visibly attached to the beginning of the stomach). In our CI session, one team used strings of yarn to represent the extent of their small intestines. We designed our small intestine to detach and unravel from the shirt allowing children to fully investigate its surprising length (*e.g.,* 450cm or 14.7 feet in five year olds [37]). See Figure 3d.

Figure 4: The design of Prototype 1 including (a-b) the heart and lung blood flow animations, and (c-d) playing with the shirt; the latter image highlights how children can explore their intestinal length via Velcro.

Evaluating Prototype 1

Prototype 1 was informally evaluated via design critiques with lab colleagues, a MakerFaire exhibit (Figure 5), feedback from our IDC demo [27], and informal demos with our CI group. Though parents, teachers, and children were excited by many aspects of our design—*e.g.,* at MakerFaire, a number of teachers and after-school coordinators gave us their contact information to volunteer for future tests—our evaluations uncovered a number of issues related to comfort, robustness, and understandability.

Lessons Learned. While attractive, the animated EL wire over the lungs was hard to see in normal room lighting and was often misinterpreted as representing *breathing* rather than blood flow. Second, though the plush, stuffed organs seemed to attract touch (*e.g.,* Figure 5a), they were heavy and encumbered movement. Third, our pulse sensor did not work reliably across wearers, occasionally failing to detect pulse altogether. Fourth, we were concerned with positional compromises made to reduce overlap between organs; teachers and MakerFaire attendees also expressed this concern. Finally, though we received positive feedback about the combination of automatic physiological sensing and on-body visualization, this feature was quite limited in Prototype 1—supporting only the heart.

Prototype 2: A New Lightweight design

Based on the above experiences, we began designing our second prototype (Figure 2b), focusing on improving the anatomical representations and reducing the weight/bulk of the shirt. Our primary concerns were on visual design, wearer comfort, and new animation approaches rather than physiological sensing. Consequently, Prototype 2 did not incorporate any physiological sensors; animations were simulated with artificial data. In contrast to Prototype 1, the anatomy was made with streamlined, flat (unstuffed) fabric organs cutout from anatomy templates. This new approach dramatically reduced weight and improved organ shape, size, proportionality, and placement (*i.e.,* organs could now appropriately overlap). We embedded a mix of LilyPad and Neopixel RGB LEDs into the heart and lungs, which were connected via conductive thread to a sewn-in Arduino

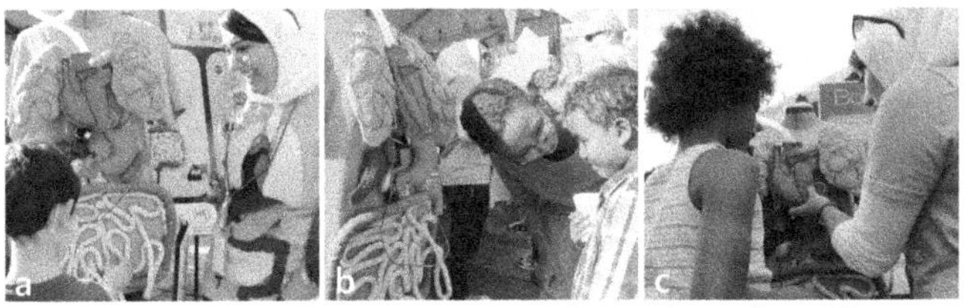

Figure 5: We demonstrated Prototype 1 and an early version of Prototype 2 at a MakerFaire exhibit. Though shirts were not worn by children, we observed interactions and elicited feedback from parents and teachers.

LilyPad. Unlike before, the lung visualizations were designed to represent *breathing*—the LEDs were intended to fill up and glow during inhalation and empty/fade during exhalation. Similar to Prototype 1, the digestive system was made solely of low-tech materials and did not animate or respond to user actions. To make the shirt easier to take on/off, we cut the back open and added snaps.

CI Session 2: Feedback Elicitation and Next Steps

For our second CI session (Figure 6), we had two primary goals: first, to get feedback on Prototypes 1 and 2 and, second, to conduct a co-design activity about how our shirts could be improved. For the first goal, two research assistants demonstrated the prototypes and elicited feedback. As Prototype 2 did not contain physiological sensors, the heart and lungs animated based on a fixed pulse and breathing rate. For the second goal, the co-design team was broken up into groups and was instructed to help design "the next generation of our shirt" using low-fidelity materials. After the design session, all groups rejoined to share their ideas and low-fidelity mockups with the team.

CI Outcomes. For the feedback elicitation, two co-design teams rotated through demonstrations of Prototype 1 and 2. At the Prototype 1 station, we observed physical activity, experimentation, and laughter. Each child wanted to try the pulse sensor and move around (*e.g.,* jump). Children not wearing the sensor would jump alongside. A few asked how the shirt worked. One child grabbed the small intestine and started unraveling it. For Prototype 2, there was less activity—probably because of the lack of sensing functionality; however, children still showed interest in the animations, the organs, and how the shirt was made. For the design activity, three of the four teams emphasized eating/digestion (Figure 6). One team, for example, thought of showing the small intestine as a "*gummy bear roller coaster*" and another designed a method of viewing food being processed and converted into waste. Others suggested updating the lungs so that they could physically inflate/deflate with breathing and help reveal differences between big and small breaths (similar to Schmidt's puppets for asthma education [31]). Teams again added sound such as "heart pumping" and "stomach grumbling."

Prototype 3: The current design

From these results, we designed and built our current prototype (Figure 2c), which is visually similar to Prototype 2 but differs in the following key ways:

Dynamically Removable Organs. While Prototype 2 had a more realistic portrayal of organs compared with Prototype 1, overlapping organs caused occlusion problems. With Prototype 3, we designed a removable organ system using conductive magnets. The heart, lungs, liver, and a portion of the stomach can be removed and reattached dynamically by the wearer or his/her peers to examine different layers of the body (Figure 7). When detached, the organ stops "working" (animating) but automatically restarts when reattached. To help with reattachment, the shirt contains organ outlines and color-coded highlighting around each connection point. Each organ is also tagged with iron-on ink labels, which help with identification and learning.

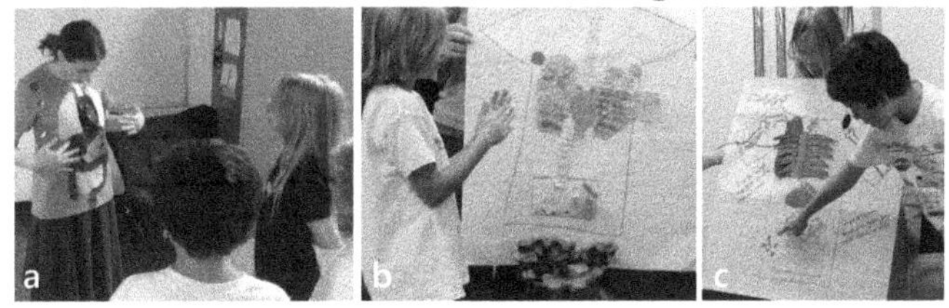

Figure 6: CI Session 2 included a (a) demonstration of Prototype 1 and 2 (2 shown) and (b-c) low-fidelity prototyping to design new shirt features.

Physiological Sensing. To expand BodyVis' physiological sensing capabilities, we added the *Zephyr Bioharness 3* [40], which is a robust body-sensing platform traditionally used in sports training and the military. Multiple independent studies have demonstrated the BioHarness' validity and reliability for measuring heart and respiratory rates [16,19]. Using a chest-worn strap, the Bioharness provides both physiological measures (*e.g.,* heartrate, breathing rate) as well as activity measures (*e.g.,* running, standing, walking). Currently, the strap is not directly sewn into the shirt and is put on independently. This decoupling between wearable sensor and visualization allowed for some unexpected explorations (as described in Study 2).

Touchscreen Stomach. For the stomach, we modified a small Android smartphone (Galaxy S3 Mini), which serves not only as the central processing unit for the shirt but also provides a flexible, programmable device for playing with sound, haptics, and visual output. The back panel and battery were removed from the device to decrease weight (from 113g to 82g). The phone's power connectors were rewired to a battery pouch on the side of the shirt, which also contained an Arduino.

Eating/Digestion. We added a button called "snack time" near the neckline to trigger digestion animations. Once pushed, food (bolus) travels down the esophagus via animated Neopixel LEDs and into the stomach, which plays an animated video of chemical secretion, muscular contractions, and food breakdown. After 18 seconds, LED-based animations continue highlighting relevant organs (*e.g.,* the liver, pancreas, and gallbladder) and showing the continued movement of food (now chyme) from the small to the large intestine. At the end of digestion, a playful flatulence sound is emitted from the smartphone. Though digestion from mouth-to-anus in children takes ~30 hours [38], BodyVis portrays it in ~35 seconds. We return to representing the body's timescales in the Discussion.

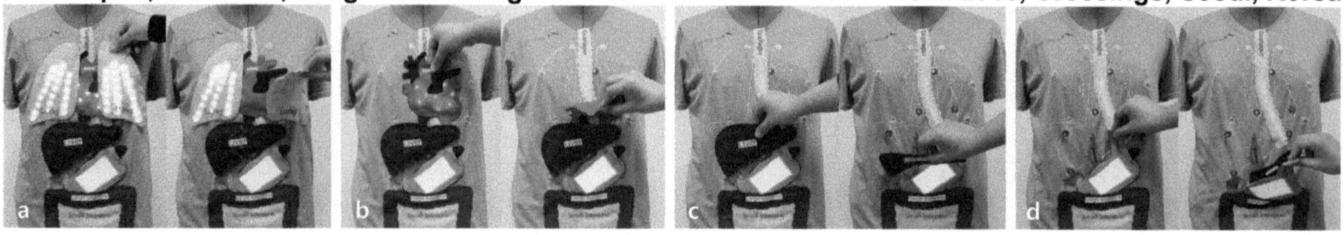

Figure 7: Using a conductive magnet approach, Prototype 3 allows for the dynamic removal and reattachment of the (a) lungs, (b) heart, (c) liver, and (d) part of the stomach, enabling learners to explore the multiple organ layers of the human body. See supplementary video for more details.

Prototype 3 System Architecture

Prototype 3 is comprised of four main technological components, which communicate over Bluetooth: (i) a Bioharness 3 that senses and transmits the wearer's biometric data to an Android smartphone (stomach); (ii) a custom BodyVis Android application that processes and wirelessly transmits the wearer's heart and breathing rate to a built-in Arduino; (iii) an Arduino that controls the LED-based animations; (iv) the "snack time" button that is hard-wired to the embedded Arduino. When pressed, digestion begins and the Arduino wirelessly communicates with the smartphone to trigger the stomach animation.

STUDY 1: TEACHER INTERVIEWS

To gain a better understanding of existing teaching methods, and to elicit feedback about BodyVis from trained educators, we conducted semi-structured interviews with seven elementary school teachers who teach anatomy. Our second study, described later, investigates children's responses and interactions with BodyVis.

Method

We recruited seven teachers (one male) through email lists, word-of-mouth, and contacts gained at MakerFaire. The participants taught science and health at elementary schools spanning 1st to 4th grade, and had a range of teaching experience from two to thirteen years. Three participants taught in the public school system; four in private school. Teacher interviews were broken into two parts: (i) a formative inquiry of teaching approaches for body learning, common body misconceptions in children, and learning challenges; and a (ii) a BodyVis design probe, where we solicited feedback to Prototypes 1 and 3. We allowed the teacher to interact with each prototype, and asked semi-structured questions including first impressions, uses in the classroom, and desired features. We also asked participants to envision scenarios with more than one BodyVis shirt.

Data and Analysis

On average, the interviews lasted 53 minutes (*SD*=15). Each interview was audio recorded and professionally transcribed. For the analysis, we pursued an iterative coding scheme with a mix of both deductive and inductive codes [6,18]. Our unit of analysis was a full response to a question. An initial codebook was derived based on topics in the body learning literature, our research questions, and our study protocol. A random transcript was then selected and coded by a single researcher. While coding, the codebook was updated to accommodate emergent themes and to clarify code descriptions. We had 16 codes in total, including learning potential, engagement, concerns (*e.g.,* cost, distraction, privacy, robustness), learning activities, and design (*e.g.,* visual design, organ representations).

To establish inter-rater reliability (IRR), a second researcher used the codebook to independently code the same interview and the resulting codes were compared using Krippendorff's alpha (*average* α=0.77; *SD=0.2; total disagreements*=22 out of 420 decisions). Krippendorff [20] suggests that scores of α < 0.667 should be discarded or recoded. In our case, 6 of the 16 codes were < 0.667. The two researchers met, resolved all 22 disagreements, and updated the codebook accordingly. Both researchers then independently coded a second random interview, establishing IRR (α=0.88, *SD=0.19*). Finally, the first researcher coded the remaining five interviews.

Findings

We present frequent patterns and emergent themes.

Part One: Existing Teaching Practices

To inform their body learning curriculum, teachers used national science standards, district requirements (for the four public school teachers), and previous teaching materials at the school. Materials included a combination of books, videos, interactive software, smartboards, transparencies, museum field trips, and 3D models (*e.g., Little Organ Annie*). To enhance learning and engagement, three teachers also incorporated physical activities—*e.g.,* T3 and T6 had children role-play as red and white blood cells in a magnified heart. T7 emphasized the importance of physicality in body learning: "*I want them to use their bodies [to learn]... if we're talking about muscles, you want them to feel their muscles.*" Similarly, T5 noted that she did not use worksheets or books for body learning and relied exclusively on hands-on activities.

When asked about learning challenges, our findings were consistent with prior work (*e.g.,* [8,17,30]). Children struggled to understand that their bodies are comprised of smaller parts (organs, bones), how these organs operate, interact, and provide benefits to the body, how food is processed, and the location of certain organs (*e.g.,* T7 found that students could often find their hearts but not stomachs).

Part Two: BodyVis Design Probe

For the design probe, teachers generally reacted positively to BodyVis. Below, we organize our findings into four areas: learning potential, proposed learning activities, teacher concerns, and suggested improvements.

Learning Potential. All teachers were positive about BodyVis' potential as a body learning tool. Common reasons included: its ability to engage children (6 teachers) and concretize otherwise invisible and/or abstract concepts (5), and the way the shirt responded to the wearer's body (4). BodyVis' use of on-body visualization to show the wearers' changing physiology, and its use of color, lights, and animations were identified as key to learner engagement. T3 described BodyVis as similar to a real life video game, and T2 emphasized the role of engagement:

> *"...the biggest thing is getting [the students] interested in [body learning]. And I think something like this would definitely get them interested and motivated to learn more about [their bodies]." (T2)*

With regard to the concretization of abstract concepts, T2 provided a representative quote:

> *"I teach the age of students [3rd grade] that's very hard for them to think in the abstract. And the inside of your body is pretty abstract unless you can really see it and this is a great way for them to be able to really see it." (T2)*

Similarly, T6 focused on how the animations overlaid on the wearer's externalized anatomy helped make invisible bodily actions more clear: "*you can really see the pathway that food's taking, that air's taking, and their pulse*." As with prior sensor-based learning approaches (*e.g.,* [5]), the coupling between *action* and *feedback* was highlighted as a primary benefit. For example, T6 stated: "*The biosensor again, that link with what's actually happening in one's own body is really fantastic.*" T5 also emphasized how the visualizations responded to one's own physiology:

> *"...[a book] describes it, the process, the steps, and then you watch a video but with this, you could actually connect to your body and see what happens in your body." (T5)*

Finally, two teachers mentioned learning opportunities for STEM topics beyond body learning. T4 suggested math activities for measuring intestines and investigating pulse. T6 suggested providing a BodyVis API so students could add sensors and program new behaviors.

BodyVis Learning Activities. When asked to design learning activities for BodyVis, three strategies emerged: physical, movement-based activities (6); peer collaboration and comparison activities (5); and as a low-tech anatomical model (4). For physical activities, teachers stressed how students could explore their bodies responding to different actions (*e.g.,* running *vs.* sitting) and contexts (*e.g.,* going outside, to the cafeteria). Five of these teachers mentioned opportunities for collaborative learning as children could observe differences and similarities between their peers. Four teachers suggested using BodyVis as a static model. Here, students would identify and learn about organs before actually wearing the shirts.

Concerns and Suggested Improvements. We identified four primary concerns: robustness and maintenance (4), cost (3), potential to distract (3), and misrepresentation of organs (3). For robustness and maintenance, teachers stated concerns both for the technology and the material. For example, T1 said: "*[if] one of the sensors stops working, how can we replace [it]*." T2 worried "*about pieces getting lost or torn.*" In terms of cost, T3 suggested there is a "*real market for [BodyVis]*," but thought that poorer schools may struggle to afford multiple shirts; others worried about the maintenance costs. Teachers also related previous struggles with technology in the classroom. T2 found that technology can be both a "positive" and a "negative," and T6 suggested that for some students BodyVis could be "*too distracting*" especially "*if they're used to worksheets.*" While teachers understood the role of simplification in focusing students' attention, three expressed concerns with our representations: *e.g.,* T7 observed that neither prototype included a trachea, and T5 questioned the gallbladder's location with respect to the liver.

In terms of improvements, suggestions included adding: details to existing organs (3), greater controls for teachers (3), stronger links between organs and organs systems (2), and more multi-sensory feedback (2). For example, T6 wanted the lungs to show the "*dispersion of gases into the alveoli*" and suggested that we "*show how different foods result in different things happening to your body*" (*e.g.,* high-sugar foods, caffeine). T4 suggested adding buttons on each organ, which would trigger audio explanations and T5 asked if each organ could play a movie like the stomach.

Summary of Study 1 Findings

Our Study 1 findings further motivate the need for interactive, physical, movement-based body learning tools and the potential benefits of BodyVis (*e.g.,* increased learner engagement, concretization). Teacher concerns and suggested improvements will help direct future work.

STUDY 2: DESIGN DEPLOYMENTS

Three single-session field deployments were conducted in local after-school programs to explore children's reactions and interactions with BodyVis. These sessions were exploratory, aimed at uncovering how children approach, understand, and react to BodyVis (*e.g.,* the questions it provokes, the social interactions that occur). See Figure 8.

Method

We recruited three after-school programs through mailing lists, word-of-mouth, and contacts acquired at MakerFaire. A total of 30 children (18 female, 12 male) aged 6-12 participated in the study. A team of two to three researchers worked with on-site staff to coordinate the sessions, which took place in large rooms with approximately 10 children per location. The study procedure included: introductions and a pre-study body knowledge questionnaire on anatomy and physiology (15 min); a 10-minute overview of BodyVis; a 30 minute interactive trial where three to four child volunteers tried on BodyVis and engaged in a small number of physical tasks; and a post-study questionnaire (15 min). Children also engaged in 15-minutes of free play with BodyVis at the end of each session. After each session, a 20-minute debrief occurred amongst the research staff and a summary of reflections and observations was composed. Parental consent and children's verbal assent were acquired, including permission to take photos and record audio/ video, prior to the study.

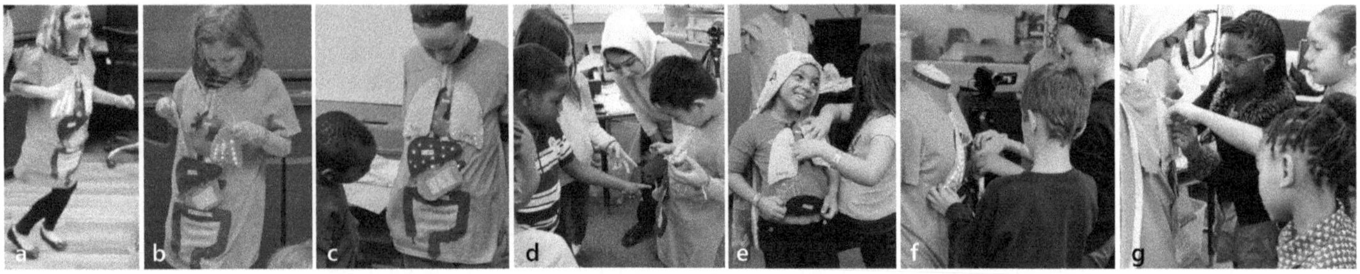

Figure 8: In Study 2, we deployed BodyVis in three after-school programs. (a) Wearers engaged in various physical activities to see how their bodies would respond and (b) touched/removed their own organs. (c-d) Wearers and non-wearers interacted together; non-wearers suggested actions, conducted activities simultaneous with wearers, and touched/asked questions about the shirt and body functions. Unexpectedly, (e) children removed BodyVis organs and placed them on their own bodies, (f) investigated BodyVis even when it was placed on a mannequin, and (g) inquired about how the shirt works.

Data and Analysis

The sessions were audio and video recorded; however, only audio was available from the third site due to technical difficulties with the video camera. We began data analysis by reviewing session video, audio, notes, and summaries; this review was used to develop an initial codebook. Using audio and video data, one researcher coded for physical actions (*e.g.,* gestures, interactions with the shirt, movements), emotional responses (*e.g.,* volume of room, facial expressions), utterances (*e.g.,* spoken questions and observations about the shirt, anatomy, and physiology), and design preferences (*e.g.,* likes, dislikes, and design ideas). A second codebook was derived using open-coding to analyze children's spoken questions. Two researchers coded this data (*average* α=0.85; *SD*=0.13).

Findings

We focus on common reactions and patterns of behavior that occurred across the three deployment sites.

Overall Reactions. Generally, children reacted positively to our prototype. As intended, the shirt elicited questions and observations about the body: *"Does the liver keep your water?"*, "*His heart is getting faster and faster!*", *"Is that what's happening inside me?"*, and "*We're looking inside his stomach!"* It also promoted body movement and inquiry ("*I wonder what would happen if...*") and engaged children in thinking about, discussing, and playing with their bodies. Wearers appeared to experience a strong connection between the shirt visualizations and their own bodies. One child, for example, pressed the snack time button after each bite of his apple. Some vocalized disgust at first ("*eewww*") and older children (*e.g.,* 10-12 years) seemed less interested; however, this changed after interactions began. A few found the BioHarness uncomfortable ("*it's itchy*").

Wearers and Non-Wearers. Though we were initially concerned with deploying a single prototype for groups of 8-12 children, wearers and non-wearers worked together to explore, play, and interact with BodyVis. While most children volunteered to wear the shirt, we could only accommodate four per site due to time constraints. However, non-wearers remained engaged throughout. They would shout out activities to the wearer (*e.g.,* jumping jacks, push-ups, "*run around us like duck-duck-goose*"), remark on physiological changes (e.g., "*[his lungs] are going faster*" and "*His heart is beating really slow*"), remove and reattach BodyVis organs, and press the "snack time" button. Because wearers could not always see the shirt, non-wearers would inform them about changes and also help them reattach organs in the proper place (*e.g.,* "*follow the color, the outlines, the magnets*"). Children would also discuss and answer each other's questions. For example, one participant asked, "*What are those yellow thingies [in the stomach]?*" Another answered: "*acid.*"

Removing/Reattaching Organs. The ability to remove and reattach organs allowed children to explore the layered nature of their bodies (*e.g.,* "*What's under the heart?"*) and also resulted in unexpected inquiry and play. For example, when a wearer removed his lung, a child asked, "*How's he going to breathe?*" Another joked: "*You're dead now!*" In one session, a wearer decided to role-play as a doctor and performed surgery on herself. Children also experimented with removing organs and reattaching them in the wrong place. One non-wearer positioned the liver as the right lung but found that the lights did not turn on. She said "*that's not right!*" and put the liver back in its correct position.

Common Questions/Observations. BodyVis elicited a wide range of observations and questions. Children made observations on changing physiology, the state of the wearer's body, and inferences about how the shirt works (*e.g.,* "*Oh, these are magnets"*). Children questioned the role of certain organs, the effect of actions on the body, and how the shirt was made and how it functions. More specifically, for the body-related questions, children asked "what happens if" inquiries (*e.g.,* "*What happens if [the heart] stops beating?*"), verification questions (*"Is that what's happening inside me?"*), questions about organs and their functions (*e.g., "what the heck is that?*" while pointing to the pancreas) and questions about the shirt's abilities "*What if I put that on, and I'm drinking this [water], would it detect where it's going*?" Though our Study 1 teachers thought that their students would be curious about the shirts' construction and operation, we were surprised with how common these questions were in in our deployments. At each session, children also asked to look inside the shirt to see its wiring and microcontroller (Figure 8g).

Disembodied BodyVis. At the end of each session BodyVis was placed on a mannequin (Figure 8f). Children would approach the mannequin and touch, play with, and explore BodyVis. At the end of one session, a non-wearer asked to wear the BioHarness. With BodyVis still on the mannequin, she performed a number of physical actions to see what would happen. Other children joined her and mimicked her behavior. So, while the coupling between sensing and visualization seems important—*i.e.,* visualizing one's changing physiology in real-time on the body—there may be interesting opportunities for visual manifestations that are physically disconnected from the sensed body (*e.g.,* a mixed reality approach where the wearer's physiology is overlaid on a virtual avatar).

Pre- and Post- Questionnaires. Though our primary intent was not to assess learning, we did examine children's pre- and post-body knowledge using body map drawings, a common assessment approach (*e.g.,* [8,11,12,35]). We analyzed organ layering, shape, position, and the addition of organs. Of the 30 participants, 22 drew at least one new organ in their post-study body maps, 17 corrected positions, 12 properly adjusted organ layers, and 10 improved organ shapes. However, 16 participants had at least one shape that was incorrect on their pre-study drawing and it remained incorrect post-study, 3 added an organ but in the wrong position, and 3 had removed organs that were correct originally. Some children remained confused about heart and lung function. Without a more rigorous evaluation (*e.g.,* with control conditions), we cannot make strong claims about these results; however, BodyVis does appear to have a positive influence on body knowledge.

DISCUSSION

As the first work exploring the combination of on-body sensing with wearable e-textile visualizations for body learning, we were encouraged by both teacher and children reactions. Below, we reflect on our study methods and findings and describe limitations and future work.

Representing the Body. Science education has diverse representational forms that abstract reality to simplify concepts and capture learner interest (*e.g.,* atomic models). Throughout the BodyVis design process we explored different ways of representing the body, not all of which were successful (*e.g.,* the heavy plush organs, EL wire for lung veins). More work is needed to understand tradeoffs between guiding a child's attention, simplifying concepts, and allowing for the accurate construction of knowledge. One design goal that we did not fully explore was combining haptics with visualization (*e.g.,* vibration for stomach rumbling, heartbeat); this may improve the wearer's connection to the shirt and increase engagement. Additionally, we did not address portraying the body's different timescales (*e.g.,* pulse *vs.* digestion). We have discussed including a "fast forward" button on the touchscreen stomach to provide additional context (*e.g.,* to describe digestion length). Surprisingly, one teacher thought of these abstractions as learning opportunities:

> *"Because this one shows it to you in under a minute, I would have [the students] compare and contrast to it and research the actual time it takes for the food to travel [through you]." (T4)*

This emphasizes the important interconnections between technology innovations and the design of learning activities.

Learning Potential. As initial research, our focus was on qualitatively assessing BodyVis rather than conducting controlled pedagogical studies. Still, our findings suggest that BodyVis has the potential to support learning and body inquiry. Teachers emphasized its ability to engage learners, concretize abstract concepts, and enable new types of learning activities. With Study 2, we observed behavior that our teachers predicted: children were active, curious, and engaged in inquiry—both about their bodies and the construction of the shirt. Still, more work is needed to examine how BodyVis affects learning. We have begun collaborating with an educational researcher with a focus on understanding how BodyVis can be used and evaluated in both formal and informal learning contexts.

Privacy and Discomfort. BodyVis is designed to facilitate social interaction and collaborative inquiry among children. As found in Study 2, non-wearers and wearers worked together to explore their bodies. These interactions included touching and comments about the body, which may make a child feel uncomfortable. This tension is one reason we pursued an iterative, participatory design approach. While these concerns did not emerge in either study, this is a critical design issue that will require continued awareness.

Cooperative Inquiry. It may seem dichotomous to work with children as co-designers on a subject in which the literature suggests they are not experts; however, their role was not to design scientifically accurate body representations but rather to help us gain a better understanding of a child's perspectives, ideas, and desires. The designs generated underscored the importance of multi-modal feedback (*e.g.,* sound, visuals), of bright distinctive colors, and of low-fi and high-fi interactivity (*e.g.,* the unraveling intestine in Prototype 1). In addition, CI includes an intergenerational mix of design partners, so adults could assist children who encountered foreign concepts.

Limitations and Future Work

We deployed BodyVis in a constrained fashion: single-session studies that were researcher facilitated. This study design is susceptible to novelty effects as well as biases that result from the designers conducting the deployments. For the teacher interviews, we had a small number of participants and the focus was on initial reactions rather than views developed from actual use. Still, the combination of methods used—iterative design, the MakerFaire exhibit, interviews, and deployments—help mitigate the effects of any one technique. Our primary future work includes: (i) improving and extending BodyVis representations; (ii) developing new physiological sensors; (iii) expanding to other parts of the body. Other long-term goals include allowing learners to investigate their bodies more broadly, exploring body systems in everyday contexts (*e.g.,* soccer matches), and making BodyVis "hackable"—allowing children to customize their BodyVis shirts.

CONCLUSION

This paper contributes new knowledge to the field of wearables and tangibles for learning. The BodyVis system demonstrated a potential to help children understand their anatomy and physiology. Our findings show that this wearable tool engages children and that teachers believe it could be an educational aid. Our vision is to transform how learners engage with and understand body concepts and to identify how wearables can be designed to support scientific inquiry and life-relevant learning more generally.

REFERENCES

1. Antle, A.N. and Wise, A.F. Getting Down to Details: Using Theories of Cognition and Learning to Inform Tangible User Interface Design. *Interacting with Computers 25*, 1 (2013), 1–20.
2. Bajura, M., Fuchs, H., and Ohbuchi, R. Merging virtual objects with the real world. *ACM Comp Graph 26*, 2 (1992), 203–210.
3. Blum, L.H. Health information via mass media: Study of the individual's concepts of the body and its parts. *Psychological Reports 40*, (1977), 991–999.
4. Blum, T., Kleeberger, V., Bichlmeier, C., and Navab, N. mirracle: An augmented reality magic mirror system for anatomy education. *2012 IEEE Virtual Reality (VR)*, 115–116.
5. Brasell, H. The effect of real-time laboratory graphing on learning graphic representations of distance and velocity. *Journal of Research in Science Teaching 24*, 4 (1987), 385–395.
6. Braun, V. and Clarke, V. Using thematic analysis in psychology. *Qualitative Research in Psychology 3*, 2 (2006), 77–101.
7. Consolvo, S., McDonald, D.W., *et al.* Activity sensing in the wild: a field trial of ubifit garden. *Proc. of CHI'08*, 1797–1806.
8. Cuthbert, A. Do Children Have a Holistic View Of Their Internal Body Maps. *The School Science Review 82*, 299 (2000), 25–32.
9. Eston, R., Rowlands, A., and Ingledew, D. Validity of heart rate, pedometry, and accelerometry for predicting the energy cost of children's activities. *J. of Appl. Physiology 84*, 1 (1998), 362–71.
10. Fjeld, M., Hobi, D., Winterthaler, L., Voegtli, B., and Juchli, P. Teaching electronegativity and dipole moment in a TUI. *IEEE Intl Conf on Adv Learning Technologies, 2004.* 792–794.
11. Garcia-Barros, S., Martínez-Losada, C., and Garrido, M. What do Children Aged Four to Seven Know about the Digestive System and the Respiratory System of the Human Being and of Other Animals? *Intl. J. of Sci Edu 33*, 15 (2011), 2095–2122.
12. Gatt, S. and Saliba, M. Young Children's Ideas About the Heart. *3rd Intl. Conference on Hands-On Science*, (2006), 17–23.
13. Gellert, E. Children's Conceptions of the Content and Functions of the Human Body. *Genetic Psych. Mono. 65*, (1962), 293–405.
14. Gillet, A., Sanner, M., Stoffler, D., Olson, A. Tangible interfaces for structural molecular biology. *Structure 13*, 3 (2005), 483–91.
15. Guha, M., Druin, A., Fails, J. Cooperative Inquiry revisited: Reflections of the past and guidelines for the future. *Intl J Child-Computer Interaction 1*, 1 (2013), 14–23.
16. Hailstone, J. and Kilding, A.E. Reliability and Validity of the Zephyr™ BioHarness™ to Measure Respiratory Responses to Exercise. *Meas. Phys Edu & Exercise Sci 15*, 4 (2011), 293–300.
17. Hmelo-Silver, C.E., Marathe, S., and Liu, L. Fish Swim, Rocks Sit, and Lungs Breathe: Expert-Novice Understanding of Complex Systems. *J. Learning Sciences 16*, 3 (2007), 307–331.
18. Hruschka, D.J., Schwartz, D., *et al.* Reliability in Coding Open-Ended Data: Lessons Learned from HIV Behavioral Research. *Field Methods 16* , 3 (2004), 307–331.
19. Kim, J.-H., Roberge, R., *et al.* Measurement Accuracy of Heart Rate and Respiratory Rate during Graded Exercise and Sustained Exercise in the Heat Using the Zephyr BioHarnessTM. *Intl. Journal of Sports Medicine 34*, 06 (2013), 497–501.
20. Krippendorff, K.H. *Content Analysis: An Introduction to Its Methodology.* Sage Publications, Inc, 2003.
21. Lam, N. and Ngo, S. Warning Signs. *NYU's ITP*, 2010. http://blog.nienlam.com/2010/12/19/warning-signs/.
22. Lee, V.R. and Drake, J. Quantified Recess: Design of an Activity for Elementary Students Involving Analyses of Their Own Movement Data. *Proc of IDC'13*, 273–276.
23. Lee, V.R. and DuMont, M. An Exploration into How Physical Activity Data-Recording Devices Could be Used in Computer-Supported Data Investigations. *International Journal of Computers for Mathematical Learning 15*, 3 (2010), 167–189.
24. Lee, V.R. and Thomas, J.M. Integrating physical activity data technologies into elementary school classrooms. *Educational Technology Research and Development 59*, 6 (2011), 865–884.
25. Marshall, P. Do tangible interfaces enhance learning? *Proc. of TEI'07*, 163–170.
26. Meng, M., Fallavollita, P., Blum, T., et al. Kinect for interactive AR anatomy learning. *Proc. of ISMA'13*, 277–278.
27. Norooz, L. and Froehlich, J. Exploring early designs for teaching anatomy and physiology to children using wearable e-textiles. *Proc. of IDC'13 (Demo Track)*, ACM Press (2013), 577–580.
28. Osborne, J., Wadsworth, P., and Black, P. *Primary SPACE Research Research Report: Processes of Life.* Liverpool University Press, Liverpool, UK, 1992.
29. Óskarsdóttir, G. The development of children's ideas about the body: How these ideas change in a teaching environment. *PhD Dissertation, Univ. of Iceland, Social Sciences*, (2006), 1–240.
30. Schmidt, C.K. Development of Children's Body Knowledge, Using Knowledge of the Lungs as An Exemplar. *Issues in Comprehensive Pediatric Nursing 24*, 3 (2001), 177–191.
31. Schmidt, C.K. Comparison of three teaching methods on 4-7 year old children's understanding of the lungs in relation to a peak flow meter in the management of asthma: A pilot study. *Journal of Asthma 39*, 7 (2002), 641–648.
32. Tinker, R.F. and Papert, S. Tools for Science Education. In J.D. Ellis, ed., *Information Technology & Sci Education. 1988 Assoc. for the Ed. of Teachers in Sci. Yearbook.* Columbus, OH, 1989.
33. Tonkin, A. Inside Story. *Nursery World*, 2007. http://www.nurseryworld.co.uk/news/722623/Inside-story.
34. Ullmer, B. and Ishii, H. Emerging frameworks for tangible user interfaces. *IBM Systems Journal 39*, 3.4 (2000), 915–931.
35. Vessey, J., Braithwaite, K., & Widemann, M. Teaching Children About Their Internal Bodies. *Ped. Nursing 16*, 1 (1990), 29–33.
36. Vessey, J.A. Comparison of two teaching methods on children's knowledge of their internal bodies. *Nursing Research 37*, 5 (1988), 262–267.
37. Weaver, L.T., Austin, S., and Cole, T.J. Small intestinal length: a factor essential for gut adaptation. *Gut 32*, 11 (1991), 1321–3.
38. Weaver, L.T. and Steiner, H. The bowel habit of young children. *Archives of Disease in Childhood 59*, 7 (1984), 649–652.
39. Yatani, K. and Truong, K.N. BodyScope: a wearable acoustic sensor for activity recognition. *Proc of UbiComp '12*, 341-350.
40. Zephyr Inc. Zephyr BioHarness 3: Model BH3. 2014. http://www.zephyranywhere.com/products/bioharness-3/.
41. Zucker, A.A., Tinker, R., *et. al.* Learning Science in Grades 3–8 Using Probeware and Computers: Findings from the TEEMSS II Project. *J. of Sci Education & Technology 17*, 1 (2007), 42–48.

Exploring Expressive Augmented Reality: The FingAR Puppet System for Social Pretend Play

Zhen Bai, Alan F. Blackwell, George Coulouris
Computer Laboratory, University of Cambridge
15 JJ Thomson Avenue, Cambridge, CB3 0FD, United Kingdom
zhen.bai, alan.blackwell, george.coulouris@cl.cam.ac.uk

(a) Enact puppet (b) Transform emotion (c) Open-ended scenery objects (d) Dramatic storyline

Figure 1. FingAR Puppet system overview.

ABSTRACT
We present "FingAR Puppet", an Augmented Reality (AR) system enhancing social pretend play by young children. Unlike goal-oriented AR systems that augment reality with informative instructions, FingAR Puppet helps children associate expressive interpretations with immediate reality. Empirical results show that FingAR Puppet promotes reasoning about emotional states, communication and divergent thinking during social pretend play for children 4-6 years old. We suggest that this study opens an interesting space for future AR systems to support complex cognitive and social development in early childhood. We also identify broader implications from using theories of cognitive development to guide the design of tangible and augmented interactions.

Author Keywords
Augmented Reality; Tangible User Interface; Pretend Play; Children.

ACM Classification Keywords
H.5.1. Information Interfaces and Presentation: Multimedia Information SystemsArtificial, augmented, and virtual realities

CHI 2015, April 18–23, 2015, Seoul, Republic of Korea.

ACM 978-1-4503-3145-6/15/04 ...$15.00.
http://dx.doi.org/10.1145/2702123.2702250

INTRODUCTION
In this paper we describe an application of the Augmented Reality (AR) paradigm that explores the capacity for AR to support complex cognitive skills. Many early research and current commercial AR applications have emphasised the value of AR for guidance and information finding in domains such as maintenance, medicine, navigation and more [37]. However, in addition to such goal-oriented tasks, AR technologies may support more complex cognitive skills. Two specific examples are divergent thinking [30], where it is necessary to think about multiple possible courses of action, and theory of mind [24], where it is necessary to think about other people's states of mind. Both of these cognitive skills are essential in early childhood development.

The developmental stages through which children shift from applying knowledge in situations with high perceptual similarity, to more general expressive and imaginative cognitive tasks, underpin essential skills in everyday life [4]. We suggest that the potential for AR to superimpose interactive virtual information onto immediate reality [1] extends beyond typical guidance and information finding, to offer support for more complex cognitive skills. This may be especially beneficial for children who have difficulty moving beyond interpretations based on high perceptual similarity. In particular, our earlier work indicates that AR can encourage children with autism to use objects more symbolically in play [2], which is closely linked with theory of mind and divergent thinking.

In this new study we developed the FingAR Puppet system to promote theory of mind and divergent thinking through social pretend play. The system employs a magic mirror metaphor to portray an imaginary AR world in which users can see themselves and their physical environment extended with augmented cues and content that bridge from immediate perception to imaginary play. These augmentations support symbolic cognition (e.g. pretending a banana is a telephone) and social cognition (e.g. constructing joint pretense among multiple players) [23, 35]. These social pretend play skills enable children to simulate and respond to acted emotions, beliefs and desires, communicate interpretation of roles, props and events [16, 17], and flexibly use play materials in response to make-believe themes[28]. These cognitive and social abilities are critical preparation for later school life [5].

We present results from an evaluation of the system in extended use by children 4-6 years old. We find that FingAR Puppet effectively promotes reasoning about emotional states, communication and divergent thinking during social pretend play. These findings open an interesting space for future AR systems to support complex cognitive and social development in early childhood. They also suggest the potential for AR to be used in a wider range of expressive and interpretive tasks. Finally, we discuss the usability implications of the magic mirror metaphor, as an approach to AR design that offers particular advantages for physical object manipulation and social interaction.

RELATED WORK

There are several interactive systems intended to assist child development in storytelling, which shares elements with social pretend play. Although various physical objects are involved in these systems, they either remain literal without any symbolic transformation (e.g. Storymat [31], Augmented Knight's Castle [10], video puppetry [3]) or simply function as tangible entities to help children interact with virtual objects more efficiently (e.g. ShadowStory [18], Puppettime [22], wIzQuebes [38]). There are other interactive systems aiming to promote children's emotion understanding. For example, StoryFaces [32] is a touch-pad based storytelling system that allows the child to watch pre-made stories involving virtual characters with his/her face, and create their own stories. It lacks support for reasoning about emotional states from other's perspectives, and reciprocal social interaction through improvisational role enactment. PUPPET [21] is a VR environment with autonomous characters with different goals and emotional states. While findings show that PUPPET help children aged 7-9 to understand characters' emotional states, further exploration is yet needed for younger children.

SYSTEM DESCRIPTION

The design of the FingAR Puppet system had two related goals: (1) to provide a complete social pretend play experience; and (2) to more specifically enhance children's emotion expression and understanding, joint pretense and divergent thinking in the context of this experience. We applied the magic mirror display metaphor [20] to support a reflected view of reality that superimposes imaginary objects and situations. The children using the system look into this magic mirror while interacting with physical objects alongside other players in a tabletop play environment (Fig.2).

Figure 2. Children interact with the FingAR Puppet system.

Design Rationale

The cognitive mechanism of pretend play is an early manifestation of theory of mind [16]. As an example of this relationship, consider these play scenarios:

Eileen pretends that the puppet is a policeman

The primary representation of reality (a puppet) is transformed via a symbolic relationship to support a secondary representation of pretense ("the puppet is a policeman"). In FingAR Puppet, this symbolic transformation is externalised through the augmentation of the play context with a pretense stimulus seen in the magic mirror.

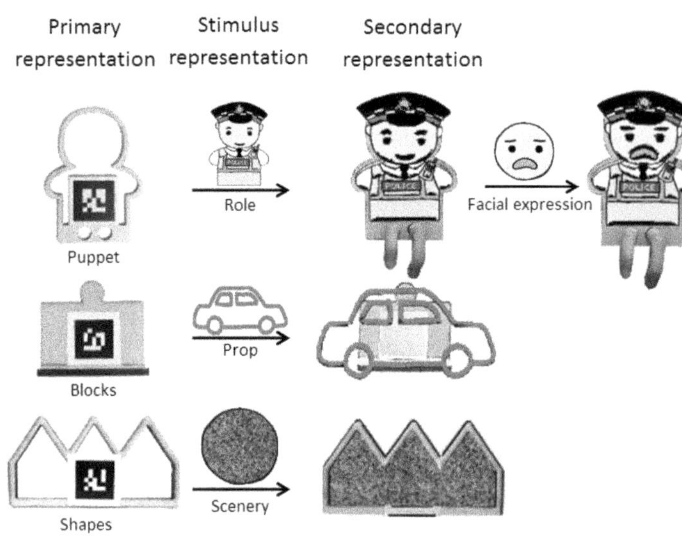

Figure 3. The FingAR Puppet design concept.

As shown in Fig.3, the primary representation of reality in the FingAR Puppet system contains physical objects: puppets, blocks and generic shapes. The stimulus representation corresponding to each type of physical referent are role (puppet), prop (block) and scenery (shapes). The design intention of these stimuli is that they should encourage the user to carry out symbolic transformation involving gradually increased mental effort. We included two types of stimuli: (1) roles and props to support specific symbolic transformations;

(a) Physical referents (b) Role representations (c) Prop and Setting representations

Figure 4. The collection of primary and stimulus representations.

(2) open-ended scenery to encourage divergent exploration [29], in which users construct their own meanings. Symbolic transformation is observed when the user assigns one of the stimulus representations to a physical referent. For example, when the user assigns the policeman role to the puppet, the secondary representation "the puppet is a policeman" was created. Similarly with emotion transformation, by assigning the "scared" facial expression to the policeman, the policeman's emotional state would be transformed to "scared".

The system supports two phases of activity: preparation and play. In the preparation phase, children set up roles, props and scenes. Each child has one puppet, several blocks, and several shapes. In the play phase, children make stories together using the AR elements they have chosen. During the play phase, children are also able to (1) change the facial expression of their puppets; (2) change role, prop or scenery whenever necessary; and (3) record a video of the play.

Interaction Design Details

Object Transformation

The collection of physical referents (puppet, block and shape) and stimulus representations (role, prop, and scenery) are shown in Fig.4.

Role/Puppet We chose to base the FingAR puppet concept on the finger-leg puppet, a familiar cheap toy for young children. Our main criterion was simplicity of operation – this form of puppet is more mobile and expressive than dolls, and easier to operate than other forms of puppet such as glove puppet, marionette and shadow puppet. The system includes 18 social and fictional based roles, all sharing the same pose and facial features (Fig.4 (b)). Based on common play themes of children's social pretend play [33], the system supported several role-specific play themes including rescue (e.g. policeman and fireman), restaurant (e.g. chef and waiter), shopping (e.g. shopkeeper), hospital (e.g. doctor, nurse), and adventure (e.g. princess, knight, pirate). We maintained a balanced number of male and female roles [11].

Prop/Block We provided wood blocks in a generic rectangular shape as the physical referent for props. The grip on top of the block was meant for the child to hold when selecting and moving the prop, in order to prevent marker occlusion. There were 12 virtual objects as the target for prop transformation (Fig.4 (c) top). These were rendered in a wireframe style and related to the specific themes of the pre-defined roles, such as fire engine with the rescue theme, cake with the dining theme, dragon with the adventure theme, etc. The child could flip the orientation of the prop by flipping the associated wood block. The wireframe style was partly motivated by our intention that in future, users should be able to draw their own target props while maintaining visual consistency with the existing props.

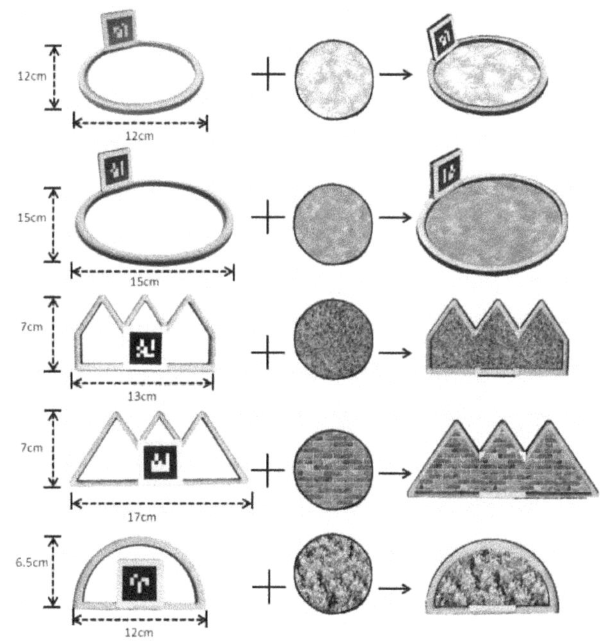

Figure 5. Scenery transformation.

Scenery/Shape We chose 12 open-ended materials to help children create meanings for physical referents (Fig.4 (c) bottom). Some materials reflected natural scenes (e.g. flower, grass, water, snow, wood and stone) or built environment scenes (e.g. brick, tile and fire). Others had more ambiguous meanings, since familiarity with stimuli affects divergent thinking processes [29]. We wished to encourage both (1) creation of different pretense interpretations using familiar materials; and (2) creation of more novel symbolic interpretations using unfamiliar materials. Materials could be associated with three types of wood shape: circle, semi-circle and sawtooth. Slight variations in size and shape were used to avoid possession conflict between players. Example combinations of shape and material are shown in Fig.5.

Transformation Action The tangible nature of the physical referent allows children to externalize their mental process of object transformation through direct manipulation [34], as demonstrated in Fig.6. To complete an object transformation, the child points the physical referent toward the target role, prop or scenery in the 'mirror'. The corresponding virtual object is then attached to or combined with the physical referent in the augmented view.

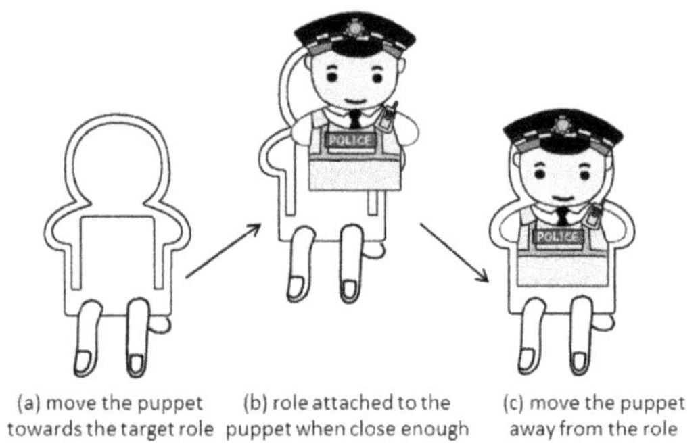

Figure 6. The action of role transformation

Emotion Transformation

Facial expression visual form We designed six facial expressions: five basic emotions (fear, surprise, happiness, anger, sadness) [9] and a neutral expression. The corresponding visual effects are seen in Fig.7.

Figure 7. The collection of facial expressions

Facial expression switch There are two important usability considerations for facial expression switching. First, the function should be easy to access, motivating children to explore this feature often in addition to other play objects. Second, the switch should be rapid to support fluency of story telling. We investigated several different expression switching methods, eventually adopting a wand-based approach (Fig.8). The user moves the wand towards the puppet to trigger an expression-switching mode. Alternative expressions are presented as a radial menu around the puppet. The user points the wand at the desired expression, then moves the wand away from the puppet to dismiss the radial menu.

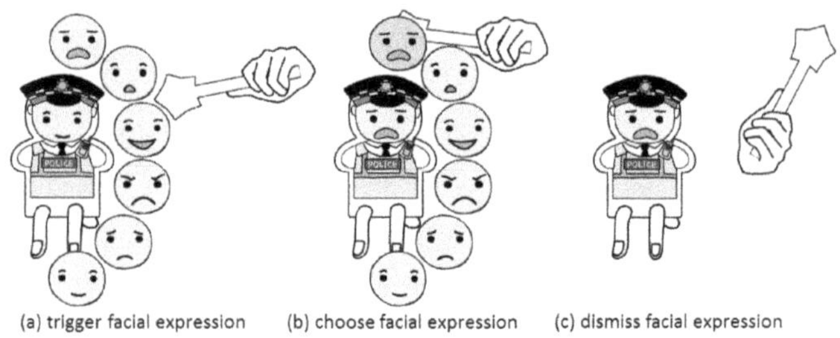

Figure 8. Action flow of wand-based switch

SYSTEM IMPLEMENTATION

We developed the FingAR Puppet system based on several open source libraries including the Microsoft XNA Game Studio 4.0 (system framework), GoblinXNA 4.1 (AR registration and rendering), ALVAR2.0 (marker tracking) and Emgu CV2.4 (image processing). We created the 3D role models from 2D images because: (1) a 2D image is easy to generate and it potentially enables user authoring in the future; and (2) the shadow details produced by the 3D model enrich the visual illustration of the role and facial expression. We implemented a "rise up" 3D effect similar to baking cookies which involved three major steps (Fig.9): (1) generate a distance transform image [26] of the original 2D image; (2) create the 3D mesh model based on the distance transform image; (3) map the original image as texture to the 3D mesh.

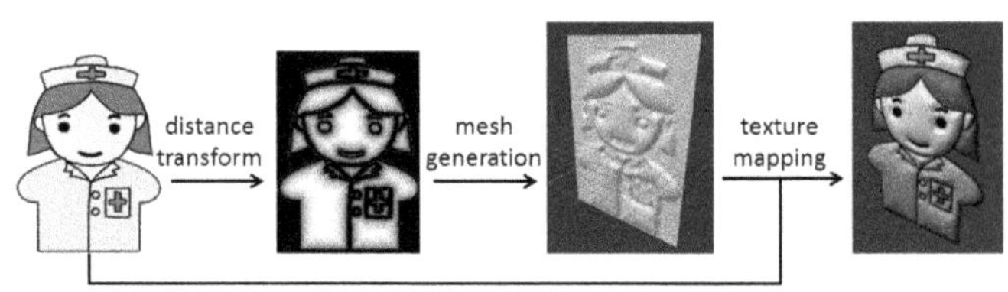

Figure 9. Implementation pipeline of the "rise up" 3D effect.

EXPERIMENT DESIGN

We designed an experiment to evaluate the effectiveness of the FingAR Puppet system in promoting reasoning about emotional states, verbal communication of shared pretense and divergent thinking. There are three null hypotheses in respect of the first three aspects:

H_{0A}: There is no significant difference in the frequency of emotional state expression between conditions with facial expression switching disabled and enabled.

H_{0B}: There is no significant difference in the frequency of causal elaboration of emotional state between conditions with facial expression switching disabled and enabled.

H_{0C}: There is no significant difference in the percentage of explicit verbal communication per object transformation between scenery selection period and role and prop selection periods.

Method

Each pair of participants interacted with the FingAR Puppet system in two conditions: facial expression switching disabled (Face_Switch_OFF) and enabled (Face_Switch_ON). This within-subjects design helped to avoid individual differences on social pretend play behaviours. The condition order was counterbalanced in order to eliminate learning and novelty effects. In both conditions participants were asked to make stories with the system for 15 minutes.

Participants

Fourteen participants from 48 to 74 months ($M = 63.00$, $SD = 8.79$) were recruited from a local primary school, eight girls and six boys. All parents of the participants signed a consent form and provided basic information about their child. Teachers paired participants into seven groups based on familiarity with each other (three mixed-gender groups, two girl-only groups and one boy-only group). Three participants used computer devices on a daily basis, and all others at least once a week. The verbal mental age of participants was from 58 to 77 months ($M = 67.14$, $SD = 7.23$) based on the British Picture Vocabulary Scale, 3rd edition. We did not record or select participants' ethnic background.

Apparatus and Data Collection

The study took place in a common room between the nursery and reception classes during normal school hours. The setup of the AR system included: (1) a Macintosh Laptop; (2) a 24-inch monitor; (3) a Logitech Webcam Pro 9000; (4) a 55*110*50cm table and (5) play materials (Fig.10 (a)). We used a video camera to record play behaviour during each session (Fig.10 (b)). Video footage from days two and three was transcribed into discrete play acts (by editing with Camtasia Studio), identifying all individual actions and speech acts.

Procedure

We conducted the experiment on three consecutive days with the support of three teaching assistants. On the first day, the experimenter taught all participants, one group at a time, how to use the AR system and let them explore the system freely for about 10 minutes. On the second day, the participants were asked to carry out play in pairs for 15 minutes in either the Face_Switch_OFF or Face_Switch_ON condition. At the beginning of each session, the experimenter gave identical instructions: "you are going to make a story together and you can play for 15 minutes." During the session, the experimenter and the teacher provided minimal prompts only when the participants were obviously not engaged in the play or had difficulty developing play ideas independently. After 15 minutes, the experimenter waited for the current play episode to finish and asked the participants to stop. The experimenter then went through a questionnaire with each participant. This procedure was repeated with the other experimental condition on the third day.

Measures

We adopted several measures from existing literature in early childhood development to design our coding scheme for emotional state [36], causal elaboration [7], and verbal communication on object transformation [12].

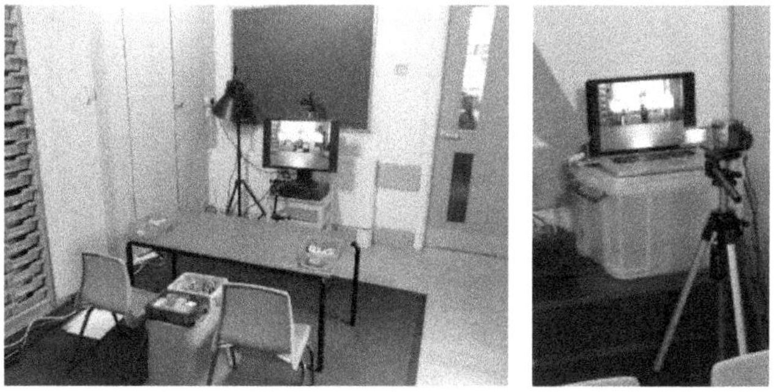

(a) interaction area (b) recording area

Figure 10. The experiment apparatus.

Emotional state Indicators of emotional states include: (1) verbal terms (e.g. happy, sad, angry, etc.); (2) behavioural terms (e.g. cry, kiss, hug, etc.); (3) tone of voice (e.g. angry voice). We counted the total number of emotional states that occurred within the play acts of each participant. If the same emotional state occurred more than once in the same play act, it was only counted once. If there was more than one different emotional state in the same play act, each one was counted independently. We divided the total number by the play time (minutes) in both conditions to calculate the frequency of emotional state occurrence. In order to make a rigid comparison between the two conditions, we excluded the facial expression switching action in the Face_Switch_ON condition from emotional state occurrence. The experimenter made the initial coding. We then randomly selected a 4-minute clip from each video (23% of the total video footage) and invited an independent rater who was not aware of the hypotheses to code the emotional state occurrence. The inter-subject agreement is highly satisfactory (Cohen's kappa = 0.98).

Causal elaboration of emotion Causal elaboration was identified as a pair of verbal or gestural play acts that revealed the cause and effect relationship of certain emotional states. Within the pair, at least one of the play acts contains emotional state. For example:

(1) child A said: "I'm *angry* now" [effect]
child B said: "because there are no customers" [cause]

(2) child A said to child B: "happy birthday" [cause]
child B made his puppet *kiss* child A's puppet and said: "thank you" [effect]

The causal elaboration could also be within one play act. For example:

(1) child A said "I'm *sad* [effect] because my dog went missing [cause]"

For each play act containing emotional state, we (1) checked if there was any causal elaboration within this play act; (2) checked all play acts 10 seconds before and after. We counted the total number of causal elaborations and divided by the play time of each group to calculate the frequency of cause elaboration. The experimenter made the initial coding, with two independent raters as before. The results demonstrated a high inter-subject agreement (average Cohen's kappa = 0.92).

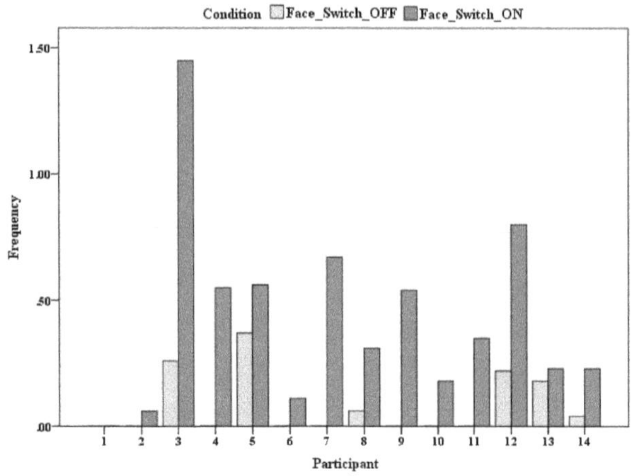

(a) Frequency of emotional state for each participant

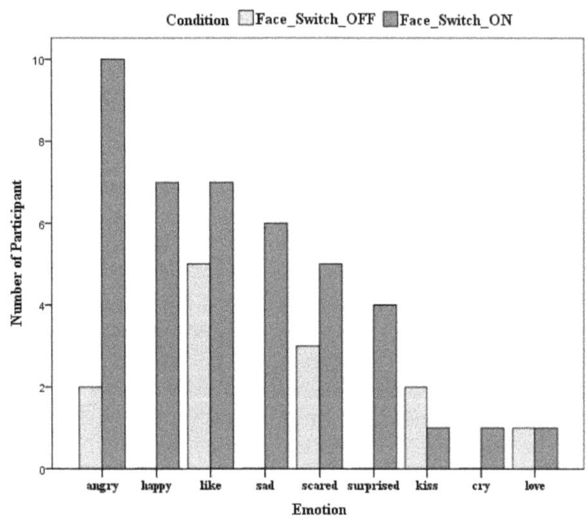

(b) Number of participants using each emotion term

Figure 11. Results of emotional states.

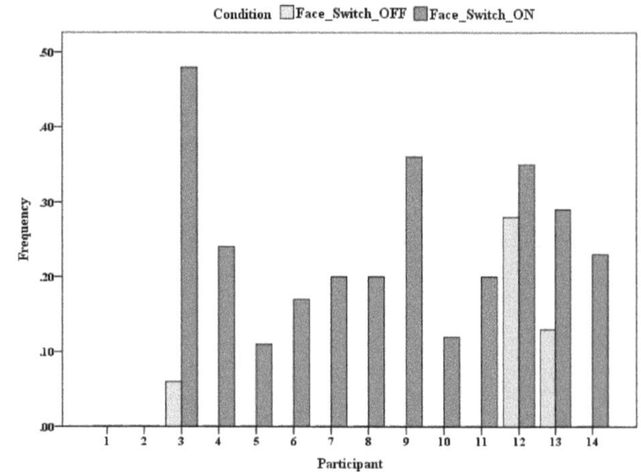

(a) Frequency of causal elaboration for each participant

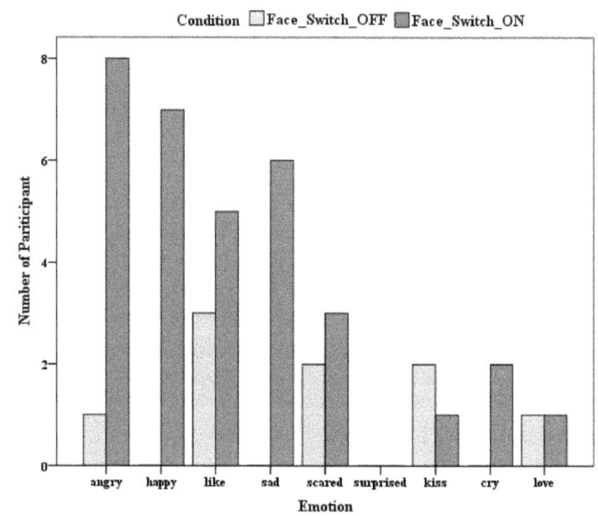

(b) Number of participants explaining each emotion term

Figure 12. Results of causal elaboration of emotion.

Verbal communication on object transformation We calculated the percentage of object transformations with explicit verbal communications during the role and prop selection period and scenery selection period. The coding steps were: (1) extracted the selection zones, which began with entering role/prop/scenery selection view and ended when exiting the selection view; (2) counted the total number of selection actions within all selection zones, and (3) counted the total number of explicit verbal communications that clarify the target of object transformation (e.g. "I'm a knight", "grass"); (4) calculated the percentage of selection actions associated with explicit verbal transformation communications.

RESULTS

Emotional States

The frequency of emotional state occurrence per participant increased in the Face_Switch_ON condition (*Mean* = 0.43, *SD* = 0.37) relative to the Face_Switch_OFF condition (*Mean* = 0.08, *SD* = 0.12). The frequency of occurrence for each participant is illustrated in Fig.11(a). The trend of individual difference is statistically significant according to the paired Wilcoxon signed-rank test ($Z = -3.18$, $p < 0.01$). The order of participants follows the group order (e.g. participant 1 (P1) and participant 2 (P2) were in group 1). All participants produced play acts involving emotional state more frequently in the Face_Switch_ON condition except for P1, who didn't generate any emotional state related play behaviour in either condition. We summarized the number of participants using each emotion term (Fig.11(b)). Besides the five non-neutral facial expressions provided by the system, other emotional terms used by the participants included like, kiss, cry and love.

Causal Elaboration of Emotion

The frequency of causal elaborations per participant was higher in the Face_Switch_ON condition (*Mean* = 0.21, *SD* = 0.13) than the Face_Switch_OFF condition (*Mean* = *0.03*, *SD* = 0.07). The difference is statistically significant according to the paired Wilcoxon signed-rank test ($Z = -3.06$, $p < 0.01$).

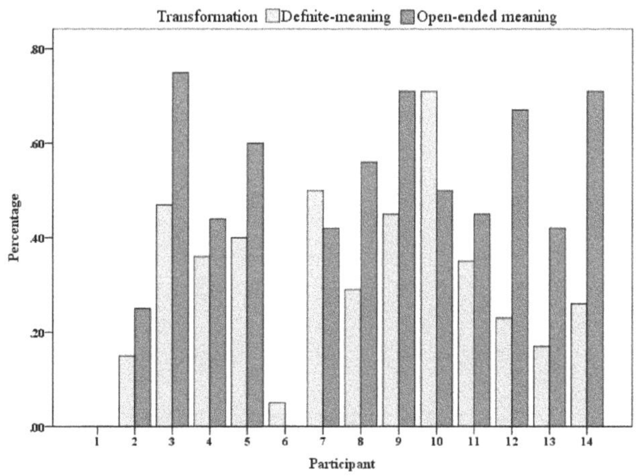

Figure 13. Percentage of verbal communication on transformation per participant.

Fig.12(a) illustrates the frequency of causal elaboration generated by each participant. There were only three participants that made some causal elaboration in the Face_Switch_OFF condition while there were twelve participants that produced causal elaboration in the Face_Switch_ON condition. We summarized the number of participants that produced play acts involving causal elaboration of different emotion terms (Fig.12(b)). It followed a similar trend as the number of participants that produced play acts involving emotional states, except no participant managed to produce any causal elaborations relating to the emotion term "surprised". The implications of the results will be explained in the discussion session.

Verbal Communication on Transformation

Participants made more verbal communications on object transformation when choosing from open-ended representations in the scenery selection period ($Mean = 0.46$, $SD = 0.24$) than the definite-meaning in the role and prop selection period ($Mean = 0.31$, $SD = 0.19$). The difference is statistically significant according to the paired Wilcoxon signed-ranks test ($Z = -2.45$, $p < 0.05$) (Fig.13). Participants carried out diverse scenery transformations. Table 1 shows representative examples of scenery transformation based on verbal reports.

Child Questionnaire

The FingAR Puppet system offered a positive user experience – the majority of participants rated the play experience as 'brilliant' in both conditions (10/14 in Face_Switch_ON and 8/14 in Face_Switch_OFF condition). When asked which play variant was more fun, all participants named the condition with facial expression switching enabled. Some representative explanations were: "it can be sad, happy, that helps to create the story", "when the character sees a shark I can change it to shocked", "when it's just one face, when you're angry you cannot change the face". Participants also confirmed that the interaction structure helped create stories: "pick character, second part (prop) whatever you want, next you choose floor, setting", "when change people, you make different story . . . like change the setting".

Table 1. Examples of scenery transformation.

	Circle	Semi-circle	Sawtooth
Green	grass, flower	grass	grass,park*
Red	fire	fire	fire
Green-red	flower		flower
Blue	swimming pool, water, sea, blue sky, big lake (with two circles combined)*		blue sky, water
White	ice rink, snow, water	snow, mountain	snow, iceberg
Brick	castle		castle
Black-white	racing flag, floor, cafe*, shield*, nurse house*		
Rock			
Golden	pancake, gold water*		
Purple		diamond	
Wood		path	
Black	black hole*		

* Symbolic ideas verbally explained in the latter play session

DISCUSSION

Emotion Expression and Understanding

These results demonstrate that the FingAR Puppet system effectively encourages children to express and understand emotion in a social play context (rejecting null hypotheses H_{0A} and H_{0B}). When the facial expression switching was enabled, users not only produced more play acts relating to emotional states, but also explained the cause and effect relationship of emotion more frequently, providing opportunities for them to reason about and respond to emotion change. Overall, participants were more likely to be emotionally aware and expressive during social pretend play when given the ability to switch the facial expression of the puppet.

The emotion terms most often used in the play explanations (Fig.11(b)) can be classified as desire-based (angry, happy, like, sad), or belief-based (scared and surprised) [27]. Understanding desire-based emotions occurs as early as two years old, while the ability to interpret people's beliefs is typically not achieved until about four years old. Our results confirm that participants were more likely to express desire-based than belief-based emotions, which corroborates the existing literature. No participants gave explanations of "surprise" confirming previous findings that children take longer to understand the complex belief-based nature of surprise [19].

Verbal Communication of Transformation

Results show that participants verbally explained their object transformation decisions during role, prop and scenery selection. Participants made more verbal explanations in relation to the open-ended representations of the scenery selection period, rather than the definite-meaning representations of the role and prop selection period. This supported our hypothesis (rejecting null hypotheses H_{0C}) that participants tend to assure both themselves and their playmates about the transformation they made by verbally clarifying the target object of the transformation when associating an open-ended representation to the physical referent.

Diverse Scenery Transformation
The result that participants generated diverse imaginary representations associated with the shapes in the scenery selection period corroborate previous research findings that open-ended tasks are effective in promoting divergent thinking [29]. We observed that participants tended to generate more imaginary representations with familiar than less familiar scenery materials. For example many participants created grass, water and flowers by assigning green, blue and green-red materials to shapes respectively. It was, however, rare to see participants creating imaginary representations beyond these obvious associations. Furthermore, participants tended to generate more novel imaginary representations with less familiar materials. For example, they created diamonds and black holes using purple and black materials respectively. They were also more likely to interpret the same AR scenery objects differently with less familiar materials. For example, by assigning the black and white material to the circle referent, participants generated different imaginary representations such as racing flag, floor, cafe, shield, and nurse house. The above observations were well explained by the theory that familiar stimuli facilitate fluency of divergent thinking while unfamiliar stimuli support originality of divergent thinking. The observations also corroborate with recent findings that allowing users to customize play scenes enriches creativity and communication in shared play activities, from a study investigating creative play between co-located users via video mediated communication [15].

Usability
Usability is a challenge in AR systems for children due to their limited cognitive and motor abilities [25]. Nevertheless, we observed that all our participants were able to interact with the FingAR Puppet system in terms of object manipulation, selection and facial expression change.

Object Manipulation
All participants manipulated the physical puppet properly by putting their fingers through the two holes on the bottom of the puppet, and acted with the puppet by moving the "legs" around. Only one participant tried to make the puppet stand on its own. For props and scenes, participants held them either with the attached grip or the body. The latter sometimes caused occlusion of the marker.

Selection
All participants understood the point-to-select mechanism for role, prop and scenery, and used the wand to choose control buttons. However, we noticed two issues with selection in the preparation phase. The first was that participants occasionally mismatched object types, for example using the prop representation object to choose scenery. Although this was infrequent, a simplified selection mechanism could be explored in future. The second issue was that some younger participants reached out towards the screen when choosing role, prop or scenery items, rather than using the world coordinate system "reflected" by the magic mirror (Fig.14).

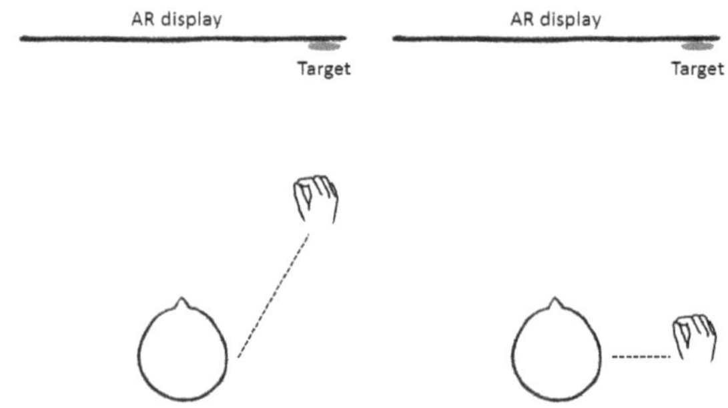

(a) Reaching towards the screen (b) Parallel with the screen

Figure 14. Illustration of participant's point-to-select behaviours using the screen as the coordinate system.

Facial Expression Change
Participants understood how to use the wand to change facial expressions. Nevertheless, this was more difficult than other actions in the FingAR Puppet system. This can be explained by the demands of bimanual manipulation. According to the kinematic chain model [13], the non-dominant hand often sets a spatial frame of reference within which the dominant hand orients fine temporal and spatial movements (e.g. in handwriting or sewing). Since participants held the puppet with their dominant hand, this meant that they had to position the wand with their non-dominant hand.

Study Limitations
There are three limitations to be aware of when interpreting these results. First, although participants produced play acts with emotional states more frequently in the Face_Switch_ON condition, these emotional states were mostly desire-based, meaning that the FingAR Puppet system may be more limited in social pretend play for complex emotions. Second, the study only examined children interacting in pairs. The limited size of the interactive space and the side-by-side seating arrangement using the AR magic mirror might become an issue with more objects or additional players. Third, this was a short-term experiment with a small sample. Although the familiarisation session on the first day was meant to eliminate learning and novelty effects, a longer-term study would be required to explore more complex emotional states and creative symbolic transformations.

Future Work
As discussed, we hope to extend our explorations into longer-term development of social-emotional knowledge, and more complex emotions such as surprise, embarrassment and pride that are especially relevant to older age groups. We would like to examine potential benefits of the FingAR Puppet system for children with autism, who often lack imaginative and social interaction skills. We would also like to observe children's different social symbolic play behaviours between using the FingAR Puppet system and in an equivalent natural play setting without computer assistance, in order to further our knowledge of the strengths and weaknesses of AR technologies in play contexts.

CONCLUSION

We presented the theoretical grounding, design and evaluation of the FingAR Puppet system, which is intended to provide an enhanced social pretend play experience for preschool children. Observations show that children are highly engaged with the FingAR puppet system. Experiment results confirm that (1) AR technology can effectively externalize the cognitive process of pretense by enabling children to transform physical referents to pretense ideas; (2) facial expression switching can encourage children to express and understand emotion in stories; and (3) open-ended representations encourage children to create diverse symbolic transformations, and to more actively communicate such ideas with a playmate as joint pretense.

This study opens an interesting space for future AR systems to support users to augment the real world with their expressive interpretation, in addition to perceiving informative augmentations that help users to obtain reality-based knowledge. Such expressive interpretations are intended to be open-ended and interpersonal, thus in turn may help reinforce key cognitive processes that shape peoples thinking pattern. Compared with technologies isolated from the immediate reality, AR helps bridge experience between computer-assisted and real life scenarios. This is especially beneficial for young children who are more capable to apply skills to situations with high perceptual similarity.

Beyond the immediate application encouraging childhood development of social pretend play, this study also points to broader implications for tangible and augmented interaction, introducing a cognitive development perspective to earlier work. The spread of ubiquitous and pervasive computing means that novel interactive systems are rapidly being deployed throughout the home and school environments in which children spend their early childhood years. New technologies have always modified the behaviours of the physical world, and past evidence is that cognitive development in early childhood is easily able to accommodate these environmental changes. However, at the same time, the embedding of digital infrastructure into our physical environment is extending the range of information media in our culture. Media literacy is increasingly delivered, not only by image, text, sound and screen, but through the novel behaviours of augmented "smart" objects.

The cognitive development perspective introduced in this paper has drawn attention to ways in which children in early-years education develop core cognitive skills in their interpretation and appropriation of augmented tangible objects. This is complementary to other ways in which the HCI community has extended its understanding of ubiquitous and pervasive interaction through turns to the social, and to embodiment, when theorising digitally augmented environments [6]. Furthermore, cognitive development is a complementary perspective to the more established computational analyses of distributed cognition and representation, by which we understand adult literacy and usability of tangible interaction [8].

During the study, children jointly produced diverse imaginary interpretations of their physical environment, encouraged by the open-ended representations of FingAR, apparently exercising the cognitive skills of theory of mind and divergent thinking. These skills lead to social and creative competence in adulthood. Deficits in these skills also have key roles in some developmental disorders, leading to inability to engage in social pretend play during childhood, and subsequent disadvantages in adult life. Although we have previously explored the use of augmented mirrors as a therapeutic aid for children with those disorders [2], in this study we have explored the ways in which new styles of literacy and competence are likely to be developed by typical children within future ubiquitous and pervasive computing environments. Our theoretically-grounded exploration of children's experience, building on prior work in developmental neuroscience and early-years education, can help to inform future understanding of the changing patterns of cognition within a culture of physically pervasive digital media [14].

ACKNOWLEDGEMENTS

We would like to thank Cambridge Overseas Trust for sponsoring this research project. We would also like to thank all psychology experts, school teachers and participants families for taking part in the study and providing insightful feedback.

REFERENCES

1. R. T. Azuma et al. A survey of augmented reality. *Presence*, 6(4):355–385, 1997.
2. Z. Bai, A. F. Blackwell, and G. Coulouris. Through the looking glass: Pretend play for children with autism. In *Mixed and Augmented Reality (ISMAR), 2013 IEEE International Symposium on*, pages 49–58. IEEE, 2013.
3. C. Barnes, D. E. Jacobs, J. Sanders, D. B. Goldman, S. Rusinkiewicz, A. Finkelstein, and M. Agrawala. Video puppetry: a performative interface for cutout animation. In *ACM Transactions on Graphics (TOG)*, volume 27, page 124. ACM, 2008.
4. A. L. Brown and M. J. Kane. Preschool children can learn to transfer: Learning to learn and learning from example. *Cognitive Psychology*, 20(4):493–523, 1988.
5. K. Coolahan, J. Fantuzzo, J. Mendez, and P. McDermott. Preschool peer interactions and readiness to learn: Relationships between classroom peer play and learning behaviors and conduct. *Journal of Educational Psychology*, 92(3):458, 2000.
6. P. Dourish. *Where the action is: the foundations of embodied interaction*. MIT press, 2004.
7. J. Dunn, J. Brown, C. Slomkowski, C. Tesla, and L. Youngblade. Young children's understanding of other people's feelings and beliefs: Individual differences and their antecedents. *Child development*, 62(6):1352–1366, 1991.
8. D. Edge, A. Blackwell, and L. Dubuc. The physical world as an abstract interface. *Contemporary Ergonomics*, pages 224–228, 2006.
9. P. Ekman. An argument for basic emotions. *Cognition & Emotion*, 6(3-4):169–200, 1992.

10. W. Farr, N. Yuill, and S. Hinske. An augmented toy and social interaction in children with autism. *International Journal of Arts and Technology*, 5(2):104–125, 2012.
11. G. G. Fein. Pretend play in childhood: An integrative review. *Child development*, pages 1095–1118, 1981.
12. C. Garvey and R. Berndt. The organization of pretend play. 1975.
13. Y. Guiard. Asymmetric division of labor in human skilled bimanual action: The kinematic chain as a model. *Journal of motor behavior*, 19(4):486–517, 1987.
14. N. K. Hayles. *How we think: Digital media and contemporary technogenesis*. University of Chicago Press, 2012.
15. S. E. Hunter, P. Maes, A. Tang, K. M. Inkpen, and S. M. Hessey. Waazam!: supporting creative play at a distance in customized video environments. In *Proceedings of the 32nd annual ACM conference on Human factors in computing systems*, pages 1197–1206. ACM, 2014.
16. A. M. Leslie. Pretense and representation: The origins of" theory of mind.". *Psychological review*, 94(4):412, 1987.
17. A. Lillard. Pretend play as twin earth: A social-cognitive analysis. *Developmental Review*, 21(4):495–531, 2001.
18. F. Lu, F. Tian, Y. Jiang, X. Cao, W. Luo, G. Li, X. Zhang, G. Dai, and H. Wang. Shadowstory: creative and collaborative digital storytelling inspired by cultural heritage. In *Proceedings of the SIGCHI Conference on Human Factors in Computing Systems*, pages 1919–1928. ACM, 2011.
19. R. MacLaren and D. Olson. Trick or treat: Children's understanding of surprise. *Cognitive development*, 8(1):27–46, 1993.
20. P. Maes, T. Darrell, B. Blumberg, and A. Pentland. The alive system: Wireless, full-body interaction with autonomous agents. *Multimedia Systems*, 5(2):105–112, 1997.
21. P. Marshall, Y. Rogers, and M. Scaife. Puppet: a virtual environment for children to act and direct interactive narratives. In *2nd international workshop on narrative and interactive learning environments*, pages 8–15, 2002.
22. M. Nitsche and S. Nayak. Cell phone puppets: turning mobile phones into performing objects. In *Entertainment Computing-ICEC 2012*, pages 363–372. Springer, 2012.
23. J. Piaget. *Play, dreams and imitation in childhood*, volume 25. Routledge, 2013.
24. D. Premack and G. Woodruff. Does the chimpanzee have a theory of mind? *Behavioral and brain sciences*, 1(04):515–526, 1978.
25. I. Radu and B. MacIntyre. Using children's developmental psychology to guide augmented-reality design and usability. In *Mixed and Augmented Reality (ISMAR), 2012 IEEE International Symposium on*, pages 227–236. IEEE, 2012.
26. A. Rosenfeld and J. L. Pfaltz. Sequential operations in digital picture processing. *Journal of the ACM (JACM)*, 13(4):471–494, 1966.
27. T. Ruffman and T. R. Keenan. The belief-based emotion of suprise: The case for a lag in understanding relative to false belief. *Developmental Psychology*, 32(1):40, 1996.
28. M. A. Runco. *Divergent thinking*. Ablex Publishing, 1991.
29. M. A. Runco and R. S. Albert. The reliability and validity of ideational originality in the divergent thinking of academically gifted and nongifted children. *Educational and Psychological Measurement*, 45(3):483–501, 1985.
30. S. W. Russ. Play, creativity, and adaptive functioning: Implications for play interventions. *Journal of Clinical Child Psychology*, 27(4):469–480, 1998.
31. K. Ryokai and J. Cassell. Computer support for children's collaborative fantasy play and storytelling. In *Proceedings of the 1999 conference on Computer support for collaborative learning*, page 63. International Society of the Learning Sciences, 1999.
32. K. Ryokai, H. Raffle, and R. Kowalski. Storyfaces: pretend-play with ebooks to support social-emotional storytelling. In *Proceedings of the 11th International Conference on Interaction Design and Children*, pages 125–133. ACM, 2012.
33. R. K. Sawyer. Levels of analysis in pretend play discourse: Metacommunication in conversational routines. *PLAY AND CULTURE STUDIES*, 5:137–158, 2003.
34. B. Shneiderman. Direct manipulation: a step beyond programming languages. *Sparks of Innovation in Human-Computer Interaction*, 17, 1993.
35. S. Smilansky. *The effects of sociodramatic play on disadvantaged preschool children*. Wiley New York, 1968.
36. H. Tager-Flusberg and K. Sullivan. Attributing mental states to story characters: A comparison of narratives produced by autistic and mentally retarded individuals. *Applied Psycholinguistics*, 16(03):241–256, 1995.
37. F. Zhou, H. B.-L. Duh, and M. Billinghurst. Trends in augmented reality tracking, interaction and display: A review of ten years of ismar. In *Proceedings of the 7th IEEE/ACM International Symposium on Mixed and Augmented Reality*, pages 193–202. IEEE Computer Society, 2008.
38. Z. Zhou, A. D. Cheok, J. Tedjokusumo, and G. S. Omer. wizqubestm–a novel tangible interface for interactive storytelling in mixed reality. *Int J Virtual Real*, 7(4):9–15, 2008.

Learning from Mixed-Reality Games: Is Shaking a Tablet as Effective as Physical Observation?

Nesra Yannier **Kenneth R. Koedinger** **Scott E. Hudson**
Human-Computer Interaction Institute
Carnegie Mellon University, 5000 Forbes Avenue, Pittsburgh PA 15213
{nyannier, krk, scott.hudson}@cs.cmu.edu

ABSTRACT
The possibility of leveraging technology to support children's learning in the real world is both appealing and technically challenging. We have been exploring factors in tangible games that may contribute to both learning and enjoyment with an eye toward technological feasibility and scalability. Previous research found that young children learned early physics principles better when interactively predicting and observing experimental comparisons on a physical earthquake table than when seeing a video of the same. Immersing children in the real world with computer vision-based feedback appears to evoke embodied cognition that enhances learning. In the current experiment, we replicated this intriguing result of the mere difference between observing the real world versus a flat-screen. Further, we explored whether a simple and scalable addition of physical control (such as shaking a tablet) would yield an increase in learning and enjoyment. Our 2x2 experiment found no evidence that adding simple forms of hands-on control enhances learning, while demonstrating a large impact of physical observation. A general implication for educational game design is that affording physical observation in the real world accompanied by real-time interactive feedback may be more important than affording simple hands-on control on a tablet.

Author Keywords
Tangible interfaces, Learning technologies, Educational games, Mixed-Reality environments.

ACM Classification Keywords
Human Factors

INTRODUCTION
As screen-based technologies such as tablets, computer games, and online videos are becoming increasingly more appealing for children, it is worth asking whether real world interaction is really needed to enhance learning or enjoyment.

CHI 2015, April 18–23, 2015, Seoul, Republic of Korea.

http://dx.doi.org/10.1145/2702123.2702397

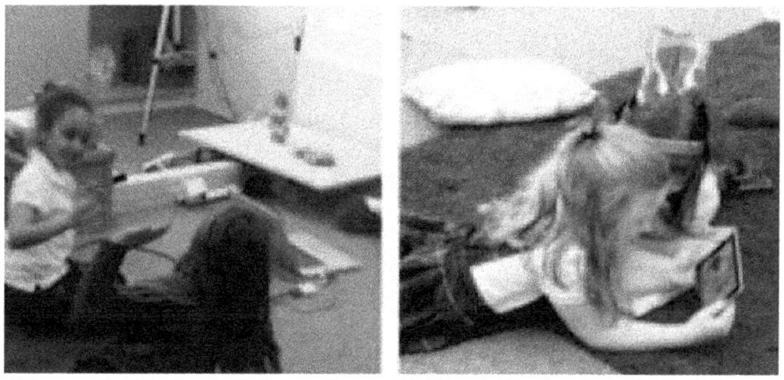

Figure 1. Students interacting with EarthShake (on the left is the mixed-reality version where children observe physical towers on the earthquake table with interactive feedback; on the right is the tablet version where they shake the tablet to shake the earthquake table on the screen)

There is little research investigating the potential advantages of real world interaction or what features may cause them [32].

Tangible interfaces and mixed-reality environments have the potential to bring together the advantages of physical and virtual worlds to enhance learning and enjoyment. Utilizing computer-vision technology to provide well-designed interactive feedback to children while they interact with physical objects in their everyday environment may be an engaging and powerful way to learn [30,17]. However one can question whether real world interaction is necessary, especially given that interactive responsiveness and feedback to real world actions is more difficult to implement. Since creating such affordances in the real world is technically challenging, it is tempting to hope that integrating easier-to-develop physical controls into a screen-based environment may improve enjoyment and learning just as well.

It is important to isolate the factors that are important for learning in mixed-reality environments. Is physical observation and experimentation with real physical objects critical to enhance learning or enjoyment? Or would it be sufficient to add simple forms of physical controls to a tablet game, such as shaking the tablet as an input? What kinds of features make tangible interfaces more enjoyable for children? What are the features that lead to more learning? We set out to address these questions and, more generally, to explore what role physical observation versus physical interaction/control plays in the learning process, especially for younger children.

Does Physical Interaction Aid Learning?

There is related research that has explored whether simple physical interaction has benefits for learning. In Montessori schools children are encouraged to play with physical items such as building blocks, shape puzzles and jigsaws in order to learn different skills. One review [15] claims that, young children have a strong attraction to sensory development apparatus and that they use physical materials with deep concentration for extended periods of time, as a result of which they advance in their critical thinking and ability to work collaboratively [15].

Piaget and Bruner showed that children had an easier time while solving problems when given concrete materials to work [5]. Locomotion can also aid children while categorizing and recalling in tasks of spatial imagery [22]. An experiment demonstrated that children were able to solve fraction problems by moving physical materials even though they were not able to solve the same problems on paper [14].

Theories of embodied cognition and situated learning have suggested that mind and body are deeply integrated in the process of producing learning and reasoning. Thought does not only happen in the mind; bodily activity can support cognition [11,18].

Nevertheless, research comparing learning from the virtual versus physical environment (without interactive feedback) has produced mixed results. 24 and 30 month olds were able to imitate the actions of an adult better after watching a live demonstration than after watching the same demonstration on TV immediately and after a 24 hour delay [10]. On the other hand, in a science learning task with fourth and fifth grade children, Klahr et al. [13] found no difference in learning from interacting with virtual objects versus physical objects. In an experiment with university students in the context of light and color, Olympiou and Zacharias also found no difference in learning from physical versus virtual interaction. However, a third condition, where students interacted with both physical and virtual materials sequentially, led to better learning from both the physical only and virtual only conditions [16]. This result suggests that physical and virtual interaction may have complementary benefits that may be combined in and further enhanced through the interactive support of a mixed-reality interface.

Mixed Reality Environments for Learning

Mixed-reality environments, including tangible interfaces, bring together the physical and virtual worlds by sensing physical interaction and providing interactive feedback [28]. They have the potential to aid learning by providing the benefits of interacting with the physical environment while leveraging computational power to give students personalized feedback and interactive instructional support.

There have been attempts to create tangible interfaces for learning. Some examples include a book with audio embedded on different pages [3], a constructive assembly system embedded with kinetic memory to record and play back physical motion [20]; a ball that displays information about acceleration [21] and a play-mat that captures stories [26]. However, most of these tangible interfaces were used for mere exploration in qualitative studies; they were not compared to a control to investigate the role of physicality.

There is some research that shows benefits for tangibles -- mostly immediate performance benefits rather than learning outcomes. Children solved puzzles more successfully when they used tangible puzzle pieces compared to a mouse [2]. A set of tangible objects provided children with a physical handle to reason about abstract sound concepts [4]. Problem solving and collaboration advantages were shown for a paper-based tangible user interface for educational simulations over mouse interaction [27]. Enhanced task performance, collaborative interactions, and sense of playfulness were demonstrated while using a tangible interface compared to a multi-touch interface [26]. Students remembered cause and effect relations in geography and climate better when they used a haptics-augmented environment compared to a solely virtual environment [29]. Rogers et al. came up with a conceptual framework for mixed reality environments, suggesting that novel mixes of physical and digital transforms facilitate exploration and reflection [24].

While these studies provide some evidence for the benefits of tangible interfaces and mixed-reality environments, there aren't enough controlled experiments that a) test whether these environments produce sustained learning benefits that yield better performance on later assessment and b) do so in comparison to simpler-to-develop and deploy flat-screen alternatives. Furthermore, these studies do not identify what it is that provides benefits for learning in these mixed-reality environments: Does observing physical phenomena play an important role for learning in an interactive setting or is it having physical/hands-on control that is critical to enhancing learning?

Factoring out the potential contributions to learning of physical observation versus physical control is not only of scientific interest (e.g., when can embodied cognition be evoked -- with or without physical activity), but is also of practical importance. Creating a system that supports one versus the other can involve substantial trade-offs in the cost of development.

Let us illustrate this factoring of physical observation versus interaction with some existing systems. In ListenReader [3], an electronically augmented paper-based book, does the hands-on action of turning pages provide any benefit? Or for BitBall [21], does the action of throwing the ball provide any learning benefits? Or is it more beneficial to observe a physical ball rather than a virtual ball on a flat-screen in order to learn the underlying principles of acceleration? To isolate the effects of each, we need randomized controlled experiments that factor out and control for these variables.

In a recent study, Yannier et al. showed that children observing physical towers in a mixed-reality game learned physics principles better and showed higher levels of enjoyment compared to students interacting with a solely virtual game on a laptop [30]. This result suggests that observing physical phenomena (along with mixed reality feedback on whether child predictions and physical results match) may enhance learning and enjoyment. But, is real world interaction necessary? Might adding simple forms of physical interaction to an easier-to-produce tablet game also increase learning and enjoyment? After all, it is intuitive to attribute potential benefits of tangible computing to physical interaction rather than physical observation.

Some argue that hands-on control and bodily movement may enhance engagement and learning [17]. These days we see a lot of games and applications on tablets for children where they move or shake the tablet to control the game. We present an experiment to investigate if adding such physical control would increase the enjoyment or learning or if observing physical phenomena is critical to enhance children's learning.

THEORETICAL BACKGROUND

The potential benefits of integrating physicality into an interactive game can be factored into the potential benefits of *observing physical phenomena* and *physical control/interaction*. Considering prior theoretical work, there are several explanations for the potential benefits of physicality. Below we discuss some possible explanations.

Benefits of experiencing physical phenomena

When children and adults learn or reason with abstract concepts, they often utilize mental simulations based on concrete motor-perceptual experiences [1]. During a physical interaction, neural patterns of brain activity are formed across modalities, integrated into a multimodal representation in memory. When such an experience is recalled from memory, the same neural patterns are reactivated with the multimodal representation [23]. For example, patterns of physically balancing the body give rise to neural patterns that are stored as a multimodal representation. This representation is activated when thinking about balance in abstract domains such as mathematics [1].

Experiencing physical phenomena in real life may help people perceive and mentally visualize the physical objects in 3D in their minds, make connections with objects they are familiar with, and as a result remember the concepts better. Yannier et al. showed that children used more meaningful gestures while explaining their predictions when they observed physical blocks in a mixed-reality game, compared to a screen-only version of the same game. This result suggests that children may be having more meaningful mental visualizations (demonstrated by the gestures they use) when they interact with 3D objects [30].

Having physical objects may trigger affordance for action, which in turn facilitates retrieval from memory. Research on embodiment has revealed that memory for actions (e.g. performing a command such as "open the book") is better than memory for the verbal description of the commands [8], suggesting that memory focuses on embodied information [9].

Research on baby media has shown that children learn vocabulary better from interacting with parents than watching matched videos, suggesting that very young children have difficulty understanding the relation between what they see on a screen and the real world [7]. In another line of research, Kahn et al. have found that in terms of heart-rate recovery from low-level stress, a glass window that afforded a view of a natural scene was more restorative than a plasma window that afforded a real-time HDTV view of essentially the same scene [12]. These studies provide evidence of cognitive benefits of observing scenes in the real world, compared to an on-screen counterpart.

Benefits of physical control/interaction

Physical interaction may further engage embodied cognition and enhance memory and learning beyond that achieved through mere physical observation [9]. In addition, having a physical control (such as shaking a tablet) in an interactive game may be inherently more engaging and enjoyable than interacting with the virtual game, which may in consequence enhance learning. This claim is supported by Montessori's theory that young children are highly engaged by sensory development apparatus [15]. There is also evidence that high engagement and enjoyment is linked positively with desirable learning outcomes such as critical thinking and grades [6].

Below we present an experiment where we have controlled for physical observation and a simple physical control in the context of an interactive game, to investigate the effect of each in turn for learning and enjoyment. We wanted to see if having a simple physical control would improve learning by producing higher enjoyment or if experiencing physical phenomena is more critical to develop deeper understanding.

EXPERIMENTAL METHOD

We conducted a 2x2 experiment, crossing mixed-reality vs. screen-only with the presence vs. absence of a simple hands-on/physical control. As outcomes, we measured enjoyment of the game and pretest to posttest learning gains, both on paper and through a hands-on task. This experiment examined EarthShake, a mixed reality game that helps children learn basic physics principles of stability and balance. In EarthShake, students make predictions about which tower will fall first when the earthquake table is shaken and then observe physical block towers with real time interactive feedback from the game [31]. The screen-only version of the game is displayed on a laptop, and includes matched videos of the physical towers shaking on the table. To investigate the effect of a physical control, we added a physical control to the mixed-reality game (children press a physical switch to shake the table) and implemented the screen-based game on a tablet with a physical control (children shake the tablet to shake the virtual table). We chose shaking the tablet and the physical switch conditions as alternatives to the screen and mixed-reality conditions in order to test if adding a potentially enjoyable experience via a physical/hands-on control would increase learning by increasing enjoyment. Observing that children loved pressing the physical switch during our pilots, we thought that giving them the physical switch might increase enjoyment (similar to how shaking a tablet might be enjoyable through a physical input experience) and in turn allow us to test if physical interaction improves learning by increasing enjoyment.

All participants interacted with the game in pairs, since no difference for learning or enjoyment was found for solo and pair conditions in a previous experiment [30].

Participants

Ninety-two 6-8 year old children (43 pairs and two groups of 3) participated. There were 22, 40, and 30 from Grades K to 2, respectively. Children were recruited from two different schools with students from mixed backgrounds with a high percentage from low-income communities. The teachers in the classroom randomly selected the pairs.

Materials

To conduct the experiment, we developed the materials and technologies to be used in the 4 different conditions: 1) mixed-reality version of EarthShake with mouse control; 2) mixed-reality version of EarthShake with physical control (pressing a physical button as input); 3) Screen-only laptop version of EarthShake with mouse control; 4) Screen-only tablet version of EarthShake with physical control (shaking the tablet as input). We discuss each in turn below.

1) Mixed-reality version of EarthShake with Mouse Control

EarthShake consists of an earthquake table, physical towers and a projected game synchronized with the real world via Kinect depth camera sensing and a specialized computer vision algorithm [31] (Figure 2). EarthShake teaches with a predict/observe/explain cycle. The game starts with the gorilla character asking students to make a prediction about which of two physical towers will fall first when he shakes the table under them [31]. The users can see the physical towers on the real earthquake table and the virtual representation (detected by our vision algorithm) of the towers in the projected interface of the game behind the table at the same time (Figure 1 left). To make a prediction, they can click on the tower (in the projected game) that they think will fall first using the mouse. The gorilla then tells the users to discuss with their partner why they think this tower will fall first. When they are done discussing, they can then click the shake button in the projected game using their mouse to shake the physical earthquake table (when

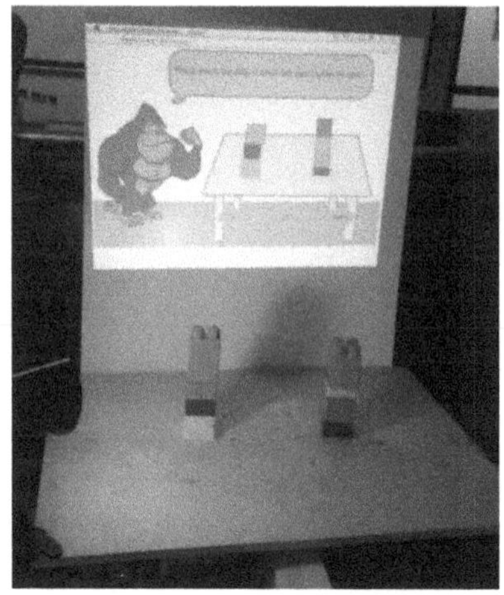

Figure 2. Mixed reality version of EarthShake. The projected game behind the towers is synchronized with the physical world via Kinect depth camera sensing.

they click the shake button on the screen, the experimenter activates the earthquake table with a switch). Once one of the towers falls down, the Kinect camera and computer vision algorithm determines the fall giving audio and visual feedback to the users. If the tower they had predicted falls first, the gorilla says: "Good job! Your hypothesis was right. Why do you think this tower fell first?" If they were wrong, he says: "Oh oh you were wrong! Why do you think this tower fell first?" This time they have to explain why this tower fell first by choosing one of the six multiple choice answers projected on the screen. The multiple menu consists of the following choices: "Because it is smaller", "Because it is taller", "Because it has more weight on top than bottom", "Because it has a wider base", "Because it is not symmetrical", "Because it has a thinner base" (Figure 5). This scenario is repeated for different contrasting cases targeting height, wide base, symmetry and center of mass principles (Figure 3).

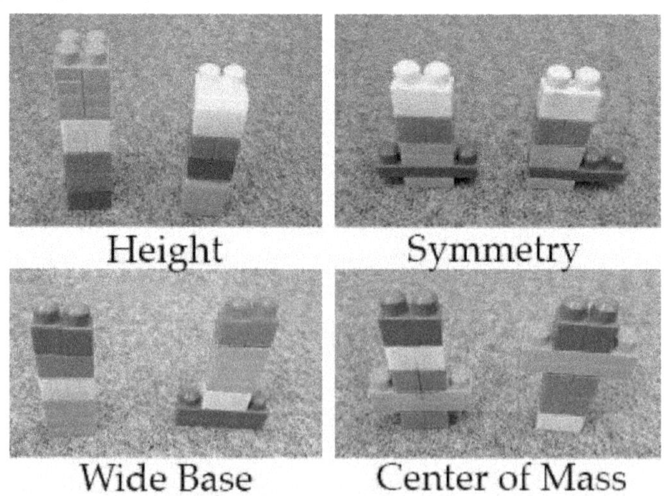

Figure 3. Contrasting cases used during the game.

During the experiment, children are asked to take turns using the mouse to select the towers and shake the table.

2) Mixed-reality version of EarthShake with Physical Control

For the second condition (mixed-reality & physical control) the same scenario as in the first condition was used. The only difference was that, children were given the physical control (a physical switch connected wirelessly to the earthquake table) to shake the table (See Figure 4).

Figure 4. Students interacting with the mixed-reality version of EarthShake with physical-control. They use a physical switch to shake the table.

In this condition, one of the children participating in the study was asked to have the physical switch to shake the table, while the other one was asked to have the mouse to control the game. They were asked to take turns to use the physical switch and the mouse. Everything else other than the control with the physical switch was kept the same as the first condition.

The switch was connected wirelessly to the motor that was used in the mechanism to drive the motion of the earthquake table. Two wireless switches (one for the participants, one for the experimenter) were connected in series, so that if one of the switches was turned off the motor would stop working. The experimenter wirelessly disabled the children's switch when it was not time to shake the table.

3) Screen-only version of EarthShake with Mouse Control

In the Laptop version of EarthShake, the same interface of the game that was projected on the screen in the mixed-reality game was used. Instead of having the live projections of the real towers, a video of the towers shaking was integrated into the interface (Figure 6). The characters, the scenario and the button controls were all kept the same as in the projected game in Condition 1 & 2. All of the game interactions were kept the same, except that pressing the "shake button" on the screen (as in Condition 1) would start the video of the table shaking instead of having the students observe the physical earthquake table.

The participants used a mouse connected to the laptop to control the game on the screen. The partners were asked to take turns using the mouse to select and shake the table during the game.

Figure 5. The scenario of the game utilizing a predict/observe/explain cycle. The video of the physical towers shaking on the earthquake table is integrated into the game interface for the screen-only conditions.

Figure 6. Laptop version of EarthShake

4) Screen-only tablet version of EarthShake with Physical Control

The tablet version of EarthShake used the same game interface as the mixed-reality and the laptop versions. Again, as in Condition 3, a video of the towers was integrated into the interface. The characters, the scenario and the button controls were all kept the same as in the projected game in Condition 1, 2 & 3. The only difference was that this time in order to shake the table, they had to shake the tablet with their hands instead of pressing the shake button as in Condition 2. Shaking the tablet would start the video of the towers shaking on the table (Figure 1 right).

In the tablet version, the partners were asked to sit on the floor next to each other in a position where both of them would be able to see the screen of the tablet. They were asked to take turns shaking the tablet and clicking the selection choices on the screen.

Measures

We measure learning with paper-based assessments and a tower construction task, using isometric pre- and post-tests. These tests were based on the NRC Framework & Asset Science Curriculum [19]. There were two different types of items included in the tests: prediction items and explanation items. First, the students were given a picture of a table with two towers on top of it and were asked to predict which tower would fall first when the table shakes by circling one of the options (Figure 7 left). Next, they were asked to explain why they chose this answer (Figure 7 right) by writing their explanation (the experimenter helped them if they had a hard time writing).

Figure 7. Examples of prediction (left) and explanation (right) items used in the paper pre/posttests.

We also used a tower pre/post test, where students built a tower given a limited number of blocks and a certain block as the base (See Figure 8). This task was the same for all the conditions, and was used as a transfer measure, to see how much their towers improved after interacting with the game.

After interacting with the game students were also given a survey to measure enjoyment. In this survey they were asked three questions as a measure of how much they enjoyed the game: "How much did you like the game?", "Would you like to play it again?" and "Would you recommend it to a friend?" For each of these questions they had to choose an answer of a 1-5 scale demonstrated with smileys (See Figure 9).

Figure 8. Children building their own towers before and after interacting with the game.

A fourth question asked "How much did you like building your tower and testing it on the earthquake table?", which was a measure of how much they enjoyed building their own towers during the tower pre/post tests.

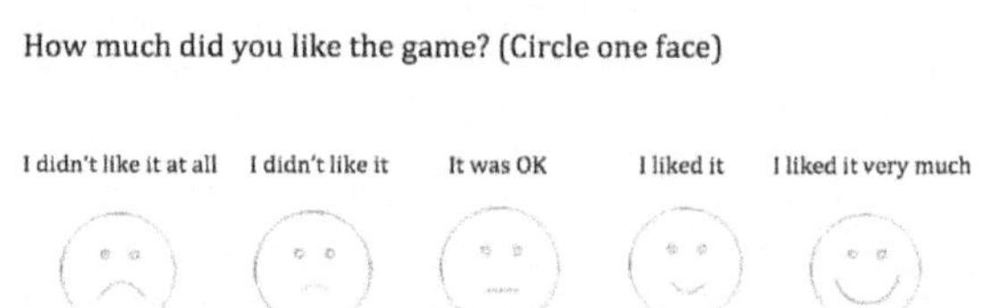

Figure 9. Example survey question measuring enjoyment.

Procedure

During the experiment, students were first given a paper pretest to see how much they already knew about the stability and balance principles introduced in the game. Then they were given a tower pretest, where they were asked by the experimenter to build a tower that would not fall down when the table shakes, using all the blocks in the provided set of blocks, and a certain block (2 by 2 square block) as the base of the tower. Then they shook the table to see if their tower would stay up. After that, they interacted with the EarthShake activity (mixed-reality or screen-only version depending on the condition they were in), which included 10 contrasting cases (Figure 3). After interacting with EarthShake, they were given the tower posttest where they were asked to build a tower again using the same rules as before. This tower was used as a measure to see if/how their towers had improved after interacting with the game. After the tower posttest, they were given a paper posttest to see how much they had learned on paper. At the end, they were given a survey as a measure of enjoyment from the game and the building activity (Figure 9). The experimenter also did a brief interview with them at the end to see what they liked/disliked about the activities and if they had any suggestions to improve the game. The same procedure was used for all 4 conditions: mixed-reality vs. screen-only crossed with physical vs. mouse control. The role of the experimenter was the same for all conditions.

RESULTS

We analyzed our paper pre and posttests, tower pre and posttests as well as the surveys that were given at the end of the game, in order to see the effects of observing physical phenomena in a mixed-reality game setting and physical control on learning and engagement.

Paper pre/post tests

A 2-way ANOVA analysis with overall pre-test score as the outcome variable confirmed no differences between the conditions at pretest (F's < .46 and p's > 0.50). To check for learning benefits, a 2-way ANCOVA was conducted with between-participant factors of control-type (mouse-control or physical control) and media-type (mixed-reality or screen-only), with pre-test score as a covariate and post-test as the outcome variable. The overall results (including both the prediction and explanation items) indicated that there was a significant effect of media-type ($F(1,91)=8.2$, $p<0.01$, $d=0.37$). The overall improvement from pre to post was 11.3 % in the mixed-reality conditions and 2.4 % in the virtual conditions. Thus, the mixed-reality game improved learning by 4.8 times compared to the screen-only alternatives. The average score on the posttests (both the prediction and explanation items) was 45% across the mixed-reality conditions and 39% across the virtual conditions. There was no effect of control type and no interaction effects. These results show that mixed-reality led to more learning than screen only, for both the mouse-control and physical-control conditions (Figure 10).

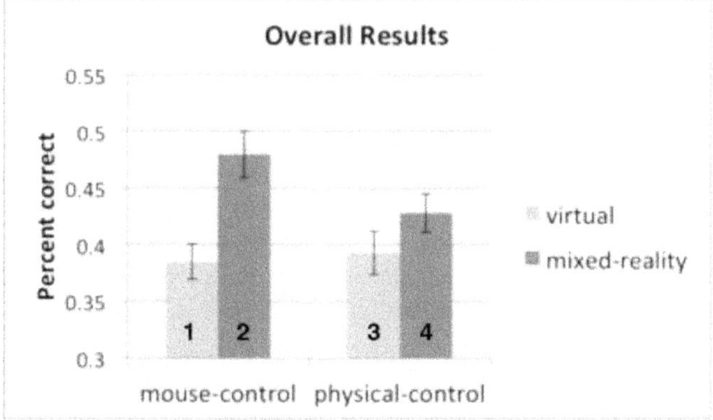

Figure 10. Overall results.

We can consider what choice improves learning most over a typical virtual, mouse-control game (#1 in Figure 10). The mixed-reality, mouse-control condition (#2) is significantly better ($p<0.05$), but the virtual, physical-control condition (#3) is not. In other words, facilitating physical observation was more powerful than facilitating physical control through shaking the tablet.

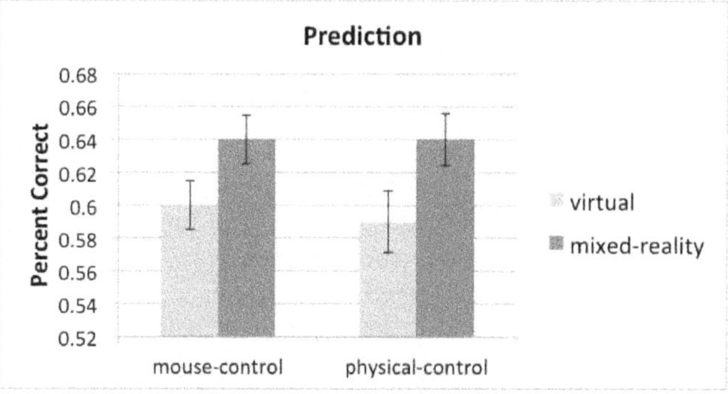

Figure 11. Percent correct for Prediction Items

Considering only the prediction items, there were again significant positive effects of the mixed-reality interface. The average of the mixed-reality condition for posttests was 64% while the average of the virtual condition was 60%. The improvement from pre to post for the prediction items was 7% in the mixed-reality conditions, whereas it was 1% in the virtual conditions ($F(1,91)=4.2$, $p<0.05$, $d=0.41$). There was no effect of control-type and no interaction effect of media-type and control-type (Figure 11).

The results were similar for the explanation items. Again a 2-way ANCOVA test showed that for the explanation items, the mixed-reality condition was learning significantly better than the virtual condition (27% vs. 18% for posttest items, $F(1,91)=4.7$, $p<0.05$, $d=0.44$). The improvement from pre to post for the explanation items was 15.5% in the mixed-reality condition, where as it was 3.7% in the virtual condition. Again there was no effect of control-type and no interaction effect ($p=0.20$) of media-type and control-type (Figure 12). However, there is an apparent trend: those in the mixed-reality with mouse-control condition seemed to be doing slightly better than those in the mixed-reality with physical-control condition. Analyzing only the mixed-reality condition on its own, we did not see a significant effect of control-type ($p=0.20$). Nevertheless, this trend makes some sense give our observation that kids having the physical switch in their hands were quite excited about pressing the button. As consequence, they may not have paid as much attention to providing explanations in the game.

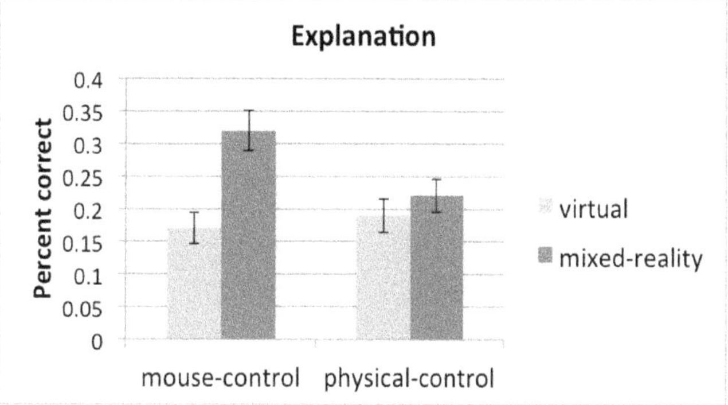

Figure 12. Percent correct for Explanation Items

Tower pre/post tests

The towers were analyzed to see if there was a difference for how much the towers had improved from pre to post in different conditions. The coding scheme, shown in Figure 13, was used to analyze the towers. Each pair of towers (pre and post) was coded according to three different principles: height, symmetry and center of mass. The fourth principle, wide base, was not used, since the base was kept the same as a constraint in the given task. If the tower pair had improved from pre to post on a certain principle, i.e. if the post tower was shorter than the pre tower, we gave them a 1. If the post tower was taller than the pre tower, we gave them a -1. If the pre and post towers had the same height we gave them a 0 for this principle. We repeated the same procedure for different principles, i.e. they got a 1 on symmetry if the post tower was more symmetrical; they got a 1 on Center of Mass if the post tower had a lower center of mass than the pre tower. After giving a score for each principle, we added up the scores to get a total score the tower pair (Figure 13). Then the total score data was analyzed to see if there was any difference for the scores between different conditions.

Figure 13. Coding scheme for Tower pre/post tests

The results of a 2 way ANCOVA show that there was a significant effect of media-type for the tower scores ($F(1,91)=6.9$, $p=0.01$, $d=0.64$). There was no significant effect for control-type and no interaction effect of media-type and control-type. Thus, the kids in the tangible condition were improving more on building stable towers than those in the virtual condition, for both the mouse-control and physical-control conditions (Figure 14). This result is particularly interesting as it demonstrates better transfer of instruction involving mere physical observing (over flat screen observing) to actual physical interaction with the blocks.

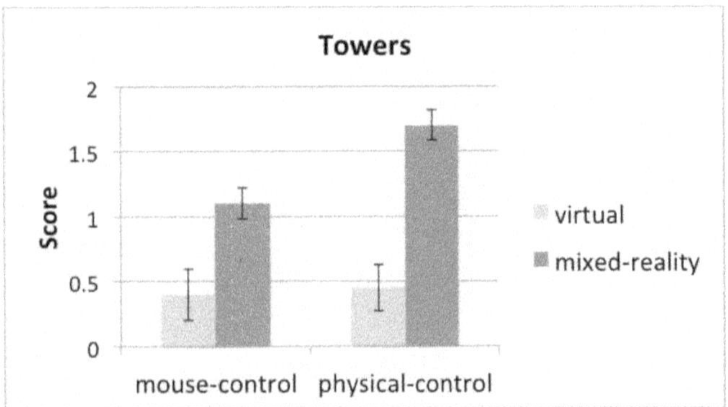

Figure 14. Tower scores

Engagement and Enjoyment

As a measure for enjoyment, the survey data was used, where the students were asked three questions (Figure 15). Comparing the scores of the children in different conditions, we saw that the students who were in the mixed-reality condition said they liked the game significantly more than those in the virtual condition ($F(1,92)=6.7$, $p=0.01$, $d=0.55$). There was no significant difference between the mouse-control and physical-control groups for enjoyment (Figure 15). There was also no interaction effect of media-type and control-type. However analyzing only those who interacted with the mixed-reality game (either with mouse-control or physical-control), we saw that there was a marginal effect of control-type ($p=0.08$, $n=45$). Thus the physical switch in the mixed-reality game was increasing enjoyment slightly. On the other hand, looking at only those interacting with the virtual game, control-type did not have any effect.

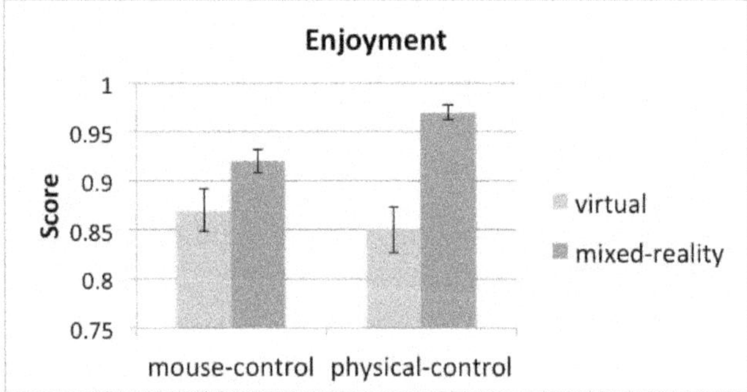

Figure 15. Enjoyment scores based on the survey

OTHER OBSERVATIONS/COMMENTS

Children seemed to be very much engaged during the game. One of the kids in the tangible condition asked if she could trade some of her toys to get an EarthShake at home. Another student said: "Can I steal your computer and set this up at home?" Some others mentioned that they would want to use this game in the circles that they do in their classrooms. Another girl said: "I never thought something we do at school could be so much fun", while another stated: "I wish all our science classes were fun like this." Another student cited that she thought this was like the next version of smart boards.

Many kids made comments indicating that the experience of seeing what actually happens in real life was better than having a computer tell them what is going to happen, which suggests that observing physical phenomena in the real world might be more believable, leading to more learning.

While kids were interacting with the game, it appeared that the explanation menu particularly helped them learn. After making a wrong prediction and observing the towers fall, many kids had an a-ha moment when they saw the menu appear behind the towers and recognized one of the items as being the reason why their prediction was wrong. The menu provided a basis for them to understand the physics principles of balance and stability (symmetry, wide base, height and center of mass). Also during our pilots we saw that children who interacted with the physical setup on its own (earthquake table and physical blocks) without any virtual component did not learn much.

Many kids mentioned that they liked building their own towers and wished there were more building activities during the game. Also, looking at the fourth question in the survey, we saw that children scored 98% on average, expressing that they liked building their own towers very much. Thus, integrating more hands-on building activities into the game may make it even more engaging.

In addition, children mentioned that they liked the gorilla character in the game, telling their friends about their *gorilla friend*. This suggests that having a character in the game made it more engaging and memorable for children.

DISCUSSION

Our experimental results provide evidence that observing physical phenomena in the context of an interactive mixed-reality game plays an important role for learning and enjoyment, while adding simple physical controls such as having the kids shake the tablet in a screen-only game or press the physical switch in a mixed-reality game does not have an effect on learning or enjoyment.

We wanted to test the claim that the learning benefit of physical observation is not just an effect of enjoyment or the novelty of the physical earthquake table, but seems to result from changes in how children better think about the physical phenomenon when they observe it in the real world. To do so, we selected out the subset children in both virtual and mixed reality groups who experienced the highest level of enjoyment (those who all scored more than 90% in the enjoyment survey). The results revealed that even for this subset there was still a significant effect of mixed reality (over virtual) on learning ($p<0.01$). Also, a 2-way ANCOVA with the enjoyment score and pre-test as covariates and post-test as the outcome variable showed that there was no significant effect of enjoyment on learning. These results suggest that enjoyment was probably not a critical mediating factor for learning (albeit a desirable independent outcome).

Comparing the mixed-reality physical switch and mouse conditions also revealed an interesting result: having the kids use the physical switch compared to the mouse increased the enjoyment marginally. However, the physical switch condition did not learn any better than the mouse condition; in contrast there was a trend in the opposite direction. Thus increasing enjoyment did not always increase learning. That's a point worth highlighting for educational technology design – adding an enjoyable feature does not always increase learning and may even be distracting in some cases.

In contrast to enjoyment as mediator, it may be that observing physical phenomena is critical to develop understanding through embodied cognition. This explanation is supported by the greater number of meaningful gestures that children made in the mixed reality condition in our prior study [30]. A similar explanation is that having a physical view of the real world phenomenon produces a sense of reality and believability that engages deeper sense making and leads to better learning. More broadly, our results are consistent with a body of theory and research suggesting that young children often fail to use information communicated to them via symbolic media including pictures, models and video [7].

These results are important since laptops and tablets are the most common tools that children interact with these days. Thus, instead of trying to integrate physical controls into screen-only environments, such as shaking the tablet, it may be worth integrating interactive instructional feedback into the physical environment, without losing the benefits of experimenting with physical objects in the real world.

CONCLUSION AND FUTURE WORK

We provided evidence that experiencing physical phenomena accompanied by interactive feedback via depth camera sensing in the real world improves learning (by approximately 5 times compared to a solely screen-based environment), while also enhancing enjoyment significantly. On the other hand, integrating simple physical controls such as shaking the tablet has little effect. Thus, mixed-reality games that support physical observation in the real world have a great potential to enhance learning and enjoyment for young children.

Although we found that adding a simple form of physical control where the hands-on actions are not relevant to the learning objectives does not have a significant effect on learning or enjoyment, a related question still remains. Do more elaborate hands-on activities where children actually build with the blocks further increase learning and/or enjoyment? Children's comments and our survey data suggest that having more building activities integrated into the game can make it more enjoyable for children. In future work, we aim to explore the role of combining more hands-on activities while maintaining the vision-based interactive learning feedback.

We also aim to expand our mixed-reality game for different content areas in education (e.g., using a balance scale rather than earthquake table) to test the generalizability of our results. Our goal is to eventually create a scalable, mixed reality platform, connecting virtual and physical worlds via affordable depth camera sensing, that can be reused for different content areas in education to improve children's science learning and enjoyment.

ACKNOWLEDGEMENTS

We would like to thank the schools and teachers that have participated in our study. We also would like to thank Eliane Stampfer Wiese and Kelly Rivers for their help.

REFERENCES

1. Antle, A. N. Research opportunities: Embodied child–computer interaction. *International Journal of Child-Computer Interaction* 1, 1 (2013), 30-36.
2. Antle, A. N., Droumeva, M., & Ha, D. Hands on what?: comparing children's mouse based and tangible-based interaction. *In Proc. IDC 2009*, ACM Press (2009), 80-88.
3. Back, M, Cohen, J, Gold, R, Harrison, S and Minneman,S, Listen Reader: an electronically augmented paper-based book. *In Proc. CHI 2001,* ACM Press (2001), 23-29.
4. Bakker, S., van den Hoven, E., & Antle, A. N. MoSo tangibles: evaluating embodied learning. In *Proc.of Tangible, embedded, and embodied interaction* 2011, ACM Press (2011), 85-92.
5. Bruner, J. Toward a Theory of Instruction. Vol. 59. Harvard University Press (1966).
6. Carini, R. M., George D. K., and Stephen P. Klein. Student engagement and student learning: Testing the linkages*. *Research in Higher Education* 47.1 (2006), 1-32
7. DeLoache, J. S., et al. "Do babies learn from baby media?." *Psychological Science* (2010).
8. Englekamp, J. & Zimmer, H. D. Memory for action events: A new field of research. *Psychological Research* 51.4 (1989), 153–157.
9. Glenberg, Arthur M. What memory is for: Creating meaning in the service of action. *Behavioral and brain sciences* 20,01 (1997), 41-50.
10. Hayne, H., Herbert, J. & Simcock, G. Imitation from television by 24- and 30-month-olds. *Developmental Science*, 6, 3 (2003), 254-261.
11. Henning, P. (1998). Everyday Cognition and Situated Learning. In Jonassen, D. (Ed.), *Handbook of Research on Educational Communications and Technology.* (2004), 829-861.
12. Kahn, P. H., Severson, R. L., & Ruckert, J. H. The human relation with nature and technological nature. *Current Directions in Psychological Science*, *18*, 1 (2009), 37-42.
13. Klahr, D., Triona, L. M., and Williams, C. Hands on what? The relative effectiveness of physical versus virtual materials in an engineering design project by middle school children. *Journal of Research in Science Teaching* 44.1 (2007), 183-203.
14. Martin, T., & Schwartz, D. L. Physically distributed learning: Adapting and reinterpreting physical environments in the development of the fraction concept. *Cognitive Science*, 29 (2005), 587–625.
15. Montessori, M. *Montessori method.* Random House Digital, Inc., (1964).
16. Olympiou, G., and Zacharias C. Z. Blending physical and virtual manipulatives: An effort to improve students' conceptual understanding through science laboratory experimentation. *Science Education* 96, 1 (2012), 21-47.
17. O'Malley, C., Stanton-Fraser, D.: Literature review in learning with tangible technologies, Nesta FutureLab Series, report 12 (2004).
18. Pouw, W. T., Van Gog, T., & Paas, F. An embedded and embodied cognition review of instructional manipulatives. *Educational Psychology Review*, *26*, 1 (2014),, 51-72.
19. Quinn, H. et al., A Framework for K-12 Science Education: Practices, Crosscutting Concepts, and Core Ideas, *The National Academies Press* (2012)
20. Raffle, Hayes Solos, Amanda J. Parkes, and Hiroshi Ishii. Topobo: a constructive assembly system with kinetic memory. *In Proc CHI 2004*, ACM Press (2004), 647-654.
21. Resnick, M., et al. Digital manipulatives: new toys to think with. *In Proc. CHI 1998,* ACM Press (1998), 281-287.
22. Rieser, J.J., Garing, A.E. and Young M.F. Imagery, action and young children's spatial orientation-it's not being there that counts, it's what one has in mind. *Child Development*, 65, 5 (1994), 1262-1278.
23. Rizzolatti, G., Craighero, L. The mirror-neuron system, *Annual Review of Neuroscience,* 27 (2004) 169–192.
24. Rogers, Y., et al. *A conceptual framework for mixed reality environments: designing novel learning activities for young children. Presence: Teleoperators and Virtual Environments* 11, 6 (2002), 677-686.
25. Ryokai, R. and Cassell, J. (1999). StoryMat: a play space for collaborative storytelling. *In Proc. CHI 1999,* ACM Press (1999), 272-273
26. Schneider, B., Jermann, P., Zufferey, G., & Dillenbourg, P. Benefits of a Tangible Interface for Collaborative Learning and Interaction. *IEEE Transactions on Learning Technologies*, 4 (2011), 222–232.
27. Shelley, T., Lyons, L., Zellner, M., & Minor, E. Evaluating the embodiment benefits of a paper-based tui for educational simulations. *Ext. Abstracts* CHI 2011, *ACM Press (2011),* 1375-1380.
28. Ullmer, B. and Ishii, H. Emerging frameworks for tangible user interfaces. *IBM Syst. J. (2000)* 915–931.
29. Yannier, N., Basdogan, C., Tasiran, S., Sen, O. L., Using Haptics to Convey Cause and Effect Relations in Climate Visualization, *IEEE Transactions on Haptics*, 1, 2 (2009), 130-141.
30. Yannier, N., Hudson. E. S, Wiese, E., Koedinger, K., Adding Physicality to an Interactive Game Improves Learning and Enjoyment: Evidence from EarthShake, *In Review*
31. Yannier, N., Koedinger, K. R. and Hudson, S. E. Tangible Collaborative Learning with a Mixed-Reality Game: EarthShake. *Artificial Intelligence in Education.* Springer Berlin Heidelberg (2013), 131-140.
32. Walker, E., & Burleson, W. Using Need Validation to Design an Intelligent Tangible Learning Environment, *Ext. Abstracts CHI 2012, ACM Press* (2012), 2123-2128.

Gauging Receptiveness to Social Microvolunteering

Erin Brady
University of Rochester
Rochester, NY USA
brady@cs.rochester.edu

Meredith Ringel Morris
Microsoft Research
Redmond, WA USA
merrie@microsoft.com

Jeffrey P. Bigham
Carnegie Mellon University
Pittsburgh, PA USA
jbigham@cmu.edu

ABSTRACT
Crowd-powered systems that help people are difficult to scale and sustain because human labor is expensive and worker pools are difficult to grow. To address this problem we introduce the idea of *social microvolunteering*, a type of intermediated friendsourcing in which a person can provide access to their friends as potential workers for microtasks supporting causes that they care about. We explore this idea by creating Visual Answers, an exemplar social microvolunteering application for Facebook that posts visual questions from people who are blind. We present results of a survey of 350 participants on the concept of social microvolunteering, and a deployment of the Visual Answers application with 91 participants, which collected 618 high-quality answers to questions asked over 12 days, illustrating the feasibility of the approach.

Author Keywords
Volunteering; SNS; friendsourcing; crowdsourcing.

ACM Classification Keywords
H.5.m. Information Interfaces and Presentation: Misc.

INTRODUCTION
Crowd-powered systems can be useful in the domain of social good. For instance, VizWiz has answered more than 70,000 visual questions for blind people [7], and Social Accessibility has made thousands of accessibility improvements to the Web [25]. Other efforts advance science [14] or promote human rights issues [27]. Scaling and sustaining these projects can be difficult given that the people powering them are generally either paid crowd workers, *e.g.,* from Amazon Mechanical Turk, or volunteers recruited via app-specific sites with limited audiences.

Two low-cost ways of accessing human resources that seem appropriate for such systems are *friendsourcing*, where users of social networking sites ask their friends to perform a small amount of work (such as answering a question), and *microvolunteering*, where people complete small online tasks for free that can benefit organizations or charities.

CHI 2015, April 18–23, 2015, Seoul, Republic of Korea.

ACM 978-1-4503-3145-6/15/04…$15.00.
http://dx.doi.org/10.1145/2702123.2702329

Previous work has considered friendsourcing and microvolunteering separately - either using one's social network for personal benefit, *e.g.,* to answer questions of personal interest, or donating one's own time, money, or resources to causes one cares about without directly involving one's social network. We introduce *social microvolunteering*, a hybrid approach that harnesses friendsourcing and microvolunteering to support crowd-powered systems with an altruistic goal.

Social microvolunteering is a type of intermediated friendsourcing in which participants provide access to their friends as a potential work force by installing an app that posts microvolunteering tasks on their social media feed, *e.g.,* answering a VizWiz question or transcribing a few seconds of audio. Friends viewing the feed who choose to perform the task can do so in-place (without leaving the social feed), thus lowering the barrier to participation [11].

Social microvolunteering offers several potential benefits over current microvolunteering paradigms. *Volunteer organizations* may *(i)* broaden their participant base to include people who may be willing to donate small amounts of time, but previously lacked the knowledge or initiative to volunteer directly, and *(ii)* improve response rate and latency for volunteer microtasks, since some of a volunteer's friends are likely to be online and available even if the original volunteer is not. The *volunteer* who installs a social microvolunteering app (and their friends who interact with the posts) can *(i)* directly help a cause either they or their friends care about by completing microtasks that support it, *(ii)* increase awareness among their social network about their chosen cause, *(iii)* strengthen social relationships with others who complete the microtasks, and *(iv)* curate their online persona in a way that may reflect positively on them by publicly engaging in acts of altruism. Finally, the ultimate *beneficiaries of the app* gain *(i)* affordable access to a pool of volunteers who can help power crowd-powered systems that they find useful, *(ii)* scalability and sustainability for apps that people care about and are willing to volunteer for, and *(iii)* higher performance because each volunteer's interest, availability, and capabilities are magnified by their network size.

This paper explores the idea of social microvolunteering. First, 350 participants completed a survey regarding their attitudes toward social microvolunteering; at the end of the survey, participants were offered a chance to install a social microvolunteering application that we built to post VizWiz-style questions to their Facebook account for 12 days. 91

participants installed the application, and we report usage data showing that, when sent to multiple users, the average time for a question to receive a first answer was 1 minute and 45 seconds, and that first answers were generally of high quality. This suggests that social microvolunteering may be capable of supporting a deployed system. We conclude with a discussion of participants' self-reported opinions of social microvolunteering and their use of our application, presenting an end-to-end examination of their reactions to the concept and reflecting on the implications for the design of future social microvolunteering apps.

RELATED WORK

Social microvolunteering is informed by prior work in the areas of social media sites and online volunteering.

Friendsourcing

Social media sites, such as Facebook and Twitter, can be a valuable resource for question asking [19, 22] since they provide a way to broadcast questions to large groups of people with whom the user has a preexisting connection and who the user trusts to provide high-quality responses. Many requests are for help with tasks that do not take much effort to complete and do not require offline action [11]. Friendsourcing can result in answers that are more tailored and trustworthy to the asker than those from traditional search engines [20], and these interactions between question askers and answerers may encourage contact with weak ties and improve bridging social capital between the users [12]. Evidence suggests that people find posts containing questions to be some of the most valuable content on social sites [1]. Mobilization requests (those that ask for an answer to a question or for a friend to do a favor) elicit more comments and faster first response times than general status updates [15].

Despite these benefits, people can be reluctant to participate in friendsourcing. Some users may not post questions on social networking sites, even if there are financial and quality incentives to doing so, believing that the social costs of bothering their friends are not worthwhile; others may rate-limit their friendsourcing activities to balance social costs [24]. Self-censorship of questions is lessened for young and active social media users, and for those highly interested in the responses [24], but it may be enhanced for people in marginalized groups (such as those with disabilities) who have to navigate additional concerns about appearing dependent [8].

Social microvolunteering is a form of intermediated friendsourcing, where the volunteers who participate ask their networks to perform tasks on behalf of a stranger or organization in need. However, it differs from traditional friendsourcing in several ways: *(i)* the altruistic gains of both the volunteer and their friends who answer, *(ii)* the self-presentation benefits for the volunteer from using the application, and *(iii)* the ability of the volunteer to answer themselves if they are online. Neither the volunteer nor their friends are direct beneficiaries of the work that is done – any benefits they may receive are more intangible.

Using social media to ask questions to strangers, rather than friends, is another active area of research; for instance, TSATracker asks Twitter users to self-report airport security line wait times [21]. However, many people viewed questions from TSATracker as spam. Social microvolunteering posts may be less likely to be perceived as spam because users are told that the posts are being shown because a specific friend is interested in a cause.

Previous research has found that applications that allow the user to post automated updates to social media can have many benefits (in the case of weight loss, accountability and support) [26]. Although there is a general sense that application posts are often perceived as spammy [6], we were unable to find any published reports quantifying user reactions to such posts. Additionally, social microvolunteering posts may differ from traditional application posts since they benefit a charitable cause instead of benefitting the user themselves or a commercial entity. This work contributes a more formal understanding of user reaction to a specific type of charitably-oriented friendsourcing application post.

Micro-activism and Online Volunteering

If someone is involved with a cause, social media sites provide a low-effort way to connect to a large group of people and share information with them. This has led to many social media users partaking in micro-activism, where the extent of their involvement in an activist cause is limited to online behaviors [17]. The impact of these activities, which can include sharing petitions or updating one's status or profile picture for a cause, have been a subject of debate, with the public press and some scholars deriding them as low-effort "slacktivism" [28] while others point to increased awareness and results [16, 27].

One example of micro-activism on social media occurred in March 2013 when the Human Rights Campaign encouraged their Facebook followers to change their profile pictures to a red 'equals' sign in support of marriage equality. Facebook reported that 120% more profile pictures than usual were changed the day after the campaign started, and the HRC reported more than 10 million visits to their web site [27]. Despite successes, micro-activism can still be viewed as low-effort and not as meaningful as traditional donations [28]. The intent of social microvolunteering is to tap into the same motivations that cause people to like and share content on Facebook while making concrete contributions for causes that are amenable to microtasks.

In addition to micro-activism on social networking sites, "microvolunteering" refers to small volunteer tasks that can be completed by a single volunteer and possibly aggregated to complete larger tasks, analogous to paid microtasks found on sites like Mechanical Turk [mturk.com]. While the concept of microvolunteering has been introduced [2],

Figure 1. The Visual Answers social microvolunteering application. When a blind user asks a visual question with VizWiz, the question is posted as the status of multiple volunteers. Comments to the thread are immediately forwarded back to the blind user as responses. Sometimes the volunteer answers the question, sometimes his or her friends answer the question, and sometimes his or her friends may enter comments that do not answer the question.

few efforts have been launched to facilitate it. As with micro-activism, attitudes toward this emerging phenomenon are mixed, with some traditional charitable organizations remaining skeptical of microvolunteering's efficacy [28].

One example of microvolunteering is Help From Home [helpfromhome.org]. Volunteers search for opportunities based on their available time or based on interest. Tasks range from playing games that help research efforts to documenting one's own efforts to save energy at home.

Microvolunteering actions are intended to be individual, rather than social, efforts, and require users to continually visit the coordinating site to look for new tasks and ways to help. As discussed earlier, *social microvolunteering* can harness the power of a user's online social network to provide additional benefits both to volunteer organizations and to individual volunteers. The tasks are also embedded in what participants are already doing (using Facebook).

APPLICATION OF SOCIAL MICROVOLUNTEERING

Technology designed to support people with disabilities often includes humans in the loop because many necessary functionalities are still beyond the reach of automated approaches [5]. Because of the value of human input in technologies for people with disabilities, and its altruistic nature, we used this as our sample domain to illustrate the potential of social microvolunteering. Here, we describe VizWiz, an application that gets microtasks from blind users, and introduce Visual Answers, our social microvolunteering application that connects VizWiz users' questions with sighted volunteers and their friends.

VizWiz

VizWiz [vizwiz.org] is a mobile phone application that allows people with visual impairments to ask questions about their environment, and receive answers quickly from sighted workers or friends [4, 7]. Users take a photograph of something they have a visual question about, record audio of their question, and then send it to crowd workers who answer it quickly. Answers are forwarded back to the user and read aloud. Other products like TapTapSee [taptapseeapp.com] provide object recognition, but VizWiz's use of human answerers supports complex or subjective questions.

VizWiz is currently free to end users, and the academic team that created the app pays the crowd workers that answer questions for each question they answer. VizWiz uses a worker retainer model, where workers are pre-recruited in order to ensure that answers can be sent back quickly [4]. Crowdworkers do not always provide high-quality answers, and so VizWiz requests redundant answers from three different workers, which further increases costs. These costs reduce sustainability and scalability.

Friendsourcing is a free way to get answers to questions, and seemed to be an appropriate way to get answers to VizWiz questions without the financial costs of using a crowdsourcing platform [8, 18]. When surveyed about using friendsourcing to get answers to visual questions, however, both visually impaired Facebook users and VizWiz users were reluctant to utilize friendsourcing within their own social networks due to concerns about response speeds and rates (possibly exacerbated by their smaller-than-average network sizes [29]) and concerns about bothering and appearing dependent upon their friends [8].

When weighing these concerns, we considered the possibility of "friendsourcing" questions to a different user's friends on social networking sites. In this way, blind users of VizWiz would still get free, useful answers to questions without incurring the perceived social costs of appearing dependent to their own friends; at the same time, the application installer and their friends who interact with the VizWiz questions may gain a sense of altruism and increased social bonds. In the next section, we describe Visual Answers, the social microvolunteering app we built to realize this concept, which allows third parties to provide access to their Facebook network as a resource for friendsourced answers to incoming VizWiz questions.

Visual Answers

We designed a Facebook application called Visual Answers to explore the potential of social microvolunteering. Visual Answers allows users to donate their Newsfeed as a venue to post visual questions from blind people using the VizWiz app. While these volunteers can (and sometimes did) answer questions themselves, they are able to magnify their contributions by providing access to their friends. Importantly, their friends may be more useful for VizWiz than the individual who installs the app could be alone. The large network of friends connected to a volunteer may help the application answer questions quickly, even when the original volunteer who installed the app is unavailable, and may open up broader pools of potential answerers whose diverse expertise may be valuable in answering questions.

Visual Answers for the Application Installer

Visual Answers takes questions as they are submitted by blind users of the VizWiz app and automatically posts them to the Facebook feed of a volunteer using the volunteer's own name and profile picture. Each post contains an explanation of the application's purpose, the text of the audio question asked by the VizWiz user, and the photo taken by the VizWiz user (Figure 2).

The volunteer's friends will see the post in their news feeds, and can comment on the post to answer the question. While the Facebook algorithm that chooses which posts are displayed on friends' news feed is unpredictable, previous research indicates that any individual post will likely be seen by 35% of a user's friends [3].

Visual Answers for the VizWiz User

In a live system, when a blind VizWiz user submits a visual question, it would be automatically posted to the Facebook feeds of multiple Visual Answers installers. When answers are received from any post, they can be instantly forwarded to the VizWiz user's phone (Figure 1).

For VizWiz users, this design provides a free source of answers that may leverage some of the benefits of traditional friendsourcing (free, high-quality answers) without exposing the user to fear of stigmatization from their own friends. This approach may also afford benefits in speed, since the app could send the same question to several users' social networks, target urgent questions toward users with larger networks or networks with more members currently online or that contain a certain type of expertise.

Figure 2. A post from Visual Answers, as seen on Facebook. The question is posted automatically from the volunteer's account, and gathers answers from the volunteer or their friends via Facebook's commenting mechanism.

SURVEY ON SOCIAL MICROVOLUNTEERING

In designing this system, we had many questions about the Facebook users' attitudes toward installing an app of this type. To determine the feasibility of the idea, we conducted an initial survey about social microvolunteering.

Respondents were first asked about their use of social networking sites (in general and to support causes they care about), their current online and offline volunteering behaviors, and obstacles to volunteering more often. Then, they were presented with a description of the Visual Answers application, and asked a series of questions to help us understand what users might think about social microvolunteering through their reactions to the description of our exemplar app. The survey had 27 questions, and took about 7 minutes. At the end of the survey, we offered an opportunity to install a pilot version of Visual Answers.

Recruitment and Demographics

Survey respondents were recruited through a series of Facebook advertisements targeted at English-speaking, U.S.-based users who were at least eighteen years old and who were interested in 'charity,' 'charitable donations,' 'volunteering,' or 'visual impairments.' We chose to target advertisements to these specific Facebook users, since we would expect this demographic to be likely early adopters of social microvolunteering in general or Visual Answers specifically. Respondents were offered a $5 Amazon gift card for completing the survey.

Facebook ads ran for 13 days in May and June 2014 in the sidebar of the Facebook interface on desktop computers. 7337 people clicked through to the survey, and 431 of those began the survey. All of the respondents were directed to the survey from facebook.com, but we could not verify whether some respondents shared the link to friends using the service; we expect that most (and likely all) respondents were directed to the survey by the ads, since we did not notice any bursts of survey activity that would be indicative of viral re-sharing, and no respondents had mutual friends who answered questions. 14 people were disqualified (either for not living in the United States or not completing the consent form properly) and 67 only partially completed the survey. 350 respondents completed the entire survey; the remainder of our survey analysis focuses on these 350.

Respondents were primarily female (63%) and middle-aged (median 44, range 18-83). This matches studies that show that Facebook users are more likely female than male, and that more older adults have joined the social network in recent years [9]. These demographics may also reflect that charitable giving increases with age up to 65 [13] and that women volunteer more frequently than men [10].

Survey Results

Social Networking Site Use

Most respondents were experienced Facebook users, with 76% having used the site for more than 3 years and an additional 19% having used the site for 1 to 3 years. Nearly all were frequent users of Facebook, logging into the site once (15%) or several times (78%) each day. Respondents were most frequently consuming content that was produced by their friends (65% read others' content several times a day) or interacting with others' content (with 45% commenting on and 59% liking others' content several times a day). Posting activity was less frequent; 19% reported posting status updates once a day, and 21% did so several times a day. Only 21% reported having ever installed a Facebook application that posted status messages on their behalf (as our Visual Answers application would).

Volunteering, Charity, and Activism

Most respondents had been involved in online activism before. 77% had participated in online activism outside of social media (online petitions, emailing politicians, etc.), and 81% had participated in activism on social media sites (*e.g.,* sharing petitions, changing profile pictures, posting statuses to draw attention to causes). Most respondents were not currently volunteering much – either never volunteering in the real world (34%) or online (59%), or doing so once a month or less in the real world (20%) or online (16%).

Many respondents explained their low levels of volunteering as being due to a lack of free time (52%) or money (42%). Others mentioned feasibility issues, such as not knowing how to find a group to match their needs (42%) or not having a group to work with nearby (15%). 11 repsondents (3%) self-identified in free-form answers that they were unable to participate in volunteering due to having a disability.

Opinions on Visual Answers

In the next section of the survey, we introduced the respondents to the concept of social microvolunteering via the concrete example of the Visual Answers application. We presented a description of how the application would work, and asked users for their opinions.

Respondents were generally receptive to the idea of installing the application (55%). Respondents were asked to indicate why they responded positively or negatively to the proposed application by selecting from a list of reasons or writing in their own. The 192 respondents who answered positively said that primary motivations would be helping people with disabilities (88%), raising awareness of disability issues to friends (69%), and feeling good about volunteering (48%). Free-form responses included both internal and external motivations such as, "*To be part of something that incredible and being disabled myself just adds to the excitement and joy*" and "*Demonstrate public service commitment.*"

For those who responded positively to installing the application, we asked about the application's potential impact on their Facebook friends. Most thought their friends would be somewhat (61%) or very (27%) happy to see the application's questions, and that friends would not be too bothered (48%) or not bothered at all (14%). When asked what posting frequencies would be acceptable, most indicated once a week (41%) or less (26%).

No clear majority appeared among reasons not to install for the 158 respondents who responded negatively, but many cited privacy concerns (40%), thinking the application would be ineffective (27%), thinking that these kind of questions are not what Facebook should be used for (14%), or concerns about annoying their friends (30%). Privacy concerns were expected, as applications that post on a user's behalf are often viewed as malicious or spam [23].

Respondents were also asked if compensation or rewards would encourage installation. Most (51%) did not think that any compensation would motivate installations, while others indicated that possibly receiving thanks from the VizWiz users (23%) or financial compensation per question posted (28%) would be a valuable reward for participation.

Discussion

Survey respondents were active users of social networking sites, and appeared to participate more in low-intensity online activism (signing petitions, changing their Facebook status or profile pictures) than real world or online volunteering. The survey results indicated that users may find social microvolunteering appealing, both because Facebook and other social networks are already being used for activism, and because they lack the time, money, or ability to participate in traditional volunteering.

While some respondents were negative about the general concept of social microvolunteering, many gave reasons why they would be wary to use Visual Answers in particular, such as, "I worry that some of my facebook friends might be jerks and misdirect a blind person."

Many respondents (53%) said that they had a family member or close friend with a disability. A few people self-indicated having a disability in their free-form responses. These personal connections to disability might have been part of the reason for the positive response to the application's description.

APPLICATION PILOT

After completing the survey, all survey respondents were offered an opportunity to install a pilot version of Visual Answers for 12 days. In this version of the application, rather than using live, unscreened VizWiz questions, we hand-selected a sample of questions from the VizWiz archive to be posted to volunteers' feeds with transcribed questions. We did not actually forward these answers to the blind users (whose questions had already been answered). This eliminated the possibility of volunteers receiving questions that might contain personal or inappropriate material and also eliminated the possibility of us sending blind users answers that might be low-quality or inappropriate – the purpose of this application pilot was to explore our hypotheses that social microvolunteering could be fast, trustworthy, and high-quality, and explore how we might design such apps to better achieve these goals.

To explore how task difficulty would impact social microvolunteering, posted questions alternated between being answerable from the photograph provided and being difficult or impossible to answer due to issues such as lighting, blur, composition, or framing, which are all common problems in blind users' photos [7].

We also varied (i) the frequency with which questions were posted (every other day, once a day, or twice a day), (ii) the explanation of the study included in the post (providing a motivation for answering, "*Answers will be forwarded directly to the blind user who asked the question,*" for research, "*Answers will be used by our research team to help develop automatic question-answering tools for blind people,*" or no motivation at all), and (iii) how we indicated to participants that questions were closed to new answers (by commenting on the post to thank people for answering, deleting the post, or doing nothing), in order to gain insight into how to post questions in the most user-friendly way.

Users

All 350 survey participants reached the page prompting them to learn more about installing Visual Answers. 188 proceeded to the next page, which described the study, and showed examples of the posts the application would make. Of these, 91 installed the application. When given the opportunity to install the application, participants were either offered a $20 Amazon gift card as additional compensation for their participation, or were offered no additional compensation. To balance the number of participants who were paid and unpaid, each survey participant who visited the page was offered the payment condition with the lowest number of active pilot users thus far. We varied the payment condition to see how it impacted potential participants' installation rates.

142 participants were offered compensation for participating, and 47 installed; the other 207 participants were not offered compensation, and 44 installed. The offer of payment was a significant factor in installations, $\chi2(1, N=350) = 6.258$, $p = 0.012$.

We associated the installations and the responses participants gave to the survey. Of the 91 who installed the application, 74 had responded positively to the application's description in the survey, while the other 17 had responded negatively. Most participants who responded positively about installing the application thought their friends or Facebook users' friends would be very (34%) or somewhat (59%) happy to answer questions from the application. Of participants who responded negatively to the application, many (35%) were opposed to the application for privacy-related reasons, such as not wanting to allow access to their information or posting permissions. However, many others cited application-related reasons – either not thinking this was an effective way to help blind people (41%), or fear that the posts would annoy their friends (35%). 8 of the 17 participants who responded negatively mentioned that financial incentives could motivate users to install.

58 of the participants who installed the application said they had a family member or close friend with a disability, and 23 said they were already involved with a charitable organizations or volunteer efforts that focused on disability.

These participants had an average of 447 friends (median 269). In the next sections, we analyze data from these 91 participants, with all names replaced with pseudonyms.

Over the duration of the pilot, 14 of the 91 participants uninstalling the application (8 in the paid condition), after an average of 4.3 days. For these participants, we used only data collected before they uninstalled.

Responses to Visual Answers Questions

24 questions were available to be posted to participants' feeds (12 easy to answer, 12 difficult to answer). Each volunteer and their friends saw any particular question only once, but across all participants each question was posted an average of 47.1 times during the 12 day study period. The average time until a first answer was received to each of the 24 questions across all users was 1 minute and 45 seconds (median of 1 minute and 28 seconds). While this confirms that near real-time speeds can be achieved by posting the same question to several volunteers' feeds simultaneously, this result was achieved when analyzing

Figure 3. Four of the questions posted by Visual Answers. (a) "Which knob, is it the left or the right, is for temperature control?", (b) "What does this bottle say?", (c) "What is in this can, please?", (d) "What's in the box?"

answers from every post during the study period – as shown in Figure 4, all 24 questions did not all have answers until posted 6 times each, and average first answer speeds decreased sharply until questions had been posted to 9 volunteers' feeds (average time of 6:27), then evened out.

Visual Answers posted 1,130 questions during the study. 479 of these questions received at least 1 comment, either from the volunteer, their Facebook friends, or both. Of 756 total comments, 618 were good-faith answers (as defined below). We break down our analysis of the answers into those from the volunteer's Facebook friends, or from the volunteers themselves.

Comments from Facebook Friends

292 of the questions posted (26%) received at least one comment from a friend, and 67 of the 91 participants received at least one comment from a friend on a question that Visual Answers had posted on their feed.

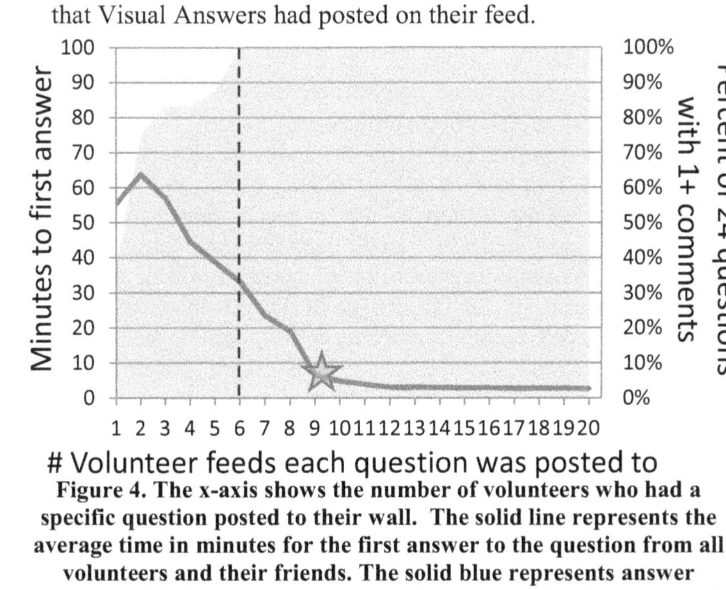

Figure 4. The x-axis shows the number of volunteers who had a specific question posted to their wall. The solid line represents the average time in minutes for the first answer to the question from all volunteers and their friends. The solid blue represents answer coverage of the 24 possible questions (the percent that had at least 1 comment). After the questions had been posted to 6 walls (dashed line), all questions had been answered at least once. After questions had been posted to 9 people (the star at 6:27), the increases in speed from posting to additional volunteers' walls grow less rapidly.

For the 292 questions that were answered by a friend, most received a small number of comments – the total number of comments from friends was 481. 156 of the questions that received comments were answerable, and the remaining 136 were unanswerable. The first answers from friends to individual posts took an average of 46.9 minutes (median 18.8 minutes), with no significant difference between first response times for answerable and unanswerable questions. In practice, questions would likely be posted as multiple volunteers' status messages, so the times reported in Figure 4 are a better estimate of experienced latency for the blind question asker.

379 of the 481 comments included *good-faith answers* – answers that either directly answered the user's question, made a helpful guess, or told the user the question could not be answered and how to improve their photograph.

198 of the good-faith comments were on answerable questions, and provided the correct answer:

> ***[in answer to "Which knob, is it the left or the right, is for temperature control?" (Figure 3a)]***
> *Left one is for Temperature. It has three settings cold to the left, 21 Celsius/70 Farenheit in the center and warm to the right.*

181 of the good-faith comments were on unanswerable questions and provided a useful guess or information on the problem and advice on taking a better photograph:

> ***[in answer to "What does this bottle say?" (Figure 3b)]***
> *The flash on the camera seems to have caused the label to be too bright white to read. Also; the picture is not centered to see the full product. My guess is that it is window/glass cleaner.*

In one case, a commenter went above and beyond to correctly answer a question we thought was unanswerable:

> ***[in answer to "What is in this can, please?" (Figure 3c)]***
> *The left one is canned pineapples. The right is petite diced canned tomatoes. (Google the bar codes; then click the WIC pdfs).*

102 of the 481 comments were not good-faith answers. Many of these comments were part of normal conversations

that occurred in the comments of the application's posts, often after a good-faith answer was received:

[in answer to: "What is this product?"]
Jenn: splenda
Jamie: Jenn, go to bed!!!
Jenn: I would if I was at home still out... just waiting for Al to pack his stuff up then we are going home promise xx

Others discussed the application ("Jess explain this to me. What is viz wiz"), interacted with previous answerers, or were just not useful as answers, such as, "Asv [sic] would a blind person be clueless; son [sic] am I." We did not distinguish between useless answers and conversational comments, since neither benefit the asker. With these few exceptions, the majority of answers from friends (78.8%) were high quality, providing correct answers or feedback.

Comments from Study Participants

In addition to receiving answers from their Facebook friends, some volunteers commented on their own statuses, either to interact with other commenters or to answer the questions themselves. 275 additional comments on the application's posts were from the volunteers themselves. These comments were posted an average of 72.3 minutes after the question was posted (median 35.8), which is significantly longer than the average time to first comments from friends, $t(477) = 3.61, p = 0.0003$.

The majority were again good-faith answers (87%). The other 36 comments were mostly conversational, answering questions about the application or thanking friends:

[in answer to "What color is my shoe?"]
Eunice: White!
Danielle [volunteer]:Thanks, this is an experimental disability app, I offered to test drive. I think it's great!

Nine volunteers received no comments from their own friends on their questions – instead, they answered a number of their own questions (4.9 answers, on average).

POST-STUDY SURVEY

After completing the twelve-day pilot of Visual Answers, all volunteers who had installed the app were invited via email to take a survey about their experiences. 61 of the 91 participants completed this survey.

Opinions of Social Microvolunteering

Nearly all participants liked the application, feeling somewhat (47%) or very (48%) positive about using it. 68% said they planned to leave the application installed after the study ended. When asked about social microvolunteering, 90% said that Facebook was a good place for social microvolunteering, and 83% said that they would want to use Facebook for social microvolunteering in the future.

From free-form answers, participants seemed to have gained the benefits of positive, altruistic feelings we hypothesized would be associated with social microvolunteering, including comments such as "It is nice to be of service," "This is an awesome application and it makes me feel good to use it," and "just that this is a great idea im [sic] glad i took the first survey."

However, there were drawbacks associated with use, too. Many criticisms focused on questions that were unanswerable, including, "Just I felt bad for them when they asked a question I could not answer" and "Why did you allow post that were illegible? Seems to be a waste of time." Other critiques focused on the application itself, such as, "Answering the questions didn't feel like there was much impact; just some random picture that popped up. People just look at pictures, and don't think of volunteering by facebook."

Friends and Impact on Facebook Use

60% of participants said that they had gotten asked questions about the application's posts during the course of the study. Despite this, most participants did not feel that using Visual Answers impacted their typical use of Facebook (65%), and only 7 said the applications' posts disrupted their news feed.

Participants said comments on their posts came mostly from personal friends (77.2%) or family members (31.6%), not from their weaker ties. For participants who had received answers from friends, the survey asked about their ties with up to 3 people who had commented on the posts. Most were friends who would usually comment on the participants' content, with only 7 of the 89 friends asked about being people who would not normally comment.

Even when there were low answer rates, participants seemed to value their friends' efforts in responding:

I personally did not get a lot of "friends" responding, but those that did were characterized by their own personal involvment [sic] in other volunteer activities and consistently responded throughout the entire study.

DISCUSSION

The survey results and application pilot demonstrate the potential of social microvolunteering to help sustain and scale crowd-powered systems designed to help people or causes. Participants were optimistic about the idea of providing access to their friends as an answering resource, and many installed the Visual Answers application (both with and without the promise of compensation) to help answer questions for blind people. Their friends engaged with the posts, quickly providing high-quality answers to a significant fraction of the questions that were posed.

Longer deployments with larger user bases will be important for answering research questions about the sustainability and impact of Visual Answers, and social microvolunteering in general. However, this initial study provides insight into the end-to-end design and deployment of a social microvolunteering app, as well as demonstrating the feasibility (in terms of both real-time performance and user attitudes) of the concept of social microvolunteering.

Feasibility

Getting high-quality answers is important for the feasibility of an application like Visual Answers. Most (81.7%) of the answers received during the pilot study were useful, either providing a correct answer or feedback on why an answer could not be obtained from the photograph. However, some had extraneous comments, resulting from users starting conversations in the comments of the applications' posts, either not realizing or not caring that their conversations might be forwarded to the blind person who posted the question. Conversational comments tended to be included after a good faith answer had already been submitted, perhaps indicating that friends felt freer to submit general comments after a real answer had been provided. Overall, 91% of the first comments posted to the 479 questions that got comments from the users or their friends were good-faith responses, significantly higher than the 65.7% of non-first comments that were good-faith ($\chi2(1, N=756) = 75.40$, $p < 0.0001$). Future work may look at detecting off-topic comments or simply only forward the first answer.

Though only 42% of individual posts received comments, across all participants all 24 questions that were posted received good-faith answers. This indicates that, while individual users and their friends cannot be guaranteed to answer any one question, distributing questions to multiple volunteers greatly expands the pool of available answerers and the likelihood of getting an answer.

Answers came back quickly when distributed to multiple volunteers, with an average first response to each question across 10 or more posts in 4 minutes, 48 seconds, and a median response time of 18 minutes on individual posts. This approaches the latency necessary for applications like VizWiz – in an analysis of the perceived urgency of VizWiz questions, most required answers within a minute (10%) or up to ten minutes (58%) [7]. In order to further reduce latency, questions could be distributed to more users at once, or targeted to volunteers with many friends currently online. Social microvolunteering could also be useful in systems without real-time demands.

Though rare, some questions from VizWiz may be inappropriate to post on Facebook, either because they contain personal information (such as a letter showing a full name and address) or even malicious content. The system could be used in a pipeline where a combination of computer vision and paid crowd workers first quickly verify that an image is appropriate for Visual Answers before the system passes it along. Alternatively, friends could flag content as inappropriate, by commenting "inappropriate" to indicate that a question should be deleted.

Bootstrapping and Sustainability

A core idea of social microvolunteering is that it may be more sustainable than paid marketplaces, but the long-term appetite for this kind of work is difficult to determine given a 12-day deployment. We have shown that a reasonable fraction of people were willing to install Visual Answers (even without monetary compensation) and that a reasonable fraction of their friends were willing to answer questions for free. This is important because a primary difficulty in sustaining crowd-powered systems is their cost.

Participants need to be recruited to install new social microvolunteering applications. For our study, we recruited survey participants and piloters through targeted advertisements on Facebook. Participants could also be recruited by advertising on mailing lists or websites for people who have an interest in a specific cause. It would be interesting to study whether social microvolunteering applications might spread virally and how app designers or individual volunteers might effectively encourage this.

Our study looked at only 12 days of use, but the long-term success of the approach requires continued interest over time. Longevity could be enhanced by posting questions infrequently (once a week or less); a larger user base would allow less frequent per-user posting. Survey respondents also indicated this would be a desired frequency.

If social microvolunteering were to become popular, it may risk being a victim of its own success, as a large number of mediated friendsourcing requests would compete for users' time and attention. To facilitate this, platform operators could adjust their newsfeed algorithms to condense or eliminate duplicate volunteering requests, or enable that functionality via APIs. Application designers could also consider this factor - if a certain percentage of a users' friends has seen a question recently, the application could defer posting for that user until a new question has come in. The challenges of the attention marketplace [24] in friendsourcing have been noted by others and merit further consideration, but are beyond the scope of our study.

Generalizability

While Visual Answers provides a compelling example of social microvolunteering, organizations could post tasks of different formats, to different social networking sites, or use different techniques to get answers. Visual Answers used image-based tasks, but social microvolunteering could deal with all types of media, ranging from simple, text-based tasks to larger, complex tasks. In traditional microwork, large tasks can be broken down into small components, with responses aggregated into complete solutions. This approach could even work to resolve some of the feasibility issues with Visual Answers – for example, having different types of microvolunteers who donate their feeds to compose an answer pipeline (checking for sensitive info, transcribing audio, answering questions, and verifying answers).

Different applications could use different strategies to get the answers they want based on their metrics of quality – speed, correctness, thoroughness, originality, or some combination of these. Tasks could be optimally routed to people with large networks for fast answers, or to networks composed of people who are likely to have correct answers (*e.g.*, health questions posted to a doctor's feed, who may have many other friends in the medical field).

Social microvolunteering could be done on various social networking sites, taking advantage of different sites' affordances and network compositions. Facebook is well-suited to multimedia tasks due to generous length limits for question text, support for embedded images/videos, user familiarity with app posts from other applications, and the network of friends and family members who can be trusted to provide quality answers. Other tasks might be better suited for platforms like Twitter, where users have a broader range of people following them, or LinkedIn, where followers might be likely to share common areas of professional expertise.

CONCLUSION

In this paper, we introduced *social microvolunteering,* where people provide access to their friends as a resource for completing microwork for causes they care about. We presented Visual Answers, a social microvolunteering application that helps blind people answer visual questions. Facebook users responded positively to the suggested application in a survey, and many went on to install the application. Overall, the questions posted to volunteer's Facebook accounts were answered correctly and quickly, and volunteers reported positive attitudes toward the application after the pilot period was complete, demonstrating the real-world feasibility of our approach.

ACKNOWLEDGEMENTS

This work was funded by NSF Award #IIS-1149709 and an Alfred P. Sloan Foundation Fellowship.

REFERENCES

1. André, P. et al. Who Gives A Tweet? Evaluating Microblog Content Value. *Proc. CSCW 2012*.
2. Bernstein, M. et al. Micro-volunteering: helping the helpers in development. *Proc. CSCW 2013*.
3. Bernstein, M.S. et al. Quantifying the Invisible Audience in Social Networks. *Proc. CHI 2013*.
4. Bigham, J.P. et al. VizWiz: Nearly Real-time Answers to Visual Questions. *Proc. UIST 2010*.
5. Bigham, J.P. et al. The Design of Human-Powered Access Technology. *Proc. ASSETS 2011*.
6. Blog, F.O. 2014. News Feed FYI: Giving People More Control Over When They Share from Apps.
7. Brady, E. et al. Visual Challenges in the Everyday Lives of Blind People. *Proc. CHI 2013*.
8. Brady, E. et al. Investigating the appropriateness of social network question asking as a resource for blind users. *Proc. CSCW 2013*.
9. Demographics of key social networking platforms: *PewResearch Internet Project,* Dec. 30, 2013.
10. Economic News Release - Volunteering in the United States, 2013: *www.bls.gov/news.release/volun.nr0.htm.*
11. Ellison, N.B. et al. Calling All Facebook Friends: Exploring Requests for Help on Facebook. *Proc. ICWSM 2013*.
12. Gray, R. et al. Who Wants to Know? Question-asking and Answering Practices among Facebook Users. *Communication Arts*. (2013).
13. Havens, J. et al. 2006. Charitable Giving: How Much, by Whom, to What, and How? *The Non-Profit Sector: A Research Handbook*. 542-567.
14. Korpela, E. et al. 2001. SETI@HOME — Massively Distributed Computing for SETI. *Computing in Science and Engineering*. (2001), 78-83.
15. Lampe, C. et al. Help is on the Way: Patterns of Responses to Resource Requests on Facebook. *Proc. CSCW 2014*.
16. Lee, Y.-hao and Hsieh, G. Does Slacktivism Hurt Activism?: The Effects of Moral Balancing and Consistency in Online Activism. *Proc. CHI 2013*.
17. Marichal, J. Political Facebook groups: Micro–activism and the digital front stage. *First Monday*. 18, 2013.
18. Martins, J. et al. 2014. Friendsourcing the Unmet Needs of People with Dementia. *W4A 2014*.
19. Morris, M.R. et al. A Comparison of Information Seeking Using Search Engines and Social Networks. *Proc. ICWSM 2010*.
20. Morris, M.R. et al. What Do People Ask Their Social Networks, and Why? A Survey Study of Status Message Q&A Behavior. *Proc. CHI 2010*.
21. Nichols, J. and Kang, J. Asking questions of targeted strangers on social networks. *Proc. CHI 2012*.
22. Paul, S.A. et al. Is Twitter a Good Place for Asking Questions ? A Characterization Study. *ICWSM 2011*.
23. Rahman, S. et al. FRAppE : Detecting Malicious Facebook Applications. *Proc. CoNEXT 2012*.
24. Rzeszotarski, J.M. and Morris, M.R. Estimating the Social Costs of Friendsourcing. *Proc. CHI 2014*.
25. Takagi, H. et al. Social Accessibility: Achieving Accessibility through Collaborative Metadata Authoring. *Proc. ASSETS 2008*.
26. Teodoro, R. and Naaman, M. Fitter with Twitter : Understanding Personal Health and Fitness Activity in Social Media. *Proc. ICWSM 2013*.
27. Vie, S. 2014. In defense of "slacktivism": The Human Rights Campaign Facebook logo as digital activism. *First Monday*. 19, 2014.
28. Voida, A. et al. Bridging Between Organizations and the Public: Volunteer Coordinators' Uneasy Relationship with Social Computing. *Proc. CHI* 2012.
29. Wu, S. and Adamic, L. Visually Impaired Users on an Online Social Network. *Proc. CHI 2014*.

Mobile Gamification for Crowdsourcing Data Collection: Leveraging the Freemium Model

Kristen Dergousoff and Regan L. Mandryk
Computer Science, University of Saskatchewan
176 Thorvaldson Building, 110 Science Place
kristen.dergousoff@usask.ca , regan.mandryk@usask.ca

ABSTRACT
Classic ways of gathering data on human behaviour are time-consuming, costly and are subject to limited participant pools. Crowdsourcing offers a reduction in operating costs and access to a diverse and large participant pool; however issues arise concerning low worker pay and questions about data quality. Gamification provides a motivation to participate, but also requires the development of specialized, research-question specific games that can be costly to produce. Our solution combines gamification and crowdsourcing in a smartphone-based system that emulates the popular Freemium model of play to motivate voluntary participation through in-game rewards, using a robust framework to study multiple unrelated research questions within the same system. We deployed our game on the Android store and compared it to a gamified laboratory version and a non-gamified laboratory version, and found that players who used the in-game rewards were motivated to do experimental tasks. There was no difference between the systems for performance on a motor task; however, performance on the cognitive task was worse for the crowdsourced game. We discuss options for improving performance on tasks requiring attention.

Author Keywords
Crowdsourcing; gamification; freemium; psychophysics

INTRODUCTION
A fundamental, and limiting, step in Human Computer Interaction research is gathering data in order to understand human behaviour. Researchers often perform costly and time-consuming user studies in laboratory environments. In academic research this usually consists of recruiting participants from a participant pool at the university, which confines participation in studies to the "boom-and-bust semester cycle" and limits the generalizability of the study to the demographic of young college students [16].

CHI 2015, April 18 - 23, 2015, Seoul, Republic of Korea
Copyright 2015 ACM 978-1-4503-3145-6/15/04©$15.00
http://dx.doi.org/10.1145/2702123.2702296

One solution that has been proposed is to crowdsource experiments. Crowdsourcing platforms such as Amazon's Mechanical Turk (AMT) have been shown to successfully recreate experimental results [12, 13] and provide additional benefits such as constant any-time access to a large and diverse participant pool, reduced operational and administrative costs, and quick experimental development [14, 16]. However issues have been raised regarding data quality because of the lack of experimental control and the ethics surrounding the low monetary incentives often provided to motivate participation [16].

Gamification is an alternate solution proposed by researchers. The gamification of experimental studies has been shown to motivate large numbers of voluntary participants [18] and to increase the enjoyability of tasks [10]. However, it is still unclear whether the results obtained through a gamified approach are as accurate as data gathered in traditional laboratory settings. Also gamified experiments are usually highly customized to the specific research question, requiring costly development of new games for each research problem that is addressed.

Our solution is to combine the motivation of gamification with the broad participant base available through crowdsourcing by leveraging the benefits of the "Freemium" model, in which players can play a game for free, but are given access to special content, features, or advertisement-free play for a fee. We created a framework in which players of a game gain in-game advantages (i.e., *powerups*) for completing experimental tasks useful to researchers (i.e., *microexperiments*). We leverage the mobile game market to target players looking to simply kill time with short gameplay sessions. The main advantage of our framework is that it separates the system for completing microexperiments from the game so that multiple experimental tasks can be deployed in a single game, or multiple games can be deployed to increase the appeal for players. In this paper, we present our framework for motivating participation in the crowdsourcing of experimental research tasks via the mobile game market, as well as Sugar Rush, our prototype Android game that we used to evaluate the efficacy of our framework.

Sugar Rush is an action-based vertical platformer that utilizes the device accelerometer. In the game, players are in control of a continuously bouncing cupcake, which they guide through platforms and enemies to collect candy, coins, and obtain a high score. Players are given the option to purchase useful powerups with in-game currency earned through the completion of microexperiments.

We evaluated our framework under three conditions to isolate the factors of gamification and crowdsourcing and examine their effects separately on the quality of data gathered (Crowdsourced Game, Laboratory Game, and Control, i.e., laboratory no game). We also analyzed usage data received from the Android market to inform the degree to which our prototype game and Freemium model motivated voluntary participation in the microexperiments. Finally, surveyed the laboratory participants who played the game to gather their opinions on the topic.

Results of the evaluation indicate that there was no difference in performance between the three conditions for the performance-based motor task (i.e., a Fitts reciprocal tapping task); however, the crowdsourced game resulted in worse performance on the attention-based cognitive task (i.e., a Cleveland and McGill information visualization judgment task). The survey results suggested that players were willing to do the tasks in return for earned in-game bonuses, would prefer the tasks over in-game advertising, and that the tasks did not detract from the play experience. The usage data shows that participants who were exposed to the powerups used them in about 21% of games, but that the majority of participants did not even try the powerups.

We discuss the opportunities of mobile crowdsourcing of data collection using gamification and present ways in which we can increase the motivation of players to complete microexperiments in a framework such as ours. In addition, we discuss game design decisions that could help improve data quality for tasks that require player attention. There are advantages to crowdsourcing data collection through mobile gamification; we provide an indication that players are willing to participate and that researchers can collect data that is of high quality for certain tasks.

RELATED WORK

We discuss crowdsourcing, gamification, and the use of games in crowdsourcing. We also present the Freemium business model and its application in mobile games.

Crowdsourcing

The term *crowdsourcing* refers to the outsourcing of a task or function to a larger network of people. Crowdsourcing has been used in many domains to assist with tasks such as solving computationally complex problems [4], generating large amounts of data [18, 19], and performing large-scale experiments [13]. In research, crowdsourcing has been increasingly adopted as an attractive alternative to laboratory-based studies. Crowdsourcing allows researchers to reach a larger, more diverse participant base at reduced operational costs [14], and the use of crowdsourcing platforms, such as Amazon's Mechanical Turk or CrowdFlower, allow researchers to streamline the experimental process by reducing the development time and administrative overhead of user studies [14, 16].

One of the largest and most well-known crowdsourcing platforms is Amazon's Mechanical Turk (AMT). Currently the AMT platform hosts more than 260,000 tasks posted by businesses and researchers [1]. AMT has been found to be an attractive alternative to lab-based behavioural studies due to its 24/7 access to an extremely large and diverse participant pool [16, 12, 14], reduced time and monetary cost of experiment administration and execution [12, 16], and its support for increased experimental scale [13, 14] and ease of experiment modification [16].

AMT has been successfully used in a number of studies illustrating that crowdsourcing research tasks is a plausible alternative. For example, Heer and Bostock [12] showed that AMT could be used to successfully recreate the results of Cleveland and McGill's classical perception study [3] as well as provide new perceptual insights with modified experimental tasks. Kamarov, et al. [13] investigated the feasibility of conducting performance-based research via AMT and found that there were no significant differences between their results obtained via laboratory experiments and those obtained from AMT, indicating that AMT can be reliable for conducting performance-based experiments.

Despite these successes, there are still some reservations regarding crowdsourcing (and the use of AMT), which prevent some researchers from adopting this approach [13]. The low rate of pay for completing tasks on AMT raises questions of ethics [16] and the loss of experimental control and low monetary incentives [8] raise questions about the quality of data that is collected from crowdsourcing.

Researchers have begun to investigate platforms that motivate participation through non-monetary incentives. One example is LabintheWild, developed by Reinecke et al [17]. LabintheWild is an online experiment platform, which incentivizes participation through a person's innate desire to learn about themselves and compare their performance with others. Instead of monetary compensation, LabintheWild provides participants with personalized feedback and reports, which they can use to gauge their performance, see how they stand up when compared with the performance of others, and share with their friends through social media platforms. In their evaluation, Reinecke et al found that the LabintheWild platform was able to attract a larger more diverse group of participants, and the non-monetary incentives did not compromise the quality of data gathered [17].

Gamification and Crowdsourced Games

"Gamification" refers to the addition of game elements in a non-gaming context in order to "create gameful and playful user experiences, motivate desired user behaviors, and generally, increase joy of use" [6]. Prior research into the effectiveness of adding game elements to work-based tasks shows that gamification can motivate participation [2], enhance performance, and increase participants' level of enjoyment [10]. Gamification has been used in a variety of projects intended to facilitate research [2, 10, 21].

Due to the motivational draw of gamification, researchers have also used games and game elements in crowdsourcing tasks as a way to motivate participation. This was largely introduced in von Ahn and Dabbish's successful GWAPs (Games With a Purpose) that have participants, as a side effect of playing, perform basic tasks that are unable to be automated by current technology [19]. The most well-known GWAP is the ESP game [18], which has participants paired up in a game where they must try to guess what word the other participant is thinking after being shown an image. The goal of this GWAP was to have participants provide accurate and descriptive labels for images on the internet. ESP managed to attract over 13,000 participants in four months and resulted in the accurate labeling of nearly 300,000 images. Crowdsourced games have been used to examine many research problems such as studying protein structures [4], improving web accessibility [20], attracting participation in relevance assessment tasks [9], and generating social network graphs [11].

Despite the benefits of gamification, it is still unknown what effects adding game elements can have on the quality of the data received from such tasks. Also the development of gamified systems can be largely time consuming, requiring that highly customized games be developed for each research problem being studied [10, 19].

Freemium Model

"Freemium" is a term coined to identify the business model where a large portion of users consume the service for free while other users pay to unlock premium features [5].

This business model can be frequently seen in today's mobile app market where it has been highly adopted by developers. This model allows developers to reach a large user base, while still covering the cost of development or even making a profit. In the context of mobile games, some freemium models provide demo levels of a game and require players to pay for additional content (e.g., Cut the Rope[1] by Chillingo). Some provide basic gameplay for free but require payment for in-game extras, such as powerups that boost gameplay, faster game progression, or costumes (e.g., Clumsy Ninja[2] by Natural Motion). Many provide ad-free game play for a price, but require players to view ads if they wish to play for free (e.g., Angry Birds Star Wars[3] by Rovio Entertainment). Developers continue to experiment with the Freemium model; for example, by requiring players to pay to avoid a cool-down period after repeated failed attempts to complete a task (e.g., Bombcats[4] by Chillingo), by requiring payment to activate a kid-friendly mode (e.g., Racing Penguin, Flying Free[5] by Top Free Games), or by leveraging access to your social network to provide you with additional content (e.g., Candy Crush Saga[6] by King.com). Payment often occurs through microtransactions, which are small payments used to make progress or unlock content or features.

Given the success of Freemium models at attracting players, we are interested in whether we can ask people to do work that benefits research (i.e., microexperiments), instead of making purchases (i.e., microtransactions), to allow them to play a mobile game for free.

A FRAMEWORK FOR CROWDSOURCED MOBILE DATA COLLECTION

The platform we developed combines both gamification and crowdsourcing techniques into a fun and compelling smartphone-based game, Sugar Rush, for delivering experimental tasks to voluntary participants. Developing a smartphone-based system allows us to leverage the small gaps in people's lives (e.g., waiting for the bus) in which they may be most willing to perform experimental tasks.

The platform is made up of two separate components: the game and the task manager. The game was developed to run on Android devices using the libGDX game development framework. The experimental task manager was developed in java and plugs in to the libGDX game. All game code and graphics were created in our lab.

Gameplay

Our game follows a genre referred to as an infinite vertical platformer, which has seen recent popularity in the mobile market (e.g., Doodle Jump[7] by Lima Sky LLC, Happy Jump[8] by Noodlecake Studios Inc., Mega Jump[9] by Get Set Games Inc.). The objective is to try to climb as high as possible without falling. We chose this game mechanic because it allows players to quickly get into or leave a play session with no need for deep menu systems, loading individual levels, or continuing previous content. This makes our game a good choice for those moments we are trying to leverage for participation in our experiment, i.e., when someone needs a quick distraction.

In our game, Sugar Rush (see Figure 1), players control a continuously bouncing avatar that they must guide through a series of pseudo-randomly generated platforms in order to collect as many coins as possible. The player controls the avatar by tilting the device left or right (which moves the avatar left or right), navigating their way to bounce on top of platforms. Players also try to gather candy and avoid enemies in an attempt to attain a new high score. If the avatar collides with an enemy or if it misses a platform, the player "dies", falls off the bottom of the screen, and the game session ends. The game maintains a local scoreboard, which is displayed after every session and contains the top five scores achieved on that device. A *game session* is defined as one round of play from the beginning of the game until the avatar 'died'.

[1] play.google.com/store/apps/details?id=com.zeptolab.ctr.ads
[2] play.google.com/store/apps/details?id=com.naturalmotion.clumsyninja
[3] play.google.com/store/apps/details?id=com.rovio.angrybirdsstarwars.ads.iap
[4] itunes.apple.com/ca/app/id595968088
[5] play.google.com/store/apps/details?id=com.topfreegames.racingpenguin
[6] play.google.com/store/apps/details?id=com.king.candycrushsaga
[7] play.google.com/store/apps/details?id=com.lima.doodlejump
[8] play.google.com/store/apps/details?id=com.noodlecake.happyjump
[9] play.google.com/store/apps/details?id=com.getsetgames.megajump

Powerup items – in-game features that boost performance – can be accessed from the main menu (see Figure 1) and "purchased" by players using in-game credits. These powerups provide players with a benefit to their game performance, such as increasing the value of each candy collected, or blasting the player through the first sections of the game, collecting a large amount of coins along the way. Once powerups have been purchased, they are automatically applied to the next session the player starts.

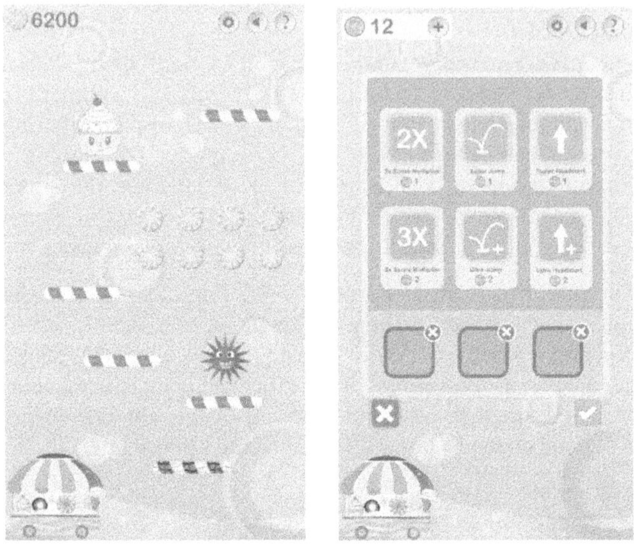

Figure 1. Sugar Rush: Gameplay (left), Powerup menu (right).

Players can earn in-game credits to purchase powerups by completing the quick experimental tasks that are included in the task manager. When the player chooses to participate in a microexperiment, the system randomly chooses one of the available experimental tasks. Upon the completion of the task, the player is awarded a single credit. The number of credits required to purchase a powerup varies between one and two credits and a player can purchase a total of three powerups at a time, providing incentives for the player to participate in multiple experimental tasks.

Task Integration

The task manager is responsible for choosing, displaying, and executing the experimental tasks.

All experimental task logic is isolated from the task manager and contained within individual task objects. These objects conform to a common Task interface, which allows the manager to notify the chosen task when it is supposed to run its programmed experiment. The task manager acts solely as a container and controller for the experimental tasks and task objects can be modified, added, or removed quickly, requiring only the development of a single object and an update pushed to the Android market.

The task manager itself is isolated from the gameplay aspect of the framework. The game has no knowledge of the tasks included in the task manager and the task manager has no knowledge of the game the player is playing or the rewards the player will receive for completing tasks. When the player taps the "add credit" button to earn more credits, the manager receives a call from the game, chooses a task, and notifies the chosen task to run its programmed experiment. Once the player has completed the microexperiment, the game receives notification from the manager; it is up to the game itself to determine what type of reward the player then receives.

Integrating the tasks in this way decouples the microexperiments from the gameplay, while still providing the motivational framework. This is important, because we wanted to ensure that the microexperiments could be modified or substituted without the need to modify the underlying game mechanics. In this way, a single game can accommodate a variety of experimental tasks, as opposed to the previous integrated approach of creating a new game for each task. Likewise this allows our task manager to potentially be integrated into many different game types utilizing different variations of the Freemium model.

Tasks

To evaluate the system, we chose two common tasks that differ in their requirements: Fitts's reciprocal tapping task [15], and Cleveland and McGill's perception task [3].

We chose a motor task and cognitive task to help determine if the system was better suited to one type of experimental task. We might expect to see degradations in the cognitive task that requires attentional resources; however, it is possible that the mobile nature of the participant as well as the small screen real estate provided by a smartphone or tablet will result in degradations in a motor task.

Motor Task

The Fitts reciprocal tapping task [15] was created to understand human motor processing and has been appropriated for computer-based aiming research. In this task, players tap on two horizontal bars in an alternating pattern (Figure 2). First, players are shown an instruction screen that explains the goal of the task, and contains what we refer to as an anchor – a button on the screen where players are asked to place their thumb to start the task. Once the player places their thumb on the anchor, the two horizontal bars are displayed and the participants are instructed to tap the bars with their opposite thumb. The anchor was included to avoid the situation where a player uses both thumbs when tapping the bars, one thumb over each bar. This behaviour would "game" the system by producing fast completion times for the task that do not conform to the expectations of a reciprocal tapping task.

There are three sizes of horizontal bars as well as three distances between bars, resulting in seven unique index of difficulties. A single combination is randomly chosen and used for a single task session. The system logs performance metrics, including the time between successive taps and the number of errors made. We chose the Fitts task because it has been well studied in the literature in human-computer interaction and represents a standard motor task.

Cognitive Task

The perception task used by Cleveland and McGill [3] was created to understand how humans perceive and respond to various ways of visually presenting quantitative data, and has been used in research in information visualization. In this task, data is presented to a user in different chart formats and users are asked to judge which category is smaller and by how much. Players are first shown a bar graph (as seen in Figure 2) and asked to identify which data category, indicated by the dots, is smaller. They are then presented with a text field and asked to estimate the percentage that the smaller bar takes up of the larger bar. Five different chart types are presented (referenced as Type 1 through Type 5). The system logs player responses along with task characteristics. We chose this task because it represents a well-studied task in the area of visual perception and has been previously used in the evaluation of crowdsourced data collection [12].

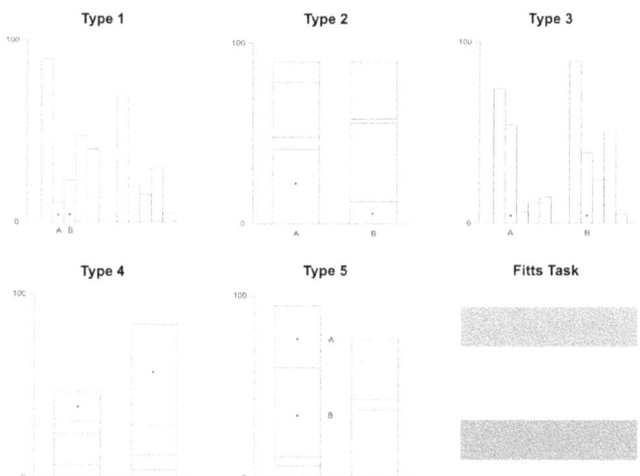

Figure 2. Top and Bottom Left: Graphs used in the cognitive task; Bottom Right: The bars in the reciprocal tapping task. The orange bar identifies the bar that is to be tapped next.

EVALUATION

To evaluate our framework we were interested in examining two main questions. First, we need to find out whether the quality of the work that they are doing meets the standards set by similar experiments conducted using more traditional approaches, such as in the lab. Second, we need to know whether participants are motivated to play our game and whether they find enough value in the powerups to "work" for them by doing tasks.

Game Versions for Experiment

To investigate these questions we developed three versions of the Sugar Rush game so that we could isolate the effects of gamification and crowdsourcing separately.

Crowdsourced Game

This is the complete version of the system that was released on the Android market. Data from the game was gathered over 5 weeks and included data from 841 unique downloads. This version is gamified and crowdsourced.

Laboratory Game

The lab version of the game is identical to the crowdsourced game except that it includes an additional starting screen that prompts the experimenter to enter the participant id, rather than have one generated by the game itself. This version is gamified, but not crowdsourced.

Control

The control version of the system removed all elements of the game from the system and instead organized the tasks into a block with 14 tasks in total – one for each unique combination of bar height and bar width in the Fitts task (9 in total) and one for each graph in the McGill task (5 in total). The tasks were identical to the ones used in the crowdsourced and lab games without any mention of the game or earning credits. The block of tasks was repeated 7 times for each participant (98 trials). Between tasks, participants were prompted to take a break if needed. The order of the tasks was randomized within each block. This version is neither gamified nor crowdsourced.

Participants and Setting

Participants were unique to each condition and each participant gave informed consent.

Crowdsourced Game

Data for the crowdsourced game was collected over a period of 5 weeks and was gathered from 841 unique downloads. The only information that was logged that was not directly related to their performance in the game was the width, height and density of the screen for their device. No other device or personal information was gathered.

Laboratory Game

Data for the lab game was collected in a university laboratory. Twenty people (8 female, ages between 18 and 35 years) participated. In terms of gaming experience, 90% of the participants indicated that they played games at least a few times per month; 75% indicated that they play games on a mobile device at least a few times per month; 7 reported being the only people who used their mobile device to play games; 11 reported that their friends, spouse, or children also use their device for playing games.

Participants were introduced to the game objects, controls, screens, as well as walked through the two task types. Participants were then left to play the game for 50 minutes. The only requirement placed on the participants during their gameplay was that between each game session they were required to complete at least one task. If the participant wanted to complete multiple tasks in order to be able to purchase and use multiple powerups within their game, they were free to do so. At the end of the 50 minutes, the participants were asked to fill out a questionnaire with demographic questions and thoughts regarding the inclusion of experimental tasks within the game.

Control

Data for the control system was collected in a university laboratory. Twenty people (11 female; aged 18 to 35, with one participant 36 to 45) participated. In terms of gaming experience, 90% indicated that they play games at least a few times per month; 90% indicated that they play games on a mobile device at least a few times per month; 13 reported being the only person to play games on their mobile device; 7 reported that their friends, spouse, children, or parents use their device for playing games.

Participants were then introduced to the system and walked through the two task types. At the end, they filled out a brief demographic questionnaire.

Data Analysis

Data collected by the crowdsourced game was temporarily stored on the players' devices and opportunistically uploaded to a document-based NoSQL server when the game detected a network connection. A python script pulled the data from the server and parsed it into a useable format. Data collected for both the lab game condition and the control condition was stored locally on the mobile device that was used in the studies. A similar python script was used to pull the data from the device and parse it into the same format used for the crowdsourcing data.

We removed participants who only played one game, i.e., opened the application and played once, but never returned to the game for a second play session (260 people), and players who had an average score of zero in their game sessions, i.e., opened the game more than once but did not play it (80 people) from further analysis.

Motor Task

In the motor task, our dependent measure was the mean movement time (MT) for a single index of difficulty (ID). Participants completed ten reciprocal taps within a trial. After removing taps that contained an error, and outlier trials in which the MT was 3 standard deviations below the mean (52/14971 trials, 0.3%), we aggregated the remaining taps, creating a measure of mean MT per trial. We then aggregated across ID to create a measure of MT for each unique ID for each participant. Although the screen sizes differed in the Crowdsourced Game, ID is calculated as a ratio of distance over width, so the seven IDs were the same across all participants in all conditions. We also conducted a linear regression of ID on MT for each of the three experimental conditions separately to determine the differences in the quality of the model fits.

Cognitive Task

In the cognitive task, our dependent measures were the mean number of errors in judgment, i.e., the number of times the participant guessed that the bar was smaller, when in fact it was larger, and vice-versa (*selection errors*), and the logarithm (base 2) of the error in the judgment of the estimation of the difference in size (*log estimation errors*). Participants completed several repeated estimates of the same chart (there were five charts presented); data were aggregated over repeated trials of a single chart for each participant to get an indicator of central tendency.

For the Crowdsourced Game, we also created a spurious trial filter to identify trials with input that clearly was not an accurate estimate. Our goal with the spurious filter was to implement heuristics that a machine could use to remove unauthentic data. Our heuristics included: repeated entry of a single value across more than 3 successive trials, values outside the range of possibility (i.e., values greater than 300% - over 100% is not a possible result), and values less than 10%. This resulted in the classification of 40% of trials as spurious (one participant was removed from further analysis for having almost entirely spurious data).

Statistical Analysis

We conducted linear mixed models to investigate differences between conditions and for the different levels of a task with a condition, i.e., ID in the motor task and graph number in the cognitive task. We used a linear mixed model instead of a RM-ANOVA to account for the lack of full coverage in the data set for each participant in both the Crowdsourced Game and Lab Game. Because the type of task and the level of the task were presented randomly in the Crowdsourced and Lab Games, not all participants completed all levels of all tasks. The linear mixed model accounts for this missing data. Alpha was set to 0.05 and pairwise comparisons used the Bonferroni method of adjusting for multiple pairwise comparisons.

RESULTS

We organize our results into two sections. First, we present results related to the quality of data, i.e., how the results for the motor and cognitive task differ across the three experimental conditions. Second, we present the results for data motivation, i.e., how often did players earn and access the powerups by doing tasks in the crowdsourced game.

Data Quality

Fitts Reciprocal Tapping Task

A linear mixed model with Index of Difficulty (seven IDs) and Condition (Crowdsourced, Lab Game, Control) as fixed effects and participant modeled as a random factor revealed a main effect of ID on MT ($F_{6,31.6}$=38.5, p<.001). As Figure 3 shows, MT increases with ID; pairwise differences were significant, except for each ID with its closest neighbours (1.32<2.00 and up, 1.58<2.33 and up, 1.70<2.47 and up, 2.00< 2.47 and up, 2.33<2.81 and up).

There was, however, no significant effect of condition on MT ($F_{2,56.5}$=1.85, p>.05) or interaction of condition and ID on MT ($F_{12,31.2}$=1.6, p>.05). Although Figure 3 shows that MTs were slightly faster in the Control condition, these differences were not significant.

Figure 3 also shows how there is less variance in the mean MT for the Control condition. This could be due to the full coverage of that data set (more points were used in the aggregation) or because there is greater consistency in the controlled, non-gamified task. We investigated how this variability affects the fit of a model regressing ID on MT for each condition separately. Results showed that the prediction of MT by ID was significant for each condition (Crowdsourced: R^2=.710, β_{ID}=.84, t=3.5, p=.017; Lab Game: R^2=.880, β_{ID}=.94, t=6.1, p=.002; Control: R^2=.985,

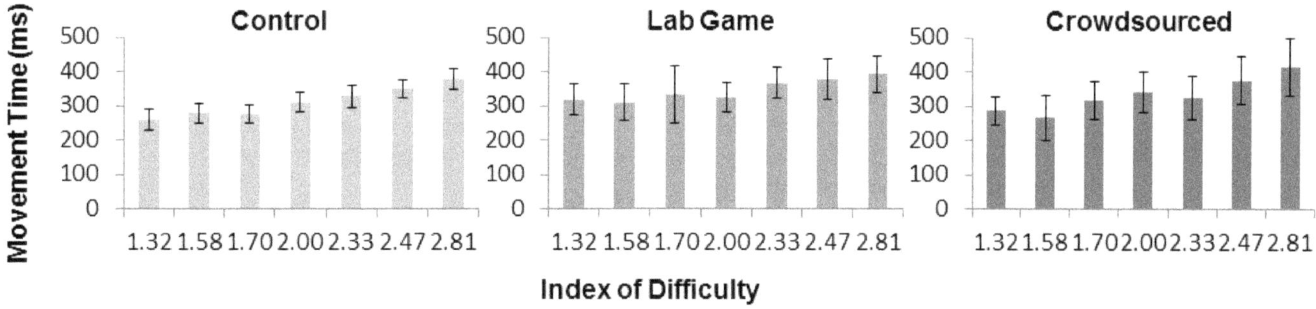

Figure 3. Mean movement time for the motor (Fitts) task across all three conditions.

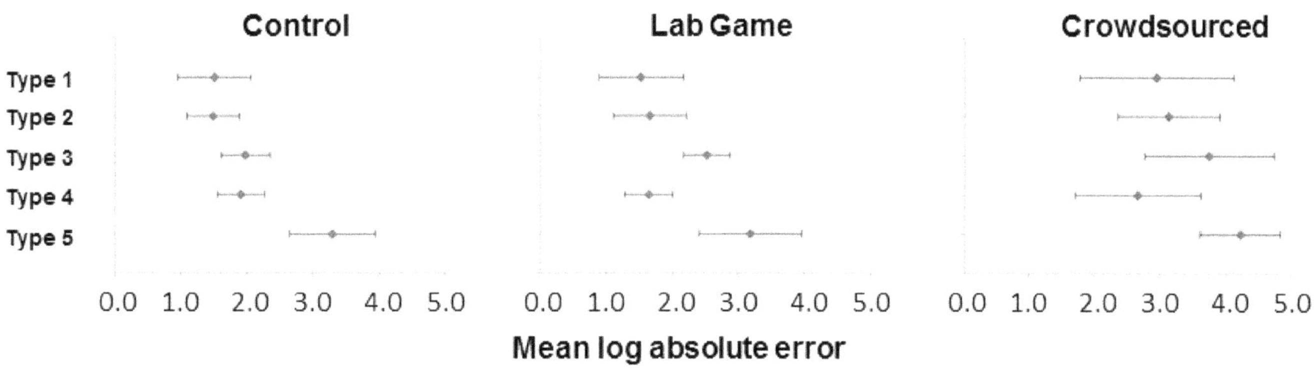

Figure 4. Mean log absolute error for the cognitive (McGill) task across all three conditions.

β_{ID}=.99, t=17.8, p<.001). However, the fit of the model was better for the Control condition than the Lab Game, which was in turn better than the fit for the Crowdsourced Game. In addition, the standardized Beta values exhibit the same relationship. As previously noted, this could be due in part to the full and repeated coverage of all IDs for all participants in the Control condition, but could also reflect the variability in performance that results from the game and from crowdsourcing the data collection.

These results show that there was no significant reduction in the performance of participants in the motor task when the task was gamified or crowdsourced; however, the regressions suggest that there is more variability in the data as a result of gamification and crowdsourcing. Whether or not this variability is due to the environment of the experiment or is an artifact of data coverage is unclear.

McGill Graph Task

A linear mixed model with graph number (Type 1 through Type 5) and experiment condition as fixed factors and participant modeled as a random factor revealed a main effect of condition on the mean number of selection errors ($F_{2,,9.2}$=6.15, p=.020), but no effect of graph type ($F_{4,4}$=5.8, p>.05) or interaction of graph type with condition ($F_{8,5.2}$=4.6, p>.05). The pairwise comparisons revealed that participants made more errors in the Crowdsourced Game than the Lab Game or Control condition (see Figure 4).

A similar linear mixed model revealed a main effect of condition on the $\log_2$ estimate error ($F_{2,44.4}$=10.1, p<.001). The pairwise comparisons revealed that participants had higher estimation error in the Crowdsourced Game than the Lab Game (p=.027) or Control condition (p<.001), see Figure 4). There was also a significant effect of graph type ($F_{4,28.2}$=18.7, p<.001), with participants performing worse with the Type 3 and Type 5 charts than the Types 1, 2, and 4 charts (see Figure 2 and Figure 4). There was a marginal interaction of condition and graph type on estimation error ($F_{8,31.1}$=2.2, p=.052). As Figure 4 suggests, the poor performance of the Type 3 chart was driven by the Lab Game and Crowdsourced conditions.

These results show that even with the spurious data filter applied, participants still performed worse (and with more variability) in the Crowdsourced Game than the Lab Game or Control condition on the cognitive task.

Motivation for Completing Tasks

We first present survey results from the Lab Game study and powerup usage data from the Crowdsourced Game.

Lab Game Survey Results

In the Lab Game condition, we asked participants for feedback on a variety of questions related to crowdsourcing experiment data collection through mobile gamification. Statements were posed for which participants rated their agreement on a 5-point scale from 1 (Strongly Disagree) to 5 (Strongly Agree). One-sample Wilcoxon Signed Ranks Tests compared the data to the hypothesized median result.

Participants significantly differed from the hypothesized median response (3.0) in their *agreement* with the following statements: I would play other games with embedded tasks if they were fun and free (median=4.0, χ^2=3.49, p<.001); Having to complete the tasks did not negatively affect my play experience (median=3.85, χ^2=3.85, p<.001); For a free game, I would rather complete tasks such as these than be forced to view advertisements (median=4.5, χ^2=3.09, p=.002); I would prefer to complete multiple tasks at a time to earn lots of credits (median=5.0, χ^2=3.70, p<.001); and, The tasks were easy to complete (median=5.0, χ^2=3.76, p<.001).

Participants significantly differed from the hypothesized median response in their *disagreement* with the following statements: I would rather not use powerups than have to complete the tasks (median=1.0, χ^2=3.01, p=.002); and Having to complete the tasks ruined the game play (median=1.0, χ^2=3.15, p=.002).

There was no difference from the hypothesized median response for the following statements: Playing Sugar Rush with the tasks made me feel like I was contributing to science (median=3.0, χ^2=1.34, p=.182); and I would pay $4.99 to play Sugar Rush without the tasks (median=1.0, χ^2=1.10, p=.272).

These results suggest that participants are open to the idea of leveraging the Freemium model for crowdsourcing data collection through gamification, that doing so does not negatively affect their play experience, and that the tasks were easy and are preferred to viewing advertisements. In this sample of participants, we asked them to complete one task for each game, and results might differ for those participants who completed the experiment in the wild.

Crowdsourced Game Use Statistics

We calculated how many players used powerups in the game. The results showed that powerups were only used in 1.1% of gameplay sessions (SD=5.9), which suggests that players were not motivated to use the powerups. However, we also discovered that only 5.3% of players (40) ever used a powerup at all. More importantly, those players who tried even a single powerup used them in 21% of gameplay sessions (SD=16.4), which is a reasonable rate of powerup usage. Our game did not expose players explicitly to the powerups, but those players who discovered powerups used them in over 1/5th of game sessions. Because players needed to earn the powerups by completing experimental tasks, our results suggest that very few experimental tasks were ever completed. In fact, the 40 players who used powerups in the game completed 1101 tasks, an average of 27.5 per person, suggesting that players who find the powerups motivating in the game are willing to complete the tasks to earn them.

Data from the Lab Game condition study suggest that exposing players to the powerups will improve their use. In that condition, players were explicitly asked to complete tasks and thus had credits available to purchase powerups for use in their game sessions. Nineteen of the twenty participants used powerups in game, and those that did used them in 69% of game sessions (SD=24). Although we would not expect to see this rate of powerup usage in the wild, there is an indication that exposing the players to the powerups might increase their appeal in the game. In the discussion we outline arguments of why players may not have used powerups and how this could be easily addressed through small changes to game design.

DISCUSSION

The results of our evaluation showed that data quality did not appear to be affected by our gamified framework for the motor task; however, crowdsourcing significantly reduced data quality for the cognitive task. Also, despite the overall usage of powerups being low, those participants who were exposed to the powerups in their gameplay used them often and, for the Lab Game condition, players reported being open to the idea of more free-to-play games that include experimental tasks for in game rewards.

In the following sections we discuss the implications of our results on the design and usage of our framework.

Separation of Game and Tasks

Because our framework separates out the game from the tasks, we are able to substitute any game for Sugar Rush and any task for the Fitts and McGill tasks that we chose. This allows us to maintain interest in the system through the release of new games and to ask any number of research questions. Our implementation only looked at research-based questions but any task – as long as the task can be deployed on a mobile phone – can be integrated with our paradigm. This would include tasks such as human computation tasks found on AMT (e.g., image labeling, object identification) or more active tasks like those associated with citizen science, where participants are involved with the collection or analysis of data.

Increasing Task Participation

In this section we discuss the effectiveness of the powerups at motivating participation and introduce alternate design strategies for increasing task participation.

Increase Exposure to the Benefits of Powerups

While the results showed that there was a small uptake in the number of players who used powerups, those players who did use powerups used them frequently. This would suggest that once players find the benefit in using the powerups, they are more likely to want to use more. There are design techniques that could be employed to increase the players' exposure to the benefits of the powerups.

Games such as Candy Crush[6] and Frozen: Free Fall[10] employ a technique whereby the player starts off with a limited number of powerups of various types. This gives the player an opportunity to try them out in their game and experience the benefits the powerups provide. The players also become used to having the powerups to use in their gameplay, increasing the likelihood that they will pay, or in our case complete tasks, in order to obtain more. This same

[10] itunes.apple.com/us/app/frozen-free-fall/id692412579

technique could be employed in Sugar Rush by giving the participants free uses of the powerups for a short while, or by starting the player off with a number of credits so they can purchase the powerups they wish to try out. Frozen: Free Fall[10] also gives players a free powerup each day they return to play the game, encouraging repeated play and getting players used to having powerups.

Another option is to include a tutorial session that walks the player through earning a credit by completing a task, and then using a powerup in a game session. This would help introduce players to the powerups, and highlight the benefits of using them in their game.

Non-Voluntary Task Integration

The current design of our framework makes the completion of tasks voluntary. Players are left to decide whether or not they participate in the tasks in order to receive game powerups. There are game designs that could be employed that would force the player to participate in tasks instead.

Some games employ mechanics that hinder the progress of the player until a requirement has been met. For example in some free-to-play games, players are required to watch an advertisement between game sessions. Other free-to-play games contain 'locked' content that will only become available to the players after they have purchased the full game or paid money to have them unlocked. These designs could be used to require players to complete experimental tasks to continue playing or gain access to content.

Variable Reward Structure

Our current implementation associates all tasks with a single reward – players get one credit when completing any of the tasks. In implementations that contain multiple experiments with different difficulties or required effort, participation in the tasks may vary. To account for this or to motivate players to participate in more time-consuming or difficult tasks, a variable reward structure could be used. To do this a standardized ranking could be associated with the task implementations within the framework, and the game could decide what type of rewards the individual ranks are to receive. For example, since the cognitive task required more effort in our implementation, the framework could notify the game that this task should receive a higher reward and the game could respond accordingly, in our case by providing more credits for task completion.

Data Quality

In this section we discuss our findings regarding the quality of the task data, the implications they have on the usage of our framework, and suggest ways to improve performance.

Effect of Task Type on Data Quality

Analysis of our results showed that data received from the motor task was able to predict movement time with relative accuracy across each condition. However, analysis of the data from the cognitive task was found to be significantly worse in the crowdsourced condition than the data received from either the lab game condition or the control condition. One possible explanation for this difference could be the uncontrolled environment in which participants are not asked to put effort into the tasks by an experimenter. Rather, the participants are more concerned with simply completing the task in order to quickly earn their credit. Because this concern of earning the credit quickly is in line with the performance-based nature of the motor task, it does not affect the quality of the results. However, because the cognitive task requires that participants take the time to make a judgment regarding the values they input, this goal of finishing as quickly as possible is detrimental to quality.

Rewarding Effort Instead of Participation

One way to motivate greater effort and accuracy by the participants in their responses is to make the rewards contingent on the effort put into the task. If entered data is identifiable as being false– such as the large sequential numbers used in the graph task or unrealistic response times – the credit reward can be withheld. Although this would only deter players from providing obviously false data, our results showed that when participants took time to enter a value, the value entered was not unreasonable. In addition, the value of the reward could be tied to the accuracy of the data, motivating participants to input quality data. Withholding rewards for obvious lack of effort or tying the value of the reward to the quality of the answer would encourage participants to spend more time in giving a response and likely result in better quality data.

LIMITATIONS AND FUTURE WORK

We released our framework on the Android market and gathered data from lab studies. We began our evaluation by isolating and investigating the factors of gamification and crowdsourcing on the quality of gathered data. To fully evaluate our framework, we need to also isolate and investigate the effect that the mobile platform has on the quality of the results. We plan to conduct a comparison study between the data gathered by our framework and data that is gathered from a non-mobile environment (i.e., desktop game in a laboratory setting, and a crowdsourced game on the AMT platform). In addition, it would be valuable to consider how our approach could be moved to a desktop environment to leverage the large computer video game market. Future work can also investigate alternative Freemium models (e.g., advertisements or unlocking additional content) to determine how best to motivate participation in tasks. One of the more popular Freemium models has players view brief advertisements; comparing how players respond to our approach versus ad viewing would provide valuable information. In our study it was found that the performance-based motor task resulted in a higher level of data quality than the cognitive task. This may have been because the goal of the performance-based task is in line with the goal of the player wanting to quickly earn a credit, or it may have been that the performance-based nature of the task was in line with the performance-based nature of the game. It would be interesting to investigate whether the type of game that is used to frame the context of the tasks has an effect on the performance results of the tasks that are included. Moving forward it would also be beneficial to determine the optimal duration of and effort required by the microexperiments to optimize willing participation and data quality.

CONCLUSION

Gathering data on human behaviour is a limiting factor in behavioural research. Crowdsourcing and gamification provide two possible solutions to this data collection problem but they each pose issues of their own. In this paper we presented our solution, which combines both gamification and crowdsourcing techniques into a smartphone-based platform to motivate voluntary participation and provide researchers with a framework that can be used to investigate multiple research questions without the need to develop costly specialized games.

Results from our evaluation showed that the quality of the motor task data did not suffer; however, the data from the cognitive task did. We feel that tying the reward to the quality of the data could improve data quality for attention-based tasks. Despite a low adoption of powerups, players that were exposed to the experimental tasks were supportive of participating in return for in-game benefits.

ACKNOWLEDGMENTS

We thank the GRAND NCE for funding, the Interaction Lab at the University of Saskatchewan for support, and Andre Doucette, Jess Richards, and Chad Jones at Push Interactions for application development and release.

REFERENCES

1. *Amazon's Mechanical Turk.* (2014). Retrieved from Amazon's Mechanical Turk: https://www.mturk.com/
2. Cechanowicz, J., Gutwin, C., Brownell, B., & Goodfellow, L. (2013). Effects of Gamification on Participation and Data Quality in a Real-World Market Research Domain. *Gamification 2013*, (pp. 58-65). Stratford, Ontario.
3. Cleveland, W. S., & McGill, R. (1984). Graphical perception: Theory, experimentation, and application to the development of graphical methods. *J. Am. Statistical Association, 79* , 531-554.
4. Cooper, S., Khatib, F., Treuille, A., Barbero, J., Lee, J., Beenen, M., et al. (2010). Predicting protein structures with a multiplayer online game. *Nature* , 756-760.
5. de la Iglesia, J. L., & Gayo, J. E. (2009). Doing Business by Selling Free Services. In *Web 2.0* (pp. 1-14).
6. Deterding, S., Björk, S., Nacke, L. E., Dixon, D., & Lawley, E. (2013). Designing Gamification: Creating Gameful and Playful Experiences. *CHI 2013: Changing Perspectives* (pp. 3263-3266). Paris, France: ACM.
7. Deterding, S., Sicart, M., Nacke, L. E., O'Hara, K., & Dixon, D. (2011). Gamification: Using Game-Design Elements in Non-Gaming Contexts. *CHI '11 Extended Abstracts on Human Factors in Computing Systems* (pp. 2425-2428). Vancouver, BC, Canada: ACM.
8. Downs, J. S., Holbrook, M. B., Sheng, S., & Cranor, L. F. (2010). Are your participants gaming the system?: Screening Mechanical Turk workers. *In Proc. CHI '10* (pp. 2399-2402). ACM.
9. Eickhoff, C., Harris, C., & de Vries, A. P. (2012). Quality through Flow and Immersion: Gamifying Crowdsourced Relevance Assessments. *SIGIR'12* (pp. 871 - 880). ACM.
10. Flatla, D. R., Gutwin, C., Nacke, L. E., Bateman, S., & Mandryk, R. L. (2011). Calibration Games: Making Calibration Tasks Enjoyable by Adding Motivating Game Elements. *UIST `11* (pp. 403-411). Santa Barabara, CA, USA: ACM.
11. Guy, I., Perer, A., Daniel, T., Greenshpan, O., & Turbahn, I. (2011). Guess Who? Enriching the Social Graph through a Crowdsourcing Game. *CHI 2011* (pp. 1373-1382). Vancouver, BC: ACM.
12. Heer, J., & Bostock, M. (2010). Crowdsourcing Graphical Perception: Using Mechanical Turk to Asses Visualization Design. *CHI 2010: Visualization* (pp. 203-212). Atlanta, GA, USA: ACM.
13. Komarov, S., Reinecke, K., & Gajos, K. Z. (2013). Crowdsourcing Performance Evaluations of User Interfaces. *CHI 2013: Changing Perspectives.* Paris, France: ACM.
14. Kraut, R., Olson, J., Banaji, M., Bruckman, A., Cohen, J., & Couper, M. (2004). Psychological Research Online: Opportunities and Challenges. *American Psychologist* , 105-117.
15. MacKenzie, S. I. (1992). Fitts' Law as a Research and Design Tool in Human-Computer Interaction. *Human-Computer Interaction, 7* , 91-139.
16. Mason, W., & Suri, S. (2012). Conducting Behavioural Research on Amazon's Mechanical Turk. *Behavior Research Methods* , 1-23.
17. Reinecke, K., & Gajos, K. LabintheWild: Conducting Large-Scale Online Experiments With Uncompensated Samples. *To appear in CSCW'15.*
18. von Ahn, L., & Dabbish, L. (2008). Designing Games With A Purpose. *Communications of the ACM* , 58-67.
19. von Ahn, L., & Dabbish, L. (2004). Labeling Images with a Computer Game. *CHI 2004* (pp. 319-326). Vienna, Austria: ACM.
20. von Ahn, L., Ginosar, S., Kedia, M., Liu, R., & Blum, M. (2006). Improving Accessibility of the Web with a Computer Game. *CHI 2006* (pp. 79-82). ACM.
21. Watson, D., Hancock, M., & Mandryk, R. (2013). Gamifying Behaviour that Leads to Learning. *Gamification '13*, (pp. 87-90).

Unequal Time for Unequal Value: Implications of Differing Motivations for Participation in Timebanking

Patrick C. Shih[1], Victoria Bellotti[2,3], Kyungsik Han[1], and John M. Carroll[1]

[1]College of Information Sciences and Technology
The Pennsylvania State University
{patshih, kuh178, jcarroll}@ist.psu.edu

[2]Palo Alto Research Center
3333 Coyote Hill Road
Palo Alto, CA, 94304
bellotti@parc.com

[3]Jack Baskin School of Computer Engineering
UC Santa Cruz, CA, USA

ABSTRACT
Timebanking is a service-based community currency, built on the principle that everyone's time is valued equally. It has potential for community building and reenergizing neighborhoods, but it faces several adoption challenges. We report on the largest investigation of timebanking practices to date by analyzing a combination of service exchange records from the three largest hOurworld timebanks with over 3,500 members with 33,000 completed service exchanges, and a survey of 446 members of over 120 hOurworld timebanks. Our findings suggest that the ideal of 'equal time, equal value' that is at the foundation of timebanking is a source of tension between members with instrumental versus idealistic and altruistic motivations. We suggest that future peer-to-peer systems must incorporate different rewards and incentives in order to accommodate users with different motivations.

Author Keywords
Timebanking; community currency; peer-to-peer service exchange; use and adoption challenges.

ACM Classification Keywords
H.5.m. Information interfaces and presentation (e.g., HCI): Miscellaneous.

INTRODUCTION
The emergence of the shared economy is disrupting conventional modes of business and transforming not only what we consume but how goods and services are exchanged, valued, and created [4]. Popular peer-to-peer (P2P) service exchange platforms such as AirBnB, Uber, TaskRabbit, and Kassi [19, 31] are rapidly changing the way we live our lives. Among these peer-to-peer (P2P) platforms, timebanking is a successful example of the P2P movement that has been around for decades. It is a service-based community currency—the time dollar—embodying the principle that everyone's time is valued equally. In other words, my hour spent mowing your lawn is as valuable as your hour spent doing my tax return. So, the work produced by the less skilled is equally valued in this system. In a timebank community, one member can earn time dollars by performing a service for another, and use the earned time dollars to request for a service from another member.

There is a long history to the development of community currencies. Like a variety of P2P services based on sharing, bartering, lending, trading, renting, gifting, swapping, etc., they are concerned with community, and social capital creation, boosting local economics and valuing marginalized labor. This enables collaborative consumption to reduce environmental impacts of current lifestyles. Seyfang and Longhurst provided a review of the lifecycle and evolution of international community currencies and organized them into four main types: service credits, mutual exchange, local currencies, and barter markets [30]. Timebanking (a form of service credits) is the oldest and the most widely adopted service-based community currency.

Prior studies have detailed timebanking's potentials in community building and reenergizing neighborhoods, but it faces several adoption challenges. For example, members prefer to offer instead of requesting services and the limited range of service on offer creates stagnation in members' ability to exchange time dollars [1, 22, 25]. The majority of the earlier timebanking studies were reported in ethnographic fashion, based on interviews and focus group data. Given advances in timebank systems that track detailed transaction data, Collom et al. suggested future researchers to leverage detailed transaction logs combined with surveys to analyze trends that influence timebank participation [13].

In this work, we employ a comprehensive survey study constructed based on conversations and 50 formal interviews with timebank founders, organizers, founders, members. The survey was distributed to approximately 10,000 members in over 120 US timebanks. With the help of timebank founders, we have also obtained database records of the three largest US timebanks. Our exploratory analysis of database service exchange records across the three largest timebanks in the US that consist of over 3,500

CHI 2015, April 18 - 23, 2015, Seoul, Republic of Korea
Copyright 2015 ACM 978-1-4503-3145-6/15/04...$15.00
http://dx.doi.org/10.1145/2702123.2702560

members with over 33,000 completed service exchanges is the most comprehensive characterization of timebank service exchanges to date.

We explore trends of member practices, only now tractable with our large dataset of service exchange transactions and survey results. In our analysis, we look for explanations of hindrances that have prevented timebanking from achieving mass adoption. Specifically, we focus on how differing self-serving and prosocial motives of timebank members affect participation. P2P services mediated by computer systems are exploding but little has yet been reported on what motivates participation (but see [3]; this venue). Here we present a close examination of an incumbent model of an established community currency practice to expose tension that could energize new designs for motivating P2P system participation in general.

RELATED WORK

Although the idea of timebanking was first conceptualized in the form of 'labor notes' in 1827 by Josiah Warren, the term 'timebanking' did not come into existence until Edgar Cahn coined it in 1986 [6] and subsequently founded the TimeBanks USA organization in 1995 [5]. Timebanking has evolved from earlier community currencies such as the Local Exchange Trading System (LETS), and a detailed history of timebanking and its predecessors can be found in [29] and [2]. In this section, we focus our review on the current understanding of timebank values and member practices in different domains, and the hindrances that prevented it from achieving mainstream adoption.

Timebanking Values and Member Practices

Since timebank transactions revolve around time-based services that require physical interaction and commitment, co-production (i.e., the provider and recipient jointly produce a service) is a direct outcome of timebank participation. In co-production, both parties engage in mutually beneficial exchanges and the shared resources and resulting social capital produce further intangible benefits to the whole community. Many see co-production and egalitarian values of timebanks as driving forces for reviving community engagement. For example, Cahn describes his vision of a successful timebank leading to "no more throw-away people" [5], and Seyfang sees timebanking as a mechanism to tackle the problem of social exclusion among the underprivileged [24].

To understand member participation, Seyfang surveyed 64 members in a timebank in South London. She found that the majority are low-income women in ethnic minority groups who are not in formal employment [25]. Over half the participants belonged to socially excluded groups, and many of them were referred to the timebank by their general practitioners for physical and mental health problems. They participate in timebanking for volunteering and informal mutual support, to access help for themselves, to get more involved in the community, to improve the neighborhood, to meet people and make friends, and to earn time credits. Gregory studied the timebank movement and its development in the UK and how it has been associated with the notion of co-production [16]. He argued that timebank-based co-production offers a tool for social policy to help deliver welfare services at a time of austerity, with potential to help re-engage and empower users of the welfare state. In both studies, timebanking has been used as a mechanism for underprivileged members of society to reengage with the community.

Besides benefiting the socially excluded, timebanking has also been appropriated in other domains. In the context of healthcare delivery to elders, Lasker et al. surveyed 160 members of a hospital-affiliated timebank [19]. They concluded that timebank participation may promote health and sense of belonging among low-income, older individuals who live alone. Timebanking has also been seen as a way to assist youth in transition. Marks found that youth participation in timebanking increased engagement and active participation in services as well as helping them gain the developmental assets they need to be successful upon discharge from formal systems [21]. In terms of sustainable consumption, Seyfang argued that timebanking offers great potential for carbon-reduction by sharing community resources and offering a supportive social network that meets participants' social and psychological needs for recognition, self-esteem, and belongingness that might otherwise be met through material consumption [28].

Basing on a set of service exchange records (i.e., hours reported) and survey data at a US timebank, Ed Collom conducted a series of analyses aiming to unpack how members' motivation affected their participation and eventual outcomes. Collom conducted a survey that assessed the motivations, engagement, outcomes, satisfaction, community experience, and demographics at this timebank [9]. He found that, in contrast to government-backed timebanks in the UK that focus on the socially excluded and underprivileged members of society, timebank members in this US timebank are predominantly well-educated, low income, politically liberal, Caucasian females who were motivated to join largely for needs and values-based reasons. Using social network and multiple regression analyses of the survey data in addition to timebank service exchange records, Collom found that needs and social-based motivations led to higher timebank participation, and lower-income and unemployed participants are more likely to gain social capital outcomes [10]. Using the same dataset, Collom identified four motivations to be the most salient predictors of differential participation: economic/instrumental, ideological/value, altruistic, and social motivations [12]. He found that economic/instrumental motivation led to higher timebank commitment, and ideological and social motivations led to more willingness to give time or money to the timebank.

These earlier studies typically concentrate analysis on a particular timebank site with a relatively small membership. This often led to inconsistent reporting of trends across different timebanks. For instance, Collom found that the elderly are underrepresented in the timebank that he studied (a mere 8% compare to 13% in the region according to US census data), and they exchange primarily with the nonelderly [11]. But many other timebank studies report a high percentage of elder participation [2, 19, 25, 33]. Given advances in timebank systems that track detailed transaction data, Collom et al. suggested future researchers to leverage detailed transaction logs combined with surveys to analyze trends that influence timebank participation at a more general level [13]. Following Collom's suggestion, this paper reports on data from detailed database records of the three largest timebanks in the US. Our analyses may provide additional insights to timebanking practices.

Issues Hindering Timebanking Adoption

Previous timebank studies have attempted to uncover barriers to timebanking adoption as an alternative currency to money. In addition to the majority of prior studies that focused on assisting those in need, Ozanne studied a timebank in a relatively affluent community in New Zealand [22]. The members of this timebank have higher than average educational level and income relative to this region. She found that timebanking members in this community are motivated to participate by altruism but have a hard time recognizing what skills they have to offer, and recognizing that their skills have value and they find it hard to ask for help from other members. However, these challenges have also been identified across different timebank communities. For example, Seyfang's study of a UK timebank identified obstacles similar to those in the more affluent communities in which people prefer to give time than spend their credits [25]. A related issue is that there exists only a limited range of services on offer. Bellotti et al. also reported similar challenges in an investigation of challenges that affected timebanking participation in US timebanks [1].

Scholars have attempted to explain the causes of these challenges from several different perspectives. The first cause is thought to be people's lack of understanding of how timebanking works. Seyfang attributed these challenges to people's unfamiliarity with the concept of timebanking compared to traditional volunteering, and to the small size of the timebank which limits range of services on offer [25]. Bellotti et al. found that aspects of the banking metaphor—for example, the prospect of going into 'debt' in order to actively ask for help—act as deterrents that compound natural reticence when it comes to asking for help [1]. The second cause has to do with people's motivation to participate in timebanking. Glynos and Speed pointed to the complexity and nuances of differing needs in timebanking [14]. They analyzed how timebanking as an initiative that enacts principles of co-production can be used in the delivery of public services. They argued that co-production in timebanking is recognition-based (i.e., strengthening community and generating social value) whereas transactions involving healthcare services are market-driven (i.e., offering paid professional help), and could cause tension in practice. Similarly, Carroll articulated the differences between service exchange and co-production scenarios for conducting timebanking on mobile personal devices such as smartphones [7]. Carroll advocated that recognition generated from participating co-production activities should be explicit and designed into future timebanking systems. Other writers attributed these challenges to lack of organization and government support. Seyfang conducted a focus group study with 12 members of a timebank with 96 members in Glasgow, Scotland [26]. She found that nearly half of the members in this timebank were organizations and institutions representing many more participants, or individual staff who participated on behalf of organizations or institutions. She found that organization-led timebanks (e.g., most UK timebanks), such as this, have the ability to boost engagement in existing community projects and activities and promote social inclusion and community development, so they outperform one-to-one exchange timebanks (e.g., most US timebanks). Seyfang refers to lack of funding, understaffing, and lack of political support in public policy as primary obstacles to the wider adoption of timebanking [27].

To address these concerns, Seyfang argued that, for a new economics of sustainable consumption to be successful, there needs to be mainstream recognition of grassroots initiatives and community action as a previously neglected site of innovation, and top-down government support is needed to enable bottom-up initiatives to thrive [28]. Gregory proposed a slightly more radical integration with national currency and argued that timebanking should be taken up as an alternative system of exchange in local economies, beyond its role as a social intervention tool for community building [15]. To assist in sustainable development, local business should consider using time credits where one person's hour equals another's, rather than using an alternative currency that can be valued in terms of the national currency. For example, instead of seeing a 'half price' meal at the café, transactions could be viewed as the cost of materials paid for in cash, and the cost of labor in time. Other researchers have attempted to facilitate timebanking adoption with technological interventions. For example, Han et al. designed a mobile timebanking smartphone app and demonstrated in a user study that convenience and ease-of-use provided by mobile technologies could reduce duration of transactions, and enable location and time-sensitive timebanking activity support, and real-time coordination [17].

The main hindrances in timebanking adoption can be generalized into the following broad categories: people are *not familiar* with the concept of timebanking as opposed to traditional volunteering, the small size of a timebank *limits the range of services* on offer, some members prefer to earn *recognition rather than time credits*, and *lack of support* from organizations and government entities. The overarching visions of these earlier timebank initiatives typically involved the following: once people are more accustomed to timebanking, they will become more comfortable requesting services, and, when there are enough community members in the timebank, its internal marketplace will contain enough tasks to be self-sustaining and ultimately grow into a viable alternative social economy to displace the real money economy [27].

However, studies such as the above that have focused on timebanking obstacles do not unpack members' differing motivations, reported in empirical studies on timebanking practices. As mentioned above, Collom found differing motivations to be the strongest predictors of differential participation [12]. In this paper, we attempt to bridge this gap by combining log data on participation with data and findings on motivations from a comprehensive survey study across over 120 US timebanks. This allows us to illustrate how differing member motivations could be a major cause of some of the aforementioned hindrances.

STUDY DESIGN

To understand user motivations and experiences with service exchange using time-based currency, we established a partnership with hOurworld, one of the largest timebank networks in the US; growing from about 8000 in 2011 to over 26,000 members in over 230 timebanks as of December, 2014. We acquired database transaction logs of hOurworld timebanking activities from the three largest timebanks in the US with a total of over 3,500 members in total. We also distributed a 120-item survey to around 10,000 timebankers in over 120 timebanks in the US between August and November, 2014.

Data collection

We obtained database transaction logs from the three largest hOurworld timebanks, located in Portland, ME (founded in September, 1997), Los Angeles, CA (founded in February, 2008), and Milwaukee, WI (founded in August, 2009). The dataset includes information about members, service types, service transactions, reported hours, and so on. Since each timebank has a different starting date, we only considered the most recent 4 ½ years worth of the data (between January 1, 2010 and Aug 31, 2014) to make the analysis comparable.

We constructed a 120-item survey [1] based on many conversations and 50 formal interviews with founders, organizers, volunteers, and members of hOurworld, TimeBanks USA and other timebanking networks. We also referred to Collom's 193-item survey and included questions that are relevant to our study [9]. The goal of our survey was to characterize timebanking practices and to obtain quantitative data to complement and reinforce our qualitative interview data. The survey contained questions that spanned over topics such as members' demographic information, motivations to request and offer services in their timebank, their experiences receiving and performing services for others, the hindrances they encountered and what mattered to them when arranging transactions. The survey items consisted mostly of Likert-scale (1 = strongly disagree, 7 = strongly agree) or categorical items followed with open-text questions for clarifications. The survey took about 30 minutes to complete, and the survey respondents received a half-hour timebank credit in their hOurworld account to compensate for their time.

Data analysis

We looked for trends, clusters, and correlations in the database transaction logs and the Likert scale survey items. Clustering is a standard way to identify statistically distinct and non-overlapping clusters in a sample [18, 31]. Since we were interested in identifying groups of people who showed similar patterns, we used k-means clustering to search for contrasting clusters among the survey respondents based on their timebanking motivations, concerns, and usage. Item intervals were normalized prior to clustering. To decide a starting point of k, we first performed the centroid hierarchical clustering on all survey items. Post-hoc multiple comparisons were made to identify specific items that contributed significantly to an overall difference.

To explore the problem of the limited range of services on offer [1, 22, 25], we coded the 367 timebank database transaction types into 13 categories as defined in previous timebanking literature [13]. As a part of this exploratory effort, detailed service exchange records by service categories will be discusses in the results section below.

Collom suggested that motivational differences could result in differential timebanking participation [12]. When coding open-ended survey questions, we coded motivations based on categories identified in previous work [12]: instrumental, idealistic, social, and altruistic. We paid close attention to differences in participants' motivations for and concerns about offering and requesting services, and how those might have affected their timebank usage. Our findings are detailed in the remaining sections of this paper.

Timebank transaction characteristics

Table 1 shows the transaction records of the three timebanks in terms of the number of members, standing offers and requests, completed service exchanges, and hours reported for the completed service exchanges.

The Portland timebank has the highest number of overall transactions and hours reported. This is because it has been around for much longer (10+ years) than the other two

[1] Due to space limitation, please contact the authors to obtain a copy of the survey items.

	Portland	Los Angeles	Milwaukee
# Members	1,433	1,274	876
# Offers	913	199	349
# Requests	157	110	177
# Transactions	18,885	12,559	1,980
# Hours Reported	52,347	36,660	12,224
# Hrs. / Trans.	2.77	2.92	6.17

Table 1: Timebank service exchange records.

timebanks and has an established practice. The timebank in Milwaukee reported far fewer transactions than the other two, but it also has the highest hours per transaction ratio. This indicates that the services being exchanged are likely to be bigger community-related projects. One trend is that all timebanks contained more standing offers than requests, indicating that members prefer to offer services rather than requesting them. This is consistent with prior literature [1, 22, 25].

Survey respondent demographics

The 120-item survey was distributed to all 10,000 hOurworld members in over 120 US timebanks between August, 2013 and November, 2013. Overall, we received a total of 446 survey responses (4.5% response rate), consisting of 44 founders, 36 coordinators, 19 affiliated staff members, 187 members; 160 respondents chose not to indicate their role or affiliation. The respondents are predominantly Caucasian (89.9%) females (77.8%) who have earned at least a Bachelor's degree (81.8%). The respondents have an average age of 49 ranging from 22-78 years old. Nearly half of the respondents (47.1%) have been actively participating in timebanks for longer than 1 year. Overall, 42.1% have received and 53.6% have performed at least 5 or more timebank services. The number of completed transactions correlates significantly with the length of respondents' membership ($r(215) = 0.57$ for received and $r(190) = 0.59$ for performed service exchanges, $p < .001$).

As with any survey, self-selection bias may be present, and our survey sample could have been more representative of more active timebankers. To test this, we compared the number of transactions between the database transaction log data and the survey responses. The log data suggests that among users who timebanked in the past year, 54.9% have received and 55.8% have performed at least 5 or more timebank transactions; in the survey, these numbers are 42.1% and 53.6% respectively. These numbers are not statistically significantly different ($t(3159)=1.25$, p=n.s.), suggesting that survey respondents' timebank usage is representative of the timebanking population as a whole.

RESULTS AND DISCUSSION

In this section, we first examined the patterns identified in the database transaction logs to show that the differences between offers and requests are not uniform across different service categories. Most notably, certified skilled labor is the most lacking in these timebanks. We then presented the differences in motivations, concerns, and timebank usage among members observed from the survey study. Based on cluster analysis, we found significant differences between high and low timebank utilizer groups. Qualitative data revealed that comparison with national currency (i.e., money) was the key source of concerns about participation in timebanking.

Timebank services by category

We first analyze log data from the three large timebanks on transactions by service category. *Event organization and program support* (e.g., assisting with community- and timebank-related project/events, attending committee meetings, etc.) are community-based events and logistics-related tasks that keep timebanks operational. They constituted 56.2% of the total hours reported, which is consistent with the percentage reported in previous timebank literature [13]. Since these community- and timebank-related events typically involve co-production activities that provide value to a community, this high percentage of reported hours is indicative of a healthy level of community engagement and participation in the three timebanks. Table 2 summarizes the remaining 43.8% non-timebank-related services (43.8% is the total, or 100%, of all the categories showing their percentages) and shows the relative percentages of the number of standing offers and requests, OR differential (standing **O**ffers minus standing **R**equests, which is indicative of the balance of supply and demand), percentage of the number of completed service exchanges, percentage of hours reported across the three timebanks, and percentage of hours reported in a deceased timebank [13]. The service categories are highlighted in green (over 10% of the service transactions), yellow (between 5-10%), and pink (below 5%) based on the level of percent hours reported.

The high percentage of *health and wellness* services (e.g., physical therapy, mental health counseling, nutrition advice, family planning, women's health, etc.) is consistent with prior literature that reported people using timebanks as a channel to receive health and mental care [16, 25]. However, some of our results differ from Collom's report of Portland West Time Dollar Exchange (2002-2006) [13]. For example, *sales and rentals of items* accounted for the highest percentage of hours reported in [13] (17.7%) but was among the lowest in our dataset. This is likely due to member adoption of other online platforms such as Craigslist and eBay that became much more popular since 2006 to fulfill similar needs. Hours reported for *Cleaning, Light Tasks, and Errands* also appeared to be much lower in our dataset (6.8%) compared to that reported in [13] (12.4%). It is likely that there exist hindrances that prevented members from effectively completing services in this category. We will explore these hindrances in more detail below.

Service Category	Offers	Requests	OR Differential	Service Exchanges	Hours	Hours [13]
Health and Wellness	9.4%	13.2%	-3.8%	21.3%	17.1%	9.2%
Tutoring, Consultation, and Personal Services	20.2%	16.9%	3.3%	13.0%	15.5%	12.0%
Transportation and Moving	6.8%	6.4%	0.3%	13.2%	12.6%	11.1%
Office and Administrative Support	14.3%	8.5%	5.8%	11.6%	11.4%	7.1%
Construction, installation, maintenance, and repair	8.6%	18.4%	-9.8%	8.5%	10.5%	8.2%
Art and Crafts Production	7.5%	7.2%	0.2%	5.2%	6.8%	6.9%
Cleaning, Light Tasks, and Errands	11.2%	12.8%	-1.6%	7.4%	6.8%	12.4%
Computer and Technology	6.2%	7.0%	-0.8%	6.0%	5.5%	3.2%
Entertainment and Social Contact	9.6%	4.1%	5.5%	5.4%	5.5%	1.9%
Food Preparation and Service	5.3%	1.8%	3.5%	5.8%	5.0%	7.3%
Sales and Rentals of Items	0.3%	0.6%	-0.2%	1.1%	2.3%	17.7%
Beauty and Spa	0.8%	2.7%	-1.9%	1.3%	0.7%	3.2%

Table 2: Percentage of standing offers and requests, service OR differential (standing offers minus standing requests), completed transactions, and hours reported by service category in Portland, Los Angeles, and Milwaukee timebanks.

Although prior literature has consistently pointed out issues that hinder timebank service exchanges such as members wanting to offer services more than request them and having a limited range of services on offer [1, 22, 25], our dataset allows us to explore these issues in more detail. Our analysis of database service exchange records shows that the differences between offers and requests are not uniform across different service categories. In Table 2, we highlight in gray the service categories that may suffer from a shortage of offers (i.e., more people are requesting than are offering). General services such as *office and administrative support*, *entertainment and social contact*, and *food preparation and service* that require lower levels of specialized skills are the categories that have a surplus of offers with fewer requests, suggesting higher supply than demand. By contrast, services such as *construction, installation, maintenance, and repair* and *health and wellness* that require certified skilled labor are in higher demand than they are in supply.

In summary, we are able to leverage the service exchange records to identify that the issue of having a shortage services on offer affects service categories that require skilled labor (especially when providers may have to be certified as in Construction, installation, maintenance, and repair). On the other hand, the issue of people preferring to make offers rather than requests is most applicable to service categories that involve lower levels of specialized skills. Below, we triangulate these findings with survey data, and aim to provide explanations for these core issues that hinder timebanking usage.

Member motivations, concerns, and timebank usage

Clustering classified the respondents into two groups (N=212 and 77, $p < 0.001$). Table 3 summarizes the differences between two groups. The two groups identified by the clustering algorithm could be generally characterized as *High* and *Low* timebank utilizers. The high utilizers are composed of 42 timebank organizers and 35 members who had been a part of a timebank for 1-3 years on average. They utilized their timebank for service exchanges at least once a month on average. Timebank service exchanges made up approximately 66.4% of their overall service exchanges among other channels exchanging services such as personal favors from friends, social welfare services, and paid professional help. As high utilizers, they have completed an average of between 10-20 service exchanges. On the other hand, the low utilizers are predominantly members (133 members vs. 79 organizers) who had been in the timebank for 6-12 months. They used the timebank once every 2-3 months. Timebank service exchanges only made up 9.71% of their overall service exchanges. They also completed fewer service exchanges (an average of 5-10). A Chi-Square test showed significant difference in membership roles ($\chi^2(1)=6.93$, $p < 0.01$).

Our survey respondents identified a variety of motivations for participating in timebanks: instrumental (53.7%), ideological (30.3%), social (9.2%), and altruistic (6.9%) reasons. Figure 1 presents motivations by membership role. Organizers tended to participate in timebanking for idealistic reasons more so than members, and members

High (77)	Low (212)	F(1,287)
Member role (0=member; 1=organizer)		
0.55 (0.50)	0.37 (0.49)	7.05**
Use length (1=less than a month; 2=1-6 months; 3=6-12 months; 4=1-3 years; 5=3-5 years; 6=more than 5 years)		
3.91 (1.37)	3.40 (1.32)	8.19**
Use frequency (1=once a year or less; 2= once every half-year; 3= once every 2-3 months; 4= once a month; 5= once every 2 weeks; 6= once a week; 7= once a day or more)		
3.79 (1.26)	3.28 (1.28)	9.13**
Use for % of all service channels		
66.4 (19.36)	9.90 (9.55)	1084.7***
# Exchanges (1=none; 2=1-5 exchanges; 3=5-10; 4=10-20 exchanges; 5=20+).		
3.83 (1.28)	2.95 (1.23)	28.02***

Note: **p < 0.01; ***p < 0.001. Results are displayed in the format of Mean (SD).

Table 3: Timebank usage of high and low timebank utilizers.

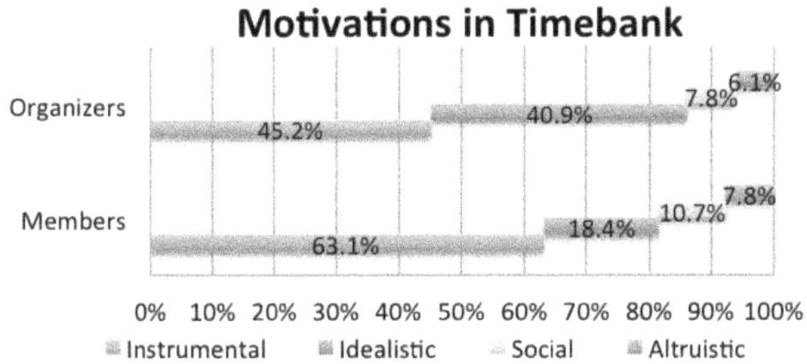

Figure 1. Motivations by Membership Role. Instrumental motivation means desire to get useful services. Idealistic motivation means drawn to timebank values of community and equal value for equal time

participated for instrumental reasons more so than organizers ($\chi^2(3)=12.97$, $p < 0.01$). This suggests that timebank organizers and members perceive the values of timebanking differently when carrying out timebank service exchanges. In the remaining portion of this section, we describe how this mismatch of motivations results in tensions and frustrations during service exchanges.

Timebanking Hindrances

Table 4 presents service exchange satisfaction and the hindrances that people encountered while they engage in these exchanges, based on the clusters of high and low timebank utilizer groups described above. Both groups reported that they are generally satisfied with their experiences and outcomes of the services that they provided and received. This is also reflected their relatively low concerns regarding service quality, trust, and inability to determine their needs in advance. In fact, those could be seen as strengths of timebanks in that these service exchanges often made members feel closer to being a part of the community, and they found other timebank members to be typically trustworthy and pleasant to deal with.

However, as the clusters showed, significant disparities between high and low timebank utilizers exist. Overall, the low timebank utilizers reported that they were significantly more concerned about different issues that hindered their ability to participate in timebank service exchanges than the high timebank utilizers. The low timebank utilizers also reported that they were less satisfied with their timebanking service exchanges than the high timebank utilizers.

Similar to their motivational differences, we wanted to see if the significant difference in membership roles affected

	High (77)	Low (212)	F(1,287)
Satisfied with Service	5.55 (0.83)	5.28 (0.98)	4.47*
Availability Issues	3.96 (1.30)	4.24 (1.21)	3.03
Inconvenience	3.47 (1.40)	4.56 (1.52)	30.05***
Lack of Trust	2.52 (1.21)	2.98 (1.24)	7.74**
Quality Concerns	2.02 (1.17)	2.93 (1.50)	23.36***
Unsure of needs	2.23 (1.45)	2.85 (1.52)	9.58**

Note: *$p < 0.05$; **$p < 0.01$; ***$p < 0.001$. Results are displayed in the format of Mean (SD). All items are 7-point Likert scale (1=strongly disagree; 7=strongly agree).

Table 4: Hindrances between high and low timebank utilizers.

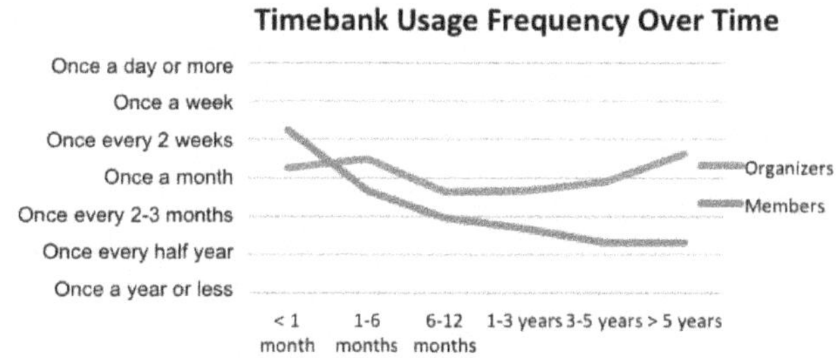

Figure 2. Timebank usage frequency over time.

people's timebank participation. Figure 2 shows the timebank usage frequency over time. Indeed, the data shows that while timebank organizers were able to sustain a relatively consistent level of activities over time, usage frequency of regular timebank members dropped from utilizing their timebank at least once every 2 weeks to once every half-year over time, and the difference is statistically significant ($F(1,386)=44.02$, $p < 0.001$).

In general, our survey results showed that regular timebank members were more concerned with issues such as inconvenience, lack of trustworthiness, quality issues, and inability to determine their needs in advance than the timebank organizers. This significantly affected regular members' ability and willingness to continue with timebanking.

Issues with Inconvenience

The issue that bothered the low timebank utilizers the most was the inconvenience of setting up and coordinating the logistics to carry out the service exchange. The majority of reports of inconvenience were due to issues having to do with transportation, and this is especially true in rural areas:

"We are a rural TimeBank and it can be hard to get in-person services conveniently as a result of distance from one another" (P74).

The inconvenience could be caused by a lack of planning or requests made on short notice:

"Sometimes I will get a last minute request for transportation needed in the next 5-10 minutes. That's hard to do. More notice would be helpful" (P17).

However, advanced planning was not always possible for timebank members because of their schedule and needs:

"I don't know my work schedule very far ahead, so it's hard to give advance notice of when I'm available. Much of the work I need help with is in my garden, so is weather dependent" (P439).

In summary, the concerns about inconvenience tended to involve transportation and schedule. This may have attributed to the relatively low hours reported in the *Cleaning, Light Tasks, and Errands* category previously mentioned above. While coordination can depend on a variety of circumstances that are difficult to predict, having a more intelligent system that is capable of making recommendations, such as service matching could mitigate some of these concerns (as suggested in [2]).

Issues with Service Availability

One issue that high and low timebank utilizers agreed on was that they shared mixed feelings about the availability of different services. This echoed issues raised in earlier research about the limited range of services on offer [22, 25]. Our earlier analysis of database service exchange records showed that there were service categories in short supply that required certified skilled labor, whereas those that required lower levels of specialized skills enjoyed a comfortable surplus of service offers. The concern of not having enough practical services on offer was commonly shared by our survey respondents:

"There aren't many really practical services available. Most services are luxury/inessential services like massage and home organization. My needs are more pragmatic" (P56).

Even when a needed skill was offered in the timebank, the service exchange could still fall through because other obligations take precedence over timebanking:

"A guy advertised that he would fix Mac computers for timebank hours. He is a professional who does this for work and was also willing to do it for the timebank. I contacted him. He said he was too busy, but I should contact him at a later date. I contacted him at the later date. He said he was still too busy and would be free after another later date, but I should feel free to hire someone else for the job. I told him I had no one else in mind and would wait. I contacted him a couple of times after the later date and received no response" (P53).

Timebank members expressed the frustration of not being able to find people who are willing to commit to provide skilled work that was in high demand because time credits were not seen to be as valuable as money.

"My requests often go unanswered, even when I request a service that has been advertised. Some of the services that I most need/want people only want to take partially in Time $, i.e., handyman, electrician, home repair services ARE more valuable than Reiki, because fewer people are skilled in home repair and everyone needs home repairs, so, the people who offer handyman services will usually only accept partial payment in Time $ and they want the rest of the payment in money (This has happened to me with at least five different people). This has made me feel discouraged, because I have lots of hours in the bank and it is difficult to spend them. As a result, I have not offered services for the past two years." (P301).

For some service providers who possess highly sought after skills, they reported that they saw timebank as an escape from work, and they did not want to work outside of work:

"If I offered my skill as a tradesperson, I would be overwhelmed with requests. And I don't like doing the work" (P312).

For others, being able to make money outside of timebanks in order to make the ends meet was too lucrative to pass up:

"For me, there's been an imbalance between providing and receiving... / Sometimes I think to myself, 'why take on client A for time dollars I won't spend, when I can take on client B for money I desperately need to pay the rent?" (P14).

Even when money was not a primary concern, the sense of equitable contribution in timebanks was still questioned by those who felt their efforts were unreciprocated:

"I sometimes feel as if I am allowing time bank members to take advantage of me, because the service I offer is quite popular (not to mention valuable, in that I would be paid well for it outside the time bank), but I have had difficulty finding members who offer the skills I had hoped to receive from the time bank" (P110).

Previous researchers such as Seyfang expressed hope that issues with the limited range of services on offer would be mitigated by mainstream adoption when people are more familiar with the concept of timebanking [25]. Based on our survey results, it is apparent that the lack of offers of certified skilled labor in timebanks is a conscious and deliberate decision made by certain timebank members. In fact, there appears to be a tension caused by the mismatch of motivations between high timebank utilizers who tended to be organizers who are more idealistic and low timebank utilizers who were mostly regular members who wished to fulfill more instrumental needs by utilizing timebank service exchanges.

DESIGN SPACE FOR TIMEBANKING

Prior work focused on timebanking as an alternative social movement. In our analysis, we reveal that the utility of an alternative currency such as time dollars depends greatly on negotiated values that are pegged to the universal monetary system. 'Equal time, equal value' is a fundamental element of time-based service exchange, and successful utilization could have a profound and transformative impact on how we engage and leverage civilian contributions at all levels of society. However, our data suggests that timebank members constantly struggle with this ideal, because of the perceived value of certified skill labor assigned by money, the universal currency.

Prior research on alternative and complementary currencies and exchanges has conceptualized the rise of different currencies as a mechanism to fulfill a variety of intrinsic human needs. Carroll and Bellotti (2015) suggest that their emergence serves to address the downsides of money [8]. Specifically, while money provides a universal platform for valuing goods and services, community currencies anchor exchange interactions and benefits in local communities

		Low Utilizers	High Utilizers
Certified Skilled Labor	Receiving	Instrumental	Instrumental / Ideological / Social
	Providing	Ideological / Altruistic	Ideological / Altruistic / Social
Low Skilled Labor	Receiving	Instrumental	Instrumental / Ideological / Social
	Providing	Ideological / Altruistic	Self-Development Ideological / Altruistic / Social

Table 5: Framework of Motivational Differences Between Timebank Members.

and timebanks facilitate equality in access to currency and exchange, and thereby in opportunities to contribute, learn and benefit. Our study elaborates Carroll and Bellotti's analysis of the strengths and weaknesses of timebanks [8]. We identify potential limits for timebanking in that, as a platform, it is effective at facilitating services that fulfill social, communal, and learning needs that demand lower levels of specialized skills, but it is less effective at providing work that requires certified skill labor. Cluster analysis reveals the existence two distinctive clusters of timebanking participation pattern that are largely distinguished by motivational differences. Table 5 represents a framework of differences between types of users. Service receivers are motivated by instrumental rewards, whereas providers have ideological and altruistic motives. High utilizers are drawn to social aspects of the experience, whereas low utilizers are not. For certified skilled individuals who are high providers, incentives must be purely ideological, altruistic and social; for low skilled individuals who are high providers, they use the timebank for self-development of personal skills as well as ideological, altruistic, and social reasons. In other words there is a missing self-development motivation for those with certified skills, which explains the short fall in those services, whereas the surplus for low skilled providers is explained by this same motive. This difference could help explain timebanking's dual personalities—equal time, equal value versus a shortage of high value services—identified in previous timebank literature [22, 25].

Value comparison between alternative currencies and money is inevitable in day-to-day service exchanges. There exists a wide spectrum of a variety of motivations such as altruistic and instrumental (personal gains oriented) drives that afford a rich design space for future complementary currency systems. Our results reveal users with both mainly self-serving and mainly other-oriented motives and lessons can be drawn from timebanking for the long-term outlook and design implications for many P2P services. Emerging peer services such as TaskRabbit, Lyft, Yerdle, Neighborgoods, etc. address these other more self-serving motivations and some have been very successful focusing more on self-interest [3]. These new P2P services offer alternative motivational frameworks to timebank ideology, especially timebanking's principle of equal value for equal time. P2P service designers must recognize the limitations of the equal time equal value model in serving instrumental ends, particularly for certified skilled members who will tend to prefer currencies that resemble conventional money—where some types of labor have higher value than others—unless highly motivated by idealistic, social, or altruistic incentives. For those that are not highly motivated in those ways, prosocial systems could offer recognition-based rewards to build reputation, but with careful design to avoid crowding out intrinsic motivations [23]. This could encourage those who are more instrumentally motivated to participate in co-production activities. They may be able to use service reviews and testimonials to build credibility of expertise in their disciplines in order to promote their businesses and attract new customers.

CONCLUSION

This study unpacks the motivational differences among timebank members that contribute to these issues. We found that the ideal of 'equal time, equal value' that is a foundation of timebanking [13] points to a tension between members with instrumental versus those with idealistic and altruistic motivations for participation. We described a framework of motivations for community currencies researchers and system developers to consider when designing future P2P systems. Future systems could incorporate different rewards and incentives such as social recognition to encourage more instrumental users to leverage timebanking services for their gain.

ACKNOWLEDGEMENTS

This work was supported by NSF IIS-1218544 and NSF IIS-1406858.

REFERENCES

1. Bellotti, V. M., Cambridge, S., Hoy, K., Shih, P. C., Handalian, L. R., Han, K., & Carroll, J. M. (2014, April). Towards community-centered support for peer-to-peer service exchange: rethinking the timebanking metaphor. In *Proc. CHI 2014*, ACM Press (2014), 2975-2984.
2. Bellotti, V., Carroll, J. M., & Han, K. Random acts of kindness: The intelligent and context-aware future of reciprocal altruism and community collaboration. In *Proc. CTS 2013*, IEEE Press (2013), 1-12.
3. Bellotti, V., Ambard, A., Turner, D., Gossmann, C., Demkova, K. & Carroll, J. M. A Muddle of Models of Motivation. For Using Peer-to-Peer Economy Systems. Forthcoming in Proc. *CHI 2015*, ACM Press (2015).
4. Botsman, R., & Rogers, R. *What's mine is yours*. HarperBusiness, New York, 2010.

5. Cahn, E.S. *No more throw-away people: The co-production imperative*. Essential Books, Washington, D.C., 2000.
6. Cahn, E. S. & Barr, N. *Service credits: a new currency for the welfare state*. Welfare State Programme Discussion Papers, WSP 008. Centre for Analysis of Social Exclusion, The London School of Economics and Political Science, London, UK, 1986.
7. Carroll, J. M. (2013). Co-production scenarios for mobile time banking. In *Proc. IS-EUD 2013*, Springer Berlin Heidelberg (2013), 137-152.
8. Carroll, J. M. & Bellotti, V. Creating Value Together: The Emerging Design Space of Peer-to-Peer Currency and Exchange. In Proc. *CSCW 2015*, ACM Press (2015).
9. Collom, E. The motivations, engagement, satisfaction, outcomes, and demographics of time bank participants: survey findings from a US system. *International Journal of Community Currency research* 11 (2007), 36-83.
10. Collom, E. Banking time in an alternative market: A quantitative case study of a local currency system. In *103rd Annual Meeting of the American Sociological Association*, Boston, 2008.
11. Collom, E. Engagement of the elderly in time banking: The potential for social capital generation in an aging society. Journal of *Aging & Social Policy*, 20, 4 (2008), 414-436.
12. Collom, E. Motivations and Differential Participation in a Community Currency System: The Dynamics Within a Local Social Movement Organization. *Sociological Forum* 26, 1 (2011), 144-168.
13. Collom, E., Lasker, J. N., & Kyriacou, C. *Equal Time, Equal Value: Community Currencies and Time Banking in the US*. Ashgate Publishing, Ltd, 2012.
14. Glynos, J., & Speed, E. Varieties of co-production in public services: time banks in a UK health policy context. *Critical Policy Studies*, 6, 4 (2012), 402-433.
15. Gregory, L. Spending time locally: the benefit of time banks for local economies. *Local Economy*, 24, 4 (2009), 323-333.
16. Gregory, L. Time in service design: exploring the use of time credits to deliver social policies. In *Cardiff School of Social Sciences Working Papers Series*, 132 (2010).
17. Han, K., Shih, P. C., Bellotti, V., & Carroll, J. M. It's Time There Was an App for That Too: An Usability Study of Mobile TimeBanking. *International Journal of Mobile Human-Computer Interaction* (2014).
18. Han, K., Shih, P. C., Rosson, M. B., & Carroll, J. M. Enhancing community awareness and participation to local heritage with an mobile application. In *Proc. CSCW 2014*, ACM Press (2014), 1144-1155.
19. Lampinen, A., Lehtinen, V., Cheshire, C., & Suhonen, E. Indebtedness and reciprocity in local online exchange. In *CSCW 2013*, ACM Press (2013), 661-672.
20. Lasker, J., Collom, E., Bealer, T., Niclaus, E., Keefe, J. Y., Kratzer, Z., ... & Perlow, K. Time banking and health: the role of a community currency organization in enhancing well-being. Health *Promotion Practice*, 12, 1 (2011), 102-115.
21. Marks, M. B. Time banking service exchange systems: A review of the research and policy and practice implications in support of youth in transition. *Children and Youth Services Review*, 34, 7 (2012), 1230-1236.
22. Ozanne, L. K. Learning to exchange time: Benefits and obstacles to time banking. *International Journal of Community Currency Research*, 14, 1 (2010), 1-16.
23. Ryan, R. M., & Deci, E. L. Self-determination theory and the facilitation of intrinsic motivation, social development, and well-being. *American Psychologist* 55 (2000), 68–78
24. Seyfang, G. Tackling social exclusion with community currencies: learning from LETS to Time Banks. *International Journal of Community Currency Research*, 6, 1 (2002), 1-11.
25. Seyfang, G. 'With a little help from my friends.' Evaluating time banks as a tool for community self-help. *Local Economy*, 18, 3 (2003), 257-264.
26. Seyfang, G. Time banks: rewarding community self-help in the inner city? *Community Development Journal*, 39, 1 (2004), 62-71.
27. Seyfang, G. Harnessing the potential of the social economy? Time banks and UK public policy. International *Journal of Sociology and Social Policy*, 26, 9/10 (2006), 430-443.
28. Seyfang, G. New economics of sustainable consumption: seeds of change. *Energy* (2009).
29. Seyfang, G. & Smith, K. *The time of our lives: Using timebanking for neighbourhood renewal and community capacity-building*. New Economics Foundation, London, 2002.
30. Seyfang, G., & Longhurst, N. Growing green money? Mapping community currencies for sustainable development. *Ecological Economics*, 86 (2013), 65-77.
31. Suhonen, E., Lampinen, A., Cheshire, C., & Antin, J. Everyday favors: a case study of a local online gift exchange system. In *GROUP 2010*, ACM Press (2010), 11-20).
32. Shih, P. C., Han, K., Poole, E. S., Rosson, M. B., & Carroll, J. M. Use and adoption challenges of wearable activity trackers. In *Proc. iConference* (2015).
33. Williams, C. C. Are Local Currencies An Effective Tool for Tackling Social Exclusion? *Town and Country Planning*, 69, 11 (2000), 323-325.

A Muddle of Models of Motivation For Using Peer-to-Peer Economy Systems

Victoria Bellotti[1,3], Alexander Ambard[1,3], Daniel Turner[1], Christina Gossmann[1], Kamila Demková[1] and John M. Carroll[2]

[1]Palo Alto Research Center
3333 Coyote Hill Road
Palo Alto, CA, 94304
bellotti@parc.com

[2]College of Information Sciences and Technology
The Pennsylvania State University
University Park, PA 16802 USA
jcarroll@ist.psu.edu

[3]Jack Baskin School of Computer Engineering
UC Santa Cruz, CA, USA

ABSTRACT
This paper reports on a study of motivations for the use of peer-to-peer or sharing economy services. We interviewed both users and providers of these systems to obtain different perspectives and to determine if providers are matching their system designs to the most important drivers of use. We found that the motivational models implicit in providers' explanations of their systems' designs do not match well with what really seems to motivate users. Providers place great emphasis on idealistic motivations such as creating a better community and increasing sustainability. Users, on the other hand are looking for services that provide what they need whilst increasing value and convenience. We discuss the divergent models of providers and users and offer design implications for peer system providers.

Author Keywords
Peer-to-peer economy, field study, user experience design.

ACM Classification Keywords
H.5.m. Information interfaces and presentation (e.g., HCI): Miscellaneous.

INTRODUCTION
This paper examines a phenomenon that, some argue, offers a promising new way of getting things done in the world. It is variously called the collaborative economy, collaborative consumption, the sharing economy, and the peer-to-peer economy. These overlapping terms, which we will collectively refer to as the *peer economy*, refer to a diverse range of *peer services*—both for-profit and non-profit—that have two common characteristics. Firstly, in most cases they are enabled by web and mobile technologies, in which power and the production of value are distributed between users. Secondly, efficient utilization of assets including labor, material goods, and knowledge is characteristic of these services [10]. It has been argued that use of such services will help avert a looming global resource depletion calamity by promoting sharing, reuse and sustainability [10,24,27,44].

CHI 2015, April 18 - 23 2015, Seoul, Republic of Korea

ACM 978-1-4503-3145-6/15/04...$15.00
http://dx.doi.org/10.1145/2702123.2702272

While advocates of the peer economy might claim these laudable alternative collectivist motivations as differentiating this new movement from the conventional economy, it is not clear how important they are when weighed against monetary and other self-interested motivations. Indeed there is already a backlash from commentators pointing out that much of the so-called sharing economy appears to have little to do with sharing [11,15,38]. So, what, then, are the real motivations for participation in the sharing economy?

Un-muddling these possible motivations is the goal of this paper. We present a qualitative investigation of peer service users' motives for participating in peer-to-peer transactions, both as providers and as receivers of value. And, unlike prior authors [17,18,34,46,50,51], we have also examined this question from the perspective of the peer service provider. We seek to understand what motivations providers believe their users have and what motivations they are trying to elicit in the design of their systems. Our inquiry took the form of 68 semi-structured interviews of individuals who used or who were founders of or employed by peer services. These services ranged from supporting entirely instrumental transactions—a means to achieve a personal goal, like renting out one's car to earn money—to apparently more purely altruistic transactions, such as giving items away for free. We frame our findings in the light of prior work on motivation, which provides theoretical foundations for our analysis.

BACKGROUND AND RELATED WORK

Theories of Motivation
There is a plethora of theories of motivation [4]. This is not surprising as understanding motivation is critical in many domains including education, the workplace, fitness, health, and marketing. In this section we discuss a selection of more influential theories that are relevant to our study.

Perhaps the most famous theory of motivations is Maslow's hierarchy of needs, represented as a pyramid with 5 or 8 levels, [35,36]. Maslow placed basic physiological needs at the bottom of the pyramid, followed by safety, then love and belonging, then esteem, and finally self-actualization at the top. Additional theories with ordered levels of needs, from basic animal up to more human aspirational, have also been proposed, with three being the most agreed upon number [32]. According to Maslow, higher level needs can only be articulated after basic needs are taken care of. But there is evidence that, in many situations, higher needs can supersede basic needs. [52]. Still, the hierarchy of needs has received support in a recent global survey of subjective well-being [47] and provides a useful framework for management and education guidance [e.g., 19,32,39]. Because of its accounting for the many possible needs that drive human activity, it is quite relevant to peer-to-peer economy participation, which offers a means to satisfy many of those needs ranging from the bottom to the top of the pyramid.

Many theories account for motivations for behavior change (e.g., see [53]). Most of these are concerned with health and wellness behaviors and assume the behavior in question, such as exercise or eating healthily, is challenging for people and depends on certain conditions (for example, coming to believe one's ability). Ajzen's Theory of Planned Behavior (TPB) [1,2] seems to be especially well developed, building on Bandura's theory of self-efficacy [5] and Ajzen and Fishbein's Theory of Reasoned Action [3]. TPB models beliefs and attitudes towards behaviors, acceptance and enforcement of those behaviors as norms, and beliefs about one's own capacity to adopt them as well as intention to do so. In a meta-analysis comparing TPB with other behavior change theories Webb et al [53] found TPB to be the most effective as a foundation for the design of internet-based behavior change interventions. Taking a behavior change perspective on motivation is valid for our work due to the fact that switching to new peer systems instead of conventional economic systems is a type of behavior change.

Self-determination Theory (SDT), another prominent theory of motivation [43], was developed in the context of education. It is founded on the surprising observation that extrinsic rewards such as money or a prize for an activity can 'crowd out' willingness to engage in the activity when not getting rewarded in subsequent trials. [23]. SDT expands on Herzberg's two-factor theory [30], which is generally referred to today as intrinsic and extrinsic motivations. SDT places motivations on a spectrum. On the leftmost extreme is complete lack of motivation. The center of the spectrum represents increasing degrees of internalization of and identification with external values. At the left—extrinsic—end of the center, one is simply responding to rewards and punishments aimed at sustaining values. At the right—intrinsic—end of the center, one has integrated those values into one's own beliefs and value system. On the rightmost extreme is intrinsic motivation, which is fully self-determined, meaning the person finds an activity rewarding in itself and is highly inclined to engage in it. The theory was highly influential in Daniel Pink's book, Drive [41], which applies the lessons from SDT to a variety of settings, especially the workplace. SDT has also been applied with predictive success in education [55], health care [56] and sports [49]. It seems applicable to peer economy participation in that services seem to range from relying on extrinsic motivations (mainly the reward of money) to depending on intrinsic drives such as amusement, curiosity or flow [21] or the simple enjoyment of being able to help others [8].

Reciprocal altruism [48] is a highly specific theory of the drive to repay favors to unrelated individuals. It is not typically counted amongst theories of motivation, and yet it is an undeniably powerful motivator [42], highly relevant to the peer economy. We might expect that participation in peer systems should be at least partially driven by a desire to reciprocate after having received a good or service.

Another relevant theory is Social Exchange Theory (SET) [31] Cook et al [20] provide a review of the importance of SET in the context of modern systems of exchange. The theory makes testable predictions (in the laboratory and in the real world) about the formation of transaction relationships and motivations to engage in exchanges in a network of actors, given variations in power of actors, value of resources, costs, and unpredictability of outcomes from exchanges. It predicts, for example, that an individual, fearing uncertainty, will tolerate significant opportunity costs to stay within an exchange relationship and that high status actors are preferred by high and low status actors as transaction partners. Reciprocity as described above plays a significant role in SET [25,26]. SET predicts that reciprocity, as a prevailing means of social exchange, is less likely than *generalized exchange* to promote solidarity or bonds of trust and affective regard. Generalized exchange is characterized by an indirect, non-reciprocal or pay-it-forward system, just as we see in many peer systems [20].

These theories informed analysis of the data collected in our study and the emergent framework that was used to analyze motivations reported by our participants.

Motivation for Participation in the Peer-to-Peer Economy

Whilst there has been considerable research on motivations for participation in online communities with some peer-to-peer characteristics, there are few publications focusing on motivations for participating in the peer economy itself, where transactions involve physical resources and services.

Suhonen et al. [46] surveyed users of a college campus lending, giving and helping service called Kassi. They found that motivations for use were primarily *altruistic* or inspired by the desire to *reciprocate* and, to a lesser extent, *instrumental*. Socializing was not listed as a motivator. Demotivators were: lack of promising opportunities for exchange, uncertainty about what to offer, and unfamiliarity with the service. Lampinen et al. [34] followed up on this work by interviewing users to reveal how they offset their sense of indebtedness for services received by "(1) offering small tokens of appreciation to exchange partners, (2) understanding and accepting the indirect nature of generalized exchange, (3) managing expectations by framing offers and requests carefully, (4) minimizing efforts needed in exchange processes, and (5) bartering and exchanging for a third party" (this last item meaning finding opportunities for transactions on behalf of friends). A limitation of this work is that it focuses on just one system, Kassi, with a user population largely made up of students.

Collom, [17,18] administered surveys to members of a time bank, finding that members were motivated by (1) personal *needs* and *wants*, i.e., self-serving needs, (2) the *values* of the timebank, and (3) by a feeling of *altruism*. Social motivations were the least important in both of these studies. His results also confirmed Knocke's [33] hypothesis that people participate most in the aspects of a system that address their motives. However, once again, this work is limited to one system, a timebank, and little open-ended, qualitative information was collected.

Van de Glind [50] conducted a qualitative interview study of participation in three peer services; a *Product Service System*, Peerby, in which users made their possessions available for usage or rent by others; a *Redistribution Market*, Shareyourmeal, in which users redistributed food by cooking for others; and a *Collaborative Lifestyle System*, Konnektid, where users could offer their skills for hire by others. He also conducted a quantitative survey of informants' estimates of how likely it was that they would use any of nine services including the three above and motivations for doing so. In his qualitative work, he found the following motivations; practicality (the most dominant), *socializing* (the second most dominant), *curiosity*, *environmentalism* and *finance*. In his quantitative study, the following incentives were statistically supported: *financial*, other people's *recommendations*, social *attitude towards the neighborhood*, *socializing* in general, and *environmentalism*. Overall, peer system users tended to be highly educated millennials, accustomed to using social media and were often early adopters of new systems. The limitation of this work, however, is that it relies on speculation about use rather than actual use of peer systems.

Finally, a recent survey of 2,500 individuals provides a ranking of 'considerations' for participation in the collaborative economy, ([51] p19). *Convenience*, followed by *price* and then *better service quality*, came out top. Again, though, this was a simple survey with fixed questions and predetermined answer options, which means interesting insights could have been missed.

Another limitation of the prior work in general is that, apart from focusing on only a few services, it does not clearly differentiate between the motives of users as receivers of goods and services and users as providers. Nor does it consider the provider's point of view on users' motivations and what motives the provider is trying to appeal to. We set out to address this gap. We also covered a larger and more diverse set of services than most studies, including for- and non-profits, ranging from primarily instrumental to primarily altruistic exchanges.

INTERVIEW STUDY OF MOTIVATIONS FOR PARTICIPATION IN THE PEER ECONOMY

We have been studying the peer economy with the goal of designing technology that will increase participation in productive exchanges, particularly in the domain of timebanking [7,8,12]. Our current work was conceived as a means to learn from the best practices of the peer economy as a whole, which is typically better resourced than timebanking in terms of its ability to create positive user experiences and to deliberately appeal to a diversity of attracting motivations.

Participants

Participants were recruited by various means, including postings on social media, snowball recruiting, and announcements on email distribution lists. We interviewed 45 users (31 female and 14 male) and 23 providers (employees or founders of organizations familiar with the user experience strategy of their company). A total of 43 different peer services were represented. The average age of users was 33.1 (SD 10.2, range 22-78) and amongst them were 10 students, 8 IT workers, 8 designers, 6 scientists, 4 managers, 2 teachers, and a few other occupations (so they resembled the well-educated participants of [50]). We did not collect demographic information from providers.

Method

We devised a semi-structured interview template that we used to collect information about motivations, roughly in line with the various stages of a *'customer journey,'* i.e., through initially being attracted to the peer service to becoming a long-term, fully engaged user and recruiting others. We also asked about problems and obstacles. The user and provider interviews contained slightly differently worded questions covering the same issues. Almost all interviews were conducted remotely using telephone or VoIP (Internet phone) and recorded for transcription. Audio problems made 5 transcripts difficult to transcribe in full, so we took notes from these and transcribed parts for quotation.

Analysis was bottom-up and focused narrowly on collecting statements from transcripts that articulated motivations for participating in peer-to-peer systems. These statements were entered by a team of researchers, one quote per row, into a shared Google Docs spreadsheet. Researchers worked synchronously and asynchronously going through transcripts and initially coded 596 quotes from the 68 interviews as being concerned with motivations. These quotes were then coded in more detail, according to an emergent motivational coding scheme that was informed by the data and prior work on motivation. This scheme will be discussed in more detail in the Analysis of Motivations section below. The coding of each quote was checked and revised as deemed necessary by at least two people. Meetings and 1-on-1 calls among coders were used to increase agreement on coding. Each quote was assigned as many motivations as were expressed (up to six at once), since people often gave multiple reasons for participation in a single quote. Motivations were also coded according to the source's role in the transaction being described by the interviewee. For users there were *user-receiver* (UR) and *user-provider* of resources (UP) roles. For providers there were service *provider* claims about *user* motivations (PU) and service *provider* describing *design* stratagems (PD) to inspire motivations. Some users talked only about the UR role, others talked about both, UR and UP and all providers talked about both PD and PU roles.

RESULTS AND DISCUSSION

In this section, we present findings with discussion and peer system design implications, since our analysis is in large part qualitative. We begin with a review of the coverage and thus representativeness of our data.

Representation

Due to providers' anonymity concerns, we obscure some company names in our analysis. In Figure 1, services are grouped into categories to show the represented distribution across 21 different types of services (43 organizations, including 6 timebanks). Eleven of these categories (shown in black in Figure 1) would fit the description of a *collaborative lifestyle* service like Konnektid described in [50], although this category is extremely diverse. Five (in diagonal hashing) are *product service systems*, like peerby in [50]. Two (in checker board pattern) are *redistribution market systems*, like Shareyourmeal in [50]. The categories shown in grey remain unclassified, being general purpose or advocacy entities.

Unsurprisingly, the two top categories are transportation and accommodation; currently the most commercially successful types of peer-to-peer business, including Uber and AirBnB. Next is 'marketplaces for selling', which may be slightly under-represented, since the popular service eBay fits this category. The general-purpose category includes services where multiple kinds of transactions are either explicitly supported or occur spontaneously in online communications. Craigslist and Nextdoor.com fit this category.

We classified 52 interviews as representing for-profit services and 15 as representing non-profits; one service did not yet have a clear business model. We also classified services as "instrumental" if they provided a financial incentive for being a resource provider (40 interviews) and "altruistic" if they supported transactions for no financial reward (35 interviews). This means that 7 interviews represented services that support both instrumental and altruistic transactions. The two platform providers could support either altruistic or instrumental applications and were classified as both. The other 5 were services that allowed people to offer resources for free or for a fee. Craigslist was classified as self-interest, rather than both, as interviewees who used it only did so for financial transactions. Timebanks were classified as primarily altruistic, even though members receive time dollars for services, since their philosophy is strongly oriented to an altruistic ideology.

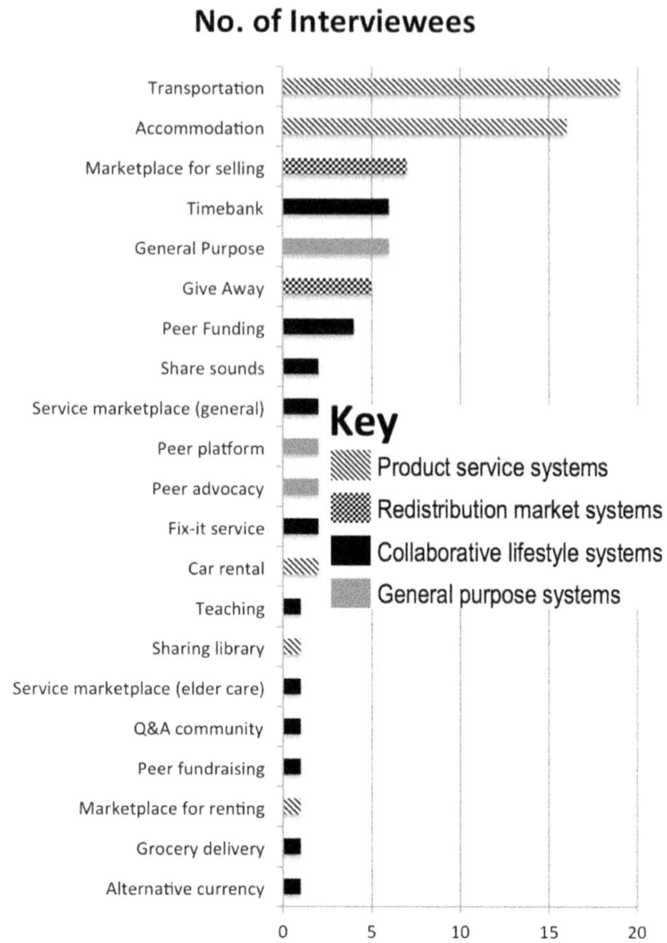

Figure 1. Number of interviewees associated with different categories of service

One challenge we experienced was obtaining interviews with individuals representing the most successful providers. Seven providers worked for somewhat-to-very-famous services. The other 16 represented less well-known or very obscure start-ups, several in beta status.

Analysis of Motivations

After a review of related work and a preliminary review of our interview transcripts, we created a rich motivational framework for data coding (see Table 1, leftmost columns). The framework lists seven theoretically informed psychological roots on the left, driving 21 variations labeled with more common terms for motivation. They are listed (following Maslow's example) roughly from more complex and uniquely human down to basic and simple motivations.

- *Value/Morality* is the drive to improve oneself or the world in terms of some value or principle including justice, equality, and wisdom [57]. Sustainability was broken out of Society/Community/Utopia, because it is often called out as a benefit of the peer economy.
- *Social influence* motives were inferred (following factors in [1,2,3,16]) when someone spoke of a normative motivation (e.g., to act like everyone else), reciprocation

Psychological Root	Common Term	User Receiver (UR)	User Provider (UP)	Provider Claims User Motivations (PU)	Service Provider Designs (PD)
Value/Morality	Self-improvement/Integrity (reduce guilt & hypocrisy)	9%	43%	24%	7%
	Society/Community/Utopia	19%	46%	85%	100%
	Sustainability	4%	23%	9%	13%
Social influence	Norm (internalized influence)	2%	3%	3%	9%
	Reciprocity (internalized morality, fear of disapproval)	1%	9%	3%	0%
	Persuasion (extrinsic influence, pressure from other)	6%	0%	21%	21%
Status/Power	Self-improvement/Increased power (future instrumentality)	7%	23%	12%	7%
	Status/Reputation/Social capital (future instrumentality)	9%	31%	26%	20%
Empathic/Altruistic	Help/Provide service to other	6%	51%	85%	36%
	Give something to other	4%	54%	24%	14%
Social connection	Social connection/Relationship	74%	100%	76%	95%
Intrinsic/Autotelic	Amusement	34%	14%	6%	5%
	Compulsion (e.g. addiction, competition)	0%	3%	3%	0%
	Interest/Engagement/Curiosity/Flow	56%	66%	44%	27%
Safety	Safety	4%	3%	6%	4%
Instrumental	Payment	2%	91%	47%	20%
	Get service/thing	100%	14%	100%	25%
	Increase value/Increase convenience	99%	31%	50%	34%
	Decrease burdens/Decrease inconvenience	18%	51%	21%	4%

Table 1. Relative frequency of code occurrence for motivations across 596 quotes from peer system users and providers. Cells show the occurrence of a code expressed as a percentage of the maximum number of instances of a code recorded for each of the 4 roles

of a resource provided by another or others, or persuasion by a contact (but not by an advertisement).

- *Status/Power* covers drives to succeed in society by gaining power and skill and by advertising such attributes through self-presentation, building reputation and acquisition of social capital over time [14,29,54].
- *Empathic/Altruistic* is based on the human instinct to empathize with others [13], which inspires the desire to assist, by providing a service or by giving something.
- *Social connection* oriented motivation comes from the human drive to start and build social relationships. It is termed 'Belonging and Love Needs' in Maslow's hierarchy [35,36].
- *Intrinsic/Autotelic* motivation, according to self-determination theory [43], is when something is done for its own sake, which could be amusement, compulsion, or interest.
- *Safety* is a basic need in our framework of motivations. It is also listed next to the bottom, above physiological needs in Maslow's hierarchy [35,36].
- *Instrumental* motivation means seeking a practical end, such as receiving a payment (of money or other valuable tokens); getting a service or thing; increasing value over prior solutions; or decreasing burdens related to prior solutions. It would include food, shelter, warmth and so on and roughly equates to Maslow's satisfaction drive at the bottom of his hierarchy of needs [35,36].

The four columns of numbered cells represent the four interviewee roles coded as user-recipient (UR), user-provider (UP), provider-claims-about-user-motives (PU), and provider-design-to-inspire-a-motivation (PD). Rather than presenting absolute numbers of instances of occurrence of each code, we present counts as percentages of the highest count of instances of a code for each column. This allows us to compare to what extent interviewees—acting in each of the roles URs, UPs, PUs, and PDs—talked about motivators, compensating for the fact that we obtained approximately twice as many UR-coded quotes, as any of the other types.

Note that Table 1 summarizes a large *qualitative* analysis. We take the obtained percentages in our data as suggesting *relative* importance to our participants, not as robust statistics. Our use of these tallies is heuristic.

We now discuss the more outstanding features of the data (summarized in Table 1) and their design implications.

Mismatched User and Provider Motivation Models

The biggest finding that Table 1 reveals is a misalignment of the motivations expressed in the different roles, suggesting that roles strongly modulate expressed motivations. In particular the greatest mismatch seems to be between system providers' design intentions (PD) and the self-reported reality for users of peer system services (UR and UP). The most important motivation category system providers talk about designing for seems to be Society/Community/Utopia—if we had not broken Sustainability out as a separate category it would have been by far the most important. Even when we dug deeper and broke out data from for-profits, non-profits, altruistic and non-altruistic services separately, this misalignment *held for all categories*.

Why might this be? We tried to compensate for selection bias in our interview study but must consider that it might be a

Figure 2. Uber advertisement for drivers on the side of a bus

contributing factor. Providers who were willing to talk to us tended to be in smaller, newer start-ups, whereas users were more often engaging the services of the giants in the peer economy. Interestingly, Figure 2 suggests that one giant, Uber (company employees declined interviews), is clear on how to motivate would-be drivers (user-providers). It is possible that only the more socially and altruistically motivated providers agreed to make time for an interview or that social desirability bias [21] influenced their responses.

Nonetheless, this striking diversity of motivations resonates with the current contention between the sharing economy cheerleaders who argue it is about creating a better world [10,24,27,44] and the skeptics who say it is self-interested business as usual [11,15,38]. We will examine the issue of self-centeredness in a later subsection. One interviewee, an AirBnB host, summed this misalignment up very crisply:

Interviewer: *And what interested you most about AirBnB?*
Interviewee: *Money. [laughter] That sounds terrible; AirBnB's whole brand is like, "This is an experience for sharing and togetherness and la-la-la-la-la-la." But I was like, I have bills to pay, and this seems like a pretty good platform to get money. [laughter]*

Providers' utopian motives would be at the top of Maslow's hierarchy [35,36] and on the more internalized end of the SDT spectrum [43]. On the other hand, user-providers are highly motivated by payments and user-receivers are far more interested in getting a service or good and increasing value (getting a better deal) than providers seem to anticipate. These motives are mostly consistent with [17,18,50 and 51] and seem to be related to more basic needs in Maslow's hierarchy; food, drink, shelter, resources, although the hierarchy does not easily map onto things like getting a better deal, for example; *"as someone who enjoys thrift shopping in general, just the concept of finding a good deal on something can be fun at times."* User-receivers' motives are very much on the extrinsic end of the SDT spectrum and very much in line with what social exchange theory would predict, due to users' evaluation of costs and value of peer services versus their competition [20,31]. User-providers' motives are apparently more mixed (see Table 1).

Design Implication: Basics Needs First

If our sample is biased towards less experienced peer system providers, at the very least, the results reported in this paper should help in refocusing their design efforts. Providers need to recognize that, while users may resonate with the ideals of a more egalitarian, helpful, and sustainable world, a user's motivation to use a peer service will often hinge upon its ability to satisfy basic needs—what Maslow called physiological and safety needs [35,36]—more effectively than the competition. Any peer service that is attempting to displace a conventional service must strive to do so more conveniently and at a lower cost to users.

Motivations to Make Social Connections

What users and providers do agree on (as suggested in Table 1) is the importance of the social element of peer systems. This is consistent with one of the previous studies [50] but not the others [17,18,34,46,51], which either do not mention it, or rate it as relatively low in importance. We find that users are attracted to systems where they can connect with other people and forge relationships or simply enjoy the company of others. Indeed, social motivations are the ones most frequently mentioned by user-providers (UPs) overall. But in breakouts we found that the UP social motive dropped off sharply in the for-profit and instrumental services.

System Providers recognize that users are motivated by this and explicitly design their systems to support it, even in the for-profit and instrumental services. As one provider put it; *"I think that there's a lot to be said for having a community of people that have shared values and being able to interact with them."* Another said; *"The whole idea is that neighbors can use it to help each other out, borrow stuff, sell stuff, prevent crime, that kind of stuff, and then ultimately build stronger relationships that help reduce crime and build better community."* There is clear understanding that people prefer to interact with others who share their values and who may be a source of help when needed.

As an example of the user perspective on the same issue, one user of Couchsurfing stated; *"I was also attracted to kind of having a social connection to a place where I had never been before and already know that there were people there who were kind of trying to meet the same kind of people, you know, people traveling. You know, you're going somewhere where you don't know anyone and then realize that there are already people there who want to get together and meet up."*

While building social relationships seems important to peer systems' success, a successful system may also foster social connections that are transient, as a ride-sharing system user described; *"we were driving and then we're talking and discovered that we're hungry and so we just tried [...] one restaurant on the way and like have a meal. I had a good fun meal. It's like you don't try to be that, you know, let's become more than friends for something longer term or something. No. It was just good and it was very fun."*

In some services, particularly those that offer accommodation for travelers, social connections may also be a means to enhance the overall value of the service; *"The interesting thing is that you stay with people or that you stay with locals or in locals'... [...] You learn about their culture. During most of the time they're really interested in you. They're interested in showing you their city and telling you about their culture. And that is for me the most thrilling part because you really get to know people's ethnicity."*

Design Implication: Go Social

Of the theories we reviewed earlier in this paper, only Maslow's hierarchy and social exchange theory (SET) explicitly deal with socialization and only SET makes predictions, related to the instrumental value of exchanges versus the costs of engaging in them [20,31]. This suggests that peer systems should support easy and positive social experiences with clear social benefits for their system users, especially experiences consistent with the needs the service addresses, since those needs are what drew the user to the system in the first place. For example, a service for gardeners who need to exchange plant seeds and cuttings should also support users in making plant-related social connections, communicating about plants, sharing pictures of plants, recommending each other for having certain horticultural skills and so on. Rather than just motivating users with the instrumental value of getting cuttings or seeds, users can be motivated by various kinds of social interactions and these enable access to instrumental and other kinds of benefits (e.g. entertainment and self-improvement through learning).

Self-interested Motivations

As mentioned above, users are motivated to participate in peer systems as receivers by the prospect of the services and things they need, especially if there is added value. These motivators count perhaps even more than social motivators. For some, in some systems, the social element doesn't matter at all compared to getting a good deal:

Interviewee: *I don't see it building more social capital as compared to Craigslist or eBay because basically there's no face-to-face interaction that's why?*

Interviewer: *Right.*

Interviewee: *It's just people coming in to find a better deal than there is on Craigslist. It's not that I'm here to make friends or be proud that I'm part of this community who recycle things.* [Later] *There's not much community feel to this and you see a very small picture of the other person. Yeah. I don't think so. It's really just a market place.*

It could be that the designers of this service have not considered the potential social aspect of their system and this may be a lost opportunity. However, the 'better deals' seem to be sufficient for the user being interviewed. For some, this may even become a compulsion as one user of a system that allowed bidding said, *"I mean if you are much of a gambler, I guess it will give you some sort of thrill to bid, out bid other people. I know some of my friends do enjoy like you can out bid people at the very last minute and then you got the deal, so…"* Notwithstanding this claim, we found little evidence of compulsive deal seeking in general in peer systems.

Increased value may not be based on price alone, but with the extra customer care that peer service providers may offer, as one user put it; *"A lot of my friends […] who are looking for a place temporarily […] they like AirBnB now, even though some might be on the more expensive side. But they'd be like, 'I wouldn't mind doing it for a couple of days, at least, because it's any day better than staying in a hotel or being secluded. Because now a lot of them give you feedback or some people even make you breakfast or take care of basic things,' which is quite nice."*

The user experience is a key part of the value proposition and multiple users mentioned the superior experience of ridesharing services compared with the competing taxi services. Superior value included higher predictability and reliability, better information for both drivers and customers (e.g. GPS visualizations) and superior customer service.

On the user-provider side, for some systems that are trying to be more altruistic in character, where the idea is that people donate items or provide services, credits or time dollars can become powerful self-centered extrinsic [23,30,43] motivators for providers. One user talked about getting a hair dryer from someone working hard for points:

Interviewer: *Why do you think she was so eager to give away her hair dryer?*

Interviewee: *Oh, she wants the credit.*

Another talked about earning *"completely pointless internet points. But nonetheless I wanted to get them."*

In both of these cases, superficially altruistic acts of giving were described—in the former case goods, and in the latter case information—but motivations were also coded as instrumental; in the former case, for the purchasing power of credits and in the latter for status, which entails the promise of future instrumental advantages [29,54]. We coded status as distinct from self-improvement—defined as increasing one's skills or abilities (power). Status was defined specifically as increasing the perception of such assets, by enhancing one's reputation and acquiring social capital. The same user who talked about the pointless points explained what they enabled; *"you gain a lot more privileges as you gain reputation for answers. You get to moderate questions, you can ban users, you can close questions, you can basically participate more in the administration of the site."* The points, in other words, are not pointless at all. Table 1 shows that self-improvement and status are moderate incentives for user providers and again, not emphasized to an equal degree when service providers explained their designs.

Other basic, self-interested motivations include safety (occasionally mentioned in relation to ride sharing and local community services) and intrinsic motivations (*autotelic*: for its own sake). User receivers and providers are drawn to interesting, engaging, and amusing experiences; peer service providers at least seem to understand that users appreciate the engagement part, but design for interest, engagement, and amusement was not apparently as high a priority for providers as it probably should be (see Table 1).

Design Implication: Make it Worth My While

Self-interest is central in social exchange theory, which predicts that humans are mainly driven to transact by this kind of motivation. Prior work also backs up this idea [17,18,50,51]. Given its primacy, service providers should consider self-interested motivations from our framework in Table 1, even if the primary objective of their service is to promote sharing and sustainable resource usage. Self-interest takes many forms other than financial rewards. For example, providers can emphasize a user's ability to learn and then advertise valuable skills through providing a service, or advertise the delights of having more space at home by giving away unwanted clutter or sharing infrequently used tools. On the other hand, providers should always be aware of the possibility of crowding out effects [43] on those who might otherwise be intrinsically motivated to participate.

Altruism and Morality

Service providers' top design priority appears to be powerfully driven by societal or utopian motives and they seemed to assume their users would be too (see Table 1). For example, when asked about what was driving his service, one said, *"... just sort of reaction to the consumer culture that has become so prevalent in our society and a desire to fight the power, if you will."* Another said, *"We are about building the community right!"* Yet another said, *"We believe in using [anon] as a way of promoting the advancement of social justice for all people in the [anon] county."* These motives clearly belong at the top of Maslow's hierarchy, being related to morality and problem solving.

Although providers talked a lot about their users helping each other (see Table 1), they said little about how their designs supported users in helping and giving. This is another mismatch, because these, although not top motivations, were important for user-providers; *"that would be a way that I could share my experience, my education with other people,"* and, *"I really liked the idea of offering accommodation for other travelers,"* and, *"I love the feeling of coming home and knowing that you've made someone's stay like really fun. So that was great. That would be one motivation."*

Another disconnect is that some user-providers (UPs) spoke of possibilities for self-improvement from a moral integrity perspective; *"it's kind of balancing my guilt for having all this other stuff that I can afford,"* and, *"I think I was opened to it because it matched my values,"* and, *"the possibility of supporting people in a car-free lifestyle."* Providers rarely mentioned designing to encourage this motivation.

Finally, in breakouts, we did find that UPs in non-profits and altruistic services talked a lot about the motive of giving to others whereas it was underemphasized by service providers. UPs mentioned this far less in the for-profits and instrumental services with payment being their top motive. Meanwhile, service providers in for-profit and instrumental services did not focus nearly so heavily on payment in talking about their designs, although they did recognize it as a motive.

Design Implication: Help Me Become My Ideal Me

The notion of moral self-improvement may be another opportunity largely missed by providers to draw people into using peer services. Appealing to identity-congruent values can influence consumer behavior [40] with large positive impacts as in the successful anti-littering campaign in Texas in the 1980's organized by Dan Syrek which appealed to the pride of the Texan male [28]. So peer system providers would do well to find out who their target users believe themselves to be and forcefully proclaim identity congruent personal ideals that can be achieved by using their service.

CONCLUSION

We conducted a unique, qualitative, interview-based study that allows us to compare the motivations that users have for participation in peer services as both receivers and providers of resources with motivations anticipated by service providers. What we have found is a number of mismatches highlighted in Table 1 that suggest areas for providers to improve their designs.

At the top level it seems fair to say that providers we talked to want to create a better world. Their model for success is to give people an opportunity to behave in a more sustainable fashion, by sharing resources and helping one another. Users, on the other hand, are operating on a model of how best to satisfy instrumental needs, particularly basic ones: just getting what they need to survive at a competitive price, with maximum convenience. It therefore seems that the sharing economy backlash [11,15,38] is grounded in an unavoidable fact that, to be successful, peer services must first serve self-interest and that a *muddle of models* will remain in play unless providers embrace what really motivates users.

Nonetheless we do see that user-providers can be motivated by altruism and moralistic impulses and that philanthropic service providers might do better to switch their focus on promoting utopian ideals and concentrate more on encouraging and rewarding these more personal motivations.

LIMITATIONS AND FUTURE WORK

Our study and report here have some limitations. First, for the sake of space, we presented different types of systems' motivations in one table, rather than breaking them apart to show some of the variations we mention in our discussion. In addition, we were unable to talk to users and providers of the exact same systems. It may be that providers of some of the services we did not cover have a deeper understanding of what users want. Certainly some have been immensely successful. But of course there may always be room for improvement and our findings may also be of value to them. Further work also remains to be done to implement some of our design ideas in some real peer systems and to collect data on pre- and post-intervention user behaviors and subjective impressions. In addition, there is more to be done to develop our analytical framework and to use it to create different ideal motivational blueprints for different kinds of service that can guide developers of peer services.

ACKNOWLEDGMENTS

Thanks to the many users and providers of peer services who gave us interviews and to Shawna Hein and Matthew Valente for conducting some of the interviews. To Josephine Giaimo for input to an early draft of the interview guideline document. This paper is based upon work funded by the National Science Foundation under Grant No. IIS-1218544.

REFERENCES

1. Ajzen, I. From intentions to actions: A theory of planned behavior. In J. Kuhl, J. Beckmann (Eds). *Action Control: From Cognition to Behavior*. Springer Berlin Heidelberg (1985), 11-39.
2. Ajzen, I. The theory of planned behavior. *Organizational Behavior and Human Decision Processes 50,2* (1991) 179–211.
3. Ajzen, I. & Fishbein, M. *Understanding attitudes and predicting social behavior*. Englewood Cliffs, NJ: Prentice-Hall, (1980).
4. Aunger, R. & Curtis, V. The Anatomy of Motivation: An Evolutionary-Ecological Approach. *Biological Theory, 7,3* (2013) 49-63.
5. Bandura, A. (1977). Self-efficacy: toward a unifying theory of behavioral change. *Psychological review,* 84,2 (1977) 191-215.
6. Bauwens, M. P2P Foundation. Category: Relational. http://p2pfoundation.net/Category:Relational
7. Bellotti, V., Carroll, J.M., & Han, K. Random Acts of Kindness: The Intelligent and Context-Aware Future of Reciprocal Altruism and Community Collaboration. In *Proc. CTS 2013,* IEEE (2013), 1-12.
8. Bellotti, V., Cambridge, S., Hoy, K., Shih, P.C., Renery Handalian, L., Han, K., & Carroll, J.M. Towards community-centered support for peer-to-peer service exchange: rethinking the timebanking metaphor. In *Proc. CHI 2014.* ACM Press, (2014) 2975-2984.
9. Botsman, R. The Sharing Economy Lacks A Shared Definition. *Fast Company Co.Exist Article* November 21, 2013. http://www.fastcoexist.com/3022028/the-sharing-economy-lacks-a-shared-definition
10. Botsman, R. and Rogers, R. (2011). *What's mine is yours. How Collaborative Consumption is changing the way we live.* HarperCollinsPublishers: London.
11. Cagle, S. The Case Against Sharing: On Access, Scarcity and Trust. Article in *The Nib*, May 27th, 2014. https://medium.com/the-nib/the-case-against-sharing-9ea5ba3d216d
12. Carroll, J.M. & Bellotti, V. Creating Value Together: The Emerging Design Space of Peer-to-Peer Currency and Exchange. To appear in *Proc. CSCW 2015*. ACM Press (2015).
13. Chakrabarti, B. & Baron-Cohen, S. Empathizing: neurocognitive developmental mechanisms and individual differences. Anders, Ende, Junghöfer, Kissler & Wildgruber (Eds.) *Progress in brain research, 156* (2006), 403-417.
14. Charlton, B.G. The inequity of inequality: egalitarian instincts and evolutionary psychology. *Journal of Health Psychology, 2* (1997), 413-425.
15. Chase, B. Sharing is caring. But not in the sharing economy. *Huffington Post, 7/25/2014.* Retrieved from http://www.huffingtonpost.com/brad-chase/sharing-is-caring-but-not-millenials_b_5618963.html
16. Cialdini, R. *Influence: The psychology of persuasion.* New York; Quill (1984).
17. Collom, E. The motivations, engagement, satisfaction, outcomes, and demographics of timebank participants: survey findings from a U.S. system. *International Journal of Community Currency Research 11*, (2007), 36-83.
18. Collom, E. Motivations and differential participation in a community currency system: The dynamics within a local social movement organization. *Sociological Forum, 26, 1* (2011), 144-168.
19. Conley, C. *Peak: How great companies get their mojo from Maslow*. Jossey-Bass, (2007).
20. Cook, K.S., Cheshire, C., Rice, E.R.W. & Nakagawa, S. Social exchange theory. In J. DeLamater & A. Ward (Eds.), *Handbook of social psychology.* Dordrecht: Springer (2013), 61-88.
21. Crowne, D., & Marlowe, D. *The approval motive: Studies in evaluative dependence.* New York: Wiley (1964).
22. Csikszentmihalyi, M. *Flow: The psychology of optimal experience.* Harper & Row (1990).
23. Deci, E. L., Koestner, R., & Ryan, R. M. A meta-analytic review of experiments examining the effects of extrinsic rewards on intrinsic motivation. *Psychological Bulletin, 125,6* (1999). 627–668.
24. Eisenstein, C. *Sacred economics: Money, gift, and society in the age of transition.* Evolver Editions, 2011.
25. Emerson,R.M. Exchange Theory, Part I: A Psychological Basis for Social Exchange and Exchange Relations in Network Structures. In *Sociological Theories in Progress*. Houghton Mifflin, Boston, MA (1972a), 38-87.
26. Emerson, R.M. Exchange Theory, Part II: A Psychological Basis for Social Exchange and Exchange Relations in Network Structures. In *Sociological Theories in Progress*. Houghton Mifflin, Boston, MA (1972b), 38-87.
27. Gansky, L. *The Mesh: Why the future of business is sharing.* Portfolio Trade, 2012.
28. Heath, C. & Heath, D. *Made to Stick: Why some ideas survive and others die*. Random House (2007).
29. Henrich J, Gil-White, F. The evolution of prestige: freely conferred deference as a mechanism for enhancing the

benefits of cultural transmission. *Evol Hum Behav, 22* (2001) 165–196.

30. Herzberg, F. (1966) *Work and the nature of man.* Cleveland, OH: World.
31. Homans, G. C. Social behavior as exchange. *American Journal of Sociology, 63*, (1958), 597–606.
32. Huitt, W. (2007). Maslow's hierarchy of needs. *Educational Psychology Interactive*. Valdosta, GA: Valdosta State University. Retrieved from, http://www.edpsycinteractive.org/topics/regsys/maslow.html
33. Knoke, David. Incentives in Collective Action Organizations. *American Sociological Review 53,3* (1988), 311–329.
34. Lampinen, A., Lehtinen, V., Cheshire, C. & Suhonen, E. Indebtedness and reciprocity in local online exchange. In *Proc. CSCW'13*. ACM Press, (2013), 661-672.
35. Maslow, A.H. A theory of human motivation. *Psychological Review, 50,4* (1943) 370–96.
36. Maslow, A. H. *Motivation and personality*. New York: Harper & Row. (1970a).
37. Molm, L. Collett, J. & Schaefer, D.R. Building Solidarity through Generalized Exchange: A Theory of Reciprocity. *American Journal of Sociology, 113,1* (2007), 205–42.
38. Morozov, E. The 'sharing economy' undermines workers' rights. *Notes EM.* Retrieved 7/13/2014 from: http://www.ft.com/intl/cms/s/0/92c3021c-34c2-11e3-8148-00144feab7de.html
39. Msroka, M. *Motivating workers in educational institutions: Adams' equity and Maslow's need hierarchy theoretical implications.* GRIN Verlag (2013).
40. Oyserman, D. Identity-based motivation: Implications for action-readiness, procedural-readiness, and consumer behavior *Journal of Consumer Psychology 19* (2009) 250–260.
41. Pink, D. H. *Drive: The surprising truth about what motivates us.* Riverhead Books (2011).
42. Regan, R. T. Effects of a favor and liking on compliance. *Journal of Experimental Social Psychology* 7 (1971), 627–639.
43. Ryan, R. M., & Deci, E. L. (2000). Self-determination theory and the facilitation of intrinsic motivation, social development, and well-being. *American Psychologist, 55,* 68–78.
44. Schor, J. B. *True Wealth: How and why millions of Americans are creating a time-rich, ecologically light, small-scale, high-satisfaction economy.* Penguin Books, (2010).
45. ServiceSpace Blog Post. *From sharing economy to gift ecology.* Posted by Nipun Mehta on May 31, 2014. http://www.servicespace.org/blog/view.php?id=14918
46. Suhonen, E., Lampinen, A., Cheshire, C. & Antin, J. Everyday favors: a case study of a local online gift exchange system. In *Proc. GROUP '10.* ACM Press, (2010), 11-20.
47. Tay, L. & Diener E. Needs and subjective well-being around the world. *J Pers Soc Psychol, 101,2* (2011) 354-65.
48. Trivers, R. L. The evolution of reciprocal altruism. *The Quarterly Review of Biology* 46, 1 (1971), 35-57.
49. Vallerand, R. J., & Fortier, M. S. Measures of intrinsic and extrinsic motivation in sport and physical activity: a review and critique. In J. Duda (Ed.), *Advancements in sport and exercise psychology measurement* (pp. 83–100). Morgantown, WV: Fitness Information Technology (1998).
50. van de Glind, P. *The consumer potential of Collaborative Consumption.* Research MSc in Sustainable Development – Environmental Governance Faculty of Geosciences, Utrecht University, the Netherlands August, (2013).
51. Vision Critical. *Sharing is the new buying. How to win in the collaborative economy* (2014). Retrieved from: http://www.visioncritical.com/sites/default/files/pdf/sharing-new-buying-collaborative-economy-report.pdf
52. Wahba, M. A., & Bridwell, L. G. (1976). Maslow reconsidered: A review of research on the need hierarchy theory. *Organizational Behavior and Human Performance, 15,2* (1976) 212–240.
53. Webb, T.L., Joseph, J., Yardley, L. & Michie, S. Using the Internet to promote health behavior change: A systematic review and meta-analysis of the impact of theoretical basis, use of behavior change techniques, and mode of delivery on efficacy. *J Med Internet Res. 12,1* (2010).
54. Willer R. Groups reward individual sacrifice: the status solution to the collective action problem. *Am Sociol Rev 74* (2009) 23–43.
55. Williams, G. C., & Deci, E. L. Internalization of biopsychosocial values by medical students: a test of self-determination theory. *J Pers Soc Psychol, 70* (1996). 767–779.
56. Williams, G. C., Grow, V. M., Freedman, Z. R., Ryan, R. M., & Deci, E. L. Motivational predictors of weight loss and weight-loss maintenance. *J Pers Soc Psychol, 70* (1996). 115–126.
57. Wright, R. *The moral animal: Why we are, the way we are: The new science of evolutionary psychology.* Vintage; Reprint edition, (1995).

Analysis of Recycling Capabilities of Individuals and Crowds to Encourage and Educate People to Separate Their Garbage Playfully

Pascal Lessel
DFKI GmbH
Saarbrücken, Germany
pascal.lessel@dfki.de

Maximilian Altmeyer
DFKI GmbH
Saarbrücken, Germany
maximilian.altmeyer@dfki.de

Antonio Krüger
DFKI GmbH
Saarbrücken, Germany
antonio.krueger@dfki.de

ABSTRACT
Sorting garbage is a relevant topic in many countries as it contributes to environmental protection. Empirical evidence suggests that not all people separate waste, potentially because they do not know how to do it correctly or are simply not motivated enough. We present the results of an online study (N=184) investigating people's capabilities for classifying waste, their capabilities to improve in this task over time and their current garbage separation behavior. The study confirms that the Wisdom of Crowds is applicable in this context as the crowd produces only half as many errors as the individual and feedback helps participants to improve. Based on this, we introduce the idea of a crowd classifying waste in a game, with their classification result then being used as feedback on gamified public trash cans to educate both the crowd playing the game and people using the trash can playfully.

Author Keywords
Gamification; Games With a Purpose; Wisdom of Crowds; Waste Separation; Behavior Change Support System

ACM Classification Keywords
H.5.m. Information Interfaces and Presentation (e.g. HCI): Miscellaneous

INTRODUCTION
Carefully handling waste is a relevant topic, as world cities in 2012 generated about 1.3 billion tonnes of solid waste per year, which will increase to 2.2 billion tonnes by 2025 [12]. In terms of recycling, in Germany, four (sometimes five) different trash bins for households are available that are designated to hold only a specific kind of trash, and in addition, glass containers (different containers for clear, green and brown glass) for non-returnable bottles can be found in all neighborhoods [9]. The situation is similar in other countries[1]. If the separation of garbage is done properly, it has a positive effect in terms of environmental protection, e.g. by reducing CO2 emissions [9] or greatly increasing the recovery rate of domestic waste [8]. Despite this obvious advantage of separating waste, not everyone seems to do it [7], resulting in the situation that the content of bins cannot be reused properly because of "contamination". There are different reasons why people do not separate waste correctly. Work conducted on this topic (e.g. [13, 24, 26]) suggests, among other reasons, that the number of bins and rules on what belongs in which of them makes it difficult to do it properly; that recycling seems not cost-effective enough to participate in; is inconvenient, if not every bin is easily reachable and that missing incentives result in a lack of motivation.

Figure 1. A German public trash can for waste separation.

In HCI, the topic of encouraging people to reflect on their recycling behavior (e.g. [27]) and waste in general (e.g. [10]) has been under investigation for a few years now. Some approaches investigate what happens if the trash cans are enhanced with technology. One prominent approach is the BinCam [21]. One part of this system is that paid crowd workers (recruited via Amazon Mechanical Turk (AMT)[2]) are meant to tag objects in pictures taken from a trash can according to waste categories. The performance of AMT was not good: in a random picture sample, 15 of 20 classifications were wrong [21]. As the focus of the work was not on the crowd, it remains unclear whether it was a problem of the crowd or only an issue of AMT, which has provided mixed results in the past (compare [2] but also e.g. [14]).

In our work, we want to focus on the crowd, as we see a big opportunity: Depending on the underlying design, individuals might, while classifying waste, also be affected by the task and adapt their behavior. To inform a system design, our goal

[1] `http://news.bbc.co.uk/2/hi/europe/4620041.stm`, last accessed on 05/01/2014

[2] https://www.mturk.com, last accessed on 05/01/2014

CHI 2015, April 18–23, 2015, Seoul, Republic of Korea.

http://dx.doi.org/10.1145/2702123.2702309

was to receive clearer insights on individuals' capabilities in classifying waste, on their attitude towards waste separation and whether they improve in this task over time while classifying. We decided to use an online questionnaire, in which participation was voluntary and without any monetary compensation, to reduce the chance of random answers to earn money faster [14], which could have been an issue before.

The results informed the design of a two component persuasive system: A public trash can, consisting of several bins (similar to Figure 1) for different types of waste, capable of taking pictures of newly discarded objects, and a display attached to it to show feedback. We decided to utilize a Gamification [5] approach for the trash can and try to motivate people to separate waste correctly by relying on a competitive setting. The second component is a mobile app which is designed as a Game With a Purpose [25] in which players lead a recycling company and one of the core activities they need to do is to classify waste (i.e. pictures the modified trash cans produce) to improve their revenue. In comparison to the BinCam, this app replaces the paid crowd by people playing the game and trying to improve their game score. The rationale behind using such a setting is that people not only in front of the trash can but also within the crowd might learn how to separate waste in a playful manner and will then do it in their "real life" more thoughtfully, even when not exposed to the game. We also present results of a first evaluation of this setting, showing that people appreciate this concept.

This paper contributes an understanding of individuals' capabilities in separating waste, shows how a crowd-based approach produces more reliable results than an individual alone and how feedback helps people to improve in this task. These findings are then transferred into a persuasive system design with the goal to educate people; this is presented afterwards.

RELATED WORK

Several approaches are available that investigate how a trash can can be modified. The effect of a trash can that is capable of taking pictures of its content is investigated in the BinCam [3, 4, 21]. Here, a bin was modified with sensors and whenever a new item was discarded, a picture was uploaded to a Facebook page. Besides the social pressure that other people on Facebook would see what was (potentially incorrectly) discarded, the authors also added some Gamification elements. For this, pictures were sent to Amazon Mechanical Turk and paid crowd workers counted the visible objects in terms of the waste category they belonged to. A competitive mechanism was added, in which the different can owners could see how well they were doing in comparison and could collect achievements. As stated, the authors mentioned that the quality of the crowd classification was not good and in conducted user studies (based on interviews with the owners), it was shown that the frequency of feedback was too coarse in the original approach, that people lose interest after some time and that there are privacy issues. We also utilize a trash can which is able to take pictures of the (newly) discarded object. In contrast to the BinCam approach, we aim for public trash cans with bins for several waste types to minimize the privacy issues occurring at home and to encourage waste separation. We will not use paid crowd workers to classify the pictures. Instead, we propose a game that should encourage people to classify such pictures and therefore have a potential positive effect on their own waste separation behavior.

Zlatow and Kelliher investigated public recycling bins, as almost 70% of the material contained in recycling bins is deemed unusable due to contamination [27]. They found that users need to be engaged on a deeper level. One proposal is the usage of a reward system in which a valid waste disposal is automatically detected and incentives are provided. Another proposal is to add educational facts around recycling to turn the act of recycling into an experience, which is also shown to be beneficial [26]. All these approaches try to make the act of throwing away, mostly done unconsciously, more conscious and engaging. With our approach we also aim for turning the usage of the trash can into an experience, e.g. by providing fast feedback and rewards.

Reif et al. [16] proposed Cleanly, an educational system, based on fieldwork and an online questionnaire. One of the results was that every second participant thinks that direct feedback would encourage them to participate in programs aimed at solving environmental problems. This, in general, is an important strategy in the area of encouraging behavioral change in sustainability (cf. for example [19]). Reif et al. introduces the holistic approach *trashducation*: the effort to educate people in their trash management by creating awareness of the trash they produce, decreasing the production of trash and endorsing proactive thinking about the environment. This is also relevant for us, as we also see education and motivation as important aspects of our system.

The work of McCarty and Shrum [15] makes clear that supporting recycling is an important topic, that the approaches in this context are relevant and that we need to understand why certain people engage in recycling while others do not, to better design programs that increase recycling behavior: For instance, the more people know about recycling, the higher the chance that they engage in recycling; or the more convenient recycling is made, the more people will recycle. Incentives also play a crucial role. All aspects have a direct impact on the work presented here, as we try to educate users, make recycling more convenient and provide virtual incentives.

Educating (by giving proper feedback) and motivating people to more thoughtfully recycle waste places this work in the area of sustainable HCI [18] and fits into the landscape provided by DiSalvo et al. [6]. The authors stated that finding new ways of engaging users and making them experts in sustainability is an emerging issue. Using game elements and social components provides individuals with further incentives on top of doing something reasonable [23]. Work, e.g. in the area of reducing energy consumption, has indicated positive effects of such approaches (e.g. [11]).

To our knowledge, none of these approaches analyzed the capabilities of a crowd in classifying waste and how their decisions could be utilized directly at a trash can. Our work tries to fill this gap by conducting an online questionnaire. The results informed the design of a mobile app game and a gamified trash can with the purpose to educate and encourage people to separate waste more thoughtfully and properly.

ONLINE USER STUDY

To inform the design of our system, we first investigated how capable people are in classifying waste, and if people make mistakes in classification, what options there are to improve their performance over time. A second aspect of the user study was to receive insights into current waste separation behavior of participants. With the study we tried to find evidence for the following hypotheses:

H1 An individual is in general not capable of classifying waste without errors.

H2 Aggregating the individual classification results leads to lower error rates in comparison to only considering individual decisions.

H3 Individuals improve over time, when they receive feedback on whether or not their past decisions were correct.

H4 Visualizing the results of other participants influences individual performance in later classification tasks.

H1 is motivated by the related work showing that people have problems classifying waste correctly. **H2** is based on the idea of the Wisdom of Crowds [20], which states that a group of people is able to come to a better decision than an individual. **H3** focuses on the educational aspect. In [22] it was shown that feedback (on wrongly separated objects) based on an analysis after the garbage was picked up has a positive impact on future decisions. We want to replicate a similar effect in our setting, but by giving immediate feedback. **H4** is based on the idea that a comparison to peer decisions might have a stronger impact, than only right-or-wrong feedback alone.

Method

We implemented a gamified online questionnaire that mimics the classification process we envisioned for the crowd in our game later on. The Gamification elements were meant to encourage people to finish the questionnaire, but were used to assess potential elements for this game as well. In general, we added points if a classification was correct and subtracted points if not. We provided bonus points if an answer was given quickly and correctly. During the classification tasks (depending on the group; see below) the participants could see how many points they needed to get to the next place on the high score list and how big the distance from the previous position on the high score list was. In the end, the participants were shown the complete list, in which only nicknames and points were displayed. As garbage separation is different between countries[3], we set up the questionnaire only in German and required that participants to have lived at least three years in Germany to participate. The questionnaire was published on student mailing lists and social networks.

[3] `http://news.bbc.co.uk/2/hi/europe/4620041.stm`, last accessed on 05/01/2014

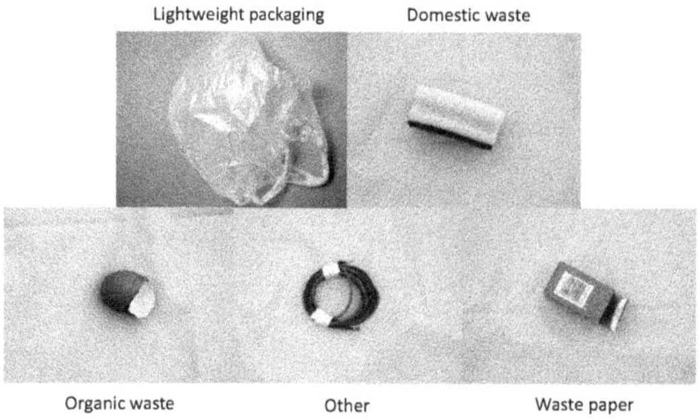

Figure 2. Example pictures for every waste category.

Behavioral Questions

After the introduction, in which we explained that the goal is to receive insights into waste separation behavior of German people, we asked the participants whether they think waste separation is easy, whether they are able to separate waste correctly and how complicated they judge waste separation to be in Germany. These questions (and all the other behavioral questions) were to be answered on a 7-point Likert scale, with labels shown on the extreme values. A set of classification tasks (see below) followed and consecutively we let participants judge their own performance in this task overall and continued with questions on the different game elements. After that, we asked questions about their waste separation behavior and collected demographic data.

Classification Task

We informed the participants that several objects would be shown, that they should classify them according to how they would be disposed of correctly in Germany and that we would assign points for their answer. The faster they provided an answer, the better for their overall score (in the case of a correct answer). For every picture they needed to decide whether the shown object belonged to domestic waste, lightweight packaging, waste paper, organic waste or none of those categories.

To acquire a ground truth for the pictures, we consulted different official material on the topic of how to separate garbage in Germany correctly and selected only pictures for which we found consensus in the material. In addition, every picture was rated by three judges beforehand in terms of its potential difficulty level and in case of incongruity, a discussion solved it (only in five cases was such a discussion necessary). The general selection of pictures was guided by the goal to have eight pictures with different representatives per difficulty category (three easy pictures, three medium pictures and two difficult pictures per category), resulting in $8 \times 5 = 40$ pictures. An example of an easy classification task was an apple (organic waste), one for a medium task was a non-returnable can (lightweight packaging), and a supermarket bill (which consists of thermal paper which should be disposed of as domestic waste) was assessed as hard to classify. Unlike the BinCam [21], we planned to use computer graphics algorithms in our system later on to extract one disposed object at a time; hence, every picture contained only one object. Figure 2 shows examples of the different waste categories.

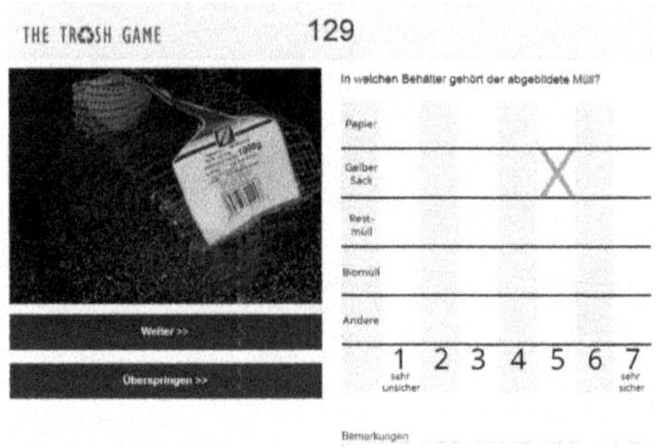

Figure 3. Example classification task of the questionnaire.

Participants could skip a classification completely and could add a comment to each of them. In addition, after they received feedback (depending on their group; see below), they also had the chance to comment on it. For every decision, participants also had to indicate how confident they were in it on a 7-point Likert scale. To simplify this, we used a grid layout in which the participants could assign a classification answer and a confidence with only one click (cf. Figure 3). We also measured the time per answer — an unusually long time might be an indicator that the participant used outside information. The order of the pictures was randomized and participants were assigned to one of five groups randomly (but equally) at the start. We varied the feedback participants received after a classification, depending on the group:

- **No feedback** (NF): Participants do not receive any feedback after their classification. They only see their overall score after all classification task and the high score list. This condition serves as a baseline.
- **Ground truth feedback** (GTF_{Only}): Participants always see whether their decision was correct or incorrect and what would be the correct answer. All gamification elements are available, i.e. they can see their points, how many points they are from the next position on the high score list, and their current placement on it.
- **Ground truth feedback with explanation** ($GTF_{Explanation}$): Same as GTF_{Only}. In addition, an explanation of how the ground truth decision was given by providing a short statement, and a reference to an official document was shown.
- **Ground truth feedback with same crowd decision** ($GTF_{CrowdSingle}$): Same as GTF_{Only}. In addition, they see how many people decided in the same way, by seeing a percentage (e.g. 12% had the same opinion).
- **Ground truth feedback with crowd decisions** ($GTF_{CrowdAll}$): Same as GTF_{Only}. In addition, they see how the crowd decided, by seeing a percentage per classification option.

Retest of false classifications

To check if any improvements were achieved due to the feedback, we asked the participants whether they wanted to improve their score by classifying a few more pictures before seeing the high score list ("bonus run"). These pictures were selected based on the errors made. The feedback group assignment remained the same for this task. In addition, we asked the participants, whether they wanted to receive an additional invitation to a follow-up study. One week after completion of the questionnaire, they received an e-mail with a new link. The questionnaire consisted of two questions (*"Did you consider the topic of waste separation more during the last week?"* and *"Do you think that you disposed of and sorted waste more thoughtfully during the last week?"*) and a set of classification tasks split in two chunks. The selection of the objects was again guided by the errors a participant made in the original questionnaire. In the first chunk, instead of a picture, we showed only the name of the object (everything else in the task remained the same). This should have minimized picture recognition effects. In the second chunk, we used the same pictures again. The order of text/pictures in both chunks was randomized and no feedback was provided.

Results

The questionnaire was accessible for four weeks and 184 people completed the questionnaire (78 female, 93 male; 13 did not specify a gender). The age distribution was skewed younger (29 <21, 124 to 21-30, 12 to 31-40, 12 to 41-50, 7 >50), due to the way we promoted the questionnaire, but which is not a problem in our case, as this fits our later target group (see system design below). Concerning the main backgrounds, 87 participants reported being students, 59 being employed and 15 working in an apprenticeship. The number of people the participants lived with was well distributed, while most (48) reported living together with 2 other persons.

Waste Separation Behavior

We asked several questions before and after the classification task to assess people's attitude towards waste separation. In general, people reported thinking waste separation is easy (M=5.11, SD=1.28, Mdn=5), that they are able to separate waste correctly (M=5.22, SD=1.27, Mdn=5), that they are in general eco-sensitive (M=5.07, SD=1.39, Mdn=5), that they separate to the best of their knowledge (M=5.42, SD=1.58, Mdn=6) and that waste separation is important to them (M=5.03, SD=1.42, Mdn=5). Participants (54) who disagreed (selecting four or less on the Likert scale) were shown potential reasons: 17% selected that it is too complicated, 30% that it is too much effort, 39% that there is too little space for waste separation at home, 31% that waste separation is useless and 26% stated that incentives are missing. In contrast, of the participants who agreed (130) 89% want to save resources and protect the environment, 35% have financial reasons and 65% also stated that it is their responsibility to protect the environment. In both cases free text answers could be provided, but were inconclusive. The participants disagreed with the statement that they seek information, if they are unsure how to dispose waste correctly (M=3.17, SD=1.58, Mdn=3) and with the statement that waste separation in Germany is difficult (M=3.46, SD=1.56, Mdn=3). After the classification task, we asked again whether they are able to separate waste and observed a small change in the self-assessment in respect to their capabilities in waste separation (M=4.9, SD=1.17, Mdn=5, $t(183)=3.35$, $p<.01$, $d=-0.25$).

Performance in the Classification Tasks

We deleted answers in the classification tasks that took longer than three times the average answering time (M=7s, SD=104s) as an explanation for this might be that participants had utilized external material. In the end, 7236 classifications in the main run were considered. Skipped classifications were counted as wrong classifications. On average an individual made M=23.37% errors (SD=7.61%, Mdn=22.5%), which supports **H1** — an individual is not able to classify waste without errors in general. We analyzed the errors per waste category and with respect to our a priori assigned difficulty level. Table 1 shows that the a priori levels fit in general (with organic waste as the only exception), i.e. medium and hard labels produced more errors than easy-rated objects and showed that some objects are harder to dispose of correctly. We analyzed the kinds of errors made more deeply, i.e. if an error was made, we checked which other category was selected. The corresponding confusion matrix is shown in Table 1 and together with the difficulty levels shows that the domestic waste objects produced the most errors. Another aspect which is also of interest is the relationship between assigned confidence value and the decision. We found that many participants utilized only the extreme values (a reason might be the time aspect to achieve more points; see limitation section). We filtered and used the remaining 88 answers for analysis. It showed that if people decided wrongly, they provided on average a lower confidence score than if they decided correctly ($M_{incorrect}$=4.89, $SD_{incorrect}$=1.00, $M_{correct}$=5.68, $SD_{correct}$=1.07, t(87)=-11.24, p<.01, d=-0.79).

	P	L	D	OR	O
Easy	5.51%	4.2%	24.05%	1.65%	8.14%
Medium	11.59%	11.01%	45.23%	21.06%	24.2%
Difficulty	25.36%	31.06%	87.77%	20.11%	67.97%
Overall error	12.75%	13.47%	48%	13.5%	29.12%

	P	L	D	OR	O	S
P	**87.29%**	4.79%	6.15%	0.55%	0.9	0.34%
L	0.83%	**86.63%**	9.57%	0%	2.83%	0.14%
D	22.36%	12.9%	**51.83%**	1.72%	10.62%	0.55%
OR	1.32%	0.13%	11.24%	**86.54%**	0.55%	0.21%
O	0.07%	11.61%	17.2%	0.0%	**70.84%**	0.27%

Table 1. Top: Errors per waste category and a priori assigned difficulty level, aggregated over all participants. Bottom: Confusion matrix showing the aggregated classification results (P=paper waste, L=lightweight packaging, D=domestic waste, OR=organic waste, O=other).

Assessing Improvements Over Time

The participants had the chance to improve over time:

- During the run: After removing outliers, we compared the error rate in the GTF-conditions (M=22.6%, SD=6%) with the NF-condition (M=25.18%, SD=8.8%), but a t-test showed no significant difference (p=0.5).

- Bonus run: 123 participants completed the bonus run. We expected an improvement in all GTF-conditions, based on the recognition of the pictures and remembering the correct answers. As the option to receive bonus points was not articulated before the classification task and answering the behavioral questions served as distractor, a better performance indicates that participants had seen the correct result and could also remember it also later on. The average error rate of the users was M=80%, SD=21% in the NF-condition and M=12%, SD=13.1% in the GTF-conditions. A one-way ANOVA showed a significant effect between condition and error rate (Welch's F(4,77.54)=68.07, p<.01, est. ω=0.83). The Games-Howell post hoc procedure was used since the homogeneity of variance assumption was not met, and revealed that every GTF-condition is significantly different from the NF-condition (every comparison with p<.01). We also checked whether the crowd-feedback had any impact on the way users performed. The rationale behind this was that users might be more likely memorize wrong classifications, if they saw how the crowd decided. However, none of the comparisons showed a significant effect.

- Follow-up run: As the bonus point run could still have only a short-term effect, we wanted to measure whether we could find evidence for improvements after a week. As a limitation, only 36 participants (NF:12, GTF:5, $GTF_{Explanation}$:3, $GTF_{CrowdSingle}$:8, $GTF_{CrowdAll}$:8) took part in this second study, limiting its expressiveness. We asked whether participants sought information about waste separation between the two questionnaires (M=2.86, SD=1.84, Mdn=2) and whether they separated waste more conscientiously (M=2.92, SD=1.86, Mdn=3). As outlined, we had two chunks of the classification task. The average error rate of users previously in the NF-condition in chunk 1 (chunk 2) was M=54.7%, SD=11.4% (M=54.3%, SD=14.3%) and of users previously in the GTF-conditions was M=33%, SD=18.2% (M=23.8%, SD=6.6%). Because of the low number of participants in $GTF_{Explanation}$, we excluded this condition in the one-way ANOVA analysis of chunk 1 and 2; additionally, one participant completed only chunk 1. We found a significant effect between group and error rate in each chunk (F(3,29)=5.61, p<.01, ω=0.54 and F(3,28)=26.3, p<.01, ω=0.84). Gabriel's post hoc procedure revealed that every GTF-condition is significantly different from the NF-condition (for chunk 1 with p<.05, for chunk 2 with p<.01), indicating that feedback was indeed helpful for subsequent classifications, even after a week. The error rates over all conditions in chunk 2 (M=34.2%, SD=17.6%) compared to chunk 1 (M=38.5%, SD=16.4%) were significantly lower (t(34)=3.71, p<.01, d=0.27) indicating that people indeed utilized recall effects, but in both chunks feedback had improved the user performance, providing evidence supporting **H3**. Again, no effect could be found by considering the crowd conditions. Hence, **H4** cannot be supported with the results made.

Crowd Performance

We tested different aggregation methods to see if a crowd-based approach produces more reliable results than individuals in this setting. We used different aggregation algorithms: a standard majority voting (MV); a weighted majority voting taking the provided confidence scores into accounts as weights (MMVC) and a weighted majority voting considering the percentage of correct decisions as weights to identify experts (WMVE). The problems with the confidence values (see above) resulted in a strict condition, in which we set the

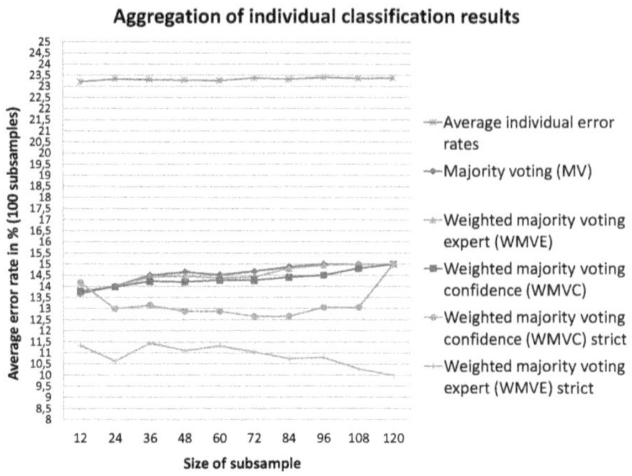

Figure 4. Crowd error rate in relation to aggregation algorithm and averaged individual error rates for different subsamples.

weights to 0 for participants who apparently did not use the confidence value properly. We also integrated a strict value for the expert rating (setting the weight to 0 for participants having a higher than average error rate). To receive more reliable results we took random subsamples of the dataset and repeated the subsample selection 100 times. Figure 4 shows the aggregated results in terms of error rates. For a better direct comparison, we also averaged over the individual (aggregated) error rate in the corresponding subsample. The result supports **H2**: the Wisdom of Crowds is applicable in this scenario, as the crowd produces a better result, independent of the specific aggregation mechanism and even at a low sample size. In our case, the strict expert metric worked best.

Perception of Feedback and Gamification Elements

For the assessment of the perception of feedback (namely true/false feedback, seeing the correct answer, justification for the ground truth answer and how the crowd has decided) and Gamification elements (seeing points, position on high score list, competition in general) we asked whether the element motivated them to classify more pictures (A), or if the participants belong to a condition in which the element was not used (B), whether it would have motivated them. The feedback elements used were seen as motivating (Mdn=5 for the different aspects in A, Mdn=6 in B); the only exception was the crowd feedback (A:n=74, M=3.5, SD=2.03, Mdn=3, B:n=110, M=3.72, SD=1.84, Mdn=4), with no significant difference between $GTF_{CrowdSingle}$ and $GTF_{CrowdAll}$. An explanation could be that such feedback is not interesting when the correct answer is also shown. Here, a follow-up study needs to investigate this further. The Gamification elements were also perceived positively (median 4 for seeing points, other 5). In all but one case participants not exposed to the corresponding element provided slightly higher scores. Always seeing the current position on the high score list is the only aspect which was perceived better by participants exposed to it (A:n=148, M=4.18, SD=2.16, Mdn=5, B:n=36, M=3.5, SD=1.76, Mdn=4). Participants were also able to add further aspects that would motivate them to classify more waste, but this was in general inconclusive.

Discussion

The study showed that individuals make errors in recycling. We provided the five major German categories and on average an individual disposes of one in five items incorrectly. The individuals classified themselves as eco-aware and capable of separating waste correctly but were not particularly interested in finding the information on how to dispose of an object correctly if unsure. In this sense, we found evidence that supports **H1** serving as additional basis to motivate the search for proper user assistance in this task, i.e. providing a system which gives immediate feedback. The conducted analysis showed that the Wisdom of Crowds is applicable in this context, as the crowd performed better than the individual (**H2**): depending on the aggregation algorithm, the crowd produces roughly only half as many errors as an individual on average. An explanation can be found in the work of Surowiecki [20], as the five rules of collective intelligence are also applicable here. In contrast to the BinCam [21], the crowd performance in our study was much better. Reasons for that might be that congruency of nationality and waste disposal rules were ensured in our case and that only one object should be classified at a time instead of counting all elements in a bin, which might be hard, as objects might be partly covered by objects above them. Our crowd was not paid and motivated to achieve a game score, which might convince them to decide more thoroughly [14]. We found evidence supporting **H3**; participants used the feedback shown and produced fewer errors not only for the same pictures but also for text-only representations after one week. Additionally, the gamification and feedback elements were perceived positively. This opens up the option for our game scenario in which not only the user in front of the trash can can improve through the feedback, but also the crowd providing it. With this setup though, we could not find supporting evidence for **H4**.

The results indicate that feedback helps people even when they are unaware of being retested. Thus a system offering a feedback mechanism and integrating it into the everyday activity of throwing something away can have a positive effect. Our study showed that an individual alone is not capable of providing sufficient feedback, but the error of a (potentially small) group of people is significantly lower. It seems possible to deploy a system that utilizes crowd feedback, but it should also integrate functionalities to educate the crowd explicitly as well. Instead of generating feedback and educating the crowd at the trash cans, we argue for using an additional system to make feedback accessible faster: an option to connect a crowd separately, also receiving feedback on their classification and with further educational options (e.g. external resources) to improve themselves, which is motivated by Gamification/game elements (as shown in our study). Integrating a Crowd as a "tool" for providing feedback at the point of interest while potentially being self-educated (and thus behaviorally influenced) is an interesting aspect for Sustainable HCI that might also be of relevance

Limitations

The study itself has limitations. First, we only investigated the waste separation behavior of German people. It remains open how this differs in other countries, which is a threat to external validity. Second, it can not be completely ruled out that the high amount of positive answers to behavior questions were influenced by social desirability or acquiescence bias. As the focus of our study was different (cf. hypotheses), this is only a minor limitation. Third, the survey used Gamification elements to motivate participants to do the (potentially) not-so-interesting task of classifying several waste pictures. As a negative side effect, people might have misjudged the time constraint and skipped through the feedback, instead of reading it thoroughly. If this is true, the effects in the feedback conditions might currently be underestimated. Forth, the selection of pictures includes uncommon objects, for the sake of the survey but the situation at a real trash can might be different. Considering that uncommon (in general, a priori labeled as medium and difficult) objects were classified worse, the performance of the crowd in a real-life situation is still questionable and will be investigated with our prototype. Fifth, the age distribution was skewed younger, limiting the expressiveness. Nonetheless, the target group for our mobile app, matches this distribution[4].

SYSTEM DESIGN

Based on our study we propose a system design consisting of two components: a modified public trash can and a mobile app. While the trash can produces images from discarded objects, the mobile app is able to present them to a crowd. Both components have the goal to get people engaged in sorting their waste: the trash can by displaying whether the object was disposed of correctly and building a competition around it and the mobile app by motivating people to improve their fictive "recycling company". A crucial component is the classification of waste. While an automated approach would be interesting it would not have helped in terms of the learning effect for the crowd, which is why it can only be seen as complementary and was not followed at this point in time.

Scenario

Alice walks through campus and encounters one of the trash cans belonging to the "Trash Game". She inspects the display and learns that her faculty has received many points in this week but is not in first place. She hopes that more people will sort their waste correctly to improve their faculty's score. Later, during a lecture, she receives a new notification on her smartphone generated by the "Trash Game" mobile app. Her fictive recycling company, WasteGoneProperly, has received a new task and needs to handle a new object. Because Alice plans to improve her company with new upgrades, she needs to gain more in-game money, so she immediately reacts to the job, as this provides her with bonus cash. She knows that the trash cans produces these pictures and provides feedback based on the opinion of the crowd. She particularly likes that, as this helps people to learn how to do it correctly. Within the game she reacts to the new picture by stating how her company would handle this kind of product. Only then does she see how other players have classified the garbage. Unfortunately, the majority of the crowd decided differently. Alice wonders about this and later in the day she decides to dive into this topic. In the meantime, certain companies have received the task to provide evidence showing that their decision was indeed correct, and Alice is able to read their statements. Some arguments and references are accepted by the community, so that she remembers how to classify the item and to do it correctly in the future.

[4]cf. **http://goo.gl/WQhaCO**, last accessed on 05/01/2014

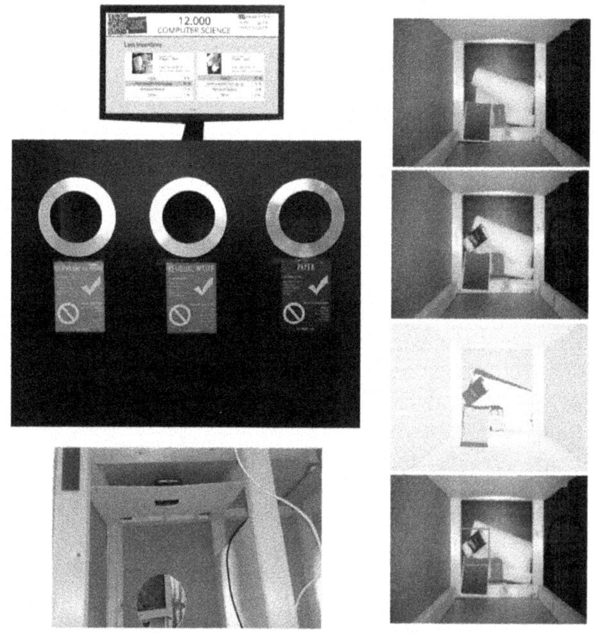

Figure 5. Left: Exterior/interior of the prototype. Right: Steps of extraction algorithm: (From top to bottom) Before insertions, after insertions, recognized differences, red rectangle showing extracted picture.

Modified Trash Can

Unlike the BinCam-approach [21] we focus on public trash cans, as people in Germany are already familiar with trash cans consisting of multiple bins in public (cf. Figure 1), potentially decreasing privacy issues. These bins are color coded, and printed pictures show prominent representatives of the corresponding categories. The design process of our trash can was guided by the realization of requirements: the can needs to recognize newly discarded objects; a picture should be generated that shows only the new object and should be made available online (in the mobile app); it should be able to receive crowd feedback and display it in a playful way by using Gamification elements.

Hardware design

We created a hardware prototype as a proof-of-concept. The basis is a wooden frame consisting of three different chambers and a smartphone attached on the ceiling of each (see Figure 5, left). The purpose of these devices is the detection of new objects and taking pictures of them. A Raspberry Pi is used to do the data handling between server and smartphones and displays the results on the trash can's display. For the persons using the trash can, the basic use stays the same — it is sufficient to throw the waste in one of the bins. The only difference visible is that this insertion is recognized and direct feedback on the display is shown.

Software design

We decided to create a competitive environment with the trash cans of the "Trash Game". Each can is associated to a group. Depending on the area of use, this could be, for example, different faculties, or divisions in a company. The smartphones are always checking for differences in the RGB pixels taken by the camera (which is more robust in comparison against changes in the lighting conditions). If a difference is recognized, a picture is taken after two seconds (to allow time for the object to fall). Subsequently, this picture is compared to the last picture taken to extract only the newly discarded object. For that, we identify areas that have changed and to reduce errors (as underlying objects might also have changed their position), we do a template matching and compare pixel arrangements of these areas with the pixel areas in the last picture and discard similar areas (see Figure 5, right). Informal tests indicated that the algorithm is robust enough to produce pictures similar to the ones used in our study. These pictures are sent to a server, which distribute them to the mobile app to get the crowd engaged. Our study has shown that even a small number of people are able to classify waste better than an individual. Currently, we consider the crowd votes after 30 seconds and if there are enough votes (20 is our current threshold) we display this as final result on the trash can's display (otherwise it is shown as preliminary, with more time being needed to come to a consensus). The display shows this counter and dynamically visualizes the distribution of votes the crowd made. If a person does not want to wait until the time is up she also has the chance to scan a barcode and is redirected to a web page showing the results afterwards.

After a correct (or incorrect) disposal (i.e. a (dis)agreement between crowd and chosen bin) the trash can receives (loses) points. The points are always clearly visible. In addition, each trash can shows the CO2 savings/production from the correctly/incorrectly separated waste inside it and the mobile game is advertised as well. Different screens are shown if nothing is currently added: A high score list shows the points of the predecessor and the successor only for the current week (so that the high score is not discouraging because the distances are too big); or the last additions are shown with the crowd voting or a screen showing common disposal hints, and the advantages of waste separation being done correctly. All the screens are chosen to get people interested in the trash can itself and to provide them with gamified feedback (to get them engaged in waste separation) as well as providing them with feedback that might improve the learning rate. Overall, we follow the design suggestions of [17].

Mobile App

The goal is to get the crowd engaged in the classification of waste, as their decisions can be used to decide if an object was sorted correctly (as shown with a low error rate). To get the individuals engaged we decided to design the mobile app as a game fitting into Games with a Purpose [25]. The prototype is implemented as a web app to ensure device-independence. By receiving feedback, people are able to get better at subsequent classifications of the same or similar objects, as shown in our study. Hence, the main idea we follow with this app is that not only are people at the location of the trash can educated, but the crowd itself also has the chance to improve.

Figure 6. Landscape classification screen of the app after a decision.

The player is head of a recycling company that tries to become the market leader by quickly and correctly disposing of specific objects. Occasionally, players receive tasks and the faster they react to them, the more money is generated, which can be spent for improving the company. This improves the market value of the company, but alters in-game mechanics as well (e.g. receiving more tasks or receiving more money per solved task). Currently, we distinguish three types of tasks, the *classification tasks*, *evidence tasks* and *knowledge tasks*. With different tasks we want to achieve a more diverse game play but also improve the data quality. A profile in the background is used which counts the times the player was correct and tracks demographic data, most importantly his country, as this moderates which tasks he receives: only pictures from bins located in the same country should be classified.

Classification tasks are triggered if a picture of a new object is taken by a trash can. Players receive a notification that a new classification task is available for them. By accepting it, they see the picture and the classification options (similar to the online questionnaire). In addition, they can provide a confidence value to their vote (cf. Figure 6). Only after they have selected an option they can see how the other companies have decided, and they will be informed about the final decision for this object. If they belong to the majority, they receive virtual money. If not, it depends on how big the difference in the voting is. If it is small (indicating that the crowd was not completely sure), no money is lost; otherwise, because the company needs to recycle the object in a more expensive way, some money is subtracted. The reason for showing the crowd distribution lies in the fact that people who see the distribution might be motivated to engage either in the seminars or in the evidence task (e.g. if they see that the vote was only slightly in favor of the other option). We used the strict expert aggregation, as this performed best in our study.

To support a deeper engagement with sorting questions, we integrated evidence tasks. Several companies are selected for this special task randomly, but can also participate in this task voluntarily. The main goal is to provide evidence (e.g. official links and/or reasonable explanations) for a previously classified object that either supports the crowd opinion or contradicts it. Similar to the Stack Exchange network[5], all players

[5]E.g. stackoverflow, `http://stackoverflow.com/`, last accessed on 05/01/2014

who participated in the crowd voting can see this discussion and up- and down-vote the different contributions, and finally accept an answer. Involved players receive a notification and potentially a (virtual) refund. In addition the company which provided the accepted evidence receives a reward that positively affects their market value. This task was created to account for crowd errors, which we also saw in our online survey, especially for uncommon objects.

The third kind of task is a task in which predefined questions are provided and players either contribute answers (e.g. "what is this object called?"or "do these pictures show the same objects?") or assess already-given answers (e.g. "Are these valid names for this object"?), which improves a knowledge base in the background. This can later serve to change the game mechanics and to inform ML-algorithms.

Besides these tasks the player has the option to attend "courses" in which commonly wrong classifications are presented with proper explanations. Attending a course provides the player a virtual certificate and bonus points, if he classifies such an object correctly in the future. To keep people engaged, we ensure that specific pictures that were already classified by the crowd (but not by the player) are given to the players even if nothing is discarded at the moment.

Preliminary Evaluation

To get an impression on how our prototypes are perceived, we presented them to university employees, students and visitors at the cafeteria foyer around lunchtime. They experienced the process by throwing an object (we provided several) into one of the bins and could also vote with the mobile app. The crowd feedback was provided in a Wizard of Oz-style experiment in which we select which feedback is shown (potentially adjusted by the participant vote). The selection was based on the results from our online study, e.g. if a supermarket bill was inserted, we presented the crowd classifications for this object, i.e. we used real values. While showing the process, we also explained the concepts of the prototypes and answered questions. Subsequently, the participants were provided with a questionnaire, consisting of several questions to be answered on a 7-point Likert scale and free-text questions.

35 people participated in our evaluation (12 female, 23 male). Questions concerning their waste separation behavior were answered similarly to our online study: Participants think that waste separation is easy (M=5.11, SD=1.23, Mdn=5), that they do it correctly (M=5.17, SD=0.923, Mdn=5) and to the best of their knowledge (M=5.6, SD=1.5, Mdn=6). They also think that waste separation in Germany is not complicated (M=3.83, SD=1.89, Mdn=4) and they do not seek more information if unsure how to separate waste correctly (M=2.71, SD=1.7, Mdn=2). Concerning the game concept, participants liked the trash can (M=5.77, SD=1.6, Mdn=6) and the mobile app (M=5.68, SD=1.57, Mdn=6). If they had the chance to decide to dispose of their waste in a normal or the augmented trash can, they would use our prototype to receive feedback (M=5.44, SD=1.66, Mdn=6). Eleven participants said this was because they liked the idea and four stated that it helps the environment. Three participants stated that the waiting time is a problem. We elaborated on this further and learned that 8 would wait, 14 would wait if feedback is provided quickly, 6 would not wait at all and 2 reported that they would wait only if unsure. Only one participant reported that he would not consider the mobile web page as an alternative if the waiting time is too long. Here, a solution could be to integrate approaches similar to [1], but with only virtual incentives. In general, the crowd feedback is judged useful (M=5.6, SD=1.33, Mdn=6) even though it could be wrong (which was also demonstrated). On the other hand, the responses were mixed for the question whether participants would also let the crowd classify their waste at home (M=3.71, SD=1.86, Mdn=4), mostly because of privacy issues, as the free-text answers showed (13), which is a replication of the results of the BinCam [21]. Concerning additional features, participants wished for further graphical elements, a variable design for different age groups, a mechanical component in which the waste is stored until the crowd has decided, and a way to achieve bonus points. Interestingly, they are undecided whether to play the mobile game (M=3.94, SD=1.9, Mdn=4). Here, a reason for this could be that only a part of the app was presented and the other functions were only explained. The answers showed that people focused more on the classification part inside the app and have not considered that these tasks are integrated into the game play. We will elaborate on this aspect further as a next step. In contrast, they liked that they could have an influence on the feedback the trash can shows (M=5.48, SD=1.56, Mdn=6). Concerning the functions, participants suggested a social media connection to compete with friends, collaboration with real recycling companies which serve as experts providing a more reliable ground truth, and that challenges should be integrated.

Discussion

Besides the goal to improve the waste separation capabilities of people at the trash can and within the crowd, the options provided by our setup might be interesting for recycling companies. The crowd provides a more reliable information on the content disposed in the bins; more specifically, through the knowledge tasks, we might also achieve a complete classification of waste inside the bin, which enables companies to better decide what should be done with the contents themselves. Moreover, with such an approach it could also be possible to learn from errors and share this knowledge with policy makers to help them to improve their own (educational) publications. In addition, it could be of interest for companies to deploy courses or publications within our app to improve crowd performance. The preliminary evaluation showed that both components are perceived well, even though participants were reluctant to play the mobile game. As a next step, we will focus on this part to receive deeper insights.

CONCLUSION

In this paper we presented results of a gamified online questionnaire which assessed people's capabilities in waste separation and found that people make errors in this task. In contrast, we demonstrated that crowd decisions in this setting produce only half as many errors as individuals. Based on the findings, we presented a novel system – the Trash Game, consisting of a trash can which is able to take photos of newly discarded objects and show feedback on whether or not the waste was separated correctly. This decision is made by utilizing a crowd which is motivated to participate by playing a mobile game in which every player is head of a recycling company and, amongst others, has the task to classify waste correctly. The core idea of both components is to achieve a learning effect, in which people in front of the trash can and within the crowd improve in recycling and will do it correctly, even if not exposed to the game components. The next step is a long-term evaluation of the mobile app. Assessing the impact on the crowd's real life will be a focus, as well seeing how large the effects are that such an approach can produce.

ACKNOWLEDGEMENTS

This work has been supported by the Cluster of Excellence on "Multimodal Computing and Interaction" funded by the German Science Foundation (DFG).

REFERENCES

1. Bernstein, M. S., Brandt, J., Miller, R. C., and Karger, D. R. Crowds in two seconds: Enabling realtime crowd-powered interfaces. In *Proc. UIST 2011*, ACM (2011), 33–42.
2. Buhrmester, M., Kwang, T., and Gosling, S. D. Amazon's Mechanical Turk: A New Source of Inexpensive, Yet High-Quality, Data? *Perspectives on Psychological Science 6*, 1 (2011), 3–5.
3. Comber, R., and Thieme, A. Designing Beyond Habit: Opening Space for Improved Recycling and Food Waste Behaviors Through Processes of Persuasion, Social Influence and Aversive Affect. *Personal Ubiquitous Computing 17*, 6 (Aug. 2013), 1197–1210.
4. Comber, R., Thieme, A., Rafiev, A., Taylor, N., Krämer, N., and Olivier, P. BinCam: Designing for Engagement with Facebook for Behavior Change. In *Proc. INTERACT 2013*, Springer Berlin Heidelberg (2013), 99–115.
5. Deterding, S., Dixon, D., Khaled, R., and Nacke, L. From Game Design Elements to Gamefulness: Defining "Gamification". In *Proc. MindTrek 2011*, ACM (2011), 9–15.
6. DiSalvo, C., Sengers, P., and Brynjarsdóttir, H. Mapping the Landscape of Sustainable HCI. In *Proc. CHI 2010*, ACM (2010), 1975–1984.
7. Environment Bureau Hong Kong. Blueprint for Sustainable Use of Resources. `http://goo.gl/JfSUZW`, May 2013. [last accessed 05/01/2014].
8. Environmental Protection Department. Programme on Source Separation of Domestic Waste. `http://goo.gl/JgxbHK`, May 2010. [last accessed 05/01/2014].
9. Federal Ministry for the Environment, Nature Conservation and Nuclear Safety. Waste Management in Germany 2013: Facts, Data, Graphics, December 2012.
10. Greengard, S. Tracking Garbage. *Commun. ACM 53*, 3 (Mar. 2010), 19–20.
11. Gustafsson, A., Katzeff, C., and Bang, M. Evaluation of a Pervasive Game for Domestic Energy Engagement Among Teenagers. *Comput. Entertain. 7*, 4 (Jan. 2010), 54:1–54:19.
12. Hoornweg, D., and Bhada-Tata, P. What a Waste: A Global Review of Solid Waste Management. *Urban Development Series*, 15 (March 2012), 1–116.
13. Hornik, J., Cherian, J., Madansky, M., and Narayana, C. Determinants of recycling behavior: A synthesis of research results. *The Journal of Socio-Economics 24*, 1 (1995), 105 – 127.
14. Ipeirotis, P. G., Provost, F., and Wang, J. Quality Management on Amazon Mechanical Turk. In *Proc. HCOMP 2010*, ACM (2010), 64–67.
15. McCarty, J. A., and Shrum, L. The recycling of solid wastes: Personal values, value orientations, and attitudes about recycling as antecedents of recycling behavior. *Journal of Business Research 30*, 1 (1994), 53 – 62.
16. Reif, I., Alt, F., Hincapié Ramos, J. D., Poteriaykina, K., and Wagner, J. Cleanly: Trashducation Urban System. In *Ext. Abstract CHI 2010*, ACM (2010), 3511–3516.
17. Schell, J. *The Art of Game Design: A Book of Lenses.* Morgan Kaufmann Publishers Inc., 2008.
18. Silberman, M. S., Nathan, L., Knowles, B., Bendor, R., Clear, A., Håkansson, M., Dillahunt, T., and Mankoff, J. Next Steps for Sustainable HCI. *Interactions 21*, 5 (Sept. 2014), 66–69.
19. Strengers, Y. A. Designing Eco-Feedback Systems for Everyday Life. In *Proc. CHI 2011*, ACM (2011), 2135–2144.
20. Surowiecki, J. *The Wisdom of Crowds.* Anchor, 2005.
21. Thieme, A., Comber, R., Miebach, J., Weeden, J., Krämer, N., Lawson, S., and Olivier, P. "We've Bin Watching You": Designing for Reflection and Social Persuasion to Promote Sustainable Lifestyles. In *Proc. CHI 2012*, ACM (2012), 2337–2346.
22. Timlett, R., and Williams, I. Public participation and recycling performance in England: A comparison of tools for behaviour change. *Resources, Conservation and Recycling 52*, 4 (2008), 622 – 634.
23. Tscheligi, M., and Reitberger, W. Persuasion as an Ingredient of Societal Interfaces. *Interactions 14*, 5 (Sept. 2007), 41–43.
24. Vining, J., and Ebreo, A. What Makes a Recycler?: A Comparison of Recyclers and Nonrecyclers. *Environment and Behavior 22*, 1 (1990), 55–73.
25. von Ahn, L., and Dabbish, L. Designing Games with a Purpose. *Commun. ACM 51*, 8 (Aug. 2008), 58–67.
26. Werner, C. M., and Makela, E. Motivations and Behaviors that Support Recycling. *Journal of Environmental Psychology 18*, 4 (1998), 373 – 386.
27. Zlatow, M., and Kelliher, A. Increasing Recycling Behaviors Through User-Centered Design. In *Proc. DUX 2007*, ACM (2007), 27:1–27:1.

Why and what did we throw out? Probing on Reflection through the Food Waste Diary

Eva Ganglbauer
Vienna University of Technology, HCI Group
1040 Vienna, Austria
eva.ganglbauer@tuwien.ac.at

Geraldine Fitzpatrick
Vienna University of Technology, HCI Group
1040 Vienna, Austria
geraldine.fitzpatrick@tuwien.ac.at

Florian Güldenpfennig
Vienna University of Technology, HCI Group
1040 Vienna, Austria
flo@igw.tuwien.ac.at

ABSTRACT
Issues of consumer food waste in industrialised countries are becoming an increasing concern and this is paralleled by a growing interest in HCI to support more sustainable consumption practices. In this paper we report on a mobile food waste diary application that was made available on app stores, with the aim of enabling motivated people to reflect on their moments of food waste and to explore rationales. Through analysis of the entries submitted by users of the diary application, we identify instances of reflection located on different levels. The intention of supporting reflection was visible in instances of submitted diary entries where deeper insights about the relationships between food waste, previous experiences, habits, knowledge, occurrences and intentions to change were offered.

Author Keywords
Food and interaction design; Food waste; Personal informatics; Reflection; Sustainability;

ACM Classification Keywords
H.5.m. Information Interfaces and Presentation (e.g. HCI): Miscellaneous

INTRODUCTION
Issues of food and wasted food are becoming an increasing concern worldwide and this is paralleled by a growing interest in HCI to support more sustainable practices [17]. To date this has largely played out in relation to energy consumption [8, 25]. However, food waste is another area of growing concern for ecological sustainability, especially considering the over-production together with the waste of food. It is estimated that around half of the food worldwide is discarded, with consumers contributing around 30% to food waste in industrialised countries [14]. The amount of food produced and finally thrown away in production and consumption greatly affect greenhouse gas emissions [6]. However, for individuals, food waste is also a personal matter and often connected with uncomfortable feelings [9, 11]. Due to a worldwide growing population we have an increased demand in food consumption, and a reasonable alternative is a more frugal handling of food. Hence food waste, for example, through overbuying or letting food spoil, unnecessarily contributes to greenhouse gas emissions, which could be avoided if the amount we produce and the amount we consume were more balanced. However, people are aware of that they throw away but often not able to report on why they discard food, nor which types, amounts or the frequency of food waste [11].

To this end this paper presents the design and use of the food waste diary as a technology intervention probing into the potential of enabling reflection on issues around food waste. The mobile food waste diary application is intended for participants to capture and reflect back on 'reasons', experiences, and occurrences connected with food waste. This paper will first describe the motivation of this case study and the intervention in more detail, and why the mobile food waste diary application was intended to support reflection. Second, the concept of reflection in personal informatics is introduced along with a framework that describes our definition of reflection and different levels of reflection. The third section presents the design of the food waste diary application, which enables people to capture various data about food waste. It will describe how the application works and what type of contents it invites.

The diary application was put online to Google Play (Android) and App Store (iOS) for free to attract interested people in downloading, installing and using the application. Through distributing the app online we were able to capture real-world authentic data from a very specific user group, genuinely interested in food waste. Fourth, the data forms the basis of a study of use of the diary. The 843 entries submitted over 18 months were analysed qualitatively and quantitatively to understand what people throw away and why; free form comments were also thematically coded, specifically looking for indications of reflection.

Finally, the findings provide deeper insights about the relationships between food waste, previous experiences, habits, knowledge, occurrences and intentions to change for people already aware of this issue and prepared to do something about it. The order of effort that people put into using the application further points to the potential value of such a tool to support those concerned about such issues.

CHI 2015, April 18–23, 2015, Seoul, Republic of Korea.

ACM 978-1-4503-3145-6/15/04 ...$15.00.
http://dx.doi.org/10.1145/2702123.2702284

MOTIVATION FOR FOOD WASTE DIARY CASE STUDY

Food waste in households is a complex issue. To date, there has been good research on how much food is thrown out by households, e.g., Schneider and Lebersorger [22] who have weighed domestic food waste. It is only more recently though that in-depth studies were conducted to explore the everyday practices around how such waste comes about in homes [9, 11]. A key insight was that the moment of throwing food away is just a final moment embedded in a number of other everyday practices that span space and time, practices such as shopping, storing, cooking, socializing and so on, where food waste becomes deeply entangled with the circumstances of everyday life [11]. For example, participants described stories of how food was wasted, determined by circumstances such as family members who would not eat as expected or how over-buying was routinely taking place in households.

Thus food waste is often described as an unintended outcome. More critically, people often feel inherently 'guilty' about wasting food [9, 11], but cannot often say why or from where these feelings emanate. As food waste is not simply the result of one occasion, person, or behaviour, it can be hard for people to understand the issues leading to waste and therefore identify issues they can influence or not. This points to an opportunity to think about how to support people reflecting on and understanding their own routines around food waste.

In the case study presented here we explore the role of digital technology and its potential in recording data to reflect on previous experiences, habits and patterns [1, 10]. A paper diary from the *Waste and Resource Action Programme* led to thinking about the potential for a digital diary. To this end we developed[1] a mobile food waste diary application for iOS and Android smart phones. This case study is intended to mainly look for reflection supported by technology, though at the same time stays open for different interpretations such as social and material cicumstances. The mobile food waste diary application was intended for participants to record instances of food waste enabling later reflections, as well as explore the rationales and experiences people would provide when throwing out food. We aimed to bridge the gap between the moment of throwing away food and the connection to previous experiences before that led to the food turning into waste. We intended to support reflection both during the recording what food was wasted, as well as when revisiting the recorded data.

REFLECTION IN PERSONAL INFORMATICS

The food waste diary can be seen as related to personal informatics, where different areas of everyday life can be recorded for reflection. Personal informatics systems are interactive applications that support users in understanding various aspects of their life, such as experiences, behaviours, patterns, habits and emotions. Advances in new sensing technologies made personal informatics a popular topic for HCI research [16] as it incorporates vast amounts of collected data for providing the user insights on their daily life. Li, Dey, and Forlizzi [16] summarized four primary life domains and information sources for personal informatics systems, namely *exercise*, *general health*, *finance* and *journaling*.

Food waste is quite different to those areas and might concern only a certain set of interested people. While many of such applications automatically gather user data, for instance, by activity trackers [7], other systems strongly rely on manual user input. Pirzadeh et al. [18] researched journaling tools as a means to improve self-knowledge and proposed a diary application as a *"support tool to help individuals record and reflect on their experiences"*. These authors stressed that the process of gaining self-knowledge include the clarification of one's own feelings . The food waste diary connects to this research by two shared assumptions. First, our proposed application takes advantage of manual data input for an in-depth *engagement* of the users with their own experiences, occurrences and feelings as opposed to more convenient but maybe unreflected automatic tracking. Second, we hypothesized that this deeper commitment would be helpful in uncovering sensible and personal reasons people provide for food waste.

Khovanskaya et. al [15] critically drew attention to the role of data mining algorithms behind the scenes of personal informatics systems and provoked their participants to critically *reflect* about the influence of these computational mechanisms. Baumer et al. [1, p.98], on the other hand, highlighted and critically remarked that the effects of reflection in most research projects were described as *"universally beneficially"* and *"wholly good"*. As the food waste diary encourages its users to reflect on a rather 'uncomfortable' issue, namely own experiences and patterns that lead to wasting precious resources like food, our proposed system adds an interesting instance to the literature that potentially can evoke negative feelings or emotions such as felt guilt, as was evident in our material.

On reflection

Reflection is a core element to many interactions being studied in HCI, from providing increasing self-knowledge through personal informatics, or changing behaviour through persuasive technologies. Digital technologies for reflection can record data automatically or require manual capture as in case of the food waste diary. In this paper, the term 'reflection' can refer to an individual mental cognitive activity in examining previous occurrences that lead to food waste. But reflection can also be thought of as social activity, e.g. examining a household's collective data about food waste together in a group [1]. Both, individual and collective approaches to reflection, are included in the definition of reflection in our paper. What both approaches of individual and collective reflection have in common, is the purpose that reflection could possibly provoke critical thoughts or alternative actions through data examination or discussion. As Baumer et al. [1] discuss,

> *"sometimes the goal of reflection is not only to increase self knowledge but to take action based on this increased*

[1]The interaction design was elaborated in group meetings where concepts and suggestions were discussed iteratively towards user experience as well as feasibility for programming. We had several meetings discussing interaction design until the programming started.

(1) (2) (3) (4) (5)

Figure 1. First screen on application start (1) to insert reason, category, optionally picture, comment and price of food product. Users can also enter the reasons why food was thrown away (2) and choose from a predefined list or generate personalised and customised reasons. Collected food waste entries can be viewed as list (3), as collected pictures of food waste (4) and as chart graph with most popular reasons (5).

awareness. Systems of reflection vary as to the extent that they support taking such action." [1, p.96]

This level of reflection is also described as *"transformative reflection"* in Fleck's and Fitzpatrick's [10] research, specifically reflection revealing an intent to change. They note that different definitions of reflection serve different purposes and present a framework for levels of reflections. These levels (R0 - R4) are presented as a means to identify reflection occurring and also to evaluate reflection later on in the findings [10, p.217 ff.]:

- *Description (R0):* Reportive account or statement about experiences and things without further explanation or reflection.
- *Reflective description (R1):* Reportive in nature with explanation or justification of reasons and experiences, without further reflection.
- *Dialogic reflection (R2):* Exploring different relationships between experiences and knowledge and considering different explanations or other viewpoints.
- *Transformative reflection (R3):* Revisiting experiences with the intention to change, re-organise or do something differently. Challenging personal assumptions and practices.
- *Critical reflection (R4):* Reported experiences are related to wider social and ethical implications. Considering the bigger picture and implications.

Different levels of reflection play out in different domains, and reflection is by far not only a core element to increasing self-knowledge or changing behaviour. Within HCI, reflective design practice described by Schön [23] is unfolding differently: From Schön's perspective, reflection on materials and design processes incorporates the processes of *"reflection-in-action"* and *"reflection-on-action"*. Reflection-in-action supports people while they are completing a task, finding out what is different and how it can change thinking and doing. Reflection-on-action entails a process that takes place after something has been done, e.g., a final reflection on an artifact where the own processes are evaluated and reflected upon.

The data submitted via the food waste diary was coded openly as well as according to the presented levels of reflection (R0 - R4) to understand if the diary was used towards reflection. This framework [10] aided in finding indicators of how different levels of reflection unfold for the subset of people who are interested in keeping a diary about their food waste.

Before moving on to the findings and elements of reflection in the data, the components and the interaction design of the food waste diary are described to provide an understanding what kind of information the food waste diary application invited to record.

FOOD WASTE DIARY APPLICATION

Food waste diary is a mobile application that allows people to capture occasions of waste. It encourages them to reflect on moments of waste and to connect to earlier experiences of discarding valuable food. The application has been developed to a stable prototype and has been freely available at Google Play (Android) and the App Store (iOS) since 7 Dec 2012. People who are genuinely interested in their food waste can download this application. Indeed, the food waste diary was installed on 1065 devices and 843 entries have been submitted in the 18 months up to 5 June 2014.

Consumers who are aware of the issue of food waste and want to collect information about how much food they actually waste and why, can do so by entering this information into the diary. We used the most common platforms Android and iOS to offer a technology that can scale and is accessible to most people living in industrialised countries, where consumer food waste is prevalent [14]. The application was made available in English and German.

The food waste diary application offers the possibility to record information and to review a history of information. To record information, the obligatory fields for an entry are the reason why food ended up in the bin and the 'type' of food. Figure 1 (2) depicts how users can choose between five predefined reasons to record why a specific item was wasted:

- *"Visibility of food stock is missing"*
- *"Over-buying"*
- *"No shopping list"*
- *"Change of cooking plans"*
- *"Special offer"*

These categories are motivated by a questionnaire study that identified the most common reasons of disposed food in households [13]. As we assumed during the design process that the mentioned reasons are not exhaustive for most users, the interface also offers the possibility for a user to specify their own explanation to capture the multifaceted nature of waste (see Figure 1 (1)). This provides a compromise between ease of use (through the pick list) and openness for interpretation (by enabling their own comments if they wish). The other obligatory field to be entered is the type of food, e.g. *"Dairy"*, *"Bakery"*, *"Fruits and vegetables"*, etc., drawn from standard food categories.

Then there are a number of non-madatory fields for 'costs' and a 'comment form' for free notes and the possibility to add a 'picture' (see Figure 1 (1)). Allowing the declaration of costs to be entered is motivated by studies [11, 20] as an incentive for consumers to waste less. The comment form for free notes was motivated simply to enable people to add more content or stories to a food waste entry. Supporting photo capture was motivated because, once included, it could be used for open engagement with the topic and further elaboration. The location of the user is automatically detected with the in-built GPS sensor, if users allow the application to do so.

After a user has submitted an entry, the screen changes to the history of submitted food waste entries, with the option of filtering for personal entries or the entries of all people using and submitting to the food waste diary. Figure 1 (3-5) presents an overview of three different views for history of food waste entries as:

- Consecutive list of entries ordered by time, Figure 1 (3).
- Pictures that have been taken from food being wasted, Figure 1 (4).
- Chart with most common reasons why food has been wasted, Figure 1 (5).

People can toggle between the individual or collective data by tapping the corresponding icon on the top left of the History screens (see upper left of screens in Figure 1 (3-5)). To consider privacy aspects, the location of submitted entries is not visible in the collective History view. The identity of the person who submitted the entry is not visible, as data is anonymised in terms of the personal details.

The trigger for people to submit entries is the incident of food being thrown away [2]. The event-triggered nature of the application implies that users have to invest additional time and energy for the mobile food waste diary in case they want to capture their waste. The aspiration at the start of the project was to provide people with a tool to support the reflective process with the mobile food waste diary application.

METHODS IN FOOD WASTE DIARY CASE STUDY

To understand real world use by people who are genuinely interested in an application that facilitates reflection on food waste, we chose to distribute food waste diary online at the Google Play and App Store on iTunes where the app could be downloaded, installed and used for free.

In the study that we describe next, we were curious whether people would download and use such a tool, and if they did, how participants would describe their waste and whether this would prompt further reflections on everyday food practices. The data presented here is a result from users who might already be aware of food waste, hence motivated enough to install the app, and possibly want to know more about the whys and hows of their waste.

The choice of app store distribution as the basis for study and data collection is becoming increasingly common [3]. It was particularly appropriate for the food waste diary as it was important for us to target people who would be genuinely self-motivated by a concern for this issue; the app store route was also informed by the experiences reported in [11] around the guilt associated with this issue, and where some recruited participants for a fridge intervention, the FridgeCam, in the end did not use it because they were not genuinely interested, despite agreeing to participate in the study. In the case of our data in the diary study, we can be more confident that all instances of use are authentic. The trade-off however is that we cannot make any claims that the findings will generalize as we have a very special self-selected subset of people genuinely interested in food waste and prepared to submit their authentic data.

As also noted by [5], there are methodological adaptations and trade-offs, as we do not have direct access to the participants. This means that we necessarily will lack some information about the participants such as demographic profiles. We cannot complement the data collected via the application with qualitative interviews to understand if and how use of the diary impacted actual practice. Hence there are limits to what we can claim about the actual reflection and/or changes enabled by the diary, rather we focus instead on indicators that might suggest possible reflection. However, we suggest that the access to authentic data from people genuinely interested in the topic provides a useful perspective on the potential of technology to support such people.

Thus, to study the use of the food waste diary we focus on analysis of the 843 submitted entries using a quantitative as well as qualitative approach. The data submitted via the food

Country	Reason	Type	Comment	cost	curre	ID
it_IT	Over-buying	vegetables	no waste	0	EUR	8d15f817d04a3b19c4e95e3b3dddd964
en_GB	was unwell	Fruits and vegetables	orange juice opened before ill. when well again had gone off. guessed cost	1	GBP	00a828affd838f66f62b84dd39716354
en_GB	Over-buying	Dairy products and eggs	bought box of 6 as 4s not available option. Cooked a quiche and a cake but unable to use last two.	0.56	GBP	00a828affd838f66f62b84dd39716354
en_GB	Visibility of food stock is missing	Drinks	last of bottle of lemon cordial open long time rediscovered in fridge	0.3	GBP	00a828affd838f66f62b84dd39716354

Figure 2. Excerpt of data entries submitted via food waste diary.

waste diary was exported to a .csv file and processed using SPSS.

As the application requires users to provide a 'rationale' and 'type' related to a food item, the most popular rationales and types of food thrown away, along with other quantitative data, is collated and presented. This quantitative analysis enabled us to get a broader picture about the most prominent reasons for and types of food thrown away, or how many entries were submitted with free comments.

Of the 843 entries, half (49,8%) have been submitted with a comment, a field that was optional and not required. Even though most of the comments were brief, they offered interesting insights and were qualitatively analysed using thematic coding [4]. A representative excerpt of entries is provided as data evidence (see Figure 2).

Concerning the data it is also important to note that users of the food waste diary were not required to enter personal information for registration; instead they were identified with a unique ID that is submitted along with an entry. The analysis is therefore based on public and anonymous data where links to individuals were removed. Due to technical reasons 182 entries were submitted without a unique ID, hence they could not be mapped to a specific user (ID). This only impacted the analysis of how many entries were submitted by the same user and how many entries were submitted from different countries. Otherwise this data is included in all other analysis.

The next section focuses on the distribution of prominent reasons for food waste, the qualitative thematic coding of these entries as well as the counted occurrences of specific instances. The codes for the qualitative coding are based on the framework for reflection [10], where the data was assigned to different levels of reflection, namely *"R0: description"*, *"R1: reflective description"* , *"R2: dialogical reflection"*, *"R3: transformative reflection"*, and *"R4: critical reflection"*. During the process of analysis an additional level of reflection emerged from the material that we named:

- *"R5: Emotional reflection"*. Emotional reflection reports on and connects specifically feelings with experiences, such as feeling guilty for throwing food away.

Besides the codes for reflection, we also identified instances of social and material circumstances in users comments about wasted food.

FINDINGS

The findings obtained by quantitative data exploration are presented first, followed by the results of the qualitative thematic analysis [4] with a focus on the levels of reflection.

Quantitative exploration

The submitted entries (N = 843) revealed trends of people's experiences and 'reasons' why food is wasted. The quantitative data exploration points to *"Over-buying"* (N = 178) as the most prominent rationale, followed by *"Visibility of food stock missing"* (N = 96) and *"Change of cooking plans"* (N = 66). Figure 3 provides more details on rationales behind wasted food. Interestingly, 414 entries and accordingly 49,1% of entries showed reasons self-defined by users without the existing categories being used. We will present patterns in these instances in the section of qualitative findings.

Further data exploration reveals that the most thrown away items were *"Fruits and vegetables"* (N = 194), followed by *"Bakery"* (N = 116) and *"Meat, fish and tofu"* (N = 111). Interestingly here again 27% of entries had self-defined food types submitted by users. These were more specific descriptions of the food types thrown away. For the existing entries with unique IDs it was technically possible to derive the country region of entries being submitted mostly from the US (N = 208), followed by Germany (N = 128), Great Britain (N = 128) and Austria (N = 128). We see a congruent pattern here as entries were submitted mainly from industrialised countries, where consumer food waste is reportedly prevalent [14].

Submitted online content usually shows a pattern from very few active users to many users who are less active. Such a pattern could be observed with the food waste diary too. The

Figure 3. Most prominent predefined 'reasons' that were submitted through the mobile food waste diary application. 49,1% of entries were self-defined by users and not using existing definitions.

user who submitted most entries had 133, followed by a user with 64 entries, another user with 38 entries, and further down a declining curve where 146 users submitted a single entry only.

Costs were submitted in 58,5% of all entries. Since this field was not obligatory in the food waste diary application (as opposed to 'reason' and 'type' that were obligatory), entering costs appeared to provide an added benefit to users. Costs were being mentioned as a reason why people want to waste less food [11, 20], and this is confirmed here where it seemed to be popular for users to add estimated costs of food waste to an entry.

Qualitative accounts

We will now describe patterns in self-defined food types and reasons, and the results from the thematic analysis of the comments. Submitted text in languages other from English has been translated to make it understandable for an international audience.

Given that 49,1% of the *reasons* submitted by users were self-defined we wanted to understand in more detail what users provided in their submitted entries. All were descriptive in nature. For example, there were many instances about the physical state of the food, such as *"leftover"*, *"overcooked"*, *"out of date"*, or *"mouldy"*.

Other submitted (custom) reasons mentioned emotions connected with discarding food such as *"don't feel like eating"*, or bodily conditions *"no appetite"* and *"migraine trigger"*. In addition, social circumstances were mentioned as reasons and submitted as self-defined text such as *"Susie didn't like it"*, or *"procrastinated about cooking"*. Connections between the busyness in life and discarded food were also evident, as time is needed to prepare and consume food at home, e.g., *"haven't been at home enough"*. This supports findings from studies about wasted food [9, 11]. Similarly, there were comments about not remembering what was there: *"forgot in the fridge"*; cases similar to this in [12] were partly attributed to lack of visibility into food storage areas and forgetting generally what food is there.

Of the submitted entries, 27% of food types were self-defined. The analysis of these entries also, expectedly, points to more specific characterisations of items being discarded. Examples were *"fish taco"*, *"rice"*, *"pizza"*, *"chinese"* or *"yogurt"*. What is interesting here is the specificity of the food type and it is interesting to speculate on what memories and meanings are implicitly entailed in these descriptions for people, e.g., remembering the particular pizza meal, why they decided to have pizza, who was there, etc. One might speculate about the memories and meanings that are implicitly entailed in these descriptions

Reflection in comments

More detail about experiences was provided in the free comment field, which was used in 414 (49,8%) of all entries. Given that this was a voluntary field, it is a statement in itself that people were prepared to make this effort in nearly 50% of entries. The comments, submitted along with the entries, provide more in-depth understanding of what people submitted in terms of thoughts, experiences, explanations and connections. Of the 414 comments, most were *descriptive (R0)* accounts (173 instances), elaborating on the type of food thrown away, e.g. *"Baked beans"*, *"Remains of roast chicken"* or *"Cheese was moulded"*. This descriptive level is reportive in nature. It may be possible that users reflected on their entries while they were making the note or at a later point when revisiting them, similar to Schön's notion of reflection-on-action, but the note itself does not provide direct access to evidence of reflection beyond awareness.

There were 58 comments that can be described as *reflective description (R1)*, a description reportive in nature but with an explanation. Illustrative excerpts were

> *"Didn't agree with me"*
> *"Salad that wasn't eaten for lunch - not hungry"*
> *"Tried gluten free pop tarts - too dry and not sweet"*

In these instances explanations about why something was thrown away were provided, from not liking something, to not being hungry, to some experienced quality of the food item itself (*"too dry and not sweet"*).

Dialogic reflection (R2) was found in 30 instances of the data and suggests deeper reflection involving the exploration of relationships between food waste, previous experiences and other circumstances. One submitted entry for example provided a comment:

> *"Over estimated fruit consumption and ripening times. Did not get to mango or avocado before off."*

The exploration of different relationships here is evident: There is a relationship between buying a product, the estimation of how long it will last and at another point of reflection, the experience that the assessment was not as estimated. Another instance where different relationships were explored reads as follows:

> *"I like buying new products. I tend to buy them without shopping list. I didn't like this taste."*

This user reflects on several experiences, habits and food waste. The user reportedly likes to try new products (a salad dressing in that case) and indicates it was impulsive buy (without a shopping list), reflecting on the connections that this might result in throwing food out and why (*"didn't like this taste"*).

A step on from dialogical reflection is *transformative reflection (R3)*, a level of reflection where the intention to change is articulated. Six instances of transformative reflection were coded in the material, such as

> *"I don't want to buy so much any more"*

This entry alone is very general but was submitted along with the food type *"Candies and Snacks"*, the reason *"Special offer"* and costs of "8 Euro". These fields connected together provide a broader picture on the intention not to buy snacks and candies any more.

The instances of *transformative reflection (R3)* share an intention to change or re-organise a habit or trying to reflect on experiences, patterns or habits that should not be repeated, such as *"Stop putting more on the plate than you can eat"*.

There is a specific instance of transformative reflection that is very interesting in terms of the various levels of reflection that come together:

> *"Wasted 1.5 bunches of kale because heard it's toxic to juice every day. Could have eaten sooner though but bought silverbeet instead and hurt back so stopped cooking etc. Don't buy 3 bunches at once."*

The comment expresses various relationships, between description and knowledge (*"heard it's toxic"*), alternative actions (*"bought silver beet instead"*), unexpected occurrences (*"hurt back"*) towards a transformative reflection (*"Don't buy 3 bunches at once"*). This comment is more like a little story in character, where the person who submitted the comment seems to not only reflect on the circumstances leading to the kale being thrown away, but already provides an alternative future action. This also reflects the complex negotiations people make in their everyday life and that food is not discarded carelessly.

Critical reflection (R4), where social and ethical circumstances are considered, were not traceable in the comments. Such deep reflection could probably be observed if we had been able to interview users of the food waste diary, asking the question if and how reflection was an issue in the use of the diary.

As described in the methods section we added another code to the levels of reflection that we described as *emotional reflection (R5)*, a code emerging out of the material. Studies on food waste have pointed to feelings of remorse and guilt when people talked about discarding food [9, 12], which resonates with the findings from this study. Comments that reflected emotions and feelings were found in 18 instances:

> *"I'm too full to finish all up. Pathetic"*

This comment was submitted along with the reason of *"Mixed food"* and *"Over-buying"*. The user submitting this entry frowns upon the discarded food; other instances even talk about being sorry for having to throw away food. One example is *"I'm very sorry but it was very disgusting and overcooked"*. Emotional reflection itself can be descriptive (R0), reflective descriptive (R1) and in some instances dialogical (R2), where an experience is related to an emotion such as being sorry but it is just not tasty. The emotion in many cases reminds of remorse or an utterance of dislike or tiredness. It suggests that the reflection on food waste triggers uncomfortable feelings when having to discard food. Hence reflection can cause *"inner discomfort"* [18].

Social and material circumstances

The data from the food waste diary also pointed to the social and material organisation of everyday life implicated in food being thrown out. Social circumstances describe broader contextual elements in the organisation of everyday life that are influenced and shaped by the people we share our lives with. The social context mattered and practices around planning, shopping, cooking, and eating are highly influenced by who else lives in the home. The food waste diary pointed to 13 instances of specific social circumstances such as *"Bad communication/no coking combination found"*. Social circumstances point to communication or throwing out food because of over-provisioning (*"packed too much for Susan's lunch"*) or having bought more than wanted *"My partner bought too much"*.

Additionally there were also material circumstances as evident from a user who noted about their egg purchase:

> *"bought box of 6 as 4s not available option. Cooked a quiche and a cake but unable to use last two."*

This quote can be interpreted in terms of the materiality of food packaging and in which quantities eggs are sold in the super-market, as eggs are only available in a pack of six but not four. The quote could as well be interpreted as concerning the social organisation of everyday life, as the user was *"unable"* to use the last two eggs for some reason. Hence the quantities, the material aspects of the package and the norm of having smallest packages of six eggs in the supermarket, also contributed to food being thrown out in the end.

DISCUSSION

Given research to date that points to the complexity of food waste and the difficulties people have in accounting for how it comes about, the focus of this paper is the design and evaluation of a mobile food waste diary to support reflection. In summary, 843 diary entries were submitted over 18 months and indicators of different levels of reflection were visible in the comments submitted with food waste entries. It is interesting to note two levels of user effort. Firstly, the entries are not passively measured or automatically added to a database. Instead they have to be entered manually, triggered by the event of wasted food, and requiring initial effort to remember to take out the application to use it. Secondly free text was added by participants not only in the comments but also about self-defined food types and reasons, despite the provision of a category list: 49,1% of entries defined their own 'reasons' for wasting food, and 27% of the food types were self-defined. Moreover half of the entries included comments additional to their entries.

This points to the significant additional effort people were prepared to put into personalising and reflecting on what food they throw away and why. It also shows the value of people wanting to be more specific, personal and detailed when manually entering data. This can enable reflection amenable for making connections as they are more personal and connected to real life. We suggest that this additional effort might encourage a more active engagement with reflection and sense-making of the data as also noted by Li et al. [16], as for many entries the predefined options were not used. This supports a design approach to offer *open-ended* and free interactions in personal informatics systems that aim to support reflection, approaches as also proposed by Baumer [1] and specifically highlighted in Sengers's and Gaver's work [24].

The focus on waste itself, as a result of the socio-technical and the conceptual intention behind the food waste diary, provides a deeper insight about food waste as being strongly connected to the social and material circumstances in which food practices are embedded. Thus the data from the mobile application enabled us to gain a deeper insight into the issue of food waste, at least as evidenced by this particular set of motivated users. In these instances social circumstances such as 'bad communication' or material circumstances of 'packaging' were reflected upon and presented as rationales for wasted food. These rationales point to the interrelated nature of everyday life and food practices. The rationales that people provided were manifested in the comments and self-defined reasons users submitted. Reportive accounts or descriptive reflections were most common, where users described in more detail what they threw away (*description (R0)*) or why (*descriptive reflection (R1)*). Instances of *dialogical (R2)* and *transformative reflections (R3)* were less often encountered but offered deeper insights about the relationships between food waste, previous experiences, habits, knowledge and intentions to change, e.g., *"I don't want to buy so much any more"*.

Processes of reflecting with technology

Schön's concepts of *reflection-in-action* and *reflection-on-action*, though concerned with design processes, are interesting here as they describe two different processes about when and how reflection can take place. *Reflection-in-action* takes place while people are enacting in an activity and making connections. Reflection-on-action takes place after a process or artifact has been completed, as a reflection on what has happened [23]. We will borrow these concepts for reflection supported by the mobile food waste diary. Reflection can take place at the moment when people are discarding food and reflecting on why they are, as reflection-in-action. While wasting, a user might already reflect on submitting the data to the food waste diary.

Schön's concept of *reflection-on-action* describes final thoughts and reflections enabling us to think back about past processes. For reflection-on-action, we can discern two different forms of reflection in the use of the food waste diary. First we could observe instances of *reflection-through-recording* when manually entering data through making connections between experiences, occurrences and why something is thrown away, how much the food costs, what different actions it might provoke and so forth. The second point of reflection-on-action can take place after an entry has been submitted through *reflection-through-revisiting*.

The speculation here, and evident in instances of the data, is that manually entering the reasons for food waste supports the reflective process through *reflection-through-recording*. We further speculate that this is likely to lead to increased understanding, addressing the barriers to reflection raised by Li et al. [16] when data is automatically recorded:

> *"Barriers in the Reflection stage prevent users from exploring and understanding information about themselves. These problems occurred because of lack of time or difficulties retrieving, exploring, and understanding information."* [16, p. 562]

Changing routines

Intentions to change certain aspects to waste less were visible in instances of *transformative reflection (R3)*, where users noted down their thoughts. Taking a critical perspective, we might argue here that the intention to change does not imply that change is going to happen, and we are only able to study the *intention to change* here.

The food waste diary application was offered to people who were genuinely interested in making visible for themselves certain aspects of food waste. As suggested by Quested [19], the availability of such a tool can be important when looking for opportunities to change and increased visibility:

> *"Opportunities to break habits have also been utilised: in addition to moments in peoples lives where they are more amenable to change [], increased visibility of food waste in the home is also a good opportunity to change behaviour. Examples include completing a food diary or placing all food waste generated over a week in a separate receptacle."* [19, p. 50]

Quested et al. suggested that major life events or a dedicated time to use a diary can elicit transformations in catching people at this point of taking an opportunity to break habits and wanting to gain more transparency on what and how much food they waste. Assuming that inherent motivation is significant, recruiting people who are genuinely interested is key and was our main motivation for this study. All in all 843 entries emphasise that there are some people who desire to reflect on food waste practices and some of the comments point to deeper reflective processes that have taken place. The entries are a testimony of people's desire and enactment of reflection on discarded food. Nevertheless, an investigation into whether personal informatics can actually enhance self-knowledge or change in everyday life, necessitates an evaluation whether personal informatics systems support such changes [18, 16]. Here we can make a start by pointing to potential indicators of such change, but as a methodological trade-off will need a different study to say how to translates to action.

Broader notions around change

We also engage here with the general critique of technology interventions aimed at individuals or households. This is important as behaviour change or motivational theories, where data is presented as feedback in a quantified way, are often critiqued [25] for singling out specific behaviours, aiming to address it without considering the broader circumstances. These approaches are often too simplistic and treat human beings as being guided by rational choice rather than negotiating the complex circumstances we live in and in which our food practices are intertwined [25]. A second point of critique is more systemic: Supporting change on any level, e.g., through reflection, carries the critique of not being radical enough for sustained change. Erickson et al. [8] speculate that a radical change in using less energy for example might only be possible through 'crisis or prices' or both at the same time. In terms of food waste, there is data that also points to this argument. For example, the 13% reduction of food waste between 2006/7 and 2010 in the UK can be connected to increased food and drink prices and reduced incomes during that time [21].

Nonetheless the fact that the application was used and seemed useful for some, suggests that we should not entirely abandon individual technology approaches; the food waste diary shows that such approaches can have benefits as well for self-motivated individuals. There is nothing inapt about supporting people who want to reflect on why, how much and which food they waste, being aware this might not lead to fundamental change and might only reach a certain set of people. The users of the food waste diary application submitted entries because they wanted to know how much they throw away and some mentioned the intention to change routines. They did so through manually capturing, making connections and reflecting on those entries.

Design considerations

As designers of interventions we have to be critical about the choices we make; in addressing individuals we should respect people's choices in the complexity of everyday life. The food waste diary application was not designed to recommend any actions, but for enabling people to capture their own connections between experiences, reasons, occurrences, types of food, or optionally costs. We argue for an approach of personal informatics where a holistic and open technology experience is offered to users, where they can creatively define, also in addition to automatic tracking of data, why and what type of data they want to enter for reflection. We also argue for it being ok to accept that we only have a view through the application, albeit a useful view, and not how the application connected to everyday life and change, as a useful trade-off for accessing authentic use and users.

The role of *emotions* as found in our material can be considered and embraced, even those that are uncomfortable [1, 18, 26]. Reflection on experiences is not just a rational and cognitive process. Experiences are always coupled with emotions and these are important in developing self-awareness. How can emotions be respected or considered in the design of such systems?

The social and material circumstances involved in the everyday negotiations and trade-offs in saving or wasting food point to the potential of technologies for helping us be more aware of these connections. An application could elicit reflection not only about the behaviour, but the *circumstances entailed* in shaping our behaviours and the connections across space and time.

Strengths, limitations and future work

As noted previously, we made a conscious decision and positive choice to offer the application worldwide at the Apple and Google Play market for free to collect data from intrinsically motivated people to use the application. We also intended to keep the threshold to use the application as low as possible, hence users were not obliged to register with email address and password. This came with the trade off that we were not able to recruit diary users for a more in-depth interview study. Such a study would enable us to gain deeper insights on reflection-through- revisiting and help us to understand if a transformation of individual or collective household actions took place after transformative reflections.

We intend therefore to carry out further research on the process of reflection-through-revisiting and as future work we intend to recruit users of the food waste diary for an interview study through a pop-up screen on the mobile application. This will enable us to understand how the diary is used as part of their broader strategies in addressing food waste and its potential for reflection in a direct conversation with participants.

CONCLUSION

The case study on the food waste diary application probes on people's food waste experiences, reasons and the connections they make. While the design intention is to open the space to instigate reflection, it also informs a richer understanding of the complexity and competing concerns that lead to wasted food. The quantitative findings inform us about 'popular' reasons for food waste ("over-buying") and that interestingly, half of the entries provided a personalised 'reason'. This points to the effort people are prepared to make and the complexity of the phenomenon of food waste, where simplistic answers to where and how something is thrown away do not exist for most cases. The complexity becomes visible in some instances of the qualitative thematic analysis of free comments, uncovering the unintended nature of food waste in everyday life through its social and material organisation and unexpected occurrences. The intention of supporting reflection was visible in some instances of submitted entries where deeper insights about the relationships between food waste, previous experiences, habits, knowledge, occurrences and intentions to change were offered. Qualitative interviews with users of the food waste diary are a subject for future research to better understand the role of reflection and how the diary facilitates it while entering the data manually (*reflection-through-recording*) and revisiting it for reflection (*reflection-through-revisiting*).

ACKNOWLEDGMENTS
We would like to thank Georg Molzer, Christoph Fischer, Petr Slovak and Francisco Nunes.

REFERENCES

1. Baumer, E. P., Khovanskaya, V., Matthews, M., Reynolds, L., Schwanda Sosik, V., and Gay, G. Reviewing reflection: On the use of reflection in interactive system design. DIS '14, ACM (New York, NY, USA, 2014), 93–102.
2. Bolger, N., Davis, A., and Rafaeli, E. Diary methods: Capturing life as it is lived. *Annual review of psychology 54*, 1 (2003), 579–616.
3. Boll, S., Henze, N., Pielot, M., Poppinga, B., and Schinke, T. My app is an experiment: Experience from user studies in mobile app stores. *Int. J. Mob. Hum. Comput. Interact. 3*, 4 (Oct. 2011), 71–91.
4. Braun, V., and Clarke, V. Using thematic analysis in psychology. *Qualitative research in psychology 3*, 2 (2006), 77–101.
5. Cramer, H., Rost, M., Bentley, F., and Shamma, D. A. 2nd workshop on research in the large. using app stores, wide distribution channels and big data in ubicomp research. UbiComp '11, ACM (New York, NY, USA, 2011), 619–620.
6. Cuellar, A. D., and Webber, M. E. Wasted food, wasted energy: The embedded energy in food waste in the united states. *Environmental Science and Technology 44*, 16 (July 2010), 6464–6469.
7. Epstein, D., Cordeiro, F., Bales, E., Fogarty, J., and Munson, S. Taming data complexity in lifelogs: Exploring visual cuts of personal informatics data. In *DIS '14*, DIS '14, ACM (New York, NY, USA, 2014), 667–676.
8. Erickson, T., Li, M., Kim, Y., Deshpande, A., Sahu, S., Chao, T., Sukaviriya, P., and Naphade, M. The dubuque electricity portal: Evaluation of a city-scale residential electricity consumption feedback system. CHI '13, ACM (New York, NY, USA, 2013), 1203–1212.
9. Evans, D. Beyond the throwaway society: Ordinary domestic practice and a sociological approach to household food waste. *Sociology 46*, 1 (2011), 41–56.
10. Fleck, R., and Fitzpatrick, G. Reflecting on reflection: framing a design landscape. OZCHI '10, ACM (New York, NY, USA, 2010), 216–223.
11. Ganglbauer, E., Fitzpatrick, G., and Comber, R. Negotiating food waste: Using a practice lens to inform design. *ACM Trans. Comput.-Hum. Interact. 20*, 2 (May 2013), 11:1–11:25.
12. Ganglbauer, E., Fitzpatrick, G., and Molzer, G. Creating visibility: Understanding the design space for food waste. MUM '12, ACM (New York, NY, USA, 2012), 1:1–1:10.
13. Glanz, R. Causes of food waste generation in households – an empirical analysis. Master's thesis, University of Natural Resources and Applied Life Sciences Vienna, 2008.
14. Gustavsson, J., Cederberg, C., Sonesson, U., van Otterdijk, R., and Meybeck, A. Global food losses and food waste. Tech. rep., FAO, 2011.
15. Khovanskaya, V., Baumer, E. P., Cosley, D., Voida, S., and Gay, G. "everybody knows what you're doing": A critical design approach to personal informatics. CHI '13, ACM (New York, NY, USA, 2013), 3403–3412.
16. Li, I., Dey, A., and Forlizzi, J. A stage-based model of personal informatics systems. CHI '10, ACM (New York, NY, USA, 2010), 557–566.
17. Pierce, J., Strengers, Y., Sengers, P., and Bødker, S. Introduction to the special issue on practice-oriented approaches to sustainable hci. *ACM Trans. Comput.-Hum. Interact. 20*, 4 (Sept. 2013), 20:1–20:8.
18. Pirzadeh, A., He, L., and Stolterman, E. Personal informatics and reflection: A critical examination of the nature of reflection. CHI EA '13, ACM (New York, NY, USA, 2013), 1979–1988.
19. Quested, T.E., M. E. S. D. P. A. Spaghetti soup: The complex world of food waste behaviours spaghetti soup: The complex world of food waste behaviours. *Resources, Conservation and Recycling 79* (October 2013), 43–51.
20. Quested, T., and Parry, A. New estimates for household food and drink waste in the uk, 2011.
21. Quested, T. E., Parry, A. D., Easteal, S., and Swannell, R. Food and drink waste from households in the uk. *Nutrition Bulletin 36*, 4 (2011), 460–467.
22. Schneider, F., and Lebersorger, S. Untersuchung der lebensmittel im restmüll in einer oberoesterreichischen region. Tech. rep., Institut fuer Abfallwirtschaft, 2009.
23. Schön, D. *Educating the Reflective Practitioner: Toward a New Design for Teaching and Learning in the Professions*. Wiley, 1987.
24. Sengers, P., and Gaver, B. Staying open to interpretation: engaging multiple meanings in design and evaluation. In *Proceedings of the 6th conference on Designing Interactive systems*, DIS '06, ACM (New York, NY, USA, 2006), 99–108.
25. Strengers, Y. Smart energy in everyday life: Are you designing for resource man? *Interactions 21*, 4 (July 2014), 24–31.
26. Williams, D. M., and Evans, D. R. Current emotion research in health behavior science. *Emotion Review 6*, 3 (2014), 277–287.

Energy Babble: Mixing Environmentally-Oriented Internet Content to Engage Community Groups

William Gaver[1], Mike Michael[2], Tobie Kerridge[1], Alex Wilkie[1], Andy Boucher[1], Liliana Ovalle[1], Matthew Plummer-Fernandez[1]

[1]Interaction Research Studio
Goldsmiths, University of London
initial.surname@gold.ac.uk

[2]Department of Sociology and Social Policy
University of Sydney
mike.michael@sydney.edu.au

ABSTRACT
The Energy Babble is a kind of automated talk-radio that is obsessed with energy and the environment. We developed it with, and deployed it to, a number of existing 'energy communities' in the UK. The system gathers content from a variety of online sources, including Twitter™ feeds from the communities, from governmental departments, and from the National Grid, and chats about it continually using a number of synthesised voices interspersed with a variety of jingles and sound effects. Designed to playfully reflect and comment on the existing state of discourse and reports of practice in the UK, the Babble can be considered both as a *product* and as a *research tool*, in which role it worked to highlight issues, understandings, practices and difficulties in the communities with whom we worked.

Author Keywords
Research through design; environmental HCI; ludic design; STS; energy communities

ACM Classification Keywords
H.5.m. Information interfaces and presentation (e.g., HCI): Miscellaneous.

General Terms
Design

INTRODUCTION
In the UK, the government has committed to a 34% cut in carbon emissions, compared to 1990 levels, by 2020, and an 80% cut by 2050, despite a prediction that global energy demand will double by 2030 [15]. This ambitious target is being approached in a number of ways, including the pursuit of low-carbon energy production and new approaches to manufacturing. In particular, a significant proportion of the saving is expected to come from reductions in domestic energy use, and thus 'energy demand reduction' is a strong theme in current government policy, including policies around research.

This stance is congruent with recent trends in 'environmental HCI'. On the face of it, the rationale for HCI's involvement in energy demand reduction is simple and convincing: Demand reduction can be supported by realtime feedback about actual energy use, according to this logic, coupled with persuasive computing approaches to encourage people to reduce their demand. Since sensing, feedback, information visualisation, persuasive computing and domestic applications are all core issues for the HCI community, it seems apparent that it could play a leading role in supporting energy demand reduction.

Over the last several years, however, the potential for simple energy demand feedback to reduce consumption has been challenged in a number of ways. First, evidence suggests that interventions produce only small and short-lived effects [1], and are prone to 'boomerang effects' in which above-average consumers may reduce their energy use, while those below-average ones increase theirs [10]. Broader concerns are raised in critiques from the social sciences. For instance, focusing on reducing resource consumption (including energy) tends to overlook the culturally embedded practices within which consumption takes place [12] and portrays the consumer as 'resource man' [14] capable of and concerned with reducing consumption as an end in itself. Dourish [5] suggests that focusing on individual behaviour change casts people as individual rational actors in a classic new-liberal way, while Brynjarsdóttir et al. [2] link persuasive approaches to modernism and its limitations and also review and identify the shortcomings of many environmental HCI projects.

In sum, despite the apparent promise of resource demand monitoring, the approach seems constrained by several factors. First, addressing individual or household consumption overlooks larger social realities that can promote or inhibit sustainable practices. Second, a narrowly instrumental approach towards reducing energy consumption is insensitive to how energy use is part of situated practices that people are unwilling or unable to change. Finally, insensitivity to diverse settings tends to lead to one-size-fits-all designs that may not fit local circumstances.

CHI 2015, April 18 - 23, 2015, Seoul, Republic of Korea
Copyright 2015 ACM 978-1-4503-3145-6/15/04…$15.00
http://dx.doi.org/10.1145/2702123.2702546

Energy, Design, STS and Communities

How can we go beyond individualistic, utilitarian and modernist approaches to design-led research on energy sustainability? The approach we describe here was conditioned by three factors that were significant in the project's framing and pursuit. First, the design work was influenced by our work on *ludic design* [6], which promotes playful engagement with ideas to offer a wide scope for interpretation [11], as well as our previous research using speculative design as a form of public engagement with science, in which designers engage with 'expert practitioners' to explore possible futures for emerging technologies [8].

Second, the project was undertaken through collaboration between Design and Science and Technology Studies (STS), with leaders representing each perspective, and team members having variable expertise in either one or both domains. Explicitly linking design work to STS emphasised an appreciation of, and engagement with, a heterogeneous mix of actors at variable scales; more generally it reflected and resulted in a shared concern with how technologies are shaped by social actors, and conversely how social realities are shaped by technologies.

A third factor important in the framing of the project came from the funding programme for which we shaped a proposal and which ultimately funded the research. Jointly supported by the UK's technology and social research agencies, the 'Energy and Communities' programme emphasised the potential importance of 'community initiatives', suggesting that 'change in energy consumption is... not simply dependent on behavioural change at the individual level but on the co-evolution of communities and the emerging technology that is available' [15]. In addition, the programme was arranged to partially and semiformally coincide and communicate with another initiative, the *Low Carbon Communities Challenge* (LCCC), which funded the work of 22 'test communities' to reduce carbon use in various ways. This meant projects funded by the 'Energy and Communities' programme were supported and encouraged to engage with a variety of 'energy communities' spread across the UK.

The Energy and Communities programme thus provided a timely opportunity for us to explore environmental issues from a mixed STS and Design approach that we labelled 'Ludic Action Research' [17]. We approached the project with a commitment to exploring and querying certain assumptions and reified notions built into the call e.g. what counts as energy-practice, what are the issues and actors at play, indeed what counts as community. This approach also sensitised the team to an expanded view of 'involvement' in the design process (e.g. [3], [16]).

In the rest of this paper, we describe the trajectory the research took in engaging with communities via a number of design-led methods, conceptualising and implementing the Energy Babble, deploying it into the communities, and assessing their responses. Finally, we reflect on the results of our study to understand the nature of the Babble both as a product and a research tool, one that illuminated the conditions and difficulties faced by the energy communities with whom we worked.

PROCESS: FROM THE COMMUNITIES TO THE BABBLE

At the outset of the project we had no plans for the sort of device we might build; instead we wanted this to emerge from our interactions with the communities. In this section we describe how we engaged with members of a number of different energy communities from the UK, the design-led methods we used to shape our relationship with them, the design explorations that eventually led to the Energy Babble concept, and how we refined the concept through software development and product design.

Forming a Network of Communities

Soon after the project was launched, we began to form a network with members of several energy communities around the UK. We met most of these at an event arranged jointly by our sponsoring research councils and the LCCC to introduce the initiatives and people involved in them to each other. Also at this event, we met representatives of the Department of Energy and Climate Change (DECC) who later took part in some of the project's activities. During the meeting, a number of LCCC participants expressed an interest in our project. We followed up these initial encounters with short visits to each site, during which we met with key members of the groups and toured the areas to see some of the projects they were pursuing.

The seven 'communities' with whom we worked[1] were by no means coextensive with their geographical settings. Typically involving small numbers of committed members who see themselves as practitioners, innovators and transition advocates, they form and reform in response to policy and funding changes, seek to enrol the communities of their villages or towns or cities, and agonise over how they will involve more people in their plans. Some were extremely well organised and funded, while others were very ad hoc and quiet. Their engagement with and characterisation of environmental issues varied as well, with key issues for them ranging from global warming to fuel poverty, and from renewable energy to conservation.

Design-Led Community Building

The initial networking meeting was effective at introducing community groups and academic researchers to each other. It also revealed potential tensions between the community groups and academic researchers, however. In discussions, it became clear that the energy communities questioned, and might resent, funding given to research that was not primarily aimed at producing direct environmental benefits, particularly given the government's changing commitments

[1] The groups were: Energise Hastings; Greening Goldsmiths; Low Carbon Living Laddock; Meadows Partnership Trust; Reepham Green Team; Sid Valley Energy Action Group; Transition New Cross.

to renewable energy and sustainability. In addition, most of the community groups were time and resource poor, and had already been subject to a great deal of scrutiny both from researchers and policy makers over the course of their operation. Now we were asking them to volunteer more time and energy to working with us. Not only did they appear somewhat jaded by the attention they had already received, it seemed that they had formed well-developed personas in presenting their work and beliefs.

These considerations influenced activities we designed to get to know more about the communities and to bring them together with each other and our research team. Most significantly, we held an 'engagement workshop' at a London museum, with participants including members of each community, and also other interested people including representatives from the funding agencies and the Department of Energy and Climate Change.

Engagement Workshop

For the workshop, we designed several playful and engaging activities, inspired by Cultural Probes, for group work. For instance, to explore participants' expectations and fears about the future, we asked them to work together to complete partially-designed front pages for imaginary periodicals, offering templates for genres such as a tabloid newspaper, a more serious looking broadsheet newspaper, and a popular science magazine (Figure 1a). To investigate people's emotional engagement with energy practices, we asked them to draw and use rubber stamps to describe the trajectory of a recent event, which resulted in annotated diagrams describing activities ranging from getting up in the morning to killing a chicken to serve at a dinner party (Figure 1b). To investigate communities both as they currently experienced them and as they imagined they might be, we gave them a diagrammatic map and a large number of stickers, asking participants to work together to create a fictional amalgamation of their communities (Figure 1c).

These activities occasioned a great deal of discussion that was informative about the participant's communities and environmental work. The primary achievement of the exercises, however, was to configure the participants' relationship with each other, and with us as researchers. By inviting the participants to engage with tasks intended to provoke creative exploration rather than to return clear social scientific data, we seemed successfully to encourage participants to forgo more formalised forms of self-presentation and to engage with us in a more personal and relaxed manner. In addition, the tasks worked to expose them to our methods and approaches as designers, and to set the tone for the design activities we pursued later.

Cultural Probes

At the end of the engagement event, we gave each participant a number of Cultural Probes kits to work with themselves and to distribute to other members of their communities. Each kit contained several items, e.g.:

- A poster for writing 'energy rules', with prompts ("It's strictly…", "Never…", "Always…")
- A form for writing an obituary for an appliance
- An unfolded envelope with a request to "confess a guilty energy use secret" before sealing it for privacy
- Cards with two devices (e.g., a clothes iron and a wind turbine) with blank speech bubbles to be filled

Participants returned the probes after several weeks. Again, part of the purpose of the probes was to encourage an informal and playful relationship with the participants. This seemed effective in encouraging returns that were revealing of the participants' attitudes and conflicts around energy use. Some (e.g. "*it's strictly energy use that defines us*") indicated that participants were zealous about sustainability. Others (e.g. confessing to "*leaving the door open and keeping the heating on*") suggested a capacity for self-deprecating humour about the contradictions in their actual practices. In general, the Probes seemed to allow us, and perhaps our participants, glimpses of the complications involved in balancing everyday life with a commitment towards environmentalism.

Our view of these complications was reinforced by our research into current energy policies and the sustainable technologies that the communities were using. We also attended energy events in the communities, where we were struck by the many different voices, affiliations, concerns and agendas in which the community actions were entangled. These discussions, the workshop, probes and observations all set the scene for our design work.

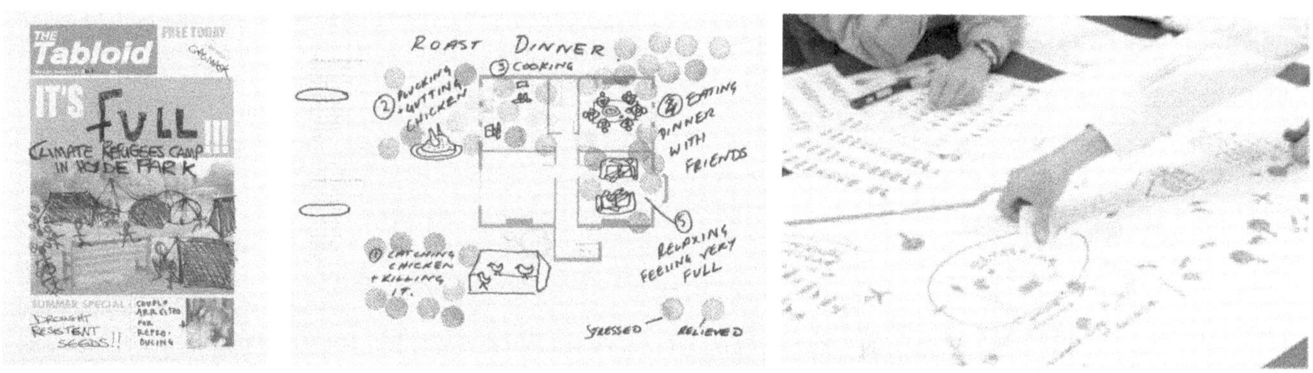

Figure 1. Engagement workshop tasks: a) imaginary periodicals; b) emotional trajectories; c) mapping communities.

Figure 2. Proposals: a) energy tourism; b) activist meter reading; c) energy awareness

From a Design Space to the Babble

As our perceptions of the energy communities and their engagements began to settle, we started to work on ideas for the systems and artefacts we might make for them. As with many of our projects, we developed numerous ideas that we captured in the form of simple evocative proposals captured in a series of design workbooks [7]. Here we outline a few to indicate avenues we explored (Figure 2):

• *Energy tourism*. Increasing concerns about sustainability brings greater visibility to previously overlooked energy infrastructures (e.g. power stations, transmission networks). Could new or obsolete energy infrastructure become sites for new forms of sightseeing?

• *Insistent activism***.** Discourse about sustainability is often channelled into predictable forms (e.g. community meetings, energy exhibitions, etc.). This may make such concerns easier to hold separate from day-to-day life. Could we design systems that would insist on such issues even in seemingly inappropriate settings?

• *Energy awareness* The desirability of supporting energy communities to share their expertise and successes was central to the funding programme. Several proposals explored ideas both in terms of functions and in terms of the socioaesthetic experiences they would afford.

Our proposals evolved over a period of months, and both reflected and spurred discussions amongst us about which best reflected our insights into the communities, what might engage the communities, and what we wanted to achieve. These culminated in the first proposal for an 'Eco Babble' (Figure 3). This was conceived as a system that would gather input from a combination of web scraping and participant input to a central server, and organise the contents in multiple ways for replay from a variety of public and domestic devices.

The Two Faces of the Babble

From the very beginning, and throughout its development and deployment, the Babble was motivated by a mixed and somewhat incommensurable set of intentions. At the time it was first suggested, our discussions did not tend to centre on what we wanted the system to achieve or how the participants might engage with it. Instead, we decided to develop it because we felt a kind of satisfaction in being able to reflect back to the participants, in a somewhat mischievous way, the complicated mix of discourse, priorities and suggestions with which we saw them contending.

As we developed the system, however, a more utilitarian perspective on its possibilities grew, as reflected by a written brief we developed to guide the work:

> Design an Energy-Babble system that displays material, collected from some combination of individual, community and public sources, to open and promote constructive affect and involvement in energy reduction issues and orientations. More specifically, the system should support understandings of, and practices related to, energy demand reduction.

Thus on the one hand, the Babble was talked about as a tool for information and communication about practices and understandings related to energy production and conservation. On the other, it was a system for portraying and even parodying the complexities of energy-related discourse. Though seldom voiced, these mixed perspectives on the Energy Babble coloured its development, surfaced more explicitly later as we described it to the community members, and ultimately inform our discussion here of how volunteers related to the system and how we understand the project.

To foreshadow our discussion, we suggest that insofar as the Babble was presented and viewed as an information and communication device, it tended to serve and be assessed as a *product*. As a reflection of energy-related discourse, in contrast, it served as a *research tool* that helped us, and ideally the participants, better understand the existing situations within which energy communities work. The correlation between utility/products and reflection/research is neither perfect nor necessary; nonetheless, distinguishing two 'faces' of the Babble—one an instrumental product, the other a reflective research tool—is useful in orienting to our intentions and results.

THE ENERGY BABBLE

Months of work separated the decision to pursue the Babble and its eventual production as 28 fully working prototypes. We do not focus on the detailed design process here both because of space constraints and because we want to explore the communities' engagement with the finished system and what this reveals both about the design and the communities (though see [18]. Instead, we fast-forward here to a description of the completed design, discussing only a few relevant aspects of our process.

The Devices

The most visible manifestation of the Energy Babble is the devices that we distributed to participants (Figure 4). These comprise a combination of two custom blown-glass components set on top of an injection-moulded base. The base houses the device's electronic components, including a Raspberry Pi microcomputer, various actuators, and a compact loudspeaker. The central glass piece serves to amplify the output of the speaker located beneath it—glass's acoustic properties make it optimal for this function—while second glass piece supports it and holds a microphone attached to the base by a coiled cable. A prominent yellow knob rotates to control volume; if turned beyond its lowest setting it plays a recorded description of the system and its operation, using the same synthesised voices as the rest of the system.

The product design of the devices was the result of a great deal of exploration and development. Starting with explorations of birdhouses and nests (to develop the theme shown in Figure 3c), attention turned to a variety of containers, and ultimately labware such as test tubes, beakers, and retorts. The final result expresses the enclosure and release of data via the glass cone in a way that we believed to be both intriguing and harmonious for everyday settings such as homes or public spaces.

The audio design of what is primarily a sound-based device also received a great deal of attention. Much time was spent reviewing off-the-shelf voice synthesisers for understandability and aesthetic acceptability, crafting a series of jingles meant to evoke contemporary music as well as news broadcasts, and designing the audio introduction to reduce the need for written documentation. In operation, the Babble plays a varying stream of messages spoken by a number of synthetic voices, and punctuated by short musical jingles reminiscent of those used in news broadcasts. These are sent to the devices via the internet from a server located in our studio.

The System

The audio stream played by the Babble devices is algorithmically constructed and represents the results of a number of modular processes. The first set of these seek new information from the web:

• *Twitter Scrape* The system scrapes messages from a variety of Twitter™ feeds, including those from the communities, from DECC, and from the National Grid.

• *Twitter Search* The system searches Twitter™ using a number of terms (e.g. 'climate change', ''energy bills', 'renewable energy') to find relevant content more broadly.

• *URL Following* If returned tweets contain 'http' and have been retweeted, the system follows the link and scrapes the first paragraph of text for output.

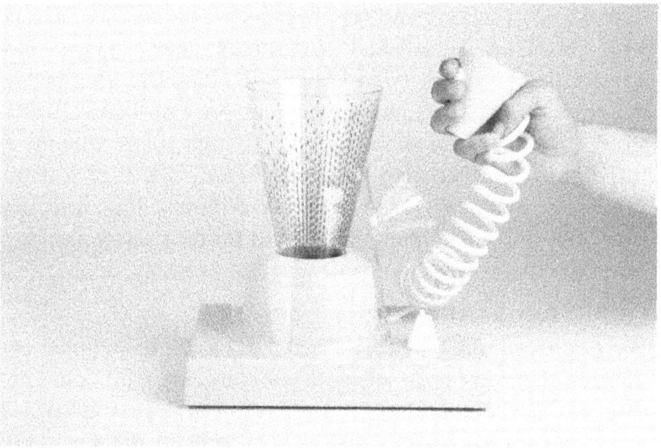

Figure 4. The Energy Babble device

• *Energy Reports* The system also tracks the National Grid, broadcasting information about current energy demand and carbon intensity, as well as changes in the amounts of energy generated by coal, gas, and wind.

• *Switched Off The...* reports hourly a list of things people tweet about having switched off (lights, heat, the internet).

A second set of modules accepts input from participants, or manipulates the existing content.

• *User Input* Users can input their own statements via the microphones on the Babble devices. Voice recordings are sent to the server, which passes them to a commercial service for speech-to-text translation, allowing them to be resynthesised both to anonymise inputs and make them congruent with the overall audio ecology. Text can also be entered directly via SMS text messaging.

• *Prompt Bot* We developed a string of generic questions (e.g. 'how do you save energy?') that were read out occasionally by the system to prompt participant responses.

• *The Voice of Babble* Markov algorithms are run on the content scraped from URLs, and separately on user inputs, to produce new text strings. Markov algorithms find word transition probabilities from a corpus; these probabilities can be used to generate new strings of words. The results tend to be locally sensible, but drift over time in a way we hoped would produce new ideas or at least be amusing.

The system orchestrated the content in a variety of ways. For instance user input was played as soon as possible, while energy reports only appeared hourly. Different voices were assigned to different streams of content, and content was repeated periodically. Distinct jingles signalled different streams of content. Finally, the output stream was arranged to be continuous but uneven, with occasional gaps followed by bursts of several messages.

The Babble Experience

The experience offered by the Babble Devices, once they are properly connected to the server and operational, is something like listening to a continuous talk radio programme. A series of voices make statements, read news items, ask questions and report energy use, all interspersed with occasional musical interludes and lapses into nonsense. The majority of content is related to energy and the environment and thus the devices present themselves as strongly focused on sustainability, though a fair amount of 'off-topic' content also creeps in from Twitter™, from following links, or from participant inputs. Our question was how our participants, all committed to environmental concerns themselves, would engage the Energy Babble.

LIVING WITH THE ENERGY BABBLE

We deployed a total of 21 Energy Babbles to members of the communities in a series of meetings at their locations (Figure 5). Each community received 3 or 4 devices, which were usually given to volunteers present at the meetings, though in a few cases extras were left for later distribution. The remaining 5 Babbles were distributed to team members, with 2 going to people more loosely connected to the project. Volunteers lived with the Babble for varying periods averaging about six months.

In the rest of this section, we briefly describe what our participants told us about their experiences with the Babbles. The majority of reports come from discussions when we deployed the devices, or several months later when we revisited the communities to pick up the devices. Others come from documentaries by an independent filmmaker hired to help us assess the field trial.

Initial Expectations and Impressions

We packaged the Energy Babbles, associated documents and equipment in custom-made cardboard boxes for transport. During deployment events, these were usually positioned visibly, but unopened, during an introductory presentation in which we reviewed the project. Then we would unpack a Babble device and describe how it worked. Because it took some time to set up one of the devices for demonstration, during these initial descriptions the group had not yet heard the system. Typically, then, initial comments and questions revealed a mix of assumptions, expectations and responses to the devices.

Initially, many participants expected us to produce a tool that would directly help them reduce energy consumption — or as G, from the Meadows, put it: '*We thought we were going to get a gizmo to save energy*'. When it became clear the Babble did not serve this purpose, they looked for other utilitarian pay-offs. In Hastings, for instance, an engineer asked '*How does this improve the social operational wellbeing of the people who use it? If I make an investment how do get a payback*?' and explained '*I wanted it to solve a problem*'. These discussions tended to encourage the news/communication interpretation of the device, which mollified many skeptics. For instance, the engineer realised it could be used to broadcast the energy output of their renewables: '*Babble could bring this information to people*'. Similarly, in Laddock a group member championed the Babble for using the British Raspberry Pi technology, and because he saw potential for it to broadcast his car battery operated DIY domestic electricity system.

Building on this, in several of the groups volunteers saw potential value in the Babbles as a kind of marketing tool for promoting their groups and environmental concerns more generally. The Hastings engineer, for instance, described broadcasting energy generation figures as *'a very powerful sales tool'*. In Sidmouth, the group speculated about deploying the Babble in a local energy shop, or using it as a recruitment platform at an Alternative Energy Vehicle show. In Reepham, the group decided that one of the devices should be free to roam, initially to the Post Office and later to a variety of environmental events.

Some people were happier to relinquish a utilitarian interpretation of the Babbles during the deployment events. For instance, after listening to the device during the Meadows deployment, D decided that they would name their Babble 'Finnegan', in a reference to James Joyce's Finnegans Wake. She explained that this was because the output is like '*a stream of consciousness*'. In New Cross, J sent an SMS message after her Babble started working: '*It's amazing! I love it so much already. The messaging system reminds me of the barbed wire telephone system in Wild West. Seriously - Google it. Thanks guys. :)* '

Installation and Accommodation

Installing the Babbles involved configuring the devices to local router settings, dealing with security, and setting it up to communicate using the router's wireless network. In many instances this proved unproblematic, but in some cases, including deployment events, it proved more difficult. While none of the problems we encountered were insurmountable, they seemed to demonstrate to potential volunteers the possible inconveniences of borrowing a Babble. More serious problems arose with some of the devices we left behind. For instance, in Reepham problems with a local firewall prevented the Babble from being installed in a local primary school. Other devices were borrowed but never installed, possibly because of the perceived difficulty of set-up. Pragmatic issues were salient even for imagined deployments: for instance, in Sidmouth ideas for showing the device at the Alternative Energy Vehicle show involved thinking about powering it via a car with solar panels, and achieving mobile internet access.

Figure 5. A deployment event.

Visual and Auditory Aesthetics

The Babble has an idiosyncratic aesthetic that extends from its physical design to its auditory output. Most of the volunteers found this appealing. For instance, in Ladock, J said she and her husband appreciated the Babble because it was '*nice, funky looking thing*'. In the Meadows, P, an art tutor, said it was a '*really nice object*' and that the microphone was a '*lovely visual element*'. This appreciation was mixed with some bemusement, however. Several people remarked on it having a 'retro' appearance, or as J from New Cross put it, the Babble looked '*like my gran could have had one*'. It also was compared to kitchen appliances. For instance G from Ladock, told us '*it looked like a food processor... a bit quirky*', while G in the Meadows told us that visitors to his home usually asked jokingly why he had a blender in his living room. The glass elements, too, attracted a mixed reception: R from Reepham described the Babble as '*beautifully made in hand blown glass*', but its fragility was a worry for the librarian of a secondary school where it was installed.

Despite some initial concerns, we received no complaints about the synthesised voices used by the Babble, and several people remarked favourably about their clarity. On the other hand, the fact of it being an audio device could be disruptive. G, in Ladock, told us he had moved it from the kitchen to the living room because it was a '*conversation stopper*' for the family. L, in Reepham, the mother of a young baby, found it '*annoying and noisy... not really for a home*'. R, her husband, told us he had relocated it to his office because of this. In the Meadows, G said the Babble '*annoys everyone*' so he turned it on when he was alone.

The intermittent nature of the output could also be unsettling. '*A few times it frightened the living crap out of me!*', J in the Meadows told us. She elaborated that once when the office was completely silent at around 9pm, the Babble had given her a fright when it unexpectedly came on. She also complained that it '*didn't talk on cue*' when she showed it to visitors, and (like other volunteers) would have liked to be able to replay interesting outputs.

Babble as a Source of Information

Volunteers often oriented to the Babbles as a potential source of information. This is not surprising given that the audio was designed in the style of an automated news broadcast, that many of the volunteers showed a propensity to seek utilitarian explanations for the device, and that we tended to encourage these explanations to reassure them about the system, rather than foregrounding a description and defence of the Babble as a playful, reflective system.

By the end of the field trial, however, many volunteers expressed disappointment in the Babble as a source of environmental news. In Ladock, G told us that he did hear information '*which was interesting*', but explained that he did not follow many alternative sources of environmental news. In contrast, his colleague J told us that she welcomed the Babble as a source of new information, but '*disappointingly, not as much as I hoped*'. '*It seemed a bit sparse,*' she explained, and '*very repetitious*'. In Reepham, R subscribes to DEC emails that he looks at in the morning: '*if they're about something I'm interested in I read them*'. He told us that the Babble never provided relevant information of which he hadn't been aware.

A recurring theme in discussing the Babble was that too much of its output was irrelevant. J, in Ladock, for instance complained that there was '*a lot more of the jumbly stuff and less of the straight stuff*'. '*I tend to be on the serious side*', she explained, and '*definitely the balance was wrong*'. Considerations such as these led to suggestions for filtering the output. For instance, R in Reepham speculated that the Babble could be more like a radio: '*you might have one stream about transport, another about food, about heating the home...*', describing the result as '*far more relevant*'. To our suggestion that mixing streams might support serendipitous connections he was doubtful: '*people's attention spans are getting shorter*', he explained, so they would get bored before putting things together themselves. J, in the Meadows, also said that the Babble gathered too much irrelevant information and that it needed a '*filter*' to focus on reporting news about communities and government, '*rather than oil and gas*'. G, also from the Meadows, echoed this, suggesting the Babble could be an app with buttons to switch on and off channels of information—a '*filtering mechanism*'.

There was no clear consensus across volunteers about which streams of information were worth hearing, suggesting that the ability to select among them would lead to a more utilitarian design. In the Meadows, for instance, P found the energy reports frustrating as they didn't mean anything to him, while G, interviewed separately, said they were '*really really good*'. In New Cross, P reported that she couldn't follow the '*technical information*', referring both to the energy reports and the information on renewable systems. For her, '*you can connect more to personal comments, to the emotional side of energy*'

Babble as a Medium for Communication

Volunteers had mixed reaction to the ability to input and hear comments using the Babble's microphone and SMS facilities, and this was reflected in the relatively few messages they left on the system (about 35 over 5 months). There was an evident reluctance to enter messages. During the first weeks of living with Babble, for instance, J in New Cross made a few contributions using the microphone. Eventually her reaction became more of an '*internal conversation*'. She reported that when she reached for the microphone she felt nervous about saying something important to the system. Similarly, R from Reepham told us that he didn't input much because he has '*controversial views*' and didn't want to '*upset anyone*'. He recounted how he had heard something on the Babble that he disagreed with, but refrained from expressing his views because he considers them quite controversial. '*I was aware that DECC might be listening, I want to come across as quite conservative, you don't know who is listening*'. In the Meadows, G was concerned to prevent his daughter from saying silly things into the microphone (when asked what those might be he responded '*are there any fit hotties out there?*'). Nonetheless, many comments diverged from clear relevance for environmental concerns, and G was annoyed by messages he thought trivial.

The reluctance to contribute to the system ran counter to appreciation for the content that did appear. For example, J from the Meadows said she would have liked to hear more from the other communities, especially '*stories and tips on how they're dealing with these issues*'. In New Cross, J enjoyed the comments: '*you can connect more to personal comments, to the emotional side of energy*'. Conversely, G in the Meadows would have liked to read out his household energy use, while P would have liked to broadcast his solar energy production; however there was little reflection about who the audience for these figures might be.

Finally, we had some indications that the lack of user inputs into the Babble reflected a lack of interest in communicating with other groups more generally. R, in Reepham, was clearest about this: he told us that while he occasionally kept track of what other communities are doing, differing circumstances meant that '*what might not be right for them, might be right for us*'. He might check for good ideas but unless something was '*revolutionary*' there wasn't much use in this. Equally, he liked telling people what worked in Reepham, but described this as '*reactive not proactive*'—his group doesn't proselytise '*the way Transition Towns do*'.

Appreciation for the Babble

Despite the lack of clear success for the Babble as a utilitarian information or communications product, all the volunteers we spoke with were largely positive about it. In part this reflected appreciation for it as a well-finished, device that could fit the home (Figure 6). In part, it stemmed from admiration for the Babble as a novel technical device. In Reepham, for instance, R found '*stimulating*' the way it uses audio rather than visual/text as a way of encountering social media. In the Meadows, P speculated about extending the Babble's technology, for instance to automatically tweet about his solar panels, or to nag him about his bad energy habits.

Admiration for the Babble as a novel technical and aesthetic device blended with its value as something to show to other people. C from Hastings, for example, was effusive about the Babble, describing the novelty of the device and the attention it had garnered at work, where she originally installed the device, and at home, where she took it later. R from Reepham described it as '*a curiosity for visitors*' that he enjoyed to members of a number of other environmental organisations with whom he worked.

Finally, several volunteers expressed appreciation for the Babble as a source of ambient awareness of environmental action. In New Cross, J told us it was reassuring to hear evidence of expertise: '*Thank God for people who know the technical bits, it's strengthening to hear that there are people out there in charge*', and more generally that the

Figure 6. Babble in a volunteer's home

Babble gave her a sense of a larger community concerned with environmental issues: '*it makes you think that you are not alone in thinking about saving the world*'. In the Meadows, J expressed a more abiding affection for the presence of the Babble: '*aw, I'll miss him actually. It was nice to have him on in the background, I'm used to it now. Its quite aptly named, Babble*'.

Babble and Wider Conversations

The accounts above all reflect discussions centred fairly closely on the Babble system as a product. What became striking to us, however, was the way that our conversations with the volunteers frequently opened from an initial concern with the Babble's usability, functionality and aesthetics to encompass the broader and more particular issues, practices and controversies with which our volunteers were living. Though these discussions may be of questionable relevance for assessing the Babble as a *product*, we suggest that these conversations and the insights they revealed can be viewed as an outcome of the Babble as a *research tool*.

For instance, at the Meadows, during a suggestion that the Babble content should be filtered to focus on communities and government '*rather than oil and gas*', J suddenly exclaimed '*except that British Gas are bastards!*', and conversation with her diverged into lengthy complaints about DECC's lack of support, British Gas call centres, and pigeon droppings building up under solar panels. In Ladock, our conversation with J about the Babble soon expanded to include her complaints about the hurdles involved in securing government funding for environmental work ('*we think they're rubbish*'), and the frustrations of not being able to give away radiator backdrops, energy monitors and LED down lighters at an Energy Fair she organized ('*it was a total failure*' that '*didn't engage the people we set out to engage*').

Also in Ladock, G described their attempts to put up a new wind turbine that was rejected by the council '*on spurious grounds*'. He attributed this to '*about half a dozen*' residents who spread '*a lot of misinformation*' about how the Low Carbon Living group were out to '*line their own pockets*', culminating in '*a minor punch-up*'. Like J, he expressed frustration at the difficulty in reaching out to dissenters within the community (there's '*no forum to talk to those people*'), and also with the government: '*lots of businesses are starting up then going to the wall because the government keeps changing the rules'*. These complaints were mixed with pride in the group's achievements. For instance, he referred to a *'story'* he put on the Babble about how on a sunny day he used his PV to charge his car and heat water: people were impressed that he could *'drive 75 miles and have hot water for absolutely nothing'*. He concluded that '*you can't depend on the government to do things, you can depend on the community to do things*'.

A notable theme that emerged from several volunteers had to do with the entanglement of energy concerns with other issues. For instance, R in Reepham told us he would be going to Buckingham Palace to be honoured for his contributions to energy efficiency, but said that he'd like to be recognised for the work he does that goes beyond that. The Babble should go beyond energy, he told us, to address fuel poverty, transport poverty, and take a '*holistic*' view. "*Energy is a key part of it but the stories are stories about many other things*' he said, '*It's too sterile if you look at only energy*'.

Similarly, in Ladock J told us that her husband refuses to be involved with Low Carbon Living because he sees their efforts as futile. *'We should be lobbying'* she said, and mentioned the social networking activist groups Avaaz and 38Degrees as effective (*'though I understand their limits'*). She also does work with Christian Aid. *'You tend to see how it all fits together - the international aspects of climate change'*. For instance, when Christian Aid pointed out that climate change harms the poorest first, she thought they were off-topic, but then realised it was true. This led her to realise that *'how we treat the world and how we treat other people, they're all linked'*.

DISCUSSION: UNDERSTANDING THE BABBLE

Taking seriously the idea that the Babble played an important role in sparking the intense discussions we had with our volunteers suggests that we move beyond assessing the system according to the utilitarian characterisation of it as an information and communication product. Turning to the reflective interpretation of the Babble instead, as a system that gathers and 'intensifies' the existing state of discourse around energy practices, may give us another perspective on how the system worked as a research tool in our meetings with the participants, by serving as an independent actor that helped shape conversations leading to better understandings of the communities and their concerns.

A simple version of this account would suggest that the Babble should be understood as a research tool that was successful, rather than simply as a utilitarian information/communication product that was less so. The distinction between these roles is not clear-cut, however. The Babble was never seen purely as a prototype product, either by the volunteers or ourselves: we never planned to produce it commercially, and they were always aware of it as part of a research project. The Babble was never solely a research tool either: it was offered seriously for long-term use, and participants engaged with it not only to further their discussion with us but to engage with the material it offered in its own right. The product and research-tool faces of the Babble are interdependent. Here we discuss several conceptual handles on how this might be understood.

To start with, it is helpful to consider the Babble in terms of the conceptual character of the 'idiot', who, in Stengers' [13] account:

> resists the consensual way in which the situation is presented and in which emergencies mobilize thought or action. This is not because the presentation would be false or because emergencies are believed to be lies, but because "there is something more important". Don't ask him why, the idiot will neither reply nor discuss the issue.... the idiot demands that we slow down, that we don't consider ourselves authorized to believe we possess the meaning of what we know (p. 994)

From this point of view, the Babble can be seen to act as an idiot within the energy communities who used it (see [17] and Michael [9]), by confounding expectations of how technologies should contribute to the communities' work. This was evident both during the deployments, when the Babble surprised and confused volunteers who were expecting some sort of demand reduction meter, or at least a clearly utilitarian design (*'I wanted to solve a problem'*), and throughout the project, as volunteers struggled to make sense of what it was doing. Instead of acquiescing to 'the consensual way in which the situation is presented', the Babble implicitly suggested that in the confused flow of messages about energy use, policy shifts, new technologies, and seeming irrelevancies "there is something more important".

But what is that 'something that is more important'? The Babble never says, but given its output this might include keeping in touch with emerging policy, sharing best practice, being aware of energy sources and demand, and joining with other communities—the very concerns identified as important by the funding programme that supported the project. But the Babble does this in the most literal, even stupid, way, and the volunteers resist it. They counter by insisting that policies are ever-changing and wilfully made difficult, that what works for one community may not work for another, that it is difficult to find meaning in statistics about energy, and that there is limited value in further contact with other communities. From this point of view, the roles are reversed: it is the Babble that presents the 'consensual way in which the situation is presented', and the community volunteers who are cast as idiots, asking the Babble, and us, and the policy-makers, to slow down, because we do not 'possess the meaning of what we know.'

Our conversations with them at the end of the field trial, then, can be seen as reflecting their pent-up responses to the obduracy of the Babble. Yes, the Babble may be right in saying that there are larger concerns at play than can be addressed by energy demand meters, but what is needed is not simply more policy, more news, and more communications. On the contrary, they told us, we need better filtering, better ways to talk about energy, better situated ways to communicate, and recognition that energy use is situated in a wider landscape of local and global issues such as inequality and sustainability. And through this, they revealed their realities, helping us to understand that these 'communities' are shifting collections of people who constantly reconfigure themselves, and who do extraordinary work to negotiate changing policy opportunities and obstacles, to filter information about new technologies, to reach out within their own communities, and to understand when it is worth communicating more closely with others.

In the end, the Babble might be understood in terms of DiSalvo's [4] account of how design can play a part in constructing publics. Following Dewey, DiSalvo suggests that publics form around issues, and that design can participate in this by bringing issues to prominence. He suggests two primary tactics for this: *projection*, in which designs suggest possible future manifestations of current trends, and *tracing*, in which design is used to make clear the history of current situations. To this, the Babble might add a third tactic: *concentration*, in which current accounts and discourses about an issue—in this case energy—are brought together to form, not just a neutral representation, but a focused stream that inundates listeners with the many different and potentially incompatible ways that that issue is discussed, legislated for, measured and worried about.

From this perspective, the Babble might form 'a public' not just via the issues that comprise it, but the issues raised by the incoherence of the babble itself. Thus the Babble begins to point toward a public that emerges out of an oscillation between different local and collective communities, variously in competition and united, informed and frustrated. Moreover, the discussions occasioned by the Babble suggests that support for situated, local communities requires better appreciation of the morass that the publics/communities must negotiate. This includes the competition/lack of communication between communities, as well as the commonalities of being placed in a relation of competition by the structure of government project funding. In highlighting these issues, the Babble may also help (re)configure a public of HCI researchers, funders and policy makers to concern itself with these realities of energy communities rather than, simply, technologies focused directly on energy demand reduction.

ACKNOWLEDGMENTS

We are deeply grateful to the energy communities for their participation in this research.This project was supported by the Economic and Social Research Council's award no. ES/I007318/1 and by the European Research Council's Advanced Investigator Award no. 22652.

REFERENCES

1. Abrahamse, W., Steg, L., Vlek, C., & Rothengatter, T. (2005). A review of intervention studies aimed at household energy conservation. *Journal of environmental psychology*, *25*(3), 273-291.
2. Brynjarsdottir, H., Hakansson, M., Pierce, J., Baumer, E., DiSalvo, C., and Sengers, P. 2012. Sustainably unpersuaded. CHI 2012, 947-956.
3. Callon, M. (2004) The Role of Hybrid Communities and Socio-Technical Arrangements in the Participatory Design. Journal of the Center for Information Studies 5(3): 3–10.
4. DiSalvo, C. (2009). Design and the Construction of Publics. Design Issues, *25*(1), 48-63.
5. Dourish, P. 2010. HCI and environmental sustainability. DIS 2010, 1-10.
6. Gaver, W. 2009. Designing for Homo Ludens, Still. In (Re)searching the Digital Bauhaus. Binder, T., Löwgren, J., and Malmborg, L. (eds.). London: Springer, pp. 163-178.
7. Gaver, W. 2011. Making spaces. CHI'11, 1551-1560.
8. Kerridge, T. (Forthcoming). Designing Debate: The Entanglement of Speculative Design and Upstream Public Engagement with Science and Technology. PhD thesis, Goldsmiths, University of London, London.
9. Michael, M. (2012). "What Are We Busy Doing?" Engaging the Idiot. Science, Technology & Human Values, 37(5), 528-554.
10. Schultz, P. W., Nolan, J. M., Cialdini, R. B., Goldstein, N. J., & Griskevicius, V. (2007). The constructive, destructive, and reconstructive power of social norms, Psychological Science, 18(5), 429–434.
11. Sengers, P. and Gaver, W. (2006). Staying Open to interpretation. Proc. DIS 2006.
12. Shove, E. (2004). Comfort, cleanliness and convenience. Berg.
13. Stengers, I. (2005). The cosmopolitical proposal. Making things public, 994-1003.
14. Strengers, Y. (2013) Smart Energy Technologies in Everyday Life: Smart Utopia? Palgrave MacMillan.
15. UK Research Council (2010), Energy and Communities call for proposals. http://web.archive.org/web/20100813103416/http://www.esrc.ac.uk/ESRCInfoCentre/opportunities/current_funding_opportunities/Energy_and_Communities_Collaborative_Venture.aspx (accessed 22.09.14).
16. Wilkie, A. (2013) Prototyping as Event: Designing the Future of Obesity, Journal of Cultural Economy: 1–17.
17. Wilkie, A., Michael, M., & Plummer-Fernandez, M. (2014). Speculative method and Twitter. The Sociological Review.
18. Wilkie, A., Michael, M., Kerridge, T., Gaver, W., Ovalle, L,. DiSalvo, C., Gabrys, J., (2012). Design, STS and cosmopolitics: From intervention to emergence in participation and sustainability. Proc. EASST 2012.

Beyond the Individual: The Contextual Wheel of Practice as a Research Framework for Sustainable HCI

Johanne Mose Entwistle
Mia Kruse Rasmussen
Alexandra Institute
(johanne.mose,mia.kruse)@alexandra.dk

Nervo Verdezoto
Robert S. Brewer
Aarhus University
(nervo,rbrewer)@cs.au.dk

Mads Schaarup Andersen
The Open University
mads.andersen@open.ac.uk

ABSTRACT
Addressing human impact on the environment by focusing on shared everyday practices, rather than just individual behavior is an approach that shows promise. However, it can be challenging to put this approach into concrete use, especially in teams unfamiliar with the practice orientation. To support the practice approach, we introduce the Contextual Wheel of Practice (COWOP), a framework that can: 1) help researchers and designers to better understand practices, 2) design effective interventions, and 3) facilitate collaboration between team members from different disciplines, who may not be familiar with the practice orientation. We describe how COWOP was developed, and our experiences using COWOP in three different cases. We then position COWOP as part of the "turn to practice" in HCI, and discuss how it can be useful to HCI researchers and be applied in domains beyond sustainability, such as healthcare and privacy.

Author Keywords
Energy; practice; practice-orientation; design; sustainable HCI; framework; collaboration

ACM Classification Keywords
H.5.m. Information interfaces and presentation (e.g., HCI): Miscellaneous.

INTRODUCTION
A dominant paradigm in addressing sustainability challenges through technology has focused on the individual. For example, electricity feedback devices are intended to reduce energy consumption by making users aware of how much electricity they use [6, 13]. Strengers describes this perspective as designing for Resource Man, an archetype for the user who is empowered by feedback and desires to control energy use through technology [39]. This perspective treats individuals as consumers of energy,

CHI 2015, April 18–23, 2015, Seoul, Republic of Korea.

ACM 978-1-4503-3145-6/15/04…$15.00
http://dx.doi.org/10.1145/2702123.2702232

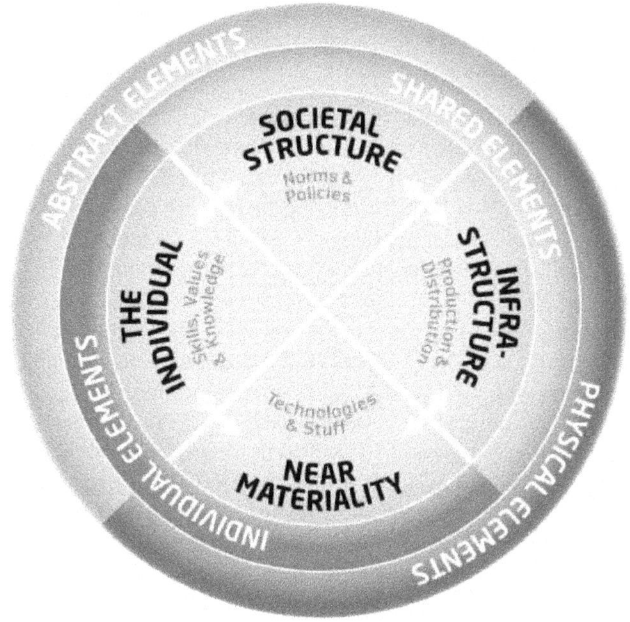

Figure 1: The Contextual Wheel of Practice.

believing that providing more information about energy use will result in the individual making informed decisions and thus using less energy.

However, a more practice-oriented worldview suggests that people do not act in the world, or think of themselves as consumers of energy. As put by Røpke, "People are practitioners who indirectly, through the performance of various practices, draw on resources" [31]. Therefore, what we should be focusing on is how people engage in the practices of everyday life, which as a *consequence* leads to the consumption of energy, if we are to truly affect their behaviors through technology. Indeed, this insight is not new to the sustainable HCI community, as there is a shift from understanding individual behaviors towards a practice-based research approach that criticizes the use of persuasive technology [5]. Aligned with this view, researchers from the sustainable HCI community have embraced a practice approach [14, 21, 26, 40] that uses practice as a unit of analysis or design for sustainable ICT rather than focusing on analyzing individual actions or changing behavior [25].

Nevertheless, we have experienced difficulties when introducing the practice orientation to colleagues on our multidisciplinary teams who are used to designing for Resource Man. Therefore, we developed the Contextual Wheel of Practice (COWOP, shown graphically in Figure 1), both as a framework for understanding practices, and as a useful point of reference to explain the practice orientation to those unfamiliar with it. COWOP is based on our experiences in multiple projects studying energy consumption, designing interventions to change energy consuming practices, and collaborating with other disciplines. COWOP lays out four constitutive elements of practices, each of which is represented as a quadrant in the wheel: *Societal Structure*, *Infrastructure*, *Near Materiality*, and *The Individual.*

Recently, Kuutti and Bannon noted that methodological tools and guidelines are needed to move towards a more practice-based research approach in HCI [22]. We aim to contribute to this turn to practice in HCI by describing our experiences understanding everyday practices with COWOP as a research framework for sustainable HCI. As such, COWOP can be seen as an *exploratory and explanatory conceptual framework*—and not as a prescriptive tool—to support HCI researchers and designers in identifying, analyzing, and understanding practices to support system design. Moreover, COWOP also serves as a useful *boundary object* [37], providing a broader overview of the practice approach when applied to a multidisciplinary research project, enabling team members from different backgrounds to come to a common understanding of the need for a broad perspective that goes beyond the usual Interaction paradigm [22] to change people's practices. Thus, the associated research questions are: how can we understand everyday practices to support system design while working on multidisciplinary project teams, and how can we support sustainable HCI researchers and designers from multiple disciplines to get this understanding?

To answer these questions, we have introduced the practice theoretical approach to multidisciplinary research projects, and iteratively developed COWOP over the last few years. These research projects are focused on energy and sustainability, and in particular, on how to foster changes in practices. Our multidisciplinary team includes anthropologists, software engineers, HCI practitioners, and designers. This multidisciplinary team enables us to base technological developments on user studies and user involvement. Through our collaboration and initial user studies, it has become clear that not all team members bought in to the practice orientation. Furthermore, we initially lacked the tools necessary to facilitate our cross-disciplinary knowledge exchange and negotiation of meaning [43] that could mediate or bridge our different perspectives.

In the following sections, we summarize practice theory and the origin of COWOP, followed by a description of the framework and its elements. We then describe our experiences using COWOP in three projects including the practices of residents at a student dormitory, and the design of new services in the energy sector. We end with a discussion on how the COWOP framework is positioned in HCI and its limitations, and how it could be used beyond the energy domain, such as in healthcare and privacy.

BACKGROUND AND RELATED WORK

During the so-called third wave HCI [2], an in-depth understanding of practices outside the workplace has become more prominent, in which the design of ICT should take into account most aspects of people's everyday life as a whole and not only isolated work practices. Rogers has named the theories in this generation as "contemporary" such as the turn to design, the turn to culture, the turn to the wild, the turn to embodiment, etc. [30]. One common theme across these different research areas is the exploration of the concept of practice that also includes interests in appropriation, digital ecologies, materiality and attempts to solve complex real-world problems [22]. Indeed, Kuutti and Bannon [22] have reported the turn to practice in HCI as the "Practice paradigm" as opposed to the traditional—so called—"Interaction paradigm" that has focused on the interaction with technology where context of use and work practice are seen as separate and static variables. In contrast to the Interaction paradigm, Kuutti and Bannon highlight the need for a more holistic practice approach in HCI that considers the importance of understanding the dynamics of new practices that emerge due to the use of technology.

Practice Theory

Practice theory evolved in the social sciences in the 1970s and 1980s [3, 16]. The main objective was to find new ways to overcome existing dualisms between actor and structure, by finding ways to give voice to human agency without neglecting structural constraints. However, these early theories did not pay much attention to the material artifacts, infrastructures, and products that shaped practices, which has later been argued as a substantial weakness [35]. Newer approaches to practice theory pay closer attention to the material and contextual dimensions of practices. Influential theorists of this movement include Reckwitz [29] and Schatzki [32] whose definitions of practice, and views on what shapes behavior, have inspired consumer research and environmental studies [26, 31, 35, 40, 42]. What these theories have in common is that they move their attention away from the individual as the focus of analysis.

While psychology and behavioral economics typically focus on individual behavior and motivation in their analyses, the practice approach looks at practices as the main unit of analysis. In particular, Reckwitz describes practices as "a routinized type of behavior which consists of several elements, interconnected to one another: forms of bodily activities, forms of mental activities, "things" and their use, a background knowledge in the form of understanding, know-how, states of emotion and motivational knowledge" [29:249]. Building on this definition, Shove et al. suggest that practices combine three types of elements: materials, competences and meanings, and that it is the connections among these elements that make, sustain, or transform practices [36:14]. Practices only exist as long as they continue to be carried out in everyday life, and therefore, we need to pay close attention to these seemingly mundane performances of everyday practices if we wish to understand them more fully [36].

Furthermore, practices are relational and contextual as "practices do not float free of technological, institutional and infrastructural contexts" [27:229]. Therefore, to study practices we need an empirical approach that takes structural, historical, and contextual elements into account and pays attention to the ways in which practices relate to each other.

To this end, several frameworks and tools have been proposed to facilitate such understandings of practice that go beyond the individual and focus on the connections between elements of practices and how they are made, sustained or broken. We will detail some of these efforts in the following subsections.

Frameworks, Concepts, and Tools

The ISM (Individual Social Material) tool is one of these models that shows how multiple contexts (the Individual, Social, and Material) affect and influence people's behavior [7]. While the individual context includes individual factors such as values, attitudes, and skills, the social context involves factors beyond the individual such as social norms, people's network and relationships as well as meanings and institutions that influence social behavior. The material context in the ISM model takes into account the existing infrastructure and technology in the environment as well as time and scheduling [7]. Although the multiple factors across the three different contexts provide a practical conceptual model for understanding people's behavior, it is a prescriptive tool that might suffer from shortcomings such as an overemphasis on the individual factors as central focus of attention.

As described in the previous section, Shove et al. propose a conceptual framework to understand social practice based on three specific elements: material, competences and meanings [36]. While the material elements encompass all the "stuff" embedded in, for example, technologies and physical objects, the meanings elements include "symbolic meanings, ideas and aspirations" and competences involve the "skill[s], know-how and technique[s]" [36]. Although this framework moves the focus of attention to practice, we argue in this paper that it might not be sufficient to fully account for the material dimensions of practices, at least in relation to energy consumption.

The Application of Practice Theory to Sustainable HCI

The theory of practice has been applied in HCI research, especially in the sustainability domain taking practices as a unit of analysis or design (e.g., [14, 21]). In particular, some researchers have used Shove's framework of social practice described above to further investigate: everyday bathing practices through "Experiments in Practice" [34], everyday repair and green-DIY practices [41], and the possible conflicts between emerging and existing heating practices [20].

Rather than applying practice theory in a prescriptive way (e.g., [21]), we aim to provide a concrete tool for applying practice theory in a more exploratory and explanatory way to support designer's reflective practices. As such, our work is aligned with the shift from "prescription to reflection" in HCI research as presented by Rogers [30]. Furthermore, we extend the related work by providing a useful boundary object for introducing and discussing practice theory with people unfamiliar with it—the COWOP framework. In the following, we describe the origin of COWOP and how it helps us understand everyday practices.

DEVELOPING THE COWOP FRAMEWORK

Based on a recent approach called Computational Environmental Ethnography (CEE) [1], we engage in multidisciplinary research projects to understand and reduce or shift energy consumption. Using CEE, we engage with qualitative data from anthropological studies, quantitative data from questionnaires, and technical data from sensors. Despite using this mixed approach (CEE), we still needed a way to help us communicate our empirical findings to project partners with a different academic background in a way that they could relate to, as well as further challenge the existing individual-focused paradigm. Yet, the findings from our anthropological field studies did not support the existing dominating assumptions about behavior and energy consumption among our partners.

Through our exploratory work with the empirical data, it became clear that practice theory would lead us to a more focused analysis [4] of specific aspects of the empirical data, such as the focus on the shifting relationships between the different constitutive elements of practices and how they can be studied from an empirical perspective.

To this end, we developed COWOP as a graphical representation of our understanding of what affects practices in relation to energy consumption (see Figure 1). In particular, we found that our analyses would benefit from a separation of material elements into two distinct categories, Near Materiality and Infrastructure, to enable us to account for the complex relationship between these elements and the different ways in which they affect practices.

COWOP has been shaped and adapted for different uses and target groups: it is still a work in progress as it evolves with the situation at hand. The current version has four elements that form a conceptual framework described in the following section.

THE CONTEXTUAL WHEEL OF PRACTICE

The Contextual Wheel of Practice shown in Figure 1 is a graphical outline of how practice theory attempts to mediate between structure and agency, the human and nonhuman, and the concrete and abstract elements that shape our daily practices. COWOP lays out four specific elements that are important for understanding practices, each of which is represented as a quadrant in the wheel. The four quadrants are (clockwise from the top): 1) *Societal Structure*, 2) *Infrastructure*, 3) *Near Materiality*, and 4) *The Individual*.

Societal Structure includes legislation, or broadly accepted social norms such as expected standards of cleanliness. The definition of Societal Structure is thus comparable with Randle and Warde's *Institutions* [27:229] and Shove et al.'s *Meanings* [36:14].

Infrastructure refers to the aspects of the physical environment that shape behavior, but are not under individual control, such as the architecture and automated processes of a building, or the means by which electricity is generated.

The Near Materiality quadrant refers to the close physical environment or technologies that are under individual control, such as a radiator in a room or the appliances plugged into wall outlets. These two categories are inspired by Geels' *technical systems* [15], and Randles and Warde's distinction between *technology* and *infrastructure* [27:229].

The last quadrant, The Individual, encompasses personal values such as a desire to live sustainably and the knowledge and skills required for that lifestyle. This category thus resembles the individual context in the ISM tool [7] and *competences* in the framework presented by Shove et al. [36].

The word *Contextual* is included in the name of the framework to stress that our actions are contextualized by the social, cultural, and material setting, and that these contexts need to be taken into account when trying to understand or affect behavior in different situations. This inclusion also helps us to better understand the scope we have for changing practices, and to design better interventions. As described in the previous section, practices are not free floating, but interrelated and affected by structural elements as well as individual motivations.

The four elements of the framework can be grouped in different ways as shown in Table 1. Societal Structure and Infrastructure deal with the elements shared across communities. On the individual level we find Near Materiality and The Individual (skills, values, and knowledge) as constitutive elements of daily practices. Besides the shared/individual groupings, COWOP also combines the elements into two other groupings. Infrastructure and Near Materiality cover the concrete physical elements that shape practices. Societal Structure and The Individual can be grouped as the abstract elements that shape practices on different levels. Therefore, COWOP mediates and encompasses elements from the very concrete to the very abstract as significant constituents of the practices that have energy consumption as a consequence.

	Shared	Individual
Abstract	Societal Structure	The Individual
Physical	Infrastructure	Near Materiality

Table 1: Two groupings of the elements in COWOP

COWOP helps us see what shapes practices and how changes in practices can occur through changes in any of the four quadrants. When using COWOP to understand practices and design interventions, it is important to appreciate how the four elements are highly interdependent For example, the state of Infrastructure will very much rely on the state of institutions and legislation (Societal Structure), and legislation will depend on Individuals' values and knowledge, but also on technological advances. Although individuals' values and knowledge are personal and internalized, they are also very much grounded in and affected by shared culture and societal structures, and as such, it becomes clear that the introduction of change is never a simple cause and effect process. Furthermore, introducing changes in one quadrant may not have the intended effect, if the targeted practice was more significantly affected and structured by elements from other quadrants. Therefore, it is crucial to look at the relationship between the different elements and how they structure practices in different situations.

USING COWOP FOR UNDERSTANDING, DESIGN, AND MULTIDISCIPLINARY COLLABORATION

In this section, we present our experiences using COWOP to understand practices, design technological interventions, and support multidisciplinary team collaboration. We present COWOP in practical use, illustrating different insights that the framework provided from three cases.

The Grundfos Dormitory Lab: Understanding Practices and Collaborating with Multidisciplinary Teams

One of our projects is built around the "Grundfos Dormitory Lab" (GDL), a highly instrumented dormitory for university students. Each of the 159 apartments in the GDL contains sensors that monitor indoor climate (temperature, humidity, CO_2 concentration), electricity, heating, and water use. The addition of sensors to the dormitory was intended to create a "living laboratory" to study how the residents use different resources, and how their behavior and the building itself could adapt to generate fewer greenhouse gas emissions. The GDL collects measurements from over 3000 sensor endpoints at approximately 5-second intervals.

To accomplish the goal of reduced emissions, we are designing interventions (such as mobile apps and physical design provocations) that will make use of the sensor data.

They will encourage the residents to reduce their carbon footprint by changing their practices. These interventions are informed by a qualitative and quantitative study of residents at the GDL [28]. We conducted two workshops with 30-60 residents, an online survey of the residents (67 valid responses), one overnight stay at the dorm, and semi-structured interviews with 20 of the residents. Through the workshops, we engaged the residents in discussions about their everyday practices and values, and their interests and attitudes towards the dorm. The online survey touched upon the same topics, and the stay gave us an impression of living at the GDL. Additional semi-structured interviews allowed us to get a deeper understanding of these themes and the practices surrounding them [28].

In the following sections, we present two types of practices we observe residents engaging in at the dorm, and how COWOP helped us to better understand these practices.

Understanding Cooking Practices at GDL

One of the main practices we try to understand is cooking. This practice is particularly interesting because it consumes so much energy that the so-called "cooking peak" strains the electricity grid in the early evening. In our studies, we have found that cooking cannot be understood as an isolated practice, but needs to be seen as part of a greater nexus of practices that constitute residents' daily lives. In this sense, cooking can be termed a "non-negotiable" practice [40] for the residents, one that is related to other practices in a way that must take place at a specific time of day, or have a certain frequency or duration.

Residents explicitly state that the energy consumption of their cooking is not a major concern for them. They have the *individual and shared knowledge* that this practice consumes energy, but they do not really see how that can be changed in any profound way without compromising the service they are trying to obtain. Therefore, they choose to use energy to obtain this service, perhaps saving elsewhere instead. Judging from these types of statements, the energy consumption related to cooking seems highly shaped by individual and shared values, and by their understandings of what is normal or desirable for them in their daily lives.

The practice of cooking, however, also has more structural and material elements that need to be considered. Cooking is perceived as highly interconnected with other practices such as physical exercise practices, and it is also impacted by Societal Structures such as educational institutions that decide when classes are held and thereby indirectly dictate when cooking is possible. Furthermore, the cooking practices in the dorm are also structured by the Infrastructure and the Near Materiality of the building. Each resident has his/her own kitchen, which offers the opportunity to cook alone in their apartment instead of together in the common room. This structural and material context potentially affects their behavior, and it affects the scope we have for change when it comes to the practice of cooking. These elements, therefore, also need to be taken into account. Even though informants might tell us that it is simply a matter of choice, the material elements affect their behaviors and thus energy consumption.

Understanding Laundry Practices at GDL

Another practice that we have examined is laundry. While cooking is considered difficult for people to shift in time due to its interconnectedness with other everyday practices, laundry is viewed as a more simple or detached practice, and therefore, easier to change. Either having the option of a postponed start on the washer or allowing people who stay up late to do their laundry during the night, would not only shift the electrical load to avoid peak load (and thereby emit fewer greenhouse gasses), it could also give the residents a greater sense of freedom. But regardless of the potential of encouraging people to do their laundry during the night, and people's apparent willingness to do so, there are structural obstacles that make such an initiative difficult in the particular context of the dormitory. The dorm rules (which are Societal Structures in this case) state that the laundry room in the dorm can only be used from 8 AM to 9 PM, because there are apartments situated above the laundry room, and they would be disturbed by the sound of laundry at night. Furthermore, even though the residents express that they are willing to air dry their clothes instead of using the dryer, this option is not available to them because the Infrastructure of the building leaves no room for air drying and they are not allowed to dry clothes in their apartments due to concerns about mold growth. This example shows us how the practice of laundry in the case of the GDL is highly structured by the *shared* elements (Societal Structure and Infrastructure) when it comes to shaping what time of day laundry is being done. Even if the residents are motivated to change their "laundry practices" they will not be able to because of shared structural constraints.

The multidisciplinary projects we come across within the IT and energy sector often take the premise that changing behavior (e.g., changing the time or way of cooking/doing laundry) is in the hands of the individual. The individual "just" needs to be motivated according to his/her personality or preferences. This understanding has been challenged by others [5] and both of our examples show that an individual's behavior is not entirely in their hands. Practices are social and negotiated, as well as structured by the physical and material context in which they unfold. Therefore, it is important to broaden the scope and take these other factors into consideration when we try to understand and affect people's practices (and energy consumption). COWOP helps us to meet this challenge in a very concrete way when developing ICT interventions in the sustainability domain. It makes it clear when such technologies may be limited in their impact and when other interventions, for example, changes in social norms and expectations or policies, need to be considered instead.

Collaborating Using the COWOP Framework
The introduction of COWOP to the dorm project with its visual and often physical manifestation in reports, presentations, internal workshops, and meetings has meant that essential changes are being introduced to both our common teamwork, but also to planned ICT interventions developed by the multidisciplinary research group.

Initially, interventions planed for the dorm were to be evaluated by simply measuring changes in energy consumption. The assumption being that if the intervention worked, energy consumption would go down and if it did not work, energy consumption would stay the same, or go up. However, this simplistic approach to effect measurement does not study how this effect (or lack of effect) comes about, and therefore, this type of effect measurement has no chance of explaining *what* actually caused an effect for *whom* and under *which* circumstances. This particular knowledge is necessary if we want to conclude anything about the effect of an intervention, just as it is essential if we want to replicate or improve an intervention. This type of knowledge is qualitative in nature and implies looking at the practice level, to *what* people actually do that consumes energy as a consequence, and *why* they do what they do? The introduction of COWOP made it clear to team members that understanding the practice level was necessary, and it is now accepted that the framework should be used for future effect measurement and cross-disciplinary analysis as suggested by CEE [1].

Furthermore, COWOP has concretely acted as an analytical tool to facilitate both design and cross-disciplinary analysis of questionnaires. The consistent use of COWOP ensures that questions in the questionnaire cover all four elements, to gain a deeper understanding of the specific context in which we engage. In the multidisciplinary CEE analysis, the hypotheses are based on the understanding that practices, and therefore, energy consumption, are shaped by all elements. Through COWOP, the combinations of questions covering different elements are being correlated with sensor data of the actual energy consumption.

Consequently, the framework has become a boundary object, providing a new, shared understanding of how energy consumption comes about, and providing ideas for how we might try to affect it in the future. It has acted as a concrete tool for us to communicate and discuss divergent understandings of human behavior and the unique characteristics of the different contexts in which we engage and given us a common frame to communicate and discuss the results of our field studies. As a consequence, the solutions that we develop in the project will have a stronger rooting in these new insights and understandings.

Developing New Services in the Energy Sector
COWOP has also proven to be valuable outside of a research context. EnergiMidt, a Danish energy company, wanted to innovate the way they approached Energy Service Company (ESCO) projects. ESCOs guarantee their customers a certain reduction in energy consumption through different types of energy reducing initiatives. The customers are often large organizations like hospitals, municipalities, or private companies. The typical assignment brief recognizes the importance of addressing the users of the buildings, but at the same time the briefs divide energy-reducing initiatives into two groups: technological initiatives and behavioral initiatives.

EnergiMidt experiences several challenges with these types of assignment briefs: how to optimize the screening of initiatives to maximize Return On Investment (ROI), how to clarify when and why behavioral initiatives are not optimal, considering the ROI, and how to differentiate EnergiMidt from other ESCOs?

We worked with EnergiMidt to address these challenges from an anthropological perspective. The introduction of COWOP revealed that categorizing initiatives as either technical or behavioral was problematic. The graphical representation of COWOP makes clear that even if an initiative is primarily concerned with technology (represented by Near Materiality or Infrastructure in COWOP depending on context), it is inseparable from the other elements that shape practices. Therefore, it does not make sense to divide energy reducing initiatives into technological and behavioral, since any technological initiative will necessarily involve thinking about behavior and practices.

Having come to this shared understanding, we changed the premise for EnergiMidt's future ESCOs by dividing initiatives into "technological" and non-technical initiatives. Another consequence is that all relevant technological initiatives will now be adapted based on insights about user practices in the buildings in question. This addition is intended to avoid undesirable circumventions of a technological initiative by users who cannot do what they want, or feel the way they want in the building. An anthropologist and an energy advisor/engineer will generate these insights about user practices through field studies.

Furthermore, EnergiMidt's ESCO projects will now divide users into "practice groups" using COWOP, with the anticipation that groups with similar practices will affect the energy consumption in a building similarly, and will also be equally affected by an initiative. To establish which types of initiatives are suitable for each group, the groups are now screened based on questions partly derived from COWOP. This screening results in the selection of categories of initiatives for each group and makes it quite clear when it will not be a good idea to use certain types of initiatives for certain groups. COWOP is also used here, because the different types of energy reducing initiatives map onto COWOP's elements. For example, consider an energy reducing campaign that focuses on The Individual element. If we are dealing with a group of users whose practices are highly structured by shared rules and norms (Societal

Structure) that do not overlap with a conscious focus on energy reduction, then this initiative is less likely to be successful for this group.

In the EnergiMidt case, COWOP was successfully adapted to address the specific needs of the case by adding another dimension into the framework: the *conscious/unconscious* level to each of the four different elements. As an example we can look at the Societal Structures quadrant (see Figure 1), which is made up of both explicit rules and laws, but also more implicit norms. Explicit rules and laws affect our lives in a more or less conscious way, whereas norms usually affect us unconsciously.

Collaborating Using the COWOP Framework

The collaboration on the EnergiMidt project spans three different disciplines: Engineering, Anthropology, and Business Development. We have used the COWOP graphical representation actively in presentations and discussions, referring to it in documents, drawing it on whiteboards, changing and adding to the contents, adapting it into new figures such as tables, etc. COWOP provided a physical manifestation of the abstract and theoretical concepts that were not common knowledge for the engineer and business developer. Working actively with and applying a theory would not have been possible without a boundary object such as COWOP. Initially, our understandings of the interplay between the individual, its context (including technology), and energy consumption were far apart. Through the use of COWOP in presentations and discussions, we have come much closer to a shared understanding that is based on practice theory. The result that speaks for itself is the actual effect that COWOP has had in our collaboration: it has become both the frame for our development process *and* an actual tool used in the new ESCO service. This collaboration has proven fruitful due to a shared curiosity, respect, and an acknowledged need for new perspectives that may not be present in all multidisciplinary teams.

The Proactive Energy Behavior Project

The Proactive Energy Behavior project (Proac) is a Danish project funded by Realdania and the Danish Ministry of Housing, Urban and Rural Affairs. The aim of the project is to develop, test, and evaluate different methods of visualizing energy consumption for residents in social housing [10]. We presented COWOP as part of a bigger development and evaluation framework in the project kick-off workshop to facilitate idea and concept development in the project groups.

Some groups were highly influenced by the contextual and practice focus provided by COWOP and came up with campaigns that aimed at changing actual practices, such as cooking and hygiene (tooth brushing and bathing), through the delivery of things relevant to the practice thus changing their Near Materiality. For example, participants were provided with a showerhead that adds air to the water and thus saves water. This campaign was an add-on to the actual energy feedback technology that was installed in each apartment, and resulted in positive attention and effects such as reduced water consumption.

COWOP also aided in the evaluation of the Proac project. The project group's initial round of evaluation found that when there were problems in a building, such as poor insulation (corresponding to the Infrastructure element), then it was difficult to motivate residents to actively participate in feedback-based initiatives. COWOP underlined the importance of taking Infrastructure into account as well as The Individual, which had initially been the sole focus of the project group.

DISCUSSION

The "Practice paradigm" is gaining currency as a starting point for system design within the HCI community [22]. As there is a need for methodological and practical tools to support the turn to practice in HCI [22] as well as designers reflective practices [38], we have not only provided empirical accounts regarding the aforementioned cases in this paper, but also presented the COWOP framework as a tool for thinking [9] based on the theory of practice to "*expand design thinking but do not prescribe design action*" [38]. In this sense, COWOP is an exploratory and explanatory framework, situated in the contemporary generation of HCI methodologies [30], that aims to support designers and researchers in their reflection and decision-making processes rather than providing a step-by-step approach such as ISM [7].

We believe that COWOP can provide the right level of abstraction of practice theory to support the understanding of everyday practices and the work of designing technical solutions in cross disciplinary teams through four important elements: Societal Structure, Infrastructure, Near Materiality and The Individual. In contrast to the ISM tool [7] that places the individual at the center, COWOP places the individual on equal footing with the other elements intended to support researchers and designers in understanding how practice theory bridges different disciplinary foci (used as a boundary object) and can support the design of sustainable interventions.

Furthermore, COWOP differs from Shove's framework [36] because it divides the material elements into Infrastructure and Near Materiality. Indeed, the COWOP elements are tightly related to previous work in HCI and CSCW that shows their importance when designing interactive technologies e.g., [11, 12, 18, 30]. However, they have not been considered and discussed as a whole for sustainable HCI. All elements establish a socio-technical conceptual framework that takes practice as unit of analysis and design to get further understanding of the dynamics of everyday practices as well as on how "*designed artifacts shape and are shaped by the contexts in which they are used*" [19].

We have shown how COWOP helps us pay attention to the specific demands of the case when understanding practices and developing technological interventions. COWOP helps us identify specific challenges that should be taken into account and provides us with a holistic view of the analyzed cases. In the following sections, we discuss the limitations of the framework, and the opportunities for using COWOP in domains beyond sustainability.

Limitations of COWOP

As a framework, COWOP necessarily simplifies some of the complexities that practice theory introduces. Therefore, COWOP should be considered only a starting point for understanding and incorporating practice theory into HCI research. We hope that COWOP's accessibility can serve as a "gateway" that guides those seeking a more in-depth understanding of practices. When collaborating with people outside HCI who are not familiar with practice theory, COWOP's simplification is an appropriate introduction for individuals who would otherwise not be exposed to this perspective.

Dividing the Wheel into four equally sized quadrants might give the impression that they all affect practices equally. As our examples show, this is not necessarily the case. Some of the elements may be more significant than others depending on the specific case at hand. The configuration of elements is dynamic, not static and this is not easily represented in the graphical representation of COWOP. However, one of the main strengths of COWOP is its representation of these elements, because they allow us to look more closely at the configurations of practices in different contexts, thereby serving as an analytical framework for exploring and explaining a specific domain under investigation beyond its empirical findings [9]. COWOP opens several opportunities to understand and support designers' and researchers' interpretative and reflective practices.

Another limitation of COWOP is that it does not explicitly include the relationship between different practices or the timeliness or contextualization of the practice itself, which is what Schatzki refers to as the "total field of practices" [33]. We believe these are important aspects, and we do work to incorporate them in our practical use of COWOP, but we have not yet found a suitable way to make it part of the graphical representation.

BEYOND SUPPORTING SUSTAINABLE HCI

COWOP is a framework that includes the material and technological surroundings that play a role in the shaping of people's practices. COWOP helps articulate the unusual characteristic of energy consumption: it is often hidden and mediated through materiality and technology. Thus, we find COWOP especially well suited for the energy domain, for which it was developed. However, COWOP is also a framework for understanding and articulating a certain perspective on the world and how people act in it, therefore COWOP is also well suited to domains beyond energy and sustainability. To use COWOP in a domain, it needs to be enriched with concepts and theories specific to that domain as well as relying on empirical studies to see its benefits. For example, for developing technology in the energy domain, COWOP is enriched with concepts from socio-technical systems, the use of scripting, mediated consumption, and non-negotiable practices. We now provide two examples of how COWOP could be used in other domains: opportunities to better understand self-care practices, and understanding privacy in computer science.

COWOP and Healthcare

An in-depth understanding of self-care practices as well as people's experiences is needed when introducing self-care technology into people's everyday life [17]. In a recent review, Fitzpatrick and Ellingsen report that there is a lack of work on conceptualization of frameworks and models for designing healthcare technology [11]. In fact, most of the existing frameworks have been inspired and reported for a specific clinical setting [8, 11]. For non-clinical settings, a conceptual framework has been proposed to understand non-functional aspects of self-monitoring technology [17]. Although this conceptual framework highlights the need to understand the material aspects of interaction and digital artifacts as well as the necessary knowledge required to perform self-care activities, a greater understanding is needed to also consider the Societal Structure and negotiations that take place between the clinical and non-clinical settings. COWOP can offer several opportunities to support designer's reflective practices and the understanding of everyday, self-care and non-negotiable practices: how people interpret and appropriate self-care technology in everyday life as well as the collaborative work among different stakeholders in healthcare; and providing a holistic view of health, disease, settings, and everyday practices to support system design.

COWOP and Privacy

The issue of privacy in computer science is often understood as providing users with the right settings to control privacy or make the individual aware of (undesired) consequences or sharing of his/her data. Thus, applying a practice-oriented approach could potentially widen the scope of understanding by taking into account context outside the individual. That privacy goes beyond the individual is recognized by Palen and Dourish [24] who state that privacy needs to be seen as a social dynamic process and Nissenbaum [23] who emphasizes social norms in privacy behavior. While broadening the scope of privacy research to include norms and social science adds invaluable knowledge to our understanding of privacy, we argue that the Infrastructure and Near Materiality elements of COWOP need to be addressed just as explicitly as the abstract elements, because sometimes the privacy problem can be resolved by drawing on the physical elements of COWOP. Therefore, we propose that COWOP can be used to build a holistic perspective on privacy.

CONCLUSION

In this paper, we presented the Contextual Wheel of Practice—a framework that bridges insights from anthropology, sociology, and HCI to better understand everyday practices, design interventions, and collaborate with others who are not familiar with the practice-oriented approach. COWOP facilitates a broader perspective beyond the individual in sustainable HCI through its four elements: Societal Structure, Infrastructure, Near Materiality, and The Individual. We developed the framework based on our experiences in several energy projects, working in multidisciplinary teams where the practice approach was new to some members and a core part of the worldview for others. These elements affect everyday practices in different ways and all of them have to be taken into account. Finally, we argued that COWOP is a useful framework outside the domain of energy, as part of the turn to practice in HCI.

We hope that COWOP can inspire researchers and designers, and contribute to the current practice-oriented research agenda in HCI. Furthermore, we encourage the HCI community to continue to move away from solutions that only focus on individual behavior towards solutions that consider a more holistic view of everyday practices.

ACKNOWLEDGMENTS

This work has been supported by The Danish Council for Strategic Research as part of the EcoSense project (11-115331) and has been partly funded by the Danish Energy Agency project: Virtual Power Plant for Smartgrid Ready Buildings (no. 12019). We would also like to thank the EcoSense & VPP4SGR teams, Yuka Nagashima, Henrik Blunck, Laura Lynggaard Nielsen, Tine Raun, Louise Lønborg Rustrup and Mette Breth Klausen.

REFERENCES

1. Blunck, H., Bouvin, N. O., Mose Entwistle, J., Grønbæk, K., Kjærgaard, M. B., Nielsen, M., Graves Petersen, M., Rasmussen, M. K. and Wüstenberg, M. Computational environmental ethnography: combining collective sensing and ethnographic inquiries to advance means for reducing environmental footprints. In *Proc. e-Energy '13*, ACM Press (2013), 87-98.
2. Bødker, S. When second wave HCI meets third wave challenges. In *Proc. NordiCHI '06*, ACM (2006), 1-8.
3. Bourdieu, P. *Outline of a Theory of Practice*. Cambridge University Press, 1977.
4. Braun, V. and Clarke, V. Using thematic analysis in psychology. *Qualitative Research in Psychology*, *3*, 2 (2006), 77-101.
5. Brynjarsdóttir, H., Håkansson, M., Pierce, J., Baumer, E. P. S., Disalvo, C. and Sengers, P. Sustainably unpersuaded: how persuasion narrows our vision of sustainability. In *Proc. CHI '12*, ACM Press (2012), 947-956.
6. Darby, S. *The effectiveness of feedback on energy consumption*. Environmental Change Institute, University of Oxford, 2006.
7. Darnton, A. and Horn, J. *Influencing Behaviours - Moving Beyond the Individual - A User Guide to the ISM Tool*. The Scottish Government, 2013.
8. Doherty, G., McKnight, J. and Luz, S. Fieldwork for requirements: Frameworks for mobile healthcare applications. *International Journal of Human-Computer Studies*, *68*, 10 (10// 2010), 760-776.
9. Dourish, P. Implications for design. In *Proc. CHI '06*, ACM Press (2006), 541-550.
10. Entwistle, J. M. and Rasmussen, M. K. The Model of Change – Understanding the How and Why of Change. In *Proc. EPIC (Ethnographic Praxis in Industry Conference)* (2014).
11. Fitzpatrick, G. and Ellingsen, G. A Review of 25 Years of CSCW Research in Healthcare: Contributions, Challenges and Future Agendas. *Comput Supported Coop Work*, *22*, 4-6 (2013), 609-665.
12. Friedman, B., Kahn, P., Jr., Borning, A. and Huldtgren, A. Value Sensitive Design and Information Systems. In N. Doorn, D. Schuurbiers, I. van de Poel and M. E. Gorman (eds.) *Early engagement and new technologies: Opening up the laboratory*, *16*, (2013), 55-95.
13. Froehlich, J., Findlater, L. and Landay, J. The design of eco-feedback technology. In *Proc. CHI '10*, ACM Press (2010), 1999-2008.
14. Ganglbauer, E., Fitzpatrick, G. and Comber, R. Negotiating food waste: Using a practice lens to inform design. *ACM Trans. Comput.-Hum. Interact.*, *20*, 2 (2013), 1-25.
15. Geels, F. W. From sectoral systems of innovation to socio-technical systems. *Research Policy*, *33*, 6-7 (2004), 897-920.
16. Giddens, A. *The Constitution of Society: Outline of the Theory of Structuration*. Polity Press, 1984.
17. Grönvall, E. and Verdezoto, N. Beyond self-monitoring: understanding non-functional aspects of home-based healthcare technology. In *Proc. UbiComp 2013*, ACM (2013), 587-596.
18. Gross, S., Bardzell, J. and Bardzell, S. Structures, forms, and stuff: the materiality and medium of interaction. *Pers Ubiquit Comput*, *18*, 3 (2014), 637-649.
19. Ingram, J., Shove, E. and Watson, M. Products and Practices: Selected Concepts from Science and Technology Studies and from Social Theories of Consumption and Practice. *Design Issues*, *23*, 2 (2007), 3-16.
20. Kuijer, L. and Jong, A. D. Identifying design opportunities for reduced household resource

consumption: exploring practices of thermal comfort. *Journal of Design Research*, *10*, 1 (2012), 67-85.

21. Kuijer, L., Jong, A. d. and Eijk, D. v. Practices as a unit of design: An exploration of theoretical guidelines in a study on bathing. *ACM Trans. Comput.-Hum. Interact.*, *20*, 4 (2013), 1-22.

22. Kuutti, K. and Bannon, L. J. The turn to practice in HCI: towards a research agenda. In *Proc. CHI 2014*, ACM Press (2014), 3543-3552.

23. Nissenbaum, H. Privacy as contextual integrity. *Wash. L. Rev.*, *79* (2004), 119-157.

24. Palen, L. and Dourish, P. Unpacking "privacy" for a networked world. In *Proc. CHI '03*, ACM Press (2003), 129-136.

25. Pierce, J., Strengers, Y., Sengers, P. and Bødker, S. Introduction to the special issue on practice-oriented approaches to sustainable HCI. *ACM Trans. Comput.-Hum. Interact.*, *20*, 4 (2013), 1-8.

26. Pink, S., Mackley, K. L., Mitchell, V., Hanratty, M., Escobar-Tello, C., Bhamra, T. and Morosanu, R. Applying the Lens of Sensory Ethnography to Sustainable HCI. *ACM Trans. Comput.-Hum. Interact.*, *20*, 4 (2013), 25:21-25:18.

27. Randles, S. and Warde, A. Consumption: the view from theories of practice. In K. Green and S. Randles (eds.) *Industrial Ecology and Spaces of Innovation*, (2006), 220-237.

28. Rasmussen, M. K., Entwistle, J. M. and Nielsen, L. L. *Understanding Energy Consumption at the Grundfos Dormitory Lab as Situated Practices*. Alexandra Institute, 2014.

29. Reckwitz, A. Toward a Theory of Social Practices: A Development in Culturalist Theorizing. *European Journal of Social Theory*, *5*, 2 (2002), 243-263.

30. Rogers, Y. *HCI Theory: Classical, Modern, and Contemporary*. Morgan & Claypool Publishers, 2012.

31. Røpke, I. Theories of practice — New inspiration for ecological economic studies on consumption. *Ecological Economics*, *68*, 10 (2009), 2409-2497.

32. Schatzki, T. R. *Social Practices: A Wittgensteinian Approach to Human Activity and the Social*. Cambridge University Press, 1996.

33. Schatzki, T. R., Cetina, K. K. and von Savigny, E., eds. *The Practice Turn in Contemporary Theory*. Routledge, 2001.

34. Scott, K., Quist, J. and Bakker, C. Co-design, social practices and sustainable innovation: involving users in a living lab exploratory study on bathing. In *Proc. Joint Actions on Climate Change Conference, Aalborg, Denmark* (2009), 8-9.

35. Shove, E. and Pantzar, M. Consumers, Producers and Practices: Understanding the invention and reinvention of Nordic walking. *Journal of Consumer Culture*, *5*, 1 (2005), 43-64.

36. Shove, E., Pantzar, M. and Watson, M. *The dynamics of social practice: everyday life and how it changes*. Sage, 2012.

37. Star, S. L. This is Not a Boundary Object: Reflections on the Origin of a Concept. *Science, Technology & Human Values*, *35*, 5 (2010), 601-617.

38. Stolterman, E. *The Nature of Design Practice and Implications for Interaction Design Research*, 2008.

39. Strengers, Y. Smart Energy in Everyday Life: Are You Designing for Resource Man? *interactions*, *21*, 4 (2014), 24-31.

40. Strengers, Y. A. A. Designing eco-feedback systems for everyday life. In *Proc. CHI '11*, ACM Press (2011), 2135-2144.

41. Wakkary, R., Desjardins, A., Hauser, S. and Maestri, L. A sustainable design fiction: Green practices. *ACM ACM Trans. Comput.-Hum. Interact*, *20*, 4 (2013), 23.

42. Warde, A. Consumption and Theories of Practice. *Journal of Consumer Culture*, *5*, 2 (2005), 131-153.

43. Wenger, E. *Communities of Practice: Learning, Meaning, and Identity*. Cambridge University Press, 1998.

Effects of Public Commitments and Accountability in a Technology-Supported Physical Activity Intervention

Sean A. Munson[1], **Erin Krupka**[2], **Caroline Richardson**[3], **Paul Resnick**[2]
[1]Human Centered Design & Engineering
DUB Group, University of Washington
smunson@uw.edu
[2]School of Information, [3]Department of Family Medicine
University of Michigan
{ekrupka,caroli,presnick}@umich.edu

ABSTRACT
Walking and other forms of physical activity have many health benefits, but people often fail to follow through on their own goals of being more active. To address gaps in current understanding of how to design technology-supported physical activity interventions, we conducted a randomized field experiment of a commitment device: making public announcements. In a control condition, weekly commitments were kept private. In two treatment conditions, they were announced on Facebook and by email. In one of the two, the announcements also included results: whether the previous week's commitment was kept. We find that, with or without public results, these posts can elicit supportive replies from the poster's social networks. People in both public announcements conditions were less likely to make commitments. We conclude that the prospect of public accountability may suppress the making of commitments in a way that counteracts the benefits of that accountability. Designers will need to address this limitation in order to make effective use of public accountability as a commitment device.

Author Keywords
Commitments; goals; performance; sharing; privacy; physical activity; social network sites; persuasive technology

INTRODUCTION
Physical activity can improve health and wellness and reduce mortality [14], but as of 2012 only 50% of US adults report achieving recommended amounts of aerobic activity and nearly 30% report no regular physical activity in their leisure time [31]. The medical, public health, and HCI communities have developed and evaluated interventions, many supported by technology, to promote physical activity. Common and effective features include goal setting [8,27], performance feedback [17], and social support [14].

CHI 2015, April 18 - 23 2015, Seoul, Republic of Korea

ACM 978-1-4503-3145-6/15/04...$15.00
http://dx.doi.org/10.1145/2702123.2702524

There has been considerable prior research into goal setting and using social network sites to solicit social support for health and wellness behaviors. Some experiments and commercial applications have deployed financial commitment devices, where people create financial rewards and punishments for themselves for keeping their commitments [2,4]. Important questions remain, however. In particular, it is not clear whether and how social accountability can be harnessed as a commitment device. The literature also offers conflicting guidance on the prospect of whether public reports of results are necessary for public commitments to create increased accountability [10,13]. Additionally, researchers have argued for the potential benefits of sharing health and wellness behavior with one's pre-existing social network, but found substantial barriers to adoption or to eliciting those benefits [18,19,21]. Previous papers offer guidance on designs for messages that might get more – as well as more supportive – replies, but these suggestions have largely been untested.

We conducted a randomized field experiment evaluating the effects of public commitments in the domain of physical activity. We compare commitments posted to the social network site Facebook and shared by email, to commitments made privately. Based on the results, we offer insights for both theory and practice. In particular, our contributions are:

- evidence that it is possible to catalyze instrumental and emotional support from people's existing social networks for a physical activity program;
- evidence against the theory that public announcements of goals without the prospect of public reporting of results will backfire and reduce motivation;
- evidence that selection effects can undermine the value of public announcements, because the potential gains from public accountability may be offset by a reduction in willingness to make commitments;
- a challenge for designers to keep the social network's interest in providing support and accountability repeatedly for the same kind of commitment;
- a challenge for designers to harness the potential gains from public support and accountability without suppressing the benefits that come from private goal setting activity.

BACKGROUND AND MOTIVATION

Physical activity is known to help reduce obesity [20] and the co-morbidities that accompany it (such as type 2 diabetes and heart disease [30]). Walking has many benefits that make it an excellent way for obese people to increase their physical activity: (1) there is no need for special equipment or training, (2) it can be done when it fits into one's schedule, and (3) it is safe and effective even when multiple risk factors for cardiovascular disease exist [11].

Objective monitoring of physical activity has been widely used in physical activity interventions (e.g., [6,7,15]). Wearing a pedometer creates an objective assessment of whether walking goals were met, and several studies have found that pedometers are a valuable tool for supporting self-monitoring and self-regulation in walking interventions [3,12,24]. It is hard, however, for people to stick with walking programs. We review relevant prior work and extract implications into a conceptual model (see Figure 1).

Social Support

Interaction with other people can increase adherence to walking programs [22] (link C→H in Figure 1) and can lead to better health outcomes [32]. Other people can provide emotional support, such as kind words in difficult times or cheers for accomplishments. They can also provide informational and instrumental support, such as practical tips on shoes and snacks, or walking together to make it more fun.

Many people already share progress reports through Facebook, Twitter, and communities on fitness tracking websites [28]. However, participants in previous studies reported limiting their posts for fear of appearing boring or boastful and experiences with the posts going unnoticed or receiving negative replies [18,19,21]. Instead, many prefer to connect to strangers on special-purpose peer support sites, where they find a more understanding, supportive and accepting audience [21].

Connections on peer support networks, however, are less able to offer instrumental support, and may offer less meaningful emotional support, because they do not have an existing, ongoing, or physically proximate relationship with the poster. Noting these limitations, prior publications urge designers and researchers to continue to explore ways to solicit support through people's existing social networks. Recommendations include supporting selective access to people's personal networks and making specific requests for what the poster wants from the audience [18,21]. Thus, in principle public announcements to people's existing online networks have the potential to elicit social support (links A→C and B→C in Figure 1), but there is a design challenge to successfully do so in practice.

Goal Setting

Self-Regulation Theory models behavior changes that require ongoing, rather than one-time, decision-making. Research shows that specific and challenging goals that are combined with timely feedback about discrepancies between desired and actual performance lead to higher performance [16]. A meta-analysis of walking interventions identified goal-setting as one of the most important components, leading to a difference in improvement over baseline of more than 2,000 daily steps when compared to interventions without goal-setting [3]. Thus, Figure 1 includes the links E→H, F→H, and G→H.

Commitment Devices

To create accountability for completing the goals that people commit to, they sometimes use "commitment devices" that create rewards or punishments for success or failure [4]. For example, on a site like stickk.com, a user can specify an amount of money to be charged to their credit card if they fail to complete a goal. As we describe in the next section, we explore social rather than financial rewards and punishments, but the expected mechanism for impact on behavior is the same.

In terms of Schelling's analysis of "anticipatory self-command" [26], there is a strategic interaction between the self who creates the commitment device and the future self who is influenced by it. Indeed, it involves a three-stage interaction among the selves at three different times: when one makes a commitment (time 1), when one chooses to engage in an activity such as deciding between walking and watching TV (time 2), and when rewards or punishments are meted out (time 3). The commitment device is entered into by the self at time 1 because s/he expects that, absent the commitment device, the self at time 2 will make a different choice than the self at time 1 wanted. The commitment device creates accountability at time 2 so that the self at time 2 makes the choice that the self at time 1 wanted. Thus, Figure 1 includes the link D→E.

One major challenge in creating effective commitment devices is establishing the credibility of consequences (rewards or punishment) [2]. To create incentives for performance, the self at time 2 has to believe that the punishment will be carried out at time 3 if the goal is not met. If a person, either the individual or some third-party monitor, has to carry out the punishment, then the more severe the punishment, the less credible the threat that it will actually be carried out. For example, if the threat is to confiscate all one's material possessions for not meeting one's walking goal, then the incentive's effect is undermined because the walker knows that the threat will not be carried out. Pedometers with upload features enable automation of the monitoring process and programs can automatically trigger actions, such as sharing of step counts with friends [1,6]. Automating monitoring and delivery of consequences removes the credibility challenge that has afflicted commitment contracts.

A second major challenge in creating effective commitment devices is self-selection. If the consequences involve punishments and the self at time 1 is not sufficiently confident that the self at time 2 will meet the commitment,

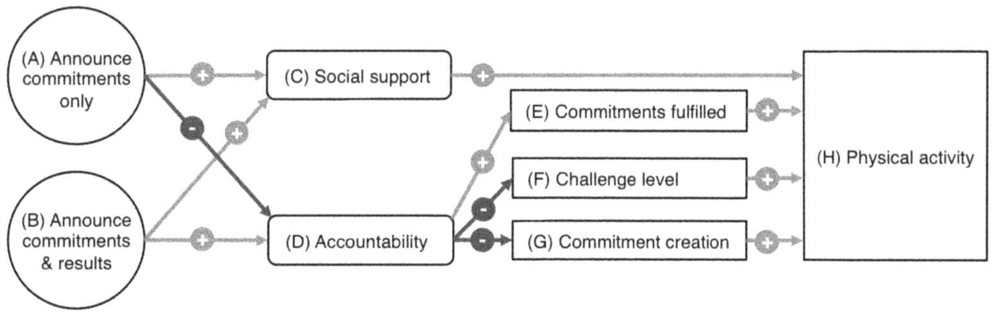

Figure 1. Conceptual model

s/he may be reluctant to voluntarily create the commitment device. In the context of our walking program, if the walker has low self-efficacy for walking, s/he may refuse to create commitments or may create less challenging commitments (links D→G and D→F in Figure 1).

Social Accountability through Public Commitments

We explore commitment devices where the rewards and punishments come from social accountability. There is conflicting theory and evidence about the effects of public announcement of goals on personal commitment to the goals and thus on performance. Some work argues that public announcement increases goal commitment, because people want to appear consistent to others [13,25]. This is especially true with a mechanism where results about completion of commitments will be automatically announced, and thus we have the link B→D in Figure 1.

Other work has found that public announcements of goals can be counterproductive to achieving stated goals if not also accompanied by public announcements of results [10]. The explanation offered is that benefits, such as being seen as the type of person who can achieve that goal, occur when the goal is announced. There is then less motivation to actually meet the goal, since all the reputation benefits have already been received. Based on this, Figure 1 includes the negative link A→D. There are other factors, however, that might make this relationship positive rather than negative. For example, public announcement of a goal might increase self-accountability [5].

Condition	time 1	time 2	time 3
Private commitment (Control)	Commitment to behavior or action.	Participants walk and are objectively monitored by FitBit devices	
Announce without results	Commitment to behavior or action, posted to Facebook and emailed to friends	Participants walk and are objectively monitored by FitBit devices	
Announce with results	Commitment to behavior or action, posted to Facebook and emailed to friends	Participants walk and are objectively monitored by FitBit devices	Prior week's outcome posted to Facebook and emailed with the next week's commitment.

x 12 weeks

Figure 2. Study design

THE STUDY

We conducted a randomized controlled trial (ClinicalTrials.gov #NCT01811407) to test the effects of including public announcements in a pedometer-based walking program. Subjects were given Fitbit pedometers that automatically upload step counts over the Internet. Each week for twelve weeks, participants had the opportunity to create a walking commitment for the upcoming week. Participants were randomized into three conditions, summarized in Figure 2.

Hypotheses

We describe the hypotheses and research questions below. Following each one, we indicate the path or paths in the conceptual model of Figure 1 that lead to the hypothesis.

H1 Social support: Public posts to people's existing social networks will catalyze responses that offer emotional, instrumental, and informational support. (A→C; B→C)

H2a "Announce without results" increases commitment creation: Announcing commitments without results will reduce accountability, and thus increase the number of commitments that are created. (A→D→G)

H2b "Announce with results" decreases commitment creation: Announcing commitments with results will increase accountability, and thus reduce the willingness to create commitments. (B→D→G)

H3a "Announce without results" increases challenge level: Announcing commitments without results reduces accountability, and thus increases the challenge level of commitments that are created. (A→D→F)

H3b "Announce with results" decreases challenge level: Announcing commitments with results increases accountability and thus decreases the challenge level of commitments that are created. (B→D→F)

H4a "Announce without results" decreases completion: Announcing commitments without results decreases accountability and thus decreases the percentage of created commitments that are completed. (A→D→E)

H4b "Announce with results" increases completion: Announcing commitments with results increases accountability, and thus increases the percentage of created commitments that are completed. (B→D→E)

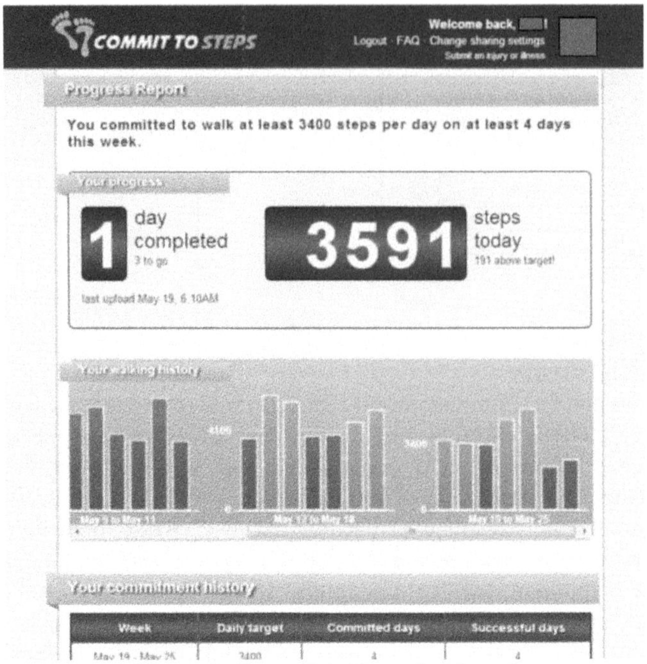

Figure 3. Commit to Steps dashboard

Figure 4. Example accountability post

Given these hypotheses about impacts on creation and completion of commitments, we do not have a clear prediction about the net effect of either treatment on physical activity levels. For example, announcing with results should reduce the number of commitments (and hence reduce physical activity) but increase the probability of completion for those that are created (and hence increase physical activity level). Thus, we describe research questions rather than specific hypotheses for the net effects.

RQ 5a: Net impact of "Announce without results" on physical activity. Do announcements of commitments without results lead to an overall positive or negative impact on physical activity outcomes? (A→D→E,F,G→H)

RQ 5b: Net impact of "Announce with results" on physical activity. Do announcements of commitments with results lead to an overall positive or negative impact on physical activity outcomes? (B→D→E,F,G→H)

APPARATUS AND PROCEDURES

We developed a custom website that interacts with the Fitbit and Facebook APIs to create a custom experience for subjects. All subjects could see graphs of their past performance and were assigned a daily target each week. The daily target changed each week. It was set automatically, based on the subject's past walking history, adjusting upward as the participant walked [23]. Targets were capped at 10,000 steps per day because it is enough to produce most of the health benefits associated with walking [29] and there may be a risk of minor injuries from overuse in people who are overly motivated to best ever-increasing targets. Subjects could not manually change their daily targets. Subjects were prompted to make a commitment each week, quantified as the number of days on which they would meet or exceed the daily step target. Subjects chose the number of days to which they committed. Figure 3 shows an example of what the web page looked like. In the example, the daily target for this week was 3,400 steps, the subject committed to exceeding that target on 4 days, and has done so on 1 day so far.

The only difference between the control and the two treatment conditions was that in the treatment conditions the commitments people made were posted to Facebook and emailed to three contacts. In the "Announce without results" treatment condition, only the next week's commitment was posted. In the other, the "Announce with results" treatment condition, both the next week's commitment and the results of the previous week's commitment were posted. The example in Figure 4 shows a post (not for a real subject) with both. The "Met my commitment..." paragraph was omitted in the "Announcements without results" condition Negative results were reported with neutral phrasing: "Fell short last week. 2 days over my daily steps target, even though I committed to 4".

Prior work suggests that social network site posts about physical activities or goals include a specific call to action for the audience [18]. Following that advice, our posts conclude with, "Please encourage me, or better yet, walk with me."

To ensure that public commitments were sufficiently "public," all participants in both treatments were asked to select at least 20 Facebook friends to whom the posts would be visible, or to make their posts visible to all of their Facebook friends. We also asked each subject to enter email addresses for three contacts, to whom our site would send weekly updates. This design choice follows recommendations from prior literature that tools which encourage sharing of health and wellness data to personal informatics sites allow users to select a subset of friends with whom to share [18,19]. We also avoid difficulties with people not setting up their support groups by making this a required step [18].

SUBJECTS

We recruited 165 adult subjects from the University of Michigan Medical system. 385 responded to invitations sent by paper mail to recent patients over 18 who were obese (BMI>=30). They completed an online form to assess eligibility. Criteria included: self-reported weight and height that implied BMI >= 30; sedentary but ambulatory and able to walk at least one block; over 18; and have more than 50 Facebook friends. 246 passed the eligibility screening. Of these, 220 consented to participation in the study.

After consent, subjects completed a registration process. This included connecting their account to Facebook and completing a questionnaire. 199 did so. After that, subjects were mailed a Fitbit with instructions. The Fitbit device was connected to an account on our custom website. We created accounts on fitbit.com for each pedometer used in the study but did not share the password for those accounts with the subjects—thus, subjects could access their step count histories only on our site, not on the Fitbit website.

After a two-week baseline period in which step counts were recorded but no commitments were made and nothing was shared with subjects' networks, subjects whose pedometers were successfully uploading step counts to the Internet were randomized to one of the three conditions. Of the 165 subjects who made it to randomization, 136 were women and 29 men, with a mean age of 47.

Subjects remained in their assigned conditions for the twelve weeks of the trial, having the option to make a commitment each week. At the end of the trial, they were asked to complete an exit questionnaire. After that, they were free to keep their pedometers and use the Fitbit website to track their ongoing walking.

Two subjects were removed from the study after randomization, due to medical conditions unrelated to the study. They are not included in the data analyses. One subject dropped out of the study after seeing what the Facebook posts looked like. That subject, and others who simply stopped participating, are included in the data analyses.

RESULTS

Overall, across all conditions, the walking program was well-received. In most online health interventions lasting several months, attrition is high, well above 50% [9]. By contrast, attrition in this study was very low: 131 of 165 subjects uploaded step counts in their twelfth week. The high continued participation occurred despite the onset of a severe winter toward the end of the twelve-week period for most participants.

Catalyzing social support and accountability

Of the participants who completed the post-study questionnaire and were in one of the two public treatments (n=81), 40 (49%) chose to limit the visibility of their posts to specific friends. The rest reported allowing the application to post to their newsfeed default. Those who customized their audience described choosing to share with close friends who they felt would be encouraging, who would not judge, and "*who could really support me*" or "*support me no matter what.*" Many also chose to share with family, but others felt it was important not to share with family or partners. A few commented that they shared with exercise partners or friends who also struggled with weight management, specifically avoiding friends who "*do not care about exercise,*" or friends who were already very fit (e.g., they ran marathons). Some described wanting to "*avoid cluttering friends' feeds.*"

Attitudes about posting commitments and results

Participants generally had positive feelings about posting commitments to Facebook. 17 of the 81 (21%) participants in one of the two treatment conditions who completed the post-study questionnaire explicitly mentioned the motivation or accountability they received as a result of sharing as the best feature of Commit to Steps, and reported mixed feelings about sharing them by email. Not all participants, though, always liked sharing their commitments. One participant mentioned deleting the automatic posts on Facebook.

Most participants had at least some positive experiences with the Facebook sharing feature, noting that it "*was also exciting to see the comments that people wrote.*" Most described receiving encouragement and support, and even walking partners:

> *"I found sharing my Commit to Steps gave me a lot of encouragement, and it even encouraged many of my friends to walk with me or to go out and walk on their own."*

> *"It did keep me motivated to keep up with my commitment and it gave me something to talk about with people."*

> *"I found it very encouraging when people had read my status and sent me comments on Facebook or in person. I felt like I was really doing something great and had a wide audience of supporters."*

They also described feeling more accountable. For example:

> *"The threat of posting my failure definitely drove me to work harder and jog around the house at night when I was short on steps. I wanted to avoid failure because my friends would see my laziness."*

> *"I felt obligated to work harder, so I didn't let anyone down."*

Two participants described being reluctant, at first, to share but enjoying the experience more as time went on:

> *"It was a little intimidating at first, but each week I was encouraged to continue."*

> *"Reticent at first, but great feedback and encouragement from people - throughout the study, in fact more as time progressed."*

For others, the experience was more neutral. Some experienced it as good when things were going well but unpleasant on weeks when they did not meet their commitment:

> *"When I made the commitments with success, it was great. It made me feel good about the efforts. However, when I was unsuccessful it was truly embarrassing for me."*

> *"I was embarrassed on weeks that listed I failed to meet my goals. At other times, it spurred me on to make those weekly goals!"*

Others felt the experience was inconsistent with what they normally share ("*Kind of odd. I like to be private*") or that the tone of the automatic post was inconsistent with how they would choose to share the content ("*asking them to support or walk with me is cheesy*"). Their friends' comments picked up on this as well:

> *"I like the idea of this accountability checker for your walking goals, but it must be an automated message as the recurring use of the word "Yay!" sort of gives it way."*

> *"I'll keep encouraging you, but dude, at least change your request up a little bit."*

One participant felt the experience was redundant to their existing, in person support ("*It was ok didn't think it was necessary for me since me support was daily from people I workout with*") and three commented that sharing was superfluous to their own motivation (e.g., "*This is a personal goal of mine. Regardless of how supportive they were, it is all up to me in the end.*"). Some additional participants said they did not remember seeing the posts or did not recall any friends replying to their posts, which was a neutral or sometimes disappointing experience.

Four participants disliked the sharing feature and would prefer not to have it. The reasons they listed were embarrassment or potential embarrassment ("*It's embarrassing and personal whether or not I achieved my goal*", "*I'm self-conscious about being overweight and did not want others to see what I'm doing*"), it was a private experience ("*It is none of their businesses how many steps per day I walk*", "*I would have preferred to not have shared this personal experience*"), or the information was boring ("*Plus, no one cares about the steps. People just get bored reading about it.*").

Experiences with email sharing were more mixed. Some participants described this sharing as comparable to Facebook, while most said they got less of a reaction to their emails than on Facebook. Because emails were more personally targeted than Facebook posts, the lack of reply was more disappointing for at least one participant. Two commented that email was more likely to annoy their friends and that Facebook was a better place.

Response characteristics

To better understand the type of support participants received, we examined the comments on participants' automated Facebook posts. The posts were noticed by subjects' Facebook friends, who responded with a variety of types of support. Figure 5 shows the mean number of likes and comments received for Facebook posts. Responses declined over time; by the last week, less than half of the posts received a comment, and the median received just one like.

The comments on posts were overwhelmingly positive. Of the 2,287 comments (this includes comments made by subjects), 1,303 comments explicitly offered emotional support. Friends cheered posters on, said missed commitments were okay and they would get back on track the next week, and offered prayers. Some offered memories of shared healthier, more active times. Several commenters called their friends' posts motivational or inspiring, and a few said that they bought fitness devices or downloaded apps to increase their own physical activity. 70 comments shared their own experiences with physical activity, sometimes in ways crafted to motivate. 28 commenters requested progress updates, which offered accountability.

Commenters also offered instrumental support. Responding to our post's request to "walk with me," 232 comments offered to set times to walk. We do not know how many of these turned into actual walks, but nearly 100 comments followed up coordinating locations and times for walks, and several other comments referenced successful meet-ups and suggested planning another. 53 comments offered to join virtually, including walking at the same time and talking on the phone, sharing fitness stats each day or week, or simply also committing to a plan to be more physically active. A smaller number of posts offered to give subjects rides to nice places to walk, to let them borrow their dogs for a walk, or to watch the participant's children so they could find time for a walk. They even offered soup when someone was sick.

Participants noted that their friends were supportive even when they did not achieve their commitment, e.g., "*It was cool, nobody really gave me a hard time for missing my goal, and everybody was supportive in some way.*" We saw this reflected in the posts, though a few comments offered tougher or more ambiguous support, such as "*you are going backward*" or "*Lol 0 days :-P.*" One commenter responded to a commitment post with "*I have my doubts,*" a reply

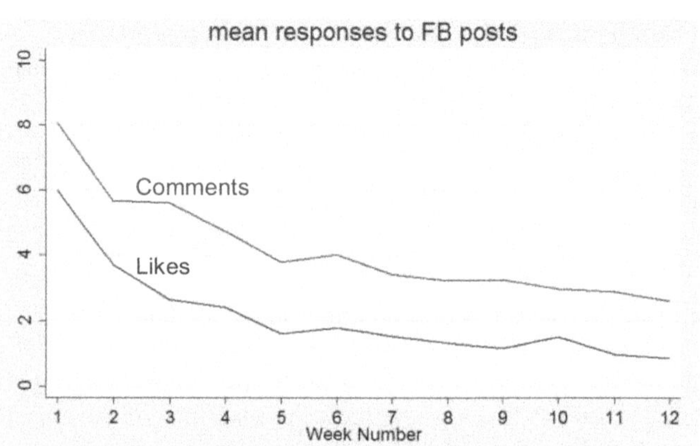

Figure 5. Responses (comments and likes) to Facebook posts declined as the study went on.

which another commenter criticized, "*C'mon {{nickname}} help {{name}} out or don't u believe in [positive motivation]?*"

Many commenters asked questions about walking (50). The most common question was how many steps are in a mile. 78 comments offered answers, and also suggestions and tips for where to walk and how to make time to walk, for remembering to wear the Fitbit, or for staying motivated. Eight additional comments offered suggestions of physical activities other than walking, though participants were sometimes resistant to these suggestions since they would not receive step count "credit" for many of those activities.

Study participants responded with "thank you" messages and progress reports. The progress reports celebrated successes and offered justifications for weeks they missed their commitments, such as being sick, forgetting to wear the Fitbit, or having trouble syncing.

Overall, we conclude that "H1 Social support" is supported. Public posts to people's existing social networks catalyzed responses that offered emotional, instrumental, and informational support.

Impact of Public Announcements on Commitment Creation

Due to a bug in our software for a couple of weeks early in the trial, it was more difficult for subjects in one of the conditions (public announcements without results) to login and thus to make commitments. To eliminate any biasing effect this may have had, we include only weeks 5-12 in our analyses of commitment creation.

Most subjects created commitments most weeks. Subjects in the private condition, however, were somewhat more likely to do so. Figure 6 shows the percentage of subjects who created commitments, by week, for each condition. Overall, in the private condition, 88.2% of all possible commitments were created, compared to 78.6% with public announcements of commitments without results, and 77.3% with public announcements of both commitments and results.

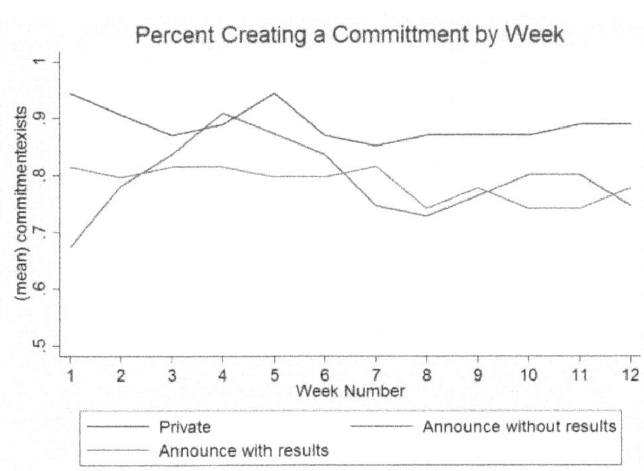

Figure 6. Commitment creation.

To test for statistical significance, we conducted a logit regression predicting the outcome in each week of creating or not creating a commitment. One advantage of the panel structure of our data, with observation of whether each subject made a commitment in eight different weeks, is that we can take into account unobserved heterogeneity in our subjects. However, our analysis has to correct for the autocorrelation among the error terms across weeks. Without a correction, our p-values would be misleadingly small. We correct by estimating a random effects logit model. In particular, this allows correction for a particular kind of autocorrelation: some subjects being more willing than others overall to create commitments, and that willingness impacting each subject in a consistent way across all periods. Even with the correction, we find that both public treatments are significantly lower than the private control treatment in the probability of making a commitment ($p<.05$).[1] We conclude that H2a is not supported but H2b is: announcement without results led to creation of fewer commitments rather than more; announcement with results led to fewer commitments, as expected.

Impact of Public Announcements on Level of Challenge

Restricting attention to only those weeks when subjects did create commitments, we now investigate whether they challenged themselves less by committing to meet the daily target on fewer days. Contingent on making a commitment, the average number of days committed to was similar across treatments: 4.16 in the Private condition, 4.14 for public announcements without results, and 4.15 for public announcements with results. We estimated a random effects regression model, and the differences between conditions were not significant. We conclude that neither H3a nor H3b is supported: the challenge level of commitments created was not higher when commitments were announced without results nor lower when announced with results.

Impact of Public Announcements on Completing Commitments

We now investigate whether subjects were more likely to succeed at completing their commitments when they were publicly announced. Here, completing the commitment means exceeding the daily target step-count on at least as many days as to which they committed. In the private control condition, subjects completed 53.8% of the commitments they created, compared to 56.0% in "Announcements without results", and 59.5% in "Announcements with results". When correcting for auto-correlation with a random effects logit regression, including week number as control variable because the probability of completing commitments decreased with time, the differences were not significant. Neither H4a nor H4b is supported: the probability of keeping commitments was not

[1] Details of all statistical analyses are available in the online appendix.

lower when commitments were announced without results nor significantly higher when announced with results.

Net Impact on physical activity

Finally, we turn our attention to the net impact on physical activity. We computed the change in daily step count for each subject from his or her baseline daily step count, as measured in the two weeks before the treatment began. As shown in Figure 7, step counts increased dramatically in the initial weeks, and declined somewhat toward the end (as the weather got worse). Considering only weeks where the pedometer was worn at least one day (i.e., daily step count > 200), the average improvement in mean daily step count in the three conditions was 957 (private), 1030 (announcements without results), and 1,407 (announcements with results). However, standard deviations were large (1374, 1679, and 1948 for the three conditions) and the differences between conditions were not statistically significant. Therefore, we are unable to conclusively answer "RQ 5: Net impact on physical activity".

DISCUSSION: IMPLICATIONS FOR THEORY

We observed an unwanted selection effect of an expectation of public accountability: people created fewer commitments when those commitments were made public. This is an especially problematic finding for situations where people repeatedly decide whether to make commitments rather than making them once, at a time when they are particularly optimistic or interested in constraining their future selves.

We did not observe a reduction in the number of days that people committed to, when they made a commitment, as we would have expected if social accountability were making people reluctant to create challenging commitments. Perhaps in a more continuous or more granular domain (e.g., if they chose their own step-count targets) we might see such a reduction. We speculate, however, that social accountability also prevents people from setting commitments that are too easy. It is also possible that people expected others to judge them on an absolute scale of how much they walked, rather than a relative scale based on the number of days they committed to, so that the number of days committed to was only a private matter even if it was publicly announced.

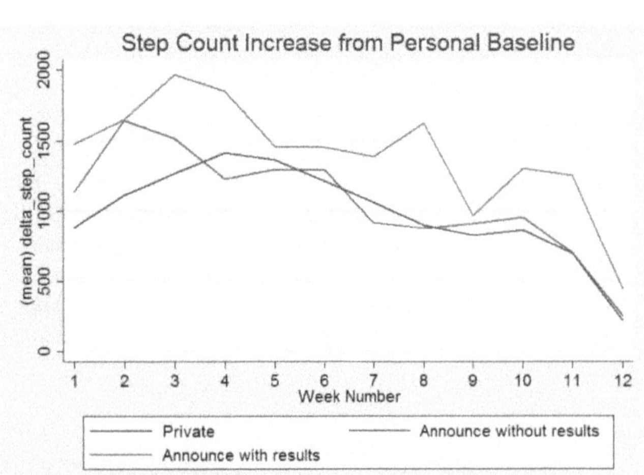

Figure 7. Week-to-week change in step count.

We did not observe statistically significant differences in the probability of keeping commitments when they were public. One possibility is that the primary benefit (if any) of public posts was the emotional, instrumental, and informational support they triggered and that, once posted, accountability or lack thereof was relatively unimportant. Although the quotes from participants reported above suggest that at least some felt the public announcements created accountability, it is also possible that most people did not perceive posts reporting fewer days than committed as embarrassing. We had considered alternative phrasings for those posts that would have been more embarrassing, but opted for a neutral phrasing in order to reduce selection effects (people not creating commitments to avoid the risk of such posts) and possible negative impacts on self-efficacy when such posts were actually made. It is possible, however, that more negative phrasing would have created more accountability.

We also did not observe statistically significant differences in overall step counts. This may be due to countervailing effects of selection (creating fewer commitments) vs. accountability (greater likelihood of keeping those commitments that were made) and support (getting mostly positive feedback from friends and family). It is also possible that each of those effects had a negligible impact on step counts.

Before overinterpreting these negative findings, however, we caution about the danger of type II errors, given the limited sample size and high variability between subjects. The sample size for the experiment was chosen to enable detection, with power > 0.8, of an effect size of an extra one-half day per week in meeting the daily step count target. This is a very large effect size, given that the daily target automatically went up for the next week when someone walked more. The effects we observed on the probability of keeping commitments and on total step counts were clinically significant, but not reliable. It may be that, with more participants, the observed effects would have been statistically significant.

We did not observe the predicted backfire effect from making commitments public without making the results public. Fewer rather than more commitments were created, and the other predicted effects were also in the wrong direction though not significant. We speculate that participants were not fully aware of whether the posts included results. Even when they knew posts did not include results, participants may have anticipated that posting the next week's commitment would prompt their friends to ask how the previous week went anyway. We observed few of these comments: two (both on the same comment) asked directly about the previous week's results while six inquired about progress during the week, and 21 others asked about progress with the program overall (were they losing weight? Feeling stronger?). It may have been sufficient, however, that participants anticipated such questions. They may also have been asked through other channels we could not observe, such as other Facebook posts, email, or face-to-face-conversations.

DISCUSSION: IMPLICATIONS FOR DESIGN

Our results offer designers challenges and guidance for the design of social features that share health and wellness activities and goals, and for the design of commitment-based health and wellness interventions.

Catalyzing support by sharing health goals and activity

Contrary to prior work, we found that the Facebook posts from Commit To Steps were effective at eliciting emotional, informational, and instrumental support, with very few negative replies from commenters. We followed recommendations from previous work: encouraging participants to select a supportive subset of their Facebook friends and including a specific ask (support or walking with them). The combination appears to have been successful, and we recommend that designers of future interventions follow these approaches.

There continue to be opportunities for improvement, however. As in previous studies, some participants were still reluctant to make commitments because they feared negative replies. Among those who posted, though, we saw very few examples of negative feedback. Participants in the public commitments conditions either received positive feedback and support and then became more open to or appreciative of the intervention, or received no feedback and became apathetic about the public posts. Assuming participants who were concerned about negative feedback would have received comparable feedback to those who did make and share commitments, future interventions might do more to help participants better anticipate positive reactions. Future interventions might also do more to match posts to respondents who may respond positively.

Other participants also reacted negatively to the specific language in the posts or their repetitiveness, and we saw a drop off in the number of replies over time. Allowing participants to customize their posts could mitigate concerns about tone and make them feel less "*cheesy*" or "*canned*" and allow people to make requests for more specific kinds of support. We had piloted such an interface but removed this ability, fearing it would overly increase the complexity of the interface. System designers could also build more variety into automated posts.

Managing tradeoffs in public commitments

There seems to be an inherent tradeoff in publicly announcing commitments that are voluntarily created. On the one hand, it deters some people from making any commitment at all. On the other hand, it encourages those who do make commitments to complete them. Alternative designs, however, might gain more of the benefits without all the costs.

First, it might be valuable to separate the announcement choice from the creation choice, so that people can create private commitments even when they do not want to accept the public accountability. For example, when setting a commitment, the interface could also present an individual with a checkbox for whether this particular commitment should be shared on Facebook.

A stronger intervention might be to pursue interventions in which people pre-commit to ongoing, system-set public commitments for an entire intervention period. For example, in Commit to Steps, participants might commit at the beginning to a 12-week program in which the system sets both their daily targets and weekly commitment to reaching them, and publicizes them each week. This, though, may have two undesirable consequences. First, it might lead people to avoid the intervention entirely. Second, a few participants who had health problems or unexpected life events that made it impossible to reach their commitments might become very frustrated when the system did not let them adjust for this; predicting busy or potentially sick times twelve weeks in advance is even less practical than anticipating them for the upcoming week.

CONCLUSION

Announcing commitments can catalyze support and accountability from existing social networks for health behavior change. However, that is not sufficient to guarantee a successful intervention. The prospect of accountability creates a selection effect that decreases the probability of making commitments. The challenge for future designers is to reduce the selection effect or reduce its consequences.

ACKNOWLEDGMENTS

This research was supported by funding from the Robert Wood Johnson Foundation and an Intel PhD Fellowship. Chanda Phelan, Michelle Draska, and Caryn McCarthy recruited participants and provided them with technical support.

REFERENCES

1. Anderson I, Maitland J, Sherwood S, Barkhuus L, Chalmers M, Hall M, Brown B, Muller H. Shakra: tracking and sharing daily activity levels with unaugmented mobile phones. *Mobile Netw Appl* 2007; 12(2-3): 185-199.
2. Ayres I. *Carrots and Sticks* 2010, New York: Bantam Books.
3. Bravata DM, Smith-Spangler C, Sundaram V, Gienger AL, Lin N, Lewis R, Stave CD, Olkin I, Sirard JR. Using pedometers to increase physical activity and improve health: a systematic review, *JAMA* 2007; 298(19): 2296-2304.
4. Bryan G, Karlan D, Nelson S, Commitment Devices. *Annu Rev Econ* 2010; 2: 671-698.
5. Cialdini RB. *Influence: Science and Practice* (5th edition) 2009. Boston: Pearson.

6. Consolvo S, Everitt K, Smith I, Landay JA. Design requirements for technologies that encourage physical activity. *CHI 2006.*
7. Consolvo S, McDonald DW, Toscos T, Chen MY, Froehlich J, Harrison B, Klasnja P, LaMarca A, LeGrand L, Libby R, Smith I, Landay JA. Activity sensing in the wild: a field trial of ubifit garden. *CHI* 2008: 1797-1806.
8. Eakin EG, Lawler SP, Vandelanotte C, Owen N. Telephone Interventions for Physical Activity & Dietary Behavior Change: A systematic review, *Am J Prev Med* 2007; 32(5): 419-434.
9. Eysenbach G. The law of attrition. *J Med Internet Res*, 2005; 7(1): e11.
10. Gollwitzer PM, Sheeran P, Michalski V, Seifert AE. When Intentions Go Public. *Psychol Sci* 2009; 20(5): 612-618.
11. Goodrich DE, Larkin AR, Lowery JC, Holleman RG, Richardson CR. Adverse events among high-risk participants in a home-based walking study: a descriptive study. *Int J Behav Nutr Phys Act* 2007; 4: 20.
12. Greaves CJ, Sheppard KE, Abraham C, Hardeman W, Roden M, Evans PH, Schwarz P. Systematic review of reviews of intervention components associated with increased effectiveness in dietary and physical activity interventions. *BMC Public Health* 2011; 11(1): 119.
13. Hollenbeck JR, Williams CR, Klein HJ. An empirical examination of the antecedents of commitment to difficult goals. *J Appl Psychol* 1989; 74(1): 18-23.
14. Kahn EB, Ramsey LT, Brownson RC, Heath GW, Howze EH, Powell KE, Stone EJ, Rajab MW, Corso P. The effectiveness of interventions to increase physical activity: A systematic review. *Am J Prev Med* 2002; 22(4): 73-107.
15. Lin JJ, Mamykina L, Lindtner S, Delajoux G, Strub HB. Fish'n'Steps: Encouraging physical activity with an interactive computer game. *UbiComp* 2006: 261-278.
16. Locke EA, Latham GP. Building a practically useful theory of goal setting and task motivation: A 35-year odyssey. *Am Psychol* 2002; 57(9): 705-717.
17. Michie S, Abraham C, Whittington C, McAteer J, Gupta S. Effective Techniques in Healthy Eating and Physical Activity Interventions: A Meta-Regression. *Health Psychol* 2009; 28(6).
18. Munson SA, Consolvo S. Exploring Goal-setting, Rewards, Self-monitoring, and Sharing to Motivate Physical Activity, *Pervasive Health* 2012.
19. Munson SA, Lauterbach D, Newman MW, Resnick P. Happier Together: Integrating a Wellness Application Into a Social Network Site, *Persuasive* 2010.
20. Murphy MH, Nevill AM, Murtagh EM, Holder RL.The effect of walking on fitness, fatness and resting blood pressure: A meta-analysis of randomised, controlled trials. *Prev Med* 2007; 44(5): 377-85.
21. Newman MW, Lauterbach D, Munson SA, Resnick P, Morris ME. "It's not that I don't have problems, I'm just not putting them on Facebook": Challenges and Opportunities in Using Online Social Networks for Health, *CSCW* 2011.
22. Richardson CR, Buis LR, Janney AW, Goodrich DE, Sen A, Hess ML, Mehari KS, Fortlage LA, Resnick PJ, Zikmund-Fisher BJ, Strecher VJ, Piette JD. An Online Community Improves Adherence in an Internet-Mediated Walking Program. Part 1: Results of a Randomized Controlled Trial. *J Med Internet Res* 2010; 12(4): e71.
23. Richardson CR, Mehari KS, McIntyre LG, Janney AW, Fortlage LA, Sen A, Strecher VJ, Piette JD. A randomized trial comparing structured and lifestyle goals in an internet-mediated walking program for people with type 2 diabetes. *Int J Behav Nutr Phys Act* 2007; 4: 59.
24. Richardson CR, Newton TL, Abraham JJ, Sen A, Jimbo M, Swartz AM. A meta-analysis of pedometer-based walking interventions and weight loss. *Ann Fam Med* 2008; 6(1): 69-77.
25. Salancik G. Commitment and the control of organizational behavior and belief. in *New directions in organizational behavior*, B. Staw and G. Salancik, eds. 1977, Krieger. 1-54.
26. Schelling TC. Self-Command in Practice, in Policy, and in a Theory of Rational Choice. *The American Economic Review* 1984; 74(2): 1-11.
27. Strecher VJ, Seijts GH, Kok GJ, Glasgow R, DeVellis B, Meertens RM, Bulger DW. Goal Setting as a Strategy for Health Behavior Change, *Health Educ Behav* 1995; 22(2).
28. Teodoro R, Naaman M. Fitter with Twitter: Understanding Personal Health and Fitness Activity in Social Media. *ICWSM* 2013.
29. Tudor-Locke C, Bassett DR, How Many Steps/Day Are Enough?: Preliminary Pedometer Indices for Public Health. *Sports Medicine* 2004; 34(1): 1-8.
30. U.S. Department of Health and Human Services, *Physical Activity and Health: A Report of the Surgeon General*, 1996, Center for Disease Control and Prevention, National Center for Chronic Disease Prevention and Health Promotion: Atlanta, GA.
31. U.S. Department of Health and Human Services. Physical activity data. *Healthy People 2020.* http://www.healthypeople.gov/2020/topicsobjectives2020/nationaldata.aspx?topicId=33.
32. Wing RR, Jeffery RW. Benefits of recruiting participants with friends and increasing social support for weight loss and maintenance. *J Consult Clin Psych* 1999; 67(1), 132.

Rare World: Towards Technology for Rare Diseases

Haley MacLeod, Kim Oakes, Danika Geisler, Kay Connelly, Katie Siek
Indiana University
{hemacleo, kimoakes, djgeisle, connelly, ksiek}@indiana.edu

ABSTRACT

Researchers have created innovative technological solutions to support people with common chronic illnesses. In this study, we investigate design opportunities for people with rare diseases who are not well studied or have smaller populations to work with, because although an individual's disease may be rare, the number of people living with a rare disease is substantial. We conducted an interview study with 19 individuals with rare diseases from around the world to understand common problems and experiences that could be supported through design. We found that communicating with friends, family, and providers about her disease were challenges for participants. Additionally, participants thought of their disease as being a large part of who they were. We discuss these findings in the context of prior work on common chronic illnesses, addressing the potential relevance of existing technological interventions for people with rare diseases.

Author Keywords

Rare diseases; chronic disease management; health.

ACM Classification Keywords

H.5.m. Information Interfaces and Presentation (e.g. HCI): Miscellaneous

INTRODUCTION

Common chronic illnesses, such a diabetes (e.g. [20]), kidney disease (e.g. [26]), cancer (e.g. [16]), and asthma (e.g. [36]) impact a large and growing subset of our population. Researchers responded with technologies that address the symptoms, causes, and management of chronic illnesses. These chronic illnesses are well studied in the medical literature and have a constrained set of symptoms and treatments to address with technology. To this end, the technologies are customised to a specific chronic illness. The research community has not found an intervention sweet spot that will work for every demographic and disease. Since there is not a one-size-fits all solution, rare diseases are left out of the health design space.

While an individual's disease may be rare, the number of people living with a rare disease is substantial. It is estimated that 10% of the world's population has a rare disease [32] (in comparison, only 3% of the world's population use Twitter[1]). If everyone with a rare disease lived in the same country, it would be the world's third most populous nation. Since some rare disease symptoms overlap with common chronic illness symptoms, we set out to investigate the common ground between rare disease populations and common chronic illness populations, and what the scope of technology could be for people with rare disease. We conducted interviews with 19 individuals living with a range of chronic rare diseases recruited from online communities. They lived around the world representing a range of health care systems. Our goal was to examine the experiences of people living with rare diseases and to identify common problems that could be addressed through design. Our main contributions are:

1. A profile of people with rare diseases;
2. A discussion of similarities and differences between rare diseases and more common chronic illnesses; and
3. How technologies could address some of these opportunities for design.

RARE DISEASES

Each country defines rare diseases slightly differently. In the US, rare diseases are those affecting less than 200,000 people (or 0.06% of the population). In most of Europe, a rare disease affects no more than 5 out of every 10,000 people (or 0.05% of the population). World wide, 10% of the population, or about 350 million people, are living with a rare disease. There are around 7,000 different rare diseases. [32] For simplicity, we relied on the NIH's list of rare diseases[2] to limit our study. Rare diseases can be challenging to diagnose — patients usually receive 2-3 misdiagnoses over five years in the UK and over seven years in the US on average before receiving a correct diagnosis [32]. Diagnosis requires visits to many different primary care physicians and specialists.

RELATED WORK

Patients as whole people & experts.

Researchers encourage us to think about people as people, instead of as patients, emphasising humanness over disease [1, 3, 19, 21]. Further, people can have an expertise that is uniquely different from clinicians' expertise [9], one that is gained through lived experiences. Researchers explore what it means to support the whole person through design [11] by acknowledging that people may prioritize life differently from clinical best practices or be unable to integrate best practices into their lives [1]. People sometimes make complex [19] and flexible [21] negotiations of their actions to accommodate their lifestyle. There is also a tension between

[1]Twitter Inc. 2Q 2014 Earnings Report. 2014.
[2]http://rarediseases.info.nih.gov/gard/categories

CHI 2015, April 18 - 23 2015, Seoul, Republic of Korea
Copyright 2015 ACM 978-1-4503-3145-6/15/04...$15.00
http://dx.doi.org/10.1145/2702123.2702494

empowering people and enabling them to make false inferences or poor decisions, and although intelligent data analysis and careful visualisations [21] can support people, there still exists a need for medical professionals in this process [18].

Social Support & Online Communities

There have been several studies on the use of online communities by people with common chronic illnesses [10–12, 27]. These online health communities tend to be disease specific and are separate from existing social media sites like Facebook or Twitter. People view sites like Facebook as too public and do not use them to share health information. Posts on Facebook or Twitter are often presented to "collapsed contexts" [4] where many environments or social groups overlap in the audience, although Pang et al. [24] found that people are hesitant to even use private messaging features to share health information — either because they were afraid they might be publicly visible or because they did not know how to create private messages. Gibson et al. [7] found that private Facebook groups worked well for support between new mothers as a privacy mechanism within an existing platform.

One exception is [31], where Suh et al. designed a Twitter-based intervention for parents to track their children's milestones, understanding that busy participants are more active on sites that are already part of their regular routine — although some participants did express concerns about sharing their information publicly. Newman et al. [23] found that conflict existed between the benefits people hoped to gain from online communities and their goal of impression management [14]. For instance, needing emotional support conflicted with a desire to have others view their health status favourably. Text message interventions were explored in the context of chronic illnesses [36] as a middle ground between convenience and privacy. Text messages may give greater control over the spread of their information, while still leveraging a medium that is part of their existing routine.

Patient-Centered Information Management

Living with a chronic condition requires a great deal of information management; people with chronic conditions often keep track of their own medical records, collect their own notes and data, and sometimes collect articles related to their condition. Given the amount of information that is managed by the patient, Pratt et al. [25] call for technologies to manage health information that focuses on the patient at the centre of the information repository. Further, Moen et al. [22] outline strategies used to manage this information in the home.

Typically, research into these patient-centred information repositories has been in the domain of Personal Health Records (PHR's), although these have been discounted in some cases for being designed from an overly "clinical perspective" [1], failing to account for the "unanchored" [16] (i.e. outside a traditional workspace) and "invisible" [34] work performed by patients during the management of a condition. A patient-centred tool that strays from this traditional clinical perspective is My Journey Compass [13], a tablet with a suite of applications, pdf informational resources, and relevant website links tailored to cancer patients.

METHOD

We conducted interviews with people who were living with a rare disease to understand their experiences and to inform possible design opportunities. This study was approved by the Institutional Review Board at Indiana University.

Recruitment

We recruited through online forums specifically targeting people with rare diseases (RareShare[3], RareConnect[4], the Rare Disease Foundation[5]). Each online forum had sub-communities for different diseases. We recruited from any that had been active within the past three months. We also recruited from Facebook groups targeting specific rare diseases. We randomly chose 30 conditions from the NIH list in different categories to target a range of diseases. 15 conditions had Facebook groups from which we were able to recruit.

Participant Information

Eligibility required a chronic rare disease diagnosis, and membership in an online community for that disease. Over 150 people responded to our recruitment notices and we selected 19 participants who represented a range of conditions. Seven participants were male (37%). Participants ranged in age from 20–66 (avg=45, sd=13). Most (53%) were living in the United States (Table 1). All recruitment notices were posted in English. All interviews were conducted in English, except one, which was conducted with the help of a translator to allow the participant to better express himself. We interviewed participants with 13 different conditions (Table 2). Two participants had more than one condition. We identify these participants using M1 and M2. We identify participants having only one condition with S1–S15.

We respected that, especially in the case of rare diseases, it can take a long time to obtain a diagnosis. We included two participants who were undiagnosed because they were active in online rare disease communities and had reported that their doctors agreed that their condition was rare. We identify these participants using U1 and U2.

Procedure

We conducted semi-structured interviews to understand participants' perceptions of their own lives. Most participants undertook a one-hour video interview (using Skype, Google Hangout or Facetime). Some were uncomfortable using video

[3]http://www.rareshare.org/
[4]http://www.rareconnect.org/
[5]http://www.rarediseasefoundation.org/

Continent	Country	Health Care System	N
Asia	Pakistan	Mostly private	1
Australia	New Zealand	Mostly public	1
Europe	England	Mostly public	2
	Ireland	Mostly public	1
	Macedonia	Mostly public	1
	Norway	Mostly public	1
North America	Canada	Mostly public	1
	United States	Mostly private	10
South America	Brazil	Mostly public	1

Table 1. Participant Locations

Disease Name	Description	Categories	N
Chiari Malformation	Dizziness, muscle weakness, numbness, vision problems, headache, balance problems	Brain Diseases	1
Ehlers-Danlos Syndrome (EDS)	Symptoms range from mildly loose joints to life-threatening complications	Connective Tissue Diseases	1
Congenital Anosmia	Lifelong inability to smell	Ear, Nose & Throat Diseases	3
Familial Amyloid Polyneuropathy (FAP)	Loss of sensation in the extremities. The autonomic and central nervous systems may be affected.	Nervous System Diseases	1
Hereditary Angioedema (HAE)	Recurrent episodes of severe swelling (e.g. the limbs, face, intestinal tract, and airway)	Immune System Diseases	1
Hereditary Spastic Paraplegia (HSP)	Increased muscle stiffness and weakness of the legs leading to difficulty walking	Musculoskeletal Diseases	1
Inclusion Body Myositis (IBM)	Progressive muscle inflammation and muscle weakness	Musculoskeletal Diseases	4
Kallmann Syndrome (KS)	Delayed puberty, abnormal development of secondary sex characteristics, and infertility	Reproductive Diseases	2
Morgellons	Abnormal skin sensations, co-existing psychiatric conditions, fibres in affected skin areas	Behavioural and Mental Disorders	1
Multifocal Motor Neuropathy (MMN)	Weakness in hands/lower arms, cramping, involuntary contractions/twitches, wasting affected muscles	Nervous System Diseases	2
Ocular Cicatricial Pemphigoid (OCP)	Chronic cicatrizing conjunctivitis. Can also affect skin/mucous membranes	Skin Diseases, Eye Diseases	1
Systemic Capillary Leak Syndrome (SCLP)	Fluid/proteins leak from capillaries resulting in dangerously low blood pressure	Blood Diseases	1
Wilson Disease	Excessive copper accumulation, leading to kidney, brain, and eye damage	Kidney/Urinary Diseases, Digestive Diseases	1

Table 2. Participant Diseases. (Note that two participants had multiple conditions, and two participants were undiagnosed)

conferencing technology, so we conducted six interviews by phone and two via instant message. We began with an informed consent process and preliminary demographic questions. The main interview was divided into four topics: experience living with the condition (When/how did you first start to notice the condition? How did you arrive at your current diagnosis? What does a good/bad day look like? How does it impact your day to day life?), relationships and support (What medical support do you get for the condition? Are you satisfied with it? How does this influence your relationship with friends or family? Do you receive support from elsewhere?), use of technology and information management (What, if anything, do you bring to medical appointments? What do you do with records or information you receive from your doctor? Do you conduct research about your condition? If so, what sources do you use? Do you find them easy to understand?), and sensemaking (How well do you feel you understand your condition? Has that changed since you were diagnosed? What do you do if you have a question or concern about your condition?). We relied on an interview guide to ensure coverage of all relevant areas, but allowed the participants' responses to guide the flow of the interview. After the interviews concluded, three participants emailed additional thoughts, which were added to their transcripts. Quotes from these additions are identified with asterisks in this paper.

Analysis

In addition to the two instant message transcripts, we transcribed the 17 interview recordings. We analysed these documents using inductive qualitative methods [29]. Three authors separately developed a set of codes based on the interview transcripts and discussed them. Each author iterated on these themes several times until converging on a set of common codes. We finalised the codes, and used them to analyse each transcript. Because of the highly sensitive nature of the interviews, all participants were given the chance to review this paper before publication to ensure they were comfortable with the content. None requested changes to this publication.

FINDINGS

Participants' conditions pervaded many aspects of their lives, and having a rare disease put them in a unique position. S13 describes the experience as *"Rare World. It's very difficult. The receptionist doesn't understand, the doctor doesn't understand. No one's heard of it. It's a really strange spot to be in."* In this section, we discuss challenges participants faced in these different aspects of their lives, and strategies they employed to overcome them.

Role As Friends

Participants varied widely in how much they shared with their friends about their experiences. Several spoke of the challenge of communicating their experiences when their diseases were both invisible and unfamiliar to others. S11 said, *"There's nothing to see. Nobody's ever heard of it. I mean, if I said I had Multiple Sclerosis everybody would know what I was talking about and they would know what to expect... It's not obvious that there is anything wrong with me at all. So I think that some people think that maybe I'm putting them on a bit."* U1 told people she had a common condition, because it was easier for them to understand. *"It's easiest just to say Lupus than anything else because people can wrap their heads around that."* Some participants had friends who tried to be supportive, but were not helpful. S13 said, *"A lot of friends would be like, 'Well just call another doctor', 'Just make an appointment with another one', 'Well, you just go tell them this.' 'You tell them you've got to do this'. I'm like, 'You don't understand, I can't find anybody else that will take me.'"*

Some participants found that, throughout the process of diagnosis and treatment, they saw who their true friends were, and that some friends handled the change in friendship better than others. S12 said, *"Some want to be there for you, but they are so scared that they don't even know how to talk to you. Then you find the friends who ... come out of the woodwork when you don't know what to do ... When shit hit the fan, some of the people who you thought would really be there actually weren't."* Several admitted to downplaying their illnesses. U1 explained, *"beyond my true true inner circle of friends ... I don't tell people. The most you'll hear from me is 'I've a little bit of arthritis.'"* S3 downplayed her own symptoms, but turned to her friends for additional support after her son was born with the same condition. *"I never complained about it because it was like a part of me and 'Okay, that's who I am.' [My friends] never realised that it can be life-threatening. When I started my fight for my son, and when I called them [for support] they would say 'We can't come because we have to go shopping' and 'we can't come because we have to go here and there.' And then I said, 'I'm having this life struggle for my baby. You guys are my friends, I expect you there.' ... So they were a little slow in understanding how important this was but it's because I never made a big fuss about it. It's who I am."*

Having a rare disease also impacted the experience of forming new relationships. S3 had previously dated people that were uncomfortable with her condition. *"But you have to tell them at the beginning. You can't go on lying to them and not telling them. When they fall in love, what are you going to do? Say, 'Okay, now, I was kidding. I have this rare disease.'"* U1 had similar experiences until she met her husband because her condition did not have a clear diagnosis or treatment.

Role As Family Members

Very few participants had friends that they considered really supportive and helpful; they relied primarily on family members for support, since family members were better able to understand what they were experiencing. Although grateful for this support, participants worried about the impact of their conditions on those around them, especially when participants did not have the disease when they first met their partners. S5 explains, *"I feel sorry for [my wife] because she has to take care of a husband who is in much worse shape than her ... So now she's had to cope with a husband who's lost a lot of his abilities and she's done very well with it ... I'm sure she doesn't like it but what are you going to do? I mean, you know, that's what marriage is about in a lot of ways."* S6, on the other hand, felt she needed support from her husband, but he was not accepting enough to be helpful. She asked him to read a book about living with her condition, but he told her he did not want to have to think about it. She said, *"Earlier I just had to tell him, 'You can stay in denial all you want to, but when I say I need you to do something ... you just have to do it.' And for a long time he used to say things like ... 'Do you really need that cane?' And I said, 'Yes I do. Stop asking me questions like that.'"*

Beyond problems with romantic partners, a genetically transmitted disease added further complications; participants who passed their conditions on to their children faced unusual challenges. Some made great sacrifices to ensure their children received necessary care — even putting their own lives at risk. S3 explained, *"I buy [medicine] for my son because our medical fund ... does not cover the medicine. So I actually have to smuggle it from other countries. For my son, one shot is around [€600 or $800] ... so I have to have three or four vials of the medicine. And I'm keeping it only for my son because I don't earn that much money that I can have a shot for me. So it's on destiny whether I will live another day."*

Role As Advocates and Patients

Participants spoke frequently of needing to advocate for themselves and for others with their conditions. Particularly in countries with predominantly public health systems, participants worked to improve access to medication. S2 described, *"the associations [for rare diseases] are united and are pressuring the government ... Health is a duty from the government and a citizen's right, but there are a lot of things that we can't reach, like expensive medications, so we need to sue for them, and this is a huge frazzle. So, we are trying to approve some laws in the [government] for this kind of medication to start to be available for the population without needing to go through the justice system to win them."* S3 was similarly engaged in advocacy and awareness campaigns, explaining, *"We can climb mountains. We can have children. We can live 100 lives. We can live 100 years. All we need is medicine."*

In addition to advocacy to governments and the general public, participants needed to advocate for themselves when dealing with medical professionals. Many told of times they felt their care was poorly handled by physicians who were ill informed about their conditions. *"I just hope and pray that, if I have an attack, what happens at the hospital is that they listen. We did have an incident where ... they tried to tell me I had a tummy bug and it wasn't until I actually passed out lying down that then they thought, 'Okay, we need to start listening to this person.'"* (S14) Such experiences often lead patients to seek replacement doctors. Not all patients had the option to simply switch doctors if they are unhappy, however, because some doctors were not willing to treat unfamiliar diseases, and health insurance or government regulations further limited options. S13 explained, *"I had to suck it up and go back because no one would take me. You'd call them, you'd tell them what you've got and they look it up, they'd say, 'Oh, no, I'm sorry we don't treat that.' I heard that over and over and over again. But I had to suck it up and go back, because no one else would take me."* S6 described how she tried to set the tone with her doctor right from the beginning. *"I just let him know right away that I was going to ask questions, I was going to read, I would come and talk to him about anything I wanted to try. And I think I kind of let him know that I was really going to be active in my care and he could either get used to it or I might move on."*

Some patients worked to reduce their reliance on doctors. S3 believed that *"Nobody wants to treat you because they know you will probably be the only patient with that rare disease that they are going to meet. So they're not very interested and motivated in working with you."* After she and her son vacationed in a different country where several doctors refused to treat them, she learned to administer shots herself. *"They were all like, 'We don't know what it is. We don't want to take this risk. So go away. We have other problems, other patients.' So I told them, 'Okay, go on Google and Google it.' 'No, no, go to somebody else's door.' So we lost a lot of hours. My son had this vomiting episode and it was very scary to have him in the car and going around . . . to find a doctor that is going to be brave enough to give him those shots. And that's when I said 'Okay, I'm going to learn to give myself the shot.'"* S3 did eventually find a doctor who was willing to treat her and her son, and like many other participants, spoke highly of doctors who, although unfamiliar with a rare condition, were willing to take the time to learn. She said, *"She had this purple hair and I thought she was a student because she didn't look very official to me. And she came with a cup of coffee and she sat down and she read the leaflet that is in the medicine . . . And she said, 'Okay, this is the first time that I am in this situation, but in the next two hours I'm going to learn everything about it.' . . . She believed me. She gave him the shot. She kept us there for two hours . . . and in the meanwhile she was on Dr. Google and she Googled it."*

While most participants had to advocate for themselves, when U2's doctors said her symptoms were psychosomatic, she had to enlist her friend's and professor's help before her doctor would take her off a medication, *"finally after six months I got my instructor and a friend to write letters, and then they commented changes they had seen in me and then the doctors told me to stop that medicine right away."* For many participants there was tension between advocating for yourself and becoming your own doctor. S13 stated, *"[The doctors] think you're crazy, like 'Oh, you don't know.' And so I think that's probably a key thing right there is you have to have sense enough to not diagnose yourself. There's a line. But you have to have sense enough to know when to keep pushing. 'cause I know some people are like, 'Oh, well I read it on the Internet', and that's it. I don't ever want to be that person, but I do want to be that person who says, 'Well I read this and I thought about this, and I just wanted to run it past you, wanted to know what you thought.'"* It is worth noting that this same participant nevertheless maintained a strong distrust of doctors. *"I was going to these doctors that I didn't trust; they didn't act like they knew what they were doing. And I would give them tests. They didn't know it, but I would ask them things like 'How do you know that this is an allergy?', and they'd say 'Well, we don't have really any way of knowing.' 'Yes you do!'"* S2 also expressed an attitude of knowing more than his doctor. *"We call it 'medical ego'. Some doctors think that they are superiors or gods, so, they don't admit that the patient knows more than them."* U2 began actively researching her symptoms after her doctor said her symptoms were all in her head and she wanted to *"prove him wrong."*

Role As Record Keepers

Because people with rare diseases often see numerous specialists, the amount of medical records can quickly multiply. Some participants kept track of their records for their own use. Due to a series of misdiagnoses and conflicts with doctors, U2 asked for personal copies of her records so she could manage them on her own. She used her lab results to research conditions that could lead to a diagnosis. S11 said she kept a *"vague journal"* of significant occurrences (e.g. bad episodes, cramps) because her symptoms slowly progressed. S13 did not methodologically maintain her records, *"but I try to keep up with like when there is a medication change, because they will always ask you when did you start it, how long were you on it, what was your dosage, and you're like 'I don't know, I can't remember what I did yesterday!'"*

For other participants, their records played a greater role in their interactions with physicians. While S6 kept a spiral notebook for personal use, she also found it helpful when she visited her doctor. *"When I first went to see the neurologist, I had this little book with me and he said 'What is that?' And I said, 'Well, this is my little book where I write down what you tell me to do, or changes that we make.' And he said, 'Oh you won't need that. We keep charts of everything and blah blah blah'. Then he started asking me all these questions, 'When did you do this? When did you do that?' So I just kind of whipped my little book out and I said, 'Okay, let me just look at my little book and I'll tell you.' It was really kind of funny."* U1 described her *"medical résumé,"* a technique she picked up from her parents who were both medical doctors. *"When I was a very young child . . . [my mother] would just hand that to the doctor. We would go in to see a specialist or an expert and she would just immediately, first thing, hand the résumé to the doctor and say, 'Read this first before we start. You might as well just read this. I'm a medical doctor, here's her medical summary, it's on two pages. Read this first and then we'll start the appointment.' And I saw the power in that . . . As I aged, I started maintaining it myself."* She further explained, *"I call it speaking surgeon-ese. The surgeons speak in very bullet point kind of language, so a patient has to get used to boiling things down to one or two sentences — to speaking in surgeon-ese, bullet-ese."*

Similar to a medical résumé, S8 made *"business cards"*. *"I've had these cards made up through the myositis association. It looks like a little gift card. It's got your name on the front . . . It tells you what to do about the disease and it's one of the greatest tools to have because when I go somewhere and if something happens to me, I just give them that card. And they've got everything there that they need."* In addition to using these cards to communicate with physicians, S8 uses them to connect with other patients for support. *"I give them to everybody actually. I left a stack of them in the physical therapy department because they had said I was their first patient with this and then I think they had two more that were diagnosed with it. So I left my card there and I was like, 'You know, if they need to talk or whatever, here's the card and I would be happy to talk to them.'"*

Role As Copers

The interview data reflects a wide range of attitudes and emotions; it was common that participants experienced anger and fear, as well as acceptance and even gratitude. Many discussed the depression they experienced, and some strategies they use to stay positive. Several discussed learning to accept their new circumstances. S5 chose to make the most of his time while he was able, since his physical condition was likely to worsen, *"I do a lot of things now. I play golf. I travel quite a bit with my wife because we know that at some point in time I won't be able to travel so much. So we kind of compress some of the plans that we might have had into a shorter time span because we don't have as much time as we'd like."* S12 also talked about learning to accept his condition, *"I do yoga. I meditate. I try to keep myself busy . . . I have realised that for whatever reason, this is a part of my story. I am walking with this. But I can't let it overcome me. And it is easy to tell you, but not easy to practice."*

Balancing a positive attitude with the negative emotions was a constant process for participants. *"I have this little mantra that if I'm in pain, I'm alive. So that's sort of how I try and twist that off, I suppose. I try to be really positive about myself. It's hard but I have a physical disability now and it does stop me from doing things."*(S4) Some participants held a sense of optimism, *"It was a big thing to understand and it sounded scary. And now I've realised, in me at least, it's going to be a lot slower progression than I originally thought and that I can keep it at bay a bit with treatment."* (S11)

Maintaining this optimism was challenging sometimes. S11 said*, *"There does not seem to be any chance that the outlook will change. No one is interested in rare diseases. They are not economically viable . . . I'm not holding my breath. No one seems to know the mechanism for MMN. So I watch my kids. That is the worst thing."* Participants were concerned about the progression of the condition and the availability of a cure. Even if no cure is possible, some participants hoped there would be more information available, *"I hope that at least. . . they'll be able to tell me why. So the biggest thing for me isn't to be able to smell, I just want to know why."*(S1)

Participants found comfort in knowing they could have worse diseases, *"I always tell people it's not great having KS, but there's people with a lot worse"*(M2). S5 and S12 both had conditions that are commonly misdiagnosed as ALS. S5 initially considered ALS to be one of many possible diagnoses, but it was ruled out fairly quickly. He said, *"At that point I immediately felt better because ALS is going to kill you pretty quickly. So there was a certain you know, 'Wow, goodie! I'm going to make it here for a while!'"* S12 was misdiagnosed with ALS for almost a full year before arriving at his current diagnosis. *"So when they tell you that you have that disease, they are pretty much saying that you're getting ready to die because most people don't make it past two years . . . That was a really bad trip. You have to deal with this huge problem all of the sudden. [When I was diagnosed with MMN instead] I was very happy. They pretty much lifted a curse off me. They told me that there's a chance you'll live your whole life."*

Role As Researchers

Participants took an active role in seeking out information about their diseases. Participants relied not only on their peers' first-hand experiences, but also turned to scientific literature for answers. Participants found academic papers through searches of Google and Google Scholar. Some participants were successful in learning about their conditions through their research. S3 described how, *"Dr. Google helped a lot because I Googled it a lot. Actually it was Google that helped me finding the medicine in the first place because no one in [my country] have ever took care of us or ever told us that actually there is a cure, because it is very expensive."*

Most participants, however, found that the information they wanted was not available. S11 explained, *"I've looked at a lot of things online...there only seems to be a very limited amount of treatments...So there's not an awful lot to look up really and no one knows what causes it anyways."* S14 felt that she understood it as well as she could, given that there was little information about it. *"I don't know what triggers it and they don't know what triggers it. And they don't know what stops it and I don't know what stops it. So what's there to know?"* U1 also felt that she understood things as well as she could, given the limited information available. *"I don't believe anybody, even the experts really have a handle on what my disease is, or what exactly is going wrong in my immune system . . . You're not going to get direct answers to your questions. . . sure, I wish I could go to some magical leprechaun and say okay, sit down with me, here's pencil and paper, draw for me exactly what's wrong with my immune system and how I can fix it. You're not going to get that. You're not going to get answers to the questions you really want answered."*

Many participants described themselves as more research literate than the general population. Twelve participants cited a reason for their knowledge or a connection to someone with a medical background - their pharmacist friend, geneticist father, researcher parents, or past career as a phlebotomist. One participant worked as a nurse for many years, while another had two parents who were both medical doctors. Some participants had less directly applicable medical background, but clung to what science background they did have. *"I present professional development to teachers for elementary science, so I know science."*(S13)

Role As Peer Supporters

Participants used online communities as a way of sharing research findings and trading resources and support. A few participants also participated in in-person groups, or had encountered other people with their diseases at symposia, conferences, or medical associations. Participants actively sought out others with whom to connect, explaining that they felt helped by *"that instant connection, and knowing you're in company who have gone through the same thing"*(M2)

Online communities were mainly used to ask questions of people with similar experiences and trade tips. Many felt that their peers were a better source of information than their doctors, who did not know or were not prepared to discuss what they wanted. S6 explained, *"None of the doctors really address . . . what you need to manage your day. So you have to rely on somebody else who has walked those steps or similar."* Sometimes participants shared tips in the groups, often in response to someone else's question. S5 explained, *"I will pipe in and say 'Well here's what I ran into and I did this about it.' ... I had to have a feeding tube and I couldn't eat. Well, turns out the feeding tube is a pain in the ass because you have to do something with it when you're not using it. And women end up tucking it in their bras, but men, you know, I ended up clipping it to my shirt... And then I saw issues like that on the Facebook thing and I typed in and said 'Here is what I did. Here is what I learned. You might want to try this.'"*

Participants who connected with others through online communities were unanimously positive about the benefits this provided. Many spoke of how this helped them feel less alone, *"It is amazing to hear other people with the same thing because when I was diagnosed they told me there was only 60 other cases in the whole world. But of course there's certainly a lot more than that."* (S14) S5 agreed, *"You sometimes think you're alone. If you have a problem and you start talking to people who have the same problem or a similar problem then all of a sudden you feel better about it, because all of the sudden you understand you're not alone."* S13 even described how excited she was the first time she met someone with the same condition. *"I'm like a child. I'm like 'I have a friend!' and she's the same way... She will email me and say, 'Have you ever had this? Have you ever had that?'"* Since there are a small number of, if any, people with the same disease locally, many people with rare diseases turn to the global community for connections. The international nature of these online communities was both a benefit and a barrier for participants. For S2, language was a barrier — he found it difficult to communicate with other people. For S8 however, the international community was a benefit, since it gave her access to research from other countries. *"I'm always online looking up different things. I just want to be informed... I know that Australia is doing an awful lot of research... the United States isn't really doing the kind of research that they are in Australia."*

Privacy was a concern to participants as well. S13, for instance, was hesitant to use a Facebook group because, *"there are platforms that you would want to say 'Hey, I've got this and here's what I deal with.' and there are others you don't. So it's for that reason that I think a lot of people are shy about it, or they're not technologically savvy, or they don't want to air their personal business."* There was concern from participants that their information was being seen by *"snake oil types that prey on desperate people and will give them all this information about how they're going to cure them and make them better and I hate those kind of people. I just really wish they would go away, but unfortunately they don't, they just get worse and worse."* (S10)

Despite these privacy concerns, participants who used Facebook groups had more positive experiences than those who used the rare disease specific online communities. Participants reported that there was little activity on these communities; we observed this throughout our recruitment process too. Most participants from these separate sites had recently registered and were disappointed by the lack of activity. M1 posted a question and did not receive any responses, *"Nobody said a word. And it isn't about me; it's just that no one is saying anything. In many communities there are one or two very active people, but relatively little activity from other members. I think there is one person who answers all of the questions for them, so I decided not to get involved with that."*

DISCUSSION

Many of the issues uncovered in our study are extreme examples of what has been seen with more common diseases. Participants expressed concerns about communicating their disease to their friends and family, and were worried about care network fatigue. We draw from literature on older adult care networks to provide recommendations on expanding this care network to reduce care network fatigue. Participants also discussed their relationship with their doctor as being particularly challenging; we identify several approaches taken in prior research and discuss how they can be extended to apply to rare disease populations.

We also found that people with rare diseases faced unique challenges that differ from previous studies of chronic illness populations. Where previous studies have encouraged researchers to focus on the whole person outside of just the disease, participants saw themselves as representatives of their disease and considered it to be part of their identity. We also found that unlike prior research, separate online communities were not effective at engaging participants.

Expanding the Care Network

Participants spoke a great deal about the toll their conditions took on relationships. It was difficult for participants to form new relationships, and it was also difficult for existing relationships to adjust to the change in dynamics following a diagnosis. Participants were frustrated by the challenges of trying to communicate what they were going through to those around them, but also worried about the fatigue their experiences were causing their informal caregivers.

This care network fatigue is something that technology can help to address. Consolvo et al. [6] describe care networks comprised of many different people (family, friends, neighbours, etc.) who play diverse roles in the care of older adults. For people with rare diseases, technology is likely to be used not so much to coordinate this care (as in [6]), but rather to communicate about these rare diseases, thereby helping to increase the size of the care network, and to reduce the burden and fatigue placed on each caregiver. **We encourage HCI researchers to design for a slow discovery process through which people with rare diseases can disseminate information about their conditions** so that their friends and family members can slowly transition from a general level of awareness (understanding what the condition is, building empathy) to a specific level of understanding (how to be helpful). This would help to gradually bring more trusted people into the care network and reduce care network fatigue.

Liu et al. [17] found that people with chronic illnesses (HIV, diabetes, and cancer), used video blogs to educate viewers about their conditions and share their own experiences in a diary-like format. This strategy could also benefit people with rare diseases as a way of helping them communicate their experiences to others. In fact, many of the experiences of people with rare diseases are extremely unique and engaging. This format could also be useful to trade tips and tricks. Participants expressed that some of their friends wanted to be helpful, but did not know how. Technology can facilitate the sharing and navigation of this information, mindful that there are likely to be case-specific limits to the extent of information deemed necessary for adequate helping. Our study draws attention to carefully balance a potential friend's informational needs with the individual's dignity and right to privacy.

A new diagnosis can cause a quick shift in the dynamics of an existing relationship — people are rapidly forced into caregiving roles they had not anticipated. S6's husband reacted to the role change by going into "complete denial," which was frustrating for S6. This story of a primary caregiver in denial, when considered in light of the higher divorce rates [8, 30] for couples where one person has a chronic illness, suggests that **we need to investigate how to help caregivers accept a new diagnosis and work towards providing them with the ability to catch up when they are ready.**

It's Who I Am

One notable difference between people with rare diseases and people with more common chronic illnesses involves their self-perceptions in relation to their conditions. Recent work in the CHI community has encouraged us to think about people as people instead of as patients, emphasising their humanness rather than their disease [1, 11, 19, 21]. To the contrary, however, participants in our study, regularly made statements saying, *"It's who I am."* (S3) or *"This is part of my story."*(S12). They spoke of themselves as ambassadors, as if they could not be understood apart from their medical conditions. This diversity of views affords the research community opportunities to use technology in a way that not only encourages people with rare diseases to think of themselves as whole people, distinct from their diseases, but also facilitates the exploration of multiple senses of self [33], particularly when rare disease communities are couched in larger social networks with mixed audiences and collapsed contexts [4, 35]. We can also leverage technology to support these individuals as advocates and help them to achieve the public awareness they are working towards.

Social media is a free mechanism with relatively low overhead and huge potential to enhance awareness of rare diseases. It is worth noting that increased awareness of rare diseases can sometimes invite unwanted comparisons with other, more common diseases. The ALS Ice Bucket Challenge, for example, has come under criticism because, although amyotrophic lateral sclerosis (ALS) is a terrible disease, it is rare and does not impact many people. Some have argued that more attention and money should be given to diseases impacting larger populations [2]. **We must investigate mechanisms people use for advocacy outreach, public response to these initiatives, and ultimately how the initiative improves the initial outreach aims** so that we can assist small groups, such as those with rare diseases, effectively and ethically raise awareness.

Leveraging Existing Platforms

We found that disease-specific types of community that have the been the subject of prior work (e.g. [11, 24, 27]) were not actively used by people with rare diseases because it is extremely difficult to achieve the critical mass necessary for these communities to be successful; rare diseases, by definition, involve small numbers of people. **We must design ways to integrate communities into platforms that people are already using to reach people with rare diseases and build that critical mass.** It may be possible to address the privacy concerns expressed by participants in our study, through closed social media groups, although [24] found that private mechanisms within social media sites were not enough. Text message based interventions, as in [36], may assuage these concerns and are worth further exploration. However, it is important to balance this desire for privacy with the desire for awareness about the condition; a possible solution might be a private platform with options to share to more public-facing platforms.

Patient-Provider Relationship

The patient-physician relationship was a major source of complaints, frustrations, and stress for participants. They reported physicians not believing them, not knowing about their diseases, not being willing or able to take time to learn about their diseases, or not being willing to treat someone with a condition with which they were unfamiliar. Especially in emergency situations, these challenges can lead to serious if not lethal health consequences. However, technology can be valuable to enable physicians to (1) more clearly differentiate empowered patients from obsessive hypochondriacs, and (2) quickly learn about unfamiliar conditions and trust the information.

Past studies of chronic illnesses populations have encouraged HCI communities to consider patients as "experts", especially in the day-to-day management [1, 19, 21]. In cases of rare diseases, the line between considering a patient as empowered and an expert and giving too much weight to someone's psychosomatic concerns is a very thin and dangerous one. If doctors are unfamiliar with the presenting symptoms of a condition, and unable to easily diagnose them, they may assume such patients have been heavily influenced by things they have read online. They are challenged to distinguish those with legitimate, but unusual complaints from those whose symptoms are purely psychosomatic, imagined, or fabricated. Technology can help make this distinction. **People could leverage technology to provide their doctors with evidence to support the diagnostic process.** For example, an individual with OCP could use photographs of the eye collected over time to observe the effectiveness of treatment. Kientz et al. [15] adopted similar approaches in their design of technologies to evaluate treatments for children with autism and help their caregivers communicate. Applying Kientz et al.'s approach to rare diseases may hold promise as an area of further study.

There is also a difference between doctors seeing patients as experts and patients seeing themselves as experts. **We can design technology that leverages the patient's perception of herself as intelligent and knowledgeable to encourage**

the adoption of new technologies and compliance with disease management practices. Participants often referred to their own medical or research background or to someone they knew who was medically knowledgeable, which indicated it was important to them to be perceived as intelligent and as experts in their own situations. Past studies of end-stage renal disease patients [26] showed similar results — participants were proud of their ability to use scientific terms, and Siek et al. recommended this eagerness be leveraged to get patients to adopt technologies.

Researchers create technologies to manage health information that focuses on the patient as the information repository [16, 22, 25]. We agree that putting patients at the centre of this information would be appropriate here as well. Participants in our study were, for the most part, highly motivated and engaged in the management of their own health. People with rare diseases, in particular those active in online communities, represent a population that is highly motivated to try new approaches and put forth effort if there are benefits to be gained. This differs from studies of chronic illness patients and data enthusiasts, which have revealed a resistance to self-tracking that requires too much effort from patients (e.g. [18, 28]). Of course, this is not to say that technology should be needlessly complicated, but there are clues that people with rare diseases may be willing to tolerate additional burden for greater returns. Putting patients at the centre of managing their medical information empowers them to feel in control.

We need to take these patient-centred information repositories a step further, enabling patients to convey knowledge about their illnesses to health professionals, and enabling health professionals to quickly learn about new illnesses from authoritative sources. **We recommend a physician-endorsed personal health record that provides a quick overview of the illness, patient care, and sources for more information.** Since the information would come from multiple sources — especially the patients — this would involve connected personal health records where people with rare diseases would use their online networks to find physicians who are trained in their conditions. These personal health records could generate multiple views depending on the need; the system could provide a layman's overview (like S8's business cards), a quick medical summary (for hospital emergency visits), a "greatest hits" view of the most pertinent information for new doctors (like U1's medical résumé), and the complete history (for deeper discovery). Current personal health records allow for navigation in a few simple ways, but allowing for more tailored information displays would be extremely helpful. We recognise that this notion of a personal health record is fraught with political and cultural challenges that need further investigation, however the growing use of tethered Personal Health Record systems might predict this to be a similarly feasible plan in the foreseeable future.

LIMITATIONS

Our decision to recruit participants through online communities gave us access to a wider range of conditions from different types of health care systems around the world. It also allowed us to explore the benefits those communities provide to people with rare diseases. However, people who are active in online communities tend to be more empowered about their health [5] and so their experiences may differ from less engaged people with rare diseases. Additionally, individuals who did not have access to online communities (either because none exist for their conditions or because they do not have access to technology) may also have a different perspective, since they would need to seek support elsewhere. Because we are interested in sociotechnical interventions, we chose to study individuals who are likely to be early adopters — they are already willing to be helped through technology.

CONCLUSION

We provide the HCI community with a glimpse inside a rare world where people with chronic rare diseases have to take on many roles — from educating to advocating to providing support for people within their immediate and broader community. People with chronic rare diseases are concerned about the toll their disease puts on their caregiver network. They constantly have to educate, advocate, and research their disease to ensure that they can effectively communicate with concerned parties about their illness and treatment. Because these diseases are so rare, there is not always the critical mass of people facing the same battle that is necessary for online health communities, and thus must risk some privacy to connect with people with similar illnesses on popular social media platforms. Some of these findings are similar to what researchers have reported on in common chronic illness populations, however based on the limited knowledge, resources, and support for people with rare diseases, the experiences presented here highlight extreme issues that can be addressed with sociotechnical systems. We expand on the current literature on chronic illness populations by illustrating how people in rare worlds think of themselves and their disease synonymously. We conclude with examples of how we can improve personal health information management for people with chronic illness so that people with rare diseases can efficiently communicate their disease to health professionals — which is imperative during emergency situations. The HCI community can use these results to create the next generation of sociotechnical tools for people with chronic illness to connect, educate, research, and share information with everyone in their care network.

REFERENCES

1. Ballegaard, S., Hansen, T., and Kyng, M. Healthcare in everyday life: designing healthcare services for daily life. In *CHI 2008* (2008), 1807–1816.
2. Belluz, J. The truth about the ice bucket challenge: Viral memes shouldn't dictate our charitable giving, 2014.
3. Bodenheimer, T., Lorig, K., Holman, H., and Grumbach, K. Patient self-management of chronic disease in primary care. *JAMA 288*, 19 (2002), 2469–2475.
4. boyd, d. Faceted id/entity: Managing representation in a digital world. Master's thesis, MIT, 2002.
5. Broom, A. Virtually he@lthy: the impact of internet use on disease experience and the doctor-patient relationship. *Qual Health Res 15*, 3 (2005), 325–345.

6. Consolvo, S., Roessler, P., Shelton, B., LaMarca, A., Schilit, B., and Bly, S. Technology for care networks of elders. *Pervasive Comput. 3*, 2 (2004), 22–29.
7. Gibson, L., and Hanson, V. 'digital motherhood': How does technology support new mothers? In *CHI 2013* (2013), 313–322.
8. Glantz, M., Chamberlain, M., Liu, Q., Hsieh, C., Edward, K., Van Horn, A., and Recht, L. Gender disparity in the rate of partner abandonment in patients with serious medical illness. *Cancer 115*, 22 (2009), 5237–5242.
9. Hartzler, A., and Pratt, W. Managing the personal side of health: how patient expertise differs from the expertise of clinicians. *JMIR 13*, 3 (2011).
10. Huh, J., and Ackerman, M. Collaborative help in chronic disease management. In *CSCW 2012* (2012), 853–862.
11. Huh, J., Patel, R., and Pratt, W. Tackling dilemmas in supporting 'the whole person' in online patient communities. In *CHI 2012* (2012), 923–926.
12. Huh, J., and Pratt, W. Weaving clinical expertise in online health communities. In *CHI 2014* (2014), 1355–1364.
13. Jacobs, M., Clawson, J., and Mynatt, E. My journey compass: a preliminary investigation of a mobile tool for cancer patients. In *CHI 2014* (2014), 663–672.
14. Joinson, A. Looking at, looking up or keeping up with people?: motives and use of facebook. In *CHI 2008* (2008), 1027–1036.
15. Kientz, J., Hayes, G., Westeyn, T., Starner, T., and Abowd, G. Pervasive computing and autism: Assisting caregivers of children with special needs. *Pervasive Comput. 6*, 1 (2007), 28–35.
16. Klasnja, P., Civan Hartzler, A., Unruh, K., and Pratt, W. Blowing in the wind: unanchored patient information work during cancer care. In *CHI 2010* (2010), 193–202.
17. Liu, L., Huh, J., Neogi, T., Inkpen, K., and Pratt, W. Health vlogger-viewer interaction in chronic illness management. In *CHI 2013* (2013), 49–58.
18. MacLeod, H., Tang, A., and Carpendale, S. Personal informatics in chronic illness management. In *GI 2013* (2013), 149–156.
19. Maitland, J., and Chalmers, M. Self-monitoring, self-awareness, and self-determination in cardiac rehabilitation. In *CHI 2010* (2010), 1213–1222.
20. Mamykina, L., Mynatt, E., Davidson, P., and Greenblatt, D. Mahi: investigation of social scaffolding for reflective thinking in diabetes management. In *CHI 2008* (2008), 477–486.
21. Mamykina, L., Mynatt, E., and Kaufman, D. Investigating health management practices of individuals with diabetes. In *CHI 2006* (2006), 927–936.
22. Moen, A., and Brennan, P. Health@ home: the work of health information management in the household (himh). *JAMIA 12*, 6 (2005), 648–656.
23. Newman, M., Lauterbach, D., Munson, S., Resnick, P., and Morris, M. "it's not that i don't have problems, i'm just not putting them on facebook": Challenges and opportunities in using online social networks for health. In *CSCW 2011* (2011).
24. Pang, C. Technology preferences and routines for sharing health information during the treatment of a chronic illness. In *CHI 2013* (2013).
25. Pratt, W., Unruh, K., Civan, A., and Skeels, M. Personal health information management. *Commun ACM 49*, 1 (2006), 51–55.
26. Siek, K., Connelly, K., and Rogers, Y. Pride and prejudice: learning how chronically ill people think about food. In *CHI 2006* (2006), 947–950.
27. Skeels, M., Unruh, K., Powell, C., and Pratt, W. Catalyzing social support for breast cancer patients. In *CHI 2010* (2010), 173–182.
28. Stone, A., Shiffman, S., Schwartz, J., Broderick, J., and Hufford, M. Patient compliance with paper and electronic diaries. *Control Clin Trials 24*, 2 (2003), 182–199.
29. Strauss, A., and Corbin, J. *Grounded theory in practice*. Sage, 1997.
30. Strine, T., Kobau, R., Chapman, D., Thurman, D., Price, P., and Balluz, L. Psychological distress, comorbidities, and health behaviors among us adults with seizures. *Epilepsia 46*, 7 (2005), 1133–1139.
31. Suh, H., Porter, J., Hiniker, A., and Kientz, J. @babysteps: design and evaluation of a system for using twitter for tracking children's developmental milestones. In *CHI 2014* (2014), 2279–2288.
32. Therapies, S. H. G. Rare disease impact report: Insights from patients and the medical community. Tech. rep., Shire Human Genetic Therapies, 2013.
33. Turkle, S. *The second self.* Simon and Schuster, 1984.
34. Unruh, K., and Pratt, W. The invisible work of being a patient and implications for health care. In *Ethnogr Prax Ind* (2008), 40–50.
35. Wesch, M. Youtube and you: Experiences of self-awareness in the context collapse of the recording webcam. *EME 8*, 2 (2009), 19–34.
36. Yun, T., and Arriaga, R. A text message a day keeps the pulmonologist away. In *CHI 2013* (2013), 1769–1778.

Looking for Respite and Support: Technological Opportunities for Spousal Caregivers

Matthieu Tixier, Myriam Lewkowicz
ICD, HETIC, Tech-CICO, Troyes University of Technology, UMR 6281, CNRS
12, rue Marie Curie - CS 42060, 10004 Troyes Cedex - France
{firstname.lastname}@utt.fr

ABSTRACT

Our research aims at informing the design of technological solutions to alleviate the stress resulting from the involvement of spouses of Alzheimer's disease patients as caregivers. For so doing, we have observed and analyzed the different offline solutions that are offered by a healthcare network in the Aube region (North-East of France). We discuss the key factors that we have identified for building an effective support network and identify five perspectives for the development of an online social support platform to lower the burden of spousal caregivers.

Author Keywords

Caregiving; spousal caregivers; respite care services; social support; support groups; Alzheimer's disease.

ACM Classification Keywords

K.4.2 Social Issues; J.3. Life and Medical Sciences, Health;

INTRODUCTION

These last years, the situation of family caregivers (family member who are voluntary taking care of an ailing relative) has begun to concentrate a significant research effort, especially in the CSCW research area [2, 8]; some researchers studied and designed solutions for experience sharing and social support among peers [9] and coordination within the heterogeneous network of professionals who intervene at home [1].

Providing help and alleviating the burden of family caregivers remains a challenge. The impact of an intervention on the health and well-being of family caregivers is hard to evaluate, and is sometimes showing no or tame effects [4]. However, several studies assessing support programs for family caregivers report that multidimensional interventions (mixing training, support groups and day care service, for instance) are the most effective ones [5].

The involvement of family in the care provided to their relatives is important whatever the disease is, but caregivers of people with Alzheimer's disease (AD) are more likely to assist with any activity of daily living. On top of that, the AARP public policy institute report [7] shows that spousal caregivers are at the same time more likely to provide assistance with medical and nursing tasks, less likely to receive support from friends or family and less likely to get support from health care professionals or aides.

In this context, our goal is then to contribute to informing the design of accessible and useful solutions to alleviate stress and increase independency of spousal caregivers. Social support models highlight the informational, emotional, tangible, and appraisal dimensions as components of supportive relations [3]. These dimensions of social support are an interesting starting point for designing technology but they need to be completed by empirical findings on how social support effectively takes place in practice. Our study aims at identifying the sources of respite and support currently found by spousal caregivers of AD patients in their daily life. For so doing, we have followed spousal caregivers of patients suffering from AD who are participating to different respite and support services provided by institutions and associations in their local context. We are thus aiming at designing relevant Information and Communication Technologies (ICT) which can complement the existing local services. In fact, the Internet appears as a promising place for spousal caregivers who are living in rural areas, or who cannot let their spouses alone. The spousal caregivers we met also explicitly mentioned that (1) they encounter issues that they would like to discuss more frequently than the activities that are planned; (2) some of the subjects they would like to speak about are difficult to discuss face to face and that they would feel less ashamed discussing that online, using a pseudonym; (3) when the AD will evolve, getting around with their ailing spouse and staying connected with their local respite and support network will be more and more difficult.

In this paper, we start presenting the field study we have conducted. We then discuss the factors we have identified that make the observed local network of services effectively

CHI 2015, April 18 - 23 2015, Seoul, Republic of Korea Copyright 2015 ACM 978-1-4503-3145-6/15/04...$15.00
http://dx.doi.org/10.1145/2702123.2702563

supportive. This allows us to identify five perspectives for the development of an online social support platform to lower the burden of spousal caregivers.

CONTEXT – A HEALTHCARE NETWORK TAKING INTO ACCOUNT FAMILY CAREGIVERS

RéGéMA is a healthcare network embracing gerontology and memory disorders. It was initiated in 2001 by a group of healthcare professionals in response to the numerous problems arising in the diagnosis and management of AD patients in the Aube region (North-East of France). The main purpose of the network is to coordinate the work of the many professionals involved in the care and support of elderly patients. The network is also responsible for informing professionals and the public of memory disorders and their treatment. RéGéMA is coordinated by a psychologist who decided to tackle seriously the burden felt by the family caregivers. She then launched several activities dedicated to providing the family caregivers some support and respite: training sessions, support group meetings, daily respite care services and an innovative community respite care service named "the Bright Spell".

DATA COLLECTION

Since 2008, we followed twenty support group meetings, ran monthly by the RéGéMA healthcare network, in the city of Troyes. Each of the meetings was lasting two hours. We have conducted semi-directive interviews with family caregivers attending the support group meetings. We focus in this paper on five interviews of spouses acting as caregivers. We then conducted 3 half-days shadowing sessions with three regular participants of the support group meetings, each session is lasting at least 3 hours. They are all female, aged between 60 and 65 years old, and take care of their husbands suffering from AD. Two of them live in the suburbs of Troyes and the other one lives in a smaller town. The three couples are mobile and regularly drive to join the different activities of the respite platform. We have conducted three individual semi-directive interviews after the shadowing sessions. These three interviews lasted from one to three hours. We have also joined the community respite care service two times, one morning and one afternoon, conducting observations of the activities of the participants. The participants were composed of 5 couples and one spouse caregiver who had recently placed her husband in an AD care unit. All but one of the caregivers were women. They were aged from 60 to 65. All these observations have been recorded also through field notes. All the observations have been recorded through field notes. The interviews have been recorded and transcribed as well.

KINDS OF SUPPORT AND RESPITE RECEIVED

Training

RéGéMA organizes training sessions for family caregivers where the different health and social professionals who intervene in the disease trajectory (neurologist, psychologist, general practitioner, speech and occupational therapist, social worker, lawyer) present their role, explain how they work and give practical advice about how to deal with patients and solve caregivers' everyday problems. Each session gathers around ten family caregivers. The training courses also provide an opportunity for meeting other people in similar situations. This training is also generally the entry point for caregivers in the use of support and respite services.

Support Group Meetings

RéGéMA runs monthly support groups for spouses and children who act as caregivers in order to provide them with a space where they can talk about their experience and discuss their problems. Two support groups exist for these two kinds of family caregivers, which correspond to common practices. The spousal caregivers' support group exists for about eight years, and mainly includes caregivers who have attended at least one session of RéGéMA training. The way these support group sessions are organized is roughly the same each time: the caregivers meet around a table at the RéGéMA office, where they are served with cakes and drinks, which are sometimes provided by the caregivers themselves. The ensuing discussions are led by the network coordinator (psychologist). She gives everybody an opportunity to speak in turn and dispenses accurate medical information.

Day Care Respite Service

For people living around the city of Troyes, a respite platform is available through the nursing home "la Roseraie". Apart from providing day care services, the respite platform also offers several activities like dance courses, yoga, gym and since this year computer literacy class. These activities are weekly organized. When possible, the care receiver can also take part to the dance or the gym sessions. Besides, the respite platform also offers in-home respite services which consist in professionals' visits for half a day in the home of the patient. The professional caregiver proposes activities and cognitive stimulation programs to the person suffering from memory disorders. During this time, the spousal caregiver can go outside with confidence or just stay at home to do all the things she/he had not the opportunity to do because of caregiving activities.

Community Respite Care Service

The Bright Spell started in June 2013. It is a respite day care service which has been initiated at the demand of four "young" AD spouse caregivers (aged 60-65) who met while taking part in the support group meetings organized by RéGéMA. These four "young" spouse caregivers expressed their frustration regarding the available day care service. They thought it did not fit their situation (even if they managed to use it). In fact, some of them are just retired, and their ailing spouse is still mobile, so they find that the activities offered by the existing day care service (mostly at retirement home) were not adapted. They were worried about their spouse being "alone" with older patients (80-90) with heavier conditions, and having difficulties to develop relationships with participants or interests in the quiet activities offered (e.g. painting, coloring pictures).

The Bright Spell is used in conjunction with the respite platform by the family caregivers we met. It is organized twice a month on Monday at a local retirement home reception and dining room. At the difference of a classic day care services where family caregivers are supposed to leave their spouses for the day, here they stay for the day. In the morning, they are used to stay at the big table and take news from each other.

FACTORS THAT MAKE THE SOCIAL SUPPORT EFFECTIVE IN THIS GROUP

Developing relationships with persons sharing a similar situation

The link between the support group members is their experience of AD from the caregiver's point of view, especially because they feel no-one else can understand what it is like: "If you have not been through it yourself, you cannot understand what it involves" was an expression which cropped up frequently when we met family caregivers. Besides being a spouse of an AD patient, the spousal caregivers we met emphasize the specificity of their situation as "young" family caregivers. They complain about their husband's need for physical and outdoor activities that classical day care services scarcely organize. Among the other possible afternoon activities at the Bright Spell, they mention they appreciate to go outside for a walk when the weather allows it. They exchange news from session to session and they feel understood by the group. One of the family caregivers calls the members of the Bright Spell her "disease friends"

Sharing Experience and Problems

Support group meetings provide a privileged opportunity for sharing practical advice with others. The tips and advice were about problems such as what to do when the patient is wandering around at night, or why, at a certain stage in the disease, it is important to keep the main doors locked at home and sometimes to close the shutters. The time shared at the Bright Spell is also an opportunity to tell the daily problems they encounter in caring for their ailing relative to persons who can understand their situation. They provide advices to each other on how to deal with the care they provide. If nobody has been confronted to a situation, they discuss to try finding possible solutions.

Joining organized activities with the care receiver

At the difference of most of the currently available respite care services, the Bright Spell offers shared activities among the family caregivers and their ailing relatives. Spousal caregivers then contribute into the definition of the activities organized by the Bright Spell as they assume they know which kind of activities could please their ailing relative. This allows them to enjoy respite through a careful balance between activities with and without the care receiver.

Counting on the group

The distributed watch-over provided by the group which meets at the Bright Spell makes possible for spousal caregivers to enjoy respite in presence of the care receivers. They can count on the group to manage the situation if their ailing relative tries to go outside or seems to be in trouble. For instance, one of the Bright Spell spousal caregiver even had a nap while the other participants were doing handwork. She felt confident in leaving her husband to the care of the group members.

Going out of the home

Even if some of the spousal caregivers we met have to drive a long way to join the Bright Spell or the other activities offered by the respite platform (e.g. 40kms for one of the couple), they appreciate to do things outside of their home. They appreciate it so much that they are used to organize trips together between two sessions at the Bright Spell. For instance, the interviewees mentioned they have done picnics during summer; they went to the bowling and invited each other for dinner. They also planned to join a journey to a historic town run by the respite care platform.

DESIGN OPPORTUNITIES

The observation and analysis of the support provided to the family caregivers allowed us to identify five perspectives for the development of an online social support platform to lower the burden of family caregivers.

Acknowledging the specificities of the caregiving situation

The fact that the family caregivers from the Bright Spell claim for their specific needs is illustrating that some dimensions are considered as important in order to be acknowledged as criteria for "sharing a similar situation": the pathology, the relationship with the care receiver (being a child, a spouse, a parent or a friend), the age, and the location. The display of this kind of information on users' profiles, as well as their use in a recommender system, is interesting in order to offer triggers for interacting with peers.

Story and experience sharing

The importance of accounts on personal experience and stories in social support leads us to the idea of a "story and experience sharing" section where an informal caregiver could post a new topic and share her/him story. Other informal caregivers would be enabled to post their personal stories under the same topic. The "story sharing" form will have to encourage reciprocity. Inside a topic, each story could have a dedicated page to underline the personal dimension of such content.

Finding the appropriate respite and support services

Transferring the experience of the Bright Spell in digital applications would be a hard task, and is a clear example of a sociotechnical gap[1] [6]. As it is the case with the Bright Spell and the RéGéMA support group, taking part to a same care service appeared as an entry point for social support exchanges among users which could be continued and sustained through an online platform. Designing relevant online information support to describe and search for such initiatives appears as an essential feature.

Easing participation to offline collective activities

Collective activities, like the trips or lunches the family caregivers have together are an important place for exchanging social support. We then identify as an interesting feature to provide means to propose trips and events to other users for them to join. A digital platform could also be a place to promote local initiatives and associations where family caregivers of patients suffering from AD are welcomed.

Enabling the participation of the care receiver

The Bright Spell illustrates that taking in charge the caregiver apart from her/his ailing relative may be a too narrow view on support and respite, especially when the caregiver is the spouse. Playing simple games or watching TV appeared as important moments for the family caregivers as they enjoy some time with their loved one. This shared focus is often difficult to achieve through conversation due to the cognitive and communication problems related to AD. Thus, providing adapted content through curated Internet video clips or interactive games on a digital platform could enable technology to meet the interest of both sides of the couple and to give opportunity for shared activities. Such content could be the ground for triggering online social support exchanges among users.

DISCUSSION

Through the observation of current support and respite practices and interviews with spousal caregivers of patients suffering from AD, our goal was to develop a better understanding of when and how these caregivers experience relief in their overwhelmed everyday life. Our findings highlight the benefits from taking part to a group as a core source of support. The group of "young" AD spouse caregivers is a mean to participate into activities without excluding the ailing relative and to share the experience of care with persons who understand the situation. These elements challenge us about the role ICT can play to maintain these supportive links when the disease evolves. In fact, this evolution raises the risk for spousal caregivers to be more isolated. Another issue lies in the solutions for enabling spousal caregivers who are not able to build or participate in such a supportive network to be and stay connected through the Internet. The proposed design opportunities are first answers in order to take into account the specific needs of spousal caregivers, while including their ailing relative and through the mobilization of existing local respite and support network(s). This leads us to a promising research challenge related to the mutual benefits between online and offline activities: how could online interaction foster face-to-face activities, or how could support group meetings find an online follow-up for some of the issues debated during the meeting?

[1] *"[the] divide between what we know we must support socially and what we can support technically"*

ACKNOWLEDGEMENTS

We thank the RéGéMA healthcare network and all the participants. This work has been supported by European Union, ANR and national solidarity fund for autonomy through AAL program (project AALI 2012-TOPIC).

REFERENCES

[1] Bossen, C., Christensen, L.R., Grönvall, E., and Vestergaard, L.S. CareCoor: Augmenting the coordination of cooperative home care work. *International Journal of Medical Informatics 82*, 5 (2013), e189–e199.

[2] Christensen, L.R. and Grönvall, E. Challenges and opportunities for collaborative technologies for home care work. *Proc. ECSCW 2011*, Springer (2011), 61–80.

[3] Heaney, C. A., & Israel, B. A. (2002). Social networks and social support. *Health behavior and health education: Theory, research, and practice*, 3, 185-209.

[4] Hinchliffe, A.C., Hyman, I.L., Blizard, B., and Livingston, G. Behavioural complications of dementia—can they be treated? *International Journal of Geriatric Psychiatry 10*, 10 (1995), 839–847.

[5] Maayan, N., Soares-Weiser, K., and Lee, H. Respite care for people with dementia and their carers. In *Cochrane Database of Systematic Reviews*, John Wiley & Sons, Ltd, 1996.

[6] Mark S. Ackerman. The Intellectual Challenge of CSCW: The Gap Between Social Requirements and Technical Feasibility. *Human-Computer Interaction 15*, 2-3 (2000), 179–203.

[7] Reinhard, S. C., Levine, C., and Samis, S. Home Alone: Family Caregivers Providing Complex Chronic Care, Washington, DC: AARP Public Policy Institute, 2012.

[8] Tellioğlu, H., Lewkowicz, M., Pinatti De Carvalho, A.F., Brešković, I., and Schorch, M. Collaboration and Coordination in the Context of Informal Care (CCCiC 2014). *Proc. Companion Publication of CSCW 2014*, ACM Press (2014), 339–342.

[9] Xie, B. Multimodal Computer-Mediated Communication and Social Support among Older Chinese Internet Users. *Journal of Computer-Mediated Communication 13*, 3 (2008), 728–750.

Barriers and Negative Nudges: Exploring Challenges in Food Journaling

Felicia Cordeiro[1], Daniel A. Epstein[1], Edison Thomaz[3], Elizabeth Bales[1,2], Arvind K. Jagannathan[3], Gregory D. Abowd[3], James Fogarty[1]

[1] Computer Science & Engineering
[2] Human Centered Design & Engineering
DUB Group, University of Washington
{felicia0, depstein, lizbales, jfogarty}
@cs.washington.edu

[3] School of Interactive Computing
College of Computing
Georgia Institute of Technology
{ethomaz, arvind.krishnaa, abowd}
@gatech.edu

ABSTRACT
Although food journaling is understood to be both important and difficult, little work has empirically documented the specific challenges people experience with food journals. We identify key challenges in a qualitative study combining a survey of 141 current and lapsed food journalers with analysis of 5,526 posts in community forums for three mobile food journals. Analyzing themes in this data, we find and discuss barriers to reliable food entry, negative nudges caused by current techniques, and challenges with social features. Our results motivate research exploring a wider range of approaches to food journal design and technology.

Author Keywords
Personal Informatics; Food Journals; Barriers; Negative Nudges.

ACM Classification Keywords
H.5.m. Information interfaces and presentation (e.g., HCI).

INTRODUCTION
Food journals are an important method for tracking food consumption and can support a variety of goals, including weight loss, healthier food choices, detecting deficiencies, identifying allergies, and determining foods that trigger other symptoms. Although food journaling is widely considered difficult and has motivated research on easing or even automating entry, little work has empirically documented why it is difficult. As a result, the field is currently missing opportunities for design and technology to improve journaling.

Our work explores key challenges people encounter in food journaling. We conduct a qualitative study combining a survey of 141 current and lapsed food journalers with analysis of 5,526 posts from community forums for three mobile food journals. Analyzing themes in this data, we find and discuss barriers to reliable food entry, negative nudges caused by current techniques, and challenges with social features. Our results support continued research in food journaling, identify specific challenges in current journals, and highlight opportunities to consider a wider range of opportunities in food journal design and technology.

CHI 2015, April 18 - 23 2015, Seoul, Republic of Korea

http://dx.doi.org/10.1145/2702123.2702155

RELATED WORK
Recent years have seen significant research in mobile food journals, which aim to improve entry or feedback relative to traditional paper methods. An early example is PmEB, which demonstrated daily calorie budget feedback computed from a mobile food journal [9]. Siek et al. studied journals for patients with chronic kidney disease, who found barcode and audio-based journals overwhelming [7]. Mamykina et al. developed MAHI, a mobile food journal to aid people with newly diagnosed diabetes in developing reflective analysis skills, essential to successful diabetes management [4].

Given the effectiveness of such systems, additional research has considered the adoption, difficulty, and everyday use of food journals. Helander et al. analyze logs from The Eatery, finding only 3% of 190,000 downloads resulted in a person using the mobile food journal for more than one week [3]. PlateMate examines minimizing burden of entry by using crowdsourcing to obtain nutritional summaries from food photos [5]. Rooksby et al. discuss challenges of personal informatics and argue for considering how tracking is intertwined with everyday life [6]. Grimes and Harper suggest that research should consider the variety of relationships people have with food [2]. Despite such interest in how food journals integrate in everyday life, relatively little is known about specific challenges people experience with food journals. We explore current challenges to inform future contributions in food journal design and technology.

DATA COLLECTION
We surveyed 141 food journalers (47 active, 94 lapsed, 105 female, 36 male, age 19 to 70, mean 34, median 30), recruited from university mailing lists, MyFitnessPal Facebook groups, and FitBit forums, randomly raffling three $20 Amazon gift cards. 117 reported journaling with mobile apps, 23 desktop / website, and 47 using paper (some using multiple methods). We also examined 5,526 posts in 627 threads in community forums for three mobile food journals (MyFitnessPal, FatSecret, CalorieCount). We quote survey respondents as P## and attribute forum posts by community.

Survey respondents answered open response questions about what made journaling difficult and what aspects of journaling they disliked. They next used a seven-point Likert scale to rate the difficulty of journaling meal types (buffet meals, ethnic food, fast food, foods served by friends, foods consumed at parties, home-cooked meals, packaged food, restaurant meals). Lapsed journalers additionally provided open responses explaining why they stopped. Responses were analyzed in an affinity diagram exercise by two members of the team, yielding themes later coded by a third.

We gathered community forum data using provided search interfaces, which allow keyword filtering of threads and posts. We initiated analysis with a set of keyword phrases targeting causes of attrition (e.g., "*stop logging*", "*no fun logging*", "*not working*", "*tired of logging*"). With these initial search phrases, we found posts such as "*It is such a slow and tedious process*" (FatSecret), which gave insight into additional keywords to use in searches (e.g., "*tedious*"). We examined posts using summative content analysis, yielding themes we had not originally specified that were consistent with our survey analysis, as well as an additional theme on challenges in social features of food journals.

RESULTS AND THEMES

Goals Drive Journaling

Journaling can end with a perceived success or at a defined endpoint. Successes included a "*goal weight*" (P46, P52, P53), understanding eating habits "*I had developed a good sense of how many calories are in the different foods I eat and in what proportions I was eating them*" (P68), or learning to make healthier food choices "*I got a grasp on what to eat and how to eat to maintain optimal health*" (P126). Endpoints included identifying a recurring problem "*I was trying to track down migraine triggers. Once we identified several triggers, I stopped*" (P50) and the end of a pregnancy "*I stopped being pregnant. :)*" (P82). Of 94 lapsed journalers, only 22 indicated they no longer needed to journal because they received enough benefit. An additional 12 reported periodic journaling: "*to audit my consumption*" (P85), "*whenever I wanted to lose weight*" (P51). A few reported journaling with no clear goal: "*I wasn't really trying to lose weight or anything but was simply curious about what I ate. Once I got a decent idea of my eating habits, I didn't really feel like continuing to journal*" (P14).

Although some journalers reach their goals or do not have a specific goal, this is a definite minority. The majority report significant challenges, sometimes leading them to abandon journaling altogether. We discuss these challenges in terms of barriers to reliable food entry, negative nudges in current journals, and challenges with social features.

Barriers to Reliable Food Entry

Our forum analysis found the effort required to journal is a major barrier: "*if I hit a rough spot or start regaining some weight I will go back to counting calories. I hate counting it's tedious but yet very important*" (FatSecret). Survey respondents also expressed this, describing food journaling as "*too much effort*", "*time-consuming*", or "*tedious*" (31, 27, 16 respondents). Looking more closely, we unpacked this theme into four barriers to reliable food entry.

What and How Much: Journalers report challenges knowing what and how much to enter in journals designed around detailed entry. P98 summarizes: "*I cook most of my own meals, so it was difficult to estimate the amounts of each ingredient (first, I loosely follow recipes, then I only eat some of what I make at a time), then find the calories (which weren't available for many of the foods I ate)*". Barriers include ingredients (e.g., "*Not knowing the exact ingredients and portions make the logging difficult*" P126, 75 others), their proportions (e.g., "*spaghetti: How much meat? How much oil? Etc…*" P107, 10 others), preparation (e.g., "*It is also difficult to know how things are cooked sometimes, did they use oil? Does that affect the calories?*" P128, 27 others), and then the portion consumed (e.g., "*I have a hard time figuring out portions*" P23, 39 others). Uncertainty regarding any undermines reliability of an entry.

Database Reliability: Many journals use a database to convert entries into calories, other components, or points. These often allow community contribution, with journalers able to publish nutritional entries themselves. Although this can enable a diverse food database, it raises concerns regarding reliability: "*the food database is put together by users, so not all entries can be considered accurate*" (P32), "*sometimes hard to find certain foods, or to know enough about the listing to know if it will be accurate*" (P129).

Databases are quite large, but journalers find categories of food missing. From our forum analysis: "*Hey all. Any tips on how to record foods not found in database? IE made from scratch, bought at a locally owned restaurant, etc. I'm finding it difficult sometimes to find something close and match it up, or to make a guess*" (FatSecret). P2 reported it harder to find healthy foods "*They don't have some of the foods I'd like to enter - like more of the healthy and organic foods.*" P40 found common foods missing "*there are large gaps particularly with foods that are only found in Canada.*"

However, continuing to grow the database presents its own barriers. Journalers report that obtaining many results from a query creates concerns for reliability "*sometimes it was even incorrect or multiple postings with all different information*" (P101), difficulty choosing "*there were too many choices and it was difficult to determine which option was the closest to reality*" (P105), and frustration with apparently irrelevant entries "*I ate some oatmeal and my options for logging it were weird. Oh, was it McDonald's oatmeal? Quaker Instant apple cinnamon oatmeal in a pouch? No. It was normal oatmeal!*" (P1). Food journal databases face a tension between providing desired foods versus overwhelming journalers.

Eating Context: Journalers report barriers entering food from restaurants, prepared by friends, from buffets, and at parties. Part of the challenge is that knowledge barriers are magnified because the journaler did not prepare the food: "*Meals at a restaurant are very difficult because you do not* *know the ingredients*" (P99), "*Foods eaten out were tricky due to the ingredients not being clear*" (P50), "*Calorie databases have some entries for chain restaurants, but finding something that might be similar to a dish at a local restaurant is difficult, if not impossible*" (P137).

Another critical challenge in these contexts is people often consume a variety of food over an extended time. P69 felt it was unreasonable to journal: "*You're simply not going to sit there with each thing you grab and log it*". This leads to delay, which leads to difficulty remembering: "*when I'm eating at a party, or at a buffet I usually eat small amounts of lots of different things. Then when I get back to my apartment and go to log it, I've often forgotten already exactly what I ate, and I'm sure I often miss things.*" (P130) and "*It was hard to log when I wasn't at home because I had to remember to when I got home*" (P112). Despite the always-available nature of mobile devices, contexts in which people eat present significant barriers to in-the-moment journaling practices that mobile journals aim to promote.

Losing the Habit: Simply forgetting to journal is a major barrier to reliable journals, and was the most-cited reason why survey respondents had missed at least one entry. But journalers further report that missed entries can lead them to abandon journaling altogether. In journals that emphasize calories or other summaries of food components, missing an entry means feedback is inaccurate: "*Half of the time, I would just log foods for half the day, so the calories totals were completely off.*" (P137). This can in turn create a feedback cycle that undermines the journaling habit: "*Every time I start I forget one meal or another so it becomes less accurate. Then I just forget completely.*" (P128). P42 noted other factors can lead to breakdowns in her journaling habit "*e.g., due to a hard deadline, travel, holiday season*", and reported "*once the habit is broken…it's hard to start again.*" Journals cannot assume continuous and complete compliance, and should instead support the journaling habit.

Negative Nudges in Current Food Journals

Nudges are features of systems that alter behavior [8]. They are typically designed to promote a desired behavior, but we found examples of unintentional negative nudges in current food journals. Journalers report the design of current journals can encourage behaviors contrary to their goals.

Contrasting Difficulty of Meal Entry: When asked to rate difficulty by meal type, respondents rated packaged food (average: 6.5) and fast food (6.3) as significantly easier to journal than home-cooked meals (4.6), buffet meals (3.7), ethnic food (3.7), restaurant meals (3.6), foods served by friends (3.2), and foods consumed at parties (2.9) (using a mixed-model analysis of variance, with participant as a random effect, applying Tukey's HSD at $p < .05$).

Journalers report databases make packaged and fast food easiest to log, with barcodes further simplifying their entry: "*It was easy to search specific brands*" (P67), "*Fast foods and prepackaged foods have calorie counts readily available*" (P86). In contrast, journalers report difficulty entering homemade food: "*took too much time, hard to track meals that aren't pre-packaged*" (P43), "*a lot of foods are difficult to track without an ingredient list or barcode*" (P45).

Many journals provide recipe builders intended to ease the difficulty of entering homemade food. Journalers were aware of this, but still considered it burdensome to enter homemade food: "*recipe builders took a long time*" (P78), "*If a particular item isn't in my app's database, I would have to deconstruct it into its constituent ingredients and then add those individually.*" (P3), "*I often had to search for lots of individual components, and I wasn't sure of the measurements*" (P47). An additional challenge with recipes is that journalers report they do not support variation in preparation: "*Even with options to create a meal and save it for later. Most of my cooking isn't that consistent.*" (P101).

This difficulty contrast creates a dilemma: "*Prepackaged meals were the easiest because of bar codes but those aren't healthy*" (P123). This can undermine the journaling habit: "*I usually stop [journaling] shortly after I made a wrap or some other type of sandwich that has a significant number of components that it would be difficult to measure and manually add*" (P105). Journalers also reported it can nudge them to eat contrary to their goals, including eating less variety "*I could make life easier by eating the same things regularly*" (P97), limiting food choice "*I just avoided eating things that were hard to log*" (P132), and avoiding healthier foods "*the time it took entering it manually made eating fresh and healthy less appealing. Easier to scan a code on some processed stuff and be done with it*" (P101). Although the mindfulness created by journaling can lead to healthier choices, the difficulty of food entry in current designs is also negatively impacting journaler food choices.

Judgment and Choosing Not to Journal: Food journalers report feelings of shame, judgment, or obsession associated with current designs. P6 reported journaling "*made me feel guilty sometimes*", while P27 noted a lack of positive feedback: "*I always felt guilty when I ate too much, and there wasn't that much pride when I was under my goal.*" Others described not wanting to journal foods they considered unhealthy or that may put them over a calorie goal: "*Sometimes I feel like not logging things because I know it's really unhealthy.* =(" (P117). Journalers report abandoning journaling due to these feelings: "*I stopped because I didn't feel a need to keep it up. I did not want to obsess about food*" (P13), "*it made me too focused and obsessive about what I was eating*" (P70), "*I think I'm obsessing about every calorie and I'm either not eating enough or eating too much*" (MyFitnessPal). P113 was especially concerned: "*it was more of an on the way to an eating disorder thing than anything else (tried to keep calories extremely low)*". Although in-the-moment feedback can be powerful, designs that create feelings of judgment can be self-defeating.

Stigma and Journaling: Journaling often takes place in the presence of others, and P37 noted "*it's not always that discreet*". Many did not want friends and colleagues to know they were tracking food "*I think I was hesitant to do the logging if not alone*" (P30) and were afraid to ask the ingredients in food "*I had more of a problem with eating out at a friend's house because I didn't want to ask for ingredients or mention that I was logging calories*" (P11). This can lead people to abandon journaling: "*I also felt embarrassed to do it in front of friends so I stopped*" (P27). Journalers also report being nudged to avoid social situations: "*It discourages you from eating out or at a friend's, even if it is healthy*" (P42). Journalers can struggle with a perceived stigma around tracking, undermining not only the reliability of their journal but also their goals and motivation.

Challenges in Social Features

The previous challenges emerged in both datasets, but our community forum analysis additionally surfaced challenges in provided social features. Journalers turn to these for social support "*please if you want to motivate me and help me out with comments and suggestions, add me as a friend*" (MyFitnessPal), and some find that support "*I have found that having friends on MFP has helped me, just having someone say good job when I do my exercise or finish under my calorie goals*" (MyFitnessPal). But others find support never materializes "*I have seen lately that I will post my diary or my progress or even some troubles and no one will comment back. How is that going to encourage me to keep going when I have no support*" (MyFitnessPal), that their motivation is undermined as friends stop journaling "*Although I used to log frequently in the past, most of my connections have stopped logging in or are no longer members, so I recently emptied my 'buddy list'*" (FatSecret), or they are discouraged by the success of others "*I hate coming on to forums and seeing how much people have lost and I have made barely any progress at all.*" (FatSecret). Embarrassment leads people to omit entries or disable sharing: "*I have logged food on here before but I get embarrassed so I made it private so only I can see and told myself be honest with yourself*" (MyFitnessPal). Social features can both support or undermine journalers, and need to be carefully considered.

DISCUSSION AND CONCLUSION

We have contributed a qualitative analysis of two datasets to empirically document specific challenges people encounter in food journaling. By unpacking "*too much effort*" into specific challenges, our findings suggest opportunities to improve food journaling design and technology.

One important opportunity is to consider journaler goals and how they relate to these challenges. For example, detailed nutritional data may be important to a journaler pursuing weight loss. But the challenges in obtaining that data might be inappropriate for a journaler looking to identify a food trigger or gain a higher-level understanding of food habits (e.g., for whom "oatmeal" is sufficient). Conversely, details of preparation might be irrelevant to a journaler interested only in calories but critical to identifying a food trigger. Instead of attempting to capture the elusive "everything", these findings suggest a diversity of journal designs to support specific goals.

Challenges with food databases suggest several opportunities. A reputation system might address reliability of community entries, and could consider goals (e.g., a journaler tracking sodium intake may find an entry more reliable if created by another journaler with a similar goal). Further, a community could vote on the accuracy of a contributed entry (e.g. "6 of 8 journalers agree with this assessment of calories"). The tension between databases providing desired foods but overwhelming journalers might be addressed using context (e.g., surface likely food at a particular restaurant), personal diets (e.g., a vegetarian's journal), routines (e.g., a person may always have the same espresso drink), or designs for lower-fidelity journals (e.g., using nutritional information from a generic "oatmeal" entry instead of strictly requiring greater disambiguation for a minor nutritional difference).

One initial promising opportunity we have pursued is a photo-based food journal, which can level the challenge of journaling different meal types, provide value in spite of missing entries, and avoid creating judgment by not emphasizing nutritional details [1]. But our findings point out a variety of challenges in food journaling and motivate future research exploring how new designs and technology can support journalers in their food-related goals.

ACKNOWLEDGMENTS

We thank Ravi Karkar, Julie Kientz, and Sean Munson for feedback and analysis. This work was funded in part by the Intel Science and Technology Center for Pervasive Computing, by the National Science Foundation under awards OAI-1028195 and SCH-1344613, and by the National Institutes of Health under award 1U54EB020404-01.

REFERENCES

1. Cordeiro F, Bales E, Cherry E, & Fogarty J. Rethinking the Mobile Food Journal: Exploring Opportunities for Lightweight Photo-Based Capture. *CHI 2015,* to Appear.
2. Grimes A & Harper R. Celebratory Technology : New Directions for Food Research in HCI. *CHI 2008*, 467–476.
3. Helander E, Kaipainen K, Korhonen I, & Wansink B. Factors Related to Sustained Use of a Free Mobile App for Dietary Self-Monitoring With Photography and Peer Feedback: Retrospective Cohort Study. *J Med Internet Res 16*, 4 (2014), e109.
4. Mamykina L, Mynatt ED, Davidson PR, & Greenblatt D. MAHI : Investigation of Social Scaffolding for Reflective Thinking in Diabetes Management. *CHI 2008*, 477–486.
5. Noronha J, Hysen E, Zhang H, & Gajos KZ. PlateMate: Crowdsourcing Nutrition Analysis from Food Photographs. *UIST 2011*, 1–12.
6. Rooksby J, Rost M, Morrison A, & Chalmers M. Personal Tracking as Lived Informatics. *CHI 2014*, 1163–1172.
7. Siek KA, Connelly KH, Rogers Y, Rohwer P, Lambert D, & Welch JL. When Do We Eat ? An Evaluation of Food Items Input into an Electronic Food Monitoring Application. *PervasiveHealth 2006*, 1–10.
8. Thaler RH & Sunstein CR. *Nudge: Improving Decisions about Health, Wealth, and Happiness.* 2008.
9. Tsai CC, Lee G, Raab F, Norman GJ, Sohn T, Griswold WG, & Patrick K. Usability and Feasibility of PmEB: A Mobile Phone Application for Monitoring Real Time Caloric Balance. *Mobile Networks and Applications 12*, 2-3 (2007), 173–184.

Computation of Interface Aesthetics

Aliaksei Miniukovich
University of Trento
Via Sommarive 9, Povo TN, Italy
miniukovich@disi.unitn.it

Antonella De Angeli
University of Trento
Via Sommarive 9, Povo TN, Italy
deangeli@disi.unitn.it

ABSTRACT
People prefer attractive interfaces. Designers strive to outmatch competitors, and create apps and websites that stand out. However, significant expenses on design are unaffordable to small companies; instead, they could adopt automatic tools of interface aesthetics evaluation, a cheaper strategy to good design. This paper describes an important step towards such a tool; it presents eight automatic metrics of graphical user interface (GUI) aesthetics. We tested the metrics in two exploratory studies – on desktop webpages (N = 62) and on iPhone apps (N = 53) – and found them to function on both GUI types and for both immediate (150ms exposure) and deliberate (4s exposure) aesthetics impressions. Our best-fit regression models explained up to 49% of variance in webpage aesthetics and up to 32% (if app genre is considered) of variance in iPhone app aesthetics. These results confirm past results and suggest the metrics are valid and reliable enough to be widely discussed, and possibly, to be embedded in our prospective GUI evaluation tool, tLight.

Author Keywords
Automatic metrics; GUI evaluation; user study; immediate impression; deliberate impression; tLight.

ACM Classification Keywords
H.5.2. Information interfaces and presentation (e.g., HCI): User interfaces – graphical user interfaces (GUI), evaluation/methodology.

INTRODUCTION
There is no doubt visual aesthetics matters in interface design. Surrounded with multiple offers of same-quality services and products, Web and app users have become selective and disregard apps and websites they do not like immediately [12]. A possible way to survive in such an environment includes carefully working out all details of visual design, making the design stand out [33]. However, small companies, start-ups and individual developers often cannot afford hiring a design agency and do their design themselves. In such cases, even well-detailed design guidelines are of limited help, since, to be applied properly, they require extensive training. Concrete GUI evaluation tools could exemplify abstract design guidelines, and drive and substantiate design choices. The tools would be based on specific quality metrics that represent specific GUI design aspects.

CHI 2015, April 18 - 23 2015, Seoul, Republic of Korea
Copyright is held by the owner/author(s). Publication rights licensed to ACM. ACM 978-1-4503-3145-6/15/04...$15.00
http://dx.doi.org/10.1145/2702123.2702575

In this paper, we extend earlier work [17, 16], and describe and test in two studies eight GUI aesthetics metrics: visual clutter, color range, number of dominant colors, figure-ground contrast, contour congestion, symmetry, and the new metrics of grid quality and white space. We based the metrics on the psychological investigations of what people see as complex and unappealing [23], and HCI investigations of webpage aesthetics [33, 14, 36, 25, 26]. The results of the present two studies replicated the results of past studies [17, 16], which suggests the metrics are solid enough to be presented to the larger CHI audience. In addition to this, we have replicated the phenomenon of consistent and lasting immediate impressions [14, 33] on two types of stimuli (webpages and mobile apps) using a between-subjects experimental design. In the rest of paper, we review related work on aesthetics in HCI and automatic aesthetics measures, and describe the eight GUI aesthetics metrics. We report Study 1, which tested metric performance on webpages, and Study 2, which tested metric performance on iPhone apps. Lastly, we summarize the results and discuss their implications for the automatic evaluation of interface aesthetics.

RELATED WORK
Past attempts [40, 39, 26, 25, 16, 17] to automatically account for visual aesthetics of GUIs consisted of two steps: gathering user scores of GUI aesthetics and matching them against computed scores of a set of automatic metrics. The first step reflects our understanding that beauty lies in the eye of the beholder, and involves conducting either carefully orchestrated in-lab user studies [14, 33, 21, 17] or large-scale crowdsourcing studies with thousands of participants [25, 25]. The second step uses the averaged user scores as the ground truth data, and tests how well various metrics and algorithms predict the scores.

Collecting Aesthetics Scores
The influence of aesthetics on the overall appreciation of GUI changes with time. Sonderegger et al. [29] conducted a longitudinal study and demonstrated the positive effect of aesthetics to almost disappear after the initial use phase. However, it is largely the initial phase that determines if a

one-time visitor converts to a user or goes to competitors [12]. While considering the initial use phase itself, aesthetics impressions could be further subdivided into the *immediate-first* (formed at a glance), *deliberate-first* (long enough for reading titles and processing images) and *overall* (after performing several tasks) impressions [30].

Several HCI studies have explored the first impression of GUI aesthetics and possible ways of collecting user scores of such impressions. In within-subjects experiments, Lindgaard et al. [14] and Tractinsky et al. [33] showed webpage screenshots to participants for half-second intervals, and asked to set a single rating per screenshot. Their experimental design allowed each participant to rate in a relatively short time a large number of stimuli, which, in turn, allowed the authors to make generalizable inferences about stimuli. Tractinsky et al. [33] then compared the half-second, immediate-first ratings with the ten-second, deliberate-first ratings of each participant and found them to strongly correlate.

Studies [13, 30] have compared the deliberate-first and overall aesthetics impressions, and their outcomes. Lee et al. [13] studied the user preferences of four websites before (deliberate-first impression) and after (overall impression) actual use, and found actual use to significantly change aesthetics appreciation. De Angeli et al. [6] explored the interplay of various qualities of two website GUIs differing in their level of aesthetics. They asked participants to perform tasks and carefully documented perceived usability, aesthetics and information quality. The effect of aesthetics in GUI appreciation was significant. Notably, both studies [6] [13] employed multi-item questionnaires for measuring aesthetics, which, one could argue, is more valid than the one-question approach. However, the whole procedure took several hours for each participant and involved studying only two [6] and four [13] GUIs.

Measuring Aesthetics Automatically

Earlier-proposed measures could be generally categorized in *element-based* and *pixel-based*. Element-based measures require knowing the organizational principles (e.g., which GUI elements can contain other elements) and basic elements of GUI (e.g., buttons, links or paragraphs of text). For example, Michailidou et al. [15] counted the number of menus, images, words and links on webpages, and found these numbers to strongly correlate with the user scores of aesthetics and visual complexity of webpages. Harper et al. [10] split each webpage in blocks of 200 × 200 pixels and counted the top-left corners of webpage elements that fell in a block. The distribution of blocks predicted user ranking of 20 webpages with 86% accuracy. Ngo et al. [19] formulated 14 arts-based measures of graphic display aesthetics. They used the positions and sizes of display elements for quantifying balance, equilibrium, symmetry, sequence, cohesion and nine other webpage characteristics. In a later test of these measures, Purchase et al. [22] used the HTML sources of 15 webpages to locate text, image and control (e.g., button) elements, and thus, to compute measure scores. A subset of the measures predicted the user ranks of webpage visual appeal. Lastly, Ivory et al. [11] suggested a number of measures of webpage design quality, which involved counting words, links, images, font types, colors of links and text, text clusters and other webpage aspects. Their metrics predicted if a webpage would be rated very low or very high on visual appeal with 65% accuracy.

Pixel-based measures take GUI screenshots as an input instead of GUI-underlying code. GUI screenshots might represent better what the user sees, which is why pixel-based metrics are considered advantageous to element-based metrics [26]. Zheng et al. [40] segmented webpage screenshots in color-homogeneous blocks to assess webpage symmetry, balance and equilibrium. A part of their measures correlated with user scores of several aesthetics sub-dimensions. Purchase et al. [21] explained nearly 25% of variance in user scores of visual complexity of various images. Their measures included computing the variance in image pixel luminance, the ratio of contour pixels to all pixels, file sizes of images in various file formats, and the number of image colors. In two large-scale online studies, Reinecke et al. [25, 26] explained up to 49% of variance in webpage aesthetics using the number of text and images blocks, mean values of hue, saturation and value of screenshot pixels, proportion of screenshot pixels of a particular color and several other measures. Finally, Wu et al. [39] listed a number of measures, both pixel-based and element-based. The pixel-based measures included decomposing webpages in visual blocks as the first step, and combining the blocks in hierarchical tree-like structures as the second step. Then, the block-average brightness, hue, saturation, texture and colorfulness were computed. These measures, combined with other element-based measures, allowed Wu et al. [39] to classify webpages with a 77% accuracy, relative to users' classifications. Notably, the webpage decomposition algorithm used in [39] was not pixel-based and still required HTML sources of webpages as an input.

Complexity Roots of Aesthetics

Psychology [23] suggested liking of everyday[1] things might arise from the ease of understanding, i.e., from the simplicity of things. Our brain has evolved to like spending less energy processing things; we see simpler objects as more familiar, and thus, safer. One might argue that complexity is only a single component of liking and conscious considerations might matter even more than complexity [1]. However, the pre-conscious perception of complexity is deemed to be universal [23] and is easier to account for than conscious considerations.

Several studies [5, 18] have explored what complexity means in HCI and listed three types of complexity: *visual complexity*, *information design complexity* and *task complexity*. Visual complexity strongly relates to immediate aesthetics perception, and many HCI studies

[1] We would like to stress that we discuss the aesthetics of everyday things, not pieces of art (cf. [32]).

focused on exploring and leveraging this type of complexity. Tuch et al. [35, 36] have asserted a strong link between visual complexity and immediate aesthetics of webpages. Several other studies [39, 25, 26] tried to measure webpage aesthetics automatically, using quantifiable aspects of HTML sources or screenshots of webpages. Despite these studies started from an assumption of a strong complexity-aesthetics link, none of them looked systematically into the underlying determinants of visual complexity, and thus, missed out several potential determinants from their analyses. Earlier work [16, 17] gave a more detailed overview of visual complexity determinants and listed eight of them, relevant to HCI (Table 1).

Visual complexity determinants	**Status**
Visual clutter	A multi-item metric[a]
Color variability	Two multi-item metrics[a] (dominant colors and color range).
Contour congestion	A single-item metric[a]
Figure-ground contrast	A single-item metric[a]
Layout quality	A multi-item metric[b] (grid quality) and single-item metric[b] (white space)
Symmetry	A single-item metric[c]
Prototypicality	*Not implemented*
Ease of grouping	*Not implemented*

[a] described in [16, 17]; [b] introduced in this paper; [c] described in [16, 17], but fully reworked here.

Table 1. The determinants of visual complexity and associated metrics.

METRICS

The metrics of clutter, color range and dominant colors have evolved from the constructs of visual clutter and color variability. Both constructs describe the amount of information on a screen; however, color variability is often measured and considered separately from clutter due to its salience: study participants always mention colors as a component of complexity [20]. Visual clutter describes the effort to introduce a new, visually prominent object to a scene [26] and is quantified with several measures (CL1-CL4, Table 2). Color variability (measures CV1-CV5, Table 2) consists of two aspects that humans perceive separately [16]: number of dominant colors (the colors a human can easily differentiate and name) and color range (the colors a human cannot differentiate without zooming in, and which are often used for smoothing edges and color gradients).

The metrics of figure-ground contrast and contour congestion reflect the constraints of the human visual system. Figure-ground contrast describes differences in luminance or color of adjacent lines. Smaller differences lead to higher mental effort needed to recognize objects or to read text [9]. As in [16, 17], we operationalized contrast as a weighted sum of number of contour pixels detected with the Canny algorithm at several consecutive levels. The Canny edge detection algorithm takes two input thresholds: high and low. In the present metric implementation, the low threshold is set to 40% of the high threshold; the high threshold varies from 10% to 70% of maximal pixel luminance (5% to 65% for the mobile app screenshots) with a step of 10%. The weights decrease from 1 to 0 with a step of .2; higher weights are assigned to edge pixels detected with lower thresholds. Finally, the weighted sum is normalized by the number of all detected edge pixels and taken as the metric of contrast.

#	Measure description
CL1	Contour density, the ratio of contour pixels to all pixels, cf. [27]
CL2	Subband Entropy [27], the amount of redundancy introduced to a scene.
CL3	Feature Congestion [27], the proportion of unused feature (e.g., color or luminance) variance.
CL4	The file size of images in the JPEG format (cf. [35, 27])
CV1	The file size of images in the PNG format.
CV2	The number of colors after color reduction: only values that occurred more than 5 (for web) or 2 (for mobile) times per image were counted.
CV3	The number of colors per dynamic cluster (see CV5).
CV4	The number of static 32-sized color clusters (the sub-cube edge size of clusters is 32 values out of possible 256, per each RGB channel). Only clusters containing more than 5 values are counted.
CV5	The number of dynamic clusters of colors after color reduction (more than 5 pixels). If a difference between two colors in a color cube is less than or equal to 3, two colors are united in the same cluster, which continues recursively for all colors. Only clusters containing more than 5 values are counted.

Table 2. The measures of visual clutter (CL1-4) and color variability (CV1-5).

Contour congestion describes the mental effort needed to differentiate spatially proximal lines. If two objects are too close to each other, a human cannot differentiate them with the peripheral vision and needs to focus on the objects [37]. As in [16, 17], we operationalized contour congestion as the proportion of congested contours to all contours. First, contour pixels are detected. Then, all contour pixels that have neighbors in a 20-pixel vicinity are marked as congested. Finally, the congested pixels are counted and normalized by the number of all edge pixels.

Well-organized information requires less cognitive effort to process. Symmetry [34, 3] and regular visual layout [2] might serve for such a purpose in HCI. In this paper, we reconsidered the past algorithm of GUI symmetry [17, 16] (in which contour symmetry was measured by looking for a match for each contour pixel across the central vertical axis). The past measure was too noisy and favored GUIs with fewer objects. Here, we measured block symmetry, which considers the position of GUI visual blocks, relative to the central vertical axis. First, we partitioned a GUI screenshot into visual blocks (the algorithm was inspired by [4]). Second, we considered separately the blocks that contained the central vertical axis and blocks that did not.

The shift of the former relative to the axis was considered as asymmetry. The shift of the latter relative to the axis and matching block (if there was a matching block) was also considered as asymmetry.

The grid quality and white space metrics describe the quality of GUI layout. Higher quality helps the user to quickly navigate within the GUI and is seen as an important aesthetic aspect of GUI [2]. We considered several existing measures of alignment and regularity of document layouts [2], and implemented those that did not require a high precision detector of GUI block positions. We first sliced a GUI screenshots in visual blocks. We then assumed the non-covered proportion of screenshot to reflect badly distributed content and took it as the white space metric. The other five block-based measures (Table 3) describe grid quality and can be combined using a factor analysis. The last measure (Table 3, G5) was added specifically to reflect the specificity of mobile GUIs: they are often organized in a single aligned column of elements, which users are tolerant of scrolling down through. Thus, the measures G1 and G2 should not apply to mobile GUIs.

#	Measure description
G1	The number of visual blocks of GUI (cf. [2]).
G2	The number of alignment points of blocks (cf. [2]).
G3	The number of block sizes, grid proportionality [2].
G4	The proportion of GUI covered by same-size blocks (cf. the cell coverage computation from [2]).
G5	The number of vertical block sizes, i.e., vertical grid proportionality.

Table 3. The measures of GUI grid quality.

STUDY 1

The first study sought to replicate the past results [16] on a bigger and more diverse sample of websites and pool of participants. In addition, we strived to extend the results from *immediate-first* to *deliberate-first* aesthetics impressions [30]. Past studies of immediate-deliberate differences [38, 33] used a within-subjects experimental design, whereas we used a between-subjects design: half of participants rated screenshots after a 150ms exposure and the other half after a 4s exposure. After we collected user ratings of aesthetics of 300 webpages, we matched the mean user scores against the scores of the automatic metrics. Additionally, we applied the resulting regression model of aesthetics to stimuli from [16].

Stimuli

A representative sample of stimuli largely determines the validity of findings. Researchers either selected websites themselves [35], relied on online collections of websites preselected for their high quality [40, 16], or asked design professionals to submit website links [14]. All these approaches implied a sample bias, either because of idiosyncratic preferences of the few people involved in the selection or because of a possible experimenter effect whereby researchers could unconsciously select the "right" stimuli. We, instead, outsourced website search and selection to a larger number of people via crowdsourcing. Over 40 workers of a crowdsourcing platform[2] looked for and reported websites in English of three website genres: corporate, eCommerce and news. We then reviewed over 300 submitted websites and filtered out those that did not match the genres we required, did not have all the page types we required (Table 4), had technical issues or required to login before displaying main content. Keeping in mind that familiarity could seriously complicate data analyses [31], we also avoided the top 500 popular websites[3] and their localized versions (e.g., amazon.it instead of amazon.com). The filtered set contained 235 websites from which we randomly selected 75 websites, 25 in each genre. Finally, we automatically took 300 screenshots of website pages (1280×800 pixels, webpage top part only, PNG format, 24-bit per pixel).

Genre	Corporate	Ecommerce	News
Page types	home	home	home
	about us	about us	about us
	contact us	details of item	piece of news
	products & services	list of items	list of news

Table 4. We took four genre-specific pages of each website.

Participants

We recruited 62 participants (mean age = 31.4 years, SD = 6.3; 22 female; 30 non Italians from all over the globe) including 7 students, 27 doctoral students, 11 postdocs and 17 full-time university employees; all were proficient in English and had normal or corrected to normal vision. Participants reported spending 6.3h a day on the Internet (SD = 3.4h); 40 participants had technical background; 21 participants indicated having significant experience in visual or GUI design. One person did not finish the test.

Design

We adopted a one-way between-subjects experimental design with exposure duration (150ms vs. 4s) as an independent factor and visual aesthetics as a continuous dependent variable. Participants were randomly assigned to either the 150ms or 4s condition. This manipulation should discern *immediate-first* from *deliberate-first* impressions: 150ms is only long enough to grasp the gist of scene [7] but not enough for reading [28], whereas 4s is long enough for up to 10 eye fixations and reading headlines. The standard duration of 500ms [33, 14] was discarded as it would allow for 1-2 eye fixations and reading 1-2 words, and would mix immediate with deliberate impressions.

Procedure

All test sessions were conducted individually, in an isolated room with a laptop and experimenter, and started with a briefing form and consent form. Participants then filled out demographics questionnaires. The study consisted of viewing (1280×800, 13-inch display) and rating 100 webpage screenshots, randomly selected from

[2] https://microworkers.com

[3] http://www.alexa.com/topsites

the pool of 300 screenshots. In each trial (cf. [16]), participants saw a fixation cross (1-1.5sec), a webpage screenshot (150ms or 4s, depending on a participant condition), and black-white noise screen (50ms) and were prompted to rate the screenshot with the key buttons from one (ugly) to seven (beautiful). We did not limit the time for rating but explicitly asked participants to do it as quickly as possible. The average completion time was below 15 minutes. At the end of test, participants were debriefed and given a small reward.

Results

In the debriefing phase, participants often noted they disliked the "broken" shopping cart pages of eCommerce websites. (Almost all shopping cart pages featured a message that the shopping cart was empty, often with the inclusion of such words as "sorry" or "unfortunately".) We did not aim at accounting for this emotional bias and decided to exclude shopping cart pages from the analysis. The ratings of one participant assigned to the 150ms condition (mean = 6.02, on a 1 to 7 scale) deviated from the mean of others by nearly three standard deviations and were excluded from further analyses. Thus, we obtained 9 to 11 ratings per screenshot.

The average score interclass correlation coefficients suggested a high consistency in user scores in both 150ms (ICC2k = .77; 95% conf. interval is .74 to 0.81; F(274, 8970) = 4.95, $p < .001$) and 4s (ICC2k = .85; 95% conf. interval is 0.83 to 0.88; F(274, 8671) = 7.08, $p < .001$) conditions. The analysis of mean scores (from now on we refer to means per screenshot) indicated our sample included both appealing and non-appealing webpages (ranging from 2.1 to 6.1 on a 1 to 7 scale, Figure 1) and was only slightly skewed in both 150ms (n = 275, mean = 3.79, SD = .8, min = 2.1, max = 6.1, skew = .48) and 4s (n = 275, mean = 3.9, SD = .89, min = 1.9, max = 6.3, skew = .24) conditions. A paired t-test revealed a small, but significant difference between the mean scores of 150ms and 4s conditions, diff. = .11, t(274) = 2.82, $p < .01$. The correlation between the mean scores of 150ms and 4s conditions was strong, r(273) = .70, $p < .001$.

We computed scores of the eight metrics for each screenshot. Four metrics (visual clutter, number of dominant colors, color range and grid quality) required combining multiple measures, for which we used maximum-likelihood factorial analyses. As in [17, 16], we expected the variance of visual clutter and color variability measures to partially overlap and wanted to cancel out the overlapping – we analyzed all the measures in a factor analysis with Varimax rotation (Table 5a). Three factors emerged. Similar to [17, 16], no measures had high cross loadings, with the exception of number of static color clusters (CV4, Table 2), which loaded on both clutter and dominant color factors. We computed Thompson's scores for the three factors. The measures of grid quality (G1-G4, Table 3) were combined in a separate factor analysis (Table 5b), in which a single factor emerged. We again estimated grid quality scores using Thompson's method.

Figure 1. The least appealing (top, 2.1 out of 7) and the most appealing (bottom, 6.1 out of 7) webpages.

A: factors \ measures	CL1	CL2	CL3	CL4	CV1	CV2	CV3	CV4	CV5
Clutter	.92	.85	.95	.92	.30		-.14	.51	.30
Color range		.20		.18	.82	.89	.72	.13	
Dominant colors	.26	.29	.24	.22	.15	.21	-.36	.65	.85

B: factors \ measures	G1	G2	G3	G4
Grid quality	.77	.67	.90	-.87

Table 5. Factor loadings of clutter and color measures (A, cumulative var. g = .83) and grid quality measures (B, cumulative var. g = .65) for webpages.

The majority of the automatic metrics generated scores that correlated with the user scores (Table 6). Please note that higher symmetry and grid quality scores correspond to less symmetric and less organized layouts, and therefore, correlate negatively with aesthetics. We then used the Akaike's Information Criterion (AIC) to select the best-fit linear models, which explained 49% (150ms condition) and 43% (4s condition) of user score variance. AIC, in addition to looking at R^2, penalizes models for each additional predictor.

Finally, we applied the factor loadings (Table 5) and linear model coefficients (Table 7, 150ms condition) from this study to the stimuli from [16], i.e., to a different data set. The amount of explained variance in the aesthetics ratings only dropped down to 42% (from 51% in [16]).

Discussion

Consistent with the past results [16], the automatic aesthetics metrics indeed captured certain aspects of webpage visual aesthetics, with clutter and color range being the strongest predictors. Two new metrics (grid quality and white space) also performed fairly well and generated scores that correlated with aesthetics ratings. Our best-fit linear regression model accounted for 49% of variance in the ratings of immediate-first aesthetics, which is comparable to the past results for similar stimuli [16]. Moreover, when applied to a different data set (from [16]), the model performed well and explained 42% of rating variance, despite significant differences in data collection of the present and former studies. Notably, we consider the factor loadings (Table 5a) as more valid, compared with the past efforts [16, 17], as they are based on a larger and more diverse sample of screenshots.

Metric	150ms exposure		4s exposure	
	r(273)	*p*	*r(273)*	*p*
Clutter	-.30	< .001	-.48	< .001
Color range	.56	< .001	.33	< .001
Dominant colors	-.08	.14	-.20	< .01
Contrast	.51	< .001	.37	< .001
Congestion	-.46	< .001	-.37	< .001
Symmetry	-.16	< .01	-.11	.07
Grid quality	-.22	< .001	-.22	< .001
White space	-.15	< .05	-.01	.90

Table 6. Pearson's correlation coefficients between metric-produced scores and user scores.

	150ms exposure		4s exposure	
Predictor	*Estimate*	*p*	*Estimate*	*p*
(Intercept)	3.79	< .001	3.90	< .001
Color range	.34	< .001	.23	< .001
Clutter	-.21	< .001	-.51	< .001
Dominant colors	-.11	< .01	-.24	< .001
Grid quality	.15	< .01	.17	< .01
Contrast	.12	< .05	--	--
Symmetry	-.14	< .01	-.08	.12
Congestion	-.12	< .01	-.07	.14
White space	-.08	.12	-.20	< .01
R^2 (adj. R^2)	.49* (.48)		.43** (.42)	

* F(8,266) = 32.52; ** F(7,267) = 29.17; both p < .001.

Table 7. Regression models of webpage visual aesthetics. (Outcome variables are aesthetics scores after 150ms and 4s exposure).

Although we cannot directly compare the results (Table 7) with the results of other similar studies [25, 39], we would like to point out that the metrics of [39], despite an impressive 77% accuracy in predicting user ranking of webpage complexity, performed only 7% better than the Feature Congestion complexity measure [27]. Feature Congestion was only one of many measures we integrated in the metrics and when we tried to use it alone to explain aesthetics ratings, R2 dropped to .11 (from .49, Table 7). The webpage aesthetics models of [25] performed fairly well (R^2 = .47), but they included several culture-dependent predictors (e.g., distaste for a particular color) and demographic predictors (age, gender, geographic location and education level), whereas we used none of them. Collecting demographics and preference data increase GUI evaluation time and cost, and makes an evaluation less affordable to small companies.

Our experimental procedure used a between-subjects experimental design, in which we collected ratings of both *immediate-first* (150ms) and *elaborate-first* (4s) impression of aesthetics. A paired t-test showed elaborate impressions to be slightly more positive than immediate impression (diff. = .11, p < .01), which was expected (cf. [24]) and could reflect a lower cognitive strain after watching screenshots for longer time [33]. The correlation between *immediate-first* and *deliberate-first* scores was strong, r(298) = .70, p < .001, which supported earlier inferences of within-subjects-design studies [33, 14]: participants do form an impression almost instantly and this impression lasts. In fact, several participants of the study explicitly mentioned that the presentation time (4s) could have been shorter and they would still rate screenshots the same. When we used the scores of immediate and elaborate impressions in regression analyses, the R^2 of the resulting models (Table 7) only differed by 6%. This seems to suggest that people rely on similar GUI aspects in judging beauty, regardless of exposure duration.

STUDY 2

A previous study [17] argued that pixel-based complexity metrics could successfully evaluate any type of GUIs, not only webpages. Study 2 sought to support the argument and replicate past studies ([17], study 1 and 2) on a bigger and more diverse sample of stimuli (iPhone apps) and pool of participants. The design of Study 2 resembled the design of Study 1; hence we only highlight the differences between the two.

Stimuli

We did not outsource stimuli selection to crowd workers due to several practical considerations. First, we could not find a service for automatic iPhone app GUI rendering and screenshot capturing, and therefore, this had to be done manually. Second, if we asked crowd workers to send us screenshots, we would receive screenshots of different sizes due to differences between various iPhone devices. In addition, we could run into privacy issues due to the possibility of screenshots containing sensitive user data. Finally, crowd tasks are designed to be short and concise, whereas we would set multiple requirements and conditions. This would make task descriptions impractically lengthy.

Instead, we crawled the Apple's app store website and selected free apps in English from three genres: business, travel and entertainment. These genres should represent well the whole of the task-fun continuum, with business apps being mainly task-oriented, entertainment apps being mainly fun-oriented, and travel apps occupying the middle. After we selected three lists of apps, we randomized the app order and considered the apps one by one from the top according to several criteria. First, we only considered apps designed for the 4-inch displays (the apps for smaller displays would render with two black areas at the top and bottom of display). Second, we avoided overly simplistic apps that had less than four visually diverse GUI layouts. Third, we avoided apps with the heavy use of cartoon graphics. Forth, we avoided apps that required a paid premium account to access their full functionality. Last, to reduce possible familiarity effects, we avoided the apps from the top 100 most popular apps list. After randomly selecting 25 apps per genre, we manually took four or more screenshots (640 × 1136 pixels; PNG format, 24-bit per pixel) per app and then randomly reduced to only four screenshots per app. Thus, we collected 300 screenshots of 75 iPhone apps.

Participants

We recruited 53 participants (mean age = 29.6 years, SD = 7.1 years; 18 female; 16 non-Italians), including 18 students, 17 doctoral students, 6 postdocs and 12 full-time university employees. All participants were proficient in English, had normal or corrected to normal vision (except one, one-eye-blind participant, whose data were later discarded) and no color blindness. All but 10 participants were very familiar with smartphones and 16 were iPhone users. In total, 34 participants had a technical background; 42 participants indicated having no significant experience in visual or GUI design.

Design & Procedure

The experimental design and procedure mirrored Study 1, with the exception of the stimuli and test device (iPhone 5C); 27 participants were assigned to the 150ms condition and 27 to the 4s condition.

Results

We excluded the data from the participant, who did not have normal or corrected to normal vision, and another participant who visibly paid no attention to the task. Each participant rated 100 randomly selected screenshots out of the pool of 300 screenshots, which resulted in seven to nine ratings per screenshot.

The average score interclass correlation coefficients suggested an acceptable consistency in user scores in the 150ms condition (ICC2k = .64; 95% conf. interval is .58 to 0.69; $F(299, 7176) = 2.91$, $p < .001$) and high consistency in the 4s condition (ICC2k = .76; 95% conf. interval is 0.72 to 0.80; $F(299, 7475) = 4.38$, $p < .001$). Mean scores (from now on we describe per screenshot means) indicated the sample of apps was not skewed and included both appealing and non-appealing apps in both 150ms (n = 300, mean = 3.71, SD = .71, min = 1.76, max = 5.81, skew = -.07) and 4s (n = 300, mean = 3.88, SD = .83, min = 1.67, max = 6.33, skew = -.05) conditions. A paired t-test suggested a small but significant difference between the mean scores of 4s and 150ms conditions, diff. = .17, $t(299) = 4.23$, $p < .001$. The mean user scores of 150ms and 4s conditions correlated strongly, $r(298) = .59$, $p < .001$.

As in Study 1, we computed scores for the eight metrics, four of which (visual clutter, number of dominant colors, color range and grid quality) needed additional maximum-likelihood factorial analyses to combine multiple measures. Three factors emerged in the factor analysis with Varimax rotation of clutter and color measures (Table 8a). One factor emerged (Table 8b) in the factor analysis of the grid quality measures relevant to mobile GUIs (G3-G5, Table 3). We then estimated the scores of corresponding metrics using Thompson's method.

	measures / factors	CL1	CL2	CL3	CL4	CV1	CV2	CV3	CV4	CV5
A	Clutter	.94	.86	.94	.89	.19	.14		.22	
	Color range	.10	.17	-.11	.31	.91	.76	.70	.22	
	Dominant colors		.23		.15	.35	.43		.69	.99
B	measures / factors	G3			G4			G5		
	Grid quality	.99			-.64			.86		

Table 8. Factor loadings of clutter and color measures (A, cumulative var. g = .82) and grid quality measures (B, cumulative var. g = .72) for iPhone apps.

The output of the symmetry metric was not normally distributed, since a large part of app layouts were almost perfectly symmetrical. We converted the output of the symmetry metric in a categorical variable: screenshots with a score < 10 were considered symmetrical (104 app layouts); screenshots with a score > 200 were considered asymmetrical (90 app layouts); the rest was considered as partially symmetrical (106 app layouts). Screenshots of the same app often varied widely on symmetry (Figure 2). A one-way ANOVA test revealed a significant effect of symmetry on user score in 4s condition ($F(2,297) = 4.62$, $p < .05$), but not in the 150ms condition ($F(2,297) = 1.01$, $p = .37$). Post-hoc comparisons using the Tukey HSD test showed participants disliked partially symmetrical layouts relative to fully symmetrical and asymmetrical layouts (Table 9b). For the rest of metrics, we estimated the correlations between their output and user scores (Table 9a). The best-fit linear models (based on the Akaike's Information Criterion) explained 13% (150ms condition) and 18% (4s condition) of user score variance (Table 10). When the effect of app genre was considered, the fit of the models went up (17% in the 150ms condition and 32% in the 4s condition).

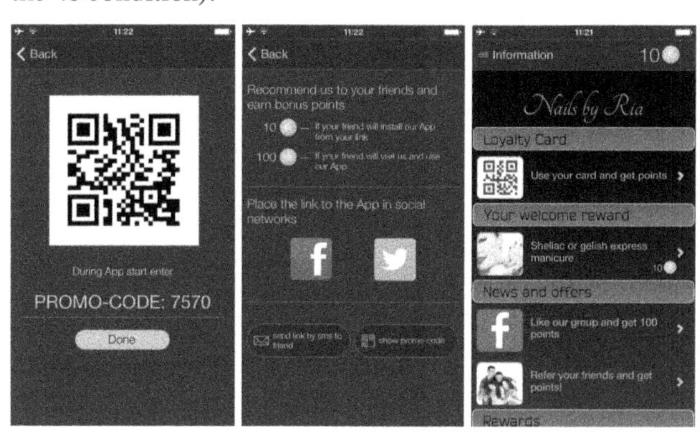

Figure 2. Symmetrical (left), partially symmetrical (center) and asymmetrical (right) screen layouts of an app.

	Metrics	150ms exposure		4s exposure	
		r(298)	*p*	*r(298)*	*p*
A	Clutter	-.22	< .001	-.30	< .001
	Color range	.26	< .001	.28	< .001
	Dominant colors	.09	.13	-.08	.18
	Contrast	.24	< .001	.26	< .001
	Congestion	-.18	< .01	-.22	< .001
	Grid quality	-.13	< .05	-.10	.07
	White space	-.01	.90	.01	.90
B	Symmetry levels	*diff.*	*p adj.*	*diff.*	*p adj.*
	Symm. – Part.Symm.	.18	.16	.32	< .05
	Symm. – Asymm.	.12	.47	.05	.92
	Part.Symm – Asymm.	- .06	.83	- .27	.05

Table 9. Pearson's correlation coefficients of user scores and continuous metrics, and between-level differences for the categorical metric of symmetry.

	150ms exposure		4s exposure	
Predictor	*Estimate*	*p*	*Estimate*	*p*
(Intercept)	3.70	< .001	3.96	< .001
Factor: part. symmetry#	--	--	- .20	.07
Factor: full symmetry#	--	--	- .02	.84
Clutter	-.13	< .01	-.20	< .001
Color range	.16	< .001	.19	< .001
Contrast	.08	.06	.05	.09
R^2 (adj. R^2)	.13* (.12)		.18 (.17)	
R^2 (app genre is included)	.17		.32	

The reference value is complete asymmetry; * F(3,296) = 14.32, ** F(5, 294) = 13.2, both p < .001.

Table 10. Linear regression models of app visual aesthetics. (Outcomes are aesthetics scores after 150ms or 4s exposure).

We also applied the factor loadings (Table 8) and linear model coefficients (Table 10, 150ms condition) from this study to the Android app screenshots from [17]. The amount of explained variance in the Android app aesthetics only dropped down to 30% relative to 36% in [17].

Discussion

Overall, the results of study 2 confirmed our expectations: the majority of the automatic metrics generated scores correlating with the user ratings of iPhone app aesthetics (Table 9). Compared with a similar study on Android apps [17], the best-fit models (Table 10) were less effective at explaining iPhone app aesthetics. However, when applied to the past dataset [17], the present study model (Table 10, the 150ms condition) explained 30% of Android app aesthetics, which demonstrated the reliability of the metrics and suggested they can be applied to both web and mobile GUIs. We consider the factor loadings (Table 8) as more valid compared with our past efforts [17], as they are based on a larger and more diverse sample of screenshots. The inclusion of app genre in the models increases R^2 (up to .32 in the 4s condition), but significantly complicates the analysis. Further studies are needed.

Study 2 used between-subjects experimental design, comparing the ratings of both *immediate-first* (150ms) and *deliberate-first* (4s) impressions of app beauty. As in Study 1, a paired t-test showed elaborate impressions to be slightly more positive than immediate impressions (diff. = .17, p < .001), which was also consistent with the past research on affective judgments [24, study 3]. However, the correlation between immediate and deliberate impression ratings remained strong (r = .58, p < .001). This further supports the claims of aesthetics impressions forming immediately and lasting [33, 14] and extends them from website-only to mobile GUIs as well.

GENERAL DISCUSSION

Study 1 and Study 2 largely converge. Using between-subjects experimental design, both studies observed a strong link between *immediate-first* and *deliberate-first* aesthetics impressions (Table 11a). This reinforces past findings [38, 33] and extends them from the web to the mobile domain (see also [17], study 1).

Passing from immediate-first to deliberate-first impression brings us closer to the real-world usage situations. (One might even argue immediate impressions are only possible in a lab.) The automatic metrics were initially designed to account only for low-level, perceptual GUI qualities, and not for high-level conscious elaborations. However, reading titles and considering images do not drastically change user scores (Table 11a) and performance of the metrics (Tables 6 & 9). We assume that the influence of GUI visual aspects carries over from the very initial, 150ms-long phase to a more elaborate, 4s-long phase.

			Web	Mobile
A	4s VS 150ms	Diff. in means	.11**	.17***
		Correlation	.70***	.58***
B	Corr. with 150ms user scores	Clutter	-.30***	-.22***
		Color range	.56***	.26***
		Dominant colors	---	---
		Contrast	.51***	.24***
		Congestion	-.46***	-.18**
		Symmetry	-.16**	---
		Grid quality	-.22***	-.13*
		White space	-.15*	---
C	R^2 of best-fit 150ms(4s) model		.49 (.43)	.13 (.18)

*** p < .001; ** p < .01; * p < .05.

Table 11. Comparison of results of studies on web and mobile GUIs.

Predicting GUI aesthetics has proven to be harder for mobile apps than for webpages, which the comparison of R^2 of regression models demonstrates clearly (Table 11c). We could attribute this to two reasons. First, visual complexity might matter much less to mobile app than to webpage evaluators, either because all apps are already designed with complexity concerns in mind (e.g., for the on-the-go use or difficult lighting conditions) or because smaller screens imply fewer details to perceive. Thus, the complexity-rooted metrics explain less of mobile aesthetics. Second, Apple reviews all iPhone apps published on their app store, which means the apps are already preselected based, in part, on their design. The iOS design guidelines[4] advices developers to "*use a family of pure, clean system colors that look good at every tint* ...", "*align text, images, and buttons to show users how information is related*" or to "*create a layout that fits the screen of an iOS device*." Following the guidelines restricts the variance in the scores of several metrics, which also reduces the chances for covariance, i.e. for stronger correlations. Indeed, the metric performance triples on Android apps (R^2 = .30), which Google Play Store publishes without review. We call for more studies on mobile apps, as they are becoming increasingly more important, and yet, rarely mentioned in literature.

The web-mobile comparison of metric performance (Table 11b) also revealed significant resemblance. Except white space, symmetry and dominant color, all metrics functioned similarly (in both, correlation direction and magnitude) for both web and mobile GUIs. The effect of dominant colors did not reach a significant level, which could reflect the overall tendency to use fewer dominant colors in mobile apps: restricted variance in dominant colors would lead to limited chances for covariance with aesthetics. The white space metric did not apply to mobile GUIs, which could follow from participants tolerating well incomplete list- or menu-like GUIs of many mobile apps. Finally, the output of symmetry metric for iPhone apps was not normally distributed (one-column layouts of apps often imply full symmetry) and was converted to a categorical variable with three levels (full symmetry, partial symmetry, and complete asymmetry). Instead of a linear drop in liking from full symmetry to complete asymmetry, we observed partial symmetry to be disliked the most (Table 9b), which was in part consistent with the recent research on slight asymmetries [8]. This might also mean complete asymmetry was perceived as an intended feature and tolerated. Overall, we conclude that the same factors matter for both web and mobile GUI aesthetics, and accordingly, the metric can be similarly applied to both web and mobile GUIs.

CONCLUSION

This paper presented two validation studies of eight automatic metrics of GUI aesthetics. The metrics performed fairly well for websites (Study 1), but were more problematic for mobile apps (Study 2). Each metric accounted for a unique GUI design aspect and could be translated in a design guideline. This work has advanced us towards the final goal of implementing the metrics in tLight, a software tool for helping non-professional designers in creating more appealing and competitive GUIs, and speeding up GUI development cycles. However, reaching the final goal requires several more steps: considering the effect of website or app genre on aesthetics; testing the metrics on aesthetics ratings gathered in more realistic usage contexts, and possibly, with users less technically literate than in the current studies; and establishing the link between approach-avoidance tendencies (e.g., buying or recommending) and the predictions of the metrics. Lastly, tLight (and similar systems) may not completely replace user studies, but can effectively complement them. Studying how user free-form feedback on designs combines with the tLight output would finalize the cycle of tLight-related research.

[4] https://developer.apple.com/design/tips

REFERENCES

1. Armstrong, T. and Detweiler-Bedel, B. Beauty as an emotion: the exhilarating prospect of mastering a challenging world. *Review of general psychology*, 12, 4 (2008), 305-329.
2. Balinsky, H. Evaluating interface aesthetics: measure of symmetry. In *Digital Publishing Conference* (San Jose 2006), International Society for Optics and Photonics.
3. Balinsky, H. Y., Wiley, A. J., & Roberts, M. C. Aesthetic measure of alignment and regularity. In *the 9th ACM symposium on Document Engineering* (Munich 2009), ACM, 56-65.
4. Cao, J., Mao, B., and Luo, J. A segmentation method for web page analysis using shrinking and dividing. *International Journal of Parallel, Emergent and Distributed Systems*, 25, 2 (2010), 93-104.
5. Choi, J. H. and Lee, H. J. Facets of simplicity for the smartphone interface: A structural model. *International Journal of Human-Computer Studies*, 70, 2 (2012), 129-142.
6. De Angeli, A., Sutcliffe, A., and Hartmann, J. Interaction, usability and aesthetics: what influences users' preferences? In *the 6th conference on Designing Interactive systems* (2006), ACM, 271-280.
7. Fei-Fei, L., Iyer, A., Koch, C., and Perona, P. What do we perceive in a glance of a real-world scene? *Journal of vision*, 7, 1 (2007), 1-29.
8. Gartus, A. and Leder, H. The small step toward asymmetry: Aesthetic judgment of broken symmetries. *i-Perception*, 4, 5 (2013), 352-355.
9. Hall, R. H. and Hanna, P. The impact of web page text-background colour combinations on readability, retention, aesthetics and behavioural intention. *Behaviour & information technology*, 23, 3 (2004), 183-195.
10. Harper, S., Michailidou, E., and Stevens, R. Toward a definition of visual complexity as an implicit measure of cognitive load. *ACM Transactions on Applied Perception*, 6, 2 (2009).
11. Ivory, M. Y., Sinha, R. R., and Hearst, M. A. Empirically validated web page design metrics. In *Proceedings of the SIGCHI conference on Human factors in computing systems* (2001), ACM, 53-60.
12. Kim, H. and Fesenmaier, D. R. Persuasive design of destination web sites: An analysis of first impression. *Journal of Travel Research.*, 47, 1 (2008), 3-13.
13. Lee, S. and Koubek, R. J. Understanding user preferences based on usability and aesthetics before

and after actual use. *Interacting with Computers*, 22, 6 (2010), 530-543.

14. Lindgaard, G., Fernandes, G., Dudek, C., and Brown, J. Attention web designers: You have 50 milliseconds to make a good first impressoin! *Behavior & information technology*, 25, 2 (2006), 115-126.
15. Michailidou, E., Harper, S., and Bechhofer, S. Visual complexity and aesthetic perception of web pages. In *the 26th annual ACM international conference on Design of communication* (2008), ACM, 215-224.
16. Miniukovich, A., De Angeli A.. Quantification of Interface Visual Complexity. In *the 2014 International Working Conference on Advanced Visual Interfaces* (2014), ACM, 153-160.
17. Miniukovich, A., De Angeli A.. Visual Impression of Mobile App Interfaces. In *Proceedings of the 8th Nordic Conference on Human-Computer Interaction: Fun, Fast, Foundational* (2014), ACM, 31-40.
18. Nadkarni, S. and Gupta, R. A Task-Based Model of Perceived Website Complexity. *Mis Quarterly*, 31, 3 (2007).
19. Ngo, D. C. L., Teo, L. S., and Byrne, J. G. Modelling interface aesthetics. *Information Sciences*, 152 (2003), 25-46.
20. Oliva, A., Mack, M. L., Shrestha, M., and Peeper, A. Identifying the perceptual dimensions of visual complexity of scenes. In *the 26th Annual Meeting of the Cognitive Science Society* (2004).
21. Purchase, H. C., Freeman, E., and Hamer, J. An exploration of visual complexity. *Digrammatic representation and inferences* (2012), 200-213.
22. Purchase, H. C., Hamer, J., Jameson, A., and Ryan, O. Investigating objective measures of web page aesthetics and usability. In *12th Australasian user interface conference (AUIC 2011)* (2011), Australian computer society, Inc., 19-28.
23. Reber, R., Schwarz, N., and Winkielman, P. Processing fluency and aesthetic pleasure: is beauty in the perceiver's processing experience? *Personality and social psychology review*, 8, 4 (2004), 364-382.
24. Reber, R., Winkielman, P., and Schwarz, N. Effects of perceptual fluency on affective judgments. *Psychological science*, 9, 5 (1998), 45-48.
25. Reinecke, K. and Gajos, K. Z. Quantifying visual preferences around the world. In *the 32nd annual ACM conference on Human factors in computing systems* (2014), ACM.
26. Reinecke, K., Yeh, T., Miratrix, L., Mardiko, R., Zhao, Y., and Liu, J., Gajos, K. Z. Predicting users' first impressions of website aesthetics with a quantification of perceived visual complexity and colorfulness. In *CHI* (2013), ACM, 2049-2058.
27. Rosenholtz, R., Li, Y., and Nakano, L. Measuring visual clutter. *Journal of vision*, 7, 2 (2007), 1-22.
28. Sereno, S. C. and Rayner, K. Measuring word recognition in reading: eye movements and event-related potentials. *Trends in cognitive sciences*, 7, 11 (2003), 489-493.
29. Sonderegger, A., Zbinden, G., Uebelbacher, A., and Sauer, J. The influence of product aesthetics and usability over the course of time: a longitudinal field experiment. *Ergonomics*, 55 (2012), 713-730.
30. Thielsch, M. T., Blotenberg, I., and Jaron, R. User evaluation of websites: From first impression to recommendation. *Interacting with Computers*, 26, 1 (2013), 89-102.
31. Tinio, P. P. and Leder, H. Just how stable are stable aesthetic features? Symmetry, complexity, and the jaws of massive familiarization. *Acta Psychologica*, 130, 3 (2009), 241-250.
32. Tractinsky, N. Visual Aesthetics. In Soegaard, Mads and Dam, Rikke Friis, eds., *The Encyclopedia of Human-Computer Interaction, 2nd Ed*. The Interaction-Design.org Foundation, Aarhus, 2013.
33. Tractinsky, N., Cokhavi, A., Kirschenbaum, M., and Sharfi, T. Evaluating the consistency of immediate aesthetic perceptions of web pages. *International journal of human-computer studies*, 64, 11 (2006), 1071-1083.
34. Tuch, A. N., Bargas-Avila, J. A., and Opwis, K. Symmetry and aesthetics in website design: It'sa man's business. *Computers in Human Behavior*, 26, 6 (2010), 1831-1837.
35. Tuch, A. N., Bargas-Avila, J. A., Opwis, K., and Wilhelm, F. H. Visual complexity of websites: effects on users' experience, physiology, perfomance, and memory. *International journal of human-computer studies*, 67 (2009), 703-715.
36. Tuch, A. N., Presslaber, E. E., Stocklin, M., Opwis, K., and Bargas-Avila, J. A. The role of visual complexity and prototypicality regarding first impression of websites: Working towards understanding aesthetic judgments. *International Journal of Human-Computer Studies*, 70 (2012), 794-811.
37. Van Den Berg, R., Cornelissen, F. W., and Roerdink, J. B. A crowding model of visual clutter. *Journal of Vision*, 9, 4 (2009), 1-11.
38. Van Schaik, P. and Ling, J. The role of context in perceptions of the aesthetics of web pages over time. *International Journal of Human-Computer Studies*, 67, 1 (2009), 79-89.
39. Wu, O., Hu, W., and Shi, L. Measuring the visual complexities of Web pages. *ACM Transactions on the Web (TWEB)*, 7, 1 (2013), 1-34.
40. Zheng, X. S., Chakraborty, I., Lin, J. J. W., and Rauschenberger, R. Correlating low-level image statistics with users-rapid aesthetic and affective judgments of web pages. In *SIGCHI Conference on Human Factors in Computing Systems* (2009), ACM, 1-10

Patina Engraver: Visualizing Activity Logs as Patina in Fashionable Trackers

Moon-Hwan Lee, Seijin Cha, Tek-Jin Nam
CIDR Lab, Department of Industrial Design, KAIST
291 Daehak-ro, Yuseong-gu, Daejeon 305-701, Republic of Korea
{moonhwan, sjcha, tjnam}@kaist.ac.kr

ABSTRACT
Despite technological improvements in commercial activity trackers, little attention has been given to their emotional, social, or fashion-related qualities, such as their visual aesthetics and their relationship to self-expression and social connection. As an alternative integrated approach incorporating HCI, fashion, and product design, our project made use of the characteristics of *patina* to improve activity trackers as fashionable wearables. We developed the Patina Engraving System, which engraves patina-like patterns on an activity tracker according to a user's activity logs. Using a piercing technique, the patina of activity logs has been made abstract, visually rich, gradually emerging, and historically accumulated. During the field trial, we found that the patina motivated the participants to increase exercises for engraving aesthetic patinas. A tracker with patina triggered spontaneous social interactions in face-to-face situations. The participants also cherished the trackers that held their own history. Based on the field trial, we discuss design implications for utilizing patina in designing future fashionable technologies.

Author Keywords
Activity tracker; patina; fashion; digital fabrication.

ACM Classification Keywords
H.5.m. Information interfaces and presentation (e.g., HCI): Miscellaneous.

INTRODUCTION
Recently, there has been a proliferation of commercial activity trackers for monitoring physical activity related to health and wellbeing, including Jawbone UP, Fitbit, Misfit Wearables, and others [23]. Most of the activity trackers collect an activity log and help users reflect on their life by visualizing the data in mobile or web applications. Related to tracking devices, the field of HCI has mainly contributed to practical issues such as how to improve sensing mechanisms and understand diverse self-monitoring methods [4, 5, 9, 26].

However, one of the important aspects of activity trackers is that they are personal fashion items that play a role in personal identity, visual aesthetics, and social communication that goes beyond technological features such as usability and sensing accuracy etc. [2, 28, 32]. Though activity trackers have been improved as a personal activity monitoring tool, it is necessary to consider issues related to HCI's third wave such as engaging user experience and the meaningfulness of digital artifacts [8]. Considering the way that activity trackers are worn in everyday life, it is especially important to investigate how they can be improved as fashion items. Since the majority of activity trackers are worn in a manner that makes them visible, customers inevitably consider not only their functionalities but also their visual appearance. Some companies have started to raise their competitiveness by cooperating with fashion brands because the technological aspects of trackers have become otherwise equivalent in the market [11].

As an alternative design approach to activity trackers, we focused on the intersection of HCI and fashionable product design. In particular, we were interested in the concept of *patina* in activity trackers. Figuratively, patina refers to any fading, darkening, or other sign of age that is felt to be natural and/or unavoidable [18]. It is known that artists and designers often deliberately use patina as a design resource for constructing aesthetic properties, lending credibility to an object or bestowing a "warm" feeling through art or product design [6, 37]. For similar purposes, we applied the concept of patina for designing activity tracking systems to improve the tracking experience of those who wear trackers to monitor activity.

In this paper, we present the Patina Engraving System (Patina Engraver and Patina Tracker), which engraves patina-like patterns on the wristband of activity trackers and thereby visualizes users' accumulated activity logs. Accordingly, the appearance of the trackers changes along with the users' tracking experience. Using the system, we conducted a field trial with 8 participants for 5 weeks to learn how the system was used in their lives.

This paper makes several contributions. First, it details a novel activity log visualization technique by applying the concept of patina. The Patina Engraving System is

CHI 2015, April 18 - 23 2015, Seoul, Republic of Korea
Copyright 2015 ACM 978-1-4503-3145-6/15/04...$15.00
http://dx.doi.org/10.1145/2702123.2702213

proposed as an example of an alternative approach to aesthetically represent an activity tracker. The process and rationale behind the system design are presented as design knowledge. The results of the field trial improve our understanding as to whether patina-like engraving enriches the tracking experience. Finally, it guides the design of future fashionable products with patina by suggesting design issues and opportunities.

BACKGROUND & RELATED WORK

This work is related to the research topics at the intersection of personal informatics and fashionable wearables. Regarding personal informatics, works on quantified-self with activity tracking and visualization of activity logs are particularly relevant. Diverse development cases also exist in the field of personalized activity tracking in fashionable wearables.

Quantified-self: General Use of Activity Trackers

The area of quantified-self movement has developed guidelines as to how to collect and use activity data, often from trackers and tracking applications [4, 5, 24, 25]. For instance, Rooksby et al. discussed various styles of tracking, including goal driven tracking and documentary tracking [30]. Li et al. found six kinds of questions that people ask about their data: Status, History, Goals, Discrepancies, Context, and Factors [25]. They also found that certain kinds of questions are more important depending on the phases of reflection: Discovery and Maintenance. The previous work in this domain contributed to our understanding of the practices of tracking systems. It emphasized the necessity of producing more than technological improvements in activity tracking, the importance of considering the emotional aspects of tracking, and the notion of developing social tracking beyond the ability to publish data to social networks [30]. Nevertheless, relatively little attention was paid to a wearable tracker. Specifically, this study takes a design approach to activity trackers as a fashionable item and attempts to improve their emotional and social qualities.

Visualization of Activity Logs: From Virtual Medium to Physical Medium

For supporting effective self-monitoring and motivating users to partake in physical activity, visualization has been a key issue in personal informatics. The majority of commercial trackers mainly target the virtual medium using numbers, graphs, and metaphors [10, 31]. Numbers and graphs take up little screen space and can be easy to interpret, however there can be usability and interpretation issues when it comes to larger data sets [36]. Some researchers suggested using virtual metaphors such as interactive art displays [9] or growing a pet according to the activity log [26]. Their research shows that this type of visualization can be engaging and fun.

Beyond the virtual medium, research has been carried out relating to the use of the physical medium for visualizing physiological and activity logs. For instance, Requena presented research projects to fabricate the physical medium as jewelry based on physiological data [29]. Related to the physical representation of activity logs, Khot et al. developed SweatAtoms, which transforms the physical activity data into 3D printed artifacts [21]. They found that a physical medium made people more conscious of their involvement in physical activity. Although the previous work showed the potential for utilizing a physical medium, there are limitations to deploying this approach in activity trackers and tracking systems. As explained in Khot et al.'s research [21], the building process using a 3D printer is a laborious and time-intensive process that is uncomfortable for general users. Additionally, because the physical object represents just one moment of tracking, users need to generate a number of objects for long-term activity logging.

In our study, we tried to exploit the advantages of the physical medium and reduce the burden of the building process. In particular, our work differs from previous research in that we exploited patina as a physical medium to visualize activity logs just as artists deliberately add patina for constructing aesthetic properties and simulating antiquity in newly-made objects.

Activity Trackers as Fashionable Wearables

The term *fashionable wearables* is used to refer to designed garments or accessories that combine aesthetics and style with functional technologies [32]. The embedding of electronics into fashion items has been investigated in research for many years, and there are even several commercial cases for supporting physical activity. Most of them mainly sense and transmit the wearer's physiological and movement data in real-time [1, 35]. As a research prototype, Social Fabric Fitness provides a glanceable shared screen on the back of a runners' shirt to increase awareness of group fitness performance [27]. Though several wearable devices have been designed to sense and monitor physical activity, they have been less than satisfactory on the fashion front. Like other wearable devices, activity trackers are generally designed as plain black (or single color) wristbands and look more like digital watch straps. To improve the quality of trackers as fashion accessories, some fitness tracker companies collaborated with luxury fashion brands [11]. Nevertheless, while the current design approach might improve trackers' visual appearance when they are worn, the design approach focusing on the visual appearance has little relationship with the main function of trackers such as activity tracking and supporting activity monitoring. Additionally, given the popularization of digital fabrication in the HCI field [20, 21, 36], there is now the potential to strengthen the diverse roles of a fashion item by allowing it to express a user's personal identity or improve social connections as well as visual aesthetics.

These cases illustrate the need for an alternative design approach that integrates activity log visualization in the area of personal informatics with an understanding of activity trackers as fashionable wearables in the fashion and product design field. This integration is important not only for improving users' physical activity, but also for supporting and engaging user experience in the long-term. To exceed the current design approach, which focuses on visual aesthetics, this research explored a design approach that utilizes activity logs for making patina-like patterns.

DESIGN EXPLORATION

We exploited the concept of patina for visualizing activity logs physically and cumulatively. In what follows, we explain the characteristics of patina, our design exploration, and the rationale behind our decisions relative to the materials and technique used to create patina.

Visualization of Activity Logs in the Form of Patina

The word *patina* refers to a thin layer that forms variously on the surface of stone, on metals, and on wooden furniture (the sheen produced by age, wear, and polishing). It can also refer to any change a surface acquires through age and exposure [18]. Patina has been used to increase the value of artifacts in art and design. Today, the terms patina and patination are used in a broader sense, denoting techniques for applying processes connected with the ageing of the surfaces of works of art or the accumulated changes in surface texture and color that result from an object's normal use. Designers have intentionally used some materials on the surface of objects to leave patina that gives a sense of history [14, 17]. Specifically, according to literature on art and culture, the characteristics of patina can be classified as below [5, 18, 37]:

- **Abstract**: Patina provides information in ambiguous ways. The abstract and subtle shape of patina may stimulate users' reflection.
- **Visually rich**: Patina is often used to make an object look aesthetically pleasing. It is often expressed on the surface of the object by changing color or texture as shown in a leather product.
- **Gradually emerging** (on a physically limited surface): Patina is created gradually in a limited space on a surface. In the long term, the patina emerges, and its expression becomes thicker and richer.
- **Historically accumulated**: Patina shows the past history of an object's use. People may leave the patina intentionally to mark an event or person. Or the patina may be unintentionally generated while the object is touched or exposed to the environment.

The characteristics of patina have already been applied in the art and design area. Some cases exist in applications of graphical interfaces that metaphorically exploit patina to provide information about user history in the HCI area [19, 33]. Few cases exist for improving the quality of a digital device. We tried to utilize physical patina in tracking systems by visualizing activity data in the form of patina and applying the patina to tracking devices and systems.

Technique and Material for Engraving Patina

With consideration given to the characteristics of patina, we tested visualization techniques in a physical medium and materials to simulate patina. In particular, inspired by stippling [34] and tattooing, we explored a piercing technique that inserts a needle into the surface, which is attached to an oscillating unit (solenoid in our case). As the unit rapidly and repeatedly drives the needles in and out of the surface, the needles leave small dots on the surface.

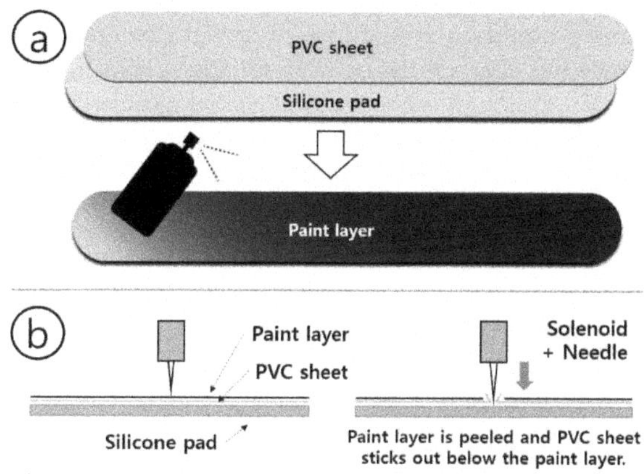

Figure 1. Material and technique for engraving patina

By exploring and comparing other fabrication techniques such as CNC milling, laser cutting, and 3D printing, we found the piercing technique has several advantages for visualizing patina. First, its expression is relatively noticeable in visual and tactile ways like the cases of tattoo or stippling arts. Second, it expresses patina gradually on a physically limited surface. Since CNC milling and laser cutting takes the surface away, and 3D printing makes the surface bigger, there are limits to the amount of patina that can be expressed on the same surface. On the contrary, piercing can express detailed and gradual traces on a limited surface. Third, the set-up and clean-up process of a piercing device is relatively convenient. CNC milling and laser cutting create lots of dust and they are risky for general customers. 3D printing takes a long time to construct objects and requires inserting materials continuously.

Throughout the process of exploring materials to pierce, such as a silicone pad, leather, etc., we developed material to maximize the visual and tactile effectiveness of the patina produced by the piercing technique (Figure 1.a). The developed material consists of three layers. The first layer at the bottom is a silicone pad (1mm). On the silicone pad, a brightly colored PVC sheet (125 μm) is attached. Then, as a third layer, a dark paint is evenly spread on the PVC sheet. When the needle reaches the painted surface, the painted layer is stripped down. This causes the bright sheet to stand out against the dark painted layer, making the pattern both visually and tactually vivid (Figure 1.b).

Visual Patterns of Patina

We also explored visual patterns for representing patina that reinforce characteristics such as *abstract, visually rich, gradually emerging,* and *historically accumulated.* Since the *abstract* and *visually rich* aspects are satisfied by the allocation of pierced dots while the *historical* aspect is satisfied by using users' activity data, we focused more on the aspect of *gradualness* on a physically limited surface.

To visualize patina on a physical surface, we applied stippling, a technique that creates a pattern simulating varying degrees of solidity or shading using small dots [34]. Throughout the exploration, we found that the piercing mechanism could be applied in three ways to our material to express the characteristics of gradualness and historicity (Figure 2). Although other types of visual patterns could be used to express patina, we selected the face, line, and fractal types that can be modified widely as basic components of visual patterns. These basic visualizing types were applied in our prototypes.

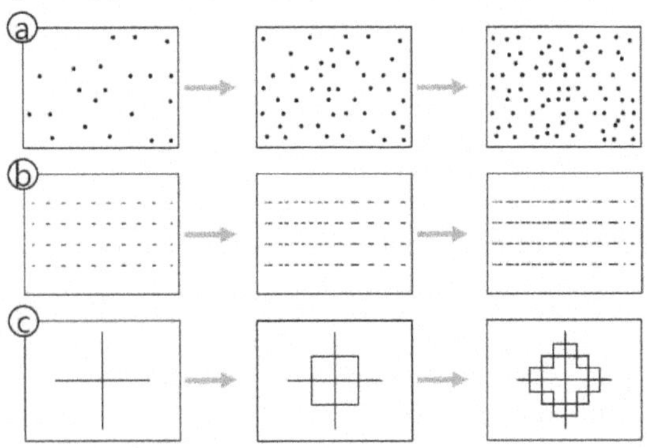

Figure 2. Visual patterns of patina: (a) Stippled face type, (b) Stippled line type, (c) Fractal type.

- Stippled face type: By filling a face with dots, it is possible to vary the color of the face.
- Stippled line type: By filling a line with dots, it is possible to make the line thicker and clearer.
- Fractal type: This type is related to a combination of lines. We especially utilized a fractal shape that is infinitely self-similar, iterated, and detailed theoretically.

PATINA ENGRAVING SYSTEM

Through the exploration of a piercing technique and material and visual patterns, we developed a prototype of the Patina Engraving System consisting of the Patina Tracker and the Patina Engraver.

Hardware of Patina Tracker and Patina Engraver

The Patina Tracker uses the three-layered material we developed in the wristband part (Figure 3). To fasten the band, magnets were attached inside at both ends. As a tracking sensor, we utilized the sensor part of Fitbit Flex [10], which was embedded at the center of the wristband. Additionally, an RFID tag was attached inside the band to identify the participant's ID and load their activity logs.

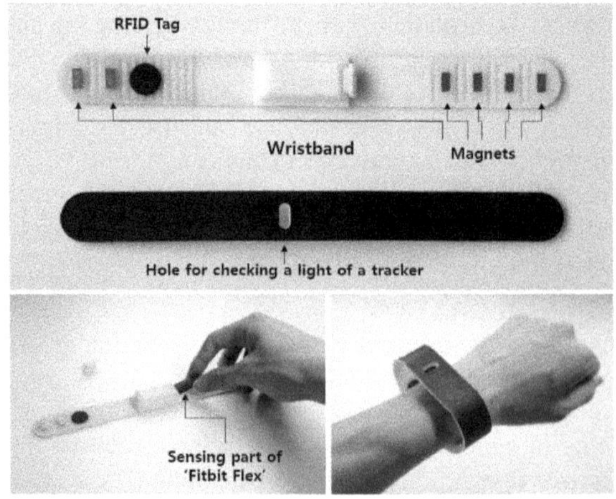

Figure 3. Patina Tracker

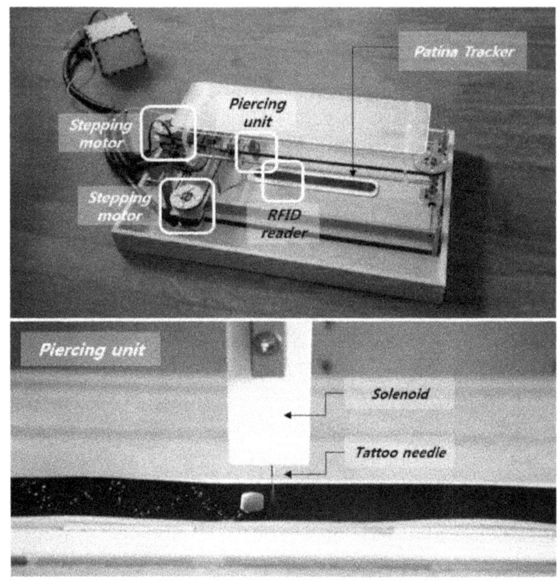

Figure 4. Patina Engraver

The Patina Engraver mainly consists of two stepper motors and a piercing unit (solenoid with a needle) (Figure 4). The piercing unit is moved in the XY-plane by two stepper motors. The piercing unit drives the needles up-down by the solenoid with the speed of 3-5 times per second. The diameter of the needle in the piercing unit was 0.35mm. During our exploration, it is found that the piercing speed and resolution vary depending on the speed of motors and the needle size. The rack at the bottom is used to place a tracker for engraving. When a tracker is put on the rack, magnets under the rack hold the tracker while it is engraved. At the same time, the RFID reader under the rack identifies whose tracker it is.

Software of Patina Engraving System

In this system, users' activity logs are periodically saved to the local computer by accessing their Fitbit account (Figure 5). If the Patina Tracker is placed on the Patina Engraver, the engraver identifies the user and loads his/her activity logs on the local computer using RFID. Then, the local computer analyzes the activity logs and sends pattern codes to the Arduino board in the Patina Engraver. The engraver moves the stepper motors and the piercing unit based on pre-defined pattern types and the pattern codes from the local computer.

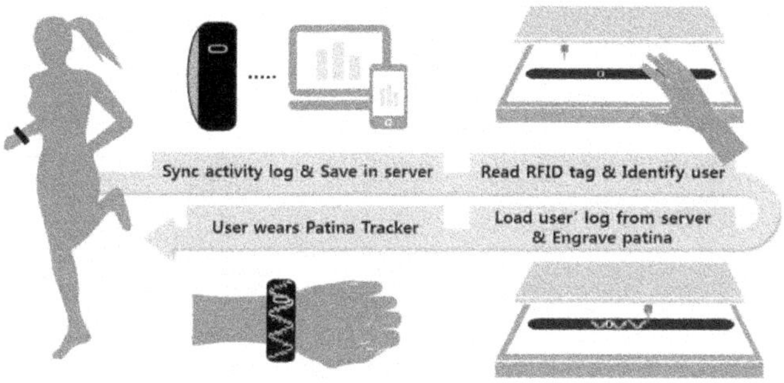

Figure 5. System overview

Patterns on Patina Tracker

The overall layout of the patina patterns on an activity tracker was decided through several phases of exploration. Firstly, we selected (i) the types of activity logs as the source data for engraving patina. Among diverse types of activity logs, we chose *steps*, *active time (minute)*, *activity calories*, *time in bed (minute)*, and *total walking distance (kilometer)* that people generally want to know when using tracking systems. Then, we considered (ii) shapes for each activity log such as zigzag, rectangle etc., (iii) visual patterns for engraving patina in the limited space (stippled face type, stippled line type, fractal type), and (iv) physical location on the surface of trackers. The pattern layout on an activity tracker was evaluated by noticeability, possible number of engravings, and visual aesthetics. Finally, each source data was mapped onto four zones (Figure 6).

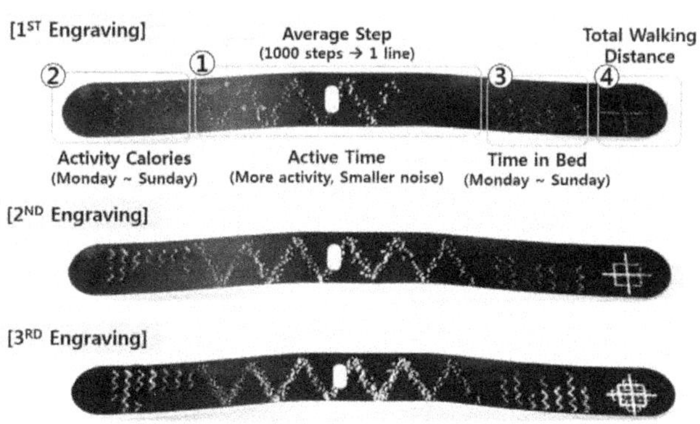

Figure 6. Designed patterns on Patina Tracker

- **Zone-1**. In this zone, average steps and active times per day are mapped to the zigzag line and engraved in the stippled face type to cover the middle surface of a tracker. Since this zone is most conspicuous when the tracker is worn, it was chosen as the area to receive steps and active times as source data. In detail, steps are mapped by the number of diagonal lines. Considering the length of the tracker and the notion that 10,000 steps a day is normal, we decided to map 1000 steps as one diagonal line. Then active times are used to define the noise on the lines. Specifically, when the active times are long, the noise value becomes smaller to engrave a more clear and vivid line. When the active times are short, the dots are engraved sporadically with bigger noise values along with diagonal lines.
- **Zone-2**. In this zone, calories per week are mapped to the length of each zigzag line. From the left to the right, the length of a line indicates the amount of activity calories from Monday to Sunday. Due to the narrow space, the stipple line type was used for engraving.
- **Zone-3**. Like Zone-2, we mapped time in bed to each line. To magnify the differences among days, patina lines were engraved when the time in bed is in the range of 240–540 minutes.
- **Zone-4.** In this zone, we mapped total walking distance using the fractal type to show distinct improvement. We divided total distance into 3 levels (lv.1: 0–20km, lv.2: 20–40km, lv.3: 40–60km). When total distance reaches a certain level, a more detailed fractal structure is drawn in three phases.

In the Patina Engraving System, the entire engraving process took about 5–10 minutes depending on the participants' activity logs.

FIELD TRIAL

We conducted an "in the wild" study [3] to understand the impacts of visualizing activity logs using patina not only on functional aspects, but also on the emotional and social aspects of the tracker and tracking experience. When participants used the Patina Engraving System, we expected that a certain amount of time would be needed for them to grow accustomed to using the new device. We also expected to find various roles of the patina engraving process and the trackers besides the natural uses. Therefore, we installed the Patina Engraver and Tracker in a natural environment for 8 participants for 5 weeks. The sample size and the length of the field trial were determined from a previous study [3] that discussed field trial methods. Given the exploratory nature of our design work, we focused on gathering a rich set of opinions rather than quantitative findings. As such, our work can be characterized as a form of cultural probing [16] and an "in the wild" study that aims to encourage reflective thinking about a system.

Participants

We contacted sports clubs to recruit a group of participants because we expected that they would be interested in exercising and activity tracking and would have a close relationship with each other. As recommended from a previous study [15], the intimate relations among participants at the same club could be a stimulus to expressing their opinions and providing a greater depth of understanding about the field context. Eventually, eight participants from the same sports club (a badminton club) were recruited for our study. There were 5 male and 3 female participants with ages varying from 22 to 28 years

(M = 24.1, SD = 2.2). All participants played badminton more than twice a week together and had close relationships. Three of the participants partook regularly in other sports such as walking, football, or golf. Participants' past experience of using trackers was also considered in the recruitment phase. Three participants had an experience of using trackers for about 1 month (M4: Misfit Shine, F1: Galaxy Gear Fit, F2: sleep tracking application). We expected that the past experience of using trackers would be useful for eliciting the potential value of our system. Throughout the paper we refer to each participant by sex and the week of the interview session (e.g. M5, week 3).

Method

During the field trial, the Patina Engraver and Trackers were used for 5 weeks. To lessen the participants' burden and observe how the system pervaded their normal lives, the Patina Engraver was installed in a building which all participants could reach within 10 minutes by foot; it was also close to the gym where the participants play badminton. After starting the study, participants were asked to set up their trackers and applications. They then created a Fitbit account with an ID and password we assigned them. Using them, we could access participants' raw activity logs. Participants were allowed to sync their logs as desired using a personal computer or mobile phone.

During the first week, participants wore the tracker without engraving patterns. Participants adapted to the tracking process and this period reduced the novelty effect of tracking itself. The first week's interviews included questions related to their biographies (ordinary practice of exercise and sleeping).

During the 2nd to 4th week, the participants visited us for interviews and used the Patina Engraver twice a week. Depending on their schedules, we met with them at intervals of 3–5 days. Among the two meetings per week, one was only for engraving and the other was for interview and engraving together. The interviews were conducted with a group of two or three participants. Since they had close relationships and attended the same sports club, they could discuss their experience spontaneously [15]. During the interview, we asked questions relating to the role of the patina and the functional, emotional, and social aspects of the Patina Engraving System. About the social impact, we asked how our system was used among acquainted and non-acquainted people.

In the 5th week, we stopped engraving tasks and participants wore a normal Fitbit tracker. In the post-use interviews, we asked what they missed the most while using the Patina Engraving System and the impacts of the engraving system compared to normal trackers. In addition, we asked them about the possibility of using patina in other contexts.

Data Collection and Analysis Method

We mainly analyzed the results based on the weekly and post-use interviews. The weekly photos of participants' trackers and their activity logs were used to identify the detailed situations users mentioned in their interviews. All interviews, for a total of 720 minutes, were audio recorded and transcribed. Interview transcription and contextual use data, including activity data and photos of participants' trackers, were categorized by our research team through iterative analytic induction. During the analysis, we considered the novelty effects and found unexpected uses and unreported results from the lead participant by referring to existing research [3].

FINDINGS

Overall, participants were receptive to the idea of engraving patina and were engaged with using their Patina Trackers and Engraver. Table 1 shows how the trackers were used for 5 weeks. The activity logs varied depending on each participant's tracking style. We also found that participants frequently forgot sleep recording, which required a mode change in the tracker. However, in general, participant's average amount of steps, active time, active calories, and time in bed tended to decrease after the 1st week as the tracking system became ordinary to them. From the weekly interviews, we also confirmed that participants become familiar with activity trackers: *"Though it was interesting to monitor my data at first, I got used to it after using the tracker several times. Now I am monitoring it less frequently than the 1st week"* (M3, week 2).

	Week 1	Week 2	Week 3	Week 4	Week 5
Steps per day	8816.3 SD = 3889.1	8688.5 SD = 3036.8	7677.4 SD = 2660.6	9085.8 SD = 3058.5	6056.2 SD = 2751
Active Time (min.) per day	81.2 SD = 33	63.5 SD = 40.1	59.1 SD = 20.9	66.6 SD = 21	52.3 SD = 23
Active Calories per day	776.4 SD = 327.2	779.2 SD = 319.7	718.6 SD = 263.7	829.9 SD = 246.1	582.4 SD = 371.2
Time in Bed (min.) per day	322.4 SD = 110.7	290.2 SD = 156.8	210.8 SD = 119.7	216.8 SD = 116.1	243.3 SD = 147.2

Table 1. Average activity logs during 5 weeks

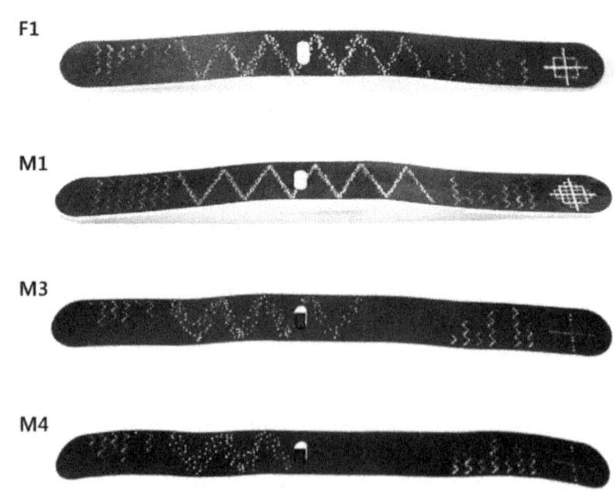

Figure 7. Participants' Patina Trackers at 3rd week (after engraving 3 times)

Meanwhile, we could observe that participants' Patina Trackers became varied after 5–6 times of engraving

(Figure 7). For instance, while the trackers of F1 and M1 were engraved with thicker patina patterns, those of M3 and M4 had less clear patina due to their relatively low level of activity. Likewise all participants' trackers became distinguishable. Next, we explain the functional, emotional, social impacts of patina engraving on the tracking experience and the perception of trackers as fashionable wearables.

Wondering about What Patina Means and Past Activities

One common feature of commercial trackers is to provide an activity log using mobile and web applications. Unlike applications that show prompt changes in physical activity, the abstract and historical aspect of patina on the trackers provided summarized information about past activities in a subtle way. After patina was engraved on the tracker, participants became curious about which parts of the tracker had changed and what kind of new patina patterns had appeared. They then tried to associate the patina with their past activities using mobile phones in the interview sessions: *"(While looking at Fitbit app) Maybe this part is vacant because I did not sleep enough for working overtime"* (F2, week 2).

During the interviews in the 4–5th weeks, several participants mentioned that they checked their activity through the mobile app or website less frequently and their activity checking period became longer as they got used to tracking. In this situation, the patina tracker became a supplement for providing summarized information: *"It became bothersome to check my activity log in mobile app. In that sense, I like this patina because it expresses approximate lifestyle"* (M3, week3), *"Though it is difficult to figure out accurate information, this provides indirect proof of my activity like a growth ring"* (F1, week 3). Several participants said they did not need to check detailed information through the app or web because they were able to expect a general tendency even without them. For them, patina was enough for checking their general life cycle.

Meanwhile, some participants mentioned the limits of patina for delivering information. Although patina could deliver information about how their activities had changed, they mention that it was not suitable for informing them about detailed changes such as differences among days or weeks: *"Because it is hard to figure out the difference as more and more patina is accumulated, it will be not good to understand my activities per day"* (F2, week 2).

Feeling Pressure for Engraving Aesthetic Patina

The patina and patina engraving put persistent pressure on participants to exercise and wear a tracker. We observed that participants made an effort to engrave more aesthetic and meaningful patina patterns. In our system, as steps and active times increase, the zigzag shape in Zone-1 is engraved more thickly in the middle of the tracker and participants considered this to be more aesthetically pleasing (Figure 6, 7). Consequently, participants were motivated to increase their exercise. Though the response about ugliness was not intentional, it seemed because vivid and flawless patterns are generally regarded as beautiful in commercial digital products. Additionally, since the patina was indelible and the engraving affected the entire aesthetics of the tracker, participants were conscious about this and mentioned that they tried to exercise more in their daily life, walking a longer route or using stairs, etc. In the case of F1, she thought her patina was ugly due to her short exercising times after the 1st patina engraving. During the next week, she mentioned that she tried to work out harder to create a more beautiful patina at the next engraving: *"Because this tracker is directly affected by my loose activity and showing it physically, it makes me regret my insufficient exercising"* (F1, week 3).

While the physical presence of patina put psychological pressure on the participants, patina engraving could also be regarded as a reward for their activities. Some participants felt fulfillment when they looked at their patina-accumulated trackers during the three weeks of patina engraving. The fact that the patina resulted from their physical activities was especially fulfilling, as they felt that the aesthetically-evolving patina was a reward for their efforts: *"If I run longer, the patina will increase and become thicker, which make me feel proud of my efforts"* (M3, week 2), *"What about using this system in the gym? If people engrave patina after working out for a week, they would feel rewarded"* (F2, week 3).

Furthermore, we found that the patina engraving affected tracker wearing habits as well. Participants were concerned about the fact that if they did not wear their trackers constantly, the patina would be irrelevant to their general lifestyle: *"Compared to other tracking devices, I tried harder to wear it regularly. This was because it is better to make patina which correspond to me"* (M4, week 2).

Having Spontaneous Co-located Interaction

Existing tracking systems support online communication by posting an activity log in social network services, showing a friend's activity log, and providing chatting functions, etc. However, in our study these functions were used less frequently at the end of the study compared to the 1st week. Most participants felt reluctant to reveal their activity history to the public. For them, it felt like vanity. Also, as they were already using other chatting platforms, they did not require that in our tracking application. Our system is different to the prevalent systems in that activity information was shown in the physical world without using a virtual medium. Using this system, participants were able to reveal their activity history quietly in the physical world. Accordingly, we observed that spontaneous interactions emerged in face-to-face situations.

Sharing and Comparing within the Participant Group

Within the participant group, which met frequently in daily life, the physical presence of patina allowed participants to access each other's activity logs easily. They said that the Patina Tracker was suitable for situations in which they exercised with sports club members in the gym without using mobile phones for accessing their activity log. Though the abstract shape of patina made it difficult to recognize details at a glance, it induced them to compare other participants' patina with their own. F1, F2, and M4 mentioned that they envied M1's tracker and were motivated and inspired by it. *"When we met in the sport club in the 2nd week, I found that Dave (M1)'s tracker was prettier than mine. And I wanted to make mine like his"* (F1, week 2). In this way, participants shared other participants' information about activities in physical spaces.

Getting Others' Attention & Conversing about Patina

Besides the social impact of patina within the participant group, we also observed social impacts on people who do not know the meaning of patina. For them, the Patina Trackers attracted attention due to the evolving nature of the accessory and the different patina that emerged periodically, thus differentiating them from static accessories. M1 said that the normal trackers, which were worn during the 1st week before the patina engraving, also attracted others attention. However, he said that in the case of the normal trackers he could only talk about the functional features of the trackers rather than personal activities related to tracking. On the other hand, the Patina Tracker with accumulated patina enabled communication about stories behind the patina and their physical activities among the people who did not know what the patina meant. In particular, participants could tell personal stories of events, growth, and achievement while exercising or sleeping: *"My colleagues ask me why the patina changed. Then I explained about each patina by associating the patina pattern with my daily activities"* (M1, week 2).

In addition, they mentioned that the abstract shape of the patina had the advantage of hiding private information from strangers: *"For people who do not know this tracker, they will consider it as just a wristband. Rather than engraving numbers or graphs, this abstract shape of patina is proper not to give details of my life"* (M4, week 4). They said they would not want to disclose their activity log to strangers.

Crafting a Symbolic Object that Holds One's Own History

All of the participants enjoyed the patina engraving process. Compared to normal tracking services, they said the engraving provided a fun experience. By actually allowing participants to engage with the patina engraving process, it promoted a sense of engagement: *"I think this engraving is similar to stitching-up in the sense that the patina emerges as I walk more"* (F1, week 4).

However, we observed that their interest in engraving faded over time, whereas their interest in the trackers lasted longer. In the interviews during the 1st week before the patina engraving, many said they would cherish their digital log more than the tracking devices. Nevertheless, through the patina engraving, they began to feel attachment toward the trackers, which contained personalized patina patterns and unique appearances. Accordingly, participants considered the Patina Trackers symbolic objects more than just a pedometer: *"If this tracker is lost and I have to get a new one without my patina, I would feel sorry about that"* (M5, week 4).

Meaningful attachment can emerge through the process of self-extension, where someone attributes important aspects of his or her self to an object [22]. In this system, the process of patina engraving helped users customize the tracker based on their activity log, which led to users symbolically extending themselves into the tracker and constructing autobiographical values: *"It (patina) is like my fingerprint. It is special in the fact that it shows who I am"* (M2, week 4), *"While patina make my tracker prettier, at the same time it strengthens symbolic meanings that I am training hard or living life to the full"* (F3, week 3).

DISCUSSION

Design Implications for Fashionable Trackers Using Patina

All fashionable items have physical, psychological, and social functions [2]. As found in our study, while aesthetically pleasing visual appearance is an integral part of fashionable trackers, it is also important to consider its psychological and social impacts, including self-expression, communication in social groups, and user experience around the trackers. In this section, we discuss research and design implications to improve the use of patina for making fashionable activity trackers.

Modifying Patina for Personally Meaningful Trackers

In our studies, participants liked the patina engraving process that customized a tracker based on their activity log, and they agreed that the patina contributed to making the tracker personally valuable. In the interviews during the 5th week, we discussed the further possibility of improving the current system to make a more meaningful tracker.

First, the selection of personally interesting types among diverse activity logs might contribute to making personalized trackers. For instance, M3 paid more attention to logs about sleep cycle, while F1 was interested in her sedentary time. Also, interpreting activity logs according to users' different lifestyles may create more meaningful trackers. In our prototype system, longer or thicker patina patterns were engraved in proportion to the absolute value of the activity logs (steps, active time, calories, time in bed). However, the same activity logs can be interpreted differently to provide meaningful information. For example, F3 wanted to engrave patina based only on the log of a specific day of the week when she took exercise regularly. If users are able to set the scope of the activity log—specific days, time slots per day, etc.—and the system utilized these to engrave patina, the tracker with patina patterns may be able to show more personal stories about their lives and deliver more useful information.

Moreover, since people have different goals when it comes to activity tracking, the patina might need to be engraved differently to meet their needs. For some users, walking

10,000 steps per day might be enough, whereas for others it might be insufficient. If the patina is engraved in proportion to the individual goals users set, the users are more likely to feel fulfilled or reflect on their lack of activities.

Using Patina for Sustained Engagement with Activity Trackers
Since activity trackers are used over a long period, designing a strategy to ensure sustained engagement is the key to their success. According to Fogg, a user needs to experience a feeling of progress toward defined goals to achieve sustained engagement in activity trackers [12, 13]. He mentioned that the success from achieving several smaller goals provides the positive momentum necessary for achieving bigger goals. In that sense, though our Patina Trackers could summarize how participants' activities changed over time, they had limitations regarding their ability to maintain users' interests and show their progress. Thus, it is necessary to consider ways of utilizing patina to motivate users in the long term. During the interviews, one of the frequently mentioned solutions for sustained use of activity trackers was to strengthen the impact of patina as a reward for completing small goals. For instance, it would be possible to engrave patina in special shapes when achieving a 100 km distance or accomplishing 20,000 steps in a day. M5 said that patina might be engraved in a way that a specific image becomes clearer gradually, which might provide a feeling of completion in the end. In this way, people would be able to gain the momentum necessary to progress. Thus, in future work, it is necessary to investigate whether the patina engraving as a reward can support sustained engagement in the trackers.

Adjusting Social Translucence of Patina
Erickson and Kellogg argued that social translucence is necessary in the digital domain [7]. As translucent property in the physical world supports graceful human-human communication in face-to-face situations, socially translucent systems can make users structure social interaction with each other and carry on coherent discussions. They worried that neither of these dimensions of social translucence are a given in the digital domain. In that sense, our system supported social translucence by engraving physical patina based on a digital activity log. By allowing users to see each other's trackers and their engraved patina and make inferences about their physical activities, the system extended the space of social interaction from the digital environment into the physical environment.

Considering the social translucence of the Patina Tracker and its effect, we could find further opportunities to develop the Patina Engraving System focusing on co-located physical activity. One of the significant qualities of the Patina Tracker is its social communication in physical space. During the last interview about the improvement of our system, several comments related to the use of the tracker for a specific group of users. For instance, M4 and M5 mentioned the patina could be engraved using both group and individual data—for example, the amount of time they exercise together or a comparison of the value of the group's activity level with that of the individual etc. Likewise, if we use this system for specific group activities, the patina on trackers may act as an emblem of the group and accordingly may strengthen peer relations and support sustained group activities.

However, it is necessary to continue exploring suitable types of information the patina can provide as well as the degree of social translucence. In our study, the Patina Engraving System visualized steps, active time, activity calories, and time in bed into the abstract shape of patina. Though the participants mentioned that the visualization in our study was fine to show to the public, they said that they would have hated it if the visualization showed details such as exact times. For example, if the tracker is too obvious, a user might feel shame about his or her lack of exercise and might worry about privacy. Since the patina would be readable for everyone including strangers, this highlights the need to tailor the types of information the patina provides, as well as the level of translucence based on the sensibilities and privacy concerns of the user.

Applying Patina to Other Contexts

Participants gave several ideas about the use of patina in devices other than activity trackers. They suggested that the patina might be helpful to achieve general health related goals like losing weight, rehabilitation exercises, or quitting smoking. M5 mentioned that people might feel a burden by exposing their smoking data to others by engraving patina on a Zippo lighter. He expected that other people would be interested in the evolving patina and support not smoking. Likewise, in future work we need to explore further whether the engraving of patina based on health relevant data can motivate people to achieve diverse health related goals and help them change their behaviors in the long term.

Also, we see opportunities for applying patina in other contexts. For instance, M3 said that it might be good to engrave patina on a credit card to warn card holders about excessive consumption. He said the patina on the credit card might force him to reflect on his spending habits. F2 mentioned that she wanted to leave physical patina on her radio that shows favorite channels. Her idea was that patina could accumulate around the tuning dial as the user frequently tunes into favorite stations. As mentioned by the participants, our design approach to combining patina with data about a user's history can be applied generally in product and interaction design. However, since the way of using various devices, users' needs, and the types of logging data differ among several cases, further research needs to be carried out to explore how patina can be applied in general interactive product design.

CONCLUSION

Our motivation for conducting this study was to make fashionable activity trackers that generate an engaging experience. Thus, in this paper, we have presented a new design approach for activity trackers by visualizing activity logs in the form of patina. Also, with the deployment of the Patina Engraving System through an "in the wild" study, we explored how participants' activity tracking experience could be affected through patina engraving. We expect this research to inspire designs for diverse tracking devices and services, as well as general fashion and product designs.

ACKNOWLEDGEMENT

This research was supported by the National Research Foundation of Korea Grant funded by the Korean Government (NRF-2014S1A5A2A01010939) and IT R&D program of MSIP/KEIT (2014, 10041313, UX-oriented Mobile SW Platform).

REFERENCES

1. Adidas miCoach Elite. http://goo.gl/qECxs3.
2. Bolton, A. *The super modern wardrobe*. New York: Harry N. Abrahms (2002).
3. Brown, B., Reeves, S. and Sherwood, S. Into the wild: challenges and opportunities for field trial methods. Proc. *CHI'11*, ACM (2011), 1657-1666.
4. Choe, E.K., et al. A. Understanding Quantified-Selfers' Practices in Collecting and Exploring Personal Data. Proc. *CHI'14*, ACM (2014) 1143-1152.
5. Consolvo, S., Everitt, K., Smith, I., and Landay, J.A. Design Requirements for Technologies that Encourage Physical Activity. Proc. *CHI'06*, ACM (2006), 457-466.
6. DeSilvey, C. Observed decay: telling stories with mutable things. *Journal of Material Culture, 11, 3* (2006), 318-338.
7. Erickson, T. and Kellogg, W. Social Translucence: An Approach to Designing Systems that Support Social Processes. *ACM Transactions on Human-Computer Interaction, 7, 1* (2000), 59-83.
8. Fallman, D. The new good: exploring the potential of philosophy of technology to contribute to human-computer interaction. In Proc. *CHI'11*, 1051-1060.
9. Fan, C., Forlizzi, J., and Dey, A. A Spark Of Activity: Exploring Informative Art As Visualization For Physical Activity. In Proc. *UbiComp'12*, ACM (2012), 81-84.
10. Fitbit. http://www.fitbit.com/.
11. Fitbit and Tory Burch. http://goo.gl/As7ce1.
12. Fogg, B.J. Persuasive Techology: Using Computers to Change What We Think and Do. *Ubiquity* (2002), 89-120.
13. Fogg, B.J. "The new rules of persuasion." RSA Digital Journal, Summer 2009. Online.
14. Fougere, T. Tyndall Table (2012). http://thomfougere.com/thomfougere-TyndallTable.
15. Frey, J., Fontana, A. The group interview in social research, *The Social Science Journal, 28(2)* (1991), 175-187.
16. Gaver, W.W., Dunne, A., and Pacenti, E. Cultural Probes. *Interactions* (1999), 21-29.
17. Heijdens's Broken White. http://goo.gl/nnMuhE.
18. Hiiop, H. *The Possibility of Patina in Contemporary Art or, Does the 'New Art' Have a Right to Get Old?* In Koht ja paik. Place and Location. Studies in Environmental Aesthetics and Semiotics VI Estonian Literary Museum, Estonian Academy of Arts (2008), 153-165.
19. Hill, W., Hollan, J., Wroblewski, D. & McCandless, T. Edit wear and read wear. Proc. *CHI'92*, ACM (1992), 3-9.
20. Jacobs, J. and Buechley, L. Codeable objects: computational design and digital fabrication for novice programmers. In Proc.*CHI'13*, ACM (2013), 1589-1598.
21. Khot, R., Hjorth, L., Mueller, F. Understanding Physical Activity through 3D Printed Material Artifacts. In Proc. *CHI'14* (2014), 3835-3844.
22. Kleine, S. S., Kleine III, R. E. and Allen, C. T. How is a possession" me" or" not me"? Characterizing types and an antecedent of material possession attachment. *Journal of Consumer Research* (1995), 327-343.
23. Ledger, D. & McCarffrey, D. *Inside Wearables,* Endeavour Partners (2014).
24. Li, I., Dey, A., and Forlizzi, J. Using Context to Reveal Factors that Affect Physical Activity. *TOCHI, 19(1)* (2012), 1-21.
25. Li, I., Dey, A.K.A., and Forlizzi, J. Understanding My Data, Myself: Supporting Self-Reflection with Ubicomp Technologies. In Proc. *UbiComp'11*, 405-414.
26. Lin, J.J., et al. Fish'n'Steps: Encouraging Physical Activity with an Interactive Computer Game. In Proc. *UbiComp'06* (2006), 261-78.
27. Mauriello, M., Gubbels, M. and Froehlich, J. Social fabric fitness: the design and evaluation of wearable E-textile displays to support group running. Proc. *CHI'14*, 2833-2842
28. Pan, Y. and Blevis, E. Fashion thinking: lessons from fashion and sustainable interaction design, concepts and issues. In Proc. *DIS'14*, ACM, 1005-1014.
29. Requena, E. LOVE PROJECT. http://goo.gl/o19avO.
30. Rooksby, J., Rost, M., et al. Personal Tracking as Lived Informatics. In Proc. *CHI 2014*, ACM, 1163-1172.
31. RunKeeper. http://runkeeper.com/.
32. Seymour, S. *Fashionable Technology: The Intersection of Design, Fashion, Science and Technology*, Springer. 2008
33. Schütte, A. A. *Patina: layering a history-of-use on digital objects*. MIT Media Laboratory (1998).
34. Simpson, I. The Encyclopedia of Drawing Techniques. London: Headline (1987), 62–64.
35. Stack, K. NFL Prospects to Wear Smart, Data Gathering Workout Shirt. Gizmodo (2011). http://goo.gl/xxbdan.
36. Swaminathan, S., et al. Supporting the design and fabrication of physical visualizations. In Proc. *CHI'14*, ACM, 3845-3854.
37. Zancheti, S. M., de Figueirôa Silva, A., Braga, A. C., Gameiro, F. G., Lira, F. B., & Costa, L. S. The patina of the city. *City & Time, 2 (2)* (2006).

Real-time Guidance Camera Interface to Enhance Photo Aesthetic Quality

Yan Xu[1], Joshua Ratcliff[1], James Scovell[2], Gheric Speiginer[3], Ronald Azuma[1]
[1]Intel Labs [2]Intel Corporation [3]Georgia Institute of Technology
{yan.xu, joshua.j.ratcliff, james.j.scovell, ronald.t.azuma}@intel.com, gheric.speiginer@gatech.edu

ABSTRACT
This paper explores whether it is effective to use real-time on-screen guidance to help users take better photos with mobile devices. Using a three-camera array, we developed a photo-taking interface that provides real-time feedback on *how* to position the subject-of-interest according to a photography composition rule: rule-of-thirds. We conduct a user study to compare the aesthetic quality of photos taken with our real-time guidance interface against a static gridline interface common to existing digital cameras. Expert photographers and Mechanical Turk workers rate the aesthetic quality of these pairs of photos. Results indicate the photos taken with our real-time guidance interface have significantly higher aesthetics scores. This study shows the potential in using camera array, computational photography, and real-time guidance interface to help non-expert users take better photos.

Author Keywords
Camera User Interface; User Evaluation; Photo Aesthetics; Camera Array.

ACM Classification Keywords
H.5.2 User Interfaces: *Evaluation*

INTRODUCTION
Digital cameras on mobile devices enable users to take photos whenever and wherever they want. However, consistently taking good quality photos requires knowledge and skill that most casual users lack. Rather than requiring users to read books or take photography classes, what if a mobile device could analyze the scene and instruct a user, in real time, on how to compose a good quality photo? Would such an interface improve the aesthetic quality of photos taken by non-expert users?

These questions are timely and important because a new generation of mobile devices with multiple cameras and advanced computational photography capabilities is just now reaching the market: examples include the *HTC One M8* smartphone (dual cameras) and the *Dell Venue 8 7000 series* tablets (three cameras). Such devices make this hypothetical camera guidance interface feasible by enabling a whole new set of scene analysis capabilities. Therefore it is now feasible and critical to test the usefulness of these interfaces. In this paper, we aim to answer the following question, *is real-time guidance an effective approach to increase the aesthetic quality of the photos?*

To answer this question, we designed and developed a camera user interface that provides real-time guidance. We focus on one photography rule: *rule-of-thirds*. We chose to implement this composition rule because it is widely adopted in photography, and it is implemented as static gridlines in many smartphone and digital cameras. Rule-of-thirds proposes that a photo should be imagined as divided into nine equal parts by two equally spaced horizontal lines and two equally spaced vertical lines, and that 1) important compositional elements should be placed along these lines or their intersection [11], and 2) the proportion of the subject of interest should be roughly one third of the total image space [12] (pp. 15–17). Our system analyzes every image frame using multiple camera inputs and gives real-time feedback according to rule-of-thirds.

We devised a user study that evaluates the effectiveness of this interface by comparing the end result—the aesthetic quality of photos taken with the real-time guidance interface and with the static gridline interface, in the specific scenario of single-person portraiture. Based on empirical data, this work reveals the potential of using camera arrays, computational photography, and real-time guidance to assist users in taking better photos.

RELATED WORK
Although photo aesthetics are subjective ("*beauty is in the eyes of the beholder*"), there are many rules and lessons from photography experts [9,11,12], which serve as a starting point for beginners to learn how to take better photos. Researchers from the image processing community leverage these photography rules, such as rule-of-thirds, simplicity, color compatibility, etc., and train classifiers using large sets of user-rated photos to distinguish between good and bad photos based on multiple aspects of aesthetic quality [2,3,5,6,7]. While most of the work is done on large datasets offline, two research projects stood out as most relevant to our work, as both gave nearly real-time feedback on photo aesthetics. Yao et al. built a mobile application that gives three kinds of feedback after a photo is taken,

CHI 2015, April 18–23, 2015, Seoul, Republic of Korea.
Copyright 2015 © ACM 978-1-4503-3145-6/15/04...$15.00.
http://dx.doi.org/10.1145/2702123.2702418

including the aesthetic quality score, color combination, and other example photos that have similar composition which is automatically selected from a high-quality photo database [13]. Pedro and Church's system maps musical feedback to the aesthetic score of smartphone camera image frames [10]. The user feedback in both systems depends on the aesthetic scores calculated from a pre-trained model. Other than the scores, there is little instructional feedback. Users must use trial and error to determine *how* to improve the photo. In contrast, we provide real-time instructional feedback through our system. Moreover, although the above two projects reported user studies, the main question remain unanswered, does the aesthetic quality of the photos increase due to the interactive feedback on photo aesthetics?

SYSTEM DESIGN

This system is tailored for our user study where users take single-person portraiture photos. We choose this scenario both because it is one of the most common scenarios for mobile device photos [4], and as it is technically feasible to implement. Our system has three main components: 1) to find the region of interest (ROI); 2) to calculate how much the ROI aligns with rule-of-thirds division lines and intersections, and whether its proportion is close to one-third; 3) to render a real-time interface that dynamically suggests which direction users should move.

To find the ROI, which is the human subject in our user study, face detection and block matching stereo disparity calculation are combined. A three-camera array (left, right, and center) is attached to the back of an Ultrabook PC (Sony VAIO Duo 11, i7-3517U). We use the stereo correspondence algorithm from OpenCV [1] to get a disparity map from the left and right cameras and rectify it to the center camera. We detect faces by Haar Feature-based Cascade Classifiers from OpenCV [1]. We segment the pixels with similar disparity values to the detected face region as the ROI. The above method fits the needs of our user study, but non-human subjects would require different approaches, such as depth-based segmentation enabled by camera arrays.

For the second step, we first multiply the ROI with a bitmap mask highlighting the rule-of-thirds grid and crossings (see Figure 1). The numerical result measures how much the subject person aligns with the rule-of-thirds grid and crossings. Secondly, we calculate the proportion of ROI by dividing the width of human subject to the image width.

The real-time guidance user interface went through several iterations. In the final version, semi-transparent arrows are rendered and animated on top of the image and on two sides. These arrows direct users to move six directions—up, down, left, right, closer, and further away. We smooth the animation of the arrows to avoid jerkiness. The arrows on the two sides direct user to move closer to or further from the subject. They start to appear when the proportion deviates from one-third beyond a small margin. The color saturation and speed of the side arrows depends on how much the difference is.

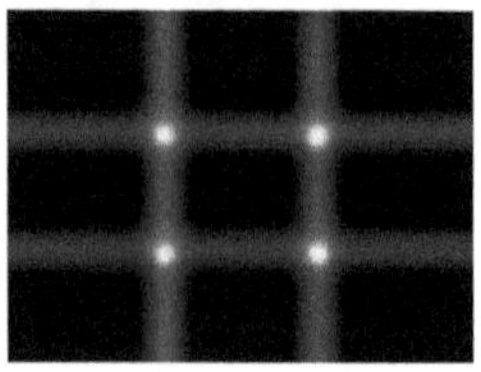

Figure 1. The bitmap mask for calculating the alignment between subject-of-interest and rule-of-thirds

Figure 2. Real-time interface with animated arrows that guide users to follow Rule-of-Thirds. Here these arrows indicate that the user should move to the lower right and further away.

USER STUDY

The goal is to find whether the real-time guidance interface can effectively enhance photo aesthetics. We hypothesize that there is a significant difference in photo aesthetic quality between photos taken with real-time guidance interface and those taken with the static gridline interface.

Procedure and Participants

We recruited forty non-expert users through several company mailing lists. These participants had not previously taken classes or read books on photography. Each used both the real-time guidance tool and a static gridline tool to take photos of a friend, as it is closer to a real-life scenario than taking photos of a stranger. The order of interfaces was alternated to counterbalance order effects. Each pair of photos shared the same subject and similar backgrounds, which helped to control for the content-related aesthetic differences.

To avoid the problem of unintentional photo snapping, each user took up to five photos and chose his or her favorite one. To avoid the variance among photo takers who may or may not know rule-of-thirds before the study, we showed users an example photo that illustrates rule-of-thirds and explained its meaning beforehand. Users were given up to 5 minutes of learning time for each interface. We could not control the subjects' facial expression, body posture, or changes in the background that was caused by different camera positions.

Figure 3. The web page for expert photographers and Mechanical Turk workers to rate photos and write comments

After these photos were taken with both interfaces, we recruited professional photographers and Mechanical Turk workers [8] to rate these 40 pairs of photos side-by-side using a 0-100 scale (Figure 3). Raters were also asked to write the main reason why they preferred one photo over the other. We recruited 24 professional photographers who specialize in portraiture with at least 2 years of full-time experience through an agency. On Mechanical Turk, we encouraged raters to review all forty pairs of photos by giving a 2-dollar bonus. We reject ratings completed in less than 10 seconds. In total, 48 of Mechanical Turk raters rated all 40 pairs of the photos. We randomize the order the photos to counterbalance any order effect.

We use within-subjects design so that individual differences in score ranges and evaluation criteria would not obscure the difference in photo aesthetic scores.

Findings

Our study shows that the aesthetic quality ratings for photos taken with the real-time guidance (RG) interface is significantly higher than those taken with the static gridline (SG) interface, according to both expert photographers and Mechanical Turk workers. Table 1 presents the means and standard deviations.

There were two independent variables, camera interface and photo-taker, and one dependent variable, photo's aesthetic rating. Using the two-factor repeated measures ANOVA, we found that expert photographers and Mechanical Turk workers (MT) rated the photos taken by RG interface to be significantly better than those taken by SG interface (expert: $F = 7.62$, $p < .05$, $\eta^2_{partial} = .249$); MT: $F = 20.41$, $p < .01$, $\eta^2_{partial} = .303$). Photo-taker is a significant factor for photo ratings (expert: $F = 5.88$, $p < .01$; MT: $F = 10.45$, $p < .01$). There is a moderate positive correlation between the average photo ratings from experts and MT raters (Pearson product-moment correlation coefficient $R = 0.68$, $p < .01$).

Raters	Real-time Guidance UI	Static Gridline UI
Expert photographers	M = 43.95 SD = 22.99	M = 40.60 SD = 22.08
Mechanical Turk workers	M = 65.98 SD = 21.87	M = 60.92 SD = 22.42

Table 1. The means and standard deviation for the photo aesthetic rating scores (range: 0-100)

Our data analysis show that users conform better to rule-of-thirds with the RG interface than with the SG interface:

- Users align the subject to the rule-of-thirds grid better with the RG interface than the SG interface (average diff = 31.76 (on a 0-250 scale), $p < .05$, one tailed paired t-test)
- The proportion of human subject's width is significantly closer to 1/3 when using the RG interface compared to the SG interface (average difference = 6%, $p < .01$, one tailed paired t-test). Users tend to have smaller subject/image ratios when using the SG interface.

There is no significant correlation between the alignment to the rule-of-thirds grid and the aesthetic quality score. There is a moderate negative correlation between the deviation from one-thirds proportion and the aesthetic quality score (Pearson product-moment correlation coefficient $R = 0.43$, $p < .01$)

To further understand the criteria that raters used, we coded user comments into different categories. 51.7% of the expert comments were about the global features of the photo, including composition (balance, camera angle and distance, rule-of-thirds etc.), lighting (exposure, evenness, shadows, etc.), and color (white balance, saturation, contrast, true to reality etc.) In contrast, only 29.8% of the Mechanical Turk raters' feedback fell into the above categories. 26% of experts' comments were about the face and body of the subject, including genuine/natural smile, mood, eye contact, glass reflection, lighting effect on the skin tone, aliveness, naturalness, movement and action, head/body proportion. 44.8% of the Mechanical Turk raters' feedback fell into those categories.

DISCUSSION

Our study demonstrates that the real-time guidance about rule-of-thirds generates significantly higher aesthetic quality portraiture photos than the static gridline interface. Moreover, the photos taken by the RG interface follow rule-of-thirds better. This shows that even when users know rules-of-thirds through instruction, the UI still makes a difference in whether users follow the rule or not. They tend not to ignore feedback when it responds to their real time motions. These findings point to a fruitful new direction to explore. By leveraging the increased scene analysis capabilities and RG interface enabled by camera arrays and computational photography, future mobile platforms can guide casual users into taking photos that look like ones taken by experts.

While this study addresses the question of *whether* RG interfaces can enhance photo aesthetic quality, the *how* and *why* questions need to be answered in future work. Our study reveals complex and intertwined factors that influence photo aesthetic quality. We find subject/image proportions close to 1/3 correlate with better aesthetic scores. This is consistent with [9] (pp.3), which points out that new photographers tend to shoot too far away from the subject and include too many distractions. But we also find that aligning the subject of interest with rule-of-thirds gridlines does not correlate with better photo aesthetics. It can be caused by other aspects of photography that are not supported by our interface. For example, a user may solely focus on rule-of-thirds when using our tool but accidentally introduce new distractions in the background. In contrast, experienced photographers attend to multiple aspects of photo-shooting at the same time. Therefore, to analyze photo aesthetics, we need to analyze multiple aspects of the scene in real time, such as depth, lighting, segmentation, semantics, etc. Full potential of this research direction will be only be unlocked with sensors that enable a greater understanding of the captured scene, both in depth and semantics. As depth sensing mobile platforms are just now reaching the market, they open up new opportunities for computational photography to change the process and outcome of photo-taking.

We collected ratings from both experts and Mechanical Turk workers. Even though they focus on different aspects of photo aesthetics, both groups rated photos taken with our real-time guidance interface to be better. They are moderately correlated with roughly a 20-point difference (with experts being stricter). This shows that although photo aesthetics are subjective, there is agreement among different user groups to some extent.

Limitations

Rule-of-thirds is just one photo composition rule. Our implementation of rule-of-thirds is one simple interpretation of the rule. Incorporating multiple rules is future work. Also, our work does not encourage creative photographic techniques that break standard composition rules.

CONCLUSION

This paper contributes to the literature by developing and evaluating a real-time photo-taking guidance interface. We present empirical evidence that this interface can enhance photo aesthetics in a constrained user scenario. It suggests that a new generation of mobile devices with camera arrays may enable breakthroughs in mobile user experiences through advanced computational photography algorithms and real-time guidance feedback.

ACKNOWLEDGEMENTS

We thank Philip Corriveau, Hannah Colett, Marisol Martinez Escobar, Audrey Younkin, Hanan Alnizami for their feedbacks on the study design and system iteration.

REFERENCES

1. Bradski, G. OpenCV Library. *Dr. Dobb's Journal of Software Tools.*
2. Datta, R. and Wang, J. ACQUINE: aesthetic quality inference engine-real-time automatic rating of photo aesthetics. *Proc. of Multimedia Information Retrieval*, ACM, (2010), 421–424.
3. Khan, S. and Vogel, Evaluating visual aesthetics in photographic portraiture. In *Proc. of Symposium on Computational Aesthetics in Graphics, Visualization, and Imaging*, ACM (2012), 1-8.
4. Kindberg, T., Spasojevic, M., Fleck, R., & Sellen, A. The Ubiquitous Camera: An In-Depth Study of Camera Phone Use. *IEEE Pervasive Computing*, *4*, 2 (2005), 42–50.
5. Li, C. and Gallagher, A. Aesthetic quality assessment of consumer photos with faces. *Proc. of Image Processing* IEEE (2010), 3–6.
6. Luo, Y., & Tang, X. Photo and video quality evaluation: F1ocusing on the subject. *In Proc. of Computer Vision–ECCV*, Springer (2008), 386–399.
7. Luo, W., Wang, X., & Tang, X. Content-based photo quality assessment. *International Conference on Computer Vision*, IEEE (2011), 2206-2213
8. Mason, W. and Suri, S. Conducting behavioral research on Amazon's Mechanical Turk. *Behavior research methods 44*, 1 (2012), 1–23.
9. Northrup, T. (2012). *How to create stunning digital photography.* Mason Press.
10. Pedro, J.S. and Church, K. The sound of light: induced synesthesia for augmenting the photography experience. *CHI'13 Extended Abstracts,* ACM (2013), 745–750.
11. Peterson, B. F. (2003). *Learning to see creatively*, Amphoto Press.
12. Smith, J. T. (1797). *Remarks on rural scenery.* Nathaniel Smith ancient Print. Cited by the Wikipedia page about rule of thirds: http://en.wikipedia.org/wiki/Rule_of_thirds (retrieved September 10, 2014)
13. Yao, L., Suryanarayan, P., and Qiao, M. Oscar: On-site composition and aesthetics feedback through exemplars for photographers. *International journal of Computer Vision*, 96, 3, Springer (2012), 353-383.

Infographic Aesthetics: Designing for the First Impression

Lane Harrison
Tufts University
lane@cs.tufts.edu

Katharina Reinecke
University of Michigan
reinecke@umich.edu

Remco Chang
Tufts University
remco@cs.tufts.edu

ABSTRACT

Information graphics, or infographics, combine elements of data visualization with design and have become an increasingly popular means for disseminating data. While several studies have suggested that aesthetics in visualization and infographics relate to desirable outcomes like engagement and memorability, it remains unknown how quickly aesthetic impressions are formed, and what it is that makes an infographic appealing. We address these questions by analyzing 1,278 participants' ratings on appeal after seeing infographics for 500ms. Our results establish that: 1) people form a reliable first impression of the appeal of an infographic based on a mere exposure effect, 2) this first impression is largely based on colorfulness and visual complexity, and 3) age, gender, and education level influence the preferred level of colorfulness and complexity. More generally, these findings suggest that outcomes such as engagement and memorability might be determined much earlier than previously thought.

Author Keywords

Visualization; Infographics; Aesthetics

ACM Classification Keywords

H.5.m. Information Interfaces and Presentation (e.g. HCI): Miscellaneous

INTRODUCTION

Information graphics, commonly called "infographics", are used to communicate complex data in an engaging manner. Defined as a collection of one or more visualizations that have been manually modified (or "adorned" [1]) to highlight specific points about the data [1, 3], infographics provide readers with an overview of a topic through data and other available information. Infographics are an effective means for telling stories about data, as they capture a reader's attention by structuring these stories using principles of graphic design.

Given these features, it is not surprising that infographics have become one of the most popular means for communicating data to large, diverse audiences [1, 3]. Companies and non-profit organizations are increasingly using infographics to attract customers and contributors. At the same time, infographics are being used to disseminate more critical information. In 2013, for example, the Centers for Disease Control (CDC) produced a series of infographics targeting health issues in the US such as high blood pressure and child vaccinations. Trends like these underscore the need for understanding the underlying factors that modulate the effectiveness of infographics.

CHI 2015, April 18–23, 2015, Seoul, Republic of Korea.

ACM 978-1-4503-3145-6/15/04$15.00
http://dx.doi.org/10.1145/2702123.2702545

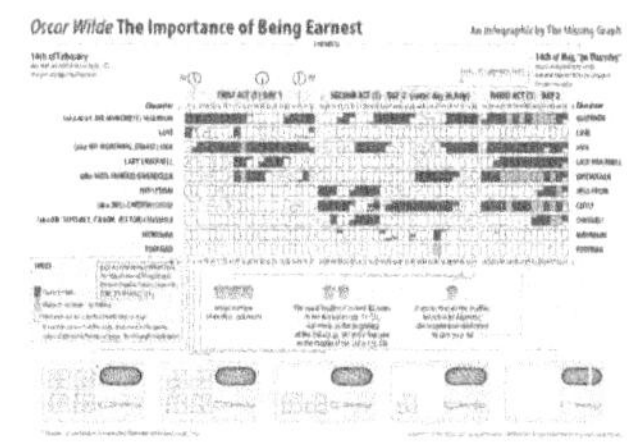

(a) m=2.68, sd=2.05

(b) m=6.50, sd=3.19

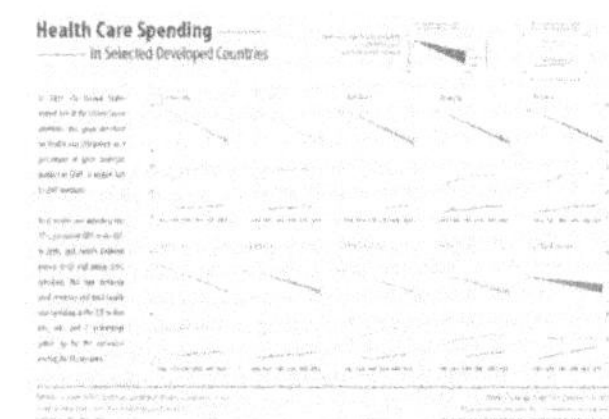

(c) m=3.35, sd=3.84

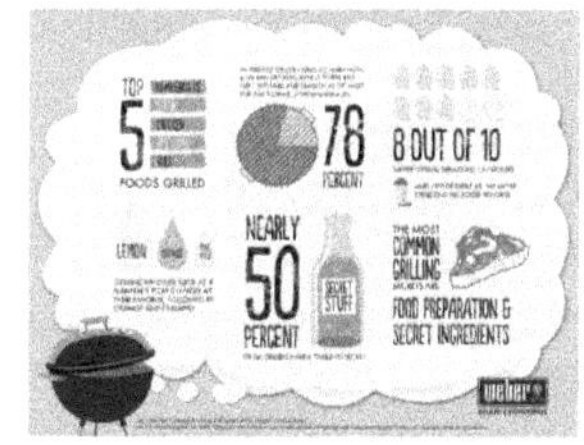

(d) m=6.69, sd=2.46

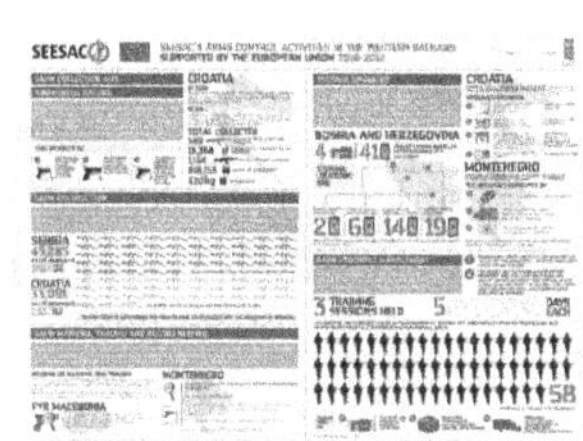

(e) m=3.70, sd=3.34

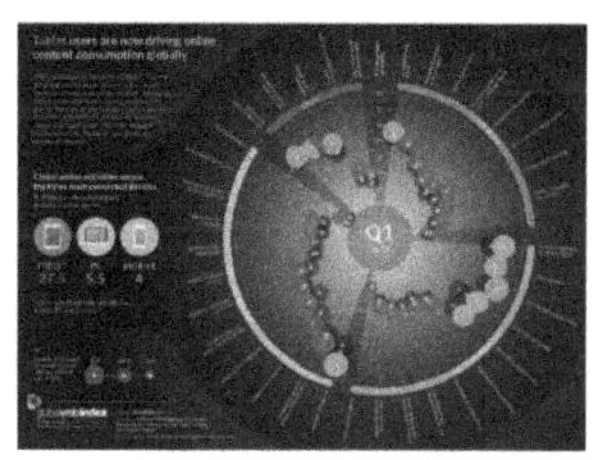

(f) m=6.60, sd=3.19

Figure 1: Infographics that resulted in the lowest (on the left) and highest (on the right) ratings of appeal (mean ratings on a 9-point Likert scale).

The heavy reliance of infographics on design has led researchers to suggest that aesthetics are among the main contributors for their success [4, 1, 3]. Infographics and data visualizations that have been rated as more aesthetically appealing have been found to have positive effects on engagement [4] and memorability [3]. However, it remains unknown how quickly these aesthetic impressions form: What is it that makes an infographic appealing to people at first sight? Are these judgements consistent within a person? What role do demographic factors play?

To investigate people's judgements of the aesthetic appeal of infographics, we conducted an online experiment with 1,278 participants, collecting approximately 83,000 ratings of appeal on a sample of 330 infographics from Visually, an online community for infographic designers. The results contribute to our understanding of aesthetics in visualization and infographics by establishing that:

- People form a reliable opinion of the appeal of an infographic within the first 500ms. Seeing that appeal is associated with engagement and memorability [4, 3], our results suggest that the first impression counts.
- Some infographics appeal broadly, but the majority produced controversial judgements. Although people are consistent in their judgements, they have strong, diverse opinions about the infographics they like/dislike.
- Demographic factors such as gender, age, and education level impact perceived appeal. We discuss how designers can optimize the first impression by adjusting the colorfulness and visual complexity of an infographic.

RELATED WORK

A key insight to the role of aesthetics in visualization and infographics is that the value of a visualization increases the more time is spent with it [10]. It follows that making visual representations of data engaging and memorable increases their value. In recent years, researchers have begun to explore the relationship between these ideas and aesthetics in information visualization [4, 1, 3]. Examining aesthetics in data visualization and task performance, Cawthon and Vande Moere found that appealing visualizations led to increased task engagement [4]. Similarly, Bateman et al. evaluated the effects of graphical embellishments (otherwise known as ChartJunk) on visualization performance, and hypothesized that the aesthetic qualities of embellished visualizations may make them more memorable [1]. Borkin et al. recently confirmed this hypothesis by identifying design techniques in visualizations and infographics that make them memorable [3].

A missing component from these studies of visualizations and infographics is to understand how aesthetic judgements form, and the factors that influence these judgements. The area of website aesthetics in human-computer interaction, in contrast, has established several methodologies for examining the aesthetic appeal of websites. The experiments of Lindgaard [6], for example, established that lasting impressions of website appeal form within 500ms of seeing it for the first time. The results of judgements like these were also shown to correlate with participant's perceptions of website usability and trustworthiness [5]. More recently, Reinecke et al. developed computational models that predict the first impression of websites using low-level image metrics of website colorfulness and complexity [9].

EXPERIMENT

Materials

To generate a representative set of stimuli, we used a two-stage process involving sampling and curation. First, we randomly chose a sample of 2,000 infographics from the approximately 40,000 available on Visually. Three coders then independently rated each infographic in this sample on representativeness (to exclude images that did not contain data visualizations or were simply images of interactive systems), content suitability (to avoid controversial infographics e.g. those concerning Israel and Palestine, or pornography), dissemination (to exclude widely known infographics), and language (to avoid the influence of non-english infographics with different language scripts). We excluded any infographic that was marked as unacceptable according to these criteria by one or more coders. The remaining 330 infographics were used in the main experiment.

Procedure

The experiment was conducted as a 10-minute online test, and advertised via online social networks. This online test included informed consent but did not collect personally identifiable information. The protocol was approved by IRBs at two institutions. As an incentive for participation, we promoted the experiment with the slogan "Do you have the eye of a designer?", and added a personalized feedback page at the end that compared a participant's ratings to the number of "likes" and "views" of the Visually community. Participants did not receive any financial compensation. Mobile users were not permitted during the experiment period.

Following the experiment procedure in [6], participants rated 30 infographics (presented in randomized order and drawn from the larger set of 330 infographics) on a 9-point Likert scale on appeal (from "not at all appealing" to "very appealing"). Infographics flashed for 500ms each, immediately followed by a screen that only showed the Likert scale. The 500s stimulus exposure time was used to capture participants' first impression of the overall aesthetics and to avoid an in-depth engagement with the information presented. The experiment started with a voluntary questionnaire collecting basic demographics information, instructions, as well as a short practice phase of five infographics, targeted at anchoring participants' responses. The main part of the experiment was divided into two phases, during which each participant was shown a random sample of 30 infographics in different randomized order. Hence, participants provided two ratings for the same 30 infographics. In-between the two phases, we presented participants with a humorous photo for distraction, and asked them to take a break. Participants were then able to add comments about possible distractions or technical issues, before being presented with their personalized results page.

Participants

A total of 1,278 participants (77.5% female) completed the experiment between June and September 2014. Participants were between 6-80 years old (m=23, sd=11 years). (Parental consent for participants under 18 years of age was waived by our IRB.) Most participants were currently enrolled in college (41.8%) or in high school or professional school (40%). Participants came from 71 countries, with the majority being based in the US (60%). Eight percent worked in a creative occupation. Since their mean ratings did not significantly differ from participants in other occupations, we did not include occupation as a factor in the analysis.

RESULTS

Consistency

To evaluate whether people form reliable first impressions of an infographic's appeal, we computed the difference between participants' ratings of the same websites between phase 1 and 2 (following Lindgaard [6] and Reinecke [9]). Of rating pairs, 37.5% were the same and 39.4% differed by 1. In contrast, only 7.9% differed by more than 2 points on the 9-point Likert scale, indicating that participants provided consistent ratings. Participants therefore form a reliable opinion of the appeal of an infographic within the first 500ms – a time that constitues a mere exposure effect [6].

Variance in an individual's aesthetic impressions

The previous result is further emphasized given that participants provided strongly varying ratings for the 30 infographics each of them saw. The mean range of a participant's ratings on the 9-point Likert scale (averaged across all participants) was 6.4 (sd=1.3), showing that individuals rated some infographics highly on appeal, while strongly disliking others. This shows that people have strong opinions about the design of infographics, which emphasizes the importance of exploring what it is that makes an infographic appealing.

Controversial infographics

While participants were consistent in their individual ratings for a given infographic between the two experiment phases, the diversity in ratings for the 330 infographics suggest that only a few infographics are universally appealing. The mean range of ratings on the 9-point Likert scale (averaged across all participants' ratings for one infographic) was 7.07 (sd=0.45), showing that what appeals to some can be highly disliked by others.

Effects of colorfulness, complexity, and demographics

Colorfulness and visual complexity explain roughly half of the variance in people's judgements of the appeal of websites [9] and are considered some of the most salient features that humans perceive within the first 500ms [6]. We therefore followed the procedure outlined in [9] to compute perceptual models of colorfulness and complexity of each of our infographics as an estimate for visual appeal. Reinecke et al.'s models [9] use a combination of several low-level image statistics: Colorfulness integrates specific colors with the saturation and number of image areas in a given image, while visual complexity is computed based on text and image areas, as well as color features that contribute to perceived complexity (see [9] for references to the full models and algorithms). The computed values for both demonstrate that our set of infographics cover a broad range of low to high colorfulness/complexity (colorfulness range=0-175, m=58, sd=27; complexity range=0-28, m=8, sd=4).

To analyze the effects of demographics on a preference for certain levels of colorfulness and complexity, we constructed a series of mixed-effects models using the *R* lme4 package [2]. ParticipantID and InfographicID were modeled as random effects, and the fixed effects Colorfulness, Complexity, and demographic variables (Age, Gender, EducationLevel, Country) were modeled to test for interactions. Demographic variables were added or excluded based on Akaikes Information Criteria (AIC) to determine which variables significantly improved the model fit.

A comparison of two models (one without demographics and one with) shows that demographic factors significantly affect ratings of appeal ($\chi^2_{45} = 118.2, p < .0001$). Country did not significantly improve the model fit (most likely because our sample size in most of the 71 countries was small), and was therefore omitted. The resulting model includes Gender, Age, and EducationLevel, and explains 34% of the variance of participants' ratings of appeal (based on an R^2 calculation using a combination of fixed and random effects [7]).

Our results indicate that the colorfulness of an infographic determines appeal more than visual complexity. This is in contrast to the finding of Reinecke et al. [9] who found that the complexity of a website plays a more important role than colorfulness as a predictor variable. One possible reason might be that infographics rely on color and color composition as a design element much more than websites.

The results also show that, in general, colorfulness is slightly positively correlated with ratings on appeal ($\beta = -0.0009, se = 0.0007, t = 1.3, p < .001$). As Figure 1 shows, some of the most highly rated infographics use a higher number, and more saturated colors (right side) than those that received some of the lowest average ratings (left side of Figure 1). However, we found a significant interaction effect of gender and colorfulness ($F_1 = 4.02, p < .001$), suggesting that the general preference for a higher colorfulness is almost reversed for male participants ($\beta = -0.0006, se = 0.0003, t = -2.4, p < .001$, see also Figure 2): While males rate colorless infographics slightly higher than females on average, they dislike highly colorful infographics more than females. Figure 1(d), for instance, was rated significantly higher by females ($m = 6.89$) than by males ($m = 6.19$) (independent t-test, $t = -2.53, p < .05$). A visual inspection of similar infographics suggests that female-preferred infographics predominantly use a higher number of different colors than those preferred by male participants.

We observed a similar effect of gender on the preferred complexity of infographics ($F_1 = 5.61, p < .001$). On average, male participants were relatively unaffected by complexity. Ratings by females, however, produced a weak negative relationship with complexity ($\beta = -0.004, se = 0.002, t = -2.4, p < .001$). Comparing Figure 1(d)—the infographic that received among the highest ratings—with Figures 1(a) and 1(e), text-heavy figures that were among the lowest

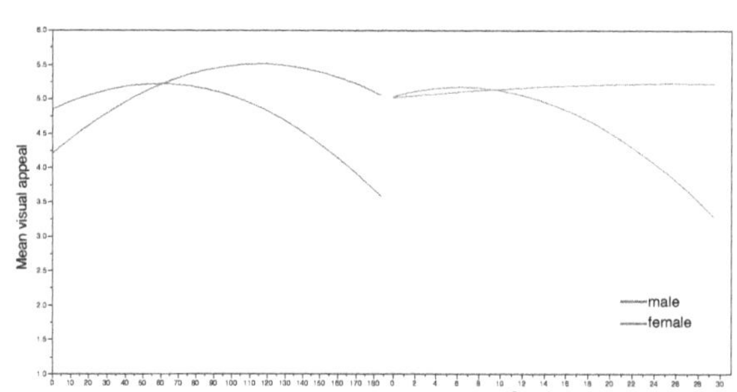

Figure 2: Average visual appeal ratings for different levels of colorfulness and complexity for females and males.

rated. While the latter two received higher ratings from males ($m = 2.94$, $m = 4.08$ respectively) than from females ($m = 2.63$, $m = 3.51$), these results were not significantly different (independent t-test, 1(a): $t = 0.877, p = 0.39$; 1(e): $t = 0.971, p = 0.35$). However, the direct comparison between these two infographics exemplifies an overall trend in our data: Men seem to be less negatively influenced by a higher number of text areas than women, who seem to generally prefer more area devoted to images.

Our analysis showed that age significantly affected participants' preferred levels of visual complexity ($F_1 = 10.9, p < .001$), but that it only has a marginal effect on the preferred colorfulness. The older participants were, the less they liked complex infographics ($\beta = -0.0004, se = 0.00004, t = -4.8, p < .001$). Previous results for websites suggested the reverse: Older participants found more complex websites more appealing [8]. However, this previous result was based on a higher sample size, and in particular, a higher average age, and might therefore not be comparable to ours.

We additionally found that participants' education level significantly affected their preference for colorfulness ($F_7 = 3.13, p < .001$) and complexity ($F_7 = 3.01, p < .001$). In general, a higher education level negatively affects the ratings of appeal for highly colorful and complex infographics, although this effect is less strong than that of gender and age.

DISCUSSION AND DESIGN GUIDELINES

One of the most important findings of this research is that people form a reliable opinion of an infographics' appeal within the first 500ms of seeing it. Given the rising use of infographics to depict important information coupled with increasing demands on user attention, this finding highlights the need for optimizing the perceived appeal of information at first sight. Furthermore, since appeal has been identified as having a positive effect on engagement and memorability, our results suggest that these effects may be formed much earlier than previously thought.

To a large extent, the first impression of appeal is based on how colorful and visually complex an infographic is. We found that colorfulness and complexity explain 34% of the variance in participants' ratings on appeal. Because colorfulness and complexity are computational metrics (see [9]), an increase in these metrics can be attributed to a number of actions a designer may take, including adding images, icons, changing the size/color of text, or by manipulating white space and layout. When optimizing the design of an infographic to make a good first impression, therefore, designers should aim for a low to medium complexity (e.g., by choosing a limited number of image and text areas), and a medium to high colorfulness (e.g., by increasing the saturation and contrast between colors). Figures 1(b), 1(d), and 1(f) are examples of an infographics that were widely judged as appealing.

Our results also show that these general guidelines can be further optimized for particular audiences, given the significant effects of age, gender, and education level. Females prefer more colorful, yet less complex infographics than males, while males generally prefer fewer and less saturated colors and are relatively unaffected by different levels of complexity. Preference for simple infographics slightly increases with age and education level. Thus, the general preference for colorful infographics with few text and image areas might appeal to most participants in our sample, but not to all.

FUTURE WORK AND CONCLUSION

This research established that people decide about an infographic's appeal based on minimal exposure, and that several demographic factors contribute to this impression. Opportunities for future work include analyzing consistency in people's ratings across a longer period of time, identifying additional factors that impact the appeal of infographics (e.g. country), and investigating how initial judgements of appeal impacts reasoning and judgements with information. As research continues to explore human-centric factors in visualization such as engagement and memorability, the results in this note provide a baseline to investigate the relationship between these factors and aesthetics.

DATASET

To facilitate future work, all stimuli, participant data, and analyses scripts are available on the authors website: http://valt.cs.tufts.edu/papers/infographic-aesthetics.

ACKNOWLEDGEMENTS

We thank Simon Warchol for help debugging the computational metrics, and Visually for providing the infographics.

REFERENCES

1. Bateman, S., Mandryk, R. L., Gutwin, C., Genest, A., McDine, D., and Brooks, C. Useful junk?: the effects of visual embellishment on comprehension and memorability of charts. In *Proc. CHI'10*, ACM (2010), 2573–2582.
2. Bates, D., Maechler, M., and Bolker, B. *lme4: Linear mixed-effects models using S4 classes*, 2013. R package version 0.999999-2.
3. Borkin, M. A., Vo, A. A., Bylinskii, Z., Isola, P., Sunkavalli, S., Oliva, A., and Pfister, H. What makes a visualization memorable? *Transactions on Visualization and Computer Graphics 19*, 12 (2013), 2306–2315.
4. Cawthon, N., and Moere, A. V. The effect of aesthetic on the usability of data visualization. In *Proc. Information Visualization'07*, IEEE (2007), 637–648.
5. Lindgaard, G., Dudek, C., Sen, D., Sumegi, L., and Noonan, P. An Exploration of Relations Between Visual Appeal, Trustworthiness and Perceived Usability of Homepages. *ACM ToCHI 18*, 1 (2011).
6. Lindgaard, G., Fernandes, G., Dudek, C., and Brown, J. Attention Web Designers: You Have 50 Milliseconds to Make a Good First Impression! *Behaviour & Information Technology 25*, 2 (2006), 115–126.
7. Nakagawa, S., and Schielzeth, H. A general and simple method for obtaining R2 from generalized linear mixed-effects models. *Methods in Ecology and Evolution 4* (2013), 133–142.
8. Reinecke, K., and Gajos, K. Z. Quantifying Visual Preferences Around the World. In *Proc. CHI'14* (2014).
9. Reinecke, K., Yeh, T., Miratrix, L., Mardiko, R., Zhao, Y., Liu, J., and Gajos, K. Predicting Users' First Impressions of Website Aesthetics With a Quantification of Perceived Visual Complexity and Colorfulness. In *Proc. CHI'13* (2013).
10. Van Wijk, J. J. The value of visualization. In *Visualization, 2005. VIS 05. IEEE*, IEEE (2005), 79–86.

ISOTYPE Visualization – Working Memory, Performance, and Engagement with Pictographs

Steve Haroz
Northwestern University
isotype@steveharoz.com

Robert Kosara
Tableau Research
rkosara@tableau.com

Steven L. Franconeri
Northwestern University
franconeri@northwestern.edu

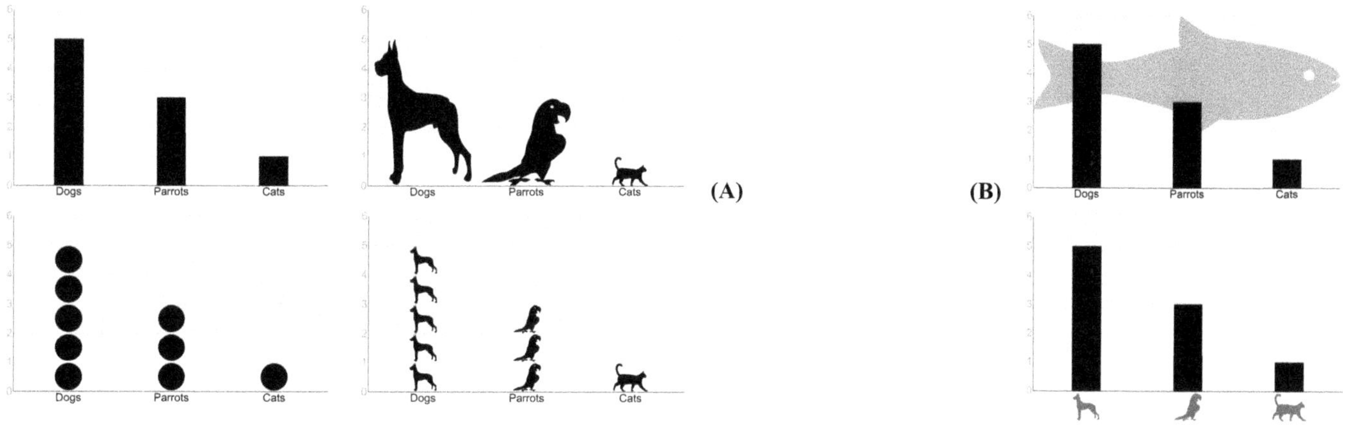

Fig. 1. Pictographic charts have been used for decades. (A) Which chart above most effectively conveys information? Which data is easiest to remember during a demanding task? Which is most engaging? (B) How integrated must a pictograph be to benefit the user? Do purely decorative background images offer the same benefits as simple axis labels? Or must they be used to convey data?

ABSTRACT
Although the infographic and design communities have used simple pictographic representations for decades, it is still unclear whether they can make visualizations more effective. Using simple charts, we tested how pictographic representations impact (1) memory for information just viewed, as well as under the load of additional information, (2) speed of finding information, and (3) engagement and preference in seeking out these visualizations. We find that superfluous images can distract. But we find no user costs – and some intriguing benefits – when pictographs are used to represent the data.

Author Keywords
Visualization; Psychophysics; Working Memory; User Performance; Pictograph; Embellishment; ISOTYPE

INTRODUCTION
The International System Of TYpographic Picture Education (ISOTYPE) uses simple pictographic elements to convey many types of information, including numerical data. Otto and Marie Neurath defined the term in the 1920s [21], though this type of chart was first described by Willard Brinton in 1914 [6]. Together with Gerd Arntz, the Neuraths created many ISOTYPE designs over several decades [1].

The goal was a universally understandable system for communicating quantities of commercial, social, or economic information (e.g., automobile production or number of children born per year). Symbols, each representing a fixed quantity, were stacked to provide an intuitive representation of a total amount (Fig. 2). Gerd Arntz's pictographs – simplified icons with minimal color – are highly recognizable and are still used in signs, traffic icons, and warning labels.

While the design community has largely embraced the simple style of ISOTYPE for pictographic embellishments [7, 17], the visualization and HCI communities tend to regard pictographs as 'chart junk' – a distraction from the data itself [24]. Here we examine how ISOTYPE-style embellishment affects viewer memory, speed, and engagement within simple visualizations.

Recent work suggests that extraneous pictographic information can indeed improve the effectiveness of visualizations. Bateman et al. found that visualizations that integrate data with illustrations yielded better memory of the data compared to minimalistic outlines of bar charts [2]. Borkin et al. found a related result – that people can better recall having seen a visualization that includes pictures [4], though it is not clear if they would better recall the data, per se. When images and clip-art are embedded in the visualization's data representation, Borgo et al. found occasional impact to work-

CHI 2015, April 18 - 23 2015, Seoul, Republic of Korea

ACM 978-1-4503-3145-6/15/04…$15.00
http://dx.doi.org/10.1145/2702123.2702275

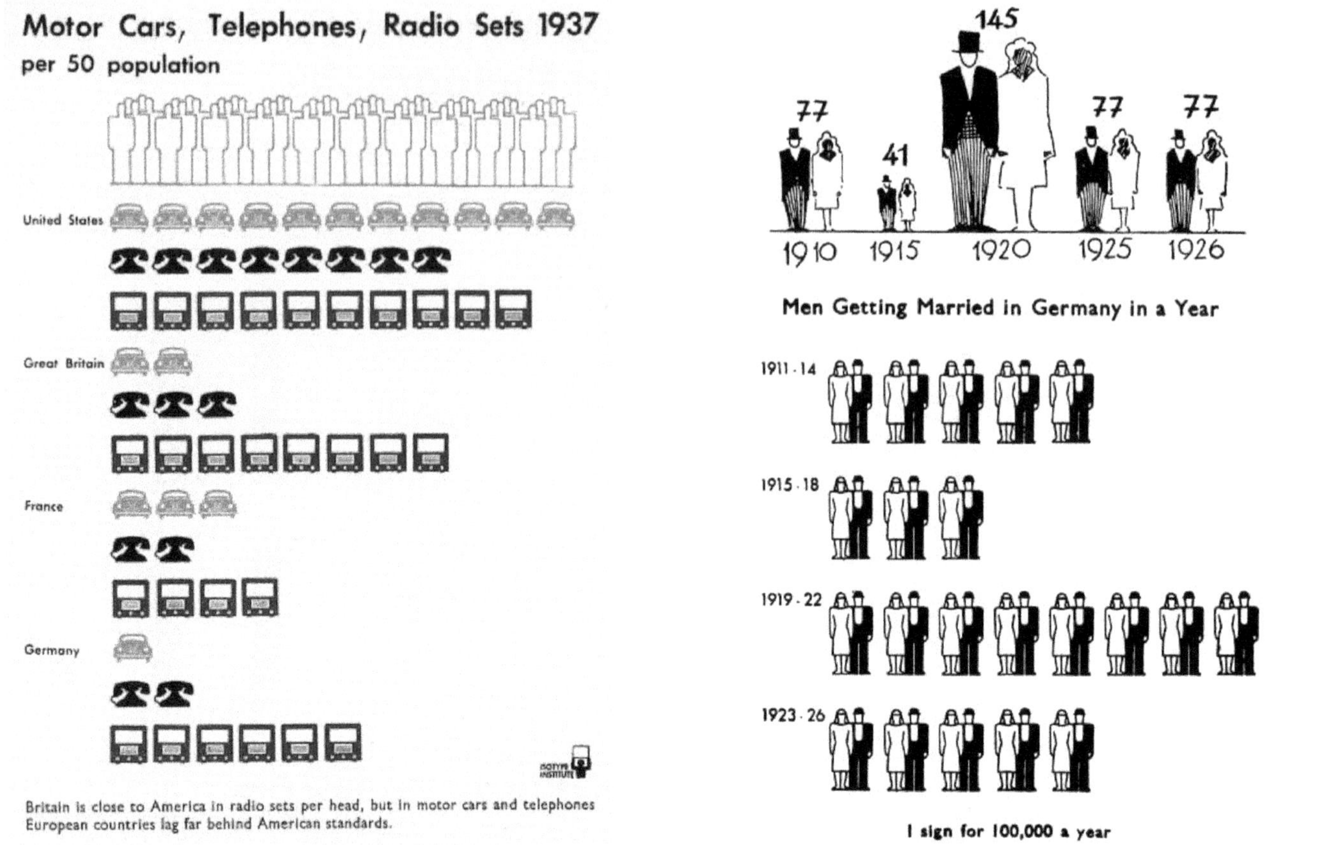

Fig. 2. Both of these example visualizations were made by Otto Neurath, a proponent of using arrays of simple pictographs to present quantitative information. The left image – published in 1937 – uses rows of pictographs to visualize the number of cars, phones, and radios in different countries. The right image – published in 1936 – shows two visualizations of the same data. Neurath insisted that stretching one pictograph (top) was inferior to stacking multiple small pictographs (bottom) [21].

ing and long term memory performance for some visualizations [3]. Other work shows that embellishing data with colors that are semantically consistent (e.g., blue for data about "oceans") can increase the speed of finding information in a visualization [19].

While past empirical research has shown that pictorial information can be beneficial, it is unclear why and when these advantages occur. In particular, we explore whether, and how, the types of pictorial cues designed by Brinton, the Neuraths, and Arntz might create more effective visualizations. Although past work has studied visualization embellishments that contain varied degrees of color [2, 3], we omit color cues and instead focus on pictorial cues carried by an object's shape

We tease apart several properties of ISOTYPE-style pictographs in our experiments in order to identify which aspects lead to costs or benefits for visualizations. For example, pictographs add identifiable symbols, which might increase memorability or engagement. Do these pictures need to be a part of the data, as in the examples in Fig. 2, or do they carry the same advantage when they merely accompany a chart in the background or as a label (Fig. 1B)? If the symbols are a part of the data, does it matter if the data value is conveyed by the number of stacked symbols, as opposed to the stretched height of a symbol, which Neurath insisted was an inferior cue (see Fig. 2, right)? If the design choice to stack or stretch matters, is that effect specific to pictographs, or would the same pattern emerge for simple non-symbolic shapes, such as a stack of circles vs. a single stretched bar (Fig. 1A, left column)?

We explore these questions across a range of sample measures: memory for previously glanced information, memory under the load of seeing intervening visualizations, speed of data extraction, and the level of observer engagement in a visualization.

CHART VARIATIONS

We manipulate several aspects of the charts independently across experiments, using the classic unembellished bar chart (Fig. 1A top-left) as a baseline.

Variation: Pictographs vs. Simple Shapes

ISOTYPE charts typically rely on pictographic representations of the real objects referred to by the data, instead of simple shapes like the rectangles of a bar chart. To test the potential costs or benefits of pictorial information, we use graphs with either ISOTYPE-style pictographs or simple shapes (see the differences across the columns of Fig. 1A).

Pictographic representation may help overcome limits on working memory, a primary bottleneck in human reasoning [9]. Pictures provide multiple cues for encoding and retrieval of memories, providing a richer set of contextual 'hooks' that allow for broader and deeper encoding of data in memory. For example, when a group of people were asked to memorize a list of words under water (while wearing scuba gear), their recall performance for the words was better when they were tested in the water, reactivating a rich set of associations between the memorized words and the sights, sounds, and emotions of their environment – compared to recalling them on land where these associations were absent [13]. Likewise, the imagery of pictographs may provide richer encoding cues, so that recalling the shape of the icon leads to more associations with the data, compared to recalling a text-based label.

We created the pictograph stimuli by making 43 sets of object categories. Each set contained four image-word pairs, chosen to reflect a category such as pets, desserts, clothes, instruments, or vehicles. All pictographs were black and white SVG files that allow for scaling (available in the demo).

Variation: Stretched vs Stacked

ISOTYPE charts typically rely on stacks of individual items to represent values (Fig. 1A bottom-right), instead of stretching the continuous extent of a single item. Because such discretizing of the values may itself impact performance, we independently manipulate this factor across both pictographs (Fig. 1A bottom-right) and simple shapes (Fig. 1A bottom-left). We also include a pictographic representation that is stretched vertically instead of being stacked (Fig. 1 top-right). We proportionally stretch the object along the x-axis to prevent distortion, but x-axis stretching is limited to prevent objects from overlapping horizontally.

Compared to stretching, stacking has the potential advantage of presenting information in a dual format - both as a height and as a number of objects. While the discrimination precision for size is typically better than for number [11], redundant encoding of both dimensions may be beneficial. In addition, for small numbers (1-4), the visual system can employ a faster and more precise mechanism for number discrimination, compared to larger ranges [8, 18]. Reliance on this more efficient system may also free up additional memory capacity for the depicted information [12]. Accuracy should therefore improve for small numbers of pictographs, even if each pictograph represents more than a single value (e.g., in Fig. 2, right, one couple represents 100,000 marriages).

Variation: Axis Labels

The use of pictographs might impact the effectiveness of a visualization because it allows a visual association for the label of the data, or more specifically, because the picture itself is used as the glyph. Would pictographic symbols have the same impact whether they are used as legend markers, allowing a visual association with the data label, or whether they are used as the markers that depict the data (either stacked or stretched)? Experiment 1 includes a condition where X-axis labels are replaced with pictographs (e.g., Fig. 1B bottom). For charts that already incorporate pictographs (stacked or stretched), the X-axis was left blank to prevent subjects from confusing the label for part of the data.

Variation: Superfluous Imagery

Perhaps pictographs impact performance merely because they affect an observer's level of engagement. While the 'axis label' variation partially distances the pictographs from the data, we also test a 'superfluous' variation that completely separates the pictograph from the data. One past study found an improved ability to recall having seen a visualization when it includes any form of picture in the image [4], but recalling the pictorial information is not the same as recalling the data behind it. Experiments 1 and 4 include the condition of a simple bar graph with a background image of the same category as the data but irrelevant to the dataset (Fig. 1B top).

EXPERIMENT 1: WORKING MEMORY CAPACITY LIMITS

Our working memory is severely limited [5, 12] and can form the bottleneck of our reasoning abilities. Visualizations that place high demand on such limited resources can be substantially more challenging to analyze [15]. Here we test whether our pictograph variations impact working memory performance.

Exp 1: Methods

Twenty-two undergraduate students (12 women) participated in this experiment in return for credit in an introductory psychology course.

In each trial, subjects viewed a chart with 3 values (each randomly selected from 1 to 5) for 1.5 seconds. The chart was then replaced with a 'response' screen that asked the subject to recall each of the values in the chart (Fig. 3). In order to test memory for the values for each category outside of the context of the graph itself, the values were queried in a random order that did not necessarily match the left-to-right ordering of the categories in the graph. For example, a chart with A=2, B=5, and C=3 may be followed by a response screen asking for B, C, and A.

The experiment was split into ten blocks – two sets for each of the five chart types specified below. One of each pair of similar blocks was in the first half and second half of the experiment, so we could analyze any fatigue or learning over a 40 minute duration (we found no change over time). Each block began with a brief reminder of the instructions and included an example chart corresponding to the block's chart type. Each block included trials with every combination of three conditions:

- *5 Charts*:
  2 Shape versus Pictograph (Fig. 1A left-right) ×
  2 Stretched versus Stacked (Fig. 1A top-bottom) +
  1 Stretched bar with a background (Fig. 1B top)
- *2 Axis styles*: whether the x-axis labels are pictographs or text (Fig. 1B bottom)
- *2 Response styles*: To avoid a potential confound of the text axis style matching the response text, we also vary

whether the response screen uses pictographs or text to identify the input fields.

The blocks were randomly ordered, as were the trials in each. Each trial was then randomly assigned one of 42 data categories. Once a category was used, it would not be reused for the at least the next 10 trials. A 43rd category was reserved to show a sample chart before each block, so subjects would know what to expect.

The experiment included 200 trials (2 block repetitions × 5 chart types × 2 axis styles × 2 response styles × 5 repetitions). The first 5 trials were considered training and thus discounted in the analysis.

Exp 1: Analysis

We compute error level by averaging the absolute error for each value in a chart. So if a chart's values are 2, 3, 4, and a subject inputs 2, 5, 5, the average error for each value is (0+2+1) / 3 = 1. Each trial therefore yields a per-value error. For each result, we computed an average per subject per condition and computed an ANOVA between these subject means followed by a Tukey HSD correction. Error bars in all figures throughout this paper (except for Fig. 4) show the standard error between subject means. All line charts show linear fits with standard error ribbons.

Compensating for Individual Differences

Fig. 4 shows the substantial differences in memory accuracy across subjects for the unembellished simple bar graph. Some had nearly perfect recall, while others were only slightly better than an optimal guess (the mean of the Y-axis range). To factor out these differences for experiments 1-4, we normalized each subject's results by their performance on the simple bar condition. That is, all subject errors are individually scaled such that simple bar charts have an error of 1.0, and other values are costs or benefits relative to that baseline.

Chart type analysis

For the chart type analysis, we omit the superfluous condition (see the Superfluous pictograph section), allowing us to split the four remaining chart types into a 2x2 combination (stretched vs. stacked; shape vs. pictograph). The result is a more diagnostic 4-way repeated-measures 2x2x2x2 ANOVA with chart segmentation type (stretched or stacked), chart depiction type (pictographic or shape), axis style (pictographic or text), and response style (pictographic or text) as factors. As there were no interactions among any of these factors (all F<1), the following section examines the main effect of each factor.

Exp 1: Results

Pictographs and stacking

As Fig. 5 shows, using pictographs instead of simple shapes led to no difference in error rates ($F[1, 21]<1$, η_p^2=0.002). But using stacked items was associated with reduced error relative to stretched items ($F[1, 21]=10.0$, $p < 0.005$, η_p^2=0.06).

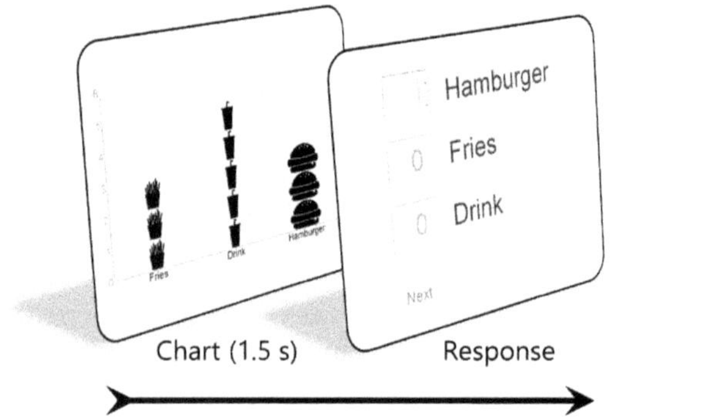

Fig. 3. In experiment 1, a chart is briefly shown then hidden. The response screen then appears where the subject enters the values. Notice that the order of the items is different in the response screen.

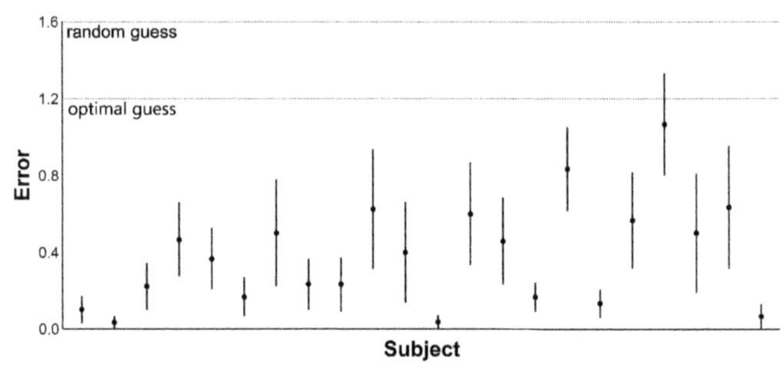

Fig. 4. Each subject's average error (difference from the correct values) for the simple bar graph condition with standard error (SE). Individual differences were large.

We were surprised at the lack of an impact from pictographs, having assumed that the rich perceptual encoding and engaging nature of pictures would be at least partly responsible for any potential advantages. The striking benefit of stacking may be explained by the cognitive advantages for small collections – the visual system has specialized mechanisms for enumerating small discrete quantities (4-5 or fewer objects [8]), and the redundant encoding of length and number may have proven beneficial to memory. Dividing length-defined objects into countable regions may have a benefit, but we predict that this benefit should only arise when stacks are smaller than 4-5 objects. The next experiment will test this prediction by introducing more numerous stacks of objects.

Axis and question pictographs

As Fig. 6 shows, using pictographs as X-axis labels resulted in more error for every type of chart ($F[1, 21]=12, p < 0.001$, η_p^2=0.07). Text labels may be recognized more quickly, as a lifetime of reading renders recognition of single words a surprisingly fast and automatic process. Alternatively, text labels may have led to better memory links between the label and the data value. Intriguingly, this advantage held regardless of whether the question was asked using text or pictograph labels, which showed no difference in performance ($F[1, 21]<1$, η_p^2=0.0003). There was also no reliable impact on error from the interaction of axis and question pictographs

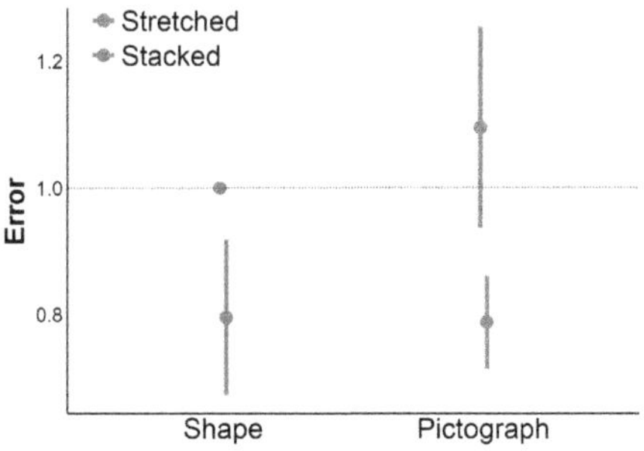

Fig. 5. Error levels are scaled relative to the error level of the simple bar chart, so it has 1.0 error for all subjects (top-left point). Charts with stacked items (blue) produced less error than those with stretched items (red). The use of simple shapes (left) or pictographs (right) had little impact.

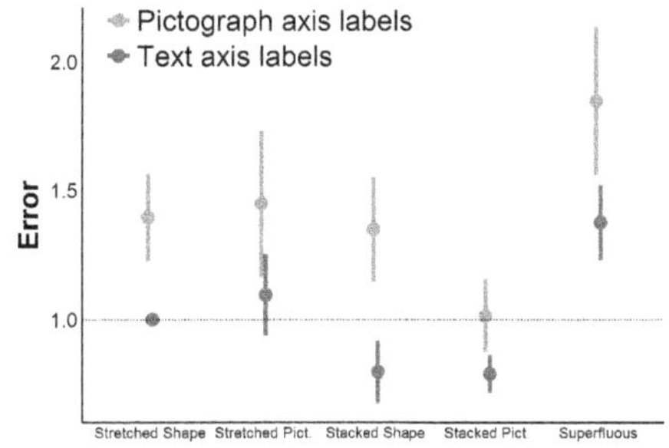

Fig. 6. For every type of chart, axes with text labels (purple) led to less error than those with pictograph labels (green).

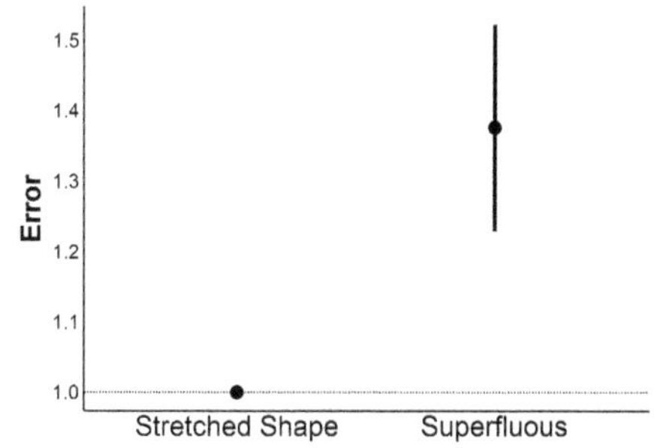

Fig. 7. An otherwise simple bar chart with a superfluous background image yields much higher error levels than an unembellished simple bar chart.

(F[1, 21]<1, η_p^2=0.002). We do note, however, that these labels were succinct and easy to read, which could have played a role in this result.

Superfluous pictograph

We also ran a 3-way repeated-measures 5x2x2 ANOVA with all five chart types, axis style (pictographic or text), and response styles (pictographic or text) as factors. There was a significant main effect of chart type (F[4, 21]=9.0, $p < 0.001$, ηp^2=0.08), driven primarily by the 45% larger error in the 'superfluous' chart type condition, relative to the mean of the other 4 conditions, (t[138]=3.39, $p < 0.001$).

As Fig. 7 shows, the addition of a superfluous pictograph – an embellishment that did not encode any data – dramatically increased recall error relative to a simple unembellished bar chart.

Left to right

Memory for the left bar was substantially more precise than the bar on the right (F[1, 21]=15, $p < 0.001$, η_p^2=0.19). Looking only at the simple bar chart trials, we scaled each subject's performance on the middle and right bar based on their error rate for the leftmost bar. The linear regression in Fig. 8 (left) shows that error level increases from left to right, suggesting that subjects are sequentially inspecting bars from left to right [10, 20] rather than simultaneously perceiving and memorizing all of them [14].

Maximum values

Because the values in the data were randomly selected, not all charts had a maximum value of 5. Some had a lower maximum. Smaller ranges may allow more precise encoding in memory. To determine if subjects were using the entire range of the axis versus the range of the data, we analyzed how the maximum data value correlated with the amount of error.

A linear regression graphed in Fig. 8 (right) shows that as the range of values increases, the amount of error increases (F[1, 21]=41, $p < 0.0001$, η_p^2=0.33). Therefore, recall from working memory becomes less accurate in proportion to the

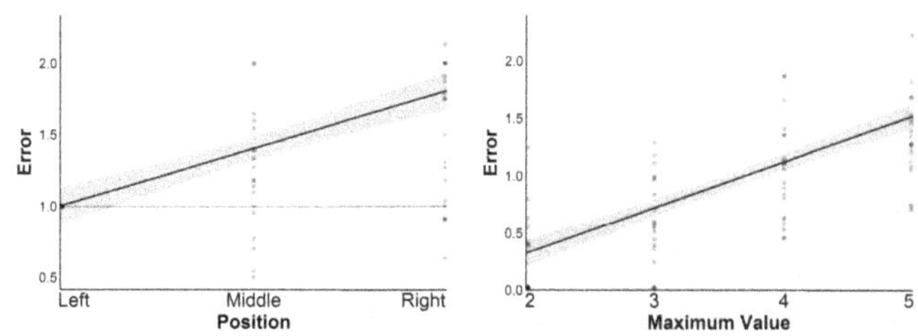

Fig. 8. (Left) Subjects strongly prioritized the leftmost values. The line is a linear fit, and the shaded region is the SE of the fit. (Right) As the maximum value – not the Y-axis range – increased, subjects made increasingly more error.

value range. The next section explores whether this effect of range on error exists at larger scales.

EXPERIMENT 2: LARGER RANGES

The visual system can quickly and precisely encode small quantities of items up to a maximum of about 4-5, an ability known as *subitizing* [8, 15, 18]. As the number of items increases beyond that range, the visual system is forced to shift to either slow counting or noisy estimation. This noisy estimation of large collections has slightly worse precision than length estimation [11].

If the improvements in working memory performance in the stacking conditions of experiment 1 are due to this advantage for number processing in small sets of items, then when larger stacks (more than 5) are displayed, performance in the stacked condition should no longer trump performance in the stretched condition, which relies on length judgment.

Exp 2: Methods

The procedure for this experiment is identical to the first experiment. The primary difference is that while the first experiment only used the range 1-5, this experiment is split into three blocks, which use the ranges 1-5, 2-10, and 3-15. The sizes of the charts on the screen were identical, only the Y-axis scale changed. We did not use a range higher than 15 because fitting more pictographs in a limited space made them difficult to discern.

We excluded the axis and question pictograph conditions, leaving all labels as text. We also excluded the superfluous pictograph condition. The experiment had 144 trials (3 ranges × 2 stacked vs stretched × 2 shape vs pictograph × 12 repetitions) blocked by range and chart type. The first 5 trials for each block were considered training and were discounted.

Due to a limited availability of undergraduate students at the time, this study was run as a web application via Amazon Mechanical Turk [16] with 30 subjects, all from the USA. It took an average of 35 minutes and paid 8 US dollars.

Exp 2: Results

We again found substantial individual differences, so we normalized the error levels by scaling all error values by the amount of error in the simple bar chart condition with a range of 1 to 5. Therefore all results represent an increase or decrease in error relative to that condition. For each result, we computed a mean per subject per condition and performed a Tukey HSD-corrected ANOVA between these subject means. There was no 3-way interaction between the three factors ($F[2, 29]<1$, $\eta_p^2=0.002$), and unless reported below, there were no significant 2-way interactions between factors.

Replicating experiment 1

The leftmost panel in Fig. 9 shows the amount of error for the 1-5 condition. This condition was very similar to experiment 1, and despite not being run in the lab, it produced very similar results. Again, stacking has a reliably large improvement on performance ($F[1, 29]=25$, $p < 0.001$, $\eta_p^2=0.22$). This time we found a small trend for a relative impairment for pictographs ($F[1, 29]=3.2$, $p > 0.05$, $\eta_p^2=0.05$), though it was tiny in comparison to the differences in error associated with different number ranges.

Smaller vs Larger Ranges

The panels in Fig. 9 show error levels for different Y-axis ranges. Although the 1–5 range shows a clear separation between stretched charts and stacked charts, an interaction between stacking and range results in the benefits of stacking disappearing with higher values ($F[2, 29]=4.5$, $p < 0.05$, $\eta_p^2=0.29$).

Maximum value

As with the previous experiment, the maximum value can be lower than the peak of the range. A linear regression of the error as a function of the maximum value (Fig. 10) showed that the maximum was correlated with error rate independent of the Y-axis scale ($F[1, 29]=470$, $p < 0.0001$, $\eta_p^2=0.4$). The lack of an interaction between the maximum and the axis range ($F[1, 29]<1$, $\eta_p^2<0.01$) supports the previous experiment's finding that people adjust their representation of scale based on the actual range of values, instead of the potential range according to the scale of the axis.

EXPERIMENT 3: MEMORY UNDER LOAD

The previous experiments tested memory for briefly glanced information, with an immediate test. Such tests might encourage verbalization strategies, such as repeating the legend names and associated numbers that are less likely to be used in the real world.

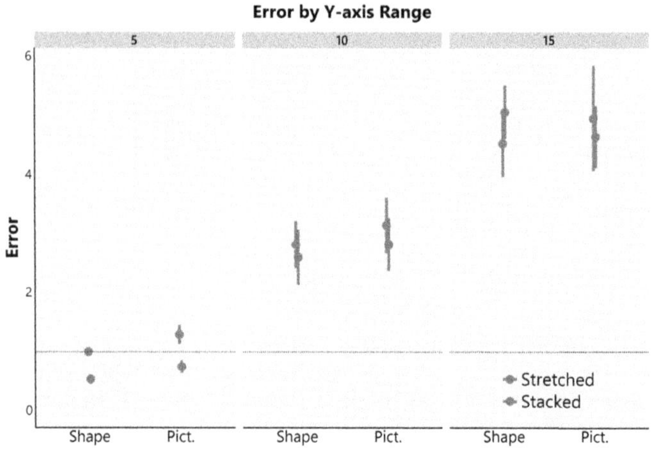

Fig. 9. Each panel shows a different Y-axis range. The amount of error for each subject is scaled by their error in the simple bar chart condition with a range of 1-5. The difference in error between the stretched (red) and stacked (blue) conditions is clear in the smaller range (left) but not for the larger ranges.

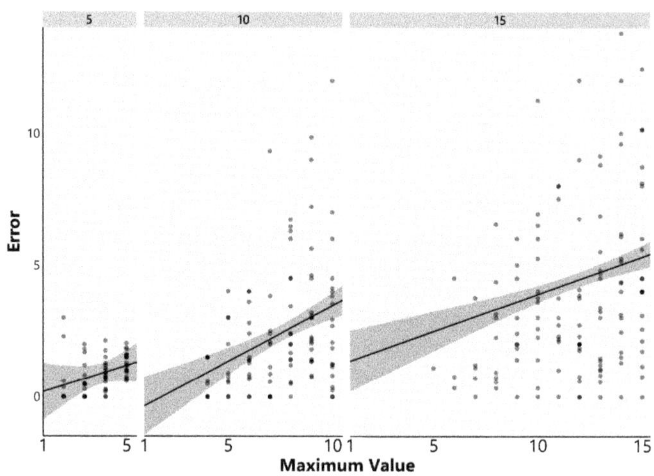

Fig. 10. The similar slopes for all Y-axis ranges show that, like in experiment 1, performance is correlated with the range of values, not just the scale of the Y-axis.

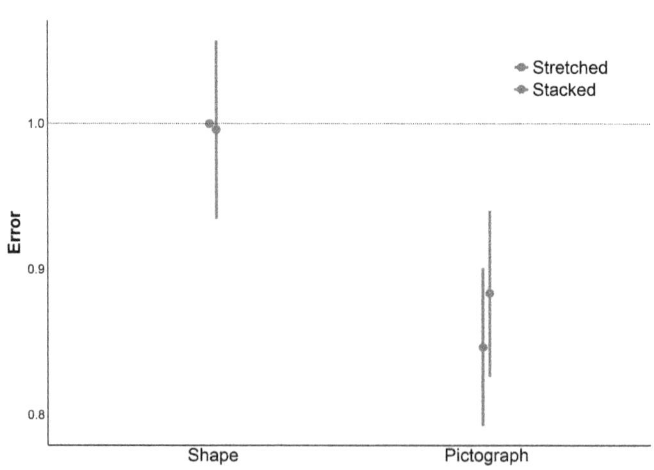

Fig. 11. In exp. 3 (1-back), pictograph charts have less error.

But a single visualization does not typically have exclusive access to working memory – other data and tasks intervene between encoding and recall. An observer might compare two visualizations, and readers of a news article might keep information from the text in mind as they examine a figure. Such situations may be less likely to encourage verbal coding of data, so that viewers rely more strongly on visual encoding of information.

Experiment 3 tests how pictographs affect memory when memory is more crowded. When memory is crowded, similar information, such as a verbal code for one set of numbers and verbal code for a second set of numbers, interferes and becomes noisy or lost [12]. Pictures may help keep information separated by expanding the information encoding space to include associations with identities and shapes that do not mutually interfere (e.g., the stack of dog icons and the stack of parrot icons in Fig 1). Research on picture memory is consistent with their support for rich and robust encoding – photographs can be recognized even after long time periods and hundreds of other viewed photographs [23], and similar recognition advantages occur for visualizations that contain rich pictorial information [4]. Therefore, experiment 3 tests whether pictographs will present an advantage over simple shapes when memory is taxed by the requirement to remember the data from an additional intervening visualization.

Exp 3 Methods

The procedure for this experiment is similar to the previous experiments but uses a *1-back* design. Subjects were asked to remember charts with a range of 1 to 5, but they were always tested on the chart *before* the one that they just saw, introducing the need to store two charts at all times. 20 subjects (12 women) participated in this experiment, which lasted an average of 25 minutes. This experiment was run in the lab, so the experimenter could confirm that subjects understood the relatively complex instructions. All subjects were undergraduates who received credit in an introductory psychology course for participating in the experiment.

For simplicity we excluded the axis and question pictograph conditions, so all labels were text. We also excluded the superfluous pictograph condition.

The experiment included 160 trials (2 stacked vs stretched × 2 shape vs pictograph × 40 repetitions) blocked by condition. The first 5 trials of each block were discounted to build up the load on memory.

Exp 3 Results

When memory is crowded, pictures help (Fig. 11). Using the same scaled measure and analysis as the previous experiments, pictograph charts led to slightly less error than charts with simple shapes ($F[1, 19]=20, p < 0.0001, \eta_p^2=0.06$).

Interestingly, the advantage found in previous experiments for stacked over stretched representations of number disappeared ($F[1, 19]<1, \eta_p^2<0.01$) and no interaction was found ($F[1, 19]=2.2, p > 0.1, \eta_p^2<0.01$). While this difference merits further study, we suspect that an increase in memory crowding shifted the performance bottleneck, such that the speed and accuracy of extracting values from the graph became less important than the ability of semantic memory to overcome competition from other datasets.

EXPERIMENT 4: SPEED AND PERFORMANCE

Do pictographs impact the speed of information recovery from a chart? Intuition might suggest that they make it easier, but they also might distract – and the results of experiment 1's axis label condition already suggest that text can trump pictographs in the context of a memory task. This experiment simulates the act of rapidly comparing the values of two known variables in a chart.

Exp 4 Methods

Subjects are presented with two targets (Fig. 12), each in the form of a pictograph with the corresponding name under it (e.g., "dog" and "parrot"). In the center is one of two questions: Which has MORE? or Which has FEWER?

A key press starts the trial and the timer. The subject views a chart with three values and presses a key to indicate which of the two pictographs or words best answers the question. The third value in the chart serves to deter people from simply selecting the tallest or shortest bar on the graph.

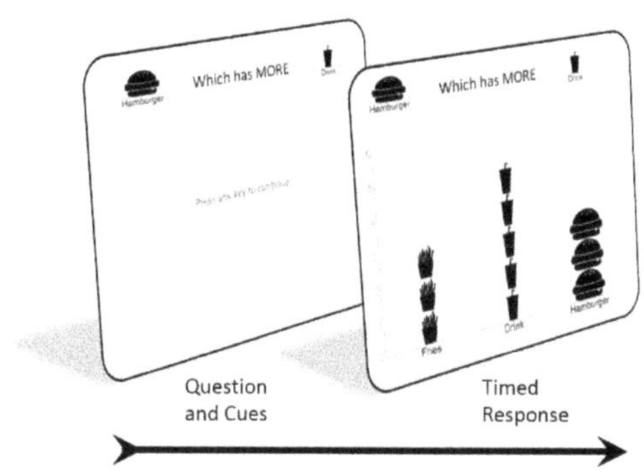

Fig. 12. The procedure for experiment 4. Notice that the order of the targets may be different from their order in the chart.

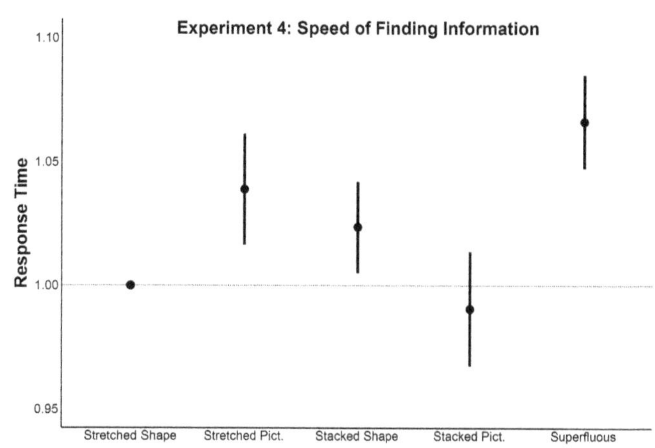

Fig. 13. How quickly subjects answered a question using the different types of charts. There is a performance cost for including a superfluous background image.

We ran 50 subjects on Amazon Mechanical Turk in 200 trials (5 chart types × 2 questions × 20 repetitions) blocked by chart type. Each subject was paid 8 US Dollars for the 30-minute study, and all participants were from the USA.

Exp 4 Results

All subjects showed over 92% accuracy, allowing incorrect responses to be dropped from analysis without substantially affecting statistical power. We also collapsed across the 'More' vs 'Fewer' condition to yield approximately 40 trials per chart type per subject. As with the previous experiments, we analyzed the results within-subject to determine the performance relative to that of the simple bar charts.

We found a main effect of graph type on response time ($F[4, 49]=20$, $p < 0.05$, $\eta_p^2=0.02$). A Tukey HSD-corrected comparison of all the graph types found that only the superfluous condition was significantly different from the standard bar graph ($p < 0.05$) as can be seen in Fig. 13.

This result combined with the results of experiment 1 show that superfluous images hurt both memorability and speed of usability of charts.

EXPERIMENT 5: INITIAL ENGAGEMENT

Although speed can be an important benchmark, the aim of some visualizations is to make people pause and look – as is often the case in news articles. Designers often rely on pictographs because they are thought to draw the attention of a reader. When perusing through a collection of articles, an enticing visualization may increase the likelihood that an article will be inspected more closely. Will an ISOTYPE visualization be better at capturing attention than a simple bar chart? We ran an experiment that simulated how visualizations are commonly encountered in a peripheral glimpse, as thumbnails among a collection of text and other visualizations competing for interest.

Exp 5 Methods

Subjects were presented with a 3x3 grid of items (Fig. 14). Each item included a short title above a small, slightly blurred thumbnail. The thumbnail was either a set of sentences about the topic from Wikipedia or a chart related to the topic. The subjects were given two minutes to look through the thumbnails. They could click whichever item interested them to view the information in full screen without pixilation or blur. Clicking again returned them to the grid, where they could repeat the process. No limit was placed on the number or duration of views for each item. However, after the trial's time had finished, everything was removed from the screen. They were then presented with a button to begin the next trial.

We selected 36 topics from the previous experiments' categories and constructed text, a bar chart, and a stacked pictograph chart for each. Throughout the experiment, each subject encountered each topic exactly once (9 items × 4 trials).

A trial included 3 bar charts, 3 stacked pictograph charts, and 3 pieces of text. We tracked the start time and duration of each view.

10 subjects (4 women) participated in this experiment. Because it was implemented as a Windows desktop application, it was run in the lab. All subjects were undergraduates and were paid 5 US dollars for the 15 minute duration.

Exp 5 Results

We binned the first minute of viewing into one-second intervals and found the portion of subjects viewing each type of item. Fig. 15 shows a linear fit of these results collapsed across trial. For the first few seconds, most are at the selection grid. However, the ISOTYPE visualization takes a quick

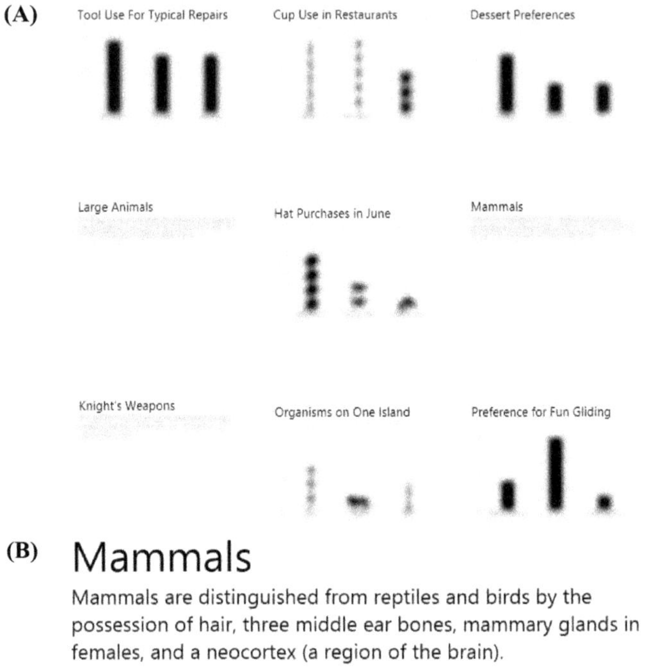

Fig. 14. (A) An example of the selection grid for experiment 5. The title is readable, but the details of the content are unrecognizable beyond the type of information. (B) An example text display that can also been seen in the middle right of the selection grid in (A).

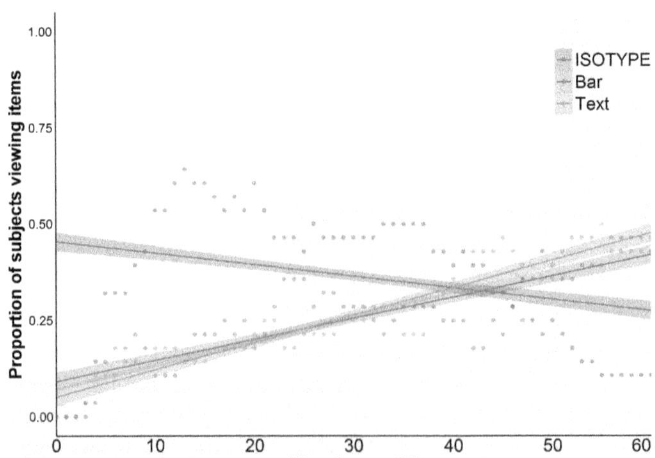

Fig. 15. ISOTYPE charts are best at initially engaging subjects to inspect information more closely.

lead and by 15 seconds has two thirds of the views. After all ISOTYPE visualizations are viewed, subjects proceed to the other items. Because most subject viewed all the items within the first minute, we discounted the second minute which had no interesting result.

Looking at the proportion viewing a given type of item, we found a main effect of item type ($F[2, 9]=61$, $p < 0.0001$, $\eta_p^2=0.1$) and an interaction between item type and time ($F[2, 9]=58$, $p < 0.0001$, $\eta_p^2=0.08$). A Tukey HSD-corrected comparison of item types found that the bar chart was indistinguishable from text (ns) and the ISOTYPE visualization was substantially different from both ($p < 0.0001$).

We also found no significant effect of trial number on ISOTYPE viewing ($F[1, 9]<1$, $\eta_p^2<0.01$), revealing that the initial interest in ISOTYPE-style charts remained consistent through the experiment. Not only are ISOTYPE visualizations highly effective at attracting initial attention, but new ISOTYPE visualizations also continue to engage.

GUIDELINES

Based on our findings in the studies, we suggest the following guidelines for using ISOTPYE displays.

(1) Superfluous pictographs are a distraction

Pictographs do not impair the viewer as long as they are used to represent data. But including an unnecessary background image in a visualization appears to be distracting, and it may divert attention away from the data. Even replacing text labels with pictographs makes encoding less efficient (at least when the text labels are unambiguous).

(2) Redundantly code length and (small) number

Break up large length-defined objects (such as the bars in a bar chart) into a few smaller items. One way of doing so is to use 'Tufte-style' gridlines [24], which are white lines superimposed over a (black) bar chart. This approach divides the bars at regular intervals allowing a user to also make a number estimate rather than only a length judgment. For small values below 4-5, number estimation is quick and accurate. However, because this performance diminishes rapidly for larger values, gridlines that break the bars into more than a few sections are unlikely to be beneficial.

(3) Use pictographs for demanding tasks

When working memory is under load, the data in ISOTYPE visualizations is recalled more accurately than with simple bar charts. Presenting successive visualizations of different information (such as visualizing sales of different products or showing food preferences in different regions) may benefit from ISOTYPE. In spite of the additional visual complexity, the information is recalled more accurately.

(4) ISOTYPE engages readers

Visualizations rarely exist in isolation. They are often embedded among additional content such as text and other visualizations that compete for a user, reader, or viewer's attention. ISOTYPE visualizations offer a way through this assortment to engage with a potential viewer. People are inclined, at least initially, to direct their focus towards a visualization with pictographic data compared with a simple bar chart or text.

CONCLUSIONS AND FUTURE WORK

Our initial exploration used simple visualizations with tightly controlled experiment parameters in hopes that this work can be extended to a more diverse set of contexts. For example, ISOTYPE visualizations have been used with multiple colors, as stacked bar charts, for fractional values, to represent vary large values, and with more than three bars. In addition, the present work uses short and abstracted tasks that allow exploration of a large parameter space. Future work should confirm that ISOTYPE visualizations help viewers better encode the relations and patterns in a dataset, extending beyond the encoding of data values that we tested here. Furthermore, because our tasks were designed to simulate communication of data, and not analytics, it is unclear whether ISOTYPE visualization would be useful for tasks such as search or group segmentation, which are common in exploration. Recent advancements in automatic pictograph selection [22] adds impetus to the need for a better understanding of how pictographs impact chart usability.

We have four main conclusions. (1) Only pictographs embedded as part of data mapping are beneficial (or at least, not harmful). Superfluous pictographs and label images are distracting and confusing. (2) Discretizing a bar into a collection of small items improves encoding and recall but only for small values. (3) Pictographs can help people remember information during demanding tasks. (4) Pictographs entice people to inspect a visualization more closely.

We found no strong evidence that using pictographs to communicate data hurts performance on any of our tasks. Our work adds more evidence to the claim that not all kinds of 'chart junk' are necessarily detrimental. The space of questions around the efficacy of embellishments in visualization is still largely unexplored, and it appears to be a fertile ground for further research.

DEMO AND CODE

Chart examples generated in D3, practice versions of the experiments, and all of the pictographs are available at:

`http://steveharoz.com/research/isotype`

ACKNOWLEDGEMENTS

Thanks to Kevin Hartstein for helping run the experiments and Darko Odic for suggesting references. This work was partly funded by NSF grants IIS-1162067 and BCS-1056730.

REFERENCES

1. Annink, E. and Bruinsma, M., eds. *gerd arntz: graphic designer.* 010 publishers, 2013.
2. Bateman, S., Mandryk, R., Gutwin, C., Genest, A., McDine, D., and Brooks, C. Useful Junk? The Effects of Visual Embellishment on Comprehension and Memorability of Charts. *ACM Conference on Human Factors in Computing Systems*, (2010), 2573–2582.

3. Borgo, R., Abdul-Rahman, A., Mohamed, F., Grant, P.W., Reppa, I., and Floridi, L. An Empirical Study on Using Visual Embellishments in Visualization. *IEEE Transactions on Visualization and Computer Graphics 18*, 12 (2012), 2759–2768.
4. Borkin, M.A., Vo, A.A., Bylinskii, Z., et al. What Makes a Visualization Memorable? *Transactions on Visualization and Computer Graphics*, 6 (2013).
5. Brady, T.F., Konkle, T., and Alvarez, G.A. A review of visual memory capacity: Beyond individual items and toward structured representations. *Journal of vision 11*, 5 (2011).
6. Brinton, W.C. *Graphic Methods for Presenting Facts.* The Engineering Magazine Company, New York, 1914.
7. Chevalier, F., Vuillemot, R., and Gali, G. Using concrete scales: a practical framework for effective visual depiction of complex measures. *IEEE transactions on visualization and computer graphics 19*, 12 (2013), 2426–35.
8. Choo, H. and Franconeri, S.L. Enumeration of small collections violates Weber's law. *Psychonomic bulletin & review 21*, 1 (2014), 93–9.
9. Cowan, N. The magical number 4 in short-term memory: a reconsideration of mental storage capacity. *The Behavioral and brain sciences 24*, (2001), 87–114; discussion 114–185.
10. Dickinson, C.A. and Intraub, H. Spatial Asymmetries in Viewing and Remembering Scenes: Consequences of an Attentional Bias? *Attention, Perception, & Psychophysics 71*, 6 (2009), 1251–1262.
11. Droit-Volet, S., Clément, A., and Fayol, M. Time, number and length: similarities and differences in discrimination in adults and children. *Quarterly journal of experimental psychology 61*, 12 (2008), 1827–46.
12. Franconeri, S.L. The nature and status of visual resources. In *Oxford handbook of cognitive psychology*. 2013.
13. Godden, D.R. and Baddeley, A.D. Context-dependent memory in two natural environments: On land and underwater. *British Journal of Psychology 66*, (1975).
14. Halberda, J., Sires, S.F., and Feigenson, L. Multiple spatially overlapping sets can be enumerated in parallel. *Psychological science 17*, 7 (2006), 572–6.
15. Haroz, S. and Whitney, D. How Capacity Limits of Attention Influence Information Visualization Effectiveness. *IEEE Transactions on Visualization and Computer Graphics 18*, 12 (2012), 2402–2410.
16. Heer, J. and Bostock, M. Crowdsourcing graphical perception. *Proceedings of the 28th international conference on Human factors in computing systems - CHI '10*, ACM Press (2010), 203–212.
17. Holmes, N. Pictograms: A view from the drawing board or, what I have learned from Otto Neurath and Gerd Arntz (and jazz). *Information design journal 10*, 2 (2001), 133–144.
18. Kaufman, E.L. and Lord, M.W. The discrimination of visual number. *The American journal of psychology 62*, 4 (1949), 498–525.
19. Lin, S., Fortuna, J., Kulkarni, C., Stone, M.C., and Heer, J. Selecting Semantically-Resonant Colors for Data Visualization. *EuroVis*, (2013), 1–10.
20. Michal, A.L. and Franconeri, S.L. The order of attentional shifts determines what visual relations we extract. *Journal of Vision 14*, 10 (2014), 1033–1033.
21. Neurath, O. *From hieroglyphs to Isotype: a visual autobiography.* Hyphen Press, 2010.
22. Setlur, V. and Mackinlay, J.D. Automatic generation of semantic icon encodings for visualizations. *Proceedings of the SIGCHI Conference on Human Factors in Computing Systems*, (2014).
23. Standing, L. Learning 10,000 pictures. *The Quarterly journal of experimental psychology 25*, 2 (1973).
24. Tufte, E.R. *The visual display of quantitative information.* Graphics press, 1983.

GEM-NI: A System For Creating and Managing Alternatives In Generative Design

Loutfouz Zaman[*], Wolfgang Stuerzlinger[†], Christian Neugebauer[‡], Robert Woodbury[†], Maher Elkhaldi[†], Naghmi Shireen[†], Michael Terry[§]

[*]York University, Toronto, Canada, zaman@cse.yorku.ca, [†]Simon Fraser University, Vancouver, Canada, [‡]University of Applied Sciences Bonn-Rhein-Sieg, Germany, [§]University of Waterloo, Canada

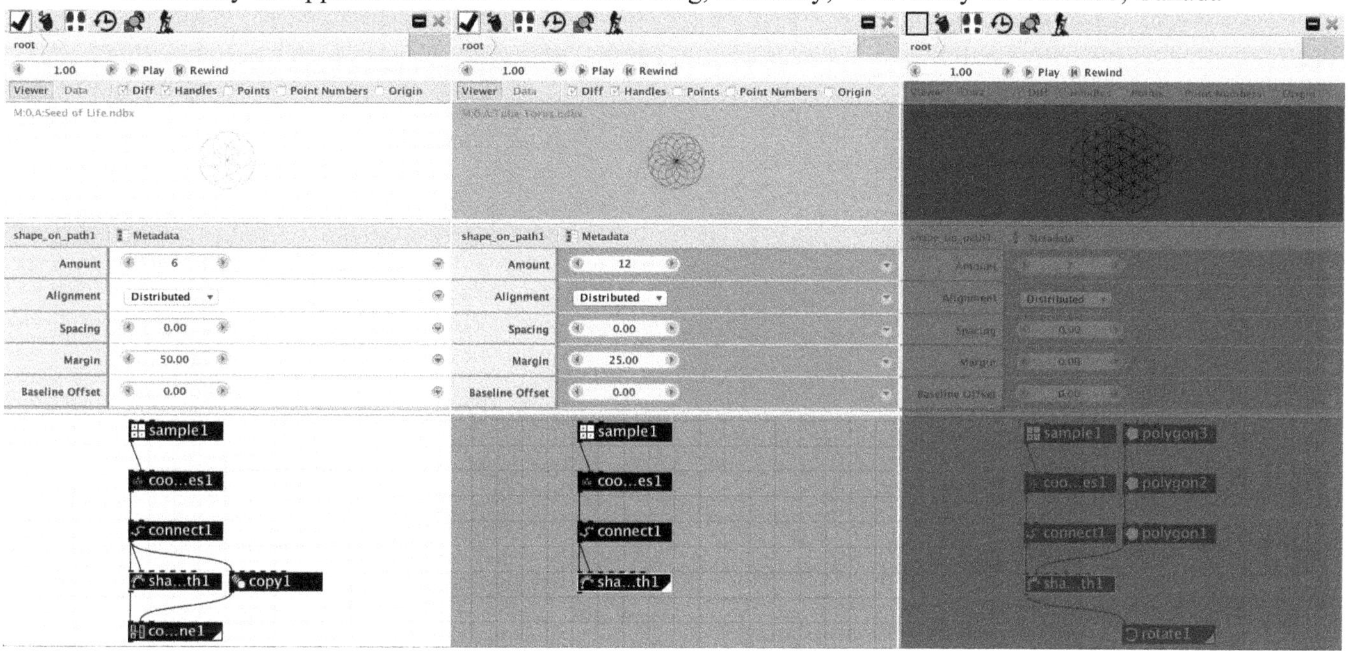

Figure 1. *GEM-NI* enables users to work with alternative generative designs simultaneously. Specifically, *GEM-NI* provides tools to manage the set of alternatives affected by edit operations, post-hoc merging of (parts of) alternatives, and several ways to create new alternatives, such as resurrection of past states with full undo lineage duplication or selection from an enhanced design gallery implementation. The leftmost alternative is the original design and is active, the center one is passive, and the rightmost one is idle.

ABSTRACT

We present *GEM-NI* – a graph-based generative-design tool that supports parallel exploration of alternative designs. Producing alternatives is a key feature of creative work, yet it is not strongly supported in most extant tools. *GEM-NI* enables various forms of exploration with alternatives such as parallel editing, recalling history, branching, merging, comparing, and Cartesian products of and for alternatives. Further, *GEM-NI* provides a modal graphical user interface and a design gallery, which both allow designers to control and manage their design exploration. We conducted an exploratory user study followed by in-depth one-on-one interviews with moderately and highly skills participants and obtained positive feedback for the system features, showing that *GEM-NI* supports creative design work well.

CHI 2015, April 18 - 23, 2015, Seoul, Republic of Korea

ACM 978-1-4503-3145-6/15/04...$15.00
http://dx.doi.org/10.1145/2702123.2702398

Author Keywords

Alternatives; generative design; parallel editing; graphical operation history; exploration; design gallery

ACM Classification Keywords

H.5.2 User Interfaces: Graphical user interfaces (GUI), I.3.4 [Graphics Utilities] – graphics editors

INTRODUCTION

Experts typically generate sets of alternative solutions when solving ill-defined problems [28]. This has been shown to result in higher quality outcomes [9]. For example, it is common practice for web designers [25], architects [1,24] and software engineers [31] to generate sketches of potential designs as they solve problems. These sketches help designers externalize knowledge, better understand the problem, and explore the space of potential solutions [2]. Due to the ease with which parameters can be varied, *parametric modeling*, where solutions are represented as models, is a particularly compelling technology to assist in exploring a design space. A *parametric* model represents the structure and hierarchy of a solution, the result of which is determined by relationships, constraints, and choices of parameter values at a given time. While building such models requires more effort, parametric modeling systems make variations easier and are now used in various domains. A prominent example is architectural design, as in the construction of the International Terminal Waterloo in London, England [37], pp. 43-45. Parametric models are often presented as networks of operations in a dataflow programming environment. As a given parametric model can quickly generate multiple options, the design process is often referred to as a *generative* one.

Parametric and generative design qualitatively changes the design process. The inherent capabilities of such systems also create new opportunities for design support tools. With generative design, it is possible to easily create a very large set of viable design options that satisfy a given set of constraints, as defined in the model. These alternatives represent points in a high-dimensional design space that must be explored, narrowed, and filtered. Current systems represent models as graphs, e.g., *AutoCAD DesignScript Studio, Grasshopper 3D*, *GenerativeComponents*, *Houdini, NodeBox,* and *Max/MSP*; or as trees, e.g., *CATIA, Inventor, ProE*, and *SpaceClaim*. Adoption is widespread in avant-garde practice and design schools and there are established textbooks and professional development courses.

In this paper, we present *GEM-NI*, a graph-based 2D design tool that supports the exploration of design alternatives in various ways. *GEM-NI* is built as a branch of *NodeBox*, a vector graphics generative design tool that uses graphs to express the computation behind the design. *NodeBox* has been used for visualization and generative art. Examples include visualizations of real-time data, evolutionary art installations that react to users, documents in a single visual style but with variations across pages, and customized wallpapers based on e-mail spam [29]. *GEM-NI* adds several novel features:

- interactive, selective post-hoc merging in alternatives;
- an enhanced interactive design gallery that explores ranges of parameters and *structural* changes to the model.

In the context of generative design, *GEM-NI* presents the following new features:

- methods to control parallel/linked editing: checkmarks and sandboxes;
- a non-destructive method for resurrecting past states from history with undo lineage, via enhanced "skating" [35];
- methods to quickly generate alternatives via branching;
- local and global undo;
- tools to manage alternatives and visually compare them;

To investigate our design choices we evaluated our system with moderately and highly skilled users.

We use the example in Figure 1 to demonstrate the capabilities of *GEM-NI*. Imagine that Ann, a designer, is tasked with creating a design for a book cover. To match the book content, she initially selects the "Seed of Life" pattern and recreates it in *GEM-NI*, by using three nodes (SAMPLE1, COORDNIATES1, CONNECT1) to create a circle. She then distributes copies of the circle along the same circular path (SHAPE_ON_PATH1), Figure 1 left. As the result does not seem complex enough, she goes back in the operation history and generates a new clone from an earlier state. After some parameter variation, she arrives at the "Tube Torus" design shown in Figure 1 center. Not entirely satisfied, she branches this design again to create a third, where she uses repeated polygons to arrange the circles in a more complex pattern, the "Flower of Life". Next, Ann creates several more alternatives using the Cartesian product (not shown in Figure 1) and uses individual and linked editing to tune the designs' parameters and manages them in the workspace. Throughout this, she uses local and global undo to correct mistakes. Merging is illustrated with another worked example below.

Encouraging exploration of a design space with parallel alternatives in design tools is a subject of current research. We are not aware of any mainstream end-user tools that yet support this approach to design exploration. Thus, we ran a user study with moderately and highly skilled users to investigate the appropriateness of our approach by gathering feedback and understanding the implications of parallel editing on their design process.

RELATED WORK

Extant Media for Exploration

Most exploration in the conceptual stage of design happens with the aid of pencil and paper—sketching is central. Its immediacy and speed enable a skilled designer to offload memory onto paper, thus greatly expanding the ability to make and consider design ideas. Buxton [5] suggests 11 qualities exhibited by (and possibly definitive of) sketching. Computer-based conceptual design systems often do not support these qualities adequately. Despite many methods proposed by researchers for the use of CAD in early stage conceptual design [17,36], CAD is still mostly used in the final stages of design, though this is changing [37].

We postulate that supporting design alternatives explicitly can capture some of the functionality seen in manual sketching, something almost entirely lacking in current CAD tools. Consider Ann, who: needs to shift focus quickly among her different designs, wants the capacity to represent, borrow, and reuse ideas across different alternatives, needs the ability to visually compare her solutions, and may even want to do parallel editing across multiple designs. *GEM-NI* provides such features.

Generative Design

We use the term *generative design* to label any computer-aided design system that provides tools to vary designs beyond direct manipulation of specific design elements.

Such systems can be understood as lying along a spectrum from direct manipulation to fully automatic design. Thus we consider parametric modeling, where changing parameters is a tool on top of manual model construction, to be a minimal generative system leaving most control with the designer. Genetic algorithms form an opposite and delegate exploration to the computer, while permitting user selection only at intermediary generations [39].

Here, we focus on the direct manipulation end of the spectrum, enabling designers to interactively control design decisions and provide "power tools" to make, modify, track, evaluate and visualize their work and to explore a larger number of design options. One of the key challenges is to facilitate the fluidity of the design process where many threads of possibilities are developed in parallel. Another challenge is a balance of features, user interactions, and workflows to enable designers to focus on exploring alternatives, as opposed to just managing them. *GEM-NI's* design gallery interface, described later, employs elements of genetic algorithms, but enhances them through Cartesian products of generative networks. The exploration facilities of *GEM-NI*, also described later, enable designers, such as Ann, to explore a much larger number of design options than what is possible through manual interaction.

Graphical Operation History

According to Shneiderman [27], history mechanisms can play an important part in the design process, supporting iterative analysis by enabling users to review, retrieve, and revisit visualization states. Many recent systems provide history-keeping mechanisms in the form of a timeline [19]. When interactive [11], graphical histories can amplify the exploration capabilities of a system. Users then can not only go back in time [13] and defer decisions [37, 38]; they have a mechanism to try out variations [35] by creating revisions [6] and versions [10] of the timeline. Moreover, history tools can help users to create reports or presentations, facilitating communication. Heer et al. [16] and Grossman et al. [13] together provide a comprehensive survey from an HCI perspective. Here we focus mainly on works that employ time sliders and graphical histories, as they are most relevant to histories in parametric design.

One of the earliest examples of graphical history is *Chimera* [20], which features an editable graphical history through panels depicting the results of each user operation. *Chronicle* [13] is a sophisticated system for exploring a document's history via a zoomable and track-based video playback metaphor. *Diffamation* [8], *a* system for text version differencing employs a *time slider* that permits the user to explore differences over time. Su [32,33] presented new pictorial visualizations for the operation history of 2D vector illustrations as interactive storyboards.

GEM-NI's new resurrection feature permits Ann to resurrect past states non-destructively as new alternatives through a simple GUI that enables her to scroll through previews of past states or to select specific operations.

Design Space Exploration

Woodbury and Burrow [38] argue that design activity is well-modeled by a network structure. This network reflects the strategies and structure of the designer's exploration. They introduce the notion of *design hysteresis*, which points out that insights are discovered not just by explicitly visiting parts of a design space, but also through re-combination of visited alternatives in said *hysterical design space*. *Design Galleries* [23] explores this space by automatically generating and organizing variations of graphics or animations produced by a parametric model. Ma [22] introduces an interactive and dynamic graph representation of a database and argues that this type of visualization enhances the user experience in exploring the data. Jankun-Kelly and Ma [18] introduce a 2D spreadsheet visualization for multi-dimensional database exploration. Terry et al.'s *Parallel Pies* [35] enhance the user experience in generating and comparing alternatives by displaying several alternatives of a model with varying parameter values simultaneously. Lunzer and Hornbæk [21] present a novel subjunctive interface with multi-state sliders for each parameter to enable parallel exploration of a parametric space. They also show multiple states of a document side-by-side and permit users to rearrange these views.

Sheikholeslami [26] realized the *Dialer* interface in Bentley Systems' *GenerativeComponents* to enable interaction with the hysterical design space. The *Dialer* comprises concentric interactive rings, one for each parameter, where the ring divisions correspond to the explored values. The outermost ring illustrates the explored parts of the hysterical space. This compact visualization is limited in the number of divisions and parameters that can be visualized.

GEM-NI extends previous work by enabling users to select an arbitrary range of parameters and parts of a generative network for a design gallery. Together with the novel ability to explore structural products of generative networks this enables designers, such as Ann, to explore the design space more quickly and widely than with other approaches.

Interacting with Alternatives

Minimal support for alternatives is found in industry tools such as Autodesk's *Showcase* and Dassault Systèmes *SolidWorks* ([37], pp. 276-277). Both focus mainly on supporting alternatives through configuration management, *alternative lineup* features and side-by-side spreadsheet-like user interfaces. *CATIA* by Dassault Systèmes shows alternatives in *Catalogs*, a static gallery of assemblies and parts. It does not support interactive exploration.

Work on subjunctive interfaces [21] supports interaction for side-by-side exploratory analysis via viewing and editing of parametric models with a multi-handle slider user interface. Terry et al. [34] presented techniques to better support systems for parametric variations; *side views* – an on-demand command preview, the *parameter spectrum* – a replacement for the traditional slider control to display a range of possible results, and the *design horizon* – a complementary design space visualization. Heer et al. describe branching history as a way to remember operations that have been undone [16]. In contrast, Terry et al. [35] describe undo as a tool for reflection-in-action, in other words, for exploring variations. In Terry's *Parallel Paths*, when users duplicate a particular variation, its lineage is also duplicated, unlike in standard cloning. This copied history enables users to create variations *after* a command: when a result is unanticipated, but still worth keeping, users can duplicate the current state and then *non-destructively* return to a previous one. Terry et al. call this *skating*.

Juxtapose [15] presents a parallel code editor and runtime parameter tuning environment for GUI alternatives. When alternatives are linked, any block of code written in one alternative is shared among the rest. Working with this system requires strong coding skills. Bueno et al. [4] use the metaphor of *rewriting history* to enable users to manage variations and explorations of a design, with support for merging, generalizing and specializing. The *d.note* tool [14] also offers alternatives, together with revision control, change tracking and annotations. A user study on computational sketching tools compared three interaction models for working with alternatives in early design: a tab interface, a layered canvas, and spatial maps [30]. They found that spatial maps better support idea reflection, as they permit side-by-side comparisons.

GEM-NI enables interaction with multiple alternatives through parallel editing, history keeping, cloning, support for non-destructive resurrection, and new methods for easy management of alternatives. To enable designers to reuse their work more easily, *GEM-NI* adds a new method for post-hoc merging of (parts of) divergent alternatives.

GEM-NI

The name *GEM-NI, Generative Many-Nodes Interpreter*, is inspired by the many-worlds interpretation in quantum physics. It implies that all possible alternative histories and futures are real, each representing an actual "world". We focused on 2D graphics, a domain that offers sufficient complexity for common issues and patterns in generative modeling to emerge, yet still practical for user studies. Also, *GEM-NI* supports exploratory design tasks widely used in the design literature and in HCI in Green's cognitive dimensions of notations [12].

We already introduced a simple usage scenario for *GEM-NI* above. Beyond this, *GEM-NI* is capable of handling a large number of alternatives, the exploration of which is only limited by screen size, processing power and memory. Each alternative is hosted in a panel. Panels are contained in one or more *workspace(s)*, which can be saved. Figure 1 shows such a workspace with three alternatives. Multiple workspaces may be open at the same time. The panel for each alternative consists of three views: output, parameter, and network view. To facilitate side-by-side viewing of alternatives, *GEM-NI's* panel layout differs from that of *NodeBox*. In *GEM-NI* views are stacked vertically: output on top, parameters in the middle, and network view at the bottom. The order in which alternatives show on screen can be re-arranged by drag and drop using a modifier key, with preview and target location highlighting. In the conceptual design phase, designers routinely generate dozens of sketches. That amount of content is difficult to fit onto a single monitor, if all alternatives are still to be viewable and editable. To aid the designer in keeping an overview of all considered alternatives, to organize them, and to view them side-by-side for visual comparison, we support multi-monitor setups in *GEM-NI*. In a preferences menu, the user can select from 1×1 to (currently) 2×3 monitors. The workspace is then re-arranged to spread all alternatives as evenly as possible for the chosen monitor arrangement. Within each monitor, horizontal space is evenly distributed.

In *GEM-NI* the creation of nodes, their positions, parameter values as well as selection state are synchronized by default across all editable alternatives. Thus, moving a node or changing a node parameter affects all of its instances in other editable alternatives. Such parallel editing can be enabled or disabled, see below. We found that uniformity in network layout makes it easier for designers to identify common elements and to compare networks visually across alternatives. E.g., SHAPE_ON_PATH1 in Figure 1 was selected in the leftmost alternative and is now selected everywhere with the corresponding parameter views. For the same reasons, zooming and panning on the network and output view are also synchronized. Every operation is accessible through the menu bar. Important ones are also accessible through GUI buttons or keyboard shortcuts.

Parallel Editing

The most common use case for parallel editing is parameter variation in a design. Ann might use parallel editing to change the size of multiple alternatives, which saves having to repeat the operation in each one. Or she might add a new node that adds a background rectangle to all designs. In *GEM-NI* she can control which alternatives are *idle*, i.e., non-editable, through *checkmarks*. Selecting an alternative makes it *active*. All other checked alternatives are *passive* and thus subject to parallel edits. Often, Ann wants to focus only on a single alternative, i.e., work in a *sandbox*.

A workspace typically contains multiple passive and idle alternatives. The active one, Figure 1 left, is shown in bright gray. Passive alternatives, Figure 1 middle, are shown in a mid-tone gray, and idle (unchecked) ones are dark gray, Figure 1 right. An alternative is activated simply by clicking anywhere on its panel, or by switching to it via the TAB key. Newly created alternatives are set to passive, permitting parallel editing. Editing an alternative makes it active and pushes changes to all passive alternatives. Idle alternatives remain unchanged. Pushed changes include operations in the network view (e.g., creating, renaming, deleting, connecting or disconnecting a node), in the parameter view (e.g., tweaking a parameter of the node), and in the output view (e.g., moving or resizing a shape by direct manipulation). Sandboxing addresses the case when the designer wants to focus her edits on only a single alternative (Figure 2). This functionality simply idles (unchecks) all other alternatives. Both checkmarks and sandboxing are accessible through GUI buttons (✔ and 🐞, see Figure 2) or through modifier keys when clicking on an alternative. The "mute" and "solo" buttons in audio and video software, such as Adobe *Audition CC* and Apple *Final Cut Pro X*, inspired our checkmarks and sandboxing.

Local and Global Undo

GEM-NI supports two types of undo: local and global. Local undo refers to undo in the currently active alternative. Global undo undoes in all checked alternatives in the workspace. Performing local undo or redo clears the global undo stack to avoid undo synchronization problems. A more powerful undo system, e.g., [11], could address this limitation. We did not implement this for simplicity.

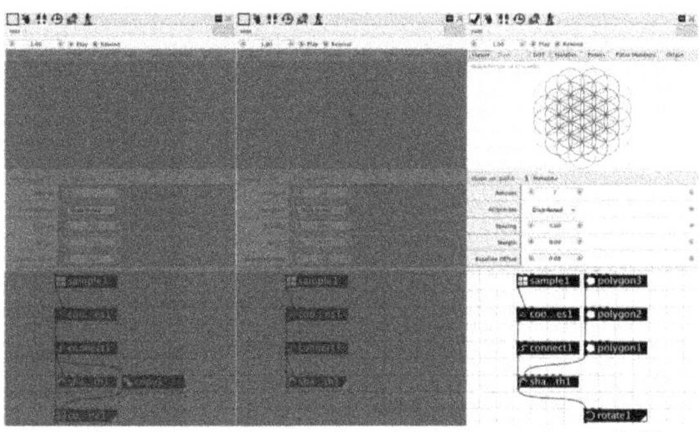

Figure 2. The alternative on the right is sandboxed. The first two alternatives are therefore idle.

Selective Merging

Designers frequently branch out to explore different alternatives. Sometimes they then want to re-use new parts in other alternatives. Figure 3 illustrates a merging scenario in *GEM-NI*. Inspired by Brownian motion, Ann first created a grid with randomly displaced ellipses (Figure 3a left). She then created an alternative that uses a compound of an ellipse and a circle (center). Subsequently she created a slightly more structured 10×10 grid of compound circles (right). Looking at this, she likes the result of the GRID1, WIGGLE1, and ELLIPSE1 nodes in the right design as well as the capability of varying the size of the grid through the new NUMBER1 node. Thus, she merges these four nodes into the other two alternatives. This overwrites the parameters of existing nodes and creates the NUMBER1 node with connections to GRID1 in the other two alternatives. Note that a copy operation would not recreate these specific connections. She then changes the size of the grid in all three alternatives to 15×15 (Figure 3b) with parallel editing.

Selective merging is a new mechanism to ensure that parts of a design can be *post-hoc* integrated into other alternatives. *GEM-NI* implements this by *overwriting* the state of the *selected* nodes across all passive alternatives. This is different from standard copy & paste, which will *duplicate* existing nodes. When merging, nodes that do not exist are created and connected suitably in the passive alternatives. Parameters of common nodes are overwritten from the active alternative. This may create conflicts, which the user needs to address later. Performing merging on the complete network essentially turns all alternatives into clones (with potentially different undo history stacks). Our technique is inspired by the corresponding functionality in source code management, mainly *Git*.

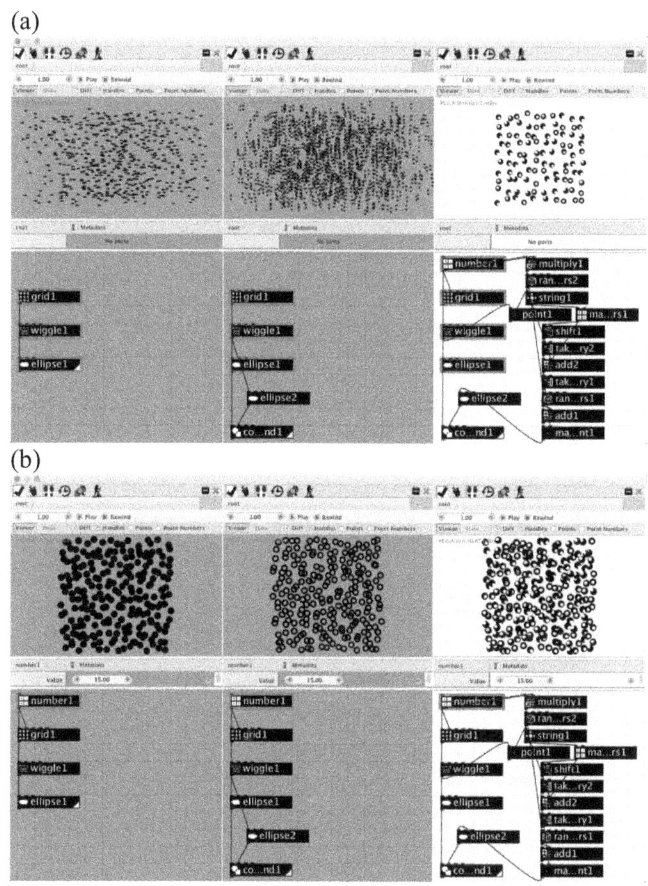

Figure 3. Merging and parallel editing: (a) Initial state with highlighted nodes selected for merging. (b) Merging replicates new nodes and connections into all other alternatives and overwrites parameters of existing nodes. The user then globally changes NUMBER1 to 15.

Creating Alternatives

Creating new empty alternatives is standard functionality. During branching/cloning, and in contrast to most other work, *GEM-NI* preserves the undo stack, which enables Ann to undo operations in both alternatives. In the example in Figure 1, Ann branched an alternative design from an intermediate version of her initial one. Usually this meant either relying on intermediate saves or using (destructive) undo to go back in time. In *GEM-NI* she can use the resurrection dialog to scroll back in time and select a starting point for a new exploration. Also, the enhanced interactive design gallery in *GEM-NI* enables Ann not only to explore the parametric design space but also to create new variations for the *structure* of the network. This makes it easier for Ann to quickly explore a larger set of designs.

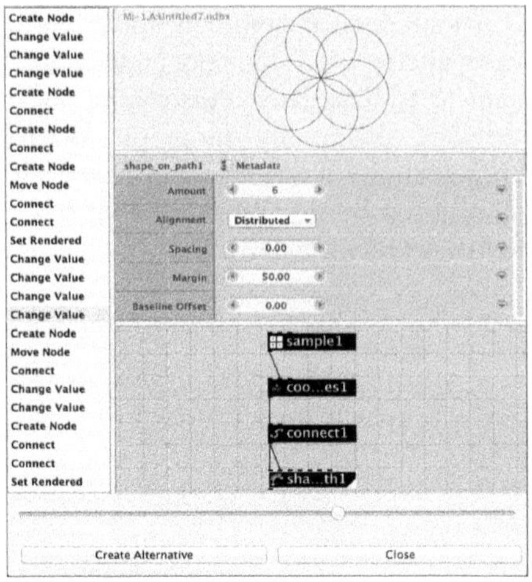

Figure 4. Dialog for creating an alternative from history: the history list on the left and the state of the alternative at that time on the right. The current entry is highlighted. The state can be selected from the list directly or by dragging the slider.

Branches

An alternative can be created as a branch through cloning, where the entire network from the active alternative is copied to the newly created alternative, along with its undo lineage. This can be interpreted as an adaptation of *skating* [35] to generative design. The new alternative then appears to the right of the active one. Preserving the undo stack upon cloning enables new use cases, as the user can now undo operations in both alternatives.

Resurrection from History

Creating alternatives from history, i.e., resurrecting past states, enables Ann to look through her past work and to select particular points in time from which she intends to "branch out" and to explore new alternatives. This happens in *GEM-NI* through a dialog (Figure 4). There, all states from the undo history are listed on the left, with a time slider on the bottom. Clicking on a list item or scrolling shows a preview of the corresponding state on the right. Clicking the "Create Alternative" button then instantiates the selected state as a new alternative in the workspace next to the active alternative. In Figure 4, the past state in the history of the left design of Figure 1 is highlighted, from which the second alternative was branched out. The dialog enables the user to create more than one alternative at a time. As with branching, *GEM-NI* clones the history stack on a resurrection from history. Together with the history previews this provides an enhanced form of *skating* [35].

Design Gallery

We implemented an interface for creating alternatives from a design gallery, inspired by the parametric Cartesian product in *Dialer* [26]. Our interface extends *Dialer* in several ways, most importantly by supporting structural products. Figure 5 shows a design gallery for Figure 1. Starting with the scenario in Figure 1, Ann now wants to explore the design space more widely. Going beyond *Dialer* [26], *GEM-NI* also enables her to specify the range over which parameters should vary. For this, Ann first selects (with a modifier key) two or more alternatives as the basis for the Cartesian product. This outlines these alternatives with a red frame. In the example in Figure 5 all three alternatives from Figure 1 are included in the product. Upon modifier key release, the main dialog appears (Figure 5a), which shows Ann all nodes of the alternatives in a nested list, with the second level denoting the parameters. To streamline the workflow, only common nodes whose parameters differ between the selected alternatives are selected for the product by default and expanded. SHAPE_ON_PATH1 is the only common node with different parameters (*Amount* and *Margin*) in the three alternatives in Figure 1. The GUI elements then permit Ann to include or exclude nodes and to specify ranges for the values of the nodes in the Cartesian product (Figure 5a). For ranges she can configure the minimum, maximum and step size.

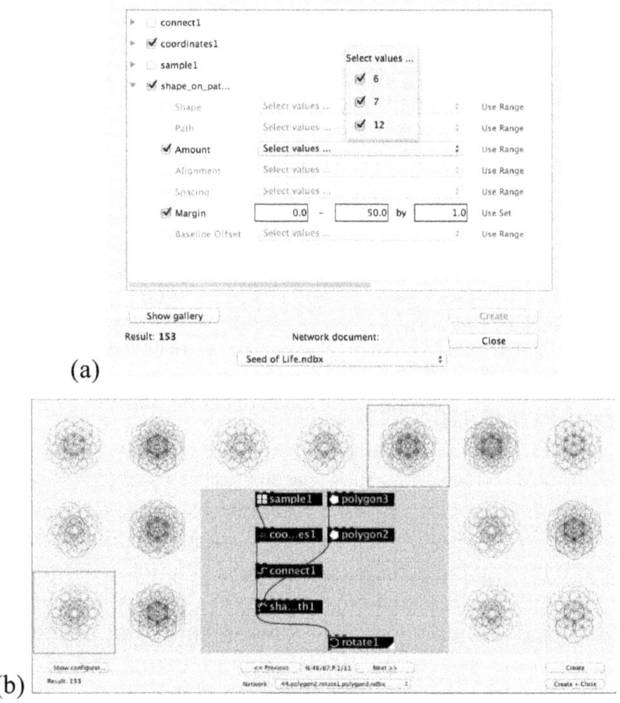

Figure 5. Design Gallery. (a) Cartesian product menu; (b) parameter range exploration preview of the selected node.

To give Ann an idea of how many potential results to expect, *GEM-NI* shows the number of designs that would be generated at the bottom left. When satisfied with the settings, Ann presses the "Show gallery" button, which displays the results of the Cartesian product (Figure 5b) in a dialog that enables the user to scroll through all pages of results with the "Previous" and "Next" buttons. She then selects two previewed designs by clicking on them and presses the "Create" button to instantiate the selected designs as new alternatives, which appends them as the last alternatives on the right side of the workspace. For reference, the design gallery shows the network of the first selected alternative in the middle, but enables Ann also to view other selected networks. Optionally, the *GEM-NI* design gallery can be invoked on a single alternative. In this case the gallery will operate in range only mode.

Finally, Ann can explore even more potential designs by exploring different *structures* for the networks of the generative model. For this our new Cartesian product first identifies all nodes that are different in the alternatives. Then *GEM-NI* constructs their power set and substitutes each into the network common to the alternatives. Since there are a total of 6 node differences among the three alternatives in Figure 1, $2^6 = 64$ networks are created. Ann can then scroll through all designs generated by varying both the network as well as the parameters or select a specific network from a drop-down list. E.g., in Figure 5b, she has selected a generated network that consists of three substituted nodes: POLYGON2, POLYGON3, and ROTATE1. In the example shown in Figure 5 there are 64 generated networks with 153 parameter variations. Thus this design gallery contains over ten thousand potential alternatives.

EVALUATION

To confirm the appropriateness of the presented techniques for the design process, we evaluated *GEM-NI* in two steps: a workshop with an exploratory design study, and follow-up in-depth interviews. The workshop introduced *NodeBox* and had the goal to gather feedback on *GEM-NI* from a user group moderately experienced in generative design.

Participants

Five unpaid participants (2 female) were recruited through a "session on new generative design tools" announcement. We targeted participants experienced with generative design. Coffee and cookies were offered as incentive. Participants design backgrounds were: architectural, sound, visual, and information design, as well as arts. One participant had to withdraw during the workshop due to an appointment. The participants were between 21 and 31 years old (μ=27.2). All were experienced designers (μ=5.7 years). One participant reported experience with generative design tools, namely *Grasshopper*, another knew *Processing*. None knew *NodeBox*. In the pre-questionnaire, all reported that they routinely create multiple alternative designs as opposed to a single solution. All stated that when they design, they regularly keep track of, review, and revisit their design iterations. For that, participants reported the following methods: saving multiple files (even for minor changes), creating files from scratch for major conceptual changes, using a stylus with a note taking application, various combinations of shuffling between files, sketches, tracing paper, and images, and keeping everything in a notebook and/or printouts, including intermediate artifacts.

Apparatus and Procedure

Workstations with dual monitors running *Windows 7* were used. Blank sketch sheets and pens were supplied. The workshop was split into two phases, followed by a one-on-one in-depth interview with participants at a later date. Along with logging and interviews, we used the Creativity Support Index (CSI) [7], a quantitative, psychometric tool in form of a survey to assess how well both systems assist creativity in the design process. In both phases participants completed the CSI questionnaire after the creative task. Collaboration was not rated.

The Workshop

In the first workshop phase participants were taught a basic version of *GEM-NI,* feature-wise equivalent to *NodeBox,* i.e., without our new contributions, and called *NodeBox* for the remainder of this section. We picked examples from a generative design book [3] as tasks. We first demonstrated how to create six designs and asked participants to recreate them on their workstations. This familiarized participants with the system to enable them to perform the main creative task. Said task was a design scenario, where participants had a client that wanted them to come up with an "algorithmic shapes" design for a small front door window, about 20×20 cm. The client expected options to choose from. Participants then used *NodeBox* to create a number of alternative designs and saved them as different files. Participants were free to sketch with pen and paper, as necessary, and were given 30 minutes for the task.

In the second phase, participants first learned how to use *GEM-NI*. All above-presented features of the system were demonstrated on the example in Figure 1, which they recreated from scratch. The second task stipulated that their client saw the alternative designs for the door window and liked them so much that she asked them to extend them to cover the entire door. Participants could reuse their designs from the first task. They were given 30 minutes to complete the task and again permitted to sketch. After completing the second CSI questionnaire they also filled the paired comparison part of the CSI. Since the tasks in our study were similar enough, we performed the CSI evaluation as a within subject tool comparison with the same task.

Results of the Workshop

The small number of participants limits our results. Also, we evaluated the tools in a fixed order. Yet, counterbalancing is difficult, as *GEM-NI* is based on *NodeBox*. Looking at the first phase, we noted that several participants had already created alternatives in a *single document* in *NodeBox* (without prompting!) through the ability to create multiple output nodes. This likely reduces the "cool tool" bias and verifies that designers already *plan for alternatives*, even in current tools. These participants had primed themselves to learn *GEM-NI* quickly. Two participants, P1 and P4 created four alternatives with *GEM-NI*. All designs of P1 differed only in parameters, but not structurally. P4 came up with several designs that were structurally different. The logs showed that both P1 and P4 used branching to create their alternatives and worked non-linearly, i.e., went back and forth between alternatives. We also logged five instances where P1 rearranged the order of alternatives. Another participant, P3, created two alternatives and accessed the history and design gallery, but did not create alternatives with those methods. Only one person was observed to use pen and paper briefly.

In-Depth Interviews

We ran in-depth interviews with three of the participants (P1-3) in the days after the workshop. At the start of the interview, participants were given a short review of the features of *NodeBox* and *GEM-NI*. Then they were asked to continue working on the second task with *GEM-NI*. In a variant of a think-aloud protocol, we asked participants to express their opinions during this, to make comments on the tools, to provide feedback on the overall workflow and experience, and to explain why they made their decisions. P1 and P2 completed the interview in a little over two hours. Participant P3 was only able to dedicate 30 minutes. Overall, participants used many more features of *GEM-NI*.

P1 created two alternatives from history. When asked about this feature, P1 pointed out "*creating alternatives from history is superior because I like the idea of being able to pick something from the actual history, which could contain ideas that were not further developed*". This is in contrast to the alternative workflow of branching and deleting of unwanted parts of the graph, where he added "*[with this] some steps might not be captured, such as creation and deletion of connectors and partial editing of nodes*". During the interview, P1 produced designs that were different both structurally and in parameters. In the end, P1 created seven designs in a non-linear way through branching. He also created an alternative from a design gallery and two from scratch. We logged deletion of six alternatives. He re-ordered alternatives 30 times and used global undo once. P2 created five designs in two workspaces and saved some of his alternatives individually and then opened them in a new workspace. He re-ordered alternatives seven times, created two alternatives from scratch and five non-linearly as branches and used merging. P2 deleted six alternatives. P2 was not able to leverage design galleries, as his design had very subtle variations in only two parameters and thus "*the results shown in the gallery were [almost] identical*". P3 created five alternatives in a single workspace in a short time, through a design gallery, which P3 found to be "*a great way to explore possibilities*". P3 deleted one alternative and rearranged alternatives 21 times.

All participants were observed using the two available monitors. It was important to their workflow to focus on a single alternative. Therefore, all dragged idle and passive alternatives to the secondary monitor, to increase the workspace for the active alternative. This generated many instances of rearranging. P1 and P2 had programming skills and stated: "*GEM-NI is like version control [systems]*". They drew on their experience with *Git* and used *GEM-NI* somewhat like a version control system for design, which enabled them to experiment more. P3 was not familiar with software version control and thus did not have the corresponding mental model. P2 demonstrated an unexpected use of our system. He created multiple sub-graphs as alternatives, where the output of all sub-graphs was rendered inside a single *GEM-NI* alternative. Then, he started using the panels as means to explore even further alternatives. In the freeform feedback, he later wrote: "*I encountered some unexpected designs while using [GEM-NI], which made things much more interesting than I had first imagined. Interactive [parallel] editing had very interesting results*". P2 worked always on a single alternative at a time and perceived parallel editing of multiple alternatives at the same time "*to be hard*", likely due to the increased cognitive effort required for such parallel tasks. This corresponds to the experience with *Juxtapose* [15], which requires strong coding skills. Only one participant was observed to use global undo.

All participants complained about aspects of *NodeBox* and to a lesser degree about *GEM-NI's* features. Most criticism revolved around the fact that focusing is not automated enough. They found rearranging panels to be hard and wished for an easier workflow. We did not focus on streamlining this specific task. Participants also asked for some difference visualization that "*would highlight changes in the rendered geometry and network*". They also preferred that sandboxing be the default work mode, and that parallel editing only be available on demand (opposite to our default). Finally, participants P2 and P3 wanted to minimize or collapse alternatives, instead of being confronted with all of them simultaneously. They suggested a side window or panel that "*shows alternatives in a way similar to the design gallery*". They also identified that they would like alternatives that are collapsed to automatically turn idle.

Task	Factor \ Scale	Enjoyment	Exploration	Expressiveness	Immersion	Results worth effort
1	Factor counts (σ)	2.5 (1.7)	3.8 (1.5)	4.0 (0.8)	2.3 (1.3)	2.5 (1.3)
1	Factor score (σ)	13 (2.5)	11.3 (2.5)	9.0 (4.3)	6.5 (1.3)	11.5 (2.4)
1	Weighted factor score (σ)	34.8 (30.6)	41.0 (15.5)	36.5 (18.4)	15.3 (9.6)	27.0 (11.2)
2	Factor counts (σ)	2.5 (1.7)	3.8 (1.5)	4.0 (0.8)	2.3 (1.3)	2.5 (1.3)
2	Factor score (σ)	14.8 (2.8)	15.8 (1.5)	14.0 (3.2)	10.0 (7.1)	13.3 (5.0)
2	Weighted factor score (σ)	37.0 (28.9)	59.8 (25.5)	56.8 (20.5)	28.8 (34.8)	32.3 (20.1)

Table 1. Average results from first task using *NodeBox (top)*; second task using *GEM-NI (bottom)*.

Results of the CSI Questionnaire and Discussion

The CSI analysis, revealed an average score of 51.5 ($\sigma = 13.5$) in the first task and a substantially higher score, 71.5 ($\sigma = 12.84$), for the one where *GEM-NI* was used ($N = 4$ for both tasks). These results depend to some degree on individual's preferences and their level of expertise with the tool. Similar to [7], we report the results with respect to average factor counts, factor score and weighted factor score (Table 1). Average counts express the number of times that participants chose a particular factor as important to the task. Expressiveness and exploration were ranked as most important. The factor score sums both agreement statement responses for a factor. A higher number indicates better supports. Weighted factor scores are more sensitive to the factors that are the most important ones for the given task. In both dimensions, *GEM-NI* scored again much higher for expressiveness and exploration.

OVERALL DISCUSSION

Here we discuss some of the consequences of the design decisions behind *GEM-NI*, as backed by the outcomes of our workshop and the in-depth interviews. *GEM-NI* supports a number of ways to create alternatives. We include adapted and enhanced variations of results from previous work, such as *Parallel Pies* [35]. We also introduced a new method for creating alternatives from a graphical history with support for lineage duplication, i.e., graphical skating, for generative design tools. The in-depth interviews indicate that this is an ideal feature to easily explore what-if scenarios. Another noteworthy way of creating alternatives in *GEM-NI* is the design gallery. This interface improves previous work [26], by enabling users to select an arbitrary range of parameters and/or parts of the generative network to use. Furthermore, we added the new ability to create alternatives from the product of generative networks, which we believe to be a great addition to design space exploration tools and found to be useful in our evaluation. Notably, participants stated that "*[they] arrived at designs that they did not expect or foresee directly*". They attributed this to both the design gallery and to parallel editing. To control the scope of parallel editing, *GEM-NI* provides checkmarks and sandboxing, which participants found very useful during our evaluation.

In *GEM-NI*, we also introduced a novel method for post-hoc merging of alternatives, inspired by branch merging in *Git*. With post-hoc merging, a designer can easily "import" the knowledge embedded in a sub-network into another alternative. Post-hoc merging is particularly useful when a designer does not remember how he/she arrived at a particular state or if someone else modified the design. Yet, we only observed and logged one participant using the technique, potentially due to the limited design complexity explored in our evaluation. Still, we believe that with time, users will realize the full potential of this feature, similar to its pervasiveness in software projects.

Two participants rearranged alternatives extensively to focus on a single one on one monitor. This justifies our decision to support multi-monitors and to use such systems in the evaluation. Participants requested minimizing and other methods to manage alternatives on dual monitors. Participants also requested difference visualizations for alternatives, and overlaid history steps. Such features have been advocated before [21]. *GEM-NI* was implemented as a branch of *NodeBox 3* by adding multiple-document model support via universal unique identifiers. This enables consistent relationships between alternatives to persist even when they are kept offline. Alternatives can then safely be included back into the workspace at a later stage, without naming conflicts. *GEM-NI* supports versioning in this way and P2 used this during the evaluation.

While the sample size of our evaluation is small, we believe it to be representative for what moderately experienced designers can achieve with *GEM-NI* compared to traditional solutions, in terms of better exploration of a design space and expressiveness. The fact that participants even created alternative-supporting schemes in existing tools, underlines the need for *GEM-NI*'s approach in generative design tools.

CONCLUSION

We presented *GEM-NI*—a new system for creating and managing alternatives in generative design. The system supports parallel editing via checkmarks and sandboxing, two new methods to control which alternatives are affected by a parallel edit. Also, we introduced a novel method for post-hoc merging of alternatives. Moreover, *GEM-NI* provides several methods to create alternatives, including a new method for resurrecting alternatives from a graphical history with previews, with full lineage preservation. Another way to create alternatives is a new design gallery, which enables users to select which ranges of parameters and/or parts of the generative network model to use for exploration. Moreover, our design gallery supports a new method to explore products of generative networks.

The feedback from participants in a workshop and in-depth interviews suggest that *GEM-NI,* and more broadly the approach behind it, indeed enables designers to work more creatively. The results indicate the direct applicability of the presented techniques for the design process also via the CSI questionnaire. While the sample size of our user study is small, it identified the potential for better creativity support through alternatives in design tools.

Future Work

We envision several extensions. Currently, the network layout is not kept consistent across versions if merging or other editing occurs. We are also planning to incorporate difference visualizations and the ability to enlarge the active alternative, and to minimize others. We will filter visually similar candidates in the design gallery. Finally, we intend to evaluate *GEM-NI* on a 2×3 multi-monitor setup.

ACKNOWLEDGEMENTS

Thanks to the helpers for the workshop and to the GRAND NCE and NSERC Discovery program for funding.

REFERENCES

1. Akin, Ö. How do architects design? *Artificial Intelligence and Pattern Recognition in Computer Aided Design*, (1978), 65–103.
2. Akin, Ö. Variants in design cognition. *Design knowing and learning: Cognition in design education*, (2001), 105–124.
3. Bohnacker, H. *Generative Design: Visualize, Program, and Create with Processing.* Princeton Architectural Press, New York, 2012.

4. Bueno, C., Crossland, S., Lutteroth, C., and Weber, G. Rewriting History: More Power to Creative People. *OzCHI 2011*, 62–71.
5. Buxton, B. *Sketching User Experiences: Getting the Design Right and the Right Design.* Morgan & Kaufmann, 2007.
6. Chen, H.-T., Wei, L.-Y., and Chang, C.-F. Nonlinear revision control for images. *ACM SIGGRAPH 2011 papers*, ACM (2011), 105:1–105:10.
7. Cherry, E. and Latulipe, C. Quantifying the Creativity Support of Digital Tools Through the Creativity Support Index. *TOCHI 2014 21*, 4 (2014), 21:1–21:25.
8. Chevalier, F., Dragicevic, P., Bezerianos, A., and Fekete, J.-D. Using text animated transitions to support navigation in document histories. *CHI 2010*, ACM (2010), 683–692.
9. Dow, S., Fortuna, J., Schwartz, D., Altringer, B., et al. Prototyping Dynamics: Sharing Multiple Designs Improves Exploration, Group Rapport, and Results. *SIGCHI' 11*, ACM (2011), 2807–2816.
10. Drucker, S.M., Petschnigg, G., and Agrawala, M. Comparing and managing multiple versions of slide presentations. *UIST 2006*, ACM (2006), 47–56.
11. Edwards, W.K., Igarashi, T., LaMarca, A., and Mynatt, E.D. A temporal model for multi-level undo and redo. *UIST 2000*, ACM (2000), 31–40.
12. Green, T.R. Cognitive dimensions of notations. *People and Computers V*, (1989), 443–460.
13. Grossman, T., Matejka, J., et al. Chronicle: capture, exploration, and playback of document workflow histories. *UIST 2010*, ACM (2010), 143–152.
14. Hartmann, B., Follmer, S., Ricciardi, A., Cardenas, T., and Klemmer, S.R. d.note: revising user interfaces through change tracking, annotations, and alternatives. *CHI 2010*, ACM (2010), 493–502.
15. Hartmann, B., Yu, L., Allison, A., Yang, Y., and Klemmer, S.R. Design as exploration: creating interface alternatives through parallel authoring and runtime tuning. *UIST 2008*, ACM (2008), 91–100.
16. Heer, J., Mackinlay, J., Stolte, C., and Agrawala, M. Graphical histories for visualization: supporting analysis, communication, and evaluation. *TVCG 14*, 6 (2008), 1189–1196.
17. Hsu, W. and Woon, I.M.Y. Current research in the conceptual design of mechanical products. *Computer-Aided Design 30*, 5 (1998), 377 – 389.
18. Jankun-Kelly, T.J. and Ma, K.-L. A spreadsheet interface for visualization exploration. *Visualization '00*, IEEE Computer Society Press (2000), 69–76.
19. Klemmer, S.R., Thomsen, M., Phelps-Goodman, E., Lee, R., and Landay, J.A. Where do web sites come from?: Capturing and interacting with design history. *CHI 2002*, ACM (2002), 1–8.
20. Kurlander, D. and Feiner, S. A visual language for browsing, undoing, and redoing graphical interface commands. In *Visual Languages and Visual Programming*, 1990, 257–275.
21. Lunzer, A. and Hornbæk, K. Subjunctive Interfaces: Extending Applications to Support Parallel Setup, Viewing and Control of Alternative Scenarios. *ACM TOCHI 14*, 4 (2008), 17:1–17:44.
22. Ma, K.-L. Image graphs - a novel approach to visual data exploration. *Visualization '99*, (1999), 81–88.
23. Marks, J., et al. Design galleries: a general approach to setting parameters for computer graphics and animation. *SIGGRAPH '97*, ACM (1997), 389–400.
24. Menezes, A. and Lawson, B. How designers perceive sketches. *Design Studies 27*, 5 (2006), 571–585.
25. Newman, M.W. and Landay, J.A. Sitemaps, Storyboards, and Specifications: A Sketch of Web Site Design Practice. *DIS 2000*, ACM (2000), 263–274.
26. Sheikholeslami, M. You can get more than you make. 2011. http://summit.sfu.ca/item/9649.
27. Shneiderman, B. The eyes have it: a task by data type taxonomy for information visualizations. *Visual Languages 1996*, IEEE (1996), 336–343.
28. Simon, H.A. *The sciences of the artificial.* MIT press, 1996.
29. Smedt, T.D., Lechat, L., and Daelemans, W. Generative Art Inspired by Nature, Using NodeBox. In *Applications of Evolutionary Computation*. Springer Berlin Heidelberg, 2011, 264–272.
30. Smith, B.N., Xu, A., and Bailey, B.P. Improving interaction models for generating and managing alternative ideas during early design work. *Graphics Interface 2010*, (2010), 121–128.
31. Stephan, M. and Cordy, J.R. A survey of model comparison approaches and applications. *Conference on Model-Driven Engineering and Software Development*, (2013), 265–277.
32. Su, S.L. Visualizing, editing, and inferring structure in 2D graphics. *Adjunct UIST 2007*, ACM (2007), 29–32.
33. Su, S.L., Paris, S., Aliaga, F., Scull, C., Johnson, S., and Durand, F. *Interactive Visual Histories for Vector Graphics.* MIT, 2009.
34. Terry, M. and Mynatt, E.D. Recognizing creative needs in user interface design. *Creativity and Cognition 2002*, ACM (2002), 38–44.
35. Terry, M., Mynatt, E.D., Nakakoji, K., and Yamamoto, Y. Variation in element and action: supporting simultaneous development of alternative solutions. *CHI 2004*, ACM (2004), 711–718.
36. Wang, L., Shen, W., Xie, H., Neelamkavil, J., and Pardasani, A. Collaborative conceptual design—state of the art and future trends. *Computer-Aided Design 34*, 13 (2002), 981 – 996.
37. Woodbury, R. *Elements of Parametric Design.* Routledge, 2010.
38. Woodbury, R.F. and Burrow, A.L. Whither design space? *Artif. Intell. Eng. Des. Anal. Manuf. 20*, 2 (2006), 63–82.
39. Xu, K., Zhang, H., Cohen-Or, D., and Chen, B. Fit and diverse: set evolution for inspiring 3D shape galleries. *ACM TOG*, *31,* 4, (2012), 57:1–57:10.

Motif: Supporting Novice Creativity through Expert Patterns

Joy Kim[1], Mira Dontcheva[2], Wilmot Li[2], Michael S. Bernstein[1], Daniela Steinsapir[2]
Stanford University[1], Adobe Research[2]
{jojo0808, msb}@cs.stanford.edu, {mirad, wilmotli, steinsap}@adobe.com

Figure 1. In Motif, a user composes each section of a video story based on patterns extracted from expert work.

ABSTRACT

Creating personal narratives helps people build meaning around their experiences. However, novices lack the knowledge and experience to create stories with strong narrative structure. Current storytelling tools often structure novice work through templates, enforcing a linear creative process that asks novices for materials they may not have. In this paper, we propose scaffolding creative work using storytelling patterns extracted from stories created by experts. Patterns are modular sets of related camera shots that expert videographers commonly use to achieve a specific narrative function. After identifying a set of patterns from high-quality storytelling videos, we created Motif, a mobile video storytelling application that allows users to construct video stories by combining these patterns. By making existing solutions used by experts available to novices, we encourage capturing shots with story structure and narrative goals in mind. In a controlled study where we asked participants to create travel video stories, videos created with patterns conveyed stronger narrative structure and were considered higher quality by expert evaluators than videos created without patterns.

Author Keywords

Novice creativity; video stories; storytelling.

ACM Classification Keywords

H.5.2. User Interfaces: User-centered design

CHI'15, April 18–April 23, 2015, Seoul, Republic of Korea.

ACM 978-1-4503-3145-6/15/04$15.00
http://dx.doi.org/10.1145/2702123.2702507

INTRODUCTION

Telling stories about personal experiences can help people reflect on their lives and build a shared history with the people around them [12]. For this reason, people often desire to create artifacts representing their personal experiences and histories in order to share them with others [18]. Today, personal stories are often accompanied by digital artifacts, such as photos or videos. However, while the prevalence of full-featured mobile devices makes it convenient to capture such artifacts, assembling them into compelling stories remains a difficult task. Expert storytellers are able to use narrative structure to guide an audience through an event, but novices typically lack consideration for narrative pacing and structure. They make mistakes such as starting and ending a story abruptly or allowing sections of the story to drag on for long periods of time.

A key challenge in creating stories with good narrative structure is capturing the right types of content. While experts typically have a narrative structure in mind and can anticipate what they might need to express that structure (e.g., footage of passing scenery on the way to an event to provide context at the beginning of a video story), novices often do not think about capturing such content in the moment and miss opportunities to do so. Moreover, even if a novice storyteller ends up capturing the right types of content, they may not know how to combine it to achieve specific narrative goals (such as highlighting a key moment by juxtaposing it with a shot of viewers' reactions).

How can novices create better stories? Existing story creation tools for non-experts, such as iMovie Trailers [3] and Animoto [1], provide templates that help novices arrange captured content in a heavily structured way. However, these tools only guide users in arranging content they already have and leave users to decide the appropriate types of content for their stories on their own. Thus, while the output from these tools contains aesthetically pleasing elements, such as stylized transitions or split-screen effects, it typically suffers from the same lack of narrative structure as amateur videos made from scratch. Another drawback of existing template-based tools is that the templates themselves are typically very rigid, forcing users to assemble a fixed number of video clips or images with specific properties in a specific order. While this prevents users from making common mistakes such as including interminable shots with very little action, this also leaves little room for novices to express their own ideas and adjust the story's structure to suit different storytelling needs.

In this paper, we propose an approach to help novices tell stories in a guided way that allows for creative freedom. Our hypothesis is that we can *scaffold novice creative work using patterns extracted from work by experts*. We explore this strategy in the domain of video story production, which is a particularly compelling application area given the prevalence of mobile video capture and sharing, and the difficulty of producing such stories well. In our approach, a *pattern* (Figure 1) is a set of related camera shots that expert videographers commonly use to achieve a specific narrative function. For example, the *Setting Out* pattern is often used at the beginning of video stories to introduce an event and why the storyteller is going to it. It typically includes a shot of scenery passing by as the storyteller travels to the event, along with narration describing where the storyteller is going and with whom. In general, pattern languages describe the knowledge of a typical creative expert in the form of a set of recurring solutions to common problems in a design domain [6]. Unlike templates, *patterns are modular ingredients that can be combined to form a larger creative solution.*

We demonstrate our approach with a video storytelling application for mobile phones called *Motif*[1] (Figure 2). Motif comprises both a story construction tool and a story capture tool. In Motif, the patterns we identified in expert videos are manifested as *story blocks*, which each consist of a set of suggested shots needed to render a pattern. In story construction mode, users can arrange these story blocks to create the outline for a video story, essentially forming a checklist of what a user needs to capture that appears while the user is in capture mode. By strongly linking the activities of capture and construction into the interface, Motif allows users to adapt their story structure as they capture content and vice-versa. In addition, these suggestions may also encourage users to record content they may not have recorded otherwise; novices are supplied with the strategies for what to capture and are only responsible for filling in the pattern with their own content without needing to manually slice video files or generate creative decisions from scratch.

In a controlled study, we asked 13 people from two different locations to create a short travel video story about popular tourist destinations in their home areas. Participants were randomly assigned to use either Motif, where stories were scaffolded by patterns extracted from expert work, or a control version of Motif where stories were not scaffolded. Through

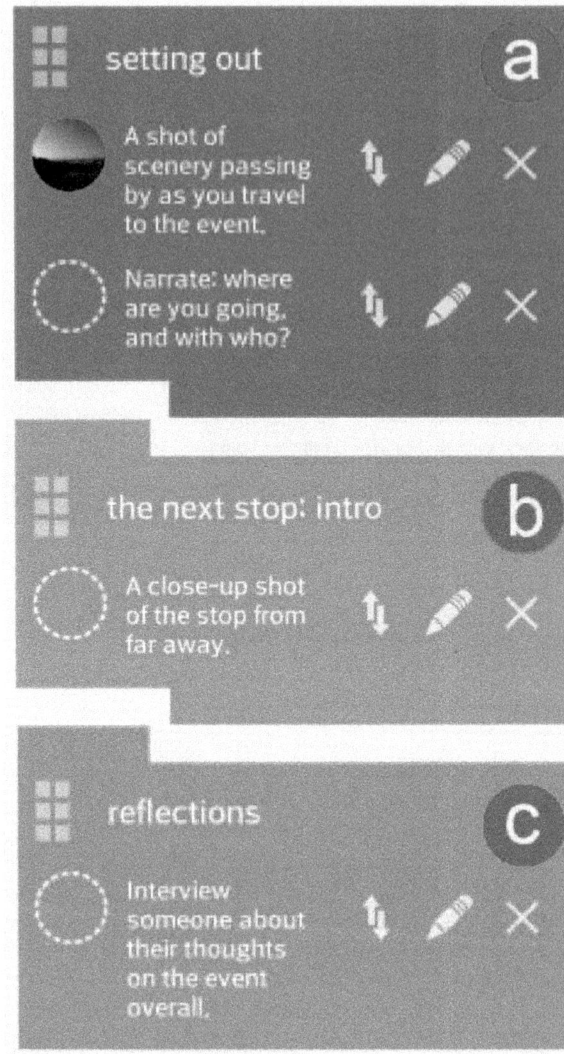

Figure 2. Stories are composed of story blocks in Motif. (a) A Beginning story block. The first shot in this block has already been filled in. (b) A Middle story block. (c) An End story block.

analysis of survey responses, interviews, and story structures present in created videos, we found that videos created using patterns were higher-quality than videos created without patterns, conveying stronger narrative structure and depicting scenes using multiple shots and angles.

RELATED WORK

There are a number of online communities and mobile applications that have made it easy to organize and capture digital artifacts. Applications such as Timehop [5] and Memoir [4] offer ways of retrieving digital content from the past and organizing them by location or time for viewing in the future. Other applications, such as Animoto and Explory [1, 2], have attempted to formalize the slideshow sharing behavior mobile users often employ when sharing photos [7] by creating tools for making narrated or text-supported slideshows.

However, these tools often focus on quick capture and attractive presentation rather than supporting story construction and

[1]`http://motifstory.stanford.edu`

planning. How-to books on home video recording or film-making often instruct readers to plan their film's visual content ahead of time with a rough outline so that moments can be anticipated and captured [15]. Veteran scrapbookers often think ahead about how they would want to make scrapbook pages about the event they're experiencing in order to make sure they capture the right photos and save the right pieces of memorabilia [19], preventing situations where they miss chances to capture something they wanted to remember. This contrasts against the way most people record their lives — without much forethought to what they would want to remember later and how they'll remember it.

Meaning-making through story construction

The capture and editing phases of a video are often considered separate activities. However, expert videographers view these two phases as intricately linked, where capture incites changes in narrative and where changes in narrative change the plan for capture. The mindful documentary model [8] captures this iterative process of story construction by using commonsense reasoning to suggest storytelling options available for a videographer in real-time. However, enabling real-time suggestions requires videographers to create text annotations for the shots they are capturing. Motif, instead, attempts to make this iterative storytelling process accessible to novices by providing mix-and-matchable patterns for use out-of-the-box.

Past work has also looked at how capturing and handling material for a story helps people construct memories of the past. The activity of building a personal history using a timeline metaphor can provide a vehicle for identifying and reminiscing on key events [17]. Asking families to create time capsules revealed that people did not create an exhaustive record of the past but instead tried to create a detailed representation of a single theme, such as "a typical day" [13]. In addition, many families constructed new artifacts for the purposes of the time capsule rather than logging past content [11]. The suggestion is that memories are not fixed but continuously reconstructed through building and interpretating narrative cues. Motif currently focuses on facilitating this relationship between reflection and story construction for story creators (rather than for an audience) by encouraging users to leave capture mode at any time to change their story's structure based on new or unexpected events.

Patterns as constraints

A pattern language describes a set of well-worn practices within a field of expertise [6]. Unlike spoken or written languages, pattern languages enable navigation of a design problem rather than communication. Motif employs a simple pattern language to guide novice work: suggestions given to novices can be thought of as a vocabulary, and the constraints Motif places on how these suggestions are put together represent a simple grammar. Use of this simple language places constraints on the creative options available to novices, which may both prevent the novice storyteller from being overwhelmed and allow novices to comfortably experiment within established boundaries [16].

STORYTELLING PATTERNS

Experienced video storytellers have developed tacit and explicit knowledge about their craft. We suggest that, like architecture [6] and web design [10], storytelling patterns can be codified and made more accessible to non-experts. In this section, we discuss the patterns we extracted from expert videos and their constituent elements. Next, we demonstrate how these patterns are instantiated within Motif.

Identifying video storytelling patterns

To develop our set of storytelling patterns, we examined 13 short video stories from the New York Times, two Rick Steves' Best of Europe travel videos, and two high-quality home videos about a group camping trip and visiting a local food festival (see supplementary materials for links). We explicitly chose a variety of videos to ensure that we generated patterns that were both common and specific across several genres of stories. We included home videos in our corpus because amateurs may have different storytelling goals than professional filmmakers; we anticipated that home videos might reveal different kinds of patterns than professionally produced videos.

Through a grounded analysis of these videos, we created a list of groups of shots that worked together to convey a coherent narrative idea or function. These groupings were detected by looking for scene changes, as they often marked where one narrative chunk ended and another began (e.g., moving from the introduction of the story to an interview with an event attendee). We also focused on repeated narrative elements, since comparing similar pieces of the story could reveal common elements between them (e.g. comparing several different interviews to identify the kinds of shots an interview typically contains). Shot groupings were selected on the basis of storytelling purpose (e.g., a pattern for how interviews are introduced) rather than on visual qualities (e.g., a pattern for showing scenery). We took note of how each shot was framed, the narrative purpose for each shot, and the length of each shot. We then consolidated groupings with similar functionality to create a list of 24 patterns.

Early iterations of the patterns were fairly general. For instance, early patterns included things like *Action/Reaction* (i.e. showing something happening and viewers' reactions to it) or *Contrast* (i.e. juxtaposing two ideas, situations, or things). We assumed that users would know when these patterns would be best appropriate. However, with early pilots of Motif, we observed that these patterns were too disconnected from the actual situations people wanted to capture. So, we instead focused patterns around specific narrative purposes. This resulted in more targeted patterns which were more easily recognizable, including: *Setting Out* (i.e., leaving for a trip), *Travel Break* (i.e. moving between two locations), and *Serve* (i.e., putting freshly-cooked food in front of people).

For each pattern, we identified the *elements* that were required. For example, a *Travel Break* pattern, which is used while travelers are enroute to a destination, requires 1) a shot of vehicles leaving the current location, and 2) a shot of the surroundings passing by, taken through the window. We noted the time lengths of each element as they appeared in

Pattern	Type	Elements	Example	Timeline
Setting Out	Beginning	■ Shot of scenery passing by as you travel to the event. ■ Narrate: where are you going, and with who? ■ Text: title of event	GCC-family (0:06–0:32)	
How to Make	Beginning	■ Shot of the final dish. ■ Text: name of dish	Cuba-Libre (0:03–0:07)	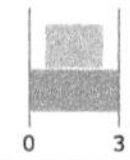
Set the Location	Beginning	■ Record yourself briefly describing the place this video will be about and why it's so great. ■ Narrate: a short outline of the trip to come. ■ Short shot showing the first part of the trip. ■ Short shot showing the second part of the trip. ■ Short shot showing another part of the trip.	RS-Italy (0:00–0:12)	
Key Moment	Middle	■ Shot of something going on during this key moment. ■ Shot of something going on during this key moment. (optional) ■ Shot showing people's reactions to the key moment.	GCC-family (28:57–30:20)	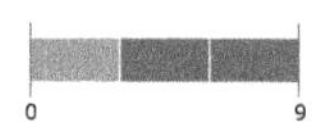
The Next Step	Middle	■ Shot of the cook grabbing the next ingredient or tool needed for this step. ■ Shot of the cook adding the ingredient or performing this step. ■ Text: name of ingredient or tool	Cuba-Libre (0:07–0:12)	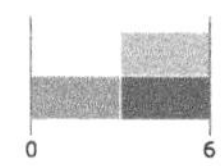
Travel Break	Middle	■ Before you head out, record a shot of vehicles heading out to your next location. ■ While you're travelling, take a shot of your surroundings through the window.	RS-Spain (27:09–27:32)	
Reflections	End	■ Interview someone on their thoughts about the event overall.	Food-Fest (3:10–5:20)	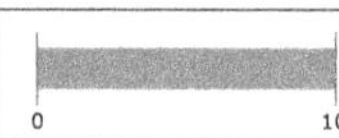
Serve	End	■ A shot of the dish being served or placed on a table.	Cuba-Libre (0:21–0:25)	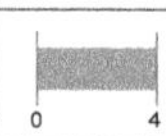
Highlight Reel	End	■ Narrate: short outline of what you did on the trip. ■ Short shot showing the first part of the trip. ■ Short shot showing the second part of the trip. ■ Short shot showing another part of the trip. (optional) ■ Record yourself describing the trip and what you got out of it.	RS-Spain (53:46–54:23)	

Table 1. A sample of story blocks and prompts available in Motif. The Example column specifies a time and expert video where the pattern can be seen (see supplementary materials).

examples and created a timeline illustrating a typical editing pattern for combining those elements into a final video (right column of Table 1).

Patterns

Table 1 presents a subset of the 24 patterns we identified. Some of them apply across a variety of story settings: for example, *Reflections*, *Set the Location* and *Key Moment* all could be used for travelogues, local events, or slice-of-life videos. Other patterns are focused on specific types of events. For example, *How to Make*, as well as *Serve*, are tailored for cooking-oriented videos, and *Travel Break* and *The Next Stop: Tips* best suit travel videos.

We classified each pattern by the narrative role it typically played in example videos. Beginning patterns often opened videos by setting the stage or providing a preview of the final goal; End patterns ensured the final part of the video had a compelling closing; Middle patterns filled in the action in between. Table 1 presents three videos of each type. Strong videos have one Beginning and one End pattern, and as many Middle patterns as necessary in order to tell the rest of the story.

Patterns not listed in Table 1 include: *How to Make Slideshow, This is Perfect for..., The Next Step (narrated), Serve (narrated), Describe Travel Plans, The Next Stop: Intro, The Next Stop: Describe, The Next Stop: Tips, The Next Stop: Mini Review, In the Action, Guests/Friends Appearing, Guests/Friends Interview, Guests/Friends Leaving, Group Shot*, and *Time Lapse*. Our supplementary materials include descriptions of all 24 patterns we identified.

MOTIF: PATTERNS IN ACTION

We manifest our use of story patterns in Motif, an Android application that uses patterns to help structure both *construction* and *capture* of video stories. In this section, we describe how Motif transforms patterns into story blocks and guides novices during the video story creation process.

Story Blocks and Prompts

In Motif, we use two user interface elements to help users make use of patterns.

Figure 3. Prompts for story blocks appear at the top of the screen while users are in capture mode.

Patterns appear as *story blocks* (Figure 2), which are used to build an outline of a video story. They can be combined according to a simple grammar: the story must start with a Beginning block, followed by as many Middle blocks as desired, then close with an End block. This grammar enforces narrative structure while leaving the user free to decide the kind of content they want their story to include. Motif's visual language suggests these constraints through the use of puzzle pieces (e.g., [14]).

The elements required for each pattern — required and optional shots, narration, and title text — are transformed into *prompts* (Figure 2). A user can tap on each prompt to insert corresponding video, audio, or text into their story. Additionally, users can use these prompts as guides during capture mode (Figure 3).

Scenario

Storytelling patterns provide guidance for the content users need to capture to achieve specific narrative goals. Reciprocally, they prioritize recognition over recall — rather than trying to remember what they've seen in past examples, novice users can now choose storytelling elements from a provided library. In this way, novices capture content they might not otherwise have captured. Below, we walk through a scenario illustrating how a user constructs a story using Motif.

Story construction through blocks

Jin is heading out for a short vacation to New York City with his friend Clara. He wants to use Motif to create a short video story about his trip so that he can share it with friends and family, as well as have a memento of the trip for the future. Having planned out his travel itinerary, Jin already has ideas for the places he wants to include in his story.

The night before he leaves, he opens Motif on his Android phone and creates a new story with a skeleton he can fill in while travelling. To start out, Jin selects a suitable Beginning block for his story. He adds the *Setting Out* story block to his story, which represents a pattern made up two elements: (a) A shot of scenery passing by as you travel to the event. (b) Narrate: where are you going, and with who?

Jin decides to add a few more story blocks for significant stops during his trip. He wants to make sure that he captures his visits to Magnolia Bakery, the Empire State Building, and Times Square, so he adds the *The Next Stop: Intro* and *The Next Stop: Describe* story blocks for each of those stops. Additionally, he adds the *The Next Stop: Mini Review* story block for the section in his story about the bakery, anticipating that his friends may want to hear his thoughts about the food and ambience he finds there. Jin continues adding a few more story blocks in this way before heading to bed. In this way, Jin is able to construct his story before any clips have been captured, in contrast to constructing a video story on a frame-by-frame basis after the trip is over.

Prompts encourage users to capture

The following day, Jin heads to the airport with Clara. While waiting at the gate, Jin checks Motif and realizes he forgot to capture the first shot for the *Setting Out* block, which suggested capturing "a shot of scenery passing by as you travel to the event". Jin decides to set the scene for travel in a different way; rather than capturing scenery passing by, he decides to capture an ambient shot of the airport near the gate.

To do this, he taps the empty circle next to the prompt, which flips the application into camera mode (Figure 3). Jin captures a 3-second shot (as suggested by the prompt), and the empty circle fills in with a thumbnail of the video clip to indicate that Jin has successfully fulfilled the prompt (Figure 2a). Motif acts as a visual checklist for Jin as he fills in his story.

Then, he looks at the next shot in the story block, which suggests "Narrate: where are you going, and with who?". Again, using the camera, he records himself briefly describing the context of his trip, and even asks his friend Clara for a few words so that she is in the video as well. When Jin is done, he quickly scans over the rest of the list to see if there is anything else he can record. He sees the rest of the story blocks can only be fulfilled at future stops on the itinerary, so he pockets his phone for now.

Jin later approaches the first major stop on his trip — the Empire State Building. He remembers having created some story blocks for this part of the trip and takes a look at Motif before he and Clara arrive there. By they time they approach the building, Jin is ready to record shots introducing and describing it. Along the way, he spots a street musician he finds interesting. Though it was not part of his plan for capture, he is able to click the "Add New Shot" button to record a few seconds of this unexpected experience on the fly. Jin can later move this uncategorized clip (Figure 4) to augment an existing story block in his story, or use the clip to fill in an empty prompt. In other words, story blocks are not rigid but can be modified to suit various situations and ideas.

Motif generates the story

In Motif, Jin is able to preview his video story at any time. When he returns to his hotel room at the end of the day, he presses the Play button to see how his video story is progressing. He notices a few things that he would like to change; he removes a shot he recorded on accident and belatedly records a clip of him picking up his backpack to remedy a jarring transition between when he left the hotel room in the morning and his visit to the Empire State Building. Once he has

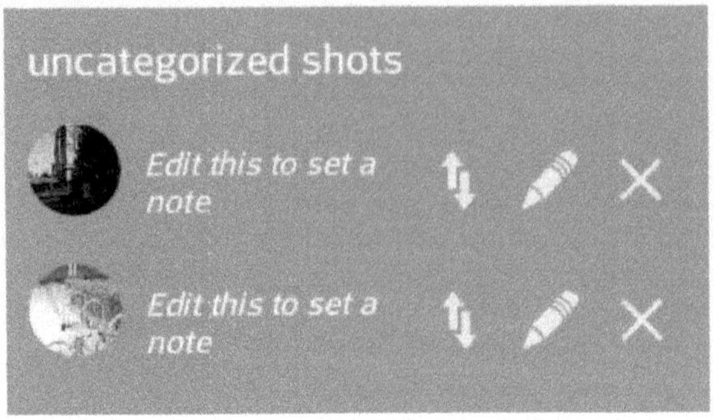

Figure 4. Users can also record shots that are not tied to a story block. These shots can be organized into story blocks later.

made modifications, Jin previews his story once again, this time finding it a much more smooth experience.

EVALUATION

Motif hypothesizes that a storytelling pattern language can support users in telling well-structured stories. In this section, we report on an evaluation exploring whether this overall strategy improves creative outcomes.

Method

We evaluated Motif through a controlled study comparing two versions of the application: the full Motif application (the Motif condition), and a version without story blocks or prompts (the control condition). The control version of the application acted like a standard camera and gallery application, with the additional ability for users to type brief notes for each captured video clip if they wished.

Thirteen participants (eight female, five male) were recruited from TaskRabbit and Craigslist in Seattle and Palo Alto for a task that lasted 1.5 hours. Six participants were recruited at the Seattle location and seven participants were recruited at the Palo Alto location.

Participants were randomly assigned to one of the study conditions and asked to use the application to create a video about a highly popular tourist spot in the area (Pike Place Market for Seattle, Stanford University for Palo Alto). The participants were first given a list of points of interest for the area as well as a map in order to ensure all participants would have some basic knowledge about available subject matter. They were then given 10–15 minutes to create a plan for what to capture using the application. Then, participants walked around the area to collect video footage according to their plans. A researcher followed participants to answer any questions about the interface and to take notes as the participant thought aloud about their video recording process. We then conducted a semi-structured interview with participants about their experience, focusing on what their criteria was for including certain shots, why they made certain design decisions, and the easiest and hardest things about creating their video. Lastly, participants filled out a short survey evaluating their experience and the video story they had created. Participants were paid $40 for their time.

To evaluate each video for quality, two researchers and one video expert used a rating rubric to independently rate each video, blind to condition, on a 7-point likert scale based on five elements:

- **Structure** ($\kappa = .867, p < .05$). Is there a clear beginning, middle, and end? Are the beginning and endings generic, or are they strongly related to the theme of the story?
- **Shot Coverage** ($\kappa = .626, p < .05$). Is there more than one shot per scene in the story? If so, do the shots cover multiple points of view and angles?
- **Shot Composition** ($\kappa = .745, p < .05$). Is the subject of the shot each clear? The shots should avoid placing subjects in the center of the shot and consider the rule of thirds. Individual shots should be as still as possible.
- **Shot Length** ($\kappa = .775, p < .05$). Are shots long enough to understand (> 2 seconds) but short enough so that it stays interesting (< 10 seconds)?
- **Audio Content** ($\kappa = .593, p < .05$). Does the video contain a smooth audio track that links the whole story together? Is narration (if any) easy to hear and understand? Is narration informative and specific?

For final decisions, disagreements in ratings were resolved through discussion. The rating rubric used was based on guidelines from a popular beginner's book about creating home video [15].

Lastly, we coded and examined survey and interview responses to look for themes in behavior between the two study conditions.

Results

Seven videos were created using the control application and six videos were created using Motif. Participants were between the ages of 22 and 60, with the average age being 36 ($SD = 12.75$). The videos created by the participants were an average of 4.8 minutes long, though total story length varied widely ($SD = 3.9$ minutes). The median video length was 3.3 minutes.

Most participants stated that they were not "video people", explaining that when travelling or sightseeing they either focused on the experience at hand, or took photos using their phones. Most participants also stated they had little experience with video editing applications, with five participants stating they had never completed a video editing project before, and six participants stating they had completed fewer than three projects in the past.

Because we gave participants a list of suggested places to visit during the study task, participants tended to visit the same areas while creating their video story. However, ideas for video stories were diverse, ranging from "a food-focused tour of local businesses" to "the story of buying flowers for my partner" to "the ghosts of Pike Place". Participants (especially those from the Seattle location) took the study as an opportunity to purchase items or pass by spots they personally found interesting about the area but had not yet had a chance to see.

In this sense, participants acted as realistic tourists; they were not experts in the area but had some knowledge of what places were famous as tourist attractions and what places were personally interesting to them. Participants also had to deal with the challenge of navigating an unfamiliar area while carrying items and recording video footage.

Story blocks helped users utilize structure of examples

The median number of story blocks in Motif video stories was five, and the median number of shots in Motif video stories was 10.5. Participants tended to use travel-related story blocks, with the top used blocks being *The Next Stop: Describe* (used in five stories), *The Next Stop: Intro* (used in four stories), *Set the Location* (used in four stories), and *Reflections* (used in three stories). This is unsurprising given the nature of the study task; most videos created by participants followed a structure where the participant moved from one point of interest to the next. Participants used a mix of patterns extracted from both the professionally produced video examples and the home video examples; the Reflections pattern was extracted from one of the home video examples.

Participants in both conditions explained that they used expert videos they had seen in the past as mental examples for the video they created. However, for participants in the Motif condition, story blocks and prompts seemed to help translate these examples into a structure for their video stories. Participants — even those that reported using video quite often to document personal experiences — noticed that this changed the way they recorded their video experience:

> *I definitely recorded different things than I normally would have. I liked the structure, how it's like a checklist, that really helps. With just the food, for example, now we're walking up to the restaurant, okay now this is the restaurant. I liked those, and normally if it were on my own, I would have done just one video [clip] and that would be it.*
>
> Participant 8, Motif condition

Participants in the control condition were less sure about how to apply elements from expert examples from the past in their own story. This was not for lack of knowledge about the area; many participants in the control condition told the researcher small stories relevant to places visited during the task when not recording (for example, describing their experience on fishing boats in Alaska while visiting the various fish stalls at Pike Place Market). Through they were given the same amount of time as Motif participants to plan their video, control participants tended to spend little time doing so, instead jumping straight into shooting whatever caught their eye. As a result, they developed a sense of a potentially good structure for their video story only after the task was finished:

> *Maybe I would put more historic facts, to tell you what these [statues] were. Or maybe I would start in the center [of the garden] and move out... I didn't have a plan... Starting was awkward and finishing was awkward.*
>
> Participant 10, control condition

At the same time, the prompts suggested by Motif did not perfectly support every participant's ideas. However, participants did modify existing story blocks to suit their own storytelling needs or recorded slightly different shots than the ones suggested by blocks:

> *I kinda had to say like, "Yeah, I guess that fits." It wasn't like, "Yeah, oh, that sounds perfect." It was like, I can kinda fit it in... I had my ideas of what I wanted and I was looking for that and I couldn't find it, so I just found the next best thing.*
>
> Participant 8, Motif condition

A Kruskal-Wallis test on experts' ratings revealed that videos created with Motif were significantly more structured according both to raters ($\chi^2(1) = 4.803, p < 0.05$) and to the expert evaluator ($\chi^2(1) = 5.09, p < 0.05$); that is, Motif videos tended not to start or end suddenly, instead having clear beginning and ending sequences. In other words, Motif successfully scaffolded the ideas participants had for their stories, guiding participants in creating plans for capture but allowing modifications to flexibly support a variety of story ideas. Participants found themselves capturing shots necessary for a larger narrative, stating they would not have captured these shots without guidance from Motif.

Story blocks reduced cognitive load during capture

Story blocks allowed users to pay an upfront cost for later benefits. Finding the right story blocks to include in the outline for their story was difficult for some participants; however, developing the story at a high-level prior to capture lessened the cognitive load for participants during the actual capture task:

> *The hardest thing was probably finding the templates, trying to fit my idea... the easiest was organizing the [video clips]. It was so nice to be like, I know that this is going go here, or I know that this is going to be the intro video. And then I knew I could record it later... I didn't have to everything in order... the organizing is done for me when I'm choosing my templates. Then I'm just filling those in.*
>
> Participant 8, Motif condition

In addition, participants did not have to generate the list of what they wanted to capture from scratch; they simply had to reconcile existing patterns with their own ideas.

> *The suggestions themselves were all well-worded, and they actually helped provide a guide for the goal that I had selected. It was like following a "choose-your-own-adventure" book... you have the free will to do a bit more of where you want to go, but eventually you're going to get to your conclusion, and it's helpful along the way to be pushed along, but gently... it was kind of a reminder, like, "What am I supposed to be doing here? Oh, right."*
>
> Participant 5, Motif condition

Participants made use of these reminders for what to capture in slightly different ways. Most participants, as described above, filled in story blocks according to the prompts given by Motif. However, one participant used story blocks as a higher-level method of keeping track of the purpose of each of their clips. Rather than creating a *The Next Stop: Describe* story block for each stop they visited, they used a single *The Next Stop: Describe* to "store" all clips they recorded where they described a new location in their tour.

Control participants, in contrast, had to mentally juggle their story idea with judgments about what to capture, making it hard to separate how they experienced the task in real-time from the order of events they wanted their story to eventually depict. This resulted in a collection of shots that were often aimless and unrelated. This became clear in one participant's use of notes in the control condition – he considered writing notes annoying but necessary to help him remember what he was capturing, as there was no structure to ground the purpose of shots:

> *I wanted to label stuff so... if I ever wanted to go back and look at things then I would, the labels, I guess they're kind of like tags that help me remember what I took videos of. If I wanted to rearrange them in the future. I guess I did it on the way because I... doing it after the fact takes more time because you have to rewatch the video.*
>
> Participant 13, control condition

Similarly, Motif participants had the most success creating structure in their stories when using story blocks that did not require them to think about a story timeline different from the way they experienced the event. As an example, one participant used the *Set the Location* and *Highlight Reel* story blocks at the beginning and end of his story, both of which call for clips showing a preview (or a review) of the spots visited during the video. Therefore, these blocks must be completed in non-linear fashion. Some of the participant expressed confusion when encountering these prompts in their story, and ignored them. Other participants explicitly removed these particular prompts.

Prompts helped with shot coverage, but not composition

A Kruskal-Wallis test observed a marginal increase in shot coverage (that is, whether participants recorded multiple shots with different points of view for a scene) for participants in the Motif condition according to raters ($\chi^2(1) = 3.6708, p = 0.056$) and the expert evaluator ($\chi^2(1) = 4.33, p < 0.05$), indicating that patterns may help novices at least think about breaking down scenes into smaller, more consumable pieces.

However, there was no difference in how well shots were composed and framed (raters: $\chi^2(1) = 0.915, n.s.$; expert: $\chi^2(1) = 1.6878, n.s.$). Videos from both conditions generally lacked still shots, with most participants capturing scenes using panoramic shots or while walking.

While neither version of the study application limited how long participants could record for each clip, the Motif application suggested along with prompts how long each clip should ideally be based on expert patterns. We expected Motif videos to comprise of many short clips, but there was no observed effect of study condition on the average length of shots per story (raters: $\chi^2(1) = 0.8767, n.s.$; expert: $\chi^2(1) = 2.4231, n.s.$). This may be due to the fact that participants from both conditions tended to narrate their thoughts in almost every shot they recorded, even for prompts that did not ask for narration. Evaluators did not see a difference in the quality of narration between conditions (raters: $\chi^2(1) = 0.8891, n.s.$, expert: $\chi^2(1) = 3.2124, n.s.$).

Motif videos ranked higher in quality overall

The expert evaluator placed participant videos in an overall ranking according to narrative and videographic quality. According to a Mann-Whitney U test, videos created by participants in the Motif condition received significantly higher ranks than videos created by participants in the control condition ($U = 38, p < 0.05$).

DISCUSSION

Through observations of participants creating video stories with and without Motif, we found that patterns extracted from expert work are able to successfully support novices in making creative decisions such as deciding on a narrative structure and making judgments about the kinds of content to capture. Further, we found that Motif videos were rated as higher quality than the control videos. In this section, we discuss the strengths and limitations of the strategy based on videos created by participants.

Supporting the what and the how

Because we generated patterns in terms of story function rather than visual aesthetic, the patterns we extracted from expert work were largely structure-oriented. That is, patterns provided templates for the kinds of shots to capture and how these shots are grouped. It is unsurprising that the areas in which Motif supported novices was in creating story structure and a unified theme in video stories.

Patterns provided by Motif did not seem to increase novice ability in *composing* the types of shots to capture; videos from both study conditions contained similar violations of videographic principles. For example, most professional videos convey a coherent picture of a subject through a series of several short shots that hold still and let subjects move in and out of the frame. However, in this study, participants employed amateur techniques such as capturing a location through 360-degree panoramas and moving the camera through a space for a long, continuous amount of time. In other words, participants knew *what* to capture, but reverted to natural habits with respect to *how* to capture.

We may be able to use the same strategy of extracting patterns from expert work to make examples of a different characteristic of video stories (such as shot composition) accessible to novices. For example, populating story blocks with visual examples rather than just text prompts may provide a more suitable scaffold for both story structure *and* creative execution. Another approach might be to apply basic machine learning techniques to detect common shot missteps (e.g., "Try holding your camera still while you take multiple shots!") and provide users with tips for improvement.

Being mindful of discovery and emotion

Though we provided participants with maps and suggested points of interest in the area about which they were making a video story, some participants were less ready to create content about the area than others. Participants found themselves sometimes unsure of how to describe a place or thing, leading some to suggest that Motif suggest not just the types of clips to capture but also the kinds of information that might be interesting to a viewer. As one participant put it, this was a clear gap in the approach Motif used (structuring novice creative work around expert patterns) and the way most people experience new places during travel or events:

> *The process of creating a video is forcing you to think about creating a video, you know, you have to think about what does the audience want to see, what's the story, what's the explanation... it's quite a different experience of being a person that's just going to somewhere for the first time and seeing it in person – you don't know what you're going to see and you're discovering things.*
>
> Participant 6, Motif condition

Instead, we may be able to use expert patterns to structure "micro-moments" in addition to the overall story. Currently, Motif depends on the participant either having some time beforehand to plan out the story blocks they anticipated using in a story, or being familiar with the types of shots Motif would ask them to capture. However, travel often includes unexpected events, changes in plans, and serendipitous meetings. Beyond just utilizing patterns evident in the end result of expert work, Motif could also embed some of the strategies experts use to anticipate and ready themselves for capturing such events.

For example, the user could indicate to the system that a certain type of event is currently happening or that they have a certain idea they want to convey. Motif could then make suggestions about how to prepare for this idea (e.g. "Is there an informational plaque nearby to help you figure what to say to viewers?") or how to prioritize capture (e.g. "Make sure you capture the audience's reaction before the performance ends!"). After the moment of discovery is over, Motif could then use its knowledge of what patterns work well together to help the user situate their captured moment in the right place within the larger story being developed.

The novice's audience

Our paper focuses on evaluation criteria surrounding narrative structure and videographic quality. However, it is likely that the social aspect of novices' storytelling goals are significantly different from that of experts. Amateurs may place significantly more weight on creating stories that are shareable with family and friends, while placing less weight on creating a video with high-quality videography that may appeal to a larger audience.

We did ask participants about shareability of the videos they created, satisfaction with the video creation process, and satisfaction with the end result through surveys and interviews, but saw no significant difference in responses between the two conditions. This makes sense: we designed a study with a realistic video capture environment, but participants were ultimately paid to make the video. As a result, participants' motivations were artificial – they created a video in a content-oriented way ("create a video about a certain place") rather than because it was an event or location they truly wanted to remember or share. While this paper focuses on aiding a novice in a certain creative task, we do note that it is important to consider how an anticipated audience affects the creative process and evaluation criteria for a novice storyteller, and leave this as future work.

Limitations

Common video editing tasks such as trimming video clips were not supported in either study condition. For similar technical reasons, Motif participants did not have access to the feature of automatically arranging their content using the timeline arragements we generated for each pattern (Table 1). Though this resulted in video stories that were less concise than if one were to use existing video editing software, we were interested less in the ability of novices to edit video and more in how patterns might play a role in helping novices make creative decisions.

The patterns we generated in this paper are not meant to comprehensively represent all strategies used by videographers; rather, we wanted to demonstrate that extracting patterns from expert work is possible and that these patterns can be made accessible to novices and support their creative work.

CONCLUSION AND FUTURE WORK

In this paper, we sought to tightly weave together *capture* and *construction* for storytelling novices. Toward this end, we identified 24 storytelling patterns such as *Setting Out*, *Key Moment* and *Travel Break* through an analysis of expert examples. Each pattern includes a set of constituent elements as well as a video timeline describing how these elements are arranged. We embedded these patterns into Motif, a mobile application that scaffolds novice creative work using story blocks and prompts. In a field experiment, we found that Motif videos were significantly better than videos created by participants without access to patterns in terms of narrative structure and overall videographic quality.

Stories are inherently social; a storyteller often develops their understanding of a story as they tell it to more and more people. Suggesting captured pictures and video that might be appropriate to share next improves narrative engagement [9]. It would be interesting to see if patterns could play a role in facilitating joint meaning-making through story with groups of people. In the domain of video production, one can imagine a group of friends acting as an informal film crew, with a system dividing creative responsibilities across each person in the group. For example, one person could be assigned to capture ambient sound in each place, another person could be assigned to capture interviews, and another person could be in charge of managing the overall story structure. Expert patterns, if broken down by these responsibilities, may be able to guide groups of users as well as individuals.

With Motif we demonstrated how pattern languages can be used in the design of end-user creative tools. While we explored supporting novices in creating short video stories in this paper, this approach could apply to other domains as well. Imagine being able to build an essay out of patterns seen in the New York Times or compose a song by mixing and matching musical strategies used by your favorite artists. Examples of creative work made by experts are everywhere; by breaking down these examples into accessible patterns, we can open up creative opportunities for all.

ACKNOWLEDGMENTS

We would like to thank our study participants for their time and valuable feedback, as well as Sebastien Robaszkiewicz and Michael Rubin for their expert perspectives on video creation. Thanks to our colleagues that participated in pilot studies and tested the Motif app during development. This material is based upon work supported by Adobe Research and the National Science Foundation Graduate Research Fellowship under Grant No. DGE-114747.

REFERENCES

1. Animoto. `http://animoto.com/`.
2. Explory. `http://www.explory.com/`.
3. iMovie. `https://www.apple.com/mac/imovie/`.
4. Memoir. `http://www.yourmemoir.com/`.
5. Timehop. `http://timehop.com/`.
6. Alexander, C., Ishikawa, S., and Silverstein, M. Pattern languages. *Center for Environmental Structure 2* (1977).
7. Balabanović, M., Chu, L. L., and Wolff, G. J. Storytelling with digital photographs. In *Proceedings of the SIGCHI Conference on Human Factors in Computing Systems*, CHI '00, ACM (New York, NY, USA, 2000), 564–571.
8. Barry, B. A. *Mindful Documentary*. PhD thesis, Cambridge, MA, USA, 2005. AAI0808503.
9. Chi, P.-Y., and Lieberman, H. Intelligent assistance for conversational storytelling using story patterns. In *Proceedings of the 16th International Conference on Intelligent User Interfaces*, IUI '11, ACM (New York, NY, USA, 2011), 217–226.
10. Duyne, D. K. V., Landay, J., and Hong, J. I. *The Design of Sites: Patterns, Principles, and Processes for Crafting a Customer-Centered Web Experience*. Addison-Wesley Longman Publishing Co., Inc., Boston, MA, USA, 2002.
11. Hodges, S., Williams, L., Berry, E., Izadi, S., Srinivasan, J., Butler, A., Smyth, G., Kapur, N., and Wood, K. Sensecam: A retrospective memory aid. In *Proceedings of the 8th International Conference on Ubiquitous Computing*, UbiComp'06, Springer-Verlag (Berlin, Heidelberg, 2006), 177–193.
12. Lindley, S. E., Durrant, A. C., Kirk, D. S., and Taylor, A. S. Collocated social practices surrounding photos. In *CHI'08 Extended Abstracts on Human Factors in Computing Systems*, ACM (2008), 3921–3924.
13. Petrelli, D., van den Hoven, E., and Whittaker, S. Making history: Intentional capture of future memories. In *Proceedings of the SIGCHI Conference on Human Factors in Computing Systems*, CHI '09, ACM (New York, NY, USA, 2009), 1723–1732.
14. Resnick, M., Maloney, J., Monroy-Hernández, A., Rusk, N., Eastmond, E., Brennan, K., Millner, A., Rosenbaum, E., Silver, J., Silverman, B., and Kafai, Y. Scratch: Programming for all. *Commun. ACM 52*, 11 (Nov. 2009), 60–67.
15. Rubin, M. *The little digital video book*. Pearson Education, 2008.
16. Stokes, P. D. *Creativity from constraints: The psychology of breakthrough*. Springer Publishing Company, 2005.
17. Thiry, E., Lindley, S., Banks, R., and Regan, T. Authoring personal histories: Exploring the timeline as a framework for meaning making. In *Proceedings of the SIGCHI Conference on Human Factors in Computing Systems*, CHI '13, ACM (New York, NY, USA, 2013), 1619–1628.
18. Van House, N., Davis, M., Takhteyev, Y., Good, N., Wilhelm, A., and Finn, M. From what? to why?: the social uses of personal photos. In *Proc. of CSCW 2004*, Citeseer (2004).
19. Wines-Reed, J., and Wines, J. *Scrapbooking for Dummies*. John Wiley & Sons, 2011.

DesignScape: Design with Interactive Layout Suggestions

Peter O'Donovan[1,2]
[1]Dept. of Computer Science
University of Toronto
odonovan@dgp.toronto.edu

Aseem Agarwala[2]
[2]Adobe Research
Seattle, WA, USA
asagarwa@adobe.com

Aaron Hertzmann[1,3]
[3]Adobe Research
San Francisco, CA, USA
hertzman@adobe.com

ABSTRACT
Creating graphic designs can be challenging for novice users. This paper presents *DesignScape*, a system which aids the design process by making interactive layout suggestions, i.e., changes in the position, scale, and alignment of elements. The system uses two distinct but complementary types of suggestions: *refinement suggestions*, which improve the current layout, and *brainstorming suggestions*, which change the style. We investigate two interfaces for interacting with suggestions. First, we develop a suggestive interface, where suggestions are previewed and can be accepted. Second, we develop an adaptive interface where elements move automatically to improve the layout. We compare both interfaces with a baseline without suggestions, and show that for novice designers, both interfaces produce significantly better layouts, as evaluated by other novices.

Author Keywords
Graphic design, suggestion interfaces, adaptive design

ACM Classification Keywords
D.2.2 Software Engineering: Design Tools and Techniques User Interfaces

INTRODUCTION
Graphic design is ubiquitous in modern life. Unfortunately, creating designs can be difficult, particularly for novices, who often wish to create simple posters, cards, or social media designs. Starting from a blank canvas can be overwhelming, and exploring alternatives is time-consuming. Novice designers also make a variety of mistakes, from misalignment to incorrect emphasis of elements. Existing tools range from simple template-based interfaces like PowerPoint, to complex systems like Illustrator. However, these tools provide no suggestions when modifying templates or designs.

This paper presents a novel system for graphic design using layout suggestions, i.e., changes in the size, position, and alignment of elements. Our system proposes two complementary types of suggestions: *refinements* which improve the current layout, and *brainstorming* suggestions which explore alternative layouts with large changes in style (see Fig. 1). Exploration and refinement are critical and complementary tasks in design. However, exploration is difficult since a designer must imagine possible layouts, and modify many elements. Refinement is also difficult, since a single modification can necessitate many other changes. Our system includes both types, allowing users to easily switch between exploring alternative layouts and refining the current layout.

Figure 1. DesignScape Interface. The central canvas allows the user to create layouts in a simple editor. On the left, the system provides *refinement suggestions*, layouts similar to the canvas, but slightly improved. On the right, the system provides *brainstorming suggestions* large-scale layout changes in a variety of styles. Photos courtesy of Wilhelm Joys Andersen and Martin Fisch.

We use an energy-based model to generate designs that encode design principles such as symmetry, alignment, and overlap. User constraints are used to infer the designer's intent, and to make refinement suggestions on the current layout. We also learn a "style space" from examples, which can be used to generate new layouts in a variety of styles, providing starting points for design. The system can also retarget layouts, allowing the user to easily modify the design size.

We also investigate different ways users can interact with suggestions. First, we develop a suggestive interface, where suggestions are previewed and accepted. Second, we develop an adaptive interface which moves elements automatically. The two modes are compared to a baseline without suggestions by novice users on Mechanical Turk, and the quality of the resulting layouts are also evaluated. Both modes produce significantly better designs than the baseline on average. Lastly, we demonstrate the system's use for tablet-based design.

RELATED WORK
Exploring alternatives is a vital part of the design process. Gross and Do [2] present a prototyping interface which allows users to sketch drawings and store alternatives. Terry et al. [7] present an interaction technique which allows users to save and embed alternatives during the design process, and easily manipulate alternatives at a later point. Dow et al. [1] find that forcing users to create multiple design alternatives, instead of refining a single design, leads to improved results. Lee

CHI 2015, April 18 - 23, 2015, Seoul, Republic of Korea
Copyright 2015 ACM 978-1-4503-3145-6/15/04
http://dx.doi.org/10.1145/2702123.2702149

Figure 2. Refinement Suggestion. Left: the user sets the current layout by positioning and scaling the elements. Note the user has locked the top-right graphic, and left-aligned the selected text block. Right: the system suggests left-aligning the three elements, and increasing the bottom graphic.

et al. [3] present a web-design interface for browsing related designs with simple attributes like background color; viewing these alternatives produced higher-quality designs. Merrel et al. [4] demonstrate interactive suggestions for furniture layouts. However, no previous work provides interactive suggestions for single-page designs like posters/advertisements.

There is little work automating single-page graphic design layouts. Most relevant is O'Donovan et al. [5], who present an energy-based design model. Unfortunately this approach takes 40 minutes to synthesize a single layout. We expand this model, increasing its efficiency substantially and introducing user constraints and style suggestions, enabling novel *interactive* interfaces.

DESIGNSCAPE OVERVIEW

We next provide a high-level view of the design interface (Fig. 1). See the Supplemental Video for demonstrations. The key goal of our interface is to provide automatic assistance during the design process, both for large-scale layout changes, as well as small improvements in position, scale, alignment, and line breaks.

Suggestive Interface. In this mode, the system shows three refinement suggestions, which vary in their similarity to the current layout. The top layout is the most conservative, only making slight modifications, whereas the bottom layout will suggest larger changes. Suggestions are easy to view and accept; the user mouses-over the suggestion to see a full-size preview in the main canvas, then clicks to accept. These suggestions also adapt to inferred user constraints. For example, if the user center-aligns two multi-line text blocks in the canvas, the interface will suggest internally center-aligning the text blocks. Fig. 2 shows an example refinement suggestion.

Adaptive Interface. The system also works in a separate adaptive mode where elements are changed automatically. This interface provides more fluid interaction, as the user does not need to view and accept changes. However, the adaptive interface is potentially frustrating if the suggestions do not match the user's desired goals.

Brainstorming Suggestions. To help users explore alternatives, the system also shows example layouts in a variety of styles. Each layout is distinct from the others, and the styles vary according to symmetry, text and graphical size, alignment preferences, etc. We describe the sampling procedure later, and provide examples. Brainstorming suggestions appear in both suggestive and adaptive modes.

Retargeting. The system can also retarget layouts to different sizes, an increasingly common task for designers. If the user modifies the canvas size, the system will move the elements to match the previous relative locations and scales, while respecting design principles such as alignment or overlap.

User Interactions

The system implements a common set of design interactions. The user can move, scale, add, or remove elements, and change text line breaks, font, colour, and alignment. The interface provides smart guidelines, which appear when two elements are close to aligned, and will snap elements together. Along with undo and redo functionality, intermediate layouts can also be saved, and are shown to the right of the canvas.

A user views the proposed layouts to the left and right of the canvas. Mousing-over the proposal previews the suggestion in the main canvas, and the user clicks to accept. The user can lock elements, which fixes the position and scale of the elements in the suggestions. However, the suggestions use the canvas layout as a soft constraint, and will try to remain similar to the canvas layout. In Fig. 2, the user has locked the top-right graphic, so this element is fixed in the suggestion.

SYNTHESIZING LAYOUTS

To synthesize layouts, we adapt the approach of O'Donovan et al. [5] which uses an energy function to model design principles. We adapt this model for the GPU, and represent elements as bounding boxes, which permits efficient computation of distances, area, and overlap. That model also segmented designs, detected alignment groups, and measured the perceptual importance of elements. Unfortunately, those techniques are time-consuming so we use simpler heuristics. We use an element's size as its perceptual importance; we find alignment between elements, but do not detect alignment groups. We measure symmetry by the difference in distances to the nearest left-most and right-most element or border.

User Constraints

To help the user specify their intent, we introduce additional constraints in the model, both inferred from user behaviour and explicitly specified. A soft constraint prefers that elements remain close to their current position and scale. However, the user can specify a hard constraint which locks an

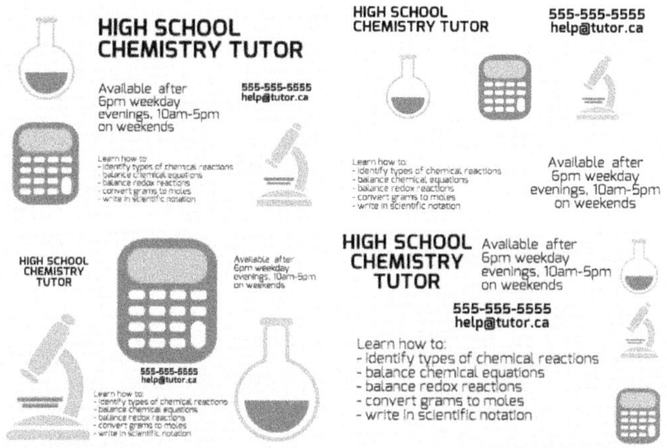

Figure 3. Brainstorming Suggestions. The system generates layouts in a variety of styles by sampling a low-dimensional parameter space learned from examples.

element's position and scale. The system also infers alignment constraints using the guide lines which automatically snap nearby elements. These lines then act as temporary constraints, with the elements in the suggested layouts matching the given alignment. The internal alignment of multi-line text blocks also changes to match these alignment lines. The user may also specify explicit size constraints, i.e., that specific elements must have the same size.

Optimization

We optimize layouts on the GPU (Nvidia GTX 770) based on the approach of Merrel et al. [4], using parallel tempering [6]. Convergence for the refinement suggestions is usually less than a second, since the canvas layout is used for initialization. Optimizing the brainstorming suggestions takes an average of 5 seconds. The system also saves brainstorming suggestions, and if pre-computed layouts are available, will display a random layout every 2 seconds. Such pre-computation is reasonable for testing; parallelization on multiple GPUs would eliminate the need for pre-computation.

Style Sampling

The brainstorming suggestions provide layouts in a variety of styles and arrangements. To generate different styles, we require different model parameters. As in O'Donovan et al. [5], we use Nonlinear Inverse Optimization (NIO) to estimate parameters given an example, but we still require a method to generalize to new styles. To accomplish this goal, we construct a low-dimensional subspace of the parameter space. We first use NIO to estimate the parameter vector for 18 example layouts, then use PCA to form a new basis. We then sample randomly in this new basis, producing layouts within the "style space" of the examples (see Fig. 3).

EVALUATION

To evaluate the adaptive and suggestive interfaces, we conducted several studies comparing them with a baseline interface without suggestions. First, novices created layouts in each interface. We then conducted two studies using AB testing: one comparing designs created using the adaptive interface to those with the baseline, and a second comparing suggestive and the baseline. Note that the baseline included snapping alignment lines and resizing constraints.

We then conducted two studies analyzing user preferences for each interface. In the first study, users used both the baseline and adaptive interfaces, then gave ratings and comments. In the second, users compared the baseline and suggestive.

Design Quality Studies

To evaluate design quality, we first had workers on Mechanical Turk (MTurk) create layouts with one of the three interfaces. Users created three layouts for a design, with no time restrictions, and could then provide comments. We used 2 designs, with 20 workers each. Workers only used a single interface (a between-subjects study), taking 2.41 minutes on average to create a layout in the baseline, versus 2.43 and 2.47 for suggestive and adaptive, respectively. Over 100 layouts were collected from each interface.

To compare layouts, we used AB testing on MTurk. For the adaptive interface study, we compared 60 adaptive layouts (randomly selected) with 4 baseline layouts (also randomly selected), and vice-versa for the baseline, producing 480 comparisons (2 interfaces $\times$ 60 layouts $\times$ 4 alternatives). Each worker evaluated a set of 20 pairs and chose their preferred layout in each pair; 10 workers completed each set. Duplicates were added and inconsistent users removed. For the suggestive interface study, we created a similar set of 480 pairs comparing suggestive and baseline designs.

Designs created by the new interfaces are generally preferred to those from the baseline. For the adaptive vs. baseline study, users voted for adaptive designs 63.4% of the time (2239 votes for adaptive designs vs. 1291 baseline votes). A χ^2 test comparing the counts to an expected frequency of 50% (1765 votes) produces $\chi^2(df = 1) = 254.59$, with $p < 0.01$. In the suggestive vs. baseline study, users voted for suggestive designs 57.7% of the time (2193 votes for suggestive vs. 1605 votes for baseline), with a $\chi^2(df = 1) = 91.03$, with $p < 0.01$. Therefore, both new interfaces help novices to create better layouts than the baseline.

We can also compare the adaptive and suggestive interfaces using a χ^2 test on the 2×2 contingency table of votes from both studies. This test shows $\chi^2(df = 1) = 24.51$, with $p < 0.01$, indicating a significant difference between the new interfaces. This difference is likely because the adaptive interface fixes many basic layout problems for novices such as overlap or misalignment. The suggestive interface is more subtle, and the user can always ignore the suggestions and treat the interface as a standard layout tool. In fact, in our study, 34.17% of the suggestive interface layouts used no suggestions. Note that for AB testing, we only used layouts where the user accepted at least one suggestion. Figure 4 shows the worst and best layouts from each interface.

Preference Studies

We next examined user preferences for the different interfaces. In a within-participant study, MTurk workers used both

Figure 4. Worst and best rated layouts from each interface. Top: baseline without suggestions. Middle: suggestive interface. Bottom: adaptive interface. We report the mean fraction of votes from AB testing.

the adaptive and baseline interface (called the "Direct" interface in the study). Users performed a short tutorial, then created two layouts with that interface. The user then switched to the other interface, completed that tutorial, and created two other layouts. The order of interfaces was random. After using both interfaces, workers provided a 5-point Likert scale rating for each, a binary preference (either baseline or adaptive), and optional comments. 40 workers completed the test.

The mean of the Likert ratings for the baseline and adaptive interfaces were 3.75 ± 0.15 and 3.81 ± 0.15 respectively, with a median of 4 for both. A Wilcoxon signed-rank test indicated no statistical difference between paired ratings. 60% of people preferred the baseline to the adaptive interface.

To compare suggestive and baseline, we completed an identical study with those interfaces. The mean ratings for the baseline and suggestive interfaces were 3.73 ± 0.14 and 3.67 ± 0.14 respectively, with a median of 4 for both; A Wilcoxon test showed no difference between the ratings. 59% preferred the baseline to the suggestive. To explain these ratings, we next examine participant feedback.

Participant Feedback

Many users reported enjoying the new interfaces: *"I really like this interface and how it automatically lines things up."* *"Great to have a decent starting point,"* *"The suggestion interface acted as a supplement to my own thought. I could find creativity and inspiration in it."* However, several users disliked the adaptive shifting of elements, e.g., *"I did not like when the picture would resize the words or pictures without my permission."* Many users preferred the baseline interface because of the greater control: *"I liked having a lot more control over the elements with the Direct Interface."* Furthermore, some users felt the suggestions constrained their creativity: *"I feel I am more creative if I use my ideas,"* *"I felt as if the suggestions were taking the human element out a little,"* *"I preferred the direct interface because I felt like the suggestions were so good, I did not feel I could make something significantly different. "*

DISCUSSION

In this paper, we present a novel system for graphic design using layout suggestions. Our key contributions are interfaces and interaction techniques allowing suggestions to aid the design process. Our adaptive interface allows users to create layouts using automatic improvements in a fluid manner. We also present a suggestive interface where users must actively accept changes. We evaluate these interfaces and find that users create better designs than a baseline interface without suggestions. However, many open problems remain, including improved exploration tools for style suggestions, more stylistic variety, and collaboration tools between users. In the Supplemental Video, we also demonstrate the system on a tablet. Suggestion-based tools are well-suited for touch interfaces where precise control of elements is difficult.

Current tools often make design tedious and time-consuming, particularly for novices. This paper presents a small step towards automating parts of the design process. However, we found that suggestions were not always desired. Some users preferred to have complete control over the design process, and found that automatic suggestions took away from their creativity. This intriguing result suggests more work investigating how suggestion-based tools are perceived by users. How can we develop tools to eliminate the tedious parts of designing, while still encouraging creative exploration?

REFERENCES

1. Dow, S. P., Glassco, A., Kass, J., Schwarz, M., Schwartz, D. L., and Klemmer, S. R. Parallel Prototyping Leads to Better Design Results, More Divergence, and Increased Self-efficacy. *ACM Trans. Comput.-Hum. Interact. 17*, 4 (2010), 18:1–18:24.
2. Gross, M. D., and Do, E. Y.-L. Ambiguous Intentions: A Paper-like Interface for Creative Design. In *Proc. UIST* (1996), 183–192.
3. Lee, B., Srivastava, S., Kumar, R., Brafman, R., and Klemmer, S. R. Designing with Interactive Example Galleries. In *Proc. CHI* (2010), 2257–2266.
4. Merrell, P., Schkufza, E., Li, Z., Agrawala, M., and Koltun, V. Interactive Furniture Layout Using Interior Design Guidelines. *ACM TOG* (2011).
5. O'Donovan, P., Agarwala, A., and Hertzmann, A. Learning Layouts for Single-Page Graphic Designs. *IEEE TVCG*, 20, 8 (2014), 1200–1213.
6. Swendsen, R. H., and Wang, J. S. Replica Monte Carlo Simulation of Spin-Glasses. *Physical Review Letters 57*, 21 (Nov. 1986), 2607–2609.
7. Terry, M., Mynatt, E. D., Nakakoji, K., and Yamamoto, Y. Variation in Element and Action. In *Proc. CHI* (2004), 711–718.

Using Game Principles in UX Research: A Board Game for Eliciting Future User Needs

Karin Slegers
CUO | Social Spaces, KU Leuven / iMinds
Parkstraat 45, Leuven, Belgium
karin.slegers@soc.kuleuven.be

Sanne Ruelens
iMinds / VUB - SMIT
Pleinlaan 9, Brussels, Belgium
sanne.ruelens@iminds.be

Jorick Vissers
CUO | Social Spaces, KU Leuven / iMinds
Parkstraat 45, Leuven, Belgium
jorick.vissers@soc.kuleuven.be

Pieter Duysburgh
iMinds / VUB - SMIT
Pleinlaan 9, Brussels, Belgium
pieter.duysburgh@vub.ac.be

ABSTRACT
This paper presents a board game approach as a UX research technique to assess potential user experiences regarding a future product. It discusses how the use of a board game may provide a) a safe research environment in which participants feel comfortable to share their thoughts and experiences in a group setting, and b) a tool to facilitate users to think about their needs regarding a future product. The use of the board game approach is illustrated by a case study in the context of developing a new train information system. The design of the board game that was used is described in detail, as well as how the game was used to elicit potential future experiences. A survey amongst the participants showed that the board game was appreciated as a surprising, pleasant and 'safe' research method.

Author Keywords
UX techniques; Board game; Future user needs; Gamification

ACM Classification Keywords
H.5.m. Information interfaces and presentation (e.g., HCI): Miscellaneous.

INTRODUCTION
Game elements are increasingly used in non-gaming contexts [2] to improve user experience (UX) or user engagement [3]. This idea, also referred to as gamification, has mostly been used in the design of new applications that aim to stimulate learning or behavior change. Building on this trend, game principles might also be used as a technique in UX research as games are considered to provide a safe environment to fail and to make mistakes [4]. Also, social influences may hinder creativity when working in groups [9], which may be mitigated by using a game. Board games seem especially interesting in this respect, as people have been familiar with this genre of games since childhood. The casual elements of a board game may act as an icebreaker, making it easier to speak one's mind.

This paper presents a game-based approach that was used to learn about possible user experiences regarding the use of a future product. Whereas more common UX research techniques, such as interviews or observations, focus on people's current and past experiences, such techniques are considered less suitable to understand potential future experiences [8]. In this respect, games were thought to provide an interesting research approach. Games usually offer a narrative [6], which could be used to provide a fictitious (but familiar) setting allowing to add futuristic elements (e.g. products or services that do not exist yet) to provide a glimpse at possible future experiences. Moreover, a board game creates a more relaxed atmosphere for exploring future scenarios, setting participants at ease, taking away some of the uneasiness they may experience when using enactment methods like role-playing.

Although examples of using game principles as a research technique have been reported (e.g. Huyghe et al. based a workshop method on the Game of the Goose, Bernhaupt et al. [1] used card games to make cultural probes more playful, and Kultima et al. [5] developed games as a tool for idea generation), overall, little literature is available providing hands-on experiences and suggestions. Where the examples mentioned above focus on idea generation and cultural probes, this paper presents a game-based research approach to bring participants into a specific setting to explore their experiences and needs regarding a future product. We illustrate the potential usefulness of this approach with an initial case study (focusing on a future 'omniscient' train information system). We discuss how we used game principles, and we illustrate what type of results one might expect when using a board game to learn about future experiences. This paper provides a game-based angle to eliciting potential future user needs and contributes to the literature on using games as a research technique by sharing

CHI 2015, April 18–23, 2015, Seoul, Republic of Korea.

http://dx.doi.org/10.1145/2702123.2702166

our game-based research approach and by inspiring other researchers to make their research more playful.

CASE STUDY: A FUTURE TRAIN INFO SYSTEM

The present case study was part of an ongoing, two-year research project aiming to develop a personalized, context-aware, multi-source train information system (TIS). More specifically, multiple sources of information (travel information as well as indirectly relevant information, such as weather, waiting times at coffee bars, or crowds in the station) are integrated into a single framework filtering the information by means of a dynamic traveller profile based on travel goals, comfort preferences, actual behavior, etc.

In the first phase of this project, qualitative user research (observations and stimulated recall interviews) was carried out to gather information on travellers' current train travel experience, and their information needs before, during and after travel. In addition to understanding current needs, we wanted to understand travellers' needs regarding our future TIS concept. We were especially interested in questions that are on train travellers' minds that are not answered by currently available information. For this purpose, we invited experienced train travellers to play a board game.

The board game was designed to represent a fictitious door-to-door train trip. The starting point was home, from which the players had to get to the train station, catch a train, connect to another train, get off the train, and reach their final destination. During the game, players could ask questions to a futuristic, omniscient TIS via a chat program on a tablet. One of the researchers would answer the questions remotely, Wizard of Oz style (players were not informed about the human nature of the TIS beforehand).

The board game workshops

The board game was first tested in a pilot session. Four of our colleagues (also frequent train travellers) played the game for half an hour. Based on their experiences, we made several small changes to the game (see below).

After the pilot, two workshops were organized with 30 participants (17 men, 13 women) recruited via a living lab research panel that is representative of the Flemish population. People who travel by train (at least occasionally) and who were interested in sharing their thoughts and expectations about future train information services were invited to participate. During the workshops, the game was played simultaneously at two or three separate tables, each moderated by a researcher who explained the rules of the game and the use of the TIS. The games lasted about 90 minutes.

Analysis

During the games, audio recordings were made, which were transcribed. Also, the questions asked to the TIS (including the answers) were logged. After the workshops, the participants were asked to fill in a short online survey. This survey included eight questions about the participants' general attitudes towards board games and their experiences during and after the workshop. The log files, as well as the transcripts were coded to identify underlying user needs. For this analysis we used the codes that emerged during the open coding of the previous user research, adding new codes when necessary. This allowed us to identify new insights that emerged from the board game study as well as to deepen our understanding of previously identified insights, and in turn to further shape the concept of the future TIS that will be developed in our project. The surveys, completed by 20 participants, were analyzed descriptively to get a feeling of the participants' experience of the board game as a research method.

The board game

Below, we describe the details of the board game (the board, the equipment and the rules). We explain the game principles we used, our approach to eliciting future experiences, and how the board game worked in practice.

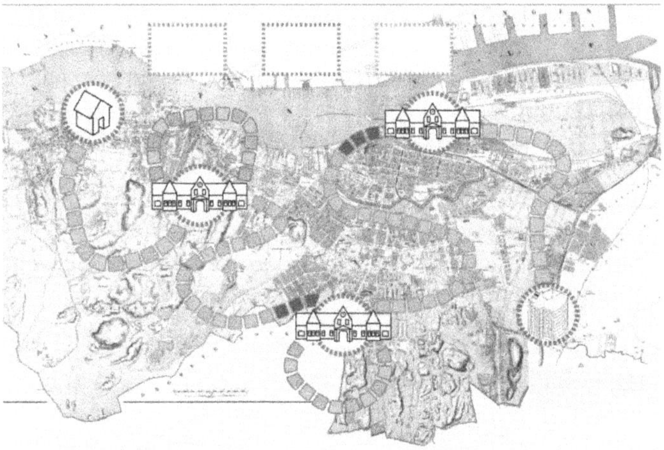

Figure 1 The board of the game used in this study.

Board game principles

The layout of the board (Figure 1) was loosely based on The Game of Life, simulating a journey by means of a **track on a board**. Our board game's track represented a train trip from home to a non-specified destination. Common phases of the journey were visualized (home to station, at the station, in the train, station to destination) to understand the questions travellers would ask the TIS in each phase. To move along the track, players threw **two dices** to determine how many squares they were allowed to move their playing piece, adding some randomness to the game.

The board track consisted of **three types of squares**: event squares, blank squares, and penalty squares. Landing on an event square meant that the players had to draw an event card (see below). A blank square allowed players to ask an open question to the TIS. Conform The Game of the Goose, players landing on a penalty square lost a turn (cf. a delay or missed connection). The different squares were aimed to add some variation to the game, giving the players a sense of unpredictable surprise in each turn, to make the game more engaging (several participants' remarks in the survey illustrate this, e.g.: *"you don't fully control the course of the game - exiting, makes you absorb in the game"* (pl.09)).

Event cards (cf. the Chance and Community Chest cards in Monopoly) were used to represent common and realistic events that might happen during each phase of a train trip (rain, overly crowded trains, unexpected delays, etc.). These cards were based on data collected in a previous series of ideation workshops where participants (as an icebreaker) had to write down several frustrating things that happened to them during recent train trips. The cards were intended to provide the players with real-life events that could serve as a specific context for asking questions to the TIS (see below). During the pilot session however, we noticed that the events steered the questions too much. We realized that we would only gain insights regarding information needs related to the specific events we included in the game. This was partially solved by creating the possibility for asking open questions when landing on a blank square. However, the use of these open questions seemed to be quite difficult for participants at times (e.g. *"Sometimes it wasn't easy to think of open questions."* (pl.09)), illustrating that thinking about possible future situations remains a difficult task.

Each **turn** consisted of several steps. First, players threw the dices and moved their playing piece accordingly. In case they landed on an event square, they drew an event card and were allowed to ask a question to the TIS based on the event described on the card. Landing on a blank square allowed players to ask an open question. When players decided to ask a question, they were allowed to throw the dice once more. At the end of each turn, all players at the table discussed the question and the train system's answer (Was it helpful? What kind of answer had they expected?).

Finally, several game principles were applied to facilitate the feeling of **competition** between players. For instance, the game had a clear goal that was representative for the journey the game aimed to enact: reaching a destination as quickly and comfortably as possible. The first team to reach the destination would win. Furthermore, the penalty squares resulted in disadvantages regarding the other players. These elements of competition intended to contribute to a playful experience, and in turn to the group atmosphere (which was appreciated by several participants, e.g.: *"A little bit of competition resulted in a good group atmosphere"* (pl.02)).

Eliciting future user experiences & needs

Players **used a mock-up of a future product**: they were allowed to ask any question they wanted to an omniscient train information system via a tablet. The answers of this system went beyond information that train travellers would currently be able to find (e.g. by linking data sources, or by providing highly personalized information), for example: "The queues at the ticket office are rather long, it'll be faster to buy a ticket at one of the machines as there are hardly any people there.". Answers such as these aimed to surprise the players and stimulate them to think more creatively about questions to ask in later turns.

Teams of two players competed against each other in each game. By working in pairs, we aimed to facilitate discussion and the generation of questions [7]. The game moderator would involve all players in the discussions by asking if the other players would have asked a similar question. Together with the couples' initial discussions, this helped us to gain insights into the needs underlying the questions. Several players indicated to appreciate this atmosphere (e.g. *"Everybody got the chance to react, not only the person whose turn it was."* (pl.14); *"Everybody got plenty opportunity to contribute."* pl.07)).

To represent several types of train travellers, and to take players out of their own standard expectations of a train trip, we introduced **fictional characters**. Players were given a specific character representing, for instance, a train commuter, an occasional train traveller, or a group of travellers. They were stimulated to assume the role of their character and to think about what their character would want to ask the TIS. During the workshops, however, we concluded that the characters did not work as well as we had anticipated. The moderators repeatedly had to remind players to use their characters, and several participants mentioned in the survey that they did not empathize with their characters (e.g: *"I had to play this character and I managed, but in reality I don't really scare so easily and so I did not say the things I would have said if I were to be myself."* (pl.13) and *"The role of a rich business man did not suit me…"* (pl.17)).

RESULTS & DISCUSSION

A game as a safe research environment

Based on our own experience as well as on the survey results, we feel that using a board game did indeed create a safe environment in our case study, making it easy to share experiences. Most participants indicated that they felt at ease while playing the game (mean score on this item in the survey (on a scale of 1 – 10) was 7.95, SD = 1.54) and that they could say what they wanted to say (mean score = 7.65, SD = 2.13). Some participants mentioned that the game facilitated discussion and sharing (*"It made it easier to talk to the other people."* (pl.03), *"Nice game which made it easier to formulate an opinion."* (pl.19)). Others indicated that they experienced the game as very pleasant (*"A pleasant and casual way of brainstorming."* (pl.04), *"A nice and playful way to share experiences"* (pl.02)).

Seventeen of the 20 participants who filled in the survey indicated that they like to play board games in general. Also, most participants indicated that they were pleasantly surprised when they first learned they were about the play a game (*"Nice, original, it definitely won't be boring like this."* (pl.07), *"This seems like a fun way to think about the topic to me."* (pl.14)). However, not everyone likes games. Three participants were disappointed when they heard they were to play a game (*"The term 'childish' went through my head."* (pl.11), *"Oh no. Monopoly déjà vu."* (pl.17)).

A game to elicit future experiences

By using a board game in our case study, we gained new insights that had not surfaced in our previous user research (using 'traditional' observations and interviews). First, the board game allowed us to focus more explicitly on what is on train travellers' minds during each phase of a train trip. The stimulated recall interviews already yielded some understanding of this, albeit a rather limited understanding as it was based on participants' recollections of one specific trip. Some questions, concerns, etc. are on train travellers' minds all the time and may become so common that they are not consciously aware of them anymore. This more implicit aspect of user experience (also referred to as tacit or latent knowledge) is difficult to assess with traditional UX research methods and requires a more generative approach [8]. We feel that the board game helped us to understand latent information needs because the setup stimulated participants to discuss many of the questions on their mind (which they could ask the TIS).

In addition, several of the needs that surfaced during the analysis of the board game study results were specifically related to the future TIS under development (and mocked-up in the board game set-up). Such 'new' needs, that were not identified in our previous research, were mainly related to one of the following categories: information regarding the train or carriage one is in (e.g. occupation rate, noise levels, storage room), facilities and services in and around the station (lockers, shops), connections to other means of transportation (e.g. availability of taxis or rental bikes), communication with train personnel, personalized travel suggestions (adapted to personal agendas or preferences, translation of announcements), and continuous, real-time information about delays and connections.

Finally, some event-related topics were repeatedly discussed during both board game workshops, but had not come up during either the interviews or the observations. One example of such a topic is the feeling of safety during a train trip. Several players asked our TIS to direct them to a safer place, or to contact railway or security personnel for them. This was obviously related to one of the event cards, but nevertheless represented an underlying need to feel safe. The topic of safety had not emerged during the observations or interviews, due to the fact that unsafe situations had not occurred. This can also be a problem when using event-based methods such as stimulated recall or the Critical Incident Technique: as long as an infrequent event does not occur, it will not be identified as important. Using a board game was a good approach in our study to yield user needs related to important, but infrequent events. However, one can only yield insights regarding the elements included in the game design. It is impossible to incorporate all events that may possibly be relevant.

CONCLUSION

In sum, the board game study described in this paper was well received by the research participants. It seemed to create a surprising and safe environment to share their thoughts and experiences in a group setting. In addition, we feel that using a board game helped us to bring research participants into a 'future state of mind', and in turn to understand latent needs that are difficult to assess with more traditional UX research methods. In this paper we carefully described how we designed and used a board game, thereby providing other researchers with inspiration and suggestions for using similar approaches in their research. As this paper describes an initial case study, further research is necessary to validate this approach.

ACKNOWLEDGMENTS

The work presented in this paper is part of TraPIST, a project co-funded by iMinds, a digital research institute founded by the Flemish Government. Project partners are Televic Rail, Be-mobile, Digitopia, TreinTramBus (all with project support from IWT) and NMBS/SNCB.

REFERENCES

1. Bernhaupt, R., Weiss, A., Obrist, M., and Tscheligi, M. Playful Probing: Making Probing More Fun. *Proc. IFIP TC 13* (2007), 606–619.
2. Deterding, S., Dixon, D., Khaled, R., and Nacke, L. From Game Design Elements to Gamefulness: Defining "Gamification."*Proc. MindTrek* (2011), 9–15.
3. Deterding, S., Sicart, M., Nacke, L., O'Hara, K., and Dixon, D. Gamification. Using Game-design Elements in Non-gaming Contexts. *CHI 2011 Extended Abstracts* (2011), 2425–2428.
4. Gee, J.P. *What Video Games Have to Teach Us About Learning and Literacy. Second Edition.* Palgrave Macmillan Trade, New York, 2007.
5. Kultima, A., Niemelä, J., Paavilainen, J., and Saarenpää, H. Designing Game Idea Generation Games. *Proc. Conf. on Future Play* (2008), 137–144.
6. Mitgutsch, K. and Alvarado, N. Purposeful by design?: a serious game design assessment framework. *Proc. Int. Conf. on the Foundations of Digital Games* (2012), 121–128.
7. Slegers, K., Duysburgh, P., and Jacobs, A. The 'Relay Ideation' Technique: Moving from Problem Understanding to Problem Solving in the Design Process. *Proc. INTERACT 2013* (2013), 651–658.
8. Visser, F.S., Stappers, P.J., van der Lugt, R., and Sanders, E.B.-N. Contextmapping: experiences from practice. *CoDesign 1*, 2 (2005), 119–149.
9. Warr, A. and O'Neill, E. Understanding Design As a Social Creative Process. *Proc. Conference on Creativity & Cognition* (2005), 118–127.

Investigating the Information Transfer Efficiency of a 3x3 Watch-back Tactile Display

Jaeyeon Lee, Jaehyun Han, Geehyuk Lee
HCI Lab, KAIST
Daejeon, 305-701, Republic of Korea
jaeyeonlee@kaist.ac.kr, jay.jaehyun@gmail.com, geehyuk@gmail.com

ABSTRACT
A watch-back tactile display (WBTD) is expected to be a viable supplement to the user interface limitations of a smartwatch. However, its design requires that many design parameters such as tactor types and stimulus patterns be determined. We conducted a series of experiments to explore the design space of a WBTD consisting of 3×3 tactors. We demonstrated that tactor types and the temporal patterns and locus of a stimulus produce statistically significant effects on the efficiency of a WBTD. The experimental results can act as a practical guideline for the design of an efficient WBTD.

Author Keywords
Watch-back tactile display; 3x3 tactor array; information transfer efficiency.

ACM Classification Keywords
H.5.2. User interfaces: Haptic I/O.

INTRODUCTION
Diverse smartwatches have recently been introduced to the market. Having computing hardware comparable with that of the mobile phones from a few years ago, smartwatches now have sufficient computing power to be a platform for many mobile applications. A more critical limitation of a smartwatch platform now seems to be its restricted user interface resulting from its small form factor. For example, displays on smartwatches are only large enough to show a few icons. In addition, considering that a touchscreen is the main user interface option for mobile devices today, a small screen also means limited input. A possible means for smartwatches to overcome these limitations may be to utilize other interface modalities such as tactile sense.

Because a smartwatch is always in contact with the wrist, it could employ a tactile display to create a constant tactile channel to supplement its limited visual display. Such a tactile display could also supplement an auditory display that is often inadequate in a mobile environment. Realizing this possibility, many researchers are studying the feasibility of a tactile display on the back of a watch. Pasquero et al. [12] showed that a piezoelectric actuator on the watch-back could be used for discrete closed-loop eyes-free interaction. Lee and Starner [7] showed that a wrist-worn tactile display having three tactors could transfer information reliably using 24 spatio-temporal patterns. Paneels et al. [11] designed a tactile display having six actuators in a circular configuration and showed that circular or alternating lateral movements aided perception. Lee and Starner [6] designed a 4×4 tactile display on the wrist and showed that it could deliver various patterns with a high average accuracy.

CHI 2015, April 18 - 23 2015, Seoul, Republic of Korea
Copyright 2015 ACM 978-1-4503-3145-6/15/04...$15.00
http://dx.doi.org/10.1145/2702123.2702530

Based on previous studies, we undertook the design of a watch-back tactile display (WBTD) consisting of 3×3 vibrotactile tactors. While testing the first prototype, we realized that many design options exist that can affect the information transfer efficiency of a WBTD. The goal of the current study therefore is to identify the best combination of design options to maximize the information transfer efficiency of a WBTD. Because many design options can be considered, we did not attempt exhaustive factorial experiments but used an exploratory approach. In three sequential experiments, we considered the effects of tactor types, spatial and temporal stimulus patterns, and stimulus positions. The remainder of this paper reports the results of the three experiments and discusses insights garnered from them.

RELATED STUDIES
Chen et al. [1] investigated the human ability to localize vibrotactile stimulation on the dorsal and volar sides of the wrist. Matscheko et al. [9] compared the case of four tactors on the wrist and that of the same four tactors around the wrist, and showed that the latter resulted in a higher information transfer rate. Oakley et al. [10] performed a point localization experiment and explored the feasibility of a 3×3 vibrotactile haptic display on the forearm regarding intensity and total contacting area. Lindeman et al. [8] presented a 3×3 vibrotactile haptic display on the back of an office chair. Cholewiak et al. [3] explored vibrotactile localization around the abdomen with a one-dimensional 12-tactor array. Jones et al. [5] conducted a point localization experiment and pattern recognition experiment with a one-dimensional 8-tactor array around the waist and a 4×4 vibrotactile haptic display on the back. With a 3×3 haptic display, Sofia et al. [13] compared localization accuracy at the different locations on the body.

These previous studies on tactile displays provide valuable background information for the design of an efficient WBTD. However, each study had a different context and explored different design options. Further empirical studies to determine the best combination of design options specifically for a WBTD are still necessary.

3X3 WATCH-BACK TACTILE DISPLAY

In a preliminary stage of this study, we conducted a two-point discrimination experiment involving three participants and observed a three-fold increase in accuracy as the distance between two tactile stimuli increased from 13 to 16 mm. In addition, we measured the sizes of the dorsal sides of their wrists and their averages were 51 mm for five males and 45 mm for five females. Based on these results, we decided to use a 3×3 tactor configuration on a 40×40 mm plate (watch-back), maintaining 15 mm center-to-center spacing between adjacent tactors.

As depicted in Figure 1, a tactile display consists of 3×3 linear resonant actuators (LRA, 170 Hz resonant frequency). The tactors are independently controlled by nine motor drivers (BD6221) and an Arduino board. A 3×1 array of tactors are on an acrylic plate with damping sponges, and these acrylic plates are connected with stretchable hinges to fit the curved surface of the wrist. A nine-hole silicon template was taped on the wrist to ensure constant 15 mm center-to-center distances between tactors and to maintain the same stimulus region within subjects. A custom-designed elastic band held the tactile display tightly with the same force (~3.26 N tension) between and within subjects.

A stimulus consists of sequential activations of a tactor or tactors along the vertical or horizontal direction. Figure 2 presents the temporal patterns of a stimulus. One cycle of a square wave (6 ms duration) was used for an activation, which feels like a light tap rather than a vibration. The amplitude of the square wave was fixed for all stimuli in the experiments. In a stimulus, time intervals between activations were chosen to 122 ms or 250 ms (depending on experimental conditions) based on background studies. The duration of all stimuli used in the experiments was the same at approximately 770 ms.

EXPERIMENTS

We recruited eight participants (three female, mean age 22.13) through an online bulletin board of our university. No participant had any prior experience with tactile display experiments. One participant was ambidextrous, but usually wore a watch on the left wrist; all other participants were right-handed. Sitting in a silent room, participants were asked to wear the tactile display on the dorsal side of the left wrist. To block any visual and auditory effects, participants maintained their left arm in a box on the desk and wore a noise-canceling headset playing white noise. Participants adjusted the volume of the noise so that it would be just loud enough to mask the tactor sounds. During the experiments, both arms were put forward on the desk in a manner similar to when using a keyboard, and stimulus names were thus consistent with those of directional keys on the keyboard (See Figure 3).

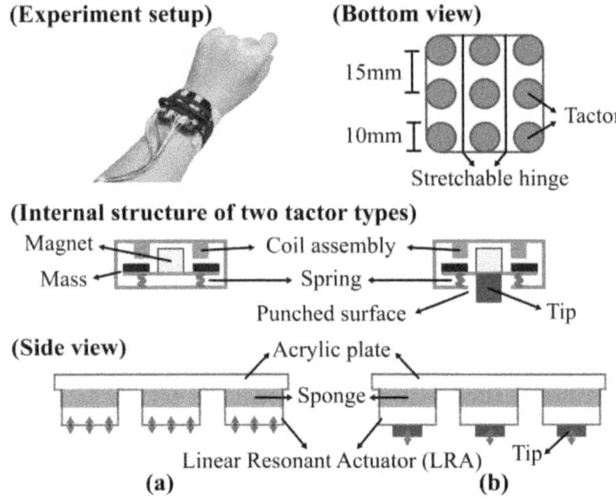

Figure 1. Prototype and structure of the two types of tactors: (a) surface type (b) tip type.

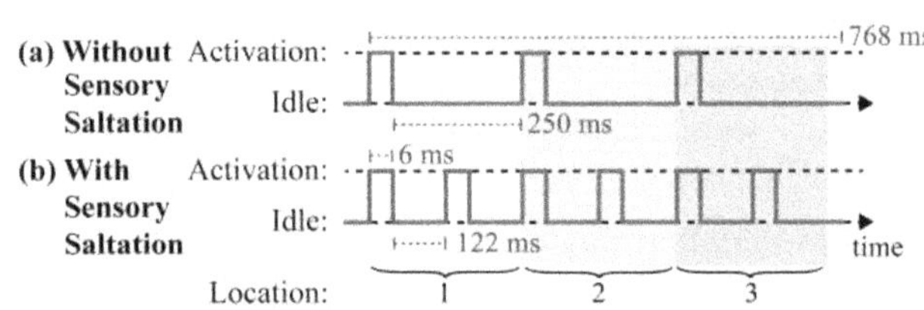

Figure 2. Temporal patterns: (a) without sensory saltation (b) with sensory saltation.

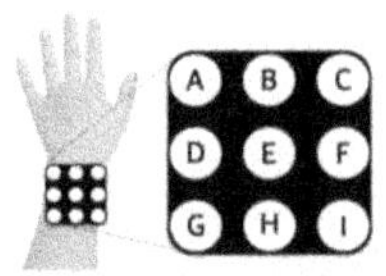

Direction	Up (U)			Right (R)		
Location	1	2	3	1	2	3
(a) Line	G-H-I	D-E-F	A-B-C	A-D-G	B-E-H	C-F-I
(b) Point	H	E	B	D	E	F
(c) Leftmost	G	D	A	D	E	F
(d) Rightmost	I	F	C	D	E	F

Down (D) and Left (L) follow along the opposite directions of Up (U) and Right (R), respectively.

Figure 3. Spatial patterns: (a) *Line*, (b) *Point*, (c) *Leftmost*, and (d) *Rightmost*.

The three experiments were of 2×2 or 1×4 within-subject design. The order of the four conditions was counter-balanced by a 4×4 Latin square. We divided the participants into four groups to experience the conditions in different orders. A test for each condition consisted of an introductory and two main sessions. In the three-minute introductory session, participants were encouraged to experience four kinds of stimuli (Up (U), Down (D), Right (R), and Left (L)) as many times as necessary. In the main session, the tactile display played 48 stimuli (4×12) in a random order. Each stimulus was played only once. After a stimulus was played, participants responded using directional keys on the keyboard. The four tests for the four conditions were continued without breaks as the experiments were not tiring. The same eight participants completed the three experiments.

In each experiment, 3072 answers were collected (4 conditions × 2 sessions × 48 stimuli × 8 participants). It took approximately one hour for a participant to complete each experiment. There were at least two-day intervals between experiments for the participants to recover from fatigue and refresh their motivation to participate.

Experiment 1: Tactor Types and Spatial Patterns

Various types of tactors were used in previous studies on tactile displays, but their effects on tactile display efficiency were not compared. We were interested in the difference between surface type [5, 6, 7, 8, 10, 12] and tip type [2, 3, 9, 11], and compared their effects in this experiment. Figure 1a shows a surface-type tactor (an LRA without any customization), while Figure 1b shows a tip-type tactor (a customized LRA with a cylindrical acrylic tip: 5-mm diameter, 2-mm extrusion). The next independent variable was spatial patterns: *Line* and *Point* patterns. The two types of patterns had a trade-off relationship in terms of perceived intensity and localization. *Line* patterns were used to maximize the perceived intensity of a stimulus [10], and *Point* patterns were used to generate a more localized stimulus. As shown in Figure 3a–b, a column or a row of tactors was activated sequentially in *Line* patterns. In *Point* patterns, however, tactors located in either a center row or center column were activated sequentially.

The overall accuracy was 81.5%. As the learning effect between the two main sessions were significant ($F(1,7) = 6.49$, $p < 0.05$), we analyzed data from the second main sessions for each condition. The stimulus-response confusion matrices and accuracy (AC, calculated as a percentage), information transfer (IT, in bits), and reaction time (RT, in seconds) are presented in Figure 4.

A two-way repeated measure ANOVA was performed on AC and IT. Tactor type exhibited a significant effect on both AC ($F(1,7) = 8.70, p < 0.05$) and IT ($F(1,7) = 7.62, p < 0.05$). No effect of the spatial patterns and no significant (tactor type) * (spatial patterns) interaction in both AC and IT were observed. The performance of the tip-type display was considerably higher and there was no significant difference between *Line* and *Point* patterns. Based on the results, we continued Experiments 2 and 3 with the tip-type display.

Experiment 2: Sensory Saltation and Spatial Patterns

By using sensory saltation [4], directional information generated by the 3-tactor array could be made comparable to the veridical directional cue produced by the 7-tactor array [2]. In this experiment, we focused on the effect of the presence and absence of sensory saltation on the perception of four directional patterns on the wrist. As shown in Figure 2b, for sensory saltation, the tactors were activated twice at the same location with the halved time interval of 122 ms. The second independent variable was spatial patterns (*Line* and *Point* patterns) because we could not determine which of the two types of patterns is better than the other based on the results of Experiment 1.

< Experiment 1 >

>80	Tactor Type: Significant effect on AC* and IT* (p<0.05)															
>70	Surface								Tip							
>60		U	D	R	L		Mean	SD		U	D	R	L		Mean	SD
Spatial Patterns: No significant effect – Line	U	69	11	9	7	AC	80.7	10.2	U	74	7	10	5	AC	85.7	12.8
	D	7	75	10	4	IT	1.27	0.30	D	5	79	5	7	IT	1.44	0.48
	R	0	13	83	0	RT	2.32	0.08	R	4	3	89	0	RT	2.24	0.13
	L	7	6	0	83				L	6	1	2	87			
Point	U	59	17	13	7	AC	78.9	12.0	U	74	8	8	6	AC	87.0	6.1
	D	6	80	9	1	IT	1.24	0.36	D	4	79	10	3	IT	1.44	0.22
	R	3	12	81	0	RT	2.34	0.14	R	0	6	90	0	RT	2.32	0.17
	L	6	7	0	83				L	2	3	0	91			

< Experiment 2 >

	Sensory Saltation (SS): Significant effect on AC* and IT* (p<0.05)															
	Without SS								With SS							
		U	D	R	L		Mean	SD		U	D	R	L		Mean	SD
Spatial Patterns: No significant effect – Line	U	148	16	18	10	AC	84.4	7.3	U	138	19	20	15	AC	86.1	9.3
	D	7	159	9	17	IT	1.33	0.29	D	10	163	11	8	IT	1.41	0.34
	R	10	20	162	0	RT	2.21	0.09	R	1	12	179	0	RT	2.22	0.17
	L	5	8	0	179				L	7	3	1	181			
Point	U	153	17	15	7	AC	86.5	12.5	U	159	16	13	4	AC	89.1	8.0
	D	14	163	6	9	IT	1.41	0.44	D	12	167	7	6	IT	1.49	0.29
	R	9	12	170	1	RT	2.16	0.09	R	7	10	173	2	RT	2.24	0.08
	L	2	12	0	178				L	1	5	1	185			

< Experiment 3 >

Locus of the Stimulus: Significant difference between Line and Leftmost on AC** and IT** (p<0.01)															
Line								Leftmost							
	U	D	R	L		Mean	SD		U	D	R	L		Mean	SD
U	153	17	15	7	AC	86.5	6.8	U	170	12	8	2	AC	92.4	5.9
D	20	156	11	5	IT	1.39	0.27	D	9	174	8	1	IT	1.63	0.23
R	4	17	171	0	RT	2.22	0.11	R	3	12	175	2	RT	2.29	0.17
L	6	2	0	184				L	1	0	0	191			
Point								Rightmost							
U	151	17	15	9	AC	88.4	8.0	U	163	12	1	16	AC	92.2	5.4
D	16	170	3	3	IT	1.50	0.24	D	9	182	1	0	IT	1.64	0.22
R	5	6	181	0	RT	2.23	0.08	R	0	3	189	0	RT	2.27	0.15
L	10	3	2	177				L	4	13	1	174			

Figure 4. The stimulus-response confusion matrices and Mean and Standard Deviations (SD) of AC, IT, and RT from the experiments.

The overall accuracy was 86.5% and no learning effect was observed in this experiment. All data from the two main sessions were analyzed. The stimulus-response confusion matrices and AC, IT, and RT are presented in Figure 4.

A two-way repeated measure ANOVA was performed on the results. The sensory saltation had a significant effect on both AC ($F(1,7) = 13.84$, $p < 0.05$) and IT ($F(1,7) = 15.93$, $p < 0.05$). No effect of spatial patterns and no significant (sensory saltation) * (spatial patterns) interaction in both AC and IT were observed. With sensory saltation, the AC and IT were considerably higher, although the patterns had a halved-time interval and the perceived speed was faster than the patterns without sensory saltation. Based on the observation that sensory saltation has a positive effect, Experiment 3 was continued with sensory saltation.

Experiment 3: Locus of a Stimulus on the Wrist

The results of the previous experiments revealed that spatial patterns (*Line* and *Point* patterns) did not produce a significant difference. However, we observed that the perceived intensity of a stimulus on the outer area of the wrist was stronger than that of the same stimulus on the inner area of the wrist. To examine the effect of the locus of a stimulus, we defined two additional spatial patterns, namely, *Leftmost* and *Rightmost* patterns (see Figure 3c–d). They are similar to *Point* patterns except that the presentation of vertical directional patterns uses the leftmost or rightmost column instead of the center column. We compared these two new types of spatial patterns with *Line* and *Point* patterns in this experiment.

The overall accuracy was 89.9%. Because no learning effect was observed, all data from the two main sessions were analyzed. The stimulus-response confusion matrices and AC, IT, and RT are presented in Figure 4.

A one-way repeated measure ANOVA was performed on the results. Locus of the stimulus exhibited a significant effect on both AC ($F(3,21) = 4.38, p < 0.05$) and IT ($F(3,21) = 6.27, p < 0.05$). A pairwise t-test with Bonferroni correction showed that only the difference between *Line* and *Leftmost* conditions was significant in AC ($t(7) = -4.23, p < 0.01$) and IT ($t(7) = -5.25, p < 0.01$). The other pairs did not have a statistically significant difference. We observed that the performance of *Leftmost* condition was considerably higher than that of *Line* condition.

DISCUSSION

In Experiment 1, the tip-type display showed a higher recognition performance compared to the surface-type display. We suspect that high pressure on the small contact area is one possible reason for the results. Higher pressure may have been applied on the skin because of the smaller contacting area of the tip-type display than that of the surface-type display. Another reason may be the different types of mechanoreceptors that different types of tactors stimulate. Our future research will include experiments to determine the reasons for these results.

In Experiment 1, we learned that tip-type tactors are better than surface-type tactors in terms of accuracy and information transfer. In Experiment 2, we learned that temporal patterns with sensory saltation can improve the performance of a WBTD. In Experiment 3, we learned that a proper choice of the locus of a stimulus on the wrist can also improve the performance of a WBTD.

CONCLUSION

Through a series of experiments, we learned that the tactor type, sensory saltation, and locus of a stimulus can affect the performance of a WBTD. Based on our findings, our recommendation for an efficient WBTD is to employ tip-type tactors, temporal patterns with sensory saltation, and point patterns on the leftmost outer area of the wrist.

ACKNOWLEDGMENTS

This work was supported by the IT R&D program of MKE/KEIT [KI10041244, SmartTV 2.0 Software Platform].

REFERENCES

1. Chen, H. Y., Santos, J., Graves, M., Kim, K., and Tan, H. Z. Tactor localization at the wrist. *Proc. EuroHaptics 2008,* Springer Berlin Heidelberg (2008), 209-218.
2. Cholewiak, R. W., and Collins, A. A. The generation of vibrotactile patterns on a linear array: Influences of body site, time, and presentation mode. *Perception & Psychophysics, 62,* 6 (2000), 1220-1235.
3. Cholewiak, R. W., and Collins, A. A. Vibrotactile localization on the arm: Effects of place, space, and age. *Perception & psychophysics 65,* 7 (2003), 1058-1077.
4. Geldard, F. A. *Sensory saltation: Metastability in the perceptual world.* Lawrence Erlbaum, Hillsdale, NJ, USA, 1975.
5. Jones, L. A., and Ray, K. Localization and pattern recognition with tactile displays. *Proc. Haptics 2008,* IEEE (2008), 33-39.
6. Lee, S. C., and Starner, T. Mobile gesture interaction using wearable tactile displays. *Ext. Abstracts CHI 2009,* ACM Press (2009), 3437-3442.
7. Lee, S. C., and Starner, T. BuzzWear: alert perception in wearable tactile displays on the wrist. *Proc. CHI 2010,* ACM Press (2010), 433-442.
8. Lindeman, R. W., and Yanagida, Y. Empirical studies for effective near-field haptics in virtual environments. *Proc. Virtual Reality 2003,* IEEE (2003), 287-288.
9. Matscheko, M., Ferscha, A., Riener, A., and Lehner, M. Tactor placement in wrist worn wearables. *Proc. ISWC 2010,* IEEE (2010), 1-8.
10. Oakley, I., Kim, Y., Lee, J., and Ryu, J. Determining the feasibility of forearm mounted vibrotactile displays. In *Proc. Haptics 2006,* IEEE (2006), 27-34.
11. Paneels, S., Anastassova, M., Strachan, S., Van, S. P., Sivacoumarane, S., and Bolzmacher, C. What's around me? Multi-actuator haptic feedback on the wrist. *Proc. WHC 2013,* IEEE (2013), 407-412.
12. Pasquero, J., Stobbe, S. J., and Stonehouse, N. A haptic wristwatch for eyes-free interactions. *Proc. CHI 2011,* ACM Press (2011), 3257-3266.
13. Sofia, K. O., and Jones, L. Mechanical and psychophysical studies of surface wave propagation during vibrotactile stimulation. *IEEE Trans. Haptics 6,* 3 (2013), 320-329.

SplitBoard: A Simple Split Soft Keyboard for Wristwatch-sized Touch Screens

Jonggi Hong[1], Seongkook Heo[1], Poika Isokoski[1,2], Geehyuk Lee[1]
[1] HCI Lab, KAIST
Daejeon 305-701, Republic of Korea
[2] TAUCHI, University of Tampere
Tampere, Finland
jonggi.hong@gmail.com, seongkook@kaist.ac.kr, poika.isokoski@uta.fi, geehyuk@gmail.com

ABSTRACT
Text entry on a smartwatch is a challenging problem due to the device's limited screen area. In this paper, we introduce the SplitBoard, which is a soft keyboard designed for a smartwatch. As the user flicks left or right on the keyboard, it switches between the left and right halves of a QWERTY keyboard. We report the results of two user experiments where the SplitBoard was compared to an ordinary QWERTY keyboard, the ZoomBoard, SlideBoard, and Qwerty-like keypad. We measured the initial performance with new users for each method. The SplitBoard outperformed all other techniques in the experiments. The SplitBoard is expected to be a viable option for smartwatch text entry because of its light processing requirements, good performance, and immediate learnability.

Author Keywords
SplitBoard; text entry; soft keyboard; smartwatch

ACM Classification Keywords
H.5.2 User Interfaces (D.2.2, H.1.2, I.3.6): Input devices and strategies (e.g., mouse, touchscreen)

INTRODUCTION
Many manufacturers have begun to produce smartwatch products. Unlike the early watch-sized computers [11], new smartwatches have the computing power and battery life comparable to early smartphones. One of the challenges in migrating applications from the smartphone to the smartwatch is the relatively smaller screen size of the smartwatch; there does not seem to be sufficient room for some GUI components, such as the soft keyboard.

It is doubtful that the QWERTY soft keyboard should be adopted on smartwatches. In order to find a soft keyboard design that is suitable for a smartwatch, we examined a diverse set of alternatives. A seemingly naïve soft keyboard design, that we call SplitBoard, implemented in this study, turned out to be a promising alternative. The SplitBoard is a scrolling QWERTY keyboard. As the user flicks left or right on the screen, the SplitBoard switches between the left and the right halves of a QWERTY keyboard. The SplitBoard layout utilizes the QWERTY layout to ensure immediate learnability. To assess the initial performance of the SplitBoard, we conducted two comparison experiments with users who had no prior exposure to the interface. The SplitBoard outperformed the four other techniques included in the experiments.

CHI 2015, April 18 – 23, 2015, Seoul, Republic of Korea
Copyright 2015 ACM 978-1-4503-3145-6/15/04…$15.00
http://dx.doi.org/10.1145/2702123.2702530

RELATED WORK
Text entry for a smartwatch can be implemented through speech recognition, handwriting recognition, a separate device such as a Bluetooth keyboard, or a few buttons in the watch frame with an encoding scheme such as MDITIM [5] or EdgeWrite [14]. However, soft keyboards are the dominant text entry technique on smartphones and tablets. We were interested to see how well soft keyboards would perform on a smartwatch.

The central theme in miniature soft keyboards is the balance between the number of keys and the ambiguity of a key press [6]. The multi-tap technique used in 12-key telephone keypads is an example of explicit, user-initiated disambiguation of ambiguous keys. The English language multi-tap requires an average of over two key presses for each character [6]. Assigning frequent characters to shorter key press sequences can reduce the number of key presses. An example of such an optimization is the QWERTY-like keypad (QLKP) used in our comparison experiments as a representative of multi-tap text entry methods. An evaluation by Hwang and Lee [2] showed that the QLKP was superior to the standard telephone character layout.

Dictionary-based disambiguation can relieve the user from explicit disambiguation by key presses. On the 12-key telephone keypad, dictionary-based disambiguation brings keystrokes per character (KSPC) down to about one [6]. A word gesture keyboard [15] combines a conventional soft keyboard with the ability to draw the key sequence on the keyboard without lifting the finger for faster entry of words. A language model is needed to disambiguate the input. Word-gesture keyboards are widely available on smartphones; however, it is not known how well they perform on the small displays of smartwatches. We did not include techniques with language databases in our experiments. Dictionary-based data can be used in diverse ways for each keyboard design, which could be an additional comparison parameter in future work.

Tapping and sliding the finger on the display can be combined on touch screens. Sliding gestures can be either straight lines akin to selecting in one-level marking menus [3] or recognized as shapes akin to handwriting [4]. A publicly available example of a tap-gesture keyboard is the MessagEase system [9]. While tap-slide combinations can save motor effort and are potentially fast for experienced users, planning the tap-slide movements is difficult for new users, which makes these movements time consuming [3, 12]. Combining a tap or key press with some other measure, such as the tilt of the device [13] or pressure applied [8], has been proposed.

Using a two-step selection technique, where the first pointer location is used as the center of the region to zoom in for a subsequent final target selection, is a well-known technique in eye-pointing [1]. This technique is used to overcome the noise in the tracker signal. Similarly, finger pointing is very noisy in extremely small devices. *ZoomBoard* [10] is a text entry technique based on this idea. In an evaluation using a tiny (16 x 6 mm) section of the iPad3 display, ZoomBoard outperformed a QWERTY soft keyboard. The superiority of ZoomBoard on the smartwatch display is not clear because the smartwatch display is usually larger than 16 x 6 mm.

SPLITBOARD

The QWERTY layout is wide; therefore, the keys become very narrow on a smartwatch. In SplitBoard, we divided the QWERTY layout into two sections: left and right. In addition to these two main sections, SplitBoard has a third component, as shown in Figure 1, for mode keys used for selecting upper case, numeric, and symbol entry modes, including an enter key. A horizontal flick gesture is used to change the section of the keyboard to be displayed.

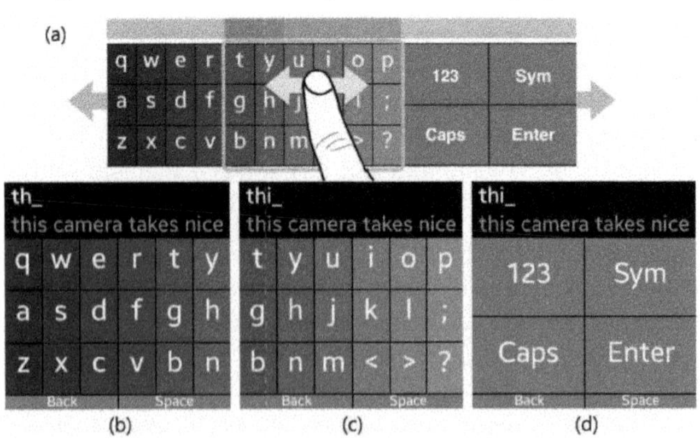

Figure 1. (a) Conceptual drawing of the SplitBoard and (b, c, and d) the three parts of the SplitBoard. When a user flicks from right to left on the part (b), the screen switches to (c).

Text can be entered by tapping on the keys. The space and backspace keys are located at the bottom of the screen. These keys are narrow but can be easily selected by touching the bezel below the screen. In our implementation of the SplitBoard, we displayed six keys per row with a two-column overlap. The number of gestures per character (GPC) changed as a function of the number of keys on a row. We conducted a simulation that estimates GPC using the 500 phrases set by Mackenzie and Soukoreff [7]. The result was approximately linear from 1.4 at 5 keys per row to 1 at 10 keys per row. We chose a two-column overlap as a compromise between key size and the number of flicks needed per character. The GPC in this case was 1.28.

EVALUATION

The conventional QWERTY keyboard (the QWERTY) is an obvious baseline for comparison. The ZoomBoard was found to be faster than the QWERTY on a very small keyboard [10]. The larger key size offered by the 12-key multi-tap technique was considered potentially important; therefore, we included the QLKP, which was found to perform better than the standard ABC keypad [2]. Finally, we wanted to include a representative of the tap-slide keyboard group. The MessagEase would have been our choice, except recent results indicate that the foreign layout causes a significant learning hurdle for new users [12]. Instead, we chose a tap-slide adaptation of the QWERTY layout that we call SlideBoard. In the SlideBoard, each key has two characters as shown in Figure 4c. We disambiguate key presses by sliding either left or right after landing on a key. A quick preliminary evaluation (3 participants, transcribing 5 phrases) showed that the SlideBoard (10.8 WPM) was faster than the MessagEase (<7.5 WPM [12]).

Before conducting the user study, we ran a simulation to compute GPC for the keyboards included in the evaluation. The results were 1.85 for both the ZoomBoard and the SlideBoard, 1.53 for the QLKP, and 1 for the QWERTY. For the ZoomBoard, the space character was counted as a single swipe gesture. For the SlideBoard, a tap and a following slide were counted as separate gestures. For the QLKP, we assumed that a user uses the space key for multi-tap segmentation when entering two characters in a same key consecutively. This result implied a better performance of the SplitBoard than other keyboards except the QWERTY.

Participants

We recruited 24 participants from our university. The participants were not native English speakers, but worked and studied in an English-speaking environment. The participants were divided into two groups of 12 participants. Participants in Group A (3 female, 9 male, mean age = 22.4) used the SplitBoard, ZoomBoard, and QWERTY. Participants in Group B (3 female, 9 male, mean age = 22.7) used the SplitBoard, QLKB, and SlideBoard.

Apparatus

The experiment was conducted on a Samsung Galaxy Gear with a 29.3 x 29.3 mm touch screen. The presented phrase and entered phrase were displayed above the keyboard area, as shown in Figure 1. The phrases were picked randomly from the 500 phrases set by Mackenzie and Soukoreff [7].

Participants wore the device on their non-dominant hand and used the index finger of the other hand to operate it.

The size of alphabetic keys was 2.9 x 5.3 mm for the QWERTY, 2.9 x 2.9 mm and 5.8 x 5.8 mm for the zoomed-out and zoomed-in ZoomBoard respectively, and 4.8 x 6.5 mm for the SplitBoard. The size of space and backspace keys on the SplitBoard was 14.5 x 1.8 mm. For keyboards used by Group B, we adjusted the positions and sizes of three function keys such that they were consistent across the three keyboards as shown in Figure 4. The size of the three function keys was 9.4 x 1.8 mm, and the sizes of the alphabetic keys in the QLKP and the SlideBoard were 9.5 x 6.4 mm and 5.6 x 6.5 mm, respectively.

Procedure

Participants entered text using the three keyboards assigned to their group. The duration of the experiment was approximately one hour per participant. Each participant completed five task blocks for each keyboard. For each block, participants were asked to transcribe five sentences. Before starting the first block for each keyboard, participants completed one sentence for practice. Participants could rest for up to 3 minutes between blocks if they felt tired. After finishing with all keyboards, participants were asked to answer a questionnaire.

Design

In each group, *Keyboards* and *Blocks* were independent variables, and a 3(*Keyboards*) x 5(*Blocks*) within-subject factorial design was used. We fully counterbalanced the order of using the keyboards. The text entry speeds in words-per-minute (WPM), total error rates (TER), and uncorrected error rates (UER) of the keyboards were measured.

Results

We statistically compared the WPMs and TERs of the keyboards in Group A and B using a repeated measures ANOVA (3 methods x 5 blocks) and a pairwise comparison with Šidák correction. The results of Group A are summarized in Figure 3 and Table 1. In Group A, there was a significant main effect of *Keyboards* on WPM ($F(2, 22) = 47.19$, $p < 0.001$). The SplitBoard was faster than the QWERTY ($p < 0.05$) and the ZoomBoard ($p < 0.001$). There was a significant main effect of *Keyboards* on TER ($F(2,22) = 62.416$, $p < 0.001$). The QWERTY caused more errors than the SplitBoard ($p < 0.001$). There was no statistically significant difference between the SplitBoard and the ZoomBoard ($p = 0.206$). The average UER of the SplitBoard was 0.58%. The QWERTY showed the same UER as the SplitBoard at 0.58%. The average UER for the ZoomBoard was 0.3%.

In the questionnaire results, 11 of 12 participants in Group A ranked the QWERTY as the least-preferred keyboard. All participants in Group A preferred the SplitBoard most, stating that the keys of the QWERTY were too small and led to numerous errors. They additionally stated that the frequent zooming of the ZoomBoard caused eyestrain. They mentioned that the SplitBoard was easy to use but it was inconvenient when a sentence required frequent switching between the keyboard parts.

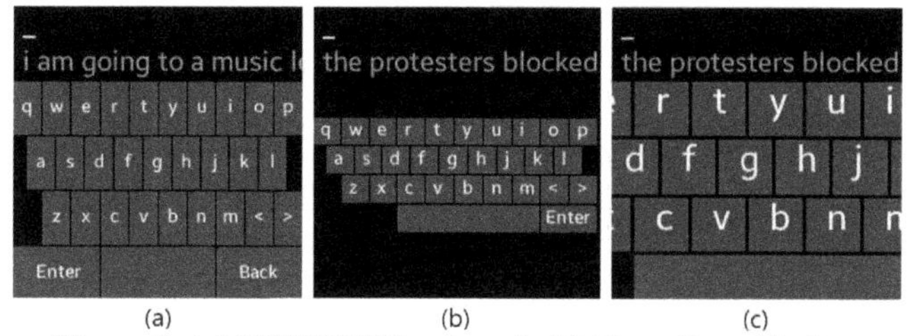

Figure 2. (a) QWERTY keyboard, (b) ZoomBoard before zooming, and (c) ZoomBoard after zooming.

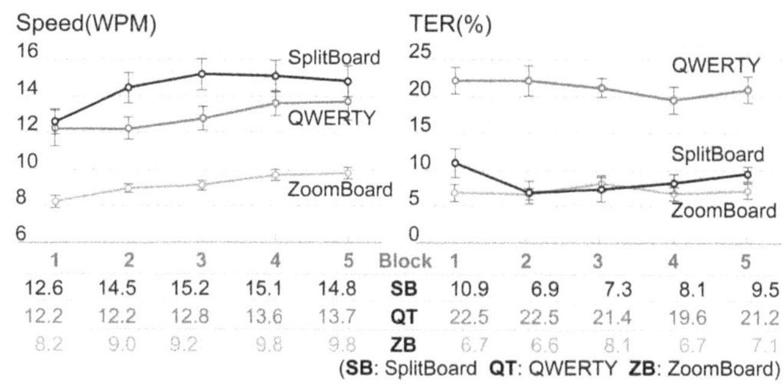

Figure 3. Average text entry rates in WPM and total error rates over five blocks in the Group A. Error bars show SEM.

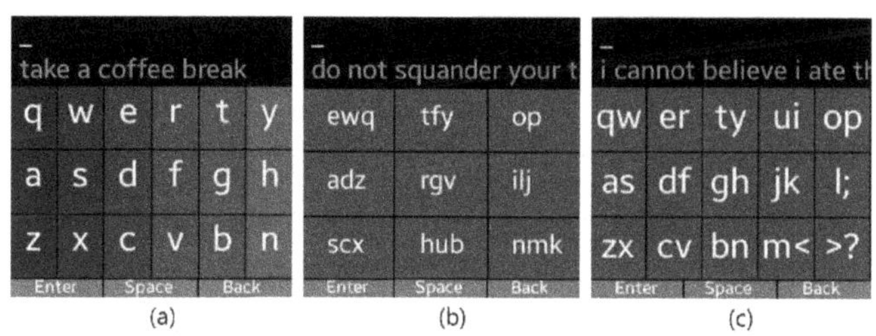

Figure 4. (a) SplitBoard, (b) QLKP, and (c) SlideBoard.

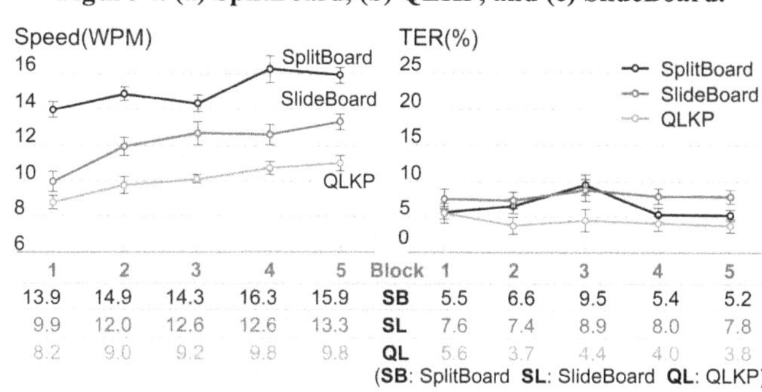

Figure 5. Average text entry rates in WPM and total error rates over five blocks in Group B. Error bars show SEM.

The results of Group B are summarized in Figure 5. There was a significant effect of *Keyboards* on WPM ($F(2, 22) = 97.382$, $p < 0.001$). The SplitBoard was faster than the QLKB ($p < 0.001$) and SlideBoard ($p < 0.001$). There was a main effect of *Keyboards* on the typing accuracy ($F(2, 22) = 10.568$, $p < 0.001$). The QLKB was more accurate than the SplitBoard ($p = 0.036$). There was no significant difference between the TERs of SplitBoard and SlideBoard. The average UERs of the SplitBoard, QLKB, and SlideBoard were 0.4%, 0.4%, and 0.7%, respectively.

Out of the 12 participants in Group B, 9 preferred the SplitBoard to the other two keyboards. In addition, 10 of 12 participants least preferred the QLKB because of both its unfamiliar layout and the 2-second timeout to discriminate keys, which often caused errors. Three participants ranked the SplitBoard as the second most preferred keyboard due to the frequent switching required for certain words.

DISCUSSION

Oney et al. [10] showed that the ZoomBoard outperforms the QWERTY for a keyboard size of 16 mm. Our results show that this is no longer true for a keyboard size of 29 mm; both the SplitBoard and QWERTY outperformed the ZoomBoard. It seems worthwhile to investigate the relative efficiency of these keyboards for different keyboard sizes.

There are additional topics to be considered as part of future work. First, we are interested in the effect of long-term learning on the efficiency of these keyboards. We measured only beginner performance in the current study and the relative efficiency of the keyboards may change when people further develop their skills. Another question relates to the efficiency of these keyboards in mobile settings. The performance of the QWERTY in the current study may be due to the stationary writing situation, and standing or walking users might not be able to hit keys equally well.

Yet another question is how the use of a language model would improve these keyboards. In this study, we avoided any dictionary-based features and focused only on the key entry efficiency of the keyboards. This is a clear shortcoming of this study, considering that every modern touchscreen keyboard uses a language model. For more practically meaningful results, it is necessary to compare these keyboards after they are augmented with a dictionary-based feature. Among the keyboards compared in the current study, we expect that the QWERTY may benefit most from a dictionary-based feature (e.g., dictionary-based auto-correction) because it suffers from the highest error rates. The QWERTY with an auto-correction feature may become a viable option considering its high WPM despite the high error rate in this study.

A language model may be also used to optimize the key layout of the SplitBoard. The bigram statistics of a language may be used to design a key layout to minimize switching between the two sides of the SplitBoard. QWERTY users may be unfamiliar with the resulting key layout, but there may exist an optimal trade-off to reduce switching while maintaining learnability.

ACKNOWLEDGMENTS

This work was supported by the IT R&D program of MKE/KEIT [KI10041244, SmartTV 2.0 Software Platform] and by the Academy of Finland [MIPI, 266285].

REFERENCES

1. Bates, R., and Istance, H. Zooming interfaces!: Enhancing the performance of eye controlled pointing devices. *Proc. Assets 2002*, ACM Press (2002), 119–126.
2. Hwang, S. and Lee, G. Qwerty-like 3x4 keypad layouts for mobile phone. *Ext. Abstracts CHI 2005*, ACM Press (2005), 1479–1482.
3. Isokoski, P. Performance of menu-augmented soft keyboards. *Proc. CHI 2004*, ACM Press (2004), 423–430.
4. Isokoski, P., Martin, B., Gandouly, P., and Stephanov, T. Motor efficiency of text entry in a combination of a soft keyboard and unistrokes. *Proc. NordiCHI 2010*, ACM Press (2010), 683–686.
5. Isokoski, P., and Raisamo, R. Device independent text input: A rationale and an example. *Proc. AVI 2000*, ACM Press (2000), 76–83.
6. MacKenzie, I. Kspc as a characteristic of text entry techniques. In *Human Computer Interaction with Mobile Devices*, F. Paterno, Ed., vol. 2411 of *LNCS*. Springer Berlin Heidelberg, 2002, 195–210.
7. MacKenzie, I. S., and Soukoreff, R. W. Phrase sets for evaluating text entry techniques. *Ext. Abstracts CHI 2003*, ACM Press (2003), 754–755.
8. McCallum, D. C., Mak, E., Irani, P., and Subramanian, S. Pressuretext: Pressure input for mobile phone text entry. *Ext. Abstracts CHI 2009*, ACM Press (2009), 4519–4524.
9. Nesbat, S. B. A system for fast, full-text entry for small electronic devices. *Proc. ICMI 2003*, ACM Press (2003), 4–11.
10. Oney, S., Harrison, C., Ogan, A., and Wiese, J. Zoomboard: A diminutive QWERTY soft keyboard using iterative zooming for ultra-small devices. *Proc. CHI 2013*, ACM Press (2013), 2799–2802.
11. Raghunath, M. T., and Narayanaswami, C. User interfaces for applications on a wrist watch. *Personal Ubiquitous Comput. 6*, 1 (2002), 17–30.
12. Thapa, A. *Beginners Performance with MessagEase and QWERTY.* Master's thesis, University of Tampere, 2013.
13. Wigdor, D., and Balakrishnan, R. Tilttext: Using tilt for text input to mobile phones. *Proc. UIST 2003*, ACM Press (2003), 81–90.
14. Wobbrock, J. O., Myers, B. A., and Kembel, J. A. Edgewrite: A stylus-based text entry method designed for high accuracy and stability of motion. *Proc. UIST 2003*, ACM Press (2003), 61–70.
15. Zhai, S., and Kristensson, P. O. The word-gesture keyboard: Reimagining keyboard interaction. *Commun. ACM 55*, 9 (Sept. 2012), 91–10.

Beats: Tapping Gestures for Smart Watches

Ian Oakley, DoYoung Lee and MD. Rasel Islam
Department of Human and Systems Engineering
Ulsan National Institute of Science and Technology, Ulsan, Korea

Augusto Esteves
Madeira-ITI, University of Madeira, Funchal, Portugal

ian.r.oakley@gmail.com, ehdud611@gmail.com, islam@unist.ac.kr, augustoeae@gmail.com

ABSTRACT
Interacting with smartwatches poses new challenges. Although capable of displaying complex content, their extremely small screens poorly match many of the touchscreen interaction techniques dominant on larger mobile devices. Addressing this problem, this paper presents *beating gestures*, a novel form of input based on pairs of simultaneous or rapidly sequential and overlapping screen taps made by the index and middle finger of one hand. Distinguished simply by their temporal sequence and relative left/right position these gestures are designed explicitly for the very small screens (approx. 40mm square) of smartwatches and to operate without interfering with regular single touch input. This paper presents the design of beating gestures and a rigorous empirical study that characterizes how users perform them – in a mean of 355ms and with an error rate of 5.5%. We also derive thresholds for reliably distinguishing between simultaneous (under 30ms) and sequential (under 400ms) pairs of screen touches or releases. We then present five interface designs and evaluate them in a qualitative study in which users report valuing the speed and ready availability of beating gestures.

Author Keywords
Wearable; Smartwatch; Multitouch; Tapping

ACM Classification Keywords
H.5.m. Information interfaces and presentation (e.g., HCI): Miscellaneous.

INTRODUCTION
Wearable technologies are entering the mainstream. Smartwatches, with a familiar and convenient wrist-mounted form-factor, are one of the main current device categories in this space. They promise to generate substantial value by enabling novel applications and services, specifically in areas such as bio-monitoring, health and the quantified self. Smartwatches can also act as helpers and adjuncts for larger mobile devices, providing notifications at a glance, the ability to remotely and conveniently issue basic commands (such as answering a call or silencing an alarm) and potentially more advanced functionality such as presenting app specific contextual menus or callouts that highlight key information [4]. Ultimately, they promise timely access to information and the ability to issue relevant responses rapidly and with minimal disruption to ongoing tasks.

CHI 2015, April 18 - 23 2015, Seoul, Republic of Korea
Copyright 2015 ACM 978-1-4503-3145-6/15/04...$15.00
http://dx.doi.org/10.1145/2702123.2702226

However, despite this potential, their small size makes effective interaction with smartwatches a challenging task. Indeed, the basic device format – the watch – is historically a purely display device and not an interactive system. Current smartwatch designs reflect these origins: sharp, vivid high-resolution screens are paired with very limited and restricted interaction spaces. Recognizing this mismatch as both a problem and an opportunity, recent research prototypes and products have focused on introducing additional input capabilities to smartwatches. Example approaches include adding physical controllers such as dials to the watch form factor (e.g. the Apple Watch, www.apple.com/watch/), using the movements of watch itself as a physical controller [19] and extending input sensing to other surfaces of the watch, such as its edge [13] or strap [15]. While these techniques tackle the core screen-size problem directly and clearly have value, they also have limitations. Specifically, we note their novel input systems may prove difficult to integrate with the currently dominant touch screen paradigm [19] and it can be practically challenging to fit additional sensing hardware in the small, constrained spaces of the watch form factor.

Given these difficulties, we argue there is value in exploring novel interaction techniques that operate with the existing input surfaces of smartwatches – the touch screens. However, this will clearly require new approaches as the extremely small size of these modules practically precludes many of the techniques that have proven successful on larger systems, such as multi-finger pinch gestures [10]. Equally, the effects of well known foundational problems with touch screen interaction, such as the fact that finger touches obscure screen contents (the fat finger problem [17]), are likely to be exacerbated on smartwatches.

As one possible way of addressing these challenges, this paper proposes a new type of multi-finger input that is specifically designed for the very small touch screens of smartwatches. It is based on what we term *beating gestures*, pairs of simultaneous or rapidly sequential touches (and optionally one or more releases) made by the index and middle finger of one hand. Essentially, instead of tapping a single finger to a screen, a beating gesture involves adjacent screen contact (and optionally release) with two fingers and in three closely controlled intervals: either simultaneously or with one event immediately preceding the other as part of a single coordinated movement. The timings and crude relative position (e.g. left or right) of this input serves to characterize each movement and the fast pace of the paired touches distinguishes it from regular single finger input [9] or noise.

The motivations for exploring this specific design space include the fact that current smartwatch systems are large enough to register two adjacent touches and the simple sequences of movements required for beating gestures may be executable rapidly and eyes-free [3], avoiding fat-finger problems. Furthermore, we suggest the technique is sufficiently expressive to control a meaningful range of functions. Finally, as it is based on standard touch-screen input, but designed to not interfere with normal single finger use, we suggest it will be easy to integrate with existing on-screen interface styles such as single finger taps, swipes, dwell and gestures. Indeed, effective integration with established input techniques was a core design goal in our work.

The remainder of this paper sets out to fully explore the potential of beating gestures. The contributions include the core idea underlying beating gestures, a thorough quantitative characterization of how beating gestures are performed, a series of prototypes showing how they can be deployed to create realistic interfaces on a smartwatch and a qualitative study of how users react to these prototypes. Taken together this work represents a well-rounded description of beating gestures that can directly inform future research and provide both inspiration and practical guidance for interface designers creating novel touch interactions for smartwatches or other small screen devices.

RELATED WORK

Smartwatches are attracting increasing research interest in HCI as the combination of their wearable form factor, growing computational power and restricted input spaces make them a ripe target for the development of new forms of interaction. One trend has been to augment the devices with novel sensing systems on alternative surfaces. Perrault *et al.* [15], for example, created a watchstrap augmented with two touch sensors that enables users to make taps and strokes all around their wrists, while Oakley and Lee [13] propose co-opting the lateral edge of a watch-like device as an input surface by covering it with an array of touch sensors. There is also a wide range of work that proposes different mechanisms and approaches for Around-Device Interaction [11]. A prominent example in this space is Harrison and Hudson's elegant use of an in-device magnetometer in conjunction with an external permanent magnet mounted on a finger to support general pointing and interface tasks [6].

However, we argue that the largest and most accessible input surface on a smartwatch remains its screen. There has been relatively little work specifically exploring touch screen interaction design on smartwatches. Early exceptions include Blasko and Fiener's [2] and Ashbrook *et al.'s* [1] studies of how a beveled edge could be used to enhance target selection performance on watch displays. More recent work has explored how sensing finger orientation with an accelerometer could create a richer input space [4] and many techniques implemented on larger devices, such as identifying finger contact point [7] or shear [8] and pressure input [14] remain relatively unexplored on watches specifically but seem likely to offer considerable benefits.

Of particular relevance for this paper is prior work that has investigated systems based on rapid sequential taps. For example, Ghomi *et al.* [5] study how users can perform rhythmic Morse code like tapping patterns for tasks such as issuing commands or switching modes. They ultimately contribute a vocabulary of 14 tapping sequences that achieve a high level of usability. Serrano *et al.* [16] extend these ideas to discuss how a series of temporally separated taps that commences on the bevel of a tablet and moves over its screen can create a unique pattern of accelerometer disturbances and screen events that can be easily disambiguated from noise or other input and be used to, for example, summon menus and issue commands. Heo *et al.* [9] describe a closely related system based on input of spatially separated and rapidly sequential on-screen touches on a phone or tablet that can also be used for controlling menus or a typing-based form of gestural input. In designing their system, Heo *et al.* point out that a rapid sequence of touches is an unusual form of input and show that it is possible to temporally disambiguate taps in their system from regular touchscreen use.

The work in this paper is inspired by these prior studies and seeks to leverage the benefits of the tapping style of interaction (in terms of its support for rapid execution of commands and the fact it does not interfere with regular touch input) and apply this to the space-restricted smartwatch form factor. In order to do so this paper adapts these ideas into beating gestures composed of a rapid pair of simultaneous or overlapping taps. It explores how users produce these gestures and how they can be deployed to create useful interfaces on a smartwatch.

USER PERFORMANCE STUDY

To investigate the potential of beating gestures, we first conducted a study to capture, analyze and understand how users perform them. The primary goal of this study was descriptive - we specifically wanted to explore the full input space of beating gestures and establish parameters such as appropriate timing thresholds to distinguish between the different touch and release beating sequences. We also sought to determine whether the gestures would interfere with existing input paradigms and measure the reliability and consistency with which users could issue the gestures.

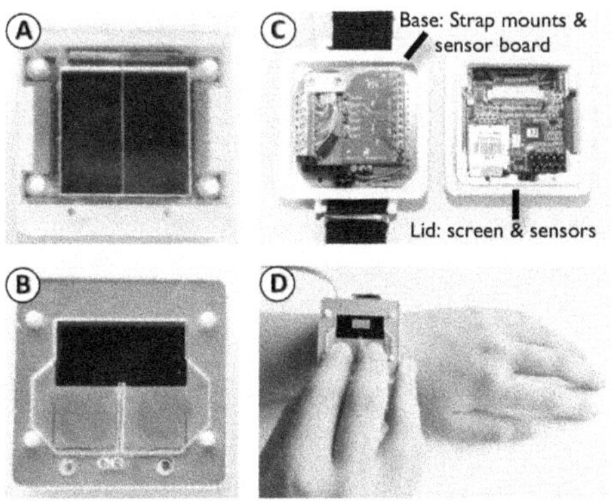

Figure 1. Watch prototype created for study. Plan views of watch screen with transparent ITO sensors (A) and half-screen PCB sensors (B). Right images show internal structure (C) and PCB prototype mounted on user's wrist with fingers touching the sensors and screen showing study UI (D).

Beats Hardware Prototype

Precise timing measurements, multi-touch input and the use of a wrist-based device were important aspects of this project. As multi-touch is not available on current watch format products, we constructed a prototype in the form factor of a smartwatch: a 3D printed 49mm by 49mm square by 25mm deep cuboid (Figure 1) with external mounting points for a standard watchband. These were sufficiently robust that the prototype could be securely attached to a user's wrist. The unit contained a 1.5inch (3.81mm) OLED screen (a 4DSystems µOLED-128-G2-GFX) and a Freescale Semiconductor MPR121 capacitive sensing microcontroller (specifically a Sparkfun MPR121 breakout board). The MPR121 was configured to report touches every four milliseconds, its highest possible update rate. Touches were captured on a pair of electrodes positioned over the surface of the screen. Two electrodes variants were developed – one full screen version based on transparent Itanium Tin Oxide (ITO) coated plastic sheets and a half-screen version using an opaque milled PCB board. While the ITO sheet offered the advantage of full visual availability of the display surface, it proved challenging to reliably calibrate its sensitivity to touches and its connections to the MPR121 board were frail and prone to failure. As such, we conducted the experimental work using the more robust and reliable PCB version of the system. A laser cut acrylic sheet was placed on top of the electrodes with holes that served to guide touches to their surfaces – without this sheet, small placement errors in single touches could result in contact with both electrodes and, thus, invalid input. Figure 1 illustrates these details.

The sensor and screen were connected via a single cable to an Arduino Mega by, respectively, I2C and RS232 communication links. The Arduino coordinated data logging and the low-level display of screen contents. It was connected by a second RS232 link to a PC and communicated sporadically (and not during touch time measurement) with a Java application that stored data and sent information about which trial contents to present.

Participants

Eighteen users completed the study (nine female, all right handed). They were undergraduate or graduate students enrolled in full time studies at UNIST in South Korea. Their mean age was 22 and they rated their experience with computers, touchscreens and smartphones to be high (4.7, 4.7 and 4.9 on a 1 to 5 scale) and their experience with smartwatches and other wearables devices to be low (1 and 1.3). Although the participant group was tech-savvy, in most cases this study was their first experience with a wearable computer. Those few with prior experience indicated they had used devices such as fitness trackers. Participants completed the study in 30-45 minutes and were compensated with approximately 10 USD in local currency.

Experimental Description and Design

The experiment sought to capture user performance in a broad set of beating gestures in order to establish both how reliably they can be produced by users and their temporal characteristics – the typical durations between each screen touch or release. As such we designed a complete set of beating gestures by systematically adjusting two variables: the sequences of finger *placement* and finger *release*. There are three possible placement sequences: the left finger followed by the right finger (*LR*), the right followed by the left (*RL*) and both together (*Dual-Tap*). There are six possible release sequences: holding both fingers on screen (*Hold*), releasing only the left finger (*L-Release*), only the right finger (*R-Release*), the left followed by the right (*LR-release*), the right followed by the left (*RL-release)* and both together (*Dual-Release*). Taken together these two variables lead to a set of 18 possible beating gestures.

The study was designed in four trial blocks. The first three each presented trials featuring a single finger-placement type (LR, RL or Dual-Tap). In each of these blocks, participants completed three trial-sets involving five randomly presented repetitions of each of the six possible finger-release sequences for a total of 90 trials. The first trial-set (e.g. the first 30 trials) were considered practice and not retained for analysis. This structure ensured that we captured participants' performance after they had gained experience with the study process and instructions and practiced each gesture for a short but sustained period of time, a manipulation intended to ensure that the results are more representative of experienced (rather than purely novice) performance. To mitigate practice effects with this structure, presentation of the finger-placement variable was fully balanced in a repeated measures design: three participants completed each of the six possible condition orders. In total, this stage of the study generated 3240 trials that were retained for analysis: 18 participants by 3 blocks by 2 trials-sets by 5 repetitions by 6 trials.

However, although we saw value in emphasizing non-novice performance, we were concerned that this study structure might lead to naturally unachievable mechanistic production of the beating gestures – simple repetition of the

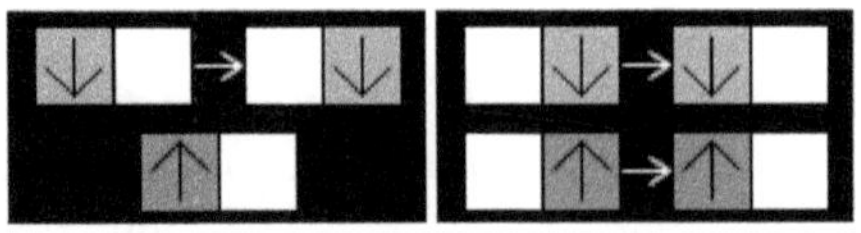

Figure 2. Two study instructions. Top row (green) indicates finger placements and bottom row (red) shows finger releases. Movement order is shown by horizontal position. The instructions are LR to L-Release (left) and RL to Release-RL (right). Participants completed practice sessions using these instructions prior in the early stages of the study.

physical motions that cannot practically scale to the context of a real-world user interface. Accordingly, in the fourth and final trial block, participants completed three runs through the complete set of 18 trials (54 total) in an entirely random order. The first run through was discarded as practice, leaving 36 trials per participant for analysis (648 trials in total). This final block enabled us to examine how participants performed the beating gestures after some experience and in a more realistic situation where finger-placement patterns fully vary from trial to trial.

Procedure

The experiment took place in a quiet room with participants seated comfortably at a desk. The experiment started with participants completing a brief demographics questionnaire, reading a set of instructions and then donning the prototype. This was always strapped to the wrist of their non-dominant hand, which was placed palm down on the surface of the desk approximately parallel to their body and in easy view of their eyes and reach of their dominant hand. All touches to the prototype were performed with their dominant hand. The experimental instructions emphasized that they were to perform the beating gestures as fast as possible while maintaining accuracy. Experimenters were available to answer any questions and demonstrated beating gestures in cases where participants had doubts about this issue. Participants then moved on the complete the main study.

Each trial in the study was structured as follows. Firstly, on-screen instructions requested participants to tap the sensors to start. After release, gesture instructions (see Figure 2 for examples) were presented alongside a centrally located green fixation spot. If participants touched the sensors during this period, the fixation spot turned red and the instructions remained on screen indefinitely. After one second without touching the sensors, the fixation spot disappeared and users followed the on-screen instructions to issue the requested beating gesture. Half a second after completing input, users were presented with feedback as to trial correctness (defined in the measures section below). Incomplete or incorrect trials timed-out after 3.5 seconds.

Measures

For each beating gesture we logged the start time of the trial and the time of each touch or release of the sensors. The key measures we extracted from this data were *beating-time*, the time between the first two touches and *release-time*, the time from the release of the first finger until the release of the second in those the nine beating gestures that require it. We also calculated *trial-time*, the time from the first touch until completion of each beating gesture with either a finger placement (for the three gestures that finish with a Hold) or the final finger release (in all other cases).

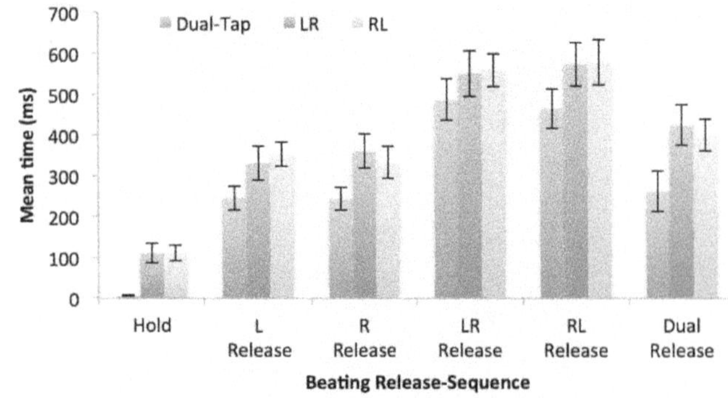

Figure 3. Mean trial-time by placement & release variables.

Errors were also logged based solely on the *sequence of touches* – if users did not produce touches in the order required by each trial within the timeout, the result was logged as an error and the trial returned to the pool still to be presented. There were no constraints, in terms of correctness, related to the timing of touches. For instance, to enter a left-right sequence, the difference between the two touches could be anywhere from 4ms, the lower bound of the touch sensor's temporal resolution, upwards. Equally, dual-tap and dual-release made no constraints on the timing involved in the dual action – both touches or releases could occur either simultaneously or one after the other and any amount of temporal separation was considered valid. This approach ensured we captured every single correctly ordered attempt to produce the beating gestures – thus representing a full picture of how users performed them.

Results

Timing Results

We first report data from the three initial conditions in the study. Overall mean trial-time was short: 355ms (Figure 3). This demonstrates beating gestures can be performed rapidly. Unsurprisingly, the data was affected strongly by the experimental variables – these entail activity that varies in quantity and complexity. A repeated-measures ANOVA, corrected for sphericity violations where appropriate, showed moderate to very strong significant effects of both finger-placement ($F (2, 34) = 12.89$, $\eta_p^2 = 0.43$) and finger release ($F (1.72, 29.1) = 131.42$, $\eta_p^2 = 0.89$), but no interaction between the two variables ($F (3.61, 61.9) = 0.14$, $\eta_p^2 = 0.1$). Post-hoc t-tests with Bonferroni CI adjustments confirmed that Dual-Tap gestures were faster than LR or RL gestures (both $p<0.01$). In terms of the release variable, gestures that did not involve finger releases (e.g. hold) were faster than those with a single finger release which were, in turn, faster than Dual-Release gestures which were, finally, faster than those with two separate finger releases (all at $p = 0.017$ or lower).

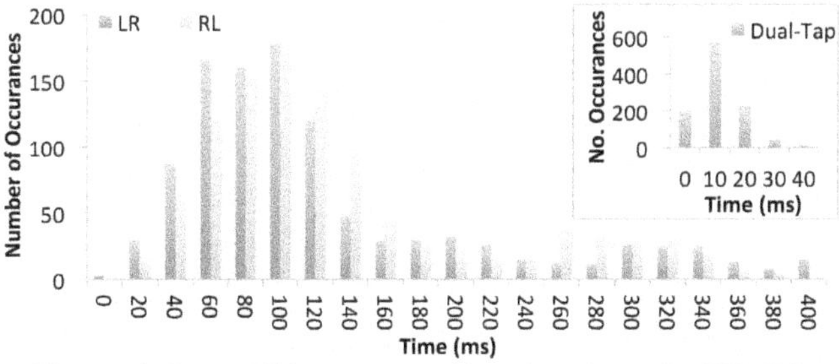

Figure 4. Overall histograms of beating-times for LR, RL and Dual-Tap placement in three main study conditions.

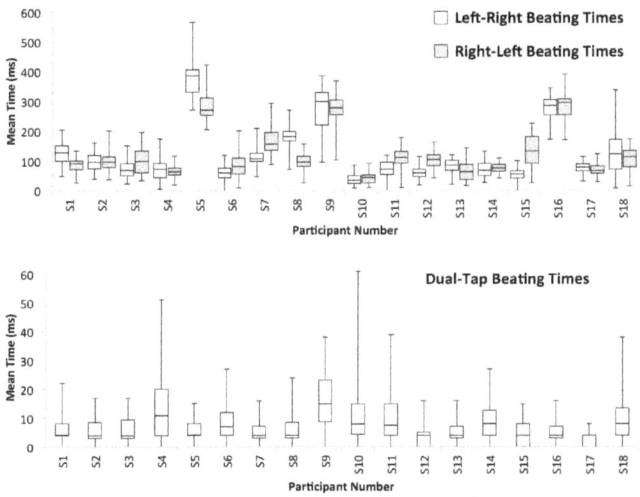

Figure 5. Median beating times shown per participant in three main conditions (outliers removed per participant) for LR and RL (top) and Dual-Tap (bottom) conditions.

More interesting are the beating-time data – the time between two finger contacts. As these distinguish between different beating gestures we examined them descriptively to characterize how distinctly, robustly and reliably they were performed. First, outliers (data in excess of three standard deviations from the mean) for each condition were excluded – a total of 36 trials or 1.1% of data. Beating-time histograms were plotted for the three finger placement sequences (Figure 4). Dual-Taps fell in a relatively narrow distribution and were completed in a mean of 7.33ms (SD 6.88) with none exceeding 35ms. LR and RL taps were completed in means of 121ms (SD 94) and 126ms (SD 82). In contrast to the Dual-Tap data, these plots show a much broader spread of data, including 159 trials (4.96% of total trials) that take place in 35ms or less – overlapping with times from the Dual-Tap condition. There is also a general rightward skew and two peaks in the data: a distinct peak at 100ms and a less prominent peak at 300ms.

To explore how much of this diversity was due to individual differences, we returned to the original dataset, removed outliers on a per participant basis (excluding 33 trials or 1% of data that was over three SD from the mean) and plotted individual box plots (Figure 5). These charts reinforce the generally reliable and consistent performance of the Dual-Tap gesture. However, LR and RL beating times were more variable. One participant (S10) produced notably more rapid times than others (mean 41ms, SD 19.2), while mean times for the majority fell in the range of 65ms to 150ms and three (S5, S9, S16) produced mean beating times that were two to three times slower – between 270ms and 340ms. Contrasting the charts, we note that two participants with positively skewed Dual-Tap times (S4, S10) also exhibit relatively rapid LR and RL times. Using this data we calculated the per-participant overlap between LR or RL and Dual-Tap input, based on a region three SDs around the Dual-Tap mean. This showed a broadly similar average misclassification rate to the aggregate data – 170 trials (5.2% of overall total) of the RL or LR trials would be misclassified as Dual-Tap. However, 133 of these trials (78%) were due to participants S4 and S10, with the misclassification rate of the remaining 16 participants running at a much lower 1.3%. This analysis suggests that the majority of users can reliably produce distinctive Dual-Tap and LR/RL input, albeit at a range of different speeds. However, a minority of users (11% in this study) exhibit an overlap in performance of these movements, which would make reliable classification of their input challenging.

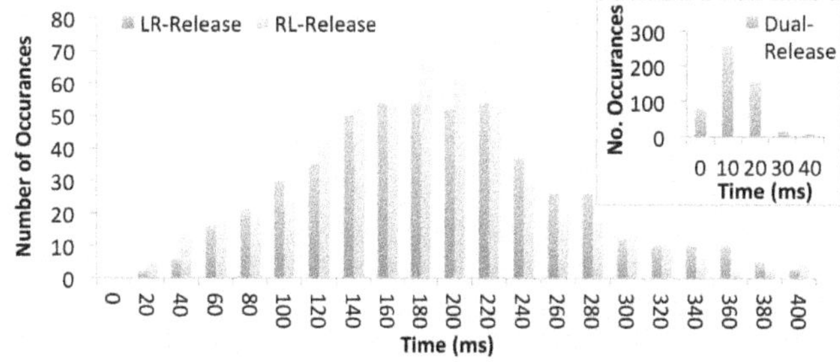

Figure 6. Histograms of release-time for Dual-Release, LR-Release and RL-Release in three main study conditions.

We analyzed release-time in a similar way. Figure 6 shows a histogram of all data from Dual, LR and RL release trials. This shows trends that broadly mirror those in the finger placement data – Dual-Release is quick and relatively homogenous while LR and RL distributions are much slower and more spread out. Means times on a per-participant basis after outlier removal (20 trials, or 1.2% of data) were as follows: Dual-Release 9.2ms (SD 3.4), LR-Release 191ms (SD 76) and RL-Release 180ms (SD 75). Also on a per participant basis, a total of 37 of the LR/RL trials (2.3% of total trials) fell within three SDs of Dual-Release mean, potentially leading to errors in classifying the beating gestures in this small proportion of trials.

Finally, we characterized performance in the final condition with that in the earlier three. Overall trial time in this block was 313ms (SD 126), a figure a t-test revealed to be significantly lower than that recorded in the initial three conditions (p=0.004). We then examined beating-times. After outlier removal (6 trials or 1% of data), means were: Dual-Tap 7.5ms (SD 3.7), LR 103ms (SD 72) and RL 110ms (SD 69). The overlap between Dual-Tap and LR/RL data was a total of 27 trials (4.1%). Release times (3 outliers, 1% of data) were: Dual-Release 11.5ms (SD 7.7), LR-Release 179ms (SD 63) and RL-Release 173ms (SD 57) with an overlap between Dual and LR/RL of 14 trials (4.3%). Overall, this performance broadly matches that in the first three conditions. This is notable because users performed a more complex task involving random variations of both finger placement and release sequences. This suggests that practice rapidly increased users' fluency with the beating task and they were then able to apply these skills to produce any of the beating gestures at any time.

Error Results

Error rates in the study were low for experimental settings. The mean error rate over the three main conditions was 5.7% (SD 4.0%) and 5.3% (SD 5.0%) in the closing condition, a difference that was not significant (t-test, p=0.44). Given the more challenging nature of the final set of trials, this similarity reinforces the idea that participants rapidly acquired the ability to execute the beating gestures fluently. Given this similarity (and for brevity) we present only an aggregate analysis of errors according to trial type and including data from all four conditions in the study.

We classified errors into two types – *extra*, or those involve making additional undesired input in the form of touches or releases of the sensors following correct completion of the required beating gesture, and *incorrect*, or simply making the wrong input. This data is plotted in Figure 7 by both finger placement (left) and finger release (right) variables and was analyzed using Repeated Measures ANOVA, adjusted for sphericity violations using Greenhouse-Geisser corrections where appropriate and followed up with *post-hoc* t-tests incorporating Bonferroni CI adjustments. The *extra* errors did not vary by finger placement type ($F(2, 34) = 0.377$, $p = 0.68$, $\eta_p^2=0.022$), but did vary significantly by finger release type ($F(2.86, 48.7) = 9.05$, $p<0.001$, $\eta_p^2 = 0.35$) and, with a weak effect size, in the interaction between these variables ($F(4.15, 70.52) = 0.377$, $p = 0.009$, $\eta_p^2=0.18$). Due to its small size, the interaction effect was hard to interpret, but the main effect was clearly revealed by the post-hoc analysis: the RL-Release and Dual-Release conditions led to reductions in *extra* errors over, respectively, the Hold (p=0.042), L-Release (p=0.015) and R-Release (p=0.004) and the Hold (p=0.035) and R-Release (p = 0.014) conditions. These results indicate that the majority of *extra* errors were due to early release of the sensors in those conditions where one or both fingers needed to remain in contact. Specifically, this occurred during the 500ms period at the end each trial after input was completed and before feedback was presented. As, in a realistic application, this time period would be minimized, or even removed, we suggest that many of these *extra* errors represent experimental artifacts – participants anticipating when to release the screen to continue to the next trial, and underestimating this time.

More serious are the *incorrect* errors. The RM-ANOVA revealed moderately powerful significant effects of the

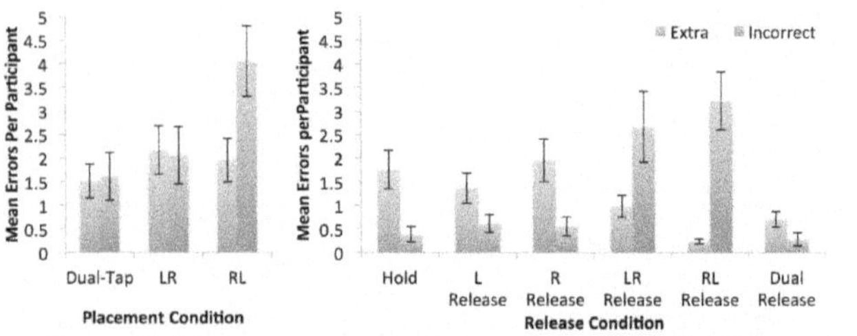

Figure 7. Mean error rates from whole study by finger placement type (left) and finger release type (right).

main effects of finger placement ($F(2, 34) = 8.97$, $p = 0.001$, $\eta_p^2=0.35$) and finger release ($F(2.04, 34.66) = 12.8$, $p < 0.001$, $\eta_p^2=0.43$) and a weak effect of the interaction between them ($F(2.91, 49.42) = 3.38$, $p = 0.026$, $\eta_p^2=0.17$). In terms of finger placement *post-hoc* tests showed Dual-Tap yielded lower errors than RL (p=0.002) while the difference between LR and RL approached significance (p=0.052). Regarding finger release, the only *post-hoc* tests to attain significance involved the RL-Release data – all other release types bar LR-Release resulted in lower errors at either p=0.002 or p=0.003. The interaction plot (not shown) suggests this effect is largely due to a near doubling of *incorrect* errors occurring in trials featuring the specific combination of RL followed by RL-Release. This suggests this particular beating gesture is challenging for users.

Discussion

The major conclusions of this study are that the majority of users performed the beating gestures rapidly (300-400ms) and reliably (approximately 5.5% overall error rate, low for experimental settings). The data compare favorably to other tapping techniques such as Bezel-Tap [16] that exhibit substantially longer task completion times (around 1.5 seconds, possible due to the accelerometer sensing system on which it is based) and larger aggregate errors rates (between 1.75% and 12%). The results also compare well to other forms of smart watch interaction, such as the touch screen radial targeting task studied by Askbrook *et al.* [1]. Although times are not reported, error rates for selecting a target from a set of 12 are stated to be 4.8% (when targets occupy 25% of the screen) – broadly similar to the 5.5% recorded in the production of one beating gesture (from a larger set of 18) recorded here. Similarly, in Harrison and Hudson's [6] discussion of around device interaction, they report that one target can be selected from 22 in around 2 seconds and with a 7.8% error rate, figures that are more than four times slower than those presented here and modestly less reliable. These comparisons provide support for the assertion that the beating gestures are a fast and accurate mechanism for interaction on smart watches.

The data also support recommendations for suitable thresholds for detecting the different beating movements. Dual-Tap and Dual-Release were fast (in the three main conditions, over all users, 28ms at the 99th percentile) indicating 30ms is an appropriate cut-off value. LR and RL were broader distributions with, respectively, figures of 401ms and 372ms at the 99th percentile. This suggests a cut off 400ms would be able to correctly capture these movements. This figure is similar to the data reported in Heo *et al.*'s [9] investigation of sequential distant taps and, as with their work, indicates that beating gestures can be easily distinguished from other forms of input, such as regular single finger taps or double taps (typically spaced at a minimum of 500ms). In this way, we argue that the beating gestures will not interfere with standard watch input in the form of single finger taps, double-taps and strokes. Furthermore, as beating input always starts with two simultaneous on screen touches, we argue it is easy to distinguish from single finger input. We also argue that the thresholds make the system relatively immune to noise – such as unintentional triggers whilst in a pocket. This is partly due to the fact that the beating gestures can rely on existing techniques to ignore on screen input – such as when the screen is turned off, or the watch orientation (as sensed by an accelerometer) is away from norms – and also because it is much more unlikely that two separate but closely timed touches would occur on the small surface of a watch that that a single touch would occur. In this way, we argue that beating input is much less likely to be accidentally triggered than standard single finger input.

However, while these 30ms and 400ms thresholds are valid general recommendations, we also noted considerable individual differences. As such, any realistic beating gestures interface should either allow users to customize thresholds (e.g. as with mouse double-click thresholds) or, adaptively adjust them to match an individual's abilities. This would be particularly important for the minority of users we observed whose data overlapped substantially between Dual-Tap and LR/RL movements – customizing the thresholds would allow these very rapid performers to tweak the system to best match their abilities. It is also worth noting that the challenges in classifying the performance of these users may be due to the study instructions (which emphasized speed) and design of the trials (which did not impose thresholds on performance). As these users logged few sequence errors, we believe they were able performers of the beating gestures who exploited the structure of the study to perform at a pace where noise was inevitable. Future studies of systems with predefined beating thresholds could confirm or refute this idea. An alternative design strategy for these users would be to create interfaces that use only Dual-Tap or LR/RL gestures, but never both, making confounding this input impossible.

The data also show that some beating gestures were harder to perform than others. Specifically, the combining RL with RL-Release led to a significant spike in the error rate, suggesting this pairing should be avoided. There is also, obviously, a clear incentive to use the simplest and shortest beating gestures in interface designs – those that involve fewer strokes are completed more rapidly and with fewer opportunities for error. This point is clearly illustrated in Figure 7 (right) where LR-Release and RL-Release account for a substantial proportion of *incorrect* errors.

BEATS INTERFACE DESIGNS

Encouraged and informed by these results and recommendations, we explored the kinds of interfaces that could be created on small screens using beating gestures. In order to achieve high-resolution multi-touch input and rich, real time graphical feedback in our designs, they were developed using the Processing programming language on a Motorola DROID RAZR XT912. Informal testing with this device indicated it reported touch events with an accuracy of approximately 10ms, sufficient to recognize beating gestures. All touch input and graphical output in the prototypes was restricted to a 30mm square zone (42.4mm or 427 pixels diagonal) in the center of the screen, a typical size for current smartwatch systems such as the Samsung Galaxy Gear (from 41.4mm to 50.1mm diagonal) and the Apple Watch (38.1mm to 43.1mm). The demos used the thresholds for classifying beating gestures derived from the empirical study – pairs of taps needed to take place within 30ms to be classified as Dual input and within 400ms to be classified as LR/RL movements. Taps separated by longer times were not considered as beating input.

Whilst designing the demonstrations we were sensitive to the limited visual space available on smartwatches. Indeed, in order to minimize on-screen clutter we designed systems that were effectively unmarked or invisible until evoked (in much the same way as swipe gestures are currently). To avoid fat-finger problems [16] of users' own bodies obscuring feedback, the designs relied on input (such as strokes) that could be made eyes-free [3] or visuals that were purposefully displaced from a user's on-screen finger [18]. To explore the diversity of the technique we sought to design interactions based on a wide range of beating gestures. Furthermore, we purposefully integrated the beating gestures with traditional input styles such as menus, pie menus and sliders/scrollbars in order to explore how beating gestures could be combined with more established touch screen interactions, one of our key initial design goals. A final design concern was the consequences of inadvertent activation – we attempted to ensure that users would be able to cancel (or reverse) the outcomes of beating input rapidly and easily. In total, we created five prototype applications.

Home Screen – Application Shortcuts. In this application, a typical watch home screen is shown (Figure 8). Touching the screen with two fingers simultaneously (Dual-Tap) causes a three-item menu to appear at the top of the screen, above the likely finger touches. Following up with an LR-Release causes the leftmost command to be activated while a Dual-Release activates the central command and an RL-Release the rightmost command. Although not implemented, stroking off-screen could have been used to cancel the menu. The idea is that users can configure applications to these commands, creating an eyes-free and readily accessible shortcut menu that could be available at all times and from any screen of the watch.

Maps – Tap Menu. In the map application, users can make short strokes to pan the map. To perform further interaction, they can activate a menu with either LR or RL touch sequence followed by releasing the last finger to touch the screen (e.g. RL followed by L-Release). A menu of four buttons then appears in a preset location under their raised finger and users can tap these icons to issue commands such as zoom in or out, or panning to specific locations. This interface is shown in Figure 9. The use of symmetric menus on the right and left of the screen (accessed by LR or RL touches) ensures the same menu is available independent of which arm the watch is worn on. The goal in this design was to provide rapid access to commonly used contextual commands without requiring that they be permanently displayed on the limited available screen space.

Messages – Stroke Menu. Driven by similar motivations, we implemented an alternative symmetric menu design on a watch screen illustrating an incoming text message. In this version, users perform either a LR or RL touch sequence and then raise the first finger that touched the screen (e.g. LR followed by L-Release). A three-quarters pie menu then appears under the finger touching the screen. Stroking towards the top, bottom or center of the screen moves over one of the menu commands and releasing the finger selects this option. In the context of this demo, we showed commands corresponding to reply-to, call-back and send-emoticon – see Figure 10. This UI allowed us to explore the use of beating input followed by simple stroke gestures.

Alarm Clock – Modes and Sliders. The alarm app in Figure 11 shows a simple digital clock. Dual-Tap followed by Dual-Release toggled between the clock and an alarm mode. When in the alarm mode, RL followed by L-Release displayed a slider over the hour digits and away from the on-screen right finger. Moving this finger up and down then adjusted the hours. Similarly, LR followed by R-Release operated similarly for minutes. Together, these enabled a user to configure an alarm time with just a few taps. Regular one finger taps in the alarm mode toggled it on and off. This design showed how beating input could issue direct commands (e.g. mode switch) and also integrate with interfaces for adjusting a pair of analogue variables.

Music Player – Navigation and Sliders. The final app was a simple music player (Figure 12). Visuals included the album artwork, playback position and play/pause state. A regular one-finger tap toggled between play and pause. A centrally positioned volume slider appeared after a Dual-Tap and subsequent vertical strokes caused changes in the displayed volume. To navigate amongst songs, users performed either a LR or RL touch sequence followed by raising the last finger to touch the screen (e.g. RL then L-Release). Subsequent taps with the raised finger moved to the previous or subsequent song, depending on whether the right or left finger was raised. This interface supported eyes free use – although on-screen state feedback was presented, there were no targets or buttons shown.

Figure 8. Demo home page (left). Dual-Tap brings up an app shortcut menu (center) and LR-Release, Dual-Release or RL-Release selects the left, center or right command respectively. In the example, RL-Release selects calendar.

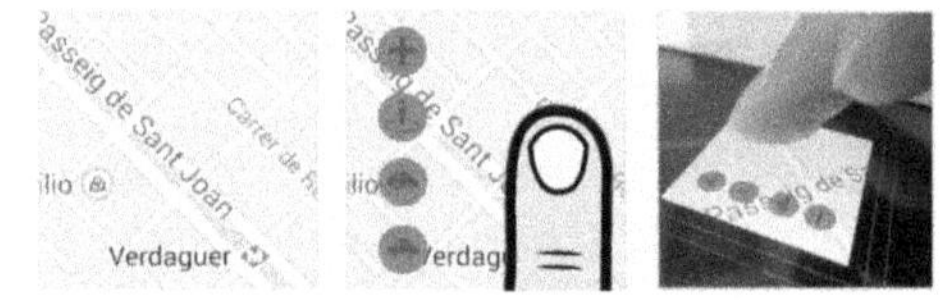

Figure 9. Demo map app (left). RL followed by L-Release shows a menu of options away from the right finger touching the screen (center and right). Subsequent taps with the raised left finger selects items.

Figure 10. Demo message app (left). LR followed by L-Release shows a menu of options under the right finger touching the screen (center and right). Stroking towards icons and releasing, as in a pie menu, selects commands.

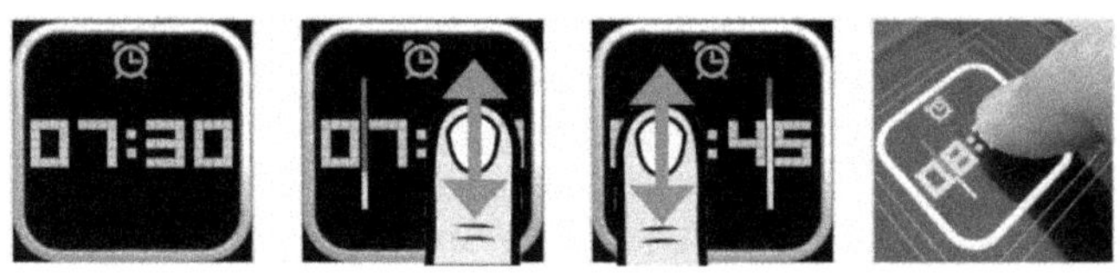

Figure 11. Demo alarm app (left). RL followed by L-Release triggers a slider and vertical strokes set hours (left-center, right). LR followed by R-Release sets minutes in a similar way (right-center). Dual-Tap followed by Dual-Release (not shown) toggles between clock & alarm modes.

Figure 12. Demo music player (left). Single taps toggle play/pause while Dual-Tap shows a volume slider adjusted by vertical movements (left-center, right). After RL followed by L-Release, subsequent taps with the left finger goes to previous songs (right-center). LR followed by R-Release enables a similar interaction for subsequent songs.

To create a final demonstration system, the five applications were implemented into a single prototype. Swipe navigation, a common technique for moving between pages of content, switched between application screens – upward and downward swipes to navigate between a sequence of the applications and a rightward swipe to return to the first home screen app irrespective of current location.

USER FEEDBACK ON BEATING GESTURES

We ran a user study to gather feedback and assess reactions to these prototypes. The goal of this study was to complement the rigorous quantitative data gathered in the first study with subjective comments and opinions regarding the interaction style when it was instantiated in functioning prototypes. Ten users (five female, a mean of 23 years old) completed the study, all students who stated they had considerable experience of computers (4.8/5), smartphones (5/5) and touchscreens (5/5) but, once again, limited experience with smartwatches (1.3) and other wearable technology (1.3). None had completed the previous study and each was compensated with approximately 10 USD in local currency. The study involved an experimenter demonstrating each application to participants and asking them to comment on the usefulness and easiness of each one. Afterwards, participants tried each system out for themselves. Audio and video (of participants hands and the prototype) were recorded and a second experimenter took live notes. The experiment took approximately 30 minutes per participant.

Results

The prototypes were generally well received. Perhaps the clearest value came in repeated statements relating to the convenience, ease or speed with which the systems could be operated. Commenting on the menu shortcuts on the home screen P3 stated that "usually there are lots of steps to access apps, but not here. Very fast." Similarly P7 liked that the zoom functions on the map were available "right away" and felt the alarm app was much quicker to operate than existing systems. P6 particularly appreciated the music player UI stating it would be useful even on a larger device such as a smartphone.

Users also tended to appreciate the interfaces that employed movements after the beating input. P1 stated that the strokes in the messages app pie menu were "easy" compared to having to "touch some specific icon" and controlling the alarm app was simple because it involved "the finger still on the screen". Similarly, P9 appreciated the "easy manipulation" of the finger placement followed by vertical strokes during setting the alarm time. P10 indicated that the Dual-Tap followed by up/down movements to set volume was "interesting and easy to use".

Conversely, participants reported difficulties in understanding how finger releases could correspond to interface events. The sequential release of both fingers to trigger apps in the home screen was reported by P1 to be "confusing" in how the finger releases related to the on screen content. P6 reiterated this sentiment and stated this movement was "difficult to understand" and that this made it hard to "catch its rhythm" or execute it correctly. Overall these issues were viewed as problems in understanding how input would relate to outcomes rather than any perceived difficulty in physical generating the movements. Those systems, such as the song navigation in the music app, that participants' felt exhibited good mapping (e.g. previous/ next mapping to left/right taps) were seen as simple and effective because, as P9 noted, "the direction of touch and [music] movement was the same".

Users also remarked on the novel nature of the input and the challenges this posed. Discussing various interfaces, P5 and P9 stated that the interface style would "need to be learnt", P7 and P8 that it was "unfamiliar" and P4 worried about the need to refer to a manual. However, these comments were tempered by the perceived simplicity of the input. For example, P6 was initially confused by the experimenter's instructions but interacting with the system "felt ok" after trying it out. Similarly P7 remarked that the message app initially seemed complex but "after a few moments" it was "easy and comfortable" and P9 felt it would be ease to become "accustomed" to the interactions.

An over-arching theme through the comments was that, although the input was easy to perform, its lack of familiarity coupled with an absence of conventional graphical cues meant that users felt it was tricky to initially pick up and might be hard to recall. These comments mirror Norman's sentiments on gestural and natural user interfaces – that a lack of familiar visual affordances negatively impact usability [12]. To address this issue users proposed solutions such as relying on a limited input vocabulary composed a few beating gestures applied systematically over a whole UI, in much the same way that swiping has been generally applied to mobile device interfaces.

Overall, the results of this study suggest were positive as to the major value that the beating gestures provide: quick, easy access to salient commands. However, like most gestural languages, care must be taken to apply the beating gestures consistently so that users can develop a general understanding of how their input will relate and connect to output. Taking advantage of their inherently simple directional (left/right) and temporal (first/second) properties and focusing more on touch than release events represent appropriate ways that designers can achieve this.

CONCLUSIONS

This paper contributes the idea and design of beating gestures: rapid sequences of screen touches and releases made by the index and middle fingers of a users hand. They were conceived as a simple mechanism for increasing the richness of input available via the touch-screens of very small devices such as smart-watches. Beyond this, we also present a user study that characterizes this novel form of gesture, numerically quantifying their performance and concluding they are a rich, rapid and reliable form of input for small screens. Building on these findings we present interaction techniques that integrate beating gestures with archetypical interface tasks such as issuing commands, interacting with menus and adjusting parameters. Our designs attempted to minimize the need for on-screen feedback or ensure clear lines of sight to critical content. A qualitative study of these designs led to generally positive user feedback regarding the convenience and speed of the techniques and concerns about their unfamiliarity. Taken together these outputs and results show the potential of beating gestures as an input technique for small screens.

There are a number of limitations to this work. Firstly, due to the small form factors of the devices, multi-touch screens are not currently common on smartwatch systems. The potential of beating gestures (and other small-screen multi-touch UIs that the community may develop) may change this in the future. Secondly, rapidly polling touch sensors increases power consumption; sensing beating gestures may negatively impact smartwatch battery life. In terms of the empirical work described here, one key, albeit common, problem is the homogeneity of the samples. Further studies that establish whether a broader population of users can readily and reliably perform beating gestures would reinforce the conclusions of this article. A second issue is the lack of formal comparisons against alternative input paradigms. Finally, in the second study, prototypes were implemented on a watch-sized portion of a mobile phone, rather than on a watch, and this lack of ecological validity may have influenced user feedback. In the future, we will develop a fully functioning watch prototype and run comparative tests in mobile scenarios.

Beyond addressing these concerns, future work should consider beating gestures on larger devices where they could be coupled with richer graphical feedback [9, 16], or in specific application areas such as security, where quick and unobtrusive input may have particular value [15]. In sum, we believe the work presented in this paper showcases the potential of beating gestures for increasing the expressivity of touch input on small devices. Furthermore, it achieves this without requiring physical changes to the watch form factor, any fundamentally new sensing hardware (unlike, many prior approaches [13, 15, 19]) or impeding or preventing existing interaction styles based on single taps, strokes, holds and pressure. We believe this demonstrates that beating gestures have the potential to be combined with these established techniques as standard elements of the touch screen interaction paradigm and look forward to exploring the novel interactions this enables.

ACKNOWLEDGEMENTS

This research was supported by Basic Science Research Program through the National Research Foundation of Korea (NRF) funded by the Ministry of Science, ICT and Future Planning (2014R1A1A1002223).

REFERENCES

1. Ashbrook, D. Lyons, K. and Starner, T. 2008. An investigation into round touchscreen wristwatch interaction. In MobileHCI '08, 311-314.
2. Blasko, G. and Feiner, S. 2004. An Interaction System for Watch Computers Using Tactile Guidance and Bidirectional Segmented Strokes. Proc. ISWC'04. IEEE.
3. Brewster, S., Lumsden, J., Bell, M., Hall, M., and Tasker, S. 2003. Multimodal 'eyes-free' interaction techniques for wearable devices. In CHI '03. 473-480.
4. Chen, X., Grossman, T., Wigdor, D.J., and Fitzmaurice, G. 2014. Duet: exploring joint interactions on a smart phone and a smart watch. In Proceedings of CHI '14.
5. Ghomi, E., Faure G., Huot, S., Chapuis, O., and Beaudouin-Lafon, M. 2012. Using rhythmic patterns as an input method. In Procs of CHI '12. 1253-1262.
6. Harrison, C. and Hudson, S.E. 2009. Abracadabra: wireless, high-precision, and unpowered finger input for very small mobile devices. In Proc. UIST '09. 121-124.
7. Harrison C., Schwarz, J., and Hudson, S.E. 2011. TapSense: enhancing finger interaction on touch surfaces. In Proceedings of UIST '11, 627-636.
8. Heo, S. and Lee, G. 2013. Indirect shear force estimation for multi-point shear force operations. In Proceedings of CHI '13. 281-284.
9. Heo, S., Gu, J., and Lee, G. 2014. Expanding touch input vocabulary by using consecutive distant taps. In Proceedings CHI '14. 2597-2606.
10. Hoggan, E., Nacenta, M., Kristensson, P.O., Williamson, J., Oulasvirta, A., and Lehtiö, A. 2013. Multi-touch pinch gestures. In Procs ITS '13. 219-222.
11. Kratz, S. and Rohs, M. 2009. HoverFlow: expanding the design space of around-device interaction. In Proceedings of MobileHCI '09.
12. Norman, D.A. 2010. Natural user interfaces are not natural. interactions 17, 3 (May 2010), 6-10.
13. Oakley, I. and Lee, D. 2014. Interaction on the edge: offset sensing for small devices. In Proceedings CHI '14. ACM, New York, NY, USA, 169-178.
14. Pedersen, E.W. and Hornbæk, K. 2014. Expressive touch: studying tapping force on tabletops. In Proceedings of CHI '14. 421-430.
15. Perrault, S.T., Lecolinet, E., Eagan, J., and Guiard, Y. 2013. Watchit: simple gestures and eyes-free interaction for wristwatches and bracelets. In Procs. of CHI '13.
16. Serrano, M., Lecolinet, E., and Guiard, Y. 2013. Bezel-Tap gestures: quick activation of commands from sleep mode on tablets. In Proceedings of CHI '13. 3027-3036.
17. Siek, K.A., Rogers, Y., and Connelly, K.H. Fat Finger Worries: How Older and Younger Users Physically Interact with PDAs. In Proc. INTERACT'05, 267–280.
18. Vogel, D. & Baudisch, P. Shift: A Technique for Operating Pen-Based Interfaces Using Touch. In Proc. CHI'07, pp. 657-666.
19. Xiao, R., Laput, G. and Harrison, C. 2014. Expanding the input expressivity of smartwatches with mechanical pan, twist, tilt and click. In Procs. of CHI '14. 193-196.

WATCHCONNECT: A Toolkit for Prototyping Smartwatch-Centric Cross-Device Applications

Steven Houben [1,2]
[1] Pervasive Interaction Technology Laboratory
IT University of Copenhagen
Rued Langgaardsvej 7, Copenhagen, DK
s.houben@ucl.ac.uk

Nicolai Marquardt [2]
[2] University College London
UCL Interaction Centre / ICRI Cities
Gower Street, London, UK
n.marquardt@ucl.ac.uk

ABSTRACT
People increasingly use smartwatches in tandem with other devices such as smartphones, laptops or tablets. This allows for novel cross-device applications that use the watch as both input device and output display. However, despite the increasing availability of smartwatches, prototyping cross-device watch-centric applications remains a challenging task. Developers are limited in the applications they can explore as available toolkits provide only limited access to different types of input sensors for cross-device interactions. To address this problem, we introduce *WatchConnect*, a toolkit for rapidly prototyping cross-device applications and interaction techniques with smartwatches. The toolkit provides developers with (i) an extendable hardware platform that emulates a smartwatch, (ii) a UI framework that integrates with an existing UI builder, and (iii) a rich set of input and output events using a range of built-in sensor mappings. We demonstrate the versatility and design space of the toolkit with five interaction techniques and applications.

Author Keywords
Smartwatch; Toolkit; Cross-Device Interaction; Rapid Prototyping; Gestural Interaction; Interface Design

ACM Classification Keywords
H.5.2. Information Interfaces. User Interfaces – input devices and strategies, prototyping.

INTRODUCTION
Smartwatches give people lightweight and immediate access to messages, notifications, and other digital data while on the go. While already powerful as standalone devices, the capabilities of smartwatches increase significantly when used in tandem with other devices that people carry, such as their phones or tablets, which allows for novel cross-device interaction techniques (e.g. [7,24]). However, so far there are only a relatively small number of explorations into *watch-centric, cross-device interaction techniques*. Building and exploring cross-device interaction techniques and applications is a difficult task, as most existing development kits have only limited support for input gesture recognition, different sensor hardware configurations, rapid interface designs, or cross-device connectivity and transfer of information.

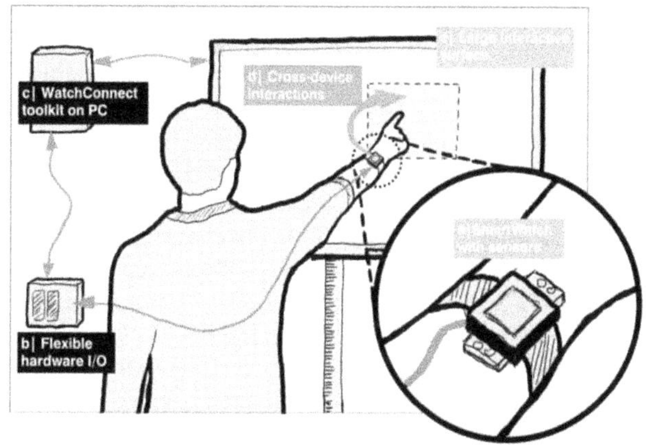

Figure 1. ***WatchConnect*** **toolkit consists of (a) wired prototyping smartwatches with sensors through a (b) flexible and extendable hardware layer, (c) a software development platform providing user interface components and a rich set of input and output events and gestures, facilitating (d) cross-device interactions with (e) other interactive surfaces.**

To bridge the gap between concept design and full implementation, we introduce *WatchConnect*, a rapid prototyping toolkit for watch-centric cross-device interaction techniques and applications (Figure 1). The toolkit provides (i) a modular and extendable hardware platform that emulates a smartwatch, (ii) a runtime system and user interface components that support quick prototyping of watch interfaces using an existing UI framework, and (iii) a rich set of input and output events and gestures using a range of built-in sensor mappings and simulators. The contribution of this paper is a *novel approach for rapidly prototyping and designing smartwatch-centric cross-device applications and interaction techniques, using simulated hardware and software building blocks.*

In this paper we first sample key related work and introduce the design of the *WatchConnect* toolkit. We proceed with the details of the architecture and components of the toolkit. Next, we demonstrate the versatility and generality of the toolkit by implementing five applications using only the basic building blocks of the toolkit. We conclude this paper with a discussion and reflection on the design and features of the toolkit, compared to other approaches.

CHI 2015, April 18 - 23 2015, Seoul, Republic of Korea
Copyright is held by the owner/author(s). Publication rights licensed to ACM.
ACM 978-1-4503-3145-6/15/04...$15.00
http://dx.doi.org/10.1145/2702123.2702215

RELATED WORK

WatchConnect builds on work on interaction techniques for smartwatches, cross-device setups, and toolkit designs.

Smartwatch Interactions

Most smartwatches allow for *touch* input. Ashbrook et al. [1] explored interaction techniques for round touch-enabled watch faces. Facet [22] allows for multi-screen interactions by expanding the watch to multiple touch-enabled watch faces arranged as a bracelet. Later, Duet [7] introduced a set of cross-device interaction techniques using both the touch screen and sensors of the watch. TouchSense [18] expanded the touch bandwidth of a watch screen, by augmenting the human finger with an IMU. Finally, Mayer et al. [24] employed the touch screen of a watch to interact with objects in the environment. A number of other approaches moved touch interaction to the *bevel* and *band* of the watch face. Blasko et al. [4] support bidirectional strokes on the frame of the watch providing tactile feedback. Oakley et al. [29] expanded this idea to the side of the bevel providing high resolution capacitive input. Xiao et al. [38] moved away from a static bevel and introduced mechanical input such as panning, twisting, tilting and clicking the bevel. Watchit [33] is the first approach that moves touch interaction and scroll gestures to the wristband. More recently, Funk et al. [8] explored using the wristband for touch-enabled text entry. Finally, Abracadabra [12] is a system that supports *above* the device interaction using a magnetic input sensor.

Other systems expanded interaction with a smartwatch by using the arm or hand for gesture or touch input. One of the first explorations into smartwatches, was Gesturewrist [35], augmenting a watch with sensors to allow for hand gesture and arm posture recognition. Gesture Watch [19] augments a watch face with sensors for the detection of swipes gestures above and around the watch. Similarly, the Haptic Wristwatch [32] allows for detection of gestures such as covering the watch, turning the bevel, or swipe over the watch. AugmentedForearm [30] took this concept further, stretching the touch display of the watch across the entire forearm. Knibbe et al. [20] augmented the watch with proximity and acoustic sensors to detect hand postures and multi-finger interactions. Finally, Skin buttons [21] project touch-enabled interface elements on the skin. Other approaches include interaction with the back of a small display [3], and with small spatial aware displays such as Siftables [25].

Cross-Device Interaction Techniques

Cross-device interaction techniques have been explored in a wide range of other device configurations. Pick and Drop [34] introduced cross-device direct manipulation. Hinckley et al. [17] allow users to bump devices together into a single workspace, using synchronized gestures. Another approach is to stitch devices together to allow for cross-device pen input [16]. Hardy et al. [11] proposed to use the back of the phone to select and interact with information on a large display. Similarly, PhoneTouch [36] allows users to interact with an interactive surface, using their phones as a personal device to configure or change the interaction with the surface. Cross-device interaction techniques were described in function of proxemics in the *gradual engagement pattern* [23]. Only recently, systems explicitly used smartwatches for cross-device interaction. Duet [7] introduced a number of interaction techniques and gestures to support distributed interaction between a watch and smartphone. Mayer et al. [24] proposed "*user interfaces beaming*" to interact with objects that are in the focus of a head-mounted display. SleeD [40] uses a sleeve display for interaction techniques distributed between the sleeve and a large interactive wall display.

Toolkits and Programming Interfaces

In recent years, a number of novel cross-device interface design toolkits have been proposed to mitigate the engineering challenges in building distributed interfaces. HydraScope [14] supports multi-surface interfaces by transforming and synchronizing existing web-based applications. Conductor [10] is a prototyping framework that allows for the construction of cross-device applications and provides task-, session-, and information-management. Panelrama [39] is a web-based toolkit for DUIs that supports built-in UI synchronization across devices by allowing developers to specify the suitability of groups of UIs (or *panels*) that are used by an algorithm to automatically distribute panels across devices. XDStudio [27] is a GUI builder that supports interactive development of cross-device interfaces through the simulation of devices, or by actual on-device authoring. The Tandem Browsing Toolkit [15] is a proxy-based online multi-display application toolkit that provides developers with a declarative framework to define multi-device web pages. XDKinect [28] is a cross-device interface toolkit that uses a Kinect depth camera to mediate interaction between different devices. The toolkit allows for proxemic-aware interaction, body tracking and multi-modal input. Finally, PolyChrome [2] is a toolkit for multi-device collaborative applications that provide support for concurrency management. A small number of commercial application programming interfaces (APIs), such as the Pebble [41], Sony SDK [42] or Apple's WatchKit [43] are available for developers.

These toolkits and APIs, however, are designed for existing hardware platforms and interfaces and provide no support for novel hardware designs, custom sensor mappings or watch-specific cross-device interfaces. Although they provide means to synchronize UIs and events, using custom hardware or designing specific gestures and postures would still require substantial engineering. While still possible to build single smartwatch applications (as seen in the related work), the challenges to build those prevent rapid prototyping and experimentation [9]. Existing commercial watch APIs require proprietary hardware and lack support for rapid prototyping of cross-device applications. In contrast, *WatchConnect* provides holistic support for the entire prototyping cycle including (i) hardware design, abstraction and mapping, (ii) built-in machine learning and gesture recognition, (iii) distributed user interface and event systems, and (iv) a high level visual programming framework and tools.

INTERACTION SPACE

To summarize the challenges of supporting interaction between a watch and an interactive surface, we present an overview on the *interaction space* that emerges when connecting the input and output space of both the watch and surface.

Watch Input Space

Prior work shows that the sensors built into smartwatches provide three interaction spaces:

W1: On the watch interaction. A watch allows for direct interaction through physical contact with the device. Users can touch the screen of the watch [1,7,18,22,24], grab and interact with the bevel of the watch face [4,29,38] for discrete touch input, or interact with a touch-enabled wristband to provide continuous input [8,33]. Combining these different modalities into one watch design provides users with a very rich input device that allows for combinations of screen, bevel and strap input.

W2: Above the watch interaction. Users can perform gestures with the non-watch-arm in the three dimensional space above the watch. Although proximity sensors and depth cameras are becoming increasingly popular, only Abracadabra [12] currently supports above the watch interaction. However, a watch equipped with distance sensors or light sensors, that are frequently used to support mid-air gestures such as in SideSight [5], can provide both continuous and discrete input. This allows for a range of gestures above the watch such as covering the watch face, hovering and holding above the edges of the watch, zooming by moving the hand closer and away from the watch face or simply using the measured distance as discrete input.

W3: Interaction via internal sensing. Integrated watch sensors can provide data on the acceleration and orientation of the device that allow for a wide range of both implicit and explicit gestures. Implicit gestures can be used to, e.g., automatically turn the watch screen on or off depending on the orientation of the watch. As demonstrated by Duet [7], TouchSense [18] and GestureWrist [35], explicit gestures allow users to switch interaction modes or express hand posture and gestures. A high granularity of input allows one to use the watch as a game controller or to express different input forms with the watch hand. Similar to other interaction spaces, the integrated sensors support both continuous and discrete input.

Interactive Surface Input Space

When wearing a watch to interact with *another touch screen* – for example a tablet or a digital whiteboard – the setup has three basic input spaces (informed by [37]):

S1: Interaction Connector Point. Because the watch hand can be recognized using the built-in sensors (as demonstrated in Duet [7]), it can be used to identify the user and to connect a specific user session to the interactive display. Identifying the user behind a touch input, as done by Schmidt et al. [36] using a mobile phone, allows applications and interaction techniques to incorporate user specific functionality, to personalize the user interface or to use the input for authentication.

S2: Interaction Collision Plane. When touching the external touch screen with the watch hand, a two dimensional input space is created that is merged with the normal touch-based input space. The screen can differentiate between touches performed with the watch hand and non-watch hand. This allows applications and interaction techniques to consider bimanual input in which specific modalities or functionality is assigned to a specific hand. Furthermore, the built-in sensors allow the screen to detect touches from the watch hand with a higher degree of granularity, thus allowing for the detection of, e.g., back of the hand, knuckle or nail touches [7].

S3: Interaction Volume. The orientation and acceleration of the watch hand can be used for expressive input, adaptive user interfaces or even mid-air gestures. Furthermore, by combining three-dimensional spatial interaction with touches from the non-watch hand, applications and interaction techniques can support advanced scenarios. Examples include navigation in three-dimensional applications, game input, gestural interaction, and gradual transitions of UI elements between devices [23].

Joint Output Space

When using the watch and interactive surface, the combination of both displays creates an output space that can be used in three configurations:

O1: Output on interactive display. The output of the interaction technique or application is shown only on the display of the interactive screen, and not on the watch. This configuration can support scenarios in which the watch is used purely as an input sensor (such as, e.g., detecting how the watch hand is touching the screen [7]) or when user-specific personalized user interface elements are shown on the display [37] based on touch input.

O2: Output on watch display. The output of the interaction with the interactive display is only shown on the small watch display. This setup can be used to provide a private or contextual view (such as, e.g., a peephole metaphor on a static map) of the data shown on the interactive surface [37].

O3: Output distributed across displays. The output or feedback of the interaction between both devices is distributed or shared across both displays [37]. This configuration allows for scenarios in which both the interactive display and the watch display are updated to reflect or visualize cross-device interactions.

Temporal Synchronized Interaction

User actions in this interaction space combine input and output spaces of both devices. By performing temporally sequenced touches, postures and gestures, users can express input and interact with the dual setup. *Temporal interactions* provide users with a fine-grained distributed interaction framework. Interaction designers can combine touches, postures or gestures in any arbitrary sequence. *WatchConnect* is designed to support the prototyping of temporal interactions.

TOOLKIT

To mitigate the challenges in designing and prototyping watch-centric cross-device interaction, we present the *WatchConnect* toolkit. The major goal of the toolkit is to provide *a fast event-driven platform* for *rapid prototyping* of *watch-centric cross-device interaction techniques and applications*. The *WatchConnect* toolkit is composed of two parts: (i) a flexible and extendable hardware platform that emulates a smartwatch, and (ii) a software platform providing user interface components and a rich set of input and output events and gestures, based on default sensor mappings. The toolkit is integrated with an existing visual user interface design tool (WPF Visual Studio) to support a rich set of existing UI components and framework, and existing platforms for rapid hardware prototyping (Phidgets [44] and Arduino [45]). In this section, we provide an overview of the architecture and components of the toolkit.

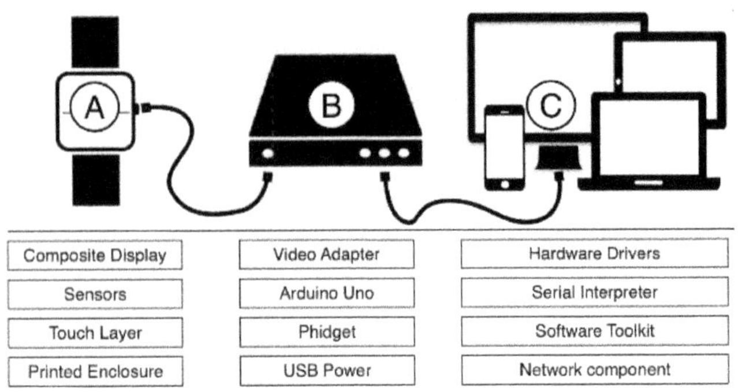

Figure 2. An overview of the *WatchConnect* toolkit.

Hardware

The *WatchConnect* toolkit is built around a wired *prototyping watch*, a smart watch emulator (Figure 2A and Figure 3) that is composed of a miniature display, a number of touch and motion sensors, and a microprocessor integrated into a form factor that *resembles a smart watch*. Using a physical cable, the *prototyping watch* is connected to the base station (Figure 2B) which converts and sends the data from the sensors and screen over a USB cable to the development computer (e.g., tablet or a large interactive surface) that runs the emulator software as well as the main toolkit (Figure 2C).

The default *prototyping watch* (Figure 3) is built around the Arduino platform and contains a light sensor, two infrared proximity sensors, an 8 channel capacitive touch sensor, a six-axis MEMS motion tracker (gyro + accelerometer), an RGB led, a flexible force sensing potentiometer and a 2 inch TFT display. The hardware components are soldered on a PCB, which slides into the 3D printed enclosure that is mounted on a wristband. Because of this setup, developers can easily extend the design with additional sensors, reconfigure the layout of the sensors or even redesign the existing watch hardware. Although the default watch uses Arduino, the toolkit also supports Phidgets to allow for fast plug and play prototyping (but somewhat bulkier components) without the need to write code for the hardware emulator.

The base station, which is connected to the development computer device using a USB and a VGA cable, consists of an Arduino microprocessor, a Phidgets interface kit, a USB power supply and VGA to component converter. All sensors are connected to either the Arduino or Phidget interface kit, which push the sensor readings over a serial protocol to the master device. The VGA converter converts the screen output from the development computer into a component signal, which is shown on the miniature display. To allow the software toolkit to analyze sensor data, a structured data exchange protocol is used which is composed of three parts: (i) a header that describes the sensor, (ii) the body that contains the sensor readings and (iii) the closing symbol that signifies the end of a package.

Figure 3. The Arduino-based watch probe with sensors.

Software

The toolkit's software architecture consists of six modules (Figure 4): (i) an *interface* library that includes a runtime and UI framework for the watch, (ii) an *input* library, providing touch, gesture and tracking input, (iii) a *hardware* and (iv) *processing* layer that abstracts the hardware and machine learning into events and gestures, (v) a *network* library that wraps REST and web socket services around the watch runtime and (vi) a *tools* library that provides applications to inspect and calibrate raw sensor data. In this section, we provide more details on the different modules.

Toolkit.Interface

The *WatchRuntime* is the central object of the toolkit in which all other toolkit components are merged into a single runtime environment that is used by developers to create a new watch application. The runtime, that can be configured and setup by using the *WatchConfiguration*, initiates all input, sensor management, processing and output into a watch window. When the hardware base station and watch probe are connected, the *Window Manager* of the runtime will push the watch window to the probe. If no hardware is connected, the runtime launches a native window to show the output. Watch applications can be designed using standard c# Windows Presentation Foundation (WPF) components in Visual Studio and the Expression Blend UI designer.

The only requirement for compatibility with *WatchConnect* is that watch applications are designed as user controls that inherit from the WatchVisual class, provided by the toolkit. Applications can be added and launched in the runtime by simply adding them as a new visual. Internally, the runtime manages all applications using a *WatchManager* that provides developers with a basic operating system-like environment to swap out watch applications. Through the *WatchRuntime,* the developer can access high level abstract gesture, touch and tracking events, which can easily be integrated into the interface design. Although we expect that most developers' needs reside in this high level abstraction space, we will later show how developers can make use of all lower level layers, right down to the hardware.

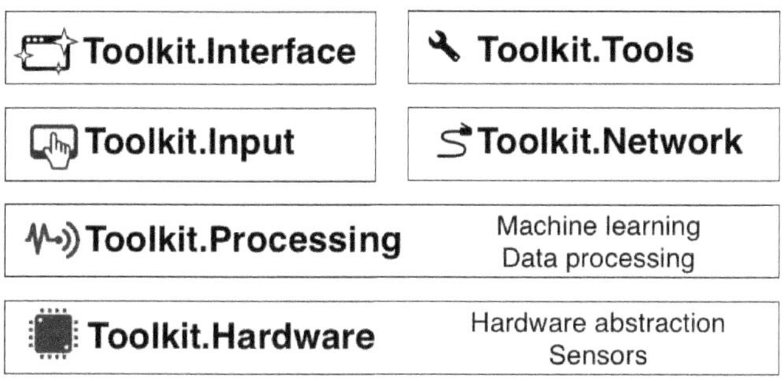

Figure 4: The architecture of the *WatchConnect* software.

Toolkit.Input

The input module provides three built-in input managers: a touch manager, gesture manager and tracker manager. First, the *TouchManager* encapsulates all "*on the device touch sensors*" - such as the *SlideTouch* device for the wristband, and a BevelTouch device - and presents the developer with high-level events including *TouchDown*, *TouchUp* and *TouchDoubleTap* events but also more complex and specialized events such as, e.g., *SliderDown*, *SliderUp* or *BevelMultiGrab*. Second, the *GestureManager* encapsulates "*above the device sensors*" – such as a light sensor and infrared proximity sensors, and tracks the internal state of the sensors using configurable thresholds and gesture detection algorithms to detect higher level gestures and postures. The abstract gesture events accessible in this manager include *SwipeLeft*, *SwipeRight*, *HoldLeft*, *HoldRight* and *Cover*. Finally, the *TrackerManager* encapsulates all the "*interaction via internal sensors*" such as the accelerometer, gyroscope and magnetometer. Similarly to the other managers, the *TrackerManager* monitors the internal state of the sensors and presents the developer with abstract high-level gestures or postures. These include an abstract IMU representation that includes the raw acceleration data, the world acceleration data, the angular motion, magnetic data and the yaw, pitch and roll. Using machine learning methods (defined in the *Toolkit.Processing* module), the manager can also detect gestures and postures that are defined by the developer who can provide training data and labels to the manager through the *WatchConfiguration.* This data can be collected using the data capture tool (provided in the *Toolkit.Tools* module). The gesture detection events provide users with the detected label as well as the probability and score of the detection. All three managers provide access to raw fused sensor data and can easily be extended by developers who can add new sensors, create new events or even add new managers (e.g., for "*on the skin sensors*"). Finally, each manager has a built-in simulator that allows developers to trigger events using simulated input such as a 3D controller or simulated data.

Toolkit.Hardware

The toolkit operates using an abstract HardwarePlatform, which can be an Arduino, Phidget or any other hardware platform that supports the *WatchConnect* protocol. The hardware module provides low level plug and play serial port management and allows managers to hook into the serial data loop to filter for specific data packets. Individual sensors are created and initiated in the managers, but use the packet definition to internally update their values. Although the toolkit supports a wide variety in sensors, there are four high-level abstract sensors: touch sensor, multi-touch sensor, proximity sensors and an IMU. These can represent a wide range of low level sensors ranging from flexible linear force resistant potentiometers to multi-channel capacitive sensors, various types of IMUs, and light and distance sensors. Although the managers provide high level events, developers can add custom lower level events directly to the sensor in order to listen or monitor changes in the internal values. Every sensor instance has an internal dynamic event mechanism that allows programmers to define events with a custom condition, which is checked and triggered from the internal value update function. This is achieved by allowing developers to inject methods into the execution body of the sensor. Finally, if new sensors are added to the setup, developers can add a new and custom hardware packet listener to the managers. This packet listener can be included in an existing manager, a newly defined manager or be used directly inside the existing watch application setup.

Toolkit.Processing

To support gesture, posture and pattern recognition, the Toolkit.Processing module provides a number of machine learning algorithms and data structures, that are built using the Accord framework and are integrated into the toolkit. The processing module includes a dynamic decision tree generator and a dynamic time warping (DTW) template engine that both use the training data and labels provided in the WatchConfiguration. The toolkit will use the training data to generate internal structures that are used by the managers to match recorded templates (e.g., for "*above the device*" proximity sensors) or monitor for gestures inside a time window.

Toolkit.Network

To allow multiple watches (connected to the same or multiple master computer devices) to interact with each other, the toolkit includes a network module that provides a websocket service that wraps the WatchRuntime and exposes all events over a real-time data connection. The module also includes *Bonjour Discovery* services to allow for zero-configuration networking support and broadcasting of watch addresses. It also provides a number of abstractions to distribute and share descriptions of the watch applications. The network module distributes watch data, meaning that each watch renders the data locally if new data is received from other watches.

Toolkit.Tools

To support developers in debugging and using the software framework, the toolkit includes a number of tools. First, the InputVisualizer provides developers with a number of visualizations that present the raw sensor data and allow for the testing of the machine learning and pattern matching data. Second, the DataRecorder provides a visual interface to record sensor data. Developers can select the data, sample rate and file location of the captured data. The recorder also allows developers to label the data as it is being recorded.

CROSS-DEVICE INTERACTION TECHNIQUES

To demonstrate the *functionality* and test the *feasibility* and *applicability* of the toolkit for the design of cross-device applications, we present five different interaction techniques implemented in realistic applications. The implementations of all applications and techniques use only the standard toolkit components, events and machine learning of the toolkit and do not include any specialized code or external tools. Table 1 provides an overview of the applications (with lines of code), and how the applications utilize the input and output of the interaction space. All applications were designed using a drag and drop editor for all UI elements, with minimal background code to link the UI to the underlying toolkit through high level objects and events. Although all applications are demonstrated on a laptop with interactive touchscreen, these techniques and applications are also usable and suitable for tablets and large horizontal or vertical surfaces. The purpose of these example applications is to demonstrate the types of advanced applications that can be constructed using only default components of the toolkit. Although these applications can be built using other methods (as demonstrated in [7,24,40]), these include custom hardware design, machine learning and other advanced computer science skills that many interaction designers do not have.

Application 1: Data Transfer

One of the core problems in multi-device information spaces is the fast, intuitive and easy transfer of files and resources across different devices [23]. A body of previous work (e.g., [23,34,36]) has explored how information can be seamlessly transferred across devices. These techniques can be expanded to smartwatches that have the potential to become *wearable mediating storage devices* that allow users to easily move their personal information to any display or device on hand. The *touch and swipe* technique allows users to connect their smartwatch to a display and use a mid-air swipe gesture to send information to the display. Users first touch the display with the watch hand to create a connection between the two devices. After the watch hand touch is recognized and the user touches an empty space, the user interface reveals a colored rectangle that is filled up over a period of two seconds. The color represents the active information on the watch, and the filling of the rectangle visualizes the time window in which the user can perform gestures to move the resource to the display. If the time window passes, the system dismisses the watch connection and treats the touch as a normal touch input. If the user performs a left to right swipe during the time window, the resource on the watch is sent to the display and shown as a touch-enabled resource (Figure 5A-B). To select which resources to send to the display, the user can use the wristband touch sensor to scroll between the different resources stored on the watch.

Application	Lines of Code	Watch			Screen			Output		
		W1: Touch	W2: Above	W3: 3D Move	S1: Identify user	S2: Multi touch	S3: 3D Space	O1: W feedback	O2: S feedback	O3: Distr. UI
Data transfer	164	•	•		•	•		•	•	•
Privacy	50			•	•			•	•	•
Navigation	98	•	•		•			•	•	•
Reading	132	•		•	•	•			•	•
UI distribution	47				•		•		•	

Table 1. Five example applications with their lines of code and how they use the interaction space.

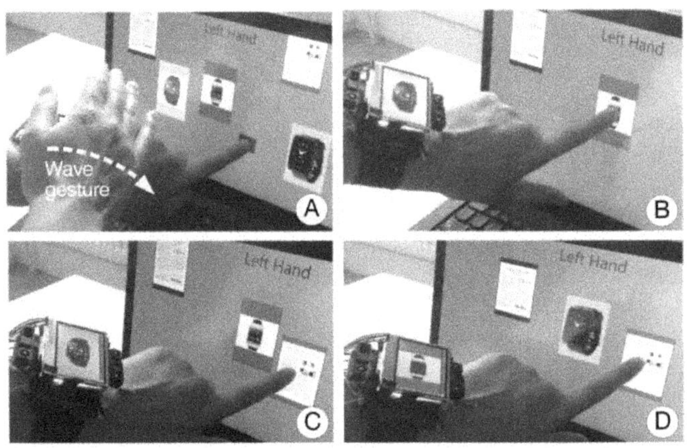

Figure 5. Users can perform gestures to move information between the display and the watch (A-B). The UI reveals part of the resource in the form of a color and shape (C-D).

If the user touches an existing resource on the display, the watch will update the UI to reveal that the watch can receive the resource, by showing a colored border on the right side of the watch (Figure 5 C-D). If the user performs a right-to-left swipe during the reveal time window, the resource is removed from the display and sent to the watch. When interacting with the resources on the surface, the UI can distinguish between left hand and right hand touches. As a consequence the UI only offers time windows to send information between devices, if a touch is linked to the watch hand.

The application leverages the entire software stack of the *WatchConnect* toolkit and was built in only 164 lines of code in a single class. It uses the built-in gesture recognizer to detect the watch hand. The UI elements are simply relocated between the watch runtime and the full screen application.

The different type of touch inputs (watch hand, non-watch hand) are channeled through events and coupled directly to the UI. The input layer on the watch automatically captures touch input on the bevel and updates the UI on the watch.

Figure 6. Users log in with the non-watch hand (A) or use the index finger or flat hand to show the password on the watch or screen (B-C). Users reset the password using the knuckle (D).

Application 2: Privacy and Password Access

The next technique facilitates access to highly private data such as passwords, bank account data or personal email. The *pose and touch* interaction technique provides users with a rich set of interactive capabilities to enter or correct a password field. Similar to the previous technique, the watch is paired to the display by touching the screen. However, in this case, the screen will monitor the posture of the hand at the moment of touching the screen. This means that the screen cannot only detect if the watch hand is touching the screen but also with which part of the hand (similarly to [7,13]). Touching the button with the non-watch hand validates the password and provides appropriate feedback (Figure 6A). The user can reveal the content of the hidden password field on the watch display, by touching the button with the index finger of the watch hand (Figure 6B), or on the touchscreen, by touching the button with the flat watch hand (Figure 6C). Users can reset the password field by touching the button with the knuckle of the watch hand (Figure 6D).

The application uses the gesture recognizer to distinguish between four different hand postures. Each posture is pushed to the UI as a different event, allowing the UI code to simply switch states and push the correct UI to the watch runtime or full screen application. This example was built in 50 lines of code and allows developers to focus only on the UI.

Application 3: Supporting Map Navigation

Interacting with maps often requires users to modify the view, find a location, or start route planning. Most maps currently provide little support for using additional devices to expand or distribute the view on the map. The *touch and push* interaction technique allows users to modify a custom secondary view on the display of the smartwatch, while using the interactive touchscreen for an overview of the general environment they want to explore. After touching the screen with the watch hand, the maps on both displays are synchronized (Figure 7A). The watch map has a default zoom level that is twice that of the main map. This allows users to quickly glance at the watch for more details as they explore the map. By touching the bevel of the watch, users can zoom in and out of the customized view, or toggle the watch map between a satellite view or the traditional map view (Figure 7C). When users interact with the map on the touchscreen, the map on the watch follows the movement, thus keeping both views synchronized. When users explore the customized view on the watch in more detail, they can synchronize the main map to that of the watch by using the *touch and swipe* gestures (Figure 7D). Finally, for selecting small targets, such as placing pushpins or route marks, the display of the watch can be used as a scope to zoom and find the exact location (Figure 7B). The user can touch the screen and press the left bevel of the watch to mark the point on the main map.

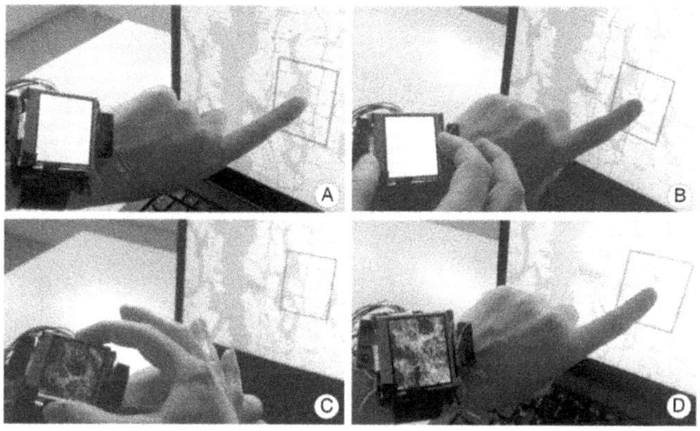

Figure 7. The watch screen shows a mini map (A), and allows users to zoom (B), change view (C) or mark locations (D).

This example was built in 98 lines of code, and utilizes the input layer to channel input from above and on the watch probe to the main interface on the surface. The application uses the temporal events to synchronize views between the watch runtime and main application, but integrates with a standard Bing maps component available in WPF / C#.

Application 4: Support Active Reading Applications

With the increasing availability of touch-enabled devices, active reading applications integrate new forms of touch-based interaction. The *gesture and touch* interaction techniques support a range of input techniques designed to create a fluid active reading application. In this application, the non-watch hand is used for *passive* browsing and reading, while the watch hand is used for *active* editing. Users can simply scroll through the text by performing on-screen swipe gestures using the non-watch hand (Figure 8A). By touching the bevel of the watch, users can browse through the menu items, thus, changing the selected option, which determines the effect of touching the screen with the watch hand (Figure 8B). The finger of the watch hand thus becomes *a reconfigurable instrument* that can be used for basic annotation with a black pen (Figure 8C), painting with a translucent brush (Figure 8D), marking text with a yellow marker (seen in Figure 8E) or as an eraser. Users can use the knuckle of the watch hand to select and copy text to a clipboard (Figure 8F).

This example was built in 132 lines of code, and again leverages the ML and processing features of the toolkit to augment a basic e-reader with advanced gestural interactions. The recognizer of the toolkit channels the recognized labels through events to the UI, which can simply be updated. Similar to all other examples, the UI itself is designed using drag and drop WPF C# components available in the Visual Studio IDE. *WatchConnect* simply connects the gestures and sensors of the watch to the already existing UI components.

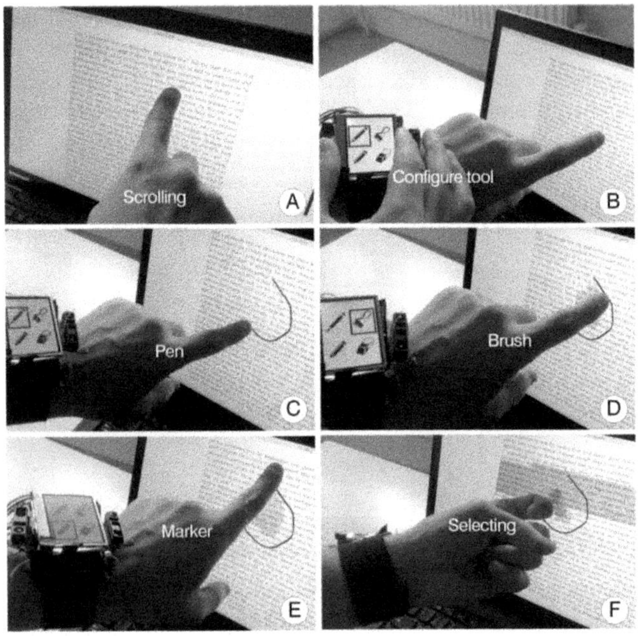

Figure 8. Users can browse text with the non-watch hand (A), configure the watch hand (B) into a pen (C), pencil (D), markers (E) or use the knuckle to select text (F).

Application 5: User Interface Beaming

One important research challenge in cross-device information spaces is how user interface elements can be seamlessly moved between different connected devices. Prior work has proposed the notion of "*user interface beaming*" [24] for mixed reality environments, or the flashlight metaphor [6] for transferring user interface elements from one device to another. Smartwatches can play a mediating role in *defining*, *exchanging* and *using* interface components or data. In this *touch and beam* technique, a UI element is initially only shown on a watch. After connecting the watch to an interactive surface by touching the display, the user interface is sent to that bigger display, to provide a bigger space for the output and utilize the potentially more advanced features provided by that device. E.g., an incoming phone call on a smart watch (Figure 9A) is simply transferred to a bigger display with better sound and camera by touching the display and connecting the watch. The hand acts like a flashlight that beams the interface on a larger canvas (Figure 9B), thus, increasing the interaction space for the user interfaces.

This example was built with 47 lines of code and uses the layout engine of the watch runtime to relay UI components based on synchronized event triggers. Designers do not need to define a multi-device context but can simply rely on the toolkit to move UI elements between the watch runtime and the main surface application.

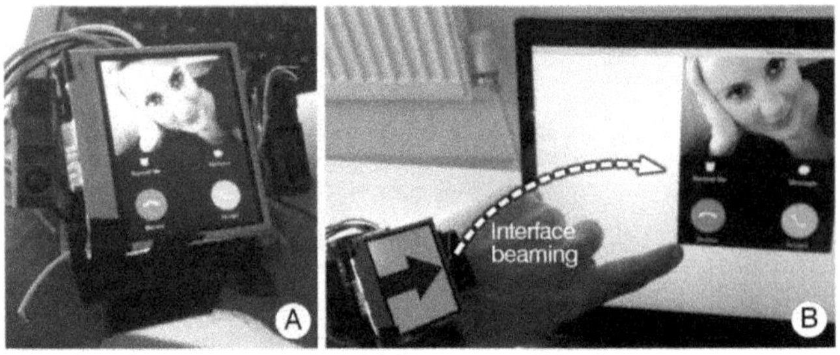

Figure 9. UI elements (A) can be beamed to the surface (B).

DISCUSSION

Designing, prototyping and testing cross-device interaction techniques with smartwatches is a complex task. To mitigate these challenges, we introduced *WatchConnect*, which uses a watch prototyping emulator to provide developers with a platform for the rapid design and prototyping of cross-device interaction techniques. Developers can create their own sensor and hardware configurations and use the software framework for easy and fast access to those hardware designs. In this section, we thematically compare *WatchConnect* to other approaches using Olsen's framework [31].

Problem Not Previously Solved

Commercial smartwatch APIs (such as [41,42,43]) provide limited support for existing hardware and single screen user interfaces. These APIs are designed to provide a *path of least resistance* towards specific UIs, but are not designed to explore novel interaction techniques and alternative designs. In contrast, *WatchConnect* allows designers to experiment, build and evaluate a range of different hardware designs, interaction techniques and gestural cross-device applications without any knowledge on distributed computing, hardware development and interfacing, data processing and sensor fusion, machine learning and networked setups. With the use of smartwatches and other mobile and wearable devices, providing tool support for designing UIs across an ecology of devices, becomes increasingly important and relevant.

Earlier cross-device UI toolkits – such as HydraScope [14], Conductor [10], or XDStudio [27] – lowered the threshold for developing applications spanning the ecology of devices. *WatchConnect* builds on top of these toolkits, and extends this work with a specialized support and focus on smartwatch specific interaction techniques, support for diverse hardware platforms, custom sensor mappings or creation of watch-centric gestural interactions. The toolkit also draws from previous work in watch-centric cross-device applications (such as Duet [7], UI Beaming [24] and SleeD [40]) to generalize these approaches and allow for rapid prototyping of complex cross-device interaction techniques using different display sizes and novel sensor input.

Reduce Solution Viscosity
Compared to other methods to develop watch-centric cross-device applications, *WatchConnect* dramatically reduces development viscosity [31] by providing a flexible architecture that allows for expressive leverage. The example applications demonstrate the range of scenarios that are supported by the toolkit. By moving all complex processes into high-level objects and events, designers can create complex gestural interactions with little overhead. However, designers with expert skills can leverage the toolkit and access, modify and create complex low level sensor mappings, custom hardware protocols and advanced machine learning approaches. Furthermore, the layered architecture allows for potential replacement of the UI layer with another existing cross-device toolkit (such as HydraScope [14], Conductor [10], or XDStudio [27]) to leverage existing multi-device features, while still using the watch-centric features of *WatchConnect*.

Empowering New Design Participants
Without adequate toolkit support, exploring watch-centric cross-device systems remained the domain of designers with highly specialized computer science skills. This is reflected in the very few watch-centric cross-device systems so far, and the number of simulation techniques used (e.g., using smartphones as watch proxies or relying on Wizard of Oz approaches). *WatchConnect* focuses in particular on making this emerging technology accessible to new, non-expert programmers. Complex applications and interaction techniques that support gestures, postures and multi-device synchronization can be designed in a short period of time without in-depth knowledge of distributed computing or machine learning. The toolkit lowers the threshold [26] for beginning the exploration of cross-device smartwatch applications, and it allows designers to focus their efforts on creative design solutions [9] for the actual cross-device user experience and interface design. In particular, the software abstracts sensor input from *above*, *on* and *in* the watch into abstract high-level events and objects for easier configuration and use. While an in-depth study of developers applying the toolkit in practice is part of our future work, we see *WatchConnect* as a fundamental step towards rapid iterative smartwatch prototyping, facilitating the exploration of novel cross-device behaviors.

Power in Combination
WatchConnect combines distributed UIs, machine learning, hardware management, data processing and simulation into one toolkit. Each building block is highly decoupled, allowing for the design of new layers or the inclusion of other approaches. The basic building blocks of *WatchConnect* can be used in complex temporal and spatial sequences that provide a power by combination [31]. *WatchConnect* integrates with C# / WPF to support a major and stable development platform that provides designer-level abstractions and a flexible and broad UI framework with numerous tools and libraries [9]. Once the design of the interaction technique or application transcends the prototyping phase and is verified and validated, designers can move the design to more permanent platforms, using standard SDKs and commercial hardware.

Generality
Using five example applications that include both novel and replications of state of the art interaction techniques, we demonstrate the versatility and generality of the toolkit, as well as the expressivity of the building block components [31]. The fundamental limitation but also strength of this toolkit is that it is based around a watch prototyping emulator and not a real – and wireless – watch. We argue that for the rapid prototyping and creative stage of the design process this is an acceptable trade-off. It brings the advantage that developers are not bound by existing hardware limitations or existing device designs, but can design and use their own setup to develop compelling and forward looking cross-device interaction techniques. We expect that in the near future more accessible smartwatch hardware platforms will emerge and future versions of the toolkit could support some of these smartwatches for prototyping. Furthermore, an in-depth testing of the toolkit and its expressive power with developers can provide us further insights into the prototyping process with smartwatch cross-device applications.

CONCLUSION
WatchConnect allows for rapid prototyping of smartwatch-centric cross-device applications and interaction techniques, using custom hardware designs and a software framework that removes complex machine learning, sensor fusion and hardware management into high level objects and events that are integrated with an existing drag and drop UI framework. The toolkit reduces development complexity and lowers the threshold for developers to design for complex device ecologies using a smartwatch as mediating instrument. The toolkit allows for future explorations of a wide range of novel multi-device interaction techniques, hardware designs and collaborative multi-surface environments. Future work includes integrating *WatchConnect* with other cross-device toolkits and smartwatch platforms to support existing frameworks and a wider set of setups and development platforms.

ACKNOWLEDGMENTS
This work was supported by the EU Marie Curie Network iCareNet under grant number 264738 and ICRI Cities. Thanks to Michael Nebeling, Sarah Gallacher and our anonymous reviewers for their feedback and helpful suggestions for the improvement of the manuscript.

REFERENCES
1. Ashbrook, D., Lyons, K., and Starner, T. An investigation into round touchscreen wristwatch interaction. *Proc. of ACM MobileHCI'08*.
2. Badam, S.K. and Elmqvist, N. PolyChrome: A Cross-Device Framework for Collaborative Web Visualization. *Proc. of ACM ITS'14*.
3. Baudisch, P. and Chu, G. Back-of-device interaction allows creating very small touch devices. *Proc. of ACM CHI'09*.
4. Blasko, G. and Feiner, S. An interaction system for watch computers using tactile guidance and bidirectional segmented strokes. *Proc. of IEEE ISWC 2004*.

5. Butler, A., Izadi, S., and Hodges, S. SideSight: multi-touch interaction around small devices. *Proc. of ACM UIST'08*.
6. Cao, X. and Balakrishnan, R. Interacting with dynamically defined information spaces using a handheld projector and a pen. *Proc. of ACM UIST'09*.
7. Chen, X., Grossman, T., Wigdor, D.J., and Fitzmaurice, G. Duet: exploring joint interactions on a smart phone and a smart watch. *Proc. of ACM CHI'14*.
8. Funk, M., Sahami, A., Henze, N., and Schmidt, A. Using a touch-sensitive wristband for text entry on smart watches. *ACM CHI'14 EA*.
9. Greenberg, S. Toolkits and interface creativity. *Multimedia Tools and Applications*, (2007).
10. Hamilton, P. and Wigdor, D.J. Conductor: enabling and understanding cross-device interaction. *Proc. of ACM CHI'14*.
11. Hardy, R. and Rukzio, E. Touch & interact: touch-based interaction of mobile phones with displays. *Proc. of ACM MobileHCI'08*.
12. Harrison, C. and Hudson, S.E. Abracadabra: wireless, high-precision, and unpowered finger input for very small mobile devices. *Proc. of ACM UIST'09*.
13. Harrison, C., Schwarz, J., and Hudson, S.E. TapSense: enhancing finger interaction on touch surfaces. *Proc. of ACM UIST'11*.
14. Hartmann, B., Beaudouin-Lafon, M., and Mackay, W.E. HydraScope: creating multi-surface meta-applications through view synchronization and input multiplexing. *Proc. of ACM PerDis'13*.
15. Heikkinen, T., Goncalves, J., Kostakos, V., Elhart, I., and Ojala, T. Tandem Browsing Toolkit: Distributed Multi-Display Interfaces with Web Technologies. *Proc. of ACM PerDis'14*.
16. Hinckley, K., Ramos, G., Guimbretiere, F., Baudisch, P., and Smith, M. Stitching: pen gestures that span multiple displays. *Proc. of ACM AVI'04*.
17. Hinckley, K. Synchronous gestures for multiple persons and computers. *Proc. of ACM UIST'03*.
18. Huang, D.-Y., Tsai, M.-C., Tung, Y.-C., et al. TouchSense: expanding touchscreen input vocabulary using different areas of users' finger pads. *Proc. of ACM CHI'14*.
19. Kim, J., He, J., Lyons, K., and Starner, T. The gesture watch: A wireless contact-free gesture based wrist interface. *Proc. of IEEE ISWC'07*,.
20. Knibbe, J., Martinez Plasencia, D., Bainbridge, C., et al. Extending interaction for smart watches: enabling bimanual around device control. *ACM CHI'14 EA*.
21. Laput, G., Xiao, R., Chen, X., Hudson, S.E., and Harrison, C. Skin buttons: cheap, small, low-powered and clickable fixed-icon laser projectors. *Proc. of ACM UIST'14*.
22. Lyons, K., Nguyen, D., Ashbrook, D., and White, S. Facet: a multi-segment wrist worn system. *Proc. of ACM UIST'12*.
23. Marquardt, N., Ballendat, T., Boring, S., Greenberg, S., and Hinckley, K. Gradual engagement: facilitating information exchange between digital devices as a function of proximity. *Proc. of ACM ITS'12*.
24. Mayer, S. and Sörös, G. User Interface Beaming - Seamless Interaction with Smart Things using Personal Wearable Computers". *Proc. of IEEE BSN 2014*.
25. Merrill, D., Kalanithi, J., and Maes, P. Siftables: towards sensor network user interfaces. *Proc. of ACM TEI'07*.
26. Myers, B., Hudson, S.E., and Pausch, R. Past, present, and future of user interface software tools. *TOCHI '00*.
27. Nebeling, M., Mintsi, T., Husmann, M., and Norrie, M. Interactive development of cross-device user interfaces. *Proc. of ACM CHI'14*.
28. Nebeling, M., Teunissen, E., Husmann, M., and Norrie, M.C. XDKinect: development framework for cross-device interaction using kinect. *Proc. of ACM EICS'14*.
29. Oakley, I. and Lee, D. Interaction on the edge: offset sensing for small devices. *Proc. of ACM CHI'14*.
30. Olberding, S., Yeo, K.P., Nanayakkara, S., and Steimle, J. AugmentedForearm: exploring the design space of a display-enhanced forearm. *Proc. of ACM AH'13*.
31. Olsen Jr, D.R. Evaluating user interface systems research. *Proc. of ACM UIST'07*.
32. Pasquero, J., Stobbe, S.J., and Stonehouse, N. A haptic wristwatch for eyes-free interactions. *Proc. of ACM CHI'11*.
33. Perrault, S.T., Lecolinet, E., Eagan, J., and Guiard, Y. Watchit: simple gestures and eyes-free interaction for wristwatches and bracelets. *Proc. of ACM CHI'13*.
34. Rekimoto, J. Pick-and-drop: a direct manipulation technique for multiple computer environments. *Proc. of ACM UIST'97*.
35. Rekimoto, J. Gesturewrist and gesturepad: Unobtrusive wearable interaction devices. *Proc. of IEEE ISWC'01*.
36. Schmidt, D., Chehimi, F., Rukzio, E., and Gellersen, H. PhoneTouch: a technique for direct phone interaction on surfaces. *Proc. of ACM UIST'10*.
37. Schmidt, D., Seifert, J., Rukzio, E., and Gellersen, H. A cross-device interaction style for mobiles and surfaces. *Proc. of ACM DIS'12*.
38. Xiao, R., Laput, G., and Harrison, C. Expanding the input expressivity of smartwatches with mechanical pan, twist, tilt and click. *Proc. of ACM CHI'14*.
39. Yang, J. and Wigdor, D. Panelrama: enabling easy specification of cross-device web applications. *Proc. of ACM CHI'14*.
40. Von Zadow, U., Büschel, W., Langner, R., and Dachselt, Raimund. SleeD: Using a Sleeve Display to Interact with Touch-sensitive Display Walls. *Proc. of ACM ITS'14*.
41. Pebble. http://developer.getpebble.com.
42. Sony Watch. http://developer.sony.com/.
43. Apple Watch. http://apple.com/watch/.
44. Phidgets. http://phidgets.com.
45. Arduino. http://arduino.cc.

It's About Time: Smartwatches as Public Displays

Jennifer Pearson, Simon Robinson, Matt Jones
Future Interaction Technology Lab, Swansea University, SA2 8PP, UK
{ j.pearson, s.n.w.robinson, matt.jones } @swansea.ac.uk

ABSTRACT
Current uses of smartwatches are focused solely around the wearer's content, viewed by the wearer alone. When worn on a wrist, however, watches are often visible to many other people, making it easy to quickly glance at their displays. We explore the possibility of extending smartwatch interactions to turn personal wearables into more public displays. We begin opening up this area by investigating fundamental aspects of this interaction form, such as the social acceptability and noticeability of looking at someone else's watch, as well as the likelihood of a watch face being visible to others. We then sketch out interaction dimensions as a design space, evaluating each aspect via a web-based study and a deployment of three potential designs. We conclude with a discussion of the findings, implications of the approach and ways in which designers in this space can approach public wrist-worn wearables.

Author Keywords
Smartwatches; public displays; wearables; mobiles.

ACM Classification Keywords
H.5.2 User Interfaces: Input devices and strategies; Interaction styles; Screen design.

INTRODUCTION
In addition to being precise timekeeping devices, wristwatches have long been regarded as anything from high-end status symbols to must-have, colour-matched fashion accessories. Despite their personal nature, however, watches have also historically acted as a useful public information resource. For example, someone not wearing a watch might ask a passerby for the time, or even just discreetly glance at another person's wrist when in a room without a visible clock.

After a trend of consumers increasingly discarding watches in favour of phones or other mobile devices [7], we now see a potential reversal with the growing focus on the smartwatch. Consumers already have the ability to link their mobile phone with wearables such as the various Android Wear, Galaxy Gear, Apple or Pebble devices, and recent estimates suggest the overall smartwatch market could expand to several hundred million units by 2020 [16]. The functionality of these devices—with content and apps often just as feature-rich as on modern smartphones—now means we have access to a vast and rich set of information and services directly from our own wrists.

So far, these devices have been marketed as an extension of our personal information spaces – that is, the watch will display a condensed version of content that is available in full on a paired phone. Consider, for example, the promotional material for the Apple Watch, which focuses around terms such as *"personal," "intimate"* and *"discreet"* to describe its capabilities.[1] Unlike the displays on more private screens, however, information given on a wrist-worn device may often be in public view. We feel that this offers a great opportunity to create a new interaction space for the presentation of content to others in close proximity to the wearer. In this research, then, we introduce the novel possibility of designing such wearables for spectators [21], turning the once inherently personal watch face into a wrist-worn public display. We imagine the display showing a range of content from the web, from the wearer, or from (and to) other people who are standing close by.

In the rest of this paper we set out our conceptualisation for this new area of personal-to-public wearables. As a first step, we explore whether the act of looking at other people's watches is socially acceptable, and whether this interaction is noticeable or disruptive in comparison to looking at one's own watch. We then investigate watch deportment via an observation study of postures and visibilities. These results are used to sketch a design space for this field, systematising five factors that will determine the way such displays are designed. We evaluate this design space in a further study that helps select the factors with the most value for current displays. We then describe three example use-case probes, which we prototype and assess in naturalistic user evaluations. Finally, we conclude with a discussion of the rich future of public personal displays.

BACKGROUND
The focus of this paper is around turning personal screens into publicly accessible information displays. While there has been much research into collaborative sharing of media by appropriating personal screens (e.g., [11, 12]), there has been surprisingly little in the area of private displays becoming public displays without direct user input. Existing research has focused around topics such as using private devices to control or place content on public displays (e.g., [4, 28]). Cheverst et al. [2], for example, allowed users who did not want their personal information placed online to leave awareness information on public screens outside their office doors. Schwarz et al. [24] moved closer to our aim with their work to automatically create large tiled displays from a collection of smaller devices. While their technology cannot be used on a single device, it is an

CHI '15, April 18–23, 2015, Seoul, Republic of Korea.

ACM 978-1-4503-3145-6/15/04...$15.00.
http://dx.doi.org/10.1145/2702123.2702247

[1] See: apple.com/watch/technology (accessed 6th Jan. 2015).

example of how personal screens can be used to create publicly accessible information displays. More related to our work, perhaps, is that of Harper and Taylor [8], whose Glancephone design let callers remotely "glance" at the person being called to see if they were available, via the camera of their phone. Similarly, in our design, the smartwatch of another person is adopted for a glancer's use, but in our case it becomes a display for any content, not just that of the wearer.

Wearable displays

A significant amount of research effort has been dedicated to personal wearable displays, with much of the focus being on providing information and services to the wearer themselves. Harrison et al. [9], for example, investigated wearable placement to ensure the quickest reaction time to visual stimuli. Of the seven different body locations evaluated, they concluded that, at least for personal use, the wrist is not only the fastest location, but also the most accurate (i.e., gave fewest errors).

The use of subtle cues on wearables to display information to the wearer has been seen in several forms for some time. Eye-q [3], for example, used peripheral LEDs mounted in eyewear to deliver discreet notifications. Other work has hinted at the possibility for more publicly visible wearables such as rings to display low-resolution information (using just three pixels) that only the wearer is able to interpret [1]. In our view, the combination of smartwatches and careful design could provide displays that are understandable by people other than the wearer in ways that are useful to both parties.

Wearable displays to provide information to others

The use of wearable displays to provide information to those other than the wearer has been touched upon previously, but usually in a more explicit manner. An early example of this is Falk and Björk [5]'s BubbleBadge, in the form of a brooch. The BubbleBadge was designed specifically to be a public wearable display, in full view of any others in the area. Falk and Björk also discuss three categories for the information provider: the wearer, the viewer, and the environment. We are interested in similar types of information source (as described later in our design space), but our approach differs to BubbleBadge's "in-your-face" scenario – our intention is to turn a personal wearable into a discreet form of public information access for those around the wearer.

Outside of HCI, public expressiveness has been studied in a range of areas, including fashion, performance and body art (see [10] for a survey), though primarily in the form of abstract and ambient displays, rather than the distinct types we explore. The value of publicly visible wearable displays for the benefit of spectators has also been explored in sport. Page and Moere [18], for example, developed a wearable system which aimed to enhance awareness and understanding of game-related data while engaging in group activities. Their TeamAwear jerseys were equipped with remotely controlled electroluminescent wires to display information such as individual fouls, scores and time alerts. Similar work on the use of wearables during group fitness activity includes Mauriello et al. [13]'s Social Fabric Fitness interface, which used eTextile screens on the back of runners' t-shirts to display information such as average pace, distance or duration to fellow runners in an attempt to increase awareness and motivate group fitness performance. Lastly, the LunarHelm [27] was an LED equipped bicycle helmet designed to provide bystanders with sensor data from the rider (e.g., for communication, expression or play). Its creators describe how wearable displays afford unique information access opportunities for those in close proximity to the wearer – a benefit we take advantage of in this work.

These sport-related examples, and other public wearables such as Waldemeyer [26]'s Twitter dress, make use of specially designed hardware (e.g., augmented helmets; eTextile displays etc.) to facilitate the behaviour they achieve. Our approach makes use of a form factor that many users already wear, however – the wristwatch. It is also worth noting here that none of these previous examples are intended for use by the wearer, as in all cases the screen is not physically visible to them. In contrast, our approach allows both public displays as well as personal displays to be offered by the same device.

How many people actually wear watches?

While media reports have regularly discussed the decline of wristwatches since the introduction of multi-function personal devices such as mobile phones,[2] market research suggests that the number of watch owners has actually remained static in recent years [15]. One study in particular, conducted by market research firm YouGov in 2011 [7], surveyed 1200 Americans about watch use, finding that 78 % owned one or more watches, and 41 % were wearing one at the time of asking. Now, with smartwatch sales increasing, it is reasonable to assume that the number of people wearing watches will either continue to remain static, as smartwatches replace or augment regular watches; or, their prevalence will increase as people resume wearing a watch with new capabilities beyond timekeeping.

The effects of personal technology on social interaction

Our focus in this paper is on the use of wearables as public, rather than private displays. It is important, therefore, to understand the extent to which such technology affects social interaction. The rise of digital wearables has generated a surge of research on the topic of social acceptability around their use. Przybylski and Weinstein [20] studied how personal mobile communication technology influences face-to-face interaction quality, demonstrating that its mere presence can interfere with social interaction, inhibiting the development of interpersonal closeness. Other investigations have focused primarily on visual appearances, such as attractiveness and comfort [6]; and, of course, on worries over how people will react to a new and possibly odd-looking wearable. It will take time for new designs and interaction methods to become socially acceptable (consider, for example, how Bluetooth headsets, now common, made wearers seem like they were talking to themselves [23]).

Some have opted to approach this issue by hiding interactions with wearables, attempting to convince passersby that the user is acting conventionally. The e-SUIT [25], for example, aimed to allow covert interactions with wearables without informing those nearby (e.g., via discreet watch notifications). Profita et al. [19] studied public wearable interactions from both social and cultural angles. With a focus on third-party attitudes

[2]E.g., bbc.co.uk/news/magazine-11634105 (accessed 6th Jan. 2015).

towards these interactions, they found that, culturally, Koreans had a higher preference for wearables that *"avoided making the user look weird or awkward"* than Americans, whose preference was for the devices to be easy to operate. Social acceptability implications of on-body actions and gestures have also been studied. Rico and Brewster [22], for example, investigated phone gestures, discovering that location and audience type had a significant impact on willingness to gesture. Similarly, McAtamney and Parker [14] studied the impact of a large head-mounted display on the conversation between two people. Non-active displays showed no effect, while active screens had a detrimental effect on the eye contact of the users in the study. While a head-mounted display is likely to be seen as more directly noticeable than a wrist-worn watch, the noticeability and perceived social impact of glancing at another person's watch during conversation are questions we investigate and report on later in this paper.

STUDY 1: THE IMPACT OF GLANCING

As a first step in assessing the viability of this new interaction area, we conducted a study to measure people's awareness of interactions with watches. Our prime focus was on whether looking at another person's watch during a conversation with them interrupted the flow of that conversation. We explored this via measuring both the perceived social acceptability of glancing at other people's watches, and also whether this action was actually noticeable or disruptive to conversation.

Primary group: public wearables

We recruited 18 participants (12F, 6M; aged 18–55) for nine 30 min paired sessions, during which one participant (the *glancer*) was prompted to look at a watch worn by the other (the *wearer*) several times without their knowledge.

Procedure

At the start of the study, participants were met separately, and led through an ethically-approved informed consent procedure. In each pair, one participant was randomly assigned to be the *glancer* and the other the *wearer*. The *wearer* was given a smartwatch to wear on their wrist (their choice of left or right), and told that the purpose of the study was to explore people's behaviours during everyday conversation, captured using the watch. They were then asked to sit at a table opposite the other participant, positioning their arm so that the watch face was visible. The *wearer* was intentionally *not* informed that the other participant would be looking at their watch.

The *glancer* was also given a smartwatch to wear on their left or right wrist, and was informed that our interest was around the impact of looking at watches during conversation. This participant was told that their secondary objective (after making conversation) was to look at the face of the other participant's watch whenever they felt their own watch vibrate. The *glancer* was asked not to mention their glancing task during the conversation unless the *wearer* asked them directly.

The primary task in the study was a short (5 min) conversation, observed by the researchers. We provided a list of example topics for participants to discuss during the study (including recent travel, work, study and news items), based on those used in [14]. Apart from the *glancer*'s instruction not to talk about their glancing task, there were no restrictions on conversation topic – participants were told that the example topics were merely suggestions and need not be followed if the conversation naturally diverged during the session. Two researchers observed the conversation from positions diagonally opposite each participant in order to record when the *glancer* looked at the other participant's watch, and note reactions and behaviours of each participant during the discussion. The vibration cue was sent automatically to the *glancer*'s watch at six intervals throughout the five-minute discussion session, and reactions were monitored by the observing researchers using an app linked to the smartwatch vibration trigger times. These intervals were randomly generated prior to the study, but were the same for every pair of participants. Both watches displayed only the current time for the duration of the conversation.

At the end of the discussion task, we performed a short semi-structured interview with the two participants. Each interview began by asking about the conversation flow, and whether anything had interrupted the discussion. The *wearer* was then directly asked whether they had noticed the *glancer* looking at the watch they were wearing. Intentionally not informing the *wearer* about the real purpose of the investigation was necessary to ensure an unbiased answer to this question (e.g., avoiding the *wearer* actively looking for watch glances from the other participant). Following this, the *wearer* was asked whether this action affected or interrupted the conversation, and the *glancer* for their perspective, such as whether they felt uncomfortable or embarrassed about checking the watch.

Participants were then asked to rate the extent to which they felt it is socially acceptable to look at (a) another person's watch; or, (b) their own watch, during a one-to-one conversation. Participants answered on a 5-point Likert-like scale from 1 (*"completely unacceptable"*) to 5 (*"completely acceptable"*). Finally, participants were asked whether they wore a watch themselves; if they had ever looked at other people's watches rather than their own; and, whether they had ever noticed other people looking at their watch. At the end of the study, each participant was compensated with £5 in return for their time.

Comparison group: personal wearables

To calibrate, we conducted a variant of the experiment to compare the effect of looking at another person's watch to the effect of looking at your own watch. We recruited 16 further participants (9F, 7M; aged 18–55) to follow a modified version of the procedure described above. In this study, only one participant wore a watch. When given a vibration cue, this participant looked at the watch on their own wrist, rather than that of the person they were talking to. As before, the other participant was told that we were investigating people's behaviours during everyday conversation, but no mention was made of the watch that their conversation partner would be wearing. All other aspects of the experiment followed the same procedure as described above.

Results

Of the 34 participants in both groups, 17 (50 %) said that they usually wore a watch, with 7 (20 %) wearing one occasionally, and the remaining 10 (30 %) never wearing a watch. 24

participants (71 %) said that they had looked at other people's watches to get the time, but only three participants (13 % of watch wearers) had noticed other people looking at their watch.

Turning now to the noticeability results. In the primary group, three participants (33 %) noticed the glancer looking at the watch that they themselves were wearing. In the comparison group, seven participants (88 %) noticed the glancer looking at their own watch. A Fisher's exact test on these values shows a significant result ($p < 0.05$), indicating that it is less noticeable to look at another person's watch than your own. Although ten participants over both groups noticed the other participant's watch glances, there were no noticeable reactions to this action (as measured by the observing researchers), and none of the participants brought up the glancing in their conversation.

The average rating for the social acceptability of looking another person's watch during a conversation was 3.32 out of 5 (s.d. 1.17), compared to 2.85 (s.d. 0.99) for looking at one's own watch. The difference between the two cases was not statistically significant (Wilcoxon signed-rank test, $p = 0.06$). However, looking at the differences between participants' ratings in more detail, it becomes apparent that in general participants felt that looking at another person's watch was more socially acceptable. That is, 15 participants (44 %) rated the acceptability of looking at another person's watch higher than looking at their own, while only 7 (21 %) said it was more acceptable to look at their own. 12 participants (35 %) saw no difference between the two cases.

This indication was supported by participants' comments. Several participants indicated that the implication of a glance at your own watch would depend on the situation (e.g., social vs. professional), but there were also many remarks about both the ease (*"it's so much easier looking at someone else's than yours"*) and acceptability (*"a quick glance is ok"*; *"I use other people's watches to tell the time instead of taking out my phone"*; *"it's a bit more unobtrusive"*) of looking at other people's watches. We believe—supported by observations, ratings, and participants' comments—these results show that it is a no more noticeable, unacceptable or even unusual practice to look at another person's watch rather than your own.

STUDY 2: WATCH FACE DEPORTMENT

The next aspect necessary in order to be able to define a design space for public watch displays is to understand the degree of visibility of watch faces in current everyday situations. We conducted a study to assess, in situations when a (non-smart) watch was visible, the degree to which watch faces could be seen by a bystander; and, in addition, to gather information on the most common deportments of these visible watches.

Procedure

We created a simple observation capturing app which was used for logging watch visibilities (as defined in Fig. 1) and positions (as shown in Table 1). Three researchers used the app over a period of seven weeks, classifying situations in which they saw people wearing a watch while engaged with others, either sitting down or standing still. People not wearing a watch were not logged. The places in which observations were captured included a wide range of homes, workplaces, third places and public spaces. For example, observations were logged in train stations, airport lounges, offices, beaches, cafés, meeting rooms, boats, public squares, restaurants, homes, hotels, visitor attractions, theatres and research laboratories. In order to be able to accurately compare visibilities, observations were logged from the perspective of a glancer positioned directly opposite the watch wearer. Each observation was classified as one of the following arm positions: by the side of the wearer; laid on a table; on the wearer's lap; by (or supporting) the wearer's head; folded arms; gesturing; in a pocket; and, any other position. Each observer followed the same classification procedure:

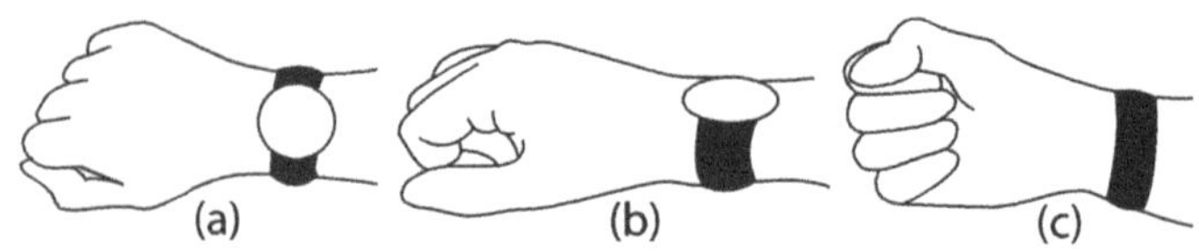

Figure 1. Visibility classifications used in the deportment study. (a) Full visibility: the watch face would be in direct view of a person sitting opposite the wearer, to the point where they would be able to read all the information displayed. (b) Partial visibility: the watch face would be partly visible to a person sitting opposite the wearer, but restricted due to, for example, display angle or clothing cover. A glancer would be able to see information on part of the screen, or distinguish a particular colour. (c) Not visible: a watch is clearly present, but a person sitting directly opposite the wearer will not be able to see any part of its face.

	Arm by side	Arm on table	Arm on lap	Arm by head	Folded arms	Arm gesturing	Hand in pocket	Other position
% Obs.	25	15	15	14	12	10	5	4

Table 1. Percentages of the 300 observations recorded in each position.

1. Select a visible area (e.g., café, platform concourse, etc.).
2. Systematically look around for people visibly wearing a watch who were engaged with at least one other person.
3. Log the visibility and deportment of the face of each watch.

Results

Over the 49-day study period, a total of 300 watch observations were captured in four European countries, over a diverse mix of international peoples and cultures. Observations spanned a wide time period (7 a.m. to 9:15 p.m.), and were captured on all seven days of the week. As can be seen from Table 1, which shows the number of observations of each deportment type that was captured, there are many different situations in which watch faces can be visible to others around the wearer.

Turning to visibility, 88 % of observations were of either fully visible (153 obs.; 51 %) or partially visible (112 obs.; 37 %) watches. Only 36 of the 300 people observed were holding the watch in a position where it was not at all visible. We did not notice any differences in positions or visibilities between times of day, days of the week, locations, cultures or countries.

Discussion – Study 2

The deportment results give a strong indication that when a person is wearing a watch that is visible, the face of that watch is likely to be able to be seen by a glancer. This is a valuable finding for the viability of future public watch displays.

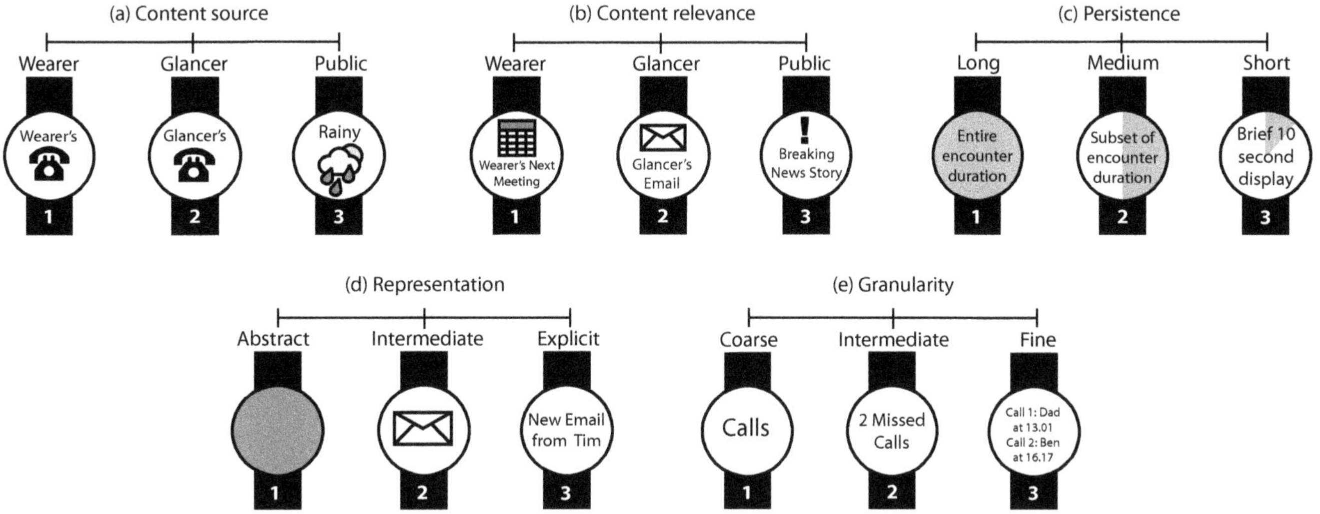

Figure 2. Content-oriented factors of the design space for public watch interactions, showing example displays of each type. Each of the five factors can be characterised on a sliding scale across the given dimension. Each scale is continuous, rather than being restricted to the three key delimiters, and allows any content-oriented aspect of the display to be described, as demonstrated later in Fig. 5. Labels (1, 2, 3) refer to the faces described in Table 2.

The positions that watch wearers' arms are held in will also be important in shaping designs in this space, as in many cases the position of a wearer's arm will directly affect the content that is displayed. While there are clearly many contextual factors that will affect a public watch display, the deportments observed in this study offer some guidance as to where different forms of displays are the most appropriate, and when.

Turning first to deciding where and when to show public watch content, the position, angle and orientation of the display will be important factors in choosing between showing information aimed at glancers or at the watch wearer themselves. When the watch is facing the wearer (supported by posture detection, a face recognition camera on the watch, or simply a tap on the screen) it might be most appropriate to default to showing the time, or other standard smartwatch content.

When the wearer's arm is on a table, by their head, or folded in front of them, there is scope for detailed, precise representations of content to be shown. When their arm is by their side, or on their lap, the screen is most likely to be only partially visible to a glancer, so these positions would perhaps be associated with abstract, iconic forms, or a low level of detail.

Arm positions and watch face visibilities will also influence the choice of display in ways that are less immediately apparent. For example, the length of time content is displayed for may be linked to externally measurable contextual variables, such as the time the watch has been held in a specific orientation (via the watch's accelerometer). Or, the distance of a glancer (via positional information or face recognition) might control the representation that is chosen, with more abstract displays (such as a single colour) used when the glancer is further away.

Other external factors, such as environmental conditions and wearer behaviours (e.g., sleeves entirely covering the display; putting hands in pockets) are clearly beyond a designer's control. However, they will directly affect the choice of both representation and granularity in many cases. For example, a watch that is only semi-visible would perhaps be most useful when displaying a coarse and abstract display, or a pictorial representation of the content. Similarly, a light sensor on the watch could influence both content duration and its representation for ease of interpretation in bright sunlight.

DESIGN SPACE: INTERACTION DIMENSIONS

Before being able to innovate in this novel space there are a number of important design factors to consider. Having explored both the acceptability and noticeability of public watch displays, and measured the real-world visibility and deportment of watches, we used these results to formalise a design space for public watch displays. We approached this by first generating an extensive set of sample design concepts covering all of the visibilities and deportments described in the previous section. These were then analysed to extract technical abstractions that systematise the properties of future designs in this space. Here, then, we present the set of interaction dimensions that we envisage will shape future public smartwatch displays. These factors revolve around the content that is displayed, and can be characterised on a scale across a dimension of its source, relevance, persistence, representation, or granularity, as illustrated in Fig. 2.

Throughout this section, we will be describing two personas (as in study 1). The *wearer* refers to the person who is wearing the smartwatch. The *glancer* refers to the intended recipient of the information displayed on the watch – for example, another person sitting or standing in close proximity to the wearer. In all cases, where specifics are given these are examples of the types of content we see as representing a particular content factor, rather than a restriction to that exact content.

Content source

The content source parameter concerns the owner of the content being displayed, and therefore where it is sourced from (see Fig. 2a). The three key delimiters on this scale are:

– *Wearer:* Information owned by the *wearer*. For example: missed call details; their next meeting time; holiday photographs; health information; contact information;
– *Glancer:* Information owned by the *glancer*. For example: missed call details; appointment times; alerts; and,
– *Public:* General information from public sources. For example: any public information that could easily be retrieved, such as the weather forceast, adverts or news.

Content relevance

This parameter concerns who the content being displayed is relevant to (see Fig. 2b). This may include anyone from the *wearer* to the *glancer* (or an intersection between the two) to the general public:

– *Wearer:* Information that is relevant to the *wearer* (but not viewed by them). For example: information about their schedule; contact details (e.g., when at a conference);
– *Glancer:* Information that is relevant to the *glancer*. For example: email or call notifications; conversation cues; and,
– *Public:* General information relevant to any person (or group of people) able to see the watch. For example: breaking news; the current time; traffic updates; stock prices.

Persistence

The duration (or longevity) of the information that is displayed (see Fig. 2c), ranging from brief alerts to very long displays:

– *Long:* For the entire duration of an encounter. For example: emergency warnings; a countdown timer to a future event;
– *Medium:* For a sub-period of an encounter's duration. For example: agenda details; a rain warning predicting when you need to walk home; and,
– *Short:* As a quick burst of information. For example: standard smartphone event alerts; adverts.

Representation

The type of presentation, ranging from entirely abstract to explicit and precise (see Fig. 2d)

– *Abstract:* Colour-based cues. For example: red for lateness to a meeting; green to indicate an important new email;
– *Intermediate:* An intermediate level of detail (such as an image). For example: an envelope icon to indicate a new email; a message sender's profile picture; and,
– *Explicit:* Clearly understandable and to-the-point, stating the information explicitly (e.g., text). For example: an alert or instruction; a message subject line; a news headline.

Granularity

The granularity of the information presented, ranging from coarse and broad to fine and narrow (see Fig. 2e):

– *Coarse:* Imprecise display of simple cues only. For example: the word "calls" to show missed calls; an email icon;
– *Intermediate:* Some but not all information. For example: number of missed calls only; an email's subject line; and,
– *Fine:* In-depth, detailed description, displaying all relevant information. For example: all missed call information (who called and at what time); an entire email body (scrolling).

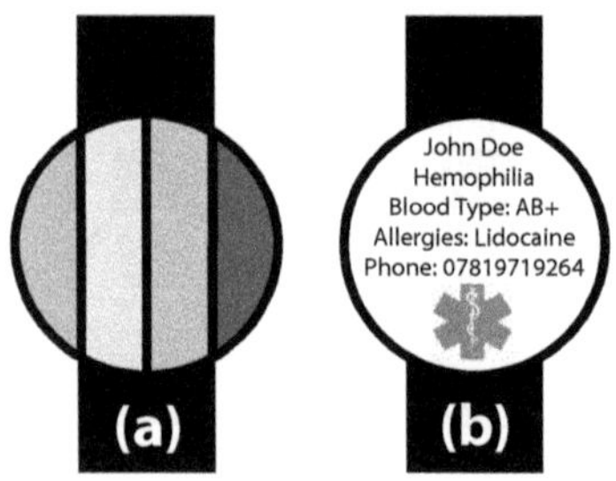

Figure 3. Potential examples of uncommon design parameter combinations. (a) An abstract representation with a fine level of granularity, showing the weather forecast across the day. (b) Content sourced from the wearer that is relevant to the public, showing the wearer's emergency health information.

Illustrative design space uses

Our aim is for these factors to help designers generate potential public watch services. We illustrate this by using them in two perhaps uncommon design parameter combinations, as illustrated in Fig. 3. Figure 3a shows the weather throughout the day, starting with clear blue skies in the morning and ending with a stormy night. This is an abstract representation (Fig. 2d.1) with a fine level of granularity (Fig. 2e.3), using colours alone to show four kinds of weather across different time periods. Figure 3b shows the wearer's emergency health information. This is content sourced from the wearer (Fig. 2a.1) that is relevant to the public (Fig. 2b.3), which could easily be captured with current smartwatches that are already used to monitor chronic health conditions.[3] While these designs are perhaps at first glance unconventional, in theory, any variation of the five design space factors could be combined to provide a type of watch face interaction.

STUDY 3: CONTENT FACTORS

After sketching out the design space of public watch interactions, we felt it valuable to investigate the usefulness of each area of the design space for potential *glancers*. We conducted a web-based study in order to determine which dimensions people find most valuable, given their expectations of current technology, and the ways in watches are currently used. 47 staff and student participants of a UK university (27F, 20M; aged 18–55) took part, completing a 10 min questionnaire.

Procedure

Participants were recruited via email, and offered a £2 gift voucher as an incentive to take part. The study began with ethically-approved informed consent and participation guidance, followed by the same questions regarding current watch use and perceived acceptability as asked in study 1. That is, participants were asked to rate the extent to which they felt it is socially acceptable to look at another person's watch; or, their own watch, during a one-to-one conversation; whether they wore a watch themselves; if they had ever looked at other people's watches rather than their own; and, whether they had ever noticed other people looking at their watch.

Participants then saw, one-by-one, each factor in Fig. 2. They were asked to rate every aspect of each factor (e.g., images Fig. 2a.1–3 through to Fig. 2e.1–3) on a Likert-like scale of 1 to 7 (7 high) for how useful this display would be to them. The three faces of the content source factor (e.g., Fig. 2a.1–3: wearer, glancer and public) were always shown first, as part of the framing and description of the concept of displaying

[3]E.g., bbc.co.uk/news/technology-28776282 (accessed 6th Jan. 2015)

Factor	Face 1	Face 2	Face 3	Significance
Source	3.2	3.2	5.1	$p < 0.0001$
Relevance	3.7	3.8	4.3	$p = 0.25$
Persistence	4.0	3.9	2.9	$p = 0.06$
Representation	2.5	4.3	3.9	$p = 0.0002$
Granularity	3.1	4.6	3.8	$p = 0.0005$

Table 2. Mean scores for each face of each factor in Fig. 2. Significance levels (Friedman tests) indicate that for content source, representation and granularity, there is a significant effect. Pairwise Bonferroni corrected post-hoc Wilcoxon signed-ranks tests on these factors show that darker green values are significant compared to lighter green values in each row (all $p < 0.001$). Unshaded values show no significance to others.

content on other people's watches. Participants were then shown each of the four remaining factors (content relevance, persistence, representation and granularity; Fig. 2b–e) one-by-one in a random order, and asked the same usefulness question about faces 1, 2 and 3 of each factor. The study ended by asking participants to rate the general usefulness of the concept to the watch *wearer*, a *glancer*, or the public.

Results

21 participants (45 %) said that they usually wore a watch, with 11 (23 %) wearing one occasionally, and 15 (32 %) never wearing a watch. 42 participants (89 %) said they had looked at other people's watches to see the time, and 20 (63 % of watch wearers) had noticed other people looking at their watch.

The average rating for the social acceptability of looking at another person's watch during a conversation was 2.40 out of 5 (s.d. 0.97), compared to 2.53 (s.d. 1.10) for looking at one's own watch. These results were not significant (Wilcoxon signed-rank test). As in study 1, however, participants generally felt that looking at another person's watch was more acceptable. 14 participants (30 %) rated the acceptability of looking at another person's watch higher than looking at their own, compared to 7 (15 %) who felt the opposite. 26 (55 %) felt there was no difference between the two actions.

Table 2 shows the average scores given for the usefulness of each design space attribute. A Friedman test shows a significant effect of content source, representation and granularity. Pairwise post-hoc Wilcoxon signed-ranks tests with Bonferroni corrections reveal the differences between each watch face option. For content source, there is a significant difference between faces 3 (public) and 1 (wearer), and also between faces 3 and 2 (glancer): participants felt public content sources were more useful. For representation, there is a significant difference between faces 2 (intermediate) and 1 (abstract), and between faces 3 (explicit) and 1: participants did not feel abstract representations were useful. Finally, for granularity, there is a significant difference between faces 2 (intermediate) and 1 (coarse): participants felt intermediate more useful than coarse granularity. Each of these pairwise comparisons was significant at $p < 0.001$ or lower.

Participants' comments reflected these preferences, particularly regarding the value of public content sources (*"useful to display public information on a watch located in a public place"*) and intermediate levels of abstraction and granularity (*"personally I would prefer an image that hints at the content rather than less or greater detail"*). Many participants were very positive about the general notion (*"I think this sort of thing would be great in a work environment to see when other people have meetings"*), while other comments highlighted the need for careful design (*"don't like colour as [it] seems to indicate danger"*). In general, while participants saw value in the displays, the low level of many of the scores suggests that an appetite for smartwatches is yet to be fired. Participants in this web-based study did not have a smartwatch for illustration of each factor, so might naturally be sceptical. However, their views indicate that the most useful representations for current users would tend towards those scoring highest in Table 2.

STUDY 4: PUBLIC WATCH DISPLAYS DEPLOYMENT

In order to test naturalistic use of public watch displays, we developed and deployed three technology probes. Each probe demonstrates how the design space factors we have described would be used to inform designs in this space.

Technology probes

We constructed three separate technology probe systems, each designed as an Android application for a Sony SmartWatch 2 (see Fig. 4, far left). We chose three different content sources as the primary consideration, and aimed to cover the majority of each of the four further design space factors.

● *Probe 1: Wearer's content*

Probe 1 displayed content sourced from the watch wearer. We designed a simple display showing the time remaining until the wearer's next meeting, automatically extracted from the calendar on their phone. The display started five minutes before a scheduled event, and began by showing a timed reminder (e.g., *"Tim's meeting is in 5 minutes"*) on a green background, as shown in Fig. 4 (far left). The display updated as the time became shorter, cycling through 4, 3, 2 and 1 minutes remaining, and through green to yellow to red for the background colour. Finally, for two minutes after the deadline the display showed a lateness warning.

Our imagined use-case for this probe was to let a glancer know the amount of time remaining before the wearer needs to leave. The factors represented by this probe are illustrated by red circle markers in Fig. 5 In this case, the content source was the wearer, and the content was relevant to some extent to both the glancer and the wearer. The content persistence was of medium length (displayed for a maximum of 7 min), and the representation was explicit, but of relatively coarse granularity.

■ *Probe 2: Glancer's content*

Probe 2 displayed content sourced from the glancer's phone. We designed a simple display that showed alert information – that is, any missed calls, emails, SMS or chat messages received by the glancer. Each alert was displayed for 30 seconds, and represented both the type of alert and its source, as shown in Fig. 4 (centre right). Messages from people marked as important were displayed on a green background; other items were displayed on a black background.

Our imagined use-case for this probe was to help a glancer evaluate whether to take out their phone to respond to alerts

Figure 4. Examples of the displays of each of the three probes. Left: the meeting reminder display as shown on a Sony SmartWatch 2. Note that the text is upside-down to the wearer, but upright for the glancer. Other images, from left to right: the wearer's content, showing two further stages of the meeting reminder; a glancer's content, showing a call alert from a person marked as important (top), and a normal email alert (bottom); and, public content, showing a news headline, and an advert.

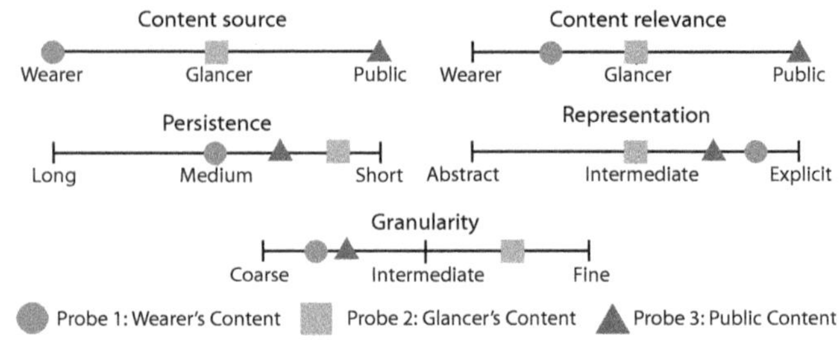

Figure 5. Overview of the design space factors represented by each probe.

(e.g., when expecting an important message). The factors afforded by this scenario are illustrated by green square markers in Fig. 5. In this case, the content source was the glancer, and the content was relevant to the glancer. The content persistence was of relatively short length (30 s), and the display was an intermediate representation (iconic and colour only), but of relatively fine granularity.

▲ *Probe 3: Public content*

Probe 3 displayed content sourced from public sources. We designed a simple display that showed local and national news, weather, and adverts, as shown in Fig. 4 (right). Our imagined use-case for this probe was as a traditional public display, showing timely information that was potentially relevant to anyone reading the screen. The factors afforded by this scenario are illustrated by blue triangle markers in Fig. 5. In this case, the content source was public, and the content was relevant to the public. The content persistence was of relatively short length (1 min), and the display was between intermediate and explicit representation, and of relatively coarse granularity.

Probe deployment

In order to test naturalistic use of the system, we deployed the three probes amongst researchers within our institution. Four participants (one each for probes 1 and 3, and two for probe 2) were asked to use the systems for between 8–12 days.

The participant for probe 1 (M; aged 46) regularly attends scheduled formal meetings with one or more people (approx. 5–10 times per day). This participant is also an author of this paper. We made this decision as it was necessary to have a very busy-scheduled person who was comfortable wearing and using the probe in their day-to-day life. However, our aim was to gather responses from third parties not involved in the deployment (i.e., glancers, rather than the wearer) – we do not focus on responses from the participant themselves. We employed this method of autoethnography—a researcher as a participant—in this probe for similar reasons to O'Kane et al. [17] who suggest that it can *"be considered as an additional method that researchers of interactive technology could employ to understand better non-routine user experiences."*

The participants for probe 2 were a married couple (M and F, aged 27) who both work and live together. Each person's phone was connected to the watch worn by the other person. We chose a close pair of participants to alleviate potential privacy concerns and issues around connecting phones to watches worn by other people, but also maximise the possibility of seeing relevant information on the other person's watch.

The participant for probe 3 (M; aged 29) regularly engages in group encounters in both professional and social capacities. We chose a socially active person to maximise the possibility of others around them seeing the public content.

Procedure

At the start of the study, each participant was given a smartwatch and briefed about the nature of the probe they would be using. All participants were fully informed about the purpose of the study, and were asked to keep the watch in a position that was visible to others (such as friends and colleagues) as much as possible whenever engaged with other people. Each participant was also asked to observe and record any reactions to the content being displayed on the watch. This information was logged via the watch itself – tapping on its screen logged an event, and participants then entered further detail using a companion app on their phone, either at the time of the event or later in the day. Participants were not paid for taking part.

Results

Probe 1: Wearer's content

The participant wore the watch for eight days, during which he had 43 scheduled meetings lasting a minimum of 30 min (45 min average). Meetings were generally one-to-one, but were not always contiguous (i.e., the watch would not necessarily display the next meeting time during each encounter).

The participant saw a correlation between observed glances at the watch and information being displayed. Of the people who were seen glancing at the watch, approximately half commented on the display. Remarks such as *"there's something on your watch"*; or, *"you're late"* were common. The watch was also a useful aid for bringing meetings to a close – pointing to the watch and stating *"as you can see, I have to go"* gave an obvious reason for ending encounters. At times, other people would bring a meeting to a close when they had seen the next meeting time was near, while on two occasions other people, upon being told that the participant needed to leave, remarked *"I know – I saw it on your watch."*

In terms of watch visibility, it was clear that other people noticed the watch screen in situations where its face was not in full view (e.g., while walking in a corridor, or when gesturing during a meeting). Finally, the participant felt that while the watch did not deter from his general working life, he would feel uncomfortable using it in external meetings, particularly in those with strangers. These results are both further evidence that watch faces need not always be in full direct view of potential glancers to be useful, and also a reminder of the need for well thought-out contextual control of the display.

Probe 2: Glancer's content

The couple wore the watches for 12 days. During this time, they tended to be in the same local area during evenings and weekends, but received only a small number of alerts while together. These participants also did not observe anyone else glancing at their watches, making the interaction entirely personal between the two of them. The need for participants to be in the vicinity of each other for messages to be received clearly affected the quantity of messages that were seen.

We designed probe 2 to be able to highlight the importance of the sender of incoming alerts (see Fig. 4), but this feature was rarely used – as one of the participants put it: *"everyone I contact is important to me."* One change in behaviour that was noted by the male participant was that his partner always knew when he was getting a call (as it was displayed on her wrist), and consequently made him answer it, which changed his typical behaviour of letting some calls go to voicemail. The female participant commented that she found herself being quite "nosy" initially, but also that the study made her realise how little she used her own phone.

In the participants' views, the key finding was that the display made each person aware that the other was receiving messages, which usually acted as a mechanism to elaborate on the content (e.g., *"who's that from?"*). The participants also found that knowing when their watch was connected to their partner's phone was helpful: *"I felt like there was an elastic between us, which was useful in the supermarket because if he went out of range I knew I had to go and find him."*

Probe 3: Public content

The participant wore the watch for 9 days, during which he was the main speaker in a two-day course, had several work meetings, sat on an interview panel and attended various social events in places such as pubs, restaurants or coffee shops.

One of the main observations from this probe was that people were far more likely to comment on the watch display in social situations than in work-based settings. For example, during one encounter in a restaurant with his family, the wearer's brother commented *"what on earth is your watch doing?"*, which prompted everyone at the table to look at his wrist, initiating a conversation about the display, and further remarks and conversations when in similar situations. These general comments about content on the watch were not seen in work situations, however. Although the participant often observed others glancing at the watch, very few commented on it. For example, while all of the seven participants in the course he ran were seen to look at the display at some point, none chose to comment at the time. After directly asking about the watch at the end of the course, two students commented that they had seen an advert for a nearby fast-food restaurant, which had sparked a conversation about where they should go for lunch.

When asked about the value to him, the participant felt that the discussions generated were interesting, but also made him feel self-conscious at times (e.g., when adverts were displayed in professional situations). He also noted the slight annoyance of not being able to read the content on his own wrist, as it was oriented for glancers rather than him as the wearer. However, he did see value in the technique for those around him, either for providing up-to-date weather reports (which one glancer was particularly interested in) or giving breaking headlines.

Discussion – Study 4

It was clear from all three probes that people around the wearer were able to see and interpret information on the watches. It was particularly encouraging that in probe 1 casual glancers not only saw the information on the watch, but also often acted on it (e.g., telling the wearer he was late for his next meeting). The third probe's finding that social situations generated more remarks than work environments is a useful contextual hint for choosing when to display publicly-sourced watch content.

CONCLUSIONS

With the increasing prevalence of smartwatches, it is certainly timely to investigate their extended use beyond the inevitable "phone-on-your-wrist" scenario. The design space and four studies in this paper have explored the concept of personal watches used as public displays. Glancing at someone else's watch is already a common social practice, with 71 % (study 1) and 89 % (study 3) doing this, often to avoid the potentially negative social signal of looking at one's own watch.

In study 1 we investigated the noticeability and social acceptability of looking at another person's watch. This action was significantly less noticeable than looking at one's own watch. In addition, social acceptability was not seen as a problem (studies 1 and 3). Turning to watch use and deportment, study 2 demonstrated that 88 % of observed watches were either fully (51 %) or partially (37 %) visible to those in close proximity to the wearer, and held in a variety of common postures.

Using the information from these initial studies, we constructed a design space, discussing in detail the different aspects and dimensions designers would need to consider before embarking on turning a personal watch into a public display. Designers wishing to construct a public watch face should consider these factors carefully, and think about any trade-offs that may need to be made across the spectrum. Our third study evaluated each factor's perceived value, then study 4 explored three potential watch displays in a naturalistic setting.

There are many aspects of public watch displays that we have not considered here. For example, setting up connections between watches and content sources may require complex Bluetooth arrangements, or linked trusted web services. There are interesting possibilities around group encounters, where there may be multiple glancers, or multiple wearers becoming glancers themselves. There will also need to be a set of general design norms for the content displayed, to ensure that the glancer is aware of the meanings in these different contexts. Battery life is a potential consideration; however, we believe that with sensible use of sensors, and activating the screen only when needed, our approach will not significantly affect battery life. Finally, as with any public display, there are many considerations around privacy and cultural norms (see Background section). We do not expect to answer all these questions in this paper; rather we have aimed to open up a new research area and highlight its potential for future work.

While previous wearable research has focused either entirely on the wearer (e.g., [3, 9]), or entirely on the glancer (e.g., [5, 18]), we allow an interchangeable approach, laying the groundwork for others to build upon. Our work not only sketches out a design space for the approach, but also investigates many of the issues and concerns over noticeability, visibility and social acceptability, generating many interesting questions and discussions relevant to the community. With the growth of wearable computing, and an expectation that smart watch sales will steadily increase, it is a perfect time to open up a new space surrounding their use.

ACKNOWLEDGMENTS

This work was funded by EPSRC grant EP/J000604/2.

REFERENCES

1. Campbell, C. and Tarasewich, P. What can you say with only three pixels? In *Proc. MobileHCI '04*, LNCS vol. 3160. Springer Berlin Heidelberg (2004), 1–12.
2. Cheverst, K., Dix, A., Fitton, D., Kray, C., Rouncefield, M., Sas, C., Saslis-Lagoudakis, G. and Sheridan, J. G. Exploring bluetooth based mobile phone interaction with the hermes photo display. In *Proc. MobileHCI '05*, ACM (2005), 47–54.
3. Costanza, E., Inverso, S. A., Pavlov, E., Allen, R. and Maes, P. Eye-q: eyeglass peripheral display for subtle intimate notifications. In *Proc. MobileHCI '06*, ACM (2006), 211–218.
4. Eriksson, E., Hansen, T. and Lykke-Olesen, A. Reclaiming public space: designing for public interaction with private devices. In *Proc. TEI '07*, ACM (2007), 31–38.
5. Falk, J. and Björk, S. The bubblebadge: a wearable public display. In *Proc. CHI EA '99*, ACM (1999), 318–319.
6. Feiner, S. K. The importance of being mobile: some social consequences of wearable augmented reality systems. In *Proc. IWAR '99*, IEEE (1999), 145–148.
7. Floyd, M. YouGov: Almost 60 % of 16–34 year olds use a phone as their primary timepiece. See: http://goo.gl/VUJ0td. 2011. Accessed 6th Jan. 2015.
8. Harper, R. and Taylor, S. Glancephone: an exploration of human expression. In *Proc. MobileHCI '09*, ACM (2009), 180–189.
9. Harrison, C., Lim, B. Y., Shick, A. and Hudson, S. E. Where to locate wearable displays?: Reaction time performance of visual alerts from tip to toe. In *Proc. CHI '09*, ACM (2009), 941–944.
10. Holgar, M., Foth, M. and Ferrero-Regis, T. Fashion as a communication medium to raise environmental awareness and sustainable practice. In *Proc. ANZCA Annual Conference '09*, ANZCA (2009), 1253–1275.
11. Kleinman, L., Carney, A. and Ma, A. Billboard: interacting with personal public displays. In *Proc. CHI EA '14*, ACM (2014), 495–498.
12. Lucero, A., Holopainen, J. and Jokela, T. Pass-them-around: collaborative use of mobile phones for photo sharing. In *Proc. CHI '11*, ACM (2011), 1787–1796.
13. Mauriello, M., Gubbels, M. and Froehlich, J. E. Social fabric fitness: the design and evaluation of wearable e-textile displays to support group running. In *Proc. CHI '14*, ACM (2014), 2833–2842.
14. McAtamney, G. and Parker, C. An examination of the effects of a wearable display on informal face-to-face communication. In *Proc. CHI '06*, ACM (2006), 45–54.
15. Mintel. Watches and Jewellery Retailing – UK – Sept. 2013. See: http://goo.gl/0JXfLv. Accessed 6th Jan. 2015.
16. NextMarket Insights. Smartwatch Forecast 2013–2020. See: http://goo.gl/3fUZLT. 2013. Accessed 6th Jan. 2015.
17. O'Kane, A., Rogers, Y. and Blandford, A. Gaining empathy for non-routine mobile device use through autoethnography. In *Proc. CHI '14*, ACM (2014), 987–990.
18. Page, M. and Moere, A. V. Evaluating a wearable display jersey for augmenting team sports awareness. In *Proc. PERVASIVE '07*, Springer-Verlag (2007), 91–108.
19. Profita, H. P., Clawson, J., Gilliland, S., Zeagler, C., Starner, T., Budd, J. and Do, E. Y.-L. Don't mind me touching my wrist: a case study of interacting with on-body technology in public. In *Proc. ISWC '13*, ACM (2013), 89–96.
20. Przybylski, A. and Weinstein, N. Can you connect with me now? How the presence of mobile communication technology influences face-to-face conversation quality. *J Soc Pers Relat* 3.10 (2012), 237–246.
21. Reeves, S., Benford, S., O'Malley, C. and Fraser, M. Designing the spectator experience. In *Proc. CHI '05*, ACM (2005), 741–750.
22. Rico, J. and Brewster, S. Gestures all around us: user differences in social acceptability perceptions of gesture based interfaces. In *MobileHCI '09 Adj.* ACM (2009).
23. Rico, J. and Brewster, S. Usable gestures for mobile interfaces: evaluating social acceptability. In *Proc. CHI '10*, ACM (2010), 887–896.
24. Schwarz, J., Klionsky, D., Harrison, C., Dietz, P. and Wilson, A. Phone as a pixel: enabling ad-hoc, large-scale displays using mobile devices. In *Proc. CHI '12*, ACM (2012), 2235–2238.
25. Toney, A., Mulley, B., Thomas, B. and Piekarski, W. Social weight: designing to minimise the social consequences arising from technology use by the mobile professional. *Pers Ubiq Comput* 7.5 (2003), 309–320.
26. Waldemeyer, M. Twitter dress. See: http://goo.gl/ABr4cw. 2010. Accessed 6th Jan. 2015.
27. Walmink, W., Chatham, A. and Mueller, F. Interaction opportunities around helmet design. In *Proc. CHI EA '14*, ACM (2014), 367–370.
28. Wouters, N., Huyghe, J. and Vande Moere, A. Openwindow: citizen-controlled content on public displays. In *Proc. PerDis '13*, ACM (2013), 121–126.

TUIkit: Evaluating Physical and Functional Experiences of Tangible User Interface Prototypes

Jorick Vissers
CUO | Social Spaces
iMinds / KU Leuven
Parkstraat 45 Bus 3605
3000 Leuven, Belgium
jorick.vissers@soc.kuleuven.be

David Geerts
CUO | Social Spaces
iMinds / KU Leuven
Parkstraat 45 Bus 3605
3000 Leuven, Belgium
david.geerts@soc.kuleuven.be

ABSTRACT
This paper describes TUIkit, a new method for evaluating both physical and functional experiences of users with early TUI prototypes. By means of a study to evaluate interactive dice prototypes, TUIkit's appropriateness for tracing the effect of different physical attributes (e.g. shape, size, weight, material, texture) on the functional and thus overall user experience was investigated. The results show that separating physical and functional experiences first and joining these afterwards, enhanced the evaluation of TUI prototypes. By applying this approach, participants became more aware of how they physically experienced the prototypes, rather than focusing solely on the functional value of the prototypes. This awareness supports earlier studies that suggest that TUIs consist of more than just interaction, and that form and materiality has a strong impact on their user experience. Finally, we suggest some future adjustments of the TUIkit method.

Author Keywords
TUI; user experience; evaluation; prototyping

ACM Classification Keywords
H.5.2. User Interfaces: Evaluation/methodology

INTRODUCTION
Tangible user interfaces (TUIs) allow us to interact with digital information in a physical way, which takes advantage of our human ability to grasp and manipulate physical objects and material [12]. However, in the design process of tangible interfaces, little attention has gone to the meaning of material qualities for TUIs, and materials are often chosen more for their availability or technical qualities, rather than for their benefits to the user. This is partly due to technical challenges in creating TUI prototypes, but also to a lack of guides or tools that support the selection of materials in function of a good user experience (UX) [4], a gap that this paper addresses.

Recent work has emphasized the importance of focusing on the materiality of TUIs (see e.g. [5] [7] [13] [22] [24]), but evaluation methods that are adapted to measure the user experience with different materials are still missing in the toolbox of the tangible interface designer [4]. As the physical form for TUIs is usually decided in an early stage, such an evaluation method should be aimed at being used in the prototyping phase, where the decision of which materials to select are being made.

In this paper, we present TUIkit, an evaluation method that can be used in the earlier phases of the design process for iteratively designing and evaluating early prototypes of tangible user interfaces. In this formative stage, evaluations are needed that can provide detailed qualitative information on how to improve the TUI prototypes in a short time frame, rather than quantitative measurements more suited for summative evaluations. Although there are several existing evaluation methods that can also be used for evaluating tangible user interfaces, so far no evaluation methods specific to TUIs have been developed [25]. While many of these methods, such as user testing, can easily be used to test various UX aspects, none of these focus on the 'Tangible Magic' [29] that TUIs should offer.

We used TUIkit to evaluate a number of prototypes for a tangible game in which physical dice are used to interact with the game. Based on these evaluations, we describe the strengths of our method, as well as suggest some aspects for improvement. The main contribution of this paper is therefore not the outcome of the evaluations of the dice prototypes, but a new qualitative method for iteratively evaluating the UX of tangible user interface prototypes.

RELATED WORK
Since their conception, tangible user interfaces have been described as combining physical form with digital information and computation [12]. The main advantage of this coupling is that the physical form of TUIs can be tailored to the users' tasks, and exploit the innate spatial skills we possess as human beings [26]. However, even though it is a crucial aspect of tangible interfaces, only

CHI 2015, April 18 - 23 2015, Seoul, Republic of Korea.

ACM 978-1-4503-3145-6/15/04...$15.00.
http://dx.doi.org/10.1145/2702123.2702478

recently more interest is going to the selection process of this physical form, mainly because of the increased ease with which tangible interfaces can be prototyped.

As the TUIkit method is to be used in this crucial prototyping phase, we will first discuss different approaches to prototyping for tangible interfaces, before looking into tangible interaction and the role of materiality.

TUI prototyping

Wiethoff et al. [27] and Hornecker et al. [11] emphasize that the culture of prototyping physical objects differs with that of prototyping digital interactive systems. This could be due to the fact that building a wireframe or paper prototype takes less time than building a prototype that needs both physical and digital interactive components [16]. Moreover, specific skills and knowledge as well as access to the right tools and materials are needed to build even low-fidelity prototypes of TUIs. However, the recent introduction of tools to support the prototyping of TUIs is making it easier for interaction designers to experiment with different forms and materials as well as interactivity in tangible user interface prototypes [1].

In contrast to several other toolkits that focus more on the technical and interactive side of tangible user interfaces by facilitating the implementation of technology that enables interaction [15, 16], Wiethoff et al. [27] present a toolkit called 'Paperbox' that supports the early exploration of different form factors and immediately provides digital interactivity for the low-fidelity TUI prototypes built with it. Wiethoff et al. [28] also created a toolkit called 'Sketch a TUI' that combines rapid creation of physical prototypes by the use of 3D cardboard objects with drawing conductive traces to make those objects interactive and functional. This combination makes it possible to create low cost tangible user interface prototypes in an iterative way within the early explorative phase. Similarly, Cookieflavors, a toolkit developed by Kimura et al. [15], consists of coin-size Bluetooth wireless components named Cookies, which can be attached to any physical object. Each component recognizes a unique motion and designers can easily assign different roles to these components, in order to create a certain interaction with every tangible object. Finally, Papier-Mâché [16] is a toolkit for developing TUI prototypes that consists of a library that supports several types of physical input related to computer vision, RFID technology, and barcodes. These types of toolkits enable designers with little or no expertise in software or hardware prototyping to develop TUI prototypes, at the same time stimulating them to explore different types of interaction and materials.

Concurrently with the emergence of these prototyping toolkits for TUIs, the increasing accessibility of hardware prototyping technologies like laser-cutters and 3D printers in for example FabLabs, also benefits and facilitates the prototyping of Tangible User Interfaces. This rise of digital fabrication expands the practices of sharing, mash-up and remix from the digital world to the physical world, making the practice of TUI prototyping accessible to a wide range of researchers and practitioners because of the low threshold in using these tools [19]. While prototypes for digital products can be more unpolished, it is argued that for physical products, the quality and finish of the prototypes have a big influence on the adoption and integration of the prototypes when being evaluated in the personal context of users, and the FabLab technologies enable designers to build more polished physical prototypes [10]. Moreover, because of the possibility to allow for faster iteration between different prototypes, and a tight coupling of the digital and the physical, new relationships between objects and (digital) interfaces can be more easily explored [18]. As these recent evolutions show, prototyping TUIs is becoming easier, cheaper, and more accessible, which stimulates a stronger focus on getting the right design by exploring several different designs, rather than getting the design right by starting from one design and refining it [3].

However, although access to prototyping tools is an important facilitator, it is not sufficient to guarantee a good user experience of TUIs. TUIkit aims to complement the rise in prototyping tools by offering a method that helps the designer choose the best combination of physical material and digital interaction, focusing equally on each of these aspects. In the next section we will explore both aspects, by showing how the user experience of tangible interaction differs from that of digital interaction, and discussing the increasing attention to the materiality of tangible interfaces.

Tangible interaction

As our method evaluates how users experience (physical) interaction with different prototypes of a TUI, we need to obtain an understanding of the meaning and components of 'tangible interaction', and what it contains. Baskinger et al. [2] describe tangible interaction as a seamless integration of computation and form, but this does not bring us any closer to understanding what its components are. A more interesting approach is to find out what the user experience of tangible interaction is like. Provost and Robert [21] identify and define the different dimensions of user experience with interactive products. They present ten UX dimensions that include physical characteristics of the product as well as the physical experiences of users, two dimensions of tangible interaction that are relevant for evaluating TUIs. Xu et al. [29] more specifically talk about a quality that is inherent in tangible interfaces called "tangible magic", which they describe as a combination of the novelty of using objects for doing unexpected things and the pleasure we gain from handling physical objects. We argue that any evaluation method that will be used for evaluating tangible user interfaces should focus on this 'tangible magic', or the physical dimensions of the user experience.

Recent work on tangible interfaces ([2], [23], [20]) emphasizes the importance of this physical dimension within tangible interaction. They describe for example how shape and form, as dimensions of physical objects, can influence how users interact with physical objects [23]. This is due to the fact that these physical attributes provide certain cues for understanding because of visual signals and physically embodied functionality [2]. Form, however, is not the only physical attribute that influences how users experience tangible interactions. Material properties have much more attributes than just shape and form [4]. Flatters et al. [7] e.g. showed in their study that texture of objects has an effect on how we grasp them. After studying the influence of three textures on how users grasped and interacted with objects, they found that low-friction surfaces caused more sequential behavior, while high-friction surfaces merged users' actions into a single 'higher-order' behavior. This calls for a more detailed analysis of material properties that goes beyond mere shape and form. In the next section, we will explore different views on materiality and how this is taken into account in our TUIkit method.

Materiality

In HCI, and more specifically in interaction design, the influence of material aspects on interactions is getting more attention, but is still in its infancy. Doering et al. [5] states that "the meaning of material qualities for tangible user interfaces has yet not been explored and investigated sufficiently", while Schmid et al. [24] claim that "we do not fully exploit the expressiveness of forms, materials and shapes of the non-digital objects we interact with." Thus, there is a clear need for methods that incorporate a focus on materiality, i.e. selecting the right materials for tangible interaction based on sound and thorough user research.

Rosner [22] argues that the design of tangible user interfaces often just adds material properties onto the designed form, rather than implementing in an authentic way the materiality of the object. She calls for researchers to take the material's attributes and restraints into consideration. Other recent work on tangible interaction also draws attention to use materiality to add value to the tangible interaction [24]. This last point is an important basis for our work presented in this paper, as we too believe that materiality adds value to tangible interaction, and there is interplay between physical and functional aspects of TUIs.

Materiality is a complex construct, and there are different perspectives on how materials are understood [9]. A first perspective sees material properties as functional affordances. This perspective links physical properties with functional aspects of tangible interaction. A second perspective focuses on computation as material, representing different states, transitions or events. In this view, the physical and the computational are interlinked, and the focus is more on the computational than on the physical. Finally, a third perspective on materiality focuses on the communicative dimension of material, where the tradition of craftsmanship brought into HCI is seen as communication between the craftspeople and the recipients of their crafts. As such, traditional materials augmented by digital properties transmit meaning to its users. Jung and Stolterman [13] distinguish form from materiality. Form is about design considerations, and can be seen as the materials that are being used, the shape this material takes or making as the process of communicating with users through craft, much like the third perspective on materiality mentioned in [9]. According to [13], materiality is about the relationship between users and the material artifact, and has two aspects: the meaning that users attach to a certain object and how different artifacts work together as a system in a broader ecology.

Our approach to evaluating the physical and functional of TUIs, focuses on the relationship between users and the interactive object, and sees material properties as affordances for functional interactions, which we conceptualize in this paper as how to handle the different functions of a specific TUI.

In conclusion, as prototyping tangible user interfaces is becoming more accessible for interaction designers, it is getting easier to explore different forms and materials. This opens opportunities to create TUIs that are creating better user experiences, but a method that helps select the right material for the interaction the TUI offers is not yet available. With this paper, we intend to fill in this gap by presenting TUIkit, a method that evaluates TUI prototypes both on the level of material properties and functional interaction, and explores the interplay between them.

TUIKIT: A METHOD FOR TUI PROTOTYPES

In the section below we describe the procedure of how to use the TUIkit UX evaluation method for Tangible User Interface prototypes. Within the four phases of this method, we also elaborate on the choices that were made to study the influence of physical attributes on users' functional experience with early TUI prototypes. After explaining the general approach of the method, we will describe how we applied the TUIkit method in a practical case study.

Introduction

In line with good research practices, the researcher starts with explaining the purpose of the study by using an informed consent that describes the planning of the session, the participant's rights, and the use of gathered data and video recordings from the session. During the introduction, the researcher also emphasizes that this is still an early phase of the design process, meaning that prototypes will be used during the session and the researchers are open for all feedback. In order to obtain this feedback, all participants are asked to verbally express all of their thoughts (either good or bad) during the whole session, by using the 'Think Aloud' method [17].

Phase 1 – Exploration

Within the first phase of the TUIkit method, users get the opportunity to explore and get an overview of all of the TUI prototypes that will be used and evaluated during the session. The goal of this phase is to make participants aware of and let them verbalize the different physical experiences with the TUIs. The researcher presents all of the prototypes at once to the participant, explains that he or she is free to explore the prototypes, and emphasizes that the focus of this phase is on the physical attributes of the prototypes rather than the functional aspects like for example how to interact with the prototype. The instruction given to the participant is: "Feel free to explore these objects and tell me what you think of them". No explanation is given yet about the functional use of the prototypes, as the goal is to let the users verbalize only their physical experiences by the use of their own vocabulary, and not yet focus on the interaction. During this phase, the researcher takes note of the words that are used by the participant to describe the physical attributes of each prototype.

Phase 2 – Differentiation

Where the goal within the explorative (first) phase is to make participants aware of their physical experience, the second phase focuses on giving more detail to this physical experience by gathering a range of terms used by the participant to describe their physical experience with the different prototypes. The approach utilized to achieve this, is based on the Repertory Grid Technique (RGT) developed by Fallman et al. [6]. They regard RGT as a methodological extension of Kelly's Personal Construct Theory [14], which states that we tend to model everything around us according to a number of personal bipolar constructs. According to Kelly, a 'construct' is a single dimension of meaning for a person allowing two phenomena to be seen as similar and thereby different from a third [14].

Just like the RGT, we opted to use an elicitation session within this phase, in which users are presented with three prototypes at a time and asked to explain how they differ from each other, in order to generate these bipolar constructs (e.g. hard vs. soft, compressible vs. solid, etc.). The amount of series of prototypes presented to the participant depends on the necessary amount to mutually compare all of the prototypes. The instructions given by the researcher to the participants are: "Describe in what way two of these three prototypes are similar and thereby different from the third. Please try to phrase this similarity and difference in one word". This approach is especially relevant for us as we can ask the participants to describe how they experience the physical differences between the various early stage prototypes. Furthermore, in order to stimulate the participant to think further than just the obvious physical attributes (e.g. size and weight), the researcher repeatedly mentions that physical attributes could be size, weight, texture, material and shape.

The outcome of this phase is a series of personal constructs and contrasts that were created by the participant and linked to the physical attributes of the prototypes. In order to capture this data, the researcher writes down each construct and contrast on separate post-its, which he jointly puts away for later use within the fourth phase.

Phase 3 - Interaction

After having evaluated purely the physical attributes of the different TUI prototypes, this phase aims to evaluate the functional or interactional aspects of the TUI prototypes. As the participant was asked within the previous two phases not to think about the functionality of the prototypes, the researcher emphasizes at the start of this phase that he/she should now focus on this functional experience. The participant gets the chance to interact with each of the prototypes in a random order. The approach, used to gather the experience of the participant during the actual use of the prototypes, is similar to the one used within the first explorative phase, i.e. by asking the participant to 'Think Aloud'. While the participant verbally expresses how he/she experiences using the different prototypes, the researcher takes notes, but more importantly asks clarifying questions to uncover the deeper meaning of the participant's experiences (e.g. *"So, you describe this prototype as more appropriate for children than for adults. Can you explain me what makes you say this?")*. The outcome of this phase consists of qualitative data about the functional use of the different TUI prototypes.

Phase 4 – Joining physical and functional experiences

The fourth phase of the TUIkit method is about colliding the data gathered from the participants within the previous phases. As mentioned earlier, the aim of the TUIkit method is to see whether the use of different physical attributes (e.g. weight, size, shape, texture, material) influences the functional experience of users, and thereby the overall UX evaluation of a TUI prototype. This aim is also communicated towards the participant in this phase. The researcher explains that, in contrast to the previous phases where the focus was either on the physical or the functional experience, combining these is the focus of this phase.

Within this fourth phase, the participant is presented with 3 tasks to conjoin their physical and functional (interactive) experiences. The first two tasks are based on the principles of the Repertory Grid Technique, building on the tasks in the second phase of the TUIkit method. Within this second phase, the participants formulated constructs and contrasts that described their physical experiences (e.g. sharp vs. round). The first task for the participant is to classify these constructs and contrasts according to 'preferred' or 'not preferred' on a giant paper table that is based on the repertory grid (see figure 1). The researcher makes notes of each classification and tries to understand the deeper reasoning, by questioning the participant about their choices.

After all constructs and contrasts are classified within the 'preferred' or 'not-preferred' column, the participant can move to the second task, which consists of marking the applicable construct or contrast (physical attributes) for each prototype that was used during the session (these are visualized at the top of the table). The participant uses the colors green or red to mark, for each prototype, whether the construct/contrast in the left (green) or the right (red) column is applicable. This marking offers, per prototype, an overview of the applicable physical attributes that were experienced by the participant.

The third and final task within this fourth phase is the ranking of all of the prototypes within a top five. The instruction the researcher gives is: *"Show me your top five of these prototypes, in which the first place ranks the best prototype and the fifth place the prototype that scored the least according to you. Also note that, for this ranking, we would like you to take into account both your physical and your functional experience with the prototypes."* The latter part of the instructions was given in order to let the participants consider the context-of-use of the TUI in the ranking, and not just the physical properties of the prototypes. After the participant finishes ranking the prototypes, the researcher questions him/her about his/her reasoning in putting the prototypes in that specific order. The outcome of this phase offers insight in on the one hand the physical attributes that are used for each prototype according to the participant, and on the other hand the preferences of the participant in terms of both physical and functional experiences with the prototypes.

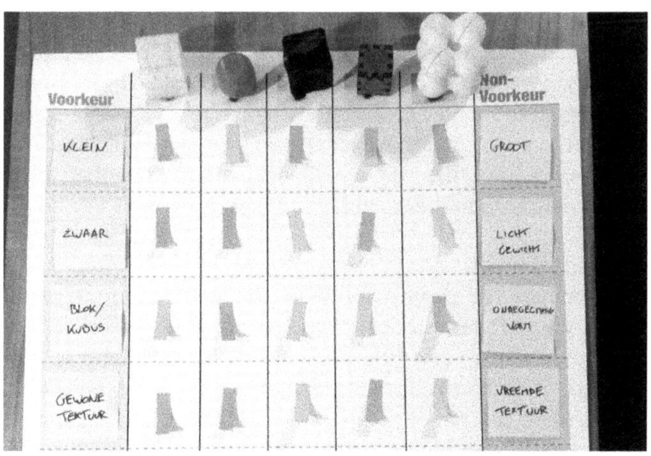

Figure 1. The Repertory Grid table

Analysis of the results

All sessions are recorded on video, and transcribed afterwards. By the use of these transcriptions and the researcher's notes, per participant, an overview can be created for each of the TUI prototypes of the words that were used to describe on the one hand their physical experience, and on the other hand their functional experience. The overall experience/evaluation of the participant is gathered from an open coding of these mapped physical and functional experiences, the classification of the physical attributes (constructs/contrasts) by preference, and finally the participant's reasoning for ranking the prototypes at the end of the sessions. The summarized experience reports of all the participants are then coded again to look for overlap. Finally, this overlap is formulated in the form of design recommendations for that specific TUI.

THE STUDY

In this part of the paper we will describe how we applied the TUIkit method in a practical case study. The aim of the study was to evaluate a series of prototypes for interactive dice, in order to identify the effect of different physical attributes on the interaction.

Use case – Interactive dice as TUI

For the use case, we chose to utilize the TUIkit method to evaluate interactive dice as a Tangible User Interface. A dice+ was used for creating the interactive link between the physical dice and the digital world. Dice+[1] is a Bluetooth-enabled gaming accessory, with built-in sensors (accelerometer, compass, gyroscope, proximity) that wirelessly communicate with iOS and Android mobile devices for dice-based gaming. Apart from serving as input device, the Dice+ also produces output by lighting up the number that was thrown. We chose this product as it has the basic properties of a TUI (integrating computation and form) and can be easily created in many different forms and shapes.

In order to investigate the effect of the different physical attributes on the user's experience, we created a series of 5 dice-shaped casings that differed from each other on a physical level (shape, size, material, and texture). On figure 2 you can see (from left to right) the prototypes, consisting of a cube shaped dice made of soft compressible material, a blue rounded dice made of rubber, a black plastic convex shaped dice, a cube shaped dice made of felt, and finally a bigger soft-plastic dice. The prototype techniques used to create these objects were laser cutting, 3D printing, and molding. The dice+ was put into these different physical casings, allowing them to be linked to a virtual board game on a tablet.

Participants

The recruitment of the participants took place through a registration form that was sent out via social media platforms (Facebook and Twitter), and which promised participants a financial incentive. We selected 8 participants, 4 women and 4 men, with ages between 24 and 34 years old. Some of the participants liked playing board games several times a week.

[1] http://www.dicepl.us

Procedure

The procedure used within this study follows the one described in the previous TUIkit method section. The session began with handing all of the dice prototypes to the participant, without giving instructions about the functional use. The participant was asked to explore the objects while verbally expressing their physical experiences to the researcher, who took notes and stimulated the participant to look for words that could describe this experience. This phase took between 5 and 10 minutes. The researcher only proceeded to the next phase of the TUIkit method, when the participant had explored all of the dice prototypes.

Figure 2. Physical prototypes for interactive dice

Within phase two, the researcher presented the participant with several series of three dice prototypes until all of the dice prototypes were mutually compared. For each series, the participant was asked to explain in what way two of these three dice prototypes were similar and thereby different from the third. These similarities and differences were formulated in two words (construct and contrast) and noted by the researcher. The duration of phase 2 was between 10 and 20 minutes.

Phase three consisted of giving the participant the opportunity to interact for an equal amount of time with each of the dice prototypes, by using them for playing a digital board game on a tablet. During this interaction, the participant was stimulated again to share his/her experiences verbally, so the researcher could take notes and dig for deeper reasoning by asking questions. The duration of phase three varied from 20 to 30 minutes.

After having focused on either the physical or functional aspects of the dice prototypes, the final phase dealt with joining them. The participant started with classifying his/her personal constructs and contrasts of phase two. For this, he/she was asked to base him/herself on the ones he/she preferred while interacting with the dice prototypes, both from a physical and a functional perspective. After the classification, the participant was asked to mark which physical construct or contrast was applicable for each dice prototype. The final task for the participant consisted of ranking the dice prototypes within a top 5, based on both his/her purely physical and his/her functional experience. The role of the researcher was to ask what the reasoning of the participant was, while ranking the dice prototypes. The total duration of this final phase, consisting of three tasks, was between 20 to 30 minutes.

RESULTS

In this section, we discuss eight main insights that emerged from our study, and that are related to the influence of physical attributes on the participants' user experience with interactive dice prototypes. The aim of these insights is to contribute to the development of future interactive dice, by sharing suggestions for physical attributes. In this paper, these results mainly serve to illustrate the type of outcome from the TUIkit method, after which we will discuss the strengths and points for improvement for our new method.

1. The rolling motion

The participants indicated that the shape of an interactive dice should be cubical, consisting of a combination of plain sides with edges and corners that are rounded outwardly. These rounded edges and corners make the dice roll more easily and thus unpredictable, while the plain sides ensure that it stops after a number of rolling motions. The majority of participants evaluated a dice that rolls too much as frustrating, as they have to wait for it to stop rolling or are forced to look for it when it rolls of the table.

2. Unpredictability is key

Several participants mentioned randomness as an important attribute for a dice. They expected a dice to be unpredictable in its movements and result, even after having practiced their rolling motion with the dice. The main physical attributes that, according to the participants, influenced this unpredictability of a dice were the material and shape. The dice that were made of softer (more compressible) material and/or had a more rounded shape seemed to move in a more bouncy and funny way. This way of moving gave the participants the impression that these dice were more unpredictable, and therefore more fair.

3. Sound aspect

As some of the prototypes were made of softer material (e.g. sponge foam, rubber), some participants remarked that these dice made very little or no sound while rolling it. The fact that it didn't produce sound did not really bother them, but most of the participants expressed that they expected a dice to make the typical sound. As opposed to these softer dice, some dice produced an overdose of noise according to the participants. They found the noise quite intrusive and imagined it would be annoying when using this extensively during a board game. The physical attributes that lead to this noise were a combination of too hard material (plastic), and a hollow non-rounded shape that is too sharp on the edges and corners.

4. Being pleasant to hold

Next to the functional value of a dice, most participants valued the feeling that a dice gives when holding it in their hand. The dice that felt more pleasant had a smaller and rounder shape, which made them more embeddable in the hand than bigger and/or cube shaped dice with sharper edges and corners. Furthermore, it seemed that a dice should be easy to grasp. This grippability depended on how much grip was offered by the shape and texture of the dice. Finally, participants mentioned that they prefer a dice with more weight, as they want to feel that they are actually holding something that they can throw.

5. Size and precaution

Especially the bigger abstract-shaped dice was experienced as too big. The rest of the dice had a better size for both rolling and holding in the hand. Participants mentioned that they felt like they needed to be too careful when rolling the bigger dice. They felt like it would break something or for example mess up the setting of a board game, when rolling this dice too hard in a real setting. Consequently, participants also mentioned that the bigger dice did not have enough rolling motion. However, we believe that this was due to the fact that they held back when throwing, because of the size leading to higher precaution.

6. Texture only effects the physical, but not the functional experience

All of the participants were (or became) aware of texture as a physical attribute of the interactive dice. However, none of the participants experienced texture as an influential factor on the actual functionality of the dice. They did value it as a physical attribute that influenced the grippability or feeling of holding it in their hands. So, texture should be taken into account for the development of future interactive dice, as it might not contribute to the functional, but does influence the physical experience.

7. Too soft materials are childish

As mentioned earlier, the material of a dice should not be too hard, as this does not benefit the fluency of the rolling motion and produces too much noise. However, the participants' feedback on the dice made of sponge foam, also pointed out that the use of too soft or compressible materials is experienced as childish. Several participants mentioned that the material reminded them of children's toys, because of the low risk for injuries. Note that this is irrespective of the fact that the participants evaluated the functional value of this dice as good.

8. Good functionality should not lead to ugly design

Within the first explorative phase, participants were free to explore the prototypes in a hands-on way. Multiple participants reached for the dice that appealed to them in a visual/aesthetic way, rather than a purely physical way. However, these dice with a higher aesthetic value often seemed to perform less on a functional level (e.g. the black plastic dice was often indicated as 'a design object' because of its shiny texture and convex shape. However, it scored badly in terms of functional experience, as it appeared that these physical attributes diminish the rolling motion and produce too much noise). Based on this experience, several participants mentioned to strive for a better balance between functional, physical and aesthetic levels. All of these aspects were equally mentioned by the participants, and thereby important for the overall experience of an interactive dice as a TUI.

Conclusion evaluation interactive dice

To conclude the evaluation study of interactive dice, we suggest that future interactive dice should consist of plain sides with slightly rounded edges and should be made of softer material that allows bounciness but does not feel too childish. These physical attributes would lead to more unpredictable movements without producing excessive noise. Furthermore participants mentioned that a dice shouldn't be too big and/or too heavy, as it needs to fit nicely into their hand and should not make them be too careful. Texture appeared to have no effect on the functional value, but participants appreciate a nice looking design object. Note for these suggestions that the TUIkit is meant for evaluating early TUI prototypes, which means that further testing throughout the design process is necessary to refine these design suggestions.

DISCUSSION ON TUIKIT AS A METHOD

After having utilized the TUIkit method in a study for the evaluation of interactive dice as a form of a TUI, we will now reflect on how this method contributed to the evaluation of both physical and functional experiences with early physical TUI prototypes. This reflection will be structured according to the four phases of the TUIkit method, whereby we aim to sum up per phase the strengths we experienced and the problems we encountered. Furthermore, we will also formulate suggestions for possible adjustments to tackle these problems in future use of this TUI evaluation method.

Phase 1 – Exploration

As the participants were instructed to explore all of the prototypes in a physical way, we noticed that several of them instantly grasped for the prototype that appealed most to them in an aesthetic way. The participants either spontaneously, or by stimulation by the researcher, explained their reasoning for exploring this specific object first. Furthermore, we noticed that, even though all of the participants were untroubled in exploring the prototypes, they were rather brief and focused on functionality in describing their first experiences to the researcher.

These findings show that the role of the researcher is crucial in this phase. In order to be able to gather a sufficient amount of data, the researcher had to emphasize on the one hand that the focus of this phase was purely physical without thinking of functionalities, and on the other hand what possible physical attributes could be relevant (e.g. size, shape, material, texture, weight). Once the participants got these instructions, they were able to describe their physical experiences with the prototypes using a wide array of physical attributes.

Phase 2 – Differentiation

In order to reflect on the appropriateness of this phase, we mapped all of the words used by the participants to formulate their constructs and contrasts during the physical differentiation. This mapping was based on the five general physical attributes (size, shape, material, texture, weight) that were mentioned by the researcher during the session. By doing so, we aimed to get insight into which physical attributes were used more or less often by the participants. The mapping pointed out that participants used all of the physical attributes during the differentiation. The majority of attributes related to shape and material, while attributes related to texture, weight and size were used less frequently. The participants tended to reuse the words that they used during the physical exploration in phase one. This gives evidence to the importance of phase one, which was to stimulate the participants to verbalize their physical experiences by the use of their own vocabulary.

However, while the first phase did stimulate users verbalizing their physical experiences, the majority of participants experienced and even expressed difficulties in having to come up with new constructs and contrasts. They often tended to use only constructs and contrasts that they already mentioned. Furthermore, this difficulty increased as the participant was presented with more series for differentiation. What we suggest for precluding this difficulty is to stimulate the participant to think further by instructing them to verbally describe what the prototypes feel like. The researcher might then adopt a supporting role, by anticipating on interesting terms used by the participant during his/her verbal expression. Another suggestion is to remove the already gathered constructs and contrasts, which were written down on post-its, from the table and placing these out of direct sight of the participants. This forces the participant to forget about the previous constructs and contrasts more easily, and thereby come up with new ones. Finally, we suggest limiting the amount of series for differentiation to a maximum of eight, as we noticed that participants started to express difficulties from the sixth series of prototypes.

Phase 3 – Interaction

To reflect on this phase, we used a similar approach as utilized within phase two, i.e. mapping all of the words (physical attributes) that the participant used to describe their functional experience (e.g. *"I think it is because of its size that this dice rolls less good than the other one"* or *"The material makes the dice bounce more, which makes it unpredictable"*). Based on this mapping we derived that the participants considered all physical attributes (shape, size, material, weight, texture) as possible influential factors on their functional experience. The fact that they spontaneously used these physical attributes to elaborate on their functional experience shows that they still bore in mind the physical focus used within the first two phases. This links directly to the goal we set for the creation of the TUIkit method, namely, bridging the physical and functional experience with TUI prototypes.

Phase 4 – Joining physical and functional experiences

Several participants mentioned during the fourth phase, in which physical and functional experiences should be conjoined, that it was challenging to find the right balance between their experiences for evaluating the prototypes. They felt like they were forced to choose either their best physical or their best functional experience, as most of the prototypes did not score well on both aspects. This trouble in balancing experiences was most noticeable in classifying the physical attributes according to preference and creating a final top 5 ranking of the prototypes, which most participants found difficult to do.

The balance between physical and functional experience did not only present challenges, but also shows the strength of the TUIkit method during this phase. When participants were asked to conjoin their experiences, we – and even the participants themselves – noticed a difference between their first impressions and the final evaluation of the prototypes. Some of the participants mentioned for example that they were very positive about some specific prototypes at the start of the session, but had to revise their judgment because it scored less on functional value during interaction.

At this point, it is important to clarify that choosing the ultimate prototype that scored best on both physical and functional levels, is not the aim of this method. The aim of the method is to detect the influence of certain physical attributes (e.g. size, shape, texture) on the functional and overall experience. This way, the ideal combination of physical attributes can be selected for particular functional experiences. Participants did try to balance their physical and functional experience, which proved that they actually became aware of these experiences, and were thereby able to indicate which combination of attributes would offer them the best functional value during interaction.

The marking of the prototypes with the applicable physical attributes (construct or contrast) in the Repertory Grid did not prove to be essential for the TUIkit method. Even though the grid offered a good overview of the physical attributes of each prototype in the end, it did not really contribute to the data analysis of the TUIkit method. Furthermore, participants indicated that this task felt contradictory, as they were forced to mark either with the construct or the contrast, which did not always correspond with their actual physical experience.

After applying this method, we formulate two suggestions for future adjustments within this phase. The first suggestion is to find an approach that is less repetitive than marking the applicable physical attributes for each prototype in the Repertory Grid. The outcome of this grid offered a good overview per prototype, but we have the impression that this data does not contribute enough to the final analysis of results in relation to the amount of effort that is required from the participants.

As a second adjustment we suggest to let the participants classify their constructs/contrasts and rank the prototypes first on a physical level and then on a functional level. By separating this evaluation of experiences first, we believe that it might be easier for the participants to find a balance in joining these two – often different – experiences.

CONCLUSION

In this paper, we began by emphasizing the lack of attention that is going to the meaning of material qualities in the design process of TUIs. Previous research suggested that materials are often chosen more for their availability or technical qualities, rather than for their benefits to the user. Our literature study revealed a lack of evaluation methods that are adapted to measure the user experience with different materials although the physical dimensions of a tangible prototype can influence how users interact with it. In our case study, we utilized a new method called TUIkit, to explore the link between both the physical and functional experience of users with interactive dice prototypes.

Our results show that participants on the one hand were able to describe their physical experience using a wide array of physical attributes, and on the other hand became aware of their physical experience and how this influenced their evaluation of the interactive dice prototypes. The outcome of the TUIkit method in the case study also consisted of actual design suggestions for the physical design of interactive dice.

However, through the case study we also noticed some points for improvement. These consisted of for example the requirement to guide participants in focusing solely on physical/functional aspects, and exploring new approaches to facilitate the difficult conjunction of both these physical and functional experiences when evaluating early TUI prototypes.

We conclude that, provided these points of improvement, the TUIkit method is a useful new method for exploring and evaluating the effect of different physical attributes (e.g. shape, size, texture, material, weight) on the functional user experience of early TUI prototypes.

FUTURE WORK

As this was an explorative study, we encourage further research to contribute to the development of a method for the evaluation of UX in TUI prototypes. To this end, it may be interesting to validate the TUIkit method's appropriateness, complexity and reliability by conducting further evaluation studies. Furthermore, testing this method in different contexts (e.g. with other age groups or for the evaluation of a broader variety of TUIs), could lead to a more refined method. Another avenue for further research on the method could be to study the effect of the order of the physical and functional evaluations by reversing the order, or providing different functionalities for the same objects.

ACKNOWLEDGMENTS

The research leading to this paper has been conducted as part of the TIII project funded by IWT with Grant no. IWT/120147/TETRA. We would like to thank our participants, as well as Jolien De Ville and Jelle Saldien for creating the prototypes.

REFERENCES

1. Antle, A. N. (2008). Inquiring materials for tangible prototyping. In *Proceedings of the 2nd International Conference on Tangible and Embedded Interaction* (pp. 139–140). Presented at the TEI'08, Bonn, Germany: ACM.
2. Baskinger, M., & Gross, M. (2010, February). Tangible interaction = form + computing. *Interactions*, *17*(1), 6–11.
3. Buxton, B. (2007). *Sketching User Experiences: Getting the Design Right and the Right Design*. Morgan Kaufmann Publishers Inc.
4. Doering, T. (n.d.). Material-centered design and evaluation of tangible user interfaces. In *Proceedings of the Fifth International Conference on Tangible, Embedded, and Embodied Interaction* (pp. 437–438). Presented at the TEI'11, New York, NY: ACM.
5. Doering, T., Sylvester, A., & Schmidt, A. (May 5-10). Exploring material-centered design concepts for tangible interaction. In *CHI '12 Extended Abstracts on Human Factors in Computing Systems* (pp. 1523–1528). Presented at the CHI EA '12, Austin, Texas: ACM.
6. Fallman, D., & Waterworth, J. (2005). Dealing with user experience and affective evaluation in hci design: A repertory grid approach. In *CHI'05 Workshop on Evaluating Affective Interfaces - Innovative Approaces*. Presented at the CHI'05, Portland.
7. Flatters, I. J., Otten, L., Witvliet, A., Henson, B., Holt, R. J., Culmer, P., … Mon-Williams, M. (2012). Predicting the Effect of Surface Texture on the Qualitative Form of Prehension. *PLOS one*, *7*(3).
8. Fuchsberger, V., Murer, M., & Tscheligi, M. (2013). Materials, materiality, and media. In *Proceedings of the SIGCHI Conference on Human Factors in Computing Systems* (pp. 2853–2862). Presented at the CHI '13, Paris, France: ACM.
9. Gross, S., Bardzell, J., & Bardzell, S. (2014). Structures, Forms, and Stuff: The Materiality and

Medium of Interaction. *Personal Ubiquitous Comput.*, *18*(3), 637–649.

10. Heller, F., & Borchers, J. (2012). Physical prototyping of an on-outlet power-consumption display. *Interactions*, *19*(1), 14–17.
11. Hornecker, E., & Psik, T. (2005). Using ARToolKit markers to build tangible prototypes and simulate other technologies. In *Proceedings of the 2005 IFIP TC13 International Conference on Human-Computer Interaction* (pp. 30–42). Presented at the INTERACT'05, Rome, Italy: Springer-Verlag.
12. Ishii, H. (2008, June). The tangible user interface and its evolution. *Communications of the ACM - Organic user interfaces*, *51*(6), 32–36.
13. Jung, H., & Stolterman, E. (2011). Form and materiality in interaction design: a new approach to HCI. In *CHI '11 Extended Abstracts on Human Factors in Computing Systems* (pp. 399–408). Presented at the CHI EA '11, Vancouver, BC, Canada: ACM.
14. Kelly, G. A. (1963). *A Theory of Personality: The Psychology of Personal Constructs*. W. W. Norton & Company.
15. Kimura, H., Tokunaga, E., Okuda, Y., & Nakajima, T. (2006). CookieFlavors: easy building blocks for wireless tangible input. In *CHI '06 Extended Abstracts on Human Factors in Computing Systems* (pp. 965–970). Presented at the CHI'06, Montréal, Québec, Canada: ACM.
16. Klemmer, S. R., Li, Z., Lin, J., & Landay, J. A. (2004). Papier-Mache: toolkit support for tangible input. In *Proceedings of the SIGCHI Conference on Human Factors in Computing Systems* (pp. 399–406). Presented at the CHI'04, Vienna, Austria: ACM.
17. Lewis, C. (1982). *Using the "thinking Aloud" Method in Cognitive Interface Design*. IBM T.J. Watson Research Center.
18. Mellis, D., Follmer, S., Hartmann, B., Buechley, L., & Gross, M. D. (2013). FAB at CHI: digital fabrication tools, design, and community. In *CHI '13 Extended Abstracts on Human Factors in Computing Systems* (pp. 3307–3310). Presented at the CHI'13, Paris, France: ACM.
19. Mota, C. (2011). The rise of personal fabrication. In *Proceedings of the 8th ACM Conference on Creativity and Cognition* (pp. 279–288). Presented at the C&C '11, Atlanta, Georgia, USA: ACM.
20. Norman, D. A. (1999, June). Affordance, conventions, and design. *Interactions*, *6*(3), 38–43.
21. Provost, G., & Robert, J. (2013). The dimensions of positive and negative user experiences with interactive products. *2nd conference on Design, User Experience, and Usability: design philosophy, methods, and tools*, *I*, pp. 399-408.
22. Rosner, D. K. (n.d.). The material practices of collaboration. In *Proceedings of the ACM 2012 Conference on Computer Supported Cooperative Work* (pp. 1155–1164). Presented at the CSCW '12, Seattle, WA, USA: ACM.
23. Sartori, L., Straulino, E., Castiello, U., & Avenanti, A. (2011). How Objects Are Grasped: The Interplay between Affordances and End-Goals. *PLOS One*, *6*(9).
24. Schmid, M., Rümelin, S., & Richter, H. (2013). Empowering materiality: inspiring the design of tangible interactions. In *Proceedings of the 7th International Conference on Tangible, Embedded and Embodied Interaction* (pp. 91–98). Presented at the TEI '13, Barcelona, Spain: ACM.
25. Shaer, O., & Hornecker, E. (2010). Tangible User Interfaces: Past, Present, and Future Directions. *Foundations and Trends in Human-Computer Interaction*, *3*(1-2), 1–137.
26. Sharlin, E., Watson, B., Kitamura, Y., Kishino, F., & Itoh, Y. (2004). On tangible user interfaces, humans and spatiality. *Personal and Ubiquitous Computing*, *8*(5), 338–346.
27. Wiethoff, A., Schneider, H., Küfner, J., Rohs, M., Butz, A., & Greenberg, S. (2013). Paperbox: a toolkit for exploring tangible interaction on interactive surfaces. In *Proceedings of the 9th ACM Conference on Creativity & Cognition Pages 64-73* (pp. 64–73). Presented at the C&C'13, Sydney, NSW, Australia: ACM.
28. Wiethoff, A., Schneider, H., Rohs, M., Butz, A., & Greenberg, S. (2012). Sketch-a-TUI: low cost prototyping of tangible interactions using cardboard and conductive ink. In *Proceedings of the Sixth International Conference on Tangible, Embedded and Embodied Interaction* (pp. 309–312). Presented at the TEI'12, Kingston, Ontario, Canada: ACM.
29. Xu, D., Read, J. C., & Sheehan, R. (2008). In search of tangible magic. In *Proceedings of the 22nd British HCI Group Annual Conference on People and Computers: Culture, Creativity, Interaction* (Vol. 2, pp. 97–100). Presented at the BCS-HCI '08, Como, Italy: British Computer Society Swinton, UK.

Lamello: Passive Acoustic Sensing for Tangible Input Components

Valkyrie Savage*†, Andrew Head†, Björn Hartmann†,
Dan B Goldman*, Gautham Mysore*, Wilmot Li*
* Adobe Research, † UC Berkeley EECS
{valkyrie,andrewhead,bjoern}@eecs.berkeley.edu, {dgoldman,gmysore,wilmotli}@adobe.com

ABSTRACT
We describe *Lamello*, an approach for creating tangible input components that recognize user interaction via passive acoustic sensing. Lamello employs comb-like structures with varying-length tines at interaction points (e.g., along slider paths). Moving a component generates tine strikes; a real-time audio processing pipeline analyzes the resultant sounds and emits high-level interaction events. Our main contributions are in the co-design of the tine structures, information encoding schemes, and audio analysis. We demonstrate 3D printed Lamello-powered buttons, sliders, and dials.

Author Keywords
3D Printing; Sound; Tangible Interaction

ACM Classification Keywords
H.5.2 User Interfaces: Prototyping

INTRODUCTION
Tangible input components have advantages over "flat" interfaces like touch screens. They are critical for eyes-free interaction and muscle memory, and can improve task speed and precision [9]. Such devices typically comprise integrated assemblies of electronics, enclosures, and microcontroller code.

Recently, researchers have begun to explore acoustically sensing interactions – such as scratching – with digitally-fabricated objects that encode information in surface textures [7, 11]. In this paper, we extend this line of work from sensing surface features to sensing interactions with tangible components that users can push, slide, and turn.

Our technique, Lamello, integrates algorithmically-generated tine structures into movable components to create passive tangible inputs (Figure 1). Manipulating these inputs creates sounds which can be captured using an inexpensive contact microphone and interpreted using real-time audio signal processing. Lamello predicts the fundamental frequency of each tine based on its geometry: thus, recognition does not require

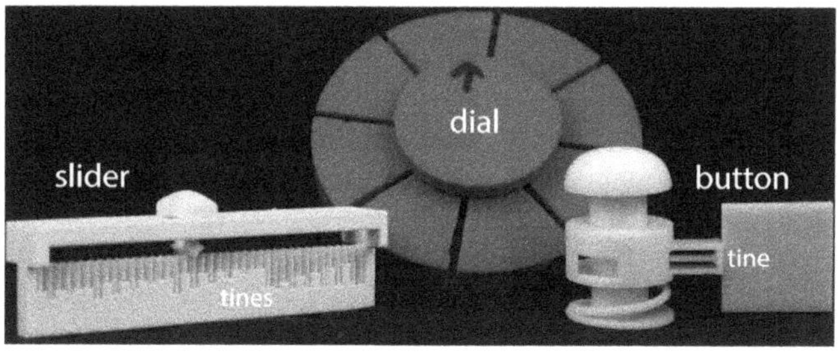

Figure 1. Passive tangible inputs that can be sensed acoustically.

training examples. The decoded high-level events can then be forwarded to interactive applications. The name "Lamello" is derived from the Lamellophone family of instruments, which create sound through vibrating tongues of varying lengths.

Recognizing mechanically-generated sound for input has important limitations – only movement generates sound, so steady state cannot be sensed – but also appealing characteristics: Components can be fabricated from a single material (e.g., 3D printed ABS plastic), and "wiring" only requires attaching a microphone. In this paper, we provide design and fabrication guidelines, and demonstrate several components that use the Lamello approach. Our evaluation shows that training-free recognition is possible, though our recognizer only has useful accuracy for a subset of tested tines.

RELATED WORK
Lamello builds on prior work in interactive device design and acoustic sensing. Recent work proposes a variety of approaches for creating interactive objects via digital fabrication: Printed Optics [16] uses printed lightpipes in optically-sensed input components; Sauron [13] modifies hollow 3D models to enable an embedded camera to sense interactions. These systems generate geometry designed to work with specific recognition techniques. We adopt a similar strategy but focus on acoustic sensing for enabling interactivity.

Passive acoustic sensing has been used for detecting mid-air gestures (SoundWave [3]), enabling touch sensing on the forearm and palm (Skinput [6]), distinguishing between different objects striking a touch surface (TapSense [5]), and recognizing stroke gestures on surfaces [4]. Active swept-frequency ultrasound sensing, which uses controlled audio output to infer interactions, can detect touch and grasp gestures on rigid objects [12]. The most relevant previous systems are Acoustic Barcodes [7] and Stane [11], which encode

CHI 2015, April 18–23, 2015, Seoul, Republic of Korea.
ACM 978-1-4503-3145-6/15/04.
http://dx.doi.org/10.1145/2702123.2702207

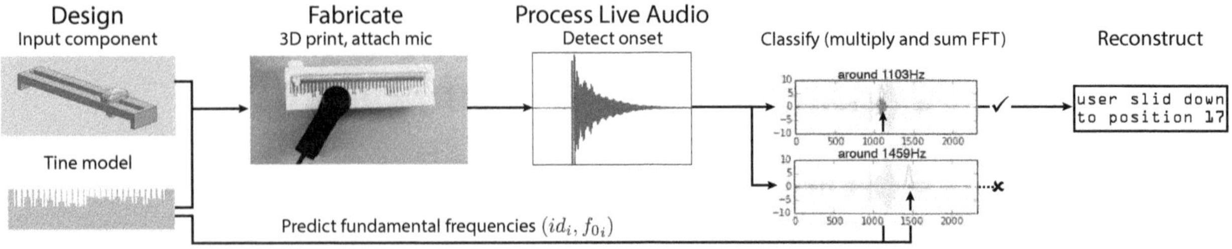

Figure 2. Lamello reuses information between the design, fabrication, and audio processing steps to allow training-free passive acoustic sensing.

information in fabricated objects that emit specific, detectable sounds during interaction. We extend their contributions: Our 3D tines encode additional information in their vibration frequencies, and we enable a wider variety of interactions than stroking or scratching. Designing specific vibration frequencies for objects has also been explored in procedurally generated metallophones [14]. Other approaches to providing passive tangible input include IR markers [15], capacitive signatures [1], and magnetic fields [8]. Audio sensing has the benefit that it does not require direct contact or line-of-sight.

LAMELLO: AUDIO GENERATION AND PROCESSING

There are two main challenges in developing a passive acoustic sensing technique that supports a variety of input controls: designing the physical mechanisms for generating sounds and developing recognition algorithms that can interpret those sounds in the intended manner (Figure 2).

Generating sounds with tines

To generate sounds, we embed tine structures in input components (Figure 1). Our tines are rectangular beams, attached at their base to the component and free to deflect at their top. Interacting with a component causes tine plucks; these vibrate the body of the component and are captured by a contact microphone. Tines can be arranged in configurations supporting different interactions (e.g., sliding, rotating, pressing).

Acoustic uniqueness: Different tines should generate unique, distinguishable sounds: we achieve this by systematically varying tine geometry. We model a vibrating tine as an ideal cantilevered beam of uniform density in free vibration [10]:

$$f_0 = \frac{1.875^2 \sqrt{\frac{E \frac{bh^3}{12}}{\rho(bh)L^4}}}{2\pi} \text{Hz}$$

Fundamental frequency (f_0) is governed by several variables: tine breadth (b), height (h), and length (L), as well as material properties (density ρ, Young's Modulus E). Our designs keep b and h constant, varying L to achieve different frequencies.

Our prototypes are 3D printed, resulting in non-uniform material deposition. To test the applicability of our model, we compared predicted and observed f_0 for several tines printed on two uPrint SE Plus FDM printers using Stratasys ABSplus-P430 thermoplastic. We find an appropriate material parameter by minimizing the error between observations and measurements. Fitted E values ranged from 9500 to 15500 based on print orientation and particular printer. The remaining error $\mu = 69.0Hz$ ($\sigma = 112.5Hz$) shows our model usefully applies to printed tines. Estimation of f_0 can be further improved by measuring post-print with calipers.

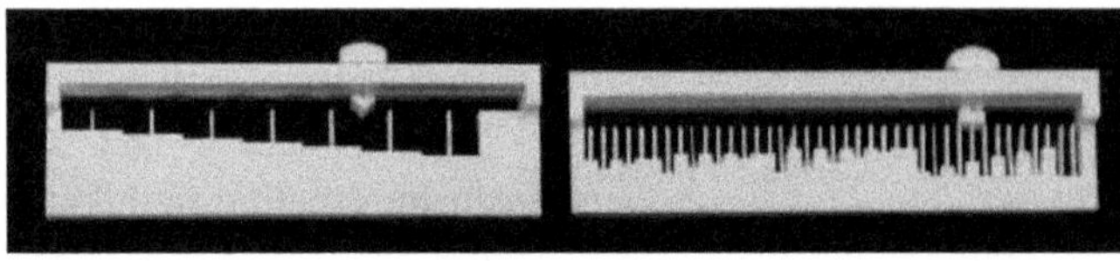

Figure 3. We experimented with two different encoding mechanisms for sliders: linearly increasing sequences (left) and de Bruijn (right). de Bruijn sequences allow classification of fewer tine lengths, but require more consecutive tine recognitions to determine position and direction.

Physical and fabrication constraints: A tine which is too thin can break or hit adjacent tines when struck, reducing recognition accuracy. A too-thick tine requires greater striking force, interfering with a user's experience. In our experience, ABS tines need 1:25 $< thickness : length <$ 1:2 to have appropriate stiffness for classification. Tine performance also depends on print orientation: on fused-deposition modeling machines, a tine is most reliable with its length laid in the printer's XY plane, as it is thus filled by a continuous extrusion. When printed in Z, tines can break as layers separate. Filleting can mitigate this problem, but may reduce the accuracy of the vibration model in predicting f_0. We fabricated tines with f_0 between $400Hz$ ($4mm$ x $50mm$ x $6mm$) and $4000Hz$ ($7.25mm$ x $6.0mm$ x $1.2mm$). Minimum tine size is determined by printer limitations: our printers have Z resolution $0.254mm$ and minimum XY feature size $1.194mm$.

Alternative fabrication techniques: Other printing or fabrication processes may not be orientation dependent. We have laser cut tines from Polyoxymethylene (Delrin) sheets, integrating these tine strips into 3D printed components. Tine sizes are similar, as laser cutting caused heat deflection in smaller feature sizes. Smaller tine sizes and higher frequencies may be achievable using different fabrication processes, e.g., injection molding or MEMS micromachining.

Encoding information: We use unique f_0s to differentiate buttons and directions on a D-pad. For position sensing, f_0 can increase across the range of motion (Figure 3 left). If more distinctions are needed than can be reliably recognized by varying f_0, we create de Bruijn patterns [2] (Figure 3 right). A de Bruijn sequence $D(k, n)$ is one which, given an alphabet size k and a subsequence length n, contains each subsequence exactly once: we can uniquely infer sequence position from n recognitions. This requires fewer f_0s, but more contiguous tine recognitions to determine user input.

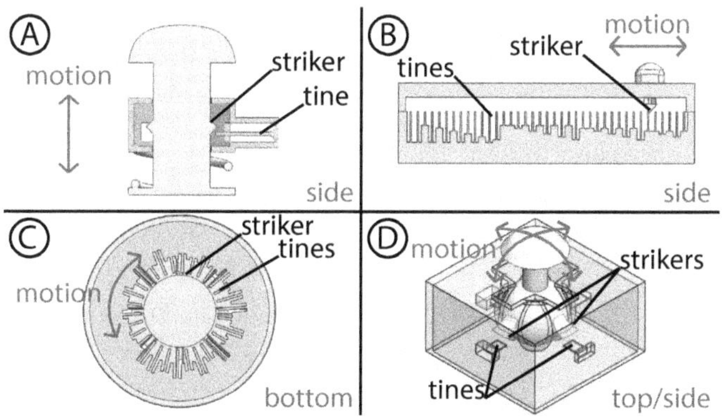

Figure 4. The Lamello technique can be used to sense a variety of physical motions, including up/down on a button, back/forward on a slider, and rotation on a dial or scroll wheel. Four tines used together can sense up, down, left, and right on a direction pad.

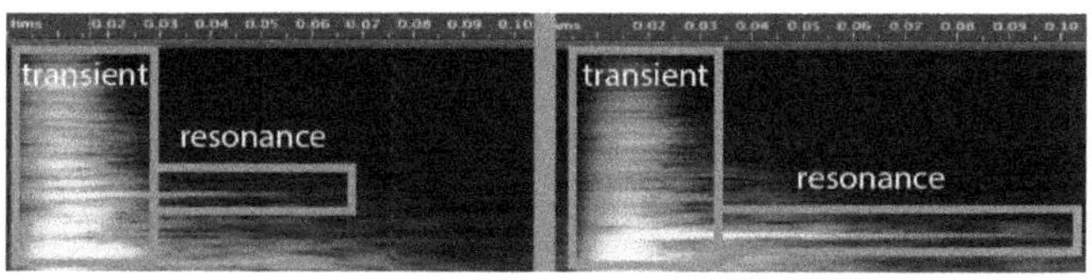

Figure 5. Two typical tine strikes (100ms): high-frequency (left) and low-frequency (right). We mark transients and resonance. Note the higher frequency has less energy (darker colors) and faster decay (shorter).

Integration of tines into larger components

We augmented several traditional input components: buttons, sliders, dials, and joysticks. Each has a "striker" attached to the user-facing "handle" (Figure 4). These strikers overlap with tine ends by $0.25 - 1mm$, balancing clear signal generation with easy interaction. Through testing, we determined that a triangular striker profile works best. The button has a rib around its shaft that strikes a tine when a user depresses it. The slider has a wiper that overlaps with the tops of tines (tines have different lengths, but are top-aligned). The dial works similarly, arranged radially rather than linearly. The D-pad derives from the button: a striker strikes a tine on the base as the user moves the handle up, down, left, or right.

Audio processing pipeline

The audio signal of a tine strike is characterized by an initial transient—a short high energy sound across a wide range of frequencies—followed by free vibration with a local long-decay energy peak at the tine's resonant frequency (Figure 5). Conceptually, our recognizer detects a transient, finds the dominant resonant frequency after the transient passes, and compares it to predicted tine frequencies.

Our audio processing pipeline, written in Python, uses basic frequency-domain features for classification. We sample our contact microphone at $16000Hz$. Our frames are 2048 samples ($128ms$), and our hop length (offset between successive, overlapping frames) is 800 samples ($50ms$), for a frame overlap of 61%. Analyzing a frame takes $5ms$, plus additional latency incurred by sound hardware. In addition to the real-time audio stream, our recognition algorithm also takes an ordered list of (id_i, f_{0i}) tuples describing the tine ordering and fundamental frequencies of a component as input.

For each frame, we first determine if a tine strike is present using a standard onset detector (with an empirically-determined amplitude threshold). Once an onset is detected, we wait 2 frame hops for the transient response to pass. We classify the subsequent frame (computation time: $5ms$). Our best-case onset-to-classification latency is therefore $2 * 50ms + 5ms = 105ms$. In practice, we have seen latency of $107.3ms$ (σ=$9.67ms$). Our sound card and driver introduce latency as they collect and report blocks: one could reduce overhead with optimized sound drivers and sample block sizes.

To classify, we compute a Fast Fourier Transform on the window, then normalize FFT bin values to represent fractions of overall audio energy. For each tine id_i, we generate a new metric: the dot product of the scaled FFT and a Gaussian centered at the bin for f_{0i}, representing the fraction of audio energy e_i in the neighborhood of f_{0i}. To account for lower energy at higher frequencies, we use a scaling factor proportional to the frequency and a σ for the Gaussians empirically determined per component, giving an adjusted list of e_{iadj}.

Mapping a recognized tine identity $id_R = argmax(e_{iadj})$ to user actions is straightforward. For buttons and joysticks, id_R maps directly to a discrete input (press, up, down, left, or right). Similarly, for dials and sliders that encode position with linearly increasing tine lengths, id_R maps to a unique position. For dials and sliders that use a de Bruijn sequence $D(k, n)$, we use each sequence of n recognized tines to determine the corresponding position within the sequence.

EVALUATION

To determine whether Lamello tines can be classified reliably and in real-time, we performed an accuracy test and built a real-time demonstration using Lamello controls.

We recorded 10 strikes for each tine on a printed dial and slider, and a laser-cut Delrin slider. Printed components were actuated with their strikers; Delrin tines were hand-plucked to determine effects of different striking methods. We classified each strike and report classification accuracy in Table 1.

We achieve promising accuracy (precision = 93%, recall = 90%) with a four-tine slider (predicted frequencies 924, 1103, 1340, and $1662Hz$). This suggests that useful interaction with Lamello is within reach. However, precision and recall rates are much lower on a set of 7 tines with frequencies above $2kHz$: the recognizer fails to classify higher f_0, which have lower energies and shorter decays (Figure 6).

To explore the utility of our technique, we used a Lamello slider and mouse emulation to control a Pong game. The achieved latency was sufficient for simple gameplay; however, Lamello may be better suited to provide input for applications such as volume or lighting control, where some latency and occasional misclassified events are acceptable.

Control	P_{4tines}	R_{4tines}	P_{7tines}	R_{7tines}
FDM Slider	93%	90%	49%	56%
FDM Dial	90%	85%	63%	54%
Plucked Delrin	98%	97%	72%	73%

Table 1. Recognition precision and recall of our printed input components using model geometry-predicted frequencies.

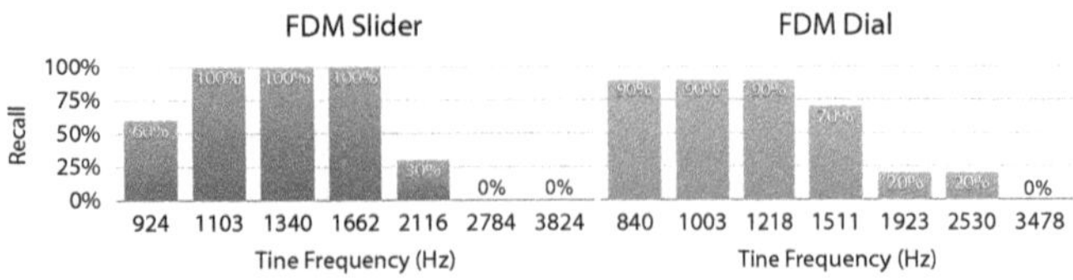

Figure 6. Per-tine recall for striking Lamello slider and dial tines. We observe high recall for low-frequency subsets of tines.

DISCUSSION AND FUTURE WORK

Initial experiments with Lamello are encouraging: components augmented with tines are easy to print and use, and tines produce unique, predictable frequencies. However, classification accuracy still needs improvement, and may require a new approach for $f_0 > 2kHz$. We identified several sources of errors to address in future work:

Striker mechanism: Finger-plucked tines having higher recognition rates than striker-actuated tines suggests that striker-created noise contributes to misclassifications.

Signal attenuation: While microphones placed at opposite ends of a printed slider produce similar overall accuracy, tines are more correctly classified by the closer microphone. Though we could not directly correlate microphone distance and signal RMS energy, this suggests minimizing distance between microphone and tines may improve accuracy.

Resonance and harmonics: Struck tines exhibit an energy peak at the predicted f_0, but their frequency spectrum is considerably more complex due to harmonics, component resonance, and other unmodeled material effects (e.g., the layered construction of 3D prints). Competing with non-fundamental vibrations is most problematic for short tines, which have lower energy. Future work can also probe optimal frequency distributions to avoid overlap between tine harmonics.

Beyond recognition rates, the Lamello approach can only detect position *changes*—it cannot sense static configurations, nor can we currently distinguish between the two directions in which a tine can be struck. In the future, we envision a library of parametric models added to larger tangible devices: we plan to leverage existing microphones in smartphones and tablets for sensing. This would open applications beyond prototyping (e.g., custom controllers for tablet games), but will require more sophisticated signal processing to filter out environmental noise and to deinterlace multiple input components manipulated simultaneously.

In conclusion, we have demonstrated the use of mechanically generated sound to support interactions beyond strokes [7] and scratches [11]. We hope our work opens a larger space of Lamellophonic input devices.

ACKNOWLEDGEMENTS

This work is supported in part by the NSF under grant DGE 1106400 and a Sloan Fellowship.

REFERENCES

1. Chan, L., Müller, S., Roudaut, A., and Baudisch, P. CapStones and ZebraWidgets: Sensing stacks of building blocks, dials and sliders on capacitive touch screens. In *CHI '12*, 2189–2192.
2. de Bruijn, N. G. A combinatorial problem. In *Koninklijke Nederlandse Akademie v. Wetenschappen 49*, Indagationes Mathematicae (1946), 758–764.
3. Gupta, S., Morris, D., Patel, S., and Tan, D. SoundWave: Using the Doppler effect to sense gestures. In *CHI '12*, 1911–1914.
4. Harrison, C., and Hudson, S. E. Scratch input: Creating large, inexpensive, unpowered and mobile finger input surfaces. In *UIST '08*, 205–208.
5. Harrison, C., Schwarz, J., and Hudson, S. E. TapSense: Enhancing finger interaction on touch surfaces. In *UIST '11*, 627–636.
6. Harrison, C., Tan, D., and Morris, D. Skinput: Appropriating the body as an input surface. In *CHI '10*, 453–462.
7. Harrison, C., Xiao, R., and Hudson, S. Acoustic barcodes: Passive, durable and inexpensive notched identification tags. In *UIST '12*, 563–568.
8. Hwang, S., Ahn, M., and Wohn, K.-y. MagGetz: Customizable passive tangible controllers on and around conventional mobile devices. In *UIST '13*, 411–416.
9. Klemmer, S. R., Hartmann, B., and Takayama, L. How bodies matter: Five themes for interaction design. In *DIS '06*, 140–149.
10. Meirovitch, L. *Analytical Methods in Vibration.* The MacMillan Company, 1967.
11. Murray-Smith, R., Williamson, J., Hughes, S., and Quaade, T. Stane: Synthesized surfaces for tactile input. In *CHI '08*, 1299–1302.
12. Ono, M., Shizuki, B., and Tanaka, J. Touch & Activate: Adding interactivity to existing objects using active acoustic sensing. In *UIST '13*, 31–40.
13. Savage, V., Chang, C., and Hartmann, B. Sauron: Embedded single-camera sensing of printed physical user interfaces. In *UIST '13*, 447–456.
14. Umetani, N., Mitani, J., and Igarashi, T. Designing custom-made metallophone with concurrent eigenanalysis. In *NIME '10*, 26–30.
15. Weiss, M., Wagner, J., Jansen, Y., Jennings, R., Khoshabeh, R., Hollan, J. D., and Borchers, J. SLAP Widgets: Bridging the gap between virtual and physical controls on tabletops. In *CHI '09*, 481–490.
16. Willis, K. D. D., Brockmeyer, E., Hudson, S., and Poupyrev, I. Printed optics: 3D printing of embedded optical elements for interactive devices. In *UIST '12*, 589–598.

WonderLens: Optical Lenses and Mirrors for Tangible Interactions on Printed Paper

Rong-Hao Liang* Chao Shen† Yu-Chien Chan† Guan-Ting Chou†
Liwei Chan* De-Nian Yang‡ Mike Y. Chen* Bing-Yu Chen*
*†National Taiwan University ‡Academia Sinica
*{rhliang, liweichan, mikechen, robin}@ntu.edu.tw ‡dnyang@iis.sinica.edu.tw

ABSTRACT
This work presents *WonderLens*, a system of optical lenses and mirrors for enabling tangible interactions on printed paper. When users perform spatial operations on the optical components, they deform the visual content that is printed on paper, and thereby provide dynamic visual feedback on user interactions without any display devices. The magnetic unit that is embedded in each lens and mirror allows the unit to be identified and tracked using an analog Hall-sensor grid that is placed behind the paper, so the system provides additional auditory and visual feedback through different levels of embodiment, further enhancing the interactivity with the printed content on the physical paper.

Author Keywords
Paper, Lens, Mirror, Optical Illusion, Tangible Interaction.

ACM Classification Keywords
H.5.2. Information Interfaces and Presentation (e.g. HCI): User Interfaces

INTRODUCTION
Tangible user interface (TUI) [6] are enabled on portable displays, such as tablet PCs [12, 20], to facilitate users' interactions with digital content. Paper, which is lightweight and versatile, is also a highly portable display. Most people still feel that physical paper are more comfortable for reading and playing than electronic displays (such as e-paper, LCDs). Paper also affords natural user interactions, because our interactions with paper builds upon our "pre-existing knowledge of the everyday, non-digital world" [7]. However, since the content that is printed on paper is static, it constrains the interactivity of printed paper.

Previous researches have increased the interactivity of printed contents on paper, for example, by applying mechanical movable structures [4] or augmenting information on the paper by using machine readable formats, such as magnetic stripes [8, 11]. Augmented Reality (AR) methods provide more seamless experiences by using a camera-projector system to project images onto paper [16, 17, 19] or provide camera-mounted handheld devices or HUDs [2] that enable users to explore the augmented visual content on the paper. Although AR-based methods support rich and interactive content, the need for additional display devices and/or external sensing mechanisms may reduce the immersion enjoyed by the interacting users. To increases immersiveness, Listen reader [1] allows users to explore the audio information that is in a specifically designed book, which is based on proximity and RFID sensing. Jabberstamp [15] enables children to associate recorded audio with paper drawings by using a stylus, which is based on electromagnetic resonance (EMR) sensing. However, without dynamic display capabilities, these systems provide only auditory feedback.

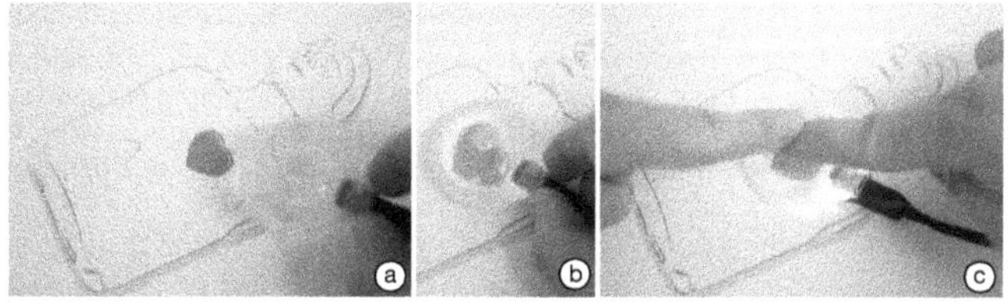
Figure 1. Immediate visual feedback provided by an LED-mounted *flexible convex lens*. (b) In a CPR learning program, the lens blinks to red to prompt the user to place the lens on the heart that is printed on the paper. (c) The heart is magnified to prompt the user to start. (d) The user presses the lens to generate pulses, making the heart contract; the progress light then changes.

This work presents *WonderLens*, a system of tangible lenses and mirrors that supports tangible interactions on printed paper. When users perform spatial operations on the lenses and mirrors, these components distort the printed content, providing dynamic visual feedback without the need for additional display devices. In each of lenses and mirrors is embedded a specifically designed magnetic unit, allowing the system to track their types and states of the optical components in real time using an analog Hall-sensor grid that is attached to the back of the paper. Accordingly, the system can improve user experiences by providing more auditory and visual information for users.

Figure 1 shows an example of interactive CPR learning to illustrate the proposed idea. When a user moves a PDMS (poly-dimethylsiloxane)-made *flexible convex lens* to a desired position, the heart that is printed on the paper becomes

CHI 2015, April 18 - April 23 2015, Seoul, Korea

http://dx.doi.org/10.1145/2702123.2702434

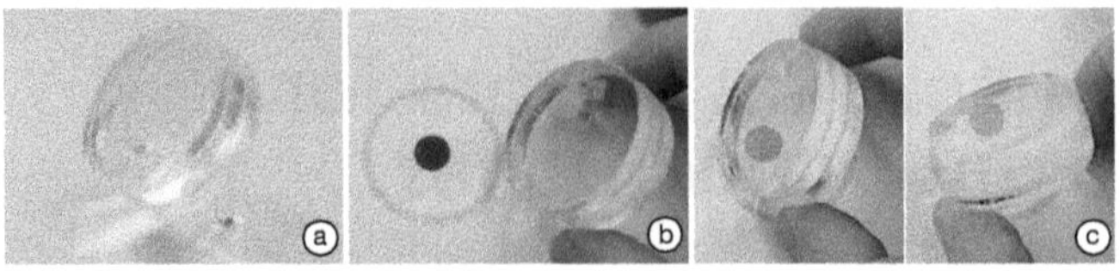

Figure 2. (a) ***Tilted cylindrical lens*****. (b) Optical refraction causes an offset on the circular symbol, and therefore displays the orientation of the lens.**

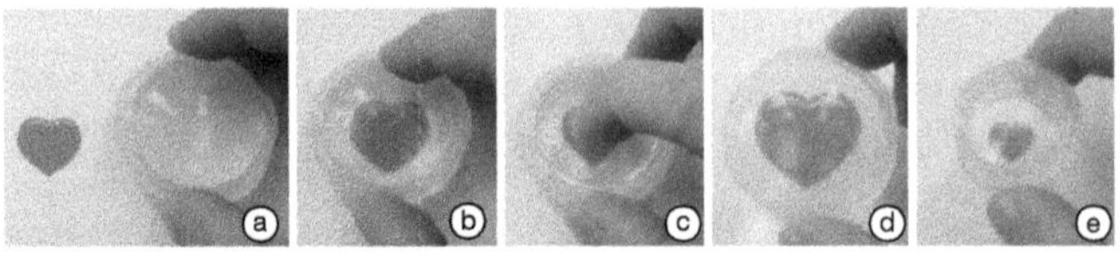

Figure 3. ***Convex lens*** **and** ***concave lens*****. (a) With an air gap beneath the convex lens, the convex lens (b) magnifies the underlying content. (c) Pressing the** ***flexible*** **convex lens reduces the magnification ratio. (d) Lifting the convex lens increases the magnification ratio. (e) Lifting the concave lens increases the shrinkage ratio.**

larger to prompt the user to continue. When the user presses and releases the lens, the user can perceive not only the printed heart contracts through the lens, but also the progress indicated by blinking point light and simultaneous heartbeat sound. This example shows that the tangible lens provides seamless user experiences of the information that is embedded in printed paper.

EXPLORING USES OF OPTICAL LENSES AND MIRRORS

This work begins with an exploration of optical lenses and mirrors. Various lenses and mirrors are fabricated by laser-cutting acrylic and molding PDMS – the material that is conventionally used to make disposable contact lenses. Analyses of their optical features and physical affordances revealed that some lenses and mirrors can provide dynamic visual feedback in the corresponding operations because of the optical illusions that they can cause. Five basic types of optical components and their corresponding visual effects are identified as the most useful and comfortable for user interactions. Simple graphical design guidelines for them are provided hereafter.

The *tilted cylindrical lens* (Figure 2) is made of a transparent acrylic cylinder. Tilting the cylinder causes it to refract the underlying graphical content, causing a small offset of that content from its actual position. The offset is proportional to both the angle of tilt and the thickness of the cylinder. Rotating the cylindrical lens results in an visual illusion of rotation, which can be perceived over a wide range of viewing angles. Circular symbols are effective for illustrating this effect.

A *convex lens* magnifies the underlying graphical content, whereas a *concave lens* shrinks the underlying graphical content, as shown in Figure 3. The size of the magnified content is proportional to the distance between the bottom of the lens and the paper. Fabricating them using PDMS and maintaining an air gap beneath them allow users to *press* them to change the magnification or shrinkage. Symbols that are smaller than the lenses are effective for illustrating this effect.

Prism (Figure 4) duplicates content in a manner that is determined by its median line. The distance between the duplicated images is determined by the angle and height of the prism, and also the distance between the bottom of prism and the paper. Translating or rotating a prism also produces optical illusions over a wide range of viewing angles. Symbols that exhibit reflective symmetry and simple lines are effective for illustrating this effect.

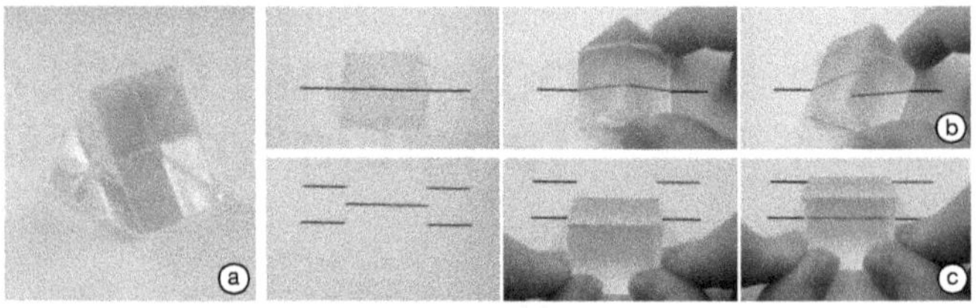

Figure 4. (a) ***Prism*****. (b) Rotating a prism on a line to break it. (c) Moving a prism on the lines to connect them.**

Figure 5. ***Angled mirrors*****. (a) $\pi/3$ angle mirror. (b) Rotate a $\pi/3$ mirror to select and complete different sectors. (c) Move a $\pi/3$ angled mirror to proportionally scale a hexagon. (d) $\pi/2$ angle mirror. (e) Move a $\pi/2$ angled mirror to generate several replicates. (f) Move a $\pi/2$ angled mirror to non-proportionally scale a rectangle.**

Angled Mirror (Figure 5), formed by two mirrors that face each other but at a certain angle rather than directly, can complete a partial content or generate several replicates of the content. The applicable principle is similar to that of a kaleidoscope: the visual effect of optical reflection is determined by the position of the angled mirror and the angle that is formed by the two mirrors. Symbols that are customized for differently angled mirrors can provide visual feedback on rotations and translations.

Based on the guidelines described above foregoing information, designers can incorporate the specified symbols into their designs of graphical content, allowing users to explore the hidden information using the lenses and mirrors.

SENSING THE LENSES, MIRRORS AND PRINTED PAPER

A sensing platform is developed to investigate the possible interactions between lenses, printed content, and digital information. To sense the near-surface interactions that are performed using optical lenses and to maintain their transparency, a specially designed permanent magnetic unit is attached to each optical lens as shown in Figure 6. The magnetic units carry essential information about the different types of lenses, including the ID, position, and orientation. The magnetic unit is also carefully located to maximize the transparency of each lens. An analog Hall-sensor grid [13] (Figure 7a), which consists of $21 \times 32 = 672$ Winson WSH136 analog Hall sensors, is measured in 2mm thick with an 21(W)$\times$16(H) cm^2 sensing area, which is placed behind

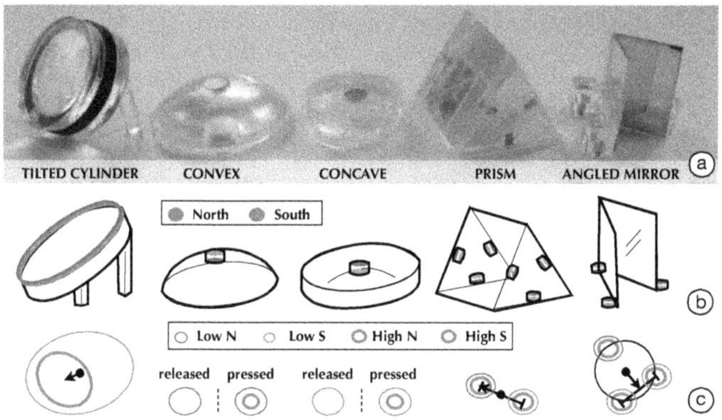

Figure 6. (a) Optical lenses and mirrors that have embedded magnetic units. (b) Placement of magnets in each of lenses and mirrors. (c) Resulting features of the magnetic field images.

Figure 7. Hardware. (a) Paper and sensing platform. Wireless and wired LED-mounted flexible convex lens.

the paper to track the magnetic unit in each lens, using the sensing algorithm that was proposed by GaussBits [12], and to identify the types of each lens from the features (e.g. blob sizes and positions) that are extracted from the magnetic-field image.

To realize the functionality of a piece of printed paper while modifying it as little as possible, to each piece of paper in this study is attached an RFID tag and two small magnets. An RFID reader and two magnets are also attached to the sensing platform to sense the presence and determine the ID, as shown in Figure 7a. The small magnets allow users to easily snap the paper onto the sensing platform for ease of alignment. The system recognizes the RFID tag of the “snapped” piece of paper and loads the corresponding digital information to enable user interactions.

ADDITIONAL AUDITORY AND VISUAL FEEDBACK

In addition to the optical illusions that are provided by the lenses and mirrors, the system can provide additional feedback that enriches interactivity and facilitate communications between the users and the system. With reference to Fishkin’s taxnomy of different levels of embodiment in TUI [3], the proposed platform provides additional auditory and visual feedback for three different levels of embodiment. With regard to auditory feedback, the system provide *environmental* sounds using the speaker of the laptop to which the sensing platform is connected. With regard to visual feedback, besides the optical illusions that are fully embodied in the lenses, an additional low-power consumption full-color LED is embedded into the LED-mounted flexible convex lenses

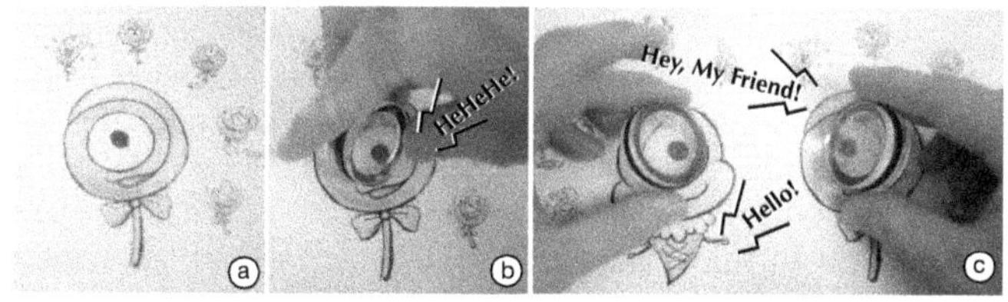

Figure 8. (a) Interactive storytelling application. A user (b) rolls the character’s eye by rotating the tilted cylindrical lens, and the character tells user what he sees. (c) Two characters chat when they are looking at each other.

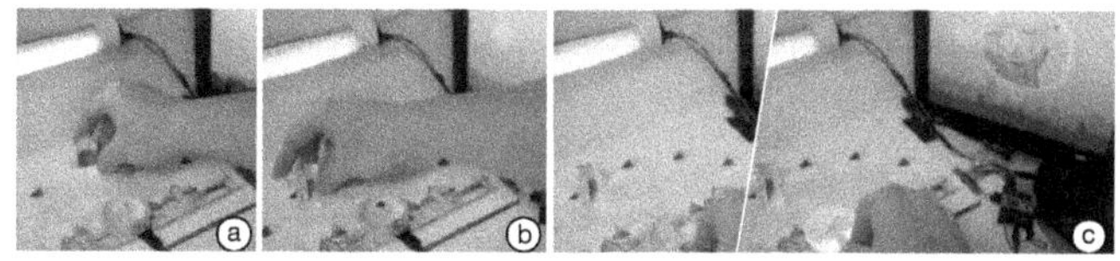

Figure 9. (a) Hide-and-Seek game. A user (b) places an angled mirror on a sun symbol to set the time to 10am, changing the ambient light and presenting the detail view on the remote display. (c) The user moves an LED-mounted convex lens to find hidden characters. Once found, the lens glows to prompt the user to check the remote display to see which character has been found.

to provide simple visual hints *nearby* the printed content, as shown in Figure 7b. Also, a full-color LED strip that can be easily attached to a lamp or a wall provides *environmental* ambient light, and a laptop display provides rich visual information that is *distant* from the users.

APPLICATION EXAMPLES

Based on the implementation described above, the utility of the lenses and the additional visual feedback are illustrated using three examples, according to the different levels of embodiment. Auditory feedback were provided for all examples.

Storytelling (Figure 8). In the interactive storytelling program, a user places a *tilted cylindrical lens* on a character’s eye. Optical refraction shifts the character’s eye to the side toward which the lens is tilted. The user rolls the character’s eye by rotating the lens, and the character vocally tells the user what he sees. When the two characters in the story look at each other, they chat. This example shows how the lens functions using *only auditory* feedback.

CPR learning (Figure 1). In the CPR learning program, a user places an LED-mounted *flexible convex lens* on a patient’s heart that is printed on the paper, and the user sees the blinking heartbeat light signals through an embedded point light, while simultaneously hearing the heartbeat. The user saves the patient by pressing and releasing the soft convex lens at a constant rate. While providing the pulses, the user can see the patient’s heart contractions and monitor progress by observing the light. This example shows how the lens works with additional visual feedback *nearby* the printed content.

Hide-and-Seek (Figure 9). In the hide-and-seek game, a user places an *angled mirror* on one of the hybrid sun (day)-and-moon (night) symbols on the paper to set the time of the story. When the angled mirror has been placed, it reflects the whole image of the selected part of the symbol, the ambient light changes in intensity and/or type, and the remote display shows an evocative scenario. In each scene, users can move an LED-mounted *convex lens* on the paper to find hidden characters out. When a character is found, the lens glows to prompt the user to check the character's details on the distant display, which is located in front of the user. Using the mirror to select another time changes hidden characters' positions again. This example demonstrates the operation of the lens and mirror with additional *environmental* and *distant* visual feedback.

CONCLUSION AND FUTURE WORK

This work has presented *WonderLens*, a system of lenses and mirrors that augments tangible interactions with printed materials. Five basic components, a proof-of-concept system, and several extensions are proposed to demonstrate possible tangible and embodied interactions. Future work should consider the fabrication of advanced lenses by CNC milling or 3D printing [14, 18] to provide more features; the use of an advanced process to manufacture analog Hall-sensor grid or 3D LC-Tag sensing [5] to reduce the cost of the sensing platform, or the combination of lenses and mirrors with circuit printing [10] and an energy harvesting mechanism [9] to further enhance the interactivity of printed paper.

ACKNOWLEDGEMENTS

We sincerely acknowledge the helpful comments of the anonymous reviewers, and thank Ying-Hsuan Yu for her assistances on implementation. This work was supported by Ministry of Science and Technology, National Taiwan University and Intel Corporation under Grants MOST102-2911-I-002-001, NTU103R7501, NTU103R104130, and MOST103-2221-E-002-158-MY3.

REFERENCES

1. Back, M., Cohen, J., Gold, R., Harrison, S., and Minneman, S. Listen reader: An electronically augmented paper-based book. In *Proc. CHI '01* (2001), 23–29.
2. Billinghurst, M., Kato, H., and Poupyrev, I. The magicbook: Moving seamlessly between reality and virtuality. *IEEE CG&A 21*, 3 (May 2001), 6–8.
3. Fishkin, K. P. A taxonomy for and analysis of tangible interfaces. *Pers. Ubiq. Comp. 8*, 5 (Sept. 2004), 347–358.
4. Hendrix, S. L., and Eisenberg, M. A. Computer-assisted pop-up design for children: Computationally enriched paper engineering. *Adv. Tech. for Learning 3*, 2, 119–127.
5. Huang, J., Takashima, K., Hashi, S., and Kitamura, Y. IM3D: Magnetic motion tracking system for dexterous 3d interactions. In *ACM SIGGRAPH '14 E-Tech* (2014), 12:1–12:1.
6. Ishii, H., and Ullmer, B. Tangible bits: towards seamless interfaces between people, bits and atoms. In *Proc. CHI '97* (1997), 234–241.
7. Jacob, R. J., Girouard, A., Hirshfield, L. M., Horn, M. S., Shaer, O., Solovey, E. T., and Zigelbaum, J. Reality-based interaction: a framework for post-WIMP interfaces. In *Proc. CHI'08* (2008), 201–210.
8. Johnson, W., Jellinek, H., Klotz, Jr., L., Rao, R., and Card, S. K. Bridging the paper and electronic worlds: The paper user interface. In *Proc. CHI '93* (1993), 507–512.
9. Karagozler, M. E., Poupyrev, I., Fedder, G. K., and Suzuki, Y. Paper generators: Harvesting energy from touching, rubbing and sliding. In *Proc. UIST '13* (2013), 23–30.
10. Kawahara, Y., Hodges, S., Cook, B. S., Zhang, C., and Abowd, G. D. Instant inkjet circuits: Lab-based inkjet printing to support rapid prototyping of ubicomp devices. In *Proc. UbiComp '13* (2013), 363–372.
11. Klemmer, S. R., Graham, J., Wolff, G. J., and Landay, J. A. Books with voices: Paper transcripts as a physical interface to oral histories. In *Proc. CHI '03* (2003), 89–96.
12. Liang, R.-H., Cheng, K.-Y., Chan, L., Peng, C.-X., Chen, M. Y., Liang, R.-H., Yang, D.-N., and Chen, B.-Y. GaussBits: Magnetic tangible bits for portable and occlusion-free near-surface tangible interactions. In *Proc. CHI '13* (2013), 1391–1400.
13. Liang, R.-H., Cheng, K.-Y., Su, C.-H., Weng, C.-T., Chen, B.-Y., and Yang, D.-N. GaussSense: Attachable stylus sensing using magnetic sensor grid. In *Proc. UIST '12* (2012), 319–326.
14. Papas, M., Houit, T., Nowrouzezahrai, D., Gross, M., and Jarosz, W. The magic lens: Refractive steganography. *ACM TOG 31*, 6 (Nov. 2012).
15. Raffle, H., Vaucelle, C., Wang, R., and Ishii, H. Jabberstamp: Embedding sound and voice in traditional drawings. In *Proc. IDC '07* (2007), 137–144.
16. Song, H., Guimbretiere, F., Grossman, T., and Fitzmaurice, G. Mouselight: Bimanual interactions on digital paper using a pen and a spatially-aware mobile projector. In *Proc. CHI '10* (2010), 2451–2460.
17. Wellner, P. Interacting with paper on the digitaldesk. *CACM 36*, 7 (July 1993), 87–96.
18. Willis, K., Brockmeyer, E., Hudson, S., and Poupyrev, I. Printed optics: 3d printing of embedded optical elements for interactive devices. In *Proc. UIST '12* (2012), 589–598.
19. Willis, K. D. D., Shiratori, T., and Mahler, M. Hideout: Mobile projector interaction with tangible objects and surfaces. In *Proc. TEI '13* (2013), 331–338.
20. Yu, N.-H., Chan, L.-W., Lau, S. Y., Tsai, S.-S., Hsiao, I.-C., Tsai, D.-J., Hsiao, F.-I., Cheng, L.-P., Chen, M., Huang, P., and Hung, Y.-P. TUIC: enabling tangible interaction on capacitive multi-touch displays. In *Proc. CHI '11* (2011), 2995–3004.

FugaciousFilm: Exploring Attentive Interaction with Ephemeral Material

Hyosun Kwon[1], Shashank Jaiswal[1], Steve Benford[1], Sue Ann Seah[2], Peter Bennett[2], Boriana Koleva[1], Holger Schnädelbach[1]
[1]School of Computer Science, University of Nottingham, UK
[2]Department of Computer Science, University of Bristol, UK
[1]{psxhsk, psxsj3, pszsdb, pszbnk, pszhms}@nottingham.ac.uk,
[2]{s.a.seah, peter.bennett}@bristol.ac.uk

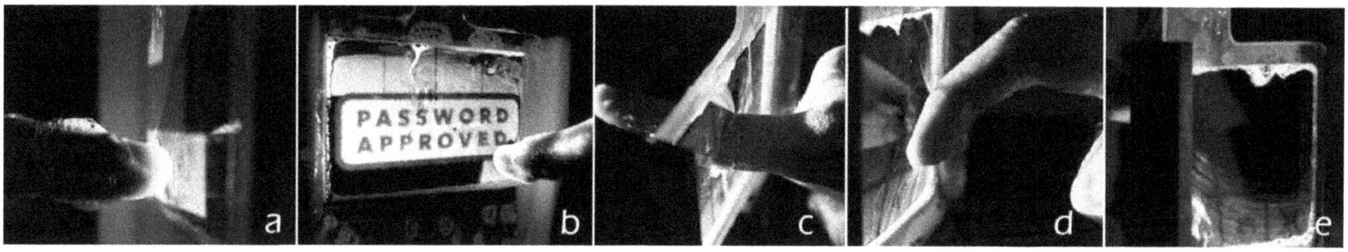

Figure 1. FugaciousFilm demonstrating attentive interactions with an ephemeral material. (a) Touching the soap film surface, (b) entering a passcode by dragging a finger across the film, (c) pushing without bursting the film, (d) hooking a finger when pulling the film, and (e) an instance of the film bursting while playing Tic-Tac-Toe game.

ABSTRACT
This paper introduces FugaciousFilm, a soap film based touch display, as a platform for *Attentive Interaction* that encourages the user to be highly focused throughout the use of the interface. Previous work on ephemeral user interfaces has primarily focused on the development of ambient and peripheral displays. In contrast, FugaciousFilm is an ephemeral display that aims to promote highly attentive interaction. We present the iterative process of developing this interface, spanning technical explorations, prototyping and a user study. We report lessons learnt when designing the interface; ranging from the soap film mixture to the impact of frames and apertures. We then describe developing the touch, push, pull and pop interactions. Our user study shows how FugaciousFilm led to focused and attentive interactions during a tournament of enhanced Tic-Tac-Toe. We then finish by discussing how the principles of vulnerability and delicacy can motivate the design of attentive ephemeral interfaces.

Author Keywords
Ephemeral User Interfaces; Tangible Interaction; Soap film; Attentive Interaction; Non-Ambient Interaction;

ACM 978-1-4503-3145-6/15/04…$15.00
http://dx.doi.org/10.1145/2702123.2702206

ACM Classification Keywords
H.5.2. Information interfaces and presentation: User Interfaces.

INTRODUCTION
The term 'fugacious' is a synonym of 'ephemeral' defined as, 'tending to disappear' or 'fleeting'. FugaciousFilm builds upon the work on Ephemeral User Interfaces, which 'employ transient materials for tangible interaction with the digital world' [25]. Ephemeral UIs adopt a stance counter to the standard HCI norms of interface stability and reliability by instead employing transience and instability [4]. The majority of Ephemeral UIs developed to date, for example, soap bubble display [21], electric-fan displays [19], candle-flame altars [27] (among others that we review below), have tended to operate as ambient displays in which the digital assumes a background role. In this paper we take a different view, proposing that the transient nature of ephemeral interfaces can also deliver highly attentive interactions in addition to peripheral and calm ones. We have therefore set out to investigate how ephemerality can be deliberately harnessed to encourage a heightened state of close attention involving suspense, tension, anticipation and excitement.

Our approach has been to develop and study a novel soap film interface in which users can touch, push, pull and pop its fragile surface as a way of interacting with digital media that are projected onto the surface. We report the lessons learned from an extended and iterative process of developing this interface that comprised three key phases:

1. Initial technical explorations to establish basic feasibility and techniques.
2. Early prototyping of concept demonstrators in order to further extend and refine these techniques.

3. A user study involving an enhanced Tic-Tac-Toe game that revealed the various ways in which our interface delivered attentive interactions.

By reflecting on this process we are able to draw out two general lessons for HCI. The first is to generalise our findings beyond FugaciousFilm by articulating the broader principles of vulnerability and fragility that explain how ephemeral interfaces can promote attentive interaction. The second is to distil specific guidelines for those who wish to work with interactive soap film interfaces in the future.

RELATED WORK

We begin by reviewing the related work that has inspired and underpinned our approach. We provide an overview of recent research into HCI's engagement with ephemerality before considering its relationship to both ambient and attentive interactions.

Ephemerality in HCI

Ephemeral User Interfaces incorporate transitory materials as a key element of interaction, and have been defined as:

"…a class of user interfaces that contain at least one UI element that is intentionally created to last for a limited time only. The durability of the UI element is determined by its intrinsic material properties in combination with its surrounding ecosystem. While their ephemeral UI element(s) exist(s), ephemeral user interfaces provide a rich and multisensory user experience. …" [4]

Transient materials such as soap bubbles, fog, wind, and ice have been employed in various tangible interactive systems to enable rich sensory experiences. In Aerial Tune [1] and Interactive Fog Screen [18] the instable nature of airflow or fog has been used as mid-air displays. Interaction in ThanatoFenestra [27] was dependent on movement of candlelight delivered by vulnerable candle flames. Bubble Cosmos [13] and Soap Bubble Interface [25] projected visual feedback onto the smoke-filled bubbles.

A small number of ephemeral interfaces have attempted to combine transitory materials with robust and functional displays and applications, some examples being: MisTable [9], a multi-touch mist display for multiple users; Desert Rain [8], an art installation of water curtain designed for mixing virtual and physical reality; Bit.Fall [17], a network based installation that physically visualized words by falling water droplets; Colloidal Display [15], a soap film display developed to achieve texture deformation for the projected image; and LOLLio [12], a flavour-changing edible interface for playing games.

However, the concept of ephemerality is not restricted to the material aspects of interfaces. Digital ephemerality has also been proposed as a solution to privacy concerns arising from the permanence of data. 'Digital forgetting', the disposal of undesirable digital possessions (e.g. photos, videos) for various reasons, has been recently proposed as a useful approach to tackle this problem [20]. Also, time-limited messaging applications such as Snapchat and Wickr that embody the concept of 'ephemeral data' have become popular [23].

In spite of these promising early developments, many questions remain unanswered as to how ephemerality can be employed in interaction design, and how the material and digital aspects of ephemerality might best be combined to create impactful user experiences.

From Ambient to Attentive Ephemerality

As noted earlier, a considerable proportion of current ephemeral UIs can be thought of as operating in an ambient or peripheral mode. We review previous works used in this ambient manner and then propose the possibility of using ephemeral UIs for non-ambient contexts.

From its inception, the field of ubiquitous computing has been concerned with how to remove the computer from the direct focus of the users' attention, by instead embedding it into the surrounding environment [28]. This has led to a surge of interest in HCI in new forms of interface that are variously described as 'ambient' [7], 'calm' [30], 'invisible' [28] or 'unremarkable computing' [26]. At first glance, the transitory and somewhat immaterial nature of ephemeral interfaces – their smokiness, fogginess or elusive flickering – appears to naturally align with this notion of ambient experience. However, we have been struck by a different inspiration. Trying to interact with ephemeral interfaces, for example trying to peer into them or touch and manipulate them, might in fact command a great deal of attention. In short, ephemerality could become a driver of highly focused and possibly even suspenseful interactions.

The traditional task-driven focus of HCI has led to a considerable focus on the nature of cognitive attention in interaction design [14]. HCI is replete with studies of, and frameworks for, managing attention and distraction with a view to supporting particular tasks, multitasking, and managing distraction and workload [3, 11]. From a different perspective, the field of virtual reality has long been concerned with how the concepts of immersion and presence might explain and inform interfaces that achieve a very particular sense of attention as people engage deeply with virtual worlds [24].

What we have in mind here is engaging users in highly attentive forms of interaction with ephemeral interfaces in which they become intensely engaged with an ongoing experience. Beyond a strong and immediate focus on the experience, this might lead them to experience tension and suspense as explored in previous breath-controlled interfaces [10], or perhaps even anxiety that might generate thrill or lead to enlightenment as discussed in recent work on 'uncomfortable interactions' [2]. With such ideas in mind, we set out to explore the relationship between ephemerality and attentive interfaces through a process of iterative prototyping.

TECHNICAL EXPLORATIONS OF FUGACIOUSFILM

We begin by summarizing early technical explorations that shaped our approach to ephemeral interaction. Building upon previous soap film projection displays, such as Colloidal Display [15] and Poppable Display [16], we developed FugaciousFilm, a soap film based ephemeral-UI. We chose to work with soap film because:

- It is well known for its fleeting nature;
- Many people will be familiar with the material experience and properties of soap film from childhood;
- It can be used as a projection surface;
- It is easily obtained;
- The duration and other important properties of the material can easily be modified in a variety of ways.

We chose to concentrate on static, or captive, soap film membranes that can be used as touchable screens rather than on free-floating soap bubbles. The implementation of FugaciousFilm therefore comprises two main parts; projection onto a soap film, and detection of interaction with the soap film. We now describe each of these in depth. The combined hardware is shown as a whole in Figure 2.

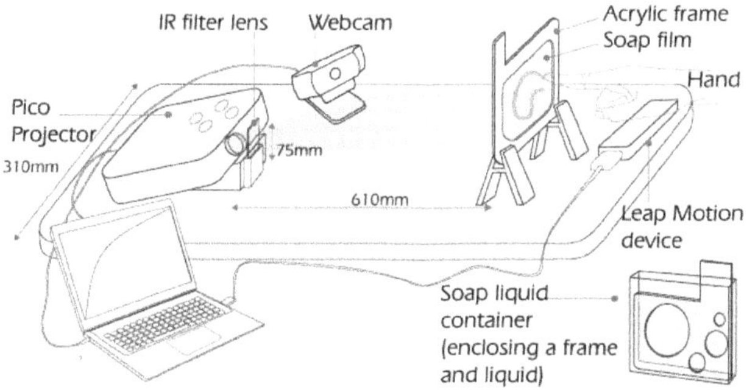

Figure 2. FugaciousFilm system setup.

Projection onto a Soap Film

Due to the transparency, in general, of soap films, projection onto the surface of the film is usually ineffective. Therefore we developed a custom-made liquid soap mixture that enables projection onto the soap film. The image can only be viewed when there are enough surfactant particles to scatter the projected light to the viewer's eyes. After experimentation, we found that mixing white solid soap and glycerin with distilled water produced an adequate film for viewing projections.

When interacting with a projection image on the soap film with a finger, we need to consider possible viewing angles for the user compared to the location of the projector. As the size of the colloidal particles may vary from 1nm to 1μm, both Rayleigh and Mie scattering occur on the surface of the soap film [5]. While light scattered via Rayleigh scattering is visible from any direction, Mie scattering projects light predominantly in the forward direction. In the case of FugaciousFilm, we found that the colloidal particles on the soap film scatter the light from the projection in all directions so that the projection image is visible from both the front and rear side of the film relative to the projector. Initial observations revealed that the vividness between front and back was similar. Therefore, we decided to use back projection in order not to interfere with the projection while interacting with the soap film.

We used an AAXA® P4-X Pico Projector (141×71×31mm, 95 Lumens) in order to keep the entire system to a compact size. As the aperture in the acrylic frame determines the shape of the film, the design and size of the frame may vary depending on the application as shown in Figure 3-a.

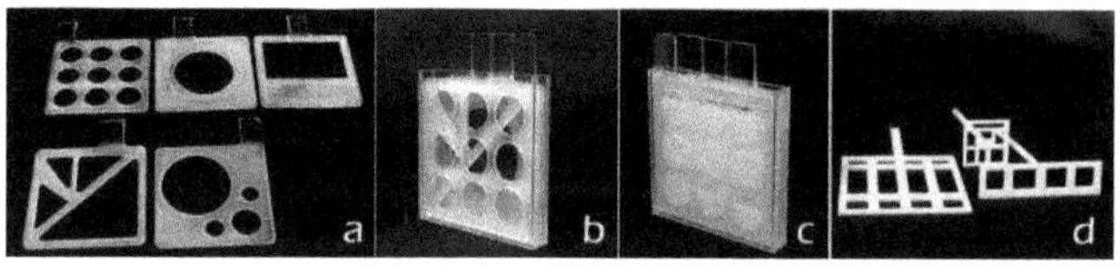

Figure 3. (a) Acrylic frames (80×80mm), (b) frames in one container, (c) container filled with soap liquid, and (d) wipers to create the soap film on the frames.

Interacting with the Soap Film

We explored two broad approaches to interact with soap film displays: creating and destroying (i.e., popping) the film and physically touching and manipulating the surface with a finger. The former requires detection of the presence/absence of the soap film in an acrylic frame, while the latter requires tracking of the user's finger in 3D space.

Soap Film Detection

The soap film in the frame may disappear either spontaneously or due to the user's interactions. To detect the presence or absence of the soap film on the frame, we implemented color tracking via a webcam. When the film is present on the frame, the color of the projection image reflected from the film (which is different from the background color) is visible to the camera. As soon as the film disappears, the background color now becomes visible and this can be used to detect the presence/absence of the soap film. We chose to use a black colored background screen as it makes the task of detecting background color much simpler. The background is detected by using a threshold on the average gray-scale pixel intensities inside the frame region. If the average value of the gray-scale intensities is less than the threshold value, this implies that the background is visible and vice-versa. One limitation of this method is that the detection of the disappearance of the soap film could be delayed if the user's hand is present close to the frame thereby blocking the visibility of the background screen. Detection occurs as soon as the user moves his/her hand away from the screen.

Fingertip Tracking

FugaciousFilm also functions as a 'penetrable' touch screen. For this purpose, we used the Leap Motion® device to accurately track the position of a person's fingertips in 3D space. We place the device in front of the soap film, where the user's fingers approach (see Figure 2). The device uses infrared LEDs and camera sensors to track the motion of the user's fingers up to an accuracy of 1/100th of a millimeter. The x, y, z coordinates of the fingertips returned by the device are used to detect the position of fingertip in relation to the soap film frame (x, y coordinates) and to determine the depth of the finger through the soap film (z coordinate). Being able to track fingertips enabled us to explore various ways of interacting with FugaciousFilm including touching (Figure 4-a), pushing (Figure 4-b) and ultimately pulling (Figure 4-c) as we describe below.

Figure 4. Various z-depth of a finger interacting on the soap film visualized with different colors. A soapy finger is (a) touching, (b) pushing and (c) pulling through the soap film.

Creating a Soap Film of Ideal Duration

Both of the approaches given above have conflicting needs of the soap film. The 'popping' technique requires that a film is pop-able, and the finger detection requires that you can at least touch the film even only briefly. We discuss below how we created a film that satisfies both of these constraints.

In general, the stability and duration of the soap films can be affected by the evaporation of water from the surface. Glycerin reduces this evaporation and so increases the lifetime. The durability of a soap film increases from seconds to many minutes for solutions with just an additional 5% glycerin and up to hours when the solution contains 50% glycerin [6]. Although adding more glycerin into the solution makes the film durable, it also makes it thicker. As a result, rather than popping in the usual way, the film breaks slowly as the surface tears. There is therefore a trade-off between durability and a clean 'popping effect' (i.e. the film disappears in an instant).

We have attempted to strike an aesthetic balance between duration and 'popping' effect. We found that the solution of 2 parts soap, 20 parts distilled water and 1 part glycerin produces a thin membrane that exists temporarily and destroys with a clean desired 'pop' effect. The average duration of a soap film created by our solution on an 80x80mm acrylic frame, when left untouched in room temperature, was 2minutes and 51seconds (n=50, SD 0.67).

EARLY PROTOTYPES

Next, we created three prototype demonstrators of FugaciousFilm in order to test its implementation as an attentive interface, better understand its capabilities, further refine our approaches, and also to inspire concepts for potential applications. We deliberately chose to explore three very different prototypes so as to reveal the potential for various ways of interacting with soap film alongside key features that would deliver a rich user experience. Developing them enabled us to learn about different aspects of interacting with an ephemeral UI including the suspense felt when handling fragile materials, harnessing randomness in a controlled manner, and multi-person interaction.

Prototype 1: Fragile Passcode

The Fragile Passcode prototype demonstrates how the skill of handling fragile material might be harnessed as a means for security in ephemeral interaction. In order to confirm their identity to a system the user must not only remember their passcode but must also remember the motor skills required to manipulate the interface in particular and subtle ways. Initially, the user needs to create a soap film on the frame by using the wiper which then reveals a projected password screen that they can touch in various ways to unlock their passcode. They touch the film with a wet fingertip to draw a pattern (Figure 5-a). Here we can add levels of difficulty into the interaction. In addition to touching the interface, we applied various z-depths beyond the film, requiring the user to find the correct depth while pushing through the film and drawing the correct code. If the passcode is entered incorrectly (Figure 5-b) once or the soap film is broken then the ability to enter the code is removed entirely. Developing this prototype inspired us to think more about the subtleties of touching, especially the depth of touch, and to reflect on the possibilities of 'dangerous' interaction techniques.

Figure 5. (a) A user unlocks the passcode by drawing a correct pattern on the film with correct depth (indicated by color). (b) Access denied by drawing a wrong pattern.

Prototype 2: Serendipitous Music Composer

The Serendipitous Music Composer prototype explored how serendipity might be harnessed by an ephemeral interface. In short, how might the random nature of an ephemeral material's decay be shaped, controlled, tamed and incorporated into attentive interaction. An acrylic frame with multiple apertures represents a single music track. However, we split the music into its constituent parts and assigned each part to a different soap film circle. When the soap film bursts, the allocated musical part for that circle starts playing (Figure 6-a). The soap film can either be popped by the user's finger or by their breath. Popping all of the films reveals the final music track, with the order of popping building up its layers in a distinct sequence. We added a 'replay' mode in which using the wiper to re-create the popped film (Figure 6-b), refreshes the screen, causing the music to stop and return to the original state (Figure 6-c). We realized that this 'refresh-ability' of soap film might help users cope with its fleeting nature and repeat or prolong experiences. It can be assigned and controlled individually.

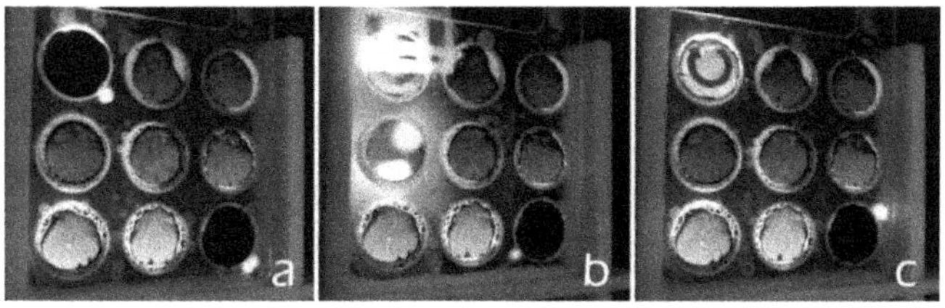

Figure 6. (a) Music is being played for two popped films (b) the user reforms the soap film with a slider on top-left corner. (c) The music mapped on the recreated film has been stopped (spinning circle disappeared).

Our initial aim for this prototype had been to demonstrate how randomness in interaction with soap film might be harnessed to deliver an aesthetic, in this case musical, experience. However, one of our important findings was that the lifetime of each soap film is not as random as we had first thought. Although the lifetime of the soap film depends on the size of the aperture and environmental conditions, it transpires that identically sized soap films also have different durability depending on their position within the wider frame. Specifically, soap films located in the bottom row usually last longer than the ones in the top row as a result of the soap liquid flowing from the top to the bottom, weakening those at the top while refreshing and therefore strengthening those at the bottom.

Prototype 3: Ephemeral TIC-TAC-TOE

The Tic-Tac-Toe prototype was designed to explore multi-user ephemeral interaction, specifically how time-critical constraints might engender a sense of precariousness when two people interact with a shared ephemeral material. We explored this idea by creating a selection of subtly different variants of the familiar game of Tic-Tac-Toe. Variations involved how the noughts and crosses were represented and how the players changed the state of the game-board.

We introduced a handicap system based around the fragility and natural breakdown of the soap film, a sense of time-criticality that is similar in principle to the use of a chess clock. A player pops the bubble (becomes a nought) while the other touches, preserves, it (becomes a cross) to make their move. However, they must complete these before any of the remaining bubbles pop of their own accord, in which case it is counted as a nought has been placed. In this regard the strength, and hence duration, of the soap film solution directly equates to the difficulty of a game. We also gave a bias to the person playing as nought because if either player breaks the film by mistake, it is counted as a 'nought' (Figure 7). However this bias in nought's favor sometimes worked adversely, as when an unintended film bursts naturally the player with nought loses his/her turn. Our explorations with this prototype revealed how the precariousness of the soap film was also affected by environmental conditions such as humidity, air currents and vibrations that could interrupt or shorten the game. We also learned how the use of a soapy finger could extend the range of interaction and maintain the lifetime of the soap film. Most importantly, we noted how players' anxious anticipation about unintended popping naturally demanded greater attention to their interactions and increased the sense of tension in the overall game experience. This provided the inspiration for our subsequent user study.

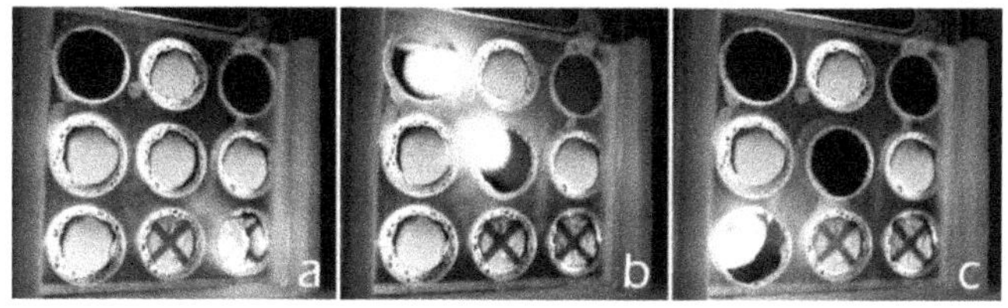

Figure 7. (a) One player is touching the bottom-right film (cross) while (b) the other player pops (nought) the center film. (c) When the user with cross breaks the film by accident, it counts as a nought that helps the opponent win the game.

USER STUDY

The final stage of our exploratory design process was to conduct a user study with a fully realized application of FugaciousFilm. We chose to further develop the Tic-Tac-Toe demonstrator as informal feedback had revealed its potential to stimulate attentiveness and tension. Tic-Tac-Toe also offered the challenge of trying to introduce tension into a relatively unexciting game of limited possibilities while also providing users with a familiar, quick and repeatable task with an inherent motivation.

Pilot Study

We began with a pilot study in order to explore the most appropriate ways in to enhance Tic-Tac-Toe through FugaciousFilm and to assess different possibilities for design of the physical soap film interface and interactions. We invited 10 university students and researchers to participate in a series of trials, each lasting 30 minutes including playing various test games and a short exit interview. Each participant played four different types of Tic-Tac-Toe game which varied in the design of the physical soap film aperture (single aperture, uniform multiple apertures, non-uniform multiple apertures), the kinds of interactions being explored (combinations of touch, pop and push) and the mapping of these to the rules of Tic-Tac-Toe as summarized by Table 1. We anticipated that the sequence of games from (a) through to (d) would involve increasing difficulty and require a progressively more sophisticated understanding of FugaciousFilm. In addition to interviewing participants, we noted their verbal expressions and finger gestures (speed, movement and cautiousness).

Encouragingly, participants clearly grasped the nature of ephemerality as the experience progressed: *"You get the sense of urgency as the time flows during the game"* and noted how this enhanced their enjoyment: *"I tried to put my cross in terms of the rule of Tic-Tac-Toe, then actually putting it without destroying the bubble becomes fun of the game."* In terms of the four different designs, the first variant (a) was the least successful due to its inherent bias towards 'noughts'. The second two were more interesting with the non-uniform apertures (c) being preferred to the uniform ones (a): *"The different sized ones were more interesting than the regular ones, because it was more difficult to pop the smaller ones"*.

Frame Design & Interface	Rules
a Uniform Apertures; c Non-Uniform Apertures — Touch / Pop	- Touch = cross / Pop = nought - Two players take alternative turns. - Accidental popping made by the player with cross counted as a nought. - Unexpected popping (by air, breath) also counted as a nought.
b Uniform Apertures (PS T T / T PS PS / T PS T); d Single Aperture (PS T T / T PS PS / T PS T) — Touch / Push	- Each of the nine sections are assigned with either touch or push. - Letters are projected visually on the film. (* Lines are projected on the film in frame-d) - Two players take alternative turns. - First player starts from anywhere with a nought. - Whoever pops the soap film loses the game. - Unexpected popping also makes the player, who's turn it is, lose the game.

Table 1. Table shows the design and the rules of four versions of the Tic-Tac-Toe game demonstrated in the pilot study.

However, it was the single large aperture (d) that generated the greatest excitement: *"Single framed game feels more devastating than the separated uniform holes (a)"*, *"I like this one (the last game) most, it adds so much more tension during the interaction."* Moreover, we also noted that participants were able to improvise some distinctive and interesting interactions with this larger film.

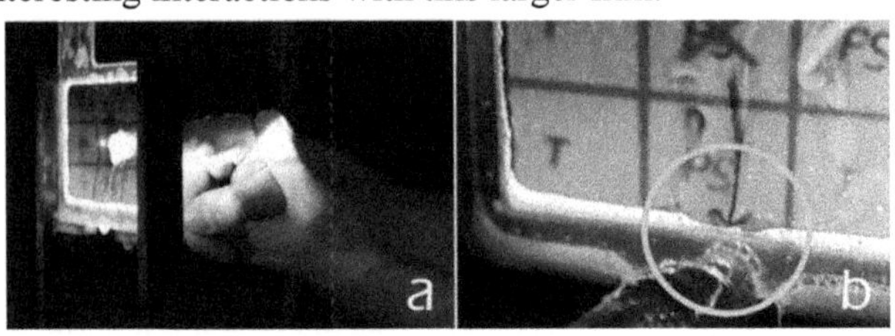

Figure 8. (a) A user holding his hand with the other hand. (b) A user drags the finger to the edge of the frame after his turn, in order to keep the film stable.

One participant held one hand with the other hand to prevent shaking while touching (Figure 8-a) while another learned to always move his finger to the bottom edge of the frame where the film is the strongest when removing it from the film so as to provide the greatest stability (Figure 8-b). Significantly, several participants also noted the good feeling and interactional potential of pulling on the soap film: "*When you put your finger through and bring it out, still doesn't break the film then it feels just great... It feels more visceral, you can see the bubble moving a lot and seems a lot more fragile.*"

Final Design Iteration – Interacting by Pulling

Inspired by our pilot participants' suggestions, we decided to extend the interactional capabilities of FugaciousFilm to include pulling and to incorporate this into the main study. The main technical challenge lay in detecting both the presence of the soap film and whether or not it is still in contact with a fingertip. We took advantage of the optical phenomenon of 'specular highlight'; a bright spot of light that is typically seen on shiny curved surfaces. When the soap film is pulled, its surface near its point of contact with the fingertip becomes slightly curved, and a specular highlight appears (Figure 9). In order to detect this spot, we employed an image processing based method, detecting blobs in images. The image of the frame captured from the camera is first converted into a gray scale image, which is then thresholded (based upon pixel intensity values) to get a binary image. Finally, the blobs are extracted by labeling the connected components [22]. The right blob representing the specular highlight can be detected by searching only for those blobs whose shape and size corresponds to that of the specular highlight.

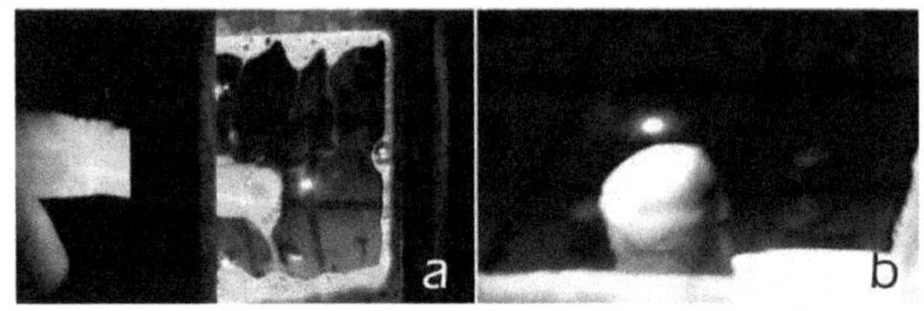

Figure 9. (a) Specular Highlight appears on the film near the finger when it's pulled. (b) Screen shots of the camera view, identifying a blob near the fingertip.

A further subtlety that needs to be considered is variation in the flexibility of the film across its surface. Surface tension of soap membrane directly applies to emotional tension that arises when pulling it. Early testing revealed that the center section could be pulled out the furthest, edge sections a medium distance and corners the least (Figure 10). We therefore tuned our pulling interaction to recognize the whole range of possible distances across the surface of our large aperture.

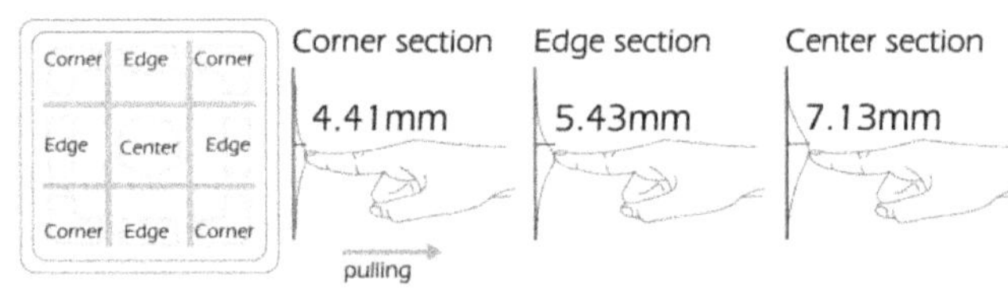

Figure 10. (Left) Regions in the soap film and (Right) an average distance from the baseline the stable soap film can reach for each section.

Main Study

Our main study took the form of a tournament where participants played our Tic-Tac-Toe game on a single soap film aperture – case (d) in Table 1. The basic rules were:

- Players alternated who goes first between games;
- The first player always starts with a 'nought'.
- When it is their turn, a player can choose to put their mark in any position, but must do so using the specified interaction type (push, pull or touch) which is visibly projected onto that section of the soap film screen;
- If player breaks the film, then they lose the game.
- Otherwise, the normal rules of Tic-Tac-Toe apply.

We created three versions of the game, varying them according to which interactions were mapped to which of the nine cells of the Tic-Tac-Toe board (Figure 11-a). We designed the study in the form of a tournament that comprised three rounds: group stages, semi-finals and a final.

In each round, the two participants involved played all 3 variants of our Tic-Tac-Toe game. After the group stages, the top 2 players in each group progressed to the semi-finals, with two players eventually progressing to the final. In total, 26 games were played since the eventual champion only required 2 games to win the final. We recruited six participants from our university network, 4 students and 2 staff (2 females and 4 males). Participants received a $13 gift voucher for participating while the overall champion and runner-up received additional $25 and $8 gift vouchers. Figure 11-b summarizes the tournament format and the progressions of the different participants who are labeled P11-P16 (P1-P10 were the participants in the pilot).

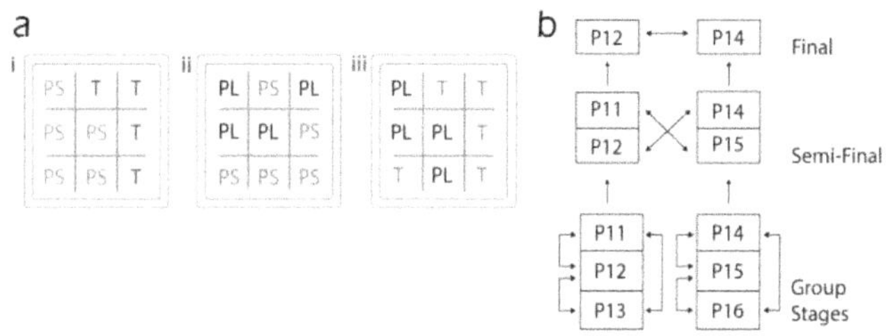

Figure 11. (a) A set of game consists of 3 versions of Tic-Tac-Toe. PS: push, PL: pull, T: touch. (b) Format of the tournament held in the user study.

The tournament lasted in 60 minutes and it was held in the empty lab space. Participants were watching and cheering as spectators while the others were playing their rounds. The whole tournament was video recorded. We have verified from the pilot test that participants express immersed emotion in two ways; through verbal utterances and gestures. Therefore, the moderator instantly marked notable verbal and behavioral feedbacks for later video analysis (Figure 12). Also, there was a final debriefing session with the whole group afterwards.

Findings

We begin with some general observations. The average game duration was 52.6 seconds (n=26, SD 31.8) and most of the games ended by the film bursting during user interaction. Overall, participants appeared to be highly engaged in the experience. They demonstrated and verbalized signs of tension and were able to develop a variety of tactics. The visceral nature of the interface affected many participants' decisions when making a finger movement and some participants developed their own tactics. In addition to putting their marks in the correct position, the fragile material clearly forced participants to be cautious in their motor control. This reflects the result that only 7 games in total were completed in a way that the players succeeded to execute interactions in every section of the film before the soap film had burst, and out of those only 2 games lasted in draw. We now drill down into specific findings. Analyzing our video-recorded observations, we focused on several indicators of attention including specific words expressing tension, finger movements and behaviors such as holding breath.

Intense Awareness of Material and Interaction

During the game, players made repeated verbal and behavioral expressions to suggest that they were very focused on handling the soap film material. Often, not only players but also spectators said, *"This is tense,"* while executing or watching the interactions. After P11 played the first round of tournament he replied, *"It's tense, but this is only round one."* In one instance, P12 sighed deeply as he visibly relaxed after he succeeded to put his cross in the right place. Reactions such as this revealed the intensity arising from having to exert fine motor control over an unstable surface. Moreover, having learned that their fingers need to be wet enough in order not to break the film, participants tended to dip their fingers into the soap solution each and every time before their turn, even when it was already wet. Participants were intensely aware of the fragility of the film when some players did not concentrate on the game tactics of Tic-Tac-Toe but instead focused entirely on executing the interaction successfully. After P15 won the game and before the film had burst, he said to P14, *"You also need to play Tic-Tac-Toe in this thing."*

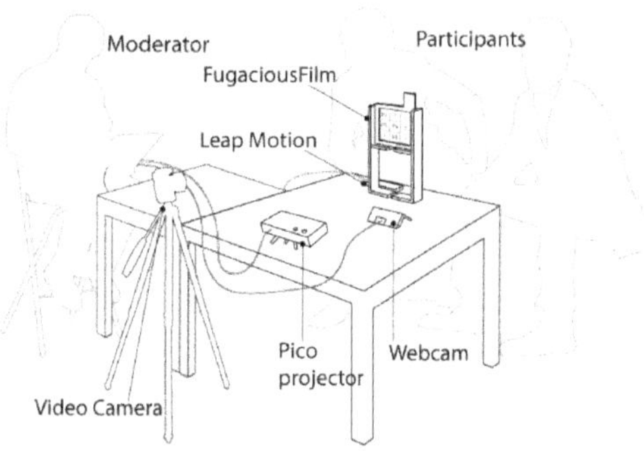

Figure 12. Study setup. Illustration shows how the study has been conducted and recorded.

Ephemerality Rules the Game

We had anticipated that the ephemerality of the interface (i.e., the sense that it might pop at any moment) would create a pressure for players to move on quickly. However, we observed the opposite in many cases. For example, P16 spent too much time at his turn hesitating where would be the 'safest' and 'correct' place to put his mark with the result that film broke before he could make any meaningful move. In a different vein, P15 used this feature of the material as one of the tactics to win the game. In one of the rounds, P15 was intentionally wasting time on his turn while commenting that, "I'm waiting for it to be breakable when it's your (P12) turn." Both cases illustrate how intensity arises from not knowing for how long the surface will remain available or stable for a given interaction, but also how this may be exploited in various ways.

Easy Touch

Participants found touching interface the easiest, initially tried to occupy the sections with 'touch' first, sometimes regardless of whether this was a good logical move in Tic-Tac-Toe. Later on, however, they figured out that touch was usually the 'safest' interaction, causing least movement to the film. This realization led to unexpected actions and reactions between the players. In the semi-final, for example, although it was obvious for P11 to defend himself and also occupy a definite chance to win by putting his cross in the center, he instead went for a touch interaction in bottom-right corner (Figure 13-a). Then P14 managed to put a winning 'nought' in the center by pulling the film (Figure 13-b). P11 responded, *"I was more concerning getting you (P14) to pull,"* suggesting that he was trying to avoid the risk of breaking the film by pulling it back.

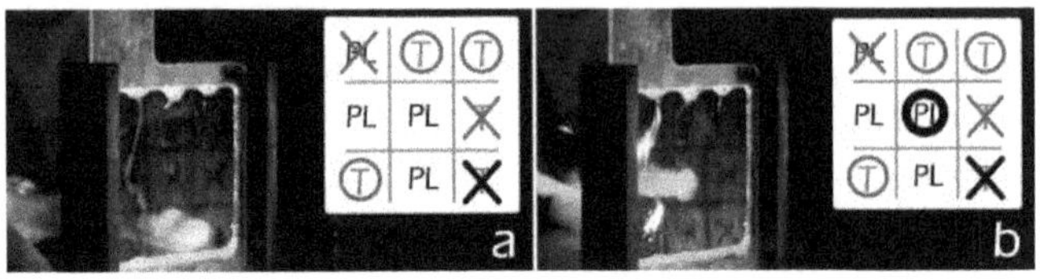

Figure 13. (a) P11 puts a cross on the bottom-left corner although he had to block the center section. (b) P14 pulls the center section successfully and wins the game.

In some instances, participants made delicate decision according to their growing knowledge of how the fragility varied across the surface and also changed over time. In Figure 14-a, P16 was trying to put cross by pushing the top left section in order to avoid the nought winning the game. But after several trials, the film became already thinner as some of liquid had evaporated while some had flowed to bottom. Then P16 changed his mind to safely put a cross on the top right corner (Figure 14-b) by 'touching'. In spite of this tactic, P15 managed to push the upper left corner and won the game (Figure 14-c).

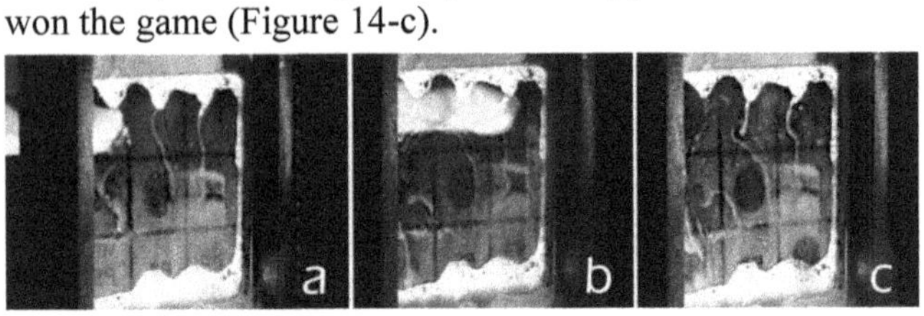

Figure 14. (a) P16 attempts to push. (b) But decides to make a safer move by touching the top-right corner. (c) Then, P15 pushes through the top-left section and wins the game.

Dangerous Push and Pull

The variant of the game involving both push and pull interactions was found to be the most demanding. Interestingly, they held opposing opinions about the difficulty of each case. P14 recalled that the vulnerability of the soap film was reinforced when it fluctuated after he pushed, *"When I push, I need to push quite further but then I also need to pull back out and it feels dangerous to burst the bubble."* Reflecting this, although participants grasped the fact that they could push a wet finger relatively far through the film, they remained especially focused, cautious and tense when performing this particular interaction compared to other interactions. One participant yelled, *"I can't put my finger anymore through"*, although he knew that he can push further and ultimately did so. This tension that participants felt on such occasions could also be seen from variations in the speed of their finger movements as players cautiously slowed down when they pulled back after pushing the film. However, some participants reported the opposite feeling. Later in the debriefing session, P11 recalled that 'pushing' was easier than 'pulling', *"If you need to pull you need to push any way."* This feedback reflected the observation that although they had to push the film to a sufficient depth to properly engage it with their finger, some participants were tend to touch slightly and then pull back.

Summary of User Study

While individual tactics and experiences varied somewhat, it was clear from the study that, in general, players:

- Were able to perform pushing, pulling and touching.
- Quickly learned the delicacy of touch required to do so.
- Also learned how the interactional properties of the soap film varied over its surface area and over time.
- Were able to tactically exploit all of this knowledge.
- Paid very close attention to the interface.
- Found this absorbing, tense and often suspenseful.

DISCUSSION

Our extended design process, from initial technical explorations, through early demonstrators, to the user study, reveals that it is possible to create an ephemeral interface from soap film that encourages highly attentive, often suspenseful interactions. From a technical perspective, we have shown that it is feasible to realize multiple forms of interaction with a soap film surface – touch, push, pop and also pull – with sufficient reliability to deliver a robust and playable game. Experientially, players found this game to be enjoyable, with the interface generating tension and excitement while also introducing new tactical possibilities. Our discussion now draws out two wider contributions from this work: (i) reflecting on how ephemeral media engenders attentive interaction through vulnerability and delicacy; (ii) distilling key techniques for interactive soap film interfaces and proposing other applications beyond games that can benefit from the ephemeral quality of the soap film.

Exploiting Vulnerability and Delicacy of Interface

Whereas previous work has explored how ephemeral media, including soap film, can be incorporated into ambient interfaces, we have shown how they might also enable highly attentive ones. We argue that these attentive, sometimes even tense, interactions arise from a combination of the inherent vulnerability of the material and the resulting delicacy of various interactions with it. This emphasis on the material qualities reflects previous discussions of uncomfortable interactions within HCI that have argued how the 'visceral' (i.e., material) qualities of interaction can enhance suspense [2].

A soap film interface is highly vulnerable. We have seen how the liquid nature of the interface makes this vulnerability dynamic. As the soap suspension flows under gravity and the moisture dries out over time, it forms stable 'black film', where the thickness became less than the wavelength of light so that it appears black [6]. The tension of the surface gradually increases until this status and therefore, it directly equates with the vulnerability of interface. Our study revealed how users also tried to anticipate the vulnerability of the interface to a degree, which further reinforces feelings of suspense. In turn, vulnerability demands a certain delicacy of interaction. Users have to manipulate the interface carefully, concentrating closely to exert fine-grained motor control over their movements. Delicate finger movements on the soap film induce tension to a positive effect requiring the user to pay especially close attention. FugaciousFilm affords a rich repertoire of interactions to play with, each introducing its own subtle forms of delicacy; touching, pushing, pulling and popping each have their own distinct 'feels'. We claim that it is the partial predictability of both vulnerability and delicacy (having a general but somewhat imprecise sense of how it varies) that is especially powerful for generating suspense in direct interactions on such fragile materials. Especially, compared to the more random behavior of free-floating bubbles introduced in previous works, enhanced use of static soap film with controlled durability opens another potential area of EUIs that has not been covered by ambient and calm interactions, though this proposal needs exploring in further research.

We expect designers may enjoy considerable flexibility with regard to how they influence durability, most notably by varying the strength of the soap solution and size and shape of the aperture, as well as by tuning software in order to apply to a wider range of interfaces. The user can also employ material techniques to enhance these interactions such as using a wet finger. Finally, the ability to refresh the soap film with the 'wiper' tool also gives these users a degree of direct control. Thus, FugaciousFilm is more than just a vulnerable material; it is an interface in which vulnerability is partially predictable and open to various forms of control by both designers and users. We propose that researchers who wish to develop other ephemeral interfaces based on different materials (we see soap film as something of a 'probe' technology in this regard) will need to ensure that they provide a similarly broad repertoire of characteristics and techniques specified in our findings.

Extending Interactions with Soap Film Displays

Our second contribution lies in extending the repertoire of techniques for designing and interacting with soap film interfaces, adding to HCI's growing body of 'craft knowledge' concerning this particular interactive material.

Balancing the Duration of the Soap Film and Experience

As discussed above, we found that designers can systematically vary the durability of the film and hence vulnerability of the display and hence the likely duration of the experience. The soap liquid solution we have created contained; 10g of a white solid soap, 100g of distilled water and 5g of glycerin, which created stable soap films that lasted for a mean average duration of just under three minutes. This average three minute duration sets a likely upper limit on the overall user experience. The longest game across the whole tournament lasted 2 minutes and 10 seconds. Further research is required to systematically explore how alternative mixtures, apertures and even environmental conditions such as temperature, humidity and air currents might affect this.

Introducing 'Pulling' Interactions to Soap Film Displays

We have extended the repertoire of interaction techniques for soap film interfaces beyond pushing, touching, and popping as demonstrated by previous projects [16, 25] to also include 'pulling'. This mode of interaction has some distinctive interactional properties. We observed that some participants tried to hold or grab the film by bending their finger like a hook (Figure 1-d) suggesting the potential to support various kinds of pulling gesture. Although it was obviously seen that the film is not quite graspable, tangibility of the material was inducing the interaction. As pulling distance physically corresponds with the degree of the surface curvature, we envision that this mode of interaction to be extended further to multi-finger gesture, such as 'pinching'.

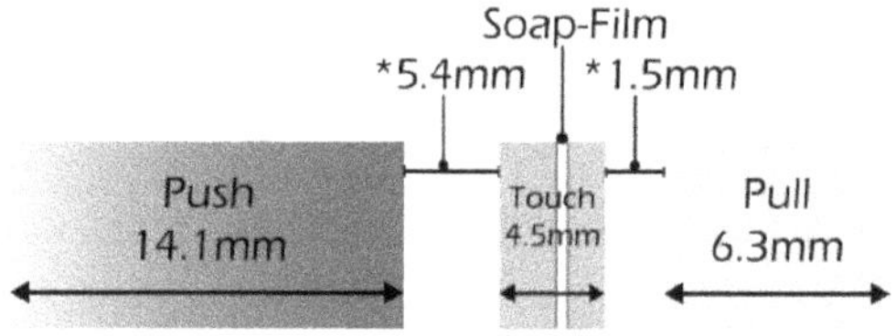

Figure 15. The ranges for push, touch, pull and *inactive regions.

Ranges for Touching, Pushing, Pulling and Inactive Regions

Our experience suggests that each of touching, pushing and pulling interface to have its own distinctive physical range of movement as summarised by Figure 15. In order to avoid a jittery interaction and also gently force the user to perform clear gestures with an appropriate delicay of touch, we found it necessary to introduce 'inactive regions' – buffer zones in which no interaction was deemed to be happening. Between touch and pull, we set the value to 1.5mm, and between touch and push we set even longer inactive region (5.4mm) in order to distinguish 'push' more clearly from 'touch' as they are continuous actions. Due to this clear gesturing, when participants perform each action, the film reacts in a typical way for that particular action (such as making large fluctuations after a pull or push). Thus, the participants deliberatuely adjusted their actions so that the result of their action wouldn't break the film.

Applications beyond Games

The games sector is a major domain for interactive technologies in its own right. Beyond our test bed Tic-Tac-Toe game, we also suggest that our approach can be applied to a wider range of games that can benefit from a variety of skillful touch interactions. There are other potential areas of application such as serendipitous music interfaces, demonstrated in one of the early prototypes. We also envisage potential applications in museums and galleries where visitors may benefit from an intense focus on delicate things. Science museums are likely to exhibit this kind of new media where hands-on experiences on various materials are appreciated. More speculatively, we suggest new approaches to engaging with increasingly ephemeral social media such as tweets and Snapchat photos by enhancing the experience of fleeting moments of interaction. The physical cue generated by the disappearing material would enhance the tension while viewing the image, before it is lost.

CONCLUSION

To conclude, our explorations with FugaciousFilm reveal that ephemeral interfaces can deliver highly attentive and even suspenseful experiences as well as ambient and calm ones, demonstrated in related works. While we have focused on soap film interfaces so far (extending their repertoire of interaction techniques as a result), we anticipate that it is possible to replicate this general approach with other ephemeral mediums and interface technologies, especially if their properties allow for the flexible control and partial predictability of both vulnerability and delicacy. From our experience designing the FugaciousFilm prototypes, we believe that ephemeral materials with such properties can be employed to build solid interactive systems that encourage focused transient interaction. Therefore, we propose FugaciousFilm as the first step towards exploring this new design space of 'attentive interaction with ephemeral material'.

ACKNOWLEGEMENTS

We thank all the participants of our study for their time and thoughtful comments. We are grateful to the EPSRC for their support through the Living with Digital Ubiquity project (EP/M000877/1).

REFERENCES

1. Alrøe, T. et al., Aerial Tunes: Exploring Interaction Qualities of Mid-air Displays. *In Proc. NordiCHI '12*. ACM Press (2012), 514–523.
2. Benford, S. et al., Uncomfortable Interactions. In *Proc. CHI'*12. ACM Press (2012), p. 2005–2014.
3. Carroll, J. M. (Ed.) (2003). HCI Models, Theories and Frameworks: Toward a Multidisciplinary Science. San Francisco: Morgan Kaufmann publishers.
4. Döring, T., Sylvester, A., Schmidt, A. A Design Space for Ephemeral User Interfaces. *In Proc. TEI '13,* ACM Press (2013). 75–82.
5. H. C. Hulst and H. C. van de Hulst, Light Scattering by Small Particles. Dover Publications, 1957.
6. Isenberg, C. The Science of Soap Films and Soap Bubbles. Dover Publications, 1978.
7. Ishii, H. and Ullmer, B. Tangible bits: towards seamless interfaces between people, bits and atoms. *In Proc. CHI'97.* ACM Press, 234-241.
8. Koleva, B. et al., "Orchestrating a Mixed Reality Performance," *In Proc. CHI'01* ACM Press, p. 38–45.
9. Martinez P, D., Joyce, E., Subramanian, S. MisTable: Reach-through Personal Screens for Tabletops, *In Proc. CHI'14*, ACM Press 3493-3502.
10. Marshall, J. et al., Breath control of amusement rides. *In Proc. CHI'11.* ACM Press (2011). 73-82.
11. Monk, A. and Gilbert, G. N. Perspectives on HCI: Diverse Approaches. Academic Press, 1995.
12. Murer, M., Aslan, I., and Tscheligi, M. LOLLio: exploring taste as playful modality. *In Proc. TEI'13,* ACM Press (2013) 299-302.
13. Nakamura, M. et al. Bubble Cosmos. *SIGGRAPH '06 Emerging Technologies*. ACM Press (2006).
14. Norman, D. 1991. Cognitive artifacts. In Designing interaction, John M. Carroll (Ed.). Cambridge University Press, 17-38.
15. Ochiai, Y., Hoshi, A.O.T. & Rekimoto, J. Reflective, deformable, colloidal display. *In Post. SIGGRAPH '13.* ACM Press (2013). 1.
16. Ochiai, Y., Hoshi, T., Oyama, A. and Rekimoto, J., "Poppable display: A display that enables popping, breaking, and tearing interactions with people," Consumer Electronics, IEEE (2013). 124-128.
17. Popp, J. Bit.Fall {Installation}. 2004. Various locations.
18. Rakkolainen, I. et al. The Interactive FogScreen. In *SIGGRAPH '05 Emerging Technologies*. ACM (2005).
19. Rydarowski, A., Samanci, O. and Mazalek, A. Murmur: kinetic relief sculpture, multi-sensory display, listening machine. In *Proc. TEI 2008*, ACM (2008), 231-238.
20. Sas, C. and Whittaker, S. Design for forgetting. In *Proc. CHI'13*, ACM Press (2013), p. 1823.
21. Seah, S A. et al. SensaBubble: a chrono-sensory mid-air display of sight and smell. *In Proc. CHI '14*. ACM, 2863-2872.
22. Shapiro, L., and Stockman, G. (2002). Computer Vision. Prentice Hall. pp. 69–73
23. Shein, E. Ephemeral Data. Commun. ACM Press (2013). 20–22.
24. Slater, M. and Wilbur, S. A Framework for Immersive Virtual Environments (FIVE): Speculations on the Role of Presence in Virtual Environments Presence 6: (1997) 603-616.
25. Sylvester, A. et al., "Liquids, Smoke, and Soap Bubbles: Reflections on Materials for Ephemeral User Interfaces". In *Proc. TEI'10*, ACM (2010). 269–270.
26. Tolmie, P. et al. Unremarkable computing. *In Proc. CHI '02*, ACM (2002). p. 399-406.
27. Uriu, D. and Okude, N. ThanatoFenestra: photographic family altar supporting a ritual to pray for the deceased. *In Proc. DIS '10*. ACM Press (2010). 422-425.
28. Weiser, M. Creating the invisible interface: (invited talk). In *Proc. UIST '94*. ACM Press (1994). 1-.
29. Weiser, M. The computer for the 21st century. *SIGMOBILE Mob. Comput. Commun. Rev.*3, ACM Press (1999). 3–11.
30. Weiser, M., Brown, J.S. The coming age of calm technology. In *Beyond calculation*, Copernicus, USA 1997. 75-85.

3D Printing Pneumatic Device Controls with Variable Activation Force Capabilities

Marynel Vázquez [1,2], Eric Brockmeyer [2], Ruta Desai [1], Chris Harrison [2,3], Scott E. Hudson [2,3]

[1]Robotics Institute
Carnegie Mellon University
Pittsburgh, PA
{marynel,rutad}
@cmu.edu

[2]Disney Research Pittsburgh
4720 Forbes Avenue
Pittsburgh, PA
eric.brockmeyer
@disneyresearch.com

[3]HCI Institute
Carnegie Mellon University
Pittsburgh, PA
{chris.harrison, scott.hudson}
@cs.cmu.edu

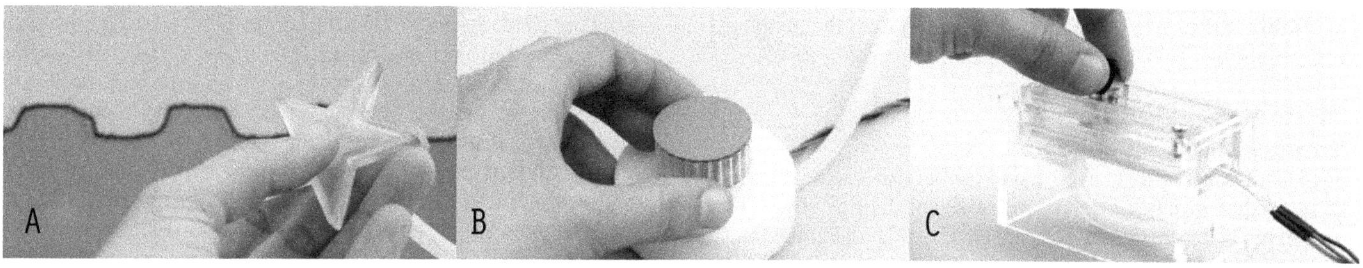

Figure 1. 3D printed pneumatic button (A), knob (B), and slider (C). We print these models with rigid and elastic materials, and in some cases add electronic components to the controls to sense user's input, such as potentiometers in the case of (B) and (C). Pressure sensing can be used to detect when users deform the elastic parts of the controls, like when they push the star. The graph behind this model shows the sensed pressure signal. We also use pressure to provide variable activation force capabilities.

ABSTRACT
We explore 3D printing physical controls whose tactile response can be manipulated programmatically through pneumatic actuation. In particular, by manipulating the internal air pressure of various pneumatic elements, we can create mechanisms that require different levels of actuation force and can also change their shape. We introduce and discuss a series of example 3D printed pneumatic controls, which demonstrate the feasibility of our approach. This includes conventional controls, such as buttons, knobs and sliders, but also extends to domains such as toys and deformable interfaces. We describe the challenges that we faced and the methods that we used to overcome some of the limitations of current 3D printing technology. We conclude with example applications and thoughts on future avenues of research.

Author Keywords
3D printing; pneumatics; physical interfaces; haptics; rapid fabrication

ACM Classification Keywords
H.5.m. Information Interfaces and Presentation (e.g. HCI): Miscellaneous

ACM 978-1-4503-3145-6/15/04...$15.00.
http://dx.doi.org/10.1145/2702123.2702569

INTRODUCTION
3D printing offers exciting new opportunities for the rapid creation of highly customized interactive components, such as pipe-based interactive objects [14] or optical elements [23]. In this work, we explore another class: a set of 3D printed physical controls whose feel and behavior can be adjusted dynamically. More specifically, we use pneumatics and standard sensing techniques for press, linear, and rotary input controls to create components with variable-activation force capabilities. These controls can be activated with light pressure, but require greater force in other circumstances. In this manner, users can receive tactile feedback through the controls based on the computational state of an interface, while providing discrete or continuous input. Additionally, some designs can be physically "highlighted" by raising them above a device surface. Illustrative examples are provided in Fig. 1.

The pneumatic controls proposed in this work are complementary to electro-mechanical variable activation force controls, such as the camera shutter of [12]. While more traditional mechanical controls may be appropriate for some applications, others may benefit from the compliance of pneumatic components. Pneumatics affords soft haptic feedback, which is harder to accomplish with mechanical actuation. In some cases it might also be easier and cheaper to route compressed air through complex geometries than to embed mechanical components inside a haptic control, such as a physical knob, button or slider. The benefits and limitations of pneumatic controls are further discussed in the paper.

We uncovered some interesting and unexpected design challenges with 3D printing technology for flexible components.

In particular, current solutions for printing support material (sacrificial material designed to hold up part of the object while it is being printed, but removed later) proved problematical in several places. Even though we expect easier-to-remove support material to become available for printing in the future, we describe current challenges and propose practical methods to mitigate them. This makes our controls easy to replicate, and facilitates their adoption and customization.

We envision that in the future we will be able to specify custom physical devices nearly as easily as we specify graphical user interfaces today – i.e., by picking components from a standardized library and editing them into a whole, functional unit. These devices could then be printed in their entirety or, in the nearer term, printed in parts and completed with simple assembly tasks. We move towards this end with the proposed, reusable set of proof of concept pneumatic components.

RELATED WORK

Pneumatic Device Controls

Harrison and Hudson used air chambers to create dynamic buttons that inflate or deflate on a visual display [6]. These chambers were manually constructed using clear acrylic, a masked glue layer, and a sheet of translucent latex. We build upon this work, and provide a more practical method for fabricating pneumatic buttons, as well as other device controls.

3D Printed Pneumatics

Slyper et al. [17] explored pneumatically sensed interactive objects based on 3D printed hollow air chambers, similar to the ones that we fabricate. One of the main differences with our work, though, is that they used the chambers passively to prototype particular manipulation affordances on robot skins, rather than actively to provide haptic feedback or render computational states. The air chambers in [17] are soft and have a hole for support material removal. This aperture is also used to sense changes in internal air pressure, which occur when users manipulate the chambers, e.g., by twisting or stretching.

Other interesting pneumatic parts have been printed. For example, [4] fabricates pneumatic flowers with multi-material 3D printing. When pressure increases inside the flowers, their petals open, making it look like they blossom. While these flowers do not have electronic components in their interior, they seem to be fabricated in a similar fashion to our controls. Another example of 3D printed pneumatic parts is the peristaltic pump of [15]. This pump uses two integrated valves, a flexible silicone tube and an actuator to displace fluids. Hobbyists have also started to explore 3D printing pneumatic components, like a one way valve [22] or a pneumatic gripper that screws to the end of a standard plastic bottle [13].

Finally, Savage et al. [14] presented a tool for routing and optimizing pipes within 3D printed structures, which can support a range of pneumatic and other applications. These explorations all suggest that 3D printing could be used to create a wide variety of pneumatic parts for interactive devices.

3D Printing vs. Alternative Fabrication Methods

While some pneumatic controls could possibly be built with other methods like manual construction, casting or injection molding, 3D printing offers a unified, flexible approach to fabrication and customization. One of the key advantages of multi-material 3D printing, in particular, is precise automatic bonding of hard and elastic materials. For pneumatics, this is where air easily leaks and models break. Alternative techniques often bond elastic material to hard substrates, complicating construction. Methods include gluing [6], plastic welding, or coating hard parts with silicone to join them with other silicone segments [24], which are all time consuming and error prone. Furthermore, silicone coating is problematic for models that need low friction for rigid moving parts, such as the haptic knobs that we fabricate. On the flip side, the most significant downside to 3D printing, at present, is cost.

It is possible to fabricate some custom pneumatic devices by pouring silicone into a 3D printed mold [1, 10]. The mold can be printed with flexible material to make it easier to remove, and its geometry can be specified using computer-aided design tools or can be automatically estimated from a target shape [16]. Electronic components can also be layered between silicone pours [18], including wire, conductive fabric, and magnetic Hall effect sensors. Modifying molds is very time consuming and prohibits rapid iteration, though.

Multi-material casting has also been demonstrated [20] and could potentially be used to create pneumatic parts with materials of different stiffness. Unfortunately, molds also limit castable forms. Some of our controls have interior geometries not possible with molds alone, requiring either multi-piece molds (which are complicated) or consumable molds that are created and broken for every control. This significantly limits the scalability of these methods in comparison to multi-material 3D printing.

Other Interactive Pneumatic Components

Pneumatic systems have become popular for creating Organic User Interfaces [21], which consider shape as a key variable of interactivity. One way of creating these interfaces is by particle jamming [5, 19], where a jammable granular material is inserted into a flexible sack. The granular material slides around in a liquid-like state when loosely packed, but hardens into custom shapes due to inter-particle friction when the sack is vacuumed. Ou et al. [11] extended the above line of work by proposing layer jamming for thin sheet interfaces. A combination of copper tape and 3M Velostat™ can be layered into these structures to measure pressure and detect deformations. Air bladders can also be used as actuation mechanisms.

Inspired by advances in soft robotics, Yao et al. [24] created pneumatic soft composites for shape-changing interfaces, which can be fabricated in laboratories, e.g., using soft lithography. Their composites can significantly alter their shape by bending, curling, or expanding, based on the properties of the underlying layered materials, such as paper or fabric. Structural changes of these interfaces can be sensed with flexible circuitry made of copper tape, fluid conductors, or inkjet conductive ink. [24] also shows how a miniature pneumatic system can be built with off-the-shelf components for their practical applications. Our pressure control system is inspired by the latter.

Haptic Feedback

The haptic sensations that we explore in this work were inspired by the interactive stylus of Lee et al. [8]. This pen generates a wide range of haptic feedback using a solenoid actuator, and has a sensitive tip to captures users' press force. In this manner, the pen can create the illusion of pressing buttons of several stiffness levels or can feel similar to pressing a two-level shutter button in a camera.

3D PRINTED VARIABLE-ACTIVATION FORCE CONTROLS

The 3D printed device controls that we explore in this work rely on changes in air pressure to alter their physical feel and behavior. These controls can provide dynamic feedback during their manipulation. For example, variable activation force knobs can change physical resistance to turning actions based on a computational state (Fig. 1B). This enables richer interactions than equivalent static control devices.

Our interactive controls achieve a tight coupling of haptic feedback and functionality based on well understood pneumatic principles. This makes them easy to control, safe and inexpensive. In addition, pneumatics allow the location where force is applied to be decoupled from actuation, which facilitates the fabrication of small devices for physically-constrained user interfaces. These properties make pneumatic devices complementary to mechanical controls.

We used an Objet Eden260V printer with a resolution of 600 dpi (42 microns) to fabricate our controls. All models were 3D printed with VeroClear (rigid material) and TangoPlus (elastic material).[1] Some models were then finished with acrylic paint. While current 3D printing materials may limit the performance of some pneumatic components (e.g., TangoPlus cannot elongate as much as Ecoflex® silicone), we expect better materials to become available in the future.

Our design considerations for these variable-activation force controls are presented in the following section, followed by our fabrication approaches. The rest of the paper is devoted to illustrative applications, as well as to the discussion of other aspects of the technology and its limitations.

Design

In general, we start our design process thinking about a desired haptic interface, its functionality and general shape. For example, we may want an interface with a haptic slider to provide input for a video game (as described in the Applications section). Then, we decide how we are going to sense user input with this device and how to incorporate air chambers with elastic parts into the geometry, such that the device can provide variable feedback. The interplay between the chosen sensing mechanism, and the shape and placement of the air chambers is key to obtaining the desired result.

Sensing User Input

We sense user interaction with pressure sensors, as well as with electrical components that operate based on connectivity and resistivity. In the first case, we attach differential pressure sensors to the pneumatic systems of the proposed physical interfaces. For illustrative purposes, consider the conceptual diagram of Fig. 2, which we built for our applications. This system is composed of a pressure source (small compressor), two solenoid valves, a pressure sensor, and a 3D printed control with an air chamber. The valves are configured so that air can be added or released from the chamber under computer control, while the sensor continuously reads air pressure within the system allowing for precise, closed-loop pressure regulation. When the valves are at rest, as in the picture, the sensor allows us to detect when users alter the volume of the air chamber, e.g., by pressing a haptic button (Fig. 1A).

In the case of electrical conductivity and resistivity, we incorporate off-the-shelf sensors into our pneumatic controls once printed. The type of sensor used depends on the desired functionality of the control. For example, we use potentiometers to get users' input in the case of knobs and sliders, but could also incorporate off-the-shelf switches to our pneumatic buttons. Since these sensors are placed inside of our control devices, they generally constrain the shape and the design of the air chambers that we use to provide haptic feedback.

Figure 3 shows two off-the-shelf potentiometers that we incorporated into our haptic physical interfaces. When these components are added to the printed models, one can think of our pneumatic controls as an approach to augment the capabilities of standard input sensors.

Conductive materials will be widely available in the future for 3D printing, making it possible to print conductive paths for electricity to flow inside of pneumatic components [9]. Although, this technology is still being researched, we simulate this result by embedding thin layers of conductive material into our printed models, such as copper tape. This is an alternative to embedding simple off-the-shelf components while printing, which provides more design freedom.

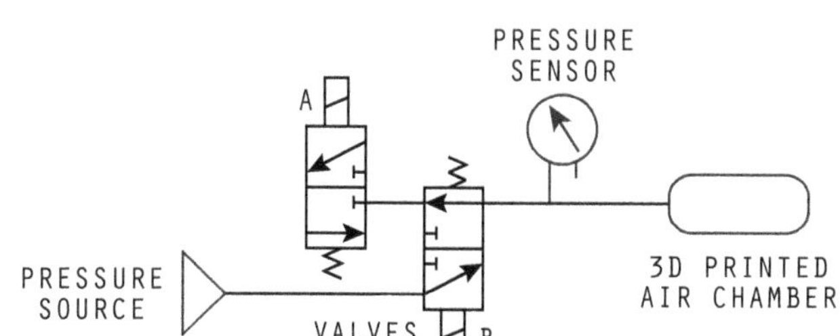

Figure 2. Prototype pneumatic system for some of our controls. The chamber is embedded in the controls and is used to provide feedback. When valves A and B are in their rest state, as in the picture, the system is closed and air cannot escape. When the valve A is actuated and B is at rest, the system is open and air is released. When B is actuated but not A, a compressor (pressure source) increases air pressure in the system.

Figure 3. Off-the-shelf potentiometers used in some of our controls: SpectraSymbol's linear sensor and wiper (A), and rotary sensor (B).

[1] A more detailed description of these materials can be found in http://www.stratasys.com/materials/

Variable Activation Force Capabilities through Air Chambers
Air tight chambers are a key element of our variable activation force controls. These chambers are compressed air reservoirs, which we use to provide variable haptic feedback.

The chambers are made with materials of several elastomer characteristics and have at least one small, open orifice for air to flow through. Hard materials are typically used to provide chambers and their controls with a consistent, well defined shape. Soft materials are essential for the elastic parts of the geometry, which deform to provide variable haptic feedback or alter the physical form of a device.

Figure 4 illustrates several air chambers that can be 3D printed. Their elastic parts expand outwards from the chamber when internal pressure increases, generating forces perpendicular to their surface. In some cases, we use this force to resist pushing and squishing of the flexible parts, such as when users press a button. In others, we use this force to generate friction between some parts of our controls. As more friction is generated, our controls provide more resistance to user's actions (e.g., knobs become harder to turn).

We can increase pressure inside the chambers in several ways in order to produce different haptic feedback. Figure 5 shows some haptic waveforms that we can reproduce with our pneumatic system (Fig. 2). We open or close the valves to generate the different dynamic pressure profiles, keeping the compressor on continuously. In Fig. 5A, we repeatedly increase, hold, reduce, and hold the internal pressure of the system. In Fig. 5B, we increase pressure more slowly over time, release air from the system, and repeat. In the bottom cases we repeatedly increase pressure by steps (Fig. 5C) or linearly (Fig. 5D), and then reduce pressure back to its original level.

The shape of the elastic part of the chambers affects their deformation and how much pressure they can hold. Printed chambers with round elastic parts, such as the one in Fig. 6, tend to be very robust. This chamber can hold up to about 7.25 psi (50 kPa) before breaking. Other printed geometries have significantly lower pressure limits, such as the star-shaped chamber of Fig. 1A. As expected, the flexible parts of the chambers tend to break in places where they connect to rigid material, and where their shape undergoes major deformations as pressure increases.

In general, we considered two types of forces during our design process. On one hand, there are *internal* forces, which we generate and control through the pneumatic system that drives our haptic controls. On the other, there are *external* forces that are present in the environment and are independent of the pneumatic system, such as gravity. The design considerations that we had with respect to the effect of these forces are further detailed the following sections, depending on the particular functionality of each control.

Fabrication
We fabricate pneumatic, variable-activation force controls using modern multi-material, photo-polymer 3D printing technology. This fabrication process is straightforward, replicable, and affordable when prototyping custom devices.

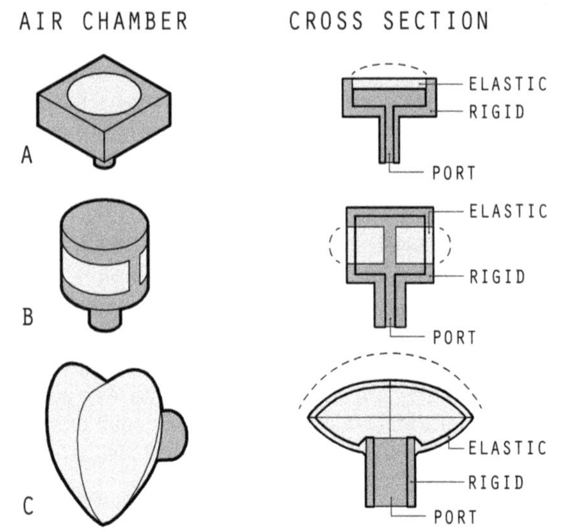

Figure 4. Several air chambers in their rest state (left) and a cross section that shows the internal flow of air (right). Air can come in or out of the chambers through the port at the bottom of each cross section. Parts made of elastic materials are colored in light gray, while rigid parts are darker. The dashed lines depict the deformation of the flexible parts when air is supplied through the ports, thus increasing internal air pressure. Our push buttons have chambers similar to (A), while our knobs have chambers like (B). 3D printing also offers the possibility of fabricating controls with more irregularly-shaped chambers, such as (C).

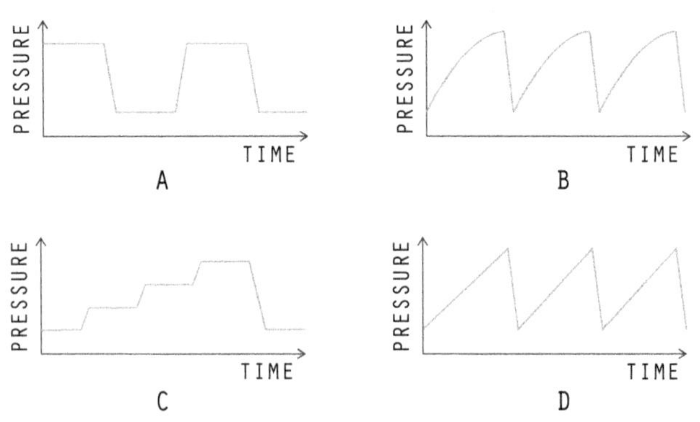

Figure 5. Dynamic pressure profiles that we can generate programmatically and render with our pneumatic controls.

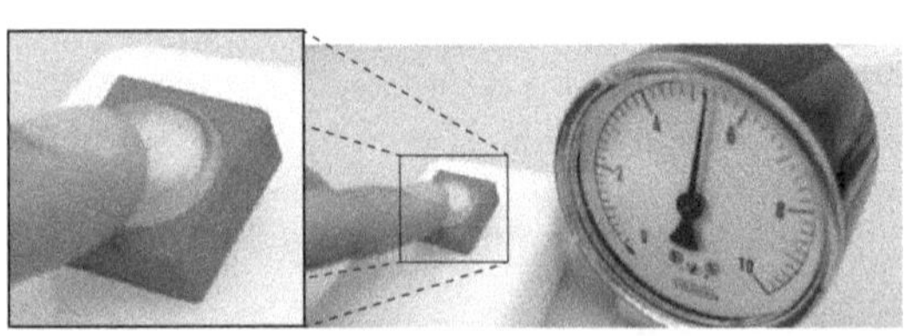

Figure 6. Printed pneumatic button (red) with an air chambers similar to Figure 4A. The button is placed on a stand (white) and is shown partially inflated, with a pressure of 5.4 psi (37.2 kPa) relative to atmospheric pressure. When the button is fully inflated at 6 psi (41.4 kPa), its top surface raises 3.5mm in comparison to its position at 0 psi. The clear and elastic top of the button has a thickness of 1mm.

The printing process starts with a digital geometric model of a control, which is then converted to slices, or layers, that are printed sequentially. Besides model materials, the printer can deposit a gel-like support material used to hold up overhanging geometry. This support material must be removed from the model after printing, e.g., with a waterjet cleaning unit or by manually rubbing it off from other materials.

Recent 3D printing technologies promise a future where all sorts of geometries for pneumatic devices and their chambers can be printed at once, immediately ready for use [3, 9]. Currently, however, these technologies are in their early stages and are not widely available. Instead, many commercial printers (like the one we use) rely on added support material to build models layer by layer.

Unfortunately, removing the support material from a printed model can be very difficult, especially when this material is inside small and tight geometries (such as tubes). Further, removing support material from soft surfaces can tear them. This is exactly what happens if we print our air chambers naively. Even after carefully trying to clean them, their interior is dirty with left-over support and their elastic parts are often broken as a result of the cleaning process. While remaining support material next to the rigid parts of the chambers does not pose much difficulty for their functionality, any support that remains next to the interior of the elastic parts can significantly affect haptic feedback since the support material is not very flexible. Another alternative to ease the cleaning process is to submerge printed models into a caustic bath, which dissolves support material. However, this technique can be a problem for embedded electronic components and, in our experience, it rarely removed all support from the models before starting to dissolve the elastic parts.

The following sections describe the approaches that we took to overcome the support material removal problem. These approaches are not mutually exclusive and should be adopted based on the desired printed geometry.

Fabricating Chambers by Parts

One approach to fabricate chambers consists of splitting the models into individual parts that can be easily assembled together. The goal of the splits should be to make the interior of the chambers more accessible. This way, we can more readily remove support material from the models once printed.

While the parts of a chamber could be put together in many ways, we found that 3D printing rigid threaded joints and assembling them with Teflon thread seal tape (or plumber's tape) was a robust approach for fabricating air-tight chambers. Due to printing resolution limitations, we opted for joints with coarse threads, which are also less likely to cross thread than finer counterparts. For example, we used threads with a major diameter between 8.5 and 50mm, and a pitch between 1.5 and 2.75mm. Sample screw models can be found in online design communities such as Thingiverse,[2] or from parts sellers such as McMaster-Carr,[3] which eases the incorporation of threaded joints into model geometry.

[2]http://www.thingiverse.com

[3]http://www.mcmaster.com

Figure 7 shows a mushroom-shaped air chamber that can be 3D printed in parts. The top part of the chamber is made of both elastic and rigid materials, while the bottom part is completely rigid. When the parts are not assembled, the split allows better access into the chamber in comparison to printing the whole mushroom at once. Note that the size of the major diameter of the screw is the main limiting factor for accessing the top part of the chamber. The bigger the diameter, the more easily we can access the interior of the top component. When the chamber is assembled with plumber's tape around the screw joint, air can only enter or leave the pneumatic component through the port at the bottom of the mushroom.

Since threaded joints are standard in pneumatic systems, we can also print parts that directly attach to industry-standard, pre-fabricated threaded pipes and fittings. For example, the top part of the chamber in Fig. 7 could potentially connect to a pipe that follows the National Pipe Thread standard, rather than connecting to the stem of the mushroom.

We could also split the heart-shaped chamber of Fig. 4C into two parts, like we did for the mushroom. In fact, we can split many sorts of chambers into parts with screw joints as long as the joints are rigid and sufficiently large to be printed with at least a few connecting threads. The former is important because flexible joints are likely to let air escape when pressure increases. The latter guarantees that there is enough contact surface to keep the parts in place once assembled.

Fabricating Chambers with Auxiliary Support

An alternative method to print air chambers dispenses with the standard gel-like support material in their interior and replaces it with auxiliary, non-printed supports. More specifically, we insert pre-made parts that provide support for further building as in [7, 23]. In addition, we use these parts to create air-tight hollow spaces for our chambers, which do not need to be cleaned after printing. As a result, pneumatic controls are less prone to breaking during fabrication. While this strategy imposes constraints on the geometry of the model, as will be explained later, it is very attractive for printing pneumatic controls with little manual labor.

We use layers of acrylic as auxiliary support in our prototypes, and never remove them from the models once printed. An illustrative air chamber with auxiliary support in presented in Fig. 8. The layers of acrylic that we use to hold up geometry are fabricated by laser-cutting acrylic sheets. The shape of these pieces is based on 2D shapes derived from the underlying 3D CAD model for the part, such that they tightly

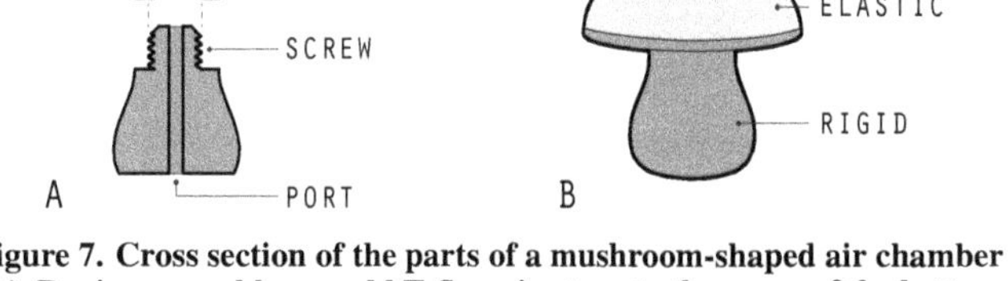

Figure 7. Cross section of the parts of a mushroom-shaped air chamber (A). During assembly, we add Teflon pipe tape to the screw of the bottom part, and insert this piece into the top one, resulting in (B).

fit printed geometry. This is important since model material may sink if gaps exist between the layers of acrylic and the printed model. When this happens, the printed geometry may deform and undesired leaks may appear in the air chambers.

When we 3D print with auxiliary support, we disable printing with the standard gel-like support material, except for adding a pedestal at the bottom of the geometry – this is necessary to remove the the model from the printing tray once finished. We then start the printing process, and pause when a hollow space for the auxiliary support is layered (such as the "enclosure" in Fig. 8A). We place the auxiliary support material flush with the current top of the model and, finally, continue printing the model on top of the added component. In some cases, we may add more than one layer of auxiliary support to a printed control. For example, we added a second piece of acrylic to the model of Fig. 8 so that it could be printed with a barbed fitting. The barb is wider than the pipe that connects it to the model and, hence, needs to be supported.

We design the hollow spaces for auxiliary support material as part of our controls. This requires thinking about the orientation of the models as they are printed, such that the auxiliary support effectively holds up overhanging geometry. For example, the model of Fig. 8 has to be printed upside down to prevent the flexible part of the chamber to fall on top of auxiliary support. When single layers of acrylic are added to a model at a time, the height of the hollow spaces follows the thickness of the acrylic parts. Besides, model material is added all around auxiliary support when it has to be placed inside of an air-tight chamber. This ensures that air cannot freely escape the chambers other than through their ports.

While this fabrication approach is practical, it imposes an important constraint on the design of the models and the way they are printed: at any point in time during the printing process, the top of the model has to be flat (even when auxiliary support is added to printed geometry). This is required because we are printing layer by layer, and the print head needs to move close to the top of the model to deposit new material. As a consequence, all the layers of acrylic that we add to our controls lie parallel to the printing tray.

Another important consideration when fabricating chambers with this approach is that auxiliary support has to be rigid enough to hold up other geometry. Therefore, any elastic material that is printed and cured on top of this support will likely lose flexibility, specially near the contact surface.

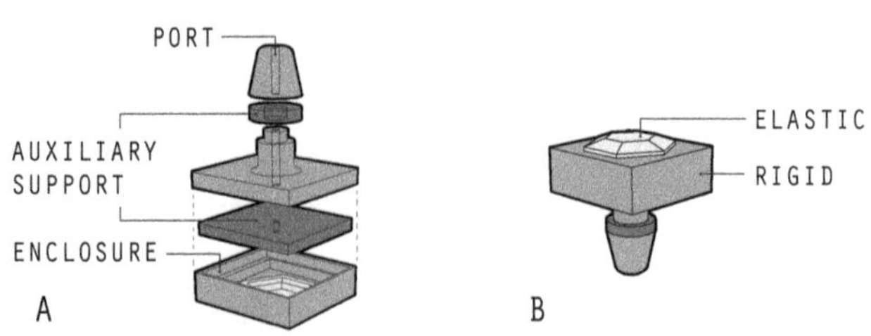

Figure 8. Auxiliary support for a pneumatic button. The model is displayed upside down in (A), as it would be 3D printed. When the bottom enclosure is printed, the first piece of auxiliary support is inserted. When the next section is layered, auxiliary support in the form of a ring is added to the pipe of the chamber to hold up the rest of the model. No manual assembly is necessary after printing the complete model (B).

Fabricating Custom Tools for Support Material Removal

We can also 3D print custom tools to remove support material from the interior of our controls. These tools can be designed based on model geometry, such that they can easily reach support material in places that are otherwise hard to access. We used one of these tools to remove support material from the chamber of a pneumatic alligator toy, as shown in Fig. 9. The alligator is later described in our Applications section.

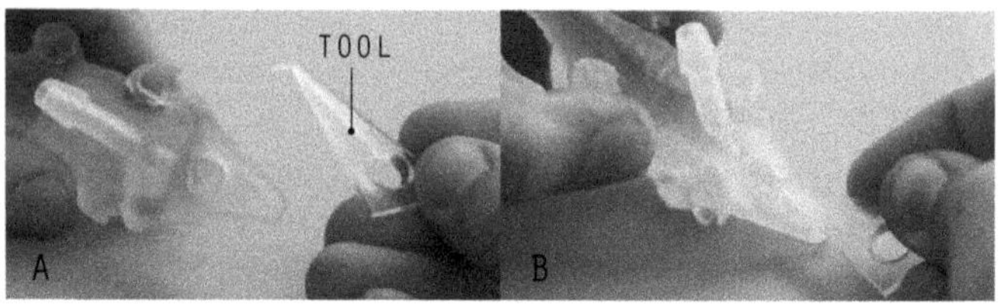

Figure 9. 3D printed tool (A) for removing support material (B)

Other Fabrication Considerations

We add 3D printed barbed connectors to all the air chambers that we fabricate, as in Figure 8. This standard connector prevents air from leaking through the ports of the chambers, and can be slightly reconfigured based on how we fabricate a model. For example, we typically make the internal diameter of the connector wider when we fabricate controls by parts, since support material has to be removed from their interior.

If a small and light component is embedded into a control while it is printed, it is likely that the head of the printer will move the component out of place when it slides on top of the model to deposit additional model material. In these cases, we add a few drops of a fast-acting cyanoacrylate-based adhesive (e.g., *superglue*) to the contact surface between the component and the part of the model that has already been printed. This extra step ensures that the component is held securely in place during the printing process.

Note that the constraints that limit the placement of layers of acrylic into our models while printing also apply to other embedded parts, including electronics. An example of embedded copper tape is presented in the next section.

Device Controls

We categorize the types of controls that we fabricate based on the type of actions that users perform to provide input:

Pressing and Squishing

We fabricate controls that can be pressed (like a standard button) and others that can be more roughly "squished". The main differences between these types of controls are their size and the roundness of their elastic parts. The bigger and rounder the elastic part of a chamber, the more "squishy".

Figure 10 shows star-shaped pneumatic buttons. User input can be sensed with a pressure sensor attached to the pneumatic system that drives the mechanisms. The curve in the background of Fig. 1A shows variations in the internal pressure of the big star as it is pressed. Note that we can scale a pneumatic control, such as in Fig. 10A, and test it immediately by simply adjusting the pressure range at which it operates. This is an advantage of pneumatics for prototyping device controls in comparison to mechanical counterparts.

We can also incorporate electronics into pneumatic buttons to sense when users fully depress their elastic top, as in Fig. 11. This allows the input to be received irrespective of pressure changes, which is useful when we provide continuous, variable haptic feedback. The button in Fig. 11 was printed with auxiliary support, and with an extra layer of acrylic that holds two thin stripes of copper tape. Additional copper tape was placed on the interior surface of the elastic part, such that it closes the circuit when it is fully depressed. As with the model of Figure 8, this button had to be printed upside down.

Furthermore, we can use the deformation of buttons to create actuated switches. To this end, we incorporated the round button of Fig. 6 into a structure with a hinge joint (Fig. 12). When pressure increases, the overhanging part of the switch raises; when pressure decreases, it lowers down due to gravity. Pneumatic controls could potentially be incorporated into more complex structures with other printed joints [2].

Turning

We fabricate knobs that resist users' turning actions with chambers similar to the one in Figure 4B. We add potentiometers inside of these controls to sense the orientation of their caps and when when users rotate them.

Figure 13 shows an illustrative knob that can provide variable feedback no matter in which direction it is turned. We printed the base (with the air chamber) independently of the cap. Even though the round shape of the chamber could very well hold a screw joint, we printed it with auxiliary support such that we did not have to remove support material from its interior. We inserted a potentiometer into the base during assembly and attached the cap to this sensor as a press-fit component. We made the elastic parts of the potentiometer slightly thicker than for the other models (1.5mm vs 1mm) since it alters the rigidity of the knob based on friction. This elastic part can still deform, though, as shown in Fig. 13C. With this deformation, we can provide at least three levels of feedback with pressures from 0 to 3.6psi (24.8 kPa).

We can also provide different feedback based on the direction in which a knob is turning. We accomplish this by adding a sawtooth pattern to the internal walls of the cap and its elastic parts (Figure 14). Counter-clockwise turns are easier than clockwise rotations with this pattern.

Sliding

In addition, we can fabricate sliders that provide variable resistance to users' actions. We offer an example mechanism in Figure 15A. This model was printed in three parts: the base chamber, the rails, and the handle; and was then assembled as shown in the picture. While we could have added an off-the-shelf slider to this device control, we opted for incorporating a linear membrane potentiometer to the model instead. This allowed us to customize the shape of the handle, showing the versatility of 3D printing.

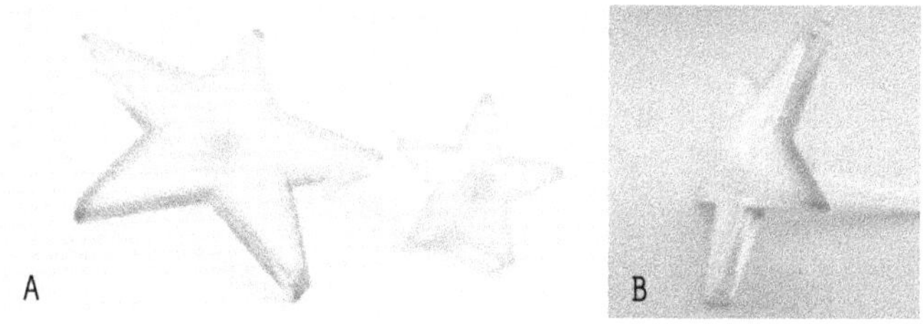

Figure 10. Star buttons fabricated with auxiliary support (A). The big star is inflated in (B) at 0.6 psi (4.1 kPa) relative to atmospheric pressure.

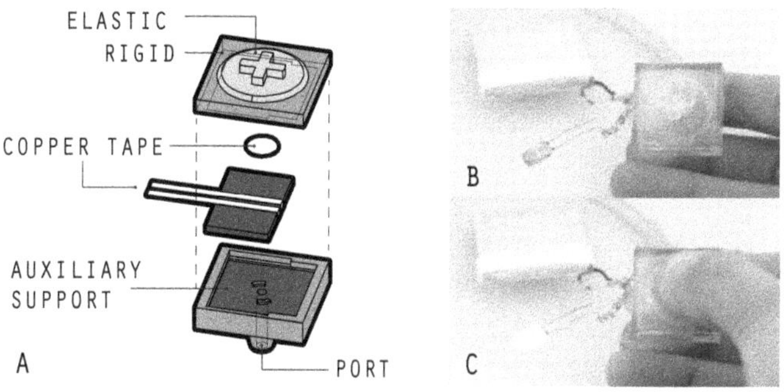

Figure 11. Pneumatic button that was printed with auxiliary support and with an internal conductive circuit made of copper tape. (A) shows the placement of copper inside the printed model, (B) shows the button in its rest state, and (C) shows the button inflated and pressed. The round piece of copper attaches to the internal bottom surface of the elastic part, and makes contact with the two copper stripes when the button is pressed. This button was printed upside down, as the one in Fig. 8.

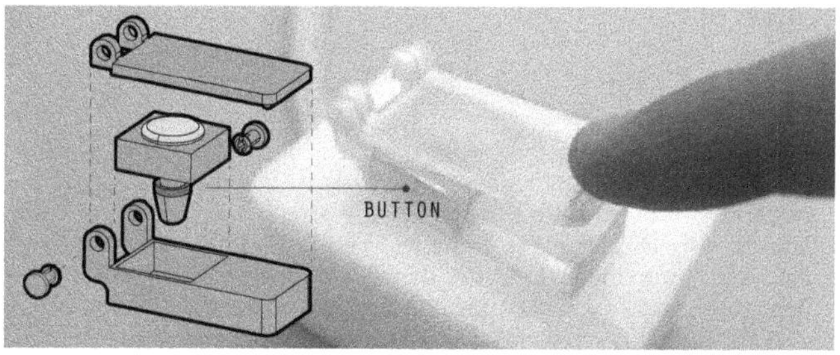

Figure 12. 3D printed switch. We inserted a button like the one in Fig. 8 into a printed structure that was fabricated by parts and assembled as in the illustration. When the button is deflated, it cannot be pressed since the rigid top of the switch is in contact with the bottom. However, when the button is inflated, the top part of the switch raises. We can then detect users' presses with a pressure sensor.

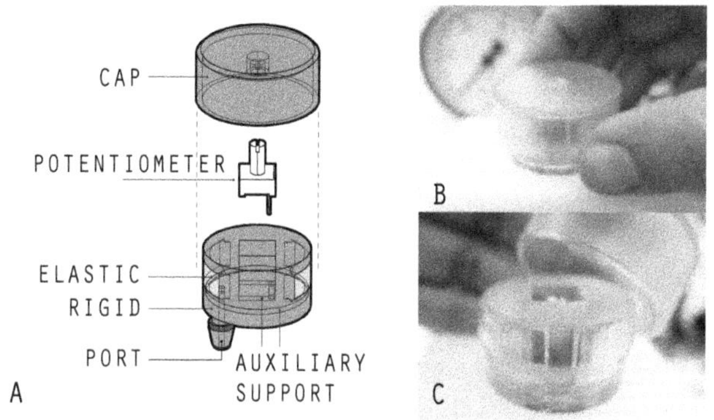

Figure 13. 3D printed knob with a chamber as in Figure 4B. (A) shows the parts that make the knob and how its assembled after printing. (B) shows the resulting component, and (C) shows the internal chamber inflated at 3.6 psi (24.8 KPa) with respect to atmospheric pressure.

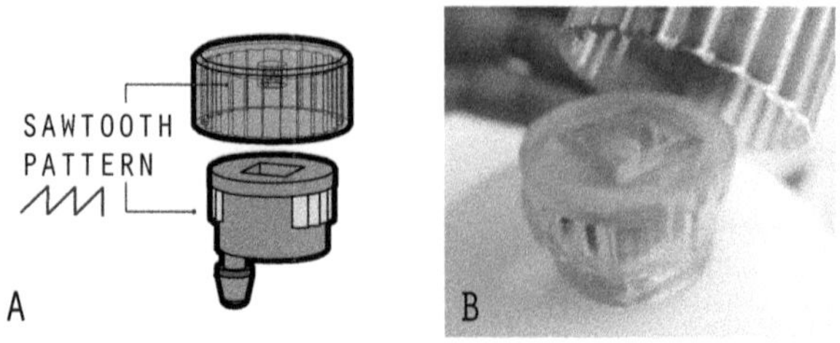

Figure 14. Sawtooth knob. The elastic walls of the chamber and the internal surface of the cap have a sawtooth pattern (A). This allows to provide different feedback based on which orientation the cap rotates. (B) shows the air chamber of the knob in its inflated state, when it can provide resistance to turning actions.

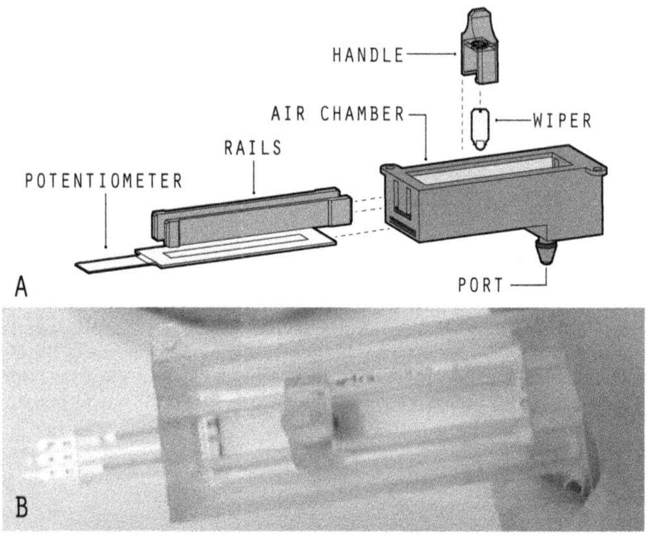

Figure 15. 3D printed slider with the linear potentiometer and wiper of Fig. 3. The base chamber was fabricated with auxiliary support independently of all other parts (A). During assembly, we screw the wiper into the handle, slide the potentiometer and rails into the base, and snap the handle onto the rails. When the elastic walls of the chamber inflate, they make pressure against the handle (B), making the slider stiffer.

The slider that we printed also locks in place - users have to push down on the handle in order to move it. We accomplished this feature by screwing a wiper with an embedded spring into the handle. This wiper also allows for precise sensing with the linear potentiometer. When air pressure increases inside the chamber, its elastic parts inflate inwards towards the handle (Fig. 15B). This generates friction that resists the linear motion of the slider. As with the knob, we were able to create three distinguishable levels of feedback at 0 psi, 0.6 psi (4.1 kPa), and 0.8 psi (5.5 kPa).

Other Device Controls

While our work spans the design space of the controls that are most often used in physical control panels, we foresee other types of pneumatic controls being fabricated akin to our prototypes. For example, one could 3D print a *pulling* control with a design similar to the chamber in Fig. 4B. Imagine replacing the hard material in the middle of the chamber with elastic material and adding a small inward curvature to the elastic walls all around. Then, it would be possible for users to provide input by pulling the top of the chamber upwards, and we would be able to provide feedback by varying pressure inside the chamber. If pressure increases, the top of the chamber would move up, thus decreasing the range of pulling motion available. Another example are *bending* controls. Consider the bending building block of [17] for prototyping manipulation affordances on robot skins. If one prints a chamber with that shape, make it air-tight, and regulate pressure inside of it, then the chamber could be used for providing both user input and haptic feedback. As pressure increases, this control would become harder to bend.

APPLICATIONS

We fabricated a set of interactive devices to illustrate potential applications for 3D printed variable activation force controls. For all of the examples that follow, we used a pneumatic configuration similar to that of Fig. 2. The specific electronic and pneumatic components that we used are depicted in Fig. 16.

Alligator Toy

We used the same operating principles of the switch of Figure 12 to make a 3D printed alligator toy. Rather than building the device with auxiliary support, we fabricated it in parts (Figure 17A). This allowed us to route air down through the alligator belly, where it is hidden from users. The elastic part of the chamber in the lower jaw of the alligator pushes the top of its head upwards when pressure increases. As a result, it looks like the alligator opens its mouth. When pressure is reduced, the top of the head falls to its rest position due to gravity. If the internal pressure of the alligator is at least 4 psi (27.6 kPa; when its mouth is slightly open), then we can sense when users press on its nose using a pressure sensor. In response, we make the alligator open and close its mouth repeatedly, e.g., with a square haptic waveform as in Figure 5A.

Responsive Lamp

We made an interactive lamp by incorporating three light emitting diodes (LEDs) into a 3D printed pneumatic device. Figure 18A shows the components of the lamp, and Figures 18B and 18C show the lamp slightly inflated and being pressed, respectively. Our lamp can respond to a variety of input gestures measured by small pressure changes. For example, long and short squeezes change its brightness, while hue is modified based on squeeze strength and duration. Haptic feedback is utilized to indicate important changes in the internal computational state of the lamp.

Volume Knob

We used the sawtooth knob from Fig. 14 to provide haptic volume control, as depicted in Fig. 19. Clockwise and counter-clockwise rotations increase and lower volume, respectively. In order to keep volume levels in a safe range, our prototype application increases pressure as the knob is rotated clockwise beyond its middle position. This alerts users that they are close to reaching unsafe volume levels. When the maximum safe volume level is reached, the chamber fully inflates, providing maximum resistance to additional clockwise rotations. Lowering the volume is still easy, though.

Side Scrolling Video Game

We used the slider from Figure 15 to provide input and haptic feedback for a side scrolling video game. In this game, users

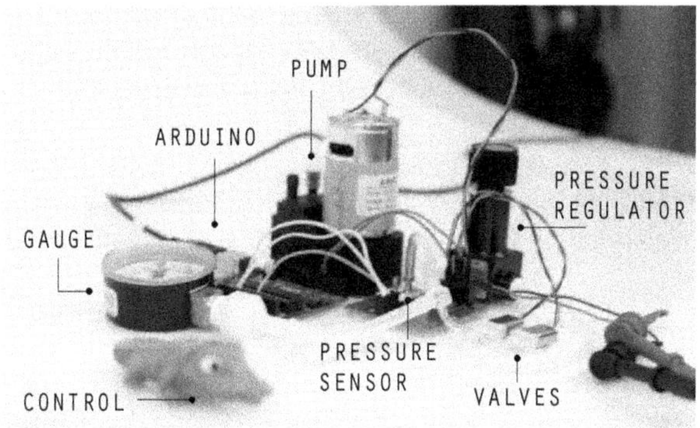

Figure 16. Pneumatic and electronic system used for all applications, which includes an AIRPO pump (model D20288), a manual pressure regulator by Airtrol, two SMC valves (model S070C), a Silicon Microstructures pressure sensor (model SM5651), a gauge, and an Arduino. The pressure regulator and the gauge are not necessary for operating our controls, but were added for safety.

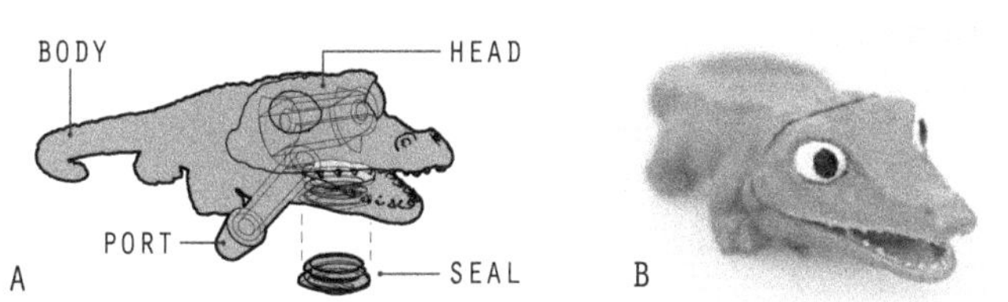

Figure 17. Alligator toy. The body, head and seal were printed independently and then assembled (A). The head snaps into the body and the seal screws into a hole in the bottom of its jaw. The elastic part on the mouth (lighter gray) inflates when pressure increases, opening the mouth (B). Fig. 9 shows the unfinished body part after printing.

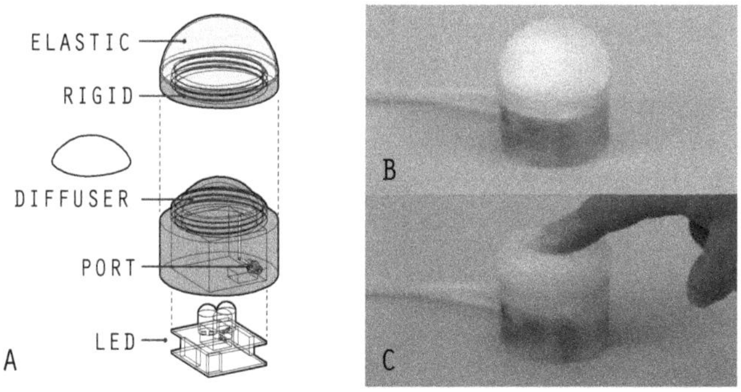

Figure 18. Pneumatic lamp. The device was printed by parts and assembled (A). We added a diffuser to the base and inserted an LED inside. (B) shows the lamp slightly inflated, and (C) shows it being pressed.

Figure 19. We use the sawtooth knob of Figure 14 to control volume in a prototype application. The current volume level is rendered real-time on the screen (as in the background of the image).

control the vertical position of an airplane as it flies through a cloudy sky (Figure 20). The slider sets the vertical velocity of the plane; in the middle position, the airplane has zero vertical velocity and simply moves horizontally. When the slider is adjusted up or down, it controls the plane's upward or downward movement in a rate controlled manner.

When the plane is flying through clear sky, the slider is set at its minimum resistance level (0 psi). To simulate little turbulence, the slider becomes harder to move when flying through smaller clouds (0.6 psi, 4.1 kPa). When the plane passes through the biggest clouds in the game, we increase the pressure of the slider to 0.8 psi (5.5 kPa; as in Fig. 15B). The slider can still be moved, but with more difficulty.

Other Applications

Other applications could benefit from variable activation force controls. For example, alarm clocks could use a pneumatic snooze button to highlight the state of the alarm, and prevent accidental presses that may shut down the alarm unintentionally. Radio tuners could also use pneumatic knobs to indicate when users reach a station. This becomes specially useful when users have to pay attention to other tasks, e.g., when they are driving and looking for a particular station. Finally, we also envision printed pneumatic components as fully-customized building blocks of free-form hardware interfaces, such as Palette.[4]

FUTURE WORK

We designed our pneumatic controls manually, based on the desired haptic feedback and sensing modality. However, this process could be semi-automated based on a set of predesigned air chambers. Making an interface to facilitate non-expert design of these controls is an important area of future work. Likewise, it would be useful to provide a computational interface for the rapid design of 3D printed tools for support material removal. This could potentially ease, even further, the fabrication of pneumatic controls.

We used acrylic as auxiliary support, but foresee other materials being used as well to hold up printed geometries. For example, one could think of 3D printing a part, e.g., an air

[4]http://palettegear.com

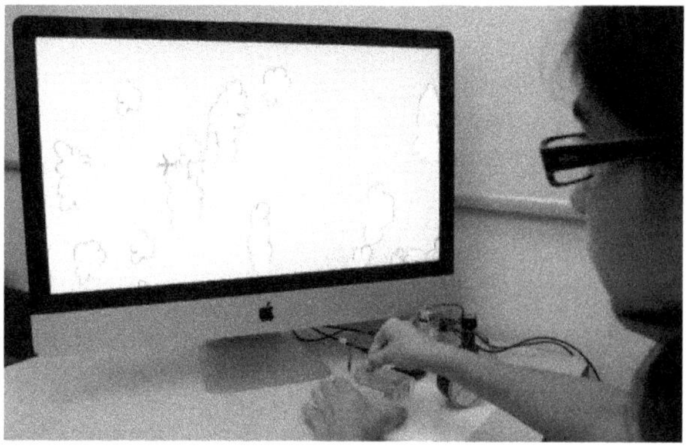

Figure 20. Flying game with pneumatic slider. The slider provides input vertical velocity for the plane as it flies through the clouds. When the plane hits turbulence, the slider becomes stiffer.

chamber, and then embedding it into another model while it is printing. This could potentially reduce the time and effort put into manually assembling printed controls, and may as well allow to create more complex air chambers.

Our work focused on the design and fabrication of devices that operate with air. While many considerations were made based on the physical properties of this compressible gas, we believe that our design rationale and fabrication approaches can guide the rapid prototyping of control devices that use other fluids, such as water. This could offer faster and less compliant feedback, which may benefit certain applications.

ACKNOWLEDGMENTS

We are thankful to Disney Research and The Walt Disney Corporation for continued support of this research effort. Thanks to Moshe Mahler for modeling the alligator.

REFERENCES

1. Borgatti, M. Thingiverse: Trefoil tentacle. `http://www.thingiverse.com/thing:92103`. Last accessed on 08/27/14.
2. Calì, J., Calian, D. A., Amati, C., Kleinberger, R., Steed, A., Kautz, J., and Weyrich, T. 3d-printing of non-assembly, articulated models. *ACM Trans. Graph. 31*, 6 (Nov. 2012).
3. Clark, L. How hair gel enables freeform 3d printing with an undo function. Wired.co.uk, July 2013. `http://www.wired.co.uk/news/archive/2013-07/25/undo-3d-printing`.
4. Clarkson, R. Blossom. `http://www.richardclarkson.com/blossom`. Last accessed on 01/02/15.
5. Follmer, S., Leithinger, D., Olwal, A., Cheng, N., and Ishii, H. Jamming user interfaces: Programmable particle stiffness and sensing for malleable and shape-changing devices. In *Proc. UIST'12* (2012).
6. Harrison, C., and Hudson, S. E. Providing dynamically changeable physical buttons on a visual display. In *Proc. CHI'09* (2009), 299–308.
7. Kataria, A., and Rosen, D. W. Building around inserts: methods for fabricating complex devices in stereolithography. *Rapid Prototyping Journal 7*, 5 (2001), 253–262.
8. Lee, J. C., Dietz, P. H., Leigh, D., Yerazunis, W. S., and Hudson, S. E. Haptic pen: A tactile feedback stylus for touch screens. In *Proc. UIST'04* (2004), 291–294.
9. Malone, E., and Lipson, H. Multi-material freeform fabrication of active systems. In *Proc. ESDA'08* (2008).
10. Mosadegh, B., Polygerinos, P., Keplinger, C., Wennstedt, S., Shepherd, R. F., Gupta, U., Shim, J., Bertoldi, K., Walsh, C. J., and Whitesides, G. M. Soft robotics: Pneumatic networks for soft robotics that actuate rapidly. *Advanced Functional Materials 24*, 2109 (2014).
11. Ou, J., Yao, L., Tauber, D., Steimle, J., Niiyama, R., and Ishii, H. jamsheets: Thin interfaces with tunable stiffness enabled by layer jamming. In *Proc. TEI'14* (2014).
12. Robins, M., and Bean, H. Variable force camera control, Oct. 4 2005. US Patent 6952528.
13. Russell, L. 3d printed pneumatic gripper. `http://getitmade.com.au/3d-Printed-Pneumatic-Gripper`. Last accessed on 08/27/14.
14. Savage, V., Schmidt, R., Grossman, T., Fitzmaurice, G., and Hartmann, B. A series of tubes: Adding interactivity to 3d prints using internal pipes. In *Proc. UIST'14* (2014).
15. Shkolnikov, V., Ramunas, J., and Santiago, J. G. A self-priming, roller-free, miniature, peristaltic pump operable with a single, reciprocating actuator. *Sensors and Actuators A: Physical 160*, 1 (2010), 141–146.
16. Skouras, M., Thomaszewski, B., Bickel, B., and Gross, M. Computational design of rubber balloons. *Proc. Eurographics* (2012).
17. Slyper, R., and Hodgins, J. Prototyping robot appearance, movement, and interactions using flexible 3d printing and air pressure sensors. In *Proc. RO-MAN'12* (2012).
18. Slyper, R., Poupyrev, I., and Hodgins, J. Sensing through structure: Designing soft silicone sensors. In *Proc. TEI'11*, ACM (New York, NY, USA, 2011), 213–220.
19. Stanley, A., Gwilliam, J., and Okamura, A. Haptic jamming: A deformable geometry, variable stiffness tactile display using pneumatics and particle jamming. In *World Haptics Conference (WHC)* (April 2013).
20. Uribe, C. D. G. Multi-material Molding and Casting Mid-sole. Master's thesis, MIT Media Lab, 2014.
21. Vertegaal, R., and Poupyrev, I. Organic user interfaces. *Communications of the ACM 51*, 6 (2008), 26–30.
22. Walus, K. Thingiverse: Adjustable one way valve. `http://www.thingiverse.com/thing:62728`. Last accessed on 08/28/14.
23. Willis, K., Brockmeyer, E., Hudson, S., and Poupyrev, I. Printed optics: 3d printing of embedded optical elements for interactive devices. In *Proc. UIST'12* (2012).
24. Yao, L., Niiyama, R., Ou, J., Follmer, S., Della Silva, C., and Ishii, H. Pneui: Pneumatically actuated soft composite materials for shape changing interfaces. In *Proc. UIST'13* (2013), 13–22.

Bridging the Theory–Practice Gap: Lessons and Challenges of Applying the Attachment Framework for Sustainable HCI Design

Christian Remy
University of Zurich
Zurich, Switzerland
remy@ifi.uzh.ch

Silke Gegenbauer
CSS Insurance
Lucerne, Switzerland
silke.gegenbauer@gmail.com

Elaine M. Huang
University of Zurich
Zurich, Switzerland
huang@ifi.uzh.ch

ABSTRACT
Despite significant progress in sustainable HCI towards theoretical frameworks to guide design, there is a gap between theory and practice, so that the impact of such frameworks is limited. As an initial exploration in bridging the theory-practice gap, we conducted a study using one well-established design framework, the Attachment Framework, to evaluate its applicability in use. We conducted a comparative study with 14 designers to explore the effect of the Attachment Framework on design, and evaluated their designs with 10 design experts using a set of six design criteria. Our results indicated a positive effect on the criterion of novelty, with mixed effects on attachment, presentation, aesthetics, usefulness, and feasibility. We contribute a set of challenges in the application of design frameworks to practice and offer a critical reflection on how researchers can more effectively communicate sustainable HCI design frameworks to practitioners.

Author Keywords
Sustainable HCI; Frameworks; Product Design; Attachment

ACM Classification Keywords
H.5.m. Information interfaces and presentation (e.g., HCI): Miscellaneous.

INTRODUCTION
Research in Human-Computer Interaction (HCI) often ends with design implications, guidelines, or frameworks that aim to guide future design. This can also be observed in the field of sustainable HCI (SHCI), which has seen a tremendous growth in design framework contributions in recent years. However, little research attention has been given to applying such design frameworks to practice [8, 29] where as a result, the practical impact of such frameworks is limited. We argue that the SHCI community should intensify its efforts to bridge the theory–practice gap in order to increase its impact on sustainability issues.

CHI 2015, April 18 - 23 2015, Seoul, Republic of Korea

ACM 978-1-4503-3145-6/15/04…$15.00
http://dx.doi.org/10.1145/2702123.2702567

As an initial exploration into this complex space, we conducted a comparative study using one well-established framework as a case study. The Attachment Framework [10, 26] is an empirically produced framework in the field of SHCI based on the concept that consumers who develop a notion of attachment to a particular device are less likely to dispose of it, ultimately leading to less obsolescence and therefore more sustainable behavior. In order to understand the applicability and value of using this framework in the design process we had 14 designers design a tablet computer that would foster such attachment, having 7 of the designers use the framework in their design and 7 not. Our main research question was: *What is the effect of using an empirically based theoretical framework from SHCI literature on the design process and outcome for SHCI?*

In order to assess the use of the framework we had 10 design experts assess the quality of the designs according to six criteria derived from the survey on product design literature [7, 23] and basic industrial design principles [37]: attachment, novelty, presentation, aesthetics, usefulness, and feasibility. Our evaluation results indicated a positive effect on novelty, where a subsequent evaluation suggested a clear link between novelty and attachment. However, we saw mixed effects of the Attachment Framework on the other five criteria. Based on a synthesis of the insights from our study as well as previous work in design research literature, we offer a deeper understanding of the challenges in applying theoretical frameworks to design practice.

We make two contributions: 1) We report on lessons learned in the application of the Attachment Framework for SHCI design, based on a set of six design criteria; 2) We identified a set of challenges in applying SHCI theory to practice. We discuss these challenges in light of design research, where our goal is to provoke rethinking of how researchers in SHCI can communicate SHCI knowledge to practitioners and designers outside of the field.

RELATED WORK
The lack of theoretical contributions being applied to design practice, commonly referred to as the "theory–practice

gap", was discussed in the last decade [e.g., 30, 36] and is still an ongoing topic [e.g., 29, 34] in the CHI community. This point has also been raised in SHCI, and some seminal works have argued for application of SHCI research to design practice [e.g., 3] or criticized the lack thereof [e.g., 8]. Previous work in SHCI has looked at successful examples of sustainable interaction design, in particular in the domain of eco-feedback technology, which has been one of the most active fields within SHCI. For example, Pierce and Roedl [27] as well as Strengers [34] looked at existing eco-feedback technology in the home, highlighting sustainable design in the wild as success stories and drawing valuable lessons for the field. Furthermore, several researchers have built prototypes for the sake of field studies in various domains, such as citizen science [e.g., 1, 20, 21] or water conversation [e.g., 2, 21] that highlight examples of SHCI design in practice, as a proof of concept and often applied by SHCI practitioners themselves.

While these efforts demonstrate that SHCI is addressing the concerns raised about HCI design principles in general (i.e., that those principles are not even applied by the researchers in the respective field itself [e.g., 30]), there is still a gap between available frameworks and their application to real-world practice. The goal of sustainable interaction design is to make environmental sustainability a central focus in design practice [3]. A variety of theoretical contributions offers opportunities for such high-impact design, e.g., design principles for sustainable mobile phones [18], more ecological use of time and travel [28], or resource consumption in the home [4], to just name a few. This design knowledge is frequently used to fuel other ideas in SHCI and these works have yielded fruitful discussion within the community – however, there is little evidence that it is being transferred to practice and little knowledge of how well it could support design. There are case studies about students [16], do-it-yourself practitioners, [20] and professional product designers [15] that investigated the use of sustainability principles being put to design practice. In this paper, we present a similar approach and report on a comparative study including an expert analysis to yield qualitative insights about the value of one SHCI theoretical framework – the Attachment Framework.

THE ATTACHMENT FRAMEWORK

One of the many problems that SHCI is trying to tackle is that of obsolescence [38, 18]. By encouraging longer use of devices, the *Attachment Framework* [26] presents a solution from SHCI research to tackle this issue. We believe that the Attachment Framework lends itself particularly well to a case study of exploring SHCI design practice as it is a well-established, empirical framework that has recently been extended, and first attempts of applying it to practice have suggested its usefulness [10]. In their initial study, Odom et al. [26] surveyed people about objects that they felt attached to, such as heirloom items, collected stories about the shared history between the object and the owner, and identified common themes for the attachment's reason. The resulting Attachment Framework offers design principles, accompanied with examples, which can be applied to new designs to achieve a similar effect. The Attachment Framework was extended by a follow-up study which in particular aimed to identify design principles for fostering attachment in the domain of consumer electronics [10], resulting in seven principles:

- **Histories**: Preserve memories connected to the device
- **Augmentation**: Re-use beyond its intended purpose
- **Engagement**: Promote physical engagement in use
- **Perceived Durability**: Long-lasting in terms of function or longevity or both
- **Earned Functionality**: Device is continued to be used because of the effort put into becoming familiar with it
- **Perceived Worth**: High perceived value of the device
- **Sufficiency**: Capable of serving its intended purpose

STUDY DESIGN

In order to understand the impact of theoretical frameworks from SHCI applied to design, we choose tablet computers for the design activity. We gave an extended version of the Attachment Framework [10] that is specifically directed towards electronic devices to designers and assessed the outcome in terms of quality of overall design as well as the understanding and interpretation of the attachment values as a means of evaluation. Using an extended version of the Attachment Framework that is directed towards electronic devices allowed us to use picturesque examples "as is", thus reducing potential bias in our study design. The benefits of using examples to foster the creation process have been studied in HCI before [17]. In the following, we will elaborate on the study design (step 1), the evaluation of design quality (step 2), and our analysis of

Step 1: Data Collection

We asked designers to create 2-4 preliminary design sketches of a tablet computer that fosters a strong bond between the device and its owner. We explained the basic concept of attachment as a way to promote environmental sustainability in a brief statement without giving away any details of the framework's design principles. Participants were then divided into two groups, with one of these groups receiving supplementary material explaining the Attachment Framework in detail, and the other group acting as control group that was not given any further advice. This ensured that both groups were on the same track with regard to their design goal, and the only difference was the framework whose value we wanted to assess. The supplementary material included a four page document with the Attachment Framework principles (engagement, earned functionality, augmentation, histories, perceived durability, perceived worth, sufficiency; cf. [10]). Each of the principles was illustrated by 2-4 non-technical examples by using unaltered participant quotes from the original study (cf. [11]). The design task was created in collaboration with

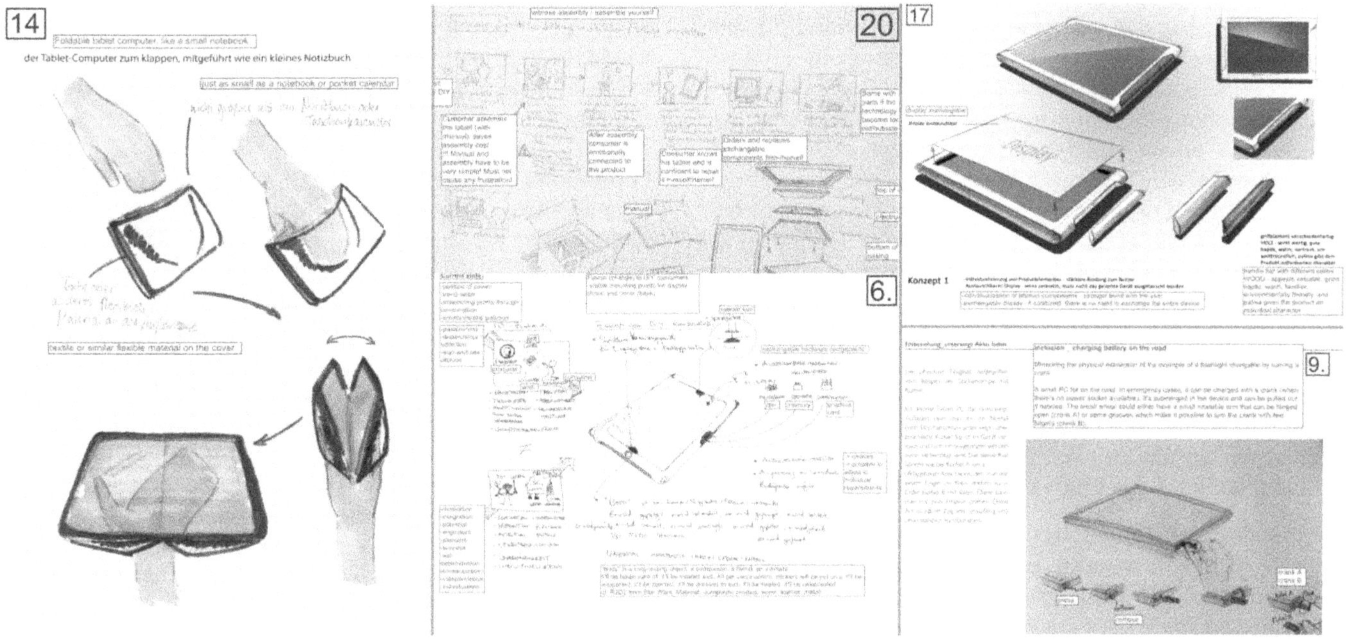

Figure 1: Four examples of the design sketches as presented to the design experts for the evaluation: designs CD5 (left), CD19 (top middle), FD 11 (bottom middle), CD12 (top right), and FD17 (bottom right).

a design expert and piloted with three designers to ensure that it did not deviate from the designers' typical process.

Fourteen participants were recruited using convenience sampling and split into two groups, having equal size of the framework group and control group (7 participants). Participants averaged 3.8 years of experience (st. dev. 1.6 years) and were compensated with an equiv. $100 US Amazon voucher. Participants' expertise was in product design, except for one participant who was an interaction designer. Their secondary expertise was in industrial design (four participants) and architectural design (two participants). Gender distribution was equal (seven female, seven male). Majority of participants were between 20 and 29 years old, and one was in his thirties. All designers were recruited in major central European cities and the study was carried out in the participants' native tongue. Based on their background information and previous experience, both groups of designers had similar experience in practice.

The designers received their task via email and sent us scanned copies of their design sketches. We asked them to include explanatory details, such as annotations, descriptions, or storyboards with the design sketches. Altogether, the participants generated 40 design sketches (21 from the group with framework, 19 from the control group), from 1 to 5 per designer. After completing the design task, all participants answered survey questions about their design background, previous experience in "green design", their typical design process, their approach for this particular task, and their thoughts about the activity (e.g., satisfaction with their sketches and difficulty of task). Four of the designs can be seen in Figure 1.

Step 2: Evaluation by Design Experts

To assess the value of the Attachment Framework and see what effects it had on the designs, we recruited ten design experts to analyze the sketches according to six different criteria. Besides the "attachment" criterion, which resembles the basic idea of the Attachment Framework itself, it is important to consider other aspects of design as well, since attachment alone does not suffice for a design to be successful or of good quality. The criteria were developed from surveying product design literature [e.g., 7, 23], product design award criteria [e.g., IDEA[1], iFDA[2], Red Dot Award[3]], and basic industrial design principles [e.g., 37]. They were refined through pilots of the evaluation with design experts, and the final criteria were:

- Attachment (does the design encourage longer use and foster attachment between the device and its owner)
- Creativity and novelty (is the design idea original)
- Presentation (is the design clearly communicated and well-presented)
- Aesthetics (how aesthetically pleasing is the design)
- Usefulness (would a product based upon this design be useful and effective)
- Feasibility and credibility (is the design idea feasible, credible, and applicable to a real-world product)

The design experts (two female, eight male) had an average of 4 years of training experience (st. dev. 1.6 years) and 7.5

[1] http://www.idsa.org/idea-2014-entry-rules-criteria-instructions

[2] http://www.ifdesign.de/awards_product_index_e

[3] http://red-dot.de/pd/jury-2012/adjudication-criteria/?lang=en

years of working experience (st. dev. 4.6 years). Participants had a diverse, often multidisciplinary background and identified their specialization as product design (7), interaction design (7), industrial design (4), and graphics design (2). While we told the evaluators that the task was to create tablet computer design sketches that fostered attachment, we did not give them the Attachment Framework itself nor told them that this was a comparative study in which one of the group received such a framework. Since pilots revealed that the evaluation takes a significant amount of time, we decided to split the designs into two groups of 20 designs each, resulting in two interchangeable sets. All annotations and descriptions on the design sketches were translated to English and were visually distinct (red text box) to distinguish our text from the original design sketch. We encouraged the experts to be critical since we did not pass the feedback to the designers.

We asked designers to select up to three designs that they felt best met each criterion and provide a justification for their choices. Pilot participants expressed concerns about exhaustion towards later criteria that might result in shorter answers, which is why we alternated the order of questions using a Counterbalanced Latin Square distribution. Participants had a choice to complete the task digitally at their computer or hand-written on paper, as the evaluation sheets were printable PDF forms. The activity was accompanied by a short eight-question survey about their background, design process approach, and experiences with regard to sustainable design. Participants received an Amazon voucher worth $50 US or 40€, as preferred.

Step 3: Analysis and Attachment Evaluation

For the analysis of the evaluation results we were mainly interested in qualitative data from the design experts' justification for their selected designs. We analyzed the data using open coding to search for common themes across the comments for each of the criteria on the quality of the design sketches, in particular themes that would only occur for either the framework or non-framework condition. Our approach was to find patterns and themes in the evaluation responses, according to the six different criteria.

The criterion "attachment" was arguably one of the most important ones to us, as it aimed to assess the core aspect of the framework and how designers interpreted it. However, most design experts indicated in their survey background questions that they had no in-depth knowledge of or experience with sustainable designs, and none of the experts had any knowledge about the Attachment Framework as such. Therefore, we added an additional evaluation step by asking three Attachment Framework experts to go through all 40 designs and, for each of the seven Attachment Framework criteria, decide whether or not they think the design exhibits this particular criterion.

We will refer to the designs as FD1 to FD21 for the designs from the framework group and CD1 to CD19 for the designs from the control group. E1 to E10 refers to comments from the evaluators. For example, E7-FD13 would be the justification provided by evaluator 7 about why she picked design number 13 (which happened to be from the framework group) for a specific criterion.

Limitations

Despite the relatively high incentive, all participants recruited for the first study were relatively young and had only a few years of working experience. One of the reasons may have been the rather substantial work load of the study (pilots indicated an estimate of four hours of work time). Another limitation was the fact that both studies were conducted remotely; however, especially for recruiting evaluators a remote study allowed us to get a diverse set of experts from all over the world. Furthermore, we only look at one specific family of devices with tablet computers, and we acknowledge that the results might not be representative findings regarding attachment for other technical devices.

RESULTS

In the following, we report on the insights from our data analysis in detail, grouped by the six design criteria that were used in the expert evaluation. While the framework seemed to have no effect on the *attachment* values communicated in the designs, there was a noticeable effect on *novelty and creativity* of the designs. However, this advantage came at the price of seemingly losing out in two other criteria, *aesthetics and presentation*, and a tie in the *usefulness* and *feasibility* criteria. Overall, the non-framework designs were mentioned slightly more often than design concepts by the framework group (85 vs. 72, not significant with $p=0.102$ for χ^2), and the qualitative results did not clearly favor one of the groups either.

Attachment

Since the task was to create a tablet computer that fostered attachment and this study is about evaluating the impact of the attachment on design, this was arguably the most important design criterion for us. Therefore, the results of this part of the evaluation were the most surprising for us: we found no evidence that the group of designers that had been given the Attachment Framework produced any better results in that regard compared to the control group. Our design experts selected eleven designs from both groups respectively that stood out as showcasing a particular idea of encouraging a stronger bond between a device and its owner. Likewise, the derived themes from the design experts' responses spanned across both groups of designs.

One design concept that was frequently mentioned was the material and its ability to develop patina or a worn-out effect over time, as was mentioned by these two evaluators: *"the use of tin as material is unconventional and nice. tin tells a story. it is used by products that proved to be able to survive under all circumstances. using materials that collect patina is essential I think.it makes a product a personal belonging" (E6-CD1)* and *"The feeling of attachment comes when something looks more aesthetic and apealing. The unique patina background will help the user with that sense of attachment. An analogy to the above is my jeans. The older it turns the more attached and more comfortable I am to that jeans" (E10-CD15).*

Similar remarks were made by other design experts (e.g., E1-CD15, E3-CD5, E4-FD12, E4-FD18, E5-CD15). Another example for a design approach that participants thought of as fostering attachment was that of being able to replace parts (FD11 and CD19, see Figure 1): *"Exchanging parts will keep the device up-to-date through more than just software updates. It is less likely to become obsolete."* (E1-FD11) and *"the possibility to exchange parts as they break or because of changing preferences helps the product to survive over a longer period of time"* (E4-CD19). Other themes that we found in our analysis were personalization of the device's hardware (E3-FD6, E5-FD11, and E8-CD10) and software (E3-CD16, E8-CD16, E9-FD5, and E10-FD21).

Evaluation by Attachment Experts

One might argue that this result is not surprising or has little validity as the design experts were no experts for sustainable design or had no knowledge of the Attachment Framework besides the short introduction provided by us. However, the evaluation of attachment criteria by the Attachment Framework experts yielded similar results: counting every single instance of attachment identified in all of the designs, the evaluators found 103 in the framework group and 77 in the non-framework group (not significant with $p=0.246$ for χ^2). This becomes even more apparent if we look at instances for which two or all three evaluators agreed on one criterion for a specific design: for eleven (framework) and eight (non-framework) designs all experts identified the same criterion; for fourteen (framework) and twelve (non-framework) designs at least two experts agreed on the same attachment value. An interesting observation was that there was less agreement on the attachment criteria than one might expect, especially given that all three evaluators had the same background.

Novelty

In terms of novelty of the design ideas, this was the only of the six design criteria where the framework-supported designs achieved clearly better results in the evaluation. The design experts deemed ten such designs as more creative and novel (17 comments), and only five of the control group (seven comments). We found three themes that were present in both groups: unusual choice of material (E7-CD1 and E10-FD6), development of patina (E6-FD18 and E10-CD15), and an adaptive user interface:

"This design concept focused on an interface that adapts to the user and gets to know her, in turn building loyality. It anticipates my needs - a big trend as we move to smarter devices and software." (E1-CD16)

"I think the thought about the computer interface that adapts to the user is quite novel and is definitely a step forward from todays UI paradigms" (E4-FD5)

A similar notion was observed by the same design expert in E4-FD21. Furthermore, two design concepts were mentioned for the non-framework group only: a foldable display (E2-CD4, E4-CD4, E5-CD5) and a design sketch that showcased multi-purpose use in context (E5-CD9), which was praised for its flexibility. Interestingly, a sketching tablet received critical acclaim for the opposite concept – a single-purpose device focusing on one task only (E6-FD9). All other themes of novel concepts (e.g., exchangeable parts, personalization, visual feedback through changing color) occurred in the framework group only. However, there was no overlap between ideas within that group either – rather, one idea per design was seen as the core novel aspect or creative design concept. Three of these novel concepts were mentioned by multiple evaluators: a tablet computer that could be re-used to serve a new purpose (FD7, mentioned by E1 and E3); a display frame that would change its color according to battery charge left (FD21, mentioned by E2, E6, and E7); and a small lever that allows for a quick emergency battery recharge by winding up (FD17, see Figure 1, mentioned by E3 and E8).

Connection between Novelty and Attachment

Upon identifying those themes, many of them resembled features that can be attributed to sustainable design, which led us to ask the question if there is a connection between the novelty aspects as identified by the evaluators and the attachment values as provided by the framework. We therefore added an additional layer of analysis: all of the evaluators' comments for the novelty aspects were analyzed with regard to values of the Attachment Framework. Three Attachment Framework experts individually decided for each comment about novelty if it resembled one (or multiple) of the attachment criteria.

Similar to the attachment evaluation, there was a strong subjectivity noticeable in the results. Only for three designs did all evaluators agree on one attachment criterion; for most of them (seven) two evaluators identified the same attachment criterion. For two designs the attachment criteria were different, and for the remaining three designs only one evaluator found that the novelty aspect was connected to attachment. Overall, 40 instances of attachment were identified in the novelty comments and only eight times was no criterion found to be present in the novelty justification, whereas at least one attachment expert saw attachment criteria present in any of the designs. Two examples for the novelty-attachment relationship can be found in Figure 1: E5 praises CD5 as *"the designer re-considers the form factor"* in the novel foldable design, while E3 points out that the *"similarity to a pocket diary/wallet would make it more likely for users to foster an attachment"*. Similarly, E1 considers FD11 to be novel as *"this design went the opposite direction [to the throw-away paradigm], emphasizing exchangeable parts"* which contribute to attachment as they *"will keep the device up-to-date"* and *"less likely to become obsolete"* (E1), and even allow for *"strong personalization"* (E5).

Presentation
The criterion of presentation quality yielded the most clear-cut result: only seven times was a design sketch from the framework group among the top three, compared to 20 from the control group. As mentioned earlier, we notified participants that we were to blame for the text clutter since we provided red-colored translations to the original designers' comments. However, the designs produced by the framework group already had a significantly higher amount of text and our added translation multiplied this clutter effect. The designs that were selected for best presentation, on the other hand, were those that came with less text and more polished graphical concepts, with two exceptions: *"Concise text. Simple reference points. Easy to understand instantly." (E6-FD9)* and *"Very well explained on how the complete flowchart would look like. Different ways to personalize your tablet is presented with good description and clearly communicated" (E10-FD6).*

The majority of comments, however, preferred sketches that were understandable without the necessity to read large amounts of text (E7-CD1: *"I don't need to read anything and I get it immediately"*) or praised good drawing skills. One evaluator even presumed that the concept was created by someone *"who knows how to render 3D objects with light + shadow"* (E1-CD13). CD12 (see Figure 1) stood out as it was praised by four different design experts for its *"good rendering"* (E2), *"detailed product design sketches"* (E4), being *"easy to understand within seconds"* (E7), and ready for *"showing [it to] a client"* (E9).

Aesthetics
Designs from the control group were more often mentioned as being particularly aesthetic (18 times) than framework designs (ten comments). Interestingly, if we were to look at the number of designs those comments were attributed to, it is evenly split among both groups (nine each) since three designs in the control group were mentioned repetitively by at least three evaluators. Four design experts (E1, E3, E6, and E8) mentioned patina as an aspect that would lead to increased aesthetics of the device. This was especially surprising as the two sketches that the evaluators referred to were produced by the control group (CD1, CD15) only. Surprising because patina was identified as a theme for the novelty and attachment criteria as well – but in those cases, stretching across both groups.

Besides other single mentions that we cannot really classify as themes (e.g., *"'easy-to-carry' style"*, E3-CD5; foldable display, E2-CD4), there were three main aspects that the design experts highlighted as particularly aesthetically pleasing. First, showcasing context of use (E5-FD7, E6-FD7, and E6-CD14), which might not appear as an aesthetic property as such, but E5 justifies it as follows: *"The idea has [s]ome poetic value, as the designer con[s]iders the device part of an environment"*. Second, exchangeable parts contributed to the aesthetics of two designs (E2-CD12, E3-FD6, and E7-CD12). Third, the most frequent pattern across all sketches that the design experts found to be aesthetically pleasing was the choice of material (e.g., E1-CD9, E4-FD16, E8-CD2, and six more). This differs from the patina theme as the evaluators' point was not about gaining a visually pleasing effect over time, but that the design came with a *"classy and high quality metal"* (E7-FD18) or *"ruggedness"* (E1-CD2) by default.

Usefulness
In raw numbers, the non-framework group was slightly ahead, with fourteen comments on this criterion, compared to twelve comments by the framework group. However, in terms of themes that emerged from our qualitative results, there was no clear winner. Several of the features that were attributed to usefulness did not fit onto overarching patterns and therefore stood out as single concepts depicted in one design, such as a sturdy and break-proof design (E1-CD9) or a wind-up crank for quick battery recharge (FD17, see Figure 1). The latter received positive comments from three evaluators: E3 liked *"the combination of such an old-fashioned mechanism with a high-tech gadget"*, especially if it were to be coupled with a *"cute charging UI"*, E5 envisions *"the user [to be] more mobile and less dependent from infrastructure"*, and E10 notes that the mechanism *"is the need of the hour [...] and can help one for longer use"*.

One theme we identified in three designs was adaptability (E1-CD16, E3-CD16, E5-FD5, and E10-FD4). E1 pointed out: *"A device that learns my needs and behavior, leading it to adapt is incredibly valuable in streamlining my life"*. While this pattern of usefulness mainly referred to software and user interface features, the most frequent themes were flexibility (six designs) and the ability to transform (five designs), originating from either group. A quote for the justification of E5-CD9, summarized the evaluators' opinion about design concepts quite well: *"A tablet that can be mounted in many different ways and places is very useful, and I liked the mention of future technology-screens that are foldable, durable and not so precious"*.

Feasibility
As with usefulness, feasibility and credibility of the design sketches was almost evenly split between the two groups (thirteen comments on eleven designs with framework, twelve comments on nine designs without). Two dominant themes emerged in our analysis: many evaluators picked designs that were about a specific material (eight designs) and pointed out that *"it could be produced today"* (E1-FD1). By relating the proposed design concept to already existing products, the design experts highlighted that some

of these ideas are *"totally feasible"*, such as E7-CD1: *"it's essentially an iPad with a leather skin."*

The other theme that had almost as many occurrences as material was software (seven designs). The design experts mentioned existing software products or concepts that would solve the main problems in bringing the design sketch to reality, such as *"Google Now"* (E1-CD16) or *"TimeHop with a diary twist"* (E6-CD14).

Summarization of the Results

We conclude that the framework had a positive effect on the novelty criterion and mixed effects on the other five criteria (attachment, presentation, aesthetics, usefulness, and feasibility). Especially surprising was that the control group had almost as many attachment criteria present in their designs as the framework group. One possible explanation might be that many of the designers expressed in their background survey having had experience in sustainable design ("green design" was a frequently mentioned term) during their studies or a personal interest in those fields, and thus possessed an already existing knowledge repository. However, the framework group's designs displayed a significantly higher quality with regard to novelty and creativity, which in turn can be linked to attachment criteria. The results indicate that the Attachment Framework might hold value for designing products that exhibit both sustainable as well as novel design.

Despite the success of our design activity in this particular aspect, the limitations of using this framework in SHCI design lies in the fact that in other five criteria – attachment, presentation, aesthetics, usefulness, and feasibility and credibility – the Attachment Framework did not perform better. Similarly, the ambiguity in evaluating the attachment criteria highlights that the framework can be interpreted in many different ways. In the following, we discuss how the insights from this study can inform future research by presenting a set of challenges that need to be addressed when applying theoretical frameworks from SHCI or similar fields to design practice.

BRIDGING THE GAP: CHALLENGES IN APPLYING SHCI THEORY TO DESIGN PRACTICE

Based on the insights from our study we identify and discuss a set of four challenges that aim to bridge the gap between SHCI theory and design practice, which can be separated into two different categories:

Category 1: The first three challenges address issues in the earlier stages of SHCI design knowledge transfer, in particular, identifying 1) the suitable target audience, 2) the appropriate stage in the process, and 3) the most effective medium of communication. Each challenge is organized as follows: first, we elaborate on how we identified the challenge based on the study insights. Second, we discuss the challenge by drawing lessons from design research literature, including fields such as product, industrial, and architectural design. Our goal is to provoke discussion and reflection on how to address these challenges.

Category 2: The fourth challenge addresses an important question in a later stage of the design process: once we have examples of SHCI research applied to design practice, how do we evaluate those instances of design in light of the given framework? We discuss this challenge based on previous SHCI research insights and the experience from our own evaluation in our study.

Challenge 1: Addressing the Right Target Audience

The potential differences in target audience became apparent when comparing the background surveys of the two different group of designers we recruited – the fourteen designers for the design activity and the ten design experts for the evaluation. While the designers had less experience in design overall in terms of years of expertise in teaching and practice, all of them expressed interest in or even experience with the design of sustainable products. The design experts, on the other hand, expressed only borderline knowledge or interest in sustainable design, but a significantly longer amount of working expertise in design practice. This sparked our interest to see if there are other differences with regard to the target audience that impact the knowledge transfer between disciplines.

Insights from Design Research

In a survey of design expertise studies, Cross [5] points out that expert designers tend to spend less time on the problem definition and more on actually developing the solution (solution-focused versus problem-focused). A survey of 103 novice designers and 52 expert designers by Gonçalves et al. [14] confirms these insights with empirical data of actual design practice. An implication would be to tailor frameworks or design guidelines to the respective stage these designers deem to be most important and spend more time on; e.g., in the case of expert designers this would be the solution generation process, while for novice designers one might focus on supporting the problem elicitation stage.

Cross concludes his survey with a warning that seems to be counter-intuitive to some HCI researchers: *"Generating a very wide range of alternatives may not be a good thing"* [5]. This is based on the fact that expert designers tend to focus on a single design quite early in the idea generation phase. Combined with his advice to be *"wary about importing behaviour from other fields"*, one should be careful to not cause any changes to the designers' practices when offering tools to support the design process – unless the designers agree to (or even ask for) the change and the benefits are clearly communicated. Otherwise, such a tool might not make its way into designer's practice and the design knowledge transfer will not be successful.

Challenge 2: Finding the Appropriate Stage in the Design Process

Another insight from the background survey of our participants was that their typical approach to design tasks differed from designer to designer. Some designers mentioned they would usually spend more time on background research – which was limited due to the time constraints in this experiment – while others did not put as much emphasis on this part of the process, mainly because the already had a repository of background from a previous, similar design task. There were also differences in their approach to brainstorming designs: most of our designers liked to sketch many different ideas and pursue one (or a few selected ones) more in-depth, while some designers mentioned they would sometimes just take the first idea that comes to their mind, sketch it in detail, and then go back and think about other ideas and repeat the process. We therefore looked into design research literature to see if there is a typical design process, if so, what it looks like, and how this changes the way we try to apply our SHCI knowledge to this process.

Insights from Design Research

The basic concept of many design disciplines looks similar to HCI's iterative design cycle [e.g., 25]. For example, for product design and engineering, Cross [6] provides a simplified four-stage model. The four different steps are exploration, generation, evaluation, and communication; the cyclic resemblance of iterative design is depicted by a repetition of generation and evaluation. For another discipline, architecture design, Lawson's model [22] is more generalized with a three-stage "analysis – synthesis – evaluation" circular process, almost identical to the HCI iterative cycle. Both authors, however, point out that as one looks closer at either of these models, the individual steps differ from discipline to discipline, product to product, and even designer to designer.

When SHCI researchers propose theoretical frameworks to be used by other disciplines, these frameworks need to fit into the target audience's work process. For example, in our study the target audience would be industrial and product designers. Looking at one more detailed model of that discipline – Kruger and Cross's expertise model of product design [19] – we highlight how complex the process, and therefore identifying the most suitable stage, is. Kruger and Cross's model is accompanied with a breakdown of eight tasks and activities: 1) Gather data, 2) Assess value and validity of data, 3) Identify constraints and requirements, 4) Model behavior and environment, 5) Define problems and possibilities, 6) Generate partial solutions, 7) Evaluate solutions, and 8) Assemble a coherent solution.

As these stages highlight, there exist different opportunities to transfer knowledge, depending on which stage is to be addressed. For example, in a design process mimicking Kruger and Cross's model, SHCI design knowledge can be fed into the first step as part of the designer's background research. This might be a stage where designers are likely to be more open towards traditional HCI design principles, as their background research process is relatively widespread at this point. But in the later steps (e.g., step six), concrete tools and applications that support the ideation process might be more helpful. Traditional guidelines are likely to be neglected at this stage in the process; however, they might be helpful if tailored to the specific stage and embedded into the tools used during the solution generation process. We therefore believe that HCI researchers have to be aware of the complex stages of the design process, consider at which stage(s) their findings may be most beneficial, and tailor their frameworks and guidelines for the appropriate stage(s) of the design process. This may significantly increase the chance of SHCI design knowledge to be applied to real-world practice.

Challenge 3: Transferring and Transforming SHCI Design Knowledge

It is important to keep in mind that the designers did not implement the Attachment Framework's principles, but their *interpretations* of those principles in the ideation phase. This matters because interpretations can be both beneficial and unfavorable: interpretation allows for less restricted thinking and enables designers to explore many different ways to apply design knowledge to their activities; but it can also lead to misinterpretation and therefore mean that it has no or even an adverse effect on design. While we do not want to limit the benefits of a framework that is open to interpretation, we need to make sure the essence of the framework communicates the same values. One approach to how this challenge can be addressed is to explore ways in which frameworks and guidelines can be presented in the designers' ideation process.

Insights from Design Research

HCI research literature often ends with implications for design, guidelines, design principles, or a framework – as in the example of the Attachment Framework that we applied in our experiment. But if such work aims to inform future design, the theoretical, text-based form of conveying the findings and insights might not be enough to reach its goal. Textual guidelines are by themselves not applicable to all stages of the design process and are not what all target audiences might prefer. There is an ongoing debate over the different impact that visual and textual stimuli have in the design process [e.g., 9, 12, 13, 24]. A balanced approach of textual and visual stimuli might present a good middle way, noting that one should rely more on visual stimuli with expert designers, as they tend to be less susceptible to be biased by these examples and make less use of text [14].

Therefore, we propose that SHCI should search for ways to not only transfer its knowledge into other domains, but also present and communicate the knowledge using representations that take the needs and practices of the target audience into account. One way to go about this is by using examples to fuel the ideation process [17]. Based on the target audience's preferences, mixing verbal examples and pictures can be useful, but if possible also including real-world objects such as end-products or prototypes; this can be especially useful for expert designers [14].

There is a variety of different ideation techniques used by designers: Smith identified 172 different techniques [31], Gonçalves et al. reported on the frequency in actual use of 14 of those [14], and Herring et al. provides an in-depth analysis of 19 [17]. If one aims to support the ideation process, SHCI design knowledge could also be integrated into tools and applications supporting these techniques instead of simply providing examples that are being used during the ideation process. While brainstorming seems to be the most frequently used and most preferred method by designers [14], there are many different ways to approach brainstorming and therefore different ways to support this process by developing tools for it. SHCI principles could be embedded into applications that facilitate the creation of checklists [14] or attribute lists [17], or serve as basis for new axes of classifications in either of these.

One has to keep in mind that the ideation process is a concrete step in only one specific stage of the design process (step 6 in the expertise model [19]). Since ideas can emerge indirectly anywhere in the cyclic design process, there might be other ways to embed design knowledge into designers' practices beyond this phase. If formulated as rules that blend into the constraints and requirements being identified in step 3 [19], abstract design implications can be turned into concrete guidance for designers. This ensures that the design process is not altered, yet the SHCI principles are considered in the design process – with equal importance to other design rules.

Challenge 4: Evaluating Applications of SHCI Design

The last challenge we encountered (as also articulated in [31]) is one that poses a more general question: *How do we evaluate the impact of our contributions in SHCI once they have been applied to practice?* To answer this question, we contrast our evaluation approach with that of Grosse-Hering et al. [15], which is to date the only evaluation of this kind.

Grosse-Hering et al. [15] performed a case study of the application of slow design principles to design. They evaluated their design by asking six participants to imagine the use of a mock-up device and report on their experience. This works because for slow design the interaction is meant to actively engage and change people's practices and thinking immediately; some of the Attachment Framework principles, however, are more subtle and require a ready-made product (sufficiency, earned functionality) or a long timeframe to be applicable (histories, perceived worth). Therefore, building prototypes and mock-ups is not a suitable strategy for evaluating attachment. Some of the designs in our study resembled storyboards or use-case scenarios (e.g., CD19, see Figure 1), but this approach does not work for all designs. This hints that a "one size fits all" solution it is unlikely to be found, but rather that every application of SHCI research requires its own evaluation, depending on its goal – which is a notion expressed by the SHCI community itself recently [32].

In our own case we used the Attachment Framework itself as an evaluation tool. This raises an additional question: *Can we use a framework that is intended to inform the design of objects for the purpose of evaluation?* The attachment experts who have had extensive experience with the framework itself did not agree on all the criteria for all the designs; in fact, there was more difference in assessing the attachment values than agreement. Despite the differences in assessing *which criterion was expressed in a certain design*, there was a general agreement on particular designs *that a design displayed some notion of attachment.* Silberman and Tomlinson [31] provided a categorization of evaluation tools, in which the Attachment Framework falls into the category of "principles" for which a certain amount of ambiguity is expected and needs to be dealt with.

The fact that both the design experts, who had no previous experience with attachment, and the attachment experts came to roughly the same results in assessing the attachment values in the designs – no clear evidence that the framework group did significantly better than the control group – might imply that the Attachment Framework holds some value to serve as a means of evaluating attachment in designs. However, the definition of the attachment principles should be phrased much more unambiguously to allow for more agreement among the evaluators. Contrary to the purpose of applying frameworks to design practice, when room for interpretation can be desirable, we argue that such frameworks should be more constrained and have as little ambiguity as possible when being used as a tool for evaluation.

We included general design criteria in our evaluation since attachment alone does not suffice as the only criterion for successful design if a product were to appeal to a broader audience. However, maybe one of the obstacles in bridging the theory-practice gap is that traditional design and evaluation criteria are not compatible to sustainable design and the emphasis for evaluating success should only be on sustainability; one of this paper's reviewers noted: "Maybe it is our notions of successful design that need to evolve".

CONCLUSION

In this paper, we investigated the application of a theoretical framework from SHCI to design practice by studying its effect on the design process and outcome. We have conducted a comparative study where half of the participants designed with the use of the framework and the other half did not. The evaluation of the produced designs was done with 10 design experts against a set of design criteria derived from the product design and industrial design literature: 1) attachment, 2) creativity and novelty, 3) presentation, 4) aesthetics, 5) usefulness, and 6) feasibility and credibility. Our evaluation results indicated a positive effect on novelty, where a subsequent evaluation suggested a clear link between novelty and attachment. However, we saw mixed effects of the Attachment Framework on the other five criteria. We believe that the lessons learned from our experiment can help inform future applications of SHCI design knowledge to design practice. In particular, we propose a set of challenges that researchers might face when frameworks are being applied to practice, and ultimately might help to re-think the way we communicate and evaluate frameworks and other theoretical contributions that emerge from SHCI research.

ACKNOWLEDGEMENTS

We thank Gunnar Harboe, Helen Ai He, Sarah Mennicken, Nemanja Memarovic, Khai Truong, Jen Mankoff, Will Odom, and all reviewers for their feedback and insightful comments, as well as all our study participants.

REFERENCES

1. Aoki, P.M., Honicky, R.J., Mainwaring, A., et al. A vehicle for research: using street sweepers to explore the landscape of environmental community action. In *Proc. CHI 2009*.
2. Arroyo, E., Bonanni, L., and Selker, T. Waterbot: Exploring feedback and persuasive techniques at the sink. In *Proc. CHI 2005*.
3. Blevis, E. Sustainable interaction design: invention & disposal, renewal & reuse. In *Proc. CHI 2007*.
4. Chetty, M., Brush, A.J.B., Meyers, B.R., and Johns, P. It's not easy being green. In *Proc. CHI 2009*.
5. Cross, N. Expertise in design: an overview. *Design Studies 25, 5 (2004)*.
6. Cross, N. *Engineering Design Methods*. J. Wiley, 2008.
7. Demirbilek, O. and Park, M. A survey of criteria for the assessment of "Good Product Design". *Proc. EAD 2001*.
8. DiSalvo, C., Sengers, P., and Brynjarsdóttir, H. Mapping the landscape of SHCI. In *Proc. CHI 2010*.
9. Eckert, C. and Stacey, M. Sources of inspiration: a language of design. *Design Studies 21, 5 (2000)*.
10. Gegenbauer, S. and Huang, E.M. Inspiring the design of longer-lived electronics through an understanding of personal attachment. In *Proc. DIS 2012*.
11. Gegenbauer, S. *The Nature of People's Attachment to Objects*, Univ. of Zurich, 2011.
12. Goldschmidt, G. and Sever, A.L. Inspiring design ideas with texts. *Design Studies 32, 2 (2011)*.
13. Goldschmidt, G. and Smolkov, M. Variances in the impact of visual stimuli on design problem solving performance. *Design Studies 27, 5 (2006)*.
14. Gonçalves, M.G., Cardoso, C., and Badke-Schaub, P. Around You: How Designers Get Inspired. In *Proc. ICED 2011*.
15. Grosse-Hering, B., Mason, J., Aliakseyeu, D., Bakker, C., and Desmet, P. Slow Design for Meaningful Interactions. In *Proc. CHI 2013*.
16. Hauser, S., Desjardins, A., and Wakkary, R. Design Activism in the HCI Classroom. *Ext. Abstr. CHI 2013*.
17. Herring, S.R., Chang, C.-C., Krantzler, J., et al. Getting Inspired!. In *Proc. CHI 2009*.
18. Huang, E.M. and Truong, K.N. Breaking the disposable technology paradigm. *In Proc. CHI 2008*.
19. Kruger, C. and Cross, N. Solution driven versus problem driven design. *Design Studies 27, 5 (2006)*.
20. Kuznetsov, S., Davis, G.N., Paulos, E., et al. Red balloon, green balloon, sensors in the sky. In *Proc. Ubicomp 2011*.
21. Kuznetsov, S. and Paulos, E. UpStream. In *Proc. CHI 2010*.
22. Lawson, B. *How Designers Think: The Design Process Demystified*. Elsevier/Architectural, 2006.
23. Morris, R. *The Fundamentals of Product Design*. AVA, 2009.
24. Muller, W. Design discipline and the significance of visuo-spatial thinking. *Design Studies 10, 1 (1989)*.
25. Nielsen, J. *Usability Engineering*. Morgan Kaufm. 1994.
26. Odom, W., Pierce, J., Stolterman, E., et al. Understanding why we preserve some things and discard others in the context of interaction design. *Proc. CHI 2009*.
27. Pierce, J. and Roedl, D. COVER STORY: Changing Energy Use Through Design. *interactions 15, 4 (2008)*.
28. Reed, C.J., Wang, H., and Blevis, E. Recognizing individual needs and desires in the case of designing an inventory of humanity-centered, sustainability-directed concepts for time and travel. In *Proc. DPPI 2005*.
29. Roedl, D.J. and Stolterman, E. Design research at CHI and its applicability to design practice. *Proc. CHI 2013*.
30. Rogers, Y. New theoretical approaches for human-computer interaction. *Annual Review of Information Science and Technology 38, 1 (2004)*.
31. Silberman, M. S. and Tomlinson, B. Toward an Ecological Sensibility. In *Ext. Abstr. CHI 2010*.
32. Silberman, M. S, Nathan, L., Knowles, B., et al. Next Steps for Sustainable HCI. *interactions 21, 5 (2014)*.
33. Smith, G.F. Idea-Generation Techniques. *Journal of Creative Behavior 32, 2 (1998)*.
34. Stolterman, E. The nature of design practice and implications for interaction design research. *Int. Journal of Design 2, 1 (2008)*.
35. Strengers, Y.A.A. Designing Eco-feedback Systems for Everyday Life. In *Proc. CHI 2011*.
36. Sutcliffe, A. On the Effective Use and Reuse of HCI Knowledge. *ACM ToCHI. 7, 2 (2000)*.
37. Ueki-Polet, K. and Klemp, K. *Less and more*. Gestalten, 2009.
38. Woolley, M. Choreographing obsolescence - ecodesign: the pleasure/dissatisfaction cycle. In *Proc. DPPI 2003*.

The Transfer of Learning as HCI Similarity: Towards an Objective Assessment of the Sensory-Motor Basis of Naturalness

François Bérard
Univ. Grenoble Alpes
LIG, Grenoble-INP
BP 53, 38041 Grenoble Cedex 9, FRANCE
francois.berard@imag.fr
+33-476-514-365

Amélie Rochet-Capellan
Univ. Grenoble Alpes
GIPSA-lab, CNRS
BP 46, 38402 Grenoble Cedex, FRANCE
amelie.rochet-capellan@gipsa-lab.grenoble-inp.fr
+33-476-574-850

ABSTRACT

Human-computer interaction should be *natural*. However, the notion of natural is questioned due to a lack of theoretical background and methods to objectively measure the *naturalness* of a HCI. A frequently cited aspect of natural HCIs is their ability to benefit from knowledge and skills that users develop in their interaction with the real (non-digital) world. Among these skills, sensory-motor abilities are essential to operate many HCIs. This suggests that the transfer of these abilities between physical and digital interactions could be used as an experimental tool to assess the sensory-motor similarity between interactions, and could be considered as an objective measurement of the sensory-motor grounding of naturalness.

In this framework, we introduce a new experimental paradigm inspired by motor learning research to assess sensory-motor similarity, as revealed by the transfer of learning. We tested this paradigm in an empirical study to question the naturalness of three HCIs: direct-touch, mouse pointing and absolute indirect-touch. The study revealed how skill learning transfers from these three digital interactions towards an equivalent physical interaction. We observed strong transfer of skill between direct-touch and physical interaction, but no transfer from the other two interactions. This work provides a first objective assessment of the sensory-motor basis of direct-touch naturalness, and a new empirical path to question HCI similarity and naturalness.

Author Keywords

transfer of learning; sensory-motor skill; interaction similarity; NUI; naturalness; empirical methods; motor learning

ACM Classification Keywords

H.5.2. User Interfaces: Evaluation/methodology;Theory and methods

CHI 2015, April 18–23, 2015, Seoul, Republic of Korea.

ACM 978-1-4503-3145-6/15/04 ...$15.00.
http://dx.doi.org/10.1145/2702123.2702359

INTRODUCTION

Human computer interaction creates sensory-motor experiences that can be more or less *natural* for the user. While often cited as a good quality of Human Computer Interactions (HCIs), naturalness is a blurred notion subject to questioning [16, 22, 23]. The term *natural* could refer to the user's expertise with a given HCI. For example, mouse interaction, can be considered as natural for many people who have been using it daily for many years. In this paper, we consider another commonly accepted aspect of natural: the ability to benefit from users' pre-existing knowledge and skills of the *physical* world (e.g. the *non-digital* world) [14]. In particular, we propose to assess the sensory-motor grounding of naturalness through an empirical measure of similarity between physical and digital interaction: the *transfer* of sensory-motor skills.

With respect to this aspect of naturalness, mouse interaction appears as less natural than direct-touch interaction. The mouse requires users to adapt to a visuomotor transformation: the mapping of the hand movement in the motor space to the displacement of the cursor in the visual space, with a dynamic gain [3]. By contrast, touch interaction on a tactile surface corresponds to a direct interaction between the user's body and the digital object. This direct interaction is supposed to benefit from the pre-existing skill of manual interaction with physical objects, which renders direct-touch pointing more natural than mouse pointing. The argument of naturalness is often used to explain the widespread success of touch-devices such as smartphone and tablet computers.

As ubiquitous computing moves the focus of HCI from designing tools that maximize *user performance* for a specific task towards the design of "*good user experiences*" [7], naturalness is becoming a central challenge of HCIs design [31]. A good user experience includes dynamical aspects such as learning cost or in situ use. These aspects are not captured by classical approaches of motor skills based on performances such as the Fitts' law [8]. New methods and investigations of human experiences are required to characterize and anticipate the experience that the user will perceive as good or natural. In particular, despite the frequent mention of skill transfer in the definition of naturalness, to our knowledge, there is no method in HCI to objectively assess the transfer of sensory-motor skills between the interaction with physical objects and the interaction with digital objects.

This work is a first effort towards an objective assessment of skills transfer between different forms of interaction, inspired from the motor learning research. This research has extensively studied the transfer of sensory-motor skills for both speech and limb movements as a "behavioral window" [25] towards the brain mechanisms that underlie human movement [2, 20, 28]. Transfer of skills is also a core question for sport and rehabilitation therapies, in particular to assess virtual reality training as a tool to enhance motor learning [12].

We propose a novel experimental paradigm as a first step towards an objective assessment of the sensory-motor grounding of naturalness. The aim is to measure the amplitude of transfer of a given skill between several interactions with digital objects and an equivalent interaction with physical objects. According to previous works in motor learning (e.g. [9, 21]), the amplitude of transfer (e.g. performance improvement) might be a function of the sensory-motor similarity between the digital and physical interactions. In other words, *gradients of transfer* should be observed as correlates of degree of sensory-motor similarity between the different interactions.

As a first implementation of this rational, we questionned the sensory-motor similarity of an interaction on a planar surface with a physical object (a small plastic token, "physical interaction"), and three equivalent interactions with a digital object (a disc the size of the plastic token, "digital interactions"): (1) direct touch pointing, (2) indirect touch (trackpad) pointing with an absolute positioning, and (3) mouse pointing with a dynamic gain. These interactions are chosen to vary the degree of sensory-motor similarity of the digital interaction with the physical interaction and thus, potentially generate a gradient of transfer. Participants are trained to a serial target acquisition task with one of the digital interactions. After a clear improvement in performances (learning effect), they are asked to do the same task with the physical interaction. The improvement of performances in the physical interaction due to the training with the digital interaction is considered as transfer effect. The amplitude of transfer is taken as an objective quantification of the sensory-motor similarity of the digital interaction with physical interaction.

After reviewing the literature on the topic of natural HCIs, we expose the main notions and methods from the motor learning literature that underlie our work. We then detail our experimental paradigm and report on an empirical study based on this paradigm. This study provides a first objective assessment of the similarity between the three tested digital interactions and the physical interaction, which is interpreted as an indication of their relative sensory-motor naturalness. We finally discuss the outcomes of the experiment and conclude.

PREVIOUS WORKS

What is a natural human-computer interaction?

With the development of ubiquitous computers and Post-WIMP interactions, the notion of *natural* is now commonly used in HCI. The notion is however broad and not well defined. Van Dam, for example, relates the naturalness of future "ideal" interactions to the naturalness of the interaction between humans, and to the ability of the interaction to become "invisible to the user" [29]. Jacob et al. extend the "Reality-Based" aspects of post-WIMP interaction to other natural human knowledge and skills (e.g. naïve physics, body, environment and social awareness and skills) [14].

Efforts of definitions and design guidelines have been made in order to better characterize and anticipate interactions that users would feel as natural [31]. *Naturalness* is however also criticized [22], in particular due to its subjective meaning and the lack of objective methods and theoretical background to understand and evaluate how and why an interaction can be felt as natural. The main issue is that "HCI researchers still do not understand why some post-WIMP designs are perceived as natural or intuitive, while others are not because there is no theory, model, or framework about the cognitive processes that let us perceive UIs this way or the other" [16] (See also [23]).

Natural HCIs commonly appear as: gestural interactions (1) that create good user experiences (2), in particular by benefitting from users' pre-existing skills (3).

A natural interaction should allow users to manipulate digital objects or communicate with digital entities through their natural interactive skills: speech and manual gestures [24]. This idea has been criticized as both speech and gestures are learned through intensive daily uses and are culturally defined [22]. Involving direct gestures in HCIs also raised a number of issues. For example, a direct transfer from a sensory-motor skill with a physical object towards an action on digital objects could end in domestic drama (e.g. the Nintendo Wii thrown on TV screens while playing bowling [22]).

HCIs were first conceived as tools to optimize a specific task. By contrast, natural interactions are based on users' feelings and experiences: the user should feel the interaction as a natural sensory-motor experience [31]. This is not the technology itself that is natural but the way users interact with it [23]. Hence, evaluation criteria progressively shift from usability and performance towards a more complex "new good", that considers the user experience [7]. This creates new interests for sensory-motor in-situ phenomena [3], embodied and situated cognition in general [11, 17] and learning and adaptation in particular [4]. However, few works have studied motor learning in HCI [4], and the way it influences the user's experience [15]. We are not aware of any work that specifically studied the transfer of sensory-motor learning from one interaction to another one.

Benefitting from user pre-existing skills. Wobbrock et al. introduced various methods to exploit users pre-existing knowledge and skills in the definition of gesture sets [32, 33], but their work was focused on finding easily *guessable* gestures rather than measuring a skill transfer. In their Reality-Based Interactions (RBI) framework, Jacob et al. expose the benefit of taking advantage of users pre-existing skills to reduce the cognitive load and the learning cost of the interaction [14]. This idea also appears in one of Wigdor et al.'s design guidelines for natural user interfaces, which is to "leverage innate talents and previously learned skills" [31].

The rational of our study is that an objective way to evaluate the *sensory-motor naturalness* of an interaction with digital objects is to measure how the sensory-motor skills involved in this interaction are influenced by similar skills in the physical world. This approach is inspired from the literature on motor learning and transfer.

Motor learning and transfer

Despite very successful application of motor control results in HCI [5, 8], uses of motor *learning* results are sparse [4]. Our study focuses on the *transfer* of *learning* of *motor skills*. Considering the broad literature on motor learning, the references below should be considered as illustrative.

The term *skill* covers a large range of phenomena from mathematical abilities to driving or running [2]. Here, we focus on interaction with real or digital objects through direct or indirect body actions: learned abilities that involved a specific control of the body via sensory-motor loops to achieve a specific task. Tennis playing and mouse pointing are classic illustrations of sensory-motor skills found in the literature on motor learning [6, 20, 34]. Pointing and reaching tasks have been extensively studies as experimental models of the upper-limb motor control and learning (e.g. [6, 19, 20, 21, 34]).

Learning of a motor skill is an "improvement, through practice, in the performance of sensory-guided motor behavior" [19].

Transfer of motor learning corresponds to a positive effect of past experiences on new ones, while negative effects are called *interferences* [20]. For example, previous expertise in typing on a QWERTY keyboard has negative effect or *interferes* with the use of an AZERTY keyboard, while learning to type with a large QWERTY keyboard may help, or *transfer*, to typing on a smaller QWERTY keyboard. Transfer and interference are extensively investigated in motor learning. These investigations not only aim at evaluating if a given training could improve the performance in another task or situation, but also at assessing the fundamental question of the nature of the representations that underlie motor control (e.g. [2, 20, 25, 28, 34]).

Motor learning and transfer of arm-movements are studied in laboratory mainly using two types of tasks: (1) common pointing/reaching tasks or speech tasks under unusual but systematic perturbation of movement or feedbacks (e.g. [13, 20, 21, 28]); (2) novel tasks, such as tracking more or less predictable trajectories [35] or pointing at targets in more or less predictable orders [10]. Our experimental task is based on the latter.

The motor learning literature indicates that skill learning is globally *specific*: in other words, to observe a transfer, the training and test situations must be very similar. However, *gradients of transfer* can be observed as correlates of the *similarity* between the training and testing experiences (e.g. [9, 21]). In our study, we attempt to observe a gradient of transfer as a correlate of the sensory-motor similarity between a physical interaction and various digital interactions. This similarity could be used as an objective evaluation of the naturalness of the digital interactions at the sensory-motor level.

AN EXPERIMENTAL PARADIGM TO STUDY THE TRANSFER OF LEARNING IN HCI

Learning and transfer of learning are assessed in controlled situations based on a paradigm that includes three mains steps [10]: (1) A *baseline phase* that allows to assess participants' performance before learning (e.g. pointing at targets in a given order A for a short period); (2) A *training phase* during which participants repeat the task (pointing in order A) for a given duration. This phase could be achieved on a single session on one day or several sessions over several days; (3) A *test phase* for transfer during which participants achieve a more or less similar task (e.g. pointing to the same targets in a new order B). Learning is assessed through the analysis of the progression of performance from the baseline to the last training period. Transfer is assessed by comparing performances in the test phase to that in the baseline.

We adapted this paradigm to the purpose of studying transfer of learning in the execution of an identical task achieved with different forms of interaction. In the remainder of this paper, we will use the expression "physical interaction" for "interaction with physical objects"; the expression "a HCI" to denote a common form of human-computer interactions such as direct touch, or mouse-pointer interaction; and the expression "a digital interaction" to denote an interaction with digital objects using a particular HCI.

Our first idea was to observe a transfer from physical interaction towards digital interaction. However, training all subjects in one condition (physical) and testing the transfer towards other conditions (the tested HCIs) present two main issues well known in the motor learning literature [10, 18, 20, 21, 28, 30]: (1) it provides no indication of the potential improvement effect for each condition. Some HCIs offer large performance improvement from training, others don't. As a result, (2) it leads to compare apples to oranges: i.e. the percentage of improvement for a given HCI-A is not equivalent to the percentage of improvement for another HCI-B. Problem (1) can be solved by introducing one control group per HCI (which makes the design more complex) but this does not solve problem (2). Therefore, the standard approach in the motor learning literature is to compare the amount of tranfer from different conditions towards a single condition. We use this "reversed" approach because it allows the indisputable *comparison* of the amount of transfer from various digital interactions towards a single physical interaction.

By reversing the experimental design, we are now observing how sensory-motor skills acquired using a particular HCI with digital objects transfer to the interaction with physical objects. This may appear as moving away from the concept of naturalness as the ability to use pre-existing skills from physical interaction. This raises the question of the *symmetry* of the transfer: if a skill acquired with a digital interaction transfers well in physical interaction, does this mean that the

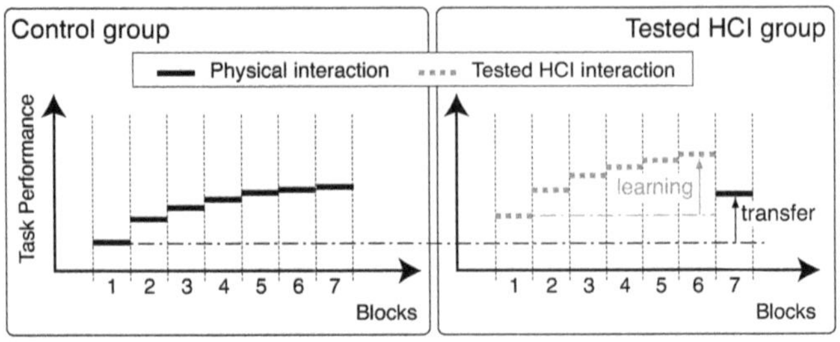

Figure 1. Observing a transfer of learning. A "Control" group of participants is trained for a novel task executed with physical interaction. The performance of another "Tested HCI" group of participants is measured after prior training on several blocks of trials on a similar task executed with the tested HCI. Transfer is observed if the performance of the tested HCI group with physical interaction is better than the initial performance of the control group.

opposite is true? While there are no obvious rational to suggest a strong asymmetry, this remains an open question that we will discuss at the end of this article. However, in our study the transfer of learning is not seen as an end but rather as a means to study the *similarity* between various forms of interaction. In this regard, observing a strong transfer of skills from a digital interaction towards physical interaction is as much an indication of the similarity of the two interactions than the opposite.

The following steps summarize our experimental paradigm:

- A *control* group of participants is trained to a novel task with a physical interaction. The initial performance of this group (i.e. block #1 of the control group in Figure 1, left) serves as the baseline;
- For each HCI, a *test* group of participants is trained to a similar task, but with digital objects moved using the tested HCI. Sensory-motor *learning* of the task is observed through performance increase over the training session (i.e. the red arrow in Figure 1);
- After a number of training blocks made of several repetition of the same task, the tested HCI group executes the task again but this time with physical interaction (i.e. block #7 on Figure 1). *Transfer* is assessed by comparing the performance in this last block with the baseline performance (black arrow on Figure 1).
- A *gradient* of transfer is observed by comparing the transfer effects from the different tested HCI to the physical interaction.

Figure 1 illustrates a case where user performance with the digital interaction is generally better than with the physical interaction. But even in the opposite case, a transfer of learning would still be demonstrated as long as the performance with the physical interaction is significantly higher in the test group than in the control group. This underscores the independence between transfer of learning and user performance.

We chose a between-subjects design because any experimental session provides some training that potentially influences participants' behavior in the following sessions. The difficulty is then to dissociate, in subjects' performances, how much is due to transfer and how much is due to repeated sessions. This is not an issue in Fitts paradigms [26] which focus on the *trained performance* (i.e. discarding the training) and mitigate transfer effects by balancing the order of presentation. This is a major problem in paradigms that measure learning and transfer. However, as the general performance of participants is variable, groups must be balanced, so that the initial performance difference between groups cannot explain the performance difference between the control group and the test groups.

THE EXPERIMENT

We conducted an empirical study based on this paradigm in order to evaluate the similarity of various HCIs with an equivalent physical interaction.

Experimental task

The task was chosen to meet the following requirements:

- the task can be performed both with a physical and digital objects, and with the different HCIs of interest;
- the task is novel to the participants, so that all participants are supposed to be similar in regard to their knowledge and practice of the task at the beginning of the experiment;
- the task is difficult enough that learning can be observed as a performance increase through training.

We chose a serial target acquisition task as previous work showed that it was appropriate to study motor learning [10]. With this kind of task, improvement in participant performance can be the result of sensory-motor learning, which depends on the interaction, but also the result of learning the sequence of targets, which is independent of the interaction. As we wanted to contrast the sensory-motor learning from various interactions, we aimed at reducing the effect of the learning of the sequence. We thus chose a very simple constant order for the target positions so that it was quickly learned in few trials. Our objective was that performance improvement would result mostly from the learning of two new *sensory-motor skills*: acquiring targets repeatedly at well known positions (e.g. by developing a proprioception of the target positions), and anticipation (e.g. using the best trajectory in the approach of a target in preparation of the acquisition of the next target).

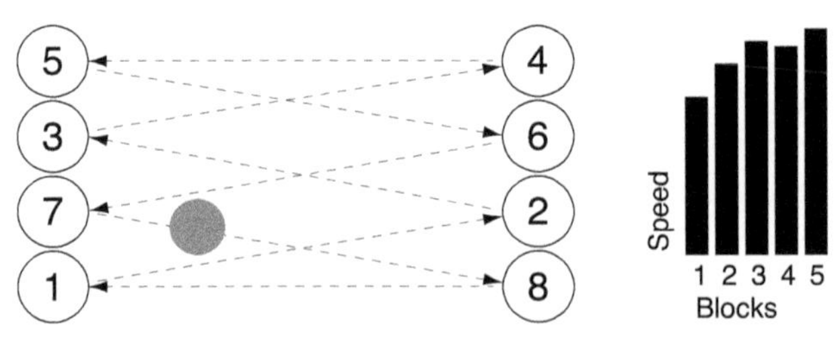

Figure 2. Left: the sequence of targets. The numbered white discs represent targets, the red disc represents the object controlled by participants. Disc size, target size and positions are represented to scale. Dashed arrows and numbers are illustrations of the order, they were not shown to the participants. Right: representation of the speed of target acquisition during pauses.

Participants had to move a red disc object (either physical or digital) on the top of a circular target which could take 8 different positions on display, as illustrated in Figure 2, left. The display was set horizontally on a desk. The outermost target centers defined a $430\,\mathrm{mm} \times 200\,\mathrm{mm}$ rectangle. Target diameter was $64\,\mathrm{mm}$, object diameter was $50\,\mathrm{mm}$. The targets were acquired when the object was entirely within the boundaries of the target, which translates in terms of Fitts' law [26] to a target size of $64 - 50 = 14\,\mathrm{mm}$. Inter-target distance was either $430\,\mathrm{mm}$ (horizontal) or $438\,\mathrm{mm}$ (diagonal). Hence, every object placement had a Fitts index of difficulty of ≈ 5 bits.

In a block of trials, participants executed a sequence of 64 target acquisitions made of 8 repetitions of the sequence presented in Figure 2, left. They initiated a block by moving the object on top of a "start area" located at position #8. Then, after a short delay, the first target appeared at position #1. The targets disappeared as soon as they were acquired, and the next target was displayed. Target acquisition was thus a *goal crossing* task [1] rather than a pointing task. In particular, target acquisition did not require the object to stop on top of the target, which fostered anticipated motion towards the next target. We also indicated the position of the next target as a hollow circle to foster anticipation and reduce the effect of learning the sequence. Participants were instructed to acquire the targets as fast as possible. They were explicitly asked to find the right speed-accuracy trade-off in order to go through each block of 64 targets as fast as possible.

After each block of trials, participants were asked to relax for 30 s. During this pause, an indication of their speed was displayed in the form of a bar chart. This is illustrated in Figure 2, right, in the case of the pause coming after the 5th block. The bar for the first block had a fixed size, the height of the other bars indicated the average speed of target selection during each block relative to the first block. The goal of this chart was to encourage participants to maintain their effort and to stay at their maximal performance across the 10 training blocks.

As a between-subjects design, any difference in groups' performances after the training session could be related either to the training, or to unbalanced average abilities between groups. In order to avoid the second possibility, the groups of participant were built according to the participants' performance in a first *group balancing* task. The group balancing task was chosen to be representative of participants' ability to quickly move the *physical* disc on top of targets. This task was also chosen so as to avoid any training to the main experiment's training task: the targets were positioned differently than in the training task (in a five arms star configuration) and anticipation was prevented by requiring the participants to move the physical disc to a start area after each target acquisition, and by displaying the next target after a varying delay (in the range 200 ms to 800 ms). The group balancing task was made of 64 target acquisitions.

Interactions

In the physical interaction, participants had to slide a plastic disc of diameter $50\,\mathrm{mm}$ and height $4\,\mathrm{mm}$. The disc had soft fabric at the bottom in order to provide smooth sliding on the surface. Soft fabric was also taped on its top side it order to improve the finger grip on the disc, as compared to bare plastic.

In this study, we focused on the two most common forms of HCI, mouse pointing and direct-touch, and on a more specific form of HCI: indirect-touch in absolute mode. We introduced the latter as an intermediate between the two formers in terms of similarity with the physical interaction. All the three HCIs were used to control the position of a red digital disc of diameter $50\,\mathrm{mm}$.

As it can be expected, the digital disc was controlled by landing a finger on its surface with *direct-touch*, and by pressing on the mouse button while the pointer was on its surface with *mouse pointing*. For the mouse interaction, participants were told that it was not necessary to maintain the mouse button depressed: once acquired, the digital disc remained under control of the mouse for the entire block. Doing so, we focused on participant's control of the mouse position and eliminated the effect of pressing on the button. Mouse pointing was used with the standard control-display transfer function of Mac OS X with "Tracking speed" set to level 3 on the 10-level scale of the control panel. Control of the digital disc with *indirect-touch* on a trackpad was more specific: we did not use a common transfer function with relative control and dynamic gain as used on most laptop computers. Instead, the trackpad was used in an *absolute* mode, similar to digitizing tablets: when a finger landed on the trackpad, the digital disc teleported to the corresponding position on the display. However, teleportation very rarely occurred during the experiment as the task was best performed with the finger remaining in contact with the trackpad during the entire block of trials. For the two *indirect* HCIs, the mouse or trackpad were placed to the left or to the right of the display surface, depending on the participant's handedness.

The rational of these choices was to create gradients of similarity between the physical interaction and the digital interactions. The tested interactions could be ordered according to their respective sensory-motor overlapping with the physical interaction as followed:

- direct-touch was the closest to the physical interaction as it involved similar visuomotor associations and arms configuration. Differences with the physical interaction included a delay in the visual feedback, the absence of somatosensorial (tactile) feedback to perceive the texture, and a difference in friction forces
- indirect-touch (trackpad) was considered as intermediate as it introduced a spatial transformation between the finger and the object motion. However, used in absolute mode, the simple linear transformation was less radical than with mouse pointing. It also involved a similar configuration of the finger;
- mouse pointing was considered the furthest to physical interaction due to the speed-dependent transformation between mouse and object motion and different finger configuration.

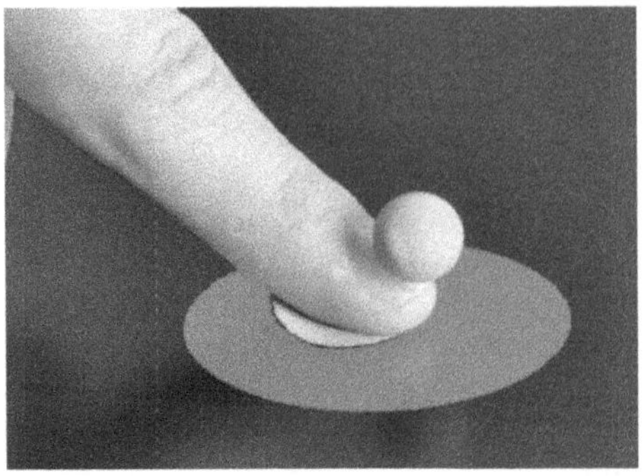

Figure 3. Implementing direct-touch with optical tracking. An optical marker is taped on the nail. A piece of soft fabric is taped underneath the finger to improve sliding.

Participants and procedure

28 volunteers (9 females, 19 males) participated in the experiment, split into the following four groups of 7 participants according to the training device:

- The control group (CTR) was trained with the physical disc, the mean age was 31.9 (range [25-41]), all participants were male,
- The touch group (TOU) was trained with direct touch, the mean age was 29.0 (range [22-39]), it included 3 females,
- The trackpad group (PAD) was trained with the trackpad, the mean age was 32.0 (range [23-43]), it included 3 females,
- The mouse group (MOU) was trained with the mouse, the mean age was 30.6 (range [21-42]), it included 3 females.

The participants were not informed about the expectations of the experiment prior the completion of the experiment. They were all graduated students or university staff used to computer, mouse or touch interactions.

Participants were instructed that the experiment was anonymous, and that it included three sessions separated with breaks:

- Group balancing session. Participants performed the 64 target acquisitions of the group balancing task. Their performance was immediately computed and they were assigned to a group so as to balance the average performance of each group.
- Training session. Participants performed 10 blocks of the training task using one of the four interactions depending on their group.
- Test (or transfer) session. After training, all participants performed 4 blocks of the training task by moving the physical disc.

Overall, participants finished the tree sessions in about half an hour.

Apparatus

The experimental tasks were performed on a 1920×1080 pixel 120 Hz LCD monitor which foot was removed so that it could be taped horizontally on a desk. The monitor was driven by custom developed software running on a 3.4 GHz workstation.

The physical disc was equipped with 3 spherical optical markers captured by 2 Flex 13 120 Hz Optitrack cameras. The outputs of the cameras were processed by the tracking software running on a dedicated 2.6 GHz workstation, the computed position was then sent over the network to the main workstation. The same optical tracking system was used to implement the direct-touch interaction on the non-touch sensitive monitor: an optical marker was attached to the pointing finger of the participant, as shown in Figure 3. In addition, a small patch of soft fabric was taped at the bottom of the finger to improve the sliding of the finger on the surface and to prevent burning sensations during the high speed dragging of the digital disc.

We used a standard wired optical mouse for the mouse pointing interaction. For indirect-touch, we used a wireless 130×110 mm Apple magic trackpad. The raw touch position on the trackpad was used to implement an absolute position mapping to the display. Only a subpart of the height of the trackpad was used in order to provide an isomorphic $x - y$ mapping on the $16/9$ display.

Results

We based our analyses on the duration of the target acquisition (in_time) measured as the time span between the appearance of a target and the first time when the disc (either physical or digital) is entirely within the target boundaries. For each subject and trial block, we withdraw trials with in_time values higher than 1.5 the interquartile range from the mean of the block. This effectively removes *failed* trials where a participant fails to acquire the target, anticipates the acquisition of the next target, and then realizes the failure and comes back to the current target.

The third block of the test session (block 13, Figure 4) of one participant in *TOU* was removed due to outlier behavior of the participant during this specific block.

The Figure 4 displays the average *in_time* values for each group and block over the whole experiment. We can observe that:

- The ability to interact with the physical object before training is equivalent for the four groups;
- The performances for MOU and PAD are worst than TOU and CTR, at the onset but also at the offset of training;
- The performances improve over the training phase for the four groups, with variable degree of improvement according to the HCIs;
- The performances are better at the onset of the transfer phase for CTR and TOU than PAD and MOU. Moreover, the progression of performances over the four blocks of the post-phase for PAD and MOU are similar to that observed over the four first blocks of training of CTR.

We will now analyze in more details these different points and their statistical reliability.

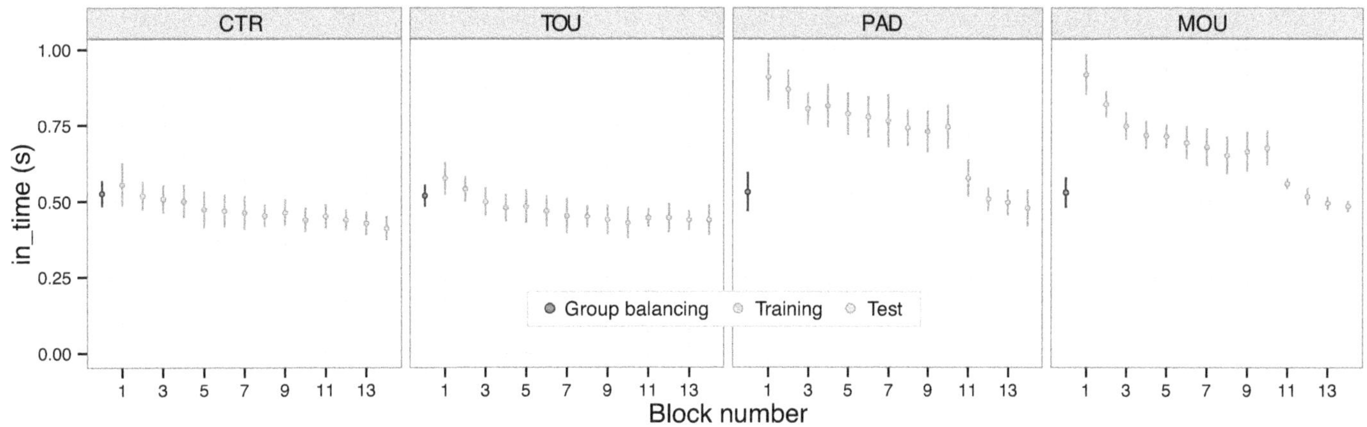

Figure 4. Mean target acquisition time, with 95% confidence intervals, for each group and each block of trials and for the three sessions.

Equivalent abilities in the physical interaction

As a result of the method used to constitute the groups, subjects' performances during the group balancing task was similar for the four groups with average in_time in the range 0.52 s to 0.53 s. A between subjects ANOVA shows no significant effect of the group on the group balancing task performances ($F(3, 24) = 0.25, p > .86$).

Training session

In order to investigate the effect of HCIs on global performances and on learning, we focused on the first and last blocks of the training session. We ran a mixed ANOVA with the group as a between subject factor and the block (1 vs. 10) as a within subject factor. It showed a significant effect of the group ($F(3, 24) = 39, p < .0001$), the block ($F(1, 24) = 221, p < .0001$) and an interaction between the two factors ($F(3, 24) = 5.5, p < .01$). We then ran post-hoc tests to evaluate differences in performance according to the HCIs and to the block (Tukey's HSD for the group factor and paired sample t.test with a Bonferroni correction for the block factor).

Different performances according to the HCI. The task required large motions of the controlled object on the display surface. As MOU and PAD both use a control-display gain to amplify the motions in motor-space, we expected smaller in_time compared to direct interactions (CTL and TOU). We actually observed the reverse: during the first block of training, the average in_time was 0.92 s for MOU, 0.91 s for PAD, 0.58 s for TOU, and 0.56 s for CTR. Even at the end of the training, in_time was still more than 0.24 s longer for PAD (0.75 s) and MOU (0.68 s) than CTR (0.44 s) and TOU (0.43 s). Comparisons between groups' performances during the first and the last block separately showed no significant differences between PAD and MOU ($p = 0.9$, for the first block and $p = .06$ for the last block). Similarly, TOU and CTR were not different in the first and last block ($p > .9$). By contrast, in_time for both TOU and CTR was significantly smaller than for MOU and PAD in all block comparisons ($p < .0001$).

Learning effect. The learning effect was significant for each group ($t(6) > 4.5$, $p < 0.05$, for all the within-subject comparisons between the first and the last block of each group after a Bonferroni correction). Over the training phase, in_time significantly decreased on average by: -0.12 s for CTR (a 21% improvement), -0.15 s for TOU (a 25% improvement), -0.16 s for PAD (a 18% improvement) and -0.24 s for MOU (a 26% improvement).

Transfer

We tested if the training with each HCI influenced participants' performances when they switched to the physical interaction. For this, we specifically focused on the first block of the training session of the control group, which indicates the *baseline* performance with the physical interaction with no training at all, and on the first block of the test session for all groups, which still indicates the performance with the physical interaction, but this time after training with various interactions depending on the group. This focus is illustrated on Figure 5. Between-subjects ANOVAs revealed a significant effect of the group, both when comparing the baseline performance ($F(3, 24) = 6.0, p < 0.01$) and the trained performance ($F(3, 24) = 12.7, p < 0.001$) of the control group with the performance after training of the test groups. Performance improved by 20% from the baseline when trained with

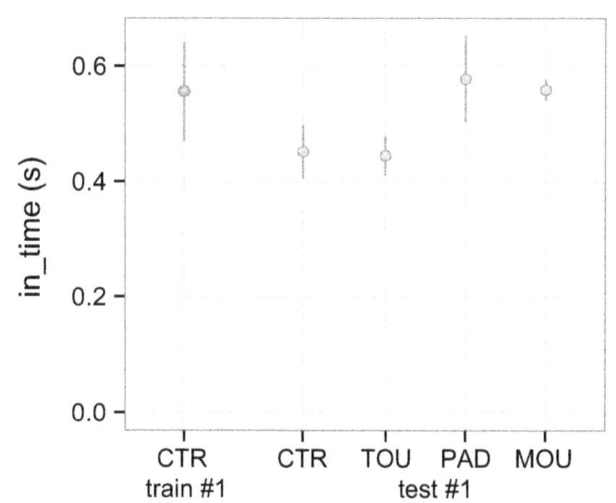

Figure 5. Close-up on Figure 4 for the first block of the training session of the control group (train #1), and the first block of the test session of all groups (test #1).

TOU ($p < 0.05$). On the contrary, no significant variation from the baseline performance was observed when training with PAD or MOU ($p > 0.9$): the initial test performance was 4% lower and less than 1% higher than the baseline for PAD and MOU, respectively. Performance after training for the CTL or the TOU groups was very similar, differing by only 1%.

DISCUSSION

The aim of this work was to propose an experimental paradigm to objectively assess the sensory-motor grounding of the naturalness of various HCIs. We use this paradigm to empirically questionned the sensory-motor naturalness of three HCIs. This paradigm rests on the rational that the naturalness of an HCI is anchored in the similarity of the sensory motor-skills involved in the HCI and those involved in the interaction with the physical world. In our paradigm, the sensory-motor similarity is operationalized in a well-known and extensively investigated phenomenon in the motor control literature: the transfer of sensory-motor learning. Using a serial target crossing task, we observe that the skills learned through training with direct-touch transfer fully to the physical interaction while no skill transfer is observed when training with indirect-touch or mouse pointing. According to our rational, this means that direct-touch is more similar to the physical interaction at a sensory-motor level, which provide an empirical and objective correlate of the widely circulated belief that direct-touch is a more natural form of interaction than mouse pointing. Taken together, the results of the experiment are not trivial: they include a number of unexpected aspects that we will now discuss and interpret.

Interpretation of the observed transfer profiles

The study was designed to observe a gradient of transfer by manipulating the sensory-motor similarity between the three tested HCIs and the physical interaction. In particular, considering the sensory-motor couplings involved in the HCIs, we were expecting the following trend in the first block of the test-session: $CTR > TOU > PAD > MOU > 0$. What we observed, however, was a binary profile of transfer with a full transfer for direct-touch and no transfer for the two other interactions: $CTR = TOU > PAD = MOU = 0$.

$CTR = TOU$

The first unexpected result concerning the transfer effect is the absence of difference between the control and the direct-touch groups. Despite substantial differences in sensory-motor associations for the two interactions (e.g. delay in visual feedback, absence of inertial mass, different tactile feedback between the display and the physical disc, different frictions), shifting from direct-touch to the physical interaction seems *transparent*: participant trained with direct-touch performed similarly than participants trained with the physical interaction. This may be explained in the current study by the limited delay of the visual feedback thanks to the high frequency/low latency tracking, and the limited friction forces of the physical token in the physical interaction. It would be interesting to study the effect of various characteristics of the direct-touch interaction, such as feedback latency or friction, to observe how they affect transfer.

$PAD = MOU = 0$

Indirect-touch and mouse pointing showed no transfer, despite the observation of a learning effect in the training session with both interactions and despite offering quite different sensory-motor controls, with the absolute PAD control arguably closer to the physical interaction than the dynamic gain control of the mouse. These results support the idea that sensory-motor transfer is very specific, as previously shown in motor learning research [21, 28]. An important repercussion of the specificity of transfer is that, when attempting to create novel *natural* interactions, designers may not be able to depart very far from a faithful reproduction of a physical interaction. Here again, it will be interesting to study more systematically how different intermediates between TOU and PAD can exhibit a transfer of learning to physical interaction. Absolute indirect-touch, for example, could be "moved" closer to physical interaction by using a control-display gain of 1 (i.e. using a pad with the same size of the display). Such study may inform about the fundamental sensory-motor requirements of natural interactions.

Previous works also showed that mouse vs. touch navigation lead to different improvements of spatial memory and that kinesthesic cues involved in touch are important for spatial memory [15, 27]. In our case, MOU and PAD may lead to different memorization of the target trajectory than the CTR condition, while the exploration with TOU may be close to CTR. More studies are required to better understand the relationship between sensory-motor experience and the cognitive aspects of naturalness [15].

Limits and improvements of the paradigm

Transfer effect vs. performance effect

The experimental task that we used was performed more efficiently with the direct interaction techniques (physical and direct-touch) compared to the indirect ones (indirect-touch and mouse). One could argue that the absence of transfer from indirect-touch and mouse is related to the bad performances in these HCIs as compare with direct-touch. However, the learning curves in Figure 4 show that performances clearly increased for these two interactions and that the higher performance of the mouse, compared to indirect-touch, did not end up in a greater transfer. Even so, it would be interesting to create an experimental task that yields better performance with mouse pointing than with direct-touch to test the independence between task performance and transfer of learning.

From digital to physical

As explained above, we chose to reverse the experimental paradigm: we measured transfer from digital to physical rather than the more intuitive opposite. We assumed that a transfer in either directions was an indication of the similarity of the sensory-motor skills involved in the two interactions, and that if two interactions use similar sensory-motor skills, then newly learned skills should transfer either way. This points to further experimentations aimed at evaluating the *symmetry* of the transfer. This could be done by measuring a baseline performance of a control group interacting with direct-touch interaction, and measuring a transfer on another group trained with physical interaction.

Beyond naturalness, why are transfer effects important for HCI

As mentioned in the "previous work" section, ubiquitous computing orients HCI towards new methods that should help evaluating what is a good user experience [7, 31]. At the same time, future HCIs might be more and more non-representational and thus intrinsically more oriented towards sensory-motor skills [11]. The consequence is that HCI designers now need to better understand sensory-motor skills, their adaptation and plasticity, especially to anticipate if and how the modern human, used to many forms of digital interactions, will be able to extend her/his sensory-motor skills to integrate novel interaction designs. Transfer of learning should thus be studied not only to and from physical interaction, but also between digital interactions.

Study of sensory-motor learning and transfer is also important at a more fundamental level: new technologies come with more and more new sensory-motor skills. These skills may interact together but also influence real word behaviors. For example, Wei et al. recently compared visuomotor learning for computer and non-computer users [30]. Using a classic direct finger pointing task, they observed greater transfer of visuomotor training with computer users than with non-computer users. This suggests that computer use, and in particular the daily exposition to the mouse visuomotor transformation, changes our subsequent visuomotor abilities in the non-digital world. This study and similar ones in motor learning, neurosciences and psychology also emphasized the relevance of studies of learning and transfer in laboratory to assess more global phenomena. As a consequence, models of sensory-motor learning may be developed and used in HCI in order to simulate the consequences of the daily use of some forms of human-computer interaction on human sensory-motor abilities.

CONCLUSION

HCI designers need theories to better understand user experience and tools to anticipate what forms of interaction would create a good user experience [7, 11, 16, 23]: interactions that will be easily integrated to user sensory-motor competences in the real world, but also that will have no negative effects on these competences. Design guidelines have been presented towards the conception of natural user interfaces [31]. However, these guidelines do not include methods to objectively assess the different rules that designers should respect to create an interaction that could be natural to the user, that will respect her/his sensory-motor abilities and extend beyond.

Facing the lack of theoretical and empirical background with regard to naturalness in HCI, our contribution was to explore the literature of sensory-motor skills learning and exploit the advances in this field to propose a first step towards an objective measurement of the sensory-motor basis of HCI naturalness. We introduce a classic paradigm in motor learning research: the transfer of sensory-motor skills.

In an empirical experiment, we found that the learning of a novel task with direct-touch interaction transferred very well to physical interaction, a first objective indication of the sensory-motor similarity of the two interactions, and an indication of the naturalness of direct-touch. We also observed that the transfer of learning may be very specific and that the design space around physical interaction is not very large for the design of novel human-computer interactions that use natural sensory-motor skills.

As mentioned elsewhere, "HCI is at a crossroads" between the digital and physical world [17]. Our feeling is that many authors look for answers in psychology or cognitive sciences [3, 16, 17] but omit what is actually one of the building blocks of HCI: sensory-motor learning. The connection with embodied and situated cognition is certainly a necessity for HCI to progress towards more and more embodied and natural interactions, but the interest for motor learning theories, models and methods will certainly be a fruitful road towards naturalness.

ACKNOWLEDGEMENTS

We would like to thank our colleagues at LIG and GIPSA-Lab for their helpful discussions and proof reading. We benefited from the facilities of the fab lab fabMSTIC to realize the experiment. This work was partially funded by the French government in the project 3DCI (FUI-AAP14) and the LabEx PERSYVAL-Lab (ANR-11-LABX-0025-01).

REFERENCES

1. Accot, J., and Zhai, S. More than dotting the i's — foundations for crossing-based interfaces. In *ACM Conference on Human Factors in Computing Systems (CHI)*, ACM (2002), 73–80.
2. Adams, J. A. Historical review and appraisal of research on the learning, retention, and transfer of human motor skills. *Psychological Bulletin 101*, 1 (1987), 41.
3. Beaudouin-Lafon, M. Designing interaction, not interfaces. In *Proceedings of the working conference on Advanced visual interfaces*, ACM (2004), 15–22.
4. Belda-Lois, J.-M., de Rosario, H., Pons, R., Poveda, R., Morón, A., Porcar, R., Gómez, A., et al. Can human movement analysis contribute to usability understanding? *Human movement science 29*, 4 (2010), 529–541.
5. Card, S., Moran, T. P., and Newell, A. *The Psychology of Human-Computer Interaction.* Lawrence Erlbaum Associates, 1983.
6. Clower, D. M., and Boussaoud, D. Selective use of perceptual recalibration versus visuomotor skill acquisition. *Journal of Neurophysiology 84*, 5 (2000), 2703–2708.
7. Fallman, D. The new good: exploring the potential of philosophy of technology to contribute to

human-computer interaction. In *Proceedings of the SIGCHI Conference on Human Factors in Computing Systems*, ACM (2011), 1051–1060.

8. Fitts, P. M. The information capacity of the human motor system in controlling the amplitude of movement. *Journal of Experimental Psychology 47*, 6 (1954), 381–391.
9. Gandolfo, F., Mussa-Ivaldi, F., and Bizzi, E. Motor learning by field approximation. *Proceedings of the National Academy of Sciences 93*, 9 (1996), 3843–3846.
10. Ghilardi, M. F., Moisello, C., Silvestri, G., Ghez, C., and Krakauer, J. W. Learning of a sequential motor skill comprises explicit and implicit components that consolidate differently. *J Neurophysiol 101*, 5 (May 2009), 2218–2229.
11. Gillies, M., and Kleinsmith, A. Non-representational interaction design. In *Contemporary Sensorimotor Theory*. Springer, 2014, 201–208.
12. Holden, M. K. Virtual environments for motor rehabilitation: review. *Cyberpsychology & behavior 8*, 3 (2005), 187–211.
13. Houde, J. F., and Jordan, M. I. Sensorimotor adaptation in speech production. *Science 279*, 5354 (1998), 1213–1216.
14. Jacob, R. J., Girouard, A., Hirshfield, L. M., Horn, M. S., Shaer, O., Solovey, E. T., and Zigelbaum, J. Reality-based interaction: a framework for post-wimp interfaces. In *Proceedings of the SIGCHI conference on Human factors in computing systems*, ACM (2008), 201–210.
15. Jetter, H.-C., Leifert, S., Gerken, J., Schubert, S., and Reiterer, H. Does (multi-)touch aid users' spatial memory and navigation in 'panning' and in 'zooming & panning' uis? In *Proceedings of AVI*, ACM (2012), 83–90.
16. Jetter, H.-C., Reiterer, H., and Geyer, F. Blended interaction: understanding natural human–computer interaction in post-wimp interactive spaces. *Personal and Ubiquitous Computing 18*, 5 (2014), 1139–1158.
17. Kirsh, D. Embodied cognition and the magical future of interaction design. *ACM Transactions on Computer-Human Interaction (TOCHI) 20*, 1 (2013), 3.
18. Krakauer, J. W., Ghez, C., and Ghilardi, M. F. Adaptation to visuomotor transformations: consolidation, interference, and forgetting. *The Journal of Neuroscience 25*, 2 (2005), 473–478.
19. Krakauer, J. W., and Mazzoni, P. Human sensorimotor learning: adaptation, skill, and beyond. *Current opinion in neurobiology 21*, 4 (2011), 636–644.
20. Krakauer, J. W., Mazzoni, P., Ghazizadeh, A., Ravindran, R., and Shadmehr, R. Generalization of motor learning depends on the history of prior action. *PLoS biology 4*, 10 (2006), e316.
21. Mattar, A. A., and Ostry, D. J. Modifiability of generalization in dynamics learning. *Journal of neurophysiology 98*, 6 (2007), 3321–3329.
22. Norman, D. A. The way i see it: Natural user interfaces are not natural. *interactions 17*, 3 (2010), 6–10.
23. O'hara, K., Harper, R., Mentis, H., Sellen, A., and Taylor, A. On the naturalness of touchless: putting the "interaction" back into nui. *ACM Transactions on Computer-Human Interaction (TOCHI) 20*, 1 (2013), 5.
24. Poddar, I., Sethi, Y., Ozyildiz, E., and Sharma, R. Toward natural gesture/speech hci: A case study of weather narration. In *Proc. Workshop on Perceptual User Interfaces (PUI)*, Citeseer (1998).
25. Shadmehr, R. Generalization as a behavioral window to the neural mechanisms of learning internal models. *Human movement science 23*, 5 (2004), 543–568.
26. Soukoreff, R. W., and MacKenzie, I. S. Towards a standard for pointing device evaluation, perspectives on 27 years of fitts' law research in hci. *International Journal of Human-Computer Studies 61*, 6 (2004), 751 – 789.
27. Tan, D. S., Pausch, R., Stefanucci, J. K., and Proffitt, D. R. Kinesthetic cues aid spatial memory. In *CHI '02 Extended Abstracts on Human Factors in Computing Systems*, ACM (2002), 806–807.
28. Tremblay, S., Houle, G., and Ostry, D. J. Specificity of speech motor learning. *The Journal of Neuroscience 28*, 10 (2008), 2426–2434.
29. Van Dam, A. Post-wimp user interfaces. *Communications of the ACM 40*, 2 (1997), 63–67.
30. Wei, K., Yan, X., Kong, G., Yin, C., Zhang, F., Wang, Q., and Kording, K. P. Computer use changes generalization of movement learning. *Current Biology 24*, 1 (2014), 82–85.
31. Wigdor, D., and Wixon, D. *Brave NUI world: designing natural user interfaces for touch and gesture*. Elsevier, 2011.
32. Wobbrock, J. O., Aung, H. H., Rothrock, B., and Myers, B. A. Maximizing the guessability of symbolic input. In *ACM Conference on Human Factors in Computing Systems (CHI) Extended Abstracts*, ACM (2005), 1869–1872.
33. Wobbrock, J. O., Morris, M. R., and Wilson, A. D. User-defined gestures for surface computing. In *ACM Conference on Human Factors in Computing Systems (CHI)*, ACM (2009), 1083–1092.
34. Wolpert, D. M., Ghahramani, Z., and Flanagan, J. R. Perspectives and problems in motor learning. *Trends in cognitive sciences 5*, 11 (2001), 487–494.
35. Zhu, F. F., Poolton, J. M., Maxwell, J. P., Fan, J. K. M., Leung, G. K. K., and Masters, R. S. W. Refining the continuous tracking paradigm to investigate implicit motor learning. *Exp Psychol 61*, 3 (2014), 196–204.

Formalizing Agreement Analysis for Elicitation Studies: New Measures, Significance Test, and Toolkit

Radu-Daniel Vatavu
University Stefan cel Mare of Suceava
Suceava 720229, Romania
vatavu@eed.usv.ro

Jacob O. Wobbrock
Information School | DUB Group
University of Washington
Seattle, WA 98195-2840 USA
wobbrock@uw.edu

ABSTRACT

We address in this work the process of agreement rate analysis for characterizing the level of consensus between participants' proposals elicited during guessability studies. Two new measures, *i.e., disagreement rate* for referents and *coagreement rate* between referents, are proposed to accompany the widely-used agreement rate formula of Wobbrock *et al.* [37] when reporting participants' consensus for symbolic input. A statistical significance test for comparing the agreement rates of $k \geq 2$ referents is presented in analogy with Cochran's success/failure Q test [5], for which we express the test statistic in terms of agreement and coagreement rates. We deliver a toolkit to assist practitioners to compute agreement, disagreement, and coagreement rates, and run statistical tests for agreement rates at p=.05, .01, and .001 levels of significance. We validate our theoretical development of agreement rate analysis in relation with several previously published elicitation studies. For example, when we present the probability distribution function of the agreement rate measure, we also use it (1) to explain the magnitude of agreement rates previously reported in the literature, and (2) to propose qualitative interpretations for agreement rates, in analogy with Cohen's guidelines for effect sizes [6]. We also re-examine previously published elicitation data from the perspective of the agreement rate test statistic, and highlight new findings on the effect of referents over agreement rates, unattainable prior to this work. We hope that our contributions will advance the current knowledge in agreement rate analysis, providing researchers and practitioners with new techniques and tools to help them understand user-elicited data at deeper levels of detail and sophistication.

Author Keywords

Guessability study, agreement rate, methodology, statistical test, user-defined gestures, disagreement, coagreement.

ACM Classification Keywords

H.5.2 Information Interfaces and Presentation: User Interfaces—*evaluation/methodology, theory and methods.*

CHI 2015, April 18–23 2015, Seoul, Republic of Korea.

ACM 978-1-4503-3145-6/15/04...$15.00
http://dx.doi.org/10.1145/2702123.2702223

INTRODUCTION

Understanding users' preferences for interacting with computing devices empowers designers and practitioners with valuable knowledge about the predominant and popular patterns of interaction. Participatory design has a long standing as a useful set of practices to collect such knowledge by involving users into the early stages of the design process [2,13]. The symbolic input elicitation methodology of Wobbrock *et al.* [37] for conducting guessability studies is one example of a practice that has emerged from participatory design. The elicitation methodology has especially found applications for gesture set design, for which it has been widely adopted to study various gesture acquisition technologies [20,22,26,27,39], input devices [1,14,15,29,31], application domains [8,16,23,24, 32,33,34], and user groups [18,33]. These studies reported valuable insights about participants' mental models of the interaction, and compiled design recommendations informed by the observed consensus among participants.

The level of participants' consensus has been measured and reported in the literature with the agreement rate formula introduced by Wobbrock *et al.* [37]. Agreement rates compute normalized values in the $[0..1]$ interval that are reflective of user consensus, *e.g.*, A=.625 denotes the overall agreement reached by 20 participants, out of which 15 suggested proposals of one form and 5 of another (see this example discussed in [37] (p. 1871) and eq. 1 showing the sum of square ratios formula for agreement rate). Since they were introduced, agreement rates have been adopted by the community and reported in many studies [1,8,14,15,16,18,20,22,23,24,26,27, 29,31,32,33,34,39]. However, there has been no attempt up to date to examine in detail the properties of the agreement rate measure, *e.g.*, what does its probability distribution function look like?, how likely is it to observe an agreement rate of .625?, or what is the relationship between agreement and disagreement? Also, there has been no attempt to strengthen agreement analysis reporting with statistical significance tests, *e.g.*, is there a significant statistical difference between the agreement rate values .625 and .595 computed from 20 participants? [37] (p. 1871). Given the wide adoption of the elicitation methodology, we believe it is high time to investigate such aspects in detail. Consequently, we are concerned in this work with formalizing agreement analysis by providing theoretical argumentation, new measures, and a statistical test for comparing agreement rates, for which we show their usefulness on previously published elicitation data from the literature.

The contributions of this work are as follows: (1) we introduce two new measures for evaluating *disagreement rate* for referents and *coagreement rate* between referents that accompany the widely-adopted *agreement rate* measure of Wobbrock *et al.* [37] for reporting participants' consensus for symbolic input; (2) a statistical significance test for comparing agreement rates for two or multiple referents derived in analogy with Cochran's Q test statistic [5] and following the χ^2 distribution; (3) an analysis of the probability distribution of the agreement rate measure, and qualitative interpretations for agreement rates, in analogy with Cohen's guidelines for effect sizes [6]; (4) a toolkit to compute agreement rates and report the statistical significance of the effect of referents over agreement rates at p=.05, .01, and .001 levels of significance; and (5) a re-examination of several published datasets collected during elicitation studies that shows the benefits of using statistical significance tests for comparing agreement rates. We hope that these contributions will advance the current knowledge in agreement rate analysis for user elicitation studies, and will prove useful to researchers and practitioners that are in search of techniques and tools to help them understand user-elicited data at deeper levels of detail and sophistication.

RELATED WORK

We review in this section previous work concerned with conducting elicitation studies and running agreement rate analysis, and we look at development of statistical techniques and tools in the Human-Computer Interaction community.

Elicitation studies

Wobbrock *et al.* [37] introduced a general methodology for maximizing the guessability of symbolic input, which was originally evaluated on the EdgeWrite alphabets. Say a practitioner wants to design a toolbar icon for an uncommon command in a spreadsheet program he calls "Shift." He asks 20 participants to draw an icon representing this command. The command itself is called a "referent," and the drawn icons are "proposals" for that referent. The designer can judge which proposals are equivalent and which are different. How much agreement is represented among the proposals is the purpose of the agreement rate calculation. Of course, real elicitation studies tend to be concerned with more than one referent, *e.g.*, eliciting proposals for every letter of the alphabet [37].

The guessability methodology consists in computing agreement rates defined as the sum of squares of the percents of participants preferring various symbols for various referents [37] (p. 1871). Since it was introduced, agreement rate analysis gained popularity, as it has been applied to evaluate consensus between users' gesture preferences for various application domains [3,8,16,23,24,26,27,29,31,32,33,34,39]. For example, Wobbrock *et al.* [39] evaluated user agreement for single-handed and bimanual gesture interaction on tabletops. Ruiz *et al.* [27] used agreement rates to characterize users' preferences for motion gestures on mobile devices. Vatavu [32,33] and Vatavu and Zaiti [34] applied the gesture elicitation methodology to reveal viewers' gesture preferences for controlling the TV set using the remote, freehand and whole body Kinect gestures, and fine finger gestures captured by the Leap Motion controller. Piumsomboon *et al.* [24] investigated users' preferences for hand gestures to be used for augmented reality interfaces. Obaid *et al.* [23] applied the gesture elicitation methodology to derive a set of commands to control the navigation of a robot. Buchanan *et al.* [3] explored users' preferences for manipulating 3-D objects on multi-touch screens, and Liang *et al.* [16] were interested in object manipulation at a distance. Seyed *et al.* [29] and Kurdyukova *et al.* [15] elicited gestures for multi-display environments, and Kray *et al.* [14] looked at gestures that span multiple devices.

These studies reported gesture sets for various application domains and gesture acquisition technologies, as well as qualitative data (*e.g.*, users' evaluations of ease of execution and fit-to-function of proposed gestures) and insights into users' conceptual models about gesture interaction. In some cases, these studies revealed surprising results, such as users preferring different gestures than those designed by experienced designers [22], or cultural and technical experience influences on users' gesture proposals [18,27,32,39]. In fact, Morris *et al.* [21] showed in a recent work that elicitation studies are often biased by users' experience with technology, such as Windows-like graphical user interfaces (*i.e.*, the legacy bias), and suggested ways to reduce this bias.

Alternative measures to evaluate agreement

The practice of running guessability studies also led to alternative ways to evaluate agreement between participants' elicited proposals. For example, Findlater *et al.* [8] proposed a variation for Wobbrock *et al.*'s original agreement rate measure [37] that evaluates to 0 when there is no agreement at all. Morris [20] introduced two new metrics to better capture the degree of agreement between participants for experimental designs that elicit multiple proposals for the same referent from the same participant: max-consensus (*i.e.*, the percent of participants suggesting the most popular proposal for a given referent) and consensus-distinct ratio (*i.e.*, the percent of distinct proposals for a given referent). Vatavu and Zaiti [34] used Kendall's W coefficient of concordance[1] in conjunction with agreement rates, and reported similar values for a gesture elicitation study involving TV control (*i.e.*, mean agreement rate was .200 and W=.254). Chong and Gellersen [4] defined the popularity of user-defined techniques for associating wireless devices as a function of the percent of participants suggesting the technique and the number of times it occurred (p. 1564). Their measure of popularity takes values in the unit interval, *e.g.*, 1 denotes the maximum level of popularity. Vatavu [33] defined the confidence value of a referent as the maximum percent of participants that were in agreement for that referent.

Contributions to statistical analysis in HCI research

In this work, we also describe a statistical significance test for evaluating the effect of referents on agreement rates. The significance test was derived from Cochran's Q test for categorical data evaluated in terms of the success or failure of treatments [5]. Our concern for providing tools to analyze the statistical significance of experimental data is not new in the Human-Computer Interaction field of study. In fact, HCI

[1] Kendall's coefficient of concordance [12] is a normalization of the Friedman statistic used to assess the agreement between multiple raters with a number ranging between 0 (no agreement at all) and 1 (perfect agreement).

researchers have made important statistics contributions in this direction, empowering practitioners with the right tools to analyze their data resulted from complex or unconventional experimental designs [11,17,38]. For example, Wobbrock *et al.* [38] introduced the Aligned Rank Transform to assist practitioners for detecting interaction effects in nonparametric data resulted from conducting multi-factor experiments. Kaptein *et al.* [11] pointed to nonparametric techniques for analyzing data collected with Likert scales, and they provided an online tool for analyzing 2×2 mixed subject designs. Kaptein and Robertson [10] were concerned with the HCI community adopting a thorough consideration of effect size magnitudes when analyzing experimental data. Martens [17] introduced Illmo, a software application that implements log-likelihood modeling to help practitioners analyze their data in an interactive way.

AGREEMENT, DISAGREEMENT, AND COAGREEMENT

Agreement rate

The definition of an *agreement rate* for a given referent r for which feedback has been elicited from multiple participants during a guessability study was introduced by Wobbrock *et al.* [37] (p. 1871) as the following sum of square ratios:

$$A(r) = \sum_{P_i \subseteq P} \left(\frac{|P_i|}{|P|} \right)^2 \quad (1)$$

where P is the set of all proposals for referent r, $|P|$ the size of the set, and P_i subsets of identical proposals from P.

However, Wobbrock *et al.* did not provide any justification for the specific mathematical formula chosen to define agreement rate in equation 1, other than a note referring to the capability of this formula to intuitively characterize differences in agreement between various partitions of P: *"for example, in 20 proposals for referent r, if 15/20 are of one form and 5/20 are of another, there should be higher agreement than if 15/20 are of one form, 3/20 are of another, and 2/20 are of a third. Equation 1 captures this."* [37] (p. 1871).

In the following, we provide a mathematical argumentation for the agreement rate formula introduced by Wobbrock *et al.* [37] (eq. 1), and we show that two correcting factors need to be applied to its current definition. Inspired by the modified calculation formula of Findlater *et al.* [8] (p. 2680), we adopt the same definition for agreement rate as the number of pairs of participants in agreement with each other divided by the total number of pairs of participants that could be in agreement:

$$\mathcal{AR}(r) = \frac{\sum_{P_i \subseteq P} \frac{1}{2} |P_i| \left(|P_i| - 1 \right)}{\frac{1}{2} |P| \left(|P| - 1 \right)} \quad (2)$$

Note the different notation $\mathcal{AR}$ (Agreement Rate) that we use in eq. 2 to differentiate from Wobbrock *et al.*'s formula [37] (eq. 1).

☞ EXAMPLE. Let's assume a number of 20 participants, from which $|P|$=20 proposals were collected for a given referent r, out of which 15/20 are of one form and 5/20 of another, *i.e.*, $|P_1|$=15 and $|P_2|$=5. The number of pairs of participants in agreement with each other is $\frac{15 \cdot 14}{2} + \frac{5 \cdot 4}{2}$, while the total number of pairs that could have been in agreement is $\frac{20 \cdot 19}{2}$. By dividing the two values, we obtain the agreement rate $\mathcal{AR}(r) = \frac{115}{190} = .605$. By comparison, the original calculation from Wobbrock *et al.* [37] would yield $\left(\frac{15}{20}\right)^2 + \left(\frac{5}{20}\right)^2 = .625$.

The definition of eq. 2 was introduced by Findlater *et al.* [8] in their touch-screen keyboards study, but the authors did not provide the connection with Wobbrock *et al.*'s initial definition of agreement rate A [37]. In the following, we fill the gap between the two papers and show how $\mathcal{AR}(r)$ is connected to $A(r)$. We also define two new measures of agreement, *i.e.*, *disagreement* and *coagreement* that we use later in the paper to introduce a statistical significance test for agreement rate and to re-examine published data from user elicitation studies.

After successive stages of simplification of eq. 2, we obtain:

$$\begin{aligned} \mathcal{AR}(r) &= \frac{1}{|P| \left(|P| - 1 \right)} \sum_{P_i \subseteq P} \left(|P_i|^2 - |P_i| \right) \\ &= \frac{1}{|P| \left(|P| - 1 \right)} \left(\sum_{P_i \subseteq P} |P_i|^2 - \sum_{P_i \subseteq P} |P_i| \right) \end{aligned}$$

and, knowing that $\sum_{P_i \subseteq P} |P_i| = |P|$, we obtain:

$$\mathcal{AR}(r) = \frac{1}{|P| \left(|P| - 1 \right)} \sum_{P_i \subseteq P} |P_i|^2 - \frac{1}{|P| - 1}$$

We continue by placing $|P|^2$ at the denominator of the values $|P_i|^2$ under the sum $\sum_{P_i \subseteq P}$ in order to arrive at a formula resembling the one introduced by Wobbrock *et al.* [37] (eq. 1):

$$\boxed{\mathcal{AR}(r) = \frac{|P|}{|P| - 1} \sum_{P_i \subseteq P} \left(\frac{|P_i|}{|P|} \right)^2 - \frac{1}{|P| - 1}} \quad (3)$$

What we find is that eq. 3 is similar to the formula proposed by Wobbrock *et al.* [37] (eq. 1), except for two correcting factors ($\frac{|P|}{|P|-1}$ and $-\frac{1}{|P|-1}$) that depend on the number of participants or, equivalently, the number of elicited proposals $|P|$. The two correcting factors are related to the number of degrees of freedom for computing the agreement rate, *i.e.*, because the sum of all ratios $|P_i|/|P|$ equals 1, the number of observations $|P_i|/|P|$ that are free to vary is one less than the number of distinct proposals. In the following, due to the many studies that have already used $A(r)$ to report agreement between participants [1,8,14,15,16,18,20,22,23,24,26,27,29, 31,32,33,34,39], we discuss the relationship between $A(r)$ and the new definition of agreement rate $\mathcal{AR}(r)$ with the two correcting factors. The following properties characterize the differences and relationship between the two definitions:

Property #1: $\mathcal{AR}(r) \in [0..1]$**, while** $A(r) \in [1/|P|..1]$.
$\mathcal{AR}$ takes values in the entire unit interval, with 0 denoting total disagreement between participants, and 1 absolute agree-

ment. Conversely, A never equals zero, having the minimum value $1/|P|$. The justification for this was that each proposal trivially agrees with itself, so zero agreement is not possible [37] (p. 1871) (except when $|P|\to\infty$, which is a purely theoretical situation). While that may be defensible conceptually, it does not create a desirable property, which is that $\min_r\{A(r)\}$ varies with $|P|$. For example, if each of $|P|$=20 participants has a distinct proposal, $\mathcal{AR}(r)$ will evaluate at 0, and $A(r)$ at .05. If the number of participants increases to 40 and they are still all in disagreement, $\mathcal{AR}(r)$ continues to evaluate at 0, while $A(r)$=.025. From this perspective, $\mathcal{AR}$ is more consistent in reporting disagreement than A.

Property #2: $\mathcal{AR}$ conserves the relative ordering of referents delivered by A, but is less optimistic.
Equation 3 describes a linear relationship between $\mathcal{AR}$ and A and, consequently, the relative ordering of referents delivered by A is left unchanged by $\mathcal{AR}$, *i.e.*, if $A(r_1)<A(r_2)$ then also $\mathcal{AR}(r_1)<\mathcal{AR}(r_2)$ for any two referents r_1 and r_2. This property is extremely important in the context of the existing body of work reporting agreement rates [1,8,14,15,16,18,20,22,23, 24,26,27,29,31,32,33,34,39], as it conserves all the referents' ordering previously reported in the literature. However, $\mathcal{AR}$ delivers less optimistic agreement rates than A:

$$\mathcal{AR}(r) \leq A(r) \quad \text{for any referent}^2 \tag{4}$$

which can be easily verified from eq. 3 knowing that $A(r)\leq 1$, which makes $|P|\cdot A(r)-1 \leq (|P|-1)\cdot A(r)$. For example, if 15 out of all the 20 proposals elicited for r are of one form, and 5 of another, $\mathcal{AR}(r)$ evaluates at .605, while $A(r)$ computes .625. If we multiply the number of proposals by a factor of 2, *i.e.*, 30/40 proposals of one form and 10/40 of another, $\mathcal{A}(r)$ remains .625, but $\mathcal{AR}(r)$ increases to .615 showing the effect of multiple participants. It is conceptually defensible that $\mathcal{AR}(r)$ should increase under these conditions given that the same agreement ratios over more participants means greater quantities of actual agreement was achieved amidst greater possibility for disagreement. The magnitudes of the two measures become close for large $|P|$ values as $\lim_{|P|\to\infty}\frac{\mathcal{AR}(r)}{A(r)}=1$ (knowing that $\lim_{|P|\to\infty}\frac{|P|}{|P|-1}=1$ and $\lim_{|P|\to\infty}\frac{1}{|P|-1}=0$).

Disagreement rate

Using the same reasoning path, we define the *disagreement rate* between participants for a given referent r as the number of pairs of participants that are in disagreement divided by the total number of pairs of participants that could be in disagreement (*i.e.*, the case of total disagreement, where all participants' proposals for a given referent are different):

$$\mathcal{DR}(r) = \frac{\frac{1}{2}\sum_{P_i\subseteq P}|P_i|\left(|P|-|P_i|\right)}{\frac{1}{2}|P|\left(|P|-1\right)} \tag{5}$$

and, after successive simplifications, we arrive at:

$$\boxed{\mathcal{DR}(r) = -\frac{|P|}{|P|-1}\sum_{P_i\subseteq P}\left(\frac{|P_i|}{|P|}\right)^2 + \frac{|P|}{|P|-1}} \tag{6}$$

[2] With equality occuring for perfect agreement, *i.e.*, $\mathcal{AR}(r)=A(r)=1$.

☞ EXAMPLE. Following the previous example, the number of pairs of participants in disagreement with each other is $\frac{1}{2}\left(15\cdot(20-15)+5\cdot(20-5)\right)$, while the total number of pairs of participants that could have been in disagreement is $\frac{20\cdot 19}{2}$. When we divide the two values, we obtain the disagreement rate for referent r as $\mathcal{DR}(r) = \frac{75}{190} = .395$. Note how the value of the disagreement rate is complementary with respect to 1.0 to the agreement rate of referent r calculated previously, *i.e.*, $\mathcal{AR}(r) = .605$.

Coagreement rate

Prior work has established agreement rates only for individual referents in isolation. However, it would be useful to know how much agreement is shared between two referents r_1 and r_2. To this end, we define the *coagreement rate* of two referents r_1 and r_2 as the number of pairs of participants that are in agreement for both r_1 and r_2 divided by the total number of pairs of participants that could have been in agreement:

$$\boxed{\mathcal{CR}(r_1, r_2) = \frac{\sum_{i=1}^{n}\delta_{i,1}\cdot\delta_{i,2}}{n}}\;, n = \frac{1}{2}|P|\left(|P|-1\right) \tag{7}$$

where $\delta_{i,1}$ takes the value of 1 if the i-th pair of participants are in agreement for referent r_1 and 0 otherwise[3], and the same applies to $\delta_{i,2}$ and referent r_2. For notation convenience, we use the variable n to denote the number of pairs of participants. Table 1 shows in a tabular form the agreement indicators $\delta_{i,1}$ and $\delta_{i,2}$ for referents r_1 and r_2 for all pairs of participants.

☞ EXAMPLE. Let's assume that referent r_1 received 3 proposals of one form (♣) and 2 proposals of another (♦) from $|P|$=5 participants, while referent r_2 received 3 proposals of one form (♠), 1 proposal of another (♥), and 1 proposal of yet another form (✿), as shown in Table 2, left. The number of pairs of participants for which we evaluate agreement is $\frac{5\cdot 4}{2} = 10$, see Table 2, right. The agreement rates of the two referents are $\mathcal{AR}(r_1) = 4/10 = .400$ and $\mathcal{AR}(r_2) = 3/10 = .300$, while the coagreement between the two referents is $\mathcal{CR}(r_1, r_2) = 1/10 = .100$.

The coagreement rate can be generalized to k>2 referents:

$$\boxed{\mathcal{CR}(r_1, r_2, ..., r_k) = \frac{1}{n}\sum_{i=1}^{n}\prod_{j=1}^{k}\delta_{i,j}}\;, n = \frac{1}{2}|P|\left(|P|-1\right) \tag{8}$$

to characterize the degree to which pairs of participants are simultaneously in agreement for referents $\{r_1, r_2, ..., r_k\}$, $2 \leq k \leq |P|$. We refer to this measure as the *k-coagreement rate*.

A SIGNIFICANCE TEST FOR AGREEMENT RATES

We derive in this section a statistical significance test for comparing two or multiple agreement rates $\mathcal{AR}$ calculated from

[3] We adopt in this section and adapt to our problem the definition of Kronecker's delta, $\delta_{i,j}$ [9] (p. 240), which is a function of two variables i and j returning 1 if the two variables are equal and 0 otherwise, *i.e.*, $\delta_{i,j} = [i = j]$.

OBSERVATION		REFERENT		DELTAS
NO.	PAIR	r_1	r_2	$\delta_{i,1} \cdot \delta_{i,2}$
1	$(1,2)$	$\delta_{1,1}$	$\delta_{1,2}$	$\delta_{1,1} \cdot \delta_{1,2}$
2	$(1,3)$	$\delta_{2,1}$	$\delta_{2,2}$	$\delta_{2,1} \cdot \delta_{2,2}$
...	...	...	...	...
n	$(\lvert P\rvert-1, \lvert P\rvert)$	$\delta_{n,1}$	$\delta_{n,2}$	$\delta_{n,1} \cdot \delta_{n,2}$
		$n \cdot \mathcal{AR}(r_1)$	$n \cdot \mathcal{AR}(r_2)$	$n \cdot \mathcal{CR}(r_1, r_2)$

Table 1: Agreement between participants for referents r_1 and r_2 expressed using the δ notation. NOTE: $\delta_{i,1}, \delta_{i,2} \in \{0, 1\}$, 1 indicates agreement and 0 disagreement; $n = \frac{1}{2}|P|\,(|P|-1)$.

PARTICIPANT NO.	r_1	r_2
1	♣	♥
2	♦	✿
3	♣	♠
4	♣	♠
5	♦	♠

OBSERVATION		REFERENT		DELTAS
NO.	PAIR	r_1	r_2	$\delta_{i,1} \cdot \delta_{i,2}$
1	$(1,2)$	0	0	0
2	$(1,3)$	1	0	0
3	$(1,4)$	1	0	0
4	$(1,5)$	0	0	0
5	$(2,3)$	0	0	0
6	$(2,4)$	0	0	0
7	$(2,5)$	1	0	0
8	$(3,4)$	1	1	1
9	$(3,5)$	0	1	0
10	$(4,5)$	0	1	0
	TOTAL	**4**	**3**	**1**

Table 2: Agreement and coagreement rate calculation example for proposals elicited from $|P|$=5 participants for two referents r_1 and r_2 (left table). The agreements for each of the 10 pairs of participants are shown in the right table as 0/1 values.

proposals elicited from the same participants, *i.e.*, repeated measures design. Toward this goal, we formulate our problem in terms of Cochran's Q test for detecting the significance of differences between $k \geq 2$ treatments [5]. Cochran's Q is a nonparametric test for analyzing experimental designs for which the outcome is a binary variable indicating the success or failure of an observation under a given treatment. For our problem, each referent $r_{i(=1..k)}$ represents a distinct treatment, for which we evaluate its success as whether agreement between participants was reached or not. Therefore, we have $n = \frac{1}{2}|P|(|P|-1)$ observations resulting from $|P|$ subjects having participated in the guessability study that we arrange in a tabular form following Cochran's method [5] (p. 257), see Table 3.

The null and alternative hypotheses for agreement rates are:

H_0: ALL REFERENTS HAVE EQUAL AGREEMENT RATES.
H_a: THERE IS A DIFFERENCE AMONG THE AGREEMENT RATES OF THE $k \geq 2$ REFERENTS.

With the notations employed in Table 3, the statistic employed by Cochran's Q test [5] (p. 266) is:

$$k(k-1)\frac{\sum_{j=1}^{k}\left(T_j - \frac{T}{k}\right)^2}{\sum_{i=1}^{n} R_i\,(k - R_i)}$$

which we successively adapt to the specifics of our problem by expressing it in terms of agreement and coagreement rates.

OBSERVATION		REFERENT				TOTAL
NO.	PAIR	r_1	r_2	...	r_k	TOTAL
1	$(1,1)$	$\delta_{1,1}$	$\delta_{1,2}$	...	$\delta_{1,k}$	R_1
2	$(1,2)$	$\delta_{2,1}$	$\delta_{2,2}$	...	$\delta_{2,k}$	R_2
...	...	...	...	...	...	...
n	$(n-1, n)$	$\delta_{n,1}$	$\delta_{n,2}$	...	$\delta_{n,k}$	R_n
	TOTAL	T_1	T_2	...	T_k	T

Table 3: Agreement between pairs of participants for $k \geq 2$ referents arranged in a tabular form. NOTE: $\delta_{i,j}$ take values 1 and 0, encoding whether the i-th pair is in agreement for referent r_j or not. T_j represents the sum of column j, R_i the sum of row i, and T the grand total of $\delta_{i,j}$; $n = \frac{1}{2}|P|\,(|P|-1)$.

The result is the V_{rd} statistic[4] (see Appendix A for the mathematical details of the calculation procedure):

$$V_{rd} = (k-1)n \cdot \frac{\sum_{j=1}^{k} \mathcal{AR}^2(r_j) - \frac{1}{k}\left(\sum_{j=1}^{k} \mathcal{AR}(r_j)\right)^2}{\sum_{j=1}^{k} \mathcal{AR}(r_j) - \frac{1}{k}\sum_{t=1}^{k}\sum_{s=1}^{k} \mathcal{CR}(r_t, r_s)} \quad (9)$$

For the case of comparing two agreement rates only (*i.e.*, $k = 2$), this formula simplifies to[5]:

$$V_{rd} = n \cdot \frac{\left(\mathcal{AR}(r_1) - \mathcal{AR}(r_2)\right)^2}{\mathcal{AR}(r_1) + \mathcal{AR}(r_2) - 2 \cdot \mathcal{CR}(r_1, r_2)} \quad (10)$$

where $n = \frac{|P|(|P|-1)}{2}$ is the number of pairs of participants.

Cochran showed that the limiting distribution of the Q statistic (under the assumption that the probability of success is the same in all samples) is χ^2 with $k-1$ degrees of freedom [5] (p. 259). Therefore, the null hypothesis H_0 is rejected at the p level if the statistic is larger than the $1-p$ quantile of χ^2:

$$\text{Reject } H_0 \text{ if } V_{rd} > \chi^2_{1-p,k-1} \quad (11)$$

For example, the critical values for 1 degrees of freedom (*i.e.*, two referents) are 3.84 and 6.63 for p=.05 and p=.01, respectively, and 7.81 and 11.34 for 3 degrees of freedom (*i.e.*, four referents). For convenience, Appendix B lists the critical values of the χ^2 distribution at the p=.05, p=.01, and p=.001 levels of significance up to 48 degrees of freedom. In the case in which the null hypothesis is rejected for $k>2$ referents, post-hoc tests can run using equation 10 but, in this case, the Bonferroni correction needs to be applied [36] (p. 261).

Testing for significance against zero

Our statistical test can also be employed to assess whether $\mathcal{AR}(r)$ is significantly greater than 0. To do that, we compare participants' agreement for referent r versus the case of absolute disagreement, which corresponds to a virtual referent $r^\star$, for which all participants would provide different proposals and, therefore, $\mathcal{AR}(r^\star)$=0. We then use the values of $\mathcal{AR}(r)$

[4] Notation V in V_{rd} stands for the *variation* between agreement rates, and the subscript rd denotes a *repeated* measures *design*.

[5] For k=2 conditions, it is customary to use McNemar's test [19]. However, McNemar's test and Cochran's Q for k=2 are equivalent [30] (p. 876).

and $\mathcal{AR}(r^{\star})$ under equation 10, which simplifies to:

$$V^{\star}_{rd} = \frac{|P| \cdot (|P| - 1)}{2} \cdot \mathcal{AR}(r) \qquad (12)$$

and decide whether to reject or not the null hypothesis (eq. 11).

☞ EXAMPLE. Let's assume referent r_1 received four distinct proposals from $|P|$=12 participants with frequencies $\{4, 4, 3, 1\}$; referent r_2 received two distinct proposals, $\{10, 2\}$; and referent r_3 received three distinct proposals, $\{5, 5, 2\}$. The agreement rates for the three referents are: $\mathcal{AR}(r_1)$=.227, $\mathcal{AR}(r_2)$=.697, and $\mathcal{AR}(r_3)$=.318. Coagreement rates are: $\mathcal{CR}(r_1, r_2)$=.152, $\mathcal{CR}(r_1, r_3)$=.045, and $\mathcal{CR}(r_2, r_3)$=.197. The V_{rd} statistic (eq. 9) is 28.964, which is significant at the p=.001 level, as indicated by the critical value for the χ^2 distribution with 3−1=2 degrees of freedom (see Appendix B). If we want to further test whether the agreement rates of pairs of referents (r_1, r_2) and (r_2, r_3) are significantly different at p=.05, we compute the statistic for these pairs (either with equation 9 or 10). The values of the V_{rd} statistic are 23.515 and 15.266 respectively, both significant at p=.001, which is below the Bonferroni corrected value of p=.05/2=.025. Furthermore, $\mathcal{AR}(r_1)$=.227 is significantly greater than 0 at p=.001 as $V^{\star}_{rd}$=14.98, which is above the critical value of 10.83 of the χ^2 distribution with 1 degree of freedom.

TOOLKIT FOR COMPUTING STATISTICAL SIGNIFICANCE TESTS FOR AGREEMENT RATES

To make computation of agreement rates and p values easy, we provide the AGATE tool (AGreement Analysis Toolkit), see Figure 1. The toolkit reads data organized in a matrix format so that each referent occupies one column, and each participant occupies one row. AGATE computes agreement, disagreement, and coagreement rates for selected referents, and reports significant effects of selected referents over agreement rates at p = .05, .01, and .001 levels of significance. The tool was implemented in C# using the .NET 4.5 framework, and is freely available to use and download at **http://depts.washington.edu/aimgroup/proj/dollar/agate.html**.

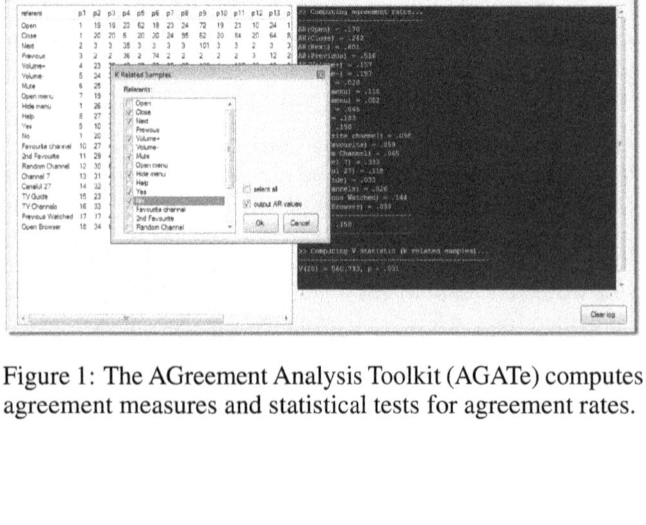

Figure 1: The AGreement Analysis Toolkit (AGATe) computes agreement measures and statistical tests for agreement rates.

CASE STUDIES

In this section, we briefly re-examine previously published data from several elicitation studies [1,24,25,34] from the perspective of our new measures. Our purpose is to show the utility of these measures and statistical test for characterizing user-elicited data in more depth. We do not attempt to be all-encompassing in our analysis, but instead our goal is to show how our measures can be employed on actual data. To this end, we pick a specific finding reported by the authors of each study, on which we then elaborate with our new measures.

Bailly *et al.* [1] (CHI '13)

In this study, 20 participants proposed gestures for 42 referents for the Metamorphé keyboard (A=.409, $\mathcal{AR}$=.336). Using our statistical test, we found an overall significant effect of referent type on agreement rate ($V_{rd(41,N=840)}$=1466.818, p<.001). Moreover, targeted statistical testing revealed more findings about users' agreement. For example, Bailly *et al.* [1] reported that *"highly directional commands (e.g., Align Left) tended to have a high gesture agreement"* (p. 567). Indeed, they did (average $\mathcal{AR}$=.809), but we also detected a significant effect of the direction of alignment (*i.e.*, left, right, bottom, and top) on the resulting agreement ($V_{rd(3,N=80)}$=121.737, p=.001), no significant difference between *Align Left* and *Align Right* (both .900), and significantly higher agreement for *Align Bottom* than for *Align Top* (.805 versus .632). To understand more, we ran coagreement analysis. The coagreement rate between *Align Left* and *Align Right* was .900, showing that all the pairs of participants that were in agreement for *Align Left* were also in agreement for *Align Right*. The coagreement between *Align Top* and *Align Bottom* was .632, indicating that all the pairs of participants in agreement for *Align Top* ($\mathcal{AR}$=.632) were also in agreement for *Align Bottom* ($\mathcal{AR}$=.900), but there were also pairs of participants that agreed on *Align Bottom* and not on *Align Top*. The k-coagreement for all the four referents was $\mathcal{CR}$=.632, showing that all participants in agreement for *Align Top* were also in agreement for the other three referents, but also that only 70% of all pairs that were in agreement for instance for *Align Left* and *Align Right* were also in agreement for *Align Bottom* and *Align Top*. Informed by these findings, the designer can now take a second, informed look at participants' proposals to understand what made the same participants agree on *Align Bottom*, but disagree on *Align Top*, for example.

Piumsomboon *et al.* [24,25] (CHI '13 and INTERACT '13)

In these studies, 20 participants proposed freehand gestures for 40 referents related to interacting with augmented reality (A=.446, $\mathcal{AR}$=.417). Using the V_{rd} test statistic, we found an overall significant effect of referent type on agreement rates ($V_{rd(39,N=800)}$=3523.962, p<.001). There were 8 referents that received high (*i.e.*, .900 and 1.000) agreement rates, and we found a significant effect of referent type over agreement rate for this subset as well ($V_{rd(7,N=160)}$=106.176, p<.001). There were 10 referents that received agreement rates below .100 ($V_{rd(9,N=200)}$=11.033, $n.s.$). Using our additional measures, we can elaborate more on some of the authors' findings. For example, the authors noted that *"we defined similar gestures as gestures that were identical or having consistent directionality although the gesture had been performed with different static hand poses. For example, in the Previous and Next tasks, participants used an open hand, an index finger, or two fingers to swipe from left to right or viceversa"* [24] (p. 958). This decision is a reasonable one, but we can now use coagreement rates to find out whether it was the same participants that used hand poses consistently or whether participants also varied their hand poses with the referent type. This investigation is important, because the authors also noted in a follow-up paper that *"variants of a single hand pose were often used across multiple participants, and sometimes even by a single participant"* [25] (p. 296). We found that coagreement equaled the agreement of the two referents ($\mathcal{CR}$=.489, $\mathcal{AR}$=.489 for *Previous* and *Next*) when we considered different hand poses as different gestures, which means that the same participants that were in agreement for *Previous* were also in agreement for *Next* and, even more, they kept their hand pose preference across the two referents. However, we found less consistency for other referents. For example, agreement rates for *Rotate-X-axis*, *Rotate-Y-axis*, and *Rotate-Z-axis* were .247, .263, and .258, while coagreements were less ($\mathcal{CR}(X,Y)$=.179, $\mathcal{CR}(X,Z)$=.153, $\mathcal{CR}(Y,Z)$=.174), showing that not all pairs of participants that agreed on rotating on the X axis necessarily agreed on the other axes as well. In fact, the coagreement rate for all three referents was .126, showing that only 70% of all pairs in agreement for *rotate-X-axis* and *rotate-Y-axis* also agreed on *rotate-Z-axis*. These results can inform further investigation into what made participants change their proposals for these referents.

Vatavu and Zaiti [32] (TVX '14)

In this study, 18 participants proposed freehand gestures to control 21 functions on Smart TVs. The authors found low agreement among participants (A=.200 and $\mathcal{AR}$=.170), explained by the many degrees of freedom of the human hand. Using our tool, we found a significant effect of referent type on agreement rate ($V_{rd(20,N=378)}$=560.793, p<.001). Vatavu and Zaiti [34] reported that *"when encountering referents with opposite effects (e.g., Next and Previous channel, Volume up and Volume down), most participants considered gestures should also be similar."* Our post-hoc tests revealed interesting findings for dichotomous referents. For example, the highest agreement rates were obtained for *Go to Next Channel* and *Go to Previous Channel* (.601 and .516), for which participants proposed hand movements to left and right, but we found a significant difference between the two ($V_{rd(1,N=36)}$=4.568, p<.05). Coagreement analysis showed that not all participants that were in agreement for *Next* were also in agreement for *Previous* ($\mathcal{CR}$=.436). When analyzing the other dichotomous referents, we found more agreement for *Open Menu* than for *Hide Menu* (.118 versus .052, $V_{rd(1,N=36)}$=4.454, p<.05), and nonsignificant differences between the agreement rates for *Volume Up* and *Volume Down* (.157 and .157, $\mathcal{CR}$=.157, showing that all the participants that agreed on *Volume Up* also agreed on *Volume Down*), and *Yes* and *No* (.183 and .150, with low coagreement $\mathcal{CR}$=.046, showing that participants that were in agreement for *Yes* were not also the ones that were in agreement for *No*). Overall, there were eight referents with agreement rates below .100, for which we did not detect significant differences ($V_{rd(7,N=144)}$=7.248, $n.s.$), suggesting the same low level of consensus for these referents.

DISCUSSION

In this section, we compare the agreement rate $\mathcal{AR}$ formula with Wobbrock *et al.*'s original A measure [37]. We also present the probability distribution function of $\mathcal{AR}$, and discuss the connection between agreement and disagreement.

The probability distribution function of $\mathcal{AR}$

Figure 2 shows the probability distribution function of $\mathcal{AR}$ that we generated by enumerating all the partitions of the integer $|P|$, which are distinct ways to write $|P|$ as a sum of positive integers, for which the order of the summands is not important [28]. For example, there are 11 distinct ways to write $|P| = 6$ as a sum of positive integers or, equivalently, the ratio $6/6$ as a sum of ratios for which the denominator is 6; see Table 4. We computed the associated agreement rates of these partitions that we binned into 100 equal intervals of $[0..1]$, and counted their frequencies (*e.g.*, the value .200 appears with frequency 2 in Table 4). The result was a discrete version of the probability function of $\mathcal{AR}$.

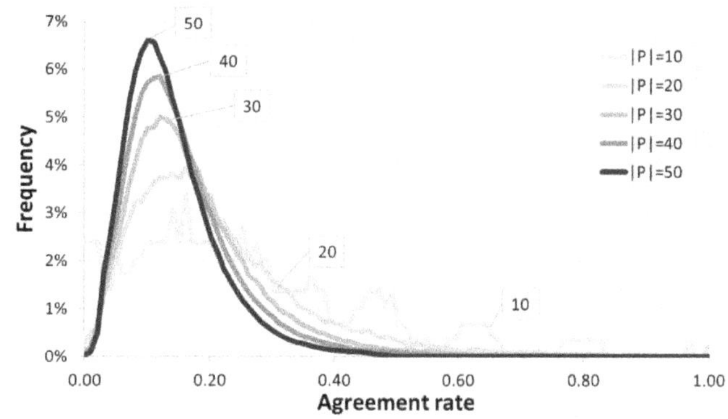

Figure 2: Probability distribution functions of $\mathcal{AR}$ computed[4] for various numbers of participants $|P|$ from 10 to 50.

When we analyze the distribution shown in Figure 2, we find that the cumulative probability of 90% is reached for $\mathcal{AR}\leq$.374, while a cumulative 99% is reached for $\mathcal{AR}\leq$.636 and $|P|$=20 participants. As the number of participants increases, there is a shift in the peak of the probability distribution toward lower values, *e.g.*, 90% cumulative probability is reached for $\mathcal{AR}\leq$.222 and 99% for $\mathcal{AR}\leq$.424 for $|P|$=50 participants. These values may seem low, but remember that we assumed each partition equally probable when we generated the probability distribution function. In the practice of guessability studies, this assumption may not hold for all referents, because some of the referents may trigger the same response from multiple participants simply due to participants' shared experience in a given field, *i.e.*, the legacy bias [21]. However, these probability distributions reflect very well current findings in the literature. For example, the average agreement rate A reported by Wobbrock *et al.* [39] for single-handed tabletop gestures is .320 (the corrected $\mathcal{AR}$ for 20 participants is .284);

[5] To compensate for the low resolution obtained for the probability distributions when bining frequencies into 100 bins at small $|P|$ values (*e.g.*, there are only 42 distinct possibilities to write $|P| = 10$ as a sum of positive integers, and 627 possibilities for $|P| = 20$), all resulted frequencies were smoothed with a central moving average using a window of size 7.

No.	Partition	$\mathcal{AR}(r)$
1	$\frac{6}{6}=\frac{1}{6}+\frac{1}{6}+\frac{1}{6}+\frac{1}{6}+\frac{1}{6}+\frac{1}{6}$	.000
2	$\frac{6}{6}=\frac{1}{6}+\frac{1}{6}+\frac{1}{6}+\frac{1}{6}+\frac{2}{6}$	.067
3	$\frac{6}{6}=\frac{1}{6}+\frac{1}{6}+\frac{1}{6}+\frac{3}{6}$	.200
4	$\frac{6}{6}=\frac{1}{6}+\frac{1}{6}+\frac{2}{6}+\frac{2}{6}$	.133
5	$\frac{6}{6}=\frac{1}{6}+\frac{1}{6}+\frac{4}{6}$	.400
6	$\frac{6}{6}=\frac{1}{6}+\frac{2}{6}+\frac{3}{6}$	.267
7	$\frac{6}{6}=\frac{1}{6}+\frac{5}{6}$	.667
8	$\frac{6}{6}=\frac{2}{6}+\frac{2}{6}+\frac{2}{6}$	.200
9	$\frac{6}{6}=\frac{2}{6}+\frac{4}{6}$	.467
10	$\frac{6}{6}=\frac{3}{6}+\frac{3}{6}$	.400
11	$\frac{6}{6}=\frac{6}{6}$	1.000

Table 4: All the 11 distinct partitions of the fraction 6/6 into sums of fractions of positive integers with denominator 6, and their associated agreement rate values.

the average rate of Ruiz *et al.* [27] for motion gestures is .260 (corrected $\mathcal{AR}$ for 20 participants is .221). Table 5 shows more average agreement rate values, all below .450.

Study	Condition	$\lvert P \rvert$	A	$\mathcal{AR}$
Bailly *et al.* [1]	Metamorphé	20	.406†	.336
Buchanan *et al.* [3]	3-D objects	14	.468†	.430
Liang *et al.* [16]	3-D objects	12	.182†	.108
Obaid *et al.* [23]	robot navigation	35	.230†	.207
Piumsomboon *et al.* [24]	augmented reality	20	.446†	.417
Pyryeskin *et al.* [26]	above the surface	16	.230	.179
Ruiz *et al.* [27]	mobile devices	20	.260†	.221
Seyed *et al.* [29]	multi-displays	17	.160	.108
Valdes *et al.* [31]	horizontal surface	19	.244	.202
Valdes *et al.* [31]	vertical surface	19	.254	.213
Vatavu [32]	TV (Kinect)	12	.415	.362
Vatavu [33]	TV (Wii)	20	.430	.400
Vatavu [33]	TV (Kinect)	20	.330	.295
Vatavu and Zaiti [34]	TV (Leap Motion)	18	.200	.170
Weigel *et al.* [35]	skin as input	22	.250†	.214
Wobbrock *et al.* [37]	EdgeWrite alphabet	20	.349	.315
Wobbrock *et al.* [39]	tabletop (1-hand)	20	.320	.284
Wobbrock *et al.* [39]	tabletop (2-hands)	20	.280	.242

† The authors did not report the average agreement rate, so we calculated (or approximated) it from the individual agreement rates reported in these papers.

Table 5: Average agreement rates A reported in the literature and corrected $\mathcal{AR}$ values. Note how the average $\mathcal{AR}$ values of these studies are less than .450 (compare with Figure 2).

Relationship between agreement and disagreement rates

It is interesting to see how agreement rate $\mathcal{AR}(r)$ compares with the disagreement rate $\mathcal{DR}(r)$ for a given referent r, knowing that the two are complementary with respect to 1, *i.e.*, $\mathcal{AR}(r)+\mathcal{DR}(r)=1$. This equation tells us that there is more agreement than disagreement for referent r if $\mathcal{AR}(r) > .500$. Figure 2 informs us that the probability of obtaining an agreement rate of this magnitude is less than 1% (under the hypothesis of equal chance partitions, see above) and, consequently, for most referents, participants are more likely to be in disagreement than in agreement (see Table 5). Another way to visualize the relationship between agreement and disagreement is to compute their ratio:

$$\frac{\mathcal{AR}(r)}{\mathcal{DR}(r)} = \frac{\mathcal{AR}(r)}{1-\mathcal{AR}(r)} \quad (13)$$

that takes values between 0 (*i.e.*, no agreement) and ∞ (absolute agreement). Figure 3 shows the values of this ratio. Informed by these results, the average agreement rates reported in the literature [3,16,23,24,26,27,29,31,32,33,39], and inspired by Cohen's guidelines for effect sizes [7], we propose qualitative interpretations for agreement rates, see Table 6.

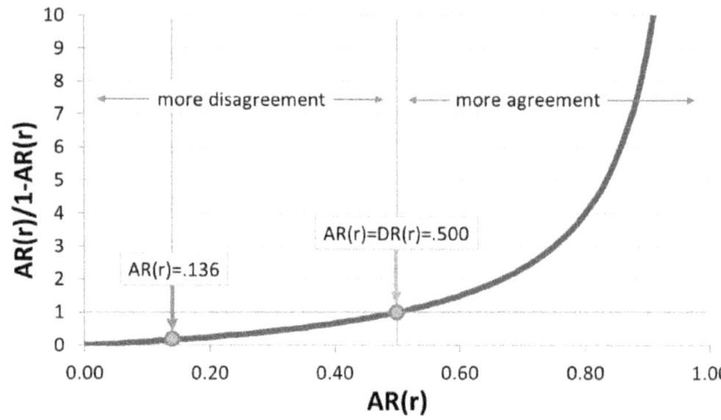

Figure 3: Relationship between agreement and disagreement rates for any referent r. Note the *theoretical* mid-point of .500 for which agreement and disagreement rates are equal, as well as the *expected* value of .136 for $\mathcal{AR}(r)$ (computed as the average of all possible agreement rate values, weighted by their probability of occurrence, according to Figure 2).

$\mathcal{AR}(r)$ Interval	Probability †	Interpretation
≤.100	22.9%	*low* agreement
.100 – .300	59.1%	*medium* agreement
.300 – .500	14.1%	*high* agreement
>.500	3.9%	*very high* agreement

† According to the probability distribution functions shown in Figure 2 and $\lvert P \rvert = 20$ participants.

Table 6: Margins for interpreting the magnitude of agreement.

CONCLUSION

We introduced in this paper new measures, a statistical test, and a companion toolkit to assist researchers and practitioners with agreement rate analysis of user-elicited data collected during guessability studies. We showed the benefits of our measures and toolkit by re-examining some published data in the literature. Further work will address new useful aspects for reporting agreement rates, such as confidence intervals, and new ways to distill agreement and coagreement into a single measure to facilitate analysis of users' consensus. We hope the contributions of this work will provide researchers and practitioners with a solid foundation for analyzing and interpreting agreement rate data and, consequently, will lead to improved user interface designs informed by more careful and in-depth examination of user-elicited data.

ACKNOWLEDGMENTS

The authors would like to thank Gilles Bailly and Thammathip Piumsomboon as well as their co-authors from [1,24,25] for kindly providing access to their gesture elicitation data. This research was conducted under the project Mobile@Old, ref. 315/2014 (PN-II-PT-PCCA-2013-4-2241), financed by MEN-UEFISCDI, Romania.

REFERENCES

1. Bailly, G., Pietrzak, T., Deber, J., and Wigdor, D. J. Métamorphe: Augmenting hotkey usage with actuated keys. In *Proc. of CHI '13*, ACM (2013), 563–572.
2. Bergvall-Kåreborn, B., and Ståhlbrost, A. Participatory design: One step back or two steps forward? In *Proc. of PDC '08*, Indiana University (2008), 102–111.
3. Buchanan, S., Floyd, B., Holderness, W., and LaViola, J. J. Towards user-defined multi-touch gestures for 3D objects. In *Proc. of ITS '13*, ACM (2013), 231–240.
4. Chong, M. K., and Gellersen, H. W. How groups of users associate wireless devices. In *Proc. of CHI '13*, ACM (2013), 1559–1568.
5. Cochran, W. G. The comparison of percentages in matched samples. *Biometrika 37*, 3/4 (1950), 256–266.
6. Cohen, J. A coefficient of agreement for nominal scales. 37–46.
7. Cohen, J. A power primer. *Psychological Bulletin 112*, 1 (1992), 155–159.
8. Findlater, L., Lee, B., and Wobbrock, J. Beyond QWERTY: Augmenting touch screen keyboards with multi-touch gestures for non-alphanumeric input. In *Proc. of CHI '12*, ACM (2012), 2679–2682.
9. James, R. C. *The Mathematics Dictionary, 5th Ed.* Chapman & Hall, New York, 1992.
10. Kaptein, M., and Robertson, J. Rethinking statistical analysis methods for CHI. In *Proc. of CHI '12*, ACM (2012), 1105–1114.
11. Kaptein, M. C., Nass, C., and Markopoulos, P. Powerful and consistent analysis of likert-type ratingscales. In *Proc. of CHI '10*, ACM (2010), 2391–2394.
12. Kendall, M. G., and Babington Smith, B. The problem of m rankings. *Annals of Math. Stats. 10*, 3 (1939), 275–287.
13. Kensing, F., and Blomberg, J. Participatory design: Issues and concerns. *Computer Supported Cooperative Work 7*, 3-4 (Jan. 1998), 167–185.
14. Kray, C., Nesbitt, D., Dawson, J., and Rohs, M. User-defined gestures for connecting mobile phones, public displays, and tabletops. In *Proc. of MobileHCI '10*, ACM (2010), 239–248.
15. Kurdyukova, E., Redlin, M., and André, E. Studying user-defined ipad gestures for interaction in multi-display environment. In *Proc. of UI '12*, ACM (2012), 93–96.
16. Liang, H.-N., Williams, C., Semegen, M., Stuerzlinger, W., and Irani, P. User-defined surface+motion gestures for 3D manipulation of objects at a distance through a mobile device. In *Proc. of APCHI '12*, ACM (2012), 299–308.
17. Martens, J.-B. Interactive statistics with illmo. *ACM Trans. Interact. Intell. Syst. 4*, 1 (Apr. 2014), 4:1–4:28.
18. Mauney, D., Howarth, J., Wirtanen, A., and Capra, M. Cultural similarities and differences in user-defined gestures for touchscreen user interfaces. In *Proc. of CHI EA '10*, ACM (2010), 4015–4020.
19. McNemar, Q. Note on the sampling error of the difference between correlated proportions or percentages. *Psychometrika 12*, 2 (June 1947), 153–157.
20. Morris, M. R. Web on the wall: Insights from a multimodal interaction elicitation study. In *Proc. of ITS '12*, ACM (2012), 95–104.
21. Morris, M. R., Danielescu, A., Drucker, S., Fisher, D., Lee, B., schraefel, m. c., and Wobbrock, J. O. Reducing legacy bias in gesture elicitation studies. *Interactions 21*, 3 (May 2014), 40–45.
22. Morris, M. R., Wobbrock, J. O., and Wilson, A. D. Understanding users' preferences for surface gestures. In *Proc. of GI '10*, Canadian Inf. Proc.Soc. (2010), 261–268.
23. Obaid, M., Häring, M., Kistler, F., Bühling, R., and André, E. User-defined body gestures for navigational control of a humanoid robot. In *Proc. of ICSR'12*, Springer-Verlag (2012), 367–377.
24. Piumsomboon, T., Clark, A., Billinghurst, M., and Cockburn, A. User-defined gestures for augmented reality. In *Proc. of CHI EA '13*, ACM (2013), 955–960.
25. Piumsomboon, T., Clark, A., Billinghurst, M., and Cockburn, A. User-defined gestures for augmented reality. In *Proc. of INTERACT '13*, Springer (2013), 282–299.
26. Pyryeskin, D., Hancock, M., and Hoey, J. Comparing elicited gestures to designer-created gestures for selection above a multitouch surface. In *Proc. of ITS '12*, ACM (2012), 1–10.
27. Ruiz, J., Li, Y., and Lank, E. User-defined motion gestures for mobile interaction. In *Proc. of CHI '11*, ACM (2011), 197–206.
28. Sedgewick, R. Permutation generation methods. *ACM Computing Surveys 9*, 2 (June 1977), 137–164.
29. Seyed, T., Burns, C., Costa Sousa, M., Maurer, F., and Tang, A. Eliciting usable gestures for multi-display environments. In *Proc. of ITS '12*, ACM (2012), 41–50.
30. Sheskin, D. J. *Handbook of Parametric and Nonparametric Statistical Procedures: Third Edition.* CRC Press, 2004.
31. Valdes, C., Eastman, D., Grote, C., Thatte, S., Shaer, O., Mazalek, A., Ullmer, B., and Konkel, M. K. Exploring the design space of gestural interaction with active tokens through user-defined gestures. In *Proc. of CHI '14*, ACM (2014), 4107–4116.
32. Vatavu, R.-D. User-defined gestures for free-hand TV control. In *Proc. of EuroiTV '12*, ACM (2012), 45–48.
33. Vatavu, R.-D. A comparative study of user-defined handheld vs. freehand gestures for home entertainment environments. *Journal of Ambient Intelligence and Smart Environments 5*, 2 (2013), 187–211.
34. Vatavu, R.-D., and Zaiti, I.-A. Leap gestures for TV: Insights from an elicitation study. In *Proc. of TVX '14*, ACM (2014), 131–138.
35. Weigel, M., Mehta, V., and Steimle, J. More than touch: Understanding how people use skin as an input surface for mobile computing. In *Proc. of CHI '14*, ACM (2014), 179–188.

df	*p*=.05	*p*=.01	*p*=.001	*df*	*p*=.05	*p*=.01	*p*=.001	*df*	*p*=.05	*p*=.01	*p*=.001	*df*	*p*=.05	*p*=.01	*p*=.001
1	3.84	6.64	10.83	13	22.36	27.69	34.53	25	37.65	44.31	52.62	37	52.19	59.89	69.35
2	5.99	9.21	13.82	14	23.69	29.14	36.12	26	38.89	45.64	54.05	38	53.38	61.16	70.70
3	7.82	11.35	16.27	15	25.00	30.58	37.70	27	40.11	46.96	55.48	39	54.57	62.43	72.06
4	9.49	13.28	18.47	16	26.30	32.00	39.25	28	41.34	48.28	56.89	40	55.76	63.69	73.40
5	11.07	15.09	20.52	17	27.59	33.41	40.79	29	42.56	49.59	58.30	41	56.94	64.95	74.75
6	12.59	16.81	22.46	18	28.87	34.81	42.31	30	43.77	50.89	59.70	42	58.12	66.21	76.08
7	14.07	18.48	24.32	19	30.14	36.19	43.82	31	44.99	52.19	61.10	43	59.30	67.46	77.42
8	15.51	20.09	26.13	20	31.41	37.57	45.32	32	46.19	53.49	62.49	44	60.48	68.71	78.75
9	16.92	21.67	27.88	21	32.67	38.93	46.80	33	47.40	54.78	63.87	45	61.66	69.96	80.08
10	18.31	23.21	29.59	22	33.92	40.29	48.27	34	48.60	56.06	65.25	46	62.83	71.20	81.40
11	19.68	24.73	31.26	23	35.17	41.64	49.73	35	49.80	57.34	66.62	47	64.00	72.44	82.72
12	21.03	26.22	32.91	24	36.42	42.98	51.18	36	51.00	58.62	67.99	48	65.17	73.68	84.04

Table 7: Critical values of the χ^2 distribution for $p = .05$, .01, and .001 levels of significance up to 48 degrees of freedom.

36. Weisstein, E. W. *CRC Concise Encyclopedia of Mathematics, 2nd Ed.* Chapman & Hall, New York, 2003.
37. Wobbrock, J. O., Aung, H. H., Rothrock, B., and Myers, B. A. Maximizing the guessability of symbolic input. In *Proc. of CHI EA '05*, ACM (2005), 1869–1872.
38. Wobbrock, J. O., Findlater, L., Gergle, D., and Higgins, J. J. The aligned rank transform for nonparametric factorial analyses using only anova procedures. In *Proc. of CHI '11*, ACM (2011), 143–146.
39. Wobbrock, J. O., Morris, M. R., and Wilson, A. D. User-defined gestures for surface computing. In *Proc. of CHI '09*, ACM (2009), 1083–1092.

APPENDIX A: TEST STATISTIC FOR REPEATED MEASURES

We start with Cochran's Q test formula (see Table 3 for the notations we employ and their relation to agreement rates):

$$k(k-1)\cdot\frac{\sum_{j=1}^{k}\left(T_j-\frac{T}{k}\right)^2}{\sum_{i=1}^{n}R_i\,(k-R_i)} \qquad (14)$$

We adapt this formula to our problem by expressing it in terms of agreement and coagreement rates.

The sum at the numerator of eq. 14 can be written as:

$$\sum_{j=1}^{k}(T_j)^2-2\frac{T}{k}\underbrace{\sum_{j=1}^{k}T_j}_{T}+\sum_{j=1}^{k}\left(\frac{T}{k}\right)^2=\sum_{j=1}^{k}(T_j)^2-\frac{T^2}{k}$$

and, knowing that $T_j = n\cdot\mathcal{AR}(r_j)$ and $T=\sum_{j=1}^{k}T_j$:

$$= n^2\sum_{j=1}^{k}\mathcal{AR}^2(r_j)-\frac{n^2}{k}\left(\sum_{j=1}^{k}\mathcal{AR}(r_j)\right)^2$$

The sum at the denominator of eq. 14 can be written as:

$$\sum_{i=1}^{n}R_i\,(k-R_i) = k\underbrace{\sum_{i=1}^{n}R_i}_{T}-\sum_{i=1}^{n}(R_i)^2=kT-\sum_{i=1}^{n}(R_i)^2$$

$$= kT-\sum_{i=1}^{n}\left(\sum_{t=1}^{k}\delta_{i,t}\right)^2$$

$$= kT-\sum_{i=1}^{n}\left(\sum_{t=1}^{k}\sum_{s=1}^{k}\delta_{i,t}\cdot\delta_{i,s}\right)$$

$$= kT-\sum_{t=1}^{k}\sum_{s=1}^{k}\underbrace{\left(\sum_{i=1}^{n}\delta_{i,t}\cdot\delta_{i,s}\right)}_{n\cdot\mathcal{CR}(r_t,r_s)}$$

$$= kn\sum_{j=1}^{k}\mathcal{AR}(r_j)-n\sum_{t=1}^{k}\sum_{s=1}^{k}\mathcal{CR}(r_t,r_s)$$

The agreement rate test statistic can then be described solely in terms of agreement and coagreement rates between the k referents, as follows:

$$k(k-1)\cdot\frac{n^2\sum_{j=1}^{k}\mathcal{AR}^2(r_j)-\frac{n^2}{k}\left(\sum_{j=1}^{k}\mathcal{AR}(r_j)\right)^2}{kn\sum_{j=1}^{k}\mathcal{AR}(r_j)-n\sum_{t=1}^{k}\sum_{s=1}^{k}\mathcal{CR}(r_t,r_s)}$$

and, after simplification by $k\cdot n$:

$$(k-1)n\cdot\frac{\sum_{j=1}^{k}\mathcal{AR}^2(r_j)-\frac{1}{k}\left(\sum_{j=1}^{k}\mathcal{AR}(r_j)\right)^2}{\sum_{j=1}^{k}\mathcal{AR}(r_j)-\frac{1}{k}\sum_{t=1}^{k}\sum_{s=1}^{k}\mathcal{CR}(r_t,r_s)}$$

where $n=\frac{1}{2}|P|\,(|P|-1)$.

APPENDIX B: CRITICAL VALUES OF THE CHI-SQUARE DISTRIBUTION

For convenience, Table 7 lists the critical values of the χ^2 distribution for p=.05, .01, and .001 significance levels for 1 to 48 degrees of freedom.

Exploring the Effect of Pre-operational Priming Intervention on Number Entry Errors

Yunqiu Li
Computer Science Department
Swansea University, UK
Yunqiu.Li@swansea.ac.uk

Patrick Oladimeji
Computer Science Department
Swansea University, UK
P.Oladimeji@Swansea.ac.uk

Harold Thimbleby
Computer Science Department
Swansea University, UK
Harold@thimbleby.net

ABSTRACT
Managing and reducing error in number entry tasks is important, especially in safety critical contexts. Understanding factors that can affect number entry accuracy could help the design of more dependable systems. We present three interventions for number entry tasks, inspired by known priming effects (where exposure to prior stimuli can impact task performance). The interventions were questions for the operator to answer before entering each number. Questions related to the value/size of the number, its structure, and the context of the number entry task respectively. Results of a within-subject study show that although there was no significant difference amongst performance across interventions, all three interventions helped to improve the accuracy of number entry by reducing entry errors (by up to 40.8%) and unnoticed errors (by up to 60.7%). These are impressive gains and suggest the importance of more work in this area.

Author Keywords
Number entry; error reduction

ACM Classification Keywords
H.5.2. Information interfaces and presentation (e.g., HCI): User interfaces — input devices and strategies.

INTRODUCTION
Number entry is ubiquitous, from kiosk machines and ticket machines to interactive medical devices. Different number entry styles encourage different types of errors, and these errors have varying severity levels [21]. In safety-critical domains, such as healthcare and aviation, number entry errors could result in system damage, injuries, and patient death. It is therefore important to seek ways to reduce error and increase accuracy.

Researchers, designers and developers have been exploring methods to detect, block or better manage number entry error in safety critical fields. Most number entry research focuses on detection and recovery from error [30, 21, 26]. In this paper, we introduce a new type of intervention, which aims to reduce the occurrence of error in the first place. We propose three interventions, all inspired by the priming technique. They are designed to help the operator better register the number they intend to enter before they enter it.

We performed experiments to evaluate user interfaces with each intervention, using healthcare as a motivating context. Our results showed this type of intervention can reduce number entry error significantly to achieve great improvement in safety. In addition, we argue that this type of intervention can work alongside existing interventions for error-recovery as an additional safety feature. Most importantly, it can be platform-independent and does not require any further alteration of the existing number entry interfaces, nor does it require the numbers to be presented differently.

RELATED WORK

Number Entry Errors
Entering numbers seems to be a routine task and can appear to be mundane. However, at the same time, number entry errors contribute to many adverse incidents and patient deaths [27]. In 2006, the death of a Canadian cancer patient, who received in 4 hours a drug (Fluorouracil) that should have lasted 4 days, revealed many design flaws of the organisational policy as well as of the interactive medical device used [1]. In 2010, an extremely skilled nurse in Seattle with a 24 year track record of excellence made an out-by-10 error (i.e., where the intended number is different from the intended number by an order of magnitude) entering a dose for a baby. The nurse subsequently committed suicide and became the "second victim" of this tragic event [2]. In 2012, a nurse in St. Luke's hospital miss-entered medication dosage in an infusion pump, which led to a fatal overdose of Heparin for her patient [10]. Unfortunately, these are just a few examples out of many. But to err is human [19], and in healthcare, errors could cost lives. A review of adult patient deaths in hospitals in England in 2009 revealed that 1 patient in 10 is affected by potentially serious medical errors, with half of them dying as a result [15]. Some of these errors are due to wrong number entry.

Post-operational Interventions for Error Recovery
Number entry tasks in healthcare, particularly related to drug administration, usually follow the standard procedure of number transcription: the user acquiring the instruction number; memorising it in short-term memory; operating a number entry interface to input the number; double-checking the entered number; finally submitting the results and proceeding with the drug administration [3, 4]. For years, researchers

CHI 2015, April 18—23, 2015, Seoul, Republic of Korea.
Copyright © ACM 978-1-4503-3145-6/15/04...$15.00.
DOI: 10.1145/2702123.2702477

have been working on different interventions to assist post-operational double-checking, so unintentional entry errors can be detected and corrected by the operator before the administration command is executed. Some of these interventions provide graphical representation of the entered number alongside the numerical representation to give the user redundant means to spot mismatches [28]. Others introduce an additional task right after entering the number but before submitting, such as a check-sum [31], to provide a secondary safety check. Though research shows that these methods are effective, they require some system modification to be used.

User Interface and Functionality Analysis

Some researchers have taken a technical approach to manage human error by improving the design of the user interface of interactive medical devices. Oladimeji et al. [22] assessed the safety of different number entry interfaces in terms of error rate and speed. Their study showed the performance of number entry interfaces is affected by the type of user interface. Their results also show that the 5-key (or directional pad) interface is safest, producing the least number of undetected errors in their study. Work by Cauchi et al. [8] explored variations in design within the same user interface layout: they identified and analysed design options for the 5-key interface using automated and simulated user trials.

Protocols and Rules as Safety Guard

Studies show that the emotional status of the user has an impact on the accuracy with which they enter numbers [7]. In safety critical fields, such as hospitals, users are often working under considerable pressure, and often in distressing situations. This may result in a higher stress level and error rate. Procedures may be in place to ensure all numbers are calculated and double-checked by at least two operators before any action starts [16, 17]. Others embed safety guards into the system, so the commands can only be executed if they fit in a safety threshold. A few programmable infusion pumps now come with drug libraries with pre-defined dosage thresholds [13]. When any extreme value is entered, the pump can alert the operator and block an infusion. In a nutshell, most of the existing research and interventions try to detect actual errors before they can cause any unrecoverable harm. These interventions are effective in increasing error recovery rate and reducing unnoticed error. However, despite such advances in technology, regulators continue to receive incident reports related to programming and administration errors [13].

Post-operational intervention can only help the operator recover from previous committed errors. Interventions aiming to reduce the occurrence of entry errors in the first place are less explored.

Priming Effect on User Performance

Our number entry interventions are inspired by the priming effect, which is where exposure to a stimulus (the prime) influences a response to a later stimulus (the target) [29]. Depending on how the prime is delivered, there are several widely studied priming models, such as repetitive priming (where the repetition of something leads to it influencing later thoughts) and semantic priming (where we process a target better if a related prime comes first). The most commonly referenced model of semantic priming is the spreading activation model [9], which sees semantic concepts as nodes in the neural network that are activated at the same time as the nodes for related concepts. In addition, dual process models distinguish between automatic (rapid, without effort, requiring no process capacity) and attentional (slow, with effort, requiring process capacity) mechanisms underlying semantic priming [23]. People have also studied priming effects on numerical tasks, mainly for the purpose of exploring priming models. Heyer and Briand found that participants were quicker to respond to 'five' after the prime 'four' than after the prime 'three', which suggested a numerical priming effect inversely proportional to the numerical distance between the prime and the target [12]. Dehaene and Akhavein's experiments [11] indicated that numbers were automatically converted mentally into quantities, even when the participants had been told to attend exclusively to their physical characteristics. Bodner and Dypvik discovered that when making odd-even judgements, a congruence effect (where the response to the target is faster when the prime and target are both even or both odd) is magnified in the block containing a high proportion of congruent pairs relative to a block containing a low proportion of such pairs, even though the prime was presented for between 42-50ms [6].

Over the years, many experiments claimed to have demonstrated priming phenomenon in lexical decision [20, 24] and other contexts relevant for behaviour change, such as social behaviour [5] and health management [32]. Though some research remains controversial [18, 25], the priming phenomenon inspired us to explore the feasibility and impact of pre-operational interventions on number entry tasks, as opposed to post-operational ones. Most numbers inputted in medical devices have two major properties: numeral structure and implied value. The former focuses on the length and composition of the number and the position of the digits. The latter usually links with physical properties such as intended dosage of a drug, volume to be administered or the rate of infusion. In addition, whenever an interactive medical device is programmed, the operator is obliged to follow the Five Rights of Medication Administration Rule [14] (right patient, drug, dose, route, and time). In other words, every number entry also comes with its own context. We believe priming interventions for such tasks, if designed appropriately, may be able to help the user attend to one of the three aspects of the instruction number (structure, value, context) better prior to the number entry task, and go deeper (in terms of the spreading activation model) to help them better register the instruction number, or be aware of the gravity of the consequences, thereby improving the expected accuracy.

THE SYSTEM AND THE INTERVENTIONS

In healthcare, particularly drug delivery systems, nurses regularly perform transcription tasks to set up drug infusions. The instruction numbers (dose, volume, rate etc) are usually on a prescription [26] for them to read, input into a device and sometimes refer to during interaction.

We designed our interventions to be an additional task the operator needs to undertake after they are prompted with a new instruction number but before they input it into the device. The interventions are questions related to the instruction number's value, structure or context. The operator needs to process the question prior to starting the number entry task.

We programmed an iPad to test the effect of our interventions. The application has 4 different user interfaces (UI). The first interface, UI1, has no intervention, but a plain number entry screen (see Figure 1), which is shared across all UIs. The number entry screen consists of two parts. On the left, there is a direct replica of legacy numeric keypad. The display of inputted number is on the top of the keypad with an undo button at the right side. A confirm button is placed at the bottom of the keypad. The instruction number appears on one side of the screen and remains accessible to participants while they interact with the keypad on the other side. It is updated with a new instruction number every time the user confirms a previous entry.

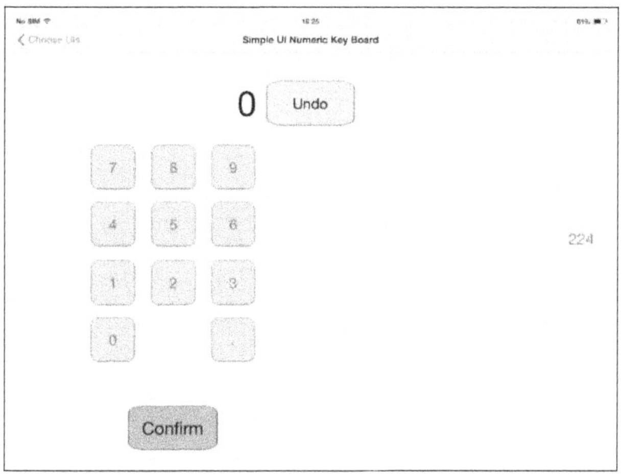

Figure 1: UI1: Numeric Keypad on Touch Screen with No Intervention

In UI2, the operator is asked to first compare the instruction number with a randomly generated round number before entering the instruction number using the number entry screen (see Figure 2a). The format of the pre-operational questions was fixed as:

> *"Compared to [a randomly generated round number], the instruction number is ... ".*

And the answers the operator can choose from are: *"Smaller"*, *"Exactly the same"* and *"Greater"*. To correctly answer the question, the operator needs to first process the value of both numbers and the relation that holds between them.

In UI3, the operator was asked a descriptive question relating to the instruction number (see Figure 2b). Here, we conducted a small scale pilot study with several researchers in the laboratory, where the authors work, to refine the design of the descriptive questions. We tested UI3 with *open questions*, such as *"How many digits are there in the instruction number?"*, *closed questions on partial feature*, such as *"Is the first digit an odd digit?"*, and *closed questions on overall structure*. Participants in the pilot study reported that the questions about the overall structure of the number were the most preferable as they felt more encouraged to analyse the instruction number as a whole, and only needed to choose from *"Yes"* and *"No"*. As a result, we avoided the *open questions* and *closed questions on partial feature* in UI3. For every number entry trial, one priming question was randomly chosen from the following four questions: *"Does the instruction number have a DECIMAL POINT?"*, *"Does the instruction number contain FOUR OR MORE digits in total?"*, *"Does the instruction number have DUPLICATE digits?"*, and *"Does the instruction number count as a WHOLE number?"*.

In UI4, the priming questions were designed to help the operator be more aware of the context of the number entry tasks, rather than the instruction number alone. Compared to previous interventions, UI4 focuses on who, when, what, where, and engages the operator's experience. As shown in Figure 2c, the operator was asked one of the following ten questions randomly prior to entry trial, and choose from *"Yes"* and *"No"*: *"Are you a student?"*, *"Is it Tuesday today?"*, *"Is it morning now?"*, *"Have you been trained to use this device?"*, *"Do you work in a hospital?"*, *"Are you a nurse?"*, *"Do you work in a university?"*, *"Have you filled in an incident report before?"*, *"Is this device an iPad?"*, and *"Are you familiar with Touch Screen Devices?"*.

Please note that questions listed here were tailored to fit for the context of our user study, which was conducted in a university, with students and staff as participants. However, the questions can be easily tailored to fit other domains.

EXPECTATIONS AND HYPOTHESES

We expect the interventions to have an impact on the participant performance. We defined some dependent variables as follows:

The operator commits an ***entry error*** if the input number was different from the instruction number. An ***unnoticed error*** is an entry error left uncorrected before the operator confirms the input. The ***error recovery rate*** is the percentage of corrected entry error in all committed entry errors. We define ***responding time*** as the time interval between when a new instruction number is presented and when the first key press of number entry occurs. ***Key press interval*** is the average time interval between every digit entry. ***Committing time*** is the time interval between when the operator has finished the last digit entry and when the confirm key is pressed.

Entry error

Both UI2 and UI3 offer intervention that prompts the operator to closely analyse the instruction number before carrying out the number entry task. UI2 primes the operator with the value of the instruction number, by encouraging them to perform an arithmetic comparison. Considering all instruction numbers are quantity related, such as medication dosage rather than identity related (e.g., phone numbers) we hypothesized the

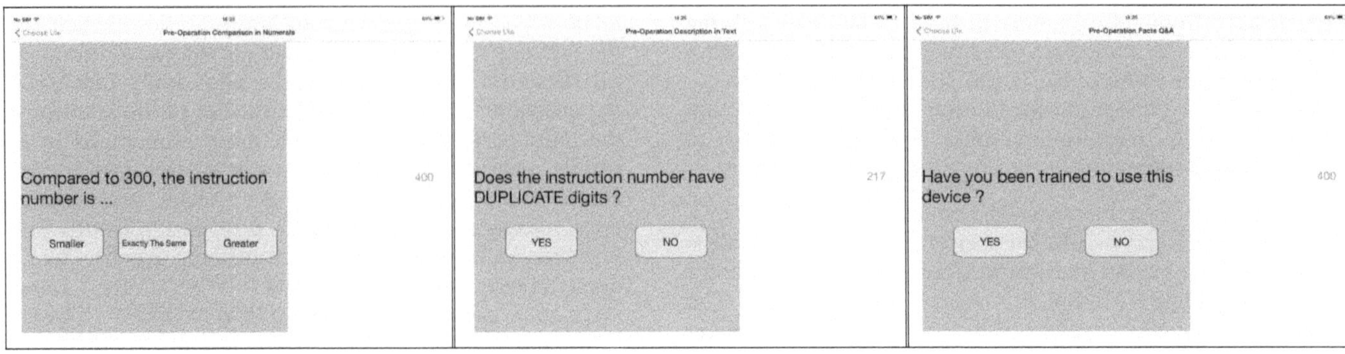

(a) UI2: Comparison with a randomly generated round number (b) UI3: Descriptive questions related to numeric structure (c) UI4: Factual questions related to the context of number entry task

Figure 2: All UIs with Pre-operational Intervention

total number of entry error committed in UI2 will be less than in UI1.

We expected to see a smaller number of entry error in UI3 than in UI1, as by the time the operator starts their number entry task, they would most likely have already analysed the structure of the instruction number, rather than seeing it as a string of digits.

We thought that context-related questions in UI4 could help the operator be more aware of the gravity of the number entry task. However, there is also the risk that these factual questions could be a distraction. Hence we expected a significantly different number of entry error in UI4 than in UI1.

Error recovery rate

Considering none of the interventions occurs during or after the actual number entry task, we were not expecting significant difference in error recovery rate in any UI.

Unnoticed error

We believe that even though the operator may still hold the same level of recovery rate, since the total number of committed entry error will be significantly lower in UI2 and UI3, the same level of reduction in unnoticed error should be expected for both UIs.

Responding time, key press interval and committing time

Speed-wise, it is reasonable to expect that the response time will be significantly shorter in UI1 than other UIs, due to the lack of pre-operational interventions. However, we expect that priming questions will only slow down the user in this criteria, and should not affect their key press interval nor committing time.

Subjective feedback

Essentially, in UI2, UI3 and UI4, participants were undertaking an additional task on top of the original number entry task. We expected that introducing pre-operational intervention to increase the perceived workload significantly. It was also expected that between UI2 and UI3, certain operators may prefer one over the other, due to their perceived arithmetic abilities.

EXPERIMENT DESIGN

To test out our hypothesis, we conducted a within-subject study. In the study, participants were asked to sit in front of a desk with the iPad placed on a stand (see Figure 3).

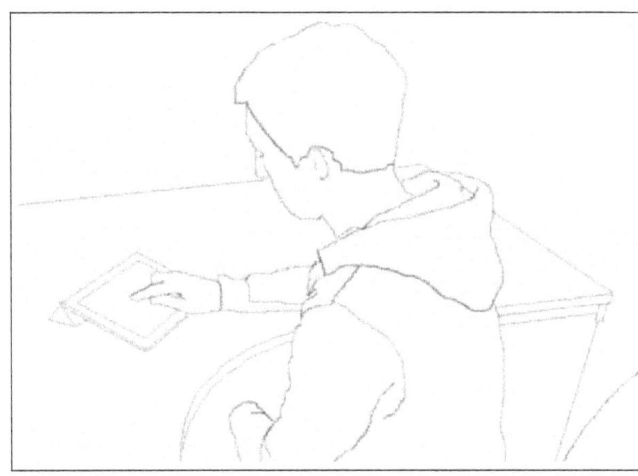

Figure 3: Study Setup

The Task

Every UI has a training block with 20 instruction numbers to help the operator familiarise themselves with the interface and the pre-operational questions (when available). Afterwards, they were asked to input 100 instruction numbers as the actual trials. To prevent fatigue and avoid rushing through, break periods were inserted in the sequence after every 20 numbers. The operators were encouraged to take a break every time they were prompted with the opportunity and go back into the trial when they were ready.

The 20 instruction numbers used in the training block were the same for all 4 UIs, but in a random order. The 100 instruction numbers for the actual trial were also the same for all 4 UIs, but randomised for each UI. All instruction numbers used were extracted from data logs of actual infusion pumps used in an acute hospital. They do not have a fixed length or format. The collection includes both whole number and numbers with decimals, with values between 1.23 to 1200.

Participants were asked to input the numbers as quickly and as accurately as they can across the 4 UIs. Whenever an intervention was used, the participants were made aware that their answers to the priming questions would be recorded only to ensure all questions were answered with consideration. The correctness of their answers would not be assessed as part of their performance.

Since the operator was entering the same set of data repeatedly using different UIs, to control the learning effect's impact on performance, a list of the 24 possible permutations of the UI sequence was generated and every sequence was assigned to 2 participants randomly. To eliminate the potential residuary effect of any previous intervention on the current UI, we broke the study into four 15-20 minute visits. Participants were advised to visit the lab no more than once a day. During each visit, only one UI was used. Before every experiment session, we demonstrated the use of the device and how to interact with it, and answered any questions raised. Printed instruction and examples were explained and available to the participants during every session.

The Participants

We recruited 48 participants within the university where the authors are based. Participants were asked to fill in an entry questionnaire prior to the study, which asks for their gender, age, native language, dominant hand, their ability to comprehend text and deal with simple arithmetic operations, experience with touch screen devices and discipline of work/study. There were 29 female participants (age: $M = 32.90$, $SD = 1.81$), and 19 male participants (age: $M = 29.39$, $SD = 1.90$). Seven were students. There were 45 right-handed participants, 2 left-handed and 1 ambidextrous. All participants were experienced touch screen users and familiar with number entry interfaces. All participants, except one, considered themselves good at comprehending text and numbers; 37 were native English speakers. However, 14 reported having better arithmetic skills, 9 considered themselves better at text comprehending. All participants received £10 Amazon vouchers in return for their time.

DATA COLLECTION AND ANALYSIS

After the participants filled in the entry questionnaire, they were introduced to the 4 UIs over the course of 4 visits to the lab. Interaction with the UIs was recorded on a keystroke and system status level.

To investigate whether participant preference influenced their subjective experience and/or had an impact on their objective performance, we designed two additional questionnaires. After using each trial, the participant was asked to fill in a NASA TLX questionnaire to measure perceived workload. This questionnaire helped us justify subjective ratings. At the end of the study, the participant was presented with screenshots of the UIs and a booklet containing all of their previous TLX questionnaires. They were asked to fill in another questionnaire, where they gave subjective ratings to every UI they had used. This 11-item questionnaire was based on Post Study System Usability Questionnaire (PSSUQ) to gather rating on overall satisfaction (6 items) and system usefulness (5 items). The original PSSUQ also covers aspects, such as information quality that were not applicable to our study.

Paired comparison was used in the end where the participant was given a scenario of a possible purchase of a device. The device would allow them either to use online banking service, or to control their medication dosage on a daily basis. The participant was required to choose one UI in the pair and to elaborate on the reason for their decisions. There were 6 UI pairs in total.

Participants' ability to correctly answer pre-operational questions was not assessed, though all answers were recorded. The results were used to determine the level of engagement with the priming question, and to ensure all questions were processed as expected, rather than quickly skipped through without consideration.

RESULTS

Data collected from the training blocks were not included in the analysis. All 48 participants encountered all 4 UIs to input 100 instruction numbers, which generated 19,200 valid trials.

For all results, we used the Shapiro-Wilk test as means of assessing normality. Since most of the repeated measures of entry error, unnoticed error and error recovery rate do not form a normal distribution, a Friedman test was used to test for difference between four groups. The alpha levels for all reported results were set at 0.05. Whenever the initial test revealed significant difference, we run post hoc analysis using Wilcoxon signed-rank tests with a Bonferroni correction applied. This resulted in a significance level set at $p < 0.008$.

Objective performance

Entry error

A Friedman test showed that UI had a significant effect on entry error ($\chi^2(3) = 25.84, p < 0.001$). Post hoc analysis showed that UI1 had significantly more errors than all other UIs (see Table 1). However, amongst all 3 interventions themselves, there was no significant difference in number of entry errors. The reduction of total number of entry errors in percentage for UI2, UI3 and UI4 were 39.5%, 40.8% and 38.7% respectively.

When compared to UI1 which had no intervention, we discovered that participants, who self-reported to be better at arithmetic operation than at text comprehension, committed significantly less entry errors when asked to do a pre-operational comparison (UI2: $p = 0.005$), but there was no significant difference in entry errors when the intervention was about the structure of instruction number (UI3: $p = 0.036$). Others, who claimed to be equally good at numbers and text comprehension, committed significantly less errors in all three cases (UI2: $p = 0.007$; UI3: $p = 0.002$; UI4: $p = 0.003$). And when there was no intervention, those who considered themselves bad at dealing with arithmetic operations committed the least number of entry errors than other participants. Figure 4 shows the average of entry errors across all UIs, clustered by self-reported arithmetic ability levels.

Entry errors of all UIs				
	UI1	UI2	UI3	UI4
	6(3.25∼9)	*3(2∼5.75)*	*3(2∼5)*	*3(2∼5.75)*
UI1		p=.001	p<.001	p<.001
UI2			p=.652	p=.476
UI3				p=.970
Unnoticed errors of all UIs				
	UI1	UI2	UI3	UI4
	2(0∼4)	*.50(0∼2.75)*	*0(0∼2)*	*0(0∼2)*
UI1		p=.014	p<.001	p=.001
UI2			p=.742	p=.386
UI3				p=.564
Error recovery rate of all UIs				
	UI1	UI2	UI3	UI4
	.67(.50∼1)	*.93(.52∼1)*	*1(.50∼1)*	*1(.52∼1)*
UI1		p=.055	p=.023	p=.043
UI2			p=.784	p=.640
UI3				p=.909

Responding time of all UIs in seconds				
	UI1	UI2	UI3	UI4
	.94(.86 ∼1.03)	*2.90(2.55 ∼3.53)*	*3.21(2.56 ∼3.73)*	*2.57(2.19 ∼3.16)*
UI1		p<.001	p<.001	p<.001
UI2			p=.317	p<.001
UI3				p<.001
Subjective rating on overall satisfaction of all UIs				
	UI1	UI2	UI3	UI4
	41(39∼42)	*34(31∼39)*	*35(32∼38)*	*36(32∼40)*
UI1		p<.001	p<.001	p<.001
UI2			p=.716	p=.234
UI3				p=.060
Subjective rating on system usefulness of all UIs				
	UI1	UI2	UI3	UI4
	31(26.75) ∼33)	*27.50(22 ∼32)*	*29(23.25 ∼31.75)*	*27(21.25 ∼30.75)*
UI1		p=.008	p=.019	p<.001
UI2			p=.233	p=.499
UI3				p=.306

Table 1: Objective performance and subjective feedback statistic results reported in *Median (IQR)* format and p-values

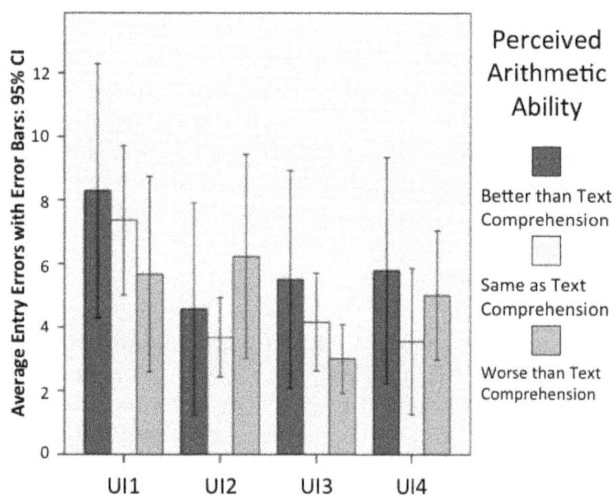

Figure 4: Average entry errors by UI, clustered by reported arithmetic ability

Unnoticed Errors

A Friedman test showed that UI had a significant effect on unnoticed error ($\chi^2(3) = 17.76, p < 0.001$). Post hoc analysis showed that only UI3 and UI4 had significantly less unnoticed error than UI1. All other pairs in the group were not significantly different (see Table 1 for details). The reduction of total number of unnoticed errors in percentage for UI2, UI3 and UI4 were 53%, 51.7% and 60.7% respectively.

Figure 5 shows the average unnoticed errors of every UI, clustered by self-reported arithmetic ability. Those with better text comprehension skills generally committed less unnoticed errors in all UIs. Though they did not achieve a significant reduction in unnoticed errors overall, their performance in UI3 was 25.1% better than in UI2. But the difference is not statistically significant. People who considered themselves equally good at dealing with arithmetic operation and text comprehension experienced significant reduction in unnoticed errors when some of the interventions were in place (UI2: $p = 0.024$, UI3: $p < 0.001$, UI4: $p < 0.001$). Participants self-reporting with better arithmetic skills performed 27.6% better when using UI2 than using UI3. However, this difference was not statistically significant.

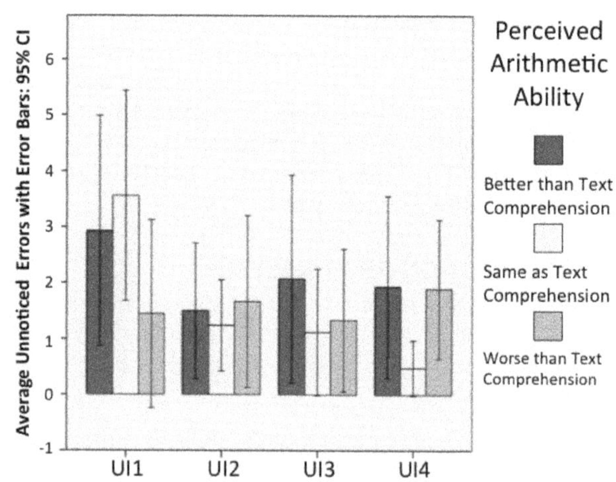

Figure 5: Average unnoticed errors by UI, clustered by reported arithmetic ability

Error recovery Rate

Though we were not expecting a significant change in error recovery rate, a Friedman test implies that it may have taken place ($\chi^2(3) = 9.35, p = 0.025$). However, post hoc analysis, as shown in Table 1, revealed that this was a Type I error.

Responding time, committing time and key press interval

	UI1 27(14.67 ~43)	UI2 44.3(27.33 ~55)	UI3 43.67(25.33 ~58)	UI4 37.67(21.67 ~50.67)
UI1		p<.001	p<.001	p=.008
UI2			p=.559	p=.028
UI3				p=.055

Table 2: Perceived workload of all UIs from TLX questionnaires reported in *Median (IQR)* format with p-values

A Friedman test showed that UI had a significant effect on responding time ($\chi^2(3) = 101.73, p < 0.001$). Table 1 shows that all UIs with intervention have significantly longer responding times than UI1. However, amongst the UIs with intervention, UI4 had the shortest responding time. The increase in responding time in percentage of UI2, UI3 and UI4 were 246%, 243% and 188% respectively.

However, the mean key press interval for UI1 was 0.38s ($SD = .09$), UI2 was 0.37 ($SD = 0.09$), UI3 was 0.38 ($SD = 0.10$) and UI4 was 0.39 ($SD = 0.09$). The committing time for UI1 was 0.48 ($SD = 0.16$), UI2 was 0.48 ($SD = 0.15$), UI3 was 0.49 ($SD = 0.18$) and UI4 was 0.50 ($SD = 0.20$). As expected, the interventions did not have any significant impact on committing time ($\chi^2(3) = 0.20, p = 0.98$), nor the keypress interval ($\chi^2(3) = 4.77, p = 0.19$).

Subjective feedback

Perceived workload

The TLX results shows that pre-operational interventions had a significant effect on perceived workload ($\chi^2(3) = 24.61, p < 0.001$). UI2 was considered to be the most demanding interface. Compared to UI1, UI2's perceived workload has increased by 42%. UI4 was the least demanding one out of the three interventions, its workload was 23% higher than UI1. UI3 sits in between with an 39.6% increase in perceived workload. However, there was no significant difference of workload amongst all UIs with intervention, as shown in Table 2.

Satisfaction and usefulness

A Friedman test showed that UI had a significant effect on satisfaction and usefulness. Participants generally rated UIs with intervention with a lower score of overall satisfaction ($\chi^2(3) = 56.65, p < 0.001$), and system usefulness ($\chi^2(3) = 17.80, p < 0.001$) (see Table 1). Compared to UI1, the overall satisfaction of UI2 was down by 14.8%, UI3 down by 14.8% and UI4 was down by 12.9%. The system usefulness of UI2 was down by 9.8%, UI3 by 8.3% and UI4 by 12%.

Subjective comments

When given a scenario of purchasing a personal device for online banking or medication dosage control, participants were asked to choose the UI they preferred in a pair of UIs and elaborate on their reasona. We found participants tended to choose the one with no intervention at all. Out of all 6 combinations, one UI could be chosen up to 3 times. The results show that UI1 was chosen 2.11 times in average ($SD = 1.07$), while UI2 and UI3 were chosen 1.40 ($SD = 1.04$) and 1.40 ($SD = 1.15$) times respectively. UI4 was the least favourite, chosen 1.06 ($SD = 0.96$) times on average.

We hand-coded all qualitative data and summarise the findings of this thematic analysis in Table 3. For every UI, a list of positive and negative attributes were presented with their distribution amongst all participants.

Some participants reported the tendency to rush through while using UI1, and that the interface was plain and the number entry tasks were not mentally engaging. But overall, participants liked the simplicity and familiarity of UI1, as well as the fact that it took significantly shorter time to accomplish a single task. However, many of the participants associated simplicity and speed with accuracy.

> *"UI1 was the quickest and easiest of the interfaces. I felt less likely to make mistakes or become distracted from the number entry task. UI1 was always the easiest interface to use with the least distraction. Therefore the lowest chance of making mistakes when working quickly." — P06*

On the other hand, some participants remained skeptical, and noticed that there may be a trade-off between speed and accuracy.

> *"UI1 is a little simplistic giving a tendency to rush. It gives the feeling of needing to be quick." — P17*

One participant also expressed the fact that with no intervention, she lost her concentration fairly quickly.

> *"[My] focus on UI1 tended to decrease as the task progressed." — P19*

UI2 was considered useful in encouraging the participant to think more about the size and the value of the number before input.

> *"The comparison question made me look properly at the value of the number. I think this made me less likely to make mistakes in entering the numbers. ... These questions were mentally challenging. I felt UI2 made me look more carefully at the number." — P07*

But not all participants considered being made to think about the instruction number a positive experience.

> *"[It is] mentally demanding, I have to study the numbers." — P24*

In addition, introducing an additional number to the system confused some participants.

> *"It was confusing as there were other numbers within the question, which could get confused with the instruction number." — P39*

UI3 was considered helpful in keeping the operator focused on the structure of the instruction number. But once again, since the intervention required additional thinking and time to process, some participants expressed frustration.

> *"... UI3 is distracting and requires more thought than UI2; I felt UI3 might improve accuracy a little, but was*

> *a bit irritating and seemed to unnecessarily slow me down." — P03*

Some participants found UI3 useful because of its relevance and focus on details.

> *"[I] had to 'read' number in a deeper way with mathematical thoughts. For me UI3 would work best as made me read number better. " — P14*

> *"[UI3] made me focus more on the actual makeup of the number. Questions are related to the number. Made me look at the number in detail — the whole number." — P32*

Participants considered UI4 less mentally demanding than other interventions. Some enjoyed the switch of focus between factual context and number entry task, and saw this as an interesting way to keep the mind focused without overloading it.

> *"[UI4] was easy to use, and the questions helped keep focus without affecting the task. Overall UI4 was the best in my opinion. It kept your brain doing difficult things by allowing it to stay focused longer." — P19*

Others considered the questions about factual context a distraction and believed it affected their performance.

> *"Irrelevant question is a bit annoying ... and it doesn't help to memorise the number, mistakes occur more than UI3." — P46*

Some participants expressed their frustration dealing with repetitive questions.

> *"UI4 has repetitive questions that make me think I am going crazy or that my answers are always wrong, because it is asked again. I didn't think of the numbers." — P02*

	Positive attributes		Negative attributes	
UI1	*Simplicity*	31	*Tendency to rush*	3
	Speed	15	*Not engaging*	1
	Single-Tasking	13		
	Familiarity	3		
UI2	*Encourage thinking and checking*	13	*Additional number*	10
	Acknowledging the value / size of the instruction number	6	*Require thinking*	5
	Engaging attention	6	*Dual-tasking*	4
	Speed	7	*Unintuitive wording*	3
	Easy-to-use	2	*Delay on speed*	2
UI3	*Encouraging thinking and checking*	16	*Require thinking*	4
	Engaging attention	6	*Delay on speed*	4
	Relevance to task	5	*Dual-tasking*	3
	Speed	5	*Loss sense of numeric value*	3
	Easy-to-use	4		
UI4	*Less mentally demanding*	11	*Irrelevance / Distraction*	13
	Engaging attention	8	*Repetitive*	5
	Speed	5	*Delay of speed*	1
	Prevent rushing	3	*Arbitrary*	1

Table 3: Subjective comments and distribution of all UIs

DISCUSSION

Interventions vs. lockout sessions

Both UI2 and UI3 offer interventions that prompt the operator to closely analyse the instruction number before entering by asking pre-operational questions. UI4 prompts the user to register the context of the number entry task. The results of the study shows that the pre-operational questions presented to the participants had an effect on improving the accuracy of number entry. However there was no significant difference amongst the effects of the three different pre-operational questions. This suggests that simply getting users to think about the magnitude or the syntactic composition of a number is not responsible for the improved accuracy in the number entry task that followed. The same effect was achieved by asking the user a non-number related question (UI4) prior to the number entry task. The common threads these UIs share include encouraging the operator to perform a pre-operational task prior to entering number, and consequently lengthening the time interval between updating the instruction number and the actual number entry. A logical question would be whether the introduction of a simple lockout period to extend the time interval between the display of instruction and the entry of the number might have the same effect on the accuracy of entry. The subjective feedback revealed an interesting common trait shared by all three interventions — *engaging attention*. We believe what the operator does during this extended period could be crucial to user performance, particularly if this lab study is moved into a simulated environment or even a real hospital ward, where distractions occur. A future study could focus on comparing the impact of a simple lockout period and a mentally demanding pre-operational intervention both in a lab study and *in situ* study.

Platform independent

Our study was conducted on a touchscreen device. However, essentially we were introducing an additional Q&A task before the actual number entry task. This process can be implemented independent of a touch screen. In our study, the answers to all priming questions were recorded in order to screen out any misuse (for example, choosing a random answer, without processing the question first). Arguably, if it can be ensured that users actually process the priming questions, it is possible to replicate UI2 and UI3 on any platform. The effect of intervention with priming questions about factual context of the number entry task is, however, in need of further investigation. With a question irrelevant to the instruction number itself, the operator may not need to look at the instruction number prior to answer the question at all. Further study is needed to verify the effect of UI4 on user performance in different settings, with domain-specific questions and users.

Informing the device and other interventions

In an environment where the digital systems and devices are not centralised nor integrated, our pre-operational interventions can further benefit the user and ensure accuracy of number entry tasks by bringing context to the number entry task. For example, if the device asks the operator to compare the instruction number to a randomly generated round number, the operator's answer can be used to set up a safety guard for the actual number entry task. If the entered number falls out of the threshold, the system can block the command from being executed until either the answer to the priming question or the inputted number is fixed. The same principle applies to UI3. For instance, if the length of the number does not match the answer to the question, the device will be alerted that there is an error somewhere. Our pre-operational intervention can easily be used alongside a post-operational intervention, such as the checksum mechanism described in [31], to ensure an overall reduction of entry errors, unnoticed errors and an improvement in error recovery rate. However, additional workload and mental demand is a drawback, which needs to be considered very carefully, but weighed against the improvement in accuracy. (Low accuracy might create much higher workload because of the adverse consequences!)

Tailor for different levels of arithmetic ability

We noticed a difference in performance between participants who considered themselves better at dealing with arithmetic operations and participants self-reported as better at text comprehension. Our study is preliminary in terms of exploring the relation between perceived arithmetic ability and performance while using numeric-value related priming interventions. Based on the data collected, people with higher perceived arithmetic ability generally perform better while using UI2, compared to using UI3. However, it would be useful to conduct further study to investigate whether this finding can be generalised, and to further explore the differences between self-reported assessments and actual objective assessment and the impact on user performance brought by the latter.

Further work

The motivation of this study was to reduce number entry errors in safety critical domains. We used real numbers from infusion pumps used in an acute hospital. However, the study was conducted in a university lab with university staff and students as participants, hence to further investigate the impact of our interventions a more situated study would be required.

In addition, it would be useful to investigate the correlation between people's perceived (or even objective) ability to deal with arithmetic operation and their performance while primed with pre-operational comparison and pre-operational descriptive questions respectively. This may give us insights on how to better tailor or choose these interventions to fit the user.

CONCLUSIONS

We have presented a series of number entry interventions inspired by the priming effect. All interventions were introduced prior to the actual number entry tasks. Our results show that these pre-operational interventions help reduce the total number of entry errors committed by up to 40.8%. Unnoticed errors were also reduced by up to 60.7%. Since these interventions do not conflict with other interventions, which can be used during or after the number entry task, we believe they can be used in conjunction with other approaches. Though we implemented these interventions on a touchscreen device, they are essentially platform-independent and can be adapted to existing workflows. As an additional task to the actual number entry task, the interventions do increase the operator's response time significantly, but they do not affect the keypress interval and the committing time of the number entry task.

Due to the additional workload and mental demand, subjective satisfaction of the user interface was reduced by up to 14.8%. Perceived usefulness was also reduced by up to 12%. These subjective measures are interesting because of the objective improvement in accuracy.

ACKNOWLEDGMENTS

With thanks to Computer Human Interaction in MEDical devices (CHI+MED), the EPSRC funded project, EP/G059063/1. Paul Cairns made many helpful comments.

REFERENCES

1. *Fluorouracil Incident Root Cause Analysis*. Institute for Safe Medication Practices Canada, 2007.
2. Aleccia, J. Nurse's suicide highlights twin tragedies of medical errors. `http://www.nbcnews.com/id/43529641/ns/health-health_care/t/nurses-suicide-highlights-twin-tragedies-medical-errors/`.
3. Barchard, K., and Pace, L. Preventing human error: The impact of data entry methods on data accuracy and statistical results. *Computer in Human Behaviour* (2011), 1834–1839.
4. Barchard, K. A., and Verenikina, Y. Improving data accuracy: Selecting the best data checking technique. *Computer in Human Behaviour* (2013), 1917–1922.
5. Bargh, J., Chen, M., and Burrows, L. Automaticity of social behavior: Direct effects of trait construct and stereotype activation on action. In *Journal of Personality and Social Psychology*, American Psychological Association (1996), 230–244.
6. Bodner, G. E., and Dypvik, A. T. Masked priming of number judgement depends on prime validity and task. *Memory and Cognition 33*, 1 (2005), 29–47.
7. Cairns, P., Pandab, P., and Power, C. The influence of emotion on number entry errors. In *Proceedings of the*

the SIGCHI Conference on Human Factors in Computing Systems, ACM Press (2014), 2293–2296.

8. Cauchi, A., Gimblett, A., Thimbleby, H., Curzon, P., and Masci, P. Safer "5-key" number entry user interfaces using differential formal analysis. In *Proceedings of the 26th Annual BCS Interaction Specialist Group Conference on People and Computers*, BCS (2012), 29–38.
9. Collins, A. M., and Loftus, E. F. A spreading-activation theory of semantic processing. *Psychological Review 82*, 6 (1975), 407–428.
10. Darragh, T. Two more patients overdosed at St. Luke's. `http://articles.mcall.com/2012-04-25/health/mc-allentown-stlukes-overdoses-again-20120425_1_hospital-nurses-nursing-errors-infusion-pumps`.
11. Dehaene, S., and Akhavein., R. Attention, automaticity, and levels of representation in number processing. *Journal of Experimental Psychology: Learning, Memory, and Cognition 21* (1995), 314–326.
12. den Heyer, K., and Briand, K. Priming single digit numbers: Automatic spreading activation dissipates as a function of semantic distance. *The American Journal of Psychology 99*, 3 (1986), 315–340.
13. "Smart" Infusion Pumps are Selectively Intelligent. `http://www.fda.gov/MedicalDevices/Safety/AlertsandNotices/TipsandArticlesonDeviceSafety/ucm245160.htm`.
14. Grissinger, M. The Five Rights: A Destination Without a Map . *Journal of Pharmacy and Terapuetics 35*, 10 (2010), 542.
15. Hogan, H., Healey, F., Neale, G., Thomson, R., Vincent, C., and Black, N. Preventable deaths due to problems in care in english acute hospitals: a retrospective case record review study. In *BMJ Qual Saf* (2012).
16. Nottingham University Hospitals NHS Trust: Medicines Code of Practice. `https://www.nuh.nhs.uk/handlers/downloads.ashx?id=13679`.
17. Princess Alexandra Hospital NHS Trust: Witnessing Medication Administration. `https://www.medicinesresources.nhs.uk/GetDocument.aspx?pageId=755928`.
18. Kahneman, D. A proposal to deal with questions about priming effects. `http://www.nature.com/polopoly_fs/7.6716.1349271308!/suppinfoFile/Kahneman%20Letter.pdf`.
19. Kohn, L., Corrigan, J., and Donaldson, M. *To Err Is Human: Building a Safer Health System*. The National Academies, 2000.
20. Meyer, D., and Schvaneveldt, R. Facilitation in recognizing pairs of words: Evidence of a dependence between retrieval operations. *Journal of Experimental Psychology 90* (1971), 227–234.
21. Oladimeji, P., Thimbleby, H., and Cox, A. Number entry interfaces and their effects on error detection. In *Proceedings of the 13th IFIP TC 13 international conference on Human-computer interaction - Volume Part IV*, Springer-Verlag, Ed. (2011), 178–185.
22. Oladimeji, P., Thimbleby, H., and Cox, A. L. A performance review of number entry interfaces. In *Human-Computer Interaction–INTERACT 2013*, Springer (2013), 365–382.
23. Posner, M., and Snyder, C. Facilitationand inhibition in the processingof signals. *In P. M. A. Rabbitt and S. Dornic (Eds.), Attention and performance V. New York: Academic Press.* (1975).
24. Schvaneveldt, R., and Meyer, D. Retrieval and comparison processes in semantic memory. In *Attention and performance IV*, New York: Academic Press (1973), 394–409.
25. Shanks, D., Newell, B., Lee, E., Balakrishnan, D., Ekelund, L., Cenac, Z., Kavvadia, F., and C.Moore. Priming intelligent behavior: an elusive phenomenon. *PLoS ONE 8*, e56515 (2013).
26. Soboczenski, F., Cairns, P., and Cox, A. Increasing accuracy by decreasing presentation quality in transcription tasks. In *Interact*, S. L. 8118, Ed. (2013), 380–394.
27. Thimbleby, H., and Cairns, P. Reducing number entry errors: solving a widespread, serious problem. *Journal of the Royal Society Interface 7*, 51 (2010), 1429–1439.
28. Tu, H., Oladimeji, P., Wiseman, S., Niezen, G., and Thimbleby, H. Employing Number-based Graphical Representations to Enhance the Effects of Visual Check on Entry Error Detection. In *to appear in International Symposium on Interaction Design and Human Factors (IDHF)* (2014).
29. Tulving, E., Schacter, D., and Stark, H. Priming effects in word fragment completion are independent of recognition memory. *Journal of Experimental Psychology: Learning, Memory and Cognition 8*, 4 (1982).
30. Wiseman, S., Cairns, P., and Cox, A. A taxonomy of number entry error. In *Proceedings of the 25th BCS Conference on Human-Computer Interaction*, British Computer Society (2011), 187–196.
31. Wiseman, S., Cox, A., Brumby, D., Gould, S., and O'Carroll, S. Using checksums to detect number entry error. In *Proceedings of the SIGCHI Conference on Human Factors in Computing Systems*, ACM Press (2013), 2403–2406.
32. Wryobeck, J., and Chen, Y. Using priming techniquesto facilitate health behaviours. *Clinical Psychologist 7* (2003), 105–108.

Comparing Person- and Process-centric Strategies for Obtaining Quality Data on Amazon Mechanical Turk

Tanushree Mitra C.J. Hutto Eric Gilbert
Georgia Institute of Technology
Atlanta, GA 30308
{tmitra3, cjhutto}@gatech.edu gilbert@cc.gatech.edu

ABSTRACT
In the past half-decade, Amazon Mechanical Turk has radically changed the way many scholars do research. The availability of a massive, distributed, anonymous crowd of individuals willing to perform general human-intelligence micro-tasks for micro-payments is a valuable resource for researchers and practitioners. This paper addresses the challenges of obtaining quality annotations for subjective judgment oriented tasks of varying difficulty. We design and conduct a large, controlled experiment (N=68,000) to measure the efficacy of selected strategies for obtaining high quality data annotations from non-experts. Our results point to the advantages of *person-oriented strategies over process-oriented strategies*. Specifically, we find that screening workers for requisite cognitive aptitudes and providing training in qualitative coding techniques is quite effective, significantly outperforming control and baseline conditions. Interestingly, such strategies can improve coder annotation accuracy above and beyond common benchmark strategies such as Bayesian Truth Serum (BTS).

Author Keywords
Human Computation, Crowd Sourcing, Mechanical Turk, Experimentation, Qualitative Coding, Micro Task

ACM Classification Keywords
H.5.2. Information interfaces and presentation (e.g., HCI) – User Interfaces: Evaluation/methodology; J.4. Social and Behavioral Sciences: Economics, Sociology

INTRODUCTION
The emergence of crowd-sourced micro labor markets like Amazon Mechanical Turk (AMT) is attractive for behavioral and empirical researchers who wish to acquire large-scale independent human judgments, without the burden of intensive recruitment effort or administration costs. Yet acquiring well-measured *high quality* judgments using an online workforce is often seen as a challenge [11,13,32,35,40]. This has led to scholarly work suggesting quality control measures to address the problem of noisy data [8,17,24,35]. Many of these studies have investigated the effectiveness of various quality-control measures as stand-alone intervention strategies on one-off tasks. How do these measures affect quality when working in tandem? What are the challenges faced in acquiring quality results when the difficulty of subjective judgments increase? The present study addresses these questions.

Building on some of the most promising strategies identified by prior work (e.g., [35]), we design and conduct a large empirical study to compare the relative impacts and interactions of 34 intervention strategies. Specifically, we collected and analyzed 68,000 human annotations across more than 280 pairwise statistical comparisons for strategies related to worker screening and selection, interpretive convergence modeling, social motivations, financial incentives, and hybrid combinations. Further, we compare these interactions against a range of representative *subjective judgment-oriented* coding activities of varying difficulty. Our study makes four principal contributions:

- We reveal several intervention strategies which have a substantial positive effect on the quality of data annotations produced by non-experts, regardless of whether correctness is defined by agreement with the most frequent annotation or as agreement with an accepted expert.
- We find that *person-oriented intervention strategies* tend to facilitate high-quality data coding among non-experts. For example, borrowing analogous concepts from the field of Qualitative Data Analysis (QDA) and adapting them for use by a massive, distributed, transient, untrained, anonymous workforce, we find that *prescreening workers for requisite cognitive aptitudes, and providing basic training* in collaborative qualitative coding methods results in better agreement and improved interpretive convergence of non-expert workers.
- We find that person-oriented strategies improve the quality of non-expert data coders above and beyond those achieved via process-oriented strategies like the Bayesian Truth Serum (BTS) technique (c.f., [30,35]).
- Finally, of particular importance for contemporary AMT researchers, we note that while our results show significant improvements in the quality of data annotation tasks over control and baseline conditions, the baseline quality has improved in recent years. In short, compared to the

CHI 2015, April 18 - 23, 2015, Seoul, Republic of Korea.

ACM 978-1-4503-3145-6/15/04…$15.00.
http://dx.doi.org/10.1145/2702123.2702553

control-level accuracies of just a few years ago [35], AMT is not nearly the "Wild West" that it used to be.

BACKGROUND AND RELATED WORK

Data Coding and Annotation

Qualitative Data Analysis (QDA)—that is, systematically analyzing non-numeric data such as interview transcripts, open-ended survey responses, field notes/observations, and a wide range of text documents, images, video, or audio data—is generally a specialized skill most often acquired through formal training. Such skills are costly, both in terms of the financial demand required to obtain the skillset (in undergraduate or graduate school, for example), and in terms of the time, labor, and expense needed to employ the skills. *Qualitative coding*, or the process of interpreting, analyzing, classifying, and labeling qualitative data (e.g., with themes, categories, concepts, observations, attributes or degree anchors, etc.) is a critical step in the larger overall QDA process. As part of qualitative data analysis, many lead researchers employ multiple skilled qualitative *coders* (individuals who perform QDA annotations), each working independently on the same data. Such a strategy makes an explicit trade-off for labor and expense for an increase in accuracy, higher reliability, and a reduction in potential coding errors. What if we could quickly, inexpensively, and yet *reliably* obtain *high-quality* annotations from a massive, distributed, untrained, anonymous, transient labor force?

Crowdsourcing Qualitative Coding & Content Analysis

Crowd-sourced labor markets are an attractive resource for researchers whose studies are conducive to online (Internet-based) participation. Research study data such as qualitative content analysis can be obtained relatively cheaply from potentially thousands of human coders in a very short time. For example, prior work by Wang, Kraut, & Levine [43] asked workers to code discussion forum messages for whether they offered information or provided emotional support. Sorokin & Forsyth [40] had coders annotate images to locate people. Hutto & Gilbert [13] asked coders to annotate the intensity of sentiments in social media texts. Soni and colleagues [39] had workers mark the degree of factuality for statements reported by journalists and bloggers. Andre, Kittur, and Dow [1] asked workers to extract thematic categories for messages shared amid Wikipedians.

Clearly, crowdsourcing does enable quick, inexpensive content analysis and data coding at large scales (c.f., [1,13,39,40,43]). However, these types of QDA activities are often quite subjective in nature. As such, they are susceptible to conflicting interpretations, dissimilar rubrics used for judgments, different levels of (mis)understanding the instructions for the task, or even opportunistic exploitation/gaming to maximize payouts while minimizing effort. Unfortunately, worker anonymity, lack of accountability, inherent transience, and fast cash disbursements can entice the online labor workforce to trade speed for quality [8]. Consequently, the collected annotations may be noisy and poor in quality. Moreover, quality can be inconsistent across different kinds of coding tasks of varying difficulty [35]. Scholars using AMT must therefore carefully consider strategies for ensuring that the codes and annotations produced by non-experts are of *high quality*—that is, ensuring that the coding produced by anonymous workers is accurate and reliable [11,13,32,35,40]. Previous research suggests several quality control measures to tackle the problem of noisy data [1,8,12,17,19,24,35,37]. Most of these earlier works, in isolation, investigate a select set of specialized interventions, often for a single (or just a few kinds of) coding or annotation tasks. Many studies also do not address the challenges associated with coding *subjective judgment* oriented tasks of varying difficulty. To address these gaps, we design and conduct a large empirical study to compare the relative impacts and interactions of numerous intervention strategies (including over 280 pairwise statistical comparisons of strategies related to worker screening and selection, interpretive convergence modeling, social motivation, financial incentives, and hybrid combinations – we discuss these strategies in greater detail later). Further, we compare these interactions against a range of coding activities that have varying degrees of subjective interpretation required.

Crowdsourcing Data Annotations for Machine Learning

Interest in high-quality human annotation is not limited to qualitative method researchers. Machine learning scholars also benefit from access to large-scale, inexpensive, human intelligence for classifying, labeling, interpreting, or otherwise annotating an assorted variety of "training" datasets. Indeed, human-annotated training data acquisition is a fundamental step towards building many learning and prediction models, albeit an expensive and time-consuming step. Here again, the emergence of micro-labor markets has provided a feasible alternative for acquiring large quantities of manual annotations at relatively low cost and within a short period of time—along with several researchers investigating ways to improve the quality of the annotations from inexpert raters [14,36,38]. For example, Snow and colleagues [38] evaluate non-expert annotations for a natural language processing task; they determined how many AMT worker responses were needed to achieve expert-level accuracy. Similarly, Sheng and colleagues [36] showed that using the most commonly selected annotation category from multiple AMT workers as training input to a machine learning classifier improved the classifier's accuracy in over a dozen different data sets. Ipeirotis, Provost, & Wang [15] use more sophisticated algorithms, which account for both per-item classification error and per-worker biases, to help manage data quality subsequent to data annotation.

Whereas these studies concentrate heavily on post-hoc techniques for identifying and filtering out low quality judgments from inexpert coders *subsequent* to data collection, we follow in the same vein as Shaw et al. [35] and focus on *a priori* techniques for encouraging workers to provide attentive, carefully considered responses in the first place. Along with the most promising strategies identified by Shaw et al. [35], we add numerous other person-centered and process-centered strategies for facilitating high quality data coding from non-experts across a range of annotation tasks. We describe these strategies in the next section.

STRATEGIES FOR ELICITING QUALITY DATA

We consider four challenges that affect the quality of crowd annotated data, and discuss strategies to mitigate issues associated with these challenges.

Challenge 1 – Undisclosed cognitive aptitudes

Certain tasks may require workers to have special knowledge, skills or abilities, the lack of which can result in lower quality work despite spending considerable time and effort on a task [16]. As in offline workforces, some workers are better suited for particular tasks than others. Asking anonymous workers with unidentifiable backgrounds to perform activities without first verifying that the worker possesses a required aptitude may result in imprecise or speculative responses, which negatively impacts quality.

Strategy 1 – Screen workers

On AMT, requesters often screen workers from performing certain Human Intelligence Tasks (HITs) unless they meet certain criteria. One very common screening tactic is to restrict participation to workers with an established reputation – e.g., by requiring workers to have already completed a minimum number of HITs (to reduce errors from novices who are unfamiliar with the system or process), and have approval ratings above a certain threshold (e.g., 95%) [2,23,29]. This approach has the benefit of being straightforward and easy for requesters to implement, but it is naive in that it does not explicitly attempt to verify or confirm that a worker actually has the requisite aptitude for performing a given task. For example, a more targeted screening activity (that is tailored more to content analysis coding or linguistic labeling tasks) would be to require workers to have a good understanding of the language of interest, or to require workers to reside in certain countries so that they are more likely to be familiar with localized social norms, customs, and colloquial expressions [13,39].

Challenge 2 – Subjective interpretation disparity

Qualitative content analysis can often be very subjective in nature, and is therefore vulnerable to differences in interpretations, dissimilar rubrics used for judgments, and different levels of (mis)understanding the instructions for the task by unfamiliar, non-expert workers.

Strategy 2 – Provide examples and train workers

Providing examples to introduce workers to a particular coding or annotation task, and modeling or demonstrating the preferred coding/annotation behaviors can help workers establish consistent rubrics (criteria and standards) for judgment decisions [44]. This is analogous to qualitative researchers sharing a common "codebook"—the compilation of codes, their content descriptions and definitions, guidelines for when the codes apply and why, and brief data examples for reference [34]. Along with the examples, requesters on AMT can then require workers to obtain a specific qualification which assesses the degree to which the worker understands how to perform the *task-specific* content analysis annotation or labeling activity. Guiding workers through the process of doing the task trains and calibrates them to the nature of desired responses. This strategy helps improve intercoder/interrater agreement, or *interpretive convergence* – i.e., the degree to which coders agree and remain consistent with their assignment of particular codes to particular data [34].

Challenge 3 – Existing financial incentives are oriented around minimizing time-on-tasks

The micro-labor market environment financially rewards those who work quickly through as many micro-tasks as possible. Consequently, there is little incentive to spend time and effort in providing thoughtfully considered quality responses. If unconsidered judgments and random, arbitrary clicking will pay just as well as thoughtful, carefully considered responses, then some workers may attempt to maximize their earnings while minimizing their effort.

Strategy 3 – Financially incentivize workers to produce high-quality results

In an effort to incentivize carefully considered responses, rewarding high quality responses has shown to improve annotation accuracy [13,35]. For every intervention strategy we examine, we include both a non-incentivized and an incentivized group, and we confirm whether financial incentives continue to have significant impacts above and beyond those of a particular intervention strategy.

Challenge 4 – Low independent (individual) agreement

There are several ways to measure the accuracy of any individual coder. A simple approach is to calculate a percent correct for codes produced by a given coder against an accepted "ground truth." Other useful metrics are Cohen's kappa statistics for nominal coding data and Pearson's correlation for ordinal or interval scales. Regardless of how accuracy is measured, the correctness of any individual coder is often less than perfect due to differences in subjective interpretations.

Strategy 4 – Aggregating, iteratively filtering, or both

One way to mitigate the problem is to use aggregated data, or by searching for congruent responses by taking advantage of the wisdom-of-the-crowd[1] and accepting only the majority agreement from multiple independent workers [13,42]. However, it is often still difficult to obtain meaningful (or at least interpretable) results when aggregated responses are noisy, or when large variance among worker judgments challenge the notion of majority agreement [41]. Prior research has addressed this challenge by adding iterative steps to the basic parallel process of collecting multiple

---

[1] *Wisdom-of-the-crowd* is the process of incorporating aggregated opinions from a collection of individuals to answer a question. The process has been found to be as good as (often better than) estimates from lone individuals, even experts [42].

judgments [11, 22]. In other words, use crowd-workers to scrutinize the responses of other workers, thereby allowing human judges (as opposed to statistical or computational processes) to identify the best quality annotations [21,23].

OUR TASKS

In order to establish a framework of strategies for obtaining high quality labeled data, we administered a combination of the above described strategies across four sets of labeling tasks: identifying the approximate number of people in a picture, sentiment analysis, word intrusion, and credibility assessments (we describe these in more depth in a moment).

Each of annotation task varied in the degree of subjective interpretation required. We deployed four HITs on AMT using a modified version of the NASA-TLX workload inventory scale to assess subjective judgment difficulty [10]. Response options ranged from "Very Low" to "Very High" on a seven-point scale. Each HIT asked 20 workers to perform the four qualitative coding tasks described below, and paid $0.75 per HIT. To account for item effects, we used different content for each annotation task in each of the four HITs. Also, to account for ordering effects, we randomized the order in which the tasks were presented. Thus, we collected a total of 80 responses regarding the difficulty of each type of task, providing us with a range of tasks that vary in their underlying subjective judgment difficulty.

TASK 1: People in Pictures (PP), median difficulty = 1

In this task, we presented workers with an image and asked them to estimate the number of people shown in the picture. This is a well-known data annotation activity in the computer vision research area [7,28]. We selected 50 images containing different numbers of people from the Creative Commons on Flickr[2]. The number of people in each image differed by orders of magnitude, and corresponded to one of five levels: None, About 2 – 7 people, About 20 – 70 people, About 200 – 700 people, and More than 2,000 people.

Expert Annotation / Ground Truth – We determined ground truth at the time we selected the image from Flickr. We purposefully selected images based on a stratified sampling technique such that exactly ten pictures were chosen for each coding/annotation category.

Figure 1: Example pictures for three of the five possible data coding/annotation categories.

TASK 2: Sentiment Analysis (SA), median difficulty = 2

In this task, we mimic a sentiment intensity rating annotation task similar to the one presented in [13] whereby we presented workers with short social media texts (tweets) and asked them to annotate the degree of positive or negative sentiment intensity of the text. We selected 50 random tweets from the public dataset provided by [13]; however, we reduced the range of rating options from nine (a scale from –4 to +4) down to five (a scale from –2 to +2), so that we maintain consistent levels of chance for coding the correct annotations across all our subjective judgment tasks.

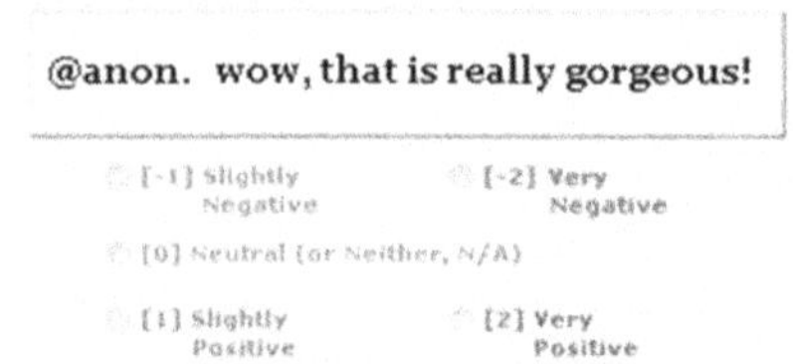

Figure 2: Example of the sentiment analysis annotation task

Expert Annotation / Ground Truth – We derived ground truth from the validated "gold standard" public dataset provided by [13], and adjusted by simple binning into a five point annotation scale (rather than the original nine point scale). One of the authors then manually verified each transformed sentiment rating's categorization into one of the five coding/annotation category options.

TASK 3: Word Intrusion (WI), median difficulty = 2

In this task, we mimic a human data annotation task that is devised to measure the semantic cohesiveness of computational topic models [5]. We presented workers with 50 "topics" (lists of words produced by a computational Latent Dirichlet Allocation (LDA) process [3]) created from a collection of 20,000 randomly selected English Wikipedia articles. LDA is a popular unsupervised probabilistic topic modeling technique which originated from the machine learning community. The topics generated by LDA are a set of related words that tend to co-occur in related documents. Following the same procedure described in [5], we inserted an "intruder word" into each of the 50 LDA topics, and asked workers to identify the word that did not belong.

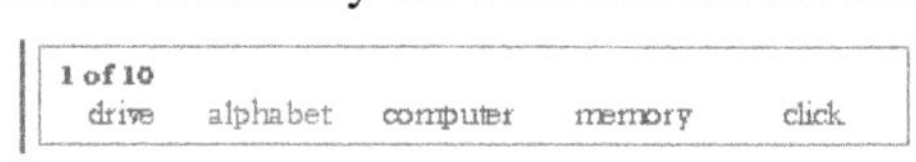

Figure 3: Example of a topic list (with the intruder word highlighted with red text for illustration purposes)

Expert Annotation / Ground Truth – A computational process (rather than a human) selected the intruder word for each topic, making this data annotation task unique among the others in that coders are asked to help establish "ground truth" for the word that least belongs. As such, there was no "expert" other than the LDA computational topic model.

TASK 4: Credibility Assessment (CA), median diff. = 3

In this task, we asked workers to read a tweet, rate its credibility level and provide a reason for their rating. This task aligns with scholarly work done on credibility annotations in social media [4,25,31]. To build a dataset of annotation items that closely resembles real-world information credibility needs, we first ensure that the dataset contains infor-

[2] https://www.flickr.com/creativecommons/by-2.0/

mation sharing tweets, specifically those mentioning real world event occurrences [26]. To this end, we borrowed existing computational approaches to filter event specific tweets from the continuous 1% sample of tweets provided by the Twitter Streaming API [4,20,45].

Figure 4: Example of a tweet along with the five credibility coding/annotation categories modeled according to existing work on credibility annotation categories [4,39].

Next, we recruited independent human annotators to decide whether a tweet was truly about an event, filtering out false positives in the process. After training the annotators to perform the task, if 8 out of 10 workers agree that a tweet is an event, we add the tweet as a potential candidate for credibility assessment. Next, the first author manually inspected the filtered list to verify the results of the filtering step before sending tweets for credibility assessments on AMT.

Expert Annotation / Ground Truth – Fact-checking services have successfully employed librarians to provide expert information [18]. We recruited three librarians from a large university library as our expert raters. The web interface used to administer the annotation questions to the librarians was similar to the one shown to AMT workers.

CONDUCT OF THE EXPERIMENTS

A full factorial design to evaluate all strategies across all coding/annotation tasks results in combinatorial explosion, making a full factorial experiment intractable. We therefore evaluate the strategies across tasks in stages. A total of 34 combinations were explored (see Table 1). We recruited non-expert content analysis data coders from Amazon Mechanical Turk, and employed a between-group experimental design to ensure we had 40 unique workers in each intervention strategy test condition (i.e., workers were prevented from performing the same data coding activity under different intervention strategies). In each test condition, we asked workers to make coding/annotation decisions for 50 different items (i.e., judgments of the number of people in pictures, sentiments of tweets, intruder words, or credibility assessments). Thus a total of 68,000 annotations were collected (50 items * 40 annotations * 34 intervention strategy combinations).

In the design of our HITs, we leverage insights from [1], who find that presenting workers with context (by having them perform multiple classifications at a time) is highly effective. To ensure workers on an average spend equal time (~ 2-5 minutes) on each HIT independent of task type, a pilot test determined the number of items to fix per HIT.

Comparative measures of correctness

We establish two measures of correctness to judge the quality of annotation in each task: (1) Accuracy compared to crowd (*Worker-to-Crowd*) and (2) Accuracy compared to experts (*Worker-to-Expert*). While the first counts the number of workers who match the most commonly selected response of the crowd (i.e., the mode), the second counts the number of workers who match the mode of experts. We purposely choose mode over other measures of central tendency to establish a strictly conservative comparison metric which can be applied consistently across all comparisons.

Statistical Analysis

For all our experimental conditions we calculate the proportion of correct responses using both metrics, and conduct χ^2 tests of independence to determine whether these proportions differ across experimental conditions. Next, as a post-hoc test, we investigate the cell-wise residuals by performing all possible pairwise comparisons. Because simultaneous comparisons are prone to increased probability of Type 1 error, we apply Bonferroni corrections to counteract the problem of multiple comparisons. Pairwise comparison tests with Bonferroni correction allow researchers to do rigorous post hoc tests following a statistically significant Chi-square omnibus test, while at the same time controlling the familywise error rate [22,33].

EXPERIMENTS

We next present two experiments. Briefly, the first experiment looks at the application of less-complex, *person-centric* a priori strategies on the three easiest subjective judgment tasks. In Experiment 2, we compare the "winner" from Experiment 1 against more complex, *process-oriented* a priori strategies such as BTS, competition, and iteration.

Experiment 1 (Strategies 1-3, Tasks 1-3)

The experimental manipulations we introduce in Experiment 1 consist of variations of intervention strategies 1 through 3, described previously, as well as a control condition that involves no intervention or incentives beyond the payment offered for completing the HIT. We next describe all control and treatment conditions used in Experiment 1.

1. **Control condition, no bonus *(Control NB)***: Workers were presented with simple instructions for completing the data coding/annotation task. No workers were screened, trained, or offered a financial incentive for high-quality annotations. "NB" stands for **N**o **B**onus.
2. **Financial incentive only *(Control Bonus-M):*** Workers were shown the same instructions and data items as the control condition, and were also told that if they closely matched the most commonly selected code/annotation from 39 other workers, they would be given a financial bonus equaling the payment of the HIT (essentially, doubling the pay rate for workers

whose deliberated responses matched the wisdom of the crowd majority). "Bonus-M" refers to bonus based on **M**ajority consensus.

3. **Baseline screening *(Baseline NB)***: Screening AMT workers according to their experience and established reputation (e.g., experience with more than 100 HITs and 95% approval ratings) is a common practice among scholars using AMT [1,6,11,27]. We include such a condition as a conservative baseline standard for comparison. Many researchers are concerned with acquiring high quality data coding/annotations, but if intervention strategies like *targeted screening for aptitude* or *task-specific training* do not substantially improve coding quality above such baseline screening techniques, then implementing the more targeted strategies may not be worth the requester's extra effort.
4. **Baseline w/ financial incentive *(Baseline Bonus-M)***: Workers were screened using the same baseline experience and reputation criteria, and were also offered the financial incentive described above for matching the wisdom of the crowd majority.
5. **Targeted screening for aptitude *(Screen Only NB)***: Prior to working on the data annotation HITs, workers were screened for their ability to pass a short standardized English reading comprehension qualification. The qualification presented the prospective worker with a paragraph of text written at an undergraduate college reading-level, and asked five questions to gauge their reading comprehension. Workers had to get 4 of the 5 questions correct to qualify for the annotation HITs.
6. **Targeted screening with financial incentive *(Screen Bonus-M)***: Workers were screened using the same targeted reading comprehension technique, and they were also offered the financial incentive for matching the majority when they performed the HIT.
7. **Task-specific annotation training *(Train Only NB)***: In comments on future work, Andre et al. [1] suggest that future research should investigate the value of training workers for specific QDA coding tasks. Lasecki et al. [19] also advocate training workers on QDA coding prior to performing the work. Therefore, prior to working on our data annotation HITs, workers in this intervention condition were required to pass a qualification which demonstrated (via several examples and descriptions) the *task-specific* coding rubrics and heuristics. We then assessed workers for how well they understood the specific analysis/annotation activity; they had to get 8 of 10 annotations correct to qualify.
8. **Task-specific annotation training with financial incentive *(Train Bonus-M)***: Workers were qualified using the same task-specific demonstration and training techniques, and they were also offered the financial incentive for matching the majority consensus.
9. **Screening and training *(Screen + Train NB)*** – This intervention strategy combined the targeted screening technique with the task-specific training technique (i.e., workers had to pass both qualifications to qualify).
10. **Screening, training, and financial incentive based on majority matching *(Screen + Train + Bonus-M)***: Prior to working on the data annotation HITs, workers had to pass both qualifications, and were also offered the financial incentive for matching the majority.

Table 1 summarizes the control and treatment conditions used for Experiment 1 (described above), and previews the test conditions for Experiment 2 (described later).

Results from Experiment 1

Table 2 shows that intervention strategies have a significant impact on the number of "correct" data annotations produced by non-experts on AMT, regardless of whether "cor rect" is defined by worker agreement with the most commonly selected annotation code from the crowd, or as agreement with an accepted expert. For example, we see from Table 2 that the χ^2 statistic related to the number of correct annotations when compared to the **crowd** is highly

	Subjective Judgment Tasks															
	People in Pictures (PP)				Sentiment Analysis (SA)				Word Intrusion (WI)				Credibility Assess (CA)			
	Median Difficulty = 1				*Median Difficulty = 2*				*Median Difficulty = 2*				*Median Difficulty = 3*			
Incentive	NB	Basis of Bonus			NB	Basis of Bonus			NB	Basis of Bonus			NB	Basis of Bonus		
Intervention		M	B	C		M	B	C		M	B	C		M	B	C
Control	✓	✓			✓	✓			✓	✓						
Baseline	✓	✓			✓	✓			✓	✓						
Screen	✓	✓			✓	✓			✓	✓						
Train	✓	✓			✓	✓			✓	✓						
Both (Screen+Train)	✓	✓			✓	✓			✓	✓				✓	✓	✓
Iterative Filtering													✓			

Table 1: Combinatorial space of experiments: Four task types varying in median subjective judgment difficulty *(People in Pictures, Sentiment Analysis, Word Intrusion, Credibility Assessment)*, **two classes of Incentives** *(NB - No Bonus, Bonus)*, **three types of bonus incentive** *(M- Majority Consensus, B – BTS, C – Competition)*, **six intervention strategies** *(Control, Baseline, Screen, Train, Both, Iterative Filtering)*. **A total of 34 combinations were explored** *(marked ✓)*.

Accuracy Metric	Task	df	N	χ^2	p
Worker-to-Crowd	All	9	59,375	388.86	$< 10^{-15}$
Worker-to-Expert	All	9	59,375	149.12	$< 10^{-15}$
Worker-to-Crowd	PP	9	20,000	345.73	$< 10^{-15}$
Worker-to-Expert	PP	9	20,000	46.66	$< 10^{-15}$
Worker-to-Crowd	SA	9	19,675	185.49	$< 10^{-15}$
Worker-to-Expert	SA	9	19,675	160.95	$< 10^{-15}$
Worker-to-Crowd	WI	9	19,700	90.74	$< 10^{-15}$
Worke-to-Expert	WI	9	19,700	59.82	$< 10^{-15}$

Table 2: χ^2 tests of independence for Experiment 1.

Likewise, the χ^2 statistic is also highly significant when comparing worker annotations to an **expert**: χ^2 (*df*=9, *N*= 59,375) = 149.12, $p < 10^{-15}$. Furthermore, Table 2 shows that these significant differences are robust across three diverse types of qualitative data coding/annotation tasks.

After seeing a statistically significant omnibus test, we perform post-hoc analyses of all pairwise comparisons using Bonferroni corrections for a more rigorous alpha criterion. Specifically, there are $\binom{10}{2} = 45$ multiple hypothesis tests, so we test statistical significance with respect to $\alpha = \frac{0.05}{45} =$ 0.001 for all paired comparisons. In other words, our between-group experimental study design supports 6 sets of 45 comparisons (i.e., $\binom{10}{2} = 45$ pairs) across 3 tasks and across 2 accuracy metrics, for a total of 45x3x2=270 pairwise comparisons; and for all pairs, p-values must be less than 0.001 in order to be deemed statistically significant.

Figure 5 depicts the percentage of correct annotations in each intervention strategy for each type of coding/annotation task, with indicators of the associated effect sizes for pairs with statistically significant differences.

Experiment 2 – Strategies S3-S4 in Task 4

The experimental manipulations of Experiment 2 are informed by the results from Experiment 1. Referring to the pairwise comparison tests from Experiment 1, we see that screening workers for task-specific aptitude and training them to use a standardized, consistent rubric for subjective judgments improves the quality of annotations. Thus we keep screening and training constant across the conditions of Experiment 2. Our Experiment 2 subjective judgment difficulty is even higher than that of the word intrusion task. Based on these observations, we repeat the ***Screen + Train + (Bonus-M)*** as a benchmark condition for Experiment 2. As test conditions, we then compare a range of incentive schemes and iterative filtering:

1. **Screening, training, and financial incentive based on majority matching (*Screen + Train + Bonus-M*)**: This condition is same as in Experiment 1 and serves as a benchmark for our second study.
2. **Screening, training, and financial incentive based on Bayesian Truth Serum or BTS (*Screen + Train + Bonus-B*)**: The effectiveness of using financial incentive schemes based on the Bayesian Truth Serum (BTS) technique is reported by Shaw et al. [35]. BTS asks people to prospectively consider other's responses to improve quality. Thus, in this intervention condition, we ask workers for their own individual responses, but we also ask them to predict the responses of their peers. They were told that their probability of getting a bonus would be higher if they submit answers *that are more surprisingly common* (the same wording as [30,35]).
3. **Screening, training, and financial incentive based on Competition (*Screen + Train + Bonus-C*)**: In this condition workers are incentivized based on their performance relative to other workers. Workers were told that their response reason pairs will be evaluated by other workers in a subsequent step to determine whether their response is the most plausible in comparison to their peers' responses. They were rewarded when their response was selected as the most plausible.
4. **Screening, training, and Iteration (*Screen + Train NB – Iteration)*)**: This strategy presented workers with the original tweets as well as the response-reason pairs collected in condition 3. Workers were asked to pick the most plausible response-reason pair. Rather than doing credibility assessments directly, workers were acting as judges on the quality of prior assessments, and helping to identify instances where the most commonly selected annotation from the crowd might not be the most accurate/appropriate – that is, they discover whether the crowd has gone astray.

Results from Experiment 2

We compare the proportion of correct response using our two measures of correctness. In Experiment 2, we find no significant difference when using *Worker-to-Expert* metric. Results are significant for *Worker-to-Crowd*: χ^2 (*df*=3, *N*= 7966) = 115.10, $p < 0.008$. To investigate the differences further we again conduct pairwise comparisons with Bonferroni correction. For our four experimental conditions, we conduct a total of $\binom{4}{2} = 6$ comparisons, thus increasing the rigor of our alpha significance criterion to $\alpha = \frac{0.05}{6} = 0.008$.

We find that across all conditions the winning strategy is the one in which workers are screened for cognitive aptitude, trained on task-specific qualitative annotation methods, and offered incentives for matching the majority consensus from the wisdom of the crowd. Surprisingly, comparing the three incentive conditions (majority-based, BTS-based, and competition-based incentives) and the iterative filtering strategy, the BTS strategy is the least effective. There is no significant difference between the effectiveness of competition versus iteration treatments. To summarize the statistical impact of each strategy:

$$S + T + BonusM > [Competition <> Iteration] > BTS$$

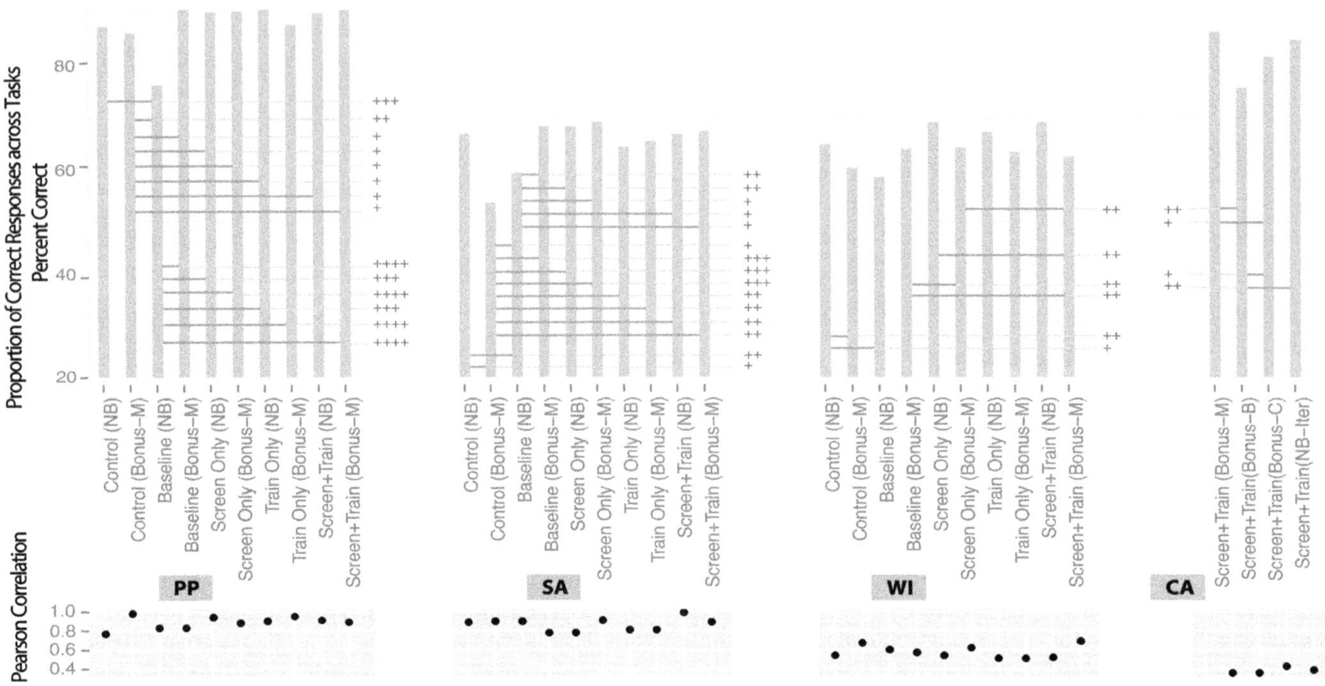

Figure 5: (Top panel) Proportion of correct responses across all tasks with respect to crowd. Pairwise comparisons which are statistically significant are shown with connecting lines (all p-values significant at 0.001 after Bonferroni correction). Effect sizes, as measured by Cramer's V coefficient, are indicated using "+" symbols at four levels: +, ++, +++, and ++++ indicate a very weak effect Cramer's V < 0.15, a weak effect Cramer's V ϵ (0.15, 0.2], a moderate effect (Cramer's V ϵ (0.2, 0.25], and moderately strong Cramer's V ϵ (0.25, 0.3]. (Bottom panel) Pearson correlation between expert and crowd annotations across all tasks.

DISCUSSION AND CONCLUSIONS

We systematically compared the relative impacts of numerous a priori strategies for improving the quality of annotations from non-experts, and we checked their robustness across a variety of different content analysis coding and data annotation tasks. We offer several reasons for focusing on a priori techniques, as opposed to complex statistical data cleaning techniques performed post-collection. First, the value of a priori strategies are not as well explored, lending novelty to our contributions. Second, a priori person-oriented strategies emulate the procedures of sharing a common QDA codebook. Our results demonstrate the value of applying a well-established method for qualitative data coding to crowd-sourced data annotations by non-experts. Third, screening and training techniques have a onetime upfront cost which soon amortizes with increases in the size of datasets, so the techniques scale exceptionally well. Fourth, person-oriented strategies are arguably more generalizable; they can be adapted to adjudicate both *objective* and *subjective* judgments. Post hoc data cleaning is suited more for objective tasks and breaks down as data becomes noisy; thus, post hoc procedures are of limited use for subjective oriented judgment tasks. Fifth, for time sensitive judgments (e.g., credibility decisions for rapidly unfolding events), simple a priori methods trump complex post hoc methods.

Crowd generated data annotations by non-experts can be reliable and of high-quality

We find that our crowd-generated data annotations have relatively high data quality (in comparison to prior research, e.g., [35]), even though we use aggressive criteria for measuring accuracy; that is, we purposely choose *exact* matching with the mode over other potential measures (e.g., mean or median) as a strict metric for all comparisons. Further, the effects of interventions are generally robust across a range of representative QDA data annotation tasks of varying difficulty and with varying degrees of subjective interpretation required. For example, the top panel of Figure 5 shows the agreement between individual coders and the crowd provided ground truth. In every task, the agreement is well above chance (20% for all tasks).

As data coding tasks become more subjectively difficult for non-experts, it gets harder to achieve interpretive convergence. This is demonstrated by the decreasing correlation trend for both the top and the bottom panels in Figure 5. When compared to an accepted expert (Figure 5, bottom), we find generally high agreement between experts and the crowd-produced accuracy measure for the two easier subjective judgment tasks (i.e., judging the number of People in Pictures [PP] and Sentiment Analysis [SA] for tweets). The subjective judgment difficulty of the Credibility Assessment (CA) task is quite high, and so correlation of the crowd to the expert librarians is understandably decreased, though still moderately strong in the 0.4 to 0.45 range. (Note: the lower correlation for the Word Intrusion [WI] task is related more to the poor performance of the computational topic model algorithm as a non-human "expert" than the ability of the crowd to match that expert).

Person-oriented strategies trump process-oriented strategies for encouraging high-quality data coding

In general, we find that screening and training workers are successful strategies for improving data annotation quality. Financial incentives do not appear to help improve quality, except in the simplest baseline condition (impact becomes negligible when stronger person-centric strategies are used).

The insightful work from Shaw and colleagues [35] noted that process-centric strategies like BTS were effective at promoting better quality annotations. An interesting finding from this study is that (in contrast to commonly employed process oriented tactics) when we target intervention strategies towards verifying or changing specific attributes of the individual worker, we see better and more consistent improvements in data annotation quality. By verifying that a person has the requisite cognitive aptitude (knowledge, skill, or ability) necessary to perform a particular qualitative data annotation task, together with training workers on qualitative data coding expectations, we can significantly improve effectiveness *above and beyond* the effects of BTS (see Figure 5, top). Person-centric strategies, such as a prior screening for requisite aptitudes and prior training on task specific coding rules and heuristics, emulate the processes of personnel selection and sharing a common "codebook". Qualitative scholars have been using such strategies for years to facilitate accurate and reliable data annotations among collaborative data coders [34]. By applying these techniques to crowd-sourced non-expert workers, researchers are more likely to achieve greater degrees of interpretive convergence – and do so more quickly, with less variation (c.f., [9]) – because workers are thinking about the data coding activity in the same ways.

Why do more to get less?

In terms of effort on behalf of both the research-requester and the worker-coder, intervention strategies such as screening and training workers have a one time up-front cost associated with their implementation, but their cost quickly becomes amortized for even moderate sized datasets. In contrast, strategies such as BTS, Competition, and Iteration require the same, sustained level of effort for every data item that needs to be coded or annotated. As such, the per-item cost for BTS, Competition, and Iteration are much heavier as the size of the dataset grows. Given that these more complex strategies actually do not perform as well as screening and training, why do more to get less quality?

Amazon is not a neutral observer; AMT is getting better

While our results show better consistency in the quality of data annotation tasks when using person-centric strategies over control and baseline conditions, we note that the quality of data obtained from AMT workers in those conditions is much higher than we initially expected, given our experience with the platform over the years. We highlight the finding that in every task across all interventions, the accuracy of crowd-produced annotation is not only well above random chance (20% for all tasks), but also well above the control condition and even the BTS treatment condition for similar subjective-oriented tasks reported in [35] just a few years ago. For example the "rank content" and "rank users" tasks from [35] are precisely the kind of subjective-oriented tasks that we are targeting with our person-centric interventions, but accuracy reported in [35] peaks at ~40% for even the best incentive category (BTS). (Note: the chance for randomly guessing the correct response for these two subjective judgment tasks was also 20%, the same as with our study). Contrast this with our results; even in the more difficult subjective judgment tasks (SA, WI, and CA), we find control condition accuracies in the 55-80% range (and our person-oriented treatment conditions are even higher, in the 65-90% range). These performance scores far exceed those reported in [35] for the two subjective judgment tasks. So it seems that compared to just a few years ago, AMT is not nearly the "Wild West" that it used to be. Interestingly, the kinds of quality control measures Amazon has enacted are also quite person-centric: e.g., requiring workers to verify their identity by providing their tax information[3], requiring workers to prove their humanity using CAPTCHAs at random intervals before accepting some HITs, and so on. (The first author even received a request from AMT to provide proof of U.S. residence by faxing a utility bill).

Our results are not intended necessarily to be prescriptive. Even in a study this size, we still focus on just a subset of potential intervention strategies, subjective judgment tasks, and various social and financial based incentives. Future work should directly compare the efficiency and effectiveness of a priori person-centric techniques to peer-centric methods (c.f., [12]) and more complex post hoc statistical consensus finding techniques (c.f., [37]). Nonetheless, the person-centric results reported in this paper help illustrate the value of applying established qualitative data analysis methods to crowd-sourced QDA coding by non-experts.

REFERENCES

1. Andre, P., Kittur, A., and Dow, S.P. Crowd synthesis: extracting categories and clusters from complex data. *CSCW* 2014, 989–998.
2. Berinsky, A.J., Huber, G.A., and Lenz, G.S. Evaluating Online Labor Markets for Experimental Research: Amazon.com's Mechanical Turk. *Political Analysis 20*, 3 2012, 351–368.
3. Blei, D., Ng, A., and Jordan, M. Latent dirichlet allocation. *J. of Machine Learning Res.3*, 2003, 993–1022.
4. Castillo, C., Mendoza, M., and Poblete, B. Information credibility on twitter. *CHI* 2011, 675–684.
5. Chang, J., Boyd-Graber, J., Gerrish, S., Wang, C., and Blei, D. Reading Tea Leaves: How Humans Interpret Topic Models. *NIPS* 2009, 288–296.
6. Crump, M.J.C., McDonnell, J.V., and Gureckis, T.M. Evaluating Amazon's Mechanical Turk as a Tool for Experimental Beh. Res. *PLoS ONE 8*, 3 2013.

[3] https://www.mturk.com/mturk/help?helpPage=worker

7. Dalal, N. and Triggs, B. Histograms of oriented gradients for human detection. *CVPR* 2005, 886–893.
8. Downs, J.S., Holbrook, M.B., Sheng, S., and Cranor, L.F. Are your participants gaming the system?: screening mechanical turk workers. *CHI* 2010, 2399–2402.
9. Gilbert, E. What if we ask a different question?: social inferences create product ratings faster. *CHI* 2014.
10. Hart, S.G. and Staveland, L.E. Development of NASA-TLX (Task Load Index): Results of empirical and theoretical research. *Adv. in psych. 52*, 1988, 139–183.
11. Heer, J. and Bostock, M. Crowdsourcing graphical perception: using mechanical turk to assess visualization design. *CHI* 2010, 203–212.
12. Huang, S.-W. and Fu, W.-T. Don't hide in the crowd!: increasing social transparency between peer workers improves crowdsourcing outcomes. *CHI* 2013.
13. Hutto, C.J. and Gilbert, E. VADER: A Parsimonious Rule-based Model for Sentiment Analysis of Social Media Text. *ICWSM* 2014, 216–255.
14. Ipeirotis, P.G. Analyzing the amazon mechanical turk marketplace. *XRDS: Crossroads17*, 2 2010, 16–21.
15. Ipeirotis, P.G., Provost, F., and Wang, J. Quality management on Amazon Mechanical Turk. *HCOMP* 2010.
16. Kazai, G., Kamps, J., and Milic-Frayling, N. Worker types and personality traits in crowdsourcing relevance labels. *CIKM* 2011, 1941–1944.
17. Kittur, A., Chi, E.H., and Suh, B. Crowdsourcing user studies with Mechanical Turk. *CHI* 2008, 453–456.
18. Kriplean, T., Bonnar, C., Borning, A., Kinney, B., and Gill, B. Integrating on-demand fact-checking with public dialogue. *CSCW* 2014, 1188–1199.
19. Lasecki, W.S., Gordon, M., Koutra, D., Jung, M.F., Dow, S.P., and Bigham, J.P. Glance: rapidly coding behavioral video with the crowd. *UIST* 2014, 551–562.
20. Lau, J.H., Collier, N., and Baldwin, T. On-line Trend Analysis with Topic Models: #twitter Trends Detection Topic Model Online. *COLING* 2012, 1519–1534.
21. Little, G., Chilton, L.B., Goldman, M., and Miller, R.C. Exploring iterative and parallel human computation processes. *CHI* 2010, 68–76.
22. MacDonald, P.L. and Gardner, R.C. Type I error rate comparisons of post hoc procedures for I j Chi-Square tables. *Ed. and Psych. Meas. 60*, 5 2000, 735–754.
23. Mason, W. and Suri, S. Conducting behavioral research on Amazon's Mechanical Turk. *Behavior research methods 44*, 1 2012, 1–23.
24. Mason, W. and Watts, D.J. Financial incentives and the performance of crowds. *ACM SIGKDD Explorations Newsletter 11*, 2 (2010), 100–108.
25. Morris, M.R., Counts, S., Roseway, A., Hoff, A., and Schwarz, J. Tweeting is believing?: understanding microblog credibility perceptions. *CSCW* 2012, 441–450.
26. Naaman, M., Boase, J., and Lai, C.-H. Is it really about me?: message content in social awareness streams. *CSCW* 2010, 189–192.
27. Paolacci, G., Chandler, J., and Ipeirotis, P.G. Running experiments on Amazon Mechanical Turk. *Judgment and Decision Making 5*, 5 2010, 411–419.
28. Papageorgiou, C. and Poggio, T. A trainable system for object detection. *Int. J. of Computer Vision 38*, 1 2000.
29. Peer, E., Vosgerau, J., and Acquisti, A. Reputation as a sufficient condition for data quality on Amazon Mechanical Turk. *Behavior Research Methods*, 2013, 1–9.
30. Prelec, D. A Bayesian truth serum for subjective data. *Science 306*, 5695 2004, 462–466.
31. Qazvinian, V., Rosengren, E., Radev, D.R., and Mei, Q. Rumor has it: Identifying misinformation in microblogs. *EMNLP*2011, 1589–1599.
32. Rashtchian, C., Young, P., Hodosh, M., and Hockenmaier, J. Collecting image annotations using Amazon's Mechanical Turk. *In Proc. NAACL HLT Workshop on Creating Speech and Language Data with Amazon's Mechanical Turk*, 139–147, 2010.
33. Rosenthal, R. and Rubin, D.B. Multiple contrasts and ordered Bonferroni procedures. *J. Ed. Psy. 76*, 6 1984.
34. Saldana, J. *The Coding Manual for Qualitative Researchers.* SAGE Publications, 2009.
35. Shaw, A.D., Horton, J.J., and Chen, D.L. Designing incentives for inexpert human raters. *CHI* 2011.
36. Sheng, V.S., Provost, F., and Ipeirotis, P.G. Get another label? improving data quality and data mining using multiple, noisy labelers. *KDD* 2008, 614–622.
37. Sheshadri, A. and Lease, M. SQUARE: A Benchmark for Research on Computing Crowd Consensus. *HCOMP* 2013, 156–164.
38. Snow, R., O'Connor, B., Jurafsky, D., and Ng, A.Y. Cheap and Fast - But is it Good? Evaluating Non-Expert Annotations for Natural Language Tasks. *EMNLP* 2008.
39. Soni, S., Mitra, T., Gilbert, E., and Eisenstein, J. Modeling Factuality Judgments in Social Media Text. *In Proc. ACL*, 415–420, 2014.
40. Sorokin, A. and Forsyth, D. Utility data annotation with Amazon Mechanical Turk. *CVPRW* 2008, 1–8.
41. Sun, Y.-A., Roy, S., and Little, G. Beyond Independent Agreement: A Tournament Selection Approach for Quality Assurance of Human Computation Tasks. *Human Computation*, 2011.
42. Surowiecki, J. *The Wisdom of Crowds.* Anchor Books, New York, NY, 2004.
43. Wang, Y.-C., Kraut, R., and Levine, J.M. To stay or leave?: the relationship of emotional and informational support to commitment in online health support groups. *CSCW* 2012, 833–842.
44. Willett, W., Heer, J., and Agrawala, M. Strategies for crowdsourcing social data analysis. *CHI* 2012.
45. Zhao, W.X., Jiang, J., Weng, J., et al. Comparing twitter and traditional media using topic models. *Advances in Information Retrieval.* Springer, 2011, 338–349.

Crowdsourced Feedback With Imagery Rather Than Text: Would Designers Use It?

David A. Robb[1] **Stefano Padilla**[1] **Britta Kalkreuter**[2] **Mike J. Chantler**[1]
[1]School of Mathematical and Computer Sciences, [2]School of Textiles and Design,
Heriot-Watt University,
Edinburgh, UK. EH14 4AS
{dar14, s.padilla, b.kalkreuter, m.j.chantler}@hw.ac.uk

ABSTRACT
Cognitive styles theories suggest that we divide into visual and verbal thinkers. In this paper we describe a method designed to encourage visual communication between designers and their audiences. This new visual feedback method is based on enabling fast intuitive selections by the crowd from image banks when responding to an idea. Visual summarization reduces the massed image choices to a small number of representative images. These summaries are then consumed at a glance by designers receiving the feedback leading to thoughtful reflection on their designs. We report an evaluation using two types of imagery for feedback. Twelve designers took part, receiving visual feedback in response to their designs. In semi-structured interviews they described their interpretation of the feedback, how it inspired them to change their designs and contrasted it with text feedback. Eleven of the twelve designers revealed that they would be enthusiastic users of a service providing this new mode of feedback.

Author Keywords
Crowdsourcing; visual; design; feedback; perceptual; emotional; imagery; image; summarization.

ACM Classification Keywords
H.5.3 [Information Interfaces and Presentation]: Group and Organization Interfaces

INTRODUCTION
For many people images are a medium preferable to text [27]. Yet, with the exception of star ratings [34], most feedback formats focus on text and they suffer from other limitations [32,17]. Work on crowdsourcing design feedback has been done and effective systems have been developed to gather it from paid non-experts [37, 19]. However, we have developed a new way to leverage participation in feedback from crowds through enabling easy, intuitive and engaging image selection as the medium. Visual feedback summaries stimulate thoughtful reflection in designers (Figure 1). We were originally motivated to apply this new feedback method (Figure 2 overleaf) to fashion design. However, in an evaluation of the method (described later), designers in the domain of interior design received the visual feedback and compared it with text. While aware of the scope for ambiguity in images the designers took inspiration from them and were motivated to make changes in their designs. They were enthusiastic to make use of a service which would provide them with more of this form of feedback.

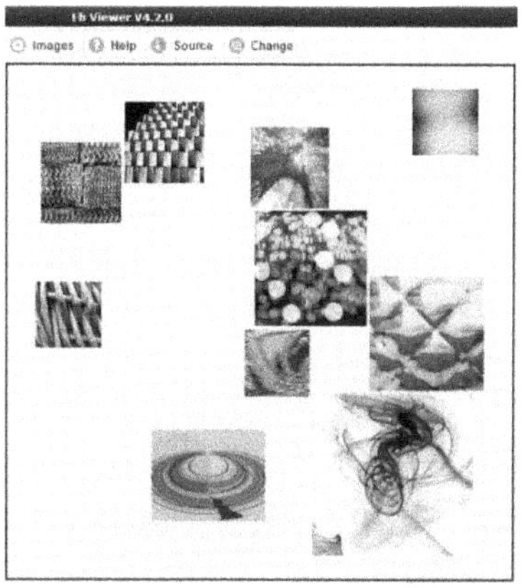

Figure 1 -Example of a visual feedback summary produced from a crowd's abstract imagery responses. This is a screenshot of feedback viewed by a designer participant during the evaluation study described in this paper.

The contributions of this paper are:

- The description of a method of obtaining image-based feedback allowing designers to elicit the intuitive perceptual and emotional reactions of a crowd to their designs in a visual format.
- The application of image summarization to the massed image selections of a crowd.
- An evaluation of this feedback method with designers who put forward their designs, viewed the visual reactions, and were given the opportunity to contrast the novel visual feedback formats with text feedback.

Figure 2 (overleaf) illustrates the visual design feedback method highlighting the areas of novel contribution. In the

CHI 2015, April 18 - 23, 2015, Seoul, Republic of Korea

ACM 978-1-4503-3145-6/15/04...$15.00
http://dx.doi.org/10.1145/2702123.2702470

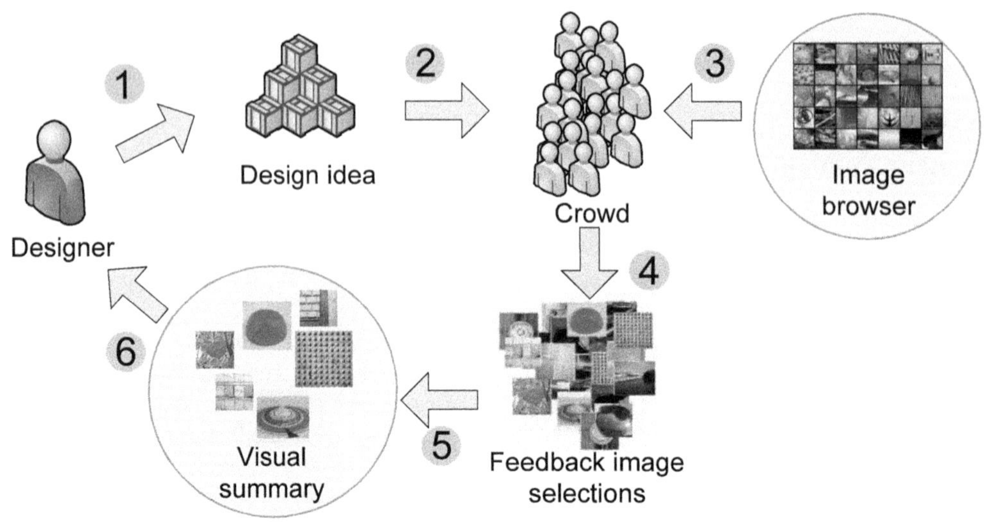

Figure 2 - The visual feedback method: 1-Designer presents design; 2-Crowd views design; 3- Crowd responds by selecting images from browser; 4- Image selections collated; 5-Visual summary generated; 6 Designer views feedback summary. The contributions are: images as a feedback medium; image summarization applied to crowd communication; an evaluation of the method.

rest of this paper, in *Background and Related Work*, we discuss areas lying behind our motivation including work on psychology and some of the drawbacks of conventional feedback. We also discuss previous work related to our implementation. In *Components of the Feedback Method* we focus on two aspects of that implementation: the image browsing interface and the generation of the visual summaries. The *Evaluation*, and *Results* sections describe how the evaluation was conducted and the results which flowed from it. Finally, in the *Discussion*, and *Conclusion* sections we discuss the implications of the results and suggest directions for the future of this novel visual crowd communication format.

BACKGROUND AND RELATED WORK

Visual Versus Verbal

Cognitive styles are frequently used in industry to predict individual performance in a range of situations [16]. They have also been used to inform aspects of teaching and learning [2]. While research since the 1950's produced several models of cognitive styles [16, 26], in a review, Riding & Cheema [27] identified two main dimensions: 1) visual-verbal and 2) holistic-analytic. It is the work in this field that lies behind a broad acceptance that some people prefer, and are more suited to, consuming information visually rather than verbally (or textually). Also, cognitive styles are independent of gender, age, and intelligence [26]. The method we describe will offer a feedback channel suited to those who prefer a visual medium.

The Importance of Intuition

Dual process theory is used to explain the apparent duality in the way that people make decisions; some decisions are arrived at slowly following a logical and analytic process, whereas intuition leads to a fast, almost effortless conclusion. The theory terms the fast intuitive process as *System 1* and the slow deliberative process as *System 2* [11]. It is actually *System 1* that takes care of most of our every-day decision making and it is this, along with its frequent unconscious involvement in our analytical decision making [11], that make it a valid feedback strategy to embrace *System 1,* by encouraging intuitive responses.

Conventional Methods for Gathering Feedback

While our motivation in developing this new method of visual feedback was a positive one, seeking a stimulating alternative to conventional methods for gathering feedback, here we briefly describe some of the shortcomings in conventional methods of computer mediated feedback.

Questionnaires can be affected by biases such as selective non-response [23]. Feedback forums also have their drawbacks. The picture they provide can suffer from overly negative responses. Customer feedback reviews via comment forums can lack input from moderate opinion holders reflecting only polarized views. Also contributors can be motivated to make their own opinion predominate [32]. If discussion on a forum develops this way, then the wisdom of the crowd as described by Surowiecki [31] is compromised as it depends on the independence of each crowd member. In addition, online reviewers are usually not encouraged to write about their emotions as subjectivity lessens the clarity of their message [17] despite the emotional impact of any product or design being an important aspect of its success.

Our new reaction method based on images, will provide an alternative which aims to avoid, or suffer less from, these drawbacks. Any selective non-response profile is likely to be different because potential respondents wary of conventional questionnaires may find responding via images more appealing and so take part. As no text is used contributors cannot argue for their view over others thus democratizing the contribution weights. Spontaneity and subjectivity will be recognized as inherent in the medium.

Crowdsourcing Design Feedback

Crowd feedback can be obtained through blogging or involvement in communities such as *Dribbble*. However, the level of commitment required to participate in such online communities [3] limits their accessibility; participants tend to be motivated to develop their own skills and status [36], thus representing more professional opinion rather than that of the eventual target audience for a given design. Alternatively paid participants can be engaged on services such as *CrowdFlower* [6]. Recent work by Xu et al. [37] describes a crowdsourcing tool for efficiently obtaining, specific, objective, feedback on graphic designs from paid crowdsourced workers in a structured way avoiding the need for a designer to have expertise in constructing human interface tasks. The feedback method we describe in this paper is intended to complement rather than compete with such systems by encouraging the participation of volunteer crowds perhaps engaged through social media.

Image Summarization

A disadvantage of images as feedback medium is that prompting a crowd to respond with visual feedback would result in a deluge of images rapidly overwhelming those receiving the feedback (assuming the crowd was large). Therefore a method of summarizing the massed image selections of a crowd is needed.

The representation of a large quantity of images by their reduction to a concise subset of representative images has been addressed in work on automated photo collage generation and for image browsing. One approach defines "representative images" as images that are interesting but different. Images are ranked by importance based on computer vision techniques such as face detection [28]. The choice of high ranking candidate images is then filtered so as to rule out near duplicate images by using similarity data based on color histogram techniques. Another approach to the reduction is by clustering the images and choosing representative images based on the cluster structure. Egorova et al [9] use source and date/time metadata as the data for clustering. Fan et al [13], in their work to improve browsing in large image collections, use tags already associated with the images to allocate images to topics. Within topics the images are then clustered based on similarity data calculated from color, texture and interest point features.

These methods all rely to some extent on computer vision techniques to measure the similarity between images. Clark et al. [1] have shown that in the case of texture images computer vision techniques produce similarity data that does not match human perceptions. Indeed the summarization methods which use metadata and tags are seeking to address the semantic gap between what can be deduced about the meaning of the image from its features and what the image actually means to a viewer. Our approach to summarization, which we describe later, uses perceptual data and thus seeks to avoid the semantic gap problem.

Abstract and Emotional Imagery

As our visual feedback method needs images for its medium we consider two types of imagery for use:

The role of emotions in intuitive thinking, decision making, and information processing is recognized in psychology literature [33, 18]. Approaches such as Kansei engineering [22] exemplify how consumer emotions can be factored into product design. Mood boards are perhaps a more established creative and analytical tool used by designers when formulating a design idea. Images and objects are arranged together to develop a mood or perceptual and emotional theme. Abstract images are often used for this to avoid specific figurative connections [14]. However, figurative images can be used to access emotions in a more specific way and can be categorized according to their affective properties [21]. Emotive images would be suitable for fast intuitive feedback as people rapidly and reliably interpret the emotion content of images [15].

Considering the above factors, we deployed two types of imagery in our evaluation: 1) a relatively abstract image set to provide a wide ranging and non-specific image pool with which designers would already be comfortable; and 2) an emotive image set built specifically to provide images communicative of emotions relevant to design conversation.

COMPONENTS OF THE FEEDBACK METHOD

In this section we focus on two steps in the feedback method as implemented for our evaluation study: intuitive image selection, and visual summary generation (steps 3 and 5 in Figure 2). We describe the construction of the image browsers along with the methods used to gather perceptual data on the image sets they hold. Then we describe the method used to generate visual summaries of image selections drawn from the browsers.

Intuitive Image Selection

Two image browsers were created to allow designers to experience two styles of image feedback, abstract and emotive, during the evaluation.

Abstract image browser

The abstract image browser was created by gathering the images, obtaining perceptual similarity data about them, and assembling them in a browser. Creative Commons licensed images tagged with the word, *abstract*, were gathered from *Flickr*. Images with writing, people, or conventionally framed objects or scenes were discarded. 500 were randomly selected from those that remained.

Obtaining the perceptual data and assembling the browser were done as described in Padilla et al. [24]. We used free sorting of 100 reference images by lab participants to generate a 100x100 similarity matrix. Then Amazon Mechanical Turk workers were asked to identify reference images that they viewed as similar to the remaining 400 query images. The query images were added incrementally to the matrix. Each time, their similarity vector was calculated as the average of chosen reference images' similarity vectors. The similarity matrix was used to train a rectangular self-organizing map (SOM) [35]. This informed the construction of an interface in which, each cell of the SOM was presented as a stack of images, the top image of each stack being the stack's centroid image. The features of this interface which make it intuitive to use when browsing are: a) stacks contain similar images, b) tapping or clicking the top image of a stack reveals the images in the stack, and c) adjacent stacks on the SOM contain images which are similar, while stacks far apart on the SOM contain dissimilar images (see Figure 3).

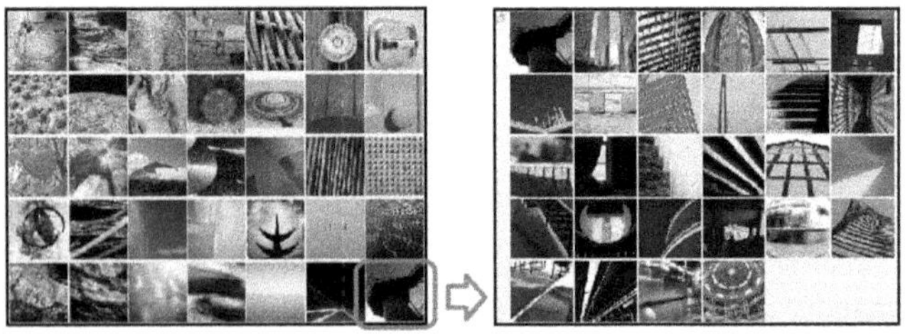

Figure 3 - SOM browser interface. Tapping or clicking the top image of a stack reveals the full stack. On the left is the top level of the SOM. On the right is the bottom left stack opened.

Emotive image browser

Although presented and organized in a similar way to the abstract browser the emotive image browser offered a different a set of images focused on emotion expressiveness. A survey, of staff and students of a design institution identified a subset of 19 terms from Plutchik's model of emotions [25] as being relevant to design feedback. 2000 Creative Commons licensed images associated with these terms were gathered from *Flickr* and *Google*. The images were then tagged with emotion terms by participants recruited via *CrowdFlower* using a drag and drop interface. This categorization produced a normalized emotion category frequency vector for each image. By filtering the images on this vector, the best 10 (approx.) images for each of the 19 emotion categories were identified. A SOM browser containing 204 images based on their emotion category vectors was assembled, resulting in image stacks containing emotionally similar images.

Visual Summary Generation

Any selection of images (or *feedback image selection)* chosen from the abstract image browser can be summarized by selecting a number of representative images; then arranging and sizing them according to the perceptual relationships and popularity within the feedback image selection. This is automated by a 4-stage algorithm:

1. Define an n dimensional similarity space (*S-space*) to describe likeness between the n images in the image set.
2. Cluster the feedback image selection in *S-space* to condense the feedback down to representative images.
3. Reduce the dimensionality of the *S-space* into a lower dimension space (3D) using multidimensional scaling (MDS) [5].
4. Project the 3D MDS space, describing the representative images, onto a 2D non-overlapping visual summary space.

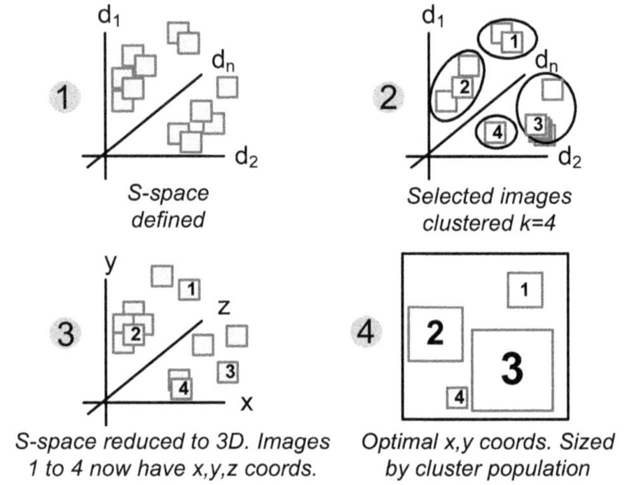

Figure 4 – The steps of the summarization algorithm.

For our evaluation experiment, the algorithm was applied as follows. 10 was chosen as k, the number of representative images; large enough to describe a spectrum within a selection but small enough to keep the summaries concise allowing display on an iPad. (Figure 4, illustrating the stages diagrammatically, uses k=4 for simplicity). The *S-space* was defined by the perceptual similarity data gathered to build the SOM browser interface. The clustering was done by applying k-means clustering [12] dividing each feedback image selection into 10 clusters. The image chosen to represent each cluster was the image closest to that cluster's centroid. In this way the summarization algorithm takes account of popular choices as a cluster's centroid is drawn towards those images chosen repeatedly. The size of each image on the summary is proportional to the cluster population. A 3D representation of the *S-space* is calculated using MDS. The summarization algorithm uses the 3D coordinates of the 10 representative images to calculate an optimized plane on which to project the 10 images. Finally the images are rendered, placing them as close as possible to their designated positions while avoiding overlaps; this being done by successively placing the images in order of popularity and applying a heuristic search of the remaining 2D summary space. Although overlapping images may be more aesthetically pleasing, it might have caused some meaningful or affecting part of an image to be obscured. Anecdotally, we have found that designers find this presentation convincing as it provides them with insight into the structure of the image set. A similar method was used to summarize selections from the emotive image browser. See examples of visual summaries in Figure 1 and Figure 6.

EVALUATION

To find out if designers would value the new visual feedback formats, we evaluated the method with a group of 12 interior design students (*designer participants*). This was done using a qualitative methodology involving semi-structured interviews and a grounded theory approach using open coding [30, 4]. Although the focus was on the views of the designers, a different 32 participants provided the feedback for the designs and we took the opportunity to ask those *feedback participants* about their preferences. All the participants (the designer participants and feedback participants) were students enrolled on a contextual studies course and received course credit for participating.

The stages of the evaluation are set out in the same sequence as the steps of the feedback method outlined previously in Figure 2.

Step 1- designer presents design

Each designer provided an image depicting one of their designs. The design domain was *interior design* and they were a diverse selection at various stages of development; they included an abstract concept design and a photo of a mobile paper sculpture fully executed. Figure 5 shows D8's prototype design for a store interior.

Figure 5 - A prototype for a store interior. (By permission D8).

Steps 2 and 3-feedback participants respond to design

Using a web application, the feedback participants representing the crowd each viewed a random selection of 6 designs. For each design, each feedback participant 1) viewed the design 2) was shown the question, "How did the design make you feel?" and 3) gave their response to the question in three formats: by selecting three images from the *abstract* browser, selecting three images from the *emotive* browser, and entering text. The order in which the three response formats were presented was randomized for each feedback participant. Each image response consisted of three images in case participants felt a combination of emotions. After completing the task, the feedback participants were asked in a questionnaire to rank the feedback formats in order of preference.

Step 4 – Collation of feedback responses

The responses of the 32 feedback participants were recorded in a database. Each had viewed half of the 12 available designs, thus the feedback responses of about 16 feedback participants were aggregated for each design. The feedback for each design, in the three different formats, was collated by running queries on the database.

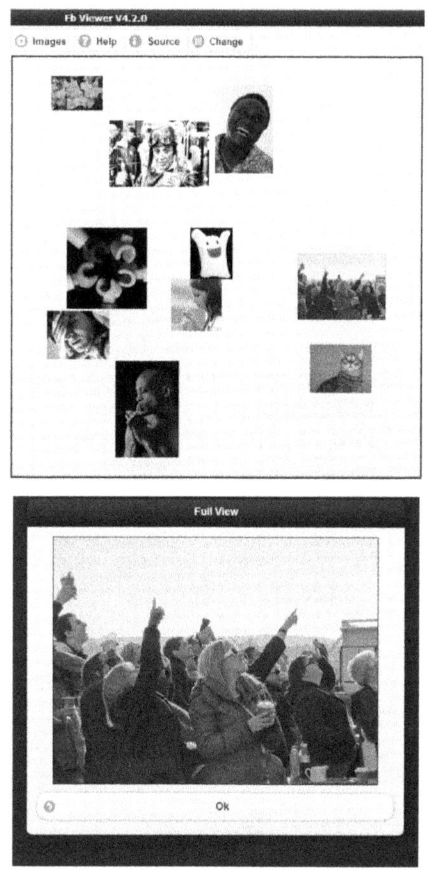

Figure 6 –Top: The visual summary of the emotive image responses to D8's design. Bottom: A component image viewed during interaction with the summary.

Step 5- Summary generation

The image responses to each design were summarized according to the algorithm described previously, producing two visual summaries to accompany each design, one of abstract and one of emotive images (Figure 6). Defining *S-space* and dimensionality reduction could be carried out beforehand as these involved calculations on the whole of each image set independent of any participant responses. The clustering was done after collection of feedback participant's image responses. (These stages of the summarization were implemented in MATLAB). The rendering of the visual summaries, was carried out by the web application used to display the summaries (implemented in JavaScript and PHP). The text responses for each design were simply collated as randomly ordered lists.

Step 6 – Designer views the feedback

In the interviews each of the 12 designer participants was shown the three forms of response gathered from the feedback participants who viewed that designer's design. A web application was used to facilitate the presentation of the response formats. The designer participants viewed them on an iPad and were encouraged to interact with them. They are interactive in that each of the component images can be viewed at full size by tapping it or clicking with a mouse. The lists of text comments were scrollable. The interviews lasted approximately 45 minutes. Each started with a 15 minute warm-up consisting of a walk-through of the two image sets, how they were constructed and how selections from them can be summarized. The designers were asked to talk about how they used images in the design process and about their designs so as to establish the development stages of the designs. During the rest of the interview the three forms of feedback were revealed to the designer in a random order, with the designer interacting with the feedback on an iPad (Figure 6) while the same feedback and their design were displayed on a monitor for discussion (Figure 7). Prepared questions probed aspects including the interpretation of component images on the summaries and their opinion of the effectiveness of a given format at communicating emotions. Additional questions followed up points raised by the designers. Audio recordings were made and transcribed.

RESULTS

This section details the main themes and evidence for them arising out of the interviews with the *designer participants*. However, first we briefly report the preferences of the *feedback participants* for the different response formats:

Feedback participant preferences

The feedback participants were asked to rank the feedback formats in order of preference in a brief post-task questionnaire. 31 of the 32 feedback participants responded (See Table 1). The highest ranked format was abstract images (average ranking 1.81); i.e. responding with images from the abstract image browser was the format ranked highest for preference overall by those giving the feedback. Thus, quantitatively, it can be seen from Table 1 that 20 out of 31 chose one of the image formats as their first preference (15 for abstract images and 5 for emotive).

Theme 1 Inspiration to make changes

An example of a designer participant being immediately inspired to make a specific change to her design is shown here, after viewing her abstract image feedback summary: "*I was looking at [it] and thinking that was earthy and very cold, it is not the environment I really wanted. So yes, it is making me think, definite change of textures, if that is how they see it as cold and mechanical. I didn't think that would be the reaction you would get but that is good though. Good feedback*" [D11]. Sometimes a less specific change was motivated. Here, after viewing emotive image feedback: *"I'd make it a nicer visual. I'd make... I'd refine it a bit more. I'd put more detail into it. I think. 'Cause it [her design image] is a bit boring."* [D6].

Rank / Format	1	2	3	No. of Responses	Average ranking
Abstract	15	7	9	31	1.81
Text	11	10	10	31	1.97
Emotive	5	14	12	31	2.23
Total	31	31	31		

Table 1 - Feedback participants' preference rankings of the formats. Abstract and Emotive were image formats. The average ranking for each format is calculated by giving each number of responses a weight equivalent to its rank, adding them and dividing by the number of responses. Note: with rankings a lower value means a higher ranking.

Designers found motivation in the visual feedback for design changes. The abstract image feedback was being read for color and texture ideas while the emotion, *boredom*, was being read from the emotive image feedback prompting change. Here the emotion being read was negative and this is discussed in another theme below, "*Negative feedback*".

Figure 7- Interview setting.

A quantitative analysis of inspiration by format perhaps indicates the potential of the image formats: 11 of the 12 participants were asked about motivated changes after the first feedback was revealed. (Other themes were pursued in the remaining interview). The order was randomized, 3 saw text first, 4 abstract images, and 4 emotive images. 5/11 described some form of change motivated by the first feedback: text 0/3; abstract 2/4; emotive 3/4. Thus, in our study, where it was possible to isolate inspiration to a single format, none were inspired by text while 5 participants drew some inspiration from images after viewing their first feedback.

Theme 2 Interpreting the Feedback

While viewing and exploring a visual feedback summary, designer participants would develop their interpretation of the feedback. Here while viewing emotive image feedback on her design for a bar interior and successively expanding the individual component images: "*Mmm. I think they are talking about the mood in this one. How, like, people here, socializing; they are happy. Something crazy going on here [little laugh]. And, [I] don't really understand this one here. Like you can just sit down by yourself and get lost in your thoughts..*"[D5].

A similar process seemed to occur with ambiguity in the text feedback with the designers assigning a message or messages to comments and groups of similar comments e.g.: *"[quoting from her text feedback]"planning and organizing, sense of group". Yeah, 'cause it's sort of the way that the chairs are laid out and stuff."*[D12].

The designers were aware of the issue of ambiguity but when encountering it they proceeded to assign a message to an image or group of images on a summary (or indeed even to text which was ambiguous).

Here D8 saw an advantage in the ambiguity of image feedback offering an escape from the harshness of text: "*People's opinions are always put across by text and whether that's a good thing or a bad thing I don't know because it gets your point across in a very direct manner?...Whereas maybe from these images especially the emotive ones, you can take out of it what you want a bit more? So maybe if you are a bit sensitive about your design you could take out the good things"*[D8].

Theme 3 Abstract image summaries as mood boards

The abstract image summaries were likened to mood boards. While talking about her abstract feedback summary:*"...Just sort of represents what is actually there [in her design]...because it is outdoor there is a lot of green and a lot of wood...Yes the look is similar to what my mood board would look like before it."* [D12]. She continued on this theme later when suggesting that she would use the abstract image feedback as a presentational tool for describing the design to others including those who commissioned the design: *"...to show like it was a presentation and you were then saying, "Well, I've actually surveyed all these people and this is what they thought of it", and then to show that [indicating the abstract summary]."* [D12]. Here two uses of the abstract image feedback are indicated. Firstly it could act as a form of reverse-engineered mood board confirming that the designer's originally planned "mood" for the design was being communicated as intended. We saw this operating in the negative when D11 (quoted in Theme 1) was motivated to make a change because she was responding to her mood-board-style reading of her abstract feedback. Secondly, the abstract feedback can be used to demonstrate perceptions of the design when presenting it to a client.

Theme 4 Negative feedback

This theme merited division into sub-themes:

Theme 4.1- Abstract imagery not seen as negative

Negative feedback was a topic arising in discussion from participants while viewing text feedback and emotive image feedback. However it was not mentioned by any participant while viewing the abstract image feedback. Combining this with the observation that changes could be motivated by the abstract feedback (see Theme 1) suggests that the abstract feedback can be inspirational without being perceived as threatening or negative.

Theme 4.2 - A tendency to focus on negative feedback

There was a tendency for participants to focus on negative feedback e.g. they would skip positive text comments and alight on the negative. This was acknowledged in discussion by one participant who had skipped to a specific negative comment: "*Just 'cause the first two sounded quite positive. [laughs]... I was enjoying reading it up to there [laughs]."* [D7]. Another participant when it was pointed out that the text list contained more positive comments than negative: *"You just can't help but read the bad stuff"*. [D6].

Negative feedback was also perceived in emotive image feedback. Participant D3's emotive image feedback summary contained only one negative image out of ten. (The image showed a man covering his eyes with his hand). The size of the images on the summaries varied with the population of the feedback cluster they represented, but the single negative image that D3 chose to dwell on only represented just 20% of the total area covered by all ten images on the summary. D3's words are quoted in Theme 4.3 below as they also apply to that theme.

We interpret this focus on negative feedback as the designers valuing the negative feedback over the positive however unpalatable it might be for them.

Theme 4.3 - The impact of negative text compared to negative emotive images.

One participant felt that negative feedback received via the emotive images was more impactful than text. Here she is referring to the single negative image in the summary: *"I think the emotive images are quite hard to look at because it is peoples' emotions towards your, design. And if an image is that big, it does kind of pull you back and like, "Why?"."* And then, *"When you look at the images, they'll be stuck to you. Whereas the writing, it doesn't really stick much to you. You just read it and you're like "Ok." But the images, you're like "Wow!" It's almost like you can see that person's emotion when they are picking this image."* [D3]. For another participant negative feedback via text was more impactful than the emotive image feedback: *"Looking at that [the emotive image summary], I'd say I'm more relaxed looking at the images than the text... this girl's bored and that guy's confused [pointing to component images in the emotive summary]. It's just less threatening than the text.... So the images are a good idea in that way."* [D6].

This difference over which format, emotive images or text was harsher for delivering negative feedback could be affected by individual participants' different cognitive styles. Alternatively it could be due to differences in the specific designs involved and their reception by the feedback crowd. Irrespective of this disagreement between the designers on whether negative feedback had more impact as text or as emotive images this does demonstrate that the designers were able to read negative feedback via the emotive image format. Thus, because they showed a keen interest in negative feedback, this indicates that the emotive image feedback would be of value to them.

Theme 5 Effectiveness at communicating emotions

When asked how well the text feedback answered the question "How did the design make you feel?", here D6 points out that the text comments had actually strayed into a critique rather than talking about feelings: *"No-one's really said how they feel really. Well, [quoting from the text feedback] "I felt uninspired" There's one. But that's it... Yeah. I think the emotive images work better than the text...'Cause it's fair enough if they were critiquing it, but they're not. They're meant to be saying how they feel and no-one's really [done that]."* [D6]. Another participant: "*What they said in the text isn't exactly feelings*" [D8]. Those designers clearly think that the emotive images have allowed those giving the feedback to focus on communicating their emotions more effectively than when using text. Another participant on the effectiveness of images for emotion: *"I like that [emotive image summary]. [be]cause it shows emotion as well, yes, mostly like emotions that people would feel...It's a good way of getting their understanding."* [D2].

Theme 6 A service offering the visual feedback

After discussing the feedback formats participants were asked if they would use an Internet service which allowed them to upload a design and receive feedback in the *visual* formats. Ten of the designers answered emphatically in the positive, one was neutral and one (D12) initially wished for text feedback but moved on to develop the idea of using the abstract feedback as a presentation tool. One participant was particularly effusive: "*I'd love that! I'd absolutely love that yeah!*" [D8]. From this it is clear that the designer participants valued the visual feedback formats and wanted more.

DISCUSSION

Before discussing the results we first point out that the nature of the sample for our evaluation means that we should be cautious about generalizing from our findings. The feedback participants may not be representative of the general population; as students in a contextual studies course it is possible they could hold some non-typical attitudes about design communication and imagery. Equally, the designer participant group might not be considered representative of all designers as they were student interior designers. However, the participants' experience of this new form of visual communication has provided a window into the likely appeal of the visual feedback formats.

Responding with images

The rankings of the response formats by the feedback participants (Table 1), giving the highest ranking to abstract images as a response format, show that for some people, perceptually organized image banks would be valued as a way of giving feedback ahead of text. The fact that some participants preferred text and some preferred images as a response format is not a surprise as this fits with the prediction of cognitive styles theory that some of the participants are likely to be more visual than verbal and vice-versa.

The two types of imagery

With designers finding the abstract imagery non-threatening yet still inspiring, and many feedback participants preferring that format, the abstract image set is the image format embraced by the participants in the study. However, the emotive imagery seemed to help the feedback participants focus on communicating their emotions rather than giving a conventional critique with text and both types of image provoked reflection in designers albeit in different ways. Cognitive factors of emotions affecting intuitive decision making [33] and being easily read in images [15] may have come into play in affecting participants' comparative impressions of the two image sets.

Scalability

The summarization algorithm allows the image selections by crowds of unlimited size to be encapsulated in a small number of representative images. Both of the two image sets are able to be augmented by adding further images or refreshed by replacing old images with new ones along with accompanying perceptual data.

Possibilities for a new service

The finding in Theme 6 that, overwhelmingly, the designer participants wished to use an internet service offering these visual formats, shows an appetite among designers for them. Figure 2 shows the possibilities for successive co-design cycles allowing presentation of a prototype, then feedback, then design changes, further feedback and so on. Indeed the designer participants were unanimous that the best use of such a service would be in developing and refining a prototype design via crowd feedback. Social networks can be a useful source of feedback on ideas [8] and could be a good conduit through which designers could use the new mode to leverage participation in feedback. In particular, photo sharing social media are likely to be frequented by users already open to responding visually.

Offering images as a response format could become popular among such users with a visual cognitive style and committed users might enjoy being involved in the development and expansion of the imagery. Visual co-design cycles may, as a design develops, accrue additional benefits. These could include the building of a following for a designer through segmentation of the visual feedback crowd. When this scenario was put to one designer participant she responded: "*That's a million dollar idea! You should get an app!*"[D1]. Another benefit could flow from adding value to any resulting product by compiling records of the co-design cycles into an attractive, visual, development narrative to be attached to the product. Such added value not only has economic benefits but because it is effectively resource-free compared to say, a garment, there is an environmental sustainability benefit when people buy fewer products on which they place higher value [29].

Applicable domains

Although originally motivated by fashion designers and evaluated with interior designs, we believe this method of feedback would work well for any aesthetic design particularly where first impressions are important; e.g. product and graphic design in automotive, food, travel and other sectors. Feedback using images need not be restricted to design conversation or co-design activities. The emotive image format might enliven or further increase the accessibility of the comments page of any web video clip for example. Another benefit of using banks of images as the medium for an online conversation would be in avoiding the cost of comment moderation. Web sites where online discussion takes place have to deal with unsuitable posts. Some automated filtering can be done but manual intervention by moderators is often required [7]. Many systems rely on users reporting abusive posts, in effect crowdsourcing the task. However, before a report is received damage will already have been done. In this new visual feedback method the feedback is drawn from given image sets, thus, the problem of unsuitable posts is avoided.

Cultural and emotional aspects of imagery

While some aspects of emotional imagery are considered universal and thus bridging cultures, such as some facial expressions [25, 10], other aspects of imagery, such as color, can vary between cultures in their emotional associations [20]. While images provide for non-verbal communication which should be language independent and thus have an advantage over text, intercultural differences may need to be taken into account. An investigation of cultural differences in the interpretation of the image banks built for the evaluation would help improve the formulation of further image banks.

CONCLUSION

In this paper we set out a novel method of enabling visual communication between crowds and designers. The crowd comments intuitively with images on an idea and these responses are summarized in succinct, visual, reports. We described an implementation of the method involving intuitive image browsers and image summarization, based on perceptual data. Two types of imagery, abstract and emotional were used. This was evaluated in a qualitative study with interior designers. These designer participants received feedback about the emotional impact of their designs and were able to contrast the visual feedback formats with text feedback. They voiced views indicating, for example, that the abstract image feedback provided an instant impression of the perceived mood in their designs and that the emotive imagery had helped those giving the feedback to focus on emotions rather than straying into conventional critiques encouraged by text. While aware of ambiguity being inherent in images, the designer participants freely interpreted the image feedback. They found motivation for change in the images while finding none in text. They were interested in the text, particularly in negative text feedback, but not inspired by it in the same way as with images. For those giving the feedback, a quantitative analysis of their preferences showed that, for some, responding with images was preferable to text (in the case of our feedback participant group the majority preferred the visual formats). While a small minority of the designer participants wished for the visual feedback to be accompanied by text, all but one desired to use an internet service that offered the visual feedback. We discussed the possibilities for this visual feedback method beyond simply being a communication medium more engaging for people with a visual cognitive style. These possibilities include use as a means of connecting designers to a following; as a tool for co-design; and adding value through narrative creation.

ACKNOWLEDGMENTS

Funded by Heriot-Watt University CDI theme. Browser images, all Creative Commons, are acknowledged here: http://www.macs.hw.ac.uk/texturelab/ack/

REFERENCES

1. Clarke, A.D., Halley, F., Newell, A.J., Griffin, L.D. and Chantler, M.J. Perceptual similarity: a texture challenge. In *Proc BMVC*, (2011).
2. Coffield, F., Moseley, D., Hall, E. and Ecclestone, K. *Should we be using learning styles?: what research has to say to practice*. Learning & Skills Research Centre. (2004).
3. Cook, E., Teasley, S.D., and Ackerman, M.S. Contribution, commercialization & audience: *understanding* participation in an online creative community. In *Proc Group2009*, ACM (2009), 41-50.
4. Corbin, J. and Strauss, A. *Basics of qualitative research: Techniques and procedures for developing grounded theory*. Sage. (2008).
5. Cox, T.F. and Cox, M.A.A. *Multidimensional Scaling (Second Edition ed.).* Chapman & Hall/CRC. (2001).

6. CrowdFlower, http://www.crowdflower.com (last accessed Sept.20th 2014)
7. Delort, J.Y., Arunasalam, B. and Paris, C. Automatic Moderation of Online Discussion Sites. *IJEC*, 15(3), (2011), 9-30.
8. Dow, S., Gerber, E., and Wong, A. A pilot study of using crowds in the classroom. In *Proc CHI2013*, ACM (2013), 227-236.
9. Egorova, M., Safonov, I. and Korobkov, N. Collage for Cover of PhotoBook. In *GraphiCon*, (2008), 160-163.
10. Ekman, P. Expression and the nature of emotion. *Approaches to emotion.* Lawrence Erlbaum Associates (1984), 319-344.
11. Evans, J. St B. T. Two minds rationality. *Thinking & Reasoning*, 20(2), Routledge (2013), 129-146.
12. Everitt B. *Cluster Analysis*. Heinemann. (1974).
13. Fan, J., Gao, Y., Luo, H., Keim, D.A. and Li, Z. A novel approach to enable semantic and visual image summarization for exploratory image search. In *Proc MIR2008,* ACM (2008), 358-365.
14. Garner, S. and McDonagh-Philp, D. Problem interpretation and resolution via visual stimuli: the use of 'mood boards' in design education. *J Art Design Educ*, 20(1), Blackwell (2001), 57-64.
15. Junghöfer, M., Bradley, M.M., Elbert, T.R. and Lang, P.J. Fleeting images: A new look at early emotion discrimination. *Psychophysiology*, 38(2), Cambridge Univ Press (2001), 175-178.
16. Kozhevnikov, M. Cognitive styles in the context of modern psychology: Toward an integrated framework of cognitive style. *Psychol Bull*, 133(3), APA (2007), 464-481.
17. Lee, J., Park, D.H. and Han, I. The effect of negative online consumer reviews on product attitude: An information processing view. *Electron Com R A*, 7(3), Elsevier (2008), 341-352.
18. Lerner, J.S., Small, D.A. and Loewenstein, G. Research Report Heart Strings and Purse Strings Carryover Effects of Emotions on Economic Decisions. *Psychological Science*, 15(5), APS (2004), 337-341.
19. Luther, K., Pavel, A., Wu, W., Tolentino, J.-l., Agrawala, M., Hartmann, B., Dow, S.P. CrowdCrit: crowdsourcing and aggregating visual design critique. In *Proc CSCW2014*, ACM (2014), 21-24.
20. McCandless, D. *Information is beautiful*, Collins. (2009).
21. Mikels, J.A., Fredrickson, B.L., Larkin, G.R., Lindberg, C.M., Maglio, S.J. and Reuter-Lorenz, P.A. Emotional category data on images from the International Affective Picture System. *Behav Res Methods*, 37(4), Springer (2005), 626-630.
22. Nagamachi M. Kansei engineering: a new ergonomic consumer-oriented technology for product development, *Int J.Industrial Ergonomics* 15(1) (1995), 3-11.
23. Oppenheim A.N. *Questionnaire Design and Attitude Measurement*, Heinemann, (1966).
24. Padilla, S., Halley, F., Robb, D. and Chantler, M.J. Intuitive Large Image Database Browsing using Perceptual Similarity Enriched by Crowds. In *Proc CAIP2013*, Springer (2013).
25. Plutchik, R. *Emotions and life : perspectives from psychology, biology, and evolution (1st ed.),* APA. (2003).
26. Riding, R.J. On the nature of cognitive style. *Educational Psychology*, 17(1-2), Routledge (1997), 29-49.
27. Riding, R.J. and Cheema, I. Cognitive Styles - an overview and integration. *Educational Psychology*, 11(3-4), Routledge (1991), 193-215.
28. Rother, C., Bordeaux, L., Hamadi, Y. and Blake, A. AutoCollage. *ACM Trans. Graph*., 25(3), (2006), 847-852.
29. Sanders, L. and Simons, G. A Social Vision for Value Co-creation in Design. (Value Co-Creation) *Open Source Business Resource*, (2009).
30. Strauss, A.L. *Qualitative analysis for social scientist,* Cambridge University Press. (1987).
31. Surowiecki, J. *The wisdom of crowds: why the many are smarter than the few and how collective wisdom shapes business, Economies, Societies and Nations*. Anchor. (2004).
32. Talwar, A., Jurca, R. and Faltings, B. Understanding user behavior in online feedback reporting. In *Proc EC2007,* ACM (2007), 132-142.
33. Tiedens, L.Z. and Linton, S. Judgment under emotional certainty and uncertainty: the effects of specific emotions on information processing. *J Pers Soc Psychol*, 81(6), APA (2001), 973.
34. Tsytsarau M. and Palpanas T. Survey on mining subjective data on the web. *Data Min Knowl Discov* 24(3), ACM (2012), 478-514.
35. Vesanto, J., Himberg, J., Alhoniemi, E. and Parhankangas, J. Self-organizing map in Matlab: the som toolbox. In *Proc. Matlab DSP Conf*, (1999), 35–40.
36. Xu, A., and Bailey, B. What do you think?: a case study of benefit, expectation, and interaction in a large online critique community. In *Proc CSCW2012*, ACM (2012), 295-304.
37. Xu, A., Huang, S.-W. and Bailey, B.P. Voyant: Generating Structured Feedback on Visual Designs Using a Crowd of Non-Experts. In *Proc CSCW2014,* ACM (2014), 37-40.

Measuring Crowdsourcing Effort with Error-Time Curves

Justin Cheng
Stanford University
jcccf@cs.stanford.edu

Jaime Teevan
Microsoft Research
teevan@microsoft.com

Michael S. Bernstein
Stanford University
msb@cs.stanford.edu

ABSTRACT

Crowdsourcing systems lack effective measures of the effort required to complete each task. Without knowing how much time workers need to execute a task well, requesters struggle to accurately structure and price their work. Objective measures of effort could better help workers identify tasks that are worth their time. We propose a data-driven effort metric, ETA (error-time area), that can be used to determine a task's fair price. It empirically models the relationship between time and error rate by manipulating the time that workers have to complete a task. ETA reports the area under the error-time curve as a continuous metric of worker effort. The curve's 10th percentile is also interpretable as the minimum time most workers require to complete the task without error, which can be used to price the task. We validate the ETA metric on ten common crowdsourcing tasks, including tagging, transcription, and search, and find that ETA closely tracks how workers would rank these tasks by effort. We also demonstrate how ETA allows requesters to rapidly iterate on task designs and measure whether the changes improve worker efficiency. Our findings can facilitate the process of designing, pricing, and allocating crowdsourcing tasks.

Author Keywords

Crowdsourcing; microtasks; task effort.

ACM Classification Keywords

H.5.m. Information Interfaces and Presentation (e.g. HCI): Miscellaneous.

INTRODUCTION

Imagine that a requester wants to use Amazon Mechanical Turk to label 10,000 images with a fixed set of tags. How much should workers be paid to label each image? Would labeling an image with twice as many tags result in a task that is twice as much effort? Should the tags be provided in a drop down list or with radio buttons? Answering these questions requires a fine-grained understanding of the amount of effort the task requires. This process today involves trial and error: requesters observe the wait time and quality on test tasks, guess what might have been causing any problems, tweak the task, and repeat. An accurate measure of the effort required to complete a crowdsourced task would enable requesters to compare different approaches to their tasks, iterate toward a better design, and price their tasks objectively. It could also help workers decide whether to accept a task, or even allow systems to offer tasks based on difficulty or time availability.

CHI 2015, April 18–23, 2015, Seoul, Republic of Korea.

ACM 978-1-4503-3145-6/15/04 ...$15.00.
http://dx.doi.org/10.1145/2702123.2702145

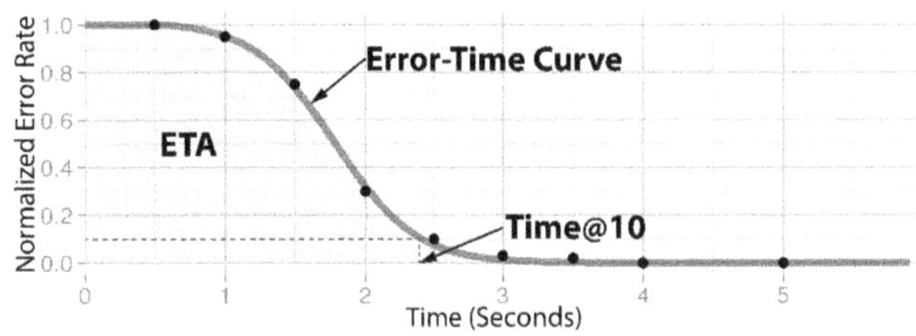

Figure 1. The ETA is defined as the area under the error-time curve.

However, despite its potential value, task effort is challenging to estimate. Workers face cognitive biases in assessing difficulty [21], while requesters cannot easily observe the process and, as experts, categorically underestimate completion times [12]. These limits suggest the need for a behavioral approach to measure effort. One approach might be to let the market identify hard tasks by reacting to the posted price [30]. However, prices cannot easily make fine distinctions in an inelastic market such as Mechanical Turk [14]. Another approach might be to use task duration as a signal of difficulty, but this is unreliable because workers regularly accept multiple tasks simultaneously and interleave work [29]. Measures such as reaction time [32] are not easy to apply to typical crowd tasks: reaction time metrics tend to use simplistic tasks (e.g., shape or color recognition), while others may be too involved for crowd work (e.g., [9]).

In this paper, we propose a data-driven behavioral measure of effort that can be easily and cheaply calculated using the crowd. Our metric, the *error time area (ETA)*, draws on cognitive psychology literature on speed-accuracy tradeoff curves [32], and represents the effort required for a worker to accurately complete a task. To create it, we first recruit workers to complete the task under different time limits. Next, we fit a curve to the collected data relating the error rate and time limit (Figure 1). Last, we compute ETA by taking the area under this error-time curve. Because ETA is calculated using a data-driven approach, task difficulty can be determined with minimal effort and without analytical modeling. Rather than measuring average duration independent of work quality, ETA computes quality as a function of duration and thus can be used to estimate a wage for a task. ETA also allows requesters to compare multiple task designs; for example, we find that tagging an image with an open textbox is less effort than choosing between a fixed list of 16 options, but more effort than choosing between a fixed list of 8 options.

After describing ETA, we explore the metric via four studies:

- *Study 1: ETA vs. other measures of effort.* For ten common microtasking primitives (e.g., multiple choice questions, long-form text entry), we show that the ETA metric represents effort better than existing measures.
- *Study 2: ETA vs. market price.* We then compare ETA as well as other measures to the market prices of these primitives on a crowdsourcing platform.
- *Study 3: Modeling perceptual costs.* By augmenting ETA with measures of perceptual effort, we find we can better model a worker's perceived difficulty of a task.
- *Study 4: Tasks without ground truth.* In order to capture how well people do a task, ETA requires ground truth. We extend the metric to also work for subjective tasks.

We then demonstrate how ETA can be used for rapidly prototyping tasks. ETA makes it possible to characterize tasks in terms of their monetary cost and human effort, and paves the way for better task design, payment, and allocation.

RELATED WORK

Measures of task difficulty or mental workload can be roughly separated into two categories: subjective and objective measures. Subjective measures include multidimensional workload assessment tools such as the NASA Task Load Index (TLX) [10] and time estimates [5]. However, such measures tend to be inaccurate and hard to capture. It is difficult for requesters to accurately estimate task difficulty, as experts categorically underestimate novices' completion times and difficulty [12, 13]. Workers are also inaccurate; subjective metrics collected from workers tend to correlate poorly with each other (e.g., between self-reported effort, self-reported difficulty, and response time [7]), and workers exhibit large variance because they use different ranges of the rating scale [11]. Worker-driven subjective task judgments sometimes appear on web sites such as Turkopticon and mTurk Grind. However, these reviews are limited in number, lag the marketplace by hours, and not available for all tasks. Our own experiments reveal that many subjective metrics, while correlated with effort, are not directly interpretable and cannot differentiate between similar tasks.

Objective measures of effort include measuring reaction time to a secondary stimulus [32] and dual task performance [33]. Physiological approaches include using EEGs [9], but these approaches are relatively involved. The pricing of tasks on Mechanical Turk can also provide a signal of the effort required for a task; survival analysis empirically models the tradeoff between pricing and rate of completion [8], and measures of how long people work on tasks can characterize a form of interface utility [30]. Still, completion rates are dependent on time of day and the presence of other tasks, and the equilibrium wage in crowdsourcing markets is low and fairly inelastic [14]. Raw task duration is another potential measure, but is a noisy signal as workers tend to switch between tasks or ignore them for periods of time [29]. Accuracy-based measures are subject to ceiling effects, especially on relatively simple tasks typical of crowdsourcing, and are not easily comparable across task types. We employ an objective approach to measuring effort, extending research on accuracy-tradeoff curves [32] to produce a more robust measure that correlates well with several subjective measures.

While our approach is data-driven, measures of effort do not inherently require a task be completed to be calculated. Machine learning can be used to estimate the difficulty of a particular input and the quality of a worker for unobserved tasks (e.g., [6]), but these approaches tend to be fairly complex and require large-scale data collection. Further, they are task-specific (e.g., multiple-choice questions [16]) and not easily comparable across tasks. Our work requires limited data and makes it possible to compare a large variety of tasks.

In addition to measuring the amount of overall effort a task requires, the effort associated with a task can also be broken down into components, for example, by separating its perceptive (e.g., reading a question), cognitive (e.g., formulating the answer), and psychomotor (e.g., writing the answer down) costs [25]. Borrowing from these models of workload, we augment our approach to explore the perceptual load of a task. We do not attempt to exactly differentiate between these component costs, but our initial experiments suggest there is value in accounting for these differences. In human factors research, analytical models for usability evaluation (e.g., ACT-R [3]) have been developed to characterize low-level processes for computer-based tasks, and can be used to predict mental workload. However, these methods require substantial training or metadata annotation to execute, which make them infeasible for many requesters. Rather than model the effort required for a task by analyzing its specific makeup, crowdsourcing allows us to do so by quickly getting workers to perform tasks and observing how they perform.

ETA: A MEASURE OF TASK EFFORT

To quantify the amount of effort a task requires for high-quality results, we measure the impact of time on the number of errors workers make. Taking inspiration from the speed-accuracy tradeoff curves developed in cognitive psychology research [26, 32], we calculate a task's *error-time* tradeoff curve by giving workers varying time constraints to finish the task and measuring the probability they make an error within each time limit. We measure the error-time area under the curve (or, simply, *ETA*) to reduce the curve to a single metric. What follows is a detailed description of this process.

Error-Time Data Collection. Cognitive psychology has demonstrated that the amount of time a person has to do a task impacts their ability to do it well [26, 32]. To calculate how much time is required to perform a crowdsourcing task well, we sample different time limits (e.g., 0.2, 2, or 20 seconds) and ask each worker within-subject to complete the task at each time limit, with the time limits presented in random order. After the time limit elapses, the task is disabled and workers cannot submit their response. By using tasks with known correct answers (gold standard tasks), we can calculate the error rate for a task within each limit. In practice, we recommend at least seven time conditions and 10 workers. For a two cent task, this comes out to under $5. To determine time limits for a task, a task designer could define them evenly spaced around an initial estimate.

The data collected for an example task can be seen in Figure 1, where the x-axis represents the amount of time workers were given, and the y-axis represents the error rate. In this example, workers have a 95% chance of getting the answer incorrect (or incomplete) when given one second to complete the task, but only a 10% chance when given about 2.5 seconds. We later demonstrate how worker consistency can be used to create these curves even without ground-truth data.

Fitting the Error-Time Curve. Next we fit a sigmoid curve to the recorded accuracies. Sigmoids (e.g., logistic curves) are a good model for performance data that undergoes a phase shift. In our data, this shift occurs at the point when the task becomes feasible to complete in the given time limit. An example error-time curve is shown fitted to the data in Figure 1. The range of potential error rates can differ across tasks; for example, a binary choice task has an observed error rate ranging from 0 (always correct) and 0.5 (random). For this reason, we scale the observed error rate to always be between 0 and 1 (and the curve clipped, if necessary, to ensure the predicted error rate is also between 0 and 1).

Calculating the ETA. Prior work exploring the tradeoff between accuracy and time in task performance has primarily focused on characterizing the functions and parameters of these curves (e.g., that they are exponential [32]), or using them to make empirical observations on a small number of very similar tasks (e.g., on different amounts of object rotations [22]). While these plots provide analytical value, they do not facilitate comparison across the wide variety of tasks found on microtask markets. Thus we extend the approach to reduce the error-time curve into a single, cross-task comparable, continuous metric.

With a model fit to the data, we reduce the curve to a single score. Many reductions are possible; we use the area under the curve (AUC). Inspired by the use of ROC AUC in machine learning, the error-time area (ETA) under the curve captures human performance under differing amounts of time. A small ETA suggests the task can be performed correctly almost instantaneously, while a large ETA suggests it is very difficult, although there are some exceptions (e.g., if a task is difficult regardless of the time limit, the ETA will be small as it measures relative, not absolute change in performance). Intuitively, each unit increase in ETA corresponds to a task requiring an additional second to achieve the same work quality. Because error is scaled, the ETA is finite and can be calculated by computing the integral at infinity.

Calculating Work Time and Wage. While ETA is interpretable, other transformations of the curve have more direct interpretations; *Time@10*, or the time it takes to achieve an error rate at the 10th percentile, reflects the amount of time a worker would need to achieve a relatively low error rate. By multiplying this time with a target pay rate (e.g., minimum wage), this metric can be used to price tasks. Such an approach may be preferable to using how long workers spend on the task, since some workers rush through tasks and care little about accuracy, while others spend more time than necessary. Time@10 can be calculated by identifying the point on the x-axis where the error-time curve crosses an error rate of 0.1 (10%) (Figure 1). Alternate thresholds (e.g., Time@5) would represent different tradeoffs between the fraction of workers able to attain the given wage rate and task price.

Code Library. A framework for computing ETA is available open-source at `http://hci.st/eta`. Users of the framework begin by collecting task-relevant data. To do this they include a Javascript library in their existing task HTML file and write a few lines of code specifying the format of the task's input and the time points desired. They then upload the modified task file to their crowdsourcing platform of choice. The library randomizes the order of the time limits, tells the worker how long they have to complete the task, and disables the answer area (but not the submit button) after the time elapses. The task's output can be analyzed using an R code library. It outputs descriptive statistics (e.g., task time), plots the error-time curve, and computes the task's ETA along with other objective and subjective measures.

This code library makes it possible to easily measure the effort a task requires via an initial HIT at the cost of a few dollars. The computed error-time curve can be used in a number of ways. Requestors can iterate on a task's design to reduce its ETA, and multiply Time@10 by an hourly wage to determine the task's payment. The ETA can also be published along with the task to facilitate task selection by workers.

While ETA grows out of a large body of cognitive science literature for measuring effort, it is important to understand how well it works in practice. For this reason, we ran a number of studies to understand when it works, when it does not, and why. Through four studies, we evaluate ETA as a measure of effort. In Studies 1 and 2, we compare ETA to other objective and subjective measures, including market price. In Study 3, we additionally model the perceptual cost of a task to account for instances where ETA does not match workers' perceived difficulty of a task. In Study 4, we extend our approach with a methodology that allows us to measure ETA without ground truth answers. Finally, we demonstrate how ETA can be used to compare effort across different versions of a task.

STUDY 1: ETA VS. OTHER MEASURES OF EFFORT

We begin by comparing ETA and other measures of difficulty (including time and subjective difficulty) across a number of common crowdsourcing tasks. After describing the experimental setup, designed to elicit the necessary data to generate error-time curves and other measures for each task, we show how closely the different measures matched.

Method

Study 1 and all subsequent experiments reported in this paper were conducted using a proprietary microtasking platform that outsources crowd work to workers on the Clickworker microtask market. The platform interface is similar to that of Amazon Mechanical Turk; users upload HTML task files, workers choose from a marketplace listing of tasks, and data is collected in CSV files. We restricted workers to those residing in the United States. Across all studies, 470 unique workers completed over 44 thousand tasks. A followup survey revealed that approximately 66% were female. We replicated Study 1 on Amazon Mechanical Turk and found empirically

Primitive	Example Question
Binary (Binary Choice)	Does this label apply to this image?
Scale (Likert Scale)	How much do you agree with this statement?
Categorize	Which category best applies to this image?
Tag	Label this image with a tag.
Describe	Describe this image.
Math	Add these two numbers together.
Transcribe	Copy this phrase exactly as presented.
Find	Find a spelling error in this sentence.
Fix	Correct the highlighted word in this sentence.
Search	Search for the answer to this question online.

Table 1. Ten primitives common to most crowdsourcing workflows.

similar results, so we only report results using Clickworker in this paper.

Primitive Crowdsourcing Task Types

We began by populating our evaluation tasks with common crowdsourcing task types, or *primitives*, that appear commonly as microtasks or parts of microtasks. To do this, we looked at the types of tasks with the most available HITs on Amazon Mechanical Turk, at reports on common crowdsourcing task types [15], and at crowdsourcing systems described in the literature (e.g., [4]). After several iterations we identified a list of ten primitives that are present in most crowdsourcing workflows (Table 1, Figure 2). For example, the Find-Fix-Verify workflow [4] could be expressed using a combination of the FIND (identify sentences which need shortening), FIX (shortening these sentences), and BINARY primitives (verifying the shortening is an improvement). In many cases, the primitives themselves (or repetitions of the same primitive) make up the entire task, and map directly to common Mechanical Turk tasks (e.g., finding facts such as phone numbers about individuals (SEARCH)).

We instantiated these primitives using a dataset of images of people performing different actions (e.g., waving, cooking) [34] and a corpus of translated Wikipedia articles selected because they tend to contain errors [1].

Experimental Design

We presented workers with a mixed series of tasks from the ten primitives and manipulated two factors: the time limit and the primitive. Each primitive had seven different possible time limits, and one untimed condition. The exact time limits were initialized using how long workers took when not under time pressure. The result was a sampled, not fully-crossed, design. For each worker we randomly selected five primitives for them to perform; for each primitive, three questions of that type were shown with each of the specified time limits. The images or text used in these questions were randomly sampled and shuffled for each worker. To minimize practice effects, workers completed three timed practice questions prior to seeing any of these conditions. The tasks were presented in randomized order, and within each primitive the time conditions were presented in randomized order. Workers were compensated $2.00 and repeat participation was disallowed.

A single task was presented on each page, allowing us to record how long workers took to submit a response. Under timed conditions, a timer started as soon as the worker advanced to the next page. Input was disabled as soon as the timer expired, regardless of what the worker was doing (e.g., typing, clicking). An example task is shown in Figure 3.

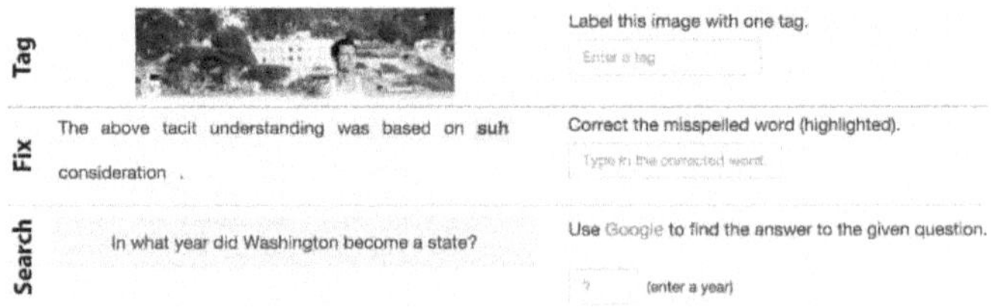

Figure 2. The tag, fix, and search tasks.

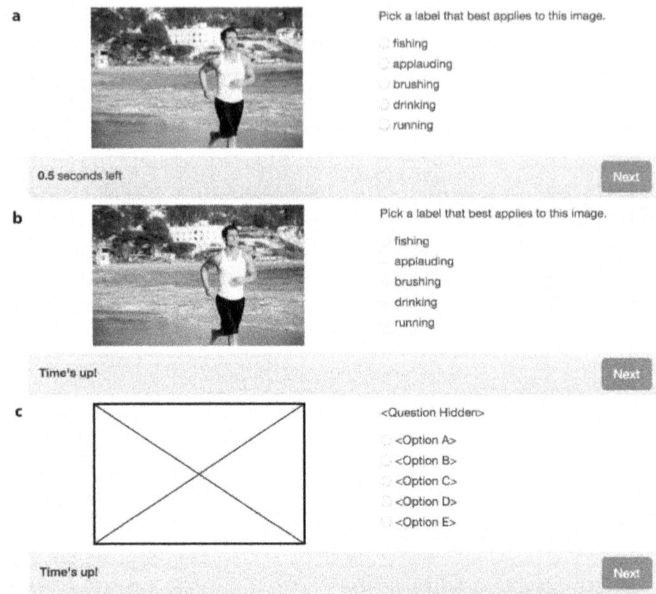

Figure 3. (a) Basic interface showing the categorize task and the countdown timer. (b) To measure effort in Studies 1, 2 and 4, questions were disabled after the timer expires. (c) To measure perceptual costs in Study 3, the question was hidden, but workers could still answer the question.

Measures

The information we logged allowed us to calculate behavioral measures for each primitive:

- *ETA.* The ETA is the area under the error-time curve.
- *Time@10.* We also calculated the time it takes to achieve an error rate at the 10th percentile.
- *Error.* We measured the error rate against ground truth for each primitive. If there were many possible correct responses, we manually judged responses while blind to condition. Automatically computing distance metrics (e.g., edit distance) resulted in empirically similar findings.
- *Time.* We measured how long workers took to complete the primitive without any time limit.

After each task block was complete, we additionally asked workers to record several subjective reflections:

- *Estimated time.* We asked workers to report how long they thought they spent on a primitive absent time pressure.

Primitive	Subj.Rank	**ETA** [conf. int.]	**Time@10** [Time@10Cost]	Error	Time			TLX	Cost	
					Time	Est.Time	RSD		Mkt.Price	Est.Cost
Binary	2.50 (1)	1.58 [1.49-1.73] (1)	2.1 [0.7] (1)	0.01 (3)	3.3 (1)	4.1 (1)	0.19 (1)	36.6 (2)	0.33 (1)	4.1 (1)
Scale	3.33 (2)	1.88 [1.73-2.05] (2)	2.7 [0.9] (3)	0.00 (2)	4.2 (3)	4.5 (3)	0.15 (3)	38.1 (3)	0.50 (2)	4.8 (3)
Categorize	3.45 (3)	1.97 [1.87-2.07] (3)	2.4 [0.8] (2)	0.00 (1)	3.9 (2)	4.4 (2)	0.19 (2)	36.2 (1)	1.00 (5)	4.3 (2)
Tag	4.30 (4)	2.91 [2.66-3.46] (4)	4.0 [1.3] (4)	0.10 (6)	5.7 (4)	6.6 (4)	0.14 (4)	44.1 (4)	1.00 (5)	5.8 (4)
Transcribe	6.40 (5)	7.62 [7.14-8.11] (8)	10.0 [3.3] (8)	0.19 (10)	11.6 (8)	10.8 (8)	-0.00 (7)	49.6 (7)	1.00 (5)	10.6 (9)
Find	6.42 (6)	3.88 [3.55-4.34] (5)	5.5 [1.8] (5)	0.13 (7)	10.9 (7)	8.1 (5)	-0.13 (9)	48.3 (5)	1.00 (5)	6.1 (5)
Fix	6.53 (7)	4.31 [3.88-4.66] (6)	6.6 [2.2] (6)	0.17 (8)	10.5 (6)	8.9 (6)	0.00 (6)	49.4 (6)	5.00 (9.5)	7.0 (6)
Add	6.90 (8)	4.92 [4.39-5.38] (7)	7.7 [2.6] (7)	0.09 (5)	9.8 (5)	9.6 (7)	0.03 (5)	51.9 (9)	5.00 (9.5)	8.2 (7)
Describe	7.15 (9)	7.78 [6.96-8.75] (9)	12.2 [4.1] (9)	0.18 (9)	15.4 (9)	11.7 (9)	-0.13 (8)	51.5 (8)	1.00 (5)	8.9 (8)
Search	8.03 (10)	11.7 [10.8-12.5] (10)	16.0 [5.3] (10)	0.04 (4)	18.8 (10)	15.2 (10)	-0.16 (10)	51.9 (10)	3.33 (8)	13.2 (10)
Kendall's Tau Coefficients (*: $p<0.05$, **: $p<0.01$)										
w/Subj.Rank	-	0.87**	0.82*	0.29	0.69*	0.82*	0.69*	0.78*	0.66*	0.78*
w/Mkt.Price	0.66*	0.56	0.51	0.20	0.41	0.51	0.41	0.56	-	0.51

Table 2. Measures of effort for ten crowdsourcing primitives (rank order in each column in brackets). ETA has the highest rank correlation with the subjective rank of a task. All prices are in cents. (Study 1, 2)

Time estimation has previously been used as an implicit signal of task difficulty [5].

- *Relative subjective duration (RSD).* RSD, a measure of how much task time is over- or underestimated [5], is obtained by dividing the difference between estimated and actual time spent by the actual time spent.
- *Task load index (TLX).* The NASA TLX [10] is a validated metric of mental workload commonly used in human factors research to assess task performance. It consists of a survey that sums six subjective dimensions (e.g., mental demand).

A separate experimental design that contained all ten primitives, where each worker completed three untimed practice questions followed by three untimed questions for each primitive (with the primitives presented in random order), was used to obtain the

- *Subjective rank.* Workers considered all of the primitives they completed and ranked them in order of effort required.

As rankings produce sharper distinctions than individual ratings [2], we consider subjective rank to represent our ground truth ranking of the primitives. However, rank would not be a deployable solution for requesters. Ranking means that workers would need to test the new task against at least $log(n)$ of the primitives, incurring a large fixed overhead. Further, ranking is ordinal, and cannot quantify small changes in effort. In contrast, ETA is an absolute ranking, can measure small changes in effort, and only needs to be measured for the target task to compare it with other tasks.

Analysis

60 workers completed Study 1, with 30 performing each primitive. We averaged our dependent measures across all 30 workers, and compared the ranking of primitives induced by each measure to the average subjective ranking (subjective rank was obtained by having 40 other workers rank all ten primitives). We used the Kendall rank correlation coefficient to capture how closely each measure approximated the

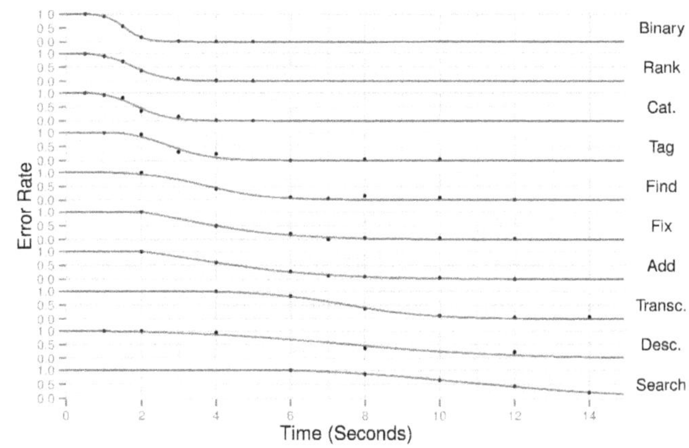

Figure 4. The error-time curves for each primitive show how the errors made decrease as more time is provided to answer a question.

workers' ranks, with Holm-corrected p-values calculated under the null hypothesis of no association. A rank correlation of 1 indicates perfect correlation; 0 indicates no correlation. Measures that capture the subjective ranking accurately can analyze new tasks types without comparing them against multiple benchmark tasks.

Results

Table 2 reports overall results for each primitive using each measure, as well as the resulting rank ordering. Bootstrap confidence intervals are also reported for ETA; their relatively small range suggests that task ranking remains fairly stable with 30 workers. Raw error-time plots, shown in Figure 4, verify that the data follows a sigmoidal pattern.

A Kendall's tau test reveals that ETA is significantly more correlated with subjective rank (τ=0.87) than other measures such as Time or TLX. It correctly lists Binary as the easiest task (ETA=1.58) followed by Scale (1.88) and Categorize (1.97), with Search being the most difficult (11.7), suggesting that the ordering of task difficulty under ETA matches workers perceptions of relative task difficulty relatively well. In fact, we find that ETA only misranks TRANSCRIBE — it was perceived as easier than other tasks that took more time.

In an upcoming section, we demonstrate how the high perception cost in this task may account for why it seemed like less effort. To understand the robustness of ETA with respect to the number of workers requested, we conducted a bootstrap analysis by subsampling from our worker pool, varying n between 1 and 30, then computing the 10th and 90th percentile of the estimated ETA for each n. We find that ETA can be reasonably estimated with a small number of workers On average, ten workers were required to obtain an ETA where 90% of the values are within 20% of the true value; with 20 workers, 95% of values are within 10% of the true value. Assuming each task costs 2 cents, it costs about $5 to generate the ETA for a task using ten workers.

The next best metrics after ETA were Time@10 (a transformation of the same error-time curve used for ETA), and estimated time. But while the relative rankings provided by Time@10 and estimated time are the same, Time@10 additionally encodes work quality. Corroborating prior research, our results suggest that time (and estimated time) can be misleading. For example, FIND takes 10.9 seconds with no time limit (and workers estimate it takes 8 seconds), but the task can be completed well in as little as 5.5 seconds (Time@10).

Previously-validated approaches were less highly correlated with subjective rank. Relative subjective duration struggled because the relative error increases as tasks take less time, making it difficult to use as an estimate across tasks of different time classes. NASA-TLX could not discriminate easy tasks well and did not order these correctly.

STUDY 2: ETA VS. MARKET PRICE

Study 1 shows that ETA is highly correlated with workers' subjective ranking of task difficulty. Measuring task difficulty is also useful because it can be used to price tasks. Thus, Study 2 attempts to estimate the market price of each task, which we then compare against our measures from Study 1.

Method

To extract the market price for our 10 primitives, we launched a set of 10 pricing tasks, one for each primitive. For each pricing task, we held the task's price constant at 10 cents, but manipulated the number of primitive tasks required to complete the pricing task. This was conducted as a between-subjects study, with each worker assigned in a round-robin fashion to a primitive and fixed number of primitive tasks to complete. This number varied between 1 and 40, with six levels used for each primitive. The exact range and values for each level depended on the primitive's difficulty.

We measured each pricing task's acceptance rate as the ratio of task accepts to task previews. When workers previewed the task, they were shown a sample primitive task and told the number of such tasks they would have to complete to get paid. Market behavior should result in more workers accepting the task if they only have to complete one repetition than if they have to complete 40. All pricing tasks remained on the market for the same 18-hour period. A mean of 20.0 (σ=3.82) people viewed each condition, with 17.3 (σ=4.38) completing a task after viewing it.

- *Market price.* We estimated the market price of each primitive by identifying the maximum number of primitive tasks where the pricing task's acceptance rate was above 90%. The mean unit cost of that primitive was then calculated by dividing 10 cents by that number.

Additionally, we consider two other measures of cost:

- *Time@10 cost.* Using Time@10, we estimated how much requesters should pay to complete each primitive, assuming continuous work and an hourly wage of $12.
- *Estimated cost.* As a rough, subjective estimate of a primitive's reservation wage, we also asked workers how much they would want to be paid for performing it once.

Results

Table 2 reports all three measures of cost, with Time@10 cost correlating best with subjective rank. While we find that market price provides some signal of effort, it is ultimately noisy and expensive to obtain. For one, the estimated market price for many primitives ended up being the same, indicating market inelasticity, making it hard to accurately rank the tasks. Further, the estimate was noisy — obtaining greater precision may require significantly more workers and conditions. With six conditions and 20 workers per condition over 18 hours, pricing data is already relatively expensive ($12 per task) and time-consuming to gather. In a paper measuring economic utility, over 20,000 jobs costing almost $1000 were run to compute the market price of three tasks (where price was varied between 1 and 6 cents) [30]. Also, market prices fluctuate; tasks that are cheap to perform at one moment may wind up being expensive later.

A Kendall's tau test reveals that only subjective rank, our previous ground truth, is significantly correlated with market price (0.66), supporting its use in Study 1. While the lack of significance with other metrics is unsurprising given the coarse-grained nature of ranking by market price, we nonetheless find that ETA and TLX are the next most highly correlated measures (0.56). These results also add an ethical dimension to market pricing as a dependent variable, as it allows requesters to estimate the wage they are paying for quality work.

STUDY 3: MODELING PERCEPTUAL COSTS WITH ETA

Study 1 suggests that ETA can accurately capture task effort, and Study 2 suggests that market price, while noisy, is correlated with subjective rank and ETA. In Study 3 we develop a model that also measures the perceptual cost of a task, to help account for the one ranking error that ETA made relative to workers' rankings. In this model, we note that effort has two components. The first, perceptual and cognitive effort, is the effort workers need to process the provided input (e.g., an image or text). The second, motor effort, is the effort spent translating their decisions into physical action (e.g., typing or clicking). Informally, workers may value their perceptual and cognitive time more than they value their motor time. By isolating the perceptual component of the task relative to the whole and estimating the time workers need to perceive the task (as opposed to the time required to complete the task), we can further improve our estimates of effort.

ETA predicted that TRANSCRIBE required more effort than workers felt it did. One important reason for the difference may lie in the relative balance of perceptual and cognitive effort. In other words, TRANSCRIBE relies heavily on low-level perception, whereas other primitives such as ADD rely on more cognition (or System 1 vs. System 2 thinking [19]). For instance, we may expect to spend a larger proportion of time reading the text provided for TRANSCRIBE as compared to SEARCH, where more time is instead spent searching for the answer than reading the provided question.

Method

For Study 3 we followed a similar design to Study 1. However, instead of randomly choosing a time limit for the entire task, we randomly chose a limit for the amount of time workers could *see* the stimulus. When the time limit expired the stimulus was hidden but workers still had to complete the task (Figure 3c). Workers were only limited in the time they could spend perceiving the task. For example, with BINARY, a worker might be shown the source image for 0.5 seconds and asked to answer whether the tag "bird" applied to the image. Workers had unlimited time to submit their response. Using the results with 60 workers, we again generated a error-time curve by fitting an exponential curve to the data, computing three metrics based on it.

- *PerceptionETA.* Similar to ETA, this measures the area under the error-time curve, but where time now corresponds to how long the stimulus was shown.
- *Perception@10.* We estimated how long the stimulus needed to be shown in order to achieve an error rate at the 10th percentile.
- *PerceptionRatio.* This measure computes the ratio of perception time, Perception@10, to total required time, Time@10. As workers have unlimited time to answer questions, Perception@10 can exceed Time@10. Nonetheless, this rarely occurs in practice.

To analyze the data, we compared the three measures of perception with the workers' subjective ranking from Study 1. We also hypothesized that ETA and measures of perception could be combined to produce an improved ranking model, and use ETA, PerceptionETA and PerceptionRatio as features in an ordered logistic regression (OLR) model.

Results

Our results in Table 3 show that ADD requires significantly less perception time (0.95) than TRANSCRIBE (5.36). This suggests that workers spend a larger proportion of time processing the perceived information for ADD. In other words, the cognitive load for ADD may be much higher than for TRANSCRIBE, albeit for a shorter amount of time. This increase may explain why ADD was perceived as more difficult than TRANSCRIBE, even though it took significantly less time to complete.

However, perception metrics alone are a poor predictor of subjective rank or market price (ranging from 0.10 to 0.47, n.s.). In other words, proportion of time spent perceiving may only have a secondary effect on the perceived difficulty

Primitive	Perception... ...ETA	...@10	...Ratio	**OLR**
Binary	0.37 (4)	0.63 (4)	0.30 (4)	1 (1)
Scale	0.40 (5)	0.65 (5)	0.24 (5)	2 (2)
Categorize	0.86 (8)	2.28 (9)	0.95 (1)	3 (3)
Tag	0.09 (1)	0.14 (1)	0.04 (8)	4 (5)
Transcribe	3.87 (10)	5.36 (10)	0.54 (2)	6 (6)
Find	1.44 (9)	2.21 (8)	0.40 (3)	3 (3)
Fix	0.42 (6)	0.67 (6)	0.10 (7)	7 (7)
Add	0.50 (7)	0.95 (7)	0.12 (6)	8 (8)
Describe	0.16 (2)	0.31 (2)	0.03 (10)	9 (9)
Search	0.31 (3)	0.49 (3)	0.03 (9)	10 (10)
Kendall's Tau Coefficients (*: $p<0.05$, **: $p<0.01$)				
w/Subj.Rank	0.07	0.11	0.47	0.90**
w/Mkt.Price	0.10	0.10	0.20	0.67*

Table 3. Measures of perceptive effort for the same primitives, as well the rankings produced by an OLR model that takes into account both ETA and these measures. (Study 4)

of a task. But by using a combined ETA-Perception OLR model, we obtain a rank correlation of 0.90 ($p<0.01$), higher than any individual metric. Models that used combinations of subjective or time-based measures were not as performant. TRANSCRIBE now appears in the right rank order, with the only confusion being that now FIND is estimated as easier than TAG and TRANSCRIBE. This same model also produces a rank correlation of 0.67 with a primitive's market price, higher than any other individual metric.

In summary, while ETA alone is a reasonable predictor of overall task effort, it can be augmented with measures of perceptual cost to attain even better predictions, at the cost of performing an additional experiment. Perceptual cost can also indicate along what dimension a task is easy or hard.

STUDY 4: MEASURING ETA WITHOUT GROUND TRUTH

To evaluate worker performance and calculate ETA we have thus far assumed that ground truth labels for a task exist. These labels are used to establish the y-axis of the error-time curve — the probability of an error when given the time limit on the x-axis. Ground truth labels may also be difficult to generate for tasks with subjective answers.

In Study 4 we create error time curves for tasks without using a ground-truth measure of quality. We explore two alternative measures of performance for subjective tasks:

- *Internal consistency.* If a worker submits the same response under a time limit as they give with no time limit, then the task can be deemed correct.
- *Between-subject variation.* If different workers submit the same responses with a given time limit, then the task can be deemed correct.

Measures of internal consistency and between-subject variation make different assumptions about a task: consistency assumes that workers will reproduce similar answers for a particular question, while variation assumes that some answers to a question are more likely than others. Both approaches can be applied to objective tasks, but it is cheaper

Primitive	Subj.Rank	Consistency		Variation		Time		TLX	Est.Cost	Perception ETA	OLR
		ETA	**Time@10**	**ETA**	**Time@10**	Time	RSD				
Obj. Scale	2.63 (1)	1.57 (1)	2.10 (1)	1.75 (1)	2.30 (1)	3.51 (2)	-0.13 (2)	29.2 (1)	10.65 (2)	0.41 (2)	1 (1)
Obj. Categorize	2.74 (2)	1.80 (2)	2.40 (2)	2.07 (2)	3.10 (2)	3.51 (1)	0.14 (1)	30.1 (2)	10.72 (3)	1.13 (4)	2 (2)
Subj. Scale	3.22 (3)	1.96 (3)	3.00 (3)	2.35 (3)	4.00 (4)	4.11 (3)	-0.25 (4)	30.8 (4)	10.40 (1)	1.25 (5)	3 (3)
Subj. Categorize	3.89 (4)	2.77 (6)	4.20 (6)	2.71 (4)	4.20 (5)	4.74 (4)	-0.31 (6)	30.4 (3)	10.79 (4)	1.55 (6)	4 (4)
Obj. Tag	3.96 (5)	2.61 (5)	4.10 (5)	3.34 (6)	4.40 (6)	5.27 (5)	-0.21 (3)	32.6 (5)	12.76 (6)	0.77 (3)	5 (5)
Subj. Tag	4.56 (6)	2.50 (4)	3.50 (4)	2.94 (5)	3.50 (3)	6.14 (6)	-0.28 (5)	35.9 (6)	11.72 (5)	0.36 (1)	6 (6)

Table 4. Task difficulty can also be measured in the absence of ground truth data. While ETA alone accurately captures the relative ranking of objective tasks, perception measures can help explain differences for subjective tasks. (Study 4)

to use ground truth when available. We use them to see if we can replicate replicate the results from Study 1 with the same primitives, and to quantify the effort required for new, subjective versions of the primitives.

Method

We focused on three primitives in Study 4: CATEGORIZE, SCALE, and TAG. For each primitive we created alternatives that were objective (i.e., identical to those in Study 1) or subjective. For example, objective CATEGORIZE asked workers which of five action labels applies to an image, while subjective CATEGORIZE asked workers which of five emotions best represented their impression of an image. Objective SCALE asked how applicable an action was, while subjective SCALE asked how applicable an emotion was to an image. Objective TAG asked workers to tag the image with an action being performed, while subjective TAG instead asked the workers for a word describing how they felt about the image.

Workers in Study 4 were shown tasks for one primitive, and first completed three practice tasks to minimize practice effects. They were then exposed to seven timed conditions, with three tasks per timed condition, sampled so that all primitives were shown the same number of times in each condition across all workers. After workers performed the tasks in the timed conditions, the exact same set of tasks was shuffled and presented under an untimed condition.

We calculated internal consistency by comparing the worker's answer on the timed categorization, scale, or tag task to the untimed answer afterwards. We defined consistency as the probability of a worker's answers being identical in both cases. Defining a distance metric for each primitive (e.g., edit distance for the tag task) results in empirically similar findings. While we find that these measures were sufficient in practice, other robust methods of measuring worker error also exist (e.g., [18]). We calculated the between-subjects variation for each task by counting the number of unique answers in the timed conditions across all workers. For both metrics, we can again generate error-time curves — in this case consistency-time curves. They are, as before, sigmoidal. We use these curves to calculate ETA and Time@10.

Similar to Study 1, we recorded task completion time, subjective cost estimates for the task, and NASA-TLX scores. Also replicating Study 1, to understand how workers subjectively ranked the primitives, we ran a separate task containing all six primitives, showing only the untimed condition. We then sorted the six tasks by workers' summative rank and compared it to the other measurements using Kendall's tau. As in Study 3, we also measured the perceptual cost of these tasks, slightly modifying the timed condition to hide the stimulus rather than disable input. 40 workers completed Study 4.

Results

As expected, the more time a worker was given to complete a task, the more likely their initial answer would be consistent with the second, untimed one ($p<.001$). In the case of objective CATEGORIZE, the error rate drops from a mean of 0.82 when workers were given half a second, to 0.03 when given five seconds. With between-subjects variation, the number of unique responses also decreases as more time is given ($p<.001$). For objective CATEGORIZE, the mean number of unique answers for an image decreased from 3.5 with half a second, to 1.2 with five seconds.

We find that the relative ordering of ETA and Time@10 for the three objective primitives is the same as when we use ground truth data in Study 1, and the absolute values of these metrics are also similar (Table 4). This suggests that both internal consistency and between-subjects variation are reasonable substitutes for ground truth data for objective tasks. However, between-subjects variation has a few advantages. It only requires each question to be asked once, and thus is significantly cheaper to run. Additionally, the rank correlation of ETA with subjective rank was better using between-subjects variation (0.87, tying Duration and TLX) than internal consistency (0.6). While the rank ordering of the objective tasks using other metrics such as RSD are also similar to what we observed in Study 1, their absolute values are substantially different — though they were correlated with effort overall, they appear difficult to interpret individually.

The perceptual cost of a task also seems to play a significant role in the case of the subjective primitives we studied. For instance, subjective TAG had the lowest perceptual cost, suggesting that while its ETA is lower than that of objective TAG, workers may perceive it as more difficult. In fact, an OLR model that combines ETA and PerceptionETA results in a completely rank-correlated prediction.

EXAMPLE APPLICATION: TASK EVALUATION

Using four studies, we showed that ETA is an accurate data-driven measure of task effort, and that it enables robust comparison across similar tasks. An accurate measure of the effort required to complete a task can enable requesters to compare different approaches to their tasks, iterate toward a bet-

		Subj.Rank	ETA	Time@10 [Time@10 Cost]	Time
Categorize	2	1.75 (1)	1.63 (1)	2.3 [0.8] (1)	3.74 (1)
	4	2.60 (2)	1.84 (2)	2.5 [0.8] (2)	4.11 (2)
	8	3.50 (4)	2.53 (3)	3.6 [1.2] (3)	5.71 (3)
	16	4.15 (5)	3.20 (5)	5.0 [1.7] (5)	6.42 (4)
Tag		3.00 (3)	3.08 (4)	4.2 [1.4] (4)	6.86 (5)

Table 5. As the number of alternatives increases, categorization tasks increase in difficulty. With 16 options, instead providing a direct tag is easier, even though it requires more time in an uncontrolled setting.

ter design, and price their task objectively. We have discussed how the measure might be transformed into price using a simple transform. We now provide an example of how it can also be used to prototype and evaluate task designs, using a similar approach to previous work that compared user interfaces by offering them for different prices on Mechanical Turk [30]. Using this same approach, task designers can iterate and make data-driven decisions about their own tasks.

In our example, we consider several alternatives to an image tagging task. There are many ways such a task could be designed. For example, workers could be asked to choose from among a number of existing tags or to enter the text of a new tag. We use ETA to decide when it is better to ask them to select tags versus enter text by comparing the TAG primitive ("Generate a label that applies to this image,") with the the CATEGORIZE primitive ("Pick the label that applies to this image,") where workers were shown 2, 4, 8, or 16 labels.

For each potential task design we collected the data necessary to calculate ETA from 20 workers, paying $2. For the purpose of this example, we also collected a subjective ranking from each worker. Relative performance information, however, is not necessary in practice to iterate on the design.

As the number of options increases, the time taken to generate a correct answer also increases (Table 5). ETA seems to increase sigmoidally, suggesting that answer strategies may change as the list of options gets longer. We also find an interesting discontinuity: asking workers to generate a tag from scratch requires more effort than asking workers to select from a list of 8 labels, but less effort than selecting from 16 options. Although workers took longer in the uncontrolled setting to generate a tag (6.9s vs 6.4s), they were able to provide the right tag within less time (4.2s vs 5.0s). In addition to the higher perceptual costs of processing more options, the paradox of choice may also partially explain the increased difficulty of selecting from more options [17].

Using other measures resulted in slight ranking differences: workers ranked tagging as easier than selecting from 8 options, but wished to get paid most for tagging. As noted previously, using subjective ranking makes comparison with other tasks difficult, and time or cost estimates tend to be noisy.

DISCUSSION

ETA represents a first step towards effectively modeling task effort. Future directions involve extending the measure and exploring alternatives, understanding the impact of monetary incentives, and exploring additional uses.

While we believe that ETA is broadly applicable, the metric has limitations. For one, it requires gold-standard responses or limited response variability. For tasks where this is not possible (e.g., written editorials) an additional crowdsourcing step could manually evaluate each response. Next, ETA measures the effort required for a task in the average case. However, perceived effort differs between workers depending on their intrinsic ability (e.g., math aptitude) [27]. Measuring ETA with respect to particular groups or individuals could account for differing expertise and help workers better select ability-appropriate tasks, as would alternative models that account for multiple dimensions of expertise (e.g., [31]). Additionally, task effort is moderated by the content of a task, not just its format. While in our experiments we focused primarily on image-based tasks, a reading comprehension multiple-choice question intuitively seems harder than choosing the right color for an image from a list for instance. Thus, in addition to differentiating primitives in general, ETA could be extended to understand different users and types of content.

Other uses of the error-time curve may reveal new dimensions of task effort. Characterizing the curve's shape could reveal subtler differences in task effort. Beyond measuring the perceptual effort of a task, ETA could also be used to capture motor costs. This would allow us to understand how effort is split between perceptive, cognitive, and motor function.

We could also study whether the ETA components associated with each primitive were additive. If the total effort required for a task is simply the sum of its constitutent primitives' ETAs, it would be easy to use the approach to iterate on complex tasks. However, tasks may have interaction effects with each other. For example, repeating a task may lead to learning effects or complacency. Interleaving different tasks may increase task time because of switching costs but potentially reduce boredom [28], and it would be valuable to extend ETA to capture these nuances.

Finally, our analysis focused on instances where workers are paid for their work. However, monetary incentives can influence task completion; paying more motivates workers to complete more tasks [24], while not paying at all tends to lead to fast but low-quality work [23]. Providing variable pay based on speed of completion could induce different points on the error-time curve, despite the fact that we saw that crowd markets were generally price-inelastic. Different approaches may be required to capture task effort using volunteers.

CONCLUSION

Crowdsourcing envisions an effective marketplace that connects interested requesters to on-demand human intelligence. However, that marketplace today is plagued with problems of quality and pricing. The Mechanical Turk market for lemons [14] may be the result of both a large number of poorly designed tasks (and hence poor quality crowd work [20]), as well as requesters' systematic underestimation of the effort required to complete tasks [12].

The error-time area (ETA) metric, which measures the effort required for crowdsourced tasks, can help improve the status quo. It accurately recovers workers' subjective rankings of task effort, and can be cheaply computed with simple instruments. The metric can be used in pricing tasks, and enables rapid task prototyping and evaluation. Given a crowdsourced library of tasks and their associated measures, requesters can benchmark their tasks against known templates. This may make it possible to identify, using ETA, task transformations that use the primitives that require the least effort. With a platform that automatically measures ETA for tasks, workers can also use these scores to figure out whether a task is worth their time. By providing requesters and workers with improved signals of effort, tools such as ETA can pave the way towards a better crowdsourcing experience.

ACKNOWLEDGMENTS

This work was supported in part by NSF award IIS-1351131.

REFERENCES

1. Japanese-English Bilingual Corpus of Wikipedia's Kyoto Articles. `http://goo.gl/4SfnUi`.
2. Alwin, D. F., and Krosnick, J. A. The measurement of values in surveys: A comparison of ratings and rankings. *Public Opinion Quarterly* (1985).
3. Anderson, J. R., Matessa, M., and Lebiere, C. ACT-R: A theory of higher level cognition and its relation to visual attention. *HCI* (1997).
4. Bernstein, M. S., et al. Soylent: a word processor with a crowd inside. In *UIST* (2010).
5. Czerwinski, M., Horvitz, E., and Cutrell, E. Subjective duration assessment: An implicit probe for software usability. In *IHM-HCI* (2001).
6. Dai, P., et al. Decision-theoretic control of crowd-sourced workflows. In *AAAI* (2010).
7. DeLeeuw, K. E., and Mayer, R. E. A comparison of three measures of cognitive load: Evidence for separable measures of intrinsic, extraneous, and germane load. *J. Educ. Psychol.* (2008).
8. Faradani, S., Hartmann, B., and Ipeirotis, P. G. What's the right price? pricing tasks for finishing on time. *Human Computation* (2011).
9. Gevins, A., and Smith, M. E. Neurophysiological measures of cognitive workload during human-computer interaction. *Theor. Issues. Ergon.* (2003).
10. Hart, S. G., and Staveland, L. E. Development of NASA-TLX (Task Load Index): Results of empirical and theoretical research. *Adv. Psychol.* (1988).
11. Herlocker, J., Konstan, J. A., and Riedl, J. An empirical analysis of design choices in neighborhood-based collaborative filtering algorithms. *Inform. Retrieval* (2002).
12. Hinds, P. J. The curse of expertise: The effects of expertise and debiasing methods on prediction of novice performance. *J. Exp. Psychol.-Appl.* (1999).
13. Impara, J. C., and Plake, B. S. Teachers' ability to estimate item difficulty: A test of the assumptions in the angoff standard setting method. *J. Educ. Meas.* (1998).
14. Ipeirotis, P. G. Mechanical Turk, low wages, and the market for lemons. `http://goo.gl/uoXA6Y`.
15. Ipeirotis, P. G. Analyzing the Amazon Mechanical Turk marketplace. *XRDS* (2010).
16. Ipeirotis, P. G., Provost, F., and Wang, J. Quality management on Amazon Mechanical Turk. In *KDD* (2010).
17. Iyengar, S. S., and Lepper, M. R. When choice is demotivating: Can one desire too much of a good thing? *J. Pers. Soc. Psychol.* (2000).
18. Joglekar, M., Garcia-Molina, H., and Parameswaran, A. Evaluating the crowd with confidence. In *KDD* (2013).
19. Kahneman, D. *Thinking, fast and slow*. 2011.
20. Kittur, A., et al. The future of crowd work. In *CSCW* (2013).
21. Kruger, J., and Dunning, D. Unskilled and unaware of it: how difficulties in recognizing one's own incompetence lead to inflated self-assessments. *J. Pers. Soc. Psychol.* (1999).
22. Lohman, D. F. The effect of speed-accuracy tradeoff on sex differences in mental rotation. *Percept. Psychophys.* (1986).
23. Mao, A., et al. Volunteering versus work for pay: Incentives and tradeoffs in crowdsourcing. In *HCOMP* (2013).
24. Mason, W., and Watts, D. J. Financial incentives and the performance of crowds. *SigKDD Explorations* (2010).
25. McCracken, J., and Aldrich, T. Analyses of selected LHX mission functions: Implications for operator workload and system automation goals. Tech. rep., 1984.
26. Pew, R. W. The speed-accuracy operating characteristic. *Acta Psychol.* (1969).
27. Robinson, P. Task complexity, task difficulty, and task production: Exploring interactions in a componential framework. *Appl. Linguist.* (2001).
28. Rzeszotarski, J. M., et al. Inserting micro-breaks into crowdsourcing workflows. In *HCOMP* (2013).
29. Rzeszotarski, J. M., and Kittur, A. Instrumenting the crowd: using implicit behavioral measures to predict task performance. In *UIST* (2011).
30. Toomim, M., Kriplean, T., Pörtner, C., and Landay, J. Utility of human-computer interactions: Toward a science of preference measurement. In *CHI* (2011).
31. Welinder, P., et al. The multidimensional wisdom of crowds. In *NIPS* (2010).
32. Wickelgren, W. A. Speed-accuracy tradeoff and information processing dynamics. *Acta Psychol.* (1977).
33. Wickens, C. D. *Processing resources in attention, dual task performance, and workload assessment.* 1981.
34. Yao, B., et al. Human action recognition by learning bases of action attributes and parts. In *ICCV* (2011).

The Effects of Sequence and Delay on Crowd Work

Walter S. Lasecki[1], Jeffrey M. Rzeszotarski[2], Adam Marcus[4], Jeffrey P. Bigham[2,3]

Computer Science Department[1]
University of Rochester
wlasecki@cs.rochester.edu

HCI[2] and LT[3] Institutes
Carnegie Mellon University
{jeffrz,jbigham}@cs.cmu.edu

Locu / GoDaddy[4]
marcua@marcua.net

ABSTRACT

A common approach in crowdsourcing is to break large tasks into small microtasks so that they can be parallelized across many crowd workers and so that redundant work can be more easily compared for quality control. In practice, this can result in the microtasks being presented out of their natural order and often introduces delays between individual microtasks. In this paper, we demonstrate in a study of 338 crowd workers that non-sequential microtasks and the introduction of delays significantly decreases worker performance. We show that interruptions where a large delay occurs between two related tasks can cause up to a 102% slowdown in completion time, and interruptions where workers are asked to perform different tasks in sequence can slow down completion time by 57%. We conclude with a set of design guidelines to improve both worker performance and realized pay, and instructions for implementing these changes in existing interfaces for crowd work.

Author Keywords

Crowdsourcing, human computation, workflows, continuity, interruptions, efficiency

ACM Classification Keywords

H.4.2 Information Interfaces & Presentation: User Interfaces

INTRODUCTION

Creating crowdsourcing workflows often involves breaking down large tasks into microtasks that can be parallelized across many crowd workers and that are amenable to redundancy-based quality control. In practice, this often results in temporal and contextual interruptions for workers that can reduce their efficiency when they want to work for longer on a single task. This is because workers must spend time recovering their working context after each change or delay.

In this paper, we identify two types of interruptions that are harmful to worker efficiency and quantify their costs: *(i)* contextual interruptions, in which workers swap between tasks of different types, and *(ii)* temporal interruptions, in which workers must wait between submitting one task and receiving the next one. Contextual interruptions can arise as a result of workflows that do not present related tasks in sequence. For example, a transcription task might ask workers to transcribe audio from different parts of a clip or different clips instead of allowing them to build on context by transcribing sequeuntial clips. Temporal interruptions can be caused by platforms that add procedural delays between tasks, *e.g.*, loading screens, steps to move to a new task, or by not using prefetching.

At first, it seems counterintuitive that task designers would present work out of sequence when a natural ordering exists, but this is quite common given that platforms commonly route workers to tasks with the least number of existing completed labels rather than sorting and delivering tasks in the order in which they were created. When requesters test the system themselves, they see the tasks presented in sequential order because they are the only ones accessing them. In practice, when many tasks are posted to a platform like Mechanical Turk, workers start at nearly the same time, so the default ordering leads workers to receive tasks out of order (Figure 1). For example, if there are n workers completing a large set of microtasks at the same rate, then the next task that each worker is asked to do will be $n-1$ tasks away from the last one they completed as no one has completed them yet. For example, if 20 workers are completing microtasks that involve transcribing 30 seconds of audio (common on platforms like Mechanical Turk), each new segment of audio received will be $30 * 19 = 570$ seconds from the previous, eliminating the context that sequential segments would provide.

In this paper, we supplement the existing literature on worker preferences with a survey of 100 Mechanical Turk workers. We find that contextual interruptions commonly result from workers switching between unrelated tasks. We then test the impact of temporal and contextual interruptions on workers

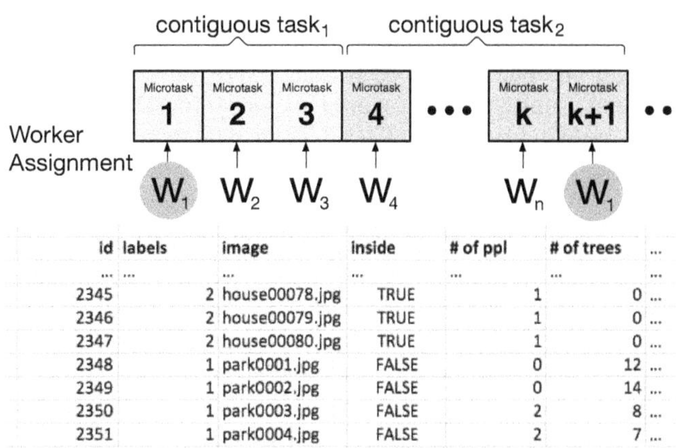

Figure 1. Crowdsourcing tasks are often delivered out of order when multiple workers accept them. Here, w_1 is asked to label a house image and is then asked to label a park image, instead of labeling images from the same group. Such context changes decrease performance and occur in many task domains that have a natural ordering.

CHI 2015, April 18–23 2015, Seoul, Republic of Korea

ACM 978-1-4503-3145-6/15/04 $15.00
http://dx.doi.org/10.1145/2702123.2702594

with 338 workers. Our results show both types of task interruptions can have significant harmful effects on completion time. Temporal interruptions can cause up to a 102% slowdown in task completion time (not counting the interruption itself), and contextual interruptions can slow down completion time by 57%. These findings suggest that both continuity and context in tasks is important for worker's productivity. We conclude with design recommendations that, by reducing interruptions, results in higher wages for workers and provide requesters with results more efficiently.

RELATED WORK

Research on workflows considers the costs and benefits of *interruptions*, or disruptions during the execution of a task. Interruptions decrease the performance of a worker shortly after an interruption [10]. This costs varies depending on the nature of the work being done, the type of interruption, and the worker's environment. Interruptions that are closely aligned with the worker's ongoing task are likely to be more disruptive regardless of how long they are, even if workers are prepared for them (which is common for microtasks) [8]. The costs of interruptions are based on cognitive load [1, 6], and workers perform poorly on the interrupting task as well [4]. We quantify the these effects in the context of microtasks.

We define interruptions not only as disruptions during execution of a single task, but also when workers are disrupted between microtasks.When workers are disrupted, they may forget some critical information and have to repeat a part of their work. For example, people who dial a phone while driving have to take moments to reexamine the road and adjust their course during interruptions [9]. In the case of microtasking, one might imagine the repeated sense-making that workers may have to do as they interleave and interrupt different varieties of tasks. They may have to re-learn how to complete a task or re-develop the necessary contextual expertise. On the other hand, tasks that underutilize cognitive resources can cause boredom that also reduces performance [13]. Continuous workflow models [11] hold the possibility of balancing worker's arousal and fatigue.

Since crowd workers are generally unknown to the requester and join or leave workflows frequently, typical task designs ensure that every task can be completed by a different, untrained and unexperienced worker. Accordingly, most work in crowdsourcing has focused on decomposable problems such as writing, editing [2], and image description [3], among others. Existing workflows focus on obtaining quality results by introducing redundancy and verification steps (e.g., answer agreement or the find-fix-verify pattern [2]).

While this approach maximizes the flexibility of the workforce by not requiring prior experience or long working periods, it disregards benefits like worker experience and memory. Because subsequent tasks are unrelated, the contextual disruptions cause a loss in specialization. Prior work has shown that despite often completing dozens of tasks per hour, workers remember task-specific details [12]. This means that discrete tasks often fail to leverage the experience workers gain over the course of completing multiple tasks [7]. Additionally, discretizing microtasks can cause a temporal disruption between the submission of one task and loading a subsequent task, which might cause workers to lose interest, move to another task completely, or earn less money for their time.

MOTIVATION

Prior research suggests that interruptions may be detrimental to workers, but workers may choose such workflows anyway. For workers, one of the draws of microtask work is flexibility. Workers might *prefer* to switch between different tasks. This means that while workflow literature may suggest this would lead to decreased performance and a likelihood of decreased pay, the variety of tasks may provide value to workers. However, workers on Mechanical Turk are known to have a selection bias towards tasks with more assignments [5].

Survey of Mechanical Turk Workers

To better understand the worker-centric factors that affect microtasking, we conducted a survey of 100 Mechanical Turk workers. The survey asked workers about their motivations, frequency of work, task or workflow preferences, and breaktaking habits. 55 respondents identified as male. 55 were aged 18-29, 34 aged 30-39, and 11 aged 40+. 85 had a university degree. 58 workers identified Mechanical Turk as a major source of income.

Worker Habits

Workers spent an average of at least four hours per day ($M = 4.47$, $SD = 2.76$) working on Mechanical Turk tasks. There was a significant difference between the working hours of those doing tasks for pocket money, as part of their living, and as a job: 3.5 (41 respondants), 5 (34 respondants), and 5.41 (21 respondants) hours on average, respectively ($F(2, 97) = 4.99$, $p < 0.01$). 64 respondents reported that they took breaks, although we found no relationship between why workers work and break-taking. Those who took breaks said they worked for 1.24 hours on average ($SD = 2.68$) and then took a break averaging 16.6 minutes ($SD = 16.9$). Thus, many workers work for long enough periods to complete many different tasks.

Of the workers who did not take breaks, 64% mentioned concerns that breaks would decrease their earnings. 11% cited issues with "flow" when transitioning between tasks, 14% cited being satisfied with natural breaks between HITs, and 11% cited time or task demands preventing them from breaking.

Our study also suggests that workers remember the kinds of HITs they complete even long after they did them, suggesting the potential for task specialization. Our results showed that 78% of participants were able to describe the HIT they did right before taking the survey, and 74% could describe a HIT they really enjoyed form the past. Many workers described HITs they completed days, weeks, or months ago. This agrees with prior work showing that workers are able to retain and apply task information to improve their performance in future tasks [12]. Workers cited novelty, ease, speed, and repeatability as traits common in preferred tasks.

EMPIRICAL EFFECTS ON WORKERS

In the previous section, we presented evidence that workers are interested in sequential microtasking and actively seek

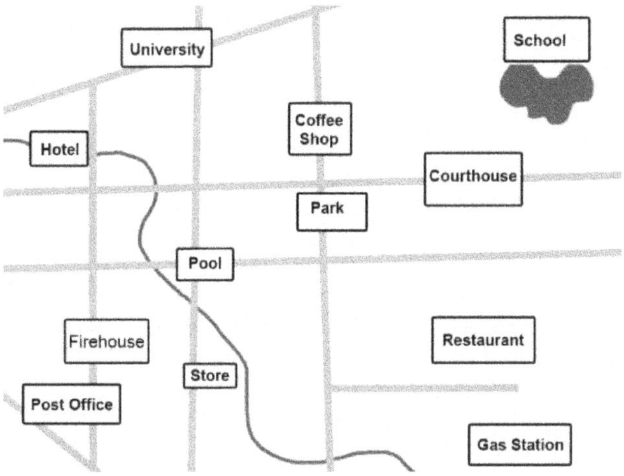

Figure 2. One of the map configurations generated for our trials. Workers were only able to see roughly $1/5^{th}$ of the map at a time through their viewport, meaning they had to scroll to find their target. Since each worker saw the same map for each of the primary search tasks, it was possible to learn the locations of the buildings over time.

it. With this in mind, we explored two common types of interruptions they may experience on a microtask platform: *temporal*, where a delay is added between tasks of the same type, and *contextual*, where different tasks are interleaved with tasks of the same type.

Experimental Setup

We created a task that asked workers to identify places on a map. Each map was larger than the user's viewport, forcing them to scroll to find a target (Figure 2). We generated a different map per worker that remained consistent across tasks so that they could remember places and geography. While we randomly placed the landmarks, all maps had the same landmarks distributed evenly in random locations. We used textual labels instead of graphical icons for clarity and to avoid cultural bias.

We varied the amount of time or type of context-based interruption. Since our tasks adhere well to the classic microtask model in which no prior expertise or context is required, workers had to eventually be able to get the correct answer to continue. Because of this, our measures focused on how long it took workers to achieve the task, rather than the degree to which they were correct.

We collected responses from 338 unique Mechanical Turk workers, and measured how long it takes them to complete tasks in different conditions and report how throughput is affected in terms of work lost. Workers were recruited half during the day in the U.S., and half during the day in India, and no recruitment filters were used. Task latency is our key measure because it captures how prepared workers were upon seeing a new task, and how their recall of the task improved their performance.

Control Task

In the control task, workers were first prompted to find and click on a particular landmark. Subsequent tasks utilized the same map but asked workers to find different landmarks. For example, a worker might be asked to click on the park. After correctly clicking on the park, they would be asked to click on the school. We expect that as workers are asked to use their map more and more, they will become more familiar with the layout of the map, and thus be able to find targets more quickly.

Temporal Interruptions

Traditional microtask interfaces often force workers to pause between tasks as a new task loads. To understand the effect of this delay, we modified the amount of time a worker had to wait between successfully completing one task and being given their next task so that it is not instantaneous as it was in the control task (C, $N = 57$). We used two delay lengths: 10 seconds (C_{short}, $N = 71$) and 30 seconds (C_{long}, $N = 67$). To avoid measuring workers time away from the task, we alert workers when the task is ready, and only measure from the time they actively begins the task. We did not find a significant difference between the average time workers spent finding landmarks in C and in C_{short} ($t(70) = 1.19$, $p = 0.24$)[1]. However, longer, 30-second breaks do have a significant effect ($t(66) = 3.40$, $p < 0.05$, Figure 3).

Contextual Interruption

On microtask platforms like Mechanical Turk task designers often provide contextually unrelated tasks to workers performing a HIT of a particular type. For example, workers captioning short audio segments from a larger recording are not necessarily given sequential pieces, but instead might be given a disjoint next piece available when they are ready for it (we discuss how this may be corrected later). To measure the effects of these contextual interruptions, we asked workers to complete a different task between each successive map task.

In the first condition (C_{map}, $N = 84$), workers who successfully identified a landmark were prompted to identify a new landmark situated on a *different* map. In the second condition (C_{image}, $N = 59$), workers who successfully identified a landmark were prompted to complete the unrelated task of image labeling (analogous to interleaving a different task in a workflow). After providing a short description of an image, workers were prompted to find another landmark on the same map as before.

For the image description distractor task, we did not find a significant difference between C and C_{image} ($t(58) = 0.31$, $p = 0.76$). As we expect from prior work, this is likely because the image description task was short and relatively disjoint from the map identification task. It does not appear to interfere with participants' performance in locating landmarks. However, the condition where workers were interrupted with a new map (C_{map}) showed a significant effect versus C ($t(83) = 4.39$, $p < 0.01$). Since this interruption was similar to the main task, it was more likely to interfere with workers' knowledge. Interestingly, this suggests that interleaving tasks is actually less of a potential detriment to workers' workflow than task design decisions. This fits with the broader picture of worker behavior discussed earlier.

[1]Since our data is not normally distributed, but is strongly log-normal, we apply a log-correction step below before running all signifigance tests.

DISCUSSION

Our results demonstrate that there can be a notable difference in performance when microtasks are presented in different workflow contexts. While the individual effects we measured initially look modest, their cumulative effect in a microtask setting can be quite large. For example, comparing the performance of participants who were shown the same kind of map landmark identification task, but with different maps interleaved as disruptions (condition C_{map}), it took 2.02 times as long on average to complete each task because participants' working knowledge and context were potentially disrupted. In our delay condition (C_{long}), even if the 30 second delay itself is completely factored out, it has the potential side effect of slowing the work conducted during active periods by a factor of 1.57, meaning workers would only get 63.7% of the work done compared to the baseline.

Our trials do not provide a comprehensive analysis of the types of tasks on crowdsourcing platforms today. However, they do provide insight into the potential effects of context and sequence delay in a microtask setting. Additionally, our experiments directly evaluation a common type of task: finding visual information (e.g., finding entries on a receipt). We believe this informs future designs for crowdsourcing tasks.

Resulting Design Guidelines

Condition C_{long} suggests that delays in task flows can seriously impact workers' performance well beyond the time lost simply because of the delay. Workers not only get bored and direct their attention elsewhere, but they may also forget their working context and need to rebuild their understanding of the task. We suggest *prefetching future tasks* in order to minimize potential delays between tasks. One simple way to do this is to simply load the next task in a hidden iframe. This has the advantage of working across a wide variety of different backend architectures. Although workers will take breaks when they feel necessary, this makes sure that the next task will load nearly instantly when they are ready.

Condition C_{map} suggests that contextual switches between tasks can confuse and interfere with workers' performance.

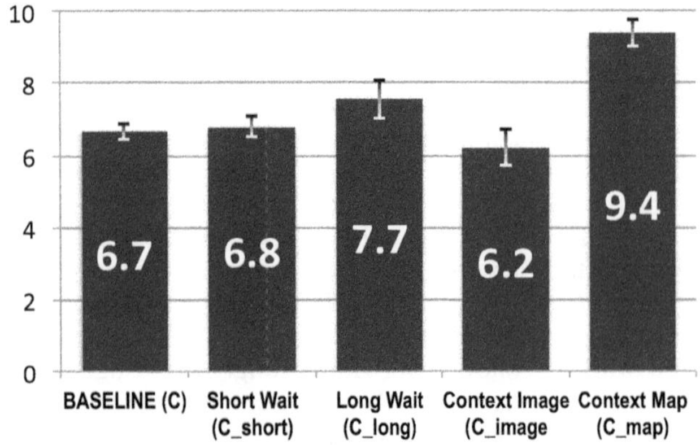

Figure 3. Task completion time increases when a worker completes different interleaved instances of a similar problem or waits for the longer period of time.

If workers are working within a batch of tasks, we suggest presenting them in a logical sequence. While there are many technical ways to achieve this, one simple approach that we use that works reasonably is to use a secondary sort by id or timestamp offset by an integer tied to the particular worker, i.e. sorting by $(id + MD5(workerid))\ \%\ n$, where n is the total number of data records. This approach has the effect of starting each worker at a different random offset in the data.

CONCLUSION

In this paper, we experimentally demonstrated the impact of temporal and contextual interruptions on microtask workers. Our findings from 338 workers indicate that these interruptions can hurt worker performance. We concluded with a set of specific guidelines to help reduce these costs in practice.

ACKNOWLEDGMENTS

This work was supported by National Science Foundation #IIS-1149709, an Alfred P. Sloan Foundation Fellowship, and two Microsoft Research Ph.D. Fellowships.

REFERENCES

1. Adamczyk, P. D., and Bailey, B. P. If not now, when?: the effects of interruption at different moments within task execution. In *CHI 2004*.
2. Bernstein, M. S., et al.Soylent: a word processor with a crowd inside. In *Proc. UIST*, pages 313–322, 2010.
3. Bigham., J. P., et. al. Vizwiz: nearly real-time answers to visual questions. In *Proc. UIST*, pages 333–342, 2010.
4. Cabon, P., Coblentz, A., and Mollard, R. Interruption of a monotonous activity with complex tasks: effects of individual differences. In *Human Factors Society*, 1990.
5. Chilton, L. B., Horton, J. J., Miller, R. C., and Azenkot, S. Task search in a human computation market. In *HCOMP 2010*.
6. Cutrell, E., Czerwinski, M., and Horvitz, E. Notification, disruption, and memory: Effects of messaging interruptions on memory and performance. In *Proc. INTERACT*, pages 263–269, 2001.
7. Dow, S., Kulkarni, A., Klemmer, S., and Hartmann, B.. Shepherding the crowd yields better work. In *Proc. CSCW*, pages 1013–1022, 2012.
8. Gillie, T. and Broadbent, D.. What makes interruptions disruptive? a study of length, similarity, and complexity. *Psychological Research*, 50:243–50, 1989.
9. Jansset, C. P., and Brumby, D. P. Strategic adaptation to performance objectives in a dualtask setting. *Cognitive Science*, 34(8):1548–1560, 2010.
10. Kreifeldt, J. G., and McCarthy, M. E. Interruption as a test of the user-computer interface. In *Proc. MC*, 1981.
11. Lasecki, W. S., Murray, K., White, S., Miller, R. C., and Bigham, J. P. Real-time crowd control of existing interfaces. In *Proc. UIST*, pages 23–32, 2011.
12. Lasecki, W. S., White, S., Murray, K. I., and Bigham, J. P. Crowd memory: Learning in the collective. In *Proc. Collective Intelligence*, 2012.
13. Pattyn, N., Neyt, X., Henderickx, D., and Soetens, E. Psychophysiological investigation of vigilance decrement: boredom or cognitive fatigue? *Physiology and Behavior*, 93(1–2):369–378, 2008.

Crowd Size, Diversity and Performance

Lionel Robert *
University of Michigan
lprobert@umich.edu

Daniel M. Romero *
University of Michigan
drom@umich.edu

ABSTRACT
Crowds are increasingly being adopted to solve complex problems. Size and diversity are two key characteristics of crowds; however their relationship to performance is often paradoxical. To better understand the effects of crowd size and diversity on crowd performance we conducted a study on the quality of 4,317 articles in the WikiProject Film community. The results of our study suggest that crowd size leads to better performance when crowds are more diverse. However, there is a break-even point – smaller, less diverse crowds can outperform more diverse crowds of similar size. Our results offer new insights into the effects of size and diversity on the performance of crowds.

Author Keywords
Wikipedia; performance; team size; diversity

ACM Classification Keywords
H.5.2 Information Systems: Information Interfaces and Presentation (e.g., HCI)—*User Interfaces: Theory and methods*; K.4.3 Computing Milieux: Computer and Society—*Organizational Impacts: Computer-supported collaborative work*

INTRODUCTION
The "wisdom of crowds'" argues that the "many are smarter than the few" [2, 8]. This concept, along with new forms of organizing, has ushered in the era of "The Crowds." Crowds are being adopted to perform work formally done by individuals. For example, crowds are being used to produce software, generate new ideas for organizations and aid in solving complex problems [2, 8]. Yet, there is still much to learn about what makes crowds more or less effective [2].

Size and diversity are two key characteristics of crowds. Yet, in the literature, their relationship to performance is often paradoxical [4]. They have been linked to increases and decreases in group performance. To better understand their effects we conducted a study on 4,317 articles in the WikiProject Film community on crowds. Our results indicate that the impact of size and diversity on crowd performance are co-dependent. That is, crowd size led to better performance when the crowds were more diverse. However, in some cases smaller, less diverse crowds outperformed similar size more diverse crowds. Results of our study offer new insights into the factors that lead to better crowd performance.

*Equal contribution

CHI 2015, April 18 – 23 2015, Seoul, Republic of Korea.

http://dx.doi.org/10.1145/2702123.2702469

Crowd Size and Crowd Diversity
Theories on the impact of group size offer conflicting views regarding the relationship between size and performance. One view states that increases in size can increase performance [4]. As size increases, more individuals are available to perform the group's task. The other view argues that increases in size can decrease performance [1]. One reason is the difficulties coordinating larger groups [8]. The group diversity literature is just as perplexing. Diversity is often labeled as the double-edge sword [20]. On one hand, diversity should lead to better performance because more diverse members offer a broader range of knowledge and skills [6, 15, 16]. On the other hand, some hypothesize that as diversity increases performance decreases because diverse members often find it difficult to work together [10, 14, 17]. This difficulty in working with diverse others often results in conflict and other types of process losses [9]. Taken together, both the literature on group diversity and group size offer conflicting views on what should lead to better crowd performance.

However, Oliver and Marwell put forth a mathematical model that posited the relationship between size and diversity in the context of collective action regarding the critical mass needed for public goods. Based on their calculations diverse groups can achieve the same level of collective action with fewer individuals than homogeneous groups [13]. Building on a similar assertion, we argue that to fully understand the effects of size and diversity both must be taken into account jointly. In other words, the effects of crowd size should depend on crowd diversity and vice versa. Specifically, we argue that size will be associated with better performance in more diverse crowds but not so in less diverse crowds. We present our arguments related to "why" in the following section.

The Effects of Crowd Size and Diversity on Performance
Increases in size should lead to better performance when crowds are more diverse for two reasons. First, as stated earlier, when diversity increases, crowds have access to a broader range of knowledge and skills [2, 14, 20]. Second, as size increases, the negative effects of diversity are likely to be diluted. The negative effects of diversity materialize when different individuals are forced to work together [9, 14, 20]. However, in larger crowds, individuals have more opportunity to find similar others to work with in the crowd. Taken

together, both claims explain why crowds are likely to benefit rather than suffer from their diversity as size increases. Therefore we propose the following:

Hypothesis: *Crowd diversity should moderate the relationship between crowd size and performance. Increases in size should be positively related to performance when crowds are diverse.*

DATA

We collected data on 4,378 articles from Wikipedia's WikiProject Film community. Article quality was our performance measure and was assessed by the Wikipedia community. In descending order of quality the article classes were *FA, GA, B, C, Start,* and *Stub*. Articles in the class *Start* and *Stub* had little information and very few editors. They were dropped from the analysis because we wanted to study active crowds. For each article, we obtained a complete list of the editors and their edits. Nearly 350,000 editors contributed at least one edit to an article.

METHOD

We considered three types of diversity based on the interest and the amount of work that editors contributed to Wikipedia. Many other factors could be related to article quality such as an editors interest and ability. We did not include these factors because our goal was to examine the relationship between crowd size and diversity and performance.

Article Quality

Each articles class was used as the performance outcome [1]. This measure has been used as a proxy for performance in other Wikipedia studies [7,8,11,18,19] and there is evidence that article class is related to the quality assessments of outside reviewers [7]. We assigned each article a digit from 1 to 4 corresponding to the C, B, GA, and FA classes, respectively. There were 123, 629, 476, and 3,089 articles in the FA, GA, B, and C classes, respectively.

Topical Diversity

We measured the similarity in topical interests of two editors on Wikipedia by the similarity of the articles they edited across Wikipedia. Given editor u, we let A_u be the set of articles u has edited on Wikipedia. For every pair of editors (u_1, u_2), we measured their Jaccard similarity as $J_{u_1,u_2} = \frac{|A_{u_1} \cap A_{u_1}|}{|A_{u_1} \cup A_{u_1}|}$. J_{u_1,u_2}. This measure indicates the overlap between the articles edited by u_1 and u_2, while controlling for the total number of articles that the pair edited. For each article a, we let P_a be the set of all pairs of editors of article a. We defineed the *topical diversity* of an article a, TD_a, as one minus the average Jaccard similarity of all pairs of editors. That is, $TD_a = 1 - \frac{1}{|P_a|} \sum_{(u_1,u_2) \in P_a} J_{u_1,u_2}$. The average topical diversity is 0.994 with standard deviation of 0.009. When TD_a is high, the editors of a tend to have low overlap in the set of articles they edit, making them a more topically diverse crowd.

[1]More details about the assessment process and quality classes can be found here: http://en.wikipedia.org/wiki/Wikipedia:WikiProject_Film/Assessment

Inner Workload Diversity

The workload among editors was not always split the same way. Some articles were characterized by having a small set of editors who made most of the edits, while other articles had editors who split the work more evenly. To measure the extent to which the editors of an article have a diverse or uniform workload, we used the Gini coefficient of their edits. We let E_a be the set of editors of article a and $W_a(e)$ be the number of times editor e contributed to article a. We defined the *inner workload diversity* of article a as the Gini coefficient of the set $\{\cup_{e \in E_a} W_a(e)\}$. An article where all editors contributed a similar number of edits had a low inner workload diversity, while an article where a few editors produced significantly more edits than the rest had a high inner workload diversity. The average inner workload diversity was 0.528 with standard deviation of 0.144.

This measure was proposed as a measure of implicit coordination [8]. We argue that it also serves as a proxy for a type of diversity. An article with high inner workload diversity has different types of editors, some who contribute very little and some who contribute a lot. An article with low inner workload diversity has only one type of editor because they all produce roughly the same amount of work.

Outer Workload

We measured the level of engagement of editors across Wikipedia. For each article a, we defined the *outer workload* of its editors as the mean number of edits they contributed to Wikipedia articles, other than a. The average outer workload was 2809 edits with standard deviation of 995.

Outer Workload Diversity

We also measured the diversity of outer workload of the editors of an article similarly to how we measured inner workload diversity. Outer Workload Diversity measures whether the article has a combination of editors who are heavy contributors to Wikipedia in general as well as editors who focus mostly on a single or very few articles, or whether most editors have about equal outer engagement. We defined the *outer workload diversity* of an article as the Gini coefficient of the number of contributions to other Wikipedia articles by each editor. The average outer workload diversity was 0.649 with standard deviation of 0.084.

Crowd Size

We measured crowd size by the log of the number of editors for each article. The average log of number of editors was 4.66 with a standard deviation of 1.22. The actual average number of editors per article was 198, with as many as 2,618.

RESULTS

The analysis was conducted using linear regression. We standardized all the independent variables. Topical diversity, inner workload diversity, crowd size, and outer workload were positively related to quality, and outer workload diversity was negatively related to quality. The R^2 was 0.22. Then we included the interactions between all the independent variables and crowd size. All interactions were significant. Table 1

Variable	Main Effects		Crowd Size Interactions	
	Coeff.	**SE**	**Coeff.**	**SE**
Topical diversity	0.041^{**}	0.013	0.056^{***}	0.014
Outer workload	0.180^{***}	0.016	0.265^{***}	0.024
Outer workload diversity	-0.098^{***}	0.011	-0.060^{*}	0.028
Inner workload diversity	0.320^{***}	0.012	0.356^{***}	0.012
Crowd size	0.322^{***}	0.019	0.330^{***}	0.021
Topical diversity X Crowd size	—	—	0.071^{***}	0.016
Outer workload X Crowd size	—	—	0.060^{***}	0.015
Outer workload diversity X Crowd size	—	—	0.046^{***}	0.014
Inner workload diversity X Crowd size	—	—	0.122^{***}	0.012

Table 1. Results of regression analysis to predict quality from diversity measures, outer workload, and crowd size. Model contains a total of $4,317$ observations. Significance key: *:p-val < 0.05, **:p-val < 0.01, ***:p-val < 0.001

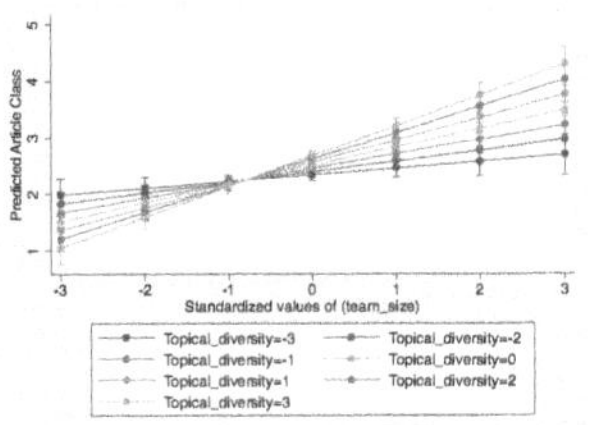

(a) Effect of topical diversity on quality by number of editors

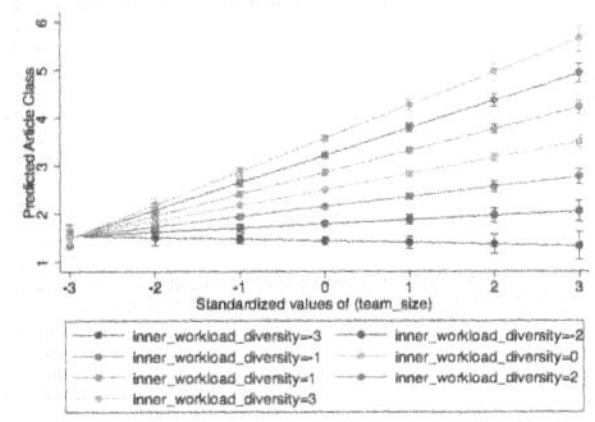

(b) Effect of inner workload diversity on quality by number of editors

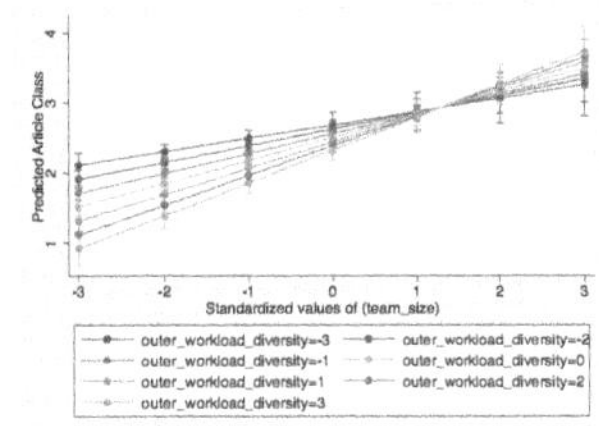

(c) Effect of outer workload diversity on quality by number of editors

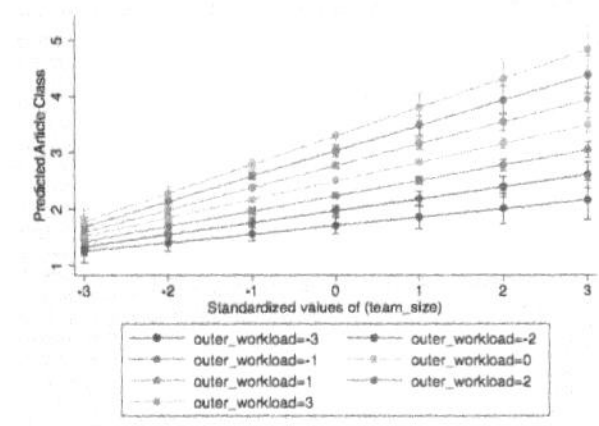

(d) Effect of outer workload on quality by number of editors

Figure 1. Interaction effects of each measure and crowd size on the quality.

shows our final model, which had an R^2 of 0.25. The increase in variance explained was significant at the 0.001 level.

These results support our hypothesis that crowd size is positively related to crowd performance in diverse crowds. Crowd size had a greater and more positive effect on performance when diversity was high. This held true for all three measures of diversity. We also found that in some cases smaller, less diverse crowds performed better than similar-size, less diverse crowds. This highlights that diversity does not always have a positive effect on performance, as previously found in the literature [2, 6, 10, 15, 17], and that crowd size may be one of the factors that determine when diversity is beneficial.

Finally, the effect of outer workload is also greater for large teams than for small teams, which suggests that larger teams benefit more from having editors who are more engaged in editing Wikipedia articles[2].

DISCUSSION

The objective of this study was to examine the relationship between crowd size and diversity and crowd performance. Results indicate that diversity is vital to understanding when crowd size leads to better performance. Crowd size is positively related to performance in highly diverse crowds but not so in less diverse crowds. The results of this study have several implications for theory and design.

Theoretical Implications

First, Figures 1(a), 1(b), and 1(c) all demonstrate that the relationship between crowd size and crowd performance is dependent on crowd diversity. Increases in size are positively related to performance when crowds are highly diverse. However, when crowds are not diverse this relationship diminishes. Based on our findings, increases in size need to be accompanied with increases in diversity. In addition, this finding also contributes to the literature on group size and diversity. Our results suggest that to better understand the effects of size and diversity on group performance future studies should take both into account jointly.

Second, our findings contribute to the work by Oliver and Marwell. Aligned with their findings, we discovered that the effects of size are dependent on diversity. However, their work focuses on public goods and explains how smaller groups can achieve the same critical mass as larger groups. Contextually, we examine large online groups, which provides an important layer of external validity.

Third, there appears to be a break-even point between size and diversity. Although the exact points differ, what is consistent across the three figures is that up to the break-even point less diverse crowds perform better than more diverse crowds. These results support our assertion that, as size increases, crowds may not be hurt by diversity because members have less chance of working with diverse others. In smaller crowds there is a greater chance of individuals having to work with diverse others. This, in turn, can lead to the negative effects of diversity that can counter the positive benefits. This explains why smaller, less diverse crowds outperform similar-size, more diverse crowds. In doing so, these results identify

[2]Since more than 70% of the articles in our data set are in quality class C, we repeated the regression analyses only using quality classes B, GA, and FA. We observed that the trends are consistent in both sets.

that the benefits of diversity may have a tipping point, which may differ depending on the type of diversity.

Design Implications

Our results have important implications for collaborative systems that support crowd work. The use of crowds is becoming increasingly common across many domains and this trend has inspired the design of recommender systems intended to maximize the benefits of large collaborations by suggesting new partnerships [3, 12]. Currently, recommendation systems use individual attributes like expertise and experience to make suggestions [3]. Our results suggest that recommender systems should also consider the number of editors and the current diversity of the crowd along with how the new member would change both the size and diversity.

Limitations

One, we found a significant interaction between crowd size and diversity on performance. However, our results were only tested on a specific Wikipedia community. More work is needed to determine whether the results hold in other crowds. We note that our measures are general enough that they can be easily applied in other domains where users contribute to multiple projects. Hence, validating our findings on other domains is a feasible extension of the present work. Two, while our results highlight the importance of size relative to diversity, we do not attempt to quantify exactly how much diversity is necessary. In fact, the amount of diversity seems to depend on the type of diversity. Therefore, future research should be directed at determining what dictates the tipping point for a particular type of diversity. Three, the teams that we studied have two important characteristics: they are online and are very large. It is unclear whether the present results have implications for offline and/or smaller teams. Finally, we standardized all the continuous variables, which is normally recommended [16]. We acknowledge that there is debate about the effectiveness associated with such action.

ACKNOWLEDGMENTS

We thank Tawanna Dillahunt, Jon Kleinberg, and Paul Resnick for useful discussions.

REFERENCES

1. Alnuaimi, O.A., Robert, L.P., and Maruping, L.M. (2010) Team size, dispersion, and social loafing in technology-supported teams: A perspective on the theory of moral disengagement. *J. of Management Information Systems*, 27(1):203–230.
2. Chen, J., Ren, Y., and Riedl, J. (2010) The Effects of Diversity on Group Productivity and Member Withdrawal in Online Volunteer Groups. Proc. CHI.
3. Cosley, D., Frankowski, D., Terveen, L., and Riedl, J. (2007) SuggestBot: using intelligent task routing to help people find work in wikipedia. Proc IUI.
4. Cummings, J.N., Kiesler, S., Zadeh, R.B., and Balakrishnan, A.D. (2013) Group Heterogeneity Increases the Risks of Large Group Size: A Longitudinal Study of Productivity in Research Groups. *Psychological Science*, 24(6):880–890.
5. Earley, P.C. and Mosakowski, E. (2000) Creating hybrid team cultures: An empirical test of transnational team functioning. *Academy of Management Journal*, 43:26–49.
6. Jehn, K.A, Northcraft, G.B., Neale, M.A. (1999) Why differences make a difference: A field study of diversity, conflict, and performance in workgroups. *Administrative Science Quarterly* 4:741.
7. Kittur, A., Chi, E., and Suh, B. (2008) Crowdsourcing for usability: Using micro-task markets for rapid, remote, and low-cost user measurements. Proc. CHI.
8. Kittur, A. and Kraut, R.E. (2008) Harnessing the wisdom of crowds in Wikipedia: quality through coordination. Proc. CSCW.
9. Van Knippenberg, D. and Schippers, M.C. (2007) Work group diversity. *Annual Review of Psychology*, 58:515–541.
10. Larson, J.R., Christensen, C., Abbott, A.S., Franz, T.M. (1996) Diagnosing groups: charting the flow of information in medical decision-making teams. *J. of Personality and Social Psychology* 2:315–330.
11. Liu, J. and Ram, S. (2011) Who does what: Collaboration patterns in the wikipedia and their impact on article quality. *ACM Trans. Manage. Inf. Sys.* 2(2):1–23.
12. McDonald, D.W. (2003) Recommending collaboration with social networks: a comparative evaluation. Proc. CHI.
13. Oliver, P. E., and Marwell, G. (1988). The Paradox of Group Size in Collective Action: A Theory of the Critical Mass. II. *American Sociological Review*. 1–8.
14. O'Reilly, C.A., Caldwell, D.F., and Barnett, W.P. (1989) Work group demography, social integration, and turnover. *Administrative Science Quarterly*. 34:21–37.
15. Page, S.E. (2007). The Difference: How the Power of Diversity Creates Better Groups, Firms, Schools, and Societies. *Princeton University Press*.
16. Robert, L.P. (2013) A multi-level analysis of the impact of shared leadership in diverse virtual teams. Proc CSCW.
17. Stasser, G., Taylor L.A., Hanna C. (1994) Information sampling in structured and unstructured discussions of three- and six-person groups. *J. Personality Social Psych.* 3
18. Stvilia, B., Twidale, M. B., Smith, L.C., and Gasser, L. (2005) Assessing information quality of a community-based encyclopedia. Proc. ICIQ.
19. Wilkinson, D.M., and Huberman, B.A. (2007) Assessing the value of cooperation in Wikipedia. *First Monday* 12(4).
20. Williams, K.Y. and O'Reilly, C.A. (1998) Demography and diversity in organizations: A review of 40 years of research. *Research in Organizational Behavior*, 20:77–140.

I Know What You Did Last Week! Do You? Dynamic Security Questions for Fallback Authentication on Smartphones

Alina Hang[1], **Alexander De Luca**[1,2,3], **Heinrich Hussmann**[1]
[1]Media Informatics Group,University of Munich (LMU), Munich, Germany
[2]DFKI GmbH, Saarbrücken, Germany, [3]Fraunhofer FKIE, Bonn, Germany
(alina.hang, alexander.de.luca, heinrich.hussmann)@ifi.lmu.de

ABSTRACT
In this paper, we present the design and evaluation of dynamic security questions for fallback authentication. In case users lose access to their device, the system asks questions about their usage behavior (e.g. calls, text messages or app usage). We performed two consecutive user studies with real users and real adversaries to identify questions that work well in the sense that they are easy to answer for the genuine user, but hard to guess for an adversary. The results show that app installations and communication are the most promising categories of questions. Using three questions from the evaluated categories was sufficient to get an accuracy of 95.5% - 100%.

Author Keywords
Fallback Authentication; Dynamic Security Questions;

ACM Classification Keywords
H.5.1. Information Interfaces and Presentation (e.g. HCI): Evaluation/methodology

INTRODUCTION
Mobile devices employ a variety of authentication schemes like PINs, alphanumeric passwords or graphical passwords to protect sensitive data (e.g. photos, contact details) on a user's device. However, fallback solutions are required when these systems fail (e.g. when users enter their PINs/passwords incorrectly for too many times). Personal Unblocking Codes (PUCs) are often used in a mobile context to enable users to regain access to their device [16]. However, they are inconvenient since users do not (and should not) carry them around all the time. Retrieving a PUC in a situation where the user is left alone, maybe in a foreign country, with the locked device, is difficult in practice. Also the fallback solutions provided by the most popular operating systems for mobile devices are very difficult to use under such circumstances, like using a specific online account for Android or connecting Apple devices to a computer running iTunes [1].

Mobile devices are often used on the go and should offer fallback solutions that can be used locally without Internet connection and which are immediately available when needed. In turn, the time needed to complete the fallback authentication process is not as critical as for primary authentication.

ACM 978-1-4503-3145-6/15/04$15.00.
http://dx.doi.org/10.1145/2702123.2702131

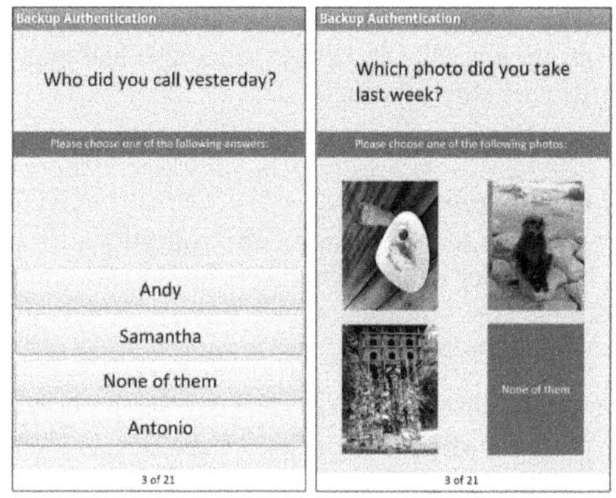

Figure 1. Screenshot of exemplary security question with four possible answers using text (left) or images (right). Translated from German.

In this work, we propose to take advantage of the enormous amount of data that is already stored on mobile devices to create dynamic security questions. This approach is immediate, does not require any additional tokens and is individual for each user. Since the questions are based on personal information and behavior, users should be able to answer them. In turn, persons who want to gain unauthorized access should not have enough knowledge to provide the correct answers.

The main contributions of this paper are the iterative design and evaluation of dynamic security questions in due consideration of different types of human adversaries (close and acquainted). Our studies indicate that privacy implications of certain questions play an important role in the design of dynamic security questions. Though certain questions were easy to remember, they turned out to be less accepted by users. Thus, different dimensions have to be taken into account when designing dynamic security questions. The study results show that the right combination of questions can yield up to 100% accuracy. In particular, questions about app usage and app installations are the most promising ones. They offered the best trade-off between usability (i.e. memorability) and security. While participants were better in answering questions about more recent activities, the performance of adversaries seem not to be influenced by the timespans used.

RELATED WORK
The most common solutions for fallback authentication are designed for web services and are often based on email or security questions.

Communication-based Password Reset

Email-based password reset is a popular approach for fallback authentication. In case of password loss, the (new) password or a link to reset the password is sent to the corresponding email account. According to Garfinkel [5], this approach works well, but comes with certain shortcomings (i.e. lack of email encryption). In a mobile context, email-based password resets do not work well as the user's only email access may be through the smartphone. Alternatives for fallback authentication have been proposed in various work. Schechter et al. [18] suggest social authentication for password reset. However, their results show that users also had memorability problems with this approach.

Security Questions

Numerous web services use security questions for password reset [4]. In order to use them, users have to answer a number of questions at set-up time, which have to be recalled during fallback authentication.

Most security questions are predefined and are based on facts (e.g. "What is your mother's maiden name?"). Though these kinds of questions seem to be easy to answer, several studies have shown that these traditional security questions are inadequate and have a bad performance in terms of usability and security (e.g. [6], [8], [15], [17]).

Since fallback authentication does not occur frequently (in the best case, never), users are often not able to recall the answers they have given due to the ambiguity of possible answers or the inapplicability of the questions. Therefore, users prefer to select easier questions, which in turn are also easier to guess for others (e.g. [15]). Haga et al. [8] and Schechter et al. [17] have shown that such questions are often correctly guessed by family members, friends or acquaintances. In particular, in times of social networks, answers to questions are often researchable by adversaries (e.g. [6], [7], [14]). Also, most security questions can be guessed by choosing the most popular answers [17].

To overcome the shortcomings of traditional security questions, some web services enable users to define their own questions [10]. However, users often lack creativity, forget the answers to their own questions or generate questions that are not secure enough [11]. Other solutions are based on the users' preferences (e.g. [9]). However, preferences might change over time and are vulnerable to insider threats: threats by adversaries that know the user well.

Dynamic Security Questions

The previous section has shown that the design of security questions is challenging. Users have to state the answer during enrolment so that the answer might not be up-to-date at the time when the actual fallback authentication is performed.

Thus, Babic et al. [2] propose the design of dynamic security questions that are based on the Internet activities of the user. Since the answers are derived automatically, no enrolment is needed and the answers are always up-to-date.

Category	Question + Timespan
SMS (out)	Who did you text [Y | LW | LM]?
SMS (in)	Who texted you [Y | LW | LM]?
Call (out)	Who did you call [Y | LW | LM]?
Call (in)	Who called you [Y | LW | LM]?
App	Which App did you use [Y | LW | LM]?
Music	Which artist did you listen to [Y | LW | LM]?
Photos	Which photo did you take [Y | LW | LM]?

Y=Yesterday; LW=Last Week; LM = Last Month

Table 1. Overview of 21 security questions used for the pre-study. One question for each category combined with three different timespans.

For a mobile context, Das et al. [3] presented an autobiographical authentication approach based on different categories (e.g. communication, technology usage, etc.). They created 13 different security questions and evaluated them in a user study. Participants performed best in answering questions about communication and were not as good in answering questions about app usage.

In order to test the security level of their security questions, Das et al. [3] introduce a theoretical adversary model that considers different types of adversaries, e.g. adversaries that know nothing, adversaries that know everything, etc. This is an interesting approach considering that studies with real adversaries are complex, time consuming and often produce high dropout rates. A theoretical model can provide hints at the security level of security questions.

Nonetheless, the model does not consider all circumstances that might influence the performance of real adversaries. Our work is similar to the work by Das et al. [3] in the sense that we analyze different types of dynamic security questions based on personal information on mobile devices. However, it is significantly different from it as we evaluate the security of those questions with human adversaries. We distinguish between close adversaries (e.g. family, friends) and acquaintances. This way, we were able to evaluate the actual security of the approach rather than a theoretical approach. For instance, with respect to true positive and true negative rates, we identified app usage as one of the best categories.

THREAT MODEL

We assume an adversary that is in possession of the smartphone. The adversary does not have the PIN or password necessary to unlock the device. Thus, the device gets blocked completely. The adversary can now use the fallback authentication mechanism to try to get access to the device. Assuming an equal distribution for each answer option, the chances for an adversary without any knowledge about the device owner to get access to the device is $(\frac{1}{x})^n$ with x being the number of possible answers for each question and n being the number of questions that have to be correctly answered.

To simulate a worst-case scenario, we consider adversaries with advanced knowledge about the user. This way, breaching the device is not plain luck. According to [13] these adversaries are very likely and thus, very interesting. The goal is to identify questions that are easily answered by users and that are, at the same time, harder to guess for these adversaries.

BRAINSTORMING

We conducted a brainstorming with four smartphone users (one female) to identify interesting information categories for the design of dynamic security questions. The participants were recruited over different channels like social networks, bulletin boards or personal communication. The participants were aged between 23-25 years (average: 24 years). All of them were students and had a technical background. Participants were invited to our lab. After a brief introduction, in which we explained the idea of dynamic security questions, they were asked to name and discuss different information categories that they thought to be suitable for the design of dynamic security questions. Participants received gift vouchers for their participation.

As a result, we identified seven categories: SMS (outgoing and incoming), call (outgoing and incoming), app, music and photos. These categories mostly agree with the results by Das et al. [3].

PRE-STUDY

In order to evaluate the seven categories, we created one question for each category. Additionally, each question was combined with the timespans *yesterday*, *last week* and *last month*. We did this to see, how far we can go back in time for the dynamic security questions. Table 1 gives an overview of all the security questions used in the pre-study.

Prototype

The prototypes consisted of two Android apps:

Logging Application

The logging app collected usage information on the user's device running in the background. Therefore, the participants did not have to cope with any changes to their smartphones. We collected information about incoming/outgoing text messages, incoming/outgoing calls (e.g. contact number), app usage (e.g. name of app) and music (e.g. artist). To ensure that our research complies with federal privacy laws, we paid particular attention to respect the participants' privacy when implementing the logging application and conducting the user studies. None of the information that were collected ever left the devices. If requested, we showed the participants a list of all the information that was logged.

Questions Application

The second app generated the actual security questions based on the logged information. The questions appeared in random order. For each of the 21 questions, 4 possible answers were provided, one of them being the option *none of them*. The incorrect answer options were generated from the logged data (excluding the correct answer). Figure 1 shows two examples on how the answer possibilities looked like. For all information categories, possible answers were provided as text (see figure 1, left). Only for the questions about photos, pictures were used instead (see figure 1, right). In case there was no logged information available to generate a question (e.g. when a user did not listen to music during a specific timespan), the corresponding question was skipped. To avoid that the questions might be too easy to guess for adversaries, we

Category	Question + Timespan
SMS (out)	Who did you text [Y | LW]?
SMS (in)	Who texted you [Y | LW]?
Call (out)	Who did you call [Y | LW]?
Call (in)	Who called you [Y | LW]?
App	Which App did you use [Y | LW]?
App Install	Which app did you install/update [Y | LW]?
Photos	Which photo did you take [Y | LW?

Y=Yesterday; LW=Last Week

Table 2. Overview of 14 security questions used for the main study. One question for each category combined with two different timespans.

excluded popular apps like Facebook or WhatsApp for the questions "Which app did you use [yesterday, last week, last month]?" The apps that were excluded are based on the data from a survey by [20], which lists the 20 most used apps in 2012 (the year in which the pre-study was conducted).

Study Design

For the pre-study, we used a within-subject design with the independent variables *category* (7 levels) and *timespan* (3 levels). This resulted in 7x3=21 different security questions (see table 1).

In order to participate in the pre-study, participants had to own an Android Smartphone. The pre-study consisted of two phases: a logging phase and a phase in which the participants had to answer questions. For the second phase, participants were asked to bring a person who knew them very well to the study. This person was asked to act as an adversary. We gave participants examples of close persons (e.g. partners and family). During the study, we also asked participants/adversaries to rate as how close they would describe their relationship.

Procedure

In the first phase of the pre-study, we sent instructions by email to our participants that informed them about the general procedure and showed them how to install the logging application that we also made available via email. The logging phase lasted for four weeks, after which we contacted the participants again and invited them to our lab.

The goal of the second phase was to let participants and adversaries answer the security questions. We installed the question app on the participant's device. Then the adversary was asked to leave the room and to wait outside. In the meantime, the participant had to answer all the questions from the question app. The questions were created in random order. This was followed by a questionnaire to gather subjective assessments. Once the participant had finished, the adversary was invited back in and had to complete the same tasks with the participant's smartphone. Participants and adversaries received gift vouchers as incentives.

Participants

Altogether, 38 persons took part in our pre-study: 19 smartphone owners and 19 persons that the smartphone owners brought along. In the remainder of the paper, smartphone owners will be referred to as participants and accompanying persons will be referred to as adversaries.

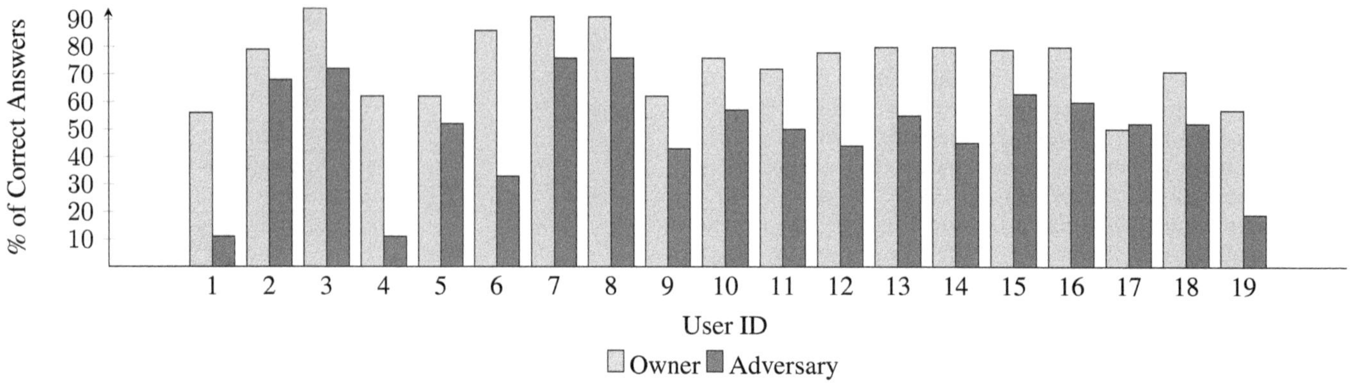

Figure 2. Overview of number of questions asked per participant and the number of correct answers by each participant as well as their corresponding adversary in the pre-study.

We recruited 19 participants (7 female) for the pre-study using mailing lists and public bulletin boards. They were aged between 20-31 years (average: 26 years). 14 of them had a college degree, 5 had a high school degree. Most of our participants had a technical background. All of them owned an Android smartphone, which was a prerequisite to participate in the study.

All participants brought one person to the study to act as an adversary. The 19 adversaries (10 female) were aged between 20-30 years (average: 24 years). 12 had a college degree, 7 a high school degree.

The relationship between participants and adversaries varied among the participants. One brought her spouse, 7 brought their partner, 8 brought a friend and three brought some acquaintances. Participant and adversary were asked to name the relationship with the respective other person in the questionnaire. Only in three cases, the relationships did not match. In those cases, the adversary considered the participant as friend, while the participant considered the adversary as an acquaintance, or the other way around. However, it is hard to draw the line between friend and acquaintances. Altogether, we can say that there is a good agreement on the relationships between participants and adversaries.

Results

We collected a total of 372 answers to dynamic security questions from participants as well as 372 answers from the adversaries. On average 20 answers were gathered per participant and per adversary.

Participants provided 275 (74%) correct answers. This is a higher percentage than can be found in similar work [3]. Adversaries gave 191 (51.3%) correct answers. The participant that performed worst only got 50% of the questions right. The best participant gave a correct answer in 94% of the cases. The best adversary reached 76% of correct answers, while the worst adversary had only 11% of correct answers. Figure 2 gives an overview of the number of correct answers for participants and their respective adversaries.

Users 3, 7 and 8 achieved over 90% of correct answers. However, their corresponding adversaries also answered over 70% of the questions correctly. Participants 7 and 8 did not only participate in our study as normal users, but they also acted as adversaries for each other. They were best friends who liked to communicate with each other using their smartphone. They told us that, in some cases, they were the answer to each other's questions. For example, for the question"Who did you call yesterday?", the adversary herself was the answer to the question. In contrast to this, there are participants who knew surprisingly little about themselves (ID 1, 17, 19). They answered less than 60% of their own questions.

Participants performed particularly well in giving correct answers to questions about text messaging: 92.8% for SMS (out) and 79% for SMS (in). However, adversaries achieved high percentages as well: 65% for SMS (out), 61.4% for SMS (in). Having a look at the other categories, adversaries achieved less than 50% of correct answers for questions about app usage, music, photos and calls (in). For the categories music and photos, participants could only answer 62.1% and 56%, respectively.

Questions about app usage showed the best trade-off between usability and security. While participants were able to answer over 70% of questions about app usage, their adversaries only achieved around 35%.

Participants tended to overestimate their performance. The difference between the number of answers they thought they had answered correctly and the actual number of correct answers was on average 3 (min=0; max=8). For adversaries the average difference between self-assessment and real performance was 4 (min=0; max=17).

Timespans

We asked participants to rate each question with respect to ease on a 5-point Likert scale, ranging from very difficult (1) to very easy (5). There were some questions that almost all participants found easy or very easy to answer (min=17 participants; max=19 participants). Interestingly, all these questions were about the timespan *yesterday*. This subjective assessment corresponds to their actual performance.

Participants had more correct answers for the timespan *yesterday* (87.3%) than for questions with the timespan *last week*

(71%). The timespans *last week* yielded more correct answers than questions about *last month* (62.3%). No tendencies were observed for adversaries (around 50% correct answers).

Perceived Security

In the questionnaire, we asked the participants to rate the perceived security of a question by assessing how easy they think certain questions could be guessed by an adversary.

Questions about music and app usage were considered as safe categories. There is no clear tendency for the other categories. We also did not find any particular timespans that participants found less or more secure.

User Stories and Comments

In general, the participants found our approach entertaining and fun. One participant in particular enjoyed the fact that she could learn more about her own usage behavior. Though some participants were concerned about the time it takes to answer all the questions, most of them found it convenient.

With respect to security, most participants thought the approach was secure against strangers, but they also assume that close persons or even acquaintances will be able to answer some of the questions.

Despite the positive feedback, there were participants who were concerned about their private data. After the study, one participant and his girlfriend jokingly said: "We just broke up - just kidding, but your study could destroy relationships. You are revealing information that you actually want to protect". They were referring to photos and communication details that we revealed as answer options during the study.

Another interesting comment was stated by two participants whose birthday was during the logging phase. One of them said: "I would have been better in answering questions about last month, if it wasn't my birthday. I received so many text messages". Thus, special events might influence the performance of a user.

MAIN STUDY

Based on the results of the pre-study, we improved the security questions and evaluated them further.

The information category music was replaced by the category app installation. This app-related category was included, since the category app usage had the best trade-off between usability and security in the pre-study. Other questions were not modified. Though questions about communication were easy to attack in the pre-study, we kept them to evaluate them in the main study with different types of adversaries (close adversary and acquainted adversary).

With respect to the timespan, we removed *last month* and kept only the timespan *yesterday* and *last week*. To enhance privacy, photos were blurred for the main study.

Study Design

The study design was similar to the pre-study. We used a within-subject design with two independent variables: *category* (7 levels) and *timespan* (two levels). Altogether, we evaluated 7x2=14 security questions (see table 2).

The study consisted of two phases: a logging phase and a phase, in which the participants had to answer security questions in random order. Again, the prerequisite to participate in the study was to own an Android smartphone.

Study Procedure

The study procedure was identical to the first study. The only difference was that we asked participants to bring two persons with them, one person that they know very well and one person they are only acquainted with. This way we were able to analyze our questions in terms of security with respect to different types of adversaries. Again, we provided participants with examples for close as well as acquainted persons and also asked participants/adversaries to rate the closeness of their relationship to each other.

Participants

Participants who took part in the pre-study were not allowed to participate again. Participants were recruited over bulletin boards, mailing list and social networks. Altogether, we recruited 18 participants for the main study. We ended the study with 11 participants (+11 close adversaries + 11 acquainted adversaries). There were different reasons for the high dropout rate, one of them being the vacation season where participants and adversaries did not show up for the second phase. Other participants had to be excluded, since the second application could not be installed on their smartphones.

The 11 participants (5 female) were aged between 19-33 years (average: 24 years). Two of them had a college degree, while 9 had a high school degree. The 11 close adversaries (three female) were aged between 19-33 years (average: 23 years). 6 of them had a college degree. 5 had a high school degree. Acquainted adversaries (two female) were aged between 19-58 years (average: 27 years). 5 of them had a college degree. 6 of them had a high school degree.

The relationship to the close adversary was manifold. Two participants brought their spouse, three brought their partner, 5 brought a very close friend and one brought her brother. There were no contradictions in the relationship between participants and their close adversary. They also all stated that they knew each other well to very well.

Eight participants brought a person they knew from college, school or work as acquainted adversaries. One of them brought a friend, two brought a friend of a close friend. Acquaintances and participants named the same relationship. There was no contradiction. Most adversary-participant pairs did not know each other well.

Results

Correct Answers to Security Questions

We created 154 dynamic security questions (14 per participant). Each of those questions had to be answered by the participants as well as their adversaries. Participants gave 135 (87.7%) correct answers. Close adversaries had 84 (54.5%) correct answers, while acquainted ones had 67 (43.5%).

The best participant had 92.9% correct answers. The worst participant achieved 78.6%. The best close adversary had

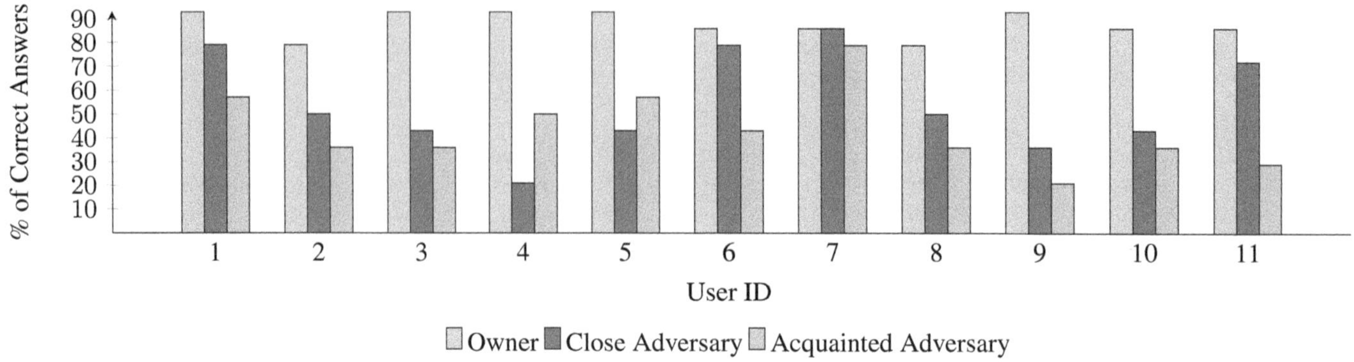

Figure 3. Overview of number of questions asked per participant and the number of correct answers by each participant as well as their corresponding adversary in the main study.

85.7%, the worst had 21.4%. The same observations can be made for acquainted adversaries. The worst had 21.4%, while the best yielded 78.6%.

An overview of the number of correct answers is shown in figure 3. Five participants had over 90% of correct answers, 4 got over 85% and 2 had over 75%. Participants were very good in answering their questions. They had only between 1-3 of 14 questions incorrect.

The results show that there are some participants that are easier to attack than others. In particular, for participants 1, 6, 7 and 11, close adversaries were good in answering their security questions. The acquainted was not as good as the close one. Participants that were hard to attack had the ID 3, 4, 9, 10. While they had a high percentage of correct answer, their adversaries, close and acquainted, yielded only a low percentage of correct answers.

The participants were good in assessing their performance. The average difference between estimation and actual performance was only 1 question (min=0; max=2;). The difference for adversaries was on average 3.

Timespans

As mentioned before, participants were good in answering questions. They made only 1-3 errors. However, they made at most one error for questions about *yesterday*. This error was always made for the question about app usage.

In general, participants achieved high percentage of correct answers for *yesterday* (94.8%) and were better in answering them than answering questions on *last week* (80.5%). Adversaries were better in answering yesterday questions than questions on *last week*. However, the differences are minimal. Close adversaries had 55.8% of correct answers for *yesterday* questions and 53.3% for questions about *last week*. In turn, acquainted adversaries achieved a lower number of correct answers than the close adversaries (44.2% for yesterday, and 42.9% for last week).

We conducted a mixed design ANOVA with the between-factor user type (user, close or acquainted adversary) and the within-factor timespan (*yesterday* and *last week*). The analysis showed no significant main effect for timespan, but a highly significant main effect for user type ($F(2,30) = 24.114$; $p < .001$). The test did not show any interaction effects between the factors timespan and user type.

The post-hoc test showed highly significant differences between user and close adversary ($p < 0.001$; *Bonferroni corrected*) and also between user and acquainted adversary ($p < 0.001$; *Bonferroni corrected*). No significant differences were found between close and acquainted adversaries.

Perceived Security

The majority of our participants found questions about communication activities and photos to be insecure. Only the information category app installation (with the timespan *yesterday*) was rated to be appropriate. The opinions for the other categories were ambiguous.

Accuracy of Security Question

Accuracy calculations are a good indicator on how well an authentication system performs. In our case, we used accuracy to calculate how well each security question worked. True positives (TP) are successful authentication attempts by legitimate users, while true negatives (TN) are unsuccessful attacks of potential adversaries. In turn, false negatives (FN) are counted when a legitimate user is accidentally rejected, while false positives (FP) depict the number of successful authentication attempts by potential adversaries. The formula for the calculation looks like this:

$$Accuracy = \frac{\sum TP + \sum TN}{\sum TP + \sum FP + \sum TN + \sum FN}$$

We will use this formula for the forthcoming analyses. The formula returns a value between 0 and 1 (or 0 and 100 in percentage). A value of 0 is bad and a rate of 1 (or 100) means that all attacks failed and the user always succeeded. Thus, a very desirable result.

Since we used two different timespans and two types of adversaries, there are four values for accuracy. This way, we can compare if the accuracy of a system depends on the timespan and type of adversary who tries to attack our questions.

Table 3 gives an overview of the calculated accuracy values that only consider the answers by users and attempted attacks by close adversaries for calculation. Table 4 shows the accuracy values that only take into account answers by users and acquainted adversaries. With respect to the close adversary,

	Close Adversary									
	Yesterday					Last Week				
Question / Category	TP	TN	FP	FN	ACC	TP	TN	FP	FN	ACC
Who did you text? / SMS (out)	11	4	7	0	68.2	9	5	6	2	63.6
Who texted you? / SMS (in)	11	5	6	0	72.7	11	2	9	0	59.1
Who did you call? / Call (out)	11	5	6	0	72.7	8	7	4	3	68.2
Who called you? / Call (in)	11	4	7	0	68.2	7	3	8	4	45.5
Which app did you install/update? / App Install)	11	7	4	0	81.8	9	6	5	2	68.2
Which app did you use? / App)	7	6	5	4	59.1	9	5	6	2	63.6
Which photo did you take?) / Photos	11	3	8	0	63.6	9	8	3	2	77.3

Table 3. True positives (TP), true negatives (TN), false positives (FP) , false negatives (FN) and accuracy (ACC; in %) of each question and the timespans yesterday, last week, taking into account answers by close adversaries.

	Acquainted Adversary									
	Yesterday					Last Week				
Question / Category	TP	TN	FP	FN	ACC	TP	TN	FP	FN	ACC
Who did you text? / SMS (out)	11	8	3	0	86.4	9	6	5	2	68.2
Who texted you? / SMS (in)	11	4	7	0	68.2	11	4	7	0	68.2
Who did you call? / Call (out)	11	8	3	0	86.2	8	6	5	3	63.6
Who called you? / Call (in)	11	8	3	0	86.4	7	6	5	4	59.1
Which app did you install/update? / App Install)	11	7	4	0	81.8	9	8	3	2	77.3
Which app did you use? / App)	7	4	7	4	50	9	6	5	2	68.2
Which photo did you take?) / Photos	11	4	7	0	68.2	9	8	3	2	77.3

Table 4. True positives (TP), true negatives (TN), false positives (FP), false negatives (FN) and accuracy (ACC, in %) of each question and the timespans yesterday, last week, taking into account answers by acquainted adversaries.

the highest accuracy was achieved for app install (*yesterday*), with over 80% (11 TP, 7 TN, 4 FP and 0 FN).

When considering the attacks by acquainted adversaries only, the highest accuracies are achieved for yesterday's SMS (out) and Call (in and out), with 86.4% (each with 11 TP, 8 TN, 3 FP and 0 FN). This is followed by App Install (yesterday) with 81.8% accuracy. This category also achieves high accuracy when combined with the timespan last week 77.3% (9 TP, 8 TN, 3 FP and 2 FN).

Best Combination

So far, we analyzed the accuracy of each individual question. However, in a fallback authentication system multiple security questions are combined to provide enhanced security. Thus, we calculated the accuracy values for all possible combinations of the 14 security questions. With n = 14, there are $\sum_{k=1}^{n} \binom{n}{k} = 16383$ possible combinations. The best combination in terms of accuracy was found for the questions: "Which app did you install yesterday?", "Who did you call yesterday?" and "Who did you text yesterday?" Table 5 gives an overview of the accuracy values for this combination. The threshold in the table depicts the number of correctly answered questions that are required to authenticate successfully. If only the attacks by close adversaries are considered, this combination can yield an accuracy of over 95%. All legitimate users were authenticated successfully (11 TP, 0 FN). Only one adversary got unauthorized access (1 FP, 10 TN). If we consider the same combination with only attacks provided by acquainted adversaries, an accuracy of 100% is achieved (11 TP, 11 TN, 0 FP, 0 FN).

Close Adversaries					
Threshold	TP	TN	FP	FN	ACC
1	11	2	9	0	59.1
2	11	4	7	0	68.2
3	11	10	1	0	95.5
Acquainted Adversaries					
Threshold	TP	TN	FP	FN	ACC
1	11	5	6	0	72.7
2	11	7	4	0	81.8
3	11	11	0	0	100

Table 5. True positives (TN), true negatives (TN), false positives (FP), false negatives (FN) and accuracy (ACC; in %) of the best combination of questions, taking into account attacks from close (top) and acquainted (bottom) adversaries, respectively. Threshold depicts the number of questions that must be answered correctly.

To achieve the reported accuracy values, users have to answer only three questions correctly (threshold = 3). There are also several other combinations with more questions that yield the same accuracy values. This is important to prevent random adversaries to succeed by chance. With only three questions (and four answer options), the chances for a random adversary is $(\frac{1}{4})^3 = 0,016$ (1.6% chance). In turn, using 7 questions will reduce the chances to 0.01% ($(\frac{1}{4})^7 = 0,000061$). For comparison: The chances of a 4-Digit PIN to be guessed by a random adversary are $\frac{1}{10000} = 0.0001$ (0.01%).

A combination with 7 questions and 95.5%/100% accuracy for close/acquainted adversaries consists of the questions "Which app did you install yesterday/last week?", "Which app did you use last week?", "Who did you call yesterday?", "Who called you last week?" and "Who texted you yesterday/last week".

DISCUSSION

Related Adversary Attack

The actual performance varied from participant to participant. There were participants who knew a lot about themselves, but we also had adversaries who were quite familiar with their usage patterns and interestingly, also made similar mistakes. This confirms our assumption that the biggest threats are persons who are very close to the user (e.g. jealous partners). We argue that such attacks are very likely [13] and thus have to be considered when designing a fallback authentication system.

Limited Device Usage

We also had participants who knew very little about themselves, but at the same time, were hard to attack. We assume that those users have very low smartphone usage with particular usage patterns (e.g. using special apps), which makes it more difficult to guess their answers. In a real-world deployment, it might be difficult to generate enough security questions for those users, since only few data is available. The same problem may arise for users who seldom install new apps.

Alternative solutions need to be provided in those cases. One might think of designing more questions within a category for which the user has enough data on the device or switch to another fallback solution. The latter approach is particularly important in case the device has been idle for some time (i.e. no usage data is available) in order to prevent adversaries to always select the option *none of them* as the correct answer.

Limiting Data Exposure

Dynamic security questions could be exploited to circumvent the primary authentication. Adversaries do not even have to get into the user's device to spy on information as some information can be leaked through dynamic questions based on usage patterns. That is why we analyzed different types of questions to gain insights on the acceptance of each question. We learned that certain questions are more accepted by participants than others.

For example, the pre-study showed that using photos was a bad idea. That is why we introduced blurred photos to evaluate whether this would reduce the privacy concerns that users have. However, the comments of the participants showed that still, they would prefer not answering photo questions at all. When designing systems with dynamic security questions, it is important to focus on data types that are personal, but that users do not mind if exposed to others. As shown by our results, different types of data on the phone have different levels of sensitivity.

Choosing Question Categories

The information categories that were related to active communication were the categories that our participants found easiest to answer. Since active communication is something that is initiated by the users (e.g. calling someone), it is probably easier to remember when being asked for it. However, these categories alone are not suitable for the design of dynamic security questions, since related adversaries are also good in answering those questions.

The categories about app usage and app installations seem to be the most promising ones. They had the best trade-off between usability and security. While participants were good in answering those questions, adversaries performed much worse for them.

In addition to this, the participants rated these categories among the safest, together with the category music. In comparison to the other categories, questions about app usage or music listening habits are less personal. Participants are probably not so reluctant to share which artist they listened to or which app they used. However, information with whom they texted or what photos they have on the device are much more sensitive. In particular photos can reveal information that better should be protected.

Though the category music was considered as safe by our participants, it is not suitable for the design of dynamic security questions due to memorability issues. Music is something one does on the go while doing other things. It is a passive activity, so that it is hard to actually remember which music one had listened to at a specific point in time. Furthermore, music is increasingly consumed through streaming services, where it is difficult to log the data.

Choosing Timespans

With respect to the timespans, the participants felt that questions about *yesterday* were easier to answer. Their actual performance for the timespan *yesterday* was also better than for other timespans. This is quite reasonable since activities that just happened a day ago, are more present in one's memory.

We got interesting insights when taking a closer look at the categories with respect to the included timespans. Some questions seem to work better with longer timespans, while others are easier to answer when they happened just recently.

For example, app installations are something that the user does consciously and thus, it will be more likely to remember the answer if it did not happen too long ago. On the other hand, using an app (if it is not newly installed) can be included in the users' routine (checking mails on the go, etc.). Though these kinds of things are done actively, they are part of an automated routine. Thus, it is easier for users to answer if the used an app during the week, instead of answering if they used it the day before.

Design for Special Events

Participants had difficulties remembering the correct answers when special events occurred (e.g. one's birthday). Two of them received too many text messages so that they could not remember who of the persons texted them. Unusual events should be taken into account when designing dynamic security questions. The identification of unusual events could be based on outlier detection. In case an event (e.g. incoming message) occurs more frequently than usual, the corresponding questions should not be asked to avoid memorability issues identified in the study. Another consideration in this case could be to invert the question (e.g. "Who didn't call you yesterday?"). However, this could cause additional social tension by highlighting that some expected event did not occur.

Adversaries and Security

Das et al. [3] showed with their theoretical model that naïve and observing adversaries performed worst in answering security questions. As examples for naïve and observing adversaries, they mentioned close family members. These are exactly the adversaries that we had in our study.

However, our results suggest that adversaries can perform quite differently. We had adversaries that performed well, but we also had adversaries who performed not as good. Altogether, the adversaries were always worse in answering the questions than the participants. How well an adversary can answer certain questions depended on how well they knew their victim. It also depended on the usage patterns of the user. In particular, participants that seldom used their smartphones were harder to attack.

Participants were better in answering the security questions in the main study. We achieved an increase of 13% of correct answers compared to the pre-study. The redesign of the security questions by removing unsuitable questions and adding promising categories seems to have positively influenced the results. The percentage of correct answers for adversaries did not change much (around 50%). Close adversaries were better than acquainted ones, which is reasonable, since close adversaries are supposed to know more than acquaintances.

Another threat by close adversaries is that they are more likely to be able to observe the behavior of the user (e.g. partner). Excluding the most popular answers from a question, is a first step to make observation more difficult, since adversaries are probably more likely to observe more regular patterns (e.g. someone using Facebook frequently). However, how easy it is for close adversaries to perform observation attacks needs to be addressed in future studies.

Real and Estimated Performance

In the first study, we found that participants overestimated their actual performance. This means that users are confident in their answers, making the overall authentication process more enjoyable and less frustrating. At the same time, being rejected even though one believes that the answers were correct might cause frustration too. Thus, it is desirable to provide a close to real experience.

Participants in the main study were very good about their estimation. Improving the security questions most likely removed error prone questions (e.g. music), reducing wrong estimates. Close adversaries and acquaintances had a good self-assessment about their performance. This could be an indicator that adversaries know quite well which answers they are able to answer and which they are not. This is a danger, in particular for close adversaries who would like to spy on information of their friend or partner. Exploiting the fact that they know which questions are missing, they might try to observe their "victim" in order to get the missing pieces.

Best Combination of Questions

The individual accuracy for each security question helped us to identify promising and problematic questions. However, the accuracy that can be achieved with one question is not sufficient due to the high number of FP and FN. The accuracy can be optimized by combining multiple questions. Using a combination of 7 questions increases security drastically. The chance for a random adversary to successfully authenticate is almost zero. Thus, our presented approach can yield a similar theoretical security level as a 4-digit PIN that is often used as primary authentication method on smartphones. This is important, since a fallback authentication mechanism needs to be at least as secure as the primary authentication. Also, the use of 7 questions seems appropriate in terms of time in the context of fallback authentication.

The best combinations contained questions about the user's communication history that were identified as privacy-intruding during the studies. However, this does not mean that one is not allowed to use these question categories. Instead, one should think of ways on how to use them, but preserve the user's privacy at the same time. For example, this could be removing the last name of the contact or even try to only give away the initials or the first three letters of a name.

Number of Attempts

The best combinations presented in this paper are very strict, meaning that users have to answer all questions correctly (within three questions) or are only allowed to make one mistake (within seven questions). While this makes it difficult for adversaries to attack, it also puts a high pressure on the user.

In case the user makes an error, one could think of an incremental approach, where with each error, more questions are asked (like in [19]). For this, the same combinations of questions can be used again, but with different answers (e.g. there may be more than one app that the user installed yesterday). However, it has to be taken into account that an incremental approach also comes with new risks (e.g. hinting at adversaries which questions have been answered incorrectly). Thus, it is important to set a limit on the incremental approach after which the user has to perform another fallback authentication (with another approach) or the authentication fails completely (similar to PUC).

LIMITATIONS AND IMPROVEMENTS

Though we collected a lot of data in our study, there was some information we could not access. For example, there are many different apps for text messaging like WhatsApp, Viber, etc. for which it was not possible to log text messaging information. This is suboptimal since those apps might have revealed further usage patterns and performances.

We had a high dropout rate for the main study, which was mostly due to the fact that participants found it hard to fulfill the requirements of bringing two people with specific properties with them for the lab study. Thus, a clear limitation of the studies is the number and age distributions of the participants. Participants were also rather tech-savvy which could have an influence on the higher app usage and thus, also limits the representativeness of our sample. We encourage additional studies with a larger and more diverse user population that take into account the different types of users, for example, in a between-groups experiment (i.e. high vs. low device usage). The study of less familiar adversaries would also be an interesting aspect to be considered in future research.

CONCLUSION

In this paper, we presented an iterative design process for dynamic security questions that are based on available (usage) data of mobile devices. We identified suitable and unsuitable categories of information conducting two user studies and tested them under the worst possible circumstances with different types of human adversaries. We identified significant differences between users and adversaries when answering dynamic security questions.

Most importantly, we showed that the design of dynamic security questions is a challenging task that does not only involve security and usability aspects, but also privacy concerns. Thus, the most usable options (i.e. categories that the user can answer best) are not necessarily the best solutions. Instead, we identified app usage and app installation as promising categories, since they have the best trade-off between usability and security. Nonetheless, they work best in combination with respect to the user's communication history, yielding over 95% to 100% accuracy.

Dynamic security questions have been proposed in the past (e.g. [2]) and are actually used in the real world (e.g. [12]). However, their privacy implications have been rarely discussed. We hope that the insights gained in this paper will inspire further discussion and research in this area. In particular, if dynamic security question are used, how can we prevent the revelation of too much personal information when their design actually relies on the personal information?

ACKNOWLEDGMENTS

We would like to thank Stephan Thalhammer and Philipp Hauptmann for their help with conducting the user studies.

REFERENCES

1. Apple Support. ios: Forgotten passcode or device disabled after entering wrong passcode. `http://support.apple.com/kb/ht1212` (Accessed: 03/03/2014).
2. Babic, A., Xiong, H., Yao, D., and Iftode, L. Building robust authentication systems with activity-based personal questions. In *Proc. SafeConfig 2009*, ACM Press (2009), 19–24.
3. Das, S., Hayashi, E., and Hong, J. I. Exploring capturable everyday memory for autobiographical authentication. In *Proc. UbiComp 2013*, ACM Press (2013), 211–220.
4. Furnell, S. An assessment of website password practices. *Computers & Security 26*, 7-8 (2007), 445 – 451.
5. Garfinkel, S. L. Email-based identification and authentication: An alternative to pki? *IEEE Security & Privacy 1*, 6 (2003), 20–26.
6. Griffith, V., and Jakobsson, M. Messin' with texas deriving mother's maiden names using public records. In *Proc. ACNS 2014*. Springer (2005), 91–103.
7. Gupta, P., Gottipati, S., Jiang, J., and Gao, D. Your love is public now: Questioning the use of personal information in authentication. In *Proc. ASIA CCS 2013*, ACM Press (2013), 49–60.
8. Haga, W. J., and Zviran, M. Question-and-answer passwords: An empirical evaluation. *Information Systems 16*, 3 (1991), 335 – 343.
9. Jakobsson, M., Stolterman, E., Wetzel, S., and Yang, L. Love and authentication. In *Proc. CHI 2008*, ACM Press (2008), 197–200.
10. Just, M. Designing and evaluating challenge-question systems. *IEEE Security & Privacy 2*, 5 (2004), 32–39.
11. Just, M., and Aspinall, D. Personal choice and challenge questions: A security and usability assessment. In *Proc. SOUPS 2009*, ACM Press (2009), 8:1–8:11.
12. Microsoft. Microsoft live mail. `https://login.live.com/` (Accessed: 04/08/2014).
13. Muslukhov, I., Boshmaf, Y., Kuo, C., Lester, J., and Beznosov, K. Know your enemy: The risk of unauthorized access in smartphones by insiders. In *Proc. MobileHCI 2013*, ACM Press (2013), 271–280.
14. Polakis, I., Lancini, M., Kontaxis, G., Maggi, F., Ioannidis, S., Keromytis, A. D., and Zanero, S. All your face are belong to us: Breaking facebook's social authentication. In *Proc. ACSAC 2012*, ACM Press (2012), 399–408.
15. Rabkin, A. Personal knowledge questions for fallback authentication: Security questions in the era of facebook. In *Proc. SOUPS 2008*, ACM Press (New York, NY, USA, 2008), 13–23.
16. Rysgaard, B. A method for protecting user data stored in memory of a mobile communication device, particularly a mobile phone, 2001. *European Patent No. EP 1107627* (2001).
17. Schechter, S., Brush, A. J. B., and Egelman, S. It's no secret: Measuring the security and reliability of authentication via 'secret' questions. In *Proc. SOUPS 2009*, ACM Press (2009), 40:1–40:1.
18. Schechter, S., Egelman, S., and Reeder, R. W. It's not what you know, but who you know: A social approach to last-resort authentication. In *Proc.CHI 2009*, ACM Press (2009), 1983–1992.
19. Schechter, S., and Reeder, R. W. 1 + 1 = you: Measuring the comprehensibility of metaphors for configuring backup authentication. In *Proc. Soups 2009*, ACM Press (2009), 9:1–9:31.
20. Statista: The Statistics Portal. Top 20 smartphone-apps in deutschland 2012. `http://de.statista.com/statistik/daten/studie/239434/umfrage/nutzeranteile-der-top-20-smartphone-apps-in-deutschland` (Accessed: 03/03/2014).

Improving Accuracy, Applicability and Usability of Keystroke Biometrics on Mobile Touchscreen Devices

Daniel Buschek[1], **Alexander De Luca**[1,2], **Florian Alt**[1]
[1]Media Informatics Group, University of Munich (LMU); [2]DFKI GmbH, Saarbrücken, Germany
{daniel.buschek, alexander.de.luca, florian.alt}@ifi.lmu.de

ABSTRACT

Authentication methods can be improved by considering implicit, individual behavioural cues. In particular, verifying users based on typing behaviour has been widely studied with physical keyboards. On mobile touchscreens, the same concepts have been applied with little adaptations so far. This paper presents the first reported study on mobile keystroke biometrics which compares touch-specific features between three different hand postures and evaluation schemes. Based on 20.160 password entries from a study with 28 participants over two weeks, we show that including spatial touch features reduces implicit authentication equal error rates (EER) by 26.4 - 36.8% relative to the previously used temporal features. We also show that authentication works better for some hand postures than others. To improve applicability and usability, we further quantify the influence of common evaluation assumptions: known attacker data, training and testing on data from a single typing session, and fixed hand postures. We show that these practices can lead to overly optimistic evaluations. In consequence, we describe evaluation recommendations, a probabilistic framework to handle unknown hand postures, and ideas for further improvements.

Author Keywords

Keystroke Dynamics; Mobile; Touch; Biometrics

ACM Classification Keywords

H.5.2 Information Interfaces and Presentation (e.g. HCI): Input devices and strategies (e.g. mouse, touchscreen)

INTRODUCTION

We use mobile devices in many tasks every day [8]. Some require access to password-protected systems, like email accounts or social networks. The device itself may also be locked with a password or PIN to protect it in cases of loss or theft [25]. Utilising device sensors and assuming a one-to-one relationship with personal devices, research proposed behavioural biometrics to enhance security [11, 16, 18, 31]. For password entry, a second, implicit security layer can observe typing *behaviour*: If an attacker knows the password or PIN, for example due to shoulder surfing [48] or a smudge-attack [2, 51], access can still be denied based on the fact that they do not type the password in the same way as the legitimate user (e.g. different rhythm, finger placement).

CHI 2015, April 18 - 23 2015, Seoul, Republic of Korea

ACM 978-1-4503-3145-6/15/04...$15.00
http://dx.doi.org/10.1145/2702123.2702252

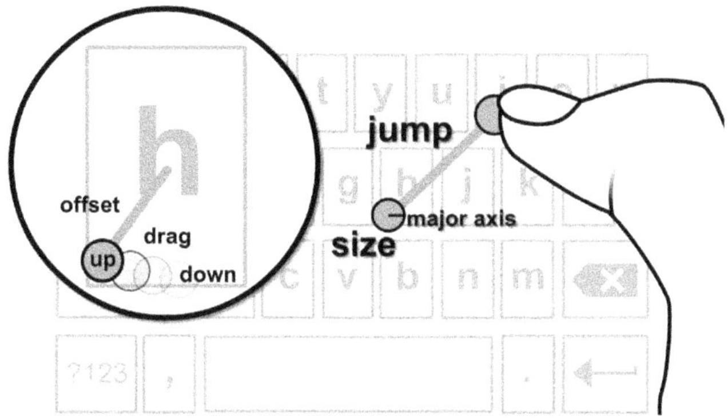

Figure 1. Touch-specific keystroke features on a mobile keyboard. In this example, the user is typing "hi". The magnified *h*-key shows touch down and up locations, the drag in between, and the offset to the key's centre. The keyboard-overlay shows touch area size and axis, as well as the "jump" vector between subsequent touches. In this paper, we analyse these touch-specific features to improve mobile keystroke biometrics.

Verifying identity based on typing behaviour (*keystroke dynamics*) has mostly been studied in terms of timing, both on physical keyboards [40, 41] and older mobile devices with physical keys [10, 14, 15, 30, 33, 38, 57]. Less work has been carried out on mobile devices with touch [32, 42, 46, 59], and without investigating touch-specific behavioural features, such as those shown in Figure 1. Recent research has successfully used similar features with gesture keyboards [11], but the potential of touch biometrics is still unknown for typing by tapping [20, 55]. Hence, to improve keystroke biometrics for the smartphone-era, this paper provides in-depth analyses of mobile-specific and touch-specific opportunities and challenges, leading to the following contributions:

1. *To improve implicit authentication accuracy, we evaluate touch-specific features for capturing individual typing behaviour.* Spatial touch features outperform the commonly used temporal features, and both can be combined to reduce equal error rates by up to 36.8%.
2. *To improve applicability, we discuss and quantify practical implications of different commonly used evaluations.* In particular, we compare results for: 1) training and testing within sessions or across sessions; 2) training on owner data only or also on data from others; 3) assuming fixed or changing hand postures. Our analyses allow for a more realistic assessment of keystroke biometrics in practice.
3. *To improve usability, we propose an approach to avoid restricting users to one typing posture.* We analyse one-thumb, two-thumb and index finger typing. We show that behaviour is highly posture-specific and present a method to handle changing hand postures.

RELATED WORK

We relate our work to touch behaviour, keystroke dynamics, and touch-based implicit identification and authentication.

Modelling Touch and Typing Behaviour

Related research reduced typing errors with keyboard personalisation based on users' individual touch distributions per key [3, 4, 13, 21, 24, 56]. Azenkot and Zhai [3] found that touch distributions for each key on a smartphone's soft keyboard varied less within users than between them. Yin et al. [56] showed that user-specific models reduce error rates further than posture- or key-specific ones. Edelmann et al. [21] also found that user-specific models led to less typing errors on a tabletop. Hence, this line of research revealed individual touch typing patterns, but none of these projects utilised this information for user authentication, which we explore here.

Research also found several influences on general touch behaviour: Individuals visually target differently with their finger tips [27], since targets are often occluded by the finger [6]. Contact areas are influenced by the finger's angle [22, 52]. Targeting offsets differ with respect to the finger's pitch, roll and yaw [28], and offset patterns [26] can better be corrected for individual users than overall [12, 53, 54]. In this paper, we examine targeting behaviour in terms of such touch offsets as a novel feature for mobile keystroke biometrics.

Behavioural Biometrics for Mobile Typing

Related work applied keystroke dynamics on mobile phones with physical keys: Zahid et al. [57] deployed a fuzzy-logic classifier observing temporal features and error counts on a keypad phone. Other researchers used neural networks to authenticate mobile phone users based on temporal typing features on keypads [15] and physical mini-QWERTY keyboards [33]. Their systems achieved 12.8% EER [15] and 12.2% EER [33], using attacker data during training.

Nauman et al. [42] enhanced password authentication for web services with keystroke dynamics on smartphones. They used keystroke latencies and key-hold times, but no touch features. Saevanee et al. [47] combined linguistic analysis with keystroke dynamics on mobile devices. The keystroke-based part of their system used key-hold times and achieved 20.8% EER. They trained classifiers in a "one-vs-rest" scheme, using data from both the legitimate user and others.

Zheng et al. [59] measured pressure and touch size for nine-key PIN unlock on smartphones. They reported EERs between 3.65%-7.34% with distance-based anomaly detection evaluated in a single session. Other authors used a Bayesian Net to authenticate phone users in a passcode entry task with a grid of 16 symbols [32]. They reported 82.18% accuracy with temporal features and distances between subsequent touches. They also applied the method to an actual keyboard, but did not consider touch features there. In contrast to these projects, we include touch offsets and touch locations.

Burgbacher and Hinrichs [11] trained Support Vector Machines (SVMs) in a "one-vs-rest" scheme to authenticate users via finger movement behaviour on gesture keyboards (see [36]). They reported 0% EER if five or more words in the message are known to the system. They targeted gesture keyboards, whereas our approach addresses typing by tapping.

Draffin et al. [20] trained neural network classifiers for keystroke authentication using touch-to-key offsets, size, pressure, drag, and hold time. Although they used features derived from exact touch locations, they did not evaluate the contribution of these new spatial features to the overall performance. This was also pointed out by Xu et al. [55], who therefore decided against using these typing features in their work on implicit authentication with mobile touch input. In contrast, we present a detailed evaluation of offsets and other touch features. We show that they outperform the temporal features, and thus should indeed be included.

Touch-based Implicit Authentication and Identification

Related work addressed verifying user identity with diverse touch measures: Shape-based phone unlock systems were enhanced with an implicit layer using touch sequence matching [1, 7, 18]. Characteristics of touch strokes from zooming and scrolling were utilised as well [23, 58]. Other work suggested to directly replace passwords with touch evidence [31, 49], for example with special touch gestures [45]. In contrast, our method addresses text-based logins and typing.

Further related research distinguished users with rear-projected tabletop systems: Holz and Baudisch [29] used a fiber optics plate to authenticate users via fingerprints during touch interaction on a multitouch table. Mock et al. [39] also captured images of finger contact areas on a tabletop. They used SVMs to identify one of twelve known typists with 97.51% accuracy, and detected unknown users with 12.3% EER, both after one keystroke. This shows that finger placement on soft keyboards provides user-specific information. However, current mobile touchscreens lack optical sensors; images of the fingers are not available. In this paper, we nevertheless utilise spatial typing touch information, solely relying on sensors available on off-the-shelf mobile devices.

Opportunities and Intended Contribution

In summary, related work on keyboard personalisation, targeting, and touch-based authentication has shown individual touch and typing behaviour. However, research on keystroke biometrics has either ignored spatial touch-specific typing features on mobile devices [15, 33, 42, 57], or only used such features on tabletops [29, 39] or with gesture-keyboards [11].

We found only one exception: Draffin et al. [20] measured touch-to-key offsets, but only tested them with one classifier, and crucially neither optimised feature sets nor evaluated the influence of the new features, as pointed out by Xu et al. [55].

In conclusion, this leaves the potential of touch features for mobile keystroke biometrics still unexplored. At the same time, related work has revealed the need to address mobile applications of keystroke biometrics and to develop novel features [5, 16, 50]. Hence, we aim to improve behavioural biometrics for mobile touch keyboards with a comprehensive analysis of touch-specific features in a password entry task.

Furthermore, we analyse common evaluation schemes in research on (mobile) keystroke biometrics to quantify the effects of potentially "optimistic" methods. We suggest alternatives which allow for more practical and usable perspectives.

THREAT MODEL

We consider that an attacker gains access to an unlocked device and additionally knows the owner's password for their email account, for a social network or for similar services and apps which require authentication. Here, keystroke information serves as an additional security layer ("password hardening" [40]): even if the attacker enters the correct password, the system can deny access due to different typing behaviour.

IMPROVING ACCURACY OF KEYSTROKE BIOMETRICS

We propose new typing features for the password entry task resulting from the described threat model. We then introduce our employed user models for implicit authentication.

Typing Features

To build user models for authentication, we need to capture individual aspects of typing behaviour. We are interested in features which vary characteristically between users, but also stay consistent for the same user over time. Formally, we describe each password entry as a feature vector, as in most related work (see e.g. [20, 42, 50]): Typing a password with n keystrokes is represented as a vector $f = (f_1, f_2, ..., f_n)^T$, the concatenation of the typing features f_t for each touch t. For example, if a system observes the two features *hold time* ht and *flight time* ft, the typing behaviour for a password entry is described as $f = (ht_1, ft_1, ht_2, ft_2, ..., ht_n, ft_n)^T$. This representation of user behaviour can then be processed by machine learning methods to authenticate users.

Related work on keystroke-based biometrics commonly uses temporal typing features (e.g. [15, 33, 42, 57]): *hold time* passes between the moment when the finger touches the screen (touch down), and the moment when the finger is lifted (touch up). Complementary, *flight time* is measured between touch up and touch down. We can also measure the time in between subsequent touch up or down events, to which we refer as *up-up* times and *down-down* times, respectively.

To complement the temporal features, we propose to consider new spatial touch-specific features (Figure 1): *exact touch locations* at touch down and up events; *offsets* between touch up and key-centres, due to typing inaccuracy; touch *"jumps"*, the distances between subsequent touches; *drag* distances/angles between touch down and up locations, due to small "natural" movements (≈ 2.1 pixels average drag in our data); touch area *sizes* and ellipses *axes*. We also evaluate touch *pressure*. Size, axes and pressure are estimated by the Android API.

User Models for Authentication

We compare models of two types: 1) anomaly detectors, which only require training data from the legitimate user; and 2) classification methods, which are trained on data from multiple users. In practice, training data can be collected in an enrolment phase or from normal use. During testing, that means whenever a password is entered correctly, these models then decide whether it was typed by the legitimate user.

Anomaly Detection: Many models for keystroke-based authentication exist [5, 34, 50]. To show that results are not model-specific, we selected methods for three common approaches: distance to training instances (here: mean distance to k=5 nearest neighbours, *kNN*); a statistical model (here: Gaussian model without covariance, *GM*); and a kernel-based method (here: Least Squares Anomaly Detection, *LSAD* [44]). We refer to the related work for detailed descriptions.

Classification: Complementary to authentication, we chose a small set of representative classifiers: k-Nearest-Neighbour classification (*kNNC*); Naïve Bayes (*NB*); and Support Vector Machines (*SVM*). We refer to related work for more details on these models [19, 43] and their applications [5, 50].

IMPROVING APPLICABILITY AND USABILITY

To improve mobile keystroke biometrics besides raw accuracy, we further target applicability and usability. Our goal is to 1) identify evaluations and assumptions that can result in too optimistic assessments of the actually applicable and usable quality of the examined systems; and to 2) propose and highlight more usable and practically relevant alternatives.

In particular, we compare conditions and quantify effects of: collecting data in a single session - or in multiple sessions; training user models on data from the owner - or also on data from others; and assuming a fixed known hand posture - or leaving the choice of postures to the user. The following sections discuss these issues in more detail and introduce our proposed improved concepts for evaluation and applications.

Evaluation Within Sessions vs Across Sessions

Typing and touch behaviour can be expected to vary over time. Therefore, training and testing on data from the same session is likely to be too optimistic, since, in practical applications, enrolment and authentication will never follow directly one after the other. However, a recent survey [50] found that 73% of examined publications on keystroke behavioural biometrics only studied data obtained in a single session.

To improve mobile keystroke biometrics for practical use, it is thus important to study the practically relevant case across sessions, and to quantify the effects of single session evaluation to inform future study design. To the best of our knowledge, this is the first reported direct comparison of evaluations within and across sessions on mobile touch keystroke data. We show that single session evaluations can lead to EERs less than half of those obtained across sessions. We thus recommend to collect data in at least two sessions.

Classification vs Anomaly Detection Methods

Two training and modelling schemes are commonly employed for keystroke-based biometrics: classification and anomaly detection (Figure 2). Classifiers are potentially more powerful, since they characterise the legitimate user in *contrast* to others, whereas anomaly detectors can only check for deviation from the legitimate user's behaviour. However, the need for data from others can make classifiers difficult or even impossible to apply in practice.

Since classifiers need training data from multiple users, their application to capture behaviour for specific passwords or PINs implies that the user's password or PIN has been typed by others and is thus known to them. In contrast to the common use of classifiers in this way [15, 32, 42, 46], we thus strongly recommend to focus on anomaly detectors instead, when adding an implicit layer for password or PIN entry.

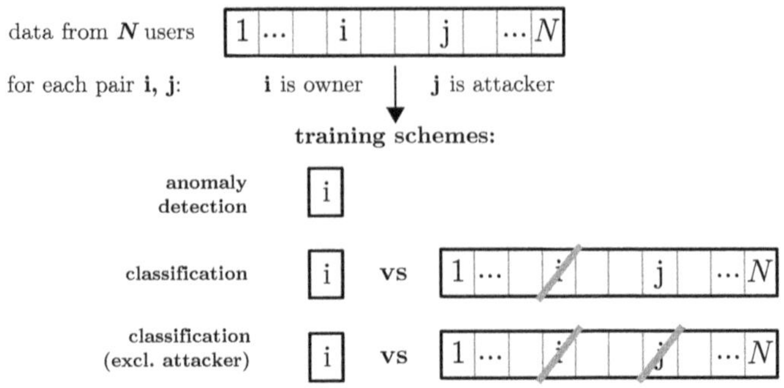

Figure 2. Three *training schemes for evaluation* of keystroke biometrics. Anomaly detectors are only trained on data from the legitimate user ("owner"). In contrast, classifiers also use pooled data from all other users. However, applications may not always have access to typing behaviour of other users in practice, especially not for specific secret passwords. Moreover, it is unrealistic to assume known data from the attacker. To address these issues, we 1) recommend anomaly detection for applications where features are extracted for secret passwords, and we 2) propose a slightly different training scheme for classifiers, which excludes the attacker from the training data for the "others"-class.

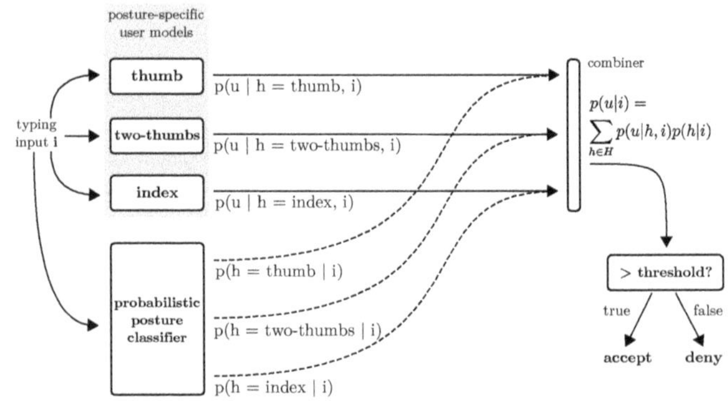

Figure 3. Probabilistic framework for usable mobile keystroke biometrics which does not restrict users to a fixed hand posture. For an entered password (input i), each posture-specific model predicts the probability $p(u|h,i)$ of the legitimate user u, assuming that the corresponding hand posture h was used. Additionally, a posture classifier estimates the probability $p(h|i)$ of each posture indeed being the one used while typing. Both sets of probabilities are then combined. The resulting probability $p(u|i)$ of the legitimate user can then be compared against a threshold.

Moreover, the dataset of others used to train classifiers often also includes data from the very participant who serves as an attacker in the current evaluation case [17]. Assuming that data from the attacker is known to the system in advance is highly unrealistic.

We address this issue with a simple alternative way of splitting the training data for evaluation of classifiers (Figure 2). In particular, we split the data into *three* parts: owner, attacker, and others (excluding the attacker). Classifiers can then be trained on data from owner and others, without assuming known data from the attacking individual.

Note that we do not argue against the use of classifiers for keystroke biometrics altogether: A system could be shipped with anonymous typing data for common words (but not passwords or PINs), collected by the developers in a user study. This data can then be used to train models against the device owner's data for the same words, observed when typing messages, e-mails, and so on (see e.g. [11, 59]). Finally, classifiers trained on "shipped data vs owner data" in this way may also be applied (even to passwords) if typing behaviour is not described per word but for example per bigram [50]. These cases are not further addressed in our study in this paper.

To the best of our knowledge, we are the first to report a direct comparison of anomaly detectors and classifiers on mobile touchscreen keystroke data. We show that classifiers lead to 28.4 - 48.1% lower EERs relative to anomaly detectors, and to 45.2 - 58.2% lower EERs, if the attacker's data is included. We thus recommend to carefully consider if classifiers are practically applicable for given use-cases. We further recommend to exclude the attackers' data from training sets when evaluating such systems.

Fixed vs Changing Hand Postures

Many studies of mobile keystroke biometrics evaluated systems with data from one hand posture or did not report the posture [14, 15, 32, 33, 57]. Some reported results for different postures [30, 59], but those were always treated separately. As a result for practical deployments, these evaluations imply systems that require fixed hand postures: the user would always have to type with the same posture for the system to work with the evaluated accuracy. This clearly restricts the user's freedom and lowers the usability of such a system.

To the best of our knowledge, this paper presents the first reported direct comparison of mobile touch keystroke biometrics for different postures. We show that entering a password in a system trained on a different posture increases EERs by up to 86.3% relative to a system assuming a fixed posture.

To address this issue and improve usability of keystroke biometrics, we propose a framework that allows users to type with different postures. We follow a probabilistic approach, utilising the fact that we do not need to *decide* for a certain posture, since we only care about correct authentication.

In summary, when a password is entered, we use a probabilistic classifier to predict a probability for each posture. We also use posture-specific user models to predict the probability of the legitimate user per posture. We then combine these probabilities, as shown in Figure 3.

In contrast to a hard decision for a specific posture, our approach always includes all training data from all postures for its predictions, and can thus better respect user-specific characteristics possibly present across postures.

Formally, we estimate the probability $p(h|i)$ of hand posture h given input i (the typing feature vector), and the probability $p(u|h,i)$ of the legitimate user u given posture h and input i. We can then integrate out the posture:

$$p(u|i) = \sum_{h \in H} p(u|h,i)p(h|i), \quad \text{for the set of postures } H$$

Any suitable models can be used to estimate $p(u|h,i)$ and $p(h|i)$. In this paper, we implement this framework as follows: For $p(u|h,i)$, we use the LSAD model, training one such model for each posture. For $p(h|i)$, we train a probabilistic SVM on the owner's data from all three postures.

Type	6 characters	8 characters
dictionary word	monkey	password
pronounceable	Igur39	Bedufo20
random	12hsVi	s5mqde3A

Table 1. Passwords used as stimuli in the user study.

STUDY AND DATA COLLECTION

We collected typing data in a user study with two sessions one week apart. The independent variables were *hand posture* and *password*. As dependent variables, we recorded keystrokes with timestamps and touch locations to derive the described features. Participants also filled in a short questionnaire.

We examined three common postures, all in portrait orientation: 1) THUMB, holding the device in the right hand, touching with the right thumb; 2) TWO-THUMBS, holding it in both hands, touching with both thumbs; and 3) INDEX finger, holding it in the left hand, touching with the right index finger.

We asked participants to repeatedly enter six passwords, shown in Table 1. These passwords were selected to cover two different lengths and three styles: dictionary words, pronounceable passwords [37], and random ones.

Participants

We recruited 28 participants with an average age of 25 years (range: 20-33). 8 were female, 20 male. All were undergraduate or graduate students. One was left-handed. All stated that they own mobile phones with touchscreens and that they (also) employ their right hand for typing. They were compensated with a €15 gift card for an online shop.

Apparatus

We used a Nexus 5 phone. Our app showed the password at the top and the entered text in a box in the centre. We used a custom touchscreen keyboard to measure all features. Style, size and functionality mirrored the default keyboard on the Nexus 5. Thus, capitalisation turned off after one keystroke and vibration issued haptic feedback on touch down.

Procedure

Each participant was invited to two sessions, with a gap of at least one week. Each session comprised three main tasks (three hand postures). The order of tasks varied between subjects according to a 3×3 latin-square design to minimise possible learning effects and fatigue. A different latin-square was used for each session to vary the order of tasks between weeks as well. Sessions lasted for about one hour. Users sat on a couch and were reminded to take breaks.

Between tasks, the app instructed users to assume the correct hand posture for the next task. The phone was held in portrait orientation. Participants were informed to neither put special emphasis on typing speed nor accuracy, but rather to touch naturally as they would do in their usual everyday typing.

For each hand posture, participants typed 6 different passwords in random order, 20 times each. Words were submitted with the return key. To advance to the next repetition, the current one had to be entered correctly without extra key presses. Otherwise, the text was cleared and the user could try again. The number of attempts was unlimited. In total, we collected 2 *sessions* × 28 *users* × 3 *postures* × 6 *passwords* × 20 *repetitions* = 20.160 correct passwords with 201.600 touches.

Feature	Authentication Equal Error Rate (%) THUMB GM	THUMB kNN	THUMB LSAD	TWO-THUMBS GM	TWO-THUMBS kNN	TWO-THUMBS LSAD	INDEX GM	INDEX kNN	INDEX LSAD
hold time	**31.98**	**32.02**	**30.87**	**26.54**	**26.47**	**25.57**	40.34	40.73	39.24
flight time	35.91	34.52	34.55	32.58	31.64	31.55	**36.92**	**36.85**	**36.60**
up-up	33.95	**32.88**	32.67	**29.91**	**28.77**	**29.45**	**37.13**	**36.71**	**36.99**
down-down	34.44	33.09	33.13	31.62	**30.63**	30.42	**37.31**	**37.04**	37.33
offset x	**33.66**	**33.06**	**31.56**	**31.65**	**31.22**	**29.82**	**39.30**	**38.71**	**37.56**
offset y	**33.28**	**32.66**	**31.31**	**30.45**	**30.07**	**29.45**	**36.21**	**35.79**	**34.07**
down x	34.12	33.55	32.23	32.40	31.42	**30.38**	39.48	39.19	37.63
down y	34.02	33.41	32.27	31.76	31.25	31.08	**36.63**	**36.29**	**35.04**
up x	**33.64**	**33.12**	**31.59**	**31.65**	**31.22**	**29.82**	**39.30**	**38.71**	**37.56**
up y	**33.62**	**33.09**	**31.99**	**31.37**	**30.90**	**31.03**	**36.40**	**36.19**	**34.82**
jump x	35.58	34.80	33.84	32.93	32.29	31.08	38.84	38.43	37.13
jump y	36.92	36.37	34.87	35.49	34.65	35.09	40.02	38.89	38.75
jump angle	37.81	37.76	36.81	33.15	32.52	31.93	39.87	39.41	38.89
jump distance	34.76	34.23	32.17	32.39	32.11	31.65	37.70	37.47	**35.64**
drag x	44.69	45.02	43.45	45.51	45.53	44.22	48.32	48.92	46.43
drag y	45.08	45.56	44.33	45.60	46.00	44.93	46.53	47.24	46.03
drag angle	45.02	45.05	45.05	44.27	44.36	44.32	45.55	45.47	45.41
drag distance	44.09	44.76	44.13	44.14	44.84	42.06	46.21	46.65	44.89
down size	**32.63**	**32.49**	**29.82**	**31.39**	**31.24**	**29.38**	**37.81**	37.51	37.21
up size	34.98	34.76	32.50	33.34	33.23	31.61	40.41	39.94	37.95
down major*	**32.63**	**32.76**	**30.62**	**31.39**	31.67	30.52	**37.81**	**36.17**	**36.03**
up major*	34.98	34.99	32.59	33.34	33.67	32.18	40.41	39.81	38.47
down pressure	**31.38**	**31.03**	**30.32**	**28.59**	**28.91**	**27.84**	**33.14**	**33.32**	**32.61**
up pressure	40.19	39.90	36.37	39.07	39.32	36.05	42.55	42.86	40.37

* The study phone estimated a spherical touch area and therefore returned identical values for major and minor axes.

Table 2. Single feature evaluation. The table shows EERs when using each feature on its own. Highlighted are the top third features (and their x/y counterparts) per model/posture combination. Overall, the best features are hold time, touch down pressure and size, and touch offsets/locations. These results show the potential of touch features.

RESULTS

Since users typed passwords they likely never used before, we considered the first three repetitions of each password as training and removed them from the evaluation. We also removed interrupted entries - those in which at least one flight time exceeded five standard deviations of all repetitions for this user and password (1.6% of each user's data per session).

In general, our evaluation setup assumes each user to be the device "owner" once. A model is trained for this user, either on data from the first session (for evaluation across sessions), or with leave-one-out cross-validation (for within session evaluation). The model is then fed the owner's testing data (i.e. data from second session, or test case from cross-validation) to record predicted probabilities for this legitimate user. Complementary, the model is fed data from all other users to record predicted probabilities for "attackers". After all users have been processed in this way, a threshold is applied to all recorded probabilities to compute global true/false acceptance rates and true/false rejection rates.

We report equal error rates (EER), obtained by varying the threshold applied to the predictions until false acceptance rate and false rejection rate are equal. We chose the EER statistic, since it provides a one-number-summary and is almost always reported in related work. We visualise results with Receiver-Operating-Characteristic (ROC) curves, which plot false positive rates against true positive rates for varying thresholds. Finally, we report comparisons of EERs in *relative* difference (e.g. 4% to 6% EER yields a 50% increase).

Feature Evaluation

To evaluate which touch and typing features are most useful to describe individual behaviour, we first examine the power of single features, before optimising feature sets.

Single Features

To assess each feature's discriminative power alone, we trained different user models on each feature on its own, as shown in Table 2. Across all three tested user models, we observed lowest EERs for hold time, touch down pressure and size, and touch offsets/locations. These results indicate that spatial touch features should be considered for mobile keystroke biometrics. Touch offsets, pressure and size almost always outperformed the flight time commonly used in related work. Typing with both thumbs was more individual than with one, as indicated by lower EERs, while the index finger was the least individual posture. Comparing models, LSAD performed best for almost all feature/posture cases.

Feature Sets

We also evaluated different sets of features to assess their combined potential for user authentication (Table 3). These sets were found with a wrapper approach [35]. Wrappers optimise feature sets by greedily adding the feature which leads to the highest improvement. We applied the wrapper to the best model from single feature evaluation (LSAD), hence the presented results for the other two models can be considered pessimistic. Table 3 shows that our proposed spatial touch features are superior to the temporal features, with 14.3 - 23.5% lower EERs. The best found sets show that offsets were the most useful features based on touch locations.

Combining spatial and temporal features outperformed feature sets consisting of only one of these dimensions: The best combined feature sets achieved 8.5 - 26.3% lower EERs than the best spatial feature sets, and 26.4 - 36.8% lower EERs than the best temporal sets. Thus, spatial and temporal features should be combined for mobile keystroke biometrics.

Although down pressure achieved the lowest EERs for single features (Table 2), it never appeared in the best sets selected from all features. An additional analysis showed that offsets resulted in 5.9 - 12.5% lower EERs than exchanging them for down pressure in the best found sets. This indicates that sensing pressure can be suitably replaced by measuring touch-to-key offsets in this context. Henceforth, we employ the best found feature set for each posture.

Comparison to Related Work

In general, a direct comparison of EERs with related work is difficult due to different devices, tasks and evaluations. Nonetheless, we can compare feature sets used in related work with the features proposed in this paper when evaluated on our data and with our models, see Figure 4. Note that our feature sets were optimised on our data and models. Nevertheless, the comparison shows the benefits of 1) considering touch-specific features and 2) optimising feature sets including touch-specific features - in contrast to related work, where these features were not considered [15, 33, 42, 55, 57] or not tested for optimal combinations [20].

Best Feature Set	Authentication EER (%) GM	kNN	LSAD
Spatial			
THUMB: offset x/y, up/down size, jump x	27.38	25.38	20.06
TWO-THUMBS: offset x/y, up/down size	23.35	21.73	18.65
INDEX: offset x/y, up/down size, jump distance	32.27	31.19	26.76
Temporal			
THUMB: hold time, up-up time	28.59	27.75	26.22
TWO-THUMBS: hold time, down-down time	24.40	23.64	21.75
INDEX: hold time, up-up time, flight time	34.57	33.72	33.25
Spatio-Temporal & Pressure			
THUMB: hold time, offset x/y, up/down size	24.32	22.63	17.00
TWO-THUMBS: hold time, offset x/y, up/down size	19.01	17.60	13.74
INDEX: hold time, offset x/y, up/down size, up-up time, jump x, jump distance	30.84	29.48	24.48

Table 3. Feature set evaluation across sessions. The table shows best found feature sets when considering only spatial, only temporal, or all features. These results show that mobile keystroke biometrics benefit from the proposed spatial touch features, including touch-to-key offsets.

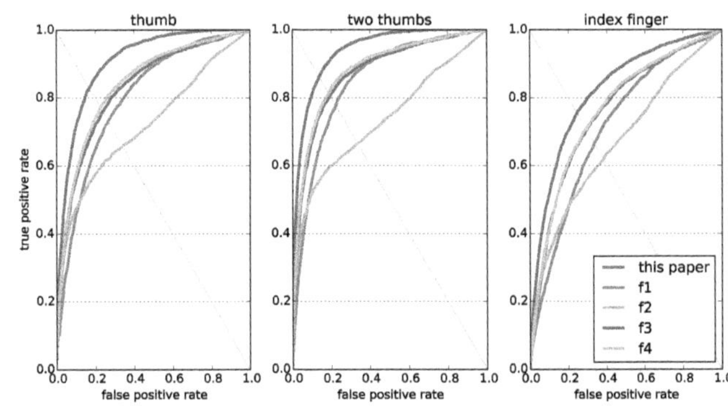

Figure 4. Comparison with feature sets from related work. The figure shows ROC curves obtained when using the LSAD model with the proposed feature sets, and when using it with feature sets occurring in related research (f1 [10, 15, 42], f2 [20], f3 [46], f4 [55, 59]). Crossings with the falling grey lines mark EERs. The results show that touch features should be included when optimising feature sets.

Within Sessions vs Across Sessions

So far, we have conducted evaluations across sessions, since user behaviour can be expected to vary over time. Table 4 now compares analyses within and across sessions: Averaged per posture, anomaly detectors achieved 40.9 - 53.3% lower EERs within sessions than across both sessions. Classifiers achieved 61.6 - 72.8% lower EERs (incl. attacker) and 51.2 - 64.0% lower EERs (excl. attacker) within sessions than across. These results show that evaluation with data collected in a single session is highly optimistic and should thus be avoided to assess the system's expected accuracy in practice.

Classification vs Anomaly Detection Methods

Table 4 also compares the three described training schemes. Averaged over all models per posture for the within session case, classifiers achieved 28.4 - 48.1% lower EERs (excl. attacker) and 45.2 - 58.2% lower EERs (incl. attacker) than anomaly detectors. Complementary, across sessions, classifiers led to 11.7 - 31.1% lower EERs (excl. attacker) and 16.8 - 38.1% lower EERs (incl. attacker). We conclude that classification evaluations yield highly optimistic results if classifiers are not applicable to the intended use-case.

Training Scheme	Equal Error Rate (%)					
	THUMB		TWO-THUMBS		INDEX	
	within	across	within	across	within	across
a) with others (incl. attacker)						
NB	9.71	19.35	10.69	22.06	14.72	37.88
kNNC	3.05	11.15	1.19	8.44	4.03	18.30
SVM	3.43	9.09	1.52	6.71	2.98	14.39
b) with others (excl. attacker)						
NB	9.96	19.58	10.71	22.14	14.78	37.88
kNNC	6.27	13.61	3.47	11.29	7.77	20.09
SVM	5.38	10.87	3.31	8.57	4.85	16.09
c) owner data only						
GM	17.04	24.32	11.71	19.01	19.77	30.84
kNN	14.02	22.63	8.89	17.60	16.55	29.48
LSAD	7.69	17.00	3.84	13.74	10.74	24.48

Table 4. EERs within and across sessions for different training schemes and models. These results reveal two insights: First, due to variance in behaviour over time, error rates obtained within a single session do not appropriately reflect the practically realistic case across sessions. Second, assuming the availability of data from others for training classifiers (cases a and b) leads to highly optimistic results compared to using only data from the legitimate user (c), especially if the specific participant used as an attacker is also included during training (compare a to b).

Comparing both classification variants, including data from the specific attacker led to 20.7 - 25.1% lower EERs (within sessions) and to 4.7 - 11.4% lower EERs (across sessions), averaged over the three tested models per posture. Hence, if classifiers are applicable in a studied use-case, evaluations should still exclude attacker data from the training sets, since it reduces errors but is most likely not available in practice.

Fixed vs Changing Hand Postures

So far, we have separated the data by hand posture, effectively assuming fixed and known postures. However, changing postures have to be considered for usable applications.

To evaluate how password typing behaviour varies between postures, we trained models on data from one posture and tested them with data from a different one. Table 5 shows the resulting EERs for all posture combinations. Averaged over all combinations and models, EERs increased by 86.3%, when models were tested with a different posture. Hence, assuming a fixed posture yields highly optimistic evaluations: Demanding a specific posture (ideally two-thumbs) improves security, but is an undesirable restriction regarding usability.

We have described a probabilistic method to enable more usable keystroke-based authentication with changing hand postures. To evaluate it, we trained models on the data from all three postures from the first session (given the ground-truth postures), and tested them with data from all three postures from the second session (without providing ground-truth postures). This resembles an application asking for all postures during enrolment, but then leaving users free to type with any of the enrolled postures without telling the system which one they are currently using.

Our proposed probabilistic framework, implemented as described in this paper, achieved 21.02% EER. Note that here we test with data from all postures. Therefore, this value also fits the expectation that a system's extension, which suitably handles changing postures, should lead to EERs between those obtained for fixed single postures (LSAD: two-thumbs 13.74% to index 24.48%). In the following, we compare our system to two simple alternatives.

	Authentication Equal Error Rate (%) Across Hand Postures		
	THUMB	TWO-THUMBS	INDEX
GM			
THUMB	24.32	38.67	40.41
TWO-THUMBS	35.66	19.01	40.76
INDEX	43.29	44.13	30.84
kNN			
THUMB	22.63	38.29	39.82
TWO-THUMBS	34.85	17.60	40.33
INDEX	42.88	43.88	29.48
LSAD			
THUMB	17.00	35.48	37.24
TWO-THUMBS	33.05	13.74	39.12
INDEX	42.45	59.07	24.48

Table 5. Equal error rates across sessions when using data of different hand postures for training (rows) and testing (columns). These results show that mobile keystroke-based biometrics are highly posture-specific.

Across postures, our framework yields a reduction in EERs by 36.4 - 64.4% compared to the values in Table 5, which correspond to a system naïvely assuming that training data from any posture is suitable for predictions for all postures.

We also compared our method to models trained on data from all postures pooled together: The best EER obtained was 27.38%, using the kNN model. In comparison, our proposed method thus reduced EER by 23.2%.

In conclusion, our probabilistic framework handles changing hand postures better than approaches, which either 1) simply ignore differences between postures (Table 5), or 2) just train a single model. In contrast, our framework estimates the probability of the legitimate user *for each posture*, in addition to the probability of each posture being indeed the one used.

SUMMARY AND IMPLICATIONS

In this section, we summarise challenges and opportunities and present implications derived from our analyses.

Challenges: We quantified the following challenges for practical and usable applications of mobile keystroke dynamics:

- *Mobile typing biometrics vary over time:* Training and testing models on data collected in a single session results in EERs less than half of the values observed across sessions.
- *Data from multiple users improves authentication accuracy, but is not applicable to password-hardening:* Evaluation with classifiers led to 11.7 - 31.1% lower EERs than employing anomaly detectors. However, classifiers using feature-vectors from different users typing a specific password impractically imply that the word is known to others.
- *Mobile typing biometrics are highly hand posture-specific:* Training and testing models on different postures increased EERs by 86.3% relative to testing with the same posture.

These challenges imply three important considerations for applicable and usable mobile keystroke dynamics: First, user studies should always include multiple sessions for each participant. Second, classifiers should only be used in evaluations if they are also applicable to the targeted threat model. This is not the case if passwords have to be revealed to others. Finally, applications of mobile keystroke biometrics have to infer postures dynamically to retain usability.

Opportunities: To improve keystroke biometrics for usable applications, we revealed and quantified these opportunities:

- *Spatial touch features outperform the traditional temporal features:* The best spatial feature sets reduced EERs by 14.3 - 23.5% relative to the best temporal sets.
- *Spatial touch features outperform pressure features:* Pressure never appeared in optimised feature sets, while offsets were always selected. They resulted in 5.9 - 12.5% lower EERs than exchanging them for pressure in the best sets.
- *Spatial and temporal features complement each other:* The best spatio-temporal feature sets reduced EERs by 8.5 - 26.3% relative to the best spatial sets, and by 26.4 - 36.8% relative to the best temporal sets.
- *Models for different hand postures can be combined to allow for changing postures:* Combining models in a probabilistic framework reduced EERs by 23.2% compared to training a single model on data from all postures, and by 36.4 - 64.4% compared to ignoring posture differences.

In consequence, we recommend to measure touch-to-key offsets to improve accuracy of mobile keystroke biometrics. Furthermore, these features should be combined with the temporal typing features known from related work. Finally, hand postures present a trade-off between security and usability: A fixed posture results in lower EERs, but restricts the user. This can be addressed by combining posture-specific models.

We expect lessons learned in this work to be useful on a broader scale beyond keystroke biometrics: Variability over time and between postures can be expected for other mobile biometrics (e.g. general touch behaviour). Moreover, potential problems regarding the use of classifiers should be considered for all behavioural biometrics related to secret tokens, not just passwords (e.g. PINs, shapes, gestures).

DISCUSSION

On our collected study data, we reduced EERs by up to 36.8% with the proposed feature sets, including touch-specific features. While a direct comparison of absolute EERs with related work is difficult due to different devices, tasks and evaluations, we showed improvements compared to feature sets employed in related work when tested with our models and data. To further improve absolute accuracy, practical systems could combine touch features with others (e.g. motion [59]), or observe mobile device usage more holistically, with typing biometrics as one part of it (multimodal biometrics [17]).

For privacy reasons, the data processing system should run on the device, not in a cloud. We analysed the study data on a PC, but also measured crucial operations on the device: Training an LSAD model is determined by computing and inverting a kernel matrix [44]. For our training set sizes and number of features, the required matrix operations took 50 ms on the Nexus 5. Authentications after password entry are simple vector multiplications, unnoticeable to users.

We highlighted that classifiers are not applicable to keystroke biometrics for password entry, if features are extracted for the specific word used: Since classifiers are trained on data from multiple users, their use implies that the password was entered by others and is thus not secret any more.

However, we do not argue against the use of classifiers in general: In this paper, we only discussed a *static* task, meaning that the system expects a fixed text (i.e. password) to be entered. For *dynamic* tasks (i.e. free text entry), typing behaviour can be described for common words [11] or for bigrams [9, 50]. In these cases, it is reasonable to assume recorded data from others to train classifiers. While we did not explicitly cover such a dynamic task in this paper, our results with classifiers show that they also benefit from the proposed touch-specific typing features.

Our analysis revealed that typing behaviour is highly posture-specific. This presents a challenge to usable applications of mobile keystroke biometrics. We proposed a probabilistic framework to allow users to type with changing postures. It outperformed models trained across all postures as well as "posture-agnostic" approaches.

LIMITATIONS

We only collected right-handed touches, limiting the observed set of postures. Our evaluations across postures can assess accuracy for changing postures between entries, or between enrolment and entry. However, they can neither assess posture changes mid-typing nor continuous changes, which might occur, for example, due to hand drift [13].

A set of three anomaly detectors and three classifiers was evaluated with six different passwords. Many more methods exist [50], and could be tested with a broader set of passwords to improve generalisability. Nevertheless, our results suggest that the proposed typing features can be suitably used by different models.

We conducted a lab study with participants sitting down in two sessions. An "in the wild" study may observe greater variability in long-term behaviour with varying contexts and phone models. Regarding touch features, related work showed that offset patterns are to some extent robust across changing conditions, and that they are highly individual on other phone models as well [12, 54].

CONCLUSION AND FUTURE WORK

In this paper, we have studied mobile-specific and touch-specific challenges and opportunities for keystroke biometrics. We have revealed, analysed and discussed different improvements for a password entry use-case and threat model. These analyses and improvements are important to advance keystroke biometrics on mobile touchscreen devices.

Overall, our results 1) improve implicit authentication accuracy through new features, 2) support realistic evaluations leading to applicable systems, and 3) improve usability with a framework to handle changing hand postures.

In summary, we first complemented existing temporal typing features with touch-specific spatial features. Second, we quantified the effect of three common assumptions, namely within-session evaluation, training on attacker data, and assuming fixed hand postures. We revealed that these practices can result in overly optimistic assessments with respect to usable applications in practice. In consequence, we addressed these issues with evaluation recommendations and a probabilistic method to account for changing hand postures.

We plan to use touch-specific features in a dynamic typing task, such as free text messaging. While related work [9, 50] extracted features per bigram in such cases (e.g. flight time from *t* to *h*), in other words features for discrete key-combinations, we will instead train regression models to map precise touch locations to feature values [12, 54].

PROJECT RESOURCES

Please contact the first author to gain access to the dataset.

ACKNOWLEDGEMENTS

This work was partially supported by funding from a Google Research Award.

REFERENCES

1. Angulo, J., and Wästlund, E. Exploring Touch-Screen Biometrics for User Identification on Smart Phones. *Privacy and Identity Management for Life 375* (2012), 130–143.

2. Aviv, A., Gibson, K., Mossop, E., Blaze, M., and Smith, J. Smudge Attacks on Smartphone Touch Screens. In *WOOT* (2010), 1–7.

3. Azenkot, S., and Zhai, S. Touch Behavior with Different Postures on Soft Smartphone Keyboards. In *MobileHCI 2012* (2012), 251–260.

4. Baldwin, T., and Chai, J. Towards Online Adaptation and Personalization of Key-Target Resizing for Mobile Devices. In *IUI 2012* (2012), 11–20.

5. Banerjee, S., and Woodard, D. Biometric Authentication and Identification using Keystroke Dynamics: A Survey. *Journal of Pattern Recognition Research 7* (2012), 116–139.

6. Baudisch, P., and Chu, G. Back-of-Device Interaction Allows Creating Very Small Touch Devices. In *CHI 2009* (2009), 1923–1932.

7. Beton, M., Marie, V., and Rosenberger, C. Biometric Secret Path for Mobile User Authentication: A Preliminary Study. In *WCCIT 2013*, Ieee (June 2013), 1–6.

8. Böhmer, M., Hecht, B., Schöning, J., Krüger, A., and Bauer, G. Falling Asleep with Angry Birds, Facebook and Kindle - A Large Scale Study on Mobile Application Usage. *MobileHCI 2011* (2011), 47–56.

9. Bours, P., and Barghouthi, H. Continuous Authentication Using Biometric Keystroke Dynamics. In *NISK* (2009), 1–12.

10. Buchoux, A., and Clarke, N. L. Deployment of Keystroke Analysis on a Smartphone. In *Australian Information Security Management Conference* (2008).

11. Burgbacher, U., and Hinrichs, K. An Implicit Author Verification System for Text Messages Based on Gesture Typing Biometrics. In *CHI 2014* (2014), 2951–2954.

12. Buschek, D., Rogers, S., and Murray-Smith, R. User-Specific Touch Models in a Cross-Device Context. In *MobileHCI 2013* (2013), 382–391.

13. Buschek, D., Schoenleben, O., and Oulasvirta, A. Improving Accuracy in Back-of-Device Multitouch Typing: A Clustering-based Approach to Keyboard Updating. In *IUI 2014* (2014), 57–66.

14. Campisi, P., Maiorana, E., Lo Bosco, M., and Neri, A. User authentication using keystroke dynamics for cellular phones. *IET Signal Processing 3*, 4 (2009), 333–341.

15. Clarke, N. L., and Furnell, S. M. Authenticating mobile phone users using keystroke analysis. *International Journal of Information Security 6*, 1 (Aug. 2006), 1–14.

16. Crawford, H. Keystroke Dynamics: Characteristics and Opportunities. In *8th International Conference on Privacy, Security and Trust* (2010), 205–212.

17. Crawford, H. A. *A Framework for Continuous, Transparent Authentication on Mobile Devices*. PhD thesis, University of Glasgow, 2012.

18. De Luca, A., Hang, A., Brudy, F., Lindner, C., and Hussmann, H. Touch me once and I know its you! Implicit Authentication based on Touch Screen Patterns. In *CHI 2012* (2012), 987–996.

19. Devroye, L., Györfi, L., and Lugosi, G. *A Probabilistic Theory of Pattern Recognition*. Springer, 1996.

20. Draffin, B., Zhu, J., and Zhang, J. KeySens: Passive User Authentication through Micro-behavior Modeling of Soft Keyboard Interaction. *Mobile Computing, Applications, and Services 130* (2014), 184–201.

21. Edelmann, J., Mock, P., Schilling, A., Gerjets, P., Rosenstiel, W., and Strasser, W. Towards the Keyboard of Oz: Learning Individual Soft-Keyboard Models from Raw Optical Sensor Data. In *ITS 2012* (2012), 163–172.

22. Forlines, C., Wigdor, D., Shen, C., and Balakrishnan, R. Direct-Touch vs. Mouse Input for Tabletop Displays. In *CHI 2007* (2007), 647–656.

23. Frank, M., Biedert, R., Ma, E., Martinovic, I., and Song, D. Touchalytics: On the Applicability of Touchscreen Input as a Behavioral Biometric for Continuous Authentication. *Information Forensics and Security 8*, 1 (2013), 126–148.

24. Goodman, J. T., Venolia, G., Steury, K., and Parker, C. Language Modeling for Soft Keyboards. In *IUI 2002* (Jan. 2002), 194–195.

25. Harbach, M., von Zezschwitz, E., Fichtner, A., De Luca, A., and Smith, M. It's a Hard Lock Life: A Field Study of Smartphone (Un) Locking Behavior and Risk Perception. In *SOUPS 2014* (2014), 213–230.

26. Henze, N., Rukzio, E., and Boll, S. 100,000,000 Taps: Analysis and Improvement of Touch Performance in the Large. In *MobileHCI 2011* (2011), 133–142.

27. Holz, C., and Baudisch, P. The Generalized Perceived Input Point Model and How to Double Touch Accuracy by Extracting Fingerprints. In *CHI 2010* (2010), 581–590.

28. Holz, C., and Baudisch, P. Understanding Touch. In *CHI 2011* (2011), 2501–2510.
29. Holz, C., and Baudisch, P. Fiberio: A Touchscreen that Senses Fingerprints. In *UIST 2013* (2013), 41–50.
30. Hwang, S.-s., Cho, S., and Park, S. Keystroke dynamics-based authentication for mobile devices. *Computers & Security 28*, 1-2 (Feb. 2009), 85–93.
31. Jakobsson, M., Shi, E., Golle, P., and Chow, R. Implicit Authentication for Mobile Devices. In *HotSec 2009* (2009).
32. Jeanjaitrong, N., and Bhattarakosol, P. Feasibility Study on Authentication Based Keystroke Dynamic over Touch-Screen Devices. In *ISCIT 2013*, Ieee (Sept. 2013), 238–242.
33. Karatzouni, S., and Clarke, N. Keystroke Analysis for Thumb-based Keyboards on Mobile Devices. In *IFIP International Federation for Information Processing*, vol. 232 (2007), 253–263.
34. Killourhy, K. S., and Maxion, R. A. Comparing Anomaly-Detection Algorithms for Keystroke Dynamics. In *Dependable Systems & Networks* (June 2009), 125–134.
35. Kohavi, Ron and John, G. H. Wrappers for feature subset selection. *Artificial Intelligence 97*, 1 (1997), 273–324.
36. Kristensson, P. O. *Discrete and Continuous Shape Writing for Text Entry and Control*. PhD thesis, Linköping University, Sweden, 2007.
37. Lau, S.-h., Siena, S., Pandey, A., Sosothikul, S., Cranor, L., Ur, B., and Shay, R. Exploring the Usability of Pronounceable Passwords. In *SOUPS Poster* (2014).
38. Maiorana, E., Campisi, P., González-Carballo, N., and Neri, A. Keystroke Dynamics Authentication for Mobile Phones. In *SAC 2011* (2011), 21–26.
39. Mock, P., Edelmann, J., Schilling, A., and Rosenstiel, W. User Identification Using Raw Sensor Data From Typing on Interactive Displays. In *IUI 2014* (2014), 67–72.
40. Monrose, F., Reiter, M., and Wetzel, S. Password Hardening Based on Keystroke Dynamics. In *Int'l. Journal of Information Security* (2002), 69–83.
41. Monrose, F., and Rubin, A. Authentication via Keystroke Dynamics. In *Computer and Communications Security* (1997), 48–56.
42. Nauman, M., Ali, T., and Rauf, A. Using trusted computing for privacy preserving keystroke-based authentication in smartphones. *Telecommunication Systems 52* (2013), 2149–2161.
43. Platt, J. C. Probabilistic Outputs for Support Vector Machines and Comparisons to Regularized Likelihood Methods. *Advances in Large Margin Classifiers 10*, 3 (1999), 61–74.
44. Quinn, J., and Sugiyama, M. A least-squares approach to anomaly detection in static and sequential data. *Pattern Recognition Letters* (2014).
45. Sae-Bae, N., Ahmed, K., Isbister, K., and Memon, N. Biometric-Rich Gestures: A Novel Approach to Authentication on Multi-touch Devices. In *CHI 2012* (2012), 977–986.
46. Saevanee, H., and Bhattarakosol, P. Authenticating user using keystroke dynamics and finger pressure. In *6th IEEE Consumer Communications and Networking Conference* (2009).
47. Saevanee, H., Clarke, N., Furnell, S., and Biscione, V. Text-Based Active Authentication for Mobile Devices. *ICT Systems Security and Privacy Protection 428* (2014), 99–112.
48. Schaub, F., Deyhle, R., and Weber, M. Password Entry Usability and Shoulder Surfing Susceptibility on Different Smartphone Platforms. In *MUM 2012* (2012), 13:1–13:10.
49. Shi, E., Niu, Y., Jakobsson, M., and Chow, R. Implicit Authentication through Learning User Behavior. *Information Security* (2011), 99–113.
50. Teh, P. S., Teoh, A. B. J., and Yue, S. A Survey of Keystroke Dynamics Biometrics. *The Scientific World Journal 2013* (2013).
51. von Zezschwitz, E., Koslow, A., De Luca, A., and Hussmann, H. Making Graphic-Based Authentication Secure against Smudge Attacks. In *IUI 2013* (2013), 277–286.
52. Wang, F., and Ren, X. Empirical Evaluation for Finger Input Properties In Multi-touch Interaction. In *CHI 2009* (2009), 1063–1072.
53. Weir, D., Buschek, D., and Rogers, S. Sparse Selection of Training Data for Touch Correction Systems. In *MobileHCI 2013* (2013), 404–407.
54. Weir, D., Rogers, S., Murray-Smith, R., and Löchtefeld, M. A User-Specific Machine Learning Approach for Improving Touch Accuracy on Mobile Devices. In *UIST 2012* (2012), 465–476.
55. Xu, H., Zhou, Y., and Lyu, M. Towards Continuous and Passive Authentication via Touch Biometrics: An Experimental Study on Smartphones. *SOUPS 2014* (2014), 187–198.
56. Yin, Y., Ouyang, T. Y., Partridge, K., and Zhai, S. Making Touchscreen Keyboards Adaptive to Keys, Hand Postures, and Individuals - A Hierarchical Spatial Backoff Model Approach. In *CHI* (2013), 2775–2784.
57. Zahid, S., Shahzad, M., Khayam, S. A., and Farooq, M. Keystroke-Based User Identification on Smart Phones. In *LNCS*, vol. 5758 (2009), 224–243.
58. Zhao, X., Feng, T., and Shi, W. Continuous Mobile Authentication Using A Novel Graphic Touch Gesture Feature. In *BTAS 2013* (2013), 1–6.
59. Zheng, N., Bai, K., Huang, H., and Wang, H. You Are How You Touch: User Verification on Smartphones via Tapping Behaviors. In *Tech. Rep. WM-CS-2012-06* (2012).

SwiPIN - Fast and Secure PIN-Entry on Smartphones

Emanuel von Zezschwitz[1], Alexander De Luca[1,2], Bruno Brunkow[1], Heinrich Hussmann[1]
[1]Media Informatics Group, University of Munich (LMU), Munich, Germany
[2]DFKI GmbH, Saarbrücken, Germany
{emanuel.von.zezschwitz, alexander.de.luca, hussmann}@ifi.lmu.de, brunkow@cip.ifi.lmu.de

ABSTRACT
In this paper, we present SwiPIN, a novel authentication system that allows input of traditional PINs using simple touch gestures like *up* or *down* and makes it secure against human observers. We present two user studies which evaluated different designs of SwiPIN and compared it against traditional PIN. The results show that SwiPIN performs adequately fast (3.7 s) to serve as an alternative input method for risky situations. Furthermore, SwiPIN is easy to use, significantly more secure against shoulder surfing attacks and switching between PIN and SwiPIN feels natural.

Author Keywords
Authentication; Mobile Devices; Shoulder Surfing

ACM Classification Keywords
H.5.m. Information Interfaces and Presentation (e.g. HCI): Miscellaneous

INTRODUCTION
As mobile devices can store and access various potentially sensitive data, user authentication on such devices has become indispensable. Despite the advance of alternative biometric mechanisms like fingerprint scanners, knowledge-based systems still represent the primary way of authentication for most users and serve as a fallback solution whenever alternative approaches fail.

PIN is commonly recognized to be a fast and easy way for daily authentication. However, the observability of the PIN-entry can open serious security holes. While some systems like ATMs can partially counter this problem by providing privacy shields and regulated environments, mobile interaction often takes place in uncontrolled (semi-)public situations which increases the threat of shoulder surfing.

A shoulder surfing attack refers to the action of intentionally getting someone's information by direct observation. While countermeasures have been researched for several years, none of these concepts has been widely deployed. Harbach et al. [3] found that observation attacks exist, but are rarely perceived critical. Therefore, we assume that most users are

CHI'15, April 18 - 23 2015, Seoul, Republic of Korea.

http://dx.doi.org/10.1145/2702123.2702212

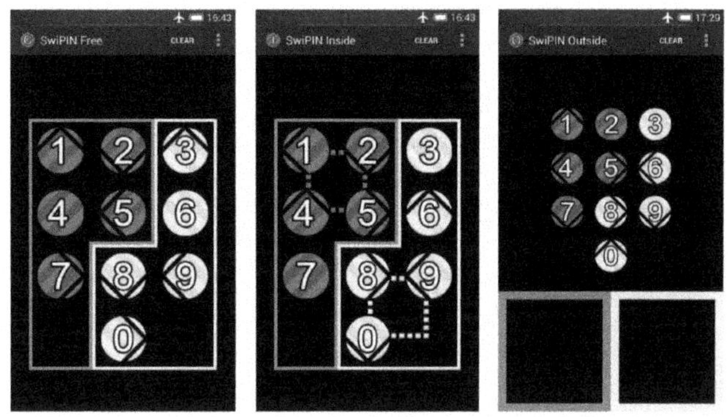

Figure 1. Three different versions of SwiPIN: *free* (left), *inside* (center) and *outside* (right). The currently assigned gesture is indicated by black arrows, no arrow meaning *tap*. To enter a "1" in SwiPIN (*free*), an *up*-gesture within the red-bordered area of the screen would be performed.

not willing to invest much effort for better protection. As it has already been suggested [5], we argue that novel approaches need to be usability-optimized, easy-to-deploy and should support the entry of traditional passwords (e.g. PIN) to have the chance of a wide user acceptance.

Bianchi et al. [1] proposed several mobile PIN-entry concepts which utilize audio or haptic cues. Roth et al. [6] developed two concepts which display digits in distinct sets. Users repeatedly indicate the respective target set, the intersection of these sets is used to determine the PIN. Similar approaches were proposed by De Luca et al. [2] and Lee [5], exploiting the limitations of the human short-term memory. Most concepts are adequately secure against human-based attacks, but authentication times are usually high (> 8 s). Kwon and Na [4] propose TinyLock which utilizes simple gestures to protect the Android pattern (un)lock from shoulder surfing and smudge attacks. TinyLock shows that simple changes in the user interface can bring significantly more security and at the same time obtain usability.

We present SwiPIN, a concept which allows PIN-entry based on simple touch gestures. Similar to TinyLock [4], it requires only little change in the user interface. SwiPIN was designed to be a fast, easy and secure input method which empowers the user to protect from shoulder surfing whenever such risk is perceived [3]. The results of two user studies show that SwiPIN is fast (M=3.7 s; SD=0.9) and secure against human-based observations. Switching between traditional PIN and SwiPIN felt natural and both approaches showed equally low error rates.

THREAT MODEL

According to our threat model, a smartphone user enters her PIN in a (semi-)public setting. An observer (attacker) standing in the user's vicinity has perfect sight on the display (no reflections, no occlusions). In the first scenario, the input is based on a traditional PIN pad. In a second scenario, the user's device is equipped with SwiPIN. As the user recognizes the potential observer, she switches to the secure mode and enters the PIN using touch gestures. After observing the PIN-entry, the attacker gets in possession of the device and tries to replicate the observed input. The observation attack takes place without additional equipment (e.g. camcorder).

SWIPIN CONCEPT

The SwiPIN concept is the result of a brainstorming with four usable security experts. We presumed that a feasible mechanism would require to support (a) fast and (b) easy input of (c) standard PINs on (d) off-the-shelf smarphones in a way that assures (e) adequate shoulder surfing protection.

SwiPIN is based on a random assignment of simple touch gestures to specific digits. To enter a digit, instead of tapping a specific button, the user performs such a gesture, usually at a different location than the respective button. As the required gesture is displayed as a black arrow on the respective digits (see Figure 1), the user does not need to memorize any additional information. The gesture mapping changes after each input. As soon as the user performs a gesture, the assignment disappears and the gestures are newly mapped. Therefore, the entry of a digit comprises two distinct steps: (a) recognizing the assigned gesture, (b) performing the recognized gesture. Thus, an attacker has to memorize the current gesture mapping to recognize an entered digit. This mapping is too complex to fit in human short-term memory, which makes the task of the observer very hard.

First designs were implemented using low-fidelity paper prototypes and high-fidelity software versions. We performed a preliminary user study and a focus group with the goal to find the best design and the right gesture set. We tested small sets with five distinct gestures and full sets with ten gestures (e.g. multi touch). Overall, the highest potential was found for the systems shown in Figure 1. The three designs use a redundant small set of five gestures (*up*, *down*, *left*, *right*, *tap*) and are based on the traditional PIN pad layout. To map ten digits to five gestures, the PIN pad was divided into two distinct areas, indicated by the colors *red* and *yellow*.

While supporting identical gesture sets, the three illustrated versions of SwiPIN provide different areas to start gesture input (gestures can end anywhere). SwiPin (*free*) (Figure 1,left) allows to start gestures anywhere in the respective half of the PIN pad. SwiPIN (*inside*) forces the user to begin the input within a certain region of the screen, which is indicated by a dotted border. Finally, SwiPIN (*outside*) requires the user to start the gesture at the bottom of the screen. Gestures were illustrated using black arrows, where no arrow meant the tap gesture. Figure 2 illustrates a participant of the user study entering a “2” on SwiPIN (*outside*). For this, a simple “down” gesture is performed. As soon as the gesture is completed, the gesture assignment in the red section changes.

USABILITY AND SECURITY STUDY

Before we compared SwiPIN against traditional PIN-entry, we analyzed the three design alternatives according to their performance, security and user perception.

The study was based on a repeated-measure within participants design. The independent variable was *system* with three levels (*free*, *inside*, *outside*). Each system was tested with three different randomly generated PINs. The sequence of *system* was counterbalanced; PINs comprised each digit only once. We measured authentication time (divided in preparation and input time), error-rate and shoulder surfing success. In addition, we collected qualitative data via questionnaires.

Procedure and Participants

The user study was held in an isolated room at our premises. We started each session by explaining the goal of the study and the SwiPIN concept. For each system, we followed the same procedure: (a) explain the characteristics of the specific design, (b) free training, (c) input of three different PINs and (d) user feedback. During training, the system allowed unlimited input of digits. Entered digits were displayed on top of the screen. Whenever the participant felt ready, the authentication task began. The user entered three different PINs. Each PIN was entered five times with a maximum of three attempts (five runs), resulting in a minimum of 15 correct and a maximum of 45 failed attempts per system. The current PIN was displayed via a pop-up message and dismissed when the user pressed start. Participant answered small questionnaires between the different concepts and filled in a final questionnaire after all systems were tested.

Participants were told to enter the PINs as fast and as error-free as possible. We did not control for hand posture (e.g. one handed), but users could use whatever felt natural. In addition, the PIN-entry was filmed for later security analysis. The whole procedure took about 20 minutes, participants were compensated with a 5 Euro shopping voucher.

We recruited 18 participants (13 male) via the university mailing list and social networks. The average age was 25 years (20-32). Eleven participants had already heard about shoulder surfing attacks. All participants were experienced touch screen users and stated to use smartphones on a daily base.

Results

We excluded the first three runs (authentication attempts) of each PIN $\times$ System combination as training. Therefore, the analysis is based on 108 samples (2 runs $\times$ 3 PINs $\times$ 18 users) per system.

Performance

The performance analysis is based on correctly entered PINs. Our data was normally distributed and allowed for parametric tests. A repeated measures ANOVA comparing the average authentication times of the two runs for each of the three PINs revealed a significant main effect for system ($F_{2,34} = 7.53, p = 0.002$). Bonferroni corrected post-hoc tests showed that SwiPIN (*inside*) (M=5.04 s; SD=0.94) was significantly slower than *outside* (M=4.32; SD=0.94) and *free* (M=4.48 s; SD=0.96; $p < 0.05$). A detailed analysis of authentication speed distinguishing preparation and input time, revealed almost equal preparation times for all systems ($p > 0.05$). After clicking start, users needed between 1.2 s (SD=0.36; *outside*) and 1.3 s (SD=0.35; *inside*) until they started with the first input. In contrast, input times differed significantly ($F_{1.44,24.50} = 13.48, p < 0.001, \epsilon = 0.72$), ranging from 3.15 s (SD=0.62; *outside*) to 3.79 s (SD=0.70; *inside*). Error-rates were low: participants failed five times (4.6%) using the SwiPIN (*free*), twelve errors (11,1%) were counted using *inside* and six (5.6%) attempts failed using *outside*.

Security

The security analysis was performed by three experienced SwiPIN users (1 female). The shoulder surfers attacked the first correct input of each PIN. Therefore, 54 (3 PINs × 3 systems × 6 users) attacks were performed by each participant. Shoulder surfers were paid 20 Euros plus 40 Cents per successfully attacked PIN. They performed shoulder surfing attacks, followed by video attacks. Therefore, we showed them videos that were cut to the respective PIN-entry. Figure 2 shows screenshots of such a video. Per attack, a maximum of three guesses was permitted. Shoulder surfing attacks were based on a one time view of the input followed by three guesses. Video attacks allowed the participant unlimited control of the video (e.g. pause and rewind). For each PIN-entry, we computed the binary success (true/false) and the relative success rate (overlap of correct digits) based on the best of the three guesses. As none of the designs was significantly secure against video attacks, only human attacks are discussed.

Outside performed best with only one exposed PIN (binary: 1 of 54; overlap: 35.6%). *Inside* was successfully attacked in five cases (binary: 5 of 54; overlap: 44.4%). In all cases, the input was slow, allowing the attacker to observe parts of the gesture mapping and guessing the remaining digit(s) by chance. *Free* was most vulnerable to observations (binary: 8 of 54; overlap: 49.5%). The main reason was that participants started their gestures on the intended digit.

Perception

Each system was rated directly after the test. We used Likert scales ranging from 1 (strongly disagree) to 5 (strongly agree). Most of the participants agreed that *free* and *outside* were easy (Mdn = 4) and fast to use (Mdn = 4). SwiPIN (*inside*) was rated lower for both aspects (Mdn=3).

In addition, users were asked to rank the respective systems. Eleven participants (61%) preferred *outside* and rated it to be the fastest and easiest system. The rest of the participants preferred *free*. SwiPIN (*inside*) was not mentioned.

FEASIBILITY STUDY

Based on the results of the first user study, we decided to select SwiPIN (*outside*) for a feasibility study. *Outside* was preferred by most participants and had the best usability and security features. The goal of this study was to compare SwiPIN (*outside*) to traditional PIN-entry in terms of performance, security and likeability. In addition, we were interested in the effects of switching between these concepts.

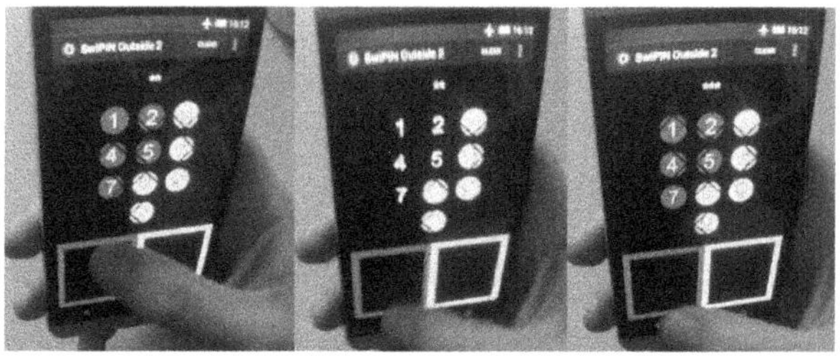

Figure 2. PIN-entry was filmed with a head-mounted camera. This sequence shows a participant entering a "2" using SwiPIN (*outside*).

The study was conducted using a repeated measure within-participants design. The independent variable *system* had the two levels SwiPIN (*outside*) and PIN (*traditional*). The dependent variables were measured at the same levels as in the previous user study. *System* was counterbalanced.

Procedure and Participants

The procedure was similar to the previous study. There were three important changes: 1) we tested only one PIN per system; 2) we had a guided training phase; 3) we added a system switching task. Therefore, we repeated the following procedure for each system: (a) introduction, (b) free training, (c) guided training, (d) PIN-entry and (d) feedback. In the guided training period, the participants were required to enter their PIN ten times, before the actual test was done. After the concepts were tested separately, we assigned a new PIN for the system switching task: (a) PIN training (10 times); (b) traditional PIN-entry (5 times); (c) SwiPIN-entry (5 times); (d) traditional PIN-entry (5 times). Users switched the methods by pressing a software button in the top right corner of the touch screen. At the end of the study, participants were given a questionnaire. The whole procedure took about 15 minutes and was compensated with a 5 Euro shopping voucher.

We used mailing lists to invite 16 participants (12 male) to our study. Their average age was 27 years (21-37). All were experienced smartphone users, eight had used SwiPIN before (within the first user study). No significant differences were found between experienced and novel users.

Results

As for the first study, the results are based on the last two PIN-entries of each device.

Performance

A two-tailed dependent t-test comparing the average authentication times of both runs of PIN and SwiPIN revealed highly significant main effects ($t_15 = 9.79, p < 0.001, r = .93$). Traditional PIN performs significantly faster (1.34 s; SD=0.3) than SwiPIN (3.66 s; SD=0.9). Error-rates were low. Within both tasks, only one failed attempt was logged (3.1%).

A repeated-measures ANOVA on the average authentication times of PIN-entry before and after switching the input method reveals that switching from PIN to SwiPIN and vice versa resulted in significantly slower authentication times ($p < 0.05$). While switching to PIN was error-free, two (12.5%) participants failed their first input on SwiPIN after PIN was used.

Security

The security analysis was equivalent to the one of the previous study. Again, the binary and relative success rates (overlap) were computed based on the best of three guesses.

Video attacks were successful in all cases and will not further be discussed. With respect to shoulder surfing attacks, PINs were correctly identified in almost all cases (binary: 14 of 16; overlap: 92.2%). The two instances that were not correctly shoulder surfed were due to very fast input. SwiPIN was correctly identified in only two instances (binary: 2 of 16; overlap: 35.9%). It has to be noted that in both cases, the attackers guessed the input based on observing the input elements. For instance, in one case, an attacker observed that the participant used the following input areas: red, yellow, red, yellow. This leaves a chance of $(\frac{1}{5})^4 = 0.16\%$ to guess the correct PIN. When observing traditional PIN-entry, we would assume a guessing probability of $\frac{1}{1}^4 = 100\%$ as an attacker could easily observe every button press.

Perception

PIN was rated very easy (Mdn=5) and very fast (Mdn=5) by most participants. SwiPIN was rated easy (Mdn=4) by most participants, but neutral (Mdn=3) in terms of speed. Most participants stated that they liked PIN (Mdn=4) and SwiPIN (Mdn=4). When asked, if they could imagine using SwiPIN in critical situations, all participants agreed. When we asked if switching to SwiPIN in front of others could be perceived as a mistrustful action, most participant disagreed (Mdn=1), one participant agreed (Mdn=4) and one was neutral (Mdn=3).

DISCUSSION

Our results show that SwiPIN (*outside*) is secure against human-based shoulder surfing and has very good usability properties. Even after very short training periods (13 inputs), SwiPIN (*outside*) users performed reasonably fast with 3.66 seconds on average. One drawback of SwiPIN lies in the fact that most people remember their PIN by muscles and this is not possible using SwiPIN. We like to note that SwiPIN was designed to be used as an additional security layer on top of PIN. That is, in low risk contexts like at home, users could opt for the faster standard PIN-entry. This way, users can still rely on muscle memory for most authentications. In addition, we assume that users are willing to accept the extra costs of SwiPIN input since it will only be activated in risky situations. In our lab setting, all participants agreed that they could imagine using SwiPIN for such scenarios. Even if this does not necessarily reflect real-world behavior, such claims are first indicators for the feasibility of the system.

The main reason for SwiPIN (*free*) being the least secure system was due to "bad lies". In these instances, the participants performed the swipes directly on top of the numbers they wanted to input. This means that the system did not take this important human factor into account. Both, SwiPIN (*inside*) and SwiPIN (*outside*) are resistant to this kind of behavior. However, with SwiPIN (*inside*) some participants reported, they felt to be forced to start on a specific position and this resulted in decreased likeability ratings. Besides preventing "bad lies", the *outside* version of SwiPIN additionally hampers observation by physically separating the presentation and the input areas. That is, the attacker had to observe two distinct areas of the screen.

Also due to this, the final system (SwiPIN *outside*) is resistant against most shoulder surfing attacks. The two instances in which it was successfully attacked in the final study were due to plain luck in combination with a clever strategy that allows to reduce the guessing space. That is, by observing the input elements, an attacker can reduce the possible digits by half. Please note that the attacker acknowledged having used that strategy and then simply guessed the PIN. Even if traditional PIN-entry would allow a guessing probability of 100%, this is a limitation as it increases the probability of a correct guess from 0.01% to 0.16%. We like to mention that using a full set of ten gestures (and only one input field) would solve this problem. However, our pre-study indicated that this strategy would also significantly reduce usability.

CONCLUSION AND FUTURE WORK

We presented SwiPIN, a concept which allows secure PIN-entry based on simple touch gestures. Fast authentication speed (3.7 s), low error-rates (3%) and shoulder surfing resistance indicate that SwiPIN is well-balanced in terms of usability and security. Therefore, we argue that it has the potential to be widely accepted as an alternative input mechanism for risky situations.

While first lab evaluations were promising, SwiPIN needs to be deployed and evaluated in the wild. By performing such field studies, we will be able to gather more insights into learning effects, real-world behavior and user acceptance.

REFERENCES

1. Bianchi, A., Oakley, I., and Kwon, D. S. Counting clicks and beeps: Exploring numerosity based haptic and audio pin entry. *Interacting with Computers 24*, 5 (2012), 409 – 422.

2. De Luca, A., Hertzschuch, K., and Hussmann, H. Colorpin: Securing pin entry through indirect input. In *Proc. CHI '10*, ACM (New York, NY, USA, 2010), 1103–1106.

3. Harbach, M., von Zezschwitz, E., Fichtner, A., De Luca, A., and Smith, M. It's a hard lock life: A field study of smartphone (un)locking behavior and risk perception. In *Proc. SOUPS 2014*, USENIX Association (Menlo Park, CA, July 2014), 213–230.

4. Kwon, T., and Na, S. Tinylock: Affordable defense against smudge attacks on smartphone pattern lock systems. *Computers & Security 42*, 0 (2014), 137 – 150.

5. Lee, M.-K. Security notions and advanced method for human shoulder-surfing resistant pin-entry. *IEEE Transactions on Information Forensics and Security 9*, 4 (April 2014), 695–708.

6. Roth, V., Richter, K., and Freidinger, R. A pin-entry method resilient against shoulder surfing. In *Proc. CCS '04*, ACM (New York, NY, USA, 2004), 236–245.

Glass Unlock: Enhancing Security of Smartphone Unlocking through Leveraging a Private Near-eye Display

Christian Winkler[1] Jan Gugenheimer[1] Alexander De Luca[2,3]
Gabriel Haas[1] Philipp Speidel[1] David Dobbelstein[1] Enrico Rukzio[1]
[1]Institute of Media Informatics, Ulm University, Ulm, Germany
[2]University of Munich (LMU), Munich, Germany; [3]DFKI GmbH, Saarbrücken, Germany
[1] *<firstname>.<lastname>@uni-ulm.de*, [2,3]*alexander.de.luca@ifi.lmu.de*

ABSTRACT
This paper presents Glass Unlock, a novel concept using smart glasses for smartphone unlocking, which is theoretically secure against smudge attacks, shoulder-surfing, and camera attacks. By introducing an additional temporary secret like the layout of digits that is only shown on the private near-eye display, attackers cannot make sense of the observed input on the almost empty phone screen. We report a user study with three alternative input methods and compare them to current state-of-the-art systems. Our findings show that Glass Unlock only moderately increases authentication times and that users favor the input method yielding the slowest input times as it avoids focus switches between displays.

Author Keywords
Smartphone; Authentication; Near-eye display; User Study

INTRODUCTION
Recent findings suggest that about 43% of smartphone users rely on some form of lock-screen to protect their phone from unwanted usage [7]. However, currently deployed smartphone authentication mechanisms like PIN and the Android unlock pattern are susceptible to different real world attacks such as smudge attacks [1], shoulder-surfing [5], or camera attacks. Especially the latter is becoming more and more of a threat with the increasing prevalence of video surveillance.

One way of protecting authentication from these attacks is to use biometric properties like fingerprints or input behavior [3]. While these are highly usable alternatives, they suffer from trust issues and the fact that they make the devices hard or impossible to share [4]. Indirect input or other kinds of software distractions [8, 9] suffer from highly reduced authentication speed and thus, negatively influence usability. As opposed to this, hardware based approaches rely on additional, external devices to provide invisible channels to the user which affect the input [2] or relocate the input to a less observable position [5]. While increasing usability, they require additional devices to be carried around.

With the advent of smart wearable devices such as smart watches and smart glasses on the consumer market, such devices are not an additional burden anymore as they are carried around anyway as part of the users' daily lives. We already see that they can be used to enhance the usability of lock-screens. For instance, Google's Android now offers to automatically disable the lock screen whenever the user's smart watch is in the near vicinity. While this may be appropriate for less concerned users, it enables new types of attacks like stealing both devices together or leveraging moments when the phone is left unattended while still in range.

CHI 2015, April 18 - 23 2015, Seoul, Republic of Korea

http://dx.doi.org/10.1145/2702123.2702316

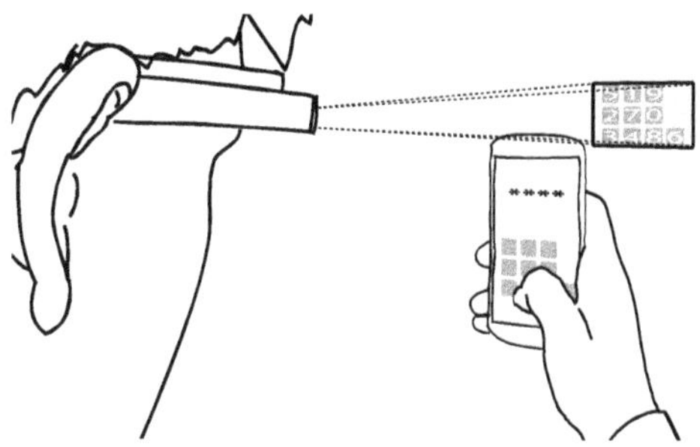

Figure 1. Glass Unlock concept: the scrambled PIN pad is only shown on the display of the user's smart glasses; input is performed on empty buttons on the smartphone, which does not give anything away to an attacker.

In this paper, we introduce a similar approach for phone unlocking, combining smart glasses with the phone's lock screen. The basic idea of Glass Unlock is to hide the lock information (e.g. PIN digits) on the phone and instead show it on the glasses' display. For instance, in a standard 10-digits PIN screen the phone would show *empty* buttons while the same layout including the digits would be visible on the glasses as shown in Figure 1. The random order of digits is required to achieve the desired security as explained later. By precluding any attackers of making sense of the users' input on the phone, Glass Unlock is secure against smudge attacks, shoulder surfing, and camera attacks.

Our main goal of this paper is to assess the additional costs of this approach compared to the state-of-the-art of unlocking. According to Harbach et al. [7], this is PIN unlocking, which about a third of all smartphone users (78% of all lock screen users) rely upon. Besides the analogue 4 out of 10 digits implementation, we further evaluated alternative variations of Glass Unlock: one that proofed to decrease the visual search time by reducing the number of digits from 10 to 6; another that proofed to support eyes-free input on the phone by requiring swipes instead of touches, thus removing any need to switch focus between the phone and the display of the glasses.

The contributions of our paper are (1) a new PIN entry concept that separates visual output from the input by moving output to the near-eye display, thereby drastically increasing unlock security; (2) a thorough study of three alternative input methods for Glass Unlock (*with* and *without* glasses). The study reveals that introducing the smart glasses for increased security only moderately increases the authentication time (by about the factor two) and users prefer the slower eyes-free input over faster alternative input methods.

GLASS UNLOCK CONCEPT
As people owning smart glasses will likely wear them most of the time, it makes sense to combine them with the people's phones to increase their security. With Glass Unlock we only look at using

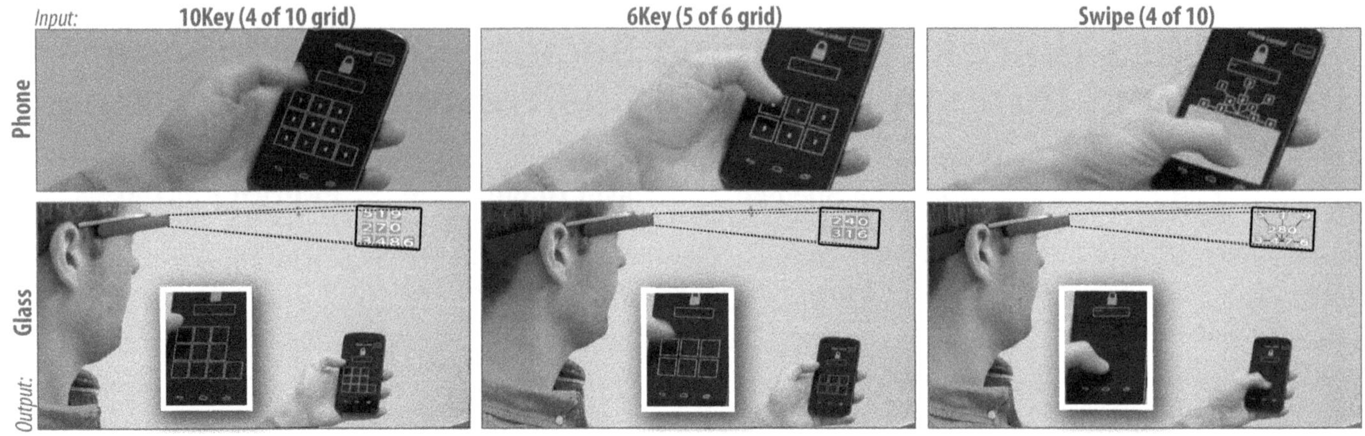

Figure 2. The 6 study systems: 3 input and 2 output methods (with and without Glass), additionally compared against standard PIN baseline (not shown).

the Glass for unlocking the phone as current smart glasses do not implement lock security so far. While the whole phone unlock could be performed on the glasses alone, users should not be forced to switch input to another device while they interact with their phone. Hence, for the Glass Unlock concept we decided to move the authentication challenge to the near-eye display while retaining authentication input on the phone. When the Glass is not available Glass Unlock gracefully degrades to scrambled PIN-entry with visible numbers on the phone.

Threat Model

Our threat model considers smudge attacks, shoulder-surfing, and camera attacks. By moving the authentication challenge from the (public) phone display to the (private) near-eye display, neither shoulder-surfing nor multiple synchronized camera observations give away the password simply because it is not shown on the phone. Small digits on the near-eye display are not visible to onlookers and cameras. In addition, Glass Unlock scrambles the order of digits after every successful unlock attempt, thus preventing attackers of merely repeating observed input on the phone, which also makes it resistant against smudge attacks.

As an attacker of Glass Unlock still has to acquire knowledge of the password, even stealing both devices together will not facilitate phone unlocking any more easily than without the glasses – this is a huge difference to previously mentioned automatic unlocking between multiple smart devices. Glass Unlock further assumes a secure Bluetooth connection between the devices, but even if the connection was compromised, an attacker of Glass Unlock would have to simultaneously record the digital transmission and observe the input on the phone. This is because no sensitive information is transmitted, only the randomized PIN layout.

By using two separate displays, Glass Unlock may require users to constantly switch between such, possibly resulting in a negative impact on completion times and user satisfaction. The following alternative input methods try to provide solutions by simplifying the visual search task or supporting eyes-free input.

Reducing Visual Search Time with *6Key*

With the standard 4 out of 10 digits PIN variant (*10Key* in Figure 2 left), users have to shift their attention multiple times between the displays unless they are able to instantly remember 4 of 10 possible positions. One possibility to decrease visual search time is to reduce the number of displayed digits (e.g. 6 digits). To maintain a large enough password space, we can increase the password length to 5 (see Figure 2 middle), resulting in 7,776 possible combinations compared to the former 10,000).

Reducing display switching time with *Swipe*

Currently available near-eye displays provide only a fixed focal length for their optics. For instance, Google Glass's virtual display is perceived in 244 cm distance while the handheld phone display is in closer proximity of only 45-60 cm to the user's eyes. Because both displays are in different focal planes, users are required to re-accommodate when switching focus between them. In our preliminary tests, this was less of an issue than initially anticipated. Yet, every focus switch adds up to the input time.

With the aforementioned 10 or 6-digit versions, focus switches are required for eye-hand coordination to hit the correct empty boxes on the phone. Relative movement such as swiping supports eyes-free input much better as touches can be performed anywhere on the screen. Swipes demand for a different mapping of the numbers, though, since these gestures are based on direction rather than position. The literature speaks against simply splitting the available space into even parts of 36 degrees because people struggle with performing eyes-free swipes of arbitrary angles [6]. We therefore designed the swipe area to consist of 5 directions (left, up/left, up, up/right, right). To increase the input space to 10 digits, all directions support two lengths, a short and a long swipe, whereby *short* is up to 1/6 of the display width and *long* anything beyond. In consequence, the input can be performed eyes-free on the phone, which in turn allows the user to focus on the glasses display all the time without having to switch attention between the displays (see Figure 2 right).

STUDY

As outlined before, we assume the presence of the Glass display and the scrambling of the PIN pad to have major negative effects on usability and input time. To test for these factors, we ran a user study with 18 participants ($M = 28$ years; $SD = 3$; 1 female). All participants were experienced smartphone users ($M = 4.39$ years; $SD = 2.05$) and 83.33% were active users of an unlock screen. Our study comprised three input techniques: *10Key*, *6Key*, and *Swipe*; and two output methods: *Phone* and *Glass* as independent variables, resulting in 6 systems overall (see Figure 2). We employed a repeated-measures design and the six systems were tested in counterbalanced order (6x6 Latin Square). In a separate entry-study, the same participants had previously provided their input to a system that mimicked a standard 4 of 10 digits PIN pad without any modification. However, participants were shortly distracted with a mental rotation task between login attempts to the 7th system to avoid input based solely on muscle memory. This study was conducted to record a baseline for each participant which we report but do not include in the statistical analysis.

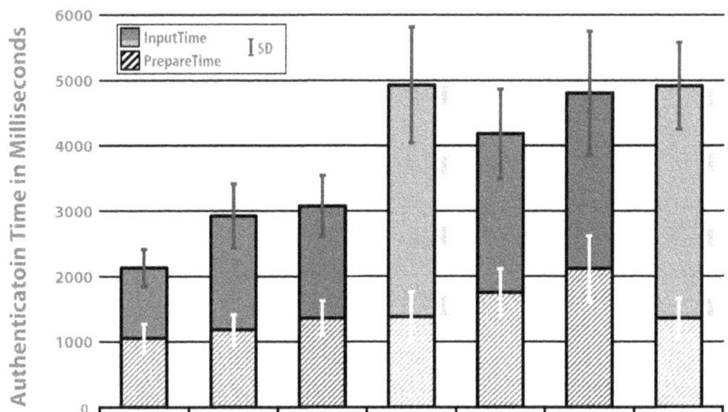

	PIN Baseline	6Key (Phone)	10Key (Phone)	Swipe (Phone)	6Key (Glass)	10Key (Glass)	Swipe (Glass)
InputTime	1078	1740	1715	3544	2426	2691	3560
ANOVA		$F_{Output}(1,17)=29.25, \eta^2=.632$		$F_{Input}(1.5,25.3)=97.96, \eta^2=.852$		$F^{Input}_{Output}(2,34)=9.66, \eta^2=.362$	
PrepareTime	1053	1182	1362	1384	1755	2115	1357
ANOVA		$F_{Output}(1,17)=41.28, \eta^2=.708$		$F_{Input}(1.5,25.7)=12.31, \eta^2=.420$		$F^{Input}_{Output}(2,34)=11.22, \eta^2=.398$	
TotalTime	2131	2122	3077	4928	4181	4806	4917
ANOVA		$F_{Output}(1,17)=87.14, \eta^2=.837$		$F_{Input}(2,34)=87.22, \eta^2=.837$		$F^{Input}_{Output}(2,34)=27.18, \eta^2=.615$	

Figure 3. Authentication times divided into preparation time (time until first touch) and input time (remaining time). Swipe input time also shows – next to it – input times per digit and preparation time in-between. An ANOVA revealed all effects to be highly significant at the $p<.001$ level.

Our prototype consists of an Android Nexus 4 and a Google Glass. On every unlock attempt, the phone sends the scrambled layout to the Glass; no transmission back to the phone is required.

Procedure

For all seven systems, participants started with a training phase. They were explained the technique and had time to train until they felt comfortable with the technique and had achieved at least two correct PIN entries in a row. Participants trained with the password they would use throughout the system *at turn*. When logging started, they were presented with 5 authentication trials, for which they each had 3 possible attempts. Passwords were chosen to consist only of unique numbers to homogenize the complexity of all possible combinations. That said, resulting times should be taken as worst case estimates. Before each attempt, the password was shown on the phone and Glass to avoid memorability issues with unfamiliar passwords during the study. Password entry started only upon touching the phone screen. When an attempt failed, the user was notified by flashing borders of phone and Glass display in red. If it was not the last failed attempt, the same scrambled layout as before was presented. When the trial was successful or had finally failed, the layout was randomized and the same password was shown again, for the next trial to start. There was no possibility to correct or undo any input in order to avoid confounding input times. Also, no instructions to approach PIN-entry were given as such would be unrealistic to enforce in a real deployment.

As any input, and scrambled PIN pads in particular, require a mental preparation time before the input can actually be performed, we logged the time between starting the attempt and performing the first touch as *preparation time* and the time between the first and last touch as *input time*, respectively. After each system, the user filled out a short questionnaire on the phone that asked for perceived speed, frustration, etc. and at the end, we asked participants to compare the systems against each other and give final feedback.

Results and Discussion

Authentication Speed

Figure 3 shows the preparation, input, and total times of the systems. First we see that the total time of the baseline was lower than total times of other phone methods. This is as expected since all other systems used a scrambled PIN pad that introduced a visual search task. An Anderson-Darling test revealed all three dependent variables to be normally distributed. Thus we averaged all 5 successful trials per user and condition and conducted a two-factorial repeated measures ANOVA on the data. Mauchly's test indicated that sphericity was violated for *input method* of preparation and input times, which were corrected using Greenhouse-Geisser estimates. The ANOVA revealed both independent variables (*input method* and *output method*) and their interaction to have a highly significant effect ($p<.001$) on all three dependent variables. Further post-hoc comparisons of means (Bonferroni corrected) indicate the success of our attempt to reduce the visual search effort with the 6Key input method as it significantly decreased ($\delta=-389.61$ ms, $p<.001$) the preparation time compared to 10Key. Furthermore, we see that the preparation times of 6Key and 10Key significantly increase ($\delta=-432.79$ ms, $p<.001$) when used with Glass, but Swipe remains almost the same. This can be attributed to Swipe's support for eyes-free input when used with the Glass. In contrast, 6Key and 10Key require users to perform a mapping to the phone once they switched their focus. This leads to a higher preparation time. Also, to minimize attention shifts, users may have tried to find and remember multiple positions from the very beginning. Swipe on the other hand allowed the input to start as soon as the first digit was discovered.

Preparation time (search time) does not only happen before the first touch, but also between touches/swipes during the input time. This explains the significant rise ($\delta=-559.53$ ms, $p<.001$) in input times between phone and Glass methods. Again, like with preparation time, the times of 6Key and 10Key increase significantly when used with Glass as display switches occur during the input as well. Very interesting for us are the high input times of Swipe. They remain almost exactly the same between output methods, which gives strong evidence that Swipe supported eyes-free input, thus was not confounded by the separation of displays. Originally we thought the high input time of Swipe must mainly stem from performing the swipes that naturally take much longer than simple touches. Further investigation of the inter-digit preparation and input times revealed, though, that performing swipes made only for about 1s of the total time (depicted to the right of Swipe bars in Figure 3). The remaining preparation time nested in the input time of Swipe was even larger than the whole input time of 6Key or 10Key, at least on the phone. A general shift of preparation time to input time for Swipe seems plausible, as there is no need to remember two positions at once. The high difference however, can possibly be explained with the unusual layout of digits during Swipe that may have hampered the visual search task even more – but this requires further research.

Authentication Errors

During the study, we collected 681 authentications. Errors were very low across all key input systems (overall 7 errors) and thus only the *Swipe* errors with and without Glass will be discussed. Most errors occurred in the length (29 errors) of the swipe – too short or too long – or the angle (14 errors) – left or right slip. Using the Glass, participants produced more errors (19) in the length of the input than without (10). This can be attributed to the eyes-free input as the works of De Luca et. al. [6] already revealed that users struggle with swipe input more when performed eyes-free. To our very surprise, introducing the Glass did not lead to any more errors with the key input methods, despite the required switching and the possible out-of-focus touching.

Qualitative System Feedback

After each system we asked participants about their perceived speed and success during the interaction. With Glass input methods, we also asked whether the participants constantly switched between displays or rather stayed on either of them (all using a positive and a negative formulation on Likert scales from 1 – strongly disagree to 5 – strongly agree which were averaged to a continuous interval scale). For speed, the output method ($F(1,16) = 10.39$, $p < .001$), input method ($F(2,32) = 12.16$, $p < .01$) and their interaction ($F(2,32) = 8.59$, $p < .001$) all turned out significant in a two-factorial ANOVA of the means of answers. Overall, 6Key ($M = 4.7$) was almost significantly ($\delta = 0.5$, $p = .059$) perceived faster than 10Key ($M = 4.4$) and significantly faster ($\delta = 0.84$, $p < .001$) perceived than Swipe ($M = 3.5$). Using Glass, 10Key ($M = 3.4$) was inferior to 6Key ($M = 4.0$), but not better than Swipe ($M = 3.6$) which scored between the others. Thus, although objectively Swipe was the slowest when used with the Glass, it was perceived better than 10Key. In contrast, participants estimated their own success in accordance with the actually measured errors. Finally, users were very sure about whether they switched between displays with almost total *dis*agreement that they switched with Swipe ($m = 1.5$) but significantly more often with 6Key ($M = 3.4$, $\delta = 1.97$, $p < .001$) and 10Key ($M = 4.3$, $\delta = 2.8$, $p < .001$). We also found a significant effect between 6Key and 10Key in favor of 6Key ($\delta = -0.83$, $p < .01$), which did not require as much display switches. This is interesting, as the number of digits to enter was even higher with 6Key. Yet, in the post-study questionnaire 5 participants explained to us that they could handle 6Key almost eyes-free which explains the results. 7 users attributed their increased success with 6Key to the larger keys (that would also facilitate eyes-free input) while only 3 mentioned the simplified search task.

Openly asked for comments about 10Key, 13 participants criticized the annoying display switches while regarding Swipe, 12 users explicitly mentioned to cherish canceling out of display switches. On the negative side, 4 reported problems with distinguishing between short and long swipes, 3 found short swipes harder to perform than long swipes, and 3 found Swipe too slow in general. Interestingly, in the final ranking of the three input methods by output method (Figure 4) participants shifted their sympathy nonetheless even more towards the Swipe technique when used with Glass, followed by 6Key gaining only half the sympathy on rank 1. Thus, display switches seem to be a very annoying factor in this new type of multi-display system and users would rather choose a slower input technique but which is less demanding on the eye. Finally, ≈65% of participants stated they would entirely replace their current lock screen with their favorite Glass Unlock variant if they owned compatible glasses and additional ≈18% would do so only for security critical apps.

CONCLUSION & FUTURE WORK

Users spend much of their time on unlocking their phones. With mobile devices becoming more and more a medium for highly sensitive data, secure unlock methods are researched that yield acceptable input times without requiring additional hardware to carry. In this paper we presented such an authentication system, Glass Unlock, that is inherently secure against the most common visual attacks against mobile phone locks while increasing the unlock time only moderately. Glass Unlock achieves this by outsourcing the security critical output to the near-eye display, which is believed to become a regular companion of many smartphone users, thus adding no additional hardware requirements. If a form of randomization is used to obfuscate the link between the displays, our quantitative results speak for the reduction of visual search tasks, for instance by performing a trade-off between the number of PIN digits and PIN length as in 6Key. But even more important seems the support of eyes-free input, either through large buttons on the phone (6Key) or through alternative input methods such as swiping, as it greatly improves the user experience.

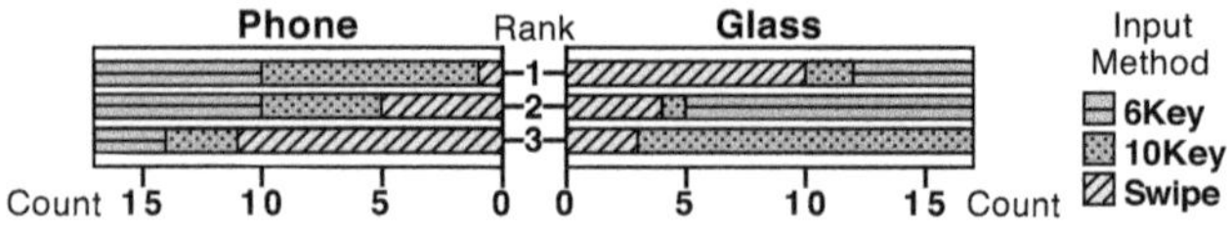

Figure 4. Final ranking of participants' preferred input method.

We also see room for future work. By comparing baseline and 10Key we have seen that scrambling of the PIN pad alone accounted for a rise of ≈44% in unlock time. Because smart glasses like the Google Glass have inbuilt proximity and motion sensors, they recognize when they are put on or off. We could take advantage of this and, instead of randomizing the PIN layout after every successful unlock attempt, only randomize it when the Glass was put off or the devices get out of range. Depending on how long the Glass is continuously worn, users may be able to memorize and adjust to the current instance of the scrambled PIN pad, thereby reducing the visual search time further. In addition, the feedback we received about improving the Swipe technique and maybe reducing it to 6 digits may lead to lower input times and fewer errors. Besides, it is important to note that the general Glass Unlock concept does not only relate to smartphone unlocking. People are required to enter secrets all the time, at the ATM, when paying with debit cards, etc. We can envision a general framework that would automatically transfer the challenge to the user's smart glasses using input methods similar to those presented in this paper.

ACKNOWLEDGMENTS

This work was conducted within the projects "Mobile Interaction with Pervasive User Interfaces" and "CompanionTechnology for Cognitive Technical Systems SFB/TRR 62" both funded by the German Research Foundation (DFG).

REFERENCES

1. Aviv, A. J., Gibson, K., Mossop, E., Blaze, M., and Smith, J. M. Smudge attacks on smartphone touch screens. In *Proc. WOOT '10*, USENIX Association (2010), 1–7.
2. Bianchi, A., Oakley, I., Kostakos, V., and Kwon, D. S. The phone lock: Audio and haptic shoulder-surfing resistant pin entry methods for mobile devices. In *Proc. TEI '11*, ACM (2011), 197–200.
3. Burgbacher, U., and Hinrichs, K. An implicit author verification system for text messages based on gesture typing biometrics. In *Proc. CHI '14*, ACM (2014), 2951–2954.
4. Coventry, L., De Angeli, A., and Johnson, G. Usability and biometric verification at the atm interface. In *Proc. CHI '03*, ACM (2003), 153–160.
5. De Luca, A., Harbach, M., von Zezschwitz, E., Maurer, M.-E., Slawik, B. E., Hussmann, H., and Smith, M. Now you see me, now you don't: Protecting smartphone authentication from shoulder surfers. In *Proc. CHI '14*, ACM (2014), 2937–2946.
6. De Luca, A., von Zezschwitz, E., Nguyen, N. D. H., Maurer, M.-E., Rubegni, E., Scipioni, M. P., and Langheinrich, M. Back-of-device authentication on smartphones. In *Proc. CHI '13*, ACM (2013), 2389–2398.
7. Harbach, M., von Zezschwitz, E., Fichtner, A., De Luca, A., and Smith, M. It's a hard lock life: A field study of smartphone (un)locking behavior and risk perception. In *Proc. SOUPS '14*, USENIX Association (July 2014), 213–230.
8. Khot, R. A., Kumaraguru, P., and Srinathan, K. WYSWYE: Shoulder Surfing Defense for Recognition Based Graphical Passwords. In *Proc. OzCHI '12*, ACM (2012), 285–294.
9. Kim, S.-H., Kim, J.-W., Kim, S.-Y., and Cho, H.-G. A new shoulder-surfing resistant password for mobile environments. In *Proc. ICUIMC '11*, ACM (2011), 27:1–27:8.

I Feel Like I'm Taking Selfies All Day! Towards Understanding Biometric Authentication on Smartphones

Alexander De Luca[1,2], **Alina Hang**[1], **Emanuel von Zezschwitz**[1], **Heinrich Hussmann**[1]
[1]Media Informatics Group, University of Munich (LMU), Munich, Germany
[2]DFKI GmbH, Saarbrücken, Germany
{alexander.de.luca, alina.hang, emanuel.von.zezschwitz, hussmann}@ifi.lmu.de

ABSTRACT
We present the results of an MTurk survey ($n = 383$) on the reasons for using and not using biometric authentication systems on smartphones. We focused on Apple's Touch ID as well as Android's Face Unlock as they are the most prevalent systems on the market. For both systems, we categorized the participants as a) current users, b) former users that deactivated it at some point and c) nonusers. The results show that usability is one of the main factors that influences the decision on whether or not to use biometric verification on the smartphone. To our surprise and as opposed to previous research on biometric authentication, privacy and trust issues were not among the most important decision factors.

Author Keywords
Biometric authentication; Face Unlock; Touch ID

ACM Classification Keywords
H.5.m. Information Interfaces and Presentation (e.g. HCI): Miscellaneous

INTRODUCTION
Biometric authentication is often referred to as the secret weapon of authentication, mainly due to the fact that the "password" (e.g. a fingerprint) cannot be forgotten [3]. This might be one of the reasons why many smartphone companies and operating system developers recently started integrating biometric authentication into their systems. The two most prominent examples are Face Unlock (introduced with Android 4.0) and Touch ID (a fingerprint scanner that was introduced with Apple's iPhone 5s). These two systems represent the first noteworthy deployment of biometric authentication in end consumer mobile devices. From a user-centered point of view, this raises a lot of interesting questions.

Despite its advantages, privacy and security issues are often mentioned as one of the main reasons or even the most important factors for a user's decision to avoid using biometric authentication in general [3]. In addition, many biometric approaches, like speaker recognition, are considered insecure by their users [7]. Recently, Chandrasekhar et al. [2] explored the usability of Touch ID and Face Unlock in a lab study and found that external factors like awkwardness when holding the device in front of the face to perform an unlock had a great negative influence on the perceived usability of the systems and the participants' willingness to use them.

CHI 2015, April 18–23, 2015, Seoul, Republic of Korea.

ACM 978-1-4503-3145-6/15/04...$15.00.
http://dx.doi.org/10.1145/2702123.2702141

In this work, we were interested in factors that cannot be evaluated in a lab study. Therefore, we performed an MTurk survey with 383 participants that own devices capable of either Face Unlock or Touch ID. We focused on the reasons that make people (not) use the biometric authentication functionalities on their own smartphones. For each authentication system we divided the results into three categories: a) activated, i.e. people that activated the system at some point and are still using it; b) deactivated, i.e. people that used the respective system but stopped using it; c) never activated, i.e. people that never activated the feature on their devices.

The main contribution of this paper consists in focused insights into reasons for using or not using biometric authentication on smartphones. We identify the main factors that influence this decision. For instance, as opposed to previous work, privacy issues were not among the main reasons for not using biometric authentication. Other factors like usability and reliability were considered much more important. These insights can help to design the systems in a way that increases user acceptance of biometric authentication on smartphones.

SURVEY
We conducted an online survey using Amazon's Mechanical Turk (MTurk) service. Even though MTurk has its limitations, MTurk studies can create meaningful and valuable results in the area of usable security if adequate measures to secure response quality are taken (e.g. control questions).

SURVEY DESIGN
As mentioned before, we decided to limit the study to Android's Face Unlock and Apple's Touch ID as they represented the most common systems at the time of this study. Therefore, we created two different MTurk tasks. The study was advertised on MTurk as being about biometric systems and Android's Face Unlock or Apple's Touch ID respectively. Workers that wanted to participate in the survey had to be US residents and needed a HIT/task approval rate (approved correct participation in previous MTurk tasks) of 90% or higher. Furthermore, the study description mentioned that they had to own a compatible device (e.g. an iPhone 5s for Touch ID).

	Touch ID			Face Unlock		
	M/F	Age	%	M/F	Age	%
activated	82/76	27 (18-47)	86.3	6/12	30 (20-51)	10
deact.	10/7	29 (20-42)	9.3	44/34	28 (18-61)	38.5
never act.	1/7	26 (20-37)	4.4	55/49	29 (18-58)	51.5
overall	93/90	27 (18-47)		105/95	28 (18-61)	

Table 1. Survey demographics and percentage of participants that have the respective system activated, deactivated it or never activated it.

The two tasks led to two different surveys hosted on our servers. The surveys were identical with the exception of the authentication mechanism they focused on. They started with a description of the respective system followed by a section about demographics. After that, the participants were asked whether they are using the respective system, have been using it or never tried it. Depending on the answer, the remainder of the survey focused on this specific context. For instance, nonusers were asked "*Why do you not use [system]?*" while participants that had used the system before and then deactivated it were asked two questions instead: "*Why did you use [system]?*" and "*Why did you stop using [system]?*".

To make sure that the participants fulfilled the requirements of the study, the survey contained control questions as well as a simple task in which the participants were asked to submit a photo of their smartphone recorded with the device itself using the front camera and a mirror. The questions as well as the photo were manually checked before approving the respective participant. Afterwards, the photos were deleted.

On average, the survey took around 20 minutes. Approved Turkers received US$ 1 for their effort, which is a common compensation for such tasks on MTurk.

Participants
The Face Unlock survey was active for 15 days until 200 submissions were approved (20 rejected). The Touch ID task was stopped after 33 days and 183 submissions were approved (28 rejected). Table 1 shows the participants' demographics.

RESULTS
For the analysis, all open-ended questions were coded using an inductive approach. Two researchers independently created codes and then met to create the final codeplan. This was then used by a third and fourth researcher to do the final coding of the responses. In all instances, saturation points of new themes were reached before the final data were coded (e.g. after 10 out of 17 participants that deactivated Touch ID). We therefore argue that our results cover the most relevant reasons for (not) using biometric authentication on smartphones.

Categories
Table 1 lists the percentage of participants that either had the respective system activated, had never activated it or had deactivated it after some time. The data reveals three noticeable trends: 1. The number of active Touch ID users is much higher than in any other category. 2. With 52%, the amount of participants that never activated Face Unlock on their devices is very high. 3. Considering the fact that the number of active users plus the number of former users represents all participants that ever used the respective system, this means that Face Unlock has a very high dropout rate of 81.3%. On the other hand, the dropout rate for Touch ID is only 9.7%.

Active Users
The results of the coding of reasons for using Face Unlock and Touch ID are listed in table 2. The main reason for using Touch ID as named by the participants is usability. Examples include speed and convenience of authentication. Many participants named it to be as easy and fast as the normal slide to unlock. Please note that reliability can be considered an important factor of usability but is listed independently in the table. For Face Unlock, usability only plays a minor role with security being the most important reason of use.

Emotion is also considered an important factor in the decision to use Touch ID. For instance, participants called it "*fun*", "*interesting*", "*joyful*" and even "*awesome*". Such positive emotional aspects were only mentioned once for Face Unlock.

In the survey, participants were also asked which authentication mechanisms they used on their smartphones before activating the respective biometric system. To gain insights into whether providing biometric authentication has a potential impact on secure behavior, we analyzed how many of them had not used an authentication mechanism before on their smartphone. For Touch ID, 24 out of 158 participants (15%) decided to use authentication due to the availability of the biometric technology. For Face Unlock, 4 out of 20 participants (20%) made this decision.

Former Users
Participants that deactivated Face Unlock or Touch ID made the decision to use the respective system at some point but then got rid of it. The reasons for this decision reveal how and why biometric systems can disappoint their users. The reasons are outlined in table 2. Even though the dropout rates for Touch ID are very low and thus the numbers have to be interpreted carefully, usability together with reliability seem to play an important role in the decision process. For Face Unlock, with 28 (36%) participants, this trend is clear and was in many instances coupled with emotional aspects like annoyance.

The main usability problems for both systems were slow speed and lack of convenience. For instance, participants that stopped using Face Unlock thought it was way too slow especially in cases when they needed quick access to their devices. In addition, correctly aligning the device in front of the face was considered unnecessarily difficult.

External factors were mentioned by 23 (29%) participants as being an important factor to stop using Face Unlock. Besides bad lighting conditions leading to bad performance, the participants mentioned social awkwardness as an important external factor that kept them from using the system. The two instances for Touch ID were due to the participant's work which negatively influenced the performance of Touch ID (e.g. oily hands) and using a protective phone case which made using the system impossible.

	Touch ID		Face Unlock	
	reason	count	reason	count
activated	Usability	110 (70%)	Security	8 (44%)
	Security	61 (39%)	Curiosity	4 (22%)
	Emotion	20 (13%)	Usability	3 (17%)
	Privacy	6 (4%)	Novelty	1 (6%)
	Novelty	6 (4%)	Emotion	1 (6%)
	Reliability	6 (4%)	Prestige	1 (6%)
			Reliability	1 (6%)
deactivated	Usability	8 (47%)	Usability	28 (36%)
	Emotion	3 (18%)	Reliability	23 (29%)
	Reliability	3 (18%)	External Factors	23 (29%)
	External Factors	2 (12%)	Emotion	12 (15%)
	Security	2 (12%)	Security	11 (14%)
			No Need	5 (6%)
			Technical Misconception	1 (1%)
never activated	Usability	3 (38%)	Ignorance	28 (27%)
	Technical Misconception	3 (38%)	No Need	24 (23%)
			Reliability	24 (23%)
	Trust	2 (25%)	Usability	23 (22%)
	Reliability	1 (13%)	Emotion	15 (14%)
	External Factors	1 (13%)	Security	8 (8%)
			Technical Misconception	7 (7%)
			External Factors	4 (4%)

Table 2. Reasons for using, not using and deactivating Touch ID and Face Unlock. Please note that participants' answers can relate to several of these categories and thus do not add up to 100%.

We also asked participants about what changes to the system would be required to make them use it again. The most important factor was usability together with reliability, which was mentioned by 36 (46%) Face Unlock and 9 (53%) Touch ID participants. Security improvements were mentioned by 29 (37%) Face Unlock participants, but were not mentioned at all in the Touch ID group.

Nonusers

The main reasons for participants that never activated the systems are listed in table 2. The results show that a high number of participants (27%) that never used Face Unlock on their devices, simply did not know that it existed (coded as "Ignorance" in the table). This number is zero for Touch ID users. Assumed reliability and usability problems as well as the group of participants that thought that their current level of protection was enough represent important factors as well.

In the small Touch ID group, technical misconception was one of the main reasons for nonuse. For instance, two participants stated that their device was used by at least one additional person. They were convinced that sharing their device would not be possible anymore once Touch ID was activated (which is not correct as the system allows to store several fingerprints). Furthermore, the only two instances of participants that did not use the system due to trust and privacy issues can be found in this group. These participants stated that they did not trust the respective company with their fingerprint data.

DISCUSSION

Usability Top Argument

In all conditions, usability was one of the top factors that influenced the decision to use or not use the respective system. Touch ID was considered as more usable than the alternatives (e.g. PIN) which made it a very convenient and useful option for the participants (even first time adopters). It seems to be better integrated into the interaction process and does not add much overhead (or even none) to the overall unlocking process. In many cases, it was considered equally fast and easy as slide to unlock. The bad usability and reliability properties of Face Unlock seem to explain the high dropout rates much more than any other factor. Please note that external factors do contribute to the usability rating as they were the reason for interaction problems in many cases.

Harbach et al. [6] recently performed a real world study on smartphone unlocking and found that users spend a significant amount of the overall device usage time on entering their PINs or unlock patterns. In most cases, securing the device was not even necessary. This explains how the increased error rate and the reduced authentication speed of Face Unlock as reported by the participants highly influence the decision to deactivate the system. It also highlights the fact that authentication systems (biometric or not) that do not provide high usability properties are not appropriate for standard authentication on smartphones.

Role of Privacy and Trust

When discussing biometric authentication from a user's point-of-view, privacy and trust are often mentioned as being one of the main reasons for not using a biometric system [3]. Users are cited as being highly critical about how their data is used and where it is stored. To our surprise, privacy and trust were only mentioned by two participants. They stated that they never activated Touch ID as they were afraid of what the smartphone and the respective company would do with their data.

Our data does not allow to fully investigate this issue but we believe that this is due to a couple of reasons. Our main hypothesis is that it can be partially attributed to the fact that smartphones are considered very private devices by their owners. This is supported by the fact that 93 (59%) of the 158 Touch ID users explicitly stated to believe that their fingerprint data is only stored locally on their device.

System developers should embrace this trust by building systems that behave this way. In addition, they should communicate transparently to their users what happens to their data.

Technical Misconception

Even though technical misconceptions were mentioned only in a few instances, they are one of the two top reasons in the (small) group of Touch ID device owners that never activated the fingerprint scanner. The interesting part is that this category represents reasons that are factually wrong but still lead the respective participant to not using a potentially helpful and useful feature. Such misconceptions should be avoided through appropriate communication and also at the interface level, for instance during the setup phase.

First Time Adopters

The analysis of the data revealed a very interesting trend. A certain number of participants (Touch ID: 15%; Face Unlock: 20%) that actively use the systems only decided to turn on authentication due to the availability of a biometric system. On their previous devices and before using Touch ID or Face Unlock, they did not use any other form of protecting their data through authentication. Please note that all of them had smartphones before they started using their current devices.

We therefore argue that the availability of a well-designed biometric authentication system can have a positive effect on the protection of the users' smartphone data. This was recently also observed by Egelman et al. [4] who reported on a study participant that only used authentication due to the convenience level provided by Touch ID.

Social Compatibility

Many external factors that made participants stop using Face Unlock were related to awkwardness when using the system in public. For instance, participants said that holding the device in front of their face made them feel weird. One user stated that "*It can be a bit embarrassing to hold your phone up in a weird position while in public just to unlock it.*". Another user noted that she would not use Face Unlock as it "*looks like I'm taking selfies all day.*". For Touch ID, no such complaints were raised.

Our results thus support the claims by Hang et al. [5] who found that social awkwardness was one of the major reasons why users in a big company were not satisfied with using their internal voice recognition system. This seems to apply even more to the smartphone context as much of the interaction with these devices takes place in public.

Advertising

Our data suggests that advertising had a big effect on the decision to activate Touch ID which was heavily advertised through all media. The lack of knowledge about the availability of Face Unlock on their devices (27% of nonusers) can be partially explained due to the fact that, with the exception of specialized media (e.g. computer magazines), this feature was not publicized at the time of our study. The importance of this is highlighted by the fact that the 8% of nonusers that mentioned security problems for not using Face Unlock were not aware of current security improvements to the system like "Wink to Unlock" which requires the user to wink to prove that the camera is not recording a static image.

Sense of Security

Even though the participants did, in many cases, not fully understand the technology of the specific system and even though they were not aware of current developments and improvements to Face Unlock, they were surprisingly good in estimating their relative security improvement/loss. For instance, all Face Unlock users were aware of the fact that it could potentially be spoofed with a photo of the user [1]. This indicates that, with respect to security, users make informed decisions and giving up security (e.g. for usability) often happens voluntarily.

CONCLUSION AND LIMITATIONS

Our survey provides first insights into the decision making process of the use of biometric authentication mechanisms on smartphones. Among others, our results show that, as opposed to previous work, trust and privacy issues are not major factors while usability is one of the top arguments for (not) using the systems. Furthermore, we provide recommendations such as considering the importance of "social compatibility" when developing biometric authentication systems for use on smartphones and thus potential public use.

Even though our study provides interesting insights into the topic, there are a few limitations that have to be considered carefully. For instance, the numbers of participants in some categories (e.g. Touch ID deactivations) is quite low. In addition, all study participants were US residents. This limits generalizability of the results. In future work, the study should be repeated with other populations to see if the results hold true for these as well.

Furthermore, at the time of the study, Face Unlock was significantly longer available than Touch ID. However, the results of the questionnaire indicate that most participants just recently started using both features with almost no early adopters in the Face Unlock group. Still, we cannot state with 100% certainty that this difference had no influence on the results. The study should be repeated in the next years to compare the results to our current insights.

REFERENCES

1. Anjos, A., and Marcel, S. Counter-measures to photo attacks in face recognition: A public database and a baseline. In *Proc. IJCB '11*, IEEE (2011), 1–7.
2. Bhagavatula, C., Iacovino, K., Kywe, S. M., Cranor, L. F., and Ur, B. Poster: Usability analysis of biometric authentication systems on mobile phones. *SOUPS Poster* (2014).
3. Coventry, L., De Angeli, A., and Johnson, G. Usability and biometric verification at the atm interface. In *Proc. CHI '03*, ACM (2003), 153–160.
4. Egelman, S., Jain, S., Portnoff, R. S., Liao, K., Consolvo, S., and Wagner, D. Are you ready to lock? understanding user motivations for smartphone locking behaviors. In *Proc. CCS '14*, ACM (2014), 750–761.
5. Hang, A., De Luca, A., Frison, K., von Zezschwitz, E., Tedesco, M., Kockmann, M., and Hussmann, H. Travel routes or geography facts? an evaluation of voice authentication user interfaces. In *Proc. INTERACT '13*, Springer (2013), 468–475.
6. Harbach, M., von Zezschwitz, E., Fichtner, A., De Luca, A., and Smith, M. It's a hard lock life: A field study of smartphone (un)locking behavior and risk perception. In *Proc. SOUPS '14*, USENIX Association (July 2014), 213–230.
7. Sieger, H., Kirschnick, N., and Möller, S. Poster: User preferences for biometric authentication methods and graded security on mobile phones. *SOUPS Poster* (2010).

Interrupt Now or Inform Later?: Comparing Immediate and Delayed Privacy Feedback *

Sameer Patil[†] **Roberto Hoyle**[♯] **Roman Schlegel**[‡] **Apu Kapadia**[♯] **Adam J. Lee**[§]
[♯]School of Informatics and Computing, Indiana University, Bloomington, IN 47408, USA
[§]Department of Computer Science, University of Pittsburgh, Pittsburgh, PA 15260, USA
[†]Yahoo Labs, 701 1st Avenue, Sunnyvale, CA 94089, USA
[‡]Corporate Research, ABB Switzerland Ltd., CH-5405 Baden-Dättwil, Switzerland
sameerpatil@yahoo-inc.com, rjhoyle@indiana.edu, roman.schlegel@ch.abb.com, kapadia@indiana.edu, adamlee@cs.pitt.edu

ABSTRACT
Feedback about privacy-affecting system operations is important for informed end-user privacy management. While feedback is most relevant if provided immediately, such delivery interrupts the user and risks disrupting ongoing tasks. The timing, volume, and nature of feedback is therefore critical for avoiding inopportune interruption. We varied the *timing* and *actionability* of feedback regarding accesses to a user's physical location. We found that the sense of privacy violation was heightened when feedback was immediate, but *not* actionable. While immediate and actionable feedback may sometimes be necessary, our findings suggest that moderately delayed feedback is often acceptable. A moderate delay may serve as a compromise to minimize interruption and avoid overly alarming reaction to immediate feedback. However, immediate and actionable feedback could still be beneficial when privacy sensitivity is high or ambiguous.

Author Keywords
Privacy; feedback; location sharing; experience sampling method; ESM.

INTRODUCTION AND RELATED WORK
With the growing adoption of technologies for interpersonal interaction, privacy has emerged as an important consideration. Yet, users typically find it difficult to understand and enact privacy preferences. Researchers have long argued for system feedback that helps users understand privacy-affecting system operations [1]. These operations include not just actions of the system but also interactive acts of the people with whom one interacts via the system [6, 7]. In particular, feedback increases system transparency and fosters the development of accurate mental models of its operations, thus helping users make more informed privacy decisions [6, 8].

Despite its usefulness, feedback also suffers from several disadvantages. In particular, feedback consumes cognitive resources and distracts users from ongoing tasks. Such disruption occurs even if feedback is purely informational, requiring no user action [3]. The resulting distraction grows with increasing feedback, eventually overwhelming the user. The demands on user attention are even greater when feedback is *actionable*, requiring the user to act on the information before the system can proceed. Inopportune interruptions resulting from actionable feedback can annoy users and may also lead them to pay less attention to the information or, worse, dismiss it altogether [2].

These challenges underscore that privacy feedback is most effective when delivered in the right manner at the right time at a manageable rate. Toward this end, researchers have tried to gauge user 'interruptibility' to avoid disrupting an ongoing task [5]. However, in the case of privacy feedback, knowing merely whether a user is interruptible may not suffice; for privacy-critical situations it might be necessary to interrupt at all times while for benign cases the most appropriate choice might be to avoid disruption even if the user is otherwise interruptible.

We carried out a user study in which we delivered feedback on privacy affecting system actions in two modes: *immediate* and *delayed*. Within each mode, we manipulated whether the feedback delivered information in a passive way or required active user action. Our results reveal important differences in the utility of privacy feedback in the different modes, suggesting that different modes may be useful for different privacy affecting situations. Our results motivate hybrid delivery of privacy feedback with varying levels of actionability and immediacy to deal with different kinds of privacy concerns.

METHOD
We built a prototype location gathering infrastructure called Locasa to conduct a study in which participants received feedback about hypothetical location inquiries by members

*A large part of this research was conducted while Sameer Patil and Roman Schlegel were researchers at Indiana University.

CHI 2015, April 18–23, 2015, Seoul, Republic of Korea.
Copyright 2015 ACM 978-1-4503-3145-6/15/04... $15.00
http://dx.doi.org/10.1145/2702123.2702165

of their social circle. We have previously provided detailed information and rationale regarding study design and procedures [4]. In this section, we summarize aspects of the study relevant for this Note.

Recruitment. We recruited participants from two communities: a college town (Bloomington, IN) and a metropolis (Pittsburgh, PA). Participation was spread over February to April 2013. To avoid priming, the study was advertised without revealing its privacy focus. The advertisement directed potential participants to a brief online screening questionnaire. Given the influence of culture on privacy, we sought to minimize cultural diversity of the sample by restricting participation to those over the age of 18 who indicated having lived in the US for at least 5 years. Since Locasa is an Android app, we further limited participation to Android users with cellular data access. We obtained informed consent from those who met these criteria.

Study setup. During setup, participants named four location recipients in the following categories: Family, Friends, Colleagues/Peers, and Acquaintances. Next, participants created any number of access-control rules based on day(s) and times(s) to specify when each group was allowed access to their location. During times not covered by the rules, location requests were denied. To ensure a stable set of rules for the study duration, we disallowed rule changes after setup. During the study, we simulated location requests from these 16 recipients. These hypothetical requests were distributed randomly throughout each day of the 15-day study period. For each request, the participant's access-control rules determined whether location would have been disclosed.

Study conditions. Participants were randomly assigned to one of two between-subject study conditions: 'actionable' vs. 'non-actionable' feedback.[1] Actionable feedback asked participants to decide whether to disclose their location to the requesting party. In contrast, non-actionable feedback *merely informed* participants whether location was disclosed to the requesting party based on the access-control rules specified during setup. Within each condition, participants received feedback in two ways: 'immediate' and 'delayed.' Immediate feedback was provided 5–6 random times throughout the day via Locasa's Android app (which also collected participants' locations at 15-minute intervals). On the other hand, delayed feedback was available by logging in to Locasa's Web interface, which showed location requests occurring since the previous login. For each study day, 8–10 randomly distributed location requests were generated for delayed feedback. In the non-actionable condition, delayed feedback informed participants whether their location was disclosed to the requesting party, just like immediate feedback. Since contextual actions are not possible with a delay, delayed feedback in the actionable condition asked participants about the actions they *would have* taken at the time of the location request.

Questionnaires. In all study conditions, a brief questionnaire accompanied each piece of feedback: participants were

[1] 'Actionable' and 'non-actionable' feedback conditions in this Note correspond respectively with the 'decision' and 'feedback' conditions reported in the previous study [4].

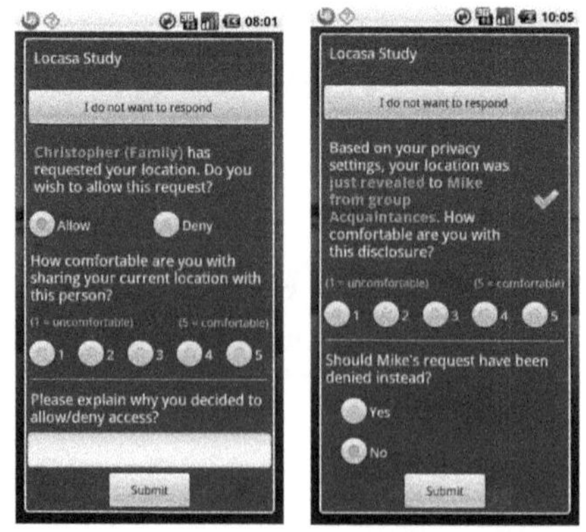

Figure 1. Immediate Feedback: Actionable (left) and Non-actionable (right).

asked to describe where they were, what they were doing, and whether their location/activity was unusual (with a five-point Likert item ranging from 'Not at all' to 'Extremely'). In the non-actionable conditions, participants could indicate whether their location should have been disclosed instead of being withheld, or vice versa, and provide open-ended explanations. In the actionable conditions, participants could enter open-ended explanations for their disclosure decisions. Figure 1 shows the questionnaires for the two conditions with immediate feedback delivered to the phone. Delayed feedback conditions presented the same questionnaires via the Web, along with a map showing where the corresponding accesses occurred.

Post-study questionnaire. At the conclusion of the 15-day study, participants completed an online post-study questionnaire that asked about experience with social media and location sharing, collected responses for scales on consumer and interpersonal privacy, and gathered demographics. We further conducted 10–15 minute semi-structured interviews with 26 participants who were willing to be interviewed.

Compensation. We used engagement based payments to ensure continued participation. Participants were paid \$3.30 for initial setup, \$0.15 for responding to a phone questionnaire, \$0.50 for responding to questionnaires via the Web at the end of each day, \$0.50 for answering *all* questionnaires on a given day, \$3.00 for answering the post-study questionnaire, and \$5.00 for the post-study interview. Participants could choose between an Amazon gift certificate and cash.

Our previous report [4] of this data was restricted to the two immediate feedback conditions delivered via the phone. This Note extends the analysis by additionally including the *delayed* versions of the respective feedback conditions.

FINDINGS

Thirty-five individuals qualified and completed the study: 19 in the non-actionable conditions and 16 in the actionable conditions. Although a majority comprised undergraduate and graduate students (aged 19–24), they spanned diverse fields of study. Many student participants were also employed part- or full-time. We did manage to recruit non-students; at least 10 participants were older than 24, with 3 older than 45.[2]

[2] We have ages for only 23 out of the 35 participants.

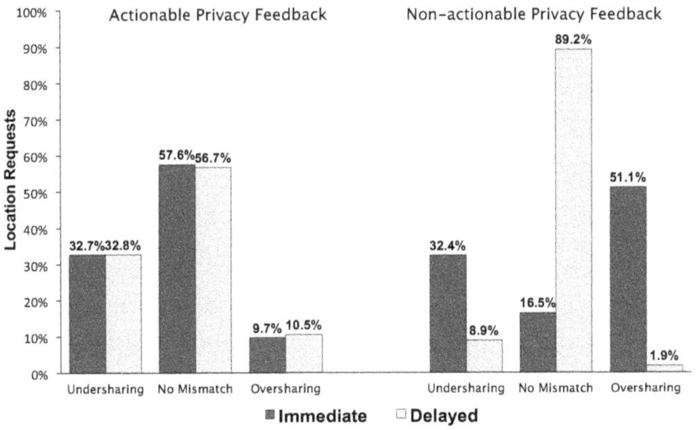

Figure 2. Mismatches between pre-specified privacy preference and contextual decision for actionable and non-actionable feedback conditions.

Across the four conditions, participants answered 5,753 questionnaires (actionable immediate: 939, actionable delayed: 1,608, non-actionable immediate: 1,095, and non-actionable delayed: 2,111). Participants in the non-actionable conditions were informed of the disclosure decision based on their access-control rules and asked for their agreement with the outcome. In contrast, participants in the actionable conditions were asked to make a disclosure decision *without being informed of the decision that would have been made by their access-control rules*.

We compared participant responses — agreement with pre-specified preferences in the non-actionable conditions and the actual decisions made in the actionable conditions — to the decisions reached by the access-control rules. Each instance where in-situ responses differed from pre-specified preferences was marked as a 'mismatch.' Mismatches were classified into two categories: 'undersharing' occurred when participants wished to reveal location even though it was withheld by pre-specified rules, while 'oversharing' occurred when participants expressed the desire to withhold location although their rules indicated otherwise.

Since the *occurrence* of mismatch and the *type* of mismatch (i.e., undersharing or oversharing) are binary, we employed binomial logistic regressions using each of these as the outcome variable. Study conditions, location context (such as recipient category and unusualness), and participant characteristics were the predictor variables. We tested for interaction among variables and included participant ID as a random effect to account for repeated measures. To obtain the most parsimonious models, we examined initial results and removed predictor variables and higher-order interactions that did not exhibit statistically significant effects.

We previously reported that for *immediate* feedback the non-actionable case evoked greater feelings of oversharing (see [4] for corresponding regression results). In this Note, we could dig deeper into this discrepancy due to the inclusion of matching study conditions with delayed feedback. Since participants in the immediate actionable condition made decisions without being informed of their initially specified privacy preference, we treated this condition as indicative of 'true' contextual desires to be employed as the comparison baseline. We then compared the baseline with the other conditions to examine the impact of the delay. As Figure 2 shows:

1. When feedback was actionable, the distribution of mismatch types stayed the same regardless of feedback timing (immediate or delayed).
2. In the case of non-actionable feedback, the feelings of oversharing almost completely disappeared when feedback was encountered after a delay.

Regression results confirmed that the distribution of mismatch type was significantly affected by feedback actionability as well as timing. There was a statistically significant interaction effect between feedback actionability and timing ($z = 8.63, p < 0.001$) indicating that mismatch distribution for non-actionable and actionable feedback was significantly different in the immediate and delayed conditions. Further, we found a statistically significant difference between immediate and delayed non-actionable feedback ($z = 11.04, p < 0.001$) but no difference for actionable feedback ($z = -0.375, p = 0.71$).

DISCUSSION AND IMPLICATIONS

As discussed in the previous section, delay affected actionable and non-actionable feedback differently. Baseline actionable feedback was unaffected by the delay. In comparison, non-actionable feedback evoked different and opposing reactions depending on the timing of delivery. When delivered immediately, it evoked a much greater sense of privacy violation. In contrast, a delay in delivery suppressed such feelings, leading to experiencing lower privacy violations than in the baseline condition. The overly alarming nature of immediate non-actionable feedback suggests that the immediate mode be reserved for the truly important and privacy-sensitive cases.

An alternative solution, of course, is to make *all* privacy feedback immediate (and actionable). The disruption resulting from such an approach makes it impractical and non-scalable. Moreover, our results show that only about 10% of requests in the baseline condition were a result of oversharing, i.e., indicative of a potential privacy violation. In other cases, immediate actionable feedback would have served no *privacy* purpose, yet would have interrupted the user. This is not to say, however, that feedback should never be immediately actionable. Such feedback is indeed necessary for avoiding oversharing. Our findings suggest several ways to keep the volume of immediate actionable feedback manageable:

- When the situation is not privacy-critical, provide feedback with a delay.
- Trigger immediate feedback at random times, particularly during initial usage when little is known about the user's contextual privacy choices.
- Utilize past decisions, along with relevant context, to detect likely cases of oversharing in order to target feedback to privacy-relevant cases.
- Examine past decisions to determine meaningful adjustments to user-specified privacy preferences that would reduce mismatches without compromising privacy.

Notably, there is a crucial framing difference between delayed feedback in the non-actionable and actionable conditions. In the case of actionable delayed feedback, participants were deciding what they would have done *at the time the location request occurred.* For non-actionable delayed feedback, however, participants answered based on their feelings about the decision *at the time of answering the question.* In other words, the reaction to non-actionable delayed feedback was influenced by hindsight and took into account whatever passed between the time of the request and the feedback. Passage of time does indeed allow various uncertainties to be resolved, thus changing prior assessments of privacy implications. In our study, passage of time typically resulted in lowering feelings of potential privacy violation.

We also point out that our findings hold methodological implications for the Experience Sampling Method (ESM). On the one hand, the lack of impact of delay in the actionable case suggests that ESM studies could conveniently gather additional data of equivalent quality via *delayed ESM*, keeping interruptions of ESM at manageable levels. On the other hand, the effect of delay on non-actionable feedback indicates that such delayed operation may be permissible when the topics involve *actions* rather than *feelings*; it seems that individuals are reasonably accurate in describing what they would have done in the recent past but find it difficult to recreate the intensity of their past feelings.

LIMITATIONS

Operational details of the study necessitated that the immediate and delayed conditions differ in terms of the feedback *interface* in addition to feedback timing. Feedback in the immediate conditions was presented via the phone while that in the delayed conditions was Web based. Therefore, it is conceivable that the results could be wholly or partially attributable to differences in the interface rather than timing. However, we believe that the contextual nature of privacy makes a strong case for attributing the findings to temporal factors.

Although we strived for breadth and diversity, a large fraction of our participants were students. Therefore, our sample cannot be considered representative of the broader US population and other cultures. On occasion, simulation resulted in queries from recipients who were either co-present with the participant or already knew the participant's location. Such scenarios would not arise in a field trial of a deployed location sharing system.

CONCLUSION

Feedback is an important and powerful mechanism for helping users understand system operation. Such transparency is particularly useful and essential for system actions that potentially impact user privacy. The contextual nature of privacy often demands immediate attention and action. Yet, this need for immediacy must be balanced with other considerations, such as disruption and/or cognitive overload, which can potentially diminish user attentiveness and undermine the utility of privacy feedback. Using the case of location sharing, our study shows that varying the timing and actionability of feedback leads to different experiences of privacy violations. Our findings suggest that immediate feedback is best reserved for the most privacy-sensitive or ambiguous situations and potentially for calibration and learning that enables a better match between privacy preferences and in-situ system decisions.

ACKNOWLEDGMENTS

We thank the study participants. We acknowledge Bart Knijnenburg for data analysis consultation and anonymous reviewers for helpful comments. This research was supported by NSF grants CNS-1016603, CNS-1252697, CNS-1017229, and CNS-1253204, and US DHS grant no. 2006-CS-001-000001, under the auspices of the Institute for Information Infrastructure Protection (I3P). The contents of this Note do not necessarily reflect the views of the sponsors.

REFERENCES

1. Bellotti, V., and Sellen, A. Design for privacy in ubiquitous computing environments. In *Proceedings of the Third European Conference on Computer-Supported Cooperative Work*, ECSCW (1993), 77–92.
2. Egelman, S., Cranor, L. F., and Hong, J. You've been warned: An empirical study of the effectiveness of Web browser phishing warnings. In *Proceedings of the ACM SIGCHI Conference on Human Factors in Computing Systems*, CHI (2008), 1065–1074.
3. Hudson, S. E., and Smith, I. Techniques for addressing fundamental privacy and disruption tradeoffs in awareness support systems. In *Proceedings of the ACM Conference on Computer Supported Cooperative Work*, CSCW (1996), 248–257.
4. Patil, S., Schlegel, R., Kapadia, A., and Lee, A. J. Reflection or action?: How feedback and control affect location sharing decisions. In *Proceedings of the ACM SIGCHI Conference on Human Factors in Computing Systems*, CHI (2014), 101–110.
5. Pejovic, V., and Musolesi, M. InterruptMe: Designing intelligent prompting mechanisms for pervasive applications. In *Proceedings of the ACM International Joint Conference on Pervasive and Ubiquitous Computing*, UbiComp (2014), 897–908.
6. Schlegel, R., Kapadia, A., and Lee, A. J. Eyeing your exposure: Quantifying and controlling information sharing for improved privacy. In *Proceedings of the Symposium on Usable Privacy and Security*, SOUPS (2011), 14:1–14:14.
7. Tsai, J. Y., Kelley, P., Drielsma, P., Cranor, L. F., Hong, J., and Sadeh, N. Who's viewed you?: The impact of feedback in a mobile location-sharing application. In *Proceedings of the ACM SIGCHI Conference on Human Factors in Computing Systems*, CHI (2009), 2003–2012.
8. Wang, Y., Leon, P. G., Scott, K., Chen, X., Acquisti, A., and Cranor, L. F. Privacy nudges for social media: An exploratory Facebook study. In *Proceedings of the 22nd International Conference on World Wide Web Companion*, WWW Companion (2013), 763–770.

From Care Plans to Care Coordination: Opportunities for Computer Support of Teamwork in Complex Healthcare

Ofra Amir[1] **Barbara J. Grosz**[1] **Krzysztof Z. Gajos**[1] **Sonja M. Swenson**[2] **Lee M. Sanders**[2]

[1]Harvard SEAS
Cambridge, MA USA
{oamir,grosz,kgajos}@seas.harvard.edu

[2]Stanford University
Stanford, CA USA
{sonjas1,leesanders}@stanford.edu

ABSTRACT
Children with complex health conditions require care from a large, diverse team of caregivers that includes multiple types of medical professionals, parents and community support organizations. Coordination of their outpatient care, essential for good outcomes, presents major challenges. Extensive healthcare research has shown that the use of integrated, team-based care plans improves care coordination, but such plans are rarely deployed in practice. This paper reports on a study of care teams treating children with complex conditions at a major university tertiary care center. This study investigated barriers to plan implementation and resultant care coordination problems. It revealed the complex nature of teamwork in complex care, which poses challenges to team coordination that extend beyond those identified in prior work and handled by existing coordination systems. The paper builds on a computational teamwork theory to identify opportunities for technology to support increased plan-based complex-care coordination and to propose design approaches for systems that enable and enhance such coordination.

Author Keywords
Care coordination; teamwork; care plan

ACM Classification Keywords
H.5.3 Group and Organization Interfaces: Computer-supported cooperative work

INTRODUCTION
The coordination of care for children with multiple, simultaneously occurring chronic conditions presents major healthcare challenges. These patients require care from multiple providers who are diverse in their expertise and work for different organizations. Despite widespread consensus on a need for greater coordination among providers, care for most of these children remains poorly coordinated [26]. As a result, they have high rates of unmet health needs, suboptimal physical functioning, and potentially preventable health care crises, and they account for a disproportionate share of health-system use and costs [31, 26].

Healthcare research has shown that effective systems of care for patients with complex chronic conditions require an *integrated care plan* that addresses patient-centered health goals and provides context for treatment decisions for all members of the care team [28, 2]. To better understand the barriers to forming and using such care plans, we conducted a study of care providers for children with complex conditions. We interviewed and observed representative team members in the Complex Primary Care Clinic (*CPCC*) at Stanford's Lucile Packard Children's Hospital, including parents of children with complex conditions, primary care providers (PCP), medical specialists, therapists and administrators.

The study revealed five characteristics of complex care that raise significant challenges to effective teamwork:

- ***F**lat-structure of team with consensus-driven plan development.*
- ***L**oosely coupled plans of individual caregivers.*
- ***E**xtended duration of plans over a child's life course.*
- ***C**ontinual distributed revision of caregivers' plans.*
- ***S**yncopated time scales of different providers.*

We more fully discuss each of these characteristics and their implications for care in the Discussion section. Taken together, they yield a teamwork setting, which we will refer to as *FLECS teamwork*.

FLECS teamwork differs fundamentally from the teamwork settings addressed by prior work in the social sciences and computer supported cooperative work (*CSCW*). A different approach is thus required for understanding and enabling effective FLECS teamwork. In this paper, we describe the use of a computational theory of collaboration, SharedPlans [19], which provides a specification of teamwork general enough to cover such teams. SharedPlans has been used in prior work to guide the design of computer agents operating as a team. We use it to identify mechanisms lacking in complex care teams and to suggest possible ways technology could provide such mechanisms.

The contributions of this paper are twofold: First, it presents a study of a broad range of members of care teams for children with complex chronic conditions. The study yields novel

CHI 2015, April 18 - 23 2015, Seoul, Republic of Korea

ACM 978-1-4503-3145-6/15/04 $ 15.00
http://dx.doi.org/10.1145/2702123.2702320

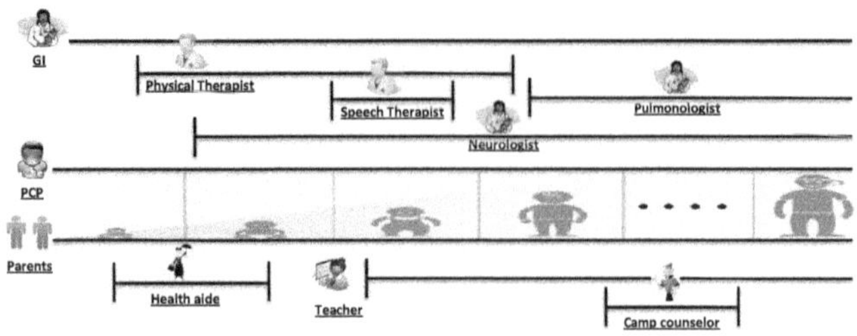

Figure 1. The complex care environment

findings specific to the challenge of implementing care plan–driven care and reveals the unique characteristics and complex nature of care teams. It also corroborates and extends prior general findings related to care coordination. Second, the paper draws on a formal computational teamwork theory to identify a set of teamwork mechanisms currently missing in teams caring for children with complex conditions, and it describes design implications for technology that could address these deficiencies and provide support for care teams' use of care plans. These design implications are also relevant to the design of technology for other teamwork settings with FLECS characteristics.

BACKGROUND AND RELATED WORK

This section describes the care environment of children with complex conditions and prior work on care coordination.

Care Teams

Children with complex conditions have multiple chronic, simultaneously occurring medical problems. Their care is significantly more complex than care for children with a single chronic disease (e.g., asthma), as it requires expertise from diverse medical specialists and other care providers whose treatments may interact. Care teams for such children are diverse and broad in scope, including not only physicians (PCPs and medical specialists) but also other types of healthcare providers (e.g., physical therapists) and people who work with the child in home and community settings (e.g., health aides, teachers). Henceforth, we refer to all caregivers who are not family members as *providers*. Providers differ in their expertise, and they address different aspects of a child's condition. Their involvement with the child's care may be continuous or intermittent, long or short term, as illustrated by the horizontal lines in Figure 1. The group of providers may change significantly over the years, either as a result of personnel changes or because the child's condition or a new developmental stage raise different needs.

Care Plans

The Chronic Care Model, which is the dominant blueprint for health-care solutions for adults and children with complex chronic conditions in the US, argues that effective patient care requires a collaborative health-care team, inclusive of an engaged, activated patient and family, supported by computer systems and with care framed by an integrated care plan [14]. According to this model, care plans should be organized around whole-person goals (e.g., school readiness) rather than organ-system goals (e.g., brain, lung).

A recent report by the Lucile Packard Foundation for Children's Health (LPFCH) [28] provides recommendations for the content of care plans and the process of developing them. It indicates that care plans should include clinical goals (e.g., feeding without a tube), family goals (e.g., going on a family trip) and "negotiated actions" (i.e., actions the team agrees upon) towards achieving the goals (e.g., starting occupational therapy, getting walking support device).

For example, a care plan might include a family-goal to travel in three months to Disneyland, and several actions toward this goal: (A1) optimize seizure medication; (A2) change feeding schedule from continuous to bolus to allow for at least 4 hours off a feeding tube; and (A3) get portable oxygen to be used during daytime naps at the park and train parents in its use. The patient status required to achieve this goal is reduced seizure frequency, lack of vomiting during bolus feeds, and parent comfort with using the portable oxygen. Persons responsible for these actions include the parent (A1, A2, A3), primary-care physician (A1, A2, A3), neurologist (A1), nutritionist (A2), lung specialist (A2, A3), home nurse (A3), and respiratory therapist (A3).

Inpatient and Outpatient Care Settings

Children with complex conditions receive most of their care in *outpatient* settings, and our study focuses on such settings. (When they need to be hospitalized their *inpatient* care is provided by a hospital-based care team.) The frequency with which these patients see particular medical providers varies depending on their conditions. The care team is distributed, and team members interact with the child and with each other less frequently than in inpatient settings. It is especially for outpatient periods that care plans need to be effectively deployed and care coordination mechanisms enhanced.

Care Coordination

Coordinated care leads to improved health outcomes for children with complex conditions and can reduce healthcare costs [15]. However, coordinating care across care teams is hard and care coordination is often not achieved [26]. O'Malley et al. [29, 10] studied medical practices' use of electronic medical records (EMR) to support care coordination. They found that while EMRs facilitate improved coordination within a single organization, they are ineffective for coordinating providers in different organizations and were also found to create information overload. According to the study, EMRs support linear processes rather than dynamic coordination processes and are optimized for billing uses rather than for provider and patient needs. In sum, current EMR systems do not provide mechanisms for supporting the coordination of team-based plans.

Human-computer interaction research has investigated systems to support patients in managing their own care [24, 6], but this work has focused on the patient alone and has not considered other care team members. The CSCW community has studied healthcare teams and developed tools for supporting them [16]. For example, prior work on coordination in inpatient settings has studied temporal and spatial coordination processes in hospital wards [7, 8], trauma-room coordi-

Role	N	Data Collection
Parents	13	Individual interviews with 4 parents (children ages ranged between 1.5 to 4 years old); focus group with 9 other parents who are also parent mentors (with children in their teens).
PCP	4	All were interviewed individually. Two of them were also observed for 2-3 hours.
Specialists	4	Individual interviews with a neurologist, pulmonologist, neonatologist and a cardiologist.
Therapists	8	3 focus groups with occupational and physical therapists (2–3 therapists in each interview).
Director of family-centered care	1	Participated in the parent focus group and in a meeting with the complex care program manager.
Care coordinator	1	Observation of 2 hours and informal conversations during that time.
Social Worker	1	Individual interview.
Program directors	2	Meeting with complex care program manager and medical director.

Table 1. Study participants.

nation [34], coordination of clinical and non-clinical staff [1], and collaborative information processes in care teams [32]. In outpatient settings, prior work has studied coordination in mobile teams (typically of therapists) and developed systems to support the loosely coupled work of such teams [30] and systems for supporting therapists' meetings [23]. While our work also addresses the need to coordinate care teams, our findings show that teamwork in complex care is significantly more complex than in these previously studied settings and thus requires new approaches for supporting coordination. We discuss these differences after presenting our findings.

RESEARCH SETTINGS AND METHODS

To better understand the challenges of care coordination and the barriers to implementing team-based care plans, we conducted a study over a period of 10 months during 2013–2014 that comprised observations and semi-structured interviews with parents and providers. Institutional Review Board approval was obtained. Most of the study was conducted in the Complex Primary Care Clinic (*CPCC*) at Stanford's Lucile Packard Children's Hospital, which operates a special complex care program. Interviews with physical and occupational therapists and a social worker were done at a nearby complex care clinic that shares many patients with the CPCC.

Participants

In the course of the study, we interviewed and observed representatives of different types of caregivers: parents, parent mentors (who are themselves parents of children with complex conditions), primary care physicians, medical specialists, therapists, a care coordinator, a social worker and administrators. Table 1 summarizes the participants by type and data collection methods. All parents we interviewed had children with complex conditions. The care teams for these children included 10–15 providers. For example, the care team for one family included a PCP, gastroenterologist (GI), neurologist, ear nose and throat doctor (ENT), a physical therapist (PT), occupational therapist (OT), speech therapist, and a school-based therapist. Another child's care team comprised 15 care providers including a PCP, cardiologist, liver transplant team, dermatologist, ENT, geneticist, GI, PT, OT, pulmonologist, and rehab specialist.

Data Collection

All interviews, focus groups and observations were conducted by the first and fourth author (some together and some separately) during visits to the CPCC in July 2013, November 2013 and March 2014. Notes were taken during interviews, focus groups and observations. The interviews with specialists and social worker and the focus groups with therapists were audio-recorded and transcribed.

Participants of the parent-mentors focus group, which lasted 2 hours, were asked to describe their experiences in managing the care for their children. They were asked to describe challenges that they face and the tools they use to manage their child's care and to brainstorm about tools that would help them better track and manage care.

In a one hour meeting with complex primary care program directors, we asked about care coordination processes and problems and about the types of support they thought would be useful to improve the use of care plans.

Individual interviews with parents lasted about an hour each. Parents were asked about the structure of the care team for their child, the use of care plans and care goals in their child's care, the tools they use to manage and track care, communication among team members and the challenges they face.

Interviews with PCPs and specialists and focus groups with therapists lasted about 45 minutes each. Interviewees were asked about their patient load, how often they see their complex patients, their use of plans and goals in care, the ways in which they gather information, their communication with parents and with other providers and the challenges they face.

In addition to interviews and observations, we collected relevant documents, including care plan templates, examples of specific care plans and patient information sheets.

Data Analysis

Analyses of interview and observation data (transcripts and notes) were done using affinity diagramming [11]. We iteratively clustered data into themes (e.g. "parents' frustration about lack of communication between providers", "physicians' view of care plans"). We discussed and revised these emerging themes over the course of several sessions.

STUDY FINDINGS

This section presents study findings on complex care teams and their use of care goals and care plans. The study revealed the complex FLECS nature of the teamwork in which care teams engage and resulting challenges to implementing long term team-based care plans. Extended duration and loosely coupled caregiver activities are inherent properties of such care. The section thus focuses on the main study findings with respect to other characteristics of FLECS teamwork. It also describes the communication deficiencies that were revealed as communication is key to teamwork.

Consensus-Driven Plan Development

Team-based care plans require that care teams, including the parents and patients (if they are old enough), reach consensus on goals for a child. Our findings indicate, to the contrary, that at present care goals are typically defined separately by individual providers. Furthermore, their use varies among providers: while for some setting and tracking goals is a regular part of their practice, others set goals only at times of major health events (e.g., new diagnosis) or do not set goals at all. Conversations between providers and parents about goals vary greatly depending on the family and the provider. Some families have a clear idea of goals whereas others do not feel confident about setting goals. Some providers discuss goals with parents regularly while others do not discuss goals at all.

Of all providers, therapists (OT and PT) are most accustomed to working with care goals. They have a more standardized process for setting and tracking them than other providers. Therapists said that they usually set 2 or 3 goals related to mobility and feeding, which are challenging areas for most infants with complex conditions. A sample PT goal is that of a child achieving the transition from sit to stand, while a sample OT goal is that of a child no longer needing a feeding tube. Therapists often define subgoals (i.e., smaller steps) toward achieving a larger goal.

When asked how he works with a family to set goals, one specialist said: "I ask parents about seizures, skin infections. I ask about quality of life – Is the kid sleeping? Is the parent sleeping? Have they developed a strategy? I also ask the parents what is their top priority. I find that single question among the most helpful I ask." For another specialist, discussions about goals usually arise when there is a life shortening diagnosis, near the end of life or when the patient is hospitalized. In these situations she asks the parents "What are [your] goals for [your] child... How much would you put them through for treating this illness." They then decide on a treatment plan depending on the desires of the family.

Many providers discussed the difficulties of setting goals with parents. One therapist said that some parents have very specific goals such as the child not tripping when walking, while other parents have very vague goals such as wanting their child "to be better". A specialist commented, "different patients have a different idea about goals. Many patients are taken aback by it... I tend to give them ideas."

Some of our findings corroborated prior work. For instance, in a study on goal settings for elderly patients [35], providers said that patients sometimes feel uncomfortable discussing goals as they expect physicians to tell them what their goals are. On the other hand, some patients felt that physicians did not have time to discuss goals and did not engage in such high-level discussions.

Our findings also reveal substantial new challenges specific to complex care teams. In particular, the different processes and approaches to goals of various providers and the lack of joint goal setting by the team create significant difficulties for parents: They need to prioritize goals because "everyone wants to work on everything", and they also need to track the various goals. While parents frequently discuss goals with therapists, they said that with some doctors "goals don't come up at all" and that they would have liked to discuss the therapists' goals with other providers. These challenges are further exacerbated by the fact that parents have little experience in goal setting: they are often uncomfortable with the idea itself and when they do finally engage, they have difficulty articulating goals that are neither too specific nor too vague.

Continual Distributed Revision of Plans

Our study revealed that current care plans are usually individual provider plans, which are not well integrated into team plans. Parents have difficulties tracking these separate plans. Given the evolving condition of children with complex conditions, plans often become obsolete, and replanning is required. According to both parents and providers, however, even when team plans are implemented, they are rarely consulted or revised.

Furthermore, the nature of care plans varies, with some being simply a list of actions without any clearly specified connection to goals. For example, one PCP's care plan included a list of diagnoses, a high-level assessment of the patient and a list of low-level treatment actions (e.g., take new medication) and required tests (e.g., conducting a sleep study). This list was not organized around goals and was not coordinated with the plans of other team members. Parents expressed frustration at the use of such plans: "sometimes the care plan is a set of tests and it is not clear what the *plan* is [emphasis ours]."

To implement team-based care plans, "Pediatric Advanced Comprehensive Care Team (PACT) chats" are being held for patients in the complex primary care clinic. PACT chats include "core members" of the care team as identified by the family. They meet together to discuss care plans for the patient. PACT chats aim to facilitate a setting for the team to create a joint, centralized planning process. As one specialist reported, however, they are "totally not scalable" as they require getting all team members together at the same time, and the meetings themselves take a long time.

When a severe acute condition arises and a child transitions to inpatient settings (i.e., is hospitalized), a "care conference" might be initiated. In care conferences, a large number of team members meet together in one room to discuss the patient's condition and decide on next treatment steps. Care conferences greatly help everyone "get on the same page", but they occur rarely, usually only when there is a severe acute condition. They mostly involve team members from within the hospital and only some outpatient providers participate.

In outpatient settings, replanning is usually done in a distributed manner. Providers might revise their individual plans when they see a patient, but typically do not coordinate with other providers when they do so. To address this problem, the complex primary care clinic has established "status chats" with a smaller number of team members to follow-up on the patient's care plan. However, as with PACT chats, these meetings are hard to coordinate and do not scale well. One specialist described an additional problem with the ongoing tracking of plans: "One of the issues with the complex care initiative is that the PACT chats and all the status chats have to be provider initiated, and so if you don't remember to do it or there's no one coordinating it, it's like where is it going, where do you even look for it?".

These findings highlight the unique difficulties care teams of children with complex conditions experience in maintaining a coordinated care plan: While team members frequently revise their individual plans for addressing a particular aspect of the child's care, there are rarely opportunities for team members to discuss their plans together, and there are currently no effective processes or tools to support them in ensuring that their distributed activities are coordinated.

Syncopated Time Scales

Providers differ in their frequency and level of involvement in the plan. PCPs see their patients 3 to 4 times a year, and possibly more during times of acute conditions. Specialists typically see patients 2 to 3 times a year (and when an acute condition occurs). While PCPs are concerned with the overall status of the child, specialists are more focused on monitoring and treating the one facet of a child's condition related to their particular speciality. Therapists meet with patients one to three times a week and are thus more involved than physicians in the delivery of day-to-day care.

As a result of their different timescales and level of involvement in a child's care, providers require different information. Parents reported synthesizing and shaping information differently depending on the provider with whom they are talking. For instance, they might share information related to seizures with the neurologist and information related to feeding with the GI, shaping their choices by what they think is most closely related to that provider's aspect of care. In addition, even when asked similar questions by providers, parents felt that different answers were expected. As one parent said, "a doctor asks if she is walking and expects a yes/no answer; a PT will ask how she is walking and how much progress she has made." Another parent said that the medical team might monitor the child's progress through swallow studies that are typically done only 1 to 3 times a year, while the occupational therapists are much more involved in day-to-day feeding therapies, and that there isn't much conversation between the two.

Providers also differ in the timelines they set for goals and the ways they track progress towards those goals. Therapists set 6–12 month goals, monitor progress and explicitly document goals and progress toward them in their reports of an evaluation that typically occurs every 6 months. Specialists, on the other hand, said that they usually do not set goal timelines. One specialist said he does not do so, because of the uncertainty about the development of the child's condition: "The timeline is the next visit [...] So much of it is beyond their [parents'] control." As for tracking goals, some specialists said they revisit goals at each clinic visit (typically every 4 or 6 months). Another said, "I like seeing my patients quarterly, because then at the sick visits you can deal with just the illness, but when you have a visit where there's nothing going on and they're happy, then you have an opportunity to talk about what the goals are [...] being honest about things."

The different timescales in which providers operate and their different involvement in care pose additional challenges for care coordination. Each of the providers has partial information about the child's status and obtains it at different times. Therefore, it is hard to establish a complete picture of the child's condition at any moment. When providers obtain new information, they need to decide whether that information should be shared with other providers without having complete knowledge of others' plans. In practice, providers reported that such communication is often deficient.

Communication Among the Care Team

We also investigated the ways providers and parents communicate and asked them how they determined the information to communicate, because these processes are essential to effective team-based care plan formation and use.

Medical providers often belong to different organizations and frequently are unable to access to each others' medical notes. Hence, they seldom have the full picture of a child's condition. Team members with access to others' records are often overwhelmed by the massive amount of information confronting them. They reported that they often miss important information. One specialist said "I use my own savvy to figure out what happened to the patient since I saw them [...] It's all manual. If something big happened I'll get a phone call."

Providers described communication with other providers as slow and deficient. Most communication between providers is asynchronous, done through email, letters and notes. Providers who are within the hospital system can copy other providers on notes they enter into the EMR. However, one specialist remarked that "figuring out exactly what [the other provider] want[s] you to read requires that you read [their] whole [individual treatment] plan", and that there is lack of feedback when sending information: "You don't know if [other providers] read it... I get stuff all the time, too, and I don't always review my chart in a timely fashion."

As a result of these communication problems, parents find themselves responsible for transmitting information between providers, and are frustrated by this situation: "We need to relay information back and forth... We wanted [the providers] to be able to talk to each other in one room." One specialist noted a problem that arises when families transmit information between providers: "The family is telling me about what has happened [since the last visit] and they say 'this happened and we went to the doctor', and I really don't know what the doctor thought." Parents are often asked about meetings with other providers but do not remember all of the details from such past meetings. In addition, when new providers join the team or when parents call after-hours, they need to re-explain their child's condition. Parents also expressed frustration at providers not sharing information with them more proactively. According to parents, communication during transitions from inpatient to outpatient settings is crucial, but often lacking. Parents described transition times as especially stressful and said that they would like to have more information to prepare them and make them more confident about taking care of the child themselves.

Our findings corroborate many prior findings, including the ineffectiveness of EMRs [29], lack of communication among providers [37], and families' frustration with this lack [38]. Our study expands these results, showing that EMRs are even less effective when providers from multiple organizations are involved, and that identifying relevant information is more difficult for providers in these settings. It also uncovered new problems, for instance, the difficulty of establishing common knowledge when communication is asynchronous and there are no means of determining whether other providers have seen information sent to them. It further identified a crucial communication gap at times of care transitions.

DISCUSSION

Our study reveals many challenges confronting care teams for children with complex conditions. In this section, we first reflect on these findings in the context of a recent report on the use of care plans in complex care [28], showing that many aspirations of the healthcare community are currently not realized. Next, we discuss the unique teamwork challenges for care teams for children with complex conditions that make the implementation of care plans especially hard in this setting. Finally, we discuss implications for design of technology support for care teams.

Care Plans: As They Are, As They Should Be

In support of the drive toward the implementation of integrated, team care plans for children with complex conditions, and to encourage their adoption and use, the Lucile Packard Foundation for children's healthcare (LPFCH) recently published a comprehensive report entitled "Achieving a Shared Plan of Care with Children and Youth with Special Health Care Needs". In their report, they outline the "10 Principles for Successful Use of a Shared Plan of Care" [28]. These principles, listed in the left column of Table 2, were identified by a panel of physicians, care coordinators and family advocates experienced in complex care and were informed by prior research on complex care coordination. This section reflects on our study findings in light of the aspirations for the use of care plans described in the LPFCH report.

Our findings reveal that many of the principles for successful implementation of care plans are currently not met, as summarized in the right column of Table 2, and that achieving them will require overcoming several barriers. These barriers cluster into four areas, which we order according to their focus on plans per se.

First, successful care plan implementation requires an integrated care plan with shared goals, implemented as a shared document that is monitored and revised over time (Principles 6, 7 and 9). Our findings reveal, however, that in current practice there are typically multiple individual plans formed by different providers, rather than a single shared team plan, and that providers are typically unaware of each other's plans. Even when team-based care plans are successfully implemented, they are rarely monitored or updated, despite the uncertainty in the outcomes of the initial plan and the inevitable, often unexpected, changes in the child's condition.

Second, successful use of care plans requires that communication among team members be clear, frequent and timely (Principle 2), as does care coordination in general. Our findings highlight many difficulties in achieving the requisite levels of communication and information sharing, including information overload, slow and unreliable communication channels and unclear communication between providers and parents. They show that providers cannot easily access or find all relevant information and thus do not have a full understanding of the child (Principles 3 and 5).

Third, care plans need to address the challenges of parent and family engagement and their integration into provision of care (Principle 1). Prior research on patient-centered care has found that patients and families are often not sufficiently engaged as a result of language barriers, cultural issues, the emotionally overwhelming situation, or providers' lack of experience with engaging parents [13, 9]. Our study revealed similar barriers (not reported in this paper as they largely replicate prior findings).

Fourth, care plans need to support transitions in care (Principle 8). In our interviews, both providers and parents described transition situations as very stressful, and families expressed the desire to be given more information and to be better prepared so they would feel more confident about meeting their new responsibilities.

Barriers to Effective Care Plan Implementation

Our study exposed the complex nature of teamwork in complex care, revealing five characteristics that, in combination, distinguish it fundamentally from other teamwork settings. In summary, these are,

- *Flat-structure, consensus driven plan development*: goal-setting requires consensus of multiple caregivers, with no single decision-maker "in charge".
- *Loosely coupled*: the activities of care providers are largely decoupled, but identifying interactions between their activities is crucial for preventing conflicts.
- *Extended duration*: care plans extend over months to years, during which a child's condition evolves.
- *Continual distributed revision*: care teams must create and frequently update well-coordinated care plans while rarely (if ever) meeting as a whole.
- *Syncopated time scales*: the timescales on which care providers interact with the child vary greatly from several times a week to once or twice a year.

These FLECS teamwork characteristics make the implementation of care plans in these settings particularly challenging. The extended duration of plans combined with uncertainty in outcomes of treatments and changes in the child's condition result in a need for ongoing revision of the goals and plans. The disparate timescales and involvement in the care plan pose difficulties for providers in keeping track of the child's current condition and plan status, and in coordinating their updated plans with others. Despite their different level of involvement in care, it is crucial that all team members reach consensus about the high-level care goals, as these goals guide their individual treatment plans. It is also important for them to be aware of changes in others' plans that might affect their own plans and to avoid undesired interactions when updating their plans. These challenges are further exacerbated by the fact that, for most providers, participating

	Principle	Study Findings
1	Children, youth and families are actively engaged in their care.	Engaging families is a complex process: families are overwhelmed by the child's condition; family engagement is a new concept and many providers do not feel comfortable with it.
2	Communication with and among their medical home team is clear, frequent and timely.	Communication is typically infrequent and slow. Providers often do not communicate among themselves, leading to lost information and to parents being responsible for transmitting information between providers.
3	Providers/team members base their patient and family assessments on a full understanding of child, youth and family needs, strengths, history, and preferences.	Team members are often focused on their aspect of the care and do not have a shared "big picture" view of the child's overarching goals.
4	Youth, families, health care providers, and their community partners have strong relationships characterized by mutual trust and respect.	Our study did not focus on this issue, but our findings show team members do not all know each other.
5	Family-centered care teams can access the information they need to make shared, informed decisions.	Team members cannot access all of the information about the patient. When they can access it, they are typically overwhelmed by the amount of information and have difficulties finding the *relevant* information.
6	Family-centered care teams use a selected plan of care characterized by shared goals and negotiated actions; all partners understand the care planning process, their individual responsibilities, and related accountabilities.	Different team members have different concepts and uses of care plans and care goals. There is no clear process for defining and revising team care plans.
7	The team monitors progress against goals, provides feedback and adjusts the plan of care on an ongoing basis to ensure that it is effectively implemented.	Progress towards goals is often not continuously monitored and care plans are not updated frequently. In addition, different providers set goals separately rather than as a team. Thus, even when monitoring is done it does not contribute much to achieving coordinated care.
8	Team members anticipate, prepare and plan for all transitions (e.g., early intervention to school; hospital to home; pediatric to adult care).	Parents feel they lack information in times of transitions, which they find especially stressful as responsibility shifts to them (e.g., in- to outpatient care) or when new providers join the team.
9	The plan of care is systematized as a common, shared document; it is used consistently by every provider within an organization and by acknowledged providers across organizations.	Different team members have different concepts and uses of care plans and care goals. Typically there are many different plans rather than a single team plan.
10	Care is subsequently well coordinated across all involved organizations/systems.	Care coordination is very hard to achieve, both between organizations and within organizations.

Table 2. Principles for successful use of care plans (left column) and findings from our study that point out the barriers in achieving them (right column).

on the care team for such patients is an exceptional situation, beyond the typical care they were trained to provide — most of their patients do not have multiple conditions nor require interaction and coordination with so many other providers. Some of the providers (e.g., PCPs in complex care clinics) are involved with many different care teams, each with a different team composition, and each operating over an extended period of time, often years.

The challenges faced by the care teams in complex care go beyond those previously studied in healthcare teamwork. In particular, the team coordination challenges they experience are not addressed by existing theories and tools. Prior studies of inpatient team coordination typically investigated the coordination of temporal activities (e.g., scheduling of operations [7]). In such settings the goals are clear (e.g., find a feasible, preferred schedule) and team members operate in the same timescale (plans are made for a specific day). When replanning is needed it is usually done in a centralized manner by a designated team member (e.g., the charge nurse might reschedule operations if an acute patient arrives [8]) and the changes are communicated by that person.

Prior work on outpatient settings has studied the coordination of mobile home care teams [30]. Such mobile teams share some characteristics with complex care teams, namely their activities are typically loosely coupled and they often do not meet together to coordinate. However, these teams are smaller than complex care teams and their high-level care plan is determined by single person (a case manager). Providers do not need to reach consensus about goals and their cooperation is not strictly required [30].

Foundations for Design of Systems to Support Complex Care Teams

For complex care teams to develop and successfully use long-term care plans, as well as for providers to operate as a team, requires systems able to support FLECS teamwork, and in particular, technology capable of supporting the collaborative, mutual consensus decision-making of a distributed, diverse team whose members operate on different timescales and seldom if ever meet as a full group. These systems must also accommodate team membership changing over the extended duration of complex-care plans.

The social science and CSCW communities have investigated teamwork extensively and developed theories and tools for supporting team coordination. Such work has studied teamwork in various domains, exploring various characteristics of the collaborative setting (e.g., mobile teams [30], co-located teams [32]), team structure (e.g., hierarchical and non-hierarchical teams [20], team homogeneity) and the nature of tasks performed by teams (e.g., loosely-coupled activities and highly interdependent tasks [22]). The FLECS teamwork characteristics exhibited by complex care teams distinguish it from the teamwork studied in prior work. As a result, existing tools and approaches do not fully address the challenges FLECS teams face.

In contrast, research in multi-agent systems (MAS) has developed several models of collaboration that more closely match the characteristics of FLECS teamwork. Each provides a formal specification for the design of computer agents able to robustly act collaboratively as members of a distributed team; they differ in the facets of teamwork they emphasize. The

Joint Intentions (JI) [27] formalization focuses on a specification of the mental attitudes required for teamwork. Planned Team Activity (PTA) [36] addresses issues of task allocation and team formation. The SharedPlans (SP) [19, 18] formalization directly represents partiality and evolution of plans. To analyze the opportunities for technology to support complex care, we chose SP, because it presumes only partial plans, distributed teams acting under uncertainty and the need for plans to evolve dynamically. (These assumptions contrast with JI and PTA which assume that the team has a complete, fully expanded plan.) SP requires certain group decision-making mechanisms, but not centralized replanning or complete knowledge of all team members' plans. It thus better fits the FLECS teamwork characteristics.

SP has been used to improve performance of multi-agent computer systems teams [39], as the model for intentional structure in dialogue systems [33], and as the basis of design for collaborative human-computer interface systems [5, 17]. While designed to guide the development of computer agents, it also provides a framework for identifying coordination mechanisms missing in complex care teams and needed to support their team-based plans.

SP is rooted in the observation that collaborative plans are not simply a collection of individual plans, but rather a tight interleaving of mutual beliefs and (coordinated) intentions of different team members. It specifies the beliefs and intentions required of team members for successful collaborative activities. In particular, SP requires that (SP1) each team member commit to (i.e., form specific intentions regarding) the team's performance of the group activity; (SP2) team members establish agreement on a "recipe" for carrying out the group action and establish mutual belief they are using that recipe; SP allows for recipes to be partial, expanded over time, and revised; (SP3) the group agrees on an allocation of tasks in the recipe according to participants' abilities to carry them out (i.e., decompose tasks and allocate work appropriately); (SP4) team members commit to performing tasks allocated to them (i.e., adopt intentions to do those tasks); (SP5) team members commit to the success of others in doing their tasks (i.e., adopt intentions that their teammates succeed).

According to SP, only the team members selected for doing a subtask determine and know in detail the recipe for that subtask. For example, the neurologist does not need to know the full details of the PT's plan for getting the child to walk, and the PT does not need to know the full details of the neurologist's plan for treating seizures. SP handles the problem of interaction among loosely coupled tasks through the required commitments to the overall team activity and to the success of teammates (SP1 and SP5) and general axioms of intention. These commitments result in several desired behaviors of team members. In particular, they necessitate communication among team members when any of them comes to believe that plans for subparts of the activity interact or when new information is obtained that could affect others' plans.

Thus, importantly, SP handles the tension between the low communication overhead of loose coupling (and the resultant lack of shared information about plan details) and coordination needs (sharing information that matters because of potential plan interactions) by requiring communication when essential, but not full sharing of all plan details by all participants. The need for such *efficient* communication was evident in our study: some of the providers we interviewed reported that when complete plans or notes are sent to them, they are unable to determine the information most important to consider, and they do not review the information in a timely manner as a result of this information overload.

We illustrate several desired behaviors engendered by SP with examples from complex care settings. The commitments to the overall team activity and to the success of teammates require that team members inform others if they learn that their plans are failing or likely to fail. For example, in the complex care domain, if the physical therapist learns in her session that the child's seizures have worsened, she should notify team members who are working toward the goal of optimizing seizure medication (in this case the PCP and the neurologist). Similarly, when team members update their plans, they should notify others about changes if their plans might affect others' plans. For example, if the GI decides to start feeding the child by mouth instead of through a tube, she should notify the nutritionist and occupational therapist who also address feeding issues. Further, although not directly involved in feeding, the respiratory therapist should also be notified because breathing and feeding often interact.

While such team behaviors and communication protocols are desired, they are hard to achieve in practice in complex care teams. The examples above assumed that team members had sufficient knowledge about others' plans and about the team's goals to realize that information should be shared. Our findings, however, show that care providers do not have this knowledge. Thus, it is unlikely that team members would exhibit the behaviors SP prescribes. However, SP also suggests ways in which technology could support care teams and help achieve desired team behaviors. The applications of SP in multi-agent systems demonstrate that it is in fact both feasible and efficient to allow individual team members to dynamically modify their individual plans and that only relatively limited communication is necessary to ensure that actions of a team members do not interfere with others' actions.

A SharedPlans-based analysis of complex care team needs suggests the following key roles for technology for supporting complex care teams:

- Make the care plan "ever present", adapting the content and form of its presentation to individual team members based on their involvement in the plan and context of use.
- Support efficient information sharing by team members.
- Enable care team members to easily adapt and expand parts of the plan, while ensuring their changes do not conflict with others' activities.

Making the care plan "ever present" will support team members in establishing and maintaining agreement and mutual belief about the high-level team plan and allocation of tasks (SP2 and SP3). Currently, these requirements do not hold in complex care teams as there are no mechanisms to support them. While care providers want their teammates to succeed, they currently do not have sufficient information about others' plans to act in a way that supports others or at least does not conflict with their activities. Efficient information sharing will help team members act in a way that does not conflict with others' plans (SP5). The partiality and dynamic nature that SP assumes, and that complex care plans exhibit, leads to the need for enabling easy plan adaptation and expansion.

Providing this support for care teams likely requires the design of intelligent interactive systems that reason about the care plan and the context of each team member in the plan to determine the parts of the plan that should be presented and the information to proactively share with each team member. Specifically, adapting the presentation of the care plan to a particular team member and context of use requires reasoning about the role of that team member in the care plan, the context of interaction (e.g., clinic visit, quick review of the patient's status), and the history of interactions with the patient (when the patient was last seen) and with the system (e.g., what information is already known).

Deciding what information to proactively share with team members requires similar reasoning. In addition, such reasoning needs to consider the importance and urgency of information about the status of the plan and changes made to it to determine when to share that information (e.g., immediately or during the next clinic visit). These information sharing challenges are beyond the current state-of-the-art in multi-agent systems research [4]. Given the limited time of care providers, it is also important to reason about interruption management [21] when making decisions about the timing of sharing information.

Lastly, to reason about the importance of information to team members, such systems will need to get sufficient details from team members about their plans. Therefore, the systems will need to incorporate mechanisms for eliciting information in a manner that fits providers' workflows and does not require much effort. The representation of plans also needs to be flexible enough to allow for team members to provide incomplete descriptions of plans that can be easily adapted with time.

CONCLUSION

In this paper, we report the findings of a study of teams providing outpatient care for children with complex conditions, focusing on their conceptualizations and use of team-based care plans, which have been shown to improve care coordination and health outcomes. We identify the FLECS characteristics of teamwork in the complex care environment, which pose challenges to team planning and coordination beyond those considered by existing theories and tools from the social sciences and CSCW. We draw on SharedPlans, a computational theory of collaboration, to suggest ways in which technology could support complex care teams and to specify capabilities that such technology will need to provide.

Our study findings also raise additional opportunities for technology to support care teams, including systems for explaining and simplifying medical information [12, 25], summarizing providers' notes [3] and supporting low-level coordination activities such as scheduling appointments and ordering equipment. However, some of the challenges revealed in our study, such as the lack of experience of both providers and parents in setting care goals, will likely require better training for providers and mentoring for families and will not be solved by technology alone.

Systems able to support FLECS teamwork have the potential to improve the coordination and effectiveness of teams in many other settings within and beyond the healthcare domain. For example, teamwork in rescue and recovery efforts, software development projects and research collaborations all exhibit some or all of the FLECS characteristics, and would benefit from greater support of team coordination.

Acknowledgments. The work was funded in part by the Nuance Foundation, a Sloan research fellowship and a CIMIT student award. We thank Stan Rosenschein for helpful discussions, and Katharina Reinecke and Roni Stern for feedback on an earlier draft of this manuscript. A special thanks goes to the study participants for sharing their experiences.

REFERENCES

1. Abraham, J., and Reddy, M. C. Moving patients around: a field study of coordination between clinical and non-clinical staff in hospitals. In *Proc. CSCW 08'*, ACM (2008), 225–228.
2. Adams, S., Cohen, E., Mahant, S., Friedman, J. N., MacCulloch, R., and Nicholas, D. B. Exploring the usefulness of comprehensive care plans for children with medical complexity (cmc): a qualitative study. *BMC Pediatrics 13*, 10 (2014).
3. Afantenos, S., Karkaletsis, V., and Stamatopoulos, P. Summarization from medical documents: a survey. *Artificial intelligence in medicine 33*, 2 (2005), 157–177.
4. Amir, O., Grosz, B. J., Law, E., and Stern, R. Collaborative health care plan support. In *Proc. AAMAS 13'*, AAMAS (2013), 793–796.
5. Babaian, T., Grosz, B. J., and Shieber, S. M. A writer's collaborative assistant. In *Proc. IUI 02'*, ACM (2002), 7–14.
6. Ballegaard, S. A., Hansen, T. R., and Kyng, M. Healthcare in everyday life: designing healthcare services for daily life. In *Proc. CHI 08'*, ACM (2008), 1807–1816.
7. Bardram, J. E. Temporal coordination–on time and coordination of collaborativeactivities at a surgical department. *CSCW 9*, 2 (2000), 157–187.
8. Bardram, J. E., and Hansen, T. R. Why the plan doesn't hold: a study of situated planning, articulation and coordination work in a surgical ward. In *Proc. CSCW 10'*, ACM (2010), 331–340.
9. Barry, M. J., and Edgman-Levitan, S. Shared decision makingthe pinnacle of patient-centered care. *New England Journal of Medicine 366*, 9 (2012), 780–781.

10. Bates, D. W. Getting in step: electronic health records and their role in care coordination. *Journal of general internal medicine 25*, 3 (2010), 174–176.
11. Beyer, H., and Holtzblatt, K. Contextual design. *interactions 6*, 1 (1999), 32–42.
12. Bickmore, T. W., Pfeifer, L. M., and Paasche-Orlow, M. K. Using computer agents to explain medical documents to patients with low health literacy. *Patient Education and Counseling 75*, 3 (2009), 315–320.
13. Carman, K. L., Dardess, P., Maurer, M., Sofaer, S., Adams, K., Bechtel, C., and Sweeney, J. Patient and family engagement: a framework for understanding the elements and developing interventions and policies. *Health Affairs 32*, 2 (2013), 223–231.
14. Coleman, K., Austin, B. T., Brach, C., and Wagner, E. H. Evidence on the chronic care model in the new millennium. *Health affairs 28*, 1 (2009), 75–85.
15. Fiks, A., Mayne, S., Localio, A., Alessandrini, E., and Guevara, J. Shared decision-making and health care expenditures among children with special health care needs. *Pediatrics 129*, 1 (2012), 99–107.
16. Fitzpatrick, G., and Ellingsen, G. A review of 25 years of cscw research in healthcare: Contributions, challenges and future agendas. *CSCW 22*, 4-6 (2013), 609–665.
17. Gal, Y., Reddy, S., Shieber, S. M., Rubin, A., and Grosz, B. J. Plan recognition in exploratory domains. *Artif. Intell. 176*, 1 (Jan. 2012), 2270–2290.
18. Grosz, B. J., and Hunsberger, L. The dynamics of intention in collaborative activity. *Cognitive Systems Research 7*, 2 (2006), 259–272.
19. Grosz, B. J., and Kraus, S. Collaborative plans for complex group action. *Artif. Intell. 86*, 2 (1996), 269–357.
20. Hinds, P., and McGrath, C. Structures that work: social structure, work structure and coordination ease in geographically distributed teams. In *Proc. CSCW 06'* , ACM (2006), 343–352.
21. Horvitz, E., and Apacible, J. Learning and reasoning about interruption. In *Proceedings of the 5th international conference on Multimodal interfaces*, ACM (2003), 20–27.
22. Hutchins, E. *Cognition in the Wild*, 8 ed. Bradford Books. University Press Group Limited, 1996.
23. Kientz, J. A., Hayes, G. R., Abowd, G. D., and Grinter, R. E. From the war room to the living room: decision support for home-based therapy teams. In *Proc. CSCW 06'*, ACM (2006), 209–218.
24. Klasnja, P., Civan Hartzler, A., Unruh, K. T., and Pratt, W. Blowing in the wind: unanchored patient information work during cancer care. In *Proc. CHI 10'*, ACM (2010), 193–202.
25. Law, E., Grosz, B. J., Sanders, L., and Fischer, S. H. SimplyPut: A Crowdware System for Improving Health Literacy. In *Proc. HAIDM Workshop*, AAMAS (2013).
26. Leape, L. *Order From Chaos: Accelerating Care Integration*. National Patient Safety Foundation, 2012.
27. Levesque, H. J., Cohen, P. R., and Nunes, J. H. *On acting together*. SRI International Menlo Park, CA 94025-3493, 1990.
28. McAllister, J. W. Achieving a shared plan of care with children and youth with special health care needs, 2014.
29. OMalley, A. S., Grossman, J. M., Cohen, G. R., Kemper, N. M., and Pham, H. H. Are electronic medical records helpful for care coordination? experiences of physician practices. *Journal of general internal medicine 25*, 3 (2010), 177–185.
30. Pinelle, D., and Gutwin, C. Loose coupling and healthcare organizations: deployment strategies for groupware. *CSCW 15*, 5-6 (2006), 537–572.
31. Quigley, L., Lacombe-Duncan, A., Adams, S., Hepburn, C. M., and Cohen, E. A qualitative analysis of information sharing for children with medical complexity within and across health care organizations. *BMC Health Services Research 14*, 283 (2014).
32. Reddy, M. C., and Spence, P. R. Collaborative information seeking: A field study of a multidisciplinary patient care team. *Information processing & management 44*, 1 (2008), 242–255.
33. Rich, C., Sidner, C. L., and Lesh, N. Collagen: Applying collaborative discourse theory to human-computer interaction.(articles). *AI magazine 22*, 4 (2001).
34. Sarcevic, A., Palen, L. A., and Burd, R. S. Coordinating time-critical work with role-tagging. In *Proc. CSCW 11'*, ACM (2011), 465–474.
35. Schulman-Green, D. J., Naik, A. D., Bradley, E. H., McCorkle, R., and Bogardus, S. T. Goal setting as a shared decision making strategy among clinicians and their older patients. *Patient education and counseling 63*, 1 (2006), 145–151.
36. Sonenberg, E., Tidhar, G., Werner, E., Kinny, D., Ljungberg, M., and Rao, A. Planned team activity. *Artificial Social Systems 890* (1992).
37. Stille, C. J., McLaughlin, T. J., Primack, W. A., Mazor, K. M., and Wasserman, R. C. Determinants and impact of generalist–specialist communication about pediatric outpatient referrals. *Pediatrics 118*, 4 (2006), 1341–1349.
38. Strickland, B., McPherson, M., Weissman, G., Van Dyck, P., Huang, Z. J., and Newacheck, P. Access to the medical home: results of the national survey of children with special health care needs. *Pediatrics 113*, Supplement 4 (2004), 1485–1492.
39. Tambe, M. Agent architecture for flexible, practical teamwork. *Proceedings of the National Conference on Artificial Intelligence* (1997), 22–28.

Engaging Pregnant Women in Kenya with a Hybrid Computer-Human SMS Communication System

Trevor Perrier† Nicola Dell† Brian DeRenzi† Richard Anderson†
John Kinuthia‡ Jennifer Unger§ Grace John-Stewart¶

†Computer Science & Engineering §Obstetrics & Gynecology ¶Epidemiology
University of Washington
{tperrier,nixdell,bderenzi,richarda,junger,gjohn}@uw.edu

‡Obstetrics & Gynecology
University of Nairobi
kinuthia@uw.edu

ABSTRACT

A growing body of HCI4D research studies the use of SMS communication to deliver health and information services to underserved populations. This paper contributes a novel dimension to this field of study by examining if a hybrid computer-human SMS system can engage pregnant women in Kenya in health-related communication. Our approach leverages the different strengths of *both* the computer and the human. The computer automates the bulk-sending of personalized messages to patients, allowing the human to read patients' replies and respond to those in need of attention. Findings from a 12-month deployment with 100 women show that our approach is capable of engaging the majority of participants in health-related conversations. We show that receiving messages from the system triggers participant communication and the amount of communication increases as participants approach their expected due date. In addition, analysis of participants' messages shows that they often contain sensitive health information conveyed through a complex mixture of languages and 'txting' abbreviations, all of which highlight the benefits of including a human in the workflow. Our findings are relevant for HCI researchers and practitioners interested in understanding or engaging underserved populations.

Author Keywords

HCI4D; ICTD; Maternal Health; SMS; Mobile; mHealth.

INTRODUCTION

The proliferation of mobile devices throughout the world, and particularly in low-income countries such as Kenya, is providing opportunities to create mobile applications that deliver health and information services to people living in poverty. Many of these applications focus on SMS, a low-cost communication channel that is supported on even the most basic mobile phones. However, the majority of existing SMS-based health applications use one-way 'push' messaging, in which generic messages are sent to large numbers of users who have no way to respond [7, 13] or they enable two-way communication between users and a server by requiring that users submit highly-structured messages that can be automatically parsed by the server [5, 16]. Although many SMS-based services would prefer to provide patients with personal attention that takes into account their specific context, they usually employ a small number of health workers who have limited amounts of time to engage in direct communication with individual users. This suggests a need for new approaches that increase the capacity of health workers and allow them to communicate effectively with a larger number of patients.

This paper makes a novel contribution to HCI4D by investigating if a hybrid computer-human SMS system can engage pregnant women in health-related conversations. Unlike prior research, our system leverages the different strengths of *both* the human and the computer and we argue that each plays a critical role in communicating with and engaging patients. The computer automates the bulk sending of personalized, time-specific messages to a large number of patients, which allows the human to spend time reading patients' replies and responding to those that have specific questions or concerns. This approach allows the human to effectively manage a much larger number of patients than would be possible if s/he was required to send all of the messages manually. Moreover, by allowing participants to send unstructured messages to the system in any format or language that they choose, we aim to allow users who may have little experience with SMS to participate and engage with the system.

We evaluate our hybrid approach through a 12-month deployment with 100 pregnant women in Kenya. Pregnant women in Kenya often have to wait for several hours at the clinic to see a nurse [18], which discourages them from attending their antenatal clinic visits and decreases the amount of advice and support that they receive during pregnancy. We use our hybrid SMS system to send pregnant women timely information that is tailored to their specific context and connect them directly to a nurse who is able to respond to their questions or concerns. This research is part of an in-progress randomized controlled trial (RCT) that aims to assess if two-way SMS communication can influence antenatal clinic visits, infant immunization rates and adoption of family planning practices. However, discussing the long-term medical outcomes of the trial is beyond the scope of this paper. Instead, we focus on understanding how low-income women use our computer-human SMS system to engage in health-related communication and we analyze the conversations that are enabled by our approach.

CHI 2015, April 18 - 23 2015, Seoul, Republic of Korea

ACM 978-1-4503-3145-6/15/04 ... $15.00
http://dx.doi.org/10.1145/2702123.2702124

Key findings from the design and evaluation of our hybrid computer-human SMS system show that, despite most participants having little prior experience with SMS, our approach successfully engages the majority of participants in meaningful health-related conversations. We show that receiving automated messages from the system triggers participant communication and that the amount of communication increases as participants approach their delivery date. Finally, although prior work has presented large-scale quantitative analyses of SMS usage data [8], to the best of our knowledge we contribute the first in-depth analysis of unstructured SMS conversations with low-income women in Kenya. We show that participants used a complex mixture of languages and 'txting' abbreviations to communicate highly personal health information over SMS. Taken together, these findings suggest that our hybrid computer-human SMS system has the potential to engage users in meaningful health-related communication.

BACKGROUND AND RELATED WORK

Our work contributes to a growing body of HCI4D literature that focuses on using SMS to communicate with users in underserved communities. The low cost of SMS compared to voice means that SMS is currently the preferred communication channel for much of Africa, including Kenya [12].

One-Way SMS Communication

A large number of prior studies have focused on one-way communication in which a server sends bulk SMS messages to a large number of recipients. Reminder systems fall under this category, including solutions designed to increase medication adherence [15], reduce missed clinic visits [13], or increase the timeliness of health worker home visits [7]. However, a major disadvantage of these systems is that the recipients have no way to send messages back to the system. For example, in one study health workers still received reminders to visit patients that had moved away from the area [7].

Another class of one-way SMS systems allow users to submit data to a server. In most cases, submitted messages must conform to a specific structure to enable automated parsing by the system. This model has been used to report stock levels [2], communicate diagnostic test results [1] or submit data [19]. However, several of these studies find that users struggle to compose properly structured messages and frequently make mistakes [19]. To overcome this limitation, other systems allow users to submit unstructured messages and then employ complex server-side processing to try and make sense of the messages. For example, Ushahidi [17] used server-side natural language processing to try and decipher submitted messages, while Hellström et al. [9] used crowdsourcing to enable users to report election incidents by SMS. However, these systems do not provide feedback to users and participants reported not using the system because they had no idea if the information they submitted made any difference [9].

Two-Way SMS Communication

To overcome the lack of feedback provided by one-way systems, several projects have designed two-way user-server SMS platforms in which users submit structured queries to a server and receive automated responses. This model has been deployed to provide users with health [16], education [5], and agricultural [23] information. However, as with one-way systems that use structured messages, many of these projects report high error rates in the messages submitted to the system. Moreover, training users to compose formatted messages is challenging and hampers the scalability of these systems.

Other systems enable two-way communication between human users. One particularly relevant example is the Weltel study [14], in which a health worker manually sent a single word message to participants who were required to respond with a single word answer. Participants that did not respond received a telephone call from the health worker. The study results show that patients who received messages had improved HIV medication adherence and lower viral loads than a control group. However, the health worker needed to manually send 273 messages and call roughly 30% of participants each week, with 62% of calls unanswered [22]. By using our hybrid SMS system, we are able to send longer, informative messages, reduce the health worker's workload, and enable meaningful SMS conversations between the health worker and participants.

Densmore [6] describes a bulk SMS platform designed to improve an NGO's communications with its clients. The system shares some similarities with our system in that it can be used to send messages to groups of users who may respond. However, unlike our system, which automatically sends tailored messages to participants at appropriate times, all of the messages in Densmore's study were manually initiated by NGO employees. In addition, all of the message senders and recipients were skilled professionals or NGO employees. Our research shows communication with low-income women drawn from the general population of Kenya, who have unknown backgrounds and varied experience with technology.

Perhaps the closest match to our hybrid human-computer communication model are 'human-in-the-loop' systems that require the input of both humans and machines. Prahalad [20] and Joshi [11] have proposed such systems in the context of rural banking and other global development efforts, though not in relation to user engagement or SMS communication.

Existing SMS Platforms

Several open-source platforms have been developed in recent years that enable the creation of SMS-based applications in low-resource environments, including FrontlineSMS[1] and RapidSMS[2]. These platforms have been widely used for a variety of applications that primarily require one-way or highly-structured two-way communication. In designing our hybrid SMS system for this study, we needed an automated solution capable of sending tailored, time-specific and dynamic messages to different groups of participants, coupled with an administrative user interface that allows a human to moderate conversations and respond to participant communication. At the time, neither FrontlineSMS nor RapidSMS supported this functionality and so we built our own prototype. However,

[1]FrontlineSMS: http://www.frontlinesms.com
[2]RapidSMS: https://www.rapidsms.org

we do not intend for our prototype to compete with these existing systems. Instead, we anticipate that they could incorporate our hybrid approach, which would allow their users to create SMS applications that better support user engagement and more nuanced communication with target populations.

A HYBRID COMPUTER-HUMAN SMS SYSTEM

The goal of our work is to use a hybrid computer-human SMS system to engage pregnant women in Kenya in health-related communication. Designing an SMS messaging system that is appropriate for maternal health settings requires that we take into account a complex and nuanced set of design criteria. For example, the date at which a woman is predicted to give birth and the date at which she actually gives birth can vary by several weeks. As a result, it is often impossible to accurately predict when a woman will give birth and automatically switch her from antenatal to postpartum messaging. To overcome challenges like this, our hybrid SMS system has been designed to incorporate input from *both* a human nurse and automated software, with each playing a critical role in the resulting communication.

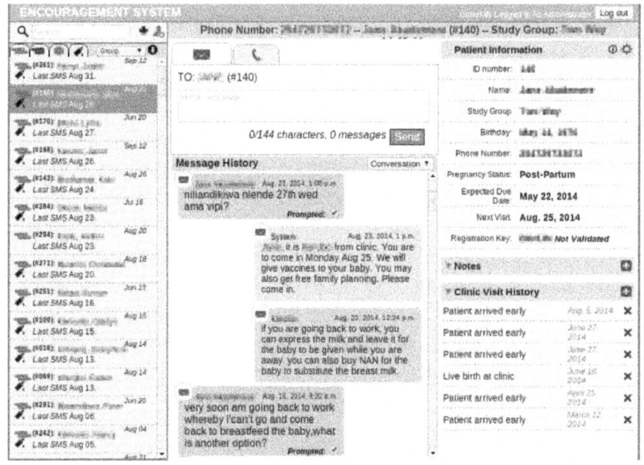

Figure 1. The laptop-based interface that the nurse uses to manage all participant communication. The system has a list of searchable contacts on the left, the communication history of the currently selected participant in the center, and mechanisms for tracking the participant's visit history and health status on the right

Design

At a high-level, our approach allows automated SMS scheduling software to handle the majority of outgoing messages. This greatly reduces the total number of messages that the nurse is required to manage, allowing her to instead spend time reading and responding to unstructured messages submitted by participants. In this way, the nurse is able to effectively communicate with a larger number of patients than would be possible if she had to send all of the messages manually. Keeping in mind the challenges of designing for maternal health settings, we identified the following criteria that influenced the design of our system:

Personalize messages

As much as possible, we personalize the content of the messages to each individual woman's specific context. We send messages that take into account gestational age and provide tailored message tracks for groups of participants with special circumstances, such as first time mothers, adolescent mothers, or women who have had previous cesarean sections. Moreover, we allow participants to choose the language (English or Swahili) that they receive messages in, and the day of the week and time of day that the messages arrive.

Encourage engagement

Our approach encourages women to engage with the system in several ways. First, each message includes a simple question relevant to the informational content of the message. Answering the question provides a natural method for engagement. Second, messages that women send to the system do not have to be structured or specially formatted in any way. Instead, women can submit questions, concerns or updates in any format and in whatever language they prefer.

Provide professional health care

Since we cannot predict the nature or content of the messages that women send to the system, it is important that responses come from qualified health professional familiar with the local culture and language. Moreover, the information in the automated messages was carefully crafted by maternal and child health experts to ensure that it was both relevant and medically accurate. Connecting underserved women directly to a health professional was one of our major goals.

Increase the nurse's capacity

To allow the nurse to easily communicate with a large number of women we designed a laptop-based interface that provides a portal through which the nurse can view and reply to messages (see Figure 1). The center of the interface depicts messages that have been sent and received by the selected participant as a conversation. Messages from the system, the nurse and the participant are displayed in different colors so that it is easy to interpret the participant's communication history. At the top of the interface is an input box that the nurse can use to send messages to the participant. The left side of the interface provides a searchable list of participants with new messages filtered to the top of the list. This allows the nurse to quickly locate and view unread messages that she has not yet responded to. Finally, the right side of the screen displays the participant's visit history and health status, such as her next scheduled clinic visit or when she is expected to give birth. Using this interface, the nurse can quickly understand a patient's prior communication, visit history and medical context and personalize her responses accordingly.

Adapt to participant circumstances

The unpredictable nature of pregnancy means that the sequence of outgoing messages may need to be dynamically adjusted based on a participant's changing circumstances. For example, if a woman gives birth earlier than expected, we need to be able to change the messages that she is receiving accordingly. Thus, rather than defining a fixed set of messages to be sent at sign-up, the messages sent to participants are instead dynamically selected according to each woman's current status at the time of sending. If the nurse changes the status of a woman in the system, the messages that she receives will automatically adapt to her new status.

Allow participants to respond only when they want to

Several prior studies [7, 14] used escalating reminder systems in which participants received a telephone call when they did not respond to a message. Our original design emulated this model. Initially, if a participant did not respond to a message, the message would be repeated every 48 hours for four days until a response was received. If no response had been received at that point, the system would prompt the nurse to call the participant. However, early feedback from focus groups with health workers and pregnant women revealed that this interaction model was overly demanding, and we changed our design to allow participants to only respond to messages when it made sense to them.

Message Content and Timing

The content of the SMS messages sent to participants was carefully crafted by maternal and child health experts using Kenya's antenatal care guidelines. In addition, we conducted focus groups with 22 pregnant women and 10 health workers prior to the start of the study to obtain feedback and iterate on the message content. Findings from these focus groups suggested that participants really wanted to feel as though someone cared about them. In addition, they wanted the messages to be directed specifically to them and take into account their personal situation. To achieve these goals, we designed the message content to include the name of the participant, with each message appearing as if it came from the study nurse (see Table 1). The messages were then further tailored to each participant based on her specific expected delivery date and covered a range of health and pregnancy related topics, including birth preparedness, factual information on what to expect, family planning, breastfeeding and immunization. The messages were then further personalized based on the participant's current pregnancy status, such as being a first time mother or adolescent. Finally, as shown in Table 1, each message that was sent by the system included a specific question designed to encourage the participant to respond.

Based on each participant's specific criteria, the system automatically selected and dispatched the relevant pre-programmed message at the appropriate time. In several cases, the final automated message was longer than the maximum size of a single SMS (140 characters) and was broken into two messages that were sent at the same time (see Table 1(b) for an example). In addition to health related information, participants also received automated appointment reminders two days before each scheduled clinic appointment (see Table 1(c)). Messages were also sent on the day of enrollment, on the day a clinic visit was recorded, and when a delivery was recorded.

Finally, women's delivery dates in Kenya are typically calculated based on the date of their last menstrual period. However, this method is frequently inaccurate and, in reality, they give birth anywhere from several weeks before to several weeks after their predicted date of delivery. Thus, if a participant had not given birth by the time all of the scheduled antenatal messages had been sent, the final antenatal message was repeated for an additional two weeks or until a birth was recorded in the system, at which point they began receiving tailored postpartum messages. In total, each participant that completed the study received approximately 35 automated messages in the seven to eight months between enrollment and completion, with at most two system messages per week.

(a) Automated message at 27 weeks pregnant [Name], this is [Nurse] from clinic. Iron helps carry nutrition to your baby. If it is low, you feel tired. Are you taking iron or do you need tablets?
(b) Automated message 8 weeks after giving birth (1) [Name] this is [Nurse] from clinic. Are you having trouble breastfeeding? Giving the baby other fluids can cause illness and weakness. (2) Please continue to only give breast milk to your baby for at least six months. How long do you plan to breastfeed?
(c) Automated clinic appointment reminder [Name], it is [Nurse] from clinic. You are to come in Friday Aug 08. We will give vaccines to your baby. You may also get free family planning. Please come in.

Table 1. Examples of automated messages sent by the system at (a) 27 weeks pregnant; (b) 8 weeks after birth; and (c) 2 days before a scheduled clinic visit. Note that, as is the case for (b), any messages longer than 140 characters were sent in two parts.

Implementation

Our system is a python-based Django web application that connects to the Kenyan telecommunication system through Shujaa Solutions[3], a third party SMS gateway that provides an API that our server can use to post outgoing messages. Incoming messages from participants are routed to our server via a callback URL. In addition, by establishing a reverse billing five-digit short code, we were able to to allow participants to send and receive messages free of charge.

EVALUATION

To understand women's engagement with our hybrid SMS system, we analyzed messages sent during a year long deployment with 100 pregnant women in Kenya. Our work is part of Mobile WACh, a larger IRB-approved clinical trial investigating maternal mobile health initiatives and behavior change. The deployment was based at Mathare North Health Center, a city council clinic located approximately 10km from Nairobi, the capital city of Kenya. Mathare provides basic health services to patients, including normal antenatal services for pregnant women, but refers all complicated cases to a higher level health facility.

Study Nurse

A dedicated nurse was hired for the duration of the study to enroll participants, respond to SMSs, keep track of anticipated and completed patient visits, monitor when participants gave birth, and conduct post study surveys. The nurse was female, computer literate and had experience reading and responding to email and participating in Skype conversations.

[3]Shujaa Solutions: http://shujaa.co.ke

We provided the nurse with a laptop and access to the system management portal so that she could communicate with participants. Prior to the start of the study, the nurse received roughly two hours of training on how to use the software.

Participant Enrollment

Starting in August 2013, pregnant women visiting the clinic for their first or second antenatal visit were invited to participate in the study. Volunteers needed to have personal or shared access to a mobile phone, be able to read and respond to messages in English or Swahili (the two national languages of Kenya) and be planning to reside in the area for the duration of their pregnancy. In addition, due to technical limitations of the SMS gateway, participants were required to possess a SIM card for the telecommunications provider Safaricom. Fortunately, the majority of Kenyans already use Safaricom. During the entire study only two people failed to meet the inclusion criteria, and this was because they did not possess a Safaricom SIM card. In total, we enrolled 100 women to receive messages from our hybrid SMS system. All participants sent and received messages using their own personal or shared mobile phones. During enrollment the nurse explained that participants would not be charged for any messages sent to the five-digit study number. All participants received a small monetary compensation for their participation.

Procedure

After screening volunteers and obtaining informed consent, the study nurse conducted a structured interview with each participant in which she collected the participant's demographic information, medical history, and current usage of and prior experience with technology. She also collected their mobile phone number and explained that they would receive one to two messages per week, starting at 20 weeks of pregnancy and continuing until 10 weeks postpartum. She explained that the messages would contain questions about their health and that they should respond, although she also made it clear that they should not use the service for emergencies. Each participant also received a business card that contained the study's five-digit short-code. After enrollment, the study nurse did not meet with participants again until several weeks after they had given birth, although participants did see other clinic nurses when they attended their normal antenatal appointments. All participant communication with the study nurse was through participants' personal mobile phones.

Data Collection and Analysis

The goal of our paper is to investigate if we are able to engage pregnant women using our hybrid computer-human SMS system and to characterize the resulting conversations that take place. To achieve this goal, we analyzed data from 100 structured interviews conducted with participants at enrollment, 3661 automated messages sent by the system, 423 messages sent by the nurse and 944 messages sent by participants, and data from two 45-minute semi-structured interviews with the study nurse that were conducted over Skype.

We began by examining the data from interviews conducted at enrollment and characterized the population of women that participated in our study, organizing them according to age, income, language, education level, employment, and their current usage of and prior experience with technology. Following this, we conducted an iterative, in-depth analysis of messages that participants sent to the system. We began by noting the language that participants sent messages in (English, Swahili or a mixture) and whether each message contained abbreviations or 'txting'. One of the authors, who speaks Swahili, translated any messages that were in Swahili into English. Then, we coded any messages that (1) answered a question posed by the system; (2) answered a question posed by the study nurse; (3) asked a question related to information sent by the system; (4) asked a new question that was not related to anything sent by the system; and (5) provided the nurse with an unprompted update or information. We further identified any messages that formed a 'conversation', which we define as a back-and-forth sequence of at least two related messages. For each identified conversation, we then further analyzed the messages that made up the conversation to identify who initiated the conversation (the system or the participant) and any themes, events or topics that caused participants to engage in conversation.

FINDINGS

Understanding Our Participants

Before analyzing participant engagement with the system, it is important to understand the characteristics of the women in our study and their prior experience with technology.

Demographic Characteristics

Our participants were all pregnant women aged between 16 and 37 years (M=24.1, SD=4.6). 38 participants reported that they had attended primary school, 51 had started (but not necessarily finished) secondary school, while 11 had some form of post-secondary education. The majority of Kenyans in Nairobi speak a complex combination of Swahili, English, slang words and local languages known as Sheng. However, since the language of education and government in Kenya is English, most of our participants prefer to receive formal communication in English as opposed to Swahili, and 97 participants chose to receive SMS messages in English. 86 participants reported that they live in single-room houses, 94 within 10km of the clinic, and 88 walked to the clinic for their appointment. 85 participants said that they were self-employed or housewives with family sizes ranging from 2 to 6 people (M=3.1, SD=1.3) with a mean monthly household income of 6500 (SD=3728) Kenyan shillings (roughly US$73). These characteristics suggest that, despite living close to Nairobi, Kenya's capital city, many of our participants are living in extreme poverty [21].

Experience with Technology

Access to mobile technology in Kenya has expanded exponentially over the past decade. All of the women screened for our study had access to a mobile phone. 76 reported that they possess their own mobile phone, while the other 24 shared a mobile phone, usually with their husband. Despite this widespread access to mobile technology, only 34 participants self-reported that they use SMS regularly, with 16 reporting that they do not use SMS at all. Moreover, only 7 participants reported ever having used the Internet. By contrast, 90% of

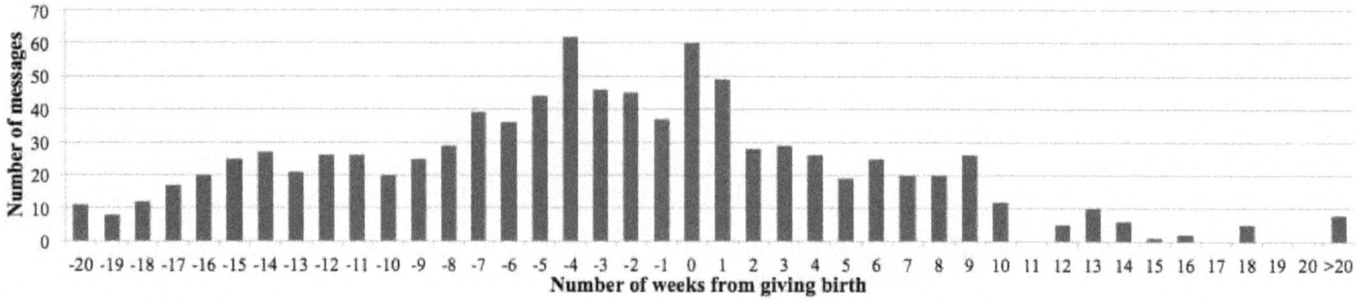

Figure 2. Total number of messages sent during each week before and after delivery. Week 0 corresponds to the week in which participants were recorded as giving birth. Week -5 depicts five weeks before giving birth while 5 shows five weeks after giving birth

participants do use their mobile phones to access mPesa, Safaricom's mobile banking service. Since mPesa requires users to navigate text-based menus and enter data, we anticipated that participants would be able to send and receive SMS messages even if they were not already frequent SMS users.

Measuring Participant Engagement

We use the number of messages that participants sent to the system as our measure of engagement. Thus, women who communicate more by sending more messages have a higher level of engagement. The total number of weeks that participants received messages from the system varied according to when they enrolled in the study and when they gave birth. To account for this variance, we divided the total number of messages that each participant sent by the number of weeks that they were receiving messages to obtain our final engagement metric, which we report as the average number of messages that each participant sent per week of participation.

The majority of participants engaged with the system

Between August 23, 2013 and August 31, 2014 we received a total of 944 SMS messages from participants. During the same time period, the system sent 3661 automated messages and the study nurse sent 423 messages to participants. On average, each participant sent 0.46 (M=0.26 SD=0.54) messages per week or two messages per month for the 7-8 months that they participated in the study, with 73 of our 100 participants sending at least one message. In addition, many participants communicated on a regular basis throughout the study (see Figure 2) with the highest amounts of engagement recorded during weeks close to participants' delivery dates. This high level of participant engagement is encouraging, particularly since the majority of our participants did not have much experience with SMS and prior work has struggled to engage these kinds of users with SMS communication [4].

Participants were more engaged close to their delivery date

To analyze how participants' communication varied throughout pregnancy, we calculated the total number of messages that participants sent in relation to when they gave birth. Our findings are shown in Figure 2. Week 0 in the graph shows the week that participants were recorded as giving birth, with values before 0 showing weeks before giving birth and values after 0 showing weeks after giving birth.

In general, participants' engagement with the system increased as they approached their delivery date. This suggests that participants were more motivated to communicate the closer that they were to giving birth. In addition, the questions that the system sent to participants in the third and fourth weeks prior to their expected delivery date specifically asked, *"Are you worried?"* and *"Do you have any questions about where to go in labor and how to get there?"* Similar open-ended questions were asked in other automated messages, however, they elicited the most responses in the weeks just prior to delivery, which indicates that this was an opportune time to provide participants with someone to whom they could direct their questions or concerns about the process of giving birth. After delivery, the number of messages that participants sent gradually decreased again, with a notable drop in messages submitted more than 10 weeks after birth. Since participants stopped receiving messages from the system at 10 weeks postpartum, it makes sense that, for the most part, they also stopped sending messages to the system.

Receiving messages triggered engagement

Figure 3 shows when participants sent messages to the system in relation to when they received messages from the system. The vast majority of messages sent by participants were on the same calendar day as they received a message from the system (705 out of a total of 944). A large number of these were direct responses to questions that the system had asked. However, many also triggered additional questions unrelated to those posed by the system, with 39 different users each submitting at least one new question. For example, one participant received the following automated message:

> *"[Name][4] this is [Nurse] from Mathare clinic. Regular, strong stomach pains are a sign of labor. If you feel strong tightening of your belly, leaking of fluid or any bleeding go to the clinic. Have you had any labor pains? How often do you feel them? Are you worried?"*

40 minutes after receiving this message, the participant sent[5],

> *"Hi,am not as such worried,but i have a little fear.i have never had any labor pains."*

[4]All names have been removed to preserve anonymity.

[5]All messages quoted in the paper show participants' original spelling and grammar.

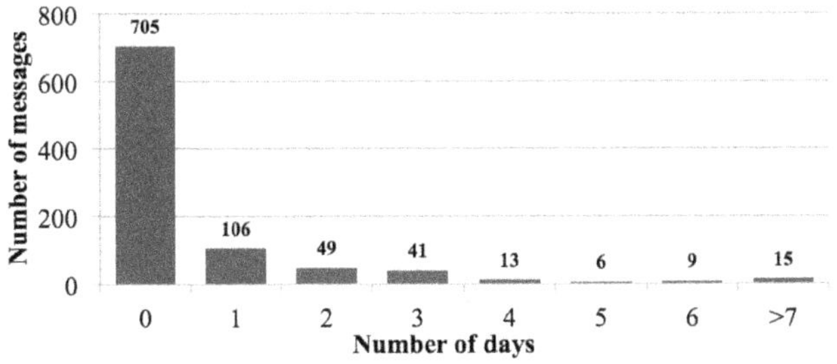

Figure 3. Summary of when participants sent messages to the system in relation to when they received messages. A value of 0 days means that the participant sent a message on the same day as receiving a message.

Then, ten minutes after sending her initial response, she sent another message to the system,

> *"Hi.madam [nurse],kindly will u state for me items that are needed when i will attend clinic during labor pains e.g clothing for the baby,basin,.and what els......."*

to which the nurse then responded,

> *"Hi [name], you need baby clothes, shawl, leso, basin, spirit, cotton wool. that is mainly it. the rest you can inquire from the nurses when you reach the hospital."*

Exchanges like this suggest that receiving messages from the system reminded participants that they had someone to whom they could direct their questions or concerns and highlight the potential for the automated messages to trigger engagement.

Some participants did not respond

Twenty-seven participants did not engage in any communication during the study. We tried to contact these participants to understand some of the reasons for their lack of response and were able to successfully reach eight participants. Three explained that they shared a phone with their husband, which made it difficult for them to read and respond to the messages. In one case, a participant said that her husband deleted the messages before she had a chance to read them. In several other cases, the person who answered the call told us that the participant had changed their phone number during the study. Moreover, several of the phone numbers that participants had provided to us appeared to be incorrect, with the number either not being a valid phone number or with the person who answered the call claiming to not know the participant.

Understanding Participants' Use of Language

Kenya has two national languages, English and Swahili, and we wanted to understand participants' use of these languages in their messages. Our findings show that participants' messages frequently included a complex mix of English, Swahili and Sheng (an informal mixture of the two), 'txt' abbreviations, and numerous spelling and grammatical errors, all of which highlight the benefit of having a human interpret and respond to messages.

Participants sent messages in a mixture of languages

Since 97 participants chose to receive messages in English, it makes sense that the majority of messages sent to the system (784 out of 944) were also in English. However, since only three participants chose to receive messages in Swahili, we were surprised to find that 41 participants sent messages that contained at least some Swahili, with 13 communicating entirely in Swahili. Follow-up conversations with the nurse showed that although some participants were more comfortable with Swahili, they feared that the messages would contain formal Swahili rather than the colloquial language that they typically use. A total of 73 participant messages were entirely in Swahili and a further 87 contained a mixture of Swahili and English. Our analysis of these messages suggests that participants mix Swahili and English freely, choosing whichever word comes to mind first. For example,

> *"my headache is ve ly pain and kizuguzugu"*

The word 'kizuguzugu' (a misspelling of 'kizunguzungu') means 'dizzy' and, although we cannot be sure, we hypothesize that this participant was either unsure of the English word for dizzy, or simply more familiar with the word in Swahili. Other participants more blatantly used Sheng, mixing English and Swahili whenever was convenient and incorporating new words not pulled from either language:

> *"My nxt visit will be on 29th may.na nina sweat sana siku hizi xana xana usiku.can u elaborate on this pliz"*

The Swahili part of this message means 'I am sweating a lot these days a lot a lot at night'. The first time the participant writes 'a lot' in Swahili, but the second and third time it is written in the slang version commonly used in Sheng. Although this complex mixing of languages may be understood by a bilingual Kenyan, it would be extremely difficult for any language processing software to interpret these messages.

Participants frequently used 'txt' abbreviations

'Txting' refers to the use of abbreviations and other techniques to craft SMS messages, often with the aim of reducing the overall length of the message [3]. Analysis of our participants' messages shows that 30% or 287 messages used 'txting' that often made the messages difficult to interpret:

> *"the 1st thing iwould like 2say hi 2u hpng dat ur fine.my qstn is dat when ivisted clnc last mnth itryd 2expose my complication 2the dctr dat the lab told 2hav some medicine coz of infctn bt they gav out 2 me some amoxil capsols 4me 2use 2x3 pa day bt whn iused them 4the 1st 4day iwas fing stomach strng pain den ijust chsn my self 2surender tkng thm did iwrng or icld cntnu usng them bcz its how they use 2cure"*

In addition, several participants appeared to not know how to input certain characters into their phone. For example, one participant responded to a question about heartburn with,

> *"yesiamhavingheartburninaweekitocurstwice"*

These findings suggest that many participants would find it difficult to compose messages that required specific formatting and it is an advantage that our system allows participants to send unstructured messages. In addition, the mix of language, 'txting', and errors highlights the importance of considering the cultural and linguistic context for automated messages and human replies.

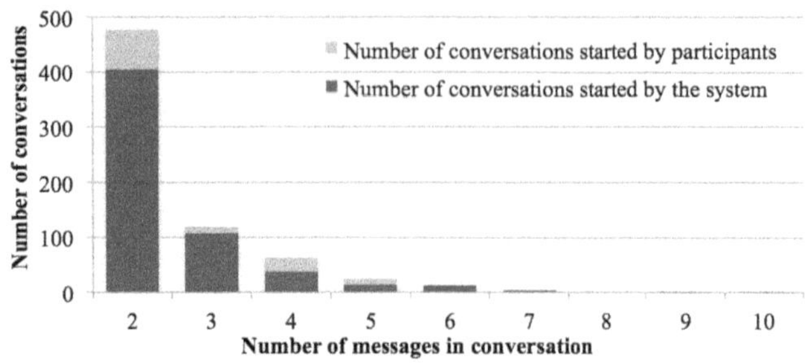

Figure 4. Graph showing the number and length of conversations (two or more related messages) started by the system and by participants.

Understanding the SMS Conversations

To understand the conversations that arose from participants' engagement with the system, we labeled any sequence of two or more related messages as a 'conversation' and analyzed the length and content of these conversations. In total, we recorded 703 conversations that took place during the study, ranging in length from two to ten messages (see Figure 4). 529 conversations were initiated by automated system messages, while the other 124 were initiated by participants.

Conversations with two messages: question and answer

The majority of two-message conversations fall into two categories: (1) the automated message asks a question and the participant responds, and (2) the participant asks a question and the nurse responds. Participant responses to system questions ranged in length and complexity from simple *'yes'* and *'no'* answers to longer, in-depth updates, such as,

> *"Am not having heartburn but am having alot of pain at the side of stormach and at the back.sometime it enter in the legs that i cant even make a single step till the pain disapear.then there is something coming up from stomach such as am unable to breath."*

There were 73 additional questions posed by participants that the nurse was able to answer with a single message. Many of these questions demonstrate the value of connecting participants to a health professional. One message asked,

> *"I have a question that is disturbing me, can a pregnant woman be dewarmed?"*

while another inquired,

> *"Hey [nurse] i ga ve birth on satudy bt my bby is cryng of stomac is it advaisable i giv ha medicine?"*

It is unlikely that these participants would be willing to wait in line for hours at the clinic just to ask these kinds of questions, which suggests that our system successfully lowers the barrier between our participants and health-related information.

Conversations with three or more messages

The majority of conversations longer than two messages were initiated by the system and then continued by the participant and the nurse. In many cases, participants would respond to a system question with a related question. For example,

> **System:** *"[Name] this is [Nurse] from Mathare clinic. When you come in for labor, we will give you a birth notification for the baby. Delivery at the hospital could save your baby's life. Do you have any questions about where to go in labor and how to get there?"*
> **Participant:** *"My worry is how 2 get in the hosp. Becoz of insecurity in our area incase labor starts at midnight. Another question is when i get at the hosp. 4 example at mathare at midnight will they able 2 open 4 me?"*
> **Nurse:** *"Hi [name], This is [nurse]. The maternity unit at Mathare operates for 24 hrs a day, so if you go there at midnight they will definitely attend to you. Thank you."*

This highlights the value of including carefully crafted questions in the automated messages that encourage participants to share their questions and concerns. Other conversations took place solely between a participant and the nurse. In these cases, a participant usually contacted the nurse seeking additional information or advice. For example,

> **Participant:** *"how about if i'give the baby other liquids,like cow milk what will happen?"*
> **Nurse:** *"Hi [name]. How old is your baby? If the baby is below 6 months, we advise you give only breast milk because the baby's digestive system is not yet fully developed to digest other foods. If i may ask. Why do you want to give cows milk?"*
> **Participant:** *"she is almost three months. very soon am going back to work whereby i'can't go and come back to breastfeed the baby,what is another option?"*
> **Nurse:** *"if you are going back to work, you can express the milk and leave it for the baby to be given while you are away. you can also buy NAN for the baby to substitute the breast milk."*

The longest conversation that we identified consisted of 10 messages in which the participant asked four different questions that were answered by the nurse. After receiving her answers, the participant concluded the conversation with,

> *"Thanks alot. Those are some of the questions that were really bothering me."*

Participants communicated sensitive personal information

Our analysis of participants' communication revealed that many were willing to communicate deeply personal health information over SMS. Several participants inquired about sexually transmitted diseases:

> *"i'was tested 4 siphilis on monday.is it posible someone can stil have other std?"*

while others asked if it was safe for them to have sex:

> *"Hi [nurse],am gud since we were 2getha.just wanted 2 ask u whetha a baby can b affected by sex while in the womb apart from sexual transmitted diseases."*

Interestingly, some participants communicated sensitive information through updates without asking a specific question:

> *"Thanks a lot.I don't have pains nor bleeding. If I can cough or sneeze I notice little urine come out. Am satisfied in early stage is okey. Am greatful for your concern."*

Participants' willingness to communicate this personal information over SMS has several potential implications. For example, since participants may be hesitant to talk about embarrassing or sensitive topics in person [10] the SMS system could provide them with a more comfortable communication channel for airing their concerns. Finally, many participants expressed gratitude for the support that they received:

> *"Dank U 2, 4 Being Consern About My Health. Am Not Realy Bad, But We R Stil Struggling With Life & Pray 2 Survive It. Coz 4 Me It's Had."*

These messages are particularly rewarding because they were unsolicited, which gives us reason to believe that participants were genuinely grateful and that it made a difference to them to feel as if someone cared about them.

Some participant questions went unanswered

For our hybrid computer-human SMS system to be successful, it is crucial that the nurse is also engaged and sends timely responses to participants (although we made it clear during enrollment that participants should *not* use the system as an emergency service). Our analysis of participant messages revealed a total of 50 questions that were never answered. In addition, in some cases the nurse responded several days after the message was received. Although the nurse's lack of response to messages did not have any observable effect on participant engagement, we plan to change the design of the interface to help the nurse do a better job of responding to messages. First, although the software made it easy to see unread messages, the nurse would often read a message but not respond immediately. However, after reading messages, it was difficult to keep track of messages that she had read but not responded to. To overcome this challenge, we plan to change the design of the system management portal so that, in addition to highlighting unread messages, it also flags messages that have not yet received a response. The nurse also described that she feared the laptop would get stolen if she carried it on public transit or left it at the clinic overnight. Thus, she frequently left the laptop at home when she went to the clinic for the day and was then unable to read and respond to messages until she got home in the evening. To overcome this issue, we plan to design a mobile version of the software that the nurse can use to read and respond to messages at any location using her personal Android phone.

DISCUSSION

Our findings clearly demonstrate the potential for hybrid computer-human SMS systems like ours to engage women in health-related communication during pregnancy and postpartum. We believe the success of our approach relies on the contributions of *both* the computer and the human. Since participants only met the nurse once at enrollment, we argue that it is not only the personal face-to-face connection to the nurse that causes them to engage with the system. Rather, it is the combination of carefully crafted personalized messages, the perceived relationship with the 'nurse' created by the automated messages *and* the messages sent by the nurse, each of which contribute to participants' motivation to communicate. The streamlined, tailored system messages provided a foundation on which further communication was built, and participants' responses to these messages suggest that they perceived the automated messages to come directly from the nurse rather than an automated system. With the system automating the bulk of the sending, the human was able to fulfill the higher order demands for advice and person-specific care. In addition, the varied topics and questions messaged by participants and the unpredictable nature of pregnancy motivate the need for a human to dynamically and adeptly control the messages that are sent. Participants often asked sensitive medical questions that require a trained professional to answer or triage to higher-level in-person care.

Taken together, these findings suggest that our system is able to supplement currently overstretched health care systems in a meaningful way. Not only do hybrid systems like ours allow for health education, appointment reminders and information dissemination, they may engage women in their own care, creating more informed patients and allowing for triage of both necessary and unnecessary in-person clinic visits. Moreover, enabling this communication requires little in terms of direct or indirect costs to the participant (*e.g.*, no travel time, transportation, waiting to see a nurse) and may decrease unnecessary visits to the clinic, which could help to reduce clinic waiting times for all patients.

The use of a hybrid messaging system does raise an interesting ethical debate: participants may think that the automated messages are being personally composed by the nurse. Our hybrid design is a compromise between an entirely automated system and a manual one. We use technology to efficiently accomplish what a human could do manually without significantly changing the process or workflow. Moreover, in our case, the outgoing automated messages have been carefully crafted by global health experts and tailored to each participant's health status. In addition, all participant messages and questions are reviewed and responded to by a qualified nurse. We believe that this approach is ethically acceptable, allowing underserved women to receive personal advice from a trained health professional, which would not be feasible if the nurse had to send all of the automated messages manually.

Our study also exposed several interesting design opportunities that we plan to explore. For example, we would like to make it easier for nurses to keep track of questions sent by women. One potential approach could be to model the web-based interface as a 'ticket management system' or email client instead of using an SMS-focused paradigm. Another interesting addition would be to allow the nurse to create and save template responses to frequently asked questions. For example, several participants asked about hospital operating hours, the safety of eating particular foods, vaccine schedules *etc*. Having template answers to these questions may help the nurse to respond more quickly and efficiently.

As we consider how to scale our hybrid system to larger deployments, we need to carefully consider how best to preserve the privacy of patients' personal health data. In our study, we explained that participants would receive messages on their own phones and we allowed them to choose the time of day that messages would arrive in part to allow them to choose a time when they would likely be alone. To avoid accidentally revealing a woman's pregnancy to her husband or family, we only began sending messages at 20 weeks of pregnancy. At the clinic, access to the messages was limited to the study nurse who logged in with a password. We hope to learn more about patients opinions on privacy through follow-up interviews at the conclusion of the ongoing medical study.

Finally, an important consideration in any HCI4D project is the sustainability of the system. Since women were able to send messages to the system for free, we are unable to tell how engagement would change if women had to pay for messages. The cost of each incoming or outgoing SMS was US$0.03. We paid for a total of 5028 messages, costing a total of US$150.84. Our biggest cost was a US$300 monthly fee to keep the SMS gateway open. However, this is a fixed fee that will not increase as the system is scaled up which means that (at least for the foreseeable future) the cost per participant will decrease as the number of participants increases. Another limitation of our study is that it involved a single nurse who managed all 100 participants at a single study site. We anticipate that additional challenges will arise as we scale the system to a large number of clinics and health workers.

CONCLUSION

This paper describes a hybrid computer-human SMS system that we designed to encourage pregnant women in Kenya to engage in health-related communication. Findings from a 12-month deployment of the system involving 100 pregnant women show that the system successfully engages the majority of participants by leveraging the different strengths of *both* the computer and the human. Moreover, analysis of the resulting conversations that took place between the system, the nurse and participants suggest that our hybrid approach provides a valuable communication channel that connects pregnant women directly to a qualified health professional. Taken together, our findings contribute a valuable and novel dimension to the growing body of HCI4D research that aims to understand and engage underserved populations.

ACKNOWLEDGMENTS

We would like to thank the study nurse and our participants for their valuable contributions and time. This work was funded in part by NSF grant IIS-1111433. Dr. Unger is supported by the Women's Reproductive Health Research (WRHR) Career Development Award NICHD, K12 HD001264-14. Dr. John-Stewart is supported by NIH/NICHD 1 K24 HD054314-06.

REFERENCES

1. Asiimwe, C., Gelvin, D., Lee, E., Amor, Y. B., Quinto, E., Katureebe, C., Sundaram, L., Bell, D., and Berg, M. Use of an Innovative, Affordable, and Open-Source Short Message ServiceBased Tool to Monitor Malaria in Remote Areas of Uganda. *American Journal of Tropical Medicine and Hygiene 85* (2011), 26–33.
2. Barrington, J., Wereko-Brobby, O., Ward, P., Mwafongo, W., and Kungulwe, S. SMS for Life: a pilot project to improve anti-malarial drug supply management in rural Tanzania using standard technology. *Malaria Journal 9* (2010), 298.
3. Carrington, V. Txting: the end of civilization (again)? *Cambridge Journal of Education 35*, 2 (2005), 161–175.
4. Crandall, A. Kenyan Farmers Use of Cell Phones: Calling Preferred over SMS. In *Mobile Communication for Development (M4D)* (2012).
5. Danis, C. M., Ellis, J. B., Kellogg, W. A., van Beijma, H., Hoefman, B., Daniels, S. D., and Loggers, J.-W. Mobile phones for health education in the developing world: SMS as a user interface. In *ACM Symposium on Computing for Development* (2010), 13:1–13:9.
6. Densmore, M. Experiences with Bulk SMS for Health Financing in Uganda. In *Extended Abstracts on Human Factors in Computing Systems* (2012), 383–398.
7. DeRenzi, B., Findlater, L., Payne, J., Birnbaum, B., Mangilima, J., Parikh, T., Borriello, G., and Lesh, N. Improving community health worker performance through automated SMS. In *Information and Communication Technologies and Development* (2012), 25–34.
8. Frias-Martinez, V., and Virseda, J. On the relationship between socio-economic factors and cell phone usage. In *Information and Communication Technologies and Development* (2012), 76–84.
9. Hellström, J., and Karefelt, A. Participation Through Mobile Phones: A Study of SMS Use During the Ugandan General Elections 2011. In *Information and Communication Technologies and Development* (2012), 249–258.
10. Johnson, T., , and Parsons, J. Interviewer effects on self-reported substance use among homeless persons. *Addict Behavior 19* (1994).
11. Joshi, A. Mobile Phones and Economic Sustainability: Perspectives from India. In *The First International Conference on Expressive Interactions for Sustainability and Empowerment* (2009).
12. Kechiche, B. Leveraging SMS to Attract the Low End of the Income Scale. *Africa and Middle East Telecom Insider 1*, 2 (2009).
13. Kunutsor, S., Walley, J., Katabira, E., Muchuro, S., Balidawa, H., Namagala, E., and Ikoona, E. Using mobile phones to improve clinic attendance amongst an antiretroviral treatment cohort in rural Uganda. *AIDS and behavior 14*, 6 (2010), 1347–1352.
14. Lester, P., Ritvo, P., Mills, E., Kariri, A., Karanja, S., Chung, M., Jack, W., Habyarimana, J., Sadatsafavi, M., Najafzadeh, M., Marra, C., Estambale, B., Ngugi, E., Ball, T., Thabane, L., Gelmon, L., Kimani, J., Ackers, M., and Plummer, F. Effects of a mobile phone short message service on antiretroviral treatment adherence in Kenya (WelTel Kenya1): a randomised trial. *The Lancet 376* (2010), 1838–1845.
15. Mbuagbaw, L., Thabane, L., Ongolo-Zogo, P., Lester, R., Mills, E., Volmink, J., Yondo, D., Essi, M., Bonono-Momnougui, R., Mba, R., Ndongo, J., N. F., and Ondoa, H. The cameroon mobile phone sms (CAMPS) trial. *Trials 12*, 1 (2011).
16. Ngabo, F., Nguimfack, J., Nwaigwe, F., Mugeni, C., Muhoza, D., Wilson, D., Kalach, J., Gakuba, R., Karema, C., and Binagwaho, A. Designing and implementing an innovative SMS-based alert system to monitor pregnancy and reduce maternal and child deaths in Rwanda. *Pan African Medical Journal 13*, 31 (2012).
17. Okolloh, O. Ushahidi or 'testimony': Web 2.0 tools for crowdsourcing crisis information. *Participatory Learning and Action 59* (2009), 65–70.
18. Ouma, P., van Eijk, A., Hamel, M., Sikuku, E., Odhiambo, F., Munguti, K., Ayisi, J., Crawford, S., Kager, P., and Slutsker, L. Research antenatal and delivery care in rural western kenya: the effect of training health care workers to provide focused antenatal care. *Reproductive Health 7*, 1 (2010).
19. Patnaik, S., Brunskill, E., and Thies, W. Evaluating the accuracy of data collection on mobile phones: forms, SMS, and voice. In *Information and Communication Technologies and Development* (2009).
20. Prahalad, C., and Fruehauf, H. *The Fortune at the Bottom of the Pyramid*. Wharton School Publishing, 2004.
21. Ravallion, M. How long will it take to lift one billion people out of poverty? *The World Bank Research Observer 28*, 2 (2013), 139–158.
22. van der Kop, M. L., Karanja, S., Thabane, L., Marra, C., Chung, M. H., Gelmon, L., Kimani, J., and Lester, R. T. In-Depth Analysis of Patient-Clinician Cell Phone Communication during the WelTel Kenya1 Antiretroviral Adherence Trial. *PLoS ONE 7*, 9, 1932–6203.
23. Veeraraghavan, R., Yasodhar, N., and Toyama, K. Warana Unwired. In *Information and Communication Technologies and Development* (2007), 1–10.

Is All About Perspective: An Exploration of Mitigating Selective Exposure with Aspect Indicators

Q. Vera Liao, Wai-Tat Fu, Sri Shilpa Mamidi
Department of Computer Science
University of Illinois at Urbana-Champaign
201 N. Goodwin Avenue, Urbana IL, 61801
liao28, wfu, mamidi1@illinois.edu

ABSTRACT

Selective exposure, the preferential seeking of confirmatory information, can potentially exacerbate fragmentation of online opinions and lead to biased decisions. We tested whether features that allowed users to better distinguish information about different issue aspects would encourage them to take different perspectives, thereby moderating the negative influence of pre-existing beliefs on information seeking. Using an information aggregator that provided drug related comments, we conducted an experiment to study the impact of aspect indicators (indicating whether the comment was about effectiveness or side effects) on moderating selective exposure. We found that, when participants were asked to decide between medications for high-risk diseases, and had preexisting biased beliefs in their effectiveness (one medication was less effective than the other), without aspect indicators they exhibited selective exposure to both types of comments (effectiveness and side effects) and were biased to choose the medication in confirmation of their pre-existing beliefs. With aspect indicators, we found reduced selective exposure to information about side effects of the medications, and as a result their overall decision bias was mitigated. However, the effect of aspect indicators in reducing selective exposure was moderated by the decision contexts, including the perceived risk of the diseases and whether the aspect was perceived to be critical to the decision.

Author Keywords

Selective exposure; confirmation bias; information seeking; decision making; biases; health.

ACM Classification Keywords

H.5.4. Information Interfaces and Presentation: Hypertext/Hypermedia-User issues.

CHI 2015, April 18–23, 2015, Seoul, Republic of Korea.

http://dx.doi.org/10.1145/2702123.2702570

INTRODUCTION

Is the glass half full or half empty? This is a question often used to demonstrate that one's perception of reality may depend on one's perspective. Indeed, individuals often differ in their beliefs in certain aspects of a situation or an issue, and they may choose to pay more or less attention to different aspects (e.g., the water in the glass, or the empty part of the glass) as they make a judgment or decision.

Research shows that prior attitudes tend to induce preferential seeking of attitude-consistent information and avoidance or ignorance of attitude-inconsistent information, a phenomenon called *selective exposure* [8, 15, 26]. Selective exposure may lead to biased judgment and decision, and, at a collective level, greater polarization and fragmentation in the society. As modern technologies make selection of information from preferred sources increasingly easy, their potential exacerbation of selective exposure has raised critics from many, calling attention to such problems as "echo chamber" [30] and "filter bubble" [28].

Meanwhile, researchers have recognized the benefits of enhancing exposure to diverse opinions could have on design of social information systems [16, 23, 24, 25, 27]. These systems not only make different opinions more accessible (e.g., often in the form of information aggregators), but they often leverage computational methods and design techniques to "nudge individuals in the direction of exposure to challenging information" [9]. The idea of *nudging*, to induce behavioral change without infringing individuals' freedom of choice, could be a critical design feature to expose people to challenging information without incurring negative user experience with the system or denial of the information itself.

Our research is in line with this *nudging* approach. Noticing that controversial issues such as "Obamacare" often have many aspects and people holding different attitudes may focus on different aspects of the issues, we see a design opportunity to improve the general reception to diverse opinions by highlighting the differences in perspectives that others take. Specifically, we are interested in testing the idea of mitigating selective exposure by distinguishing information on different aspects of a controversial topic, thus potentially reducing information seekers' resistance to arguments put forward by the other side, but on "non-conflicting aspects" where they do not have strong biased beliefs. To this end, we conducted an experiment to explore how aspect indicators, i.e., interface features indicating the focused issue aspect of information, impact users' information seeking in a system providing diverse opinions.

We studied the effects of aspect indicators in the context of medical decision-making: a common situation where someone may have had or heard about negative opinions on a medication and consider switching to a different option by browsing other patients' comments online. Such decision is controversial if neither option has definite advantages but largely depends on an individual's preferences.

The reasons we chose such a context were twofold. First, medical decisions naturally involve multiple aspects (e.g., effectiveness and side effects) that are established, distinctive, and often consistently defined [12]. This allowed us to study aspect indicators without concerning the possible difference in the definition of aspects across topics and individuals. For example, imagine a patient is concerned about the *effectiveness* of a medication and intends to seek evidence for rejection. In such situations, we are interested in whether the patient may show selective exposure to information, i.e., preferentially seeking negative information on both the *effectiveness* and *side effects* of the medication; and if so, whether the presence of aspect indicators will moderate the selective exposure.

Moreover, our study contributes to the emerging literature on studying biases in online health information seeking. Identified to be the most common cause of decision errors in clinical decisions [3], selective exposure could cause more harm to patients seeking information online as they are more likely to form incorrect beliefs, and selective exposure is found to increase their illusory confidence in them and result in inferior decisions [14, 15, 17, 31]. Our study sets to further understand this problem by exploring the tendency of selective exposure to information in medical decision-making supported by web technology.

Another key question is whether it makes a difference if the aspect in which one has a biased belief is a *critical* or *uncritical* aspect for the controversial topic. As theories in multi-attribute decision-making suggest, varying weights given to different attributes (i.e., aspects) may influence one's motivation to seek relevant information [34]. While we chose to study aspect indicators distinguishing effectiveness and side effects of treatments, we were aware that they might not be given equal consideration in different situations. Importantly, as [2] suggests, when choosing treatment for high-risk diseases, effectiveness is likely to be the critical aspect and given more consideration than side effects, while it may be the contrary for low-risk diseases. One may ask, e.g., if two patients with life-threatening diseases both have negative attitudes towards a medication, while one is concerned about its effectiveness that is vital to his life, the other is concerned about certain side effects that one can usually endure for a life-saving medication, would they exhibit differences in selective exposure tendency?

To the best of our knowledge, such questions have not yet been well explored in the selective exposure literature. Specific to medical decision, it is unclear whether concerns on a critical aspect of the decision may motivate people to deliberatively seek accurate information, and as a result, reduce selective exposure [11], or whether it may incur a higher level of anxiety when making possibly irreversible decisions, thereby increase selective exposure [8, 24]. To study this, we conducted an experiment where participants had biased belief in different aspects (*side effects* or *effectiveness*) and made decisions regarding diseases with varied levels of perceived risk (high/low).

In this paper, we define:

- *attitude* as one's pre-existing preference between treatment options to be compared.
- *attitude-consistent* (*inconsistent*) information as information that supports (opposes) the attitude.
- *belief* as the detailed, aspect specific existing opinions, e.g., one treatment may cause bad side effects.
- *biased aspect* as the aspect (effectiveness/side effect) where one has pre-existing biased belief; and *unbiased aspect* as where one does not.
- *critical aspect* as the aspect perceived to be critical to the decision; and *uncritical aspect* if otherwise.

To summarize, we were interested in understanding how aspect indicators in an opinion-diverse system influenced information seeking and decision making of users with pre-existing biased beliefs in certain aspects of a controversial topic. We also examined the impact of perceived criticalness of the aspect where one had biased beliefs. We explored the research questions in a medical decision-making context, and chose treatments' effectiveness and side effects to be the two studied aspects. Specifically, we ask the following research questions:

RQ1: How do aspect indicators influence selection of comments on effectiveness or side effects for users having preexisting biased beliefs in one of the two aspects?

RQ2: How do aspect indicators influence selection of comments on effectiveness or side effects when making decision regarding high versus low risk diseases?

RQ3: How do aspect indicators influence the decision outcomes for users having pre-existing biased beliefs in effectiveness or side effects, and for decision regarding high versus low risk diseases?

RQ4: How do perceived disease risk and biased aspect influence selective exposure tendency in seeking medical information online? How does the selective exposure, if any, influence the decision outcomes? How do aspect indicators impact the process?

RELATED WORK

Selective exposure has been mainly studied based on Festinger's cognitive dissonance theory [6, 7, 8]. According to the theory, when committed to a belief or decision, people are driven to seek supportive information and avoid or ignore unsupportive information in order to eliminate the negative state of cognitive dissonance. Therefore, to mitigate selective exposure, the key lies in reducing the cognitive dissonance one experiences when processing attitude-inconsistent information [8, 9, 30].

Given that many controversial topics involve multiple aspects or dimensions, narrowing down information seeker's perceived conflicts to only a subset of them could potentially reduce the overall cognitive dissonance. Consistent with this idea, previous research found that people are more likely to interact with others holding dissimilar attitudes if they share common ground on some aspects of the topic [1, 10, 23]. Similarly, a strategy adopted by decision-making support systems (DSS) to "de-bias" users with strongly held biases is to first partially acknowledge or endorse certain aspects of their positions before bringing in attitude-challenging information on other aspects [20]. These results suggest that, selective exposure could potentially be reduced by explicitly showing that attitude-challenging information focuses on aspects where the information seeker does not have conflicting beliefs. We are interested in testing the idea in this paper.

Interfaces that present information by aspects are pervasive. Many algorithms have been developed to extract and classify aspects of information in various domains [13, 19, 33]. Relevant to our study, tools have been developed to show how information sources with different biases (e.g. media, politicians) focus on different aspects of controversial issues [1, 27] to assist users in sense making and deliberation. While a number of previous studies examined users' navigation of such interfaces, e.g., tag-based [29] or multi-facet [19] ones, to the best of our knowledge, we are among the first to study how presenting information by aspects influences seeking of attitude consistent versus attitude inconsistent information.

While online selective exposure has been frequently studied in the political domain [9, 10, 16, 25] due to the deep concern of polarized society. A few recent studies drew attention to the problem in online health information seeking. In particular, research on "Cyberchondria" [18, 31, 32], a term referring to people's escalation of medical concerns after performing online information search, suggests that Internet may potentially reinforce selective exposure. For instance, search engines often use algorithms favoring satisfying searchers rather than accuracy, hence tend to provide confirmatory information that strengthens users' pre-existing beliefs. Consistent with findings from psychological research [7], this line of research also indicates that anxiety associated with medical decisions may exacerbate online selective exposure by drawing attention to alarming terminologies [31].

Meanwhile, patients' selective seeking and avoidance of medical information has been broadly explored in more general (offline) contexts (e.g., [21]). Avoidance of new, challenging information was found to be a common coping strategy used by patients to manage fear and uncertainty, especially among those with serious, life-threatening diseases such as cancer [4, 5].

A few studies have explored designs that integrate de-biasing techniques in health information search interfaces to mitigate the negative impact of biased beliefs. For example, [17] employed an anchor de-biasing intervention that asks users to assemble evidence for and against a proposition before they commit to a decision. [29] used a social tagging interface that presented popular terms supporting different positions of controversial health topics, and found it to raise awareness of different perspectives. In this paper, we conducted an experiment based on this general idea by testing how information seekers select diverse drug related comments with labeled aspects.

METHODOLOGY

Platform and Task

We created CompareMed, a system supporting comparative medical decision by aggregating patients' comments from social media. To help a user compare two treatments, the system presents comments on each treatment side by side. For each treatment, it presents a list of comment snippets (with usernames), which one can click to read the whole message. Each snippet is shown with a star rating, which reflects how negative or positive the comment is, using a 1 (negative) to 5 (positive) scale. In the experimental conditions (Figure 1(a)), the system presents *aspect indicators*- star signs that not only show comment sentiment, but also, by the labels ("side effects" and "NO side effects", or "ineffective" and "effective"), indicate whether the comment focuses on the effectiveness or side effects of the treatment. Different color schemes were also used to further differentiate the two kinds of comments. In the control condition, only one kind of star sign was used, with generic labels ("bad" and "good")(Figure 1(b)). This format, including the star signs, and separate ratings given to effectiveness or side effects of a medication, is commonly seen on drug-review websites.

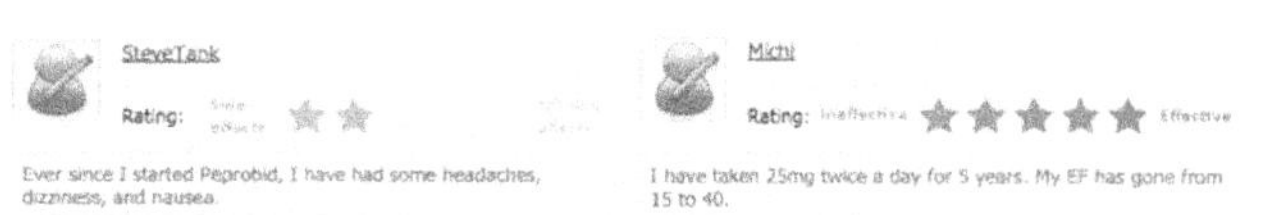

Figure 1(a). Snippets of side effects comment (left) and effectiveness comment (right) for experimental conditions

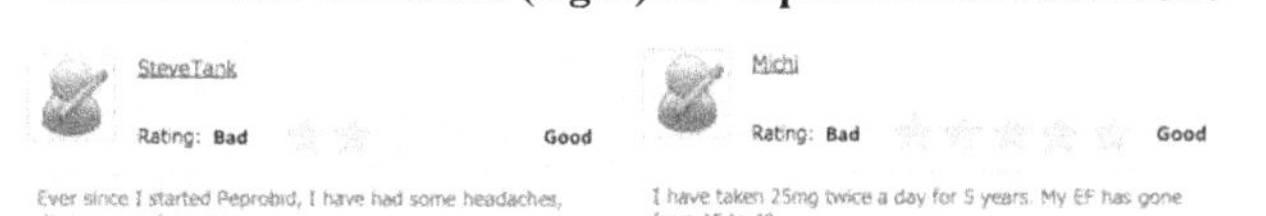

Figure 1(b). Snippets for control conditions

To introduce "pre-existing biased beliefs" in the experiment, for each task, participants were given a scenario to imagine that a close friend was having negative experience with a treatment they just initiated, and facing the decision of switching to an alternative treatment, which the friend had heard might work better. The participant was asked to use CompareMed to learn about the two options and provide suggestions. We expected that it would introduce biased beliefs favoring one treatment (*alternative*) to the other (*current*).

Participants were asked to freely browse the system until they were ready to give suggestions. Then they proceeded to the survey page to rate their preference between the treatments and wrote down suggestions for the friend.

Experimental Design

The experiment included two between-subjects variables: biased aspect (effectiveness/ side effects), presence of aspect indicator (presence/ absent); and one within-subject variable: disease risk (high/ low). In other words, participants were randomly assigned to one of four conditions: having biased beliefs in effectiveness/side effects and with or without aspect indicators. Each participants were given 6 decision-making tasks, half of which were about high-risk diseases that could be potentially life-threatening and needed to be cautiously controlled: congestive heart failure (CHF), deep venous thrombosis (DVT) and acute asthma attack; the other three were low-risk minor diseases that were commonly seen and could be treated or controlled by over-the-counter medicines: diarrhea, back pain and heartburn (acid reflux).

Material

Comments

For each disease, we chose two medicines that received similar user ratings on WebMD as candidate treatments to be compared in the experiment. Their names and other identifying information were replaced to avoid recognition.

For each medication, we collected 50-60 comments from the "user comments" section of popular drug information websites (e.g., WebMD.com, rxlist.com), and medical discussion forums, e.g., medhelp.org. We were conscious about having a balanced number of positive and negative comments, and comments regarding effectiveness and side effects. We intentionally excluded comments that did not have a clear focus on either aspect.

Two researchers independently rated comments for their sentiment (positive/ negative) and focused aspects (effectiveness/ side effects). We excluded comments that they disagreed on and ended up with 32 comments for each medicine, with *evenly* distributed sentiment and aspects to create a "controversial" decision where the information does not significantly favor one option over the other. Table 1 presents examples of each type of comment.

Scenario

An important step in the experiment was to introduce biased beliefs by giving participants a scenario of a disfavored current treatment and a potentially better alternative. To manipulate the biased aspect, two versions of scenario were created for each of the 12 medicines (2 for 6 tasks): one mentioning lack of effectiveness, and the other complaining about side effects of the current medication. To make it coherent, the scenario mentioned side effects that also appeared in some of the negative comments.

To strengthen the negative opinion on the current option, we included an image with each scenario, picturing a patient suffering from the disease (for biased belief in effectiveness) or side effects mentioned (for biased belief in side effects). Pictures were intentionally chosen to have no excessive information but portrait of a single patient.

To strengthen the difference in the perceived risk, for the high-risk disease, the scenario mentioned the disease could be life threatening and needed to be attended very cautiously, while for the low-risk diseases it mentioned it might not be a serious problem.

For randomization purpose, in each experiment session, one of the two medications was randomly chosen to be the current option, by randomly loading one of the two created scenarios. On the screen, the current and alternative option were randomly placed on the left or right side, with the current option labeled as "currently taking" on the heading. The order of the 6 disease tasks was also randomized.

Aspect	Sentiment	Example
Effective -ness	Positive	Dosage currently 25mg of Peprobid twice a day and I am feeling pretty great. My EF is up to 50-55% from 20%. And my BP is 130/85, which is a great improvement from 208/182. My heart doctor and my PCP both told me that this will be a miracle medicine and they were right
	Negative	Diagnosed with Congestive Heart Failure, It was hoped this would reduce my BP and help me avoid worse conditions up ahead. Now I have been taking Peprobid for the last 3 months, I really can not say it has made me feel one bit better.
Side effects	Positive	After being on Atenolol for 5 years, switching to Peprobid was a vast improvement. I used to jitter and feel exhausted all the time with the other meds. No side effects so far with Peprobid.
	Negative	I am only on 12.5 mg of Peprobid but I sleep all night & day, if I am not sleeping I am so exhausted I can not move with out becoming so short of breath I have to stop and sit not moving for at least 15-29 min. The side effects are dragging me down.

Table 1. Example of comments for the medicine "Peprobid" treating congestive heart failure

Measurement
We are interested in participants' information selection (i.e., comments that they clicked to read) and their decision outcomes. The experimental platform recorded participants' clicks on comments, and we used them to analyze the number of selections for each type of comment.

To measure decision outcomes, after each browsing session participant was asked to rate two statements: 1) The alternative is a better option; and 2) I would like to switch to the alternative; based on a 1 (disagree) to 5 (agree) Likert scale. The ratings were averaged to create *decision index*, which reflects participants' preference for the alternative over the current option.

Participants
We recruited 67 participants from the Urbana-Champaign community by using online job boards and a campus-wide mailing list for faculties and university staff. Participants' average age is 26.58 (SD=11.58), including 21 male and 13 with post-graduate degree. There was no significant difference in age, gender and education of participants assigned to the four experimental groups. We measured participants' experience with seeking health information online by asking them rate how often they look online for: 1) information about medicines; 2) disease related information; 3) healthy lifestyle related information; and 4) health related social media. We also measured their self-rated knowledge for all the diseases used in the experiment. We did not observe significant difference of the two measurements among the experimental groups.

RESULTS
To report on the results, we will first test whether aspect indicators influenced the selection of comments on effectiveness or side effects for participants who had biased beliefs in one or the other aspect (R1). Then we will examine whether aspect indicators influenced information selection differently for participants concerned about high versus low-risk diseases (R2). In the last part, we will explore how these factors - disease risk, biased aspect and aspect indicators - impacted participants' decision outcomes (R3), and if so, attempt to understand the causes by examining the presence of selective exposure (R4).

Biased Aspects on Selection of Comments on Different Aspects
To test whether the aspect indicators impacted the selection of comments on effectiveness or side effects, we started by calculating the selection percentage of effectiveness/side effects related comments (divided by the total number of selected comments) for each task, by each participant.

We ran a mixed effect linear regression model on the selection percentage of comments, by including comment aspect (effectiveness/side effects), participant's biased aspect (effectiveness/side effects), and presence of aspect indicators (present/absent) as fixed-effect independent variables[1]. We found a significant three-way interaction among all the fixed-effect variables (*β=0.13, t(64)=2.43, p=0.02*). We illustrate the interactive effect by plotting the average selection percentages of effectiveness and side effects related comments in Figure 2.

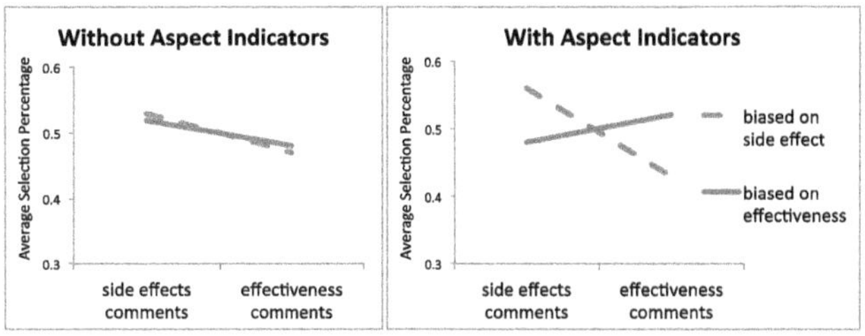

Figure 2. Selection percentages of side effects/effectiveness comments for participants with different biased aspects

The figure shows that, the aspect indicators led to participants' preferential selection of comments on the aspect where they had biased beliefs. In the control conditions where there was no aspect indicator, thus harder to identify the focused aspect of comment (whereas not impossible, given the snippet), they did not discriminate the selection between the two types of comment. To confirm the conclusion, we tested the interactive effect between biased aspect and comment aspect in the condition with or without aspect indicators separately. As expected, we found it to be significant in the experimental conditions with aspect indicators (*β=0.16, t(32)=3.98, p<0.01*), but not in the control conditions (*β=0.04, t(31)=1.12, p=0.26*).

This result suggested that aspect indicators facilitated participants to explore more about the aspect that they were concerned about in their pre-existing beliefs. It could also be seen as a validation of our manipulation to introduce biased beliefs in different aspects of the topic, as participants in the two experimental conditions (biased on side effect or effectiveness) responded differently in their information seeking on the two aspects.

Disease Risk on Selection of Comments on Different Aspects
Given that previous research [2] suggests that people tend to put more weight on effectiveness related information for high-risk diseases, but side effects for low-risk diseases, we were interested in testing whether the aspect indicators would facilitate this tendency.

We ran a mixed-effect linear regression on the selection percentage of side effect/ effectiveness comments by including comment aspect, disease risk (high/low), and presence of aspect indicators as fixed-effect independent variables. We found a significant three-way interaction among them (*β=0.21, t(64)=3.93, p<0.01*). In Figure 3, we

[1] For all the mixed-effect regression analyses in this paper, participant was included as random-effect.

illustrate this three-way interaction by plotting the average selection percentages of each type of comment.

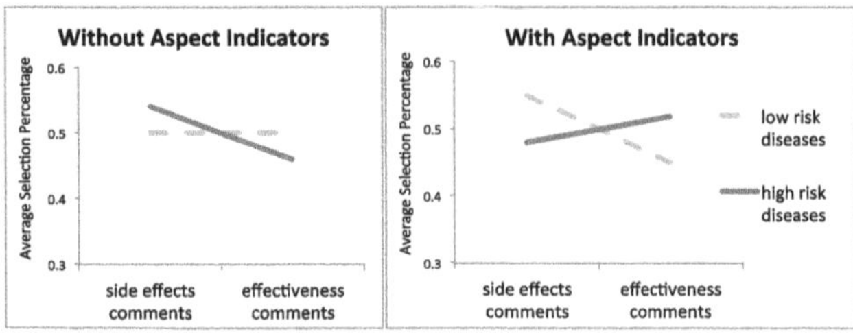

Figure 3. Selection percentages of side effects/effectiveness comments for treating high versus low risk diseases

Figure 3 suggests that, with the assistance of aspect indicators, participants were more interested in seeking effectiveness related information for high-risk diseases, but side effects for low-risk diseases. The conclusion is confirmed by the significant two-way interaction between comment aspect and disease risk found in the conditions with aspect indicators (*β=0.10, t(32)=2.35, p=0.02*).

The tendency is consistent with what was found in [2], suggesting that effectiveness, rather than side effects, is likely the *critical aspect* when considering treatment options for high-risk disease; although this tendency tends to be reduced, or even reversed for low-risk diseases.

Decision Outcome

As discussed earlier, we measured decision outcome in the post-task survey by two 5-point Likert-scale items, and created the *decision index* by averaging the ratings of the two. The value reflects the preference for the alternative over the current option, i.e., a decision bias consistent with the pre-existing attitude, with higher value indicating higher preference. For quality control reason, we excluded 10% of the results where the ratings to the two questions differed by larger than 2.

We ran a mixed effect linear regression model on the decision index, by including disease risk, biased aspect and presence of aspect indicators as fixed-effect independent variables. We found a significant three-way interaction among all of them (*β=-1.32, t(64)=-2.06, p=0.04*), and a two-way interaction between disease risk and biased aspect (*β=0.91, t (64)=2.00, p=0.05*).

The results suggested that whether participants had pre-existing biased belief on effectiveness or side effects had different impact on decision bias for high versus low risk diseases. The presence of aspect indicator, however, seemed to moderate such difference. To further understand it, we tested the interactive effect between disease risk and biased aspect separately for the control and experimental conditions. As expected, we found it to be significant without aspect indicators (*β=-0.94, t(62)=2.12,p=0.03*), but not significant when aspect indicators were presented (*β=-0.40, t(65)=-0.86, p=0.40*). To illustrate the interaction, we plot the average decision index in Figure 4.

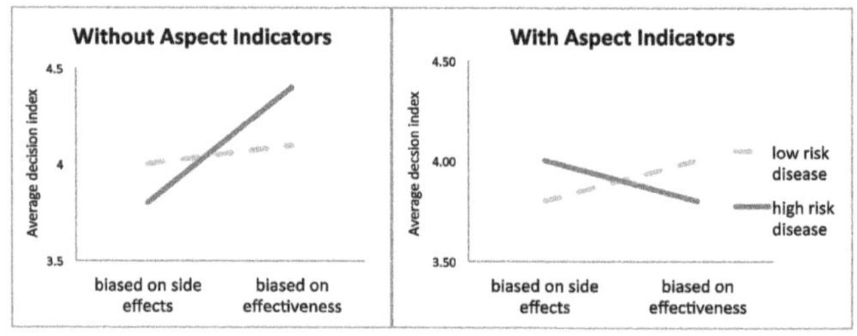

Figure 4. Decision Index for participants with biased beliefs on side effects versus effectiveness

Figure 4 suggests that, in the control conditions, when making decisions for high-risk diseases, participants who had biased beliefs in the effectiveness of treatment options were most likely to make biased decision consistent with pre-existing attitude after performing information seeking in the system. This tendency, however, was moderated by the presence of aspect indicators, leading to no statistically significant difference in the decision outcomes among all conditions with different biased aspects and disease risk. We will attempt to uncover the potential causes of such differences in decision outcomes in the next section by examining participants' selective exposure tendency.

Selective Exposure

For the rest of the paper, we are interested in understanding selective exposure, i.e., the preferential selection of attitude consistent over inconsistent information. In particular, we will focus on exploring the potential causes of the difference in decision outcomes we observed.

To start with, we coded *attitude consistency* for each comment as an independent variable. Given the introduced bias of "a disfavored current treatment and a potentially better alternative", we coded negative comments on the current and positive on the alternative treatment to be *attitude consistent.* We coded positive comments on the current and negative on the alternative to be *attitude inconsistent.* Therefore, for each task, there are four types of comment: attitude consistent/inconsistent comments on effectiveness/side effects.

To verify that participants' decision outcomes were influenced by their selective exposure, we started by testing the effect of selective exposure on decision outcomes. For each task performed by each participant, we quantified the extent of selective exposure, by the number of attitude consistent comments minus that of attitude inconsistent comments selected, and tested its main effect on the decision index. As expected, we found a significant positive effect of selective exposure on the decision outcomes (*β=1.06, t(66)=4.62, p<0.01*), i.e., the preference for the alternative option. It confirmed that participants' biased decisions were associated with selective exposure tendency in their information seeking process.

Given that we have identified the interactive effects of biased aspect, disease risk and presence of aspect indicators on the decision outcomes, we focused on exploring their effects on participants' selective exposure tendency. We first calculated the selection percentage of different types of comment (attitude consistent/inconsistent, on side effects/effectiveness) among all comments selected. We ran a mixed-effect linear regression model on the selection percentage, by including comment attitude consistency, comment aspect, participants' biased aspect, disease risk and presence of aspect indicators as fixed-effect independent variables.

We found a significant three-way interaction among attitude consistency, biased aspect and disease risk (*β=0.07, t(63)=2.10, p=0.04*), and a significant four-way interaction among attitude consistency, comment aspect, presence of aspect indicator and disease risk (*β=0.14, t(63)=2.22, p=0.03*)[2]. In the following section, we will focus on interpreting these interactive effects to unfold how these variables impacted participants' selective exposure.

Effects of Biased Aspect and Disease Risk on Selective Exposure

The three-way interaction among attitude consistency, biased aspect and disease risk suggests that biased aspect affected selective exposure tendency differently for seeking information for high-risk versus low-risk diseases. To illustrate the interaction, we plot the average selection percentages of each type of comment for decision regarding low versus high-risk diseases in Figure 5.

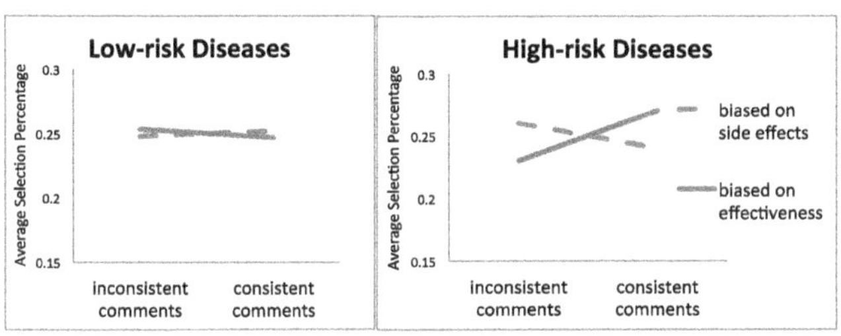

Figure 5. Selection percentages of different comments for participants with biased beliefs on side effects or effectiveness

The figures show that, when participants had biased beliefs in the effectiveness of medications treating high-risk diseases, they exhibited significant selective exposure tendency, by selecting more attitude consistent comments than inconsistent comments. They did not show such bias when making decision for treating low-risk diseases, nor when they were only concerned about side effects of medicines treating high-risk diseases. The conclusion is confirmed by the significant interaction between biased aspect and comment consistency for high-risk diseases (*β=0.06, t(65)=2.28, p=0.02*), but not for low-risk diseases (*β=-0.01, t(65)=-0.50, p=0.62*).

The result suggests that, information seekers with biased beliefs in the effectiveness of medications treating high-risk diseases are most likely subject to selective exposure. It can be understood from the fact that they may be especially prone to anxiety when seeking information regarding a critical aspect of a potentially irreversible, life-concerning decision. Comparatively, concerns on side effects of a life-saving drug, or treatment choice for a low-risk minor disease, are likely less vital situations and thus may not induce the same level of selective exposure tendency.

The results may shed light on the finding in previous section that, in the control condition, participants are most likely to make biased decision when they had biased beliefs in the effectiveness aspect for high-risk diseases- because it led to most significant selective exposure. However, to understand why this decision bias was moderated by the presence of aspect indicator, we may need to examine how they impacted participants' selective exposure tendency on different aspects, which we will discuss in the next section.

In short, we found that participants exhibited significant selective exposure tendency when they had biased beliefs in the effectiveness of medications treating high-risk diseases.

Effects of Disease Risk and Aspect Indicator on Selective Exposure to Information of Different Aspects

The four-way interaction suggests that the aspect indicators had different impact on participants' selective exposure when seeking information on the aspect of effectiveness or side effects, and it differed for treating high versus low risk diseases. To unpack the four-way interaction, we tested the three-way interaction among attitude consistency, comment aspect and presence of aspect indicators for high-risk and low-risk disease separately.

When seeking information to make treatment decisions for high-risk diseases, we found the above mentioned three-way interaction to be significant (*β =0.12, t(64)=2.51, p=0.01*). We illustrate it in Figure 6 by plotting the average selection percentages of different types of comment.

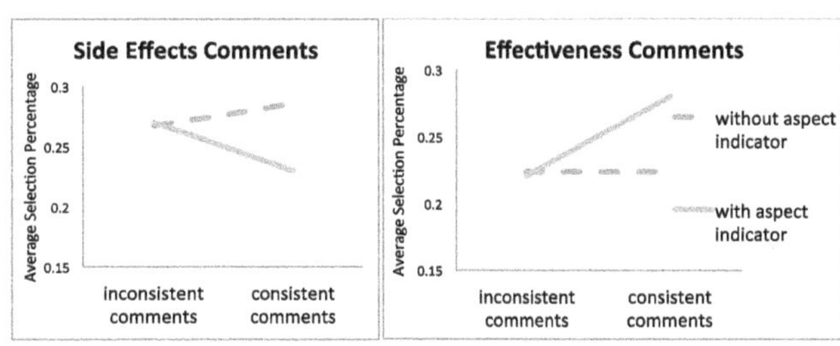

Figure 6. Selection percentage of different types of comment for treating high-risk diseases

Figure 6 suggests that, when seeking information for treatments of high-risk diseases, the presence of aspect indicators increased the preferential selection of attitude consistent comments, i.e., selective exposure tendency, for seeking effectiveness related information, but decreased it for seeking side effects related information. To verify, we tested the interactive effect between presence of aspect indicators and comment consistency for selecting side effects or effectiveness related comments separately.

[2] The three-way interaction among biased aspect, comment aspect and presence of aspect indicator is still significant.

Indeed, we found a significant interaction for selection of effectiveness related comments ($\beta=0.06$, $t(65)=2.00$, $p=0.04$) and a reverse marginal one for side effects ($\beta=-0.06$, $t(65)=-1.57$, $p=0.10$).

We did not find either the similar three-way interaction ($\beta=-0.02$, $t(64)=-0.53$, $p=0.59$), or other significant effects for information seeking tasks regarding low risk diseases, suggesting that the aspect indicators did not significantly impact the selective exposure tendency when participants were only concerned about low-risk diseases.

The above results seem to suggest that, by distinguishing the focused aspect of information, it may increase selective exposure for seeking information related to effectiveness, the *critical aspect*, for treating high-risk diseases, and decrease it for side effect-the *uncritical aspect* in this case.

Now we can revisit the difference that aspect indicators made on the decision outcomes- the fact that it reduced the decision bias for participants who had biased beliefs on effectiveness of medications treating high-risk diseases. We plot the average selection percentages of different comments in the particular situation (biased on effectiveness, for high-risk diseases) in Figure 7.

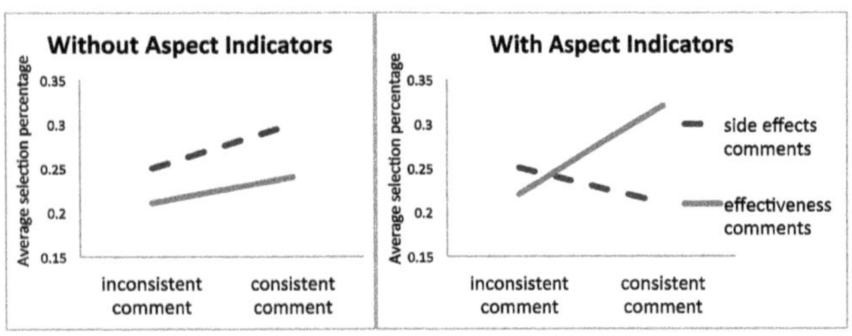

Figure 7. Selection percentage of different comments in the situation of "biased on effectiveness, high-risk diseases"

The figure suggests that, in the control condition where participants could not easily discriminate the focused aspects of comments, they exhibited selective exposure for seeking both effectiveness and side effects related comments, even though they had biased beliefs in only the effectiveness aspect. In the experimental condition, the aspect indicators helped participants to distinguish the two kinds of comment at the information selection stage, and hence "nudged" them to only show selective exposure on the effectiveness aspect but not the side effect aspect, which could potentially have caused the moderated decision bias we observed. To verify that selective exposure in seeking side effects related comments was decreased, we tested the interactive effect of attitude consistency and presence of aspect indicators on the selection percentage of side-effects related comments in the situation, and found it to be marginally significant ($\beta=-0.07$, $t(32)=-2.02$, $p=0.08$).

This is an encouraging finding by suggesting that, as we hypothesized, highlighting the focused issue aspects may encourage people to consciously seek information from different perspectives, and potentially alleviate perceived conflicts on aspect where they do not have strong biases, at least when it is an *uncritical aspect* to the decision. Imagine someone with negative opinions on the effectiveness of a treatment, if s/he indiscriminately seeks biased information for different aspects, s/he may conclude that the treatment is both ineffective and causes bad side effects. This could be especially problematic in medical decisions as they often involve trade-offs made between different aspects [12].

However, when we looked at the effect of aspect indicators on moderating selective exposure on *unbiased aspect* in another situation- when participants had biased beliefs in side effects of treatments for high-risk diseases- we did not find the same interactive effect between presence of aspect indicators and attitude consistency on selection of effectiveness related comments ($\beta=0.02$, $t(31)=0.42$, $p=0.68$). It suggests that aspect indicators may not be as effective in reducing selective exposure on *unbiased aspect* if it happens to be the *critical aspect* to the decision, as it could be overridden by the tendency to seek confirmatory information on the critical aspects of decisions.

In short, we found that, for participants who had biased beliefs about the medication in one aspect- the effectiveness-in treating high-risk disease, the aspect indicators assisted them to differentiate comments on the other aspect- its side effects, where they did not have biased beliefs, and reduced their selective exposure on seeking the latter. By assisting participants to assess different aspects of the decision more accurately, aspect indicators hence helped moderate their decision bias.

CONCLUSION AND DISCUSSION

To summarize, we conducted an experiment to study how aspect indicators- interface features that distinguish between comments on effectiveness and side effects of medications - influenced users' interaction with a medical-decision support tool that aggregates online drug related comments. Particularly, we were interested in testing whether aspect indicator could assist users to recognize issue aspects in which they did not have preexisting biased beliefs, thereby reducing their selective exposure to information in these aspects. We found that:1) aspect indicators facilitated users to seek information on aspects that they were more concerned about, such as aspects in which they had biased beliefs, and aspects that were critical to the decision, e.g., effectiveness of medications for treating high-risk diseases; 2)in the context of medical decision, people who had biased beliefs in the effectiveness of medications treating high-risk diseases were most likely subject to selective exposure, which resulted in biased decision; 3) aspect indicators could mitigate the above-mentioned problems, by assisting users to distinguish between information on different aspects, and thus to reduce their selective exposure on aspect where they did not have biased beliefs. The decrease in selective exposure to a subset of issue aspects resulted in less overall decision bias.

Most importantly, we interpret the results as evidence supporting the idea that interface cues showing issue aspects of information can be a useful feature that "nudges" users towards diversity-seeking, as it can potentially narrow down information seekers' biased beliefs to a subset of issue aspects, thereby reducing potential cognitive dissonance. It may therefore reduce their resistance to diverse opinions and encourage them to seek information about the issue from different perspectives.

However, the aspect indicator should be used with caution, as its effectiveness may depend on the criticality of the aspect. At least in the context of medical decision for treating high-risk diseases, aspect indicators' moderation of selective exposure on unbiased aspect seems to be less effective when it happens to be the critical aspect (i.e., effectiveness) of the decision. We should point out, however, that more research is needed to understand the generalizability of this conclusion. It is possible that the above mentioned reduced effect was due to the tightened anxiety associated with seeking effective treatment for high-risk diseases, and we do not know whether it applies to other contexts or domains, e.g., in political debates. Moreover, the selective exposure tendency in this situation, where one is only concerned about side effects of a life-saving drug, seems to be low in general, and that could also lead to the absence of the additional positive effects of aspect indicators.

With the same goal of distinguishing non-conflicting aspects, a variation of the idea is to highlight aspects on which a user and an attitude-inconsistent source may agree. For example, in a political forum, a feature that enables users to see "topics you agree on" of other members can potentially reduce the barriers of interactions among users with different opinions or ideology. Another similar idea is to reconstruct messages that support a disagreeable position by aspects, and bring forward the non-contradicting aspects before introducing more attitude-challenging ones.

To achieve these goals, a diversity-enhancing or "de-biasing" system should ideally be able to identify in which aspects of a controversial issue a particular user may have strong biased beliefs. Existing techniques that can extract aspects from users' previous contents could be applied [1, 13]. Our study also suggests that techniques to partition a topic into aspects and methods to infer individuals' varying weights giving to different issue aspects could also be useful for developing fine-grained systems that gradually "nudge" users to take different perspectives.

Our study also contributes to the literature on biases in online health information seeking. Consistent with previous research [4, 31], we found that health information seekers tend to seek more confirmatory information in anxiety prone situation such as when one is concerned about a life-threatening condition. Therefore, de-biasing techniques should be taken into consideration for design of medical decision-support systems. Our study also suggests that, while medical decision is typically a multi-attribute decision, information seekers may not be able to recognize or explicitly seek information to accurately assess all the different attributes. Aspect indicators, or other kinds of design feature that encourage users to seek information for different aspects may be useful to facilitate informed decision-making. A more advanced decision-support system could also integrate the varying weights that are supposed to be given to different aspects, based on the decision context and/or user profile.

LIMITATIONS

The current study has two limitations: 1) This is a laboratory experiment relying on artificially introduced "biases". While this approach is widely used in the selective exposure research [7, 8] allowing tighter control on unwanted noises such as prior experience, it is unknown how such bias differs from personal beliefs that develop over time, or for people who have rich knowledge in the decision context. We plan to conduct field experiments with real patients in the future. Nevertheless, we believe our experimental setup represented a valid context of novice patients performing exploratory information seeking. 2) We acknowledge that peer comments may not be the only type of medical information that people seek online, and there may be other issues, such as information credibility, concerned with which comment is sought and considered. We want to point out that the experiment is intended to be an exploratory "case study" to identify a potential problem and a possible solution for online health information seekers. More studies are needed to demonstrate the general functionality of such a tool for assisting online medical decision-making.

REFERENCES

1. Awadallah, R., Ramanath, M., & Weikum, G. Opinionetit: understanding the opinions-people network for politically controversial topics. In *CIKM 2011*, ACM Press (2011), 2481-2484.

2. Bergus, G. R., Levin, I. P., & Elstein, A. S. Presenting risks and benefits to patients. *Journal of General Internal Medicine*, 17, 8 (2002), 612-617.

3. Bornstein, B. H., & Emler, A. C. Rationality in medical decision making: a review of the literature on doctors' decision-making biases. *Journal of Evaluation in Clinical Practice*, 7, 2 (2001), 97-107.

4. Brashers, D. E., Goldsmith, D. J., & Hsieh, E. Information seeking and avoiding in health contexts. *Human Communication Research*, 28, 2 (2002), 258-271.

5. Evans, M., Shaw, A., Thompson, E. A., Falk, S., Turton, P., Thompson, T., & Sharp, D. Decisions to use complementary and alternative medicine (CAM) by male cancer patients: information-seeking roles and types of evidence used. *BMC Complementary and Alternative Medicine*, 7, 1(2007), 25.

6. Festinger, L. (1962). *A theory of cognitive dissonance* (Vol. 2). Stanford University Press.

7. Fischer, P., Kastenmüller, A., Greitemeyer, T., Fischer, J., Frey, D., & Crelley, D. Threat and selective exposure: The moderating role of threat and decision context on confirmatory information search after decisions. *Journal of Experimental Psychology: General*, 140(1), 51
8. Frey, D. Recent Research on Selective Exposure to Information. *Advances in Experimental Social Psychology* 19 (1986), 41-80
9. Garrett, R., Resnick, P. Resisting Political Fragmentation on the Internet. *Daedalus* 140, 4 (2011) 108-120.
10. Grevet, C., Terveen, L. G., & Gilbert, E. Managing political differences in social media. In *CSCW 2013*, ACM Press (2014), 1400-1408.
11. Hart, W., Albarracín, D., Eagly, A. H., Brechan, I., Lindberg, M. J., & Merrill, L. Feeling validated versus being correct: a meta-analysis of selective exposure to information. *Psychological Bulletin*, 135, 4 (2009), 555.
12. Hibbard, J. H., & Peters, E. Supporting informed consumer health care decisions: data presentation approaches that facilitate the use of information in choice. *Annual Review of Public Health*, 24, 1(2003), 413-433.
13. Jiang, Y., Liao, Q., Cheng, Q., Berlin, R., Schatz, B. Designing and Evaluating a Clustering System for Organizing and Integrating Patient Drug Outcomes in Personal Health Messages. In *AMIA 2012*, 417.
14. Keselman, A., Browne, A. C., & Kaufman, D. R. Consumer health information seeking as hypothesis testing. *Journal of the American Medical Informatics Association*, 15, 4 (2008), 484-495.
15. Klayman, J. Varieties of confirmation bias. *Psychology of Learning and Motivation*, 32(1995), 385-418.
16. Kriplean, T., Morgan, J., Freelon, D., Borning, A., & Bennett, L. Supporting reflective public thought with considerit. In *CSCW 2012*, ACM Press (2012), 265-274.
17. Lau, A., & Coiera, E. W. Can cognitive biases during consumer health information searches be reduced to improve decision making? *Journal of the American Medical Informatics Association*, 16, 1(2009), 54-65.
18. Lauckner, C., & Hsieh, G. The presentation of health-related search results and its impact on negative emotional outcomes. In *CHI 2013*, ACM Press (2013), 333-342.
19. Lee, B., Smith, G., Robertson, G. G., Czerwinski, M., & Tan, D. S. FacetLens: exposing trends and relationships to support sensemaking within faceted datasets. In *CHI 2009*, ACM Press (2009),1293-1302.
20. Lewandowsky, S., Ecker, U. K., Seifert, C. M., Schwarz, N., & Cook, J. Misinformation and its correction continued influence and successful debiasing. *Psychological Science in the Public Interest*, 13, 3(2012), 106-131.
21. Leydon, G. M., Boulton, M., Moynihan, C., Jones, A., Mossman, J., Boudioni, M., & McPherson, K. Cancer patients' information needs and information seeking behavior: in depth interview study. *Bmj*, 320 7239 (2000), 909-913.
22. Liao, Q. V., & Fu, W. T. Beyond the filter bubble: interactive effects of perceived threat and topic involvement on selective exposure to information. In *CHI 2013*, ACM Press (2013), 2359-2368.
23. Liao, Q. V., & Fu, W. T. Can you hear me now?: mitigating the echo chamber effect by source position indicators. In *CSCW 2014*, ACM Press (2014), 184-196
24. Liao, Q. V., & Fu, W. T. Expert voices in echo chambers: effects of source expertise indicators on exposure to diverse opinions. In *CHI 2014*, ACM Press (2014), 2745-2754.
25. Munson, S. & Resnick P. Presenting Diverse Political Opinions: How and How Much. In *CHI 2010*, ACM Press (2010), 1457-1466.
26. Nickerson, R. S. Confirmation bias: A ubiquitous phenomenon in many guises. *Review of General Psychology*, 2, 2 (1998), 175.
27. Park, S., Kang, S., Chung, S., Song, J. NewsCube: Delivering Multiple Aspects of News to Mitigate Media Bias. In *CHI2009*, ACM Press (2009), 443-452.
28. Pariser, Eli. *The Filter Bubble: What the Internet Is Hiding from You*, Penguin Press, 2011
29. Schweiger, S., Oeberst, A., & Cress, U. Confirmation Bias in Web-Based Search: A Randomized Online Study on the Effects of Expert Information and Social Tags on Information Search and Evaluation. *Journal of Medical Internet Research*, 16, 3(1998).
30. Sunstein, C. R. (2009). *Republic. com 2.0.* Princeton University Press.
31. White, R. W., Horvitz, E. "Cyberchondria: studies of the escalation of medical concerns in web search." *ACM TOIS*, 27, 4 (2009), 23.
32. White, R. W. Beliefs and Biases in Web Search. In *SIGIR 2013.* ACM Press (2013), 3-12.
33. Yee, K. P., Swearingen, K., Li, K., & Hearst, M. Faceted metadata for image search and browsing. In *CHI 2003,* ACM Press (2003), 401-408.
34. Zeleny, M. (1982). *Multiple criteria decision making* (Vol. 25). J. L. Cochrane (Ed.). New York: McGraw-Hil

Storytelling in Information Visualizations: Does it Engage Users to Explore Data?

Jeremy Boy
Inria, Telecom ParisTech,
EnsadLab
Saclay, Paris
myjyby@gmail.com

Françoise Detienne
CNRS, Telecom ParisTech
Paris
francoise.detienne@telecom-paristech.fr

Jean-Daniel Fekete
Inria
Saclay
jean-daniel.fekete@inria.fr

ABSTRACT
We present the results of three web-based field experiments, in which we evaluate the impact of using initial narrative visualization techniques and storytelling on user-engagement with exploratory information visualizations. We conducted these experiments on a popular news and opinion outlet, and on a popular visualization gallery website. While data-journalism exposes visualizations to a large public, we do not know how effectively this public makes sense of interactive graphics, and in particular if people explore them to gain additional insight to that provided by the journalists. In contrast to our hypotheses, our results indicate that augmenting exploratory visualizations with introductory 'stories' does not seem to increase user-engagement in exploration.

Author Keywords
Narrative visualization; storytelling; social data analysis; engagement

ACM Classification Keywords
H.5.m. Information Interfaces and Presentation (e.g. HCI): Miscellaneous

INTRODUCTION
In this article, our interest is to assess whether augmenting exploratory information visualizations with initial narrative visualization techniques and storytelling can help engage users in exploration. Many online data graphics use narrative design elements to explain a given dataset in a straightforward and compelling way. According to New York Times graphic editors Mike Bostock and Shan Carter [5], these *explanatory graphics* are preferable for data-journalism, as they have the advantage of exposing up-front what the main insights from the data are, without making people "have to work for them." However, most only provide limited interactivity [24, Fig.7], which reduces the potential for personal extraction of insight.

In essence and by definition, Information visualization (Infovis) is interactive and exploratory. Thus, finding ways to make *exploratory graphics* more accessible and engaging to people is important, because if open/public/civic data is to truly empower people, then these people should be able to use appropriate tools to gain their own insights and knowledge—not only that provided by journalists in articles written or designed from a specific perspective. Here, we explore the potential of narrative visualization techniques and storytelling to trigger this desired user-engagement. By engagement, we specifically mean a user's investment in the exploration of a visualization. We present the results of three web-based field experiments, in which we compare user-behavior on a series of exploratory visualization webpages we designed that either included an initial 'story', or did not.

After the background section of this article, we describe the design of our first experiment, present our analysis of user-behavior, and discuss our results. In Section 4, we present the design of our two follow-up experiments, and discuss our results. Finally, in Section 5, we conclude with the implications of these results, and give perspectives for future work.

CHI 2015, April 18 - 23 2015, Seoul, Republic of Korea.
Copyright © 2015 ACM 978-1-4503-3145-6/15/04$15.00.
http://dx.doi.org/10.1145/2702123.2702452

BACKGROUND
One of the main purposes of Infovis is insight [18], which is usually gained through data exploration. Yet, to trigger an exploratory behavior, North suggests that users need to have initial questions; after that, they can go "beyond those initial questions in depth and unexpectedness" [18]. Exploratory behavior is related to question articulation in what Marchionini calls "information seeking" [16], where the process of question articulation, interaction with the query system, and reflective consideration of the outcome is the basis for "information tasks" [16]. An *information task* is *"the manifestation of an information seeker's problem and is what drives information seeking actions."* However, exploring an information-rich environment is rarely a single task activity, but rather a process in which each new action is the result of a set of intricate decision points derived from the previous action [25].

Toms describes this *information interaction* [25] process as a loop that cycles until a satisfactory amount of information is retrieved and integrated. According to Toms, users can initiate the interaction either by formulating a goal, or simply by deciding to examine a body of information. They then select or query a subset of this information, and scan it. When a cue is detected, they stop to examine the data, and if it is relevant, they extract and integrate it. Users can then recycle in multiple, nonlinear ways through each step.

While these models nicely conceptualize the process of exploring an interactive-information-rich environment, they assume that users have a relatively clear initial intent or questions in mind, and that they are capable of formulating appropriate queries using the interface. However, in the context of an online exploratory visualization, where viewers may not have specific background knowledge about the data or about visualization systems, question articulation and data querying may be problematic. As such, designers and researchers [12, 15, 17, 23, 24] have suggested that storytelling can be used to trigger user-interaction and exploration, as it can provide the preliminary questions [24].

Narrative Visualizations

Hullman & Diakoplous define narrative information visualizations as *"a style of visualization that often explores the interplay between aspects of both explorative and communicative visualization. They typically rely on a combination of persuasive, rhetorical techniques to convey an intended story to users as well as exploratory, dialectic strategies aimed at providing the user with control over the insights she gains from interaction"* [15]. This interplay raises a tension previously identified by Segel & Heer between author-driven and reader-driven scenarios [24]. *Author-driven* scenarios follow a linear structure intended by the author. In their most extreme incarnation, they provide no interaction. On the contrary, *reader-driven* scenarios give control to the person receiving the information by providing an open system, and allowing free interaction. Note that interactive narrative visualizations rarely fall directly into either of these categories, but rather somewhere along a spectrum between the two. In this article, we investigate whether author-driven scenarios can help initiate reader-driven ones.

Segel & Heer also propose a design space for narrative design elements [24, Fig.7], and identify three common structures of interactive narrative visualizations: the Martini Glass structure, the Interactive Slideshow, and the Drill-Down story. Here, we focus on the first two. The *Martini Glass* has a two-stage structure: first, the user goes through a relatively heavily author-driven scenario, in which the visualization is introduced through the use of text, annotations, nicely crafted animations, or interesting and evocative views. Second, when the author's intended narrative is complete, the user is put in charge and can actively explore the visualization following whichever path s/he considers most interesting. Thus, the authoring segment should function as a "jumping off point for the reader's interaction" [24]. The *Interactive Slideshow* structure follows a standard slideshow format, and allows for mid-narrative interaction within each slide. These may follow the Martini Glass structure by presenting the author's intended story before inviting the user to interact with the display. Thus, this structure is more balanced between the author- and reader-driven approaches.

While these frameworks are very useful for matters of design, it is still unclear whether the use of narrative visualization techniques in an introductory author-driven scenario can effectively lead to user engagement in a later more reader-driven scenario. Segel & Heer report some results of the deployment of a narrative visualization (The Minneasota Employment Explorer) [24], but the intent of the study was to create and measure social engagement in the annotation of data with personal stories, rather than personal engagement in the exploration of provided data. Although we agree with Segel & Heer that an author-driven scenario is likely to help users articulate initial questions for exploration, we question whether it is sufficient for going "beyond those initial questions in depth and unexpectedness" [18].

User-Centered Metrics and Behavior

Measuring a user's level of engagement in the exploration of data is a complex matter, specially when it comes to online mass-media. Acquiring the necessary qualitative information is impractical, if not impossible. As such, we need to find appropriate behavioral proxies that can describe an analytical and/or exploratory intent.

Gotz & Wen have modeled patterns of user-behavior in terms of analytic actions [14]. They identify four common patterns: Scan, Flip, Swap, and Drill-Down. A *Scan pattern* describes an iterative set of inspection actions of similar data objects, and indicates a user's intent to compare attributes of these objects. A *Flip pattern* describes an iterative set of changes in filter constraints, and indicates a user's intent to compare multiple sets of the data. A *Swap pattern* describes an iterative set of rearrangements of the order in which dimensions of the data are presented, and indicates a user's intent to find correlations between various dimensions. Finally, a *Drill-Down pattern* describes an iterative set of filter operations on orthogonal dimensions of the data, and indicates a user's intent to narrow the analytic focus to a targeted subset of the data.

From a broader perspective, Rodden et al. have proposed a set of user-centered metrics for Web analytics, which they categorize in the HEART framework: Happiness, Engagement, Adoption, Retention, and Task success [21]. Some of these metrics are attitudinal and subjective, and do not fit our present needs. Others however, are behavioral and seem adequate for assessing a user's involvement with the webpage. Typically, Engagement is measured with metrics such as frequency, intensity, and depth of interaction.

While choosing appropriate metrics is essential for revealing underlying qualitative traits, these need to be related to a *goal*, and must be identifiable through different *signals* [21]. Here, our goal is to see whether augmenting exploratory information visualizations with initial narrative visualization techniques and storytelling can help engage users in exploration; we use low-level user-activity traces as signals, and we focus on analytic actions (which we refer to as *semantic operations*), and engagement—typically *depth of interaction*, which we interpret as the number of interactions a user performs that have a direct and perceivable impact on the display.

CASE 1: THE CO_2 POLLUTION EXPLORER

In the rest of this article, we describe the design and results of our three field experiments. For each, we created a specific exploratory visualization webpage with two versions: one that included an introductory *narrative component*, which told a short 'story' about the topic and context of the data, provided initial insights and unanswered questions, and introduced the different visual encodings; and another that did not. Each version, which we respectively refer to as the Storytelling (ST) version and the no-ST version, was alternately assigned to new browser connections; returning connections were reassigned the same version using a Cookie. Thus, our experimental design was between-subjects.

By comparing user-behavior between versions, we seek to determine whether augmenting such a visualization with an introductory 'story' can help engage users in exploration. Our first field experiment was conducted with the CO_2 Pollution Explorer [1], which was first published in English on **visualizing.org**, a popular online visualization gallery, then in French on Mediapart, a popular French news and opinion outlet. The visualization was referenced as one of the "Best of the visualisation web... January 2014" on **visualisingdata.com**, and was curated in the "Visualizing Highlights: March 2014" on **visualizing.org**. It was also picked up by bloggers on **reddit.com**, **citylab.com**, various other sites, and social media. Altogether, the webpage received roughly four thousand unique browser connections between January and June 2014.

Design

The CO_2 Pollution Explorer presented a dataset on the yearly evolution of CO_2 emissions in different countries of the OECD. The two main graphical components were a CO_2 Pollution Map [6], showing the emission of each country as an animated smoke cloud, and a line graph, showing the evolution of emissions over time. The narrative component in the ST version was designed as a heavily author-driven (although "user-directed") slideshow with messaging, that included five stimulating default views (or *sections*). These were sequenced using a set of stepper-buttons, which triggered various animated transitions [24, Fig.7]. Each section followed the general layout shown in Fig.1a, and interactions were limited to clicking on the stepper-buttons and hovering over the graphic—this displayed an inspector with country names and/or total CO_2 emissions. This design was directly inspired by many well accepted and highly acclaimed NY-Times graphics [22]. After the narrative component, the webpage 'opened up' (similarly to the Martini Glass structure) to an *Explore section*, which included only a small amount of messaging, and introduced several extra interactive features that visitors could freely use to explore the dataset. This section followed the layout shown in Fig.1b, and was what visitors assigned to the no-ST version were shown.

Metrics

Using the categories of interaction described by Yi et al. [27] and inspired by Gotz & Wen's analytic actions [14], we created the following taxonomy of semantic operations users could perform with the CO_2 Pollution Explorer. Each level corresponds to one or several low-level interactions with specific features of the interface (presented in brackets).

- **inspect:** show the specifics of the data [*hover line graph, hover line graph dot, hover map*]
- **connect:** show related items [*hover list*]

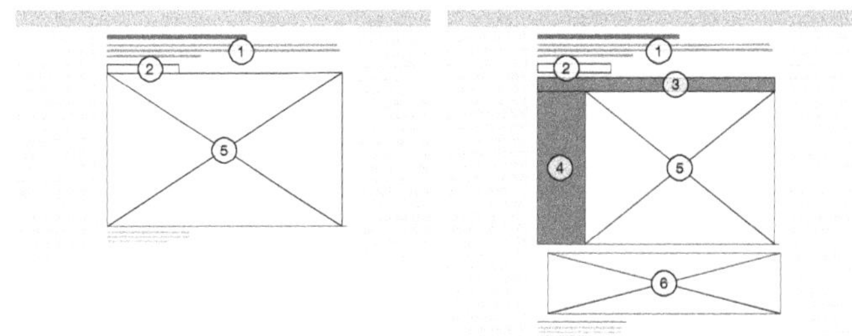

(a) (b)

Figure 1: General layouts for sections in the narrative component (a), and for the Explore section (b). 1) short descriptive paragraph (messaging), 2) stepper-buttons (to navigate between sections—only in the ST version), 3) query-buttons, 4) list of country names and query checkboxes, 5) main graphic, and 6) secondary graphic. Additional interactive features in the Explore section are highlighted in red.

- **select:** mark something to keep track of it [*click line graph, click line graph dot, click map, click list label*]
- **filter:** show something conditionally [*click list checkbox, click "Show All Countries/Remove All Countries" button*]
- **explore:** show something else [*click query-button*]
- **narrate:** show a different section [*click stepper-button*]

To make sense of the four thousand sessions we collected, we performed some initial filtering and manipulations: 1) Since the webpage was designed for desktop browsers, we removed all mobile device connections. While displayable on such devices, the visualization offered certain interactive capabilities that touch displays do not handle (*e. g.,* hovering). In addition, mobile device displays are generally smaller than desktop ones, and we could not assert that the visualization fully fitted the screen resolution, or that if it did, it would not be too small to read and interact with. 2) While several sessions were those of returning browser connections, we considered each of them individually. Return is a good indicator for user-engagement [21]. However, analyzing aggregated sessions would have created major outliers for other metrics such as uptime or depth of interaction. In addition, while it may be conceivable that certain users opened the page, read or explored it for a moment, then turned to another activity, only to later come back and finish their exploration, our traces do not show whether users remembered what they had previously done or that they were not distracted by some external factor. In line with this, we also set a ten minute threshold for inactivity within sessions. Each session in which two consecutive traces were separated by ten or more minutes were split in two. 3) We removed all browser connections that had arrived to the webpage through social media and personal blogs. This allowed us to categorize two different visitor populations: on the one hand, we had visitors coming from visualization gallery websites, which we consider to be a *visualization-savvy population*, and on the other hand, we had visitors coming from Mediapart, which we consider to be an *information-savvy population*, but with *a priori* no particular interest in visualizations—since Mediapart very rarely publishes interactive data-graphics. 4) Finally, several of the browser connections in our traces were ours, as we had originally used the live version for debugging and demoing. Unfortunately, we had no direct method for removing these sessions, since UUIDs were random and anonymous. However, we never communicated the URL directly, and it was hard to guess or remember. Therefore, to filter out our own sessions, we removed all connections that had no previous page URL. In the end, this procedure resulted in a subset of **2975 sessions.**

To obtain practical metrics, we coded the visitor-activity traces in the following way: 1) We attributed session IDs to each returning session and computed the uptime of all sessions. We also separated out the time visitors in the ST version spent in the narrative component and the time they spent in the Explore section. 2) We counted the total amount of click and hover interactions, and extracted all *meaningful interactions*. We define *meaningful hover interactions* as *hover interactions that affect the display (e. g., an inspector overlay) and that last longer than 250ms, so that the user can perceive its effect on the display;* and *meaningful click interactions* as *click interactions that occur on interactive features of the display (i. e., not random clicks anywhere on the display).* We then added these meaningful interactions to get a *total meaningful interactions* count per session. 3) We separated out the different semantic operations, and we repeated the interactions coding procedure for the Explore section alone (in the ST version). This provided us with comparable values for identical settings in both versions. 4) Finally, we coded the sections visitors inspected in the ST version in a dichotomous way: inspected sections were coded 1 and all others 0; and we controlled for linear sequencing of these sections by looking for the pattern [1, 2, 3, 4, 5, Explore] and coding 1 when matched, and 0 otherwise.

Hypotheses

Our analysis was driven by two qualitative hypotheses. The first was that *the narrative component should effectively immerse users in the ST version,* resulting in the fact that they should read through the whole 'story' at least once in a linear fashion, and the second, that *the presence of this narrative component should effectively engage users in the exploration of the data,* resulting in higher user-activity levels in the Explore section of the ST version than in the whole no-ST version. However, verifying such qualitative hypotheses in a web-based field experiment is impractical. Therefore, we operationalized them with the following six quantitative hypotheses:

- **H1.1 (whole webpage):** Visitors in the ST version spend more time on the webpage than those in the no-ST version,
- **H1.2 (whole webpage):** Visitors in the ST version perform more meaningful interactions with the webpage than visitors in the no-ST version,
- **H2.1 (ST version only):** A majority of visitors in the ST version inspect all six sections of the webpage,
- **H2.2 (ST version only):** A majority of visitors in the ST version inspect the six sections in a linear fashion,
- **H3.1 (Explore section only):** Visitors in the ST version spend more time in the Explore section than visitors in the no-ST version, and
- **H3.2 (Explore section only):** Visitors in the ST version perform more semantic operations in the Explore section than visitors in the no-ST version.

We conducted separate analyses for the two populations mentioned above; each was composed of three phases. First, we looked at the general differences between the ST and the no-ST versions. Then, we inspected the ways in which visitors in the ST version inspected the narrative component. Finally, we compared the ways in which visitors behaved in the Explore section between versions.

Results

In the following subsections, we present the results for the information-savvy population (**1270** sessions). In the subsequent Discussion section, we simply report the similarities and discrepancies we found with the visualization-savvy population (**1705** sessions). With respect to the concerns and recommendations in [4, 9, 11], we base all our analyses and discussions on estimation, *i. e.,* effect sizes with confidence intervals (95% CI). Effect sizes are reported as ratios between values for the ST version and values for the no-ST version. All point estimates and 95% CI are based on 10000 percentile bootstrap replicates of the statistic applied to the data [7].

Whole Web-Page Analysis

The first part of our analysis focused on standard aggregated Web analytics (*i. e.,* total uptime and click-count). We began by inspecting the webpage's uptime in both versions. We applied a logarithmic (log) transformation to the data in an attempt to normalize their distributions. Nevertheless, the dashed histogram in Fig. 2 shows a bimodal distribution, and the one in Fig. 3 is skewed. To explain this, we looked at the day of the week and the time of the day at which visitors connected to the webpage, expecting that during working hours, sessions would be shorter. This was not the case. Pursuing, we considered that the abnormality of the distributions might be due to bouncing behaviors. The Google Analytics Help page [13] defines *bounce rate* as *the percentage of single-page visits.* While this definition is not directly applicable in our case, since we use a single dynamic page, we interpret this metric as *the percentage of visitors who perform no click interaction on the page*—since seeing different pages of a website boils down to clicking on a series of hyperlinks[1]. We emphasize that this interpretation strictly concerns the absence of click interactions, since hover interactions may be incidental.

[step 1] 19.2% of sessions in the ST version and **14.6%** in the no-ST version showed a bouncing behavior. The geometric mean (GM) durations of these sessions were **9.5 seconds (s)** and **17.9s**, respectively. We expected this to be the result of returning users who had already read the story and/or seen the visualization. However, the return IDs showed that **88/122** (71.9%) bounces occurred in first-time connections in the ST version, and **65/93** (70.4%) in the no-ST version.

[1] In some cases, the bounce rate is not a "negative" metric: visitors may just find the information they need on the first page without having to perform an interaction. However, in our case, the amount of information readily available on page-load is quite low.

[step 2] We removed all bounced sessions from further analysis, and plotted the uptime distributions again. The solid histograms in Figs. 2 and 3 show that they are now near-normal.

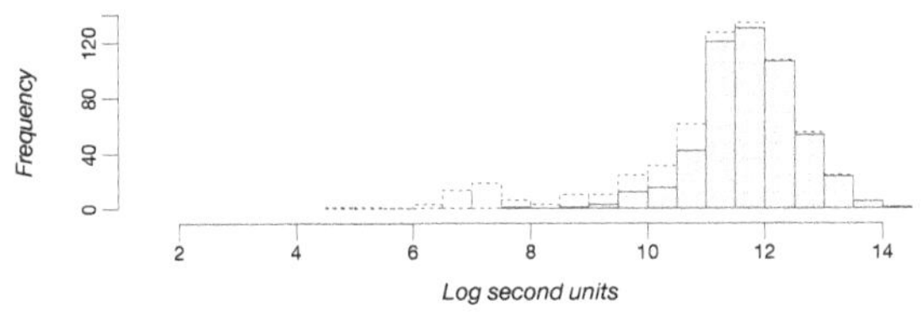

Figure 2: Log uptime distribution in the ST version.

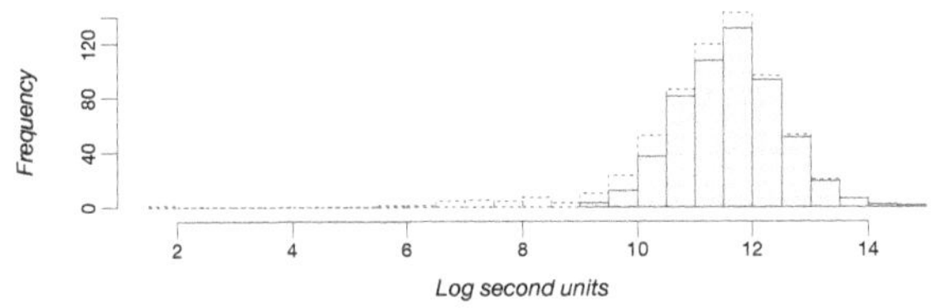

Figure 3: Log uptime distribution in the no-ST version. In both of these Figures, dashed histograms represent distributions before removal of bounced session, and solid histograms represent distributions after removal.

[step 3] We then compared uptime in both versions. Fig. 4 provides evidence that visitors in the ST version spent more time on the webpage (GM = **123.8s,** 95% CI [115.3, 132.9]) than visitors in the no-ST version (GM = **101.6s,** 95% CI [101.6, 117.1]), since the ratio is above 1.

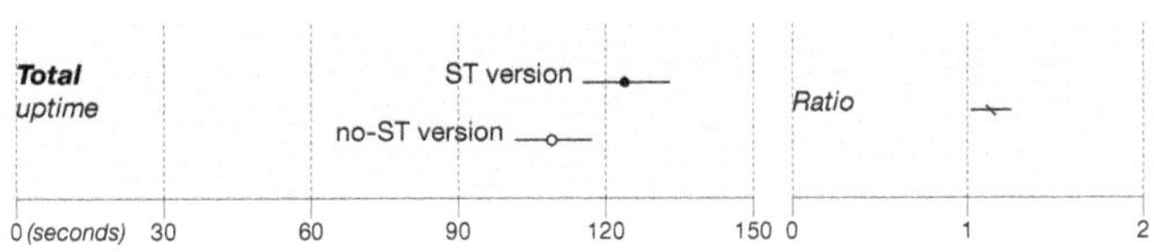

Figure 4: Geometric mean uptime with 95% CI and ratio.

[step 4] Next, we turned to the number of meaningful interactions. Visitors performed on average **42.7 meaningful interactions,** 95% CI [39.3, 46.3] in the ST version, and **43.7,** 95% CI [40.3, 47.3] in the no-ST version (Fig. 5). This provides no real evidence of a difference between versions.

[step 5] We then conducted separate comparisons of the meaningful hover and click interactions. Fig. 5 provides little evidence that visitors in the no-ST version performed more meaningful hover interactions. However, it provides good evidence that visitors in the ST version performed more meaningful click interactions.

Narrative Framework Analysis

The second part of our analysis focused on the narrative framework, and the way visitors in the ST version navigated through the different sections of the narrative component and the Explore section.

[step 6] We began by looking at the number of sections visitors had inspected. In all sessions, visitors saw more than one section; in **77.5%,** they saw the Explore section; and in **71.7%,** they saw all six sections. Similarly to the bounce rate, we expected that the sessions in which visitors did not inspect

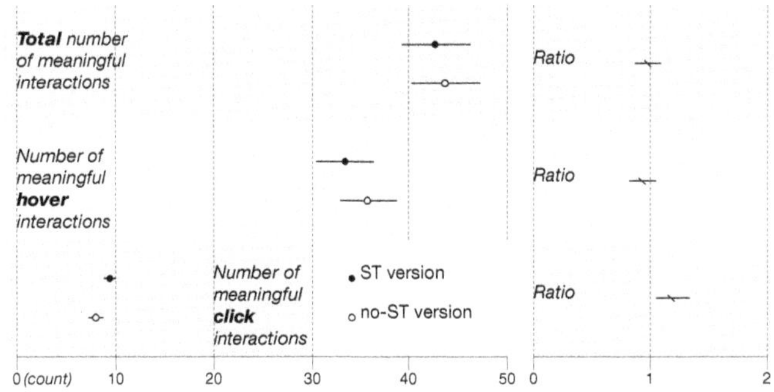

Figure 5: [steps 4 and 5] Meaningful interaction means with 95% CI and ratios for the whole webpage.

all sections would be returning visits, where visitors would have already seen some (if not all) of the content. However, the return IDs showed that **125/145** (86,2%) of these sessions were first-timers.

[step 7] We removed all sessions in which all six sections had not been inspected from further analysis, and turned to the number of sessions in which the narrative component and the Explore section had been inspected in a linear fashion. Only **130/367** (35.4%) met this requirement.

Explore Section Analysis

The last part of our analysis focused on comparing visitors' behavior in the Explore section between versions. Remember that in the no-ST version, visitors were only shown the Explore section, so the time they spent and the interactions they performed in this section are the same as those for the whole webpage [steps 1 through 5].

[step 8] We began by looking at the time visitors spent in the Explore section. These durations were normally distributed (once log transformed) for both versions, and their geometric means and 95% CI (Fig. 6) provide good evidence that visitors in the no-ST version spent twice as much time in Explore section as visitors in the ST version did (**108.8s>54s**).

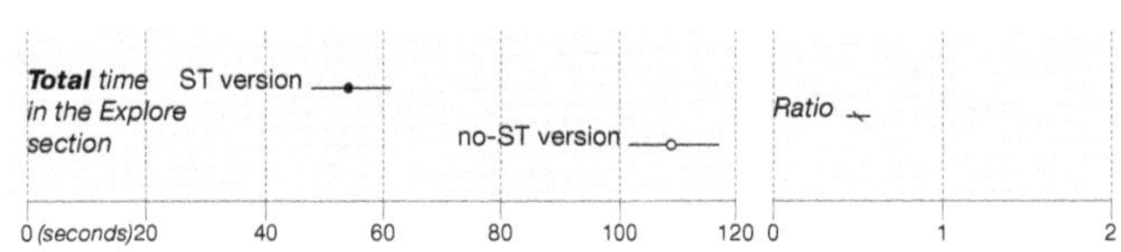

Figure 6: Geometric mean time spent in the Explore section with 95% CI and ratio.

[step 9] Next, we compared the amount of meaningful interactions. Fig. 7 provides good evidence that visitors in the no-ST version performed more hover and click interactions than visitors in the ST version.

[step 10] After that, we turned to the semantic operations visitors performed. We did not consider *narrate* operations here, as they were not available in the no-ST version. A summary is given in Fig. 8. All CI and effect sizes, except for *connect* operations, provide good evidence that visitors in the no-ST version performed more semantic operations than visitors in

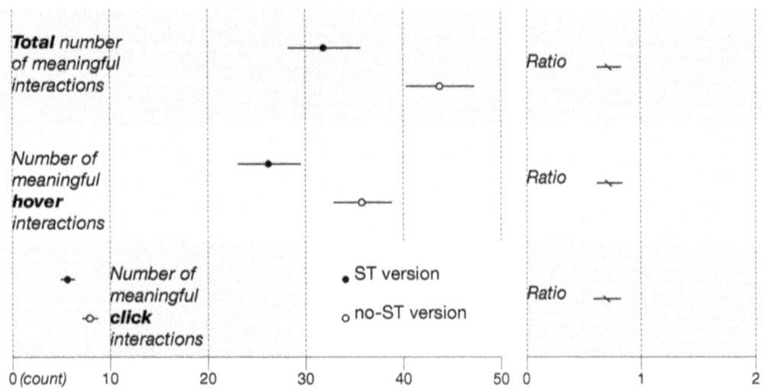

Figure 7: Meaningful interaction means with 95% CI and ratios for the Explore section alone.

the ST version. The figure also provides good evidence that in both versions, visitors mainly performed *inspect* operations. However, the most surprising finding here is that nearly no visitor at all performed *filter* operations.

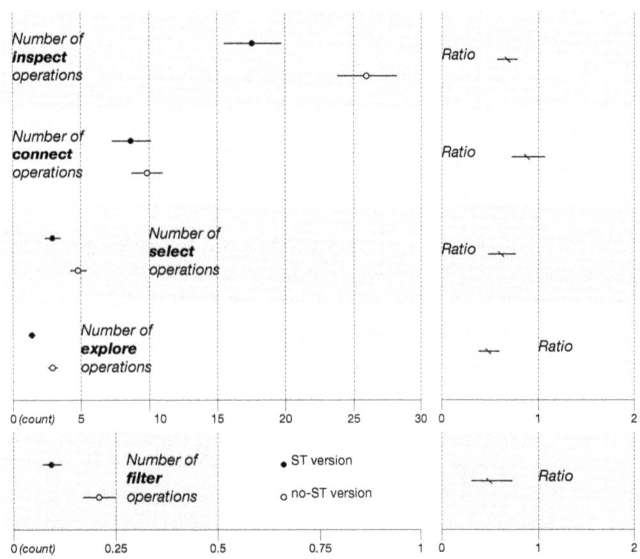

Figure 8: Semantic operation means with 95% CI and ratios for the Explore section alone. The numbers of *filter* operations are plotted with a different scale, as they are very small.

Discussion

H1.1 is confirmed by our results [step 3]. However, the 20% bounce rate in the ST version [step 1] might indicate a certain miscomprehension of the purpose of the stepper-buttons: visitors may not have realized that it was possible to display other content. While we did not pilot-test the usability of these buttons *per se*, we did show the ST version to several people before publishing the webpage (including our editor at Mediapart), and the stepper was not an issue. Thus, another explanation, when considering the 15% bounce rate in the no-ST version and the fact that most bounces in both versions were first-time sessions, might simply be that visitors had trouble displaying the webpage; one visitor reported this, and attributed it to the browser extension Ad Block Plus (ABP).

H1.2 is only partially confirmed, as visitors in the ST version only performed more click interactions [step5]. Although these two conclusions seem rather obvious (since there was more content in the ST version), and it may be argued that on this level, the two versions are difficult to compare, this information can be valuable for a publisher, who may simply want to know what format will increase the uptime and click-count of his/her article.

H2.1 is also confirmed [step 6]. To estimate whether these visitors actually read the textual content of the narrative component, we conducted a post-hoc analysis to determine their word per minute (wpm) score. *wpm* is a standard metric for reading speed [8, p.78], and according to [20], the average French reader's score is between 200 and 250 wpm. Visitors spent roughly 78s (GM) in the narrative component, where there were altogether 269 words to read. Their average wpm is thus **207,** which makes it plausible to assume that they read the story, even if they spent extra time inspecting the graphics.

H2.2 however, is not confirmed [step 7]. This reinforces our idea of a possible miscomprehension of the purpose of the stepper-buttons. *These may not have been explicit enough to convey the idea of a linear narrative* (P1) [2].

H3.1 and H3.2 are not confirmed either [steps 8 and 10]. It should be noted however, that the interaction counts in the no-ST version are likely to include erroneous interactions, *i. e.,* interactions that visitors performed just to get used to the interface, without any specific analytical intent. Nevertheless, we consider these negligible, since the only operations that visitors in the ST version could have gotten 'used to' in the narrative component were *inspect* operations; and, even though the evidence is low, it seems visitors in the no-ST version performed altogether more hover interactions [step 5].

Overall, these results invalidate our qualitative hypotheses: the narrative component did not immerse visitors in the way we expected it to, since they did not inspect the 'story' in a linear fashion; and it did not increase visitors' engagement in exploration in the Explore section. This suggest that augmenting an exploratory visualization with initial narrative visualization techniques and storytelling does not increase user-engagement in exploration. Nevertheless, it does not mean that visitors in the ST version retrieved less information from the webpage than visitors in the no-ST version did: our results simply do not account for this. In fact, since the narrative component provided several important insights, it is possible that visitors in the ST version actually got more information out of the webpage. However, this was information we provided, not personal insight.

As visitors in both versions mainly performed *inspect* operations [step 12], it seems that the Scan pattern was predominant [14], and that visitors' main analytical intent was to simply compare the specific amounts of CO_2 emitted by the countries displayed by default at a single point in time. A possible explanation for this limited exploratory behavior after having inspected the narrative component in the ST version is that *visitors may have considered the information pre-*

[2] We point out possible design or usability problems uncovered by our analysis in this section, and discuss how we fixed them for our follow-up experiment in the next section.

sented in the 'story' to be sufficient (P2). Alternatively, it may be that *our design of the narrative component was not compelling enough to help them articulate questions about the data* (P3), and *did not sufficiently 'train' them to use the interactive features of the Explore section* (P4). It is also possible that *visitors did not perceive the dataset as being rich enough for them to spend extra time exploring it* (P5)—one visitor commented that "the graphic is interesting, but it lacks a key piece of information necessary to a political solution for the reduction of greenhouse gases: the emission rate per capita!" [1, on Mediapart]. Visitors may have indeed had too much *a priori* knowledge of the topic. A final explanation we can think of is that the visualization itself may not have been appealing enough. Toms reports that "the interface must rationally and emotionally engage the user for satisfactory resolution of the goal. [...] content alone is not sufficient" [25]. *The interactive features of the CO_2 Pollution Explorer may not have been explicit enough or may have been perceived as too limited* (P6)—as suggested by the general absence of *filter* operations [step 11].

Nevertheless, the webpage did generate some interesting debate in the Comments sections of the websites it was picked up by—typically on `citylab.com`, visitors discussed "who's responsible for cleaning up our past?", as well as possible solutions for the future, such as "a Manhattan Project for clean energy production" [1, on `citylab.com`]; but unfortunately, it is impossible to tell which version these people had seen.

Finally, while we had expected that the behavior of the visualization-savvy population would be different, specially concerning interactive-behavior, it was overall very similar; uptime was slightly shorter and interactions count smaller, but the general trends were the same—as illustrated by the ratio comparisons in Fig. 9, with the minor exception of the number of *connect* operations, for which there is good evidence here that visitors in the no-ST version performed more.

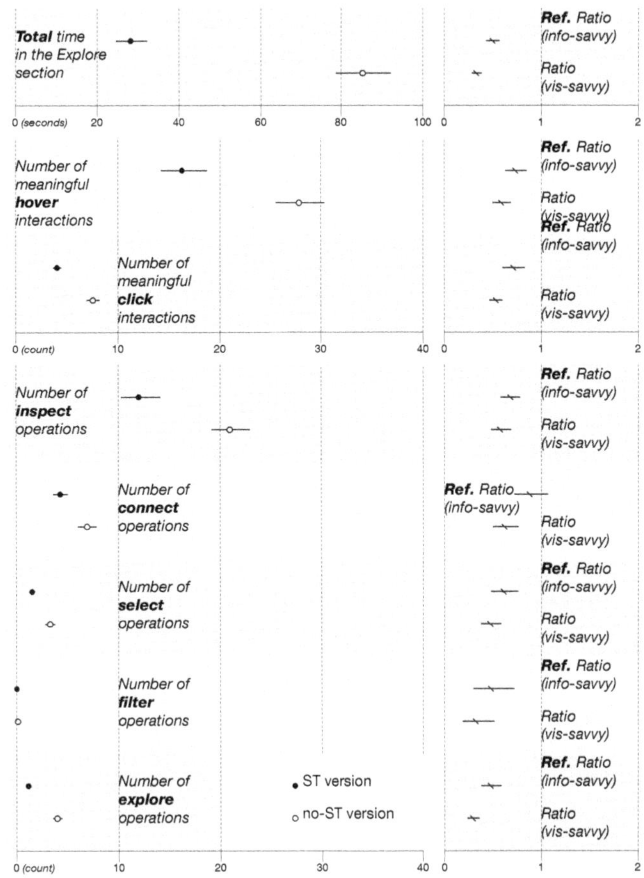

Figure 9: Activity comparisons between versions for the visualization-savvy (vis-savvy) population in the Explore section alone. Ratios for the information-savvy (info-savvy) population are also shown for reference.

CASES 2 & 3: THE ECONOMIC RETURN ON EDUCATION EXPLORER AND THE NUCLEAR POWER GRID

To ensure these unexpected results were not confounded by the possible design or usability problems pointed out in the previous section, we conducted a follow-up study with two other exploratory visualization webpages—The Economic Return on Education Explorer [2] and the Nuclear Power Grid [3]—for which we recreated the two alternately assigned versions (ST and no-ST), thus respecting the between-subjects experimental design. In these, we attempted to solve the listed problems, which we summarize below. For each, we give a design rationale and the solution we adopted.

P1. A minority of visitors inspected the six sections in a linear fashion. **Rationale:** People should be aware that the stepper corresponds to a linear sequencing of the sections of the 'story.' **Solution:** We added a mention beneath the descriptive paragraph of the first slide to tell people that each step corresponds to a section of the 'story,' and that they can read through section using the stepper-buttons.

P2. The narrative component may have provided too many insights, which may have hindered visitors' incentive to explore the visualization. **Rationale:** To foster exploration, the 'story' should serve as a means, a "jumping-off point," not as an end. **Solution:** We told the 'story' from a specific perspective, creating a particular theme, which left more room for discovery of important insights outside of the theme.

P3. Visitors may have been unable to articulate initial questions about the data, even with the help of the narrative component. **Rationale:** People need explicit help to articulate questions if they are not familiar with the data. **Solution:** We added explicit questions in the Explore section for visitors to answer.

P4. Visitors may not have been sufficiently 'trained' to use the interactive features of the Explore section. **Rationale:** The narrative component should also provide an explicit tutorial for the visualization. **Solution:** We added a bolded instruction for each new interactive feature made available in the narrative component.

P5. The data may not have been rich enough for visitors to truly engage in exploration. **Rationale:** The dataset should hold the promise of finding interesting information for people to engage in information interaction. **Solution:** We used a richer dataset for one of the new webpages, and a simpler dataset for the other to act as a baseline.

P6. Visitors may have considered that the interactive potential of the interface was too limited. **Rationale:** People should find the interface appealing, and should be able to easily distinguish and use its different interactive features. **Solution:** On the richer dataset webpage, we added several interactive features, including direct manipulation of data objects.

We emphasize that these problems and design solutions are not necessarily new, nor are they standard. We simply point them out here, as we believed they might have confounded our previous results.

Like the CO_2 Pollution Explorer, we published both new webpages first in English on `visualizing.org`, then in French on Mediapart. The Economic Return on Education Explorer was soon exhibited in the "Visualizing Highlights: August 2014" on `visualizing.org`, and it received a total of roughly 1300 unique browser connections in one weekend. Unfortunately, the Nuclear Power Grid did not meet the same success; it received only 119 browser connections from Mediapart, and 131 from visualization galleries.

Design

The Economic Return on Education Explorer (which we refer to as the *richer visualization*) used a rich dataset on the lifetime costs and benefits of investing in different levels of education in the OECD area; its main graphical component was an interactive stacked bar chart. There were four sections in the narrative component in the ST version, which followed the layout shown in Fig.1a; the Explore section followed a similar layout to Fig.1b, except it included only one graphic.

The Nuclear Power Grid (which we refer to as the *simpler visualization*) used a simple dataset on nuclear energy production and consumption in the OECD area; its main graphical component was a table in which each cell contained a numeric value, a bar chart, a pie chart, and an illustration of a cooling tower. There were three sections in the narrative component, and the layouts were again the same, except that the Explore section did not include the list (Fig.1b(4)), and query-buttons (Fig.1b(3)) were replaced by a drop-down menu.

Metrics

We created the following taxonomies of semantic operations for each visualization:

Semantic Operations for the Richer Visualization

- **inspect:** show the specifics of the data, [*hover label, hover stacked bars*]
- **filter:** show something conditionally, [*click list checkbox, click "Show All Countries/Remove All Countries" button*]
- **explore:** show something else, [*click query-button*]
- **reconfigure:** show a different arrangement, [*click stacked bars*]
- **narrate:** show a different section, [*click stepper-button*]

Semantic Operations for the Simpler Visualization

- **inspect:** show the specifics of the data, [*hover background bar, hover pie chart*]
- **reconfigure:** show a different arrangement, [*select from drop-down menu*]
- **narrate:** show a different section, [*click stepper-button*]

Since we received fewer visits for the simpler visualization, and since our previous results had shown that there was no important difference in trends between the information-savvy and the visualization-savvy populations, we aggregated the data of both populations for the two visualizations. We performed all initial filtering and coding in the exact same way as in the CO_2 Pollution Explorer case; in the end, we kept subsets of **1178 sessions** for the richer visualization, and of **160 sessions** for the simpler visualization. While this last number is quite small compared to those of the other cases, it is still big enough for estimation of user-behavior.

Hypotheses

We maintained the same qualitative hypotheses as for the CO_2 Pollution Explorer, and thus the same quantitative hypotheses. However, the purpose of having created two new webpages was to see whether the richness of the dataset might affect the impact of the narrative component on user-engagement in exploration. Thus, we added a third qualitative hypothesis: *the impact of the narrative component on user-engagement in exploration should be more pronounced when the visualization presents a richer dataset,* resulting in higher user-activity levels in the Explore section of the richer visualization than in that of the simpler visualization.

Results

For both webpages, we conducted the exact same analysis as before. We began by removing all bounced sessions—**27.9%** in the richer visualization case, and **33.1%** in the other—, and plotted all results of the whole webpage and Explore section analyses [steps 3 to 5 and 8 to 10] in Fig. 10. These are compared to those of the information-savvy population in the CO_2 Pollution Explorer case.

Narrative Framework of the Richer Visualization Analysis

[step 6-BIS] In **92.2%** of all sessions, visitors saw more than one section; in **57.4%,** they saw the Explore section; and in **53.7%,** they saw all five sections. The return IDs showed that **157/191** (82.2%) sessions in which visitors did not inspect all sections were first-time connections.

[step 7-BIS] We removed these sessions from further analysis ([steps 7-BIS to 10-BIS]). In **91/222** (40.9%) remaining sessions, visitors inspected all four sections and the Explore section in a linear fashion.

Narrative Framework of the Simpler Visualization Analysis

[step 6-TER] In all sessions, visitors saw more than one section; in **80%,** they saw the Explore section; and in **75.7%,** they saw all four sections. The return IDs showed that **4/17** (23.5%) sessions in which visitors did not inspect all sections were first-time connections.

[step 7-TER] We removed these sessions from further analysis ([steps 7-TER to 10-TER]). In **22/53** (41.5%) remaining sessions, visitors inspected all three sections and the Explore section in a linear fashion.

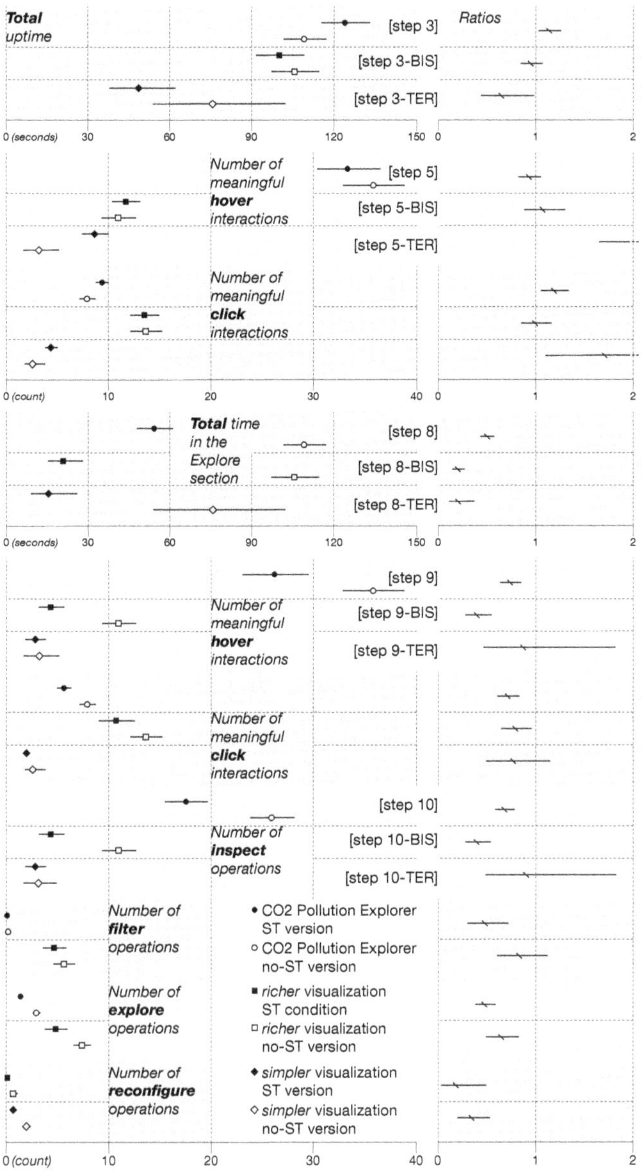

Figure 10: Activity comparisons between versions for the richer and simpler visualizations. Values for the CO_2 Pollution Explorer are also shown for reference.

Discussion

In the richer visualization case, none of the 'whole webpage' and 'Explore section only' hypotheses are confirmed (H1.1, H1.2, H3.1, H3.2). In fact, there is even no evidence of a difference in total uptime, or in number of meaningful hover and click interactions between versions on the whole webpage level—as attested by the ratio 95% CI that all overlap 1 [steps 3-BIS, and 5-BIS] (Fig. 10).

In the simpler visualization case, none of the 'whole webpage' and 'Explore section only' hypotheses are confirmed either, with the exception of H1.2. However, these results are to be considered cautiously, since they show a lot of variability in the data—as attested by the very wide 95% CI. This can be attributed to the smaller sample size. Nevertheless, since we are not directly interested in effect sizes, but rather in simply seeing if there is a difference between versions, the ratio 95% CI that do not overlap 1 (Fig. 10) provide sufficient information for our needs. Overall, visitors spent the least amount of time and performed the least amount of interactions in this case, be it on the whole webpage level or in the Explore section alone—this was expected, as the dataset and interactive potential of the visualization were not as rich as in the other cases.

Finally, in both cases, H2.1 is confirmed, but H2.2 is not. While the percentages of sessions in which visitors inspected all sections of the narrative component in a linear fashion are higher than in the CO_2 Pollution Explorer case, they are still below 50%.

Overall, these results invalidate once again our two main qualitative hypotheses, and confirm those of the CO_2 Pollution Explorer: the narrative components did not immerse visitors in the way we expected them to in either cases; and they did not increase visitors' engagement in exploration in the Explore sections. Furthermore, while there is evidence that visitors of the richer visualization performed more meaningful click interactions in the Explore section than visitors of the simpler visualization did—which seems normal, since there were many more clickable features in the richer visualization; there is no real evidence that they spent more time there, or that they performed more meaningful hover interactions—as shown by the 95% CI for the analysis of the Explore sections of the ST versions in [steps 8-BIS, 8-TER, 9-BIS and 9-TER] (Fig. 10). Thus, there is no real evidence that the narrative component in the richer visualization case had a bigger effect on user-engagement in exploration than the one in the simpler visualization case—this invalidates our third qualitative hypothesis. However, from a broader perspective, confirming this third hypothesis would have been pointless, since each of our experiments have shown that including a narrative component does not increase user-engagement in exploration.

CONCLUSION

In this article, we have shown that augmenting exploratory information visualizations with initial narrative visualization techniques and storytelling does not help engage users in exploration. Nevertheless, our results are not entirely negative. The CO_2 Pollution Explorer and the Economic Return on Education Explorer were successful webpages that did engage people in a certain way: both received a relatively high number of visits, and the average uptime was well-above web standards, whatever the version. They were also curated in referential online visualization galleries. Thus, beyond the spectrum of this study, it is important that the concept of engagement in Infovis be better defined. Here, we consider it from a behavioral perspective as an investment in exploration, which may lead to insight. However, engagement can also be considered from an emotional perspective as an aesthetic experience, as is done with certain *casual information visualizations* [19, 26].

Ultimately, our goal is to understand how to engage people with exploratory visualizations on the web. While this study may have failed due to the simple fact that people have a limited attention span on the internet, and that if they read through an introductory narrative component, they will not spend extra time exploring a visualization, we still claim that 'pushing' observations, unanswered questions, and themes from a narratorial point of view in the form of an introductory 'story' does not seem to encourage people to dig further for personal insights. In the future, we will continue to investigate new/other strategies for fostering exploratory behavior (like the one taken by the Game-y Infographics [10]) to allow switching from author-driven visualizations to reader-driven ones on the web.

ACKNOWLEDGEMENTS
The authors would like to thank Sophie Dufau, journalist and editor at Mediapart, for publishing the visualizations; all readers of Mediapart who took part in these experiments; Pierre Dragicevic for sharing his R code for calculating 95% CI, and for his help with the analysis of the collected data; Petra Isenberg for proof-reading this article; and Google for the Research Award that funded this work.

REFERENCES
1. The CO_2 Pollution Explorer. On Mediapart: `http://blogs.mediapart.fr/blog/la-redaction-de-mediapart/180314/co2-la-carte-de-la-pollution-mondiale`; on visualizing.org: `http://visualizing.org/visualizations/where-are-big-polluters-1971`; on citylab.com: `http://www.citylab.com/work/2014/03/map-historys-biggest-greenhouse-gas-polluters/8657/`.
2. The Economic Return on Education Explorer. On Mediapart: `http://blogs.mediapart.fr/blog/la-redaction-de-mediapart/180914/les-diplomes-est-ce-que-ca-paye`; on visualizing.org: `http://visualizing.org/visualizations/there-financial-interest-investing-longer-studies`.
3. The Nuclear Power Grid. On Mediapart: `http://blogs.mediapart.fr/blog/la-redaction-de-mediapart/190914/le-poids-du-nucleaire-dans-le-monde`; on visualizing.org: `http://visualizing.org/visualizations/what-part-nuclear-energy`.
4. American Psychological Association. *The Publication manual of the American psychological association (6th ed.)*. Washington, DC, 2010.
5. Bertini, E., and Stefaner, M. Data Stories #22. `http://tiny.cc/datastories`.
6. Boy, J., and Fekete, J.-D. The CO_2 Pollution Map: Lessons Learned from Designing a Visualization that Bridges the Gap between Visual Communication and Information Visualization [Poster paper]. In *Proc. of IEEE VIS'14* (Nov. 2014).
7. Canty, A., and Ripley, B. *Boostrap Functions*, 2014.
8. Carver, R. *The Causes of High and Low Reading Achievement*. Taylor & Francis, 2000.
9. Cumming, G. The new statistics: Why and how. *Psychological science 25*, 1 (2014), 7–29.
10. Diakopoulos, N., Kivran-Swaine, F., and Naaman, M. Playable data: Characterizing the design space of game-y infographics. In *Proc. of CHI'11* (2011), 1717–1726.
11. Dragicevic, P., Chevalier, F., and Huot, S. Running an hci experiment in multiple parallel universes. In *CHI '14 Extended Abstracts* (2014), 607–618.
12. Franchi, F. On visual storytelling and new languages in journalism. `http://www.brainpickings.org/2012/02/06/francesco-franchi-visual-storytelling/`.
13. Google analytics. `https://support.google.com/analytics/answer/1009409?hl=en`.
14. Gotz, D., and Wen, Z. Behavior-driven visualization recommendation. IUI '09, ACM (New York, NY, USA, 2009), 315–324.
15. Hullman, J., and Diakopoulos, N. Visualization rhetoric: Framing effects in narrative visualization. *IEEE TVCG 17*, 12 (Dec. 2011), 2231–2240.
16. Marchionini, G. *Information Seeking in Electronic Environments*. Cambridge Series on Human-Computer Interaction. Cambridge University Press, 1997.
17. Murray, S. Engaging audiences with data visualization. `http://www.oreilly.com/pub/e/2584`.
18. North, C. Toward measuring visualization insight. *IEEE CG&A 26*, 3 (2006), 6–9.
19. Pousman, Z., Stasko, J., and Mateas, M. Casual information visualization: Depictions of data in everyday life. *IEEE TVCG 13*, 6 (Nov. 2007), 1145–1152.
20. Richaudeau, F. *Méthode de Lecture rapide*. Retz, 2004.
21. Rodden, K., Hutchinson, H., and Fu, X. Measuring the user experience on a large scale: User-centered metrics for web applications. In *Proc. of CHI'10* (2010).
22. Rooze, M. Interactive News Graphics. `http://tinyurl.com/NYTimes-collection`.
23. Satyanarayan, A., and Heer, J. Authoring narrative visualizations with ellipsis. *Proc. EuroVis'14* (2014).
24. Segel, E., and Heer, J. Narrative visualization: Telling stories with data. *IEEE TVCG 16*, 6 (Nov. 2010), 1139–1148.
25. Toms, E. G. Information interaction: Providing a framework for information architecture. *J. Am. Soc. Inf. Sci. Technol. 53*, 10 (Aug. 2002), 855–862.
26. Wood, J., Isenberg, P., Isenberg, T., Dykes, J., Boukhelifa, N., and Slingsby, A. Sketchy rendering for information visualization. *IEEE TVCG 18*, 12 (2012), 2749–2758.
27. Yi, J. S., Kang, Y. a., Stasko, J., and Jacko, J. A. Toward a deeper understanding of the role of interaction in information visualization. *IEEE TVCG 13*, 6 (2007), 1224–1231.

Understanding Data Videos: Looking at Narrative Visualization through the Cinematography Lens

Fereshteh Amini[1], Nathalie Henry Riche[2], Bongshin Lee[2], Christophe Hurter[3], Pourang Irani[1]

[1]University of Manitoba
Winnipeg, MB, Canada
{amini,irani}@cs.umanitoba.ca

[2]Microsoft Research
Redmond, WA, US
{nath,bongshin}@microsoft.com

[3]ENAC, University of Toulouse
Toulouse, France
christophe.hurter@enac.fr

ABSTRACT
Data videos, motion graphics that incorporate visualizations about facts, are increasingly gaining popularity as a means of telling stories with data. However, very little is systematically recorded about (a) what elements are featured in data videos and (b) the processes used to create them. In this article, we provide initial insights to build this knowledge. We first report on a qualitative analysis of 50 professionally designed data videos, extracting and exposing their most salient constituents. Second, we report on a series of workshops with experienced storytellers from cinematography, graphics design and screenplay writing. We provided them with a set of data facts and visualizations and observed them create storyboards for data videos. From these exploratory studies, we derive broader implications for the design of an authoring tool to enable a wide audience to create data videos. Our findings highlight the importance of providing a flexible tool supporting a non-linear creation process and allowing users to iteratively go back to different phases of the process.

Author Keywords
Information visualization; narrative visualization; data storytelling; data video; qualitative analysis.

ACM Classification Keywords
H.5.m. Information interfaces and presentation (e.g., HCI): Miscellaneous.

INTRODUCTION
Storytelling with data is rapidly becoming prominent both in practice and academia. Leading media outlets such as the New York Times and the Guardian are increasingly exposing the general public to stories with visual depictions of data, or narrative visualizations [20, 27]. *Data videos* – custom motion graphics combining both visual and auditory stimuli to promote a data story – are one among the seven genres of narrative visualizations [27]. The popularity of data videos could be attributed to the diverse forms of narrative structures and the wide range of visuals they expose an audience to within a short presentation time. As a result, researchers have argued that data videos can be highly impactful, making it a particularly interesting form of narrative visualization to study.

Despite the great potential that data videos can offer, we know very little about their constituent characteristics to help create narratives using this medium. Such knowledge can be instrumental in allowing a broader audience to design and craft data videos. We consider this work as a first step toward understanding data videos and a basis for developing, in the future, novel tools geared towards generating compelling data stories using this medium.

As empirical knowledge can be the cornerstone for early design implications [11], we attain our goals with two exploratory studies. In a first exploration, we identify the *high-level narrative structures* found in professionally created data videos and expose their key components. We carry out a qualitative examination of the narrative structures in 50 professional data videos collected from a range of reputable sources through the lens of established disciplines such as film theory and cinematography [13, 15]. Our findings are structured around the four narrative categories classically used in cinematography: Establisher, Initial, Peak, and Release [13, 25]. We report on the different types of narrative structures formed by the sequencing of these categories and characterize the videos' contents through the varied types of data visualizations, and attention cues used.

Furthermore, to gain an understanding of the various strategies used in the *process* of creating visual narratives, we observed professional storytellers create storyboards from data and visualizations we provided them. We gain valuable insights through a series of workshops we conducted with 13 experienced storytellers, such as screenwriters, video makers, and motion graphics designers. We describe our observations on the most common processes they employ to build a narrative structure and their consultations for making their video storyboards visually compelling.

CHI 2015, April 18 - 23, 2015, Seoul, Republic of Korea
Copyright 2015 ACM 978-1-4503-3145-6/15/04$15.00
http://dx.doi.org/10.1145/2702123.2702431

RELATED WORK

While the perspective of using data visualizations as a means to communicate is not a recent topic [4], storytelling with data has recently begun to gain more attention in the research community [20, 22, 27]. In particular, the spread of infographics to a wide audience and the development of fields like data journalism create unique opportunities for research in information visualization [16, 23, 29].

Many researchers have taken a step towards filling the gap between data exploration to gain insights and tell stories from these insights. Examples of these efforts include the expansion of data exploration tools to support storytelling scenarios such as GeoTime Stories [14] or Tableau Story Points [18]. Furthermore, several visual analytics systems have integrated storytelling into their designs [18, 28], to allow analysts to annotate stories within the exploratory visual process for example.

Research pieces directly aimed at providing solutions to help people craft narrative visualizations are scarce [12, 21]. We believe that our community needs to develop a larger body of knowledge on narrative visualizations, characterizing their key components but also studying the process to craft them. Such knowledge will inform the design of tools that would help a wide range of people consume and craft stories with data visualization.

Segel and Heer [27] initiated a first step in identifying genres of narrative visualizations by conducting an analysis of 58 narrative visualizations. They proposed a broad view of narrative visualizations integrating in their analysis static infographics, comics, slide-shows, video, and animations. Their insights offer a general sense of the range of visual and narrative components used in storytelling with data.

More focused studies of narrative visualizations have explored specific genres or aspects of narrative visualizations. Bateman et al. [9] and Borkin et al. [10] specifically focused on understanding infographics and what makes them appealing or memorable to a large audience. Hullman et al. [19] discussed categories of rhetorical techniques drawn from an online journalism corpus. The more relevant to ours is Hullman et al.'s [20] work on the analysis of sequences in storytelling with data. While this work focused on specific transitions between visuals, we take a more holistic view of the narrative structure and characterize higher-level structure in data videos.

While these previous studies have deepened our knowledge on the composition of narrative visualizations, identifying what makes them compelling or memorable, none of these studies have looked at the process involved in crafting them. We also aim to fill this gap and report insights on the creation process involved in crafting data videos.

Even though research is sparse regarding the structure of storytelling with data visualizations, there is a wealth of research on narrative story structure in other fields such as literature [15], cinematography [24], or comics [13, 25]. We aimed at building on this body of work, looking at the composition of data videos through this lens. In particular, we analyzed data videos using the theory of visual narrative structures described by Cohn [13]. This approach attempts to unify different perspectives on narrative structures in different genres. Derived from the structure of comics, we also believe it particularly suited to analyzing stories featuring data visualizations.

STUDY 1: ANALYSIS OF DATA VIDEOS

To better understand the *content* and *structure* of data videos, we conducted a qualitative analysis of 50 data videos from 8 reputable online sources. A complete list of the videos is included in a companion website[1].

Methodology

Data Video Selection

To ensure videos collected have a good quality and likely to have been created by experienced professionals, we selected several from a range of reputable sources as well as those with a high number of views on YouTube.com and Vimeo.com. We collected data via online magazines, government and research center websites, graphic design company websites, and visualization blogs.

In addition, a data video had to meet the following three inclusion criteria to be added to our dataset: 1) it contains a core message and presents arguments supported by data; 2) it includes at least one data visualization; and 3) it follows a narrative format which refers to the spoken or written account of connected events given in a sequence [3].

Data Video Analysis

We conducted both open [17] and close [26] coding of the data. In the first phase, the lead researcher used an open-coding approach to *characterize the content* of 10 (20%) of the videos. Through the discussion of these codes among three researchers over three sessions, we selected two dimensions: *Data Visualization Type* and *Attention Cues*. Since our final code-set was composed of well-defined types such as bar charts and scatterplots for visualizations or animation and highlighting for attention cues, the lead researcher completed the coding on the remaining set.

In the second phase, we sought to characterize the *Narrative Structure* of data videos. Looking at this data through the cinematography lens [13], we opted to analyze the data around four main narrative categories: *Establisher, Initial, Peak,* and *Release*. We analyzed the type of content included. Two researchers independently coded five (10%) data videos and refined the coding until they had reached agreement on the segmentation of each sequence (at about 2 seconds precision) and their codes. The lead researcher completed the coding on the remaining videos.

[1]http://hci.cs.umanitoba.ca/projects-and-research/details/data-videos

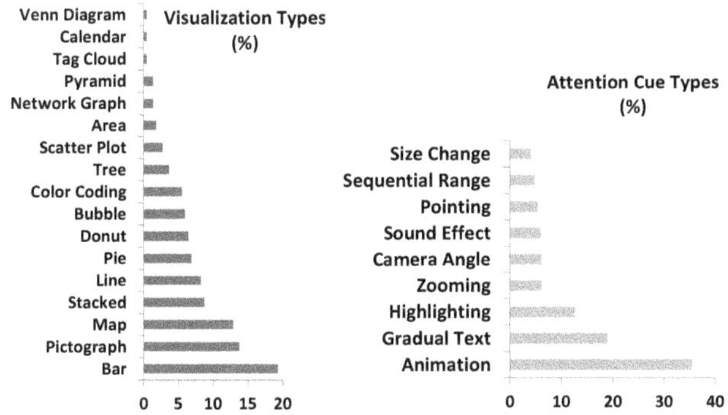

Figure 2. Percentage of visualization types (left), and attention cue types (right) coded.

Characterizing the Content of Data Videos

We describe the content of data videos along the two identified dimensions: *Data Visualization Types* and the types of *Attention Cues.*

Data Visualizations

In data videos, visual data representations are the primary means for conveying a story. Overall, data videos we collected present a large amount of visuals in a short amount of time. While the average duration of a data video was found to be 3 minutes (ranging from 1 to 7.5 minutes), the average number of data visualizations presented is six (ranging from 1 to 19 visualizations). On average, 48% of the total duration of a data video is dedicated to data visualizations. However, despite this high content dedicated to visualizations, 72% of the data videos tend to rely on only 5 different types of visualizations on average (Figure 2-left). For example, more than half of the data video duration in [7] contains data visualizations but they are limited to only 3 types of representations (scatter plots, bar charts, and maps).

Attention Cues

One of the most important and unique design dimensions with regards to data videos are Attention Cues or tactics used to keep viewers engaged during the delivery of a story. We identified nine major types of visual and auditory effects, aimed at drawing the viewer's attention. These include camera motion effects such as zooming, building tension in the story via soundtracks, and emphasizing salient information via gradual text appearance or highlighting (Figure 2-right). The top three most commonly used effects were animation, appearing/disappearing, and highlighting (e.g., the data video in [6] includes several attention cues). Surprisingly, we did not identify many cues specifically related to data visualizations except for animated sequential data presentation.

Characterizing the Narrative Structure of Data Videos

Narrative is defined as a spoken or written account of connected events [3]. The organization and ordering, in which these connected events are presented (i.e., the narrative structure) may greatly impact the understanding of the narrative and, in case of data videos, the viewing experience. In this section, we present our findings regarding the narrative structure of data videos. We analyzed them through the lens of the dramatic structure as initially defined by Freytag [15] and further refined for visual narratives by Cohn [13]. Below we describe different types of narrative structures encountered, and present findings regarding their content.

Narrative Structure and Categories

Following Cohn's theory of visual narrative structure, we split data videos into temporal sequences and coded these sequences regarding their role in the narrative. We used Cohn's definitions for the four major narrative categories:

- *Establisher* (E): sequences that "provide referential information without engaging them in the actions or events of a narrative."
- *Initial* (I): sequences that "set the action or event in motion."
- *Peak* (P): sequences where "the most important things happen; the culmination of an event or the confluence of numerous events."
- *Release* (R): sequences that show "the aftermath of the Peak."

As described by Cohn, we observed that data video categories are also hierarchical and can be further decomposed into units: sequences that put forward different points contributing to a single category. Figure 3 describes the coding of an example data video [8].

Narrative Structure Patterns

A given sequencing of categories and the number of units composing them form a narrative structure pattern. Our analysis revealed many different patterns (Figure 1). Even though some are subsets of others, we show them to demonstrate variety. We labelled these patterns using regular expressions composed of narrative categories: [Element+] where Element is one of {E,I,P,R} and the "+" sign indicates repetition of the preceding element. Among these, three recurrent patterns emerged and we could loosely correlate them to the types of message they convey.

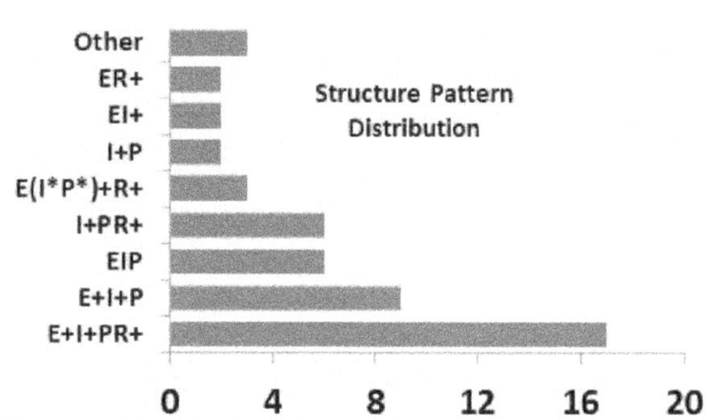

Figure 1. Distribution of narrative structures patterns.

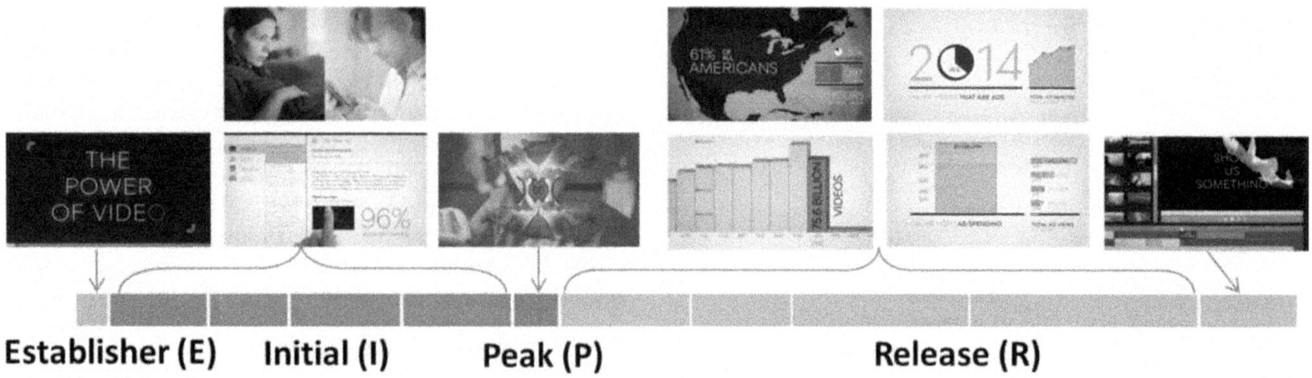

Figure 3. Coding of an example data video [8] about exploration of the power of online video. Screen captures from the video are associated with the corresponding narrative category.

This data video is 2.07 minutes long and follows the (EI+PR+) narrative structure pattern; the combination of voice narration, video footage, data visualizations, and attention cues provides a balanced video with a powerful story about our evolving relationship with media. The Establisher unit sets up the video indicating that the video is about "the power of video", quickly transitioning to the Initial category that includes 4 units. The first 3 Initial units each include a new fact such as stats about the rising use of video. At the beginning of the forth Initial unit, the narrator asks "why video?" followed by footage of everyday people and by reflecting on the information already presented, builds the tension for the Peak unit that answers the question in one sentence. The Peak ends with drastic audio and animation effects to grab the viewer's attention. The video then continues by presenting more facts that supports the answer given in the Peak. This is done through 4 Release units, all of which include data visualizations (i.e., bar, pie, line, and stacked charts, and a map). Animated charts, highlighting a single bar in the bar chart, and sequential change of the year range are amongst attention cues used within the data visualizations. The fifth and last unit in the Release includes a take away message which asks the viewers to create videos: "Show Us Something".

The most common pattern we identified in 34% of the videos is the "E+I+PR+" pattern. Videos following this pattern are usually well-balanced, solidly grounding their story with several units in *Establisher* (E+), building some tension with several units in *Initial* (I+) and leading to a single *Peak* (P), usually occurring around the middle of the video. The multiple *Release* units (R+) ensure ample time for conveying the take away message.

Two other dominant patterns are "E+I+P" and its subset pattern of "EIP"; these structures contain a single *Peak* unit (P) without any *Release* units. Cohn [13] refers to this complex structure as the left-branching tree not commonly seen in comics. Data videos of this narrative structure finish the narrative by leaving the viewer with a "question" or "something to think about" after presenting some facts within the data (e.g., [5]).

We also observed structures that break away from the common pattern with an escalating tension followed by a single *Peak* [15]. First is "E(I*P*)+R+" which depicts data videos including multiple *Peak* units proceeded by multiple *Initial* units. The videos pertaining to this pattern are longer in duration when compared to other patterns and include alternative visualizations of the same aspect of the data or multiple new facts all having the same tension level. Two other surprising patterns are somewhat similar: "EI+" and "ER+," both of which do not contain a distinct *Peak* unit in the narrative structure. The data videos following these patterns present "multiple problems" or "multiple solutions," respectively.

Composition of Narrative Categories

To gain an overview of the relative importance of these categories, we report on the proportion of average time devoted to each category as well as the proportion of data visualizations and attention cues in each of these.

We note that the *Initial* category is the most prominent in data videos (Figure 4) implying that the structures in the data videos break away from the traditional narrative structures in which the Initial category is shorter in duration stretching up to the middle of the narrative where the Peak is (e.g., Buster Keaton's silent film, the general [2], perfectly aligns with the traditional structure). Figure 5 shows that on average about 60% of the Initial category of units contain some type of data visualization. This finding suggests that data visualizations are used even for setting events in motion and not necessarily for only presenting closing facts, as might be the case when they are used in the *Peak* or *Release* categories of the narrative.

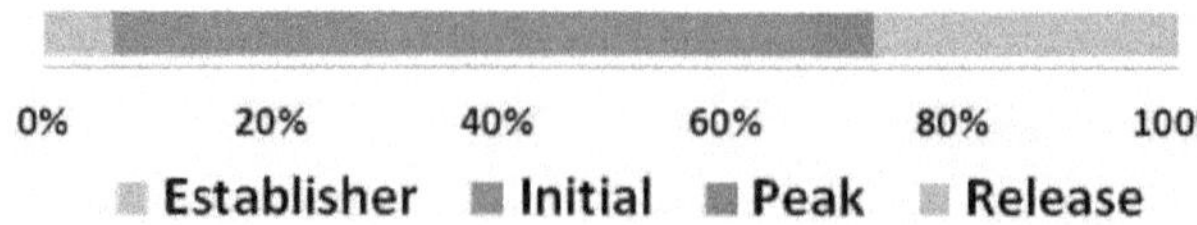

Figure 4. Average duration percentages of narrative categories out of the total duration of the video

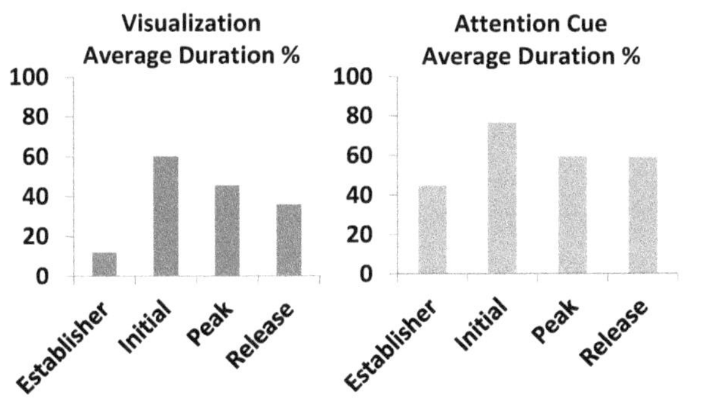

Figure 5. Left: the average duration percentage of data visualizations, and Right: the average duration percentage of attention cues out of total duration of each category.

In addition, the proportion of attention cues in each category follows a distribution similar to data visualizations suggesting that they could be directly related and that data visualizations are usually accompanied by some type of attention cue to guide viewers' attention to the most interesting insight. Attention cues are also used when transitioning between narrative category units to guide viewers' attention from one scene to the other.

Figure 6 presents the duration distribution of different types of content for each category. As it can be expected, we observed that it is common to initiate the narrative with a question (20%), and conclude the narrative with a spoken or written take away message (30%). Our analysis also revealed that data videos contain a large amount of repetitions: 46% of new facts are accompanied by a repetition. While it may be expected that these repetitions occur later in the video, a good proportion is present in the Initial category (22%). It is also worth noting that several videos introduce new facts in the Release or the last category of the narrative (27%). For example the video in Figure 1 includes new facts in Release units as further evidence of the claim made in the peak.

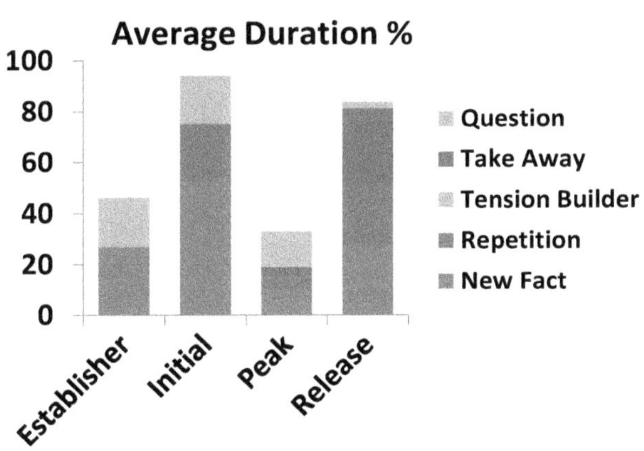

Figure 6. Average percentages of new fact, question, and repetition occurrences in each narrative category.

STUDY 2: ANALYSIS OF STORYBOARDING PROCESS

Continuing our mission for understanding data videos and to complement our findings from Study 1, we conducted a second study to gain insights on the process of creating data videos. We designed a series of workshops to observe how professional storytellers create data video storyboards.

Methodology

Participants

We recruited 13 experienced storytellers (5 female and 8 male, aged 27 to 65 years) for our study, asking them to create storyboards for data videos. We recruited participants with formal training and significant experience crafting stories for a wide audience through motion graphics with or without data visualizations (4 participants), cinematographic pieces including trailers, advertisements, TV series, and movies (5 participants), and other storytelling format such as screenplay, novels, comics, and infographics (4 participants). We conducted five sessions with pairs having the same background and three sessions with a single participant. Participants were unfamiliar with one another.

Study Material

We opted to provide all of our participants with a set of facts and visualizations to select from to create a data video storyboard. We selected data of general interest on marriage and divorce [1]. We hypothesized that such data could lead to polarized take away messages such as advocating for or against marriage, stimulating discussions between participants and possibly leading to different design or narrative structures.

Using our findings in Study 1 and four pilots with one pair and three single students in cinematography and human-computer interaction, we refined the facts and visualizations to use. We extracted a set of 12 different data facts covering several distinct topics in hopes of providing enough material for participants to create different stories. Examples of facts we provided are "the majority of divorces happen between ages 40 and 44", "the average duration of marriage before divorce is 10 years", "there are peaks in the number of divorces after world war 2 in 1945 and after the divorce reform act in 1971". To illustrate each of the facts, we used 22 data visualizations and infographics all of which were amongst the most common types found through our first study and extracted from blogs or news websites covering these stories such as the Guardian; or created from the raw data using Excel.

Procedure

We conducted 3-hour sessions including a 15 to 20 minutes break in the middle. We initiated the session with a presentation of the study and a collection of demographics. Participants watched two data videos and we presented a hand-drawn storyboard we created for one of them to illustrate the type of output we expected. To motivate them to create the most compelling data video, we told them they would enter a contest with other groups. The most compelling storyboard would win a prize.

Figure 7. Example Storyboard (Royal Wedding UK).

The first panel features a video clip from William and Kate's royal wedding and voice over stating that marriage rates were about 49% in 2012. The next panel features a video clip from Charles and Diana's wedding, 20 years earlier with the voice overstating that marriage rates were 62% then. The third panel stars a bar chart, representing the trends in marriage rates over by different heights of wedding cakes. The fourth panel shows a cupcake representing the projected low rates 30 years from now. The final panel invites the viewer to turn this trend around, featuring an animation where cake layers are added below the cupcake.

An experimenter was present in the experimental room at all times, to introduce the data and later play the role of the data analyst, answering questions about data and visualizations. The experimenter instructed participants to build their story from the data given to them, not allowing them to search or make up new information. The experimenter also informed the participants that data visualizations were provided as examples only and they were encouraged to design or alter the visual representations to best fit their story. Participants built their storyboards on pen and paper, using pens, pencils, markers, rulers, scissors, and colored sticky notes. We asked them to provide enough details for us to create the actual video from the storyboard. We also instructed them to "think aloud" (if single) and video recorded the session. Finally, the experimenter conducted a semi-structured interview, asking participants to describe the video they envisioned from the storyboard, to comment on their design process, and gather their impression on the quality of their story. Participants received two software gratuities.

Session and Storyboard Analysis

We collected 10 storyboards and recorded over 24 hours of video from the eight storyboarding sessions we conducted. We analyzed videos of the sessions using an open-coding approach as well as the narrative structure codes from Study 1. Two researchers (who had observed and conducted sessions) developed two initial code-sets independently, and reached to an agreement on a final code-set by iteratively coding 10% of the videos. Based on these codes, one researcher proceeded to code the remaining videos.

Characterizing Storyboard Elements/Appearance

We collected a diverse set of storyboards, differing not only in their form but in their content and general intent. In this section, we do not present a deep analysis of their structure as storyboards collected were not finalized but report on key observations on their content. As an example of the artefacts we collected, Figure 7 shows a short storyboard (S10) calling viewers to action, such as collectively working toward reducing divorce rates.

Narrative Structure

We were generally surprised by the variety of stories that could be told with the same data. We gathered the intent and take away message during the final walkthrough and reported them in Table 1. All finished storyboards could be matched to narrative structure patterns we identified in study 1. For example, factual stories employed an EI+ narrative structure without any *peak,* but rather going over a subset of facts in order. In contrast, the storyboards building tension, or reflecting participants' viewpoints featured a *peak* towards the second third of the storyboard, utilizing E+I+P, one of the most common narrative structure pattern.

Story Type	Storyboard Content
Factual (3)	S1 & S2. Presents temporal trends in marriage and divorce rates S3. Presents temporal trends in marriage and divorce rates and speculate on reasons
Tension builders (2)	S4. Unveils only part of the trends then reveal recent changes. S5. "Are they going to divorce?". Sets up a married couple undergoing therapy.
View points (3)	S6. "Marriage is not inevitable". Advocates that lower marriage rates correspond to a positive societal change where unmarried people are better accepted. S7. "Marriages can still work out". Advocates that even if divorces are going up, there are marriages that last. S10. "Marriage rates are going down, let's turn this around".
Inciting Reflection (2)	S8. "Marriage is not about couples, it is about individuals". Demonstrate that higher divorce rates today from the fact that it is less advantageous for individuals to be married. S9. Advocates that in a world increasingly materialist, husbands and wives become disposable commodities, leading to higher divorce rates.

Table 1. Content of the 10 storyboards created by participants.

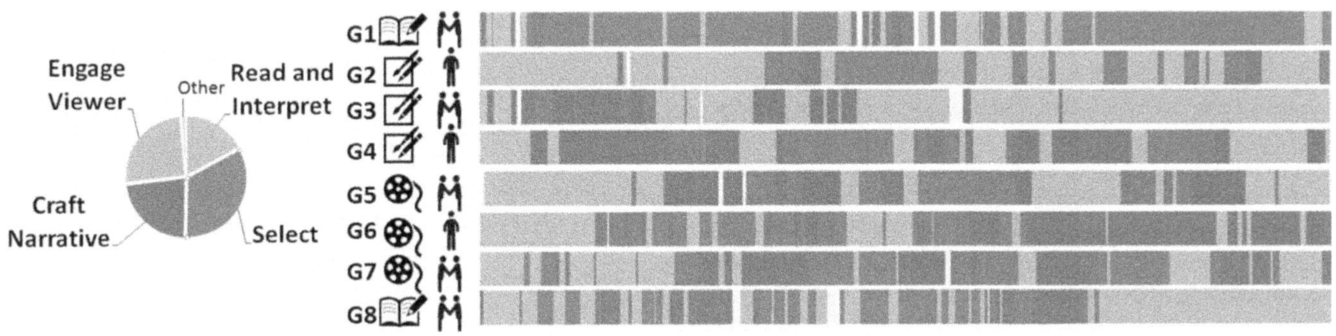

Figure 8. The proportion of time spent on each storyboarding activity over all 8 session groups (G1-G8) (left). Temporal sequence of activities shown for 8 separate storyboarding workshop sessions each lasting about 3 hours (right). The icons indicate group vs. individual sessions and participant backgrounds (Writer, Graphic/Motion Graphic Designer, and Cinematographer).

Strategies to Engage Viewers

As most storyboards we collected were not polished (due to time limitations), we do not report the detailed account on visual effects or animations used in them. However, we identified a recurring viewer engagement strategy: the degree of personification of the story. Participants in 4 sessions explicitly discussed introducing recurrent human figures or topic-related recognizable objects (e.g., wedding ring or cake) to raise the degree of personification of the video and help the viewer relate to the message and project themselves in the video. In fact, only 2 storyboards did not feature these elements; and for one of them the participant commented that she did not add human characters by lack of time. The remaining storyboards had varying personification degrees, from a few pictograms and icons to the integration of realistic objects or human acted video footage.

Characterizing the Storyboarding Process

Our analysis of the session videos revealed four main activities participants engaged with during the session. We first describe what these activities encompass and report our findings on their temporal sequencing.

Four Main Activities

The first category of activities we identified dealt with **reading and interpreting data** and the corresponding visualizations. As all participants had to do this before they start building their story (see green segments in Figure 8), it is not surprising that they dedicated the beginning of the session to these activities. Interestingly, in 3 out of 5 pairs, this task was mostly achieved by one participant while the other took notes or started composing a narrative structure.

The second category of activities we observed centered on **selecting data** and corresponding visualizations and physically grouping them into piles of interest (see blue segments in Figure 8). This process was closely coupled with the *read and interpret* process in 5 of the cases. Participants in 4 of the sessions made a first round of decisions on which information to use or to discard, even before discussing a general story line. For example, one participant referred to this process as *"looking for inspiration for a story."* It is also interesting to note that a common criterion for selecting data visualizations was its complexity and the estimated low visual literacy of a broad audience. Two participants pointed out the need to *"simplify and appeal to a very broad audience."* This finding correlates with our analysis of visualization types in study 1.

The third category of activities focused on discussing and **crafting the narrative structure** and the content of its different categories (see red segments in Figure 8). Amongst activities belonging to this category, about 30% of the time on average was dedicated to identifying the general theme, figuring out a logical flow and identifying meaningful connections between scenes. 49% of the time on average was devoted to identifying a Peak, the ending scene and discussing the take-away message. Most interesting discussions revolved around the creation of a rhythm in the video. Specifically, finding a good opening scene to hook the viewer and integrating salient points distributed throughout the video to keep the viewer watching until the end of the video were discussed in 7 sessions. Hooks people discussed dealt with posing questions that a general audience could have, identifying a controversial point or a statement contradictory to popular belief. Participants also discussed the need of several *Peaks* in the story, where important points are clearly stated, repeated or summarized.

Finally, a set of activities was dedicated to **integrating strategies to engage viewers** (see orange segments in Figure 8). Participants felt that it was crucial to include such strategies to avoid overwhelming the viewers with massive amounts of data referred to by one participant (G2) as "information dump". The line is sometimes blurred between activities for making the narrative structure more compelling and activities aiming at story material to engage viewers. In coding activities in this category, we focused exclusively on discussions and design of techniques that can be dissociated from the story content such as the addition of animation, sound effects or various visual effects. Groups with "graphic/motion graphic design" background spent significantly more time on this process (20 minutes more).

Non-Linear and Iterative Process

While participants devoted about the same amount of time for each set of activities overall (Figure 8-left), our detailed analysis of the activities during the sessions (Figure 8-right) confirmed that the creation process was **non-linear**. Participants in all eight sessions alternated between different set of activities. For example G3 (3rd sequence from top in Figure 8) closely coupled selecting data and crafting the narrative structure (blue and red segments) and later in the session alternated between crafting the narrative structure and integrating strategies to engage viewers (red and orange segments). We were surprised to observe some participants (e.g. G3) incorporating user engagement strategies early in the session, before having crafted an end-to-end narrative structure or even before deciding on a take-away message.

We also observed that the process was **iterative**. Participants may craft an end-to-end narrative structure with a first set of data and visualizations and iteratively add to their storyboard. This could either be done by selecting additional data visualization to expand on some points, or by altering the narrative structure to integrate elements to engage viewers. Semi-structured interviews at the end of the session revealed two types of iterative process. A writer in G1 explained that she works in waves, as she write novels: first crafting a logical flow from end-to-end, second reviewing this flow to extract the most exciting plot, adding and removing elements, third integrating engaging elements such as humor or recurring characters and fourth designing visual materials to provide a consistent feel. In contrast, a motion graphics designer in G3 explained that he would build a complete vision in his head, capture it through a rough draft and iterate on this draft to turn it into a product.

DESIGN IMPLICATIONS

We summarize our main findings regarding common practices for data videos design and derive a set of implications for data video authoring tool for novices.

Data Video Content

Visualization types: It is not surprising that the designers of data videos heavily rely on data visualizations to present the facts within data (48% of the total duration on average). However, despite the viewers' general impression that data videos each feature diverse custom visualizations, most videos rely on only a few types of well-known visualizations (e.g. bar charts, pictographs, and maps).

Limiting novice designers to a small set of commonly used visualization types but giving them the flexibility to customize their rendering options and color palette would appear as a good strategy to enable the creation of data videos that may be comprehensible to a large audience. Along this line, one of the most powerfully customizable, yet easily understood visual representations is certainly the pictograph, composed of icons representing data units. While most visual analytics tools and commercial charting tools do not offer much support to create these visualizations, they are heavily present in data videos and certainly should feature in data video authoring software.

Whether an authoring tool should also support the creation of more advanced visual representations, or even help authors design their own custom visual encodings remains an open question. We believe that such a direction could prove beneficial but would require assisting the author into creating an accompanying set of visuals and attention cues to help a general viewer correctly decode and understand the visualization. Further research is needed to understand how to preserve viewer engagement while respecting the general level of visual literacy as seen in our current day society.

Attention Cues: Attention cues are used throughout data videos to guide viewer attention, highlight specific parts of the data, or help a seamless transition between different aspects of data. While camera effects, highlighting, and text animations are commonly integrated in presentation software such as PowerPoint, data video authoring should also provide support for including voice narration and soundtrack which are present in almost all data videos we studied. Enabling authors to carefully time these different cues to support the narrative rather than obfuscating the facts poses a challenge. By guiding authors into using an explicit narrative structure for their videos, hints on the type, frequency and strength of attention cues they can use, based on concrete examples as from our sample list, can help authors achieve the right balance.

We were also surprised that only few of these attention cues were tightly coupled with the data (mostly highlighting and filtering). Other cues such as gradually changing the layout or visual encoding according to different data attributes could enhance data videos with data-driven attention cues.

Engaging Viewers: Our observations in both studies indicate that the audience is more engaged if facts told in the story relate to something they know. Observations from workshops hinted at several degrees of personification, such as including human figures or object icons, introducing recurring characters or human-acted video footages (e.g., initiating the video on marriage statistics by the video footage of the UK royal wedding in Figure 7). Supporting authors in finding such assets and enabling them to tightly couple them with visualizations (e.g., animating a pie chart into a wedding ring, using the wedding ring in a pictograph) would ease one of the most tedious part of visual editing. In addition, providing features to tie the video together, such as including recurring animated characters or objects (e.g., whiteboard sketching hand as in the VideoScribe software) could help create more engaging videos.

Narrative Structure

Narrative Categories: We believe that identifying different building blocks of a narrative (Establisher, Initial, Peak, and Release) could play a central role in a data video authoring tool. Making these building blocks explicit and suggesting the types of content commonly used in them, as well as their duration, could certainly streamline the process. In particular, we observed that authors of data videos generally include a small number of different facts about the data but tend to repeat these facts with alternate visualizations. Supporting authors in clearly identifying the data facts they introduce and providing features to ease the generation of repetitions of these facts with alternative representations would streamline the process. By providing statistics on common practices and making the video structure more explicit, authors may reflect on the video content they are creating and adjust the information density to their audience.

Narrative Structure: We observed that there are many different arrangements for the units composing the narrative. Thus, it seems important to provide flexible narrative structure, allowing authors to generate their own patterns. It would be also useful to provide sample templates based on our observations that guide the author through a selected narrative structure by making sure the right narrative units are defined and sequenced according to common practices. In particular, showcasing patterns that tend to be associated with different types of videos (e.g., "call-to-action" or "educational" videos) may guide authors in making well-structured videos for their intended messages. For example, a call-to-action could benefit from building tension through repeating several units of the *Initial* narrative category, concluding with a single *Peak* unit. Educational data videos, on the other hand, may have multiple *Peak* units for teaching about different aspects of the topic.

One-of-a-kind Data Video: There is a trade-off between encouraging novices to follow common practices and enabling them to create a one-of-a-kind engaging and memorable data video. We believe that a successful authoring tool will limit authors in some dimensions (e.g., types of visualizations, narrative categories) to ensure they create comprehensible narratives; while enabling them to customize other dimensions (e.g., visual rendering, narrative structure pattern) to create unique one-of-a-kind videos. In particular, we believe that suggesting alternatives at the right time of the video creation process can stimulate creativity by giving authors a glimpse of other possible choices. This could be achieved by incorporating video sample examples (by analogy to code examples in programming environments) to show a diverse set of designs and inspire authors.

Authoring Process

Non-linear and Iterative Process: We collected evidence that crafting data video storyboards is a non-linear process and requires going back to the data throughout the process. We expect it to be even more common if we enable end-users to create data video. This process is also dependent on the authors' background and work practices. Some authors envision everything at once including the story, custom-made graphics, and animation while others build a logical flow with abstractions of the facts (e.g., outline notes, default visualizations, etc.), go back to add elements that will engage viewers, return to edit the visualizations, and finally take another iteration to dissociate the logical flow from the story plot and the story material. An authoring tool with storyboarding facilities based on rapid sketching may help in capturing the authors' initial vision and allow iterative refinement. Such a tool can also integrate features to enable authors to easily go back and forth between different storyboarding activities.

DISCUSSION AND LIMITATIONS

Findings from study 1 are reported from our analysis of a limited corpus of videos. While we believe results from study 1 are likely to generalize to other online data videos provided for the general public consumption, further studies are required to examine data videos designed for a specific audience or targeted to a specific discipline or industry. We expect that further research will expand our corpus and build on our findings.

We decided on several criteria to include data videos from the limited inventory of available videos online, such as number of views or rank in the search results. However, assessing their actual quality, whether or not they comply with best design practices, or the level of engagement of their audience remains an open research question. More research on audience reactions is needed to develop appropriate metrics for evaluating these data videos and their reception by the audience. A key challenge is that such evaluation metrics depend on factors such as intended message, audience background as well as accurate measures to capture engagement. Creating such metrics could help advance storytelling research and pursue exciting questions such as investigating most compelling narrative structures.

Considering study 2, we originally aimed at recruiting experienced designers of data videos. However, since data video storytelling is a relatively new phenomenon, recruiting enough participants specializing in this medium proved challenging. We broadened our selection criteria and recruited participants with formal training (i.e., having a degree or certificate) and significant experience creating stories with and without videos. We believe that triangulating the perspectives of these experienced "storytellers" with diverse backgrounds is still valuable to understand the creation process.

As with all laboratory studies there are tradeoffs in studying experts outside of their working environment in a relatively short period of time. While longitudinal studies with individuals in work settings may be necessary to deeply understand each step of the creation process, our goal was rather to gain an overview of design practices and understand if and how they may vary amongst different individuals or professions. Engaging with 13 of these experts over 3-hour sessions shed some light on the diversity and breadth in crafting storyboards and enabled us to derive a set of general implications for supporting the creation process of novices.

CONCLUSION

Data videos are a relatively new yet popular medium for storytelling with data. Our research community can benefit from in-depth studies than help to catalog our knowledge on this exciting medium. Such knowledge can also inform the design of tools to make it possible for a broader audience to craft compelling ones. We consider our work a step toward this goal. Through two exploratory studies, we advance the body of knowledge on what constitutes data videos as well as provide insights on the processes involved to create them. We first reported on the qualitative analysis of 50 data videos, extracting their most salient elements including types of visualizations and attention cues. We also examined their narrative structure and described the wide range of patterns used in data videos. Finally, we observed how experienced storytellers from cinematography and screenplay writing design storyboards for data videos and reported on their process. We concluded on a set of broader implications for the design of data video authoring tools to enable general users to create the necessary pieces. In the future, we plan to iteratively design a data video authoring tool to assist novice users in creating engaging and memorable one-of-a-kind data videos.

ACKNOWLEDGMENTS

We acknowledge a NSERC grant awarded to the last author for part of this work. We also thank MSR for recruiting participants and Ashkan Hagshenas for helping with Study2.

REFERENCES

1. Divorces in 2012. http://www.ons.gov.uk/ons/rel/vsob1/divorces-in-england-and-wales/index.html.
2. The general (1926). http://explore.bfi.org.uk/4ce2b6aae85f3.
3. Oxford online dictionary. http://www.oxforddictionaries.com.
4. Use a picture. it's worth a thousand words. Speakers Give Sound Advice, Syracuse Post Standard (page 18), March 28, 1911.
5. 99% v 1%: the data behind the occupy movement. http://www.theguardian.com/news/datablog/video/2011/nov/16/99-v-1-occupy-data-animation, 2012.
6. Global air traffic. http://www.rightcolours.com/portfolio2.html, 2012.
7. Racing against history. http://www.nytimes.com/interactive/2012/08/01/sports/olympics/racing-against-history.html?_r=0, 2012.
8. An infographic exploration of online video. http://www.shutterstock.com/blog/an-infographic-exploration-of-online-video, Shutterstock, 2014.
9. Bateman, S., Mandryk, R. L., Gutwin, C., Genest, A., McDine, D., and Brooks, C. Useful junk?: the effects of visual embellishment on comprehension and memorability of charts. *Proc. CHI*, 2573–2582, 2010.
10. Borkin, M. A., Vo, A. A., Bylinskii, Z., Isola, P., Sunkavalli, S., Oliva, A., and Pfister, H. What makes a visualization memorable? *IEEE TVCG (InfoVis '13) 19*, 12 (2013), 2306–2315.
11. Brehmer, M., Carpendale, S., Lee, B., and Tory, M. Pre-design empiricism for information visualization: Scenarios, methods, and challenges. *Proc. BELIV Workshop*, ACM Press (2014), 147–151.
12. Satyanarayan, A. and Heer, J. Authoring narrative visualizations with ellipsis. *Proc. EuroVis*, (2014).
13. Cohn, N. Visual narrative structure. *Cognitive science 37*, 3 (2013), 413–452.
14. Eccles, R., Kapler, T., Harper, R., and Wright, W. Stories in geotime. *Information Visualization 7*, 1 (2008), 3–17.
15. Freytag, G. Technique of the Drama: An Exposition of Dramatic Composition and Art. University Press of the Pacific, 1904.
16. Gershon, N., and Page, W. What storytelling can do for information visualization. *CACM 44*, 8 (2001), 31–37.
17. Glaser, B. G., and Strauss, A. L. The discovery of grounded theory: Strategies for qualitative research. Transaction Publishers, 2009.
18. Heer, J., Mackinlay, J., Stolte, C., and Agrawala, M. Graphical histories for visualization: Supporting analysis, communication, and evaluation. *IEEE TVCG (InfoVis '08) 14*, 6 (2008), 1189–1196.
19. Hullman, J., and Diakopoulos, N. Visualization rhetoric: Framing effects in narrative visualization. *IEEE TVCG (InfoVis '11) 17*, 12 (2011), 2231–2240.
20. Hullman, J., Drucker, S., Riche, N. H., Lee, B., Fisher, D., and Adar, E. A deeper understanding of sequence in narrative visualization. *IEEE TVCG (InfoVis '13) 19*, 12 (2013), 2406–2415.
21. Jern, M., Rogstadius, J., Astrom, T., and Ynnerman, A. Visual analytics presentation tools applied in html documents. *Proc. IV*, IEEE (2008), pp. 200–207.
22. Kosara, R., and Mackinlay, J. Storytelling: The next step for visualization. *IEEE Computer 46*, 5 (2013), 44–50.
23. Ma, K.-L., Liao, I., Frazier, J., Hauser, H., and Kostis, H.-N. Scientific storytelling using visualization. *IEEE CG&A 32*, 1 (2012), 12–19.
24. Mascelli, J. V. The five C's of cinematography.
25. McCloud, S. Understanding comics: The invisible art. William Morrow Paperbacks, 1994.
26. Richards, L. Handling qualitative data: A practical guide. Sage Publications, 2009.
27. Segel, E., and Heer, J. Narrative visualization: Telling stories with data. *IEEE TVCG (InfoVis '10) 16*, 6 (2010), 1139–1148.
28. Viegas, F. B., Wattenberg, M., van Ham, F., Kriss, J., and McKeon, M. Manyeyes: a site for visualization at internet scale. *IEEE TVCG (InfoVis '07) 13*, 6 (2007), 1121–1128.
29. Wojtkowski, W. and Wojtkowski, W. G. Storytelling: its role in information visualization. *European Systems Science Congress* (2002).

How Deceptive are Deceptive Visualizations?: An Empirical Analysis of Common Distortion Techniques

Anshul Vikram Pandey
School of Engineering,
New York University
anshul.pandey@nyu.edu

Katharina Rall
School of Law,
New York University
kr1326@nyu.edu

Margaret L. Satterthwaite
School of Law,
New York University
satterth@exchange.law.nyu.edu

Oded Nov
School of Engineering,
New York University
onov@nyu.edu

Enrico Bertini
School of Engineering,
New York University
enrico.bertini@nyu.edu

ABSTRACT
In this paper, we present an empirical analysis of deceptive visualizations. We start with an in-depth analysis of what deception means in the context of data visualization, and categorize deceptive visualizations based on the type of deception they lead to. We identify popular distortion techniques and the type of visualizations those distortions can be applied to, and formalize why deception occurs with those distortions. We create four deceptive visualizations using the selected distortion techniques, and run a crowdsourced user study to identify the deceptiveness of those visualizations. We then present the findings of our study and show how deceptive each of these visual distortion techniques are, and for what kind of questions the misinterpretation occurs. We also analyze individual differences among participants and present the effect of some of those variables on participants' responses. This paper presents a first step in empirically studying deceptive visualizations, and will pave the way for more research in this direction.

Author Keywords
Deceptive Visualization; Empirical Analysis; Evaluation.

ACM Classification Keywords
H.5.m. Information Interfaces and Presentation (e.g. HCI): Miscellaneous

INTRODUCTION
In recent years, data visualization has gained popularity as a powerful communication tool to support arguments with numbers while still making messages accessible. In fields as disparate as business, policy analysis, human rights, and journalism [14, 35], specialists and laypersons are using data to shape compelling, informative, and convincing narratives, conveyed through or supported by visualizations. While the use of such visual depictions as persuasion devices is not new, the popular use of visualizations has undoubtedly increased due in part to user-friendly software that allows non-experts to create visualizations. As such practices become more widespread and accessible, important new challenges and questions arise. If visualizations can make messages more accessible, comprehensible and persuasive [27, 37], visual representations can also be easily misused and misunderstood - even by their creators.

This problem has been known for a long time and it is not limited to visual representations but more to the general problem of communicating through numbers and statistics. Darrell Huff's "How to Lie with Statistics", published in 1954, popularized the problem and warned against the many traps of using statistics and charts in communication [15]. In the 1980s, Edward Tufte introduced the concept of *graphical integrity* in his classic "Visual Display of Quantitative Information" and succinctly explained the many subtle ways in which data graphics can distort information [38].

Despite their influence, these seminal works have not prevented distortion through data visualization. If anything, the heightened popularity of data visualization may have actually increased the prevalence of such cases and the impact they have on the population at large. Examples abound in popular media, TV and the Internet [4]. Some examples collected from popular sources [3, 1, 2] involve notorious distortions, such as manipulation of axis orientation/scale (Figure 1[a,c]), use of disproportionate sizes (Figure 1[f]), incorrect representation (Figure 1[d]) and non-linear scales (Figure 1[b,e]).

Misrepresentations may result from a lack of expert knowledge, as appears to be the case in distorted representations collected from human rights organizations. However, the possibility of influencing the audience can also create an incentive to use distortions intentionally - either in a zeal to convince, in the case of advocates, or in an attempt to mislead, in the case of unethical marketing firms. While jour-

CHI 2015, April 18–23, 2015, Seoul, Republic of Korea.

http://dx.doi.org/10.1145/2702123.2702608

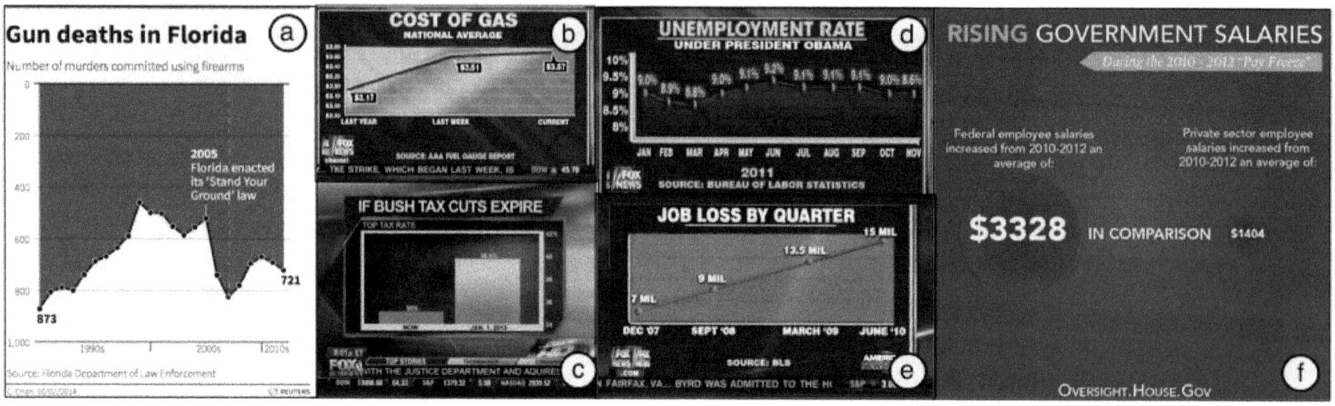

Figure 1. Some of the real-world data visualization examples which might lead to misinterpretation of message, hence to deception.

nalists may run the risk of accidentally distorting visualizations due to their significant time constraints, some very obvious examples of media misrepresentations suggest that distorted visualizations are sometimes used intentionally. While the motives behind these types of distortion differ dramatically from an ethical point of view, their visual characteristics and perception by the audience are largely the same. In this work we take a step toward understanding the extent to which audiences are deceived and whether there is a relationship between deception and individual differences among people. While the literature cited above, and many newly available works [4], warn against the danger of deceptive visualizations, we are surprisingly not aware of any empirical work aimed at assessing the severity of deception. To close this gap, we designed and ran a series of crowdsourced studies aimed at understanding the deceptive effect of distortion techniques.

Our studies stem from a preliminary analysis of existing deceptive visualizations which led us to (1) categorize deceptive visualization effects and focus on two main classes: *message reversal* and *message exaggeration/understatement* and (2) derive synthetic examples to reproduce these effects in a controlled environment.

In the studies, we selected a set of common misrepresentation techniques from the classes we identified as frequent and created deceptive and non-deceptive versions of the same charts. We also collected personal traits of participants related to *education*, *chart familiarity* and *visual ability* to examine whether these traits play a role as co-factors on deception. Our results show that deceptive charts have a major impact on how people interpret a message and that in some cases this effect is modulated by some personal attributes we included in the study.

The main contributions of our work are: (1) the definition and classification of deceptive methods in visualization; (2) the empirical confirmation and measurement of some of the well-known graphical distortion techniques; and (3) the empirical analysis of the effect of personal attributes on the deceptive effect.

We believe this is an important first step toward a better characterization and understanding of how visualizations impact their readers. By studying the deceptive effect we expand some of the recent research on the cognitive and social effects of visualization, including research on bias [16], memorability [7, 9], literacy [11], and persuasion [27].

RELATED WORKS

The fact that it is possible to "lie" with statistics and visual representations has been known for a very long time in areas related to data analysis and representation. The 1950s classic "How to Lie with Statistics" introduced numerous methods through statistical communication can lead to misinformation [15]. In the 1980s, Tufte developed the concept of *graphical integrity* and the *lie factor* to describe how visual representation can distort information and deceive the reader [38]. Similar in spirit, and building upon them, are two more recent books on the same topics: "How to Lie with Charts" [17], which focuses mostly on the use of charts in business environments, and "How to Lie with Maps" [24], with focuses on geographical visual representations. While all of these works expose common deception patterns and provide guidelines to spot and avoid them, we are not aware of studies that test the deception effect in a controlled experiment.

Visualization researchers have, however, studied how visual encoding can distort information at level of perception. Particularly relevant is research on visual encoding which establishes how data is perceived and compared when represented with different visual channels such as position, size, color, angle. Bertin [8] introduced the concept of visual encoding and visual channels and provided guidelines on how to best use them. Cleveland and McGill in their famous experiments on *graphical perception* discovered that some visual channels lead to more accurate comparisons of quantitative information than others [13] (e.g., position along a common scale being the best one and area a poor one). Color, if not used properly, can lead to numerous distortions. The seminal work "How not to lie with visualization" [33], the more recent "Rainbow color map (still) considered harmful" [10] and numerous experiments on the topic show how poor color selection can lead to numerous distortions [12, 21]. The perception of correlation in scatter plots and parallel coordinates can also be problematic: when asked to estimate correlations, participants typically underestimate the positive correlations and overestimate the negative correlations in parallel coordinate plots [22, 31]. Mapping a numeric quantity to the radius of a circle rather than area is another popular technique that leads to distortion, and the use of area size has been found to be problematic also when rectangles are used [19].

All these studies focus mostly on visual effectiveness and are based on the careful selection and testing of specific perceptual tasks. For instance, Cleveland and McGill asked participants to compare two bars marked with a dot in a bar chart. While this is of course useful, we are more interested in studying deception effects at the *message level* of visualization because it better simulates what happens in the real world when a reader is presented with a new chart (e.g., in a newspaper, book, or presentation). Therefore, rather than asking participants to compare two bars in a chart, our studies ask participants to compare quantities between real-world objects using the domain language, as described in the User Study section. This, as explained in graph comprehension theory [36], is a crucial difference as part of the tasks the reader will need to perform is the translation between the question and the mapping between the domain concepts and the graphical representation (what Pinker calls *graphical schemata* [30]). Since the deceptive effect may well happen during this translation and mapping phase of graph comprehension, we determined it would be important to run studies that focus on the message level of data visualization.

DECEPTION AND DECEPTIVE VISUALIZATIONS

In data visualization, the classic adage "*do not lie to your users*" [34] is fading fast. Designers and communicators are utilizing the power of data visualization to augment their messages, which in turn has an effect on how users perceive the original message. While we are not aware of any study which discusses the trade-off between how much augmentation is good enough, or what is the maximum extent to which a communicator may augment through additional information without distorting the underlying message, there are strong proponents and opponents of deceptive designs that we would classify as deceptive.

Webster's Dictionary describes deception as "*the act of making someone believe something that is not true*" [5], which implies that deception necessarily involves an intent to mislead. However, as Adar et al. [6] maintain, "*deceptive(ness)* does not require intent", i.e., one may induce deception without lying. There are numerous examples of data visualizations and infographics which are deceptive, but which may not have involved an intent by the communicator to deceive. For example, while omitting outliers and other data points to show a best-fit regression line leads to a deceptive visualization with intent by a statistician, such poor practice may also result from novice use of statistics. Similarly, not following best practices of visualization design, such as truncating the axes, may lead to a deceptive visualization either *with* or *without* intent, depending on the level of sophistication of the creator.

To shed some more light on the origins of these problems in one particular field we conducted interviews with experts working at the intersection of data and human rights. These interviews suggested that while statistical literacy remains relatively low within the human rights advocacy world, the power of data-driven advocacy exerts an increasing pull to use data visualization. Human rights experts readily agree that there is little tailored evidence to guide decisions about how best to design data visualization to support human rights messages. Further, human rights organizations frequently lack sufficient personnel with specialist training in data analysis and visualization. This mismatch between strong incentives to use visualization and gaps in capacity can lead to the accidental construction of distorted visualizations, which can in turn mislead target audiences.

Based on these findings and the definitions introduced in the previous work [32], we put forth a working definition of deceptive visualization as "**a graphical depiction of information, designed with or without an intent to deceive, that may create a belief about the message and/or its components, which varies from the actual message**". Instead of focusing on the intent of the creator, we are interested in analyzing aspects of deceptive visualization such as distortion techniques, deception severity, etc., and thus do not explore the boundary of intentional vs. unintentional deceptiveness.

In visualization, deception may occur at two levels - the *chart level*, where the user reads the chart incorrectly, and/or processes an incorrect estimate of the data presented; and the *message level*, where users interpret the message incorrectly. Chart level deceptions occur at the visual encoding level, and are mostly modulated by the ability or inability of the user to read the chart correctly. The user's visual literacy, ability, and chart familiarity play an important role in neutralizing the deceptive effect of the visualization. Message level deceptions occur at message interpretation level, and may lead to creating false beliefs about the message and/or its components.

In the real world, visualizations are usually accompanied by a message, hence, it is interesting to study how visualizations lead to a message level deception. As this is the first experimental study that explores visualization deceptiveness, we chose to narrow our scope to focus only on message level deceptions. There are various ways to visually deceive viewers even at the message level, e.g., presentation of deliberate misinformation, distractions, information overload, or through deceptive techniques applied on the level of visual encoding. In our study, we decided to start from the common types of graphical distortions without including deceiving effects that do not stem from choices made at the visual encoding level (e.g., we excluded deliberate data manipulation). Starting with complete data, we identified two broad classes of message level deception - Message Exaggeration/Understatement, and Message Reversal, as described below.

Message Exaggeration/Understatement

This kind of deception happens when the fact is not distorted, however, but the extent of the presented fact is tweaked, i.e., the fact is exaggerated. For example, if a chart compares two quantities - A and B, where *A is bigger than B*, but the users are presented with the fact that *A is bigger than B*, but the extent is exaggerated. This type of deception affects the "**How**

much" type of questions, such as "*How much do you think is quantity A bigger than quantity B?*"

Message Reversal

This type of deception happens when a visualization encourages users to interpret the fact in the message incorrectly. For example, if a chart compares two quantities - A and B, where *A is bigger than B*, the users perceive the message as *A is smaller than B*. Thus, users perceive the incorrect message due to a distorted visualization, even though the actual data is presented. This type of deception affects the "**What**" type of questions, such as "*What does the chart show?*".

STUDY RATIONALE AND METHODS

Given the limited empirical literature on deceptive visualization, we set out here some of the design rationale that made up the groundwork of this study. The main experiment design choices that are necessary for this kind of study include the selection of distortion and affected visualization techniques, the mechanism to create deceptive visualizations to study the effect, a way to detect/measure the deceptive effect, and a measure of additional attributes that might impact users' responses.

Selecting Distortion and Visualization Techniques

In "How to lie with Charts" Jones says: "Almost all visualizations are prone to distortion or lie" [17]. However, distortion techniques are visualization specific: one type of distortion technique may not affect all visualizations. For some visualizations, colors play a role in deception, for others truncated axes or missing labels add the deceiving layer. This research focuses on some of the visualization techniques that are widely used. Our focus on those techniques that reach broad audiences allowed us to exclude complex visualization techniques such as heatmaps or network maps in favor of focusing on simpler charts used extensively by journalists, human rights activists, and policy makers. We chose four distortion techniques: *truncated axis, area as quantity, aspect ratio, and inverted axis* that we identified as having been used in these realms.

Creating Treatments

Based on the distortion and visualization techniques, we created two set of treatments or visualizations, one control and one deceptive, for each of the distortion techniques mentioned above. In the following, we present the illustration of treatments we created for each of the distortion techniques.

Truncated Axis

In the truncated axis visual distortion, one or more of the axes of a chart are altered by changing the minimum and maximum values presented on the scale, as shown in Figure 2. Such alteration of the axis range leads to exaggeration or understatement of the quantities presented, thus directly affecting the user's response to the "how much" type of questions. For example, in Figure 2, users' responses to the question "*How much do you think Y is bigger than X?*" is likely to be dependent on the type of chart (control/deceptive) presented. It is important to note that all chart types that are axis-based are susceptible to this type of distortion. In this research, we use this distortion technique with bar-charts only.

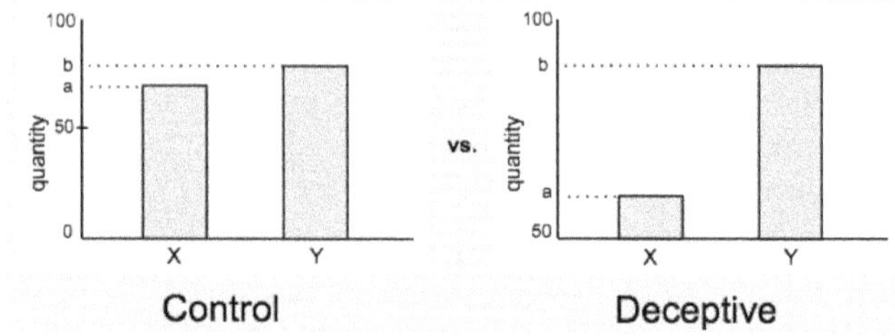

Figure 2. Illustration showing Truncated Axis distortion, which leads to message exaggeration/understatement type of deception.

Area as Quantity

Encoding quantitative data with size has faced serious criticisms in the visualization community, and is a process that requires careful mapping of data with graphics. Although no guidelines are available about how to map the actual data with graphical area, it is believed that a one-to-one mapping between the data and the graphical area is least prone to distortion. This is also one of the six graphical integrity principles suggested by Tufte [38]. However, it is not uncommon to see data mapped with one of the variables in the graphics that affect the graphical representation exponentially. This induces the message exaggeration/understatement type of deception. For example, from Figure 3 one may conclude that Y is "a lot" bigger than X, when the quantity is mapped to the radius of the circle (in the deceptive visualization). Other area-based charts are also prone to this type of distortion. When the quantity is mapped to the area, as in the control condition, the visualization is less susceptible to deception.

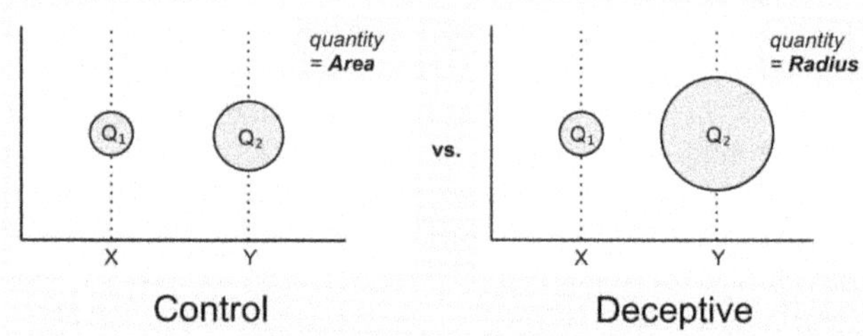

Figure 3. Illustration showing Area as Quantity distortion, which leads to message exaggeration/understatement type of deception.

Aspect Ratio

This type of distortion primarily affects line-charts as it directly impacts the rate of increase or decrease of one quantity over another. While one may argue that aspect ratio may impact other visualizations such as bar-charts where the width-to-height ratio of the bars may create a similar effect, we apply this distortion to only line-charts as they appear more frequently with this type of charts. Another way of looking at this type of distortion is the angle of inclination/declination of the lines that are affected because of the changes in the aspect ratio. As shown in fig 4, by widening the scales on one of the axes, the angle can be distorted. Hence, the rate at which the quantity appears to increase seems slower in the deceptive visualization condition as compared to the control condition. This type of distortion also leads to message exaggeration/understatement.

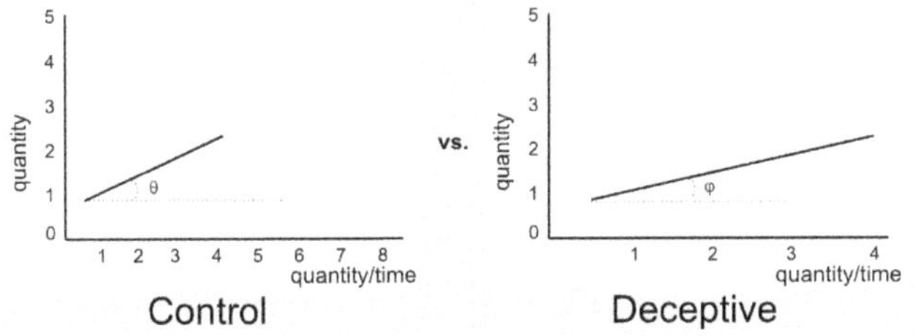

Figure 4. Illustration showing altered angle of the trend responsible for "rate of increase/decrease" due to Aspect Ratio distortion, which leads to message exaggeration/understatement type of deception.

Inverted Axis

Human beings relate directions with trends, such as: upwards - increase, downwards - decrease, right - front/progress, left - back/receding [17]. This directional interpretation makes *inverted axis* one the most common distortion techniques that leads to reversal of the message, and makes the users susceptible to drawing *false* conclusions. In other words, here deception occurs due to reversal of the message instead of exaggeration or understatement. This type of distortion also affects almost all visualization techniques that are axis-dependent. Figure 5 shows two chart conditions (control and deceptive) showing an increase in the quantity on the y-axis by quantity on the x-axis, however, the latter gives an impression that the quantity is decreasing because of the inverted y-axis.

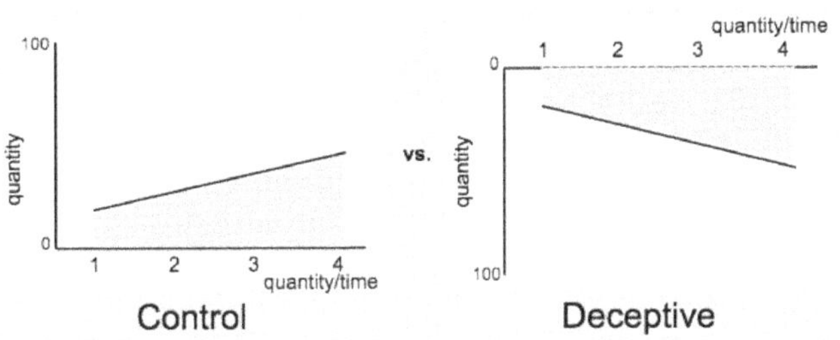

Figure 5. Illustration showing Inverted Axis distortion, which leads to message reversal type of deception.

Detecting Deception

In the scope of this research, we are only concerned with the deception that occurs through visual misrepresentation of information, which has an effect at the message level. As mentioned earlier, we categorized two types of message level deceptions - Message Exaggeration/Understatement, and Message Reversal, as follows:

Message Exaggeration/Understatement

These questions were created to detect whether the participants received the message in its original or exaggerated/understated form. As mentioned earlier, in this type of deception the fact of the message is not distorted, but is exaggerated. We detect this exaggeration/understatement by asking the "*how much*" type of question with a context, such as "*How much better do you think the condition of safe drinking water access in Silvatown is as compared to that in Wilowtown?*", where the users would reply on a 5-item Likert scale ranging from *slightly better* to *substantially better*. As this type of deception is unidirectional, i.e., it is extremely rare that the user would find smaller quantity bigger, the question and scale were designed to capture the single-tailed effect. To detect and study the extent of exaggeration/understatement, we compared the results of the correctly represented and misrepresented charts through a between-subject analysis.

Message Reversal

These questions were created to detect whether the users received the fact in the message correctly or not. Unlike *message exaggeration* where the fact in the message is not distorted, here the deceit occurs at the message level, distorting it. Instead of asking the "*how much*" question, we ask a multiple-choice "*what*" type of question, such as "*What can you say about the access to safe drinking water by the majority ethnic group in Silvatown, between 1995 and 2010?*". We provide three answer choices to the participants, including two interpretations of the message (one correct, and one incorrect, which the visual distortion would lead to), and "uncertain" as the third answer choice. A comparison of accuracy and between-subject analysis of the response gives an estimate of whether or not there is an effect of distortion.

Measure of Individual Differences

One of the most important aspects of studying visualization impact on human perception is understanding the ability of the target population to read and process the information presented, and form an interpretation of the underlying message. We included this aspect by using a two stage process to analyze participant's familiarity with basic charts, and their ability to process the information. To quantify familiarity, we used a 5-Likert scale question: "*How familiar are you with the chart shown below?*", with responses ranging from "not familiar at all" to "very familiar", presuming that higher chart familiarity means better ability of the participant to detect deception.

Another important variable to determine individual differences is "Need for Cognition". Need for cognition is a personality trait studied in social psychology to characterize the extent to which individuals are inclined towards effortful cognitive activities. This factor goes hand-in-hand with visual ability in profiling an individual based on his cognitive abilities and desire to process graphical information. Petty and Cacioppo define it as: "*the tendency to engage in and enjoy effortful cognitive endeavors*". In our study, we use their short 18-item test [29], which is one of the most popular scales to measure need for cognition. Apart from these, participants' demographic information, such as *age*, *gender* and *education* were recorded, while we primarily analyzed *education* as higher education may lead to higher visual literacy and ability to reason with statistics and graphs.

USER STUDY

We started our analysis by conducting two pilot studies. The first study was aimed at identifying whether or not there is a noticeable effect of distortion techniques on participants' responses, leading to deception. We used a real world deceptive visualization example (Figure 1[a]) and asked questions to detect any misinterpretation of the presented information. We found that such distorted visualizations can deceive users.

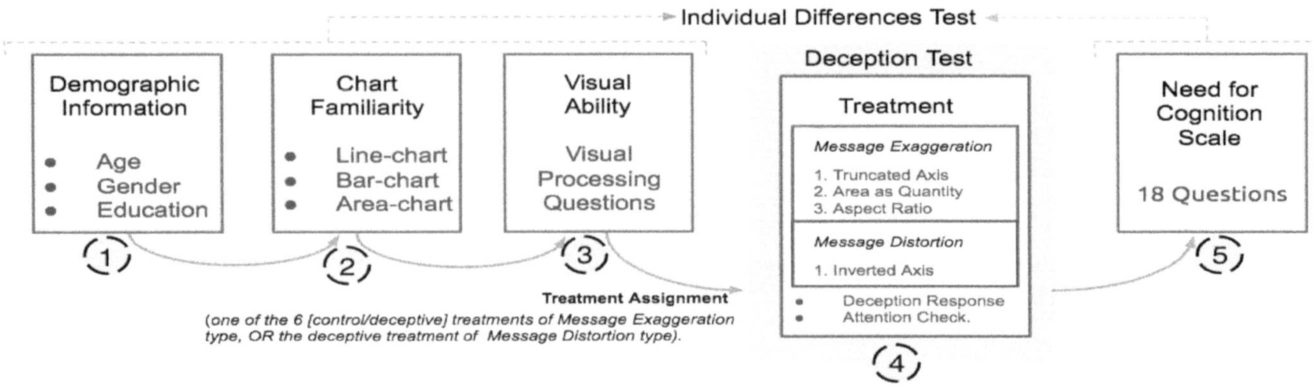

Figure 6. Various stages of the experiment. Stages 1, 2, 3 and 5 correspond to the individual differences test, while 4 corresponds to deception test.

In the second study, we wanted to understand whether an artificially generated scenario and data can lead to a similar deceptive effect under the same distortion techniques. Similar to the first pilot study, the participants were deceived, however, we did not find any noticeable difference between the responses when real or artificial scenario/data were used. The final user study was designed based on the findings of these two pilot studies.

In the final study, we conducted two types of experiments targeted to assess each of the two deception types - Message Exaggeration/Understatement, and Message Reversal. In the first type of experiment, we conducted tests on three deceptive visualization cases, one for each of the three distortion techniques - "truncated axis", "aspect ratio", and "area", individually. For the second type of experiment, we conducted tests on the "inverted axis" type of distortion technique. All the experiments were performed in a crowd-based setting with the primary goal to find an effect of distortion on users' responses, and additionally capture other interesting trends. The following section describes the experiments in detail.

Experiment Setup

The experiment consisting of four individual visual distortions (three for message exaggeration/understatement type of deception; the other for message reversal type of deception) was conducted using Amazon Mechanical Turk (MT). We chose MT as our primary experimental platform because it allowed us to conduct parallel studies on a diverse subject pool in an iterative fashion, allowing us to quickly test and refine our hypotheses. While conducting behavioral research based on self-reported measures on a crowdsourced platform may be considered problematic, several researchers have demonstrated the viability of MT as a reliable data collection platform [18, 26]. For instance, Paolacci et al. [28] compared results of classic experiments in judgment and decision-making using traditional and crowdsourcing methods and found that participants behave consistently.

For our final user study, we recruited 330 unique participants from MT who self-reported a United States location and whose previous task approval rate was equal to or exceeded 99%. Each experiment took 5-10 minutes and the participants were paid US $0.30 for participation.

Procedure

To take part in the study, the participants clicked on the link provided in the description of our task on MT. The link redirected the participants to a webpage hosted on our internal servers, where they undertook various stages of the experiment, as shown in Figure 6. Participants were provided a consent form with the description of the study, the data we would collect, and the tasks they would need to perform. Upon agreeing to the terms, we presented a personal information form (stage 1) to collect the basic demographic information about the participants, such as age, gender and education level. The next page presented a visual ability test (stage 2). The test was designed to include visual processing tasks [23, 20]. Next, the participants were presented a chart familiarity test (stage 3) where we asked how familiar they were with the specific types of charts: bar-charts, line-charts, and area-charts. We added a simple chart example to each of the familiarity questions. The participants provided their answer on a 5 point Likert scale, ranging from 1 (not familiar at all) to 5 (very familiar). Once the participants clicked "Proceed", one of the 6 treatments was assigned to them - control or deceptive from one of the 3 distortion types - in the message exaggeration/understatement focused experiment, or one of the 2 treatments - control or deceptive from the inverted axis distortion type - in the message reversal focused experiment.

On the treatment page (stage 4), we presented a brief **overview** about the chart, the actual **chart**, a message level **deception test** question, and an **attention check** question. The question to detect message level deception was designed to ensure that the participant did not have to perform any estimation tasks, avoiding the graph comprehension problem. For the bar-charts and bubble-charts, we asked the participants to **compare** the quantities presented, by asking *"how much better do you think is [quantity A] as compared to [quantity B] in terms of [the context]"*. Similarly, for the line-charts, we asked the participants to detect **improvement** of a quantity over time, by asking *"how much do you think [quantity A] has improved in terms of [the context] between [time period]"*. For the line-area-charts of the message reversal type of deception, we asked *"what can you say about the effect of [quantity A] over [quantity B]?"*. It is important to note that in each of the presented treatments, the actual numbers/data were presented on the chart as we were interested in detecting deception due to visual representation even in the presence of accurate data. Based on the information presented in the chart, we asked an attention check question to filter out random clickers. Finally, at stage 5, the participants responded to a simplified need for cognition scale. Once the study was successfully complete, the participants were paid through Amazon Payments. We later used the responses collected at stages 1, 2, 3 and 5 to determine individual differences, and those collected at stage 4 to detect deception.

In our study design, *distortion type* is the main independent variable, whereas *user response* to the deception test question is the only dependent variable we take into account for the statistical analysis purposes. For the individual differences test, we consider three factors - *chart familiarity, visual ability, and need for cognition*, which may play a confounding role in modulating the *user response*. Other variables derived from *user response* are *response accuracy* - the percentage of correct responses - used to detect message reversal type of deception, and *mean/average user response* - the average of *user response* for the given condition.

RESULTS

We conducted a series of crowdsourced user studies to explore deceptive visualizations, and to determine how severe different distortion techniques are in terms of deceiving the user. We studied two types of deception: Message Exaggeration/Understatement and Message Reversal by applying relevant distortion techniques on commonly used visualizations and asking "How much" and "What" types of questions to detect the two types of deception, respectively. As the two studies are dissimilar on various aspects, we analyzed the data separately. In this section, we first present findings on the message exaggeration/understatement type of deception, and later on the message reversal type of deception.

Message Exaggeration/Understatement

We chose three distortion techniques - Truncated Axis (bar chart), Area as Quantity (bubble chart), and Aspect Ratio (line chart) - to study this type of deception. For each distortion technique, we created two treatments: control and deceptive. The deceptive visualization examples from the actual study are shown in Figure 7[a,b,c].

We recruited 250 unique participants for this study and assigned one of the six treatments to each of them. As a step to filter out the noise and retain the data quality, we filtered out those participants who did not provide a response to the attention check question or incorrectly answered it. The final distribution of the participants by distortion technique and treatment is shown in Table 1.

Treatment	Truncated Axis	Area as Quantity	Aspect Ratio
Control	37	40	38
Deceptive	43	40	42

Table 1. Distribution of participants (*who answered all the attention check questions correctly*) by treatment (Control, Deceptive) and distortion technique (Truncated Axis, Area as Quantity, Aspect Ratio).

Effect of Distortion on Response

Across all chart types, we found a significant effect of distortion on participants' responses. We found that participants who saw the deceptive visualization perceived the underlying message in its exaggerated form, and responded higher on the 5-Likert scale when asked the "**How much**" question. Table 2 shows the average participant response when exposed to one of the 6 treatments, and Figure 8 shows the distribution with 95% confidence interval.

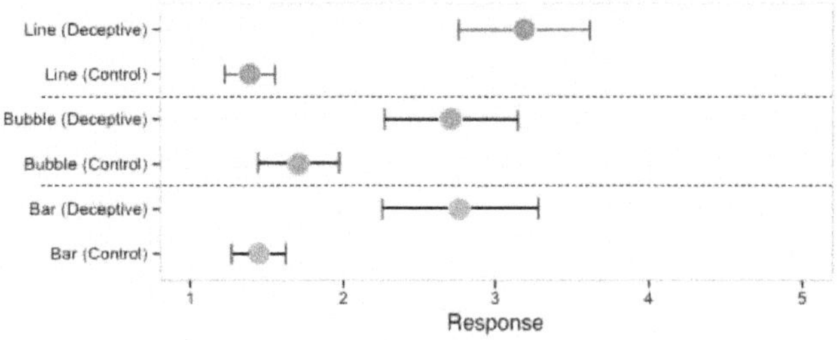

Figure 8. Average participant response with 95% confidence interval, when exposed to a treatment.

Treatment	Distortion Technique	Average Response
Line (Deceptive)	Aspect Ratio	3.19, 95% CI [2.76, 3.62]
Line (Control)	Aspect Ratio	1.39, 95% CI [1.23, 1.55]
Bubble (Deceptive)	Area as Quantity	2.71, 95% CI [2.27, 3.15]
Bubble (Control)	Area as Quantity	1.71, 95% CI [1.45, 1.98]
Bar (Deceptive)	Truncated Axis	2.77, 95% CI [2.26, 3.28]
Bar (Control)	Truncated Axis	1.45, 95% CI [1.27, 1.62]

Table 2. Average participant response (with 95% CI) to the "how much" question, by treatment (Control, Deceptive) and distortion technique (Truncated Axis, Area as Quantity, Aspect Ratio). *(minimum = 1, maximum = 5)*

We ran a Mann-Whitney's U test (one-tailed) to evaluate the difference in the responses of our 5-item Likert scale question, for each of the treatment categories (Line, Bubble, Bar). We found a significant effect of distortion for all three treatment categories. For the treatments with bar-charts, the "truncated axis" distortion led to difference in the responses between the control condition and the deceptive visualization condition. We found the difference in participants' responses highly significant ($p < 0.001$) for control/deceptive conditions across all the distortion types. For the "aspect ratio" distortion type, the mean ranks of Line (Control) and Line (Deceptive) were 24.42 and 55.04, respectively; $U = 1409$, $Z = 5.88$, $p < 0.0001$, $r = 0.66$. Similarly, for the treatments with bubble-charts where the "area as quantity" distortion plays a role, the mean ranks of Bubble (Control) and Bubble (Deceptive) were 32.47 and 48.52, respectively; $U = 1121$, $Z = 3.08$, $p = 0.0007$, $r = 0.34$. The treatments that involved bar-charts (affected by the "truncated axis" distortion), the mean ranks of Bar (Control) and Bar (Deceptive) were 31.08 and 48.60, respectively; $U = 1144$, $Z = 3.36$, $p = 0.0003$, $r = 0.37$.

Message Reversal

We chose a single yet common distortion technique - Inverted Axis - to study this type of deception. We applied this distortion technique on a line-area-chart where the representation distorted the underlying message. This led the participants to interpret the fact ("**what**" type of question)

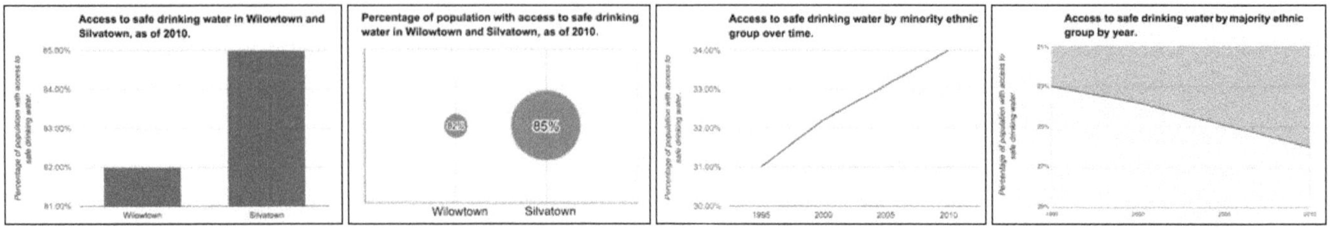

a. Truncated Axis b. Area as Quantity c. Aspect Ratio d. Inverted Axis

Figure 7. Deceptive visualization examples with corresponding distortion technique used in the study. Examples (a), (b) and (c) are used for message exaggeration/understatement technique, and (d) for message reversal.

presented in the message wrong, unlike the previous deception type where participants would misinterpret only the extent ("**how much**" type of question) of the presented fact. In other words, this distortion technique facilitates an estimation of accuracy in participants' responses, hence it can be tested in a between-subject design. We created only 2 treatments (control/deceptive) to study this distortion. Each treatment accompanies a deception test question to calculate response accuracy - the variable which we later used for all analysis purposes. The deceptive visualization example from the actual study is shown in Figure 7[d].

We recruited 80 unique participants for this study and randomly assigned one of the two treatments (control/deceptive) to them. We applied the same filtration mechanism to eliminate noise from the data. Out of the 80 participants, 78 passed our filtration criteria and were included in the dataset for further analysis. 38 of those participants were shown the deceptive visualization and 40 were shown the control condition.

Effect of Distortion on Response

Based on the information presented in Figure 7[d], we asked the participants "***what** can you say about the condition of access to safe drinking water by majority ethnic group over time?*", and provided a correct interpretation ("improved"), an incorrect interpretation ("declined") and an uncertain ("I do not know") answer choice.

Out of the 38 selected participants who saw the deceptive visualization, 30 responded incorrectly, 7 correctly and one chose the uncertain response. For the 40 participants who saw the control condition, 39 responded correctly, 1 responded incorrectly and no participant reported uncertainty. The response distribution by treatment type is shown in Table .

Treatment	Selected	Correct	Incorrect	Uncertain
Control	**40**	39 (97.50%)	1 (2.5%)	0
Deceptive	**38**	7 (18.42%)	30 (78.95%)	1 (0.02%)

Table 3. Response distribution (Correct, Incorrect, Uncertain) by treatment type for the *Inverted Axis* distortion.

To test for statistical significance of the differences in response we use the Freeman-Halton extension of Fisher's Exact Test, testing the null hypothesis that distortion has no effect on the participants' response. The findings were statistically highly significant ($p < 0.0001$), showing the effect of distortion on participants' response, hence, rejecting the null hypothesis.

Attribute	Level	Line chart	Bubble chart	Bar chart
Education	Low	3.93, [3,29, 4.56]	3.07, [2.42, 3.72]	2.73, [1.91, 3.54]
	High	2.85, [2.36, 3.33]	2.50, [1.93, 3.05]	2.73, [2.20, 3.24]
Chart Familiarity	Low	2.72, [1.91, 3.53]	2.60, [1.73, 4.49]	4.34, [3.98, 4.69]
	High	3.41, [2.96, 3.89]	2.71, [2.22, 3.21]	2.42, [1.93, 2.94]
Visual Ability	Low	2.88, [1.95, 3.79]	2.72, [1.75, 3.69]	4.07, [3.36, 4.79]
	High	3.33, [2.86, 3.79]	2.68, [2.21, 3.18]	2.23, [1.73, 2.74]
Need for Cognition	Low	3.40, [2.63, 4.20]	3.10, [2.08, 4.15]	3.22, [2.10, 4.32]
	High	3.18, [2.71, 3.68]	2.56, [2.10, 3.03]	2.67, [2.12, 3.20]

Table 4. Average participant response (with 95% CI) across various individual differences attributes, grouped by the deceptive chart type.

Analyzing Individual Differences

As explained in Section , we collected relevant participant data (stages 1,2,3 and 5 in Figure 6) to identify individual differences. Our main goal was to see whether some of these personal attributes have an impact on how susceptible a person is to the deceptive effect. Here we provide the results of our analysis on the four main individual difference proxies we used: *education level* (collected as part of the demographic data), *chart familiarity*, *visual ability*, and *need for cognition*.

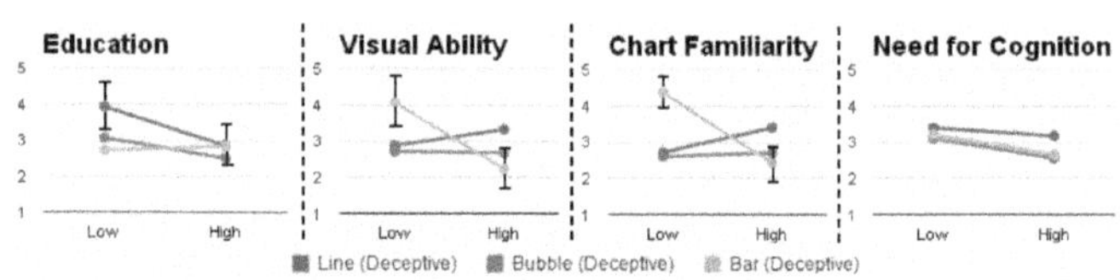

Figure 9. Comparison of average user response across deceptive charts, by the low/high level of individual differences factors.

Individual differences are studied largely in behavioral research where personal attributes of the user have an effect on his response [25]. Following this line of research, we conducted a quantitative analysis on the effect of individual differences on participants' responses, and also correlation between each of these factors to test for their independence. To facilitate our analysis and the communication of the main results, we binned the values obtained from individual differences into "high" and "low" values. For example, out of the 5 education levels (primary, secondary, undergraduate, graduate, doctorate), we regarded "primary" and "secondary" as "low education", and the rest as "high education". Participants who correctly responded to more than three questions on the visual ability test were tagged as "high visual ability", and the remaining ones as "low visual ability" participants. Similarly, those who self-reported a chart familiarity of 4 or 5 were tagged as "high chart familiarity", and those with 3 or below as "low chart familiarity" participants. Participants with overall "Need for Cognition" (range = [18, 90]) less than

54 were tagged as "low need for cognition", and greater or equal to 54 were tagged as "high need for cognition".

The results are presented in Figure 9. Table 4 presents all the effect sizes for individual differences with confidence intervals. Each chart in Figure 9 represents the effect of one individual difference factor (*education*, *visual ability*, *chart familiarity* and *need for cognition* from left to right). Within each chart, a line represents the effect size (that is the deceptive effect) obtained when the individual difference factor is low (left side) and high (right side). Line color represents the distortion effects we tested: *line*, *bubble*, *bar*.

As one can see from the figure, no clear trends exist between individual differences and participants' responses, across all chart types. The only major trend we observed was the effect of *visual ability* and *chart familiarity* on deception when a bar chart is shown (yellow line). *Education* also seemed to have an effect when a line chart was used, although the confidence intervals overlap. For the other charts, the effect was not clear as the confidence intervals are wide and overlap substantially, and hence are not shown in the figure. As the two charts provide very similar results, we also performed a correlation analysis between *visual ability* and *chart familiarity*, which revealed low correlation ($p = 0.171$) between the two factors. While *education* and *need for cognition* seem to follow a similar trend across chart type, the confidence intervals overlap substantially, making it hard to provide strong conclusions on these effects. We also performed a correlation analysis between all the individual difference factors and none of them showed strong correlation. Despite our expectations the analysis on individual differences did not provide definite conclusions.

DISCUSSION

The main goal of this study was to investigate whether and to what extent people are deceived by a number of well-known distortion techniques employed in graphical presentation of data and statistics. We also set out to see whether this effect is modulated by a set of individual differences we selected for the study.

The results confirm that these techniques do lead to major misinterpretation from the reader's side and that the effects are also rather large. When asked to compare two entities or variables by answering on a scale between 1 and 5, the distorted charts lead to responses between 58.5% and 129.5% bigger than the control condition. Out of the three charts that use a *message exaggeration/understatement* technique, the line chart is the one with the biggest effect, followed by the bars and then bubble, suggesting that these type of charts may have a more pronounced effect. The same is true for the conditions covering *message reversal* in which the deceptive condition led to 97.5% incorrect responses whereas the control condition led to only 18.4% incorrect responses.

Our analysis of the individual differences did not provide any conclusive information. However, some of the individual differences attributes seemed to have en effect for a particular type of chart. Further research is needed to disentangle the relationship between deception technique, chart type and individual differences. More precisely, it is necessary to understand if the effects depend on the chart type or only on distortion technique used. Another interesting direction is to take into account the general graphical literacy of the participants, and see whether it correlates with the response. The visualization literacy test developed by Boy et al. [11], can be employed for this purpose. While our study includes an elements that can be considered a proxy for literacy, e.g., *chart familiarity*, an objective measure of literacy may lead to more interesting results.

It is also important to discuss the main implications of this study. While deception through visualization has been known and discussed for a long time, our study allows a solid foundation for such discussions. It is important to advance the science of visualization and to help visualization practitioners with visualization principles and guidelines. It is also necessary to devise strategies to cope with the problem we identified and discussed in this study. It is necessary to educate readers and increase their ability to spot problematic and potentially deceiving information.

At last, we put forth a series of questions regarding real world visualizations. Are they designed intentionally to deceive? How can we distinguish between the intentionally and unintentionally created misrepresentations? Analyzing the root causes that lead to the publication of this kind of charts would lead to a better understanding of the phenomenon and hopefully to better solutions to the problem.

CONCLUSION

We presented in this study a first step in empirical analysis of deceptive visualizations. We started with a formal definition of deceptive visualization, outlining what deception means in the context of data visualization, what its types are, and what kind of distortion techniques are used to induce certain types of deception. We conducted a series of user studies to propose, test and establish the hypothesis that visual distortion indeed has an effect on participants' responses. Finally, we examined the effect of individual differences on participants' responses, followed by a discussion of how severe various distortion techniques are based on the quantitative analysis of the collected responses. We believe that future research will benefit from our work as it provides a foundation for further exploration of the space of deceptive visualizations.

ACKNOWLEDGMENTS

This work was partially supported by NSF Award IIS-1149745 and NYU-Poly Seed Fund Grant for Collaborative Research.

REFERENCES

1. Business Insider. `http://read.bi/1esYzVd/`, 2014.
2. Flickr. `https://www.flickr.com/photos/oversight/8475012926/in/photostream/`, 2014.
3. Media Matters. `http://mediamatters.org/research/2012/10/01/a-history-of-dishonest-fox-charts/190225/`, 2014.
4. Visualising Advocacy. `https://visualisingadvocacy.org/blog/`

`disinformation-visualization-how-lie-datavis/`, 2014.

5. Webster's Dictionary. `http://www.merriam-webster.com/dictionary/deception/`, 2014.
6. Adar, E., Tan, D. S., and Teevan, J. Benevolent deception in human computer interaction. In *Proceedings of CHI*, ACM (2013), 1863–1872.
7. Bateman, S., Mandryk, R. L., Gutwin, C., Genest, A., McDine, D., and Brooks, C. Useful junk?: the effects of visual embellishment on comprehension and memorability of charts. In *Proceedings of CHI*, ACM (2010), 2573–2582.
8. Bertin, J. *Semiology of graphics: diagrams, networks, maps*. esri press, 1983.
9. Borkin, M. A., Vo, A. A., Bylinskii, Z., Isola, P., Sunkavalli, S., Oliva, A., and Pfister, H. What makes a visualization memorable? *IEEE Transactions on Visualization and Computer Graphics (Proceedings of InfoVis 2013)* (2013).
10. Borland, D., and Taylor II, R. M. Rainbow color map (still) considered harmful. *IEEE computer graphics and applications 27*, 2 (2007), 14–17.
11. Boy, J., Rensink, R., Bertini, E., and Fekete, J. A principled way of assessing visualization literacy.
12. Brewer, C. A. Spectral schemes: Controversial color use on maps. *Cartography and Geographic Information Systems 24*, 4 (1997), 203–220.
13. Cleveland, W. S., and McGill, R. Graphical perception: Theory, experimentation, and application to the development of graphical methods. *Journal of the American Statistical Association 79*, 387 (1984), 531–554.
14. Emerson, J. *Visualizing information for advocacy*. Tactical Technology Collective, 2013.
15. Huff, D. *How to lie with statistics*. WW Norton & Company, 1954.
16. Hullman, J., Adar, E., and Shah, P. The impact of social information on visual judgments. In *Proceedings of CHI*, ACM (2011), 1461–1470.
17. Jones, G. E. *How to lie with charts*. LaPuerta Books and Media, 2011.
18. Kittur, A., Chi, E. H., and Suh, B. Crowdsourcing user studies with mechanical turk. In *Proceedings of CHI*, ACM (2008), 453–456.
19. Kong, N., Heer, J., and Agrawala, M. Perceptual guidelines for creating rectangular treemaps. *Visualization and Computer Graphics, IEEE Transactions on 16*, 6 (2010), 990–998.
20. Lengler, R. Identifying the competencies of'visual literacy'-a prerequisite for knowledge visualization. In *IV* (2006), 232–236.
21. Levkowitz, H., and Herman, G. T. Color scales for image data. *IEEE Computer Graphics and Applications 12*, 1 (1992), 72–80.
22. Li, J., Martens, J.-B., and Van Wijk, J. J. Judging correlation from scatterplots and parallel coordinate plots. *Information Visualization 9*, 1 (2010), 13–30.
23. Micallef, L., Dragicevic, P., and Fekete, J. Assessing the effect of visualizations on bayesian reasoning through crowdsourcing. *Visualization and Computer Graphics, IEEE Transactions on 18*, 12 (2012), 2536–2545.
24. Monmonier, M. How to lie with maps.
25. Nov, O., and Arazy, O. Personality-targeted design: theory, experimental procedure, and preliminary results. In *Proceedings of the 2013 conference on Computer supported cooperative work*, ACM (2013), 977–984.
26. Nov, O., Arazy, O., López, C., and Brusilovsky, P. Exploring personality-targeted ui design in online social participation systems. In *Proceedings of CHI*, ACM (2013), 361–370.
27. Pandey, A., Manivannan, A., Nov, O., Satterthwaite, M., and Bertini, E. The persuasive power of data visualization. *Visualization and Computer Graphics, IEEE Transactions on 20*, 12 (Dec 2014), 2211–2220.
28. Paolacci, G., Chandler, J., and Ipeirotis, P. G. Running experiments on amazon mechanical turk. *Judgment and Decision making 5*, 5 (2010), 411–419.
29. Petty, R. E., and Cacioppo, J. T. *Communication and persuasion: Central and peripheral routes to attitude change*. Springer-Verlag New York, 1986.
30. Pinker, S. A theory of graph comprehension. *Artificial intelligence and the future of testing* (1990), 73–126.
31. Rensink, R. A., and Baldridge, G. The perception of correlation in scatterplots. In *Computer Graphics Forum*, vol. 29, Wiley Online Library (2010), 1203–1210.
32. Richards, J. *Deceptive advertising: Behavioral study of a legal concept*. Routledge, 2013.
33. Rogowitz, B. E., Treinish, L. A., Bryson, S., et al. How not to lie with visualization. *Computers in Physics 10*, 3 (1996), 268–273.
34. Rubinstein, R., and Hersh, H. *The human factor: Designing computer systems for people*. Morgan Kaufmann Publishers Inc., 1987.
35. Segel, E., and Heer, J. Narrative visualization: Telling stories with data. *IEEE Transactions on Visualization and Computer Graphics 16*, 6 (2010), 1139–1148.
36. Shah, P., and Hoeffner, J. Review of graph comprehension research: Implications for instruction. *Educational Psychology Review 14*, 1 (2002), 47–69.
37. Tal, A., and Wansink, B. Blinded with science: Trivial graphs and formulas increase ad persuasiveness and belief in product efficacy. *Public Understanding of Science* (2014), 0963662514549688.
38. Tufte, E. R., and Graves-Morris, P. *The visual display of quantitative information*, vol. 2. Graphics press Cheshire, CT, 1983.

STRATOS: Using Visualization to Support Decisions in Strategic Software Release Planning

Bon Adriel Aseniero, Tiffany Wun, David Ledo, Guenther Ruhe, Anthony Tang, Sheelagh Carpendale
Department of Computer Science
University of Calgary
{baasenie, twwun, dledomai, ruhe, tonyt, sheelagh}@ucalgary.ca

ABSTRACT
Software is typically developed incrementally and released in stages. Planning these releases involves deciding which features of the system should be implemented for each release. This is a complex planning process involving numerous trade-offs—constraints and factors that often make decisions difficult. Since the success of a product depends on this plan, it is important to understand the trade-offs between different release plans in order to make an informed choice. We present STRATOS, a tool that simultaneously visualizes several software release plans. The visualization shows several attributes about each plan that are important to planners. Multiple plans are shown in a single layout to help planners find and understand the trade-offs between alternative plans. We evaluated our tool via a qualitative study and found that STRATOS enables a range of decision-making processes, helping participants decide on which plan is most optimal.

Author Keywords
Information Visualization; Release Planning; Software Engineering.

ACM Classification Keywords
H.5. Information Interfaces & Presentation; H.4.2. Information Systems Applications: Decision Support.

INTRODUCTION
Different models of software development have been used in industry, including iterative and incremental practices, as well as newer, agile methodologies. Companies trying to deliver a product work under several constraints (e.g. time, budget, personpower), and often have to contend with fluctuating and growing sets of customer requirements. Thus, it is important for large projects to make effective and efficient decisions concerning the use of resources—that is, deciding on a development plan such that it articulates what order features should be developed, which features should be postponed, how resources should be divided, etc. The process of structuring and managing project plans to balance between factors such as *stakeholder satisfaction, resource allocation, feature dependencies, etc.* is known as *release planning* [1]. The goal of release planning is to find an optimal release plan which balances these factors desirably—a decision-making process which typically requires the involvement of a human *planner* (e.g. project managers).

To support planners in this decision-making process, we created a tool called STRATOS (STRATegic release planning Oversight Support). STRATOS uses a hybrid visualization showing several potential release plans, revealing strengths and trade-offs within a single layout. It is designed to help planners choose an optimal plan by visualizing the interrelated factors and constraints. Our intention is to enhance the decision-making process of planners by allowing them to use different problem solving strategies while facilitating an easier way to account for multiple factors and trade-offs among alternative plans.

We make two contributions in this work:
1. First, we present the design and implementation of STRATOS, an interactive hybrid visualization which supports decision-making in software release planning;
2. Second, we outline and discuss the results of a qualitative study of this tool, in which we identified the scope of what a visualization tool like STRATOS could enable and support in software release planning.

The next section gives a brief explanation of the practice of release planning to help explain the motivation of our research, followed by a survey of related literature on visualization tools for software engineering and release planning. We then explain the design and implementation of STRATOS, outline its qualitative study, and discuss its results and implications. Finally, we explore some avenues for future work.

Practice of Release Planning
One method of release planning, EVOLVE II [9], makes use of standard planning procedures to arrive at a *release plan* containing the prioritization of features, timing of releases,

CHI 2015, April 18 - 23 2015, Seoul, Republic of Korea
Copyright 2015 ACM 978-1-4503-3145-6/15/04…$15.00
http://dx.doi.org/10.1145/2702123.2702426

and allocation of resources. This method is realized in ReleasePlanner™[1] which is an industry-grade online decision support tool for release planning [3]. Planners, stakeholders, and development team members work together in planning their project using ReleasePlanner; the iterative standard planning procedures include:

1. Studying and classifying the characteristics of the project. This involves defining the project *features* – different components and capabilities of the software, and available *resources* – supplies needed for the implementation of features (e.g. budget, hours of labour, risk, etc. [15]).

2. Identifying the *stakeholders* and their influence. Stakeholders are people who have a vested interest in the project and have a say on the importance of features and the use of resources. In ReleasePlanner, stakeholders are given a *weight* signifying their influence level and they vote on the priority of each feature using a nine-point scale. These votes are used to predict how satisfied they will be regarding a plan. Stakeholder satisfaction ranges from *very excited* to *very disappointed,* and includes *very surprised* and *surprised*—excitement (positive) occurs when high priority features are released early within a plan, disappointment (negative) occurs when features with high priority gets postponed, and surprise (neither positive nor negative) occurs when a feature with low priority gets released earlier than expected. This stakeholder satisfaction is further summarized in conjunction with feature prioritization into the Stakeholder Feature Points (SHFP) which summarizes the degree of optimality for the plan.

3. Examining multiple plan scenarios with varying values of constraints and factors and choosing the best one. This involves creating possible groupings of features to be implemented within a development cycle or *release.* Depending on the grouping of features, releases will have different resource requirements and the planner has to assess whether resources are going to be used appropriately. Typically, some features are postponed because of resource limitations.

Instead of having planners create multiple plan scenarios, ReleasePlanner uses an automated genetic algorithm to provide a small solution set of optimized release plans for analysis. In this method, planners still decide which plan in the solution set is best for their project. Our research focused on supporting these first three procedures since understanding the benefits and trade-offs of each plan by thoroughly examining resource constraints, stakeholder satisfaction, and feature implementation can quickly grow in complexity [12,15].

The next three steps—4. Executing the chosen plan, 5. Analysing the outcome of the executed plan after each release and adjusting the plan accordingly, and 6. Recording the analysis from Procedure 5 for reference—occur after planning and are thus not in the current focus.

[1] http://releaseplanner.com

Alternative Plans	1	2	3	4	5
Implemented Features (out of 27)	16	21	21	18	19
Resources not used in Release 1	$2,200 109 hrs	$600 73 hrs	$500 64 hrs	$2,800 119 hrs	$2,500 128 hrs
Resources not used in Release 2	94 hrs	114 hrs	123 hrs	107 hrs	87 hrs
Resources not met in Release 2	$2,200	$600	$500	$2,000	$2,500
Stakeholder Feature Points (SHFP)	98.3%	98.2%	97.9%	96.2%	94.9%
"Very disappointed" stakeholder points	0	1	1	0	0

Table 1: Summary of an example solution set. Values of the main factors are shown for each alternative.

Example Solution Set

Table 1 shows a simplified overview of an example solution set which contains five alternatives each having different benefits and trade-offs (as a result of Procedure 3); Alternative 1 contains the highest excitement from the SHFP and has no *very disappointed* score, but the number of total features released is the lowest. Alternatives 2 and 3 contain the best balance of resources between releases and tied for the most features released, differing only in that Alternative 2 has a higher SHFP. Both, however, contains a *very disappointed* stakeholder point. Alternative 4 contains no disappointment score, while having more features released than alternative 1. Lastly, Alternative 5 is what we considered as the least optimal plan. It contains the lowest SHFP and resource imbalance, even though it has the second highest amount of features released.

Alternative 2 is the most balanced alternative in terms of all of the constraints and factors as it maintains a high degree of optimality (>95%) while having 1 *very disappointed* stakeholder point, and it has good resource allocation. Nevertheless, as Table 1 illustrates, each solution has merits, and it is precisely because each alternative has advantages and disadvantages that human decision-making is important in understanding and articulating these trade-offs. Therefore, there is a need for tools that support planners.

Working closely with a release planning domain expert, who also spearheaded the development of ReleasePlanner, we developed STRATOS to help planners examine optimal plans through a hybrid visualization. Our tool complements ReleasePlanner by providing a visualization for the data generated by ReleasePlanner in spreadsheet format. However, planners can also visualize their own data by following the required spreadsheet format.

RELATED WORK

To set the stage, we first outline related work in visualization used in software engineering and development. We then discuss visualizations that have been previously created specifically for release planning. We also discuss visualizations that we have drawn from in designing STRATOS.

Visualizations for General Software Development

Visualizations have been previously used in software engineering. For example, UML (Unified Modelling Language) [16] is commonly used to capture and portray requirements during the software development process. Although UML provides developers with constructs to build object-oriented models close to real-world models [8], UML focuses primarily on software architecture rather than management (e.g. budget, development schedule).

In contrast, Gantt charts visualize the development schedule, allowing planners to chart and hierarchically see dependencies between related feature components [5]. This makes these charts effective at executing plans with minimal confusion [5]. Similarly, Wnuk et al. explored how one can represent feature life cycles in a two dimensional graph [23]. Kanban visualizes workflow of a development team [2]. It depicts just-in-time development process, where features are only implemented when there is an explicit customer request; as a consequence, development is represented as a large number of small deliverables. These deliverables are depicted with cards that can be moved along a board signifying where it is in the development cycle. While Gantt charts and Kanban are effective at visualizing development progress, they both rely on a flexible plan that is already decided on earlier. Putting these in perspective, we envision our tool to coexist with these pre-existing kinds of visualizations. This is because our tool supports the decision-making process to come up with a plan before development begins, and possibly when a change in plan is needed or when a new development cycle begins.

Visualizations for Release Planning

The goal of introducing visualization in release planning is often the same: to increase the transparency of solutions, showing why certain plans are suggested, and what the trade-offs look like between alternatives [1]. While some release planning tools like ReleasePlanner provide basic visualizations (e.g. bar graphs, line graphs, etc.)[3,23], these are typically focused on simple bivariate relationships, unable to depict the complex, multivariate relationships inherent in release planning. Several researchers have explored using different visual representations to support release planning. For example, Feather et al. provided several representations that showed the requirements and risks for the planning of a release [6]. Their tool provided different basic visualization views for comparing risks and exploring the solution space as a trade-off between cost and benefit. While each view is useful, switching between them to in order to accomplish tasks can be cumbersome as it relies on mentally integrating information across several views to answer questions. STRATOS begins with the premise that several variables need to be visually accessible simultaneously to show their interrelatedness and reduce this burden.

Carlshamre et al. illustrated ways to represent feature dependencies, including coupling, precedence, multiplicative cost and multiplicative value through a graph that resembled a directed node-link graph [4]. Herrmann's Rational-Based Analysis Tool allows for the representation of use cases, multiple releases, and the features related to them by showing the subclass–superclass relationship through *knowledge nuggets*—objects which contain information pertaining to plans. It also allows for modification of releases or plans [10]. These provided a good basis for STRATOS in representing hierarchical relationships. However, while these are useful for showing functional dependencies (for development planning), they do not account for the broader factors that impact release planning (e.g. resource allocation and stakeholder preferences) which are important in determining how to arrange releases such that they would arrive to market in the most effective way possible.

Visualizations that Influenced the Design of STRATOS

We were inspired by several existing visualizations that we leverage in our work. The Sankey diagram [17] is based on Minard's drawing of Napoleon's Russian Campaign of 1812—to which he claimed to promptly convey *"the relation not given quickly by numbers"* [22]. Sankey diagrams have been used for depicting energy and material balances of complex production systems (e.g. Steam-Engine production) [16,17]. Reihmann et al. furthered this development by making Sankey diagrams interactive and useful for planning alternative flow scenarios [14].

While the Sankey diagram is effective for depicting resource consumption, our data has other properties that have led us to examine other visualizations as well. One aspect of our data is that it is highly comparative, containing information about several plans, releases, and features. Features, in particular, remain constant among all of the plans in a solution set, with the difference being their priority. This makes it akin to multivariate data, hence we turned to using Parallel Coordinates [11] for its depiction. We took inspiration from these works to create a hybrid visualization tool that supports the decision-making process of release planning.

Parallel Sets [13] bears a striking resemblance to our visualization. Parallel sets is a visualization which combines parallel coordinates and frequency displays. It was designed specifically for showing categorical information as independent dimensions, while STRATOS depicts alternatives. STRATOS was designed with a more practical goal in mind—the comparison of alternative release plans to support planners in choosing the best plan. Nevertheless, parallel sets have been shown to help identify relationships in the data which reinforces our use of a similar visualization to depict relationships among release planning factors and constraints.

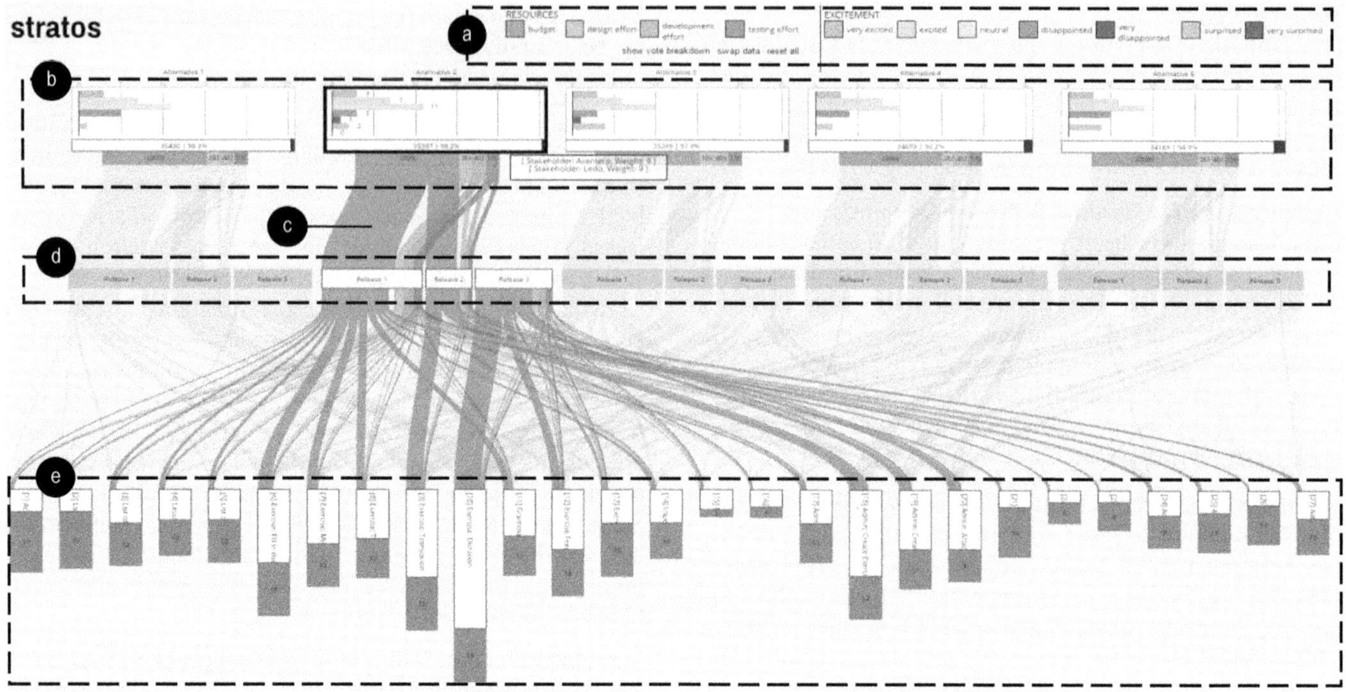

Figure 1: STRATOS' view of a release planning solution set summarized in Table 1. (a) Legend for the colour representations of resources and excitement levels. (b) The boxes representing the alternative plans in the solution set. (c) The flow diagram visualizing the flow of resources into the (d) alternative's releases, and eventually to the (e) features.

STRATOS

Our goal in designing STRATOS (Figure 1) is to support planners in their release planning decision-making process through visualization. Our solution combines the flow visualization of Sankey diagrams with the multivariate illustration of Parallel Coordinates. Our data set is inherently hierarchical, with plans containing releases and releases containing features, thus we opted to use a forest or multiple tree layout [7]. STRATOS visualizes the important factors of release planning in a unified, single layout. This ensures that all of the factors are readily available to the planner. We also implemented interactive brushing, allowing components to interactively reveal relationships in the data. Our design process relied on gaining knowledge and feedback from a release planning domain expert.

Design Process and Guidelines

We used a method akin to Sedlmair's et al. design study methodology [18]. We worked closely with a release planning domain expert who emphasized that a visualization could help planners in release planning. He helped identify important patterns and relationships, providing guidance for the development of STRATOS. We iterated on several visualization designs specifically to highlight these relationships which were not readily apparent with basic visualizations. The underlying design guidelines for STRATOS are:

1. *Consider as many as possible factors.* Knowing the conditions of multiple factors and constraints of release planning is important for planners to be able to make good and well-informed decisions. The visualization design must take into account visualizing as many factors as possible.
2. *Provide a holistic view.* The visualization must also be able to show how the factors and constraints relate to each other. A holistic view allows planners to consider most of the factors with considerable ease rather than trying to do so while switching between views. Hybrid visualization brings together different aspects of existing visualization techniques to create something novel. We bring the advantages of several techniques together to make data comparisons more transparent.
3. *Support comparison between plans.* While plans will be shown as distinct, consistency across representations must be used to support comparison between plans.
4. *Support different strategies for decision-making.* Different planners often have different ways of deciding what is the best plan regarding their project. An interactive visualization should allow planners to explore the data however they prefer (e.g. allowing a planner to start their exploration of the data anywhere in the visualization).
5. *Support both individual and collaborative exploration of data.* Release planning can be performed either as an individual or as a team. This extends Guideline 4 in case of collaborative planning.
6. *Support details-on-demand* [19]. While visually conveying information allows planners to do simple comparisons at-a-glance, they must be able to access detailed information for fine-grained analysis.
7. *Minimize required interactions.* Minimizing interaction overhead by avoiding deeply nested menus and other complicated actions while still providing full visualization and data access could help simplify the planner's task.

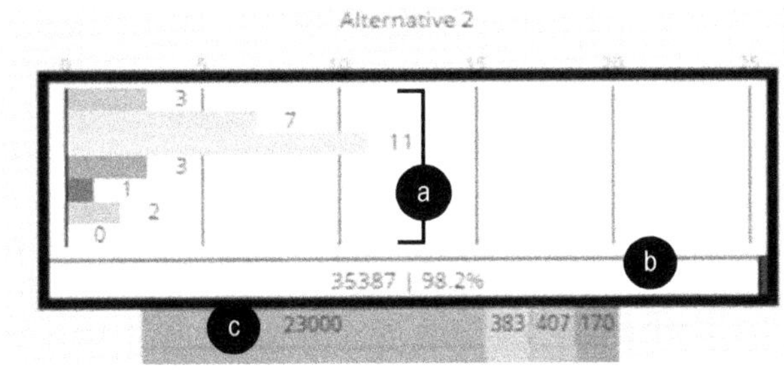

Figure 2: Header of one alternative plan tree, showing (a) stakeholder excitement levels, and (b) the SHFP degree of optimality. (c) Initial resource flow.

Visual Representation

As previously mentioned, STRATOS is a hybrid visualization that integrates Sankey diagrams and parallel coordinates in a multiple tree layout. Figure 1 shows an overview of STRATOS. At the top right hand side (Figure 1.a) are two legends: (1) resources and (2) stakeholder satisfaction levels. Each plan can be thought of as a hierarchy that contains resources, releases and features. The overall view is a small forest, with one tree representing an alternative plan. The hierarchy shows alternative headers at the top (Figure 1.b), releases in the middle (Figure 1.d), and the features at the bottom (Figure 1.e). Since all alternatives contain the same set of features—though they have been given different implementation order—the trees representing the plans also share the same set of features. This visually depicts that the plans are alternatives for the same software. The flow or graph edges represent resource allocation. Their thickness is mapped to the crucial factor of available (or required) amount of the resource each represents. The flow of resources shown from the plan to the releases and from the releases to the features (Figure 1.c) function similar to parallel coordinates where plans, releases, and features are the axes.

Figure 2.a shows the bar chart representation of the stakeholder satisfaction. Figure 2.b (white bar) shows the degree of optimality for a plan (SHFP). Figure 2.c shows the top of the resource flow visual element. The amount of available resources are shown here (dark blue: budget, light blue: design effort, pink: development effort, red: testing effort).

Figure 3.a shows the flow of resources into release 1. Each release's width (named white bar) corresponds to the total amount of resources needed to implement all the features included in the release. The incoming flow to the release shows the amount of resources allocated for the release, while the flow coming out of the release shows the amount of resources required to implement the features scheduled for implementation in that development cycle (see Figure 3). Here, planners can immediately see discrepancies between the allocated resources and the required resources (see Figures 3.c, 3.d). In the data visualized in Figure 1 (and enlarged in Figure 3) each alternative contains 3 releases: Release 1, contains the set of features to be released at first launch of the software; Release 2 contains the set of features to be released at a later time (e.g. during a patch update); and Release 3

Figure 3: The flow diagram shows the allocation of resources as (a) the initial allocated amount of resources, (b) the actual amount needed (for budget). (c) Gaps in the incoming resources mean that the release needs more of that resource, while (d) gaps in the outgoing resources mean it needs less of that resource allocated to it.

contains the remaining subset of features which are postponed due to resource constraints. This is why, as seen in Figure 3, Release 3 does not receive any incoming resources.

At the bottom of the visualization, we show the set of features of the software (see Figure 1.e). This list of features works like a stacked bar chart where each feature is represented by a stacked bar. The white bar (Figure 4.b) represents the amount of resources the feature requires (i.e. the longer it is, the more resources the feature needs), while the blue bar (Figure 4.d) represents the consolidated stakeholder votes on the priority of the feature. The breakdown of these votes per stakeholder can be seen in its tooltip (Figure 4.e). When comparing a plan or a release, amber dots appear at the bottom of some features signifying the number of plans or releases it belongs to among those being compared. For example, when two releases are being compared, one amber dot under a feature means that the feature belongs to only one of the highlighted releases, while two dots means it is in both.

Interaction

Through interaction, a planner can have access to all the details of the data. Following our guidelines, a planner can begin his/her interaction anywhere in the visualization. To describe the different interactions in STRATOS, this section

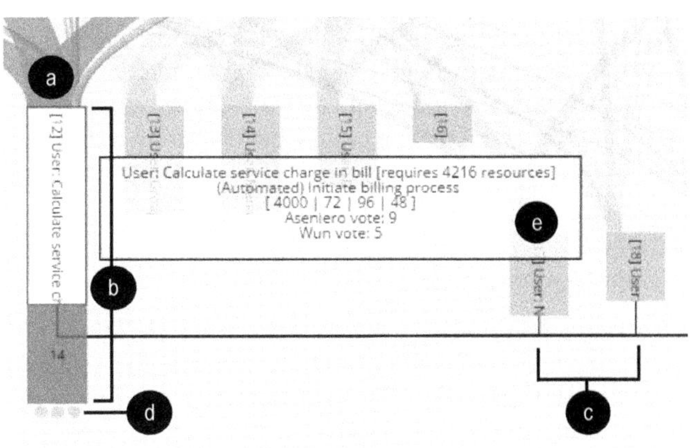

Figure 4: A feature represented by a stacked bar. (a) The flow of resources to the feature. (b) The amount of required resources. Clicking on the feature shows (c) dependent features and (d) the stakeholder votes. (e) Tooltip displaying detailed information including the breakdown of the stakeholder votes on the feature.

describes each interaction from top to bottom regarding the different parts of the visualization.

At the top of the visualization, tapping an alternative plan header highlights the flow of resources, releases, and features related to that alternative plan (as seen on Figure 1, with Alternative 2 being highlighted). Tapping again deselects the alternative, removing the highlighting. Pressing and holding (for ~1s) on an alternative shows the stakeholder weights.

The same interaction also applies to the releases in the middle of the visualization (Figure 1.d). In this case, the highlighted elements will be all the features that belong to that release, the alternative header it belongs to (but not the other releases in the alternative), and the flow of resources coming in and out of the release. Planners can highlight multiple releases from different alternatives simultaneously to compare them (e.g. they could look at the differences of two releases regarding the features they implement). Pressing and holding shows a tooltip containing the actual amount of resources the release requires and the amount allocated to it. As before, tapping on a release puts it in focus until it is tapped again.

Tapping on any feature highlights all of the releases it belongs to within all alternatives. It also highlights the feature, revealing the bar representing the stakeholder votes it received. The tooltip for each feature shows the full name of the feature, the amount of resources it requires, and the breakdown of the stakeholder votes it received (see Figure 4.e). Tapping on a feature puts it in focus until it is tapped again. It also shows the other features that are dependent on it. These dependent features will move slightly downwards and be connected by a line that links them to the feature in focus on which they depend (see Figure 4.c).

We designed several other interactions. First, resources available for highlighting can be chosen by marking them on the legend. If a resource type is marked with an "x" on the legend, then that type will not highlight. This can be used by planners should they wish to focus on a specific type of resource(s). Second, we implemented a "reset all" button that clears all highlighted items, since a planner may want to clear all highlighting rapidly to examine the data from a different focus, rather than tapping to toggle off all existing highlights.

Implementation

We implemented STRATOS as a web application using HTML5 and JavaScript.

STUDYING RELEASE PLANNING WITH STRATOS

We conducted a qualitative study to evaluate the scope of what a visualization like STRATOS can support in the decision-making involved in release planning. In our study, we focused on discovering important factors in planners' decision-making processes such as: identifying their decision strategies, and examining how a visualization of a solution set reflecting real-life complexity affects these strategies. In doing so, we took note of whether our underlying guidelines were justified, and if planners arrived at what is considered a good decision. We also used this study as an opportunity to find strengths and weaknesses in our current implementation, and to find further requirements to ease the complexity of this decision-making process. Our method involved observing participants' behaviours and decision-making processes.

Participants

Participants who had a background in software engineering and release planning were carefully selected through a recruitment process involving the help of the domain expert. We studied 15 participants (five female and ten male): twelve were graduate students with computer science, electrical, computer, and or software engineering backgrounds; and three participants were industry-based software developers whose work involves software release management. They had varying levels of experience with software release planning: nine participants had at least one or more years of experience, and six had less than a year of experience. Two participants had experience in using ReleasePlanner.

Setup

We ran STRATOS on a 72", 2K HD SMARTboard during the study, showing the visualization on a large screen and allowing touch and pen interaction. This also allowed the researchers to observe each participant's interactions with STRATOS. We used an HD webcam positioned directly in front of the SMARTboard to record each session.

Procedure

We ran participants through the study individually, with each session running for about an hour. At the beginning, we asked them to fill out a demographic questionnaire about their background with release planning, and experience with similar visualizations (like Sankey Diagrams) and other visualizations for software release planning. We then introduced STRATOS, explaining each component of the visualization and how to interact with it.

The study was composed of two phases: a *familiarization phase*, and an *exploration phase*. The first phase's purpose was to help participants build familiarity with the visualization and its interactivity. We visualized a simple solution set containing three alternatives and asked participants to perform a set of simple tasks. We encouraged the participants to ask questions whenever they get confused and we provided assistance as necessary. The tasks in the first phase were:

1. Naming a feature and stating the amount of resources it requires, as well as any dependent features.
2. Reporting to which releases the feature from Task 1 belongs to for each alternative.
3. Choosing a release and indicating the amount of features planned to be implemented in it.
4. Finding the feature that requires the most resources.
5. Finding which feature has the top priority according to the stakeholders.
6. Reporting the amount of resources allocated for a plan.
7. Selecting which alternative has the most positive response from the stakeholders.

In the second phase, we asked our participants to take on the role of a project manager (a planner) in a scenario in which they were to explore a new dataset and choose an optimal plan. For this phase, the software being planned for was a standard language learning software, with all of its features labelled and described. We used the previously described solution set (the example in this paper's introduction) with five plans pre-generated from ReleasePlanner (see Figure 1). In this phase, the participants interacted with STRATOS on their own, but encouraged to think aloud as they worked. Once they had chosen an alternative, we asked them to explain why they believed their chosen alternative was the best plan.

At the end of the study, we asked participants to fill out a post-study questionnaire about their overall thoughts on STRATOS. We asked them to rate STRATOS on how easy it was to use and read, and their confidence on their chosen alternative. We also asked them about which parts of the visualization helped them most, their criticisms, and suggestions.

RESULTS

Our participants did not have any trouble with any task during the familiarization phase. Although, some had difficulty with the last task, Task 7. This asks participants to find a balance between the different satisfaction levels (i.e. identifying and resolving the issue of plans that have more *very excited* with some *very disappointed* score, against a plan that has less *very excited* but no *very disappointed* scores) which already involves a form of decision-making. For the remainder of the study, we took note of the distribution of participants between their chosen alternative plans. As seen on Figure 5, seven out of 15 chose the most balanced alternative (Alternative 2), while only one participant (Participant 8) was not able to make a choice. Assessment of each participant's confidence over their chosen plan(s) showed that 13 of 15 positively agreed that they chose the optimal plan, and according

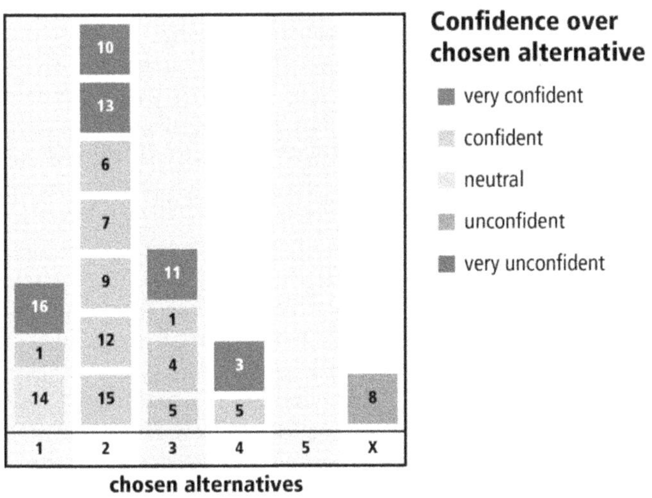

Figure 5: Stacked chart showing the number of participants (one per square) who chose each plan. When a participant had a split vote, their square is divided. Colours represent participant's confidence level.

to the post-study questionnaires, participants felt more or less comfortable with using and reading STRATOS.

We found consistency in participants' justifications for their choices. Alternative 1 was chosen primarily because of its high SHFP, its zero *very disappointed* stakeholder point, and the number of its implemented features. Alternative 2 was chosen for its efficiency with resource allocation, high SHFP, and the number of its implemented features. Alternative 3 was chosen for its balanced resource allocation. Alternative 4 was chosen because certain features postponed in other alternatives were implemented in it.

Decision Strategies

Based on our observations, we outline several strategies that our participants employed to choose an alternative plan based on common reasons in their justification. While we treat these strategies as separate, most participants used one of these as their main justification for choosing an alternative plan but also used some aspects of other strategies.

Strategy 1: Resource-allocation-based decision strategy. Some participants focused on how the resources are handled within each alternative. They tried to find discrepancies in the resource allocation such as surplus or insufficient budget.

Strategy 2: Stakeholder-excitement-based decision strategy. Some participants focused on how happy the stakeholders would be with each alternative. They mostly examined stakeholder satisfaction levels. Some also examined which features were rated highly by stakeholders and whether those features were scheduled to be released as soon as possible.

Strategy 3: Feature-based decision strategy. Some participants preferred to look at which features are implemented or postponed within each alternative. For example, participant 11 made her own ranking of the features and then chose the plan that she believed to implement more features that were important to her. Similarly, Participant 8 focused on the feature hierarchy, trying to find which plan implements features that had many dependent features.

Participant Inclination

We identified certain inclinations that our participants had while interacting with STRATOS. This was done by open-coding our observations of participant behaviours during the second phase of the study. In particular, we focused on which elements of the visualization participants seemed to be most drawn to and any repeating actions. We noticed that they were inclined to use either visual or numeric cues, or a mix of both. We observed each participant's behaviours and categorized them accordingly. Of the 15 participants, nine had visual, three had numeric, and three had mixed inclination (see Figure 6). This is important because even if two participants used the same decision strategy in choosing an alternative, if they have different inclinations, their method of using STRATOS differed as well. This could lead to them choosing different plans altogether. For example, Participants 3 (visual) and 14 (numeric) both used resource-allocation-based

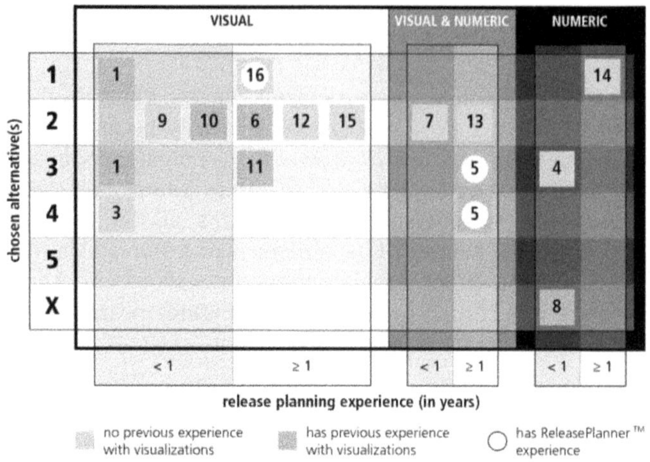

Figure 6: Participant distribution in inclination categories. This also shows details about the participants (each square with the participant number) such as the alternative(s) they chose, length of release planning experience, and experience with visualizations similar to STRATOS.

decision strategy, but they chose different plans—with Participant 3 choosing Alternative 4, and Participant 14 choosing Alternative 1.

Visual Inclination. Participants with a visual inclination looked at the data primarily using visual cues. They understood visualization techniques easily and used the visual representations to examine and compare alternative plans. We found STRATOS' flow visualization effectively supported participants who used the Resource-allocation-based decision strategy with this inclination. Those who used this strategy looked at the flow visualization to get an overview of how resources are divided among releases. In particular, they focused on comparing the thickness and gaps between the flow visual elements to find insufficient or surplus resources. Those who used the Feature-based decision strategy used the flow visualization like parallel coordinates; using the flow lines from the features as lines pointing to which releases they are scheduled for implementation. Those who used the Stakeholder-satisfaction-based decision strategy mainly used the top portion of the visualization (plan headers) displaying the stakeholder satisfaction levels, and the stakeholder vote representation at the bottom of each feature.

Numeric Inclination. Participants with a numeric inclination used actual numbers in order to examine and compare alternative plans. Using the visual representations only to locate tooltips showing the represented data as numbers on which they heavily relied. Some used the SMARTboard pen to write down these numbers to remember them when they needed to calculate. For example, Participant 4 who used the Resource-allocation-based strategy wrote down the amount of resources in each alternative and then calculated the difference between them.

Mixed Inclination. Participants with a mixed inclination used the visual representations similar to those with a visual inclination; however, they equally used numeric data to compare visual representations that looked similar. As those with visual inclination, participants with mixed inclination were supported by STRATOS. Their inclination also encouraged them to examine the details of the data rather than simply relying on what they visually perceived. Nevertheless, they also shared the disadvantages of those with a numeric inclination.

Most participants who had a visual or mixed inclination chose Alternative 2, while those with a numeric inclination were more varied in their choices; however, none of them chose Alternative 2. This can be attributed to the visualization showing Alternative 2's balanced resource allocation which gave advantage to those who had a visual inclination and used a Resource-allocation-based decision strategy. Evidence for this can be found in the participants' justifications—with Alternative 2's efficient handling of resources being a frequent reason for choosing it. This could also be the reason why participants who were confident with their choice(s) tended to have a visual inclination. Moreover, if a participant thought that the visualization was easy to read, she/he was more likely to be confident in her/his choice(s).

DISCUSSION

Regarding the Inclinations

The inclinations we identified may be a form of personal inclination; however, they could also be artefacts stemming from STRATOS being designed as a visualization tool. In our data, participants who have no previous experience with similar visualizations were more dispersed in their inclinations, while those with previous exposure to similar visualizations were more visually inclined. This suggests that the inclinations stem from both STRATOS' design and personal experience. Supporting these inclinations should therefore be taken into account in designing future tools like STRATOS.

Regarding the Strategies

From our observations, while it may be that most of our participants came in with resource-allocation-based strategy (Strategy 1) as their pre-established strategy for decision-making, it was interesting to see a connection with the use of Strategy 1 and the way STRATOS is designed. Because STRATOS' main visualization is a flow diagram of resources, it is arguable that participants who had a visual or mixed inclination found it easier to assess each alternative based on their resource allocation. However, it is also possible that they may have been urged to employ this strategy as their main decision due to the visual cues because the most prominent visual cue in STRATOS is the resource flow diagram. Since release planning is often subjective, it is good that STRATOS' allowed for the exploration of the different alternatives. What matters is that none of the participants chose Alternative 5, which we deemed to be the least balanced plan in the solution set. Hence, despite the fact that some participants did not choose Alternative 2, they were able to make informed decisions, and the visualization did not lead them towards a detrimental solution. This shows that STRATOS showcased the different alternatives and did not bias the participants to fixate on one alternative.

Regarding the Design Guidelines

The unified layout of STRATOS showed all of the factors and how they relate with each other, providing a holistic view (Guideline 2) and allowing participants to compare alternatives (Guideline 3). The hybrid visualization of STRATOS has also been shown to support multiple decision-making strategies (Guideline 4). We found that all strategies of the participants involved some form of examining most factors of release planning. This suggests that STRATOS' visual elements allowed the planners to consider as many release planning factors as they could (Guideline 1). However, the study showed that while a single layout could help in easing the mental load coming from view switching, this gives its own type of mental load and that training time (approximately 20 minutes) was necessary for the participants to be able to use STRATOS comfortably and effectively. This issue raises a question on whether compartmentalizing the single view into several visualization widgets (one visualization per factor) and updating all whenever one is interacted with by the planner, could lower the mental load. Arriving at a good balance would require additional future work. Nevertheless, the choice of combining Sankey diagrams and parallel coordinates in a tree view hybrid visualization proved useful in supporting participants who had visual or mixed inclinations.

To some extent, STRATOS also supported those with a numeric inclination via details-on-demand (Guideline 6). STRATOS provides the ability to drill down to actual data through tooltips—and numerically inclined participants did use the structure of STRATOS to find the right tooltips—there are some aspects of this numerical approach that the design of STRATOS did not effectively support. For example, participants who used the Stakeholder-satisfaction-based decision strategy with a numeric inclination were not able to draw out numeric data composing the stakeholder satisfaction levels. On the other hand, Participant 8, who used a Feature-based decision strategy—focusing mostly on stakeholder votes for each features, dependent features, and when they are implemented—had to go through each of the features to see their details in the tooltips. This put a heavy mental load on the participant which hindered him finding the best plan.

It is hard to say whether these difficulties are due to the participants not understanding the visualization enough or because some type of support was lacking, since our post-study questionnaire data showed that most numerically inclined participants still agreed that the visualization was easy to read. Nevertheless, rather than having the participants dig for numerical information through tooltips, it is advisable to specifically design ways of how to integrate numerical data within the same view of the visualization. Minimizing the required interactions for all the inclinations is imperative to ensure they are all well-supported (Guideline 7). Simplifying required interactions can be extended to the feature visual elements as well. For instance, rather than showing a single bar for the stakeholder votes with its breakdown shown in the tooltip, the domain expert suggested that it would be more meaningful to see the vote breakdown as separate parts of the stacked bar. This is because some stakeholders have a higher weight than others, and seeing the vote of a targeted stakeholder at-a-glance can add more utility to the visualization. Finding features dependencies can also be simplified by arranging the features in space based on their dependencies.

Limitations

One limitation of our qualitative study is our participant sample. While our participants had at least graduate level experience with release planning, the majority were still students with only a handful of planners from industry. While this participant sample is seldom perfect, this study's participants' skill set was both representative and sufficient for the study's purpose. The goal of our study was to understand the scope of what a visualization like STRATOS potentially supports, and not to evaluate STRATOS (in its current prototype form) as a tool used in industry. Nevertheless, a study involving industry planners could shed light into how visualizations like STRATOS might perform in the wild. It could also lead to the identification of other decision strategies and inclinations, and inform how this type of visualization can be integrated with existing management practices. Furthermore, the study was performed individually between participants, and as such, it did not investigate what roles STRATOS could take on as part of a development team dynamics (Guideline 5). Investigating this could inform us about group decision-making strategies, how they relate to individual decision strategies and inclinations, and how to support them.

FUTURE WORK

We derived several ways in which STRATOS can be improved by reflecting over the lessons from our study together with the release planning expert. One way is to improve support for planners with a numeric inclination. The domain expert suggested this type of inclination can be better supported by implementing a type of dashboard that integrates the visual elements of STRATOS with the spreadsheet containing the numerical data. Dashboards have been shown to provide better awareness of both high-level and low-level aspects of data [21], suggesting its incorporation with the visualization of STRATOS would be beneficial. Moreover, to reduce the mental load stemming from the single layout of STRATOS, he suggested implementing a feature which guides the planner along a series of steps to analyse the data. This would enable the planner to focus on a certain portion of the visualization, while the rest of the visualization is rendered out-of-focus to reduce visual clutter but maintain overall awareness. It would need to be possible for the planner to override this feature at any time to retain the *freedom of choice* afforded by STRATOS' design guideline 4.

There are also other things that could be implemented to turn STRATOS from a simple visualization tool into a full visual analytics tool. *Direct manipulation*, or being able to modify the data on the spot [20] (e.g. changing values for budget, adding and removing features, etc. and seeing the visuals update accordingly) could further increase decision support.

Furthermore, embedded analysis of the data could highlight areas of the data that could be missed due to human error.

CONCLUSION

In this paper we presented STRATOS, a visualization tool that supports the decision-making process involved in software release planning. We outlined how we used a hybrid visualization combining Sankey diagrams and parallel coordinates in a tree view for its design and implementation, and the qualitative study we conducted to study its scope. In brief we contribute: (1) STRATOS: a decision support visualization tool; and (2) the study where we identified three decision strategies (resource-allocation-based, stakeholder-satisfaction-based and feature-based) and three inclinations (visual, numeric, and mixed). We observed that while most participants had a main strategy for their decision, they also made use of other strategies, indicating that supporting multiple strategies is useful for decision-making support.

We argued that STRATOS is able to support multiple processes and suggested that similar visualizations could help planners in decision-making. Our future work suggestions could open up more support for decision-making. In broader terms, we would like to extend the lessons learned from STRATOS to the design of other visualizations supporting decision-making beyond the area of software release planning.

Acknowledgements

We would like to thank the following organizations for providing funding and equipment for this research: Alberta Innovates Technology Futures (AITF), Natural Sciences and Engineering Research Council of Canada (NSERC), Graphics Animation and New Media (GRAND), SurfNet, and SMART technologies.

REFERENCES

1. Amandeep, Ruhe, G., and Stanford, M. Intelligent Support for Software Release Planning. In F. Bomarius and H. Iida, eds., *Product Focused Software Process Improvement*. Springer Berlin Heidelberg, 2004, 248–262.
2. Anderson, D.J. *Kanban.* Blue Hole Press, 2010.
3. Bhawnani, P. and Ruhe, G. ReleasePlanner-Planning new Releases for Software Maintenance and Evolution. *ICSM (Industrial and Tool Volume)*, (2005), 73–76.
4. Carlshamre, P., Sandahl, K., Lindvall, M., Regnell, B., and Natt och Dag, J. An Industrial Survey of Requirements Interdependencies in Software Product Release Planning. In *Proc. Fifth IEEE International Symposium on Requirements Engineering*, (2001), 84 –91.
5. Clark, W. and Gantt, H.L. *The Gantt Chart, a Working Tool of Management.* New York, Ronald Press, 1923.
6. Feather, M.S., Cornford, S.L., Kiper, J.D., and Menzies, T. Experiences using Visualization Techniques to Present Requirements, Risks to Them, and Options for Risk Mitigation. *First International Workshop on Requirements Engineering Visualization, REV '06*, (2006), 10.
7. Feiner, S. Seeing the Forest for the Trees: Hierarchical Displays of Hypertext Structures. In *Proc. ACM SIGOIS and IEEECS TC-OA 1988 Conference on Office Information Systems*, ACM (1988), 205–212.
8. France, R., Evans, A., Lano, K., and Rumpe, B. The UML as a Formal Modeling Notation. *Computer Standards & Interfaces 19*, 7 (1998), 325–334.
9. Greer, D. and Ruhe, G. Software Release Planning: An Evolutionary and Iterative Approach. *Information and Software Technology 46*, 4 (2004), 243–253.
10. Herrmann, K. Visualization of Release Planning. *First International Workshop on Requirements Engineering Visualization, 2006. REV '06*, (2006), 8–8.
11. Inselberg, A. and Dimsdale, B. Parallel Coordinates: A Tool for Visualizing Multi-dimensional Geometry. In *Proc. 1st Conference on Visualization '90*, IEEE (1990), 361–378.
12. Jantunen, S., Lehtola, L., Gause, D.C., Dumdum, U.R., and Barnes, R.J. The Challenge of Release Planning. *Fifth International Workshop on Software Product Management (IWSPM)*, (2011), 36–45.
13. Kosara, R., Bendix, F., and Hauser, H. Parallel Sets: Interactive Exploration and Visual Analysis of Categorical Data. *IEEE Transactions on Visualization and Computer Graphics 12*, 4 (2006), 558–568.
14. Riehmann, P., Hanfler, M., and Froehlich, B. Interactive Sankey Diagrams. *IEEE INFOVIS*, (2005), 233–240.
15. Ruhe, G. *Product Release Planning: Methods, Tools and Applications.* CRC Press, 2011.
16. Rumbaugh, J., Jacobson, I., and Booch, G. *The Unified Modeling Language Reference Manual (2nd Edition).* Pearson Higher Education, 2004.
17. Sankey, H.R. The Thermal Efficiency of Steam-Engines. *Minutes of the Proceedings 125*, 1896 (1896), 182–212.
18. Sedlmair, M., Meyer, M., and Munzner, T. Design Study Methodology: Reflections from the Trenches and the Stacks. *IEEE Transactions on Visualization and Computer Graphics 18*, 12 (2012), 2431–2440.
19. Shneiderman, B. The Eyes Have It: A Task By Data Type Taxonomy for Information Visualizations. In *Proc. Visual Languages*, IEEE (1996), 336–343.
20. Shneiderman, B. and Maes, P. Direct Manipulation vs. Interface Agents. *Interactions 4*, 6 (1997), 42–61.
21. Treude, C. and Storey, M. Awareness 2.0: Staying Aware of Projects, Developers and Tasks Using Dashboards and Feeds. *ACM/IEEE 32nd International Conference on Software Engineering*, (2010), 365–374.
22. Tufte, E.R. *The Visual Display of Quantitative Information.* Graphics Press, Cheshire, CT, 1983.
23. Wnuk, K., Regnell, B., and Karlsson, L. Visualization of Feature Survival in Platform-Based Embedded Systems Development for Improved Understanding of Scope Dynamics. *Requirements Engineering Visualization, REV '08*, (2008), 41–50.

Supporting Subtlety with Deceptive Devices and Illusory Interactions

Fraser Anderson[1], Tovi Grossman[1], Daniel Wigdor[2], George Fitzmaurice[1]
[1]Autodesk Research, User Interface Group
{first.last}@autodesk.com
[2]University of Toronto
dwigdor@dgp.toronto.edu

Figure 1: Examples of subtle interactions achieved through the use of the presented gimmicks. From left to right: reading text messages, composing an email, and checking the time.

ABSTRACT
Mobile devices offer constant connectivity to the world, which can negatively affect in-person interaction. Current approaches to minimizing the social disruption and improving the subtlety of interactions tend to focus on the development of inconspicuous devices that provide basic input or output. This paper presents a more general approach to subtle interaction and demonstrates how a number of principles from magic can be leveraged to improve subtlety. It also presents a framework that can be used to classify subtle interfaces along with a modular set of novel interfaces that fit within this framework. Lastly, the paper presents a new evaluation paradigm specifically designed to assess the subtlety of interactions. This paradigm is used to compare traditional approaches to our new subtle approaches. We find our new approaches are over five times more subtle than traditional interactions, even when participants are aware of the technologies being used.

INTRODUCTION
Mobile devices enable always-available access to information, supplying a perpetual connection to the world outside our immediate surroundings. While compelling, it is often inappropriate to use one's phone or other electronic device, be it for privacy or social reasons [22, 23, 29]. In many situations, users wishing to access their mobile device resort to simplistic methods, such as hiding their phone under a desk or turning down the screen brightness, to avoid detection. These methods have limited effectiveness as observers often notice such behaviors.

CHI 2015, April 18 - 23, 2015, Seoul, Republic of Korea

ACM 978-1-4503-3145-6/15/04 $15.00

Our work focuses on the development of technologies that enable *subtle interaction* (Figure 1). We define subtle interaction as *providing input to, or receiving output from, systems without being observed.* The primary goal is the development of a suite of technologies that enable users to leverage always-available computing without compromising privacy or social interaction.

Previous commercial and research efforts have investigated approaches to subtle interaction. These efforts typically focus on miniaturization, or decreasing the cognitive load of interactions [3, 29]. Further, these efforts have largely produced technologies, which once known to an observer, are no longer subtle – that is, they can be readily noticed and observed. In contrast, our work focuses on developing technologies and techniques, which even if known, would not telegraph their use to others.

Efforts to advance subtle interfaces have also been hampered somewhat by a lack of systematic identification of the space of subtle interaction or guiding principles for the design of the devices. To help us in developing these, we focused on the related domain of magic and illusion. Magicians have been developing and perfecting means of deceiving observers for centuries, amassing a vast quantity of knowledge. Their effects rely on established methods and principles that can be combined in various ways to conceal their true intent. While specific magic tricks are of little value to designers of subtle interfaces, the principles upon which they are built can be leveraged for subtle interactions.

This paper makes several contributions to the area of subtle interfaces. First, we present a survey of the techniques that users currently employ in the wild to achieve subtle interaction. Next, we provide design guidelines for subtle interfaces that are derived from established magic principles. We also provide a framework for the classification of subtle interfaces. Leveraging the guidelines and framework, we developed a system of subtle interfaces comprised of input and output devices. Lastly, we present an evaluation method that can be used to quantify the subtlety of interactions.

RELATED WORK

The present work is inspired by research from intersection of magic and human-computer interaction (HCI) as well as within wearable and ubiquitous computing.

Illusion and Deception in Human-Computer Interaction

Stage magic and HCI have many parallels [26], such as a need for consistency, the use of metaphors, and smoothness throughout the interactions. Busk et al. separated magical knowledge into three layers of *effects*, *methods*, and *principles* that can be used as a framework for magic-inspired interfaces [7]. Marshall, Benford, and Pridmore described a technology-based magic trick that applied the principles of misdirecting attention and creating false expectations to deceive the user [19]. This prior work focuses on high-level similarities between HCI and magic, rather than adapting magical knowledge for subtle interactions.

Adar, Tan, and Teevan discuss the uses and morality of deception in computer interfaces [1]. They argue that deception can be a useful feature of design, as in placebo buttons, which give the operator a sense of control and decrease user frustration [30]. In contrast, our work focuses on systems that are designed to aid users in deceiving others, rather than systems that are designed to deceive the user.

Subtle Wearable and Ubiquitous Interfaces

Subtle interactions for wearable interfaces typically focus on actions with low cognitive load, so they can be performed without a perceived loss of attention, or small and fast movements, so they can be performed before observers notice them [4]. Ashbrook introduced microinteractions for mobile interfaces [5], which can be initiated and completed in under four seconds. Holleis et al. evaluated the placement of fabric-based capacitive sensors, identifying locations that are quick and easy to access, but not necessarily subtle [14]. Constanza developed a video-based technique for evaluating the subtlety of a muscle-driven interface [9].

A number of approaches provide subtle, low-bandwidth input through novel hardware designs. ShoeSense made use of a depth camera mounted on a shoe to sense gestures made by users [6], while ShoeSoleSense made use of pressure sensors and vibrotactile feedback to provide input and output [20]. An approach by Sumitomo et al. used a strain sensor placed around the waist to allow users to input sequences by contracting their abdomen [25]. Electromyogram sensors have been used to enable users to interact hands-free, or without visibly moving [10, 24]. Nenya was a magnetic ring that could be tracked by a wrist-worn sensor to allow users to subtly access menu items [3]. In other work, covert 'duress' signals were built into authentication schemes, allowing users to signal that the authentication is not genuine using a small modification of their input sequence [18]. Clawson et al. described a scenario where devices could be used to subtly send a signal from one party to the other [8].

With respect to subtle output, several approaches have made use of small LEDs to provide low-bandwidth information channels without being visible to observers [11, 13]. Toney et al. described a suit that integrated LEDs, vibrotactile feedback and an interactive watch [27]. Similarly, Lee developed wearable tactile displays that relayed alerts to the user [15]. To disguise output, Worddit and Timesify provide tools that modify how Reddit and gossip websites were rendered so they appeared to be Microsoft Word or the New York Times webpage, respectively [31, 32].

While these approaches contribute to the development of novel devices, the use of the individual devices is not sufficient for truly subtle interaction. In contrast to prior work, we address the greater context of subtle interaction, and provide guidelines derived from magic principles. We also explicitly evaluate the subtlety of our approaches. Lastly, we describe how a system of devices can work together to improve the overall subtlety of the interactions.

SURVEY OF EXISTING PRACTICES

To increase our understanding of how technology is used subtly today, a crowd-sourced, online survey was conducted. The survey was intended to gauge interest in subtle interaction, as well as understand how users currently utilize their technology when they are attempting to be subtle. It also provided information on common use cases, enabling the design of an evaluation that reflects realistic settings.

Survey Instrument

The survey consisted of 19 questions with Likert-scale, binary, and free form responses regarding aspects of subtle interaction. The tasks people currently attempt to perform subtly were probed, for example, as were the steps they take to conceal their interactions, and their emotions towards people who use technology subtly. The questions focused on both social and professional context and was posted on classified sites (e.g., Craigslist), as well as Mechanical Turk.

Responses

In total, 227 responses were received. The age of respondents ranged from 14-69 years (M = 30; 124 male), with respondents located in North America (143), Asia (61), Europe (20), and South America (3).

When asked which tasks were frequently performed, checking the time, texting, and taking photos were the most common (Figure 2). Most respondents, i.e., 86%, reported that they attempt to use their mobile devices undetected during meetings for tasks unrelated to the meeting, while 94% reported doing the same during social events. A less frequent, but commonly reported behavior was pretending to receive a call or text message to leave a situation (73%).

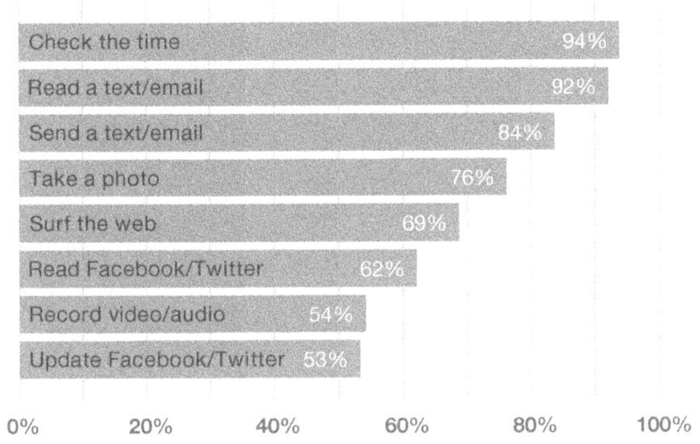

Figure 2: Proportion of respondents who reported performing each task subtly.

Nearly all respondents (94%) reported being 'caught' using technology where they were not supposed to (e.g., where interaction was prohibited by laws, employers, or social norms). When asked about the primary reason for attempting to using technology discreetly, the most frequent response was to avoid violating social norms (35%) followed by prohibition by their employers (25%) and prohibition by location (e.g., at a museum, 18%). Almost all respondents (94%) responded that they would use technology to help them interact with their devices more subtly.

When asked about the most common situations where subtle interaction was used, three general themes were evident. Respondents reported using technology subtly to *distract themselves* from undesirable situations (e.g., "during moments when things get boring or awkward"). Another common purpose was to *record events or information* (e.g., "record a video from a meeting … I needed evidence"). Finally, several participants used subtle interactions to *keep others informed* of their current situation (e.g., "I used [my] mobile phone to message my wife about the situation").

Respondents also reported a variety of techniques they adopted to facilitate subtle interaction. Respondents reported *hiding the device* out of sight (e.g., "check the phone under the desk") or *leave the area* where they may be caught ("At work, I go to the washroom"). Others *disguise their interactions* (e.g., "I pretend I'm trying to get reception … in actuality I am snapping a photo").

The responses to the survey, indicated that users attempt to use technology subtly in many scenarios, and that they desire technology that provides them with more discretion. Additionally, the responses demonstrate that users are willing to put conscious effort into concealing their interactions from others to prevent others from being disturbed or upset that they are using technology.

DESIGNING FOR SUBTLETY

As users desire technology that can disguise their actions, we looked to magic to inform the design of these technologies. As magic requires expertise in deception and illusion, we consulted with professional magicians, as well as the magic literature, to explore how magic can be leveraged for the design of subtle interactions. We present guidelines derived from a subset of magic principles: *user customization, modularity, simulation and dissimulation*, *separating cause and effect* and *user training*. These principles were chosen because of their broad applicability to many subtle designs.

P1) User Customization

we don't need any more new tricks … we do need more tricks fitting the specific personalities.

D. Fitzkee [12]

For a convincing performance, magicians customize and tailor their tricks to their routine and character. A construction worker may look out of place wearing a large ring that conceals a vibrotactile motor. However, if the vibrotactile motor was contained within a more generic form-factor, it could be integrated into a pair of safety glasses or other object that is consistent with the user's character. More importantly, devices that are not customizable will be easily recognized once they are widely available. If a manufacturer develops a smart-ring with a distinctive look, its functionality will be known and observers will be weary of the users' interactions with it.

P2) Modularity

If the magician performs the same trick twice for the same audience, there is an increased chance that the audience will identify the method.

S. Macknik et al. [16]

Using the same method to misdirect the audience's attention can lead to revelation of the magician's methods. Likewise, repeated use of a subtle device is likely to raise suspicion from observers. By varying the location, modality, and method of input, users of subtle interfaces can improve their ability to interact undetected. For instance, if the user has a joystick that can be concealed in a pocket, up a sleeve, or within a lapel, they can move the joystick between locations to prevent observers from becoming suspicious of the continued manipulation of their pocket, for example. Thus, a modular system that provides redundancies allows users to vary their behavior and select the interaction technique most subtle for a given transaction. This, however, adds complexity to interactions with the system

P3) Simulation and Dissimulation

Where simulation is disguising a thing to make it appear similar to something else, dissimulation is the act of making something appear to be dissimilar to what it truly is.

D. Fitzkee [12]

If a magician is attempting to convince the audience that a box is empty, he must interact with the box and behave as if it were empty and weightless. Similarly, users who wish to interact subtly must conceal the true nature of their devices and integrate their interactions with their natural behaviours. If a sensor is concealed within a baseball cap, then the interactions should be extensions of natural manipulations of the cap, such as adjusting the angle of the brim. Additionally, if users leverage existing technology to interact subtly, then efforts should be made to interact overtly with the device when it is appropriate to do so. This will lead observers to believe their device is normal and unremarkable which will aid in concealing its subtle functionality.

P4) Separating Cause and Effect

... introduce delays between the method behind a trick and its effect, preventing you from causally linking the two ... the magician must separate the method from the magical effect.

S. Macknik & S. Martinez-Conde [17]

Just as magicians introduce delays to misdirect the audience, designers of subtle interfaces can introduce temporal and spatial separations between an action and resultant effect to misdirect observers. If a user adjusts his watchband and the screen immediately changes, observers may correlate the watchband manipulation with the change in output. However, if the user adjusts his watchband and thirty seconds later his phone displays a notification, observers would have difficulty associating the input, which was unremarkable at the time, with the output.

This separation is counter to traditional user-interface guidelines, which promote a tight coupling between cause and effect to minimize the gulf of evaluation [21]. By implementing this separation, interactions can become more subtle, but the user interface may become more cumbersome and usability may suffer as a result.

P5) User Training

I promise never to perform any illusion for any non-magician without first practicing the effect until I can perform it well enough to maintain the illusion of magic.

Magician's oath [17]

Practice is a critical component in the performance of magic, as well as in subtle interaction. Clumsy, untrained movements can cause erroneous input and be spotted by observers quickly. To circumvent this, users should be aware of the necessity of training and be provided with tools to support that training. Guides can help train users on how to efficiently provide input, such that behaviours become automatic and require less of the users' attention.

DEVICE FRAMEWORK

While there are several devices that enable subtle interaction, there is no framework that can describe or categorize them in a useful manner that will facilitate future developments. We have identified five factors that describe the functionality of an interaction technique within the context of subtle interfaces: the *type of device*, *customizability*, *device visibility*, *interaction observability*, and *task transparency*.

The *type of device* references whether the interface provides *input* or *output* capabilities.

The *customizability* refers to the degree that the interface can be tailored by the end user. Techniques may be re-configured *on-the-fly* for each *user* or *not customizable*.

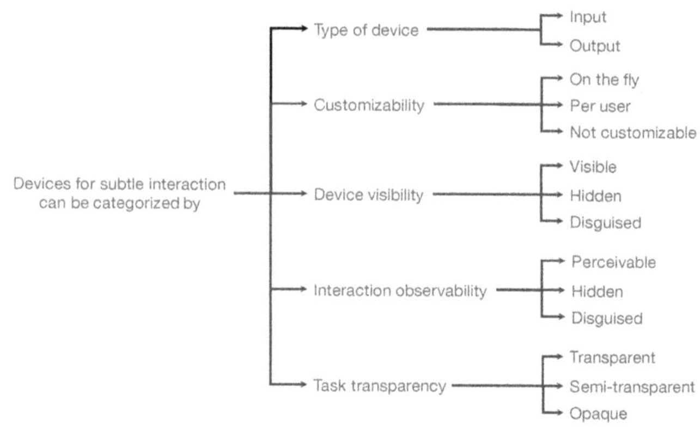

Figure 3: Overview of the framework for subtle devices.

Device visibility represents whether or not the hardware associated with the device is *visible*, *hidden*, or *disguised.* Visible devices, e.g., a traditional smartphone, are the least subtle and must be used sparingly. Hidden devices are those that can be used while out of sight of the observers, e.g., within a pocket or a shoe. These are the most subtle but also have limited bandwidth and can be difficult for the user to operate. Disguised devices are those that are visible to the observer, but provide functionality beyond their appearance.

Interaction observability refers to how the observers may perceive the user's interaction. This could be *perceivable, hidden*, or *disguised.* Perceivable interactions are those that are noticeable by observers, but may enable subtle interaction if performed quickly enough. Hidden interactions are not able to be detected by observers, and as with hidden devices, often provide maximal subtlety with minimal bandwidth. Disguised interactions may be observable but could be identified as a normal behaviour.

Task transparency refers to how readily observers can detect the task that is being performed by the user. This is important, as some tasks may be acceptable for a given scenario and others may not. Thus, by obscuring the task, the user may be afforded additional subtlety. The task may be *transparent,* in the case of a traditional watch with a single function, or it may be *opaque,* in the case of a smart phone that possesses a wide range of functionality. The task may also be *semi-transparent* if observers can identify a subset of potential tasks (e.g., they can observe that the user is receiving a notification, but cannot determine the type).

SAMPLE DECEPTIVE DEVICES

To explore the framework, several representative input and output devices were constructed (Figure 4). Used collectively, these devices demonstrate the utility of the design principle of Modularity (**P2**).

Input Devices

Super Sneaky Spyglasses

A small camera mounted inside a pair of glasses (Figure 4A) can allow the user to take photographs or record video. This *disguised device* can be triggered through *hidden interactions*, i.e., orienting their head then pressing a button that is tethered to the frame of the glasses and concealed within a sleeve or a pocket of the user. The task is *transparent* and not obfuscated at all, as knowledgeable observers will be aware of the sole function of the device. The current form factor is *not customizable*. The success of this device relies on the user's use of *dissimulation* (**P3**) when using the device, as they must treat the glasses as they would unmodified glasses - they must not touch them excessively or prolong eye contact while taking photos. To implement the Super Sneaky Spyglasses commercial spyglasses[1] were modified to include a tethered button rather than the more obvious button mounted on their frame.

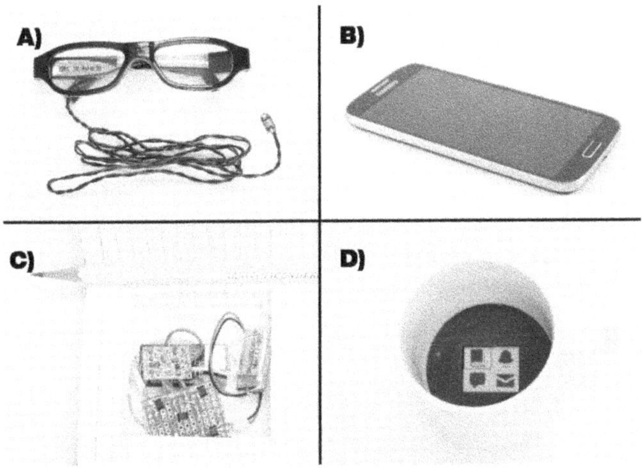

Figure 4: Subtle devices. A) Super Sneaky Spyglasses, B) Samsung Galaxy S5 running Phony Phone, C) Magput in a book, and D) Lil LCD in a mug

Phony Phone

Phony Phone is a mobile application that renders a black screen on the cell phone (Figure 4B), providing the appearance of a sleeping phone while still allowing input to be recorded and processed. Users can interact with the device by swiping and tapping on the black screen, *disguising* their interactions as idle fidgeting. Phony Phone is a *disguised* device, the task is *semi-transparent*, as a knowing observer could determine that the user was providing input but could not identify the specific task. Phony Phone can provide a full range of input supported by modern touch screen phones (touches, swipes, gestural input) and can be *customizable* by the end user (i.e., the application can be deployed on their phone and does not require a specific, identifiable piece of hardware). This device enables subtle interaction through the spatial *separation of input and output* (**P4**); the touches on the screen have no visible effect on the device itself.

To implement Phony Phone, an Android application was developed and was run on a Samsung Galaxy S5.

Magput

Five linear Hall Effect sensors mounted in an 'x' shape can be used to sense the location of a magnet over the grid enabling continuous 2D or gestural input via EdgeWrite [28] in a small space (Figure 4C). Magput can be placed within many common objects to provide an input device that is easily disguisable. For example, the device can be placed within a book with a magnet inside of a pen, or it could be mounted inside a jacket pocket with a magnet placed beneath an adhesive bandage. In both cases, the sensors and magnet are *disguised*, and the users' interaction is *disguised* as idle doodling or casual fidgeting with the device. As with Phony Phone, the task is *semi-transparent* as expert observers could determine that the user is providing input to the system but could not determine the nature of the input. Magput can be *customized on-the-fly* (**P1**) by moving it between various locations on the user's body, or amongst their accessories. To subtly interact using EdgeWrite gestures, users must *practice* (**P5**) prior to use. To aid in this, a small, physical training guide was developed that can be placed over top of the sensor to provide the user with tactile cues to guide them to the correct locations. While this is a simple device, training systems that are more complex could be implemented (e.g., [2]). In our implementation, the sensors are connected to a Femtoduino BLE[2], which relays sensor data via an RF link to an Arduino Uno, which relays the data to a PC which is tethered to the mobile phone via Bluetooth.

Output Devices

Lil LCD

Small, modular displays can be leveraged to provide repositionable, high-bandwidth output that could be concealed within innocuous objects. These displays can be hidden inside a coffee cup form factor (Figure 4D), for example, and allow for the subtle viewing of information during a meeting. The device, as well as the interactions with it, are *disguised*, as the user can place it out of sight and casually glance at it when appropriate. If noticed, the task is *semi-transparent*, observers are aware that there is some information being obtained, but are not able to determine what that information is from a distance. Lil LCD is customizable *on-the-fly*, as the display can be relocated with relative ease. By *separating the output* (**P4**) from the interaction, observers will have difficulty identifying when the user is interacting. In our implementation, the module is comprised of a waterproof Sony Smartwatch 2 display that is tethered via Bluetooth to a mobile phone. To aid in concealment, custom 3D printed 'shells' were printed and affixed to the module.

[1] http://www.newegg.com/Product/Product.aspx?Item=9SIA34P0ZN7835

[2] www.femtoduino.com

Numerical Sonification

To disguise numerical data, an audio alert can be used to encode numbers in a manner that could be mistaken for a message or calendar notification. Four notes of increasing pitch can be used to signify the numbers 30, 15, 5, and 1 respectively and can be summed together to derive the encoded number. For instance, the note sequence 'A C E E G G' could inform the user that it is 57 minutes past the hour (30 + 15 + 5 + 5 + 1 + 1 = 57). The device used in this approach is *customizable per-user* (**P1**) and *disguised,* as it is deployed on the user's own mobile phone. Users can further customize it by changing the timbre of the audio tones to be more consistent with their existing notifications. The interactions with the device are *disguised* and the task is *semi-transparent* as observers may be aware that the tones convey information, but would not know if the information was the time, a sports score, or the number of unread emails in the user's inbox. To provide misdirection, the audio is *separated temporally* (**P4**) from the input that triggers it by adding a delay of five seconds. To develop and test Numerical Sonification a number of audio files were created and the playback functionality was integrated into the Phony Phone application.

Usability of Sample Devices

A brief pilot study was conducted to provide an initial understanding of the usability of the proposed devices. After being shown the devices and their operation, four participants responded to 7 point usability-focused Likert items for each device. Three participants stated they could use the interfaces with only a few minutes of training (median of 6), with one participant indicating that Magput would require more training. All participants described all devices as 'easy to use' (median of 6), with Magput scoring lower than the other interfaces. As the primary contribution of this work is the subtlety, a rigorous usability study was omitted in favour of the development of a technique to evaluate the subtlety of the interactions.

MANAGING ILLUSIONS

As the context of use rapidly changes with wearable and mobile interactions, it is imperative that users have their technology tailored to their immediate situation. The use of a large number of highly configurable modules and devices has the potential to overwhelm new users with the volume of potential combinations of devices. To address this, a configuration system (Figure 5) was developed to allow users to assign actions and data to their various devices.

The user begins the configuration process by creating a new preset. A preset represents a set of mappings that are suitable for the given context. For instance, the user may have one preset for casual meetings or social events where some use of technology is appropriate, and another for formal meetings where interaction is restricted.

With each preset, users can create mappings between input triggers, a list of pre-defined data streams (e.g., incoming text messages, sports scores, or the weather), and output devices (e.g., the Lil LCD or Numerical Sonification). The functional capabilities of each device (e.g., what type of data it is capable of generating or displaying) are encoded within the program logic and simplify the user experience. As a user selects a particular data stream, only those devices capable of triggering or displaying the data stream become active. While this interface does not expose the complete functionality of the modular system, it provides enough flexibility to satisfy many common use cases.

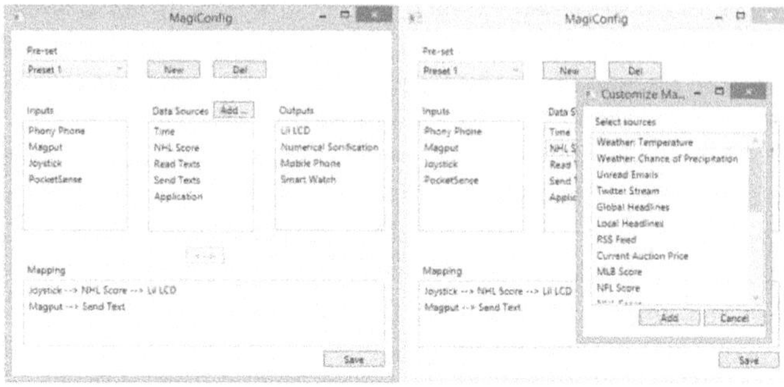

Figure 5: Configuration interface showing mappings between input devices, data, and output devices.

EVALUATION

In this section, we propose a novel evaluation methodology centered on the real-world context of a round-table meeting (Figure 6). This approach is similar to Constanza et al. [9] in that it uses a video-based methodology, but focuses on a real-world scenario rather than a highly controlled scene.

Figure 6: Sample frame from the staged meeting videos.

We recorded video of a staged five-person meeting from the perspective of one of the meeting attendees (Figure 6). During the meeting, which was divided into a series of two-minute clips, the four attendees (actors) within the view of the camera would subtly interact with technology in some way. After all recordings had been completed, the crowd-sourced participants viewed the resultant videos and assessed when the attendees were interacting with technology. In contrast to the prior evaluation methods [9], this method better reflects a real-world use case of subtle interaction and allows for a wider range of hypotheses to be tested. Additionally, our survey identified workplace meetings as one a common scenario where subtle interaction is desired.

Recording Procedure

Two blocks of ten two minute clips were recorded, resulting in twenty total video clips. The content of each of the two-minute clips was a game of 'twenty questions' played by all five attendees. During eight of the ten clips in each block, one of the on-camera attendees would interact with technology, while the remaining two rounds did not contain any interaction. The actors were instructed to behave naturally and to perform the tasks as they would in a regular meeting (e.g., relatively discreetly). For each block each actor was assigned two interaction techniques and was given time to familiarize themselves with their operation and to practice using them subtly. Between blocks, actors were re-assigned interaction techniques to ensure that the measured subtlety was not due to an actor's performance. The meetings were recorded at 1080p, via a camera positioned at eye-level, which captured all attendees within the frame (Figure 6).

Subtle Tasks and Devices

Four tasks were analyzed in the evaluation: checking the time (*check time*), reading a text (*read text*), sending a text (*send text*), and taking a picture (*picture*). These tasks are representative of the range of input and output tasks most commonly performed subtly today (Figure 2). Each of the four tasks was completed using currently available technology (*traditional*) as well as using interactions designed to support subtle interaction (*subtle*).

Using *traditional* interaction, checking the time was accomplished using a wristwatch, while reading and sending texts, as well as taking photos was accomplished using mobile phones (i.e., Samsung Galaxy Nexus, iPhone 4, and Nokia Lumia 1020). Unlock passcodes were removed from the phones to minimize the amount of interaction needed. While a smartwatch may provide many opportunities for achieving subtle interactions, it was not included in the study as smartwatches are not nearly as ubiquitous as mobile devices at the current time. However, the current paradigm can be used to evaluate the subtlety of smartwatches and other wearable interfaces in the future.

To evaluate the *subtle* interactions, checking the time was accomplished using numerical sonification in combination with Phony Phone – the attendee tapped the black screen and five seconds later, a tone encoding the time played. Reading a text was accomplished using a modular display affixed to the inside of a coffee cup. Sending a text was done using EdgeWrite-based input with Magput. The sensors were placed inside a hollowed-out notebook and activated by a magnet that was embedded in the back of a pencil or underneath an adhesive bandage on the finger. Taking a picture was accomplished using the Super Sneaky Spyglasses with the tethered button resting in the lap.

Participants

Sixty participants, age 21-55 years (M = 34 years; 27 male) were recruited via crowd-sourcing to watch the videos and determine when an actor was interacting with a device.

Design

A three-factor, mixed study design was used with a between-subjects factor of Condition (i.e., *no knowledge*, *module knowledge*, and *customization knowledge*) and within-subject factors of Task (i.e., *check time, read time, send text, picture*) and InteractionType (i.e., *subtle*, *traditional*).

For each condition, a different introductory video was shown. For participants in the *no knowledge* condition, an introductory video explained their task and informed them that they should be monitoring for technology use in addition to paying attention to the meeting content. Participants in the *module knowledge* condition were also shown the various subtle modules that would be used (e.g., the Magput, the Lil LCD, etc.). Participants in the *customization knowledge* condition were also shown how those modules would be used within the experiment (e.g., inside a book, cup, etc).

Each participant watched a single block of ten videos, which included two instances of each task (*subtle* and *traditional*), along with two videos with no interactions. The presentation order of the videos was counterbalanced across participants.

Procedure

After watching each video, participants indicated which meeting attendant, if any, interacted with technology during the clip. Participants were also asked to specify the device, the interaction, as well as the task that was being completed by the identified attendant. Participants were asked to guess the item being described by the 20 questions. This ensured that they were not focusing their attention solely on detecting technology use, which better reflects a real-world scenario.

RESULTS

Responses to the post-video questionnaire were collected, and where appropriate, free-form text was manually coded.

Measures

Three measures were captured to analyze the subtlety of each interaction technique: *device subtlety*, *interaction subtlety*, and *task subtlety*. Task subtlety is defined as the proportion of trials in which the participant correctly identifies the task that was being performed subtly. Device subtlety is defined as the proportion of trials in which the device that was being used was correctly identified. Interaction subtlety is defined as the proportion of trials in which the observer correctly identified the attendee performing the interaction technique.

The results aggregated across task and condition (Figure 7) demonstrated that participants had trouble correctly identifying the task in comparison to identification of the device or the interactions. This is because it is difficult to observe the content of the phone's screen from the viewpoint of another meeting attendee so participants would have to guess if the attendee was reading texts, sending texts, or just surfing the web. In contrast, the device and the interaction were identified more readily, as they are recognizable from the vantage point of the recorded video. In addition, the identification rates for both device and interaction were nearly identical, as observers have to see both the device and interaction to realize that the attendee is using technology.

While participants had difficulty identifying the task being performed across all interaction techniques, they were more accurate in determining the direction of the interaction (i.e., input or output) with the subtle devices. As input and output were separated for many of the techniques, they could, for example, identify movements of the pencil on the book as being used to input data, but could not identify whether the attendee was texting or triggering another device.

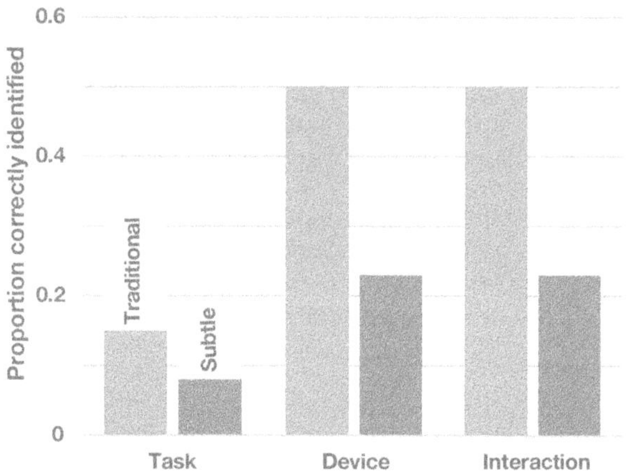

Figure 7: Correct identifications of task, device, and interactions by device type, aggregated over all knowledge conditions.

In the analyses that follow, we consider an interaction to be correctly identified if the participant correctly identified either the device or the interaction.

Analysis

A loglinear analysis was conducted in SPSS on the cell frequencies for the correct identification of the interaction using the factors of Condition (i.e., *no knowledge, module knowledge, customization knowledge*), Task (i.e., *check time, read text, send text, picture*), and InteractionType (i.e., *traditional, subtle*). The analysis demonstrated significant main effects of Condition ($\chi^2(2) = 53.99$; $p < 0.001$), Task ($\chi^2(3) = 22.63$; $p < 0.001$) and InteractionType ($\chi^2(1) = 43.85$; $p < 0.001$), as well as significant interactions between InteractionType and Condition ($\chi^2(2) = 14.72$; $p < 0.001$) and InteractionType and Task ($\chi^2(3) = 34.17$; $p < 0.001$). Due to the interaction effects, the main effects of Condition, Task and InteractionType were not analyzed further.

To examine the interaction between InteractionType and Condition (Figure 8), three separate Chi-square tests were performed for each of the three conditions. The analyses found significant differences between the noticeability of traditional and subtle interaction for the no knowledge and module knowledge conditions ($\chi^2(1) = 25.31$; $p < 0.001$; $\chi^2(1) = 25.58$; $p < 0.001$ respectively). There was, however, no significant difference between the traditional and subtle interaction types within the customization knowledge condition ($\chi^2(1) = 1.26$; $p = 0.26$). It thus appears that the amount of knowledge a participant was given influenced how well they noticed the interactions. Those participants with no knowledge, or knowledge of only the modules, were not able to reliably identify the subtle interactions, with participants only noticing 8-9% of interactions. In contrast, those same participants were able to notice 44% of traditional interactions, representing a five-fold increase in subtlety with the new approaches. It is worth noting that the correct identifications of the subtle interactions in the no knowledge condition stem from Numerical Sonification.

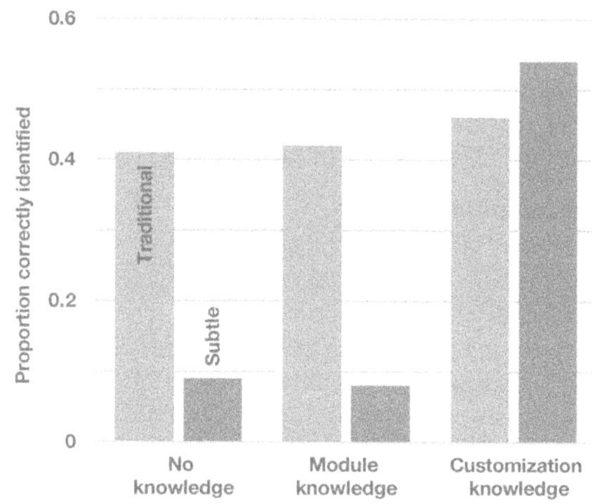

Figure 8: Correct identifications by knowledge condition and interaction type, aggregated over task.

To examine the interaction between InteractionType and Task (Figure 9) separate Chi-square tests were performed. Task was found to significantly affect the identification of traditional interactions, with checking the time being identified significantly less often than the other tasks ($\chi^2(3) = 25.73$; $p < 0.001$). Task also affected noticeability of subtle interactions, with taking a photo being significantly less noticeable than the other tasks ($\chi^2(3) = 19.19$; $p < 0.001$).

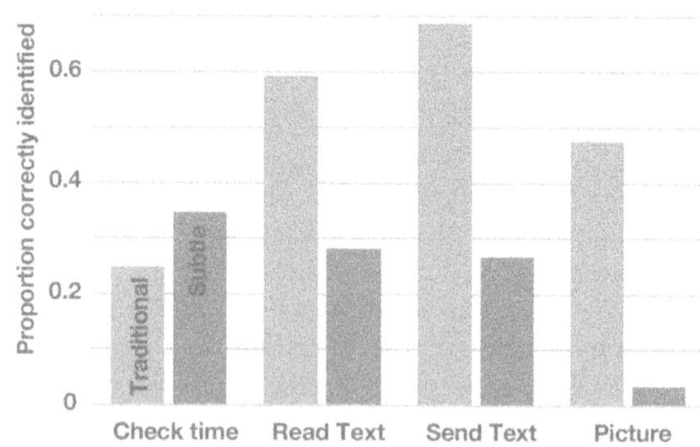

Figure 9: Correct identifications by interaction type and task, aggregated over all knowledge conditions.

The interactions with the watch to check the time were very subtle and rarely noticed, as the meeting attendees could glance down at the watch briefly. Similarly, taking photos with the spyglasses required only a quick press of a button.

In contrast, checking text messages required prolonged manipulation of the device in a relatively overt manner. With the exception of checking the time, the subtle techniques were less conspicuous than the traditional techniques. This is because the numerical sonification technique required touching a mobile device followed by an audible tone. In our evaluation paradigm, this stood out to observers, as none of the other technology generated audio notifications. However, in real-world use we expect this to be less noticeable.

DISCUSSION

Our results show that the proposed method can quantify the subtlety of various forms of interaction, and distinguish these techniques with regards to their level of subtlety. The results also show that the majority of the new approaches to subtle interaction are successful in deceiving observers.

Knowledge of the Observers

The results for *module knowledge* are of particular interest as they demonstrate that end-user customization is a powerful tool for subtle interactions. Despite being shown all of the devices, participants were not able to imagine using them in the manner that they were used in the video, allowing the meeting attendees to interact without being noticed. In contrast, once participants were aware of the customization, they were able to identify the subtle interactions at nearly the same rate as the traditional interactions, with the exception of the spyglasses, which remained nearly imperceptible.

Participants in the *customization knowledge* condition identified more of the traditional interactions then participants in the *module* or *no knowledge* conditions. This could be the result of the participants being more attentive as they had a greater proportion of trials where they could successfully identify an interaction. It is possible that if modular subtle devices become prevalent, that the set of possible customizations may also become well known, and therefore easier for observers to spot. However, if this should happen, then the set of possible customizations will be so great as to make observers suspicious of everyday actions.

Supporting Devices

Situational awareness and the knowledge of observer's attention is essential for successful subtle interaction, thus we explored support devices for subtle interaction. While the role of input and output devices is clear, these support devices are used in conjunction with other devices to increase the resulting subtlety of interactions. Support devices are unexplored in the literature, and here we provide two examples which may be used to drive future research. The first alerts the users when observers may be perceiving their interaction, the second provides smoother transitions into and out of social situations.

If a user is engaged with their device, their attention may be diverted from their environment. If an observer approaches the user from behind, the user may be unaware and may continue to interact with their device while the observer monitors their actions. To prevent this, a proximity sensor is placed on the user's shoulder facing away from the user and provides pulsing vibrotactile feedback if an observer approaches the user. As the approaching observer moves closer the frequency of pulsing increases, giving the user an awareness of the speed and distance of the observer.

As the use of technology diverts the user's attention from the current situation, it may be difficult to follow and rejoin conversations when the interaction is complete. To enable a more fluid transition in and out of social contexts, our buffered audio technique records audio in a short buffer, and replays it at 1.5x speed through a bone-conduction speaker on demand. This technique provides contextual awareness of the situation, and helps conceal the user's diverted attention using a deceptive device by bringing them back "up-to-speed" with the current conversation.

Ethics of Deception

Adar et al. [1] discuss well-meaning uses of deception for interaction. What is being proposed with subtle interaction, however, could be perceived as ill meaning. Deceiving observers into believing you are cognitively present while you attend to remote information can have consequences. We believe users will interact with their devices regardless of the subtlety of the interaction. By supporting interactions that are more secretive, we increase the probability that the interactions go unnoticed and observers remain un-offended. Advances in subtle interaction could be beneficial as users could check the time, for example, without seeming as if they are bored with the current situation.

Evaluation Limitations

While the study captures the visual and audio aspects of interactions as well as changes in the user's attention, it is not able to capture whether or not the behavior is consistent with the user's personality. To capture this, a study would have to intentionally deceive participants that were known to the experimenter. This type of study is logistically difficult and the results would be subjective. Additionally, the study did not assess the utility of using a number of devices rather than a single device. With a number of devices, we suspect the overall subtlety of the interaction will increase as users can interact with the most subtle interface given their situation. Lastly, although the video-approach is more convenient and repeatable than in-person studies, it is still artificial. Participants are actively monitoring for deceptive behaviours and anomalies in the participants actions and movements.

Future work

This work should serve as a basis for the development of many future subtle interaction techniques that leverage the presented magical principles to improve the subtlety of the interfaces. We hope that researchers and practitioners seek out magical principles and methods beyond what is presented here to develop novel interactions. Truly subtle interaction relies on the existence of a multitude of customizable modules to be successful, so the development of new approaches is critical to its success.

CONCLUSION

The design of subtle interfaces extends beyond the design of imperceptible input and output devices. Driven by a desire from users for more subtle interactions, we have leveraged knowledge and techniques from the domain of magic to inform the design of subtle interfaces. We developed a framework to classify the various devices and techniques that support subtle interaction, and have built representative interfaces that sample areas of the framework. Lastly, we provided an evaluation paradigm by which the subtlety of interactions can be explored and understood.

REFERENCES

1. Adar, E., Tan, D.S., & Teevan, J. (2013). Benevolent Deception in Human Computer Interaction. *CHI*, 1863-1872.
2. Anderson, F., Grossman, T., Matejka, J., & Fitzmaurice, G. (2013). YouMove: Enhancing Movement Training with an Augmented Reality Mirror. *UIST*, 311-320.
3. Ashbrook, D., Baudisch, P., & White, S. (2011). Nenya: Subtle and Eyes-free Mobile Input with a Magnetically-tracked Finger Ring. *CHI*, 2043-2046.
4. Ashbrook, D.L., Clawson, J.R., Lyons, K., Starner, T.E., & Patel, N. (2008). Quickdraw: The Impact of Mobility and On-body Placement on Device Access Time. *CHI*, 219-222.
5. Ashbrook, D.L. (2010). Enabling mobile microinteractions. https://smartech.gatech.edu/handle/1853/33986.
6. Bailly, G., Müller, J., Rohs, M., Wigdor, D., & Kratz, S. (2012) ShoeSense: A New Perspective on Gestural Interaction and Wearable Applications. *CHI*, 1239-1248.
7. Busk, N.K., Forstholm, J.S., Lessél, L.S., & Sørensen, S.G. (2012). Introducing Magical Experiences in UX. *SIDeR*, 21-24.
8. Clawson, J., Patel, N., & Starner, T. (2010). Digital kick in the shin: on-body communication tools for couples trapped in face-to-face group conversations. *Workshop on Ensembles of On-Body Devices, MobileHCI*.
9. Costanza, E., Inverso, S.A., Allen, R., & Maes, P. (2007). Intimate Interfaces in Action: Assessing the Usability and Subtlety of Emg-based Motionless Gestures. *CHI*, 819-828.
10. Costanza, E., Inverso, S.A., & Allen, R. (2005). Toward Subtle Intimate Interfaces for Mobile Devices Using an EMG Controller. *CHI*, 481-489.
11. Costanza, E., Inverso, S.A., Pavlov, E., Allen, R., & Maes, P. (2006). Eye-q: Eyeglass Peripheral Display for Subtle Intimate Notifications. *MobileHCI*, 211-218.
12. Fitzkee, D. (1945). *Magic by Misdirection*. Saint Raphael House.
13. Hansson, R. & Ljungstrand, P. (2000). The Reminder Bracelet: Subtle Notification Cues for Mobile Devices. *CHI EA*, 323-324.
14. Holleis, P., Otto, F., Hussmann, H., & Schmidt, A. (2007). Keystroke-level model for advanced mobile phone interaction. *CHI*, 1505-1514.
15. Lee, S. & Starner, T. (2010). BuzzWear: Alert Perception in Wearable Tactile Displays on the Wrist. *CHI*, 433-442.
16. Macknik, S.L., King, M., Randi, J., Robbins, A., Teller, Thompson, J & Martinez-Conde S. (2008). Attention and awareness in stage magic: turning tricks into research. *Nature Reviews Neuroscience 9*, 11, 871-879.
17. Macknik, S.L., Martinez-Conde, S., & Blakeslee, S. (2010). *Sleights of mind*. Macmillan.
18. Marques, D., Carrico, L., & Guerreiro, T. (2014). Duress Unlock: Using Covert Signals to Restrict Access to Mobile Devices. *CHI EA*.
19. Marshall, J., Benford, S., & Pridmore, T. (2010). Deception and Magic in Collaborative Interaction. *CHI*, 567-576.
20. Matthies, D.J.C., Müller, F., Anthes, C., & Kranzlmüller, D. (2013). ShoeSoleSense: Proof of Concept for a Wearable Foot Interface for Virtual and Real Environments. *VRST*, 93-96.
21. Norman, D.A. (2002). *The design of everyday things*. Basic books.
22. Profita, H.P. (2011). Social acceptability of wearable technology use in public: an exploration of the societal perceptions of a gesture-based mobile textile interface. Thesis, *Georgia Institute of Technology*.
23. Reeves, S., Benford, S. O'Malley, C., & Fraser, M. (2005). Designing the Spectator Experience. *CHI*, 741-750.
24. Saponas, T.S., Tan, D.S., Morris, D., Balakrishnan, R., Turner, J., & Landay, J.A. (2009). Enabling Always-available Input with Muscle-computer Interfaces. *UIST*, 167-176.
25. Sumitomo, H., Katayama, T., Terada, T., & Tsukamoto, M. (2014). Implementation and Evaluation on a Concealed Interface Using Abdominal Circumference. *AH*, 51:1-51:8.
26. Tognazzini, B. (1993). Principles, Techniques, and Ethics of Stage Magic and Their Application to Human Interface Design. *CHI*, 355-362.
27. Toney, A., Mulley, B., Thomas, B.H., & Piekarski, W. (2002). Minimal social weight user interactions for wearable computers in business suits. *ISWC*, 57-64.
28. Wobbrock, J., Myers, B. & Kembel, J. (2003) EdgeWrite: a stylus-based text entry method designed for high accuracy and stability of motion. *UIST*, 61-70.
29. Yi, B., Cao, X., Fjeld, M., & Zhao, S. (2012). Exploring User Motivations for Eyes-free Interaction on Mobile Devices. *CHI*, 2789-2792.
30. "Dummy" Thermostats Cool Down Tempers, Not Temperatures. http://news.thomasnet.com/IMT/2003/04/11/dummy_thermostat.
31. Timesify. http://www.timesify.com/.
32. Worddit. http://pcottle.github.io/MSWorddit

Understanding Users' Touch Behavior on Large Mobile Touch-Screens and Assisted Targeting by Tilting Gesture

Youli Chang **Sehi L'Yi** **Kyle Koh** **Jinwook Seo**
Human-Computer Interaction Laboratory, Department of Computer Science and Engineering
Seoul National University, 1 Gwanak-ro, Gwanak-gu, Seoul 151-744, Korea
{ylchang, shlyi, kyle}@hcil.snu.ac.kr, jseo@snu.ac.kr

ABSTRACT
As large-screen smartphones are trending, they bring a new set of challenges such as acquiring unreachable screen targets using one hand. To understand users' touch behavior on large mobile touchscreens, we conducted an empirical experiment to discover their usage patterns of tilting devices toward their thumbs to touch screen regions. Exploiting this natural tilting behavior, we designed three novel mobile interaction techniques: *TiltSlide*, *TiltReduction*, and *TiltCursor*. We conducted a controlled experiment to compare our methods with other existing methods, and then evaluated them in real mobile phone scenarios such as sending an e-mail and web surfing. We constructed a design space for one-hand targeting interactions and proposed design considerations for one-hand targeting in real mobile phone circumstances.

Author Keywords
Large mobile screen; One-hand interaction; Tilting gesture

ACM Classification Keywords
H.5.2. User Interfaces: Input devices and strategies, Interaction styles, Screen design.

INTRODUCTION
With the ever increasing size of touchscreen mobile devices, a new category of devices called "phablets" (for phone-tablet) is emerging. Apple has also joined the trend by releasing a large iPhone 6/6+ [1]. Such large devices provide enough screen display, delivering a stream of applications that take advantage of the new space. However, it is inevitable that some parts of the screen become unreachable when used with one hand. People often encounter the situation where only one hand is available to control the device while the other hand is occupied with other operations. This brings us the challenge of acquiring unreachable targets in large-screen mobile devices.

There have been several attempts to address the issue. Some investigated a feasible region for users' thumbs [3,13], and others proposed innovative one-hand targeting methods to assist selecting far-targets [1,2,10,11,12,14,15,16,18,19,22, 23,24,25]. However, there has not been any research on understanding users' touch behaviors in terms of tilting devices and exploiting them to design novel mobile interactions to reach uncomfortable regions.

CHI 2015, April 18–23, 2015, Seoul, Republic of Korea.

ACM 978-1-4503-3145-6/15/04...$15.00.
http://dx.doi.org/10.1145/2702123.2702425

In this paper, we presented an empirical analysis of users' tilting behavior when touching large mobile screens with one-hand using their thumbs. We introduced three novel mobile interaction techniques using the tilting gesture to touch targets in uncomfortable regions on large screen smartphones. To validate their performance and preference, we conducted a controlled experiment to compare them with other techniques introduced before.

The new interaction techniques had to blend with existing and more conventional interactions in current mobile applications. For such reason, we conducted a user study on ordinary mobile phone scenarios to verify their feasibilities. Also, we proposed a design space for one-hand targeting interactions and discussed design considerations based on the results of the user study.

RELATED WORK
As an endeavor to assist the user in real mobile phone scenarios, one-hand targeting interactions have to be taken into consideration by their trigger mechanisms as well as their targeting mechanisms (we verified this through our Experiment 3). Thus, we constructed a design space by *Trigger Mechanisms* versus *Targeting Mechanisms* in Table 1. The *Targeting Mechanisms* could be further categorized into *Assisted Touch* and *Cursor*. *Assisted Touch* mechanism can directly touch targets with the thumb by improving the reachability of the target either by transforming the screen space (*Screen Transform*) or by introducing a proxy space for the screen (*Proxy Region*), while *Cursor* mechanism involves a pseudo-fingertip like a remote cursor.

AppLens [12] is one of the methods using the *Screen Transform* mechanism. It is a tabular fisheye interface that is invented to show multiple applications in different levels of details simultaneously. *AppLens* brings an application screen closer to the thumb by allowing users navigate applications by a rectangle cursor (called object cursor) that can be moved by predefined set of gestures or a physical joystick embedded on a PDA. The gestures are designed inside of the thumb's accessible area to facilitate one-handed device use. *ThumbSpace* [14] is one of the methods

Trigger Mechanisms \ Targeting Mechanisms		Assisted Touch (Touch with user's thumb)		Cursor (Called pseudo-fingertip)	
		Screen Transform	Proxy Region	Same Direction	Opposite Direction
Always On		*AppLens [12]*	*ThumbSpace [14]*		
Tapping			*TapTap [18]*	*Offset Cursor [16,19]*	
Dragging	Edge (Bezel)	*ES [15]*		*EC [15] (Called ETEC)*	
			BezelSpace, CornerSpace [25]	*BezelSpace, CornerSpace [25]*	
	Anywhere	*LS [15]*		*Adaptive Horizontal Offset [10]*	*MagStick [18], LC [15]*
				TiltCursor	
Mode Change	Tilting Gesture	*TiltReduction, TiltSlide*		*TiltCursor*	
	Physical button	*iPhone6/6+ [1]*	*"enhanced" ThumbSpace[11]*	*A Piece of Butter [22]*	
	Touch Gesture	*One-handed operation mode[2]*			
Back-Side Touch				*Behind-the-Display Cursor [23,24]*	
Long Touch / Double Touch					

Table 1. A design space by *Trigger Mechanisms* versus *Targeting Mechanisms* for one-hand targeting interactions.

using the *Proxy Region* mechanism. It uses an empty semitransparent proxy view where all available targets on the screen are mapped. The proxy view is placed in a comfortable region for the user's thumb. However, both methods are activated at all times, even for targets located in comfortable regions. Thus, Karlson et al. improved their method in "enhanced" *ThumbSpace* [11] triggered only by pressing a button (the center of the DPad) and combined *Shift* [21] to solve the occlusion of targets from a thumb.

Newly released large smartphones are equipped with a *Screen Transform* mechanism as a reachability feature to support one-hand interaction. *iPhone 6/6+* [1] enables users to pan down the screen by half by double-tapping the home button. After an item on the screen is touched, the screen returns back to the original position. However, it cannot address the reachability problem of bottom uncomfortable regions and is not efficient to successively touch multiple far-targets. *One-handed operation mode* [2] of Samsung Galaxy Note3 shrinks the screen to make it comfortable for one-hand targeting by a pre-defined touch gesture, i.e., swiping from the bezel to the center and going back to the bezel at once. It renders the actual screen to help users identify targets, and we took a similar approach in our *TiltReduction* method.

On the other hand, the methods using the *Cursor* mechanism can be further categorized by the direction of cursor movement. *Same Direction* methods shift a cursor in the same direction as the thumb, while *Opposite Direction* methods shift it in the opposite direction.

As the *Same Direction* methods, *Offset Cursor* [16,19] (called take-off paradigm) appears at a fixed distance above the tapping point until the thumb is lifted. For acquiring a target, users tap the screen and drag their finger until the cursor is located on top of the target. However, users cannot guess a distance to a target before tapping. Thus, *Adaptive Horizontal Offset* [10] proposed an improvement by adjusting horizontal distance dynamically. However, either cannot acquire the target that is placed under users' thumbs.

TapTap and *MagStick* [18] are designed to improve one-hand targeting on small touch screens; nonetheless, they can help with far-targets' accessibility. *TapTap* shows a zoomed-in pop-up view at the center of a screen when users touch on a region where targets are densely positioned. It brings far-targets to the center of a screen by touching the area near the target. *MagStick* shows a cursor at the touched position and then moves it in the direction opposite a thumb movement. Such *Opposite Direction* methods can avoid occlusion from a thumb, but reverse direction movements may involve awkwardness. The cursor of *MagStick* also attracts targets, so it sticks to the nearest target that is closer than the pre-defined threshold. The magnetized cursor could speed up target acquisition, but it is not effective for densely populated targets.

Kim et al. [15] presented four targeting methods by combining two trigger techniques (a bezel swipe or a wide area touch by the pad of the thumb) and two support techniques (sliding screen or extendible cursor). *Edge trigger with Sliding screen* (*ES*) and *Large-touch trigger with Sliding screen* (*LS*) slides screen towards a thumb as much as drag movement of the thumb to get far-targets closer, while *Edge Trigger with Extendible Cursor* (*ETEC*) and *Large-touch trigger with extendible Cursor* (*LC*) use an extendible cursor multiplying thumb movements to reach far-targets. Among these methods, *ETEC* showed significant improvements in terms of speed and accuracy. We adopt a similar approach in our *TiltCursor* method by using an extendible cursor in the same direction as a thumb.

BezelSpace and *CornerSpace* [25] utilize the benefits of the *Cursor* mechanism and the *Proxy Region* mechanism. When a user perform bezel swipe, *BezelSpace* generates a cursor and a proxy region under the thumb. The user can move the cursor inside the proxy region. Likewise, by bezel swipe, *CornerSpace* generates four corner buttons (denoting each corner of a screen) and a cancel button at the lift-up position of the thumb. By selecting a corner button, a cursor appears from the corner of the screen and a proxy region instead of the buttons.

A Piece of Butter [22] also uses the *Cursor* mechanism to select an item from a fixed menu. A cursor moves along the direction of the tilt by that much of the tilting angle. Usage of a tilt sensor is similar to our methods, but adjusting the cursor by tilting is hard for accurate targeting. Apart from using built-in sensors, *Behind-the-Display Cursor* [23,24] added sensors such as touch pad and optical sensor mounted on the back side of a mobile device to adjust a cursor to select hard-to-reach items by the forefinger. However, such methods requires additional hardware, making it hard to be adopted in current smartphones as it is.

UNDERSTANDING USERS' BEHAVIOR (EXPERIMENT 1)

First, we were interested in users' behavior of tilting the large screen smartphones towards their thumbs using the palm and the rest of fingers when they had to directly touch far-targets located outside the thumb's naturally reachable region. We presumed that the direction of tilting depended only on the position of the target and not on the distance from the thumb. In relation to this issue, GripSense [9] used rotational movement as a factor to detect which side of the user's hand holds the device. However, there has not been any empirical evidence to our knowledge to determine the direction and amount of tilting to touch far-targets on large mobile screens.

Second, we also noted the degree of uncomfortableness (called uncomfortable degree) of touch gestures for target acquisition. Karlson et al. [13] discussed the issue in various handheld devices. However, the results cannot be directly applied to the devices currently available in the market because of differences, including but not limited to screen size/ratio, thickness, and weight. Moreover, because even the largest screen tested in their study was smaller than the smallest device used for our experiment, we found it necessary to re-evaluate state-of-the-art large devices.

We designed an empirical experiment reflecting our observations. We recorded data from a built-in gyroscope sensor at the precise moment of target acquisition. We also collected task completion time between start action and target acquisition. We examined uncomfortable degree for all areas of a touchscreen through the questionnaire.

Participants

We recruited 11 participants (5 females) through an online reservation system announced on a campus bulletin board. Their age ranged from 20 to 29 years (M = 24.4, SD = 2.9). We screened participants so that all were right-handed and had experience with touchscreen mobile devices for more than three months. We did not require any previous experience with large mobile devices because we wanted to examine the general tendency of users' touch behaviors.

Apparatus

We conducted a controlled experiment using two large touchscreen mobile devices: (1) Samsung Galaxy S4 (136.6 × 69.8 × 7.9 mm, 5" screen) and (2) Samsung Galaxy Note3 (151.2 × 79.2 × 8.3 mm, 5.7" screen). The former is considered large screen smartphones, whereas the latter reaches the new category of "phablets".

Task

The participants were asked to hold the device in their right hands (dominant hands). Since their grip posture could change during the task, we enforced them to go back to their original state by having them press the Start button before each targeting task in order to prevent the functional area of the thumb from being affected [3]. We chose the Start button to be positioned where the thumb could reach naturally (The position of the Start button was empirically determined through a pilot study. We verified in the Results section that the position was within the comfortable region). They initiated the task by touching the red Start button and tapping on targets that appear in random regions using their thumb. The width of each square target was 7mm resulting in a 7 × 12 (84 cells) grid for Galaxy S4 and an 8 × 14 grid (112 cells) for Galaxy Note3. The target cells were highlighted one at a time in random order.

(A)

38.4	33.5	27.8	22.1	19.8	21.1	13.3	11.9
30.0	23.5	25.8	17.6	19.0	9.5	13.8	9.8
26.2	24.8	17.4	17.2	13.9	12.3	7.8	5.4
24.9	24.4	14.1	9.4	7.3	6.5	3.4	1.2
26.8	17.6	11.9	7.6	10.2	2.1	-0.8	-3.4
19.6	11.2	7.2	8.2	0.1	-0.7	1.1	0.3
17.0	9.8	6.0	7.1	0.0	-1.7	-2.4	-2.4
16.9	12.2	6.5	-0.5	1.3	-1.6	-6.0	-7.0
10.6	9.8	4.8	2.8	-2.9	-5.4	-7.6	-10.8
10.3	4.5	2.0	-1.4	-1.6	-5.0	-6.2	-13.9
11.5	8.4	4.6	2.4	-5.5	-5.3	-8.9	-12.0
19.0	7.9	2.7	-0.6	-5.2	-7.3	-12.4	-13.1
20.1	5.9	7.7	-2.1	-5.6	-9.0	-9.5	-18.3
21.3	7.4	4.5	-4.0	-9.8	-13.1	-15.7	-18.9

(B)

12.7	12.5	13.6	14.8	15.7	12.6	15.0	10.1
9.7	14.6	14.8	11.9	13.1	12.3	12.6	13.2
14.0	14.1	13.0	10.1	10.4	10.8	14.0	9.7
10.5	9.3	9.6	14.7	8.2	11.2	8.2	7.2
7.7	9.9	9.8	8.5	6.4	3.6	4.6	0.4
6.8	11.4	5.8	0.7	3.9	-2.1	-2.7	-1.4
0.0	5.3	5.0	-0.5	0.0	2.0	0.5	-0.6
2.7	-2.8	-4.7	4.0	-2.0	-3.7	-1.9	-4.3
-0.9	-12.1	-10.2	-7.9	-1.2	-8.9	-6.3	-10.8
-7.3	-7.3	-7.9	-10.2	-9.8	-12.6	-13.0	-11.4
-13.3	-14.4	-16.3	-16.2	-7.5	-16.1	-18.9	-14.7
-26.0	-17.1	-18.8	-22.1	-16.4	-15.9	-20.3	-16.7
-28.0	-26.0	-31.1	-20.7	-20.8	-23.5	-22.2	-22.7
-35.1	-30.9	-33.4	-33.3	-23.0	-27.6	-29.8	-27.8

Figure 1. Degree of tilting converted from gyroscope data relative to Start button for x-axis (A) and y-axis (B) when acquiring targets on Samsung Galaxy Note3. The red squares denote the position of Start button.

Procedure

At the beginning, we measured the length of each participant's thumb and palm size since they are important factors to determine the ability of the thumb to reach. The thumb length ranged from 53mm to 73mm (M = 62mm, SD = 6.8mm) and the average palm size was 81.5mm (palm length, SD = 7.1mm) × 105.8mm (palm breadth, SD = 8.6mm).

All participants performed the tasks for all cells of the grid once on Galaxy S4 first and then on Galaxy Note3. The devices' specific order was chosen from the device with mild reachability problem to severe. Before beginning the experiment with each device, they had a training session that consisted of tapping 16 targets, which were equally distributed across all regions of the screen. This allowed them to have a relative perception of comfortableness of reaching various regions of the device. For the main task, after tapping a target, they were asked to verbally report the rating of uncomfortableness of touching the target. The rating ranged from 1 to 3 (1 for <Natural for a thumb>, 2 for <Somewhat uncomfortable because of bending or stretching of the thumb>, and 3 for <Very uncomfortable because of too much bending or stretching of the thumb>).

Results

The larger touchscreen device (5.7" screen)

We aggregated the gyroscope data for touching each region and showed the results in a heat map (Figure 1). We calibrated all values to be aligned with the gyroscope value

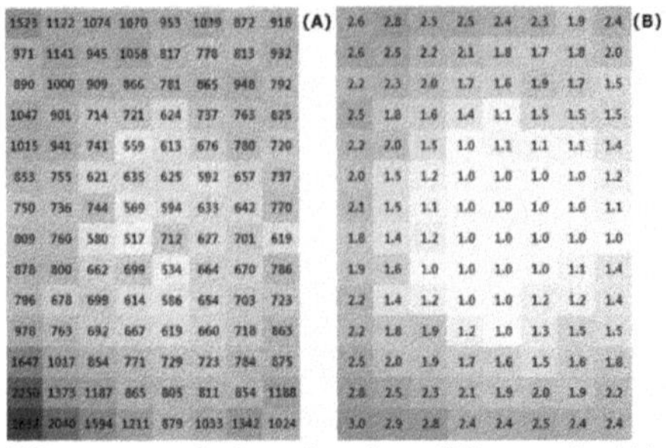

Figure 2. Mean completion time in milliseconds (A) and mean degree of uncomfortableness (B) on Samsung Galaxy Note3.

acquired upon touching the Start button where users could touch naturally when they are holding the device at their front-facing angle.

Figure 1(A) indicates the amount of left-right (or x-axis) tilting. The red color (positive value) means users tilted the devices to the right side, whereas the blue color (negative value) means they tilted the devices to the left side. Figure 1(B) indicates the amount of top-bottom (or y-axis) tilting. The red color (positive value) denotes the devices were tilted to make the top of the devices closer to the user, and the blue color (negative value) means the devices were tilted to make the bottom of devices closer to the user. The darker the color is, the more tilted the device is.

We confirmed that users tilted the devices much more on both axis when they had to touch farther targets by using linear regression to check the correlation between the amount of tilting and the distance of targets from the Start button. The tilting amount correlated significantly with distance for both x-axis (r = 0.584, p = 0.000) and y-axis (r = 0.735, p = 0.000).

Additionally, we confirmed that the tilting direction depended on the location of targets. First, for the targets placed on the left side, the tilting direction of y-axis was the opposite for top-left and bottom-left ones. Also, we verified that users tilted significantly more on x-axis for tapping the top-left than the bottom-left ($F_{1,10}$ = 15.315, $p < .005$) using RM-ANOVA. Second, for the targets placed on the right side, the tilting direction of x-axis was the opposite for top-right and bottom-right ones. We inferred that the ergonomical limitation of the thumb being rather difficult to bend downward may have resulted in such behavior. Although tilting directions for far-targets varied, they all were attempts to bring the target closer to their thumb.

We aggregated task completion time and uncomfortable degree of participants and represented the results using a heat map (Figure 2). We confirmed that the center of the screen was comfortable for all participants where the Start button was positioned. We also discovered that some targets near the right side edge were uncomfortable. The targets were within reach of a thumb but too close, so they required participants to bend their thumbs. Through these results, we found that not all uncomfortable targets were equally far. We verified task completion time has significant correlation with uncomfortable degree (r = 0.788,

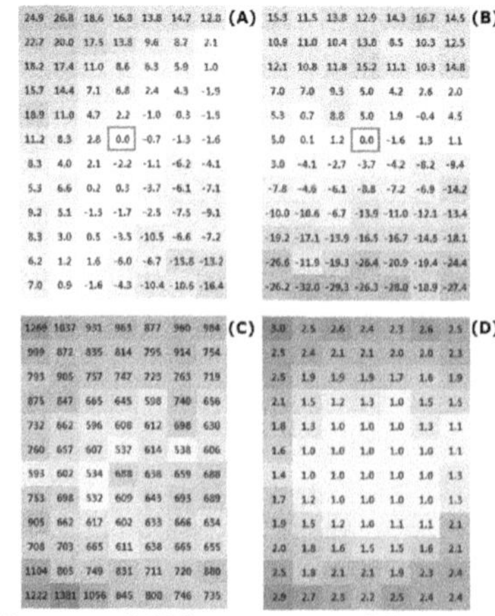

Figure 3. Degree of tilting converted from gyroscope data relative to Start button for x-axis (A) and y-axis (B), mean completion time in milliseconds (C), and mean degree of uncomfortableness from questionnaire (D) on Samsung Galaxy S4. The red squares denote the position of Start button.

p = 0.000) using linear regression. Namely, participansts tilted the devices when they felt uncomfortable at tapping the targets even when they were close.

Also, we discovered that the targets at the bottom-left region took significantly more time to touch than the targets at the top-left region ($F_{1,10}$ = 6.125, $p < .05$) using RM-ANOVA. Also, we confirmed that the bottom-left targets was significantly more uncomfortable than the top-left targets (Z = -2.000, $p < .05$) using Wilcoxon signed-rank test. We discuss this phenomenon by comparing them with the results on smaller devices.

The smaller touchscreen device (5" screen)

We observed similar results on a smaller screen device, the Galaxy S4 (Figure 3). The tilting amount correlated significantly with the distance for both x-axis (r = 0.592, p = 0.000) and y-axis (r = 0.738, p = 0.000), namely, users tilted the devices much more for farther targets regardless of the screen size if they were larger than five inches.

We also found that task completion time has significant correlation with uncomfortable degree (r = 0.823, p = 0.000) using linear regression and the targets near the right edge were uncomfortable because they were too close.

Interestingly, aligning the two results from smaller Galaxy S4 and larger Galaxy Note3 by the Start buttons excluding the non-existent targets, we found that they matched well in terms of both tilting direction and tilting amount for the targets in the same location. We verified strong correlations for both x-axis tilting (Pearson correlation coefficient of 0.958) and y-axis tilting (0.953). We also verified strong correlation for uncomfortable degree of two devices (0.918). It would be interesting to see if this concordance can be generalized into even larger devices.

The most interesting finding was that, in contrast with the result of larger Galaxy Note3, the targets at bottom-left region had no significant difference from the targets at top-

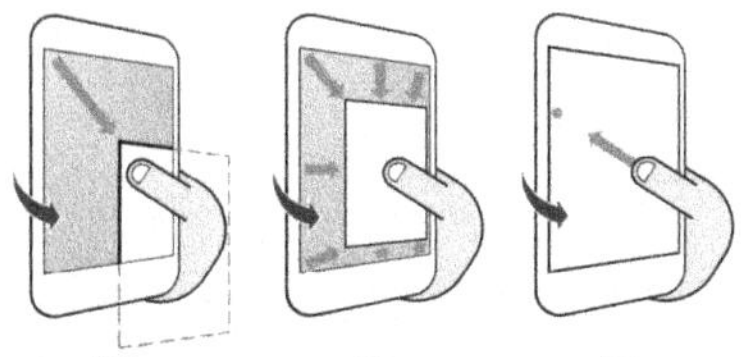

Figure 4. Three mobile interaction techniques using tilting gesture: *TiltSlide* (A), *TiltReduction* (B), and *TiltCursor* (C).

left region in task completion time ($F_{1,10}$ = 0.062, ns) and uncomfortable degree (Z = -1.000, ns). We could suspect that the uncomfortableness of the bottom-left area was due to the larger size of the screen. From this result, we suggest that we need to be careful when putting targets in the bottom-left area on a large mobile screen.

ONE-THUMBED INTERACTION BASED ON TILTING

We verified that users use the strategy of tilting the devices to bring the targets at uncomfortable regions closer to their thumbs. Tilting gesture in mobile devices has been actively evaluated, from exploring the effectiveness of combinations of tilt and drag directions [20] and the effective discretization of tilt angle [17] to evaluating the suitability of tilt to control pointers on large displays [5]. However, there have not been any researches on the tilting gesture for one-hand targeting on large mobile touchscreen. We first designed three novel mobile interaction techniques using tilting gesture: *TiltSlide*, *TiltReduction*, and *TiltCursor*.

TiltSlide (*TS*): When a user tilts a device, the screen slides to the tilting direction (Figure 4A). This method resembles iPhone 6/6+'s Reachability feature [1] although it only brings the screen down to one direction, i.e. *down*, whereas *TS* supports eight different directions depending on the way the device was tilted, i.e., *right-down*, *right*, *right-up*, *up*, *left-up*, *left*, *left-down*, and *down*. The screen slides until any of its edges hits the center of the physical screen.

TiltReduction (*TR*): When a user tilts a device, the screen shrinks to fit into a customized comfort region (Figure 4B). Inspired by *ThumbSpace* [14], we enable users to determine the comfort region as a rectangle that they diagonally draw by dragging their thumbs from top-left to bottom-right. The rectangle's aspect ratio is maintained to that of the screen to avoid distortion. While dragging, users can preview a shrunk-sized screen rendered within the rectangle. They were allowed to draw the rectangle repeatedly until their thumb could comfortably reach the entire rectangle.

TiltCursor (*TC*): A cursor appears when a user starts to drag while a device is being tilted (Figure 4C). At first, the cursor appears under the thumb and moves to the same direction as the dragging gesture. It also moves faster than the thumb movement to reach even far-targets by manipulating within the thumb's comfort region. The cursor does not exceed the boundary of the screen to be helpful especially on reaching four corners, since the width of a target at the corner goes infinite considering Fitts' law [8]. The target underneath the cursor is selected upon lifting.

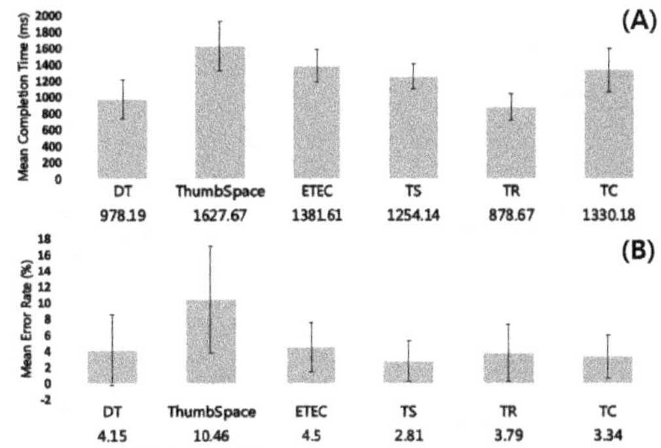

Figure 5. Mean completion time (A) and mean error rate (B) for one targeting. Error bars denote standard deviation.

In our first prototype, the amount of "slide" for *TS* was determined by the degree of x-axis tilting. However, we got the feedback that it was too sensitive, and it was difficult to control the degree of tilting. Thus, we changed *TS* to slide the screen to the point where any of edges hit the center of the screen, when the degree of tilting exceeds the predetermined thresholds of each eight direction. Also, the speed of a cursor was set to be 2.5 times that of a thumb after careful calibration. The tilting thresholds to "trigger" our methods used an average of the gyroscope value from the first experiment and were further adjusted heuristically through pilot study to better fit users' intention; 35 degrees on x-axis for *TR* and *TC*.

EXPERIMENTAL EVALUATION (EXPERIMENT 2)

To validate the effectiveness of our methods, we conducted a controlled and comparative experiment with three other methods: *Direct-Touch* (*DT*) (a normal method without an assistant), *ThumbSpace* [14], and *ETEC* [15]. We chose them since they suggest different methodologies such as a proxy region and an edge cursor. We chose *ETEC* over other cursor methods for the comparison, since it allows access to the entire area of a screen (while *Offset Cursor* [16,19] and *Adaptive Horizontal Offset* [10] do not). Also, *MagStick* [18] was not considered because its weakness for densely located targets may interfere with the result. We also excluded *TapTap* [18] because its main goal is to assist accurate target acquisition.

Hypotheses

We made hypotheses about the results from two different perspectives: method and region.

Comparison of the method

TR and *TS* would be faster than *ThumbSpace* (**H1**). Though they all use *Assisted Touch*, i.e., directly touching the target, *ThumbSpace* needs additional cognitive effort to determine the relative position of a target on an empty proxy view. We inferred that these additional costs would result in extra time. We also hypothesized that *Assisted Touch* (*TR*, *TS*) would be faster and more accurate than *Cursor* (*ETEC*, *TC*) (**H2**), since dragging a cursor until it reaches a target would take more time than directly touching the target with the thumb. Also, when the user lifts his/her thumb for selection,

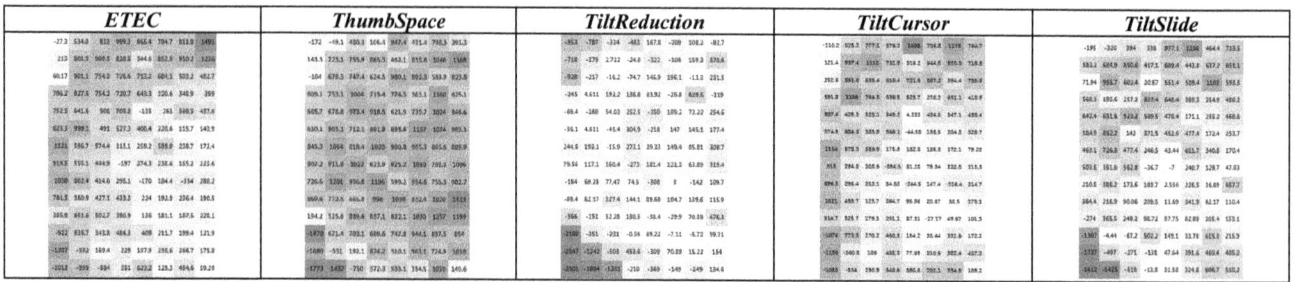

Table 2. The differences between each method and *Direct Touch* (Value$_{method}$ - Value$_{DT}$) in task completion time. The red color (positive value) denotes the region took more time than *DT*, and the blue color (negative value) denotes the region took less time than *DT*. The white color means there were no differences.

a slight disposition of the cursor could make an inaccurate target acquisition. In *Cursor*, *TC* would be faster than *ETEC* (**H3**) because *TC* enables users to start dragging nearer targets, while *ETEC* has to start dragging only from predetermined bezel locations. Since *TR* has reduced target size from shrinking the screen size to fit into the comfort region, *TR* would be less accurate than *DT* and *TS* (**H4**).

Comparison of the region

ThumbSpace would result in uniform task completion time among most regions (**H5**) since a user has to utilize a proxy view for every target; the targets in comfortable regions as well as in uncomfortable regions.

Participants

We recruited 18 participants (10 females) through an online reservation system announced on a campus bulletin board. Their age ranged from 20 to 30 (M = 24 and SD = 3.2). We screened participants to be right-handed and to have had experience with touchscreen mobile devices for more than one years. They were given $10 for their time.

Apparatus

We used Samsung Galaxy Note3 (151.2 × 79.2 × 8.3 mm, 5.7" screen). We developed an Android application [7] that implemented six methods: *TS*, *TR*, *TC*, *DT*, *ETEC*, and *ThumbSpace*. We collected task completion time and the number of errors through the application.

Task

The participants were asked to acquire a target as fast as and as accurate as possible while holding a device in their right hands. Targets were located in an 8 × 14 grid (112 cells) on screen and the width of each square target was 7mm. Each cell was activated and highlighted to be a target, and we counted the number of errors when non-highlighted cells were touched. We asked participants to sit straight on a chair and not to lean forward to control other external factors such as posture.

Procedure

The participants performed the target acquisition tasks using the six methods by five trials each. One trial contained 30 targets at randomly activated regions while maintaining the same total thumb-travel distance. We used a Latin Square design to eliminate ordering effects. A five-minute training session for each method was performed before they started the first trial to get themselves familiar with each method. They were allowed to have a five-minute break after five trials were completed. Seven questions were given upon completion of the experiment.

Results

We analyzed results (Figure 5) using RM-ANOVA and found significant main effects on task completion time ($F_{5,85} = 24.59$, $p < .01$) and error rate ($F_{5,85} = 9.65$, $p < .01$). Post hoc analysis using Bonferroni correction allowed us to rank the methods as follows: the fastest *TR* (878.67ms) and *DT* (978.19ms); *TS* (1254.14ms), *TC* (1330.18ms), and *ETEC* (1381.61ms); the slowest *ThumbSpace* (1627.67ms). Namely, only *TR* showed competitive performance with *DT*.

TR and *TS* were significantly faster than *ThumbSpace*; 1.9 and 1.3 times respectively ($p < .001$ for both), confirming **H1**. Only *TR* was significantly faster than *Cursor* (*ETEC*, *TC*); 1.6 and 1.5 times respectively ($p < .001$ for both). Also, only *ThumbSpace* (10.46%) had significantly more errors than all other methods; *TS* (2.81%), *TC* (3.34%), *TR* (3.79%), *DT* (4.15%), and *ETEC* (4.5%) ($p < .001$ for all), thus partially confirming **H2**. We suppose that difficulty in determining a slide direction took more time than expected for *TS*. We could not confirm **H3**; we speculate that the more complex method for the trigger of *TC* may have counter-affected performance in time, since *TC* requires a combination of two gestures (tilt and drag), while *ETEC* requires only one (drag). We could not confirm **H4**; even with its reduced size, the accuracy for *TR* was as good as *DT* and *TS*. We assume that showing a preview of reduced targets for *TR* while defining a customized comfort region might prevent making targets too small to touch accurately.

We show the mean task completion time of each method relative to that of *DT* for all areas of the screen in a heat map (Table 2). *ThumbSpace* generally performed worse than *DT* over most regions, confirming **H5**. Interestingly, all methods outperformed *DT* in the bottom-left region; it is consistent with the previous finding that bottom-left is the hardest region for direct touch and has to use assistive methods to get over a difficulty.

Actually, during the experiment, participants had a hard time and often dropped the device in an attempt to touch a

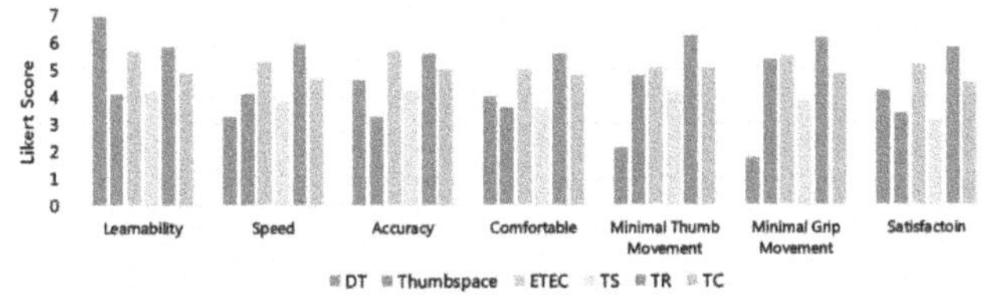

Figure 6. Questionnaire results (means)

bottom-left target with *DT*. One participant had to rotate the device 180 degrees to touch bottom-left and top-left targets. However, while using other assistive methods, none of the participants dropped or rotated the device.

We analyzed questionnaire results (Figure 6) using Friedman test; thumb movement ($\chi^2 = 44.25, p < .001$) and learnability ($\chi^2 = 44.85, p < .001$). *DT* was significantly less preferred than all other methods in thumb/grip movement (mean = 2.1/1.7 respectively) ($p < .001$ for all); however, *DT* (6.9) was preferred than all other methods except *TR* (5.8) in terms of learnability ($p < .05$ for all). In summary, compared to *DT*, *TR* showed a promising result because it required less thumb/grip movement with comparable performance in speed, accuracy, and learnability.

REAL SCENARIO EVALUATION (EXPERIMENT 3)

We confirmed that our tilting methods had potential for acquiring targets in an uncomfortable region. However, we cannot apply the result directly to real mobile phone circumstances because we excluded several factors in the previous experiment: (1) Mechanisms of our methods could be in conflict with conventional mobile interactions such as long touch, double tap, swipe, scroll, and drag; and (2) Though we ascertained that a reduced screen size had not shown any difference in accuracy for acquiring the target, there could be overlooked factors such as small font size or figures that might be difficult to see the details when reduced in size.

We noted that one-hand targeting interactions used different trigger mechanisms. We speculated that they could show different performance in real mobile phone scenarios because of conflicts with their trigger mechanisms and existing mobile interactions. Also, smartphone usage could require frequent re-triggers to perform a series of real-world tasks (e.g. tapping a far-target in reduced screen size and checking details in original large screen size using the reduced-screen method). Thus, the time required for trigger becomes more crucial in real mobile phone scenarios.

We designed a user study to evaluate one-hand targeting interactions triggered by different mechanisms in real mobile application scenarios. We chose two among our methods: *TR* (triggered by tilting gesture) and *TC* (triggered by both tilting gesture and dragging). We excluded *TS* since it used the same trigger mechanism as *TR* with worse performance than *TR* in our Experiment 2. We compared our methods with others introduced in previous research. *ETEC* (triggered by dragging) was included for comparison with *TC*, namely we wanted to investigate the effect of

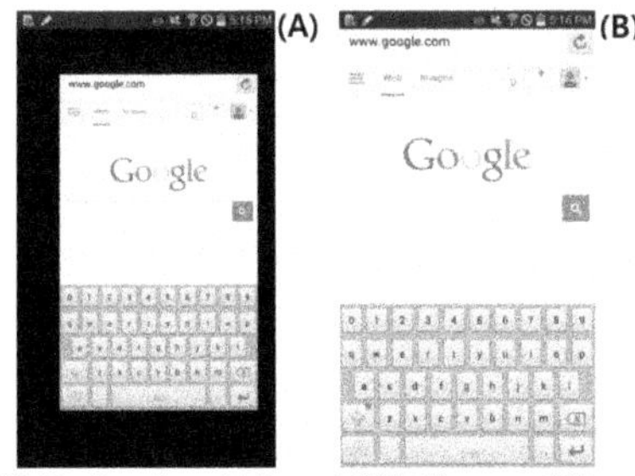

Figure 7. *TiltReduction* (A) and *TiltCursor* (B) on the Android application developed to similar to common web browsers.

trigger mechanisms for the same *Cursor* methods. We also chose *One-handed operation mode* [2] (triggered by touch gesture) for comparison with *TR*, since they used the same reduced-screen method to assist one-hand targeting. In short, we conducted experiments using five methods: *Direct Touch*, *TR*, *TC*, *ETEC*, and *One-handed operation mode*.

We also chose the tasks that could represent real mobile phone usage. Bohmer et al. [4] logged mobile phone usage and uncovered patterns of application usage during a day. Among them, we chose two frequently used tasks in our daily usage of smartphones: typing and search. For typing tasks, we asked participants to compose and send an e-mail. For search tasks, we asked participants to do web surfing.

Participants

We recruited 15 participants (4 females) through an online reservation system announced on a campus bulletin board. We screened participants to be right-handed and to have had experience with touchscreen mobile devices for more than one year. We recruited only those who usually used QWERTY software keyboard as their primary input method on mobile devices and who mainly used Google Search /Gmail as web browser and e-mail to eliminate possible learning effects. Their age ranged from 20 to 29 years (M = 23.8, SD = 2.6). They were compensated with $10 for an hour, total experiment time.

Apparatus

We chose Samsung Galaxy Note3 (5.7" screen) to compare the result with our previous experiments. We developed an Android application whose appearance was similar to common web browsers in smartphones. We used WebView (an Android control) and built a custom software keyboard designed to function similarly to other common smartphone QWERTY keyboards (Figure 7). It should be noted that no correction algorithms were applied to typing. We collected task completion time, the number of "Delete" key presses on the software keyboard, and touch coordinates.

Task

The participants performed two tasks: sending an e-mail and web surfing. For the e-mail task, they navigated the Google homepage upon launching the application, and they were asked to navigate Gmail and read a randomly chosen, pre-designated e-mail out of 15. The e-mail consisted of 12 small letters that could only be recognized on a normal size

Q1	Go to Notice, and find out opening hours for <Name> Café.
Q2	Go to News, and find out the ratio of Asian students in internationalization chart.
Q3	Go to Events, and find out who directed the movie showing on October 16.
Q4	Go to Academic-College of Engineering-Dept. of Computer Science and Engineering, and list the name of a seminar on September 15.
Q5	Go to About-Symbols, and find out School Bird.

Table 3. Questions given for web surfing tasks.

screen (not on a reduced size screen). The 12 letters were compounded with random alphabets (e.g., qUeK xHaP wYcI) to have no meaning, while maintaining the same average amount of uncomfortable degree based on the first experiment (we ensured that all the e-mails had no significant difference in time for typing their letters using direct touch (*DT*) through a pilot study). We asked the participant to reply to an e-mail with the same sequence of the letters by memorizing a chunk of four letters at a time before typing, so that he/she has to consistently change between the normal size and the reduced size for every e-mail. Also he/she was asked to perform the tasks as quickly and as accurately as possible.

For the web surfing task, the participants performed without any restriction in time and action. They were given a question before starting and asked to find an answer by surfing the web. The questions are summarized in Table 3. We utilized our university website because navigating the website required various mobile interactions such as swipe and horizontal and vertical scrolling.

Procedure

The participants were asked to hold the devices in their right hands and use all five methods one at a time. The five methods were assigned to subjects using a Latin Square to eliminate ordering effects. Before performing e-mail and web surfing tasks using each method, the participants had a training session long enough to get used to the method and the e-mail task. And then they were asked to perform a web surfing task using the method as frequently as possible, since we wanted them to have enough experience for insightful feedback. Lastly, they performed an e-mail task three times for the method and were asked to use the method only for touching uncomfortable targets. Upon completion of the experiment using all methods, the participants completed a questionnaire with seven questions for subjective evaluation using a seven point Likert scale [Rating: 1 = strongly disagree, 7 = strongly agree].

Hypotheses

For the e-mail task, we hypothesized that *TR* would be faster than *One-handed operation mode*, since *One-handed operation mode* needs additional time to be triggered (**H1**). Furthermore, *TR* would not have a significant difference with *DT* on task completion time, considering that trigger by tilting gesture requires less time (**H2**). *Cursor* (*ETEC*, *TC*) would be slower than *Assisted Touch* (*TR*, *One-handed operation mode*) since *Cursor* requires a separate trigger

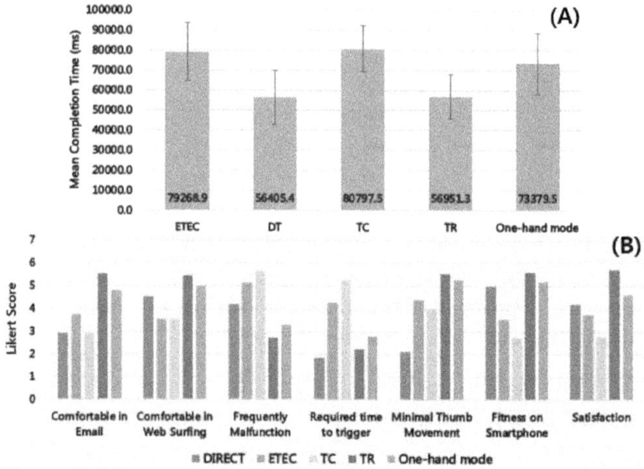

Figure 8. Mean completion time for e-mail tasks (A) and mean results of each question (B).

action for each target acquisition, whereas *Assisted Touch* allows users to select multiple targets once it is triggered (**H3**). *DT* would have more errors than other methods, because directly touching a far target may result in miss-pressing (**H4**). For the web surfing task, *Cursor* (*ETEC*, *TC*) would be preferred less than *Assisted Touch* (*TR*, *One-handed operation mode*) since dragging a cursor conflicts with swiping or scrolling in web browsers (**H5**).

Results

E-mail task

We analyzed results (Figure 8) using RM-ANOVA and found a significant main effect on task completion time ($F_{4, 56} = 27.22, p < .001$) and the number of errors ($F_{4, 56} = 4.81$, $p < .01$). We treated the number of pressing the "Delete" key as the number of errors. Post hoc analysis using Bonferroni correction allowed us to rank the methods as follows: *DT* (56405ms) and *TR* (56951ms); *One-handed operation mode* (73379ms), *ETEC* (79268ms), and *TC* (80797ms).

TR was significantly faster than *One-handed operation mode*; almost 1.3 times ($p < .001$), confirming **H1**. From the result, though both *TR* and *One-handed operation mode* used mode-change mechanisms to trigger reduced screen, tilting gesture was significantly faster than touch gesture. We also confirmed **H2**; all other methods except *TR* were significantly slower than *DT* ($p = .001$ for *One-hand operation mode*, otherwise $p < .001$). Though *TR* was frequently re-triggered during the e-mail task, it showed competitive performance in time with *DT*, like the result of Experiment 2. For such reason, we were able to verify tilting gesture requires less time. Only *TR* was significantly faster than *Cursor* (*ETEC*, *TC*); almost 1.4 times ($p < .001$ for both), partially confirming **H3**. In other words, the fewer number of trigger by touch gesture (because of multiple target selection in a trigger) requires as much time as the more number of trigger by dragging.

DT (mean = 1.82 errors) had significantly more errors than *TR* (0.4) ($p < .05$) excluding other methods: *ETEC* (0.69),

TC (0.91), and *One-handed operation mode* (1.09); partially confirming **H4**. Comparing this result with the accuracy result of Experiment 2, some trigger mechanisms such as dragging and touch gesture could have as many errors as *DT* in real mobile phone circumstances because of conflicts with existing mobile interactions. We assume that touch action for the trigger might be mis-classified as direct touch.

We analyzed questionnaire results on comfortableness for e-mail task ($\chi^2 = 31.45$, $p < .001$) using Friedman test. *TR* (mean = 5.5) and *One-handed operation mode* (4.8) were significantly preferred than all other methods ($p < .05$ for all). The dragging mechanism for *TC* (2.9) or *ETEC* (3.7) was felt as uncomfortable as *DT* (2.9), which does not assist targeting at all for e-mail task on a large smartphone.

Web surfing task

We confirmed **H5** by analyzing questionnaire results on comfortableness for web surfing task ($\chi^2 = 27.87$, $p < .001$). *Cursor* (*ETEC*, *TC*: 3.5/3.5 respectively) was preferred significantly less than *Assisted Touch* (*TR*, *One-handed operation mode*: 5.5/5.0 respectively) and even *DT* (4.5) ($p < .05$ for all). We verified that participants felt that they activated unintended actions significantly more with *Cursor* (5.1/5.7) than *Assisted Touch* (2.7/3.3) ($p < .01$ for all). They rated the appropriateness and preference of *Cursor* (3.5/2.7 and 3.7/2.8) on smartphones to be lower than those of *Assisted Touch* (5.6/5.2 and 5.7/4.6) ($p < .01$ for all).

We got interesting feedbacks from interviews after the user study; most participants (86%) reported the difficulty of dragging gesture with the device tilted. We also verified through the questionnaire results that they felt *TC* (5.3) required significantly more time to trigger than *ETEC* (4.3) ($p < .05$). These are kinds of feedbacks not found in the previous study, implying that they might be confused to deal with three factors: tilting, dragging, and conventional mobile interactions such as scrolling. They also said that the typing using *Cursor* was especially annoying since they wanted to type in the way they were already familiar with.

DISCUSSION

In evaluating one-hand targeting methods in real mobile phone scenarios, we verified that their trigger mechanisms were important factors as assisting techniques on large mobile devices. In Table 1, the *Trigger Mechanisms* can be categorized into *Always On* (always staying as "triggered"), *Tapping*, *Dragging*, *Mode Change* (switching use/non-use of targeting mechanism), and *Back-Side Touch* (using a touch pad attached on the back side). Furthermore, there could be other mechanisms for trigger such as *Long Touch* and *Double Touch*, but they had not been explored in the past to our knowledge. It might be because of conflicts with conventional touch interactions in mobile phones.

We verified that *ThumbSpace* [14] could be helpful for some targets in uncomfortable regions, but generally showed bad performance among most regions including comfortable regions. Therefore, the *Always On* mechanism has to be used for targeting methods designed to support both uncomfortable regions and comfortable regions.

Since the *Tapping* mechanism overlaps with direct touch in mobile phones, targeting methods using this mechanism have to block the direct touch (e.g. *Offset Cursor* [16,19]) or use other means of resolving the ambiguity (e.g., *TapTap* [18] is triggered only by touching the region that has two targets in close proximity).

The *Dragging* mechanism can be divided into dragging *anywhere* and dragging from the *edge*. Targeting methods using *Dragging anywhere* [10,15,18] conflict with dragging interactions generally used in mobile phones. Thus, they have to block the conventional dragging or utilize other conditions, e.g., *TC* provides a cursor by dragging while the device is tilted. However, the results of our Experiment 3 showed that users felt it difficult to satisfy both conditions. Hence, we suggest that combining several mechanisms has to be designed and applied with care.

The *Mode Change* mechanism utilizes various modalities such as pressing a *physical button* [1,11,22], defining a unique *touch gesture* [2], or using a built-in sensor, e.g., *tilting gesture*. Through Experiment 3, we verified that *tilting gesture* was significantly faster than *touch gesture*, which is considered one of the most efficient modes of touch [6]. However, the targeting methods using sensors must consider false positive issues and endeavor to stabilize them. In order to stabilize our tilting mechanism, we mainly relied on the gyroscope sensor to detect triggers (rather than an accelerometer sensor) and used the threshold angles which are beyond the normal shake while typing and walking, except only rare circumstances, e.g., recklessly driven public buses. We verified them through an informal in-lab experiment by constantly using our custom-built web browser from Experiment 3.

Overall, we verified that while using a cursor can assist in acquiring far-targets, it is slower than touching with a thumb. Therefore, targeting methods using *Cursor* will be useful if used with direct touch in comfortable regions.

CONCLUSION AND FUTURE WORK

In this paper, we explored users' touch behavior using tilting devices on large mobile touchscreens. We also investigated the thumb's comfortable region with state-of-the-art large mobile devices and proposed that the bottom-left region is yet to be explored for further optimization. Based on our observations, we designed three novel mobile interaction techniques using tilting gesture to facilitate one-hand targeting. We analyzed them with other methods of related works in a controlled environment and real mobile phone scenarios. We found that the trigger mechanism of one-hand targeting methods was an important factor for time, accuracy, or preference. Based on the analysis, we proposed design considerations as our design space for one-hand targeting interactions.

We could not evaluate our methods with the recently released iPhone6/6+'s method. It may be effective for upper half screen; thus, we may compare it with our methods in the future. Also, we would like to empirically analyze false positive trigger issues. From the first experiment, we found that tilting patterns of a smaller device matched well with those of a larger device for same regions. It will be interesting to expand the experiment to other larger or smaller devices to see if we can generalize such pattern.

ACKNOWLEDGEMENTS

This work was supported by the National Research Foundation of Korea (NRF) grant funded by the Korea government (MSIP) (NRF-2014R1A2A2A03006998) and also supported by the Basic Science Research Program through the National Research Foundation of Korea (NRF) funded by the Ministry of Education, Science and Technology (NRF-2013R1A1A3006706).

REFERENCES

1. https://www.apple.com/iphone-6/design/ Retrieved on Sept. 19, 2014.
2. http://www.androidcentral.com/how-shrink-galaxy-note-3-s-display Retrieved on Sept. 20, 2014.
3. Bergstrom-Lehtovirta, J. and Oulasvirta, A. Modeling Functional Area of the Thumb on Mobile Touchscreen Surfaces. *Proc. CHI'14*. 1991-2000. 2014.
4. Bohmer, M., Hecht, B., Schoning, J., Kruger, A., and Bauer, G. Falling Asleep with Angry Birds, Facebook and Kindle: a large scale study on mobile application usage. *Proc. MobileHCI'11*. 47-56. 2011.
5. Boring, S., Jurmu, M., and Butz, A. Scroll, Tilt or Move It: Using Mobile Phones to Continuously Control Pointers on Large Public Displays. *Proc. OzCHI'09*. 161-168. 2009.
6. Bragdon, A., Nelson, E., Li, Y., and Hinckley, K. Experimental Analysis of Touch-Screen Gesture Designs in Mobile Environments. *Proc. CHI'11*. 403-412. 2011.
7. Chang, Y., L'Yi, S., and Seo, J. Reaching Targets on Discomfort Region Using Tilting Gesture. *Proc. UIST'14*. 115-116. 2014.
8. Fitts, P.M. The information capacity of the human motor system in controlling the amplitude of movement. *Journal of Experimental Psychology*, 47, 381-391. 1954.
9. Goel, M., Wobbrock, J.O., and Patel, S.N. GripSense: Using Built-In Sensors to Detect Hand Posture and Pressure on Commodity Mobile Phones. *Proc. UIST'12*. 545-554. 2012.
10. Huot, S. and Lecolinet, E. Focus+Context Visualization Techniques for Displaying Large Lists with Multiple Points of Interest on Small Tactile Screens. *Proc. Interact'07*. 2007.
11. Karlson, A.K. and Bederson, B.B. One-Handed Touchscreen Input for Legacy Applications. *Proc. CHI'08*. 1399-1408. 2008.
12. Karlson, A.K., Bederson, B.B., and SanGiovanni, J. AppLens and LaunchTile: Two Designs for One-Handed Thumb Use on Small Devices. *Proc. CHI'05*. 201-210. 2005.
13. Karlson, A.K., Bederson, B.B., and Contreras-Vidal, J.L. Understanding Single-Handed Mobile Device Interaction. *Tech Report HCIL-2006-02.*
14. Karlson, A.K. and Bederson, B.B. ThumbSpace: Generalized One-Handed Input for Touchscreen-Based Mobile Devices. *Proc. Interact'07*. 324-339. 2007.
15. Kim, S., Yu, J., and Lee, G. Interaction Techniques for Unreachable Objects on the Touchscreen. *Proc. OzCHI'12*. 295-298. 2012.
16. Potter, R.L., Weldon, L.J., and Shneiderman, B. Improving the accuracy of touch screens: an experimental evaluation of three strategies. *Proc. CHI'88*. 27-32. 1988.
17. Rahman, M., Gustafson, S., Irani, P., and Subramanian, S. Tilt Techniques: Investigating the Dexterity of Wrist-Based Input. *Proc. CHI'09*. 2009.
18. Roudaut, A., Huot, S., and Lecolinet, E. TapTap and MagStick: Improving One-Handed Target Acquisition on Small Touchscreens. *Proc. AVI'08*. 146-153. 2008.
19. Sears, A. and Shneiderman, B. High Precision Touch-screens: Design Strategies and Comparison with a Mouse. *International Journal of Man-Machine Studies*. 593-613. 1991.
20. Tsandilas, T., Appert, C., Bezerianos, A., and Bonnet, D. Coordination of Tilt and Touch in One- and Two-Handed Use. *Proc. CHI'14*. 2001-2004. 2014.
21. Vogel, D. and Baudisch, P. Shift: A Technique for Operating Pen-Based Interfaces Using Touch. *Proc. CHI'07*. 657-666. 2007.
22. Weberg, L., Brange, T., and Hansson, A.W. A Piece of Butter on the PDA Display. *CHI'01 Extended Abstracts*. 435-436. 2001.
23. Yang, X.D., Irani, P., Boulanger, P., and Bischof, W.F. One-Handed Behind-the-Display Cursor Input on Mobile Devices. *CHI EA'09*. 4501-4506. 2009.
24. Yang, X.D., Mak, E., Irani, P., and Bischof, W.F. Dual-Surface Input: Augmenting One-Handed Interaction with Coordinated Front and Behind-the-screen Input. *Proc. MobileHCI'09*. 1-10. 2009.
25. Yu, N.-H., Huang, D.-Y., Hsu, J.-J., and Hung, Y.-P. Rapid Selection of Hard-to-Access Targets by Thumb on Mobile Touch-Screens. *Proc. MobileHCI'13*. 400-403. 2013.

One-Handed Bend Interactions with Deformable Smartphones

Audrey Girouard[1], Jessica Lo[1], Md Riyadh[1], Farshad Daliri[1], Alexander Keith Eady[1] and Jerome Pasquero[2,3]

[1]Carleton University
Ottawa, Canada

[2]Blackberry Limited
Waterloo, Canada

[3]Motsai
Montreal, Canada

{audrey.girouard, jessica.lo, md.riyadh, farshad.daliri, alex.eady}@carleton.ca, j.pasquero@motsai.com

ABSTRACT
Smartphones are becoming larger, mainly because bigger screens offer a better experience for viewing content. One drawback of larger screens is that they make single-hand interactions difficult because of hard to reach touch targets and of the need to re-grip the device, both factors significantly reducing their usability. Flexible smartphones offer an opportunity for addressing this issue. We first set out to determine the use of common single-hand mobile interactions through an online survey. Then, we designed and evaluated one-handed deformable gestures that offer the potential for addressing the finger reach limitation on large smartphones. We identified that the top right up bend and the center squeeze up gestures are the fastest and preferred gestures. We found no hand preference, which indicates that the gestures could be implemented to fit the needs of a wider range of the population, instead of favoring right-handed users. Finally, we discuss the impact on deformable gestures on one-handed interactions issues.

Author Keywords
Deformable user interfaces; flexible displays; one-handed interactions; bend gestures; mobile; HCI;

ACM Classification Keywords
H.5.2. Information interfaces and presentation: *User Interfaces – Interaction styles, user-centered design.*

INTRODUCTION
Large screen smartphones are becoming increasingly popular in the mobile phone arena, mainly because larger screens offer a better experience for viewing content. One drawback of larger screens is that they make single-hand touch interactions more difficult as they significantly limit the reach of the interacting finger(s) [4,9,12,29]. Single-hand interactions are performed using one hand which both holds and interacts with the device, as opposed to gestures performed while the device is on a table. Figure 1 illustrates a typical case for one-handed touch interactions.

CHI 2015, April 18 - 23 2015, Seoul, Republic of Korea

ACM 978-1-4503-3145-6/15/04…$15.00
http://dx.doi.org/10.1145/2702123.2702513

Figure 1. When used with one hand, current phones have a limited functional interaction zone (in green, on left). We explore bending the device to augment one-handed, open-air interactions (right).

Several usability issues occur with one-handed touch interactions, the main ones being the presence of unreachable touch targets, thumb screen occlusion, and constant change of grip, which sometimes lead to the need to use two hands, or to drop the phone [3]. While researchers have proposed new interaction to maximize thumb input [9,12,19,29], or the use of alternate sensors for input [18,21,22,27], the problem of one-handed interactions remains.

Deformable devices offer an opportunity to address some of these issues. Flexible displays promotes mobility [26], which leverages the comfortable use of smartphones in mobile environment. The deformability of flexible displays offers novel interaction techniques, such as bending a corner up or down which has been shown to be a feasible and effective input method for flexible handheld devices [10,13,16,20,24,25]. They can be particularly suited for continuous bipolar, as well as quick response actions [1].

In this paper, we explore the potential of deformable devices to address one-handed interaction issues with smartphones. We first set out to determine the use of common single-hand mobile interactions through an online survey. Then, we designed and evaluated one-handed deformable gestures that offer the potential for addressing the finger reach limitation on large smartphones. We identify the fastest and preferred gestures to propose the best gestures for single or repeated rapid actions, and discuss their impact on typical one-handed interactions problems.

RELATED WORK

To study one-handed deformable gestures for flexible smartphones, we explored two groups of prior research: deformable interactions on flexible devices, and one-handed interactions on rigid smartphones.

Deformable Interactions on Flexible Devices

Early works [2,20] explored the conceptual idea of bendable interactions and successfully proved these interactions to be viable. In most recent years, deformable interaction research has broadened across various areas, such as interaction techniques [7,16,23], applications [10,13,15,28] and the physical characteristics of flexible devices [6,11,14].

PaperPhone [13] was the first prototype to use an actual flexible electrophoretic E Ink display. Lahey et al. studied the use of bend gestures with common smartphone interactions such as navigating a contact list or browsing through a music player. The participants held the flexible prototype with their left hand, and used their right to interact with the right half of the prototype. The authors found that users preferred bend gestures that were conceptually simple and less physically demanding.

Kildal et al. [10] presented the first fully flexible prototype with the Kinetic device. They implemented two main interactions, bending and twisting the whole device, both performed by holding the landscape device with both hands. They propose a set of initial design guidelines, including that bend and twist deformations are more easily performed using two hands, especially for larger devices.

We found two prior works that proposed interactions that can be performed with a single hand. Gallant et al. [7] presented interaction techniques for foldable user interfaces. Among the techniques, two can be performed using only one hand: the scoop technique, which consists of holding the device on the bottom side and creating a crease with the thumb, and the squeeze technique, done by holding both sides of the device with one hand, and creating a concave or convex shape. Unfortunately, they do not propose any evaluation of those techniques. FlexView [5] examined z-axis navigation on a touch-enabled flexible mobile device. Their interaction language consisted of leafing and squeezing the device as well as using touch, the latter being performed using a single hand. The results showed squeezing to be faster than touch input in the pan-and-zoom task.

More recently, Ahmaniemi et al. [1] tried to answer the question "What is a device bend gesture really good for?". They evaluated gestures and use-case pairing for a landscape flexible device similar to the Kinetic. Their initial study identified the actions of zooming and list browsing to be best performed with device-deformation gestures, as opposed to map navigation, web browsing and horizontal sliders. They found that bend gestures are optimal for continuous bipolar parameters and when quick reactions are required, such as calendar alarms, calls, switching the device on/off, or switching applications on/off.

These prior works introduced deformable one- and two-handed gesture patterns, and evaluated them for a variety of tasks. However, little work exists in examining the details of one-handed usage of flexible handheld devices.

One-Handed Interactions on Rigid Devices

Due to the increase in device size of current smartphones, touch input often requires bimanual operation, one hand to hold the device and the other to perform gestures [13]. However, in many mobile environments, one-handed input is desired but often difficult to achieve given the ergonomics of unimanual operations [3,4,9,12,29]. Because of the limited reach of the thumb when the device is held with one hand, common problems with one-handed touch input on smartphones include unreachable targets and screen occlusion caused by the thumb, resulting in limited input capabilities with one hand without re-gripping. In response, researchers have proposed various strategies to address these problems such as maximizing thumb input, using pressure as an input or other sensors for interaction.

While there are a number of ways to hold a mobile device with one hand, the most practical one that limits usability issues is to place it in the palm of the hand with fingers on the sides, as illustrated in Figure 1 on the left [3]. To extend thumb interaction while using this grip, researchers have looked at how to maximize the use of the thumb input. Yu et al. [29] propose BezelSpace and CornerSpace, a tailored user interface for thumb interaction designed to access difficult targets. In the first design, the user swipes from the bezel without lifting the thumb and activates an extended cursor. The user then can manipulate the cursor to unreachable targets from within the thumb's reachable area. The second design involves swiping from the bezel and lifting the thumb. Once lifted, a four-way navigation button appears at that location, which allows users to select the four corners. Boring et al. [4] present Fat Thumb, which uses the thumb's contact size as a form of simulated pressure and integrate it as a means to pan and zoom. This interaction replaces the pinch gesture, which is difficult to execute with one hand.

Aside from touch input, the use of pressure sensors is also commonly found in prior works. GraspZoom [18] placed a force sensitive resistor on the back of the device to detect the pressure applied by touch input on the front. They apply this scheme to zooming and scrolling. Spelmezan et al. [22] placed pressure sensors on both sides of their SidePress prototype and offered it as an alternative input method to scrollbars, drag-and-flick or pinch-to-zoom. Their results suggest that users can precisely and efficiently control SidePress, and it is more efficient than the drag-and-flick gesture when scrolling large documents. Brewster et al. [27] conducted initial exploration in using the pressure inputs with the fingers on the sides of a device.

In addition to these methods, other interesting strategies include using different sensors and altering the physical movement of the device for interaction. Spelmezan et al.

[21] designed a power-up button on the smartphone. It is a physical button placed on the upper left side of the device and can detect pressure as well as proximity. This enables gesture interaction with one thumb without interacting with the touch display. In parallel, Holman et al. [8] also proposed measuring the pressure on the side of the phone to detect finger position.

These prior works suggest a clear call to order to investigate strategies to enable one-handed interactions in handheld devices. In this paper, we extend beyond current rigid devices and explore the possibilities of flexible devices using deformable interactions.

SURVEY ON ONE-HANDED USAGE PATTERNS

We conducted an online survey to investigate one-handed usage patterns on smartphones. Our goal was to identify user's preferred handedness for one-handed tasks in smartphones, where they find themselves most often having to perform one-handed tasks (e.g. walking, sitting), and which tasks are typically performed with a single hand. With this survey, we aimed to make an informed decision about our users for the experiment to follow.

Our survey was administered online during a 2 week period. We used social media to find participants. We drew two $10 gift cards among the participants.

Participants

158 participants (65 females) completed our questionnaire, with an average age of 26 years fold (18-61 range). Most participants reported being right handed (87.34%), while the rest was split between left handed (6.96%) or ambidextrous (5.70%).

The top 10 phone models possessed by participants were the Samsung Galaxy S2 and S3, the iPhones 4, 4S, 5 and 5S, the Google Nexus 4 and 5, the HTC One and the Blackberry Bold. The two most popular models are the iPhone 4S (12.67%) and the Galaxy S3 (11.39%).

Types of One-handed Interactions

The majority of participants (72.15%) preferred to use their right hand when performing one-handed tasks on their phones. The rest were divided between using their left hand (8.86%), using either hand with no preference (8.23%), or using both hands equally (10.76%). When reclassified using handedness, these values hold true: 70.89% of participants preferred using their dominant hand for one-handed interactions, with 10.13% using their non-dominant hand.

Many participants explained that they adapted their device usage to the phone's UI. One participant found that "most UI for applications cater to the thumb being on the right side of the screen". Another participant (left handed, but uses their right hand for one-handed tasks) claims that "software is designed for right handed people". Participants also mentioned the placement of icons and buttons on a device, which guide a user to operate their phone with a certain hand (typically the right). Finally, a right handed participant mentioned choosing to use his left hand to operate their phone to leave their dominant hand free for other things if need be.

Locations of One-handed Interactions

Our survey results also show that the participants use their smartphones with one hand in a variety of scenarios: 48.10% of participants use them while walking, 43.04% while standing, 32.38% while sitting, 24.68% while resting the smartphone on a surface (both arms on a table), and 31.65% without any preference.

Of the 105 participants that provided an explanation for where they use one handed interactions, 8.57% claim to primarily use their phones with one hand and will only use two when necessary. For users who prefer to only use one hand, some claimed that "two hands has too much screen occlusion", it is "not comfortable", and that "the actions required to operate the phone usually requires only one hand." Other users resort to using their phones with one hand when they are multitasking and using the other for something else, with one user specifying that they "only use two hands if [they] need stability or for certain gestures such as pinching" or "to type". 11.43% of participants will use one hand as a precautionary measure. Interestingly, two third of these users will not use their devices with one hand as they fear dropping their phones, while the other third will use their devices with one hand for their own safety – in case they trip, for example. One participant who uses her phone with one hand while walking says she "can concentrate on maintaining [her] balance with the other hand whilst walking", another said if she "falls, trips or slides on ice, [she] wants to be able to break [her] fall".

On the contrary, 7.62% of users explicitly expressed primarily using two hands when operating their phones and will only use one when necessary, such as for "notification checking". Some participants said they use two hands because of the large size of their devices. One user claimed they "rarely use [their] phone in one hand since it's usually too large to perform tasks and [they] need both hands; one to hold [their] phone and the other to perform a task".

Tasks for One-handed Interactions

Finally, we inquired about common high level one-handed tasks in smartphones. The tasks most commonly performed with one hand are those which involve a single tap or a short swipe on the screen: the most popular tasks are unlocking the phone (81.65%), selecting an app (77.85%), scrolling through websites (75.95%), and viewing pictures (73.42%). Other common tasks include using the dial pad (60.76%) and finding a contact name (62.03%).

There is a drop in the proportion of users who perform tasks one handed when the task requires a variety of rapid gestures, or gestures requiring more than one finger. Participants do not report often texting with one hand (34.18%), likely attributed to the lack of speed. Zooming on a map is not popular with one hand (17.09%), since two fingers are

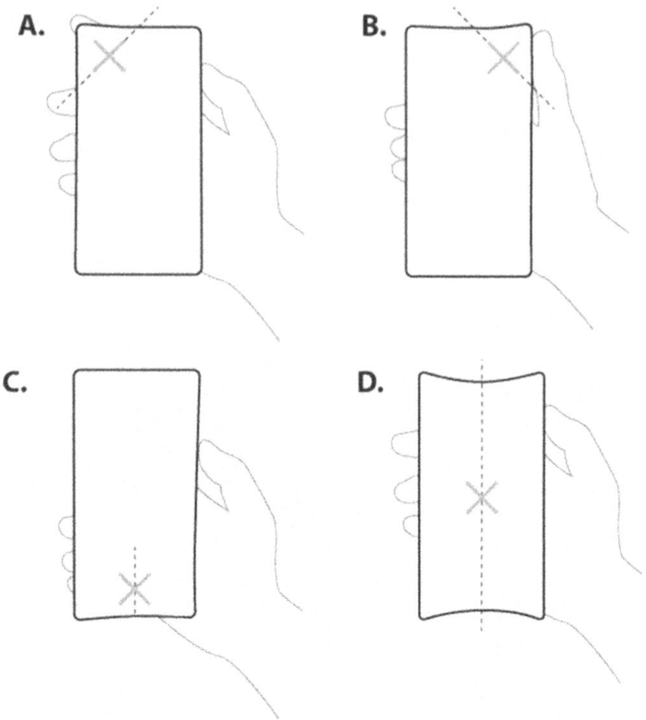

Figure 2. One-handed deformable gestures locations, with the right hand, performed up: A) top left corner, B) top right corner, C) lower bottom, and D) center.

required to perform a pinching gesture, which is physically awkward to do using one hand while holding the device with that hand. Finally, the task of panning a map is only performed with one hand by 31.01% of users. While this might be surprising given its similarity to the gesture performed when scrolling through websites, its low use is probably due to the combination of map tasks, pan and zoom, for which the latter requires two fingers.

Limitations

The social networks of researchers who disseminated the survey invitation include contacts living outside of Canada, and we assume that a proportion of those participated. However, without geographical data from participants, we do not know the exact composition of the participants.

We also acknowledge that self-reported common tasks may not be an accurate reflection of actual tasks. Many common operations are sub-tasks, and users may not consciously notice them, which could affect their reporting. Still, we believe this has minimal impact, since our high level survey produced useful information that will influence our gesture and experiment designs.

Summary of Results

This survey provides us with background information on one-handed gestures, which we will use to guide the design of our one-handed bend gesture experiment.

The large majority of users use their right hand to hold and interact with their rigid smartphone with a single hand, indicating that our bend gestures must be able to be performed with the right hand. However, a quarter of participants used their left hand exclusively or interchangeably. This indicates that a non-negligible proportion of the population could still benefit from left-handed bend gestures.

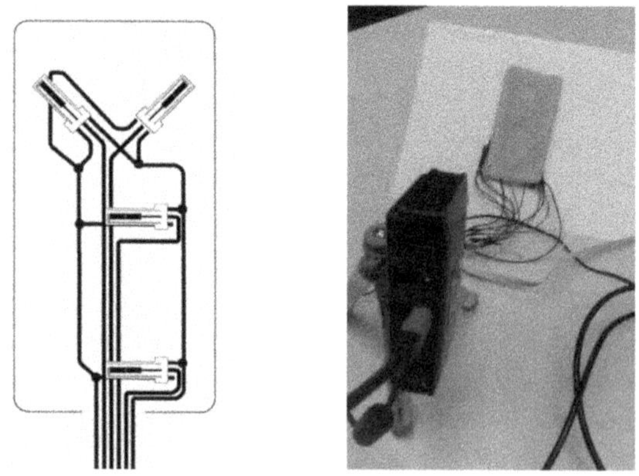

Figure 3: Our flexible circuit contains four bi-directional sensors (left), and the experimental setup (right).

One-handed usage of smartphones is more common in mobile scenarios (i.e., walking, standing) than in relatively more stationary situations. The one-handed gestures are typically single, unique touch events, or identical events that are repeated quickly. This information will help us design and conduct our experiment.

ONE-HANDED DEFORMABLE GESTURES

Prior to the experiment, we gathered a small group of expert HCI researchers to generate a set of possible gestures given a flexible mockup prototype using one hand. Our mockup prototype was made of silicone, and approximated the size of current large smartphones. From all the collected gestures, we selected a subset to evaluate by considering ergonomic constrains, hand sizes and dexterity. For instance, gestures that were only possible for users with very large hands were discarded. We also selected single gestures, i.e. bending one part of the display at once, as complex, or multi gestures required too much dexterity for most users.

The selected gestures are performed in four locations (top-left corner, top-right corner, central bend along the vertical axis, and lower bottom bend along the vertical axis) and in both directions (up and down, which can be referred to as concave and convex, respectively) for a total of eight gestures (Figure 2). To keep a consistent mental model across location, the direction is based on the movement exhibited by the sides of the device. This classification by location and direction is based on the two most popular bend characteristics in prior work [13,24].

ONE-HANDED DEFORMABLE PROTOTYPE

We fabricated a flexible prototype using the dimensions of a representative popular phone, the Samsung Galaxy S3. Our prototype measured 4 mm x 70 mm x 136 mm. We constructed the prototype out of silicone, and augmented it with four Flexpoint 1" bidirectional bend sensors to detect the eight gestures (Figure 3). We connected the prototype to an Arduino microcontroller, and developed an application that recognizes our 8 pre-defined deformable gestures from the sensor's raw data and provides users with instructions and visual feedback about their interactions. We used a Pico projector to create an interactive display on the prototype.

We followed a similar process as the one outlined by Lo and Girouard [17]. Prior the experiments, we tested mock prototypes made out of different material hardness and selected a flexibility that was most suitable for one-handed deformation. The resulting prototype is 60A shore hardness. A two-part mold was machined to cast the silicone mold. The flexible circuit was placed in the middle of the molds and silicone was cast on both sides. This process created a uniform, comfortable prototype.

EXPERIMENT FOR ONE-HANDED BEND GESTURES

We designed a study to investigate the performance of the 8 one-handed deformable gestures. Specifically, we were interested in learning about how gestures are performed with each hand, which gestures are faster, and which are more comfortable, and finally whether the gestures are appropriate in varying scenarios. We evaluated the effect of handedness on the gestures, as both hands are used for one-handed mobile use by a significant proportion of the population, as shown in the survey.

We chose to mimic mobile scenarios preferred by users for one-handed interactions. Participants were in sitting condition to minimize overall fatigue, but they were required to hold the flexible smartphone prototype in the air while performing the gestures, without their arms or elbows resting on the table.

Task

We developed two tasks for participants: the single event task, and the repeated event task. Figure 4 illustrates the visual feedback provided for each event.

The **single event** is designed to determine which gestures are the quickest to perform. These gestures would be useful for short interactions, such as notification dismissal, selection, answering a phone call. To accomplish a single event task, participants performed the correct bend gesture once.

The **repeated event** illustrates scenarios where one handed gestures are repeated a number of times, such as when browsing photos, navigating a music library, or scrolling a webpage. In the repeated event task, participants were required to perform the correct bend gesture repeatedly nine times. Participants received a visual feedback for each successful repetition.

Study Design

To evaluate the gestures, we designed 2x2x4x2 factorial repeated measures within-subject design, with the factors: *hand* (left, right), *task* (single event, repeated event), *gesture location* (top-left corner, top-right corner, central squeeze, and bottom squeeze) and *gesture direction* (up, down). We conducted three trials for each condition in the

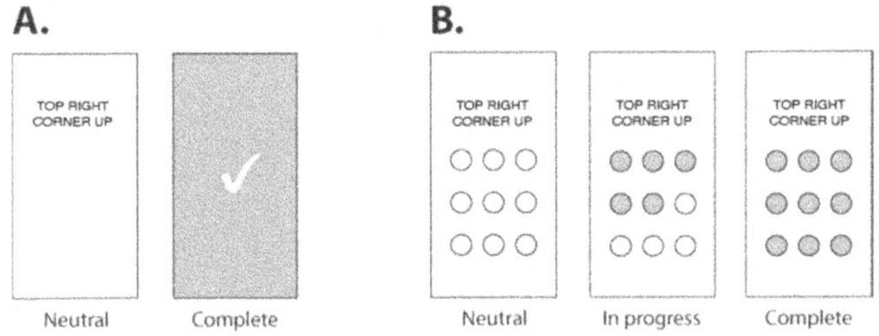

Figure 4. Visual feedback for single event task (A), and repeated event task (B)

single event. We counterbalanced by hand and task, and randomized by gesture.

We measured the duration of each gesture and the number of errors. The duration of a gesture is measured from the time the gesture name appears on the screen to the time the gesture is correctly performed and recognized by the system, which may include time to change grip. Participants rated their level of preference ("I like performing this gesture") and comfort ("I find this gesture comfortable to perform") on a 5-point Likert scale, where 1 is strongly disagree and 5 is strongly agree.

The experiment started with a training period, where participants could practice every gesture. They received a simple feedback that indicated which gesture was activated: e.g., the top left corner turned blue when the top left gesture was performed up, and it turned orange when it was performed down. Participants told the experimenter when they were comfortable with the gestures and were ready to proceed.

Participants

18 participants (10 males) completed our study (mean age of 28.8 years old). Two had previously participated in a flexible display study. 15 participants were right handed, and an equal number (though a different subset) reported using their right hand when handling their mobile device one-handed. This followed the same proportion of users found in the survey. Participants were given a $10 gift card as compensation.

Results

Single Event

We aggregated the results of the three trials and we ran a 3-way within-subject repeated measured ANOVA using the factors *hand*, *gesture location*, and *gesture direction* on the duration and error.

We found a significant effect of gesture location ($F_{3,51}$ = 9.33, $p < 0.001$, $\eta^2 = 0.35$) and gesture direction ($F_{1,17}$ = 18.39, $p < 0.001$, $\eta^2 = 0.52$) on duration. Pair-wise post-hoc comparisons found the central squeeze to be significantly faster than all other gesture locations (center: M = 4425.58 ms; top right: M = 5600.03 ms; top left: M = 5857.37 ms; bottom: M = 6325.51 ms). Gestures up were significantly faster (M = 4958.02 ms) than gestures down (M = 6146.02 ms). All pair-wise comparisons performed are Bonferroni corrected ($p < 0.05$).

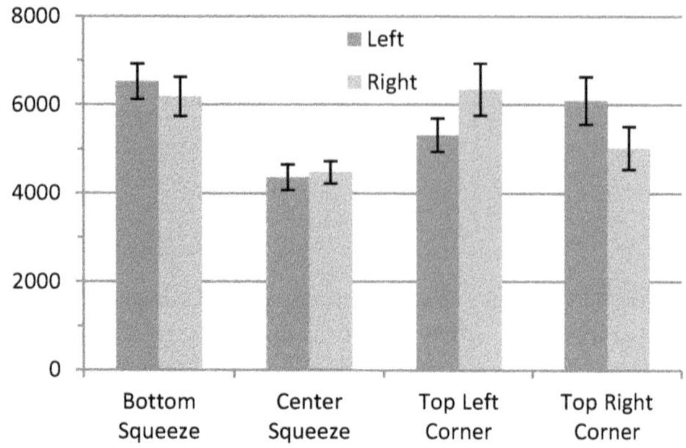

Figure 5. Duration (in ms) for the 4 locations by hand, for the single event task. Error bars show standard error.

We also observe a significant interaction of hand and gesture location on duration ($F_{3,51} = 3.30$, $p = 0.046$, $\eta^2 = 0.16$), as illustrated in Figure 5. Pair-wise post-hoc comparisons identified that in the left hand, the central squeeze location is significantly different from the bottom squeeze location as well as from the top right location. In the right hand, the central squeeze location is significantly different from the bottom squeeze and the top left location.

The interaction of location and direction on duration is also significant ($F_{3,51}$=5.06, $p = 0.006$, $\eta^2 = 0.23$). Figure 6 displays the duration this interaction. Pair-wise post-hoc comparisons found that the bottom location and the top right location are significantly different between directions.

Finally, we found 3-way significant interaction of hand, location and direction on number of errors ($F_{3,51}$=4.40, $p = 0.010$, $\eta^2 = 0.04$). The top-right down gesture with the left hand obtained the highest number of error (M = 0.99, SD = 0.30), followed by the top-left down gesture with the right hand (M = 0.70, SD = 0.21). This is the only significant factor or interaction with the number of errors.

For every error that occurred, the system recorded the ges-

Table 1. Average number of errors by location and direction. Cell shading indicates importance.

Gestures asked		Top Left Corner D	Top Left Corner U	Top Right Corner D	Top Right Corner U	Center Squeeze D	Center Squeeze U	Bottom Squeeze D	Bottom Squeeze U
Top Left Corner	D	0.00	0.11	0.10	0.01	0.17	0.12	0.02	0.00
	U	0.03	0.00	0.01	0.11	0.01	0.14	0.00	0.10
Top Right Corner	D	0.00	0.04	0.00	0.04	0.43	0.09	0.00	0.01
	U	0.00	0.07	0.00	0.00	0.00	0.25	0.00	0.00
Center Squeeze	D	0.01	0.00	0.04	0.00	0.00	0.02	0.07	0.03
	U	0.00	0.00	0.00	0.00	0.04	0.00	0.00	0.30
Bottom Squeeze	D	0.00	0.01	0.00	0.00	0.16	0.01	0.00	0.27
	U	0.00	0.00	0.00	0.00	0.03	0.07	0.07	0.00

(Column headings: Gestures recorded.)

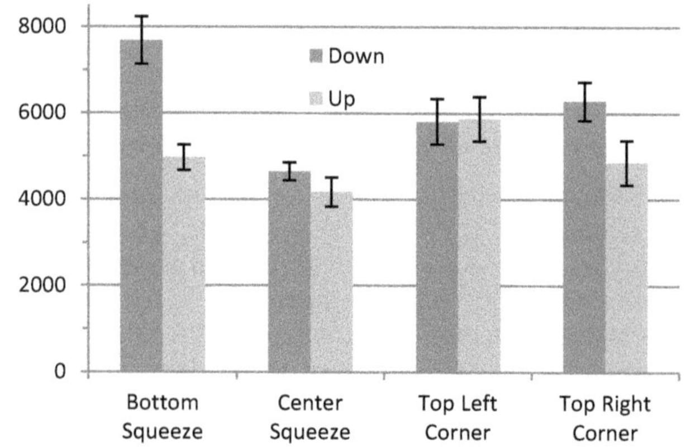

Figure 6. Duration (in ms) for the 4 location, by direction, for the single event task. Error bars show standard error.

ture that was wrongfully produced. Table 1 displays the number of each type of wrong gesture produced for every gesture asked. The table does not differentiate between the type of error, mainly between participants who made a mistake and choose to produce the wrong gesture (participant error), and between situations where the wrong sensor is activated because the gesture was not performed correctly (prototype error). However, given that our sensors only produce a single value, which we use to determine their direction, any error in direction only must be participant error. An example of this situation occurs, if the gesture asked is a top left corner down and the recorded gesture is a top left gesture up (12 errors total of this nature in Table 1).

Repeated Event

In analysing the gestures from the repeated event, we noticed that the first repetition of this event followed closely the values of the gestures in the single event, but that repetitions 2 to 9 did not: the single event gestures averaged 6285.47 ms on the first trial, and the repeated event gestures averaged 6696.51 ms on the first repetition, while the other 8 reps averaged 1789.49 ms. This result is reasonable, since the first repetition is essentially the same task as the single event task. Given this pattern, we chose to only analyse repetitions 2 to 9.

We aggregated the results of the 8 repetitions, and ran a 3-way within-subject repeated measured ANOVA using the factors *hand*, *gesture location*, and *gesture direction* on the duration and number of errors. We found no significant factor or interaction in this analysis, indicating that the variables hand, gesture location nor gesture direction contributed to the variability in the duration or the number of errors.

Questionnaires

We performed Friedman tests on the questionnaire data with the factors *task*, *hand*, *gesture location* and *gesture direction*. For the preference question, we found significance for the factors event ($\chi^2 = 14.67$, $p < 0.001$), location ($\chi^2 = 62.53$, $p < 0.001$), and direction ($\chi^2 = 158.06$, $p < 0.001$). The repeated event yielded stronger agreement (M = 3.29, SD = 1.25) than the single event (M = 3.15, SD = 1.33). The bottom location had the lowest preference (M =

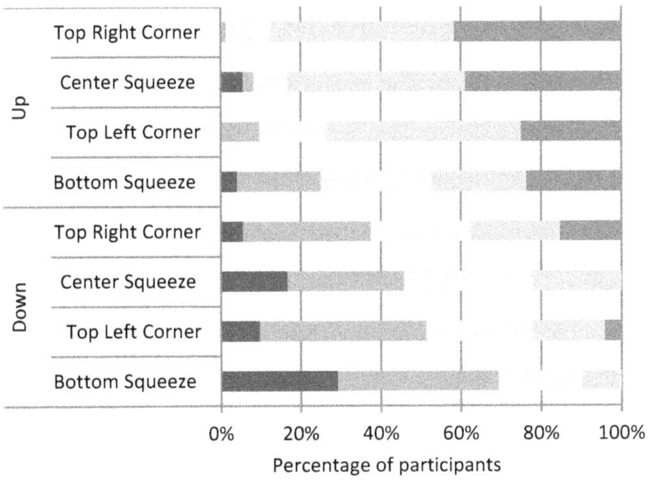

Figure 7. Distribution of Likert scale responses for the question on physical comfort "I find this gesture comfortable to perform", ordered by the level of agreement.

2.70, SD = 1.33), followed by the top left (M = 3.24, SD = 1.21), the central (M = 3.37, SD = 1.31) and the top right location (M = 3.57, SD = 1.18). Finally, the up direction obtained stronger agreement (M = 3.83, SD = 1.10) than the down direction (M = 2.60, SD = 1.19).

The results are almost identical for the physical comfort question, with the factors location ($\chi^2 = 65.63$, $p < 0.001$) and direction ($\chi^2 = 172.27$, $p < 0.001$) being significant. The bottom location is least comfortable (M = 2.76, SD = 1.26), followed by the top left (M = 3.27, SD = 1.14), the center (M = 3.34, SD = 1.27) and the top right location (M = 3.69, SD = 1.13). The up direction is also more comfortable (M = 3.92, SD = 1.02) than the down direction (M = 2.61, SD = 1.10). Figure 7 shows the distribution of the responses for the physical comfort question, which is representative of the data of both questions.

Observations

Throughout the experiment, we observed the interactions the participants had with the prototype and the gestures. Figure 8 illustrates some of the grips and gestures that participants performed.

While users had no trouble differentiating the corner gestures from each other (though some confused left and right on occasion) and from the center and bottom squeezes, participants seemed to have trouble separating the center and bottom squeezes from each other, occasionally persisting in spite of feedback indicating an error. In addition, these interactions sometimes resulted in a false activation of another (wrong) sensor. For instance, very large bottom bends sometimes resulted in activations of the center sensor.

The directionality of the gestures (up/down) can be problematic for device-spanning interactions (center and bottom gestures), depending on whether the participant perceived

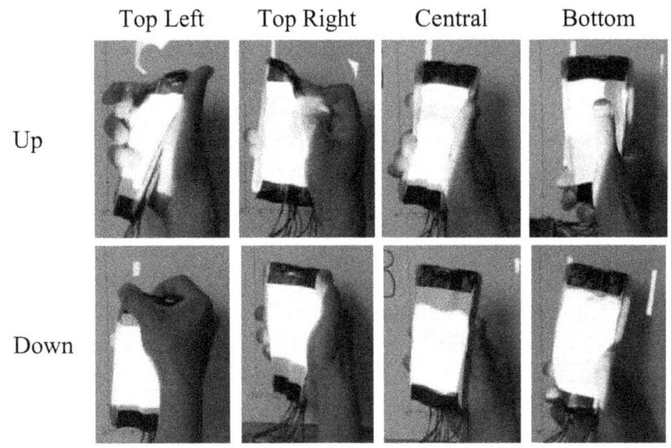

Figure 8. Examples of the gestures performed by our participants.

the up gesture as moving the center or the sides of the prototype towards them. Some users understood pushing the sides of the device upwards to constitute up (creating a concave shape), and moving the sides in the opposite direction to mean down (convex shape), while others used the center of the device as their reference point, effectively reversing the interaction in their mental model. Feedback from the device allowed users to correct erroneous gestures, but they re-occurred frequently. Participants seemed evenly split on whether they found our assignment to align with their understanding of the device. Our directionality labelling was based on prior work [1,13], but we do acknowledge that it may be somewhat arbitrary.

The degree of fine motor control possible when interacting with the device with one hand also influenced the variety of possible interactions. Many participants had difficulty activating the corner opposite their thumb (e.g. the right corner while holding with the left hand) and were forced to change their grip to interact with this corner, only to return to their original grip afterwards.

Users exhibited a variety of grips when trying to interact with certain gestures: some occluded the screen significantly (e.g. the top left down gesture in Figure 8), some resulting in an unstable hold during the change of grip; some users dropped the device or some activated different sensors. Many users voiced displeasure and frustration with having to change grip, and voiced a preference for maintaining the same grip for all interactions. We observed that many users adapted to re-gripping by bracing the prototype against the desk to stabilize the prototype during re-gripping - an option that would not always be available in practical applications.

Hand size influenced how the device was gripped, and the ability to reach corners (very small hands) or to control how they bent corners (very large hands). Users with large hands were able to adopt a pinching grip - activating the device using their index finger and thumb instead of using their whole hand. Almost all participants used their pointer finger to put pressure on the back of the device to achieve a squeeze in the downward direction. To achieve the bottom squeeze gestures, almost all users had to change their grip on the device, moving their hand downwards on the device. They then changed their grip again to perform the following gesture (unless it was a bottom squeeze gesture again).

DISCUSSION

Our investigation with the one-handed deformable prototype produced useful insight about how participants performed various gestures. We found the central squeeze gesture to be the fastest of the four locations in the single event task. It is also one of the two preferred gesture. It is easy to perform, and does not require a really specific grip, which means it can be done quickly in a variety of hold scenarios. It gathered a high level of agreement for comfort. We recommend to associate quick and important actions with this central gesture.

Second in speed are the two top locations. It is important to note that the two top location gestures are performed differently by each hand: with the left hand, the top-left gesture is done using the thumb finger, but it is done using the index finger when performed with the right hand. In our analysis, we kept the grouping by location, and not by which finger performed the gesture, so the interface would be consistent no matter which hand is used, similarly to current touch interfaces. For instance, dismissing a notification would be done using a top right corner bend up, no matter whether it would be performed using the left or right hand. Yet, our post-hoc analysis revealed a difference in performance through the interaction of hand and location. For the top locations, the gesture performed with the thumb (illustrated in Figure 2B) is faster than the one performed with the index (Figure 2A). This result is also consistent with the questionnaire data as well as our observations. Given that most users are likely to use their right hand to perform the one-handed gesture based on our survey results, we recommend placing important actions in the top right location, as they could be accomplished in a similar speed range as with the central squeeze.

The interaction of hand and gesture location leads us to wonder about whether we should create interfaces that keep constant the set of actions, or the gestures performed. We can easily imagine a smartphone that could detect the hand that is holding it, and adjusts the expected gesture accordingly. It would bank on muscle memory transferability among hands, yet might confuse the user by lack of coherence. A follow up study would clarify this.

In general, the bottom gestures did not obtain particularly high notes from the preference data, mainly due to the fact that participants had to change their grip to accomplish this gesture. We also notice that a large number of errors with the squeezing gestures come from them being mistaken: a bottom gesture recognized as a central gesture (28 errors), and central gesture being recognized as a bottom gesture (41 errors). We have confidence that the inability for users to differentiate the squeezes relates more to their inability to deform the device correctly with one hand than to a sensor issue. We noticed that it is difficult for users to perform a bottom squeeze without also squeezing the center of the device. Given that the bottom squeeze was fast in the down direction, we propose two solutions. An improved sensor placement and recognition algorithm may better recognize the two gestures distinctively, eliminating some error cases. Alternatively, we suggest the merge of the two gestures: a bottom or a central squeeze would produce the same result in the latter solution.

The duration data and the questionnaires point to the fact that up gestures are superior to down gestures: they are faster, and they are more liked. This result is consistent with prior work [13,24]. In this case, it is due to the fact that the hand is placed behind the device, so the user has to simply push to activate. Upwards gestures required less re-gripping, which is preferred by users. Re-gripping requires a higher focus of attention, and sometimes a second hand, both of which lead to a higher cost of execution [3].

An interesting result comes from the lack of significance for the factor hand in both the duration and questionnaire data. While this does not indicate a lack of difference between the hands, it does indicate that the two hands offer somewhat of an equivalent experience performing single handed bend gestures. This means that we can offer left handed interactions at almost no loss of performance, which might benefit a quarter of the user population, based on the number of participants who reported using the left hand, both or either hands to currently perform one handed interactions with their smartphone. This provides deformable devices a considerable advantage over rigid, touch-only devices.

The repeated event yielded no significant results. In this context, this indicates that once users position their hand correctly, they can perform any gesture repeatedly at approximately the same speed. This indicates that designers can use other criteria to select the gesture to be used to scroll a website or browse pictures, since individual gestures do not matter for speed. However, users performed repeated actions at a much faster pace than new actions (3.6 times faster). This suggests that designers should keep the same gesture for subsequent actions of the same nature, whether it being associated to the same action (changing page on an eBook reader), or with different actions that should be performed consecutively (opening the camera application and taking a picture).

Occlusion is an important issue with thumb interaction, as the thumb can restricts the user from viewing the screen, missing specific targets or important information. While we can notice occlusion in the top-left gesture in Figure 8, this mostly occurred with the top gesture location located under the index, for down gestures (the top-left down gesture with the right hand, and the top-right down gesture with the left hand). As these gestures did not obtained a stronger performance or preference from the participants, we do not believe occlusion to be a main issue with one-handed bend gestures as it can be for one-handed touch gestures. In addition, better, more sen-

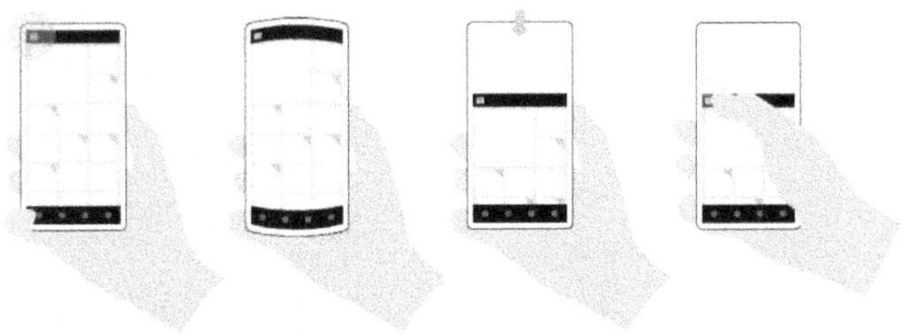

Figure 9. A squeeze gesture could pan down the entire GUI to access an area otherwise unreachable without re-gripping the device, in this case an element of the top menu bar.

sitive sensors and gesture recognition algorithms might alleviate this issue further.

Potential Application

To illustrate our results, we propose a potential application of the deformable gestures that will ease the shortcoming of reachability of current touch phones with our deformable gestures. We make use of the suggestion to merge the central and bottom squeeze gesture, and create a single squeeze gesture, with up and down directions.

This squeeze gesture up seem suited for triggering a down pan motion of the entire GUI so that all its top active elements are reachable without the need to overextend one's finger of change hand posture (Figure 9). When the user cannot reach a top left button with his finger in a one-handed situation, he could simply squeeze up the device to scroll the GUI down until he can reach it. He would then be able to interact with the GUI at the right height, and squeeze again to have the GUI automatically scroll back up. With this potential application, the user has now performed an interaction that is currently difficult to perform on current handheld devices without having to change his grip.

Limitations

We acknowledge the possibility that bends might mistrigger touch operations when offered conjointly. However, our goal with this work was not to integrate the two input modalities in a functional device, though this would be an interesting future work. Instead, we focused on simple and fast tasks such as unlocking or answering the phone, where typically there are no other commands available, so the chance of accidental touches is low. Also, while the presence of a touch screen might have changed users grip slightly, we believe that general positioning would be similar, so our results should hold.

Our experimental design had a higher ratio of top to bottom gesture, based on prior work [e.g. 13,24] as well as ergonomic constraints: it is simply hard to perform precise and different gestures on the bottom. However, our questionnaires asked about gestures individually, to minimize this experimental bias.

Among the limitations of our device, we have already pointed to the fact that some gestures generated a false positive when a very large bend was produced, such as a top right corner registering a central gesture. A better gesture recognition algorithm should take care of this issue. A confound to this finding was a warping of the prototype through the study, which potentially made bends in the down direction more difficult. The lack of interactive display on the prototype may have affected the experience. However, to minimize this issue, we did not project any information that required a detailed placement, everything was located on the center of the display. Finally, while we tried to produce a flexible printed circuit, it was not strong enough to withstand experimentation, and we create a prototype with wires. This may have influenced the gesture performance, but we expect that the effect would have been the same over every gesture.

CONCLUSION

This paper explored one-handed deformable interactions for flexible smartphones. First, we inquired about current one-handed interactions in rigid cellphones through an online survey. Most of our 158 participants used their cellphone one-handed using their right hand, in context of mobile scenarios, to do single, short tasks. We then identified 8 deformable gestures, based on four locations (top left corner, top right corner, squeezing the central location vertically, or squeezing the bottom location vertically), and two directions (up and down). Finally, we ran an experiment to evaluate those 8 gestures performed with each hand, in the context of single tasks and repeated tasks.

Our results show promise for one handed gestures, and warrant further exploration. The two best gestures were the top right up and the center squeeze up, which were faster, preferred, and more comfortable than the rest. We found no hand preference, which indicates that the gestures could be implemented to fit the needs of a wider range of the population, instead of favoring right-handers. We noticed that occlusion, one of touch's weaknesses, is not a problem for deformable gestures. While the experiment did not explicitly measure changes in hand posture and grips, we observed that almost all participants had to re-grip to perform certain gestures. Well-designed bend gestures would likely minimize the overall need for repositioning one's hand(s) on the device. Hence, we believe that one-handed deformable gestures are an interesting, complementary interaction to touch, as they can alleviate some of one-handed touch's issues.

In addition to exploring more complex gestures and improving on the gesture recognition algorithm, the main future work for one-handed bend gestures concerns the implementation of the gestures with real applications. For instance, it would be worth exploring them in the context of applications, such as answering a phone call, browsing an article, dismissing notifications. An insitu evaluation of the gestures would also provide important information concerning their use.

ACKNOWLEGMENTS

We thank Taryn Laurendeau for her analysis of the survey data. This work was supported and funded by the National Sciences and Engineering Research Council of Canada through an Engage grant (453812/2013) and a Discovery grant (402494/2011).

REFERENCES

1. Ahmaniemi, T., Kildal, J., and Haveri, M. What is a device bend gesture really good for? *Proc. CHI*, (2014), 3503–3512.
2. Balakrishnan, R. and Fitzmaurice, G. Exploring interactive curve and surface manipulation using a bend and twist sensitive input strip. *Proc. Interactive 3D graphics*, (1999), 111–119.
3. Bergstrom-Lehtovirta, J. and Oulasvirta, A. Modeling the functional area of the thumb on mobile touchscreen surfaces. *Proc. CHI*, (2014), 1991–2000.
4. Boring, S., Ledo, D., Chen, X.A., Marquardt, N., Tang, A., and Greenberg, S. The Fat Thumb: Using the Thumb's Contact Size for Single-Handed Mobile Interaction. *Proc. MobileHCI*, (2012), 39–48.
5. Burstyn, J. FlexView: An Evaluation of Depth Navigation on Deformable Mobile Devices. *Proc. TEI*, (2012), 193–200.
6. Dijkstra, R., Perez, C., and Vertegaal, R. Evaluating effects of structural holds on pointing and dragging performance with flexible displays. *Proc. CHI*, (2011), 1293–1302.
7. Gallant, D., Seniuk, A., and Vertegaal, R. Towards more paper-like input: flexible input devices for foldable interaction styles. *Proc. UIST*, (2008), 283–286.
8. Holman, D., Hollatz, A., Banerjee, A., and Vertegaal, R. Unifone: Designing for auxiliary finger input in one-handed mobile interactions. *Proc. TEI*, (2013), 177–184.
9. Karlson, A. and Bederson, B. ThumbSpace: Generalized One-handed Input for Touchscreen-based Mobile Devices. *Proc. INTERACT*, (2007), 324–338.
10. Kildal, J., Paasovaara, S., and Aaltonen, V. Kinetic Device : Designing Interactions with a Deformable Mobile Interface. *Proc. CHI EA*, (2012), 1871–1876.
11. Kildal, J. Interacting with deformable user interfaces: effect of material stiffness and type of deformation gesture. *Haptic and Audio Interaction Design*, (2012), 71–80.
12. Kim, S., Yu, J., and Lee, G. Interaction Techniques for Unreachable Objects on the Touchscreen. *Proc. OzCHI*, (2012), 295–298.
13. Lahey, B., Girouard, A., Burleson, W., and Vertegaal, R. PaperPhone: Understanding the Use of Bend Gestures in Mobile Devices with Flexible Electronic Paper Displays. *Proc. CHI*, (2011), 1303–1312.
14. Lee, S., Lim, Y., and Lee, K.-P. Exploring the effects of size on deformable user interfaces. *Proc. CHI*, (2012), 89.
15. Lee, S., Maeng, S., Kim, D., Lee, K., and Lee, W. FlexRemote: Exploring the effectiveness of deformable user interface as an input device for TV. *Proc. HCII*, (2011), 62–65.
16. Lee, S.-S., Kim, S., Jin, B., et al. How Users Manipulate Deformable Displays as Input Devices. *Proc. CHI*, (2010), 1647.
17. Lo, J. and Girouard, A. Fabricating Bendy: Design and Development of Deformable Prototypes. *IEEE Pervasive Special Issue on Fabrication and Printing 13*, 3 (2014), 40–46.
18. Miyaki, T. and Rekimoto, J. GraspZoom: zooming and scrolling control model for single-handed mobile interaction. *Proc. MobileHCI*, (2009).
19. Roudaut, A. and Huot, S. TapTap and MagStick : Improving One-Handed Target Acquisition on Small Touch-screens. *Proc. AVI*, (2008), 146–153.
20. Schwesig, C., Poupyrev, I., and Mori, E. Gummi: A Bendable Computer. *Proc. CHI*, (2004), 263–270.
21. Spelmezan, D., Appert, C., Chapuis, O., and Pietriga, E. Controlling widgets with one power-up button. *Proc. UIST*, (2013), 71–74.
22. Spelmezan, D., Appert, C., Chapuis, O., and Pietriga, E. Side pressure for bidirectional navigation on small devices. *Proc. MobileHCI*, (2013), 11–20.
23. Steimle, J., Jordt, A., and Maes, P. Flexpad : Highly Flexible Bending Interactions for Projected Handheld Displays. *Proc. CHI*, (2013).
24. Warren, K., Lo, J., Vadgama, V., and Girouard, A. Bending the Rules: Bend Gesture Classification for Flexible Displays. *Proc. CHI*, (2013).
25. Watanabe, J., Mochizuki, A., and Horry, Y. Bookisheet: Bendable Device for Browsing Content Using the Metaphor of Leafing Through the Pages. *Proc. UbiComp*, (2008), 360–369.
26. Wightman, D., Ginn, T., and Vertegaal, R. BendFlip: Examining Input Techniques for Electronic Book Readers with Flexible Form Factors. *Proc. INTERACT*, (2011), 117–133.
27. Wilson, G., Brewster, S., and Halvey, M. Towards utilising one-handed multi-digit pressure input. *Proc. CHI EA*, (2013), 1317–1322.
28. Ye, Z. and Khalid, H. Cobra: Flexible Displays for Mobile Gaming Scenarios. *Proc. CHI EA*, (2010), 4363–4367.
29. Yu, N.-H., Huang, D.-Y., Hsu, J.-J., and Hung, Y.-P. Rapid Selection of Hard-to-Access Targets by Thumb on Mobile Touch-Screens. *Proc. MobileHCI*, (2013), 400.

Grip Change as an Information Side Channel for Mobile Touch Interaction

Matei Negulescu, Joanna McGrenere
Department of Computer Science, University of British Columbia
{mnegules, joanna}@cs.ubc.ca

ABSTRACT
In order to reach targets with one hand on common large mobile touch displays, users tilt and shift the device in their hand. In this work, we use this grip change as a continuous information stream for detecting where the user will touch while their finger is still en-route. We refer to this as in the air prediction. We show that grip change detected using standard mobile motion sensors produces similar in the air touch point predictions to techniques that use auxiliary sensor arrays, even in varying physical scenarios such as interacting in a moving vehicle. Finally, our model that combines grip change and the resulting touch point predicted where users *intended* to land, lowering error rates by 41%.

Author Keywords
Adaptive interface; mobile device; predictive model; touch; grip; display size

ACM Classification Keywords
H.5.2. User Interfaces: Input devices and strategies

INTRODUCTION
With the growing popularity of mobile devices, researchers have searched for ways of improving input accuracy on touch displays. Of note, researchers have identified a number of factors that affect touch patterns in systematic ways: hand posture used to touch a target (e.g., a one-handed posture that uses the dominant thumb rather than two thumbs to type) [1,4]; the location of the target on the screen [6]; physical activity, such as walking [3] versus sitting at a desk; and even whether or not users are interacting while carrying items in the other hand [8]. These are all significant factors that impact touch patterns and therefore touch accuracy on mobile devices. Adaptive systems take advantage of systematic patterns of user touch interaction under these conditions to adjust where the user touched to where they *intended* to land. For example, Yin et al. [10] and Goel et al. [4,5] showed improved touch accuracy using adaptive soft keyboards that take into consideration systematic offsets caused by hand posture and individual differences.

CHI 2015, April 18 - 23 2015, Seoul, Republic of Korea

ACM978-1-4503-3145-6/15/04…$15.00
http://dx.doi.org/10.1145/2702123.2702185

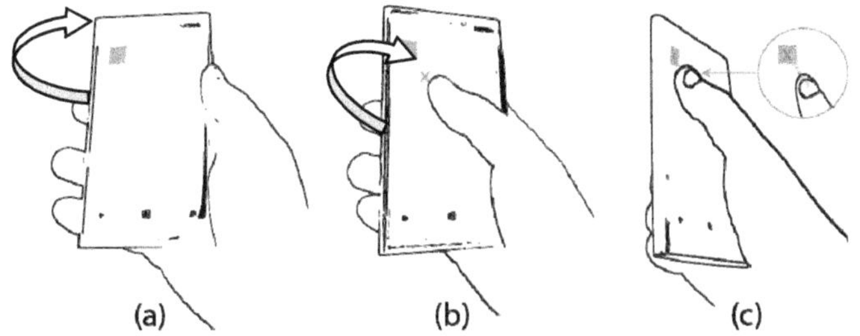

Figure 1. Grip change as the user reaches for the target (blue square): (a) device lays flat in palm, then (b) device is tilted towards the thumb by the other fingers enabling in the air prediction of an area (green circle) around a likely touch point (green X), and finally (c) at thumb touchdown, prediction can adjust actual input to intended target (red X).

The need for these adaptations has, if anything, increased with the variability of form factors spanning compact 3.5 inch displays (e.g. Nokia M8) and phone/tablet hybrids with near-6 inch touchscreens (e.g. Samsung Galaxy Note 3). As mobile displays get larger, the ability to accurately target, especially with one hand, around the screen suffers. Bergstrom-Lehtovirta et al. adaptively modeled users' reach to define a functional area describing the maximum reach of their current hand posture [2].

When users need to reach targets on the edge and outside their functional area with one hand, they change their grip of the phone. As Figure 1 shows, users tend to shift the device in their hand, extending the thumb's reach. As Noor et al. showed, this grip change can be used to predict the touch point [7], or rather a likely area around it (Figure 1b in green), while the finger is still en-route. We refer to this as *in the air prediction.* Beyond in the air prediction, grip change can also be an indicator of where the user *intended* to land at the moment they touchdown. We refer to this as *on touchdown prediction.* The target may be outside the user's functional area even at maximum reach, so their touch point might miss a target but be close to one or more viable targets (Figure 1c). The grip change motion preceding the touch is indicative of intent to reach to further targets. In other words, a model that uses both the grip change and where the user touches down can better predict where the user intended to land than models that only consider one of these factors.

Past work has detected physical grip and grip change over time through *adding extra hardware* – additional sensor arrays on the back or side of the device (e.g. [7,9]). Noor et al. used the grip change—as measured while the user reaches for the target—to predict the resulting touchdown point while the finger is still en route (in the air) [7]. However, we wondered whether an auxiliary sensor array is critical to in the air prediction, or whether internal motion sensors (i.e. common accelerometers and gyroscopes) can achieve similar results. Given the potential predictive power of grip change on touch accuracy, it is additionally important to understand how detection of grip change is affected by common physical scenarios such as walking or interacting while in a moving vehicle. This is not addressed in the literature.

We explore using solely the motion sensors internal to today's devices to detect grip change and then use it to make in the air predictions of touch points. We verify prediction results in four different physical scenarios: interacting while sitting at a desk, standing without support, while walking, and while on a moving bus. As proof of concept, we use test our models using a single thumb posture. Our first study shows in the air prediction rates similar to Noor et al. A second study shows that a model that adjusts users' touches using both grip change and their touchdown point lowers touch errors by 41% consistently throughout the four physical scenarios tested.

In short, grip change can be used to continuously provide information about users' intent, in the air and on touchdown, beyond where they actually touch. Predicting where the user will touch prior to touchdown allows for a potential virtual hover space for mobile devices, while touchdown models take into consideration user intent in lowering touch errors.

STUDY 1 – IN THE AIR PREDICTION USING MOBILE MOTION SENSORS

To verify that hand grip change can be reliably detected in the air using solely mobile motion sensors (i.e. accelerometer and gyroscope), we ran a study that largely replicates Noor et al.'s touch target prediction experiment [7]. Participants were asked to touch the single on-screen square target to complete a trial. The target size was chosen to be physically identical to Noor et al.'s setup on the mobile device (1cm^2). The target was randomly placed on the surface of the display for each trial with a uniform distribution. As in Noor et al., once the user successfully clicked on the target, the next target was displayed after an enforced 500ms delay.

Participants and Apparatus

Eight participants (mean age 26.3, SD=3.6, 7 males), all right-handed, were asked to perform 1000 trials each (8000 trials in all), using the phone in their right hand and interacting with the thumb (i.e. a one-handed posture). All participants were regular and frequent mobile phone users.

Participants were presented with a custom application on a Nokia Lumia 920 with a 4.5" display at a 1280x720 resolution. Of note is that this device is significantly larger than the one used in Noor et al. (a Nokia N9 with a 3.9" display), which makes a direct comparison of prediction accuracy non-trivial. The application recorded 2D touch points on the display, and 3-axis accelerometer and gyroscope readings at a sampling rate of 50Hz.

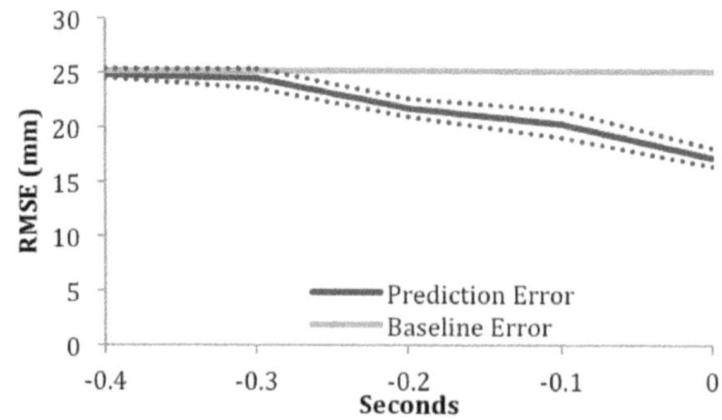

Figure 2. Root mean square error (and ± standard error in dashed lines) of touch point prediction before touch contact using mobile sensor detected hand grip change.

Results

To predict where participants touched based on hand grip change, we used the raw, time ordered accelerometer and gyroscope measures of the 500ms before touch as features. As with Noor et al. [7], we used Gaussian Process (GP) Regression to generate a nonlinear model that maps motion sensor values to 2D screen coordinates. Using Matlab's *gpml* package, the models were built independently for each axis and were defined using a squared exponential covariance function for smoothness and a constant mean function (with a prior of 0). The hyperparameters for these functions were learned from the data. Due to individual differences in how users grip and move the phone in their hand, the model was created on a per-user basis. Participant data was split between training and test sets using 10-fold cross validation.

As Figure 2 shows, the resulting models (in blue) provide a root mean square error (RMSE) smaller than a baseline model that simply picks the center of the available area for its prediction (in red). Predicting 0.1s before the touch provides a RMSE of 20.3mm, and 21.8mm at 0.2s. Though our much larger device makes comparison difficult, our grip change model provides similar results to Noor et al.'s 18mm (at 0.2s before touch) using only internal sensors. However, while motion sensor detected grip change can be satisfactory in some scenarios, more complex interactions (e.g. a virtual hover space) may require combining mobile sensors with high precision auxiliary sensor arrays such as Noor et al.'s.

STUDY 2 – GRIP CHANGE ON THE MOVE

The second study had two goals: (1) show how in the air prediction using motion sensor detected grip change performs in a more representative task and under various physical conditions (e.g. while walking); and (2) show how grip change can provide information on users' intent.

Methodology

The experiment was designed to gather touch and motion data from participants in a common task from every-day device use: selecting a particular target from an array of homescreen icons. In contrast to the first study, the participant selected one target, highlighted red, out of the always-visible array of 5x4 targets that simulate a Google

Android and Apple iOS homescreen. Each target was 99x99 pixels, which corresponds to the Google Android recommended size for icons for the Lumia 920's resolution and physical size.

In order to see how well a grip change prediction model works under common motion scenarios, participants performed the study in four physical conditions:

a) *Sit*: seated at a table, with their phone-handling (right) hand partially resting on the table for stability

b) *Stand*: free standing without any stability support

c) *Walk*: walking around a closed outdoors course at a constant, researcher defined comfortable walking speed

d) *Bus*: seated on a moving bus

Each trial highlighted one out of the 20 targets available at random with a uniform distribution. To simulate realistic, continuous interaction, the application moved to the next trial as soon as the participant touched the screen, without the enforced delay of the first study. The study was designed to be 1 hour in duration, which allowed 200 trials per condition. During the Bus scenario, data was only collected while the bus was moving – participants were asked to pause while the vehicle was stationary.

Participants and Apparatus

Twelve new participants (mean age 26.1, SD=2.2, 7 males), all right handed each completed 200 trials for each of the four conditions (9600 touch trials in all) using a one-handed posture. All participants were regular, frequent mobile users.

The custom experiment application ran on the same Nokia Lumia 920 device as in the first study. The application collected 2D touch coordinates for each trial, and 3-axis accelerometer and gyroscope readings sampled at 50Hz.

Results – In the Air Prediction on the Move

To verify whether target prediction is possible in different physical conditions, we again trained user-specific GP regression models mapping mobile motion sensor sequences to touch coordinates. Figure 3 shows touch prediction results using 10-fold cross validation for each condition, with the baseline model – always guessing in the center of the application area – shown in red. Note that the baseline error is higher (29mm) than the first experiment due to the static set of available targets to select from. As in Study 1, the prediction models created in the stationary conditions (Sit and Stand) have a lower RMSE than the baseline model. At 0.1s before touch, the GP regression model created in the Sit condition had a RMSE of 23.7mm (with Stand at 22.9mm), still lower than the baseline model (29.0mm).

Specifically comparing the results between the two studies shows that Study 1's result was better; it produced an RMSE of 20.3mm at 0.1s before touch, whereas in Study 2 for Sit it was 23.7mm. This can be explained by our more conservative approach in Study 2. We used a more realistic task and did not enforce a delay between trials. At times,

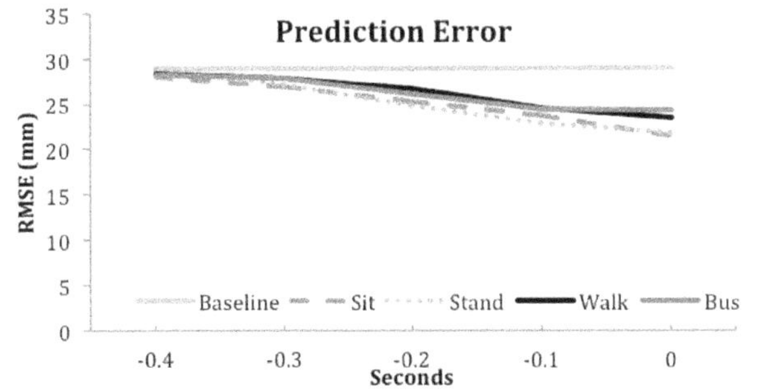

Figure 3. Root mean square error for the predicted touch points in Study 2's four different physical conditions.

more than one target was clicked within the 500ms prior to touchdown, which resulted in a lack of clear segmentation between touches. We also had a more limited data set (200 trials per user, per condition). Altogether, prediction RMSE in the Sit condition is thus higher than the first study. This more realistic scenario shows how in the air prediction using grip change degrades in a freeform homescreen task.

Lastly, unpredictable motion such as interacting in a bus, leads to higher prediction RMSE (24.4mm at 0.1s before touch) than sitting at a table (23.7mm at 0.1s), though critically, still lower than baseline models (29.0mm). This shows that, even with a relatively small amount of prior data, touch prediction using hand grip change is viable in high motion, unpredictable physical conditions.

Results – On Touchdown Prediction of Touch Intent

The secondary goal of the study was to verify whether grip change can improve touch performance by providing insight into targeting intent at the point of touchdown.

In order to separate user intent from their inherent touch patterns, we first built a baseline regression model mapping the 2D touch coordinates to the center of the highlighted target (referred to as the *XY Model*). We use the center of the highlighted target as an approximation of where the user intended to touch. This model takes into consideration individual touch behavior but uses no other information other than touchdown to infer user intent.

Next, we built a GP regression model that uses where the user touched, and the grip change as measured by the motion sensor readings of the 500ms prior to touchdown (*XY+Grip Model*). Again, the model attempts to map these features to the center of the highlighted target. We test the two models against the raw touch points (*Raw*). The models' goal is to improve on Raw accuracy by inferring where the user intended to touch rather than where they actually touched. To build and test the models, we use 10-fold cross validation.

An analysis of variance with *Model* (XY, XY+Grip, Raw) and *Physical Condition* (Sit, Stand, Walk, and Bus) as within-subject factors found a significant main effect of *Model* on touch accuracy ($F_{2,22}$ = 25.162, $p < 0.001$). Bonferroni correction showed significant differences between all pairs of *Models*. As Figure 4 shows, participants had a Raw accuracy of 83% over all physical conditions. The

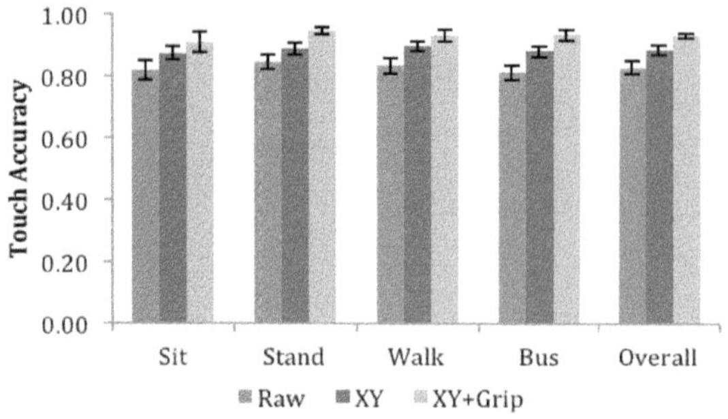

Figure 4. Touch accuracy comparing the three models per physical condition; Overall aggregates across all the data.

XY Model which took into consideration user-specific touch behaviour improved accuracy to 88%. Our XY+Grip Model further boosted accuracy to 93% consistently over all physical conditions—a 41% reduction in error rates over the XY Model alone.

CONCLUSIONS AND FUTURE WORK

In contrast to more static models that take into consideration individual touch behaviour (e.g. hand posture), we consider grip change as a continuous information stream, useful at multiple points in the interaction sequence. Prior to touchdown, grip change detected using standard mobile motion sensors can help estimate a touchdown point, useful for a virtual hover space and providing interactive support (e.g. continuous feedback of a user's touchdown point). On touchdown, grip change that preceded a touch point can be a useful predictor of where users intended to land, rather than where they touched. Although performance degrades in high motion scenarios, our results show that grip change can make reasonable touch predictions and reliably improves touch accuracy, reducing error rates by 41%.

Our study trained a model to infer intent by having full knowledge of the intended target. A question remains of how well such models can be trained and perform during everyday use where the intended target may not be known; some touches will hit an actual target, but one that was not intended. While our second study did not filter out any movement+touch sequence, more work is needed to verify the impact of such accidental touches in real world use cases. Additionally, our models only considered movement data that ends with a touch. More work is needed to filter out false positive movements and to design interactions that will fail gracefully (i.e., never permanently modify the interface state based on an expected touchdown).

Furthermore, our models were evaluated offline, and it remains to be seen how users adapt their touches when encountering a system that is itself adapting based on inferred intent (i.e., online). Continuous visual feedback of the model's predicted touch point may be critical to help users correct their targeting motion.

Finally, grip change was detected through data gathered on a relatively large smartphone and with a single thumb hand posture. While the current trend is one of increasing display sizes, more work is needed to verify how grip change varies for different phone-to-hand ratios, and whether smaller devices and other common hand postures have detectable and useful grip variations Past work on automatically detected hand posture using internal sensors (e.g. [4,5]) may be critical pre-processing for adaptive grip change models.

In conclusion, our studies show that grip change is a promising information side channel that is detectable with internal motion sensors, even when there is movement due to physical activity. Models using mobile sensor-detected grip change make useful in the air predictions and may complement techniques that use auxiliary sensor arrays to create more complex interactions. Additionally, the grip change measured right before touchdown provides insight into where the user intended to land. Leveraging this information significantly improves touch accuracy beyond models that adjust based solely on the touchdown point.

ACKNOWLEDGEMENTS

This work was funded by NSERC and the GRAND NCE.

REFERENCES

1. Azenkot, S. and Zhai, S. Touch behavior with different postures on soft smartphone keyboards. *Proc. of MobileHCI'12*, 2012, 251–260.
2. Bergstrom-Lehtovirta, J. and Oulasvirta, A. Modeling the Functional Area of the Thumb on Mobile Touchscreen Surfaces. *Proc. of CHI'14* ACM (2014), 1991–2000.
3. Goel, M., Findlater, L., and Wobbrock, J. WalkType: using accelerometer data to accomodate situational impairments in mobile touch screen text entry. *Proc. of CHI'12*, ACM (2012), 2687–2696.
4. Goel, M., Jansen, A., Mandel, T., Patel, S.N., and Wobbrock, J.O. ContextType: Using Hand Posture Information to Improve Mobile Touch Screen Text Entry. *Proc. of CHI'13*, ACM (2013), 2795–2798.
5. Goel, M., Wobbrock, J., and Patel, S. GripSense: Using Built-in Sensors to Detect Hand Posture and Pressure on Commodity Mobile Phones. *Proc. of UIST'12*, 2012, 545–554.
6. Henze, N., Rukzio, E., and Boll, S. 100,000,000 taps: analysis and improvement of touch performance in the large. *Proc. of MobileHCI'11*, ACM (2011), 133–142.
7. Mohd Noor, M.F., Ramsay, A., Hughes, S., Rogers, S., Williamson, J., and Murray-Smith, R. 28 Frames Later: Predicting Screen Touches from Back-of-device Grip Changes. *Proc. of CHI'14*, ACM (2014), 2005–2008.
8. Ng, A., Brewster, S.A., and Williamson, J.H. Investigating the Effects of Encumbrance on One- and Two- Handed Interactions with Mobile Devices. *Proc. of CHI'14*, ACM (2014), 1981–1990.
9. Wimmer, R. and Boring, S. HandSense: Discriminating Different Ways of Grasping and Holding a Tangible User Interface. *Proc. of TEI'09*, ACM (2009), 359–362.
10. Yin, Y., Ouyang, T.Y., Partridge, K., and Zhai, S. Making touchscreen keyboards adaptive to keys, hand postures, and individuals: a hierarchical spatial backoff model approach. *Proc. of CHI'13*, ACM (2013), 2775–2784.

An Experimental Comparison of Vertical and Horizontal Dynamic Peephole Navigation

Jens Müller[1], Roman Rädle[1], Hans-Christian Jetter[2], Harald Reiterer[1]
[1] Human-Computer Interaction Group, University of Konstanz, Germany
{Jens.Mueller,Roman.Raedle,Harald.Reiterer}@uni-konstanz.de
[2] Intel ICRI Cities, University College London, London, United Kingdom
h.jetter@ucl.ac.uk

ABSTRACT
Dynamic peephole navigation represents a technique for navigating large information spaces in an egocentric way. Studies have shown cognitive benefits for a vertical peephole orientation, when compared to non-egocentric interaction styles. To see how the aspect of canvas orientation effects user performance, we conducted a study (N=16) which revealed that canvas orientation has no significant effect on either navigation performance or spatial memory. We also found a significantly lower physical demand and a higher mental demand in the horizontal orientation. For short-term activities we therefore propose a vertical orientation, while for long-term activities horizontal dynamic peephole navigation is more suitable.

Author Keywords
Dynamic peephole navigation; canvas orientation; spatial memory; subjective workload; navigation performance.

ACM Classification Keywords
H.5.2. User Interfaces: input devices and strategies. Evaluation/methodology.

INTRODUCTION
One way to handle large datasets is by provisioning movable viewports, so-called dynamic peepholes, which allow the user to explore information spaces in an egocentric way. Instead of panning the screen content (e.g. a city map), the user physically moves to off-screen content (e.g. a neighboring city) as if it were situated in physical space (Figure 1). Studies on this technique (e.g. [3,4,5]) show cognitive benefits for a vertical peephole canvas when compared to non-egocentric interaction styles. In some situations, however, a horizontal orientation may be more practical. Consider the following scenario:

Figure 1. Navigating a virtual map on a vertical (left) and a horizontal (right) peephole canvas. A tablet serves as a peephole which can be moved to explore off-screen content.

A multidisciplinary team of urban planners[1] meets in an office to work on a large project. The meeting is supported by a horizontally oriented, large-scale peephole canvas which shows the construction site. Via a tablet, each team member navigates the site and works on their individual spot. The architect privately evaluates their drafts of a barrier-free entrance of a particular building on their tablet. The architect then publishes one design on the canvas so that others can see it. The civil engineer, who is dependent on the architect's design, now sees the published design on the peephole canvas and picks it up to work on it later at the office. At the end of the meeting, all modifications are highlighted on the canvas and are discussed by the team.

Scenarios like the one above may require a large peephole canvas. In this case, a horizontal canvas orientation seems more practical than a vertical one, because the canvas size is not restricted by the persons' reach height (Figure 1, left). In addition, a horizontal canvas orientation does not occlude as much of the interaction space as a vertical orientation does (compare Figure 1, left and right).

[1] https://www.planning.org/aboutplanning/

CHI 2015, April 18 - 23 2015, Seoul, Republic of Korea
Copyright 2015 ACM 978-1-4503-3145-6/15/04...$15.00
http://dx.doi.org/10.1145/2702123.2702227

While some properties of peephole navigation are well explored (e.g. peephole size and the optimal number of horizontal canvas layers [8]), the aspect of canvas orientation and its effects on human cognition is still unexplored. This note reports findings of an experimental comparison on a single-user navigation task between vertically and horizontally oriented canvases.

BACKGROUND AND RELATED WORK

In 1993 Fitzmaurice [1] introduced the Chameleon prototype, a spatially-aware palmtop that served as a dynamic peephole to navigate virtual information spaces. As a continuation of the Chameleon, Yee [11] presented a peephole prototype to create and manipulate virtual objects. A usability test showed that the technique "can be more effective than current methods for navigating information on handheld computers." Spindler et al. [10] presented PaperLens, a projection-based peephole prototype to navigate information spaces spanned above the tabletop.

Comparative studies (egocentric vs. non-egocentric)

Mehra et al. [4] compared the perception of line lengths for static and dynamic peepholes and found that dynamic peephole navigation results in a significantly better line length discrimination. Kaufman and Ahlström [3] compared user performance of vertical peephole interaction (via a projector phone) with touch-based input (via a smartphone). While there were no significant differences in navigation performance, spatial memory performance was significantly better when participants navigated with the projector phone. Rädle et al. [5] compared vertical dynamic peephole navigation with touch navigation. Their study revealed an effect on navigation performance and long-term spatial memory in favor of egocentric navigation. Spindler et al. [9] investigated navigation speed for both traditional Pinch-Drag-Flick gestures and egocentric manipulation using a tablet and a smartphone. Their results show that spatial manipulation can significantly outperform traditional Pinch-Drag-Flick. Scarr et al. [7] provide an overview on spatial memory in user interfaces and discuss spatial reference systems as a crucial cognitive factor.

Studies on the properties of dynamic peephole interaction

Spindler et al. [8] investigated user performance for multi-layer interaction above the table. For horizontal search tasks they identified 44 layers as the maximal number. Rädle et al. [6] investigated the effect of the peephole size on a vertical canvas. They identified the tablet as "sweet spot" in terms of peephole size and both user navigation performance and user task load.

Thus, assuming that 1) dynamic peephole navigation on a vertical canvas provides cognitive benefits compared to non-egocentric techniques and that 2) a horizontal canvas orientation has practical advantages in certain scenarios, the question raised by this paper is how the orientation of the peephole canvas affects user performance.

EXPERIMENT

We conducted a controlled lab experiment to study the influence of the canvas orientation on user performance and task load. The experiment was designed as a counter-balanced within-subjects design with the peephole canvas orientation being the independent variable (Figure 2).

Figure 2. Two study conditions: Horizontal orientation of the peephole canvas (top) vs. vertical orientation (bottom).

In each condition participants were tasked to find a sequence of predefined symbols for which they had to navigate through the canvas by moving the peephole. For a peephole we used a tablet as it represents a sweet spot in terms of peephole size and both navigation performance and task load [6]. In contrast to [6] we did not simulate the peephole with a proxy device but used a real tablet in favor of external validity. The dependent variables are user task load (NASA TLX), navigation path length, navigation time, spatial memory, and qualitative data from a concluding, semi-structured interview and from video recordings.

Participants

16 participants (8 female, 8 male) were recruited for the experiment. The mean age was 25.5 years (SD = 4.39, min = 20 years, max = 38 years). 13 participants were students of which only one had a background in computer science; the other 3 were administrative staff.

Study Apparatus & Environment

As a tablet we used a Microsoft Surface 2 device (208ppi, 984 g, 1920*x*1080 pixels on 10.6"). The tablet was equipped with passive markers and tracked with an OptiTrack 3D motion capturing system (24 cameras, tracking rate = 100 Hz, tracking mean error < .5 mm).

Depending on the study condition, the orientation of the peephole canvas was either horizontal (parallel to the ground) or vertical (parallel to the wall; Figure 2). Canvases had a physical dimension of 292*x*82 cm, a resolution of 23891*x*6709 pixels and a control-display gain of 1 to make navigation as natural as possible. In contrast to [6], rotation was enabled around the axis orthogonal to the canvas.

Task Design

Each canvas contained 20 distinct symbols (*targets*). From the 20 targets only 8 were defined as *search targets*, all others served as distractors. For the targets we used symbols from the Wingdings font as in [5]. The study task consisted of a search task and a reconstruction task.

In the *search task*, participants had to find the 8 search targets in a pre-defined order (8 targets = 8 trials = 1 block). To confirm a search target and to continue with the next trial, participants had to center the matching target on the tablet display (Figure 2, center right) and touch the display. Each block was repeated 8 times resulting in 64 trials.

In the *reconstruction task*, participants had to recall and reconstruct the location of the 8 search targets, again using the tablet. They were exposed to a plain canvas, i.e. all targets had been removed from the canvas. The search targets were displayed on the border of the tablet display and participants had to physically move and "drop" each search target at its presumed location. Locations could be changed by re-dropping a target at a different location.

Procedure

First, participants filled out a demographic questionnaire. We then asked the participants to hold the tablet up in the air to individually optimize the position of the vertical peephole canvas. Afterwards the task was introduced to the participants. To make sure that participants were able to adequately perform the study task from the beginning, they were provided a training phase (approx. 3 min.) in which they could familiarize themselves with the technique.

Participants then began with the study task (approx. 14 min. in each condition). Afterwards, they were provided the NASA TLX questionnaire. Attached to the questionnaire there were several paper-based mazes. They were given 5 minutes to fill out the questionnaire and to continue with the mazes in case they finished the TLX early. The mazes were meant to distract participants from keeping the locations for the subsequent reconstruction task in their short term or working memory. After 5 minutes, participants were asked to reconstruct the locations of the search targets (approx. 14 min.). After participants had finished the reconstruction task, the study task was repeated in the respective other condition. After the completion of the study task in both study conditions, participants were asked about their preferred canvas orientation by a semi-structured interview. The entire procedure took approx. 60 minutes. Participants were compensated with 10 Euros.

RESULTS

For *user task load*, a pairwise comparison in the NASA-TLX revealed a significantly lower mental demand ($p < .05$) in the vertical condition (M = 37.81, SD = 20.24) than in the horizontal condition, (M = 50.31, SD = 22.09) whereas the physical demand was lower ($p = .017$) in the horizontal condition (M = 29.69, SD = 20.36) than in the vertical condition (M = 47.81, SD = 24.21) (Figure 3). The mean values of all other dimensions were not significantly different.

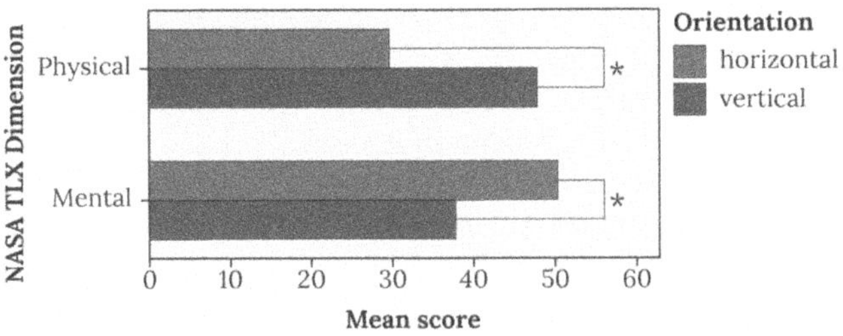

Figure 3. Task Load in the two dimensions in which significant differences occurred.

For *path length* an ANOVA showed that the peephole canvas orientation had no significant effect ($F_{1,15} = 1.468$, $p = .244$, *partial* $\eta^2 = .089$) (Figure 4).

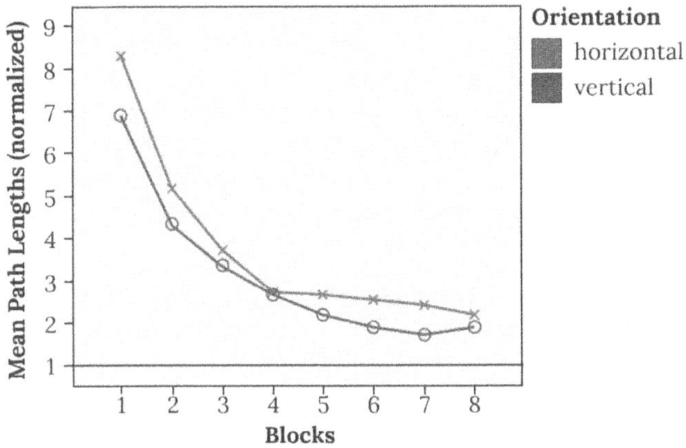

Figure 4. Normalized path lengths across all 8 blocks.

For *navigation time* an ANOVA showed that peephole canvas orientation had no significant effect ($F_{1,15} = 1.680$, $p = .214$, *partial* $\eta^2 = .101$).

For *spatial memory* an ANOVA showed that peephole canvas orientation had no significant effect ($F_{1,15} = 3.854$, $p = .068$, *partial* $\eta^2 = .204$).

Analysis of *qualitative data* revealed that 10 out of 16 participants preferred the vertical condition, with 7 reporting that less freedom of movement provided them with better orientation. From the 6 participants who preferred the horizontal condition, 4 justified this with a more comfortable operation and 2 with a higher degree of freedom. As an orientation-independent *recall strategy*, 5 participants reported having actively used the boundaries of the peephole canvas. In the vertical condition 5 participants reported to have mentally subdivided the canvas (e.g. left/right, upper/lower half). In the horizontal condition, 3 participants reported that the sequence of footsteps helped in retaining the target location and 3 reported that they tried to retain the directions between the angles of the targets.

Analysis of video recordings yielded two major *movement patterns* in the horizontal condition: 13 of 16 participants did not use rotation at the beginning of the search task; instead they moved either sideways or back and forth. 9 of these 13 participants started to use rotation at some point, stating afterwards that they first had to attain a mental map of the canvas before moving freely (*'I first started turning around when I had the map in my head'*; *'As I achieved an overview at some time, I broke out and became more playful'*). 4 participants did not use rotation at all in the horizontal condition, as they feared to lose orientation (*'I would have lost orientation, if I had turned around'*).

DISCUSSION AND LIMITATION

In the vertical orientation, navigation was based on two major components: walking along the virtual canvas and vertically moving the tablet. In the horizontal orientation, however, only walking was required to navigate the entire canvas. This probably caused a lower *physical demand* in the horizontal orientation. The increased *mental demand* in the horizontal orientation resonates with both the observed movement patterns (participants initially avoided rotations) and participants' report on an initial lack of orientation. It can therefore be hypothesized that the increased *mental demand* results from an additional degree of freedom (yaw rotation) and decreases with the establishment of a mental map. This could be subject of further research.

The limitation of this study refers to the aspect of physical reference systems [7]: In fact, we sought to minimize their effect (e.g. by providing a homogenous physical background of the canvases). Yet, we cannot guarantee that some remaining features (e.g. window frames) might have been more conducive to either of the two conditions.

IMPLICATIONS

For short-term activities that do not require much space, a vertical canvas orientation is more suitable than a horizontal one as the physical demand plays a minor role and quick orientation keeps the mental demand at a low level. For long-term activities that require vast spaces–e.g. spatial planning activities–a horizontal canvas orientation is more suitable due to the lower physical demand. Supporting the establishment of a mental map, however, is crucial to reduce mental effort at an early stage. This could be achieved by providing the user a virtual reference system such as the Wedge visualization technique [2].

CONCLUSION

In this paper we compared the effects of the peephole canvas orientation on user task load, navigation, and spatial memory performance. The results of our study suggest that the differences in navigation performance and spatial memory are minor. In addition, navigating the horizontal canvas was reported to be less physical demanding than the vertical canvas. For long-term activities that require a large canvas we therefore consider a horizontal canvas orientation a promising alternative. Yet, horizontal navigation yielded a higher mental demand due to an initial lack of orientation, which, however appeared to decrease with a growing mental map of the canvas. For short-term activities that do not require a large canvas we therefore propose a vertical canvas orientation.

REFERENCES

1. Fitzmaurice, G.W. Situated information spaces and spatially aware palmtop computers. *Communications of the ACM*, 1993, 39–49.
2. Gustafson, S., Baudisch, P., and Gutwin, C. Wedge: Clutter-Free Visualization of Off-Screen Locations. *Proc. of CHI '08*, 787–796.
3. Kaufmann, B. and Ahlström, D. Studying Spatial Memory and Map Navigation Performance on Projector Phones with Peephole Interaction. *Proc. of CHI '13*, 3173–3176.
4. Mehra, S., Werkhoven, P., and Worring, M. Navigating on Handheld Displays: Dynamic versus Static Peephole Navigation. *ACM Transactions on Computer-Human Interaction 13*, 4 (2006), 448–457.
5. Rädle, R., Jetter, H., Butscher, S., and Reiterer, H. The Effect of Egocentric Body Movements on Users' Navigation Performance and Spatial Memory in Zoomable User Interfaces. *Proc. of ITS '13*, 23–32.
6. Rädle, R., Jetter, H., Müller, J., and Reiterer, H. Bigger is not always better: Display Size, Performance, and Task Load during Peephole Map Navigation. *Proc. of CHI '14*, 4127–1436.
7. Scarr, J., Cockburn, A., and Gutwin, C. Supporting and Exploiting Spatial Memory in User Interfaces. *Foundations and Trends® in Human–Computer Interaction 6*, 1 (2012), 1–84.
8. Spindler, M., Martsch, M., and Dachselt, R. Going Beyond the Surface : Studying Multi-Layer Interaction Above the Tabletop. *Proc. of CHI '12*, 1277–1286.
9. Spindler, M., Schuessler, M., Martsch, M., and Dachselt, R. Pinch - Drag - Flick vs . Spatial Input: Rethinking Zoom & Pan on Mobile Displays. *Proc. of CHI '14*, 1113–1122.
10. Spindler, M., Stellmach, S., and Dachselt, R. PaperLens: Advanced Magic Lens Interaction Above the Tabletop. *Proc. of ITS '09*, 69–76.
11. Yee, K. Peephole Displays: Pen Interaction on Spatially Aware Handheld Computers. *Proc. of CHI '03*, 1–8.

Author Index

www.ingramcontent.com/pod-product-compliance
Ingram Content Group UK Ltd.
Pitfield, Milton Keynes, MK11 3LW, UK
UKHW051418290926
15471UKWH00009B/1664